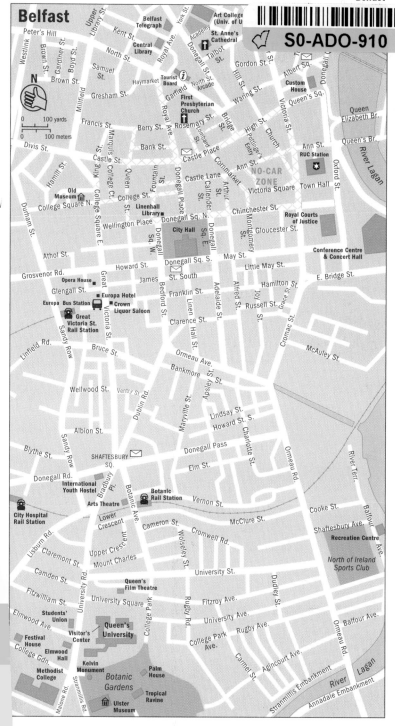

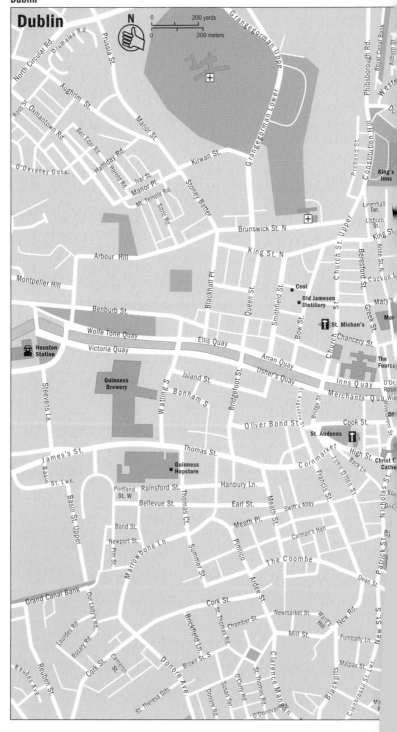

Dublin

Dublin

Cork and Galway

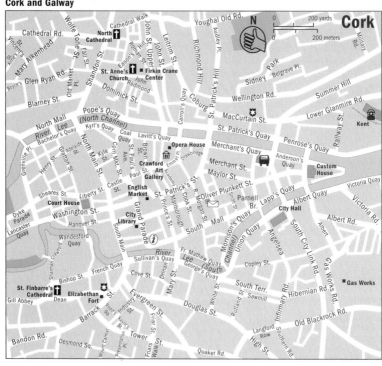

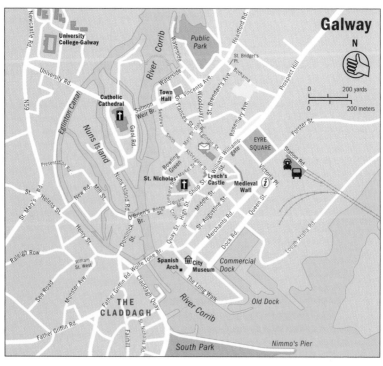

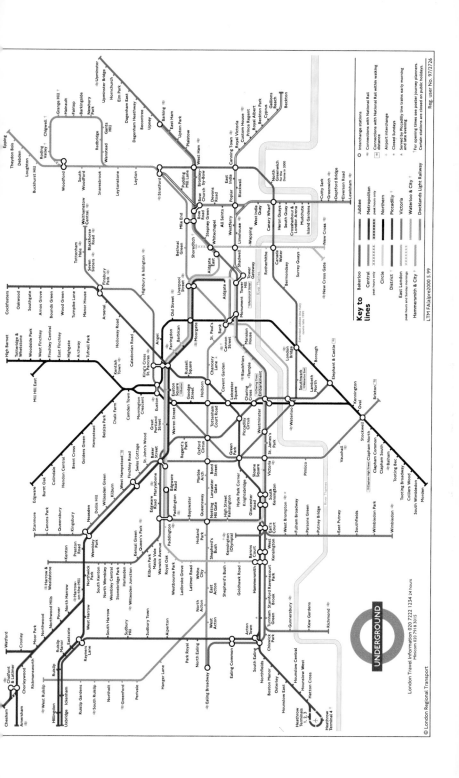

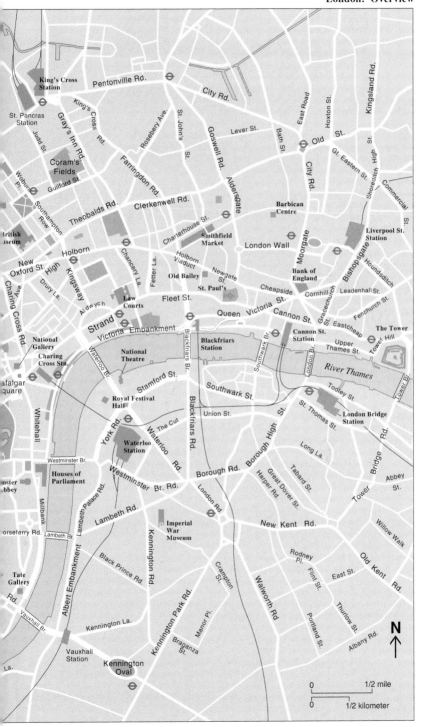

London: Westminster and Whitehall

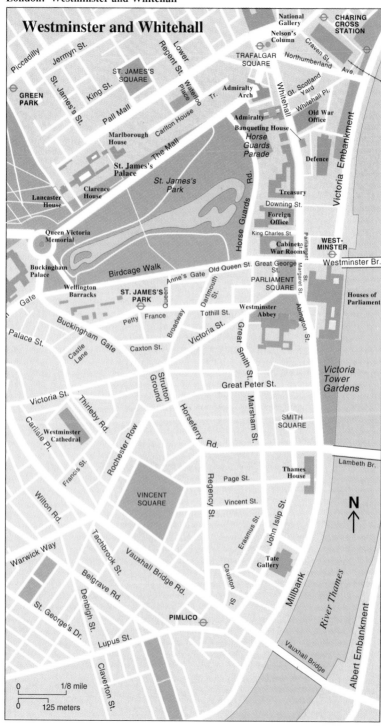

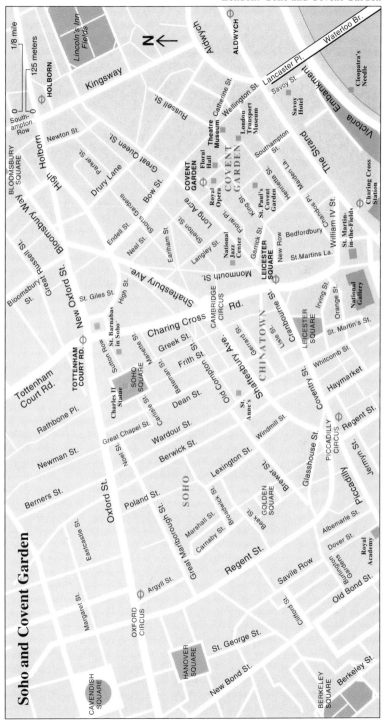

London: Soho and Covent Garden

Soho and Covent Garden

1/8 mile
meters
0
125

Southampton Row

HOLBORN

Lincoln's Inn Fields

Kingsway

ALDWYCH
ALDWYCH

Waterloo Br.

Newton St.
Russell St.
Catherine St.
Wellington St.
Lancaster Pl.
Savoy St.

Cleopatra's Needle

Victoria Embankment

Holborn
High

BLOOMSBURY SQUARE

Great Queen St.
Parker St.
Drury Lane
Bow St.
Theatre Museum
London Transport Museum
Savoy Hotel
The Strand

Bloomsbury Way

Great Russell St.
Bloomsbury St.

Endell St.
Shorts Gardens
Neal St.
Earlham St.
Langley St.
Shelton St.
Long Acre
Floral Pl.
Floral Hall
COVENT GARDEN
Royal Opera
COVENT GARDEN
King St.
Southampton St.
Henrietta St.
Maiden La.
St. Paul's Covent Garden
New Row
Bedfordbury
St.Martins La.
Chandos Pl.
William IV St.
St. Martin-in-the-Fields
Charing Cross Station

New Oxford St.
TOTTENHAM COURT RD.
Tottenham Court Rd.
Rathbone Pl.

St. Giles St.
High St.
Shaftesbury Ave.
Monmouth St.
Mercer St.
St. Barnabas in Soho
Sutton Row
National Jazz Center
Garrick St.
LEICESTER SQUARE
CAMBRIDGE CIRCUS
Charing Cross Rd.
Greek St.
Bateman St.
Frith St.
Old Compton
Dean St.
St. Anne's
Shaftesbury Ave.
CHINATOWN
Gerrard St.
Lisle St.
Cranbourne St.
LEICESTER SQUARE
Irving St.
Orange St.
St. Martin's St.
National Gallery

Charles II Statue
SOHO SQUARE
Carlisle St.

Newman St.
Berners St.
Eastcastle St.
Margaret St.

Great Chapel St.
Noel St.
Wardour St.
Berwick St.
Poland St.
Oxford St.
SOHO
Lexington St.
Brewer St.
Marshall St.
Broadwick St.
Beak St.
GOLDEN SQUARE
Windmill St.
Glasshouse St.
Coventry St.
Whitcomb St.
Haymarket
PICCADILLY CIRCUS
Regent St.
Jermyn St.
Piccadilly

Great Marlborough St.
Carnaby St.
Regent St.
Savile Row
Albemarle St.
Dover St.
Old Bond St.
New Bond St.
Royal Academy
Bruton St.
Berkeley St.

OXFORD CIRCUS
Argyll St.
HANOVER SQUARE
St. George St.
BERKELEY SQUARE

CAVENDISH SQUARE

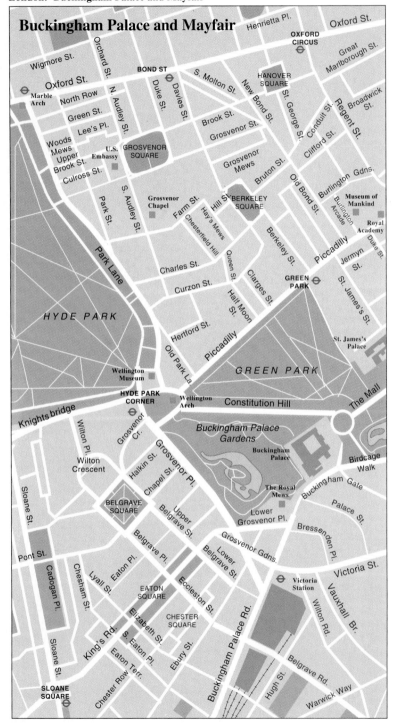

Buckingham Palace and Mayfair

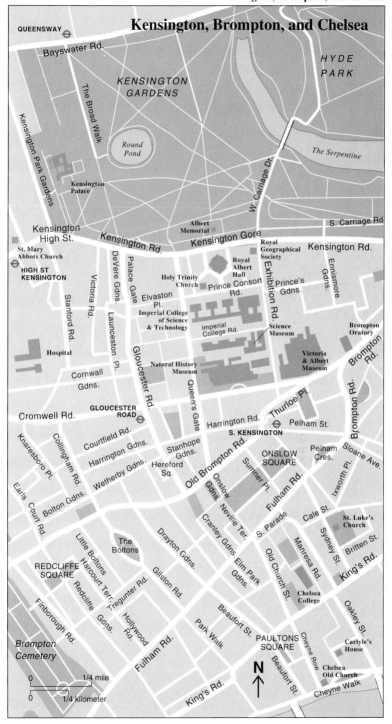

Kensington, Brompton, and Chelsea

QUEENSWAY

Bayswater Rd.

KENSINGTON GARDENS

HYDE PARK

The Broad Walk

Kensington Park Gardens

Round Pond

The Serpentine

Kensington Palace

W. Carriage Dr.

Kensington High St.

Kensington Rd.

Kensington Gore

Albert Memorial

S. Carriage Rd.

Kensington Rd.

St. Mary Abbots Church

HIGH ST KENSINGTON

DeVere Gdns.

Palace Gate

Holy Trinity Church

Royal Albert Hall

Royal Geographical Society

Ennismore Gdns.

Prince Consort Rd.

Prince's Gdns.

Exhibition Rd.

Victoria Rd.

Stanford Rd.

Launceston Pl.

Elvaston Pl.

Imperial College of Science & Technology

Imperial College Rd.

Science Museum

Brompton Oratory

Hospital

Gloucester Rd.

Natural History Museum

Victoria & Albert Museum

Brompton Rd.

Cornwall Gdns.

Cromwell Rd.

GLOUCESTER ROAD

Queen's Gate

Harrington Rd.

Thurloe Pl.

Pelham St.

S. KENSINGTON

Knaresboro Pl.

Collingham Rd.

Courtfield Rd.

Harrington Gdns.

Stanhope Gdns.

ONSLOW SQUARE

Pelham Cres.

Sloane Ave.

Wetherby Gdns.

Hereford Sq.

Summer Pl.

Fulham Rd.

Ixworth Pl.

Earls Court Rd.

Bolton Gdns.

Old Brompton Rd.

Onslow Gdns.

Neville Ter.

S. Parade

Cale St.

St. Luke's Church

Little Boltons

Drayton Gdns.

Cranley Gdns.

Elm Park Gdns.

Old Church St.

Manresa Rd.

Sydney St.

Britten St.

King's Rd.

The Boltons

REDCLIFFE SQUARE

Harcourt Terr.

Redcliffe Gdns.

Tregunter Rd.

Gilston Rd.

Hollywood Rd.

Chelsea College

Oakley St.

Finborough Rd.

Fulham Rd.

Park Walk

Beaufort St.

PAULTONS SQUARE

Cheyne Row

Carlyle's House

Brompton Cemetery

King's Rd.

Beaufort St.

Chelsea Old Church

Cheyne Walk

N

0   1/4 mile

0   1/4 kilometer

London: City of London

The City

N

Leman St.
Mansell St.
Commercial St.
ALDGATE EAST
Middlesex St.
Widegate St.
Houndsditch
Minories
Royal Mint St.
E. Smithfield
St. Katharine's Way
Tower Br. Approach
Tower Br.
ALDGATE
Aldgate
Fenchurch St. Station
Pepys St.
TOWER HILL
TRINITY SQUARE
Tower Hill
Liverpool St. Station
St. Mary Axe
Seething La.
All Hallows
The Tower
Tower Pier
Bishopsgate
Old Broad St.
Fenchurch St.
Lloyd's
St. Olave's
Mark La.
Mincing La.
St. Dunstan's
Gt. Tower St.
Lower Thames St.
HMS Belfast
London Stock Exchange
Leadenhall St.
Leadenhall Market
Lime St.
St. Mary at Hill
Billingsgate Market
Sun St.
South Pl.
Throgmorton Ave.
St. Margaret's
Threadneedle St.
Bank of England
Cornhill
Lombard St.
Eastcheap
The Monument
Monument St.
St. Magnus Martyr
London Br.
MOORGATE
FINSBURY CIRCUS
Moorfields
London Wall
Throgmorton St.
Lothbury St.
BANK
Princes St.
King William St.
St. Mary Abchurch
Walbrook
MONUMENT
Chiswell St.
Ropemaker St.
Coleman St.
Basinghall Ave.
Moorgate
Poultry
Mansion House
St. Stephen Walbrook
Temple of Mithras
CANNON
Cloak La.
Cannon St. Station
Southwark Br.
Silk St.
Fore St.
Basinghall St.
King St.
St. Mary le Bow
Watling St.
St. Mary Aldermary
Cannon St.
Queen St.
Beech St.
Guildhall
Gresham St.
Milk St.
Cheapside
Bread St.
MANSION HOUSE
Upper Thames St.
River Thames
Barbican Centre
St. Giles without Cripplegate
Museum of London
Wood St.
New Change
Cannon St.
Queen Victoria St.
St. Benet's
BARBICAN
Aldersgate St.
St. Bartholomew the Great
Little Britain
St. Martin's-Le-Grand
ST. PAUL'S
St. Paul's Cathedral
St. Andrew-by-the-Wardrobe
Puddle Dock
Blackfriars Station
West Smithfield
Lloyd La.
Snow Hill
Holborn Viaduct Station
Warwick La.
Old Bailey
Fleet La.
St. John St.
FARRINGDON
Cowcross St.
Smithfield Market
Gillspur St.
Holborn Viaduct
Farringdon Rd.
Ludgate Hill
LUDGATE CIRCUS
New Bridge St.
BLACKFRIARS
Blackfriars Br.
1/4 mile
1/4 km
Clerkenwell Rd.
Hatton Garden
Greville St.
Ely Pl.
Farringdon Rd.
Shoe Lane
New Fetter La.
Fetter La.
St. Bride St.
Fleet St.
GOUGH SQ.
Tudor St.
Temple Ave.
Temple Church
Middle Temple La.
The Temple
Victoria Embankment

Let's Go writers travel on your budget.

"Guides that penetrate the veneer of the holiday brochures and mine the grit of real life."

—*The Economist*

"The writers seem to have experienced every rooster-packed bus and lunar-surfaced mattress about which they write."

—*The New York Times*

"All the dirt, dirt cheap."

—*People*

Great for independent travelers.

"The guides are aimed not only at young budget travelers but at the independent traveler; a sort of streetwise cookbook for traveling alone."

—*The New York Times*

"Flush with candor and irreverence, chock full of budget travel advice."

—*The Des Moines Register*

"An indispensible resource, *Let's Go*'s practical information can be used by every traveler."

—*The Chattanooga Free Press*

Let's Go is completely revised each year.

"Only *Let's Go* has the zeal to annually update every title on its list."

—*The Boston Globe*

"Unbeatable: good sightseeing advice; up-to-date info on restaurants, hotels, and inns; a commitment to money-saving travel; and a wry style that brightens nearly every page."

—*The Washington Post*

All the important information you need.

"*Let's Go* authors provide a comedic element while still providing concise information and thorough coverage of the country. Anything you need to know about budget traveling is detailed in this book."

—*The Chicago Sun-Times*

"Value-packed, unbeatable, accurate, and comprehensive."

—*Los Angeles Times*

Let's Go Publications

Let's Go: Alaska & the Pacific Northwest 2001
Let's Go: Australia 2001
Let's Go: Austria & Switzerland 2001
Let's Go: Boston 2001 **New Title!**
Let's Go: Britain & Ireland 2001
Let's Go: California 2001
Let's Go: Central America 2001
Let's Go: China 2001
Let's Go: Eastern Europe 2001
Let's Go: Europe 2001
Let's Go: France 2001
Let's Go: Germany 2001
Let's Go: Greece 2001
Let's Go: India & Nepal 2001
Let's Go: Ireland 2001
Let's Go: Israel 2001
Let's Go: Italy 2001
Let's Go: London 2001
Let's Go: Mexico 2001
Let's Go: Middle East 2001
Let's Go: New York City 2001
Let's Go: New Zealand 2001
Let's Go: Paris 2001
Let's Go: Peru, Bolivia & Ecuador 2001 **New Title!**
Let's Go: Rome 2001
Let's Go: San Francisco 2001 **New Title!**
Let's Go: South Africa 2001
Let's Go: Southeast Asia 2001
Let's Go: Spain & Portugal 2001
Let's Go: Turkey 2001
Let's Go: USA 2001
Let's Go: Washington, D.C. 2001
Let's Go: Western Europe 2001 **New Title!**

Let's Go *Map Guides*

Amsterdam	New Orleans
Berlin	New York City
Boston	Paris
Chicago	Prague
Florence	Rome
Hong Kong	San Francisco
London	Seattle
Los Angeles	Sydney
Madrid	Washington, D.C.

Coming Soon: *Dublin* and *Venice*

Let's Go

BRITAIN & IRELAND

2001

Johs Pierce editor
Lisa M. Herman associate editor
Mike Durcak map editor

researcher-writers
Teresa Crockett
Emily A. Harrison
Winnie Li
Kate D. Nesin
Jason Schwartz

St. Martin's Press ≈ New York

Maps by David Lindroth copyright © 2001, 2000, 1999, 1998, 1997, 1996, 1995, 1994, 1993, 1992, 1991, 1990, 1989, 1988 by St. Martin's Press.

Distributed outside the USA and Canada by Macmillan.

ISBN: 0-312-24569-6

First edition
10 9 8 7 6 5 4 3 2 1

Let's Go: Britain & Ireland is written by Let's Go Publications, 67 Mount Auburn Street, Cambridge, MA 02138, USA.

Let's Go® and the thumb logo are trademarks of Let's Go, Inc.
Printed in the USA on recycled paper with biodegradable soy ink.

HOW TO USE THIS BOOK

"Goddag! Erik Bloodaxe the Norseman here. Some Viking mates of mine and I set sail on the North Sea for a bit of a cruise a while back, and before we knew it we were here in Britannia, and we figured we might as well loot and pillage a bit, just to prove we'd actually been somewhere on our vacation, and not just been sailing the high seas aimlessly, drinking mead and mucking about. (You know how it is—the folks back home always demand souvenirs and mementos, plundered gold, charred wood from torched cottages, that sort of thing.) Turns out we liked this Britannia tolerably well, so we figured we'd stay a while.

"And once you get here, so should you! Just look at what you're holding—this, my friends, is a copy of *Let's Go: Britain and Ireland 2001*, the most comprehensive budget travel guide ever written about these isles. I wish I'd had one of these when I arrived. All my mates and I had was longswords and a boat. We didn't know how to greet the natives, so we burned their towns! You, on the other hand, are armed with a handy-dandy yellow book, so you shouldn't make our mistake. The first chapter, **Discover Britain and Ireland,** provides you with an overview of these rain-driven plots o' land, including the **Suggested Itineraries.** The **Essentials** section is full of vital information about where to get the leak in your ship mended and how to spend your gold so it lasts longer. If my comrades Olaf and Thorleifur could read, I'd make them read it! Learn something about this strange and sheep-strewn land and its strange and sheep-strewn people in the next section, **Great Britain,** featuring Vikings and all our historical friends (not to mention some enemies), as well as news on what verses the bards have been reciting lately. Introductory chapters specific to **Scotland, Wales, Northern Ireland,** and **Ireland** follow later.

"The remainder of the book is divided into places that we Vikings have raided and settled in, and places that we haven't. Well, actually, there aren't any that we haven't raided, but we didn't settle in Wales. For instance, **England,** land of lush valleys, adorable little villages, and monasteries ripe for the taking, we sacked. **Wales,** home to windy, sand beaches, we looted, but not for long. **Scotland,** birthplace of haggis, we also looted, but for considerably longer. **Northern Ireland** we plundered. **Ireland,** land of bogs, we greedily robbed of everything we could find, then settled in Dublin. The **black tabs** in the margins will help you to navigate between chapters quickly and easily, while the **Appendix** contains useful **conversions** and a **glossary** of handy phrases in the many semi-intelligible languages these barbarians speak.

"My Viking friends and I have arranged all the information about towns in an elegant, easy-to-plunder manner for your gold-seeking pleasure. In each section (accommodations, food, sights, entertainment, and so on), we list sleeping barns, meadhouses, forts, and minstrel fairs in order from best to not-quite-as-super. Our absolute favorites are so denoted by the highest honor given out, the *Let's Go* thumbs-up (🖐). I would have preferred a two-horned helmet in miniature rather than some silly thumb, but there you have it. The **phone code** for each region, city, or town appears opposite the name and is denoted by the ☎ icon. **Phone numbers** in text are also preceded by the ☎ icon. **Grayboxes** at times provide wonderful cultural insight, at times simply crude humor. We Vikings like crude humor. We're so crude we drink mead out of skulls! **Whiteboxes,** on the other hand, provide important practical information, such as warnings (⚠) and helpful hints and further resources (🔍). I think that's about it for now. Happy looting and pillaging!"

A NOTE TO OUR READERS The information for this book was gathered by *Let's Go* researchers from May through August of 2000. Each listing is based on one researcher's opinion, formed during his or her visit at a particular time. Those traveling at other times may have different experiences since prices, dates, hours, and conditions are always subject to change. You are urged to check the facts presented in this book beforehand to avoid inconvenience and surprises.

CONTENTS

MAPS

RESEARCHER-WRITERS

Teresa Crockett *Midlands, Northwest England, Southern and Central Scotland*

From Oxford canal-jumping to Fort William canyoning, Teresa dove into her itinerary with energetic abandon, leaving no depth un-plunged in her pursuit of the next great adventure. A veteran of *Let's Go: California 2000*, she demonstrated her dedication by so enjoying National Health Service research that she went back for more. Just a few days before deadline, Teresa waltzed into the office with a Cadbury chocolate box bigger than her backpack—the only things we thanked her for more profusely were her meticulous research and utterly dependable copy.

Emily A. Harrison *Wales, Midlands, Northwest England*

Enchanted by Wales and enchanting the Welsh, Em sped through her itinerary at a record pace, delighting us with side-splitting marginalia, insightful prose, careful research, and enthusiasm that fairly leapt off the page. We looked forward to her weekly phone calls with glee and were never disappointed, hearing tales of Em frightening the sheep, scaring the bus driver, and finding her family roots in a cave. And all we had to do in return was tell her the Red Sox scores! It hardly seemed a fair trade, but we'd make it again in a heartbeat, and we know Em would, too.

Winnie Li *Edinburgh, Central Scotland, Highlands and Islands*

Jetting around her real homeland with the zeal of a long-lost daughter returning to native shores, Winnie dodged divebombing Shetland birds, motored in fits and starts along steep Highland roads, and fell in with the locals from Fife to the Outer Hebrides. A veteran of *Let's Go: Germany 1999*, this scholar of Scottish folklore significantly rearranged and expanded our coverage of Edinburgh and the Highlands. We thank Winnie for her stellar writing, for her big heart, and for improving the book in ways that promise to benefit readers for many years to come.

Kate D. Nesin *East Anglia, Midlands, Northeast and Northwest England*

Ever-reliable Kate zoomed through East Anglia and the northeast in search of the perfect cybercafe and the perfect tearoom, sending back reams of beautifully penned, rock-solid copy detailing her efforts. Exploring hilltop cathedrals from Lincoln to Durham, savoring Evensong from Cambridge to York, and charming peacocks everywhere, she reported on everything she saw with a keen eye for detail and an even keener appreciation of the beauty all around her. We were only too happy to send plucky Kate the Skittles she needed to keep going.

Jason Schwartz *South and Southwest England*

Putting his scientific training to good use, Jason commented on the many places he visited with clinical precision, and his state-of-the-art grayboxes impressed us with their imaginative wordplay. On his journey the length of southern England, he unearthed hidden gems in Bristol, ate like a king in Brighton, and wandered the beach in Bournemouth, all the while battling stubborn ankles and even more stubborn bus timetables before heading north for some well-deserved recuperation.

John T. Reuland	*Editor, London*
Maja Groff	*Editor, Ireland*
Derek (Teddy) Wayne	*Associate Editor, Ireland*
Whitney K. Bryant	*London*
Daryl Sng	*London*
Tobie E. Whitman	*London*
Mandy Davis	*Northern Ireland, Republic of Ireland*
Sarah C. Haskins	*Republic of Ireland*
Kalen Ingram	*Republic of Ireland*
Ian T. McClure	*Northern Ireland, Republic of Ireland*

ACKNOWLEDGMENTS

TEAM B&I LTD. THANKS: Teresa, Em, Winnie, Kate, and Jason, for braving the rain and the injured feet to send us all the words. Jonathan, for simply stellar MEing, quick and meticulous edits, thoughtful comments, hilarious demeanor, and tireless work till (yes, till) the very end. All officemates who helped out at the last minute. Podmates—Nick, for BBQing, kickballing, and running the good ship *Let's Go* so smoothly; Maja, for speaking Danish; Teddy, for punning; shoeless Alice, for serious (but mostly not-so-serious) football discussions; all four, for keeping things loose. Team Ireland, for the speedy crunching. Anne and everyone in the office; it's been great. All editors and RWs who went before us; we salute you.

JOHS THANKS: Lisa, for unflagging commitment, superb editing, a vigilant eye for detail, and boundless good cheer. I wouldn't have had a different co-editor for all the fountains in Kansas City. Daryl, for sending me to Wales. Charley, Thomas, and all Harvard friends and teachers, for four great years. William Wordsworth and the River Duddon, both for flowing. Uncle Norman A., for generosity. Uncle Norman B., for always being just a short drive away. Grandma and Grandpa, Betty and Charlie Pierce, and Mormor and Morfar, Ruth and Hilmar Kjær, for all their love. Holly, Bheka, and Britta, for all the good years to come.

LISA THANKS: Johs, for teaching me about football and bucktoothed berserkers while still dedicating so much time and effort to this book. Thrylos! Lisa P. and Susie, for keeping in touch from across the globe. Dawn and JoRel, for friendship closer to home. Karen, Jeff, Matt, Megan, Siobhan, and Sunny, for all those days in the office. Dan, for making this summer even better just by being around. And, of course, Mom, Dad, Greg and the rest of my family for encouraging and supporting me, even when I decided to spend yet another few months away from home.

Editor
Johs Pierce
Associate Editor
Lisa M. Herman
Managing Editor
Daryush Jonathan Dawid
Map Editor
Mike Durcak

Publishing Director
Kaya Stone
Editor-in-Chief
Kate McCarthy
Production Manager
Melissa Rudolph
Cartography Manager
John Fiore
Editorial Managers
Alice Farmer, Ankur Ghosh,
Aarup Kubal, Anup Kubal
Financial Manager
Bede Sheppard
Low-Season Manager
Melissa Gibson
Marketing & Publicity Managers
Olivia L. Cowley, Esti Iturralde
New Media Manager
Daryush Jonathan Dawid
Personnel Manager
Nicholas Grossman
Photo Editor
Dara Cho
Production Associates
Sanjay Mavinkurve, Nicholas
Murphy, Rosalinda Rosalez,
Matthew Daniels, Rachel Mason,
Daniel Visel
Some Design
Matthew Daniels
Office Coordinators
Sarah Jacoby, Chris Russell

Director of Advertising Sales
Cindy Rodriguez
Senior Advertising Associates
Adam Grant, Rebecca Rendell
Advertising Artwork Editor
Palmer Truelson

President
Andrew M. Murphy
General Manager
Robert B. Rombauer
Assistant General Manager
Anne E. Chisholm

Britain & Ireland: Points of Interest

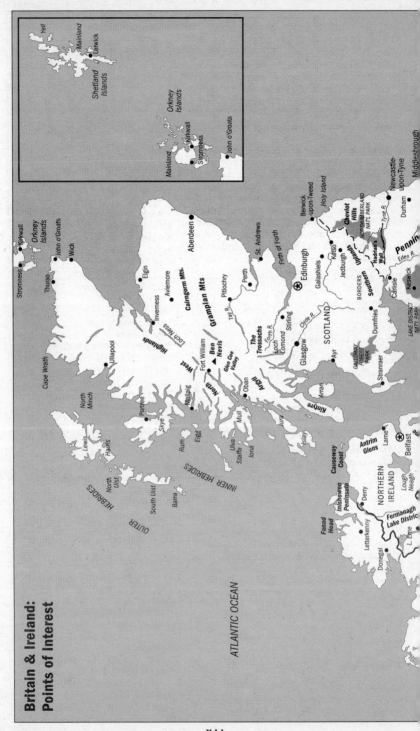

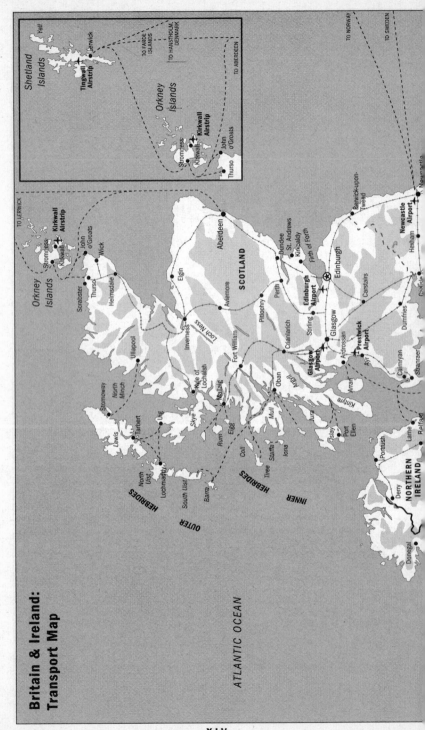

Britain & Ireland: Transport Map

ATLANTIC OCEAN

NORTHERN IRELAND

OUTER HEBRIDES

INNER HEBRIDES

SCOTLAND

Shetland Islands

Orkney Islands

Lewis
Stornoway
North Minch
Tarbert
North Uist
Lochmaddy
South Uist
Barra
Uig
Skye
Kyle of Lochalsh
Mallaig
Rum
Eigg
Coll
Tiree
Staffa
Iona
Mull
Oban
Jura
Islay
Port Ellen
Kintyre
Arran
Ardrossan
Ayr
Prestwick Airport
Stranraer
Cairnryan
Larne
Belfast
Portrush
Derry
Donegal

Ullapool
Scrabster
Stromness
Kirkwall
Kirkwall Airstrip
John o'Groats
Thurso
Wick
Helmsdale
Inverness
LOCH NESS
Fort William
Crianlarich
Stirling
Glasgow
Glasgow Airport
Dumfries
Carlisle

Elgin
Aviemore
Pitlochry
Perth
Aberdeen
Dundee
St. Andrews
Kirkcaldy
Firth of Forth
Edinburgh
Edinburgh Airport
Carstairs
Hexham
Newcastle
Newcastle Airport
Berwick-upon-Tweed

TO LERWICK
TO NORWAY
TO SWEDEN

Inset: Shetland Islands / Orkney Islands

Shetland Islands
Yell
Lerwick
Tingwall Airstrip

Orkney Islands
Stromness
Kirkwall
Kirkwall Airstrip
John o'Groats
Thurso

TO FAROE ISLANDS
TO HANSTHOLM, DENMARK
TO ABERDEEN
TO NORWAY
TO SWEDEN

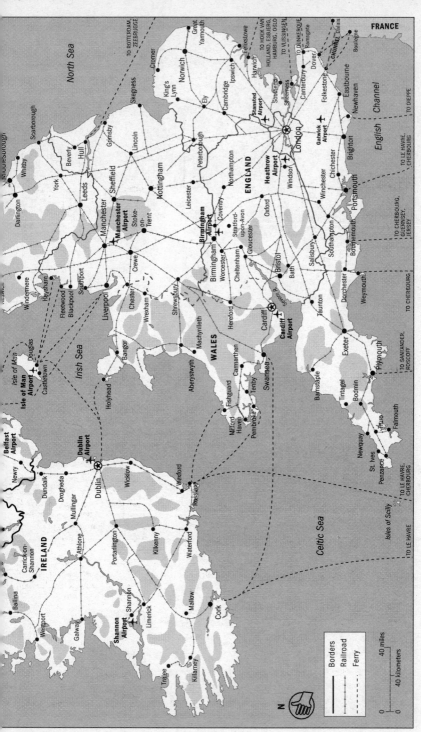

XV

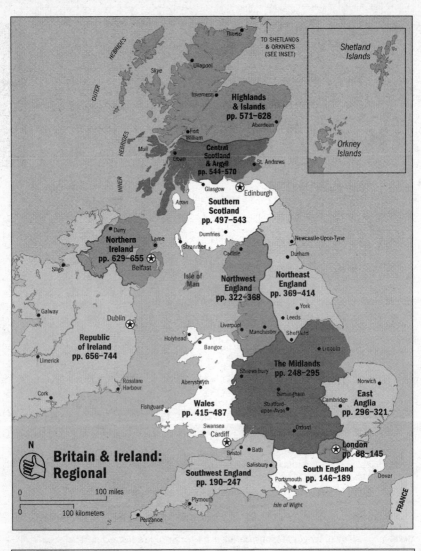

To Shetlands & Orkneys (SEE INSET)

HEBRIDES

Thurso

Ullapool

Skye

Inverness

OUTER

HEBRIDES

Highlands & Islands
pp. 571–628

Fort William

Aberdeen

Mull

Central Scotland & Argyll
pp. 544–570

Oban

St. Andrews

INNER

Glasgow

Edinburgh

Arran

Southern Scotland
pp. 497–543

Derry

Larne

Northern Ireland
pp. 629–655

Dumfries

Belfast

Newcastle-Upon-Tyne

Sligo

Stranraer

Carlisle

Durham

Isle of Man

Northwest England
pp. 322–368

Northeast England
pp. 369–414

Galway

Dublin

York

Leeds

Liverpool

Sheffield

Manchester

Republic of Ireland
pp. 656–744

Holyhead

Bangor

Lincoln

Limerick

Aberystwyth

Shrewsbury

The Midlands
pp. 248–295

Norwich

Rosslare Harbour

Birmingham

Cambridge

East Anglia
pp. 296–321

Cork

Fishguard

Wales
pp. 415–487

Stratford-upon-Avon

Oxford

Swansea

Cardiff

London
pp. 88–145

N

Britain & Ireland: Regional

Bristol

Bath

Salisbury

South England
pp. 146–189

Dover

0   100 miles

Southwest England
pp. 190–247

Portsmouth

0   100 kilometers

Plymouth

Isle of Wight

FRANCE

Penzance

Shetland Islands

Orkney Islands

DISCOVER BRITAIN AND IRELAND

For a small island nation of just under 60 million people, alone in a cold northern sea, Britain's worldwide influence—in language, literature, culture, politics, economics, and science—astounds. English, borne to the corners of the earth by British ships, is today a true *lingua franca*. Because of Britain's historical roles as colonial ruler of far-flung lands and spearhead of the Industrial Revolution, and contemporary roles as cultural beacon and immigration destination, it is the rare visitor who arrives on British shores without some connection to the land. Today, though the Union Jack no longer flies over two-fifths of the earth's surface, the residue of Empire continues to shape British society: a cosmopolitan and multiethnic country, modern Britain constantly challenges the traditional pastoral stereotypes associated with the island. Brits eat kebabs as often as they do lemon curd and scones; five-story dance clubs in gritty urban settings attract as many visitors as do the most majestic ruined castles or the prettiest villages full of gabled cottages and herbaceous borders. Britain enchants not just for its scenic splendor, not just for its remarkable history, not just for its engaging culture, but for the incredible array of sensations to be experienced in all those areas, and more, in a land you can travel the length of in a day or two.

Travelers who come to Ireland with images from poetry or film in mind will not be disappointed: spectacular, windswept scenery wraps around the coast, mist shrouds the peaks of dramatic mountains, and the dazzling green hues of Ireland's hills and vales demonstrate that the moniker "Emerald Isle" is no exaggeration. Traditional music and pub culture thrive in villages and cities, and despite the ever-pervasive influences of globalization in one of Europe's fastest-growing economies, the voices—literary, mythical, joke-cracking—of an older Ireland still sound out loud and strong.

FACTS AND FIGURES

CAPITALS London (UK and England), Cardiff (Wales), Edinburgh (Scotland), Belfast (Northern Ireland), Dublin (Republic of Ireland).

LANDS England and Scotland are kingdoms, Wales a principality, and Northern Ireland a constituent part of the United Kingdom. Ireland is a republic.

LAND AREA Great Britain 94,251 sq. mi. (244,110 sq. km). Northern Ireland 5,452 sq. mi. (14,120 sq. km.). Ireland 27,137 sq. mi. (70,285 sq. km).

POPULATIONS England 49.1 million, Wales 2.9 million, Scotland 5.1 million, Northern Ireland 1.6 million, Republic of Ireland 3.8 million.

WHEN TO GO

The popularity of Britain and Ireland as tourist destinations makes it wise to plan around the multitudes that descend upon the Isles during the high season. While the weather is at its most hospitable from June to August, hostels, B&Bs, and sights will be packed. Spring or autumn (Apr.-May and Sept.-Oct.) may provide better experiences; the weather is still reasonable and flights less expensive. If you intend to visit large cities and stay indoors visiting museums and watching theater, traveling during the off-season (Nov.-Mar., excluding holidays), when airfares and rooms are cheaper, will further reduce the damage to your bank account. However, sights, accommodations (particularly hostels), and tourist information centres often run reduced hours or even close, especially in rural regions.

WEATHER. The weather in Britain and Ireland is subject to frequent changes but few extremes (except at high altitudes and in northern Scotland), with an average temperature in the mid-60°s Fahrenheit (15-20°C) in the summer and in the low 40°s Fahrenheit (5-7°C) during the winter. Regardless of when you choose to go, the infamously fickle weather means that it *will* rain. At least it gives people something to talk about. Scotland, Wales, and Ireland are especially soggy; you should be prepared with warm, waterproof clothing at all times. Relatively speaking, April is the driest month in Ireland, especially on the east coast near Dublin. For a temperature chart, see **Climate,** p. 745. Another factor to consider is hours of **daylight**, particularly if you're going to Scotland—Edinburgh, after all, is on roughly the same line of latitude as Nova Scotia. In winter, the sun sets around 4pm, depending on how far north you are. People planning outdoor activities should come in summer to enjoy the best conditions, but in Scotland the warm weather also brings out annoying blood-sucking midges (gnats).

THINGS TO DO

Visitors to Britain and Ireland enjoy a panoply of opportunities for exploration within a relatively compact space; for instance, the clubs of Manchester are only an hour by train from the sparkling waters and craggy peaks of the Lake District. For more specific regional attractions, see the **Highlights** section at the beginning of each chapter.

NATURAL WONDERS

Skip the satanic mills and head to the green and pleasant hills. The **West Highland Railway** (p. 590) is a wonder of engineering, slicing through the lochs and moors of Scotland's Highlands. Discover the romantic (or the Romantic) in you in the surprisingly peaceful **Lake District** (p. 356). Wales meets the Atlantic Ocean at the **Pembrokeshire Coast National Park** (p. 448) in the form of stunning cliffs and beautiful, beautiful beaches. The **Shetland Islands** (p. 624), closer to Norway than to Great Britain, have a remote mystique. The bizarre honeycomb columns of **Giant's Causeway** (p. 651) in Northern Ireland spill out from the Antrim coast, a long strip of rocky crags and white beaches. The **Ring of Kerry** (p. 711) in southwest Ireland encircles a peninsula speckled with mountains, waterfalls, and cliffs; its natural phenomena are most densely packaged in **Killarney National Park** (p. 709).

HISTORY, PRE-1066

Well, how far back do you want to go? Stone Age sites litter Britain and Ireland, none more famous than **Stonehenge** (p. 196). Farther southwest are the **quoits** (ancient burial chambers) of Cornwall (p. 247). In Co. Meath in Ireland, the 5000-year-old passage-grave at **Newgrange** (p. 694) is an architectural feat that stumps present-day engineers. On the limestone **Rock of Cashel** (p. 698), a mish-mosh of early Christian structures pop up across the skyline, including a medieval cathedral and a Celtic cross. The **Isle of Anglesey** (p. 477) off Wales has equally ancient sites, such as **Bryn Celli Ddu** (p. 478), a Neolithic burial tomb in the middle of a farm, of all places. **Hadrian's Wall** (p. 410) marks a Roman emperor's frustration with his pesky neighbors to the north, while the baths at **Bath** (p. 198) hint at more relaxed moments for the Romans. And William the Conqueror tops off this quick history, earning his nickname at the Battle of **Hastings** (p. 161).

CASTLES AND CATHEDRALS

The defensive fortifications scattered throughout Britain and Ireland point to the tumultuous past of the Isles. Edward I of England had a tough time containing the Welsh; his massive castles in north Wales include the spectacular ones at **Beaumaris** (p. 479), **Caernarfon** (p. 473), **Conwy** (p. 480), and **Harlech** (p. 461), all an easy swing across the northwest. Two castles, equally grand, stand atop volcanoes in Scotland, one in **Edinburgh** (p. 498), and one in **Stirling** (p. 545). It's good to be Queen, especially when you get to stay in **Windsor** (p. 260) and survey the land. Or the Legoland, if you prefer. Across the Irish Sea, **Kilkenny Castle** (p. 695) is a stunning, well-preserved medieval work. If you want to stay in one and play knight for a night (or dame for a day), **Durham Castle** (p. 401) lets out its rooms, and there's a hostel in **St. Briavel's Castle** (p. 432). Not strictly castles, the elegant mansions of **Castle Howard** (p. 390) and **Blenheim Palace** (p. 260), are still good places at which to gape at how the other 0.001% lives.

In northeast England, **York Minster** (p. 388), the country's largest Gothic cathedral, competes with **Durham Cathedral** (p. 401) for the title of "most imposing." **The Salisbury Stake** (p. 195) is not a dinner but the tallest spire in England. In London, thousands flock to **Westminster Abbey** (p. 117) and to **St. Paul's Cathedral** (p. 107), where Poets' Corner and the Whispering Gallery are breathtaking. The quiet of **Christ Church Cathedral** (p. 679) in Dublin belies its contested history.

LITERARY LANDMARKS

Almost every corner of the islands has been captured in print. **Virginia Woolf** drew inspiration for her novel *To the Lighthouse* from St. Ives (p. 245). **Jane Austen** grew up in Winchester (p. 182), wrote in Bath (p. 198), took the odd trip to the Cobb in Lyme Regis (p. 217), and immortalized all the areas in her novels. **Sir Arthur Conan Doyle** set Sherlock Holmes's house on 221b Baker St. in London (p. 122), but sent the sleuth to Dartmoor (p. 225) to find the Hound of the Baskervilles. **Thomas Hardy** was a Dorchester (p. 213) man, whose fictional county of Wessex mirrored southwest England perfectly. Stratford-upon-Avon (p. 262) has never forgotten **William Shakespeare**, long after he shuffled off this mortal coil. Farther north, the Brontës—Charlotte, Emily, and Anne—lived in the parsonage in Haworth (p. 376), and vividly captured the wildness of Yorkshire's moors (p. 391). **Wordsworth** and **Coleridge** lived in the Lake District (p. 356), and much of their poetry was inspired by walks near its waters and along its mountain ridges. The Welsh **Dylan Thomas** grew up in Swansea (p. 441), moved to Laugharne (p. 448), and always drew inspiration from his homeland. Scotland's national poet is **Robbie Burns,** and every town in Dumfries and Galloway (p. 522) pays tribute to him. Among famous Dubliners was **James Joyce,** a colossus among novelists (p. 682). **W.B. Yeats** scattered his poetic settings throughout Ireland, but chose Co. Sligo (p. 735) for his gravesite. Oh, and **Salman Rushdie** has come out of hiding, but we don't know where he is. London, apparently.

A SPORTS FAN'S PARADISE

Football (soccer, if you must) fanaticism is everywhere: the Queen Mum is an Arsenal fan and Salman Rushdie guns for Tottenham. At the **football grounds** (p. 139) around London, become a gunner for a day at Highbury, cheer the Spurs at White Hart Lane, or follow the rich kids in Chelsea. Then head up to **Old Trafford** (p. 339),

Manchester United's grounds on Sir Matt Busby Way, named after their legendary football manager, or go west to the grounds of bitter rivals **Everton** and **Liverpool** (p. 332). **Rugby** scrums take place in the **Millennium Stadium,** Cardiff (p. 428). Discouraged by the terrace yobs and the mud? **Cricket** is altogether more refined—watch the men in white at London's **Lords** grounds (p. 140). **Tennis,** too, demands a more genteel conduct, and the strawberries and cream at **Wimbledon** (p. 140) are a perfect example, especially when the English rain holds off.

But you want to join in, eh? The surf is up all along the Atlantic coast at **Newquay** (p. 243), **St. Ives** (p. 245), and **Lewis** (p. 603). Go canyoning or whitewater rafting at **Fort William** (p. 590), or try the more sedate punting in **Oxford** (p. 249) or **Cambridge** (p. 297). Try **Snowdonia National Park** (p. 467) for hiking. And of course, every national park has its mountain bike rental stores, and any town worth its boots will see kickabouts taking place—go forth, young traveler, and seek your game.

FESTIVALS

Festivals pepper the British calendar. The **Edinburgh International Festival** (p. 514) brings to Scotland's capital a cornucopia of performances, from top-class theater to the experimental work of the Fringe. **Mardi Gras** (p. 339) in Manchester's Gay Village is a party and a half, as is the **Glastonbury Festival** (p. 211)—if you can get tickets and if it doesn't get muddy. London's Chinatown erupts in celebration during the **Chinese New Year festival** (p. 113). The **Royal National Eisteddfod** in Llangollen, Wales (p. 486), continues the Welsh bardic tradition.

In the warmer months, virtually every small village in Ireland finds reason to gather its sheep for show, pull pints, and tune its fiddles. Joycean scholars take part on an 18-hour ramble through Dublin's streets every year on June 16, **Bloomsday** (p. 687). In late April, Galway gathers international bards for its **Poetry and Literature Festival** (p. 729). Around August, every set in Ireland tunes in to the nationally televised **Rose of Tralee Festival and Pageant** (p. 715).

▨ LET'S GO PICKS

BEST BIG LUMPS OF STONE One of the world's geological marvels, the **Giant's Causeway** (p. 651) towers in Northern Ireland. The **Callanish Stones** (p. 605), dumped on the Isle of Lewis by prehistoric people, are less overrun than Stonehenge. **Avebury** (p. 197) is a whole damn village of the humongous rocks—how the hell did they carry those things?

BEST SUNSETS The walled Welsh city of **Caernarfon** (p. 473) sits on the water, ready to sail to the western horizon. In Ireland, Yeats still can't get enough of the views from **Drumcliff** (p. 737) towards Benbulben. The extreme northern location of the **Shetlands** (p. 624) makes for breathtaking skies.

BEST BEACHES Newquay (p. 243), on the dazzling Cornwall coast, is a bizarre amalgam of Californian surfer dude and Cornish staid dowager. Or try Provence-esque **Tenby** (p. 445), in southwest Wales, for a more serene experience. Unspoiled, deserted white beaches line Ireland's **Inishowen Peninsula** (p. 743).

BEST PUB CRAWLS Tradition mandates a pub crawl in **Edinburgh** (p. 498); troop down the **Royal Mile,** or muster up the stamina for the **Rose St.** stumble. If the blonde in the black skirt is your drink of choice, the pubs of **Dublin's Grafton St.** (p. 684), not to mention of all Ireland, serve up copious pints of Guinness.

BEST NIGHTLIFE SCENES Home of the Beatles, **Liverpool** (p. 333) comes together every night, especially at top club Cream. Students take over pretty much all of **Newcastle** (p. 403)—there's not much else to do there anyway. **Manchester's Gay Village** (p. 340) is a great place even if you're straight. And **London** (p. 142) has the odd club, too.

BEST QUIRKY MUSEUMS A collection of antiquities and architectural marvels, **Sir John Soane's Museum** (p. 133) is worth a look. Not strictly quirky, but decidedly different, is Sheffield's **National Centre for Pop Music** (p. 374), an interactive paean to the joys of pop, rock, dance, and other incarnations of modern music.

SUGGESTED ITINERARIES

THE BEST OF BRITAIN AND IRELAND (1 MONTH) In **London** (4 days; p. 88), you'll spin around from museums to theater to a quiet pint to clubbing all in the space of a day. Next is **Oxford** (2 days; p. 249), for the University and Blenheim Palace, and **Stratford-upon-Avon** (1 day; p. 262), Shakespeare's hometown. On to **Liverpool** (2 days; p. 328), home of the Beatles; or **Conwy** and **Caernarfon** (2 days; p. 473) for the grand Welsh castles, then to the ferry port of Holyhead (p. 479). Cross from there to **Dublin** (3 days; p. 667), home to Joyce and Guinness. Don't forget a day-trip to the **Wicklow Mountains** (p. 691). **Cork** (1 day; p. 703) offers the diversions of a university town. Rural Ireland calls? Answer the **Ring of Kerry** (1 day; p. 711) then. **Galway** (1½ days; p. 725), a center of Irish culture, is also close to the **Cliffs of Moher** and the moon-like **Burren** (p. 722). **Donegal** (1½ days; p. 737) serves as a base to see Slieve League, Europe's highest sea cliffs. Enter Northern Ireland through boisterous **Derry** (1 day; p. 652), enjoy the gorgeous scenery of **Giant's Causeway** (1 day; p. 651), and head for politically-divided and exciting **Belfast** (2 days; p. 636). Then back across the Irish Sea to Stranraer (p. 527), where a train leads to **Glasgow** (1 day; p. 529) and nearby **Loch Lomond** (p. 548). The **Isle of Mull** (1 day; p. 567) offers rural diversions, and you'll need the rest before you enter stately **Edinburgh** (3 days; p. 498). The **Lake District** (2 days; p. 356) holds scenic diversions; historic **York** (1 day; p. 385) and **Cambridge** (1 day; p. 297) complete the southbound journey. Time left? Take a trip to see the stunning cathedral of **Ely** (p. 309). And back to London to kick back, maybe with a West End play.

ENGLAND (3 WEEKS) All-encompassing England, simultaneously urban and pastoral, modern and traditional, offers highlight after highlight. Start in **London** (4 days; p. 88), the huge cosmopolitan center of everything in England and arguably the world—culture, nightlife, this city has it all. Head south to **Brighton** (2 days; p. 162), with its pumping nightlife by the sea. **Salisbury** (2 days; p. 192) offers a magnificent cathedral and is a good base for exploring the stone circles at **Stonehenge** (p. 196) or the less-visited **Avebury** (p. 197). For even more rustic charm, head west to **Dartmoor** (1 day; p. 225) or **Bodmin Moor** (1 day; p. 234), countryside areas long immortalized in literature. **Newquay** (1 day; p. 243) offers an incongruous slice of surfer culture. Return back north through **Bath** (1 day; p. 198) and villages in the **Cotswolds** (1 day; p. 272). Head on to **Oxford** (2 days; p. 249), which holds the University, as well as beautiful Blenheim Palace. Catch a play at **Stratford-upon-Avon** (1 day; p. 262), Shakespeare's hometown. After you've checked out the Bard's former lodgings, make a day-trip to breathtaking **Warwick Castle** (1 day; p. 267). The northern cities have their charms, too; **Liverpool** (2 days; p. 328) has Beatles sites, plus exuberant nightlife. Partied too hard? Go north to the **Lake District** (2 days; p. 356), which admittedly is where all tourists go. Still, there's space for everyone if you look. Continue northeast to **Hadrian's Wall** (p. 410) before making your way back south to **York** (1 day; p. 385); a city for history buffs, with preserved city walls and England's largest Gothic cathedral. **Sheffield** (1 day; p. 372) features the hip National Centre for Popular Music. Heading south, punt next to the University of **Cambridge** (2 days; p. 297). A quick train ride brings you back to London.

SCOTLAND (2 WEEKS) Not just men in kilts, Scotland combines remote romantic glens and islands with lively cities. **Edinburgh** (4 days; p. 498) has an amazing Festival in August, and it's festive year-round, with the historic Royal Mile and unbeatable pubs. Then westward ho to its rival, **Glasgow** (2 days; p. 529), which holds fabulous museums and hip nightlife, and allows a daytrip to the bonnie bonnie banks of **Loch Lomond** (p. 548). From Glasgow, a trip to the **Isle of Skye** (2 days; p. 596), through Mallaig, is worth the

Suggested Itineraries

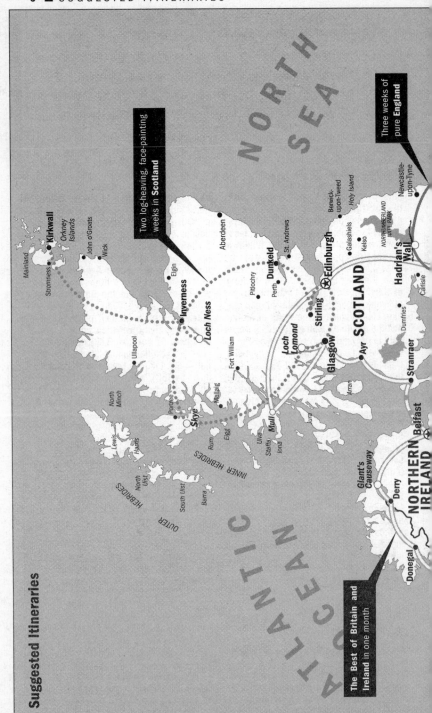

Two log-heaving, face-painting weeks in **Scotland**

Three weeks of pure **England**

The Best of **Britain and Ireland** in one month

NORTH SEA

ATLANTIC OCEAN

Orkney Islands
Kirkwall
Mainland
Stronness

John o'Groats
Wick

Elgin
Inverness
Loch Ness
Aberdeen

Ullapool

North Minch

Fort William
Mallaig
Portree
Skye

Lewis
Harris
North Uist
South Uist
Barra

OUTER HEBRIDES

INNER HEBRIDES
Rum
Eigg
Uva
Staffa
Iona
Mull
Jura

Pitlochry
Perth
Dunkeld
St. Andrews
Stirling
Loch Lomond
Glasgow
SCOTLAND
Ayr
Arran
Stranraer
Dumfries

Edinburgh
Galashiels
Kelso
Berwick-upon-Tweed
Holy Island
Newcastle-upon-Tyne
NORTHUMBERLAND NAT'L PARK
Hadrian's Wall
Carlisle

Giant's Causeway
Derry
NORTHERN IRELAND
Belfast
Donegal

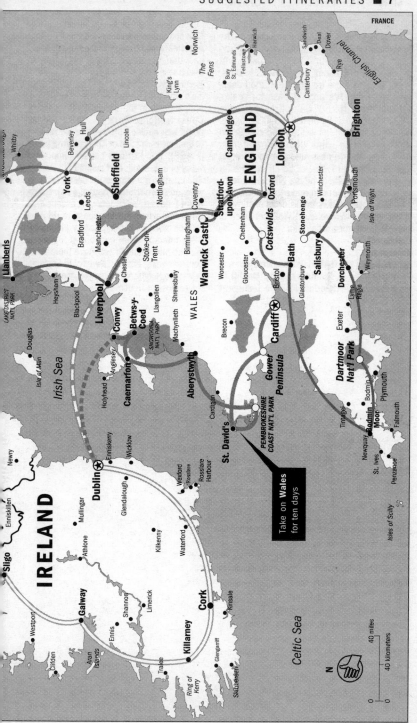

FRANCE

English Channel

Sandwich
Deal
Dover
Rye

Norwich

The Fens

Bury St. Edmunds

Harwich
Felixstowe

Canterbury

King's Lynn

Brighton

Beverley
Hull

ENGLAND

Cambridge

London ✪

Portsmouth

Isle of Wight

Whitby

York

Lincoln

Leeds

Sheffield

Nottingham

Coventry

Oxford

Winchester

Llanberis

Bradford

Manchester

Stoke-on-Trent

Birmingham

Stratford-upon-Avon

Cheltenham

Cotswolds ○

Stonehenge

LAKE DISTRICT NAT'L PARK

Chester

Shrewsbury

Warwick Castle

Worcester

Gloucester

Bath

Salisbury

Dorchester

Weymouth

Heysham

Blackpool

Liverpool

Conwy

Betws-y-Coed

Llangollen

Machynlleth

WALES

Bristol

Glastonbury

Lyme Regis

Exeter

Irish Sea

Holyhead

Anglesey

SNOWDONIA NAT'L PARK

Caernarfon

Brecon

Cardiff ✪

Dartmoor Nat'l Park

Isle of Man

Douglas

Aberystwyth

Cardigan

Gower Peninsula ○

St. David's

PEMBROKESHIRE COAST NAT'L PARK

Bodmin

Plymouth

Tintagel

Bodmin Moor

Newry

Enniskillen

Enniskerry

Dublin ✪

Wicklow

Wexford

Rosslare

Rosslare Harbour

Newquay

St. Ives

Penzance

Falmouth

Take on **Wales** for ten days

Sligo

IRELAND

Mullingar

Athlone

Glendalough

Kilkenny

Waterford

Isles of Scilly

Westport

Clifden

Galway

Shannon

Ennis

Limerick

Celtic Sea

Tralee

Killarney

Ring of Kerry

Glengarriff

Skibbereen

Kinsale

Cork

Aran Islands

N

40 miles

40 kilometers

0
0

effort for a dramatic view of the Cuillins. Or choose one of the other islands in the **Hebrides** (including Mull, Lewis, and Harris). Continue north to the remote and beautiful Highlands. **Inverness** (1½ days; p. 583) is more transport hub than destination, but it's a good base for seeing **Loch Ness** (p. 587). The **Orkney Islands** (2 days; p. 618) offer Kirkwall's magnificent cathedral, as well as traces of Stone Age, Pictish, and Viking inhabitants. Return via Inverness, and stop by **Dunkeld** and **Birnam** (1 day; p. 557), which offer splendid views, or by the **Fife Seaside** (1 day; p. 554) for sun and seafood. **Stirling** (1 day; p. 545) is proud of its castle and of William "Braveheart" Wallace. Back to Edinburgh for a wee dram.

WALES (10 DAYS) Wales offers acres of remarkable undisturbed country. **Cardiff** (2 days; p. 423), capital of the resurgent nation, has impressive castles nearby. The **Gower Peninsula** (1 day; p. 444) offers beaches while nearby **Swansea** (p. 441) has students and nightlife. On to **Tenby,** beach resort town with flair (1 day; p. 445). Magical **St. David's** (1 day; p. 452), Britain's smallest city, has an impressive cathedral; it's also in the scenic **Pembrokeshire Coast National Park** (p. 448). Farther north, kick back on the seaside promenade of the university town of **Aberystwyth** (1 day; p. 456). Tiny **Harlech** boasts panoramic views of sea, sand, and summits (1 day; p. 461). On to the impressive castle and city walls of **Caernarfon** (1 day; p. 473). **Llanberis** (1 day; p. 470) lets you ascend **Mt. Snowdon**, whether you choose to do it by foot or by train. Finally, **Conwy** (1 day; p. 480) offers another castle and a bevy of curious attractions. If you have more time, consider going east to Liverpool in England, or west to **Holyhead,** where you can take the ferry across to Dublin.

ESSENTIALS

DOCUMENTS AND FORMALITIES

CONSULAR SERVICES

ENTRANCE REQUIREMENTS

Passport (p. 11). All foreign nationals need a passport to travel into Britain or Ireland, though EU citizens may not have them checked.

Visa (p. 12). Citizens of the US, Australia, New Zealand, South Africa, and many other western countries do not need visas to enter Britain or Ireland. If you are unsure, call your local embassy or complete an online enquiry form at www.visa.fco.gov.uk.

Inoculations: No inoculations are necessary for visiting Britain or Ireland.

Work and Study Permits (p. 12). Work or study permits are required for all non-EU citizens planning to work or study in either Britain or Ireland.

Driving Permit (p. 43). A valid foreign driver's license or an International Driving Permit is required for all those planning to drive.

UK EMBASSIES AND CONSULATES ABROAD

For addresses of British embassies in countries not listed here, check with the **Foreign and Commonwealth Office** (☎ (020) 7238 4503; www.fco.gov.uk/directory/posts.asp), or check your local telephone directory. Some large cities (e.g. New York) have a local British consulate, which can handle most of the same functions as an embassy.

Australia: British High Commission, Commonwealth Ave., Yarralumla, Canberra, ACT 2600 (☎ (02) 6270 6666; fax (02) 6273 3236; www.uk.emb.gov.au). Consulate-General, Level 10, SAP House, Canberra Center, Canberra, ACT 2601 (☎ (19) 0294 1555). Consulates-General in Brisbane, Melbourne, Perth, and Sydney; Consulate in Adelaide.

Canada: British High Commission, 80 Elgin St., Ottawa, K1P 5K7 (☎ (613) 237-1530; www.britain-in-canada.org). British Consulate-General, 777 Bay St., Suite 2800, Toronto, Ont. M5G 2G2 (☎ (416) 593-1290). Consulates-General also in Montreal and Vancouver; Consulates in Halifax, St. John's, Quebec City, and Winnipeg.

France: British Embassy, 35 Rue du Faubourg-St-Honoré, 75383 Paris CEDEX 08 (☎ 01 44 51 31 00; www.amb-grandebretagne.fr); British Consulate-General, 18 bis rue d'Anjou, 75008 Paris (☎ 01 44 51 31 02). Consulates-General also in Bordeaux, Lille, Lyon, and Marseille.

Ireland: British Embassy, 29 Merrion Rd., Ballsbridge, Dublin 4 (☎ (01) 205 3700; www.britishembassy.ie).

New Zealand: British High Commission, 44 Hill St., Thorndon, Wellington 1 (☎ (04) 472 6049; www.brithighcomm.org.nz). Consulate-General, 17th floor, Fay Richwhite Building, 151 Queen St., Auckland 1 (☎ (09) 303 2973).

South Africa: British High Commission, 91 Parliament St., Cape Town 8001 (☎ (021) 461 7220); also at 255 Hill St., Arcadia 0083, Pretoria (☎ (012) 483 1200; www.britain.org.za). Consulates-General in Johannesburg and Cape Town; Consulates in Port Elizabeth and Durban.

US: British Embassy, 3100 Massachusetts Ave. NW, Washington, D.C. 20008 (☎ (202) 588-6500; www.britainusa.com/bis/embassy/embassy.stm). Consulate-General, 845 3rd Ave., New York, NY 10022 (☎ (212) 745-0200). Other Consulates-

General in Atlanta, Boston, Chicago, Houston, Los Angeles, and San Francisco. Consulates in Anchorage, Dallas, Kansas City, Miami, Minneapolis, Nashville, New Orleans, Phoenix, Pittsburgh, Portland, Salt Lake City, San Diego, Seattle, St. Louis, and Puerto Rico.

IRISH EMBASSIES AND CONSULATES ABROAD

Australia: Irish Embassy, 20 Arkana St., Yarralumla ACT 2615 (☎ (00612) 6273 3022).

Canada: Irish Embassy, Suite 1105, 130 Albert St., Ottawa, Ont. K1P 5G4 (☎ (613) 233-6281; emb.ireland@sympatico.ca).

France: Irish Embassy, 12 Avenue Foch, 75116 Paris (☎ 01 44 17 67 60).

New Zealand: Consulate-General, Dingwall Bldg., 2nd Fl., 87 Queen St., P.O. Box 279, Auckland 1 (☎ (09) 302 2867).

South Africa: Irish Embassy, Delheim Suite, Tulbagh Center, 1234 Church St., Colbyn 0083, Pretoria (☎ (012) 342 5062).

UK: 17 Grosvenor Pl., London SW1X 7HR (☎ (020) 7235 2171).

US: Irish Embassy, 2234 Massachusetts Ave. NW, Washington, D.C. 20008 (☎ (202) 462-3939; www.irelandemb.org). Consulate, 345 Park Ave., 17th floor, New York, NY 10154 (☎ (212) 319-2555). Other Consulates in Chicago, San Francisco, and Boston.

EMBASSIES AND CONSULATES IN THE UK

Australia: Australian Embassy, Australia House, The Strand, London WC2B 4LA (☎ (020) 7379 4334; www.australia.org.uk).

Canada: Canada House, Trafalgar Sq. #5, London SW1Y 5BJ (☎ (020) 7258 6600).

France: French Embassy, 58 Knightsbridge, London SW1X 7JT (☎ (020) 7201 1000); Consulate-General, 6A Cromwell Pl., London SW7 2EW (☎ (020) 7838 2000; www.ambafrance.org.uk).

Ireland: See **Irish Embassies and Consulates Abroad,** above.

New Zealand: New Zealand High Commission (consular section), New Zealand House, 80 Haymarket, London SW1Y 4TQ (☎ (020) 7930 8422; www.newzealandhc.org.uk).

South Africa: South African High Commission (consular section), 15 Whitehall, London SW1A 2DD (☎ (020) 7925 8900; www.southafricahouse.com).

US: American Embassy, 24 Grosvenor Sq., London W1A 1AE (☎ (020) 7499 9000; www.usembassy.org.uk). Consulates in **Scotland** at 3 Regent Terrace, Edinburgh EH7 5BW (☎ (0131) 556 8315), and in **Northern Ireland** at Queens House, 14 Queens St., Belfast BT1 6EQ (☎ (028) 9032 8239).

EMBASSIES AND CONSULATES IN IRELAND

Australia: Australian Embassy, Fitzwilton House, 2nd fl., Wilton Terr., Dublin 2 (☎ (01) 676 1517).

Canada: Canadian Embassy, Canada House, 65/68 St. Stephens Green, Dublin 2 (☎ (01) 478 1988).

France: French Embassy, 36 Ailesbury Rd., Dublin 4 (☎ (01) 260 1666).

New Zealand: Consulate-General, 37 Leeson Park, Dublin 6 (☎ (01) 660 4233; fax 660 4228).

South Africa: South African Embassy, Alexandra House, 2nd fl., Earlsfort Terr., Dublin 2 (☎ (01) 661 5553).

UK: See **UK Embassies and Consulates Abroad,** above.

US: American Embassy, 42 Elgin Rd., Ballsbridge, Dublin 4 (☎ (01) 668 7122; after hours ☎ (01) 668 9612).

PASSPORTS

REQUIREMENTS. Citizens of all countries need valid passports to enter Britain and/or Ireland and to re-enter their own country. EU citizens (including Irish visitors to Britain and vice-versa) should carry their passports, even though they will probably not be checked upon entry. Depending on your nationality, you may be prevented from entering either country if you have less than six months left before your passport expires; check with your local consulate or embassy. Arriving home with an expired passport is always illegal, and may result in a fine.

PHOTOCOPIES. Be sure to photocopy the page of your passport with your photo, passport number, and other identifying information, as well as any visas, travel insurance policies, plane tickets, or traveler's check serial numbers. Carry one set of copies in a safe place, apart from the originals, and leave another set at home. Consulates also recommend that you carry an expired passport or an official copy of your birth certificate in a part of your baggage separate from other documents.

LOST PASSPORTS. If you lose your passport, immediately notify the local police and the nearest embassy or consulate of your home government. To expedite its replacement, you will need to know all information previously recorded and show identification and proof of citizenship. In some cases, a replacement may take weeks to process, and may be valid only for a limited time. Any visas stamped in your old passport will be irretrievably lost. In an emergency, ask your embassy for immediate temporary traveling papers that will permit you to re-enter your home country. Your passport is a public document belonging to your nation's government. You may have to surrender it to a foreign government official, but if you don't get it back in a reasonable amount of time, inform the nearest mission of your home country.

NEW PASSPORTS. File any new passport or renewal applications well in advance of your departure date. Most passport offices offer rush services for a steep fee. Citizens living abroad who need a passport or renewal should contact the nearest consular service of their home country.

Australia: Info ☎ 13 12 32; passports.australia@dfat.gov.au; www.dfat.gov.au/passports. Apply for a passport at a post office, passport office (in Adelaide, Brisbane, Canberra, Darwin, Hobart, Melbourne, Newcastle, Perth, or Sydney), or overseas diplomatic mission. Passports AUS$128 (32-page) or AUS$192 (64-page); valid for 10 years. Children AUS$64 (32-page) or AUS$96 (64-page); valid for 5 years.

Canada: Canadian Passport Office, Department of Foreign Affairs and International Trade, Ottawa, ON K1A 0G3 (☎ (613) 994 3500 or (800) 567 6868; www.dfait-maeci.gc.ca/passport). Applications available at passport offices, Canadian missions, and post offices. Passports CDN$60; valid for 5 years (non-renewable).

Ireland: Pick up an application at a *Garda* station or post office, or request one from a passport office. Then apply by mail to the Department of Foreign Affairs, Passport Office, Molesworth St., Dublin 2 (☎ (01) 671 1633; fax 671 1092; www.irlgov.ie/iveagh), or the Passport Office, Irish Life Building, 1A South Mall, Cork (☎ (021) 27 25 25). Passports IR£45; valid for 10 years. Under 18 or over 65 IR£10; valid for 3 years.

New Zealand: Send applications to the Passport Office, Department of International Affairs, P.O. Box 10526, Wellington, New Zealand (☎ (0800) 22 50 50 or (4) 474 8100; fax (4) 474 8010; www.passports.govt.nz; email passports@dia.govt.nz). Standard processing time is 10 working days. Passports NZ$80; valid for 10 years. Children NZ$40; valid for 5 years. 3 day "urgent service" NZ$160; children NZ $120.

South Africa: Department of Home Affairs. Passports are issued only in Pretoria, but all applications must still be submitted or forwarded to the nearest South African consulate. Processing time is 3 months or more. Passports around SAR80; valid for 10 years. Under 16 around SAR60; valid for 5 years. For more information, check out http://usaembassy.southafrica.net/VisaForms/Passport/Passport2000.html.

ESSENTIALS

UK: Info ☎ (0870) 521 0410; www.ukpa.gov.uk. Get an application from a passport office, main post office, travel agent, or online (for UK residents only) at www.ukpa.gov.uk/forms/f_app_pack.htm. Then apply by mail to or in person at one of the passport offices, located in London, Liverpool, Newport, Peterborough, Glasgow, or Belfast. Passports UK£28; valid for 10 years. Under 15 UK£14.80; valid for 5 years. The process takes about 4 weeks; faster service (by personal visit to the offices listed above) costs an additional £12.

US: Info ☎ (202) 647-0518; www.travel.state.gov/passport_services.html. Apply at any federal or state courthouse, authorized post office, or US Passport Agency (in most major cities); see the "US Government, State Department" section of the telephone book or a post office for addresses. Processing takes 3-4 weeks. New passports US$60; valid for 10 years. Under 15 US$40; valid for 5 years. Passports may be renewed by mail or in person for US$40. Add US$35 for 3-day expedited service.

VISAS AND PERMITS

VISAS. EU citizens do not need a visa to enter Britain or Ireland. For visits of less than six months, citizens of Australia, Canada, New Zealand, South Africa, and the US do not need a visa; neither do citizens of Iceland, Israel, Japan, Malaysia, Mexico, Norway, Singapore, Switzerland, and some Eastern European, Caribbean and Pacific countries. Citizens of most other countries need a visa to enter Britain and Ireland. Tourist visas cost £33 for a one-time pass and allow you to spend up to six months in the UK. Visas can be purchased from your nearest British consulate. US citizens can take advantage of the **Center for International Business and Travel** (CIBT; ☎ (800) 925-2428), which secures visas for travel to almost all countries for a variable service charge. If you need a **visa extension** while in the UK, contact the Home Office, Immigration and Nationality Department (☎ (020) 8686 0688).

WORK PERMITS. Admission as a visitor does not include the right to work, which is authorized only by a work permit. Entering Britain or Ireland to study requires a special visa. For more information, see **Alternatives to Tourism,** p. 61.

IDENTIFICATION

When you travel, always carry two or more forms of identification on your person, including at least one photo ID; a passport combined with a driver's license or birth certificate is usually adequate. Many establishments, especially banks, may require several IDs in order to cash traveler's checks. Never carry all your forms of ID together; split them up in case of theft or loss. It is useful to bring extra passport-size photos to affix to the various IDs or passes you may acquire along the way. Most central London Tube stations have photo booths (£2.50 for four photos).

STUDENT AND TEACHER IDENTIFICATION. The **International Student Identity Card (ISIC),** the most widely accepted form of student ID, provides discounts on sights, accommodations, food, and transport. ISIC cards are preferable to institution-specific cards (such as a University ID) because tourism personnel in Britain and Ireland are instructed to recognize the former. All cardholders have access to a 24hr. emergency helpline for medical, legal, and financial emergencies (in the UK and elsewhere call London collect ☎ (020) 8666 9025), and US cardholders are also eligible for insurance benefits (see **Insurance,** p. 26). Many student travel agencies issue ISICs, including Campus Travel and STA Travel in the UK; they are also issued on the web (www.counciltravel.com/idcards/index.htm). The card is valid from September of one year to December of the following year and costs £5, AUS$15, CDN$15, or US$20. Applicants must be degree-seeking students of a secondary or post-secondary school and must be of at least 12 years of age. Because of the proliferation of fake ISICs, some services (particularly airlines) require additional proof of student identity, such as a school ID or a letter attesting to your student status, signed by your registrar and stamped with your school seal. The **International Teacher Identity Card**

(ITIC) offers the same insurance coverage as well as similar but limited discounts. The fee is £5, AUS$13, or US$20. For more info, contact the **International Student Travel Confederation (ISTC)**, Herengracht 479, 1017 BS Amsterdam, Netherlands (☎ +31 (20) 421 28 00; fax 421 28 10; istcinfo@istc.org; www.istc.org).

YOUTH IDENTIFICATION. The International Student Travel Confederation issues a discount card to travelers who are 26 years old or under, but are not students. This one-year **International Youth Travel Card (IYTC)** offers many of the same benefits as the ISIC. Most organizations that sell the ISIC also sell the IYTC (US$20).

TOURIST SERVICES

ABOUT BRITAIN

BRITISH TOURIST AUTHORITY (BTA). The BTA (www.visitbritain.com) is an umbrella organization coordinating the activities of the four separate UK tourist boards outside the UK; it also sells the **Great British Heritage Pass** (p. 14). In addition to those listed below, the BTA has many branches in Western Europe and throughout the rest of the world.

> **Australia:** Level 16, Gateway, 1 Macquarie Pl., Circular Quay, Sydney NSW 2000 (☎ (02) 9377 4400; www.visitbritain.com/au).
>
> **Canada:** Air Transat Bldg., 5915 Airport Rd., Suite 120, Mississauga, Ont. L4V 1T1 (☎ (888) 847-4885 or (905) 405-1840; www.visitbritain.com/ca).
>
> **Ireland:** 18-19 College Green, Dublin 2 (☎ (02) 670 8000).
>
> **New Zealand:** 17th Fl., Fay Richwhite Building, 151 Queen Street, Auckland 1 (☎ (09) 303 1446).
>
> **South Africa:** Lancaster Gate, Hyde Park Ln., Hyde Park, Sandton 2196 (☎ (011) 325 0343).
>
> **US:** 551 Fifth Ave. #701, New York, NY 10176 (☎ (800) 462-2748 or (212) 986-2200; www.travelbritain.com).

WITHIN THE UK. The Scottish, Welsh, Northern Irish, and Irish tourist boards all have additional locations at the Britain Visitor Centre (see English Board below).

> **English Tourist Board**, Britain Visitor Centre, 1 Regent St., Piccadilly Circus, London SW1 4XT (www.travelengland.org.uk).
>
> **Scottish Tourist Board**, 23 Ravelston Terr., Edinburgh EH4 3EU (☎ (0131) 332 2433; www.holiday.scotland.net).
>
> **Welsh Tourist Board**, Brunel House, 2 Fitzalan Rd., Cardiff CF24 0UY (☎ (029) 2049 9909; www.visitwales.com).
>
> **Northern Ireland Tourist Board**, 59 North St., Belfast BT1 1NB (☎ (028) 9024 6609; www.ni-tourism.com).

ABOUT IRELAND

IRISH TOURIST BOARD (BORD FÁILTE). Bord Fáilte (bored FAHL-tshah; UK ☎ (020) 7493 3201; from rest of world ☎ +353 (01) 666 1258; www.ireland.travel.ie). The head office is at Baggot St. Bridge, Dublin 2 (☎ (01850) 230 330).

> **Australia:** Level 5, 36 Carrington St., Sydney NSW 2000 (☎ (02) 9299 6177; fax 9299 6323).
>
> **Canada:** 2 Bloor St. W., Toronto, ON M4W 3E2 (☎ (416) 925-6368; fax 961-2175).
>
> **New Zealand:** Dingwall Building, 87 Queen St., Auckland (☎ (09) 379 3708; fax 302 2420).

South Africa: Everite House, 20 De Korte St., Braamfontein, Johannesburg (☎ (011) 339 4865; fax 339 2474).

UK: 150 New Bond St., London W1Y 0AQ (☎ (020) 7493 3201; fax 7493 9065).

US: 345 Park Ave., New York, NY 10154 (☎ (800) 223-6470, ☎ (212) 418-0800; fax (212) 371-9052; www.irelandvacations.com).

SIGHTS

Most sights in Britain and Ireland list **concession** prices among their admission prices; these are usually the prices for students, seniors (called Old Age Pensioners, "OAPs"), the disabled, and children (although children often have an even lower rate). *Let's Go* lists "concessions" when visitors in all those categories are charged the same reduced price. Often, the last admission into many sights is 30 minutes before the listed closing time; *Let's Go* notes unusually early last admissions. Sites listing "summer" hours are usually referring to tourist **high season**, normally from Easter to September or October. These date ranges often vary, especially in small towns. The organizations listed below run many of the major historical sights in Britain and Ireland; most sell **special passes** which save those intending to sight-hop a fair bit of money.

Cadw, The "Heritage in Wales" Membership Department, FREEPOST, CF1142/9, Cardiff CF1 1YW (☎ (0800) 0743121; main switchboard (029) 2050 0200). Runs many Welsh sights, including most of Edward I's grand castles. Yearly membership £24, seniors £16, youth (16-20) £15, under 16 £12, adult couple £40, family £42.

English Heritage, Fortress House, 23 Savile Row, London W1X 1AB (☎ (01793) 414910; www.english-heritage.org.uk). Sells an **Overseas Visitor Pass**, which lets you into any English Heritage sight. Seven-day pass £12.50, two adults £23.50, families £27.50. 14-day pass £16, two adults £30.50, families £35.

The Great British Heritage Pass is an extremely useful pass that gets you into all National Trust, English Heritage, Historic Scotland, and Cadw properties throughout Britain (7-day £32, US$54; 15-day £45, $75; month £60, $102). Purchase it at any British Tourist Authority office or at the Britain Visitor Centre (p. 13).

Historic Scotland, Longmore House, Salisbury Pl., Edinburgh EH9 1SH (☎ (0131) 668 8600; www.historic-scotland.gov.uk) runs many sights in Scotland, including Edinburgh Castle. The Scottish Short Break and Explorer tickets, available at any of their sights or at Scottish tourist information centres, gives access to all their attractions. Three-day ticket £10, seniors and children £7.50, families £20; 7-day £15, £11 and £30; 14-day £20, £14 and £40.

The National Trust, National Trust Membership Department, P.O. Box 39, Bromley, Kent BR1 3XL (☎ (020) 8315 1111; www.nationaltrust.org.uk). Dedicated to preserving the countryside and historic homes in England, Wales, and Northern Ireland. The **National Trust for Scotland,** 28 Charlotte Sq., Edinburgh EH2 4ET (☎ (0131) 243 9300; www.nts.org.uk) maintains the countryside and properties north of the border. Members of either receive free entry to over 300 Trust sites. (Membership £30, ages 13-25 £15.) US and Canadian residents should contact **The Royal Oak Foundation,** 285 West Broadway #400, New York, NY 10013 (☎ (212) 966-6565; membership US$45; families US$70), the National Trust's North American membership branch.

CUSTOMS

ENTERING BRITAIN AND IRELAND

Upon entering Britain or Ireland, you must declare certain items from abroad and pay a duty on the value of those articles that exceed the allowance established by Her Majesty's Customs or by the Irish authorities. It is wise to make a list, including serial numbers, of any valuables that you carry with you from home; if you register this list with customs before your departure and have an official stamp it, you will avoid import duty charges and ensure an easy passage upon your return. Be especially careful to document items manufactured abroad. **Do not bring dogs, cats, or other pets into the United Kingdom or Ireland.** Strict anti-rabies laws mean that Fido will be kept in quarantine for 6 months. If you are arriving in Britain from a western European nation, however, and wish to bring along your pet, you may be able to avoid having to place the pet in quarantine by participating in the new **PETS** "pet passport" trial scheme. Provided you are able to have your pooch or feline friend microchipped, vaccinated, blood-tested, and certified against tapeworm and ticks six months before entering the UK, you should be able to avoid pet quarantine. Consult www.maff.gov.uk/animalh/quarantine for more details.

EUROPEAN CUSTOMS As well as freedom of movement of people within the European Union (except when crossing into the United Kingdom from anywhere other than Ireland!), travelers can also take advantage of the freedom of movement of goods. This means that there are no customs controls at internal EU borders, in this case at the Channel Tunnel or when arriving at British or Irish airports from another EU country (take the blue customs channel), and travelers are free to transport whatever legal substances they like as long as it is for their own personal (non-commercial) use—up to 800 cigarettes, 10L of spirits, 90L of wine (60L of sparkling wine), and 110L of beer. You should also be aware that **duty-free** was abolished on June 30, 1999 for travel between EU member states; however, travelers between the EU and the rest of the world still get a duty-free allowance when passing through customs.

LEAVING BRITAIN AND IRELAND

If you're leaving for a non-EU country, you can claim back any **Value Added Tax** paid (see p. 20). Keeping receipts for purchases made abroad will help establish values when you return. Upon returning home, you must declare all articles acquired abroad and pay a **duty** on the value of articles that exceed the allowance established by your country's customs service. Goods and gifts purchased at **duty-free** shops abroad are not exempt from duty or sales tax at your point of return; you must declare these items as well. "Duty-free" merely means that you need not pay a tax in the country of purchase. For more specific information on customs requirements, contact the following information centers:

Australia: Australian Customs National Information Line (in Australia call ☎ 1 300 363 263, from elsewhere call ☎ +61 (2) 6275 6666; www.customs.gov.au).

Canada: Canadian Customs, 2265 St. Laurent Blvd., Ottawa, ON K1G 4K3 (☎ (800) 461- 9999 (24hr.) or (613) 993-0534; www.ccra-adrc.gc.ca).

Ireland: Customs Information Office, Irish Life Centre, Lower Abbey St., Dublin 1 (☎ (01) 878 8811; fax 878 0836; taxes@revenue.iol.ie; www.revenue.ie/customs.htm).

New Zealand: New Zealand Customhouse, 17-21 Whitmore St., Box 2218, Wellington (☎ (04) 473 6099; fax 473 7370; www.customs.govt.nz).

South Africa: Commissioner for Customs and Excise, Private Bag X47, Pretoria 0001 (☎ (012) 314 9911; fax 328 6478; www.gov.za).

UK: Her Majesty's Customs and Excise, Passenger Enquiry Team, Wayfarer House, Great South West Road, Feltham, Middlesex TW14 8NP (☎ (020) 8910 3744; fax 8910 3933; www.hmce.gov.uk).

US: US Customs Service, 1330 Pennsylvania Ave. NW, Washington, D.C. 20229 (☎ (202) 354-1000; fax 354-1010; www.customs.gov).

ESSENTIALS

MONEY

Britain is expensive. Even if you stay in hostels and prepare your own food, you can still expect to spend anywhere from £15-30 per person per day, depending on where you choose to visit. Accommodations start at about £6 a night for a bed in a hostel in rural areas, or £13-14 per night in a B&B, while a basic sit-down meal at a pub costs about £5. London in particular is a budget-buster, with £25-35 a day being the bare minimum for accommodations, food, and transport, without even including the costs of visiting sights or going out at night. Don't let that daunt you, however. Bargains exist—top-quality theater, for example, is fairly inexpensive. In Ireland you can expect to spend about IR£20-30 a day.

CURRENCY AND EXCHANGE

Carrying **cash** with you is risky, even in a money belt, but necessary; foreign personal checks are never accepted and even traveler's checks may not be accepted in some locations. The **Pound Sterling** is the main unit of currency in the **United Kingdom,** including Northern Ireland. It is divided into 100 pence, issued in standard denominations of 1p, 2p, 5p, 10p, 20p, 50p, and £1 in coins, and £5, £10, £20, and £50 in notes. (Scotland uses a £1 note, and you may still see the discontinued £2 coin around.) Northern Ireland and Scotland have their own bank notes, which can be used interchangeably with English currency, though you may occasionally have difficulty using Scottish £1 notes outside Scotland, and Northern Irish notes are not generally accepted outside Northern Ireland. In the **Republic of Ireland,** the monetary unit is the **Irish pound** or "punt," which may share a similar name with its British counterpart but is not interchangeable. Resident of both nations refer to pounds as "bob" or "quid," as in "ten quid" (never "quids").

The currency chart below is based on August 2000 exchange rates between local currency and US dollars (US$), Canadian dollars (CDN$), British pounds (UK£), Irish pounds (IR£), Australian dollars (AUS$), New Zealand dollars (NZ$), South African Rand (SAR), and European Union euros (EUR€). Check a large newspaper or the web (try www.letsgo.com) for the latest exchange rates.

THE BRITISH POUND	£1 =
IR£1 = £0.77	= IR£1.29
US$1 = £0.67	= US$1.50
CDN$1 = £0.45	= CDN$2.22
AUS$1 = £0.39	= AUS$2.54
NZ$1 = £0.30	= NZ$3.32
SAR1 = £0.10	= SAR10.42
EUR€1 = £0.61	= EUR€1.64

THE IRISH POUND	IR£1 =
UK£1 = £1.29	= UK£0.77
US$1 = £0.86	= US$1.16
CDN$1 = £0.58	= CDN$1.72
AUS$1 = £0.51	= AUS$1.97
NZ$1 = £0.39	= NZ$2.57
SAR1 = £0.12	= SAR8.08
EUR€1 = £0.79	= EUR€1.27

As a rule, it's cheaper to convert money in Britain or Ireland than at home. However, you should bring enough foreign currency to last for the first 24 to 72 hours of a trip to avoid being penniless should you arrive after bank hours or on a holiday.

When changing money abroad, try to go only to banks or bureaux de change that have at most a 5% margin between their buy and sell prices. Since you lose money with every transaction, convert as much as you think prudence allows.

If you use traveler's checks or bills, carry some in small denominations (the equivalent of US$50 or less) for times when you are forced to exchange money at disadvantageous rates, but bring a range of denominations since charges may be levied per check cashed. Store your money in a variety of forms; ideally, you will at any given time be carrying cash, traveler's checks, and a cash and/or credit card.

TRAVELER'S CHECKS

Traveler's checks (**American Express, Thomas Cook,** and **Visa** are the most recognized) are one of the safest and least troublesome means of carrying funds. Several agencies and banks sell them for a small commission, though members of the American Automobile Association, and some banks and credit unions, can get American Express checks commission-free (see p. 43). Each agency provides refunds if your checks are lost or stolen, and many provide additional services, such as toll-free refund hotlines abroad, emergency messages, and stolen credit card assistance.

While traveling, keep check receipts and a record of which checks you've cashed separate from the checks themselves. Also leave a list of check numbers with someone at home. Never countersign checks until you're ready to cash them, and always bring your passport with you to cash them. If your checks are lost or stolen, immediately contact a refund center (of the company that issued your checks) to be reimbursed; they may require a police report verifying the loss or theft. Ask about toll-free refund hotlines and the location of refund centers when purchasing checks, and always carry emergency cash.

American Express: In Australia call ☎ (800) 251 902; in New Zealand ☎ (0800) 441 068; in the UK ☎ (0800) 521313; in the US and Canada ☎ (800) 221-7282. Elsewhere call the US collect ☎ +1 (801) 964-6665; www.aexp.com. Traveler's checks are available in British pounds as well as US dollars at 1-4% commission at AmEx offices and banks, commission-free at AAA offices (p. 43). *Cheques for Two* can be signed by either of 2 people traveling together.

Citicorp: In the US and Canada call ☎ (800) 645-6556; in Europe, the Middle East, or Africa call the UK ☎ +44 (20) 7508 7007; elsewhere call the US collect ☎ +1 (813) 623-1709. Traveler's checks available in 7 currencies at 1-2% commission. Call 24hr.

Thomas Cook MasterCard: In the US and Canada call ☎ (800) 223-7373; in the UK call ☎ (0800) 62 21 01; elsewhere call the UK collect ☎ +44 (1733) 31 89 50. Checks available in 13 currencies at 2% commission. Checks cashed commission-free.

Visa: In the US call ☎ (800) 227-6811; in the UK call ☎ (0800) 89 50 78; elsewhere call the UK collect ☎ +44 (1733) 31 89 49. Call for the location of their nearest office.

CREDIT CARDS

Credit cards are accepted in many businesses in Britain and Ireland. However, small establishments—including many B&Bs—will often either not accept them, or add a surcharge. Where they are accepted, credit cards offer superior exchange rates. Credit cards may also offer services such as insurance or emergency help, and are sometimes required to reserve hotel rooms or rental cars. **MasterCard** (a.k.a. **Access** in Britain) and **Visa** (a.k.a. **Barclaycard**) are widely accepted; **American Express** cards work at some cash machines, AmEx offices, and major airports.

Credit cards are also useful for **cash advances,** which allow you to withdraw pounds from associated banks and cash machines throughout Britain and Ireland instantly. However, transaction fees for all credit card advances (up to US$10 per advance, plus 2-3% extra on foreign transactions after conversion) tend to make credit cards a more costly way of withdrawing cash than cash machines or trav-

ESSENTIALS

Money From Home In Minutes.

If you're stuck for cash on your travels, don't panic. Millions of people trust Western Union to transfer money in minutes to 176 countries and over 78,000 locations worldwide. Our record of safety and reliability is second to none. For more information, call Western Union: USA 1-800-325-6000, Canada 1-800-235-0000. Wherever you are, you're never far from home.

www.westernunion.com

WESTERN | MONEY
UNION | TRANSFER

The fastest way to send money worldwide.

eler's checks. In an emergency, however, the transaction fee may prove worth the cost. To be eligible for an advance, you'll need to get a four-digit **Personal Identification Number (PIN)** from your credit card company (see **Cash Cards,** below). If you already have a PIN, check with the company to make sure it will work in Britain and/or Ireland; also ask about any foreign transaction fees that they may charge.

Visa: (US ☎ (800) 336-8472). Issued in cooperation with banks and other organizations. For lost cards, call ☎ (0800) 891725 in Britain or ☎ (1800) 558 002 in Ireland.

MasterCard: (US ☎ (800) 307-7309). Issued in cooperation with banks. For lost cards, call ☎ (0800) 964767 in Britain or ☎ (1800) 557 378 in Ireland.

American Express: (UK ☎ (01273) 620555; US ☎ (800) 843-2273). Annual fee of up to US$55. AmEx cardholders may cash personal checks at AmEx offices abroad and access an emergency medical and legal assistance hotline (24hr.; UK ☎ (012) 2266 5555, from Ireland call the UK at ☎ 00 44 12 2266 5555, elsewhere call US collect ☎ +1 (202) 554-2639). Members also enjoy American Express Travel Service benefits (including plane, hotel, and car rental reservation changes; baggage loss and flight insurance; mailgram and international cable services; and held mail).

CASH CARDS

Cash cards—called ATM cards in the USA—are widespread in both Britain and Ireland, and you can assume that all banks listed in *Let's Go* have 24hr. cash machines (sometimes called "cashpoints") outside unless otherwise stated. Depending on the system that your home bank uses, you can probably access your personal bank account from abroad. Cash machines get the same wholesale exchange rate as credit cards, but there is often a limit on the amount of money you can withdraw per day (around US$500), and computer networks sometimes fail. There is typically also a surcharge of US$1-5 per withdrawal. Be sure to memorize your PIN code in numeric form since machines elsewhere often don't have letters on their keys (see "Please Sir, May I Have Some More?" p. 20). Also, if your PIN is longer than four digits, ask your bank whether you need a new number.

The two major international money networks are **Cirrus** (US ☎ (800) 424-7787) and **PLUS** (US ☎ (800) 843-7587). The cash machines of all major British and Irish banks (including Barclays, HSBC, Lloyds TSB, National Westminster, Royal Bank of Scotland, Bank of Scotland, Allied Ireland Bank (AIB), and Ulster Bank) usually accept both networks. To locate cash machines in Britain and Ireland, call the above numbers, or consult www.visa.com/pd/atm or www.mastercard.com/atm.

Visa TravelMoney (for customer assistance call ☎ (0800) 963833 in Britain; ☎ (1800) 559345 in Ireland) is a system allowing you to access money from any Visa cash machine. You deposit an amount before you travel (plus a small administration fee), and you can withdraw up to that sum. The cards, which give you the same favorable exchange rate for withdrawals as a regular Visa, are especially useful if you plan to travel through many countries. Check with your local bank to see if it issues TravelMoney cards. **Road Cash** (US ☎ (877) 762-3227; www.roadcash.com) issues cards in the US with a minimum US$300 deposit.

GETTING MONEY FROM HOME

AMERICAN EXPRESS. Cardholders can withdraw cash from their checking accounts at any of AmEx's major offices and many representative offices (up to US$1000 every 21 days; no service charge, no interest). "Express Cash" withdrawals from any cash machine that takes AmEx in Britain and Ireland are automatically debited from the cardholder's checking account or line of credit. Green- card holders may withdraw up to US$1000 in any seven-day period (2% transaction fee; minimum US$2.50, maximum US$20). To enroll in Express Cash, cardmembers may call (800) 227-4669 in the US; elsewhere call US collect ☎ +1 (336) 668-5041. The AmEx national number in Britain is ☎ (0800) 521313 and in Ireland ☎ (1800) 626000.

ESSENTIALS

PLEASE SIR, MAY I HAVE SOME MORE? To use a cash or credit card to withdraw money from a cash machine in Europe, you must have a four-digit **Personal Identification Number (PIN)**. If your PIN is longer than four digits, ask your bank whether can just use the first four, or whether you'll need a new one. **Credit cards** in North America don't usually come with PINs, so if you intend to hit up cash machines in Europe with a credit card to get cash advances, call your credit card company before leaving to request one.

People with alphabetic, rather than numerical, PINs may also be thrown off by the lack of letters on European cash machines. The following handy chart gives the corresponding numbers to use: 1=QZ; 2=ABC; 3=DEF; 4=GHI; 5=JKL; 6=MNO; 7=PRS; 8=TUV; and 9= WXY. Note that if you mistakenly punch the wrong code into the machine three times, it will swallow your card for good.

WESTERN UNION. Travelers from the US, Canada, and the UK can wire money abroad through Western Union's international money transfer services. In the US, call ☎ (800) 325-6000; in Canada, ☎ (800) 235-0000; in the UK, ☎ (0800) 833833. The rates for sending cash are generally US$10-11 cheaper than with a credit card, and the money is usually available at the place you're sending it to within an hour. To locate the nearest Western Union location, consult www.westernunion.com.

US STATE DEPARTMENT (US CITIZENS ONLY). In dire emergencies only, the US State Department will forward money within hours to the nearest consular office, which will then disburse it according to instructions for a US$15 fee. Contact the Overseas Citizens Service, American Citizens Services, Consular Affairs, Room 4811, US Department of State, Washington, D.C. 20520 (☎ (202) 647-5225; nights, Sundays, and holidays 647-4000; http://travel.state.gov).

TIPPING AND BARGAINING

Tips in restaurants are usually included in the bill (sometimes as a "service charge"), but check; if gratuity is not included, you should tip 10-15%. Tipping the barman in pubs is not at all expected and almost never done, though a waiter or waitress should be tipped. Tour guides and theater ushers are also rarely tipped. Taxi drivers should receive a 10% tip, and bellhops and chambermaids usually expect somewhere between £1 and £3.

If you're at an outdoor market, bargaining is sometimes acceptable. A general rule is that if there is a price tag, don't bargain, but if there is no indication of price then bartering is fair game. Don't expect to barter anywhere else.

TAXES

Both Britain and Ireland have a 17.5% **Value Added Tax (VAT),** a sales tax applied to everything except food, books, medicine, and children's clothing. The tax is **included** within the price indicated on the price tag—no extra expenses should be added at the register. The prices stated in *Let's Go* include VAT unless otherwise specified. Non-EU citizens can reclaim VAT through the **Retail Export Scheme** upon exiting Britain, though this is a complex procedure only worth doing for large purchases. Not all shops participate in the scheme, and of those that do, many have a purchase minimum of £50 before they will offer refunds. An administrative fee will often be deducted from your refund. Shops that do give refunds will fill out a form, which must be presented with the goods and receipts to customs upon departure (look for the TaxFree Refund desk at the airport). At peak hours, this additional process can take as long as an hour, so plan accordingly. Once you have checked in and passed security, you may receive your refund directly. To obtain the refund by check or credit card, send the form (stamped by customs) back in the envelope provided; the shopkeeper will then credit your refund. You must leave the country within three months of your purchase in order to claim a VAT refund, but you cannot receive a refund unless you apply for it before leaving the UK. You cannot receive a refund on accommodations and meals.

SAFETY AND SECURITY

 The **national emergency number** in both Britain and Ireland for police, ambulance, fire, and (in appropriate areas) coastguard and mountain rescue services is **999**. The **112** EU-wide number will also work.

If you keep your wits about you, traveling in Britain and Ireland is considered relatively safe. Be alert about your belongings, surroundings, and companions, and exercise caution in larger cities. Both **muggers** and **pickpockets** are present in big-city transport systems. Certain areas of larger cities are dangerous at night—don't walk alone, don't wear revealing clothing, and don't carry valuables. Check with the reception at hostels or hotels for information on dangerous areas. You may want to carry a **whistle** to scare off attackers or attract attention. If you're by yourself, be sure that someone at home knows your itinerary. In the **countryside,** take care along roads without sidewalks during the day and don't do so at night. Walk so that you face oncoming traffic. This way, you will be able to see the cars coming toward you, and the motorists will be able to make eye contact with you.

To avoid unwanted attention, try to blend in as much as possible. The gawking camera-toter is a more obvious target than the low-profile traveler. Wearing a backpack on both shoulders, a baseball cap, or a fanny-pack (always called a bumbag in Britain; see **Language,** p. 746) immediately marks you as a foreigner. When traveling in Britain's bigger cities, avoid stopping suddenly in the middle of the sidewalk or at the exit to the Underground to stare at something new—if you're really interested come back and look later. Familiarize yourself with your surroundings before setting out; if you must check a map, duck into a cafe or shop.

TERRORISM

Terrorist groups in Northern Ireland have attacked cities throughout Britain over the past several decades. It is obviously difficult to predict where or when these attacks will occur. Most Irish terrorist organizations set out to cause maximum monetary damage but minimum casualty. Britain deals with terrorism by asking the population to stay alert—if you see **unattended packages** on public transport, notify the driver or a guard immediately. The following government offices provide travel information and advisories over the phone, by fax, or on their websites: **Australian Department of Foreign Affairs and Trade** (☎ (2) 6261 1111; www.dfat.gov.au); **Canadian Department of Foreign Affairs and International Trade (DFAIT)** (☎ (800) 267 6788 in Canada; elsewhere call ☎ +1 (613) 944-6788; www.dfait-maeci.gc.ca); **New Zealand Ministry of Foreign Affairs** (☎ (04) 494 8500; fax 494 8511; www.mft.govt.nz/trav.html); **UK Foreign and Commonwealth Office** (☎ (020) 7238 4503; fax 7238 4545; www.fco.gov.uk); and the **US Department of State** (☎ (202) 647-5225; auto faxback (202) 647-3000; http://travel.state.gov). Check for updates on the situation at www.state.gov or www.visitbritain.com.

SAFETY ON THE ROAD

DRIVING. Driving in Britain and Ireland is considered relatively safe, and the roads and highways are for the most part in excellent condition. Britons and the Irish drive on the left—if you come from a country that drives on the right then expect to spend a few hours becoming accustomed to driving on the other side of the road and to having the steering wheel on the right side of the car.

You must wear a **seatbelt** in the front of the car, and in the back provided the car has them fitted. The driver is responsible for ensuring that all passengers under age 18 are wearing seatbelts. Children under 40lbs. should ride only in a specially designed carseat, available for a small fee from most car rental agencies. Study route maps before you hit the road, especially in Northern Scotland, where shoulders, motorways, and gas stations are rare. For long drives in desolate areas invest in a cellular phone and a **roadside assistance program** such as the RAC or the A.A. (see p. 42). **Sleeping in your car** is one of the most dangerous (and often illegal) ways to get your rest. If your car breaks down on a motorway, call ☎ 999 and wait for the police to assist you. For more infromation, see **By Car**, p. 42.

CYCLING. If you're cycling, take some challenging day-long rides at home to prepare yourself before you leave, and have your bike tuned up if you're taking it with you. Wear reflective clothing, drink plenty of water (even if you're not thirsty), and ride on the same side as the traffic. Learn the international signals for turns, and use them. Know how to fix a modern derailleur-equipped chain mount and change a tire, and practice on your own bike; a few simple tools and a good bike manual will be invaluable. **Cycling on a motorway is illegal and highly dangerous.**

PUBLIC TRANSPORTATION. Britain's system of public transport is well developed and considered a relatively safe system. Avoid getting into train or Underground carriages by yourself late at night, and try to stick to the more populated parts of the platform when waiting for a train. **Night buses** are a reliable if unsavory way of traveling around big cities; though you may be accompanied by drunken revelers, the drivers are well aware of potential problems and usually throw troublemakers off the bus before problems start up. Taxis fall into two groups—government-licensed **taxis** and freelance **minicabs**. The former is usually the safer option: while there are some excellent, reputable minicab firms that *Let's Go* lists, others may not be reliable and may compromise your safety.

Let's Go does not recommend **hitchhiking** under any circumstances, particularly for women—see **Getting Around** (p. 36) for more information.

SELF DEFENSE

There is no sure-fire way to avoid all the threatening situations you might encounter when you travel, but a good self-defense course will give you concrete ways to react to unwanted advances. **Impact, Prepare, and Model Mugging** can refer you to local self-defense courses in the US (☎ (800) 345-5425) and Vancouver, Canada (☎ (604) 878-3838). Workshops (2-3hr.) start at US$50; full courses run US$350-500.

FINANCIAL SECURITY

PROTECTING YOUR VALUABLES. Theft in Britain and Ireland is not exceptionally common, but this does not mean you should let your guard down. Hostels, train stations, and tourist sights are some of the most common areas for petty theft. Buy a few combination **padlocks** to secure your belongings either in your pack—which you should **never leave unattended**—or in a hostel or train station locker. **Don't put a wallet in your back pocket, or in the back of your backpack,** and never count your money in public. **Carry as little cash as possible;** instead carry traveler's checks, cash cards, and credit cards, keeping them in a **money belt**—not a bum-bag—along with your passport and ID cards. **Keep a small cash reserve separate from your primary stash.** This should entail about US$50 sewn into or stored in the depths of your pack, along with your traveler's check numbers and important photocopies.

CON ARTISTS AND PICKPOCKETS. Among the more colorful aspects of large cities are **con artists.** They often work in groups, and children are among the most effective. They possess an innumerable range of ruses. Beware of certain classics: sob stories that require money, rolls of bills "found" on the street, mustard spilled (or saliva spit) onto your shoulder to distract you while they snatch your bag. Don't ever hand over your passport to someone whose authority you question (ask to accompany them to a police station if they insist), and

don't ever let your passport out of your sight. Similarly, don't let your bag out of sight; never trust a "station-porter" who insists on carrying your bag or stowing it in the baggage compartment or a "new friend" who offers to guard your bag while you buy a train ticket or use the toilet. Beware of **pickpockets** in city crowds, especially on public transportation. Take special care between 8-10am and 4-6pm—rush hour is no excuse for strangers to press up against you on the Tube or on buses. Be alert in public telephone booths. If you must say your calling card number, do so very quietly; if you punch it in, make sure no one can look over your shoulder.

ACCOMMODATIONS AND TRANSPORTATION. Never leave your belongings unattended; crime occurs in even the most demure-looking hostel or hotel. Bring your own **padlock** for hostel lockers, and don't ever store valuables in any locker. Most hotels also provide lock boxes free or for a minimal fee.

Be particularly careful on **buses** and **trains;** determined thieves wait for travelers to fall asleep. Carry your pack in front of you where you can see it. When traveling with others, sleep in alternate shifts. When alone, use good judgement in selecting a train compartment: never stay in an empty one, and use a lock to secure your pack to the luggage rack. Try to sleep on top bunks with your luggage stored above you (if not in bed with you), and keep documents and valuables on your person.

If traveling by **car,** don't leave valuables (such as radios or luggage) in it while you are away. If your tape deck or radio is removable, hide it in the trunk or take it with you. If it isn't, at least conceal it. Similarly, hide baggage in the trunk—although savvy thieves can tell if a car is heavily loaded by the way it sits on its tires.

HEALTH

 Call the local police station for the nearest doctor or hospital casualty department. In England and Wales you can also call **NHS Direct**, a 24hr. advice service staffed by nurses (☎ 0845 4647). In Scotland, the NHS **Helpline** (☎ (0800) 224488) offers information on health services. In more serious emergencies, the emergency number for ambulance assistance is ☎ **999** in both Britain and Ireland, and the EU-wide ☎ **112** works as well.

In both Britain and Ireland, medical aid is readily available and of the quality you would expect in major Western countries. For minor ailments, **chemists** (drugstores) are plentiful. Individual chemists often hang green, symmetrical crosses outside their stores, whereas the **Boots** chain has a blue logo and can be found in almost every town. **Late night pharmacies** are rare, even in big cities. If you are in need of more serious attention, most major hospitals have **24-hour emergency rooms** (called "casualty departments" or "A&E," short for Accident and Emergency). Call the numbers listed in the box above for assistance.

In Britain, the state-run **National Health Service (NHS)** encompasses the majority of health-care centers. There are a few private hospitals in bigger cities, but these cater to the wealthy and are not often equipped with full surgical staff or complete casualty units. Citizens of EU countries and certain Commonwealth countries are entitled to free medical care in the UK at any NHS hospital or clinic. EU nationals also receive free medical care in Ireland. **Health insurance** is a must for all others visiting either Britain or Ireland, who will be charged for all medical services. If you are working or studying legally in the UK, however, NHS tax is deducted from your wages, and care is free. Most travel insurance covers health care, while most American health-insurance plans (except Medicare) cover members' medical emergencies during trips abroad; check with your insurance carrier to be sure. For more information, see **Insurance,** p. 26.

BEFORE YOU GO

Preparation can help minimize the likelihood of contracting a disease and maximize the chances of receiving effective health care in the event of an emergency. For tips on packing a basic **first-aid kit** and other health essentials, see p. 27.

In your passport, write the names of people you wish to be contacted in case of a medical emergency, and also list any allergies or medical conditions of which you would want doctors to be aware. Matching a prescription to its British or Irish equivalent is not always easy, safe, or possible. Carry up-to-date, legible prescriptions or a statement from your doctor stating the medication's trade name, manufacturer, chemical name, and dosage. While traveling, be sure to keep all medication with you in your carry-on luggage.

IMMUNIZATIONS AND PRECAUTIONS

Travelers over two years old should be sure that the following vaccines are up-to-date: MMR (for measles, mumps, and rubella); DTaP or Td (for diptheria, tetanus, and pertussis), OPV (for polio), HbCV (for haemophilus influenza B), and HBV (for hepatitis B). No injections are specifically required for entry into the UK, though protection against hepatitis B and tetanus is highly recommended. Your home country may require further vaccinations for reentry.

USEFUL ORGANIZATIONS. The **US Centers for Disease Control and Prevention** (CDC; ☎ (877) FYI-TRIP; www.cdc.gov/travel), which are an excellent source of information for travelers, also maintain an international fax information service. The CDC's comprehensive booklet *Health Information for International Travelers*, an annual rundown of disease, immunization, and general health advice, is free on the website or US$22 via the Government Printing Office (☎ (202) 512-1800). The **US State Department** (http://travel.state.gov) compiles Consular Information Sheets on health, entry requirements, and other issues for various countries. For quick information on health and other travel warnings, call **Overseas Citizens' Services** (☎ (202) 647-5225; after hours ☎ 647-4000).

ENVIRONMENTAL HAZARDS

While the weather has a reputation for overcast skies, the possibility of **sunburn** is always present. Remember that while British and Irish beaches may not be gloriously sun-drenched, the sun can beat down even through the clouds. If you're prone to sunburn, apply sunscreen liberally and often to avoid burns and lower the risk of skin cancer; protect eyes with sunglasses to avoid damaging exposure to ultraviolet rays. If you get sunburned, drink more fluids than usual and apply calamine or an aloe-based lotion.

Travelers to the Scottish Highlands during the winter, and anyone attempting to climb mountains, should take precautions against the cold. A rapid drop in body temperature is the clearest warning sign of **hypothermia.** Victims may also shiver, feel exhausted, have poor coordination or slurred speech, hallucinate, or suffer amnesia. Seek medical help, and *do not let hypothermia victims fall asleep—* their body temperature will continue to drop and they may die. To avoid hypothermia, keep dry, wear layers, and stay out of the wind. In wet weather, **wool** and **synthetics** such as pile retain heat. Most other fabrics, especially cotton, will make you colder. If a region of skin turns white, waxy, and cold, do not rub the area; it may be a sign of **frostbite.** Drink warm beverages, get dry, and slowly warm the area with dry fabric or steady body contact until a doctor can be found.

The common European **stinging nettle** is an annoyance rather than a serious health risk. Tiny skin-puncturing hairs on the plant's stem and leaves are filled with stinging fluid. They are found almost everywhere plants can grow from early spring to late autumn, and can be identified by their serrated leaves. Clusters of tiny green flowers also appear in the summer. Getting caught up in nettles entails a stinging feeling followed by a small reddish swelling and possible numbness.

PREVENTING DISEASE

INSECT AND TICK-BORNE DISEASES

Be aware of insects—particularly fleas and lice—in wet or forested areas. Natural repellents can be useful: taking vitamin B-12 regularly can eventually make you smelly to insects, as can garlic pills. Calamine lotion or topical cortisones (like Cortaid) stop bites from itching, as can a bath with half a cup of baking soda.

Ticks can be particularly dangerous in rural and forested regions. Pause periodically while walking to brush off ticks using a fine-toothed comb on your neck, scalp, and legs. **Lyme disease,** carried by ticks, is a bacterial infection marked by a circular bull's-eye rash of two inches or more that appears around the bite. Later symptoms include fever, headache, fatigue, and aches. Antibiotics are effective if administered early. Left untreated, it can cause problems in joints, the heart, and the nervous system. If you find a tick attached to your skin, grasp its head parts with tweezers as close to your skin as possible and apply slow, steady traction. Do not remove ticks by burning them or coating them with nail polish remover or petroleum jelly. Removing a tick within 24hr. greatly reduces the risk of infection.

FOOD- AND WATER-BORNE DISEASES

Prevention is the best cure: be sure that everything you eat is cooked properly and that the water you drink is clean. Tap water throughout Britain and Ireland is safe; water at campgrounds is not so trustworthy. To be on the safe side, you can purify your own water by bringing it to a rolling boil or treating it with **iodine tablets,** available at any camping goods store. Other culprits are raw shellfish, unpasteurized milk, and sauces containing raw eggs.

Parasites such as microbes and tapeworms hide in unsafe water and food. **Giardia,** for example, is acquired by drinking untreated water from streams or lakes. Symptoms of parasitic infections in general include swollen glands or lymph nodes, fever, rashes or itchiness, digestive problems, eye problems, and anemia. When **camping,** boil your water, wear shoes, and eat only cooked food.

AIDS, HIV, AND STDS

For detailed information on **Acquired Immune Deficiency Syndrome (AIDS)** in Britain or Ireland, call the **US Centers for Disease Control's** 24hr. hotline at (800) 342-2437, or contact the **Joint United Nations Programme on HIV/AIDS (UNAIDS),** 20 av. Appia 20, CH-1211 Geneva 27, Switzerland (☎ +41 (22) 791 36 66, fax 791 41 87). The brochure *Travel Safe: AIDS and International Travel* is available at all Council Travel offices and on their website (www.ciee.org/Isp/safety/travelsafe.htm). Currently the UK has restrictions on **HIV-positive travelers;** if you appear unwell you may be tested on entrance and a positive result may block your entrance to Britain. Contact your local British consulate or embassy (see p. 9) for details.

Sexually Transmitted Diseases (STDs) such as gonorrhea, chlamydia, genital warts, syphilis, herpes, and hepatitis B are easier to catch than HIV, and some can be just as deadly. Warning signs for STDs include: swelling, sores, bumps, or blisters on sexual organs, rectum, or mouth; burning and pain during urination and bowel movements; itching around sexual organs; swelling or redness in the throat; and flu-like symptoms with fever, chills, and aches. If these symptoms develop, see a doctor immediately. When having sex, latex **condoms** (the most common and reliable British brands are Durex and Mates) may protect you from certain STDs, but oral or even tactile contact can lead to transmission.

WOMEN'S HEALTH

Women traveling are vulnerable to **urinary tract** and **bladder infections,** which can cause a burning sensation and painful and frequent urination. To try to avoid these, drink plenty of vitamin C-rich juice and clean water, and urinate frequently, especially right after intercourse. Women are also susceptible to **vaginal yeast**

ESSENTIALS

infections, which are likely to flare up in hot and humid weather; wear loosely fitting trousers and cotton underwear. **Tampons** and **pads** are easily available, and reliable **contraceptive devices** are also relatively easy to find. Women on the Pill should bring enough supplies to allow for possible loss or extended stays, or should bring their prescription. Women who need an **abortion** while in the UK should contact the **International Planned Parenthood Federation,** European Regional Office, Regent's College, Inner Circle, Regent's Park, London NW1 4NS (☎ (020) 7487 7900), for more information. Abortions are illegal in Ireland; call the London office if you need help. For **further information,** consult the *Handbook for Women Travellers,* by Maggie and Gemma Moss (Piatkus Books, £8 or US$15).

INSURANCE

Travel insurance generally covers four basic areas: medical problems, property loss, trip cancellation/interruption, and emergency evacuation. Although your regular insurance may well extend to travel-related accidents, you may consider purchasing travel insurance if the cost of potential trip cancellation/interruption is greater than you can absorb. Travel insurance purchased separately generally runs US$50 per week for full coverage, while trip cancellation/interruption may be purchased separately for about US$5.50 per US$100 of coverage.

Medical insurance (especially US university policies) often covers costs incurred abroad; check with your provider. **Americans** should note that Medicare does *not* cover foreign travel. **Australians** traveling in the UK are entitled to many of the services that they would receive at home as part of the Reciprocal Health Care Agreement. **Canadians** are protected by their home province's health insurance plan for up to 90 days after leaving the country; check with the provincial Ministry of Health or Health Plan Headquarters. **Homeowners' insurance** (or your family's coverage) often covers theft during travel and loss of travel documents (passport, plane ticket, railpass, etc.) up to US$500.

US-issued **ISIC** and **ITIC** (p. 12) provide basic insurance, including US$100 per day of in-hospital sickness for up to 60 days, US$3000 of accident-related medical reimbursement, and US$25,000 for emergency medical transport. Cardholders have access to a toll-free 24hr. helpline for medical, legal, and financial emergencies overseas (US and Canada ☎ (800) 626-2427, elsewhere call US collect ☎ +1 (713) 267-2525). **American Express** (US ☎ (800) 528-4800) grants most cardholders automatic car-rental insurance (collision and theft, but not liability) and ground travel-accident coverage of US$100,000 on flight purchases made with the card.

INSURANCE PROVIDERS. Council and **STA** (p. 31) offer a range of plans that can supplement your basic coverage. Other private insurance providers in the **US** and **Canada** include: **Access America** (☎ (800) 284-8300); **Berkely Group/Carefree Travel Insurance** (☎ (800) 323-3149; www.berkely.com); **Globalcare Travel Insurance** (☎ (800) 821-2488; www.globalcare-cocco.com); and **Travel Assistance International** (☎ (800) 821-2828; www.worldwide-assistance.com). Providers in the **UK** include **Campus Travel** (☎ (01865) 258 000) and **Columbus Travel Insurance** (☎ (020) 7375 0011). In **Australia,** try **CIC Insurance** (☎ 9202 8000).

PACKING

You should be able to purchase most things you need in Britain and in Ireland, so **pack light:** a good rule is to lay out only what you absolutely need, then take half the clothes and twice the money. The less you have, the less you have to lose, store, or carry, plus you'll have space for the souvenirs you will inevitably buy.

LUGGAGE. If you plan to cover most of your itinerary by foot, a sturdy frame backpack is unbeatable. See **Backpacks,** p. 51, for details on how to select a good pack. Before you leave, pack your bag, strap it on, and imagine yourself walking uphill on hot asphalt for three hours; this should give you a sense of how important it is to pack lightly. Remember also to bring a good raincover for the backpack. Toting trunks or a suitcase is fine if you plan to live in one or two cities and explore from there, but a very bad idea if you're going to be moving around a lot.

DAYPACKS. In addition to your main piece of luggage, a small backpack, rucksack, or courier bag may be useful as a daypack for sight-seeing expeditions; it doubles as an airplane carry-on. Packing an empty, lightweight **duffel bag** inside your luggage allows you to fill your luggage with purchases and keep your dirty clothes in the duffel.

SLEEPSACKS. Some hostels require that you have your own sleepsack or rent one of theirs. To avoid paying linen charges, you can make the requisite sleepsack yourself (fold a full-size sheet in half the long way, then sew it closed along the open long side and one of the short sides), or buy it at a camping store.

CLOTHING. While temperatures in Britain and Ireland never reach arctic levels, it's still a good idea to bring a **warm jacket** or wool sweater. No matter when you're traveling, bring a **rain jacket**, sturdy shoes, and thick socks. Remember that wool will keep you warm even when soaked through, whereas wet cotton is colder than wearing nothing at all. Include a pair of **flip-flops** or sandals for when you take showers. If you plan to be doing a lot of hiking, see **Outdoors**, p. 51, for other items to pack. Those intending to go out at night should include a **dressier outfit** (and a nicer pair of shoes if space permits) in case dress codes are in place.

WASHING CLOTHES. *Let's Go* provides information on launderettes (laundromats) in the **Practical Information** sections of some cities, but sometimes it may be cheaper and easier to use a sink. Bring a small bar or tube of detergent soap and a travel clothes line.

ELECTRIC CURRENT. In both Britain and Ireland, electricity is **240 volts AC**, enough to fry any 110V North American appliance; most European 220V appliances are fine. Visit a hardware store for an adapter (which changes the shape of the plug to the three-square-pin one used in the UK) and a transformer (which changes the voltage). Don't make the mistake of using only an adapter, unless appliance instructions explicitly state otherwise.

CONTACT LENSES. Contact lens wearers should bring an extra pair, a copy of their prescription, a pair of glasses, extra solution, and eyedrops. American machines which heat-disinfect contact lenses will require a 240V transformer (about US$20). Consider switching temporarily to a chemical disinfection system.

FIRST-AID KIT. For a basic first-aid kit, pack bandages, aspirin or other painkillers, antibiotic cream, a thermometer, a Swiss Army knife, tweezers, moleskin, decongestant, motion-sickness remedy, diarrhea or upset-stomach medication (Pepto Bismol or Immodium), an antihistamine, sunscreen, insect repellent, burn ointment, and a syringe for emergencies (get an explanatory letter from your doctor).

FILM. Film in Britain generally costs £4 for a roll of 24 color exposures; film in Ireland costs around IR£4. Developing film in the UK usually costs about half of what it does in the US. Since you're likely to get overcast conditions, you should use film marked ISO 200 or higher. Less serious photographers might consider bringing a **disposable camera** or two rather than an expensive permanent one. Despite disclaimers, airport security X-rays *can* fog film, so either buy a lead-lined pouch, sold at camera stores, or ask the security to hand inspect it. Always pack film in your carry-on luggage, since higher-intensity X-rays are used on checked luggage.

OTHER USEFUL ITEMS. For **safety** purposes, you should carry a whistle, a moneybelt for carrying valuables, and a padlock. Some **basic outdoors equipment** (compass; waterproof matches; pocketknife; insect repellent) and **sun gear** (sunscreen; sunglasses; hat) may prove useful, even if you don't intend to spend much time outdoors. **Quick repairs** can be done with a needle and thread and electrical tape for patching tears. **Miscellaneous** items you should remember: alarm clock; earplugs; flashlight; rubber bands; safety pins; string; tweezers; garbage bags; sealable plastic bags; small calculator for currency conversion; umbrella; and water bottle.

ESSENTIALS

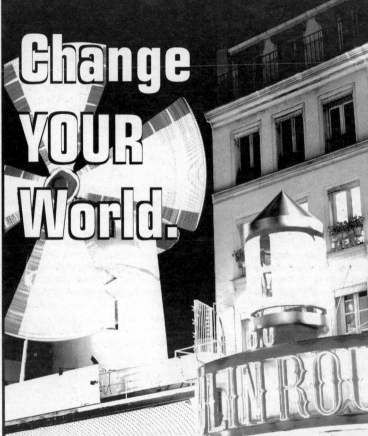

STUDENT TRAVEL

Change YOUR World.

THE WORLD LEADER IN STUDENT TRAVEL

meet imagine touch see learn wonder feel live listen
INDIVIDUAL INDEPENDENCE SEE LEARN ENJOY MEET
experience meet chan
LISTEN DO ENJOY RELA

STA TRAVEL
WE'VE BEEN THERE.

CST #1017560-60

800.777.0112

www.statravel.com

GETTING THERE

BY PLANE

When it comes to airfare, a little effort can save you a bundle. If your plans are flexible enough to deal with the restrictions, courier fares are the cheapest. Those flying to Britain or Ireland from within Europe should look into **discount airlines** (p. 32). Tickets bought from consolidators and standby seating are also good deals, but last-minute specials, airfare wars, and charter flights often beat these fares. The key is to hunt around, to be flexible, and to ask persistently about discounts. Students, seniors, and those under 26 should never pay full price for a ticket.

DETAILS AND TIPS

Timing: Airfares to Britain and Ireland peak between June and Sept.; holidays (such as Christmas and Easter) are also expensive. Midweek (M-Th morning) round-trip flights run US$40-50 cheaper than weekend flights, but are generally more crowded and less likely to permit frequent-flier upgrades. Return-date flexibility is usually not an option for the budget traveler; traveling with an open return ticket can be pricier than fixing a return date when buying the ticket and paying later to change it.

Airports: Most long-haul flights into Britain land in one of the two major London airports, Heathrow or Gatwick. Some fly directly to regional airports, such as Manchester, Glasgow, or Edinburgh. Flights to Ireland usually land in Dublin or Shannon.

Route: Round-trip flights are by far the cheapest; open-jaw tickets (arriving in and departing from different cities) tend to be pricier. Patching one-way flights together is the most expensive way to travel.

Round-the-World (RTW): If Britain or Ireland is only one stop on a more extensive globe-hop, consider a RTW ticket. Tickets usually include at least 5 stops and are valid for about a year; prices range US$1200-5000. Try **Northwest Airlines/KLM** (US ☎ (800) 447-4747; www.nwa.com) or **Star Alliance,** a consortium of 13 airlines including United Airlines (US ☎ (800) 241-6522; www.star-alliance.com).

Boarding: Confirm international flights by phone within 72hr. of departure. Most airlines require that passengers arrive at the airport at least 2hr. before departure for long-haul flights, 1hr. for intra-European flights. One carry-on item and 2 checked bags is the norm for long-haul flights; within Europe there's usually a 20kg weight limit per bag.

Fares: Round-trip fares to London from the US range from US$160-350 (during the off-season) to US$200-550 (during the summer). Round-trip fares to Dublin from the US range from US$400-$600.

Useful Websites: A2bAirports (www.a2bairports.com) and **BAA** (www.baa.co.uk) are online guides to airports in Britain and Ireland, including flight arrival information. **Microsoft Expedia** (www.expedia.com or www.expedia.co.uk) and **Travelocity** (www.travelocity.com or www.travelocity.co.uk) let you compare flight fares, look at maps, and make reservations on the web. **TravelHUB** (www.travelhub.com) is a directory of travel agents that includes a searchable database of fares from over 500 consolidators. **VirginNet** (www.virgin.net/travel) details cheap flights into the UK from many North American destinations, as well as a UK hotel finder.

Further Reading: *The Official Airline Guide,* an expensive tome available at libraries, has schedules, fares, and reservation numbers. For further information, see *The Worldwide Guide to Cheap Airfares,* by Michael McColl (Insider Publications, US$15); *Discount Airfares: The Insider's Guide,* by George Hobart (Priceless Publications, US$14); or *Fly Cheap,* by Kelly Monaghan (Intrepid Traveler Publications, US$14.95).

BUDGET AND STUDENT TRAVEL AGENCIES

While knowledgeable agents specializing in flights to Britain and Ireland can make your life easier and help you save, they may not spend the time to find you the lowest possible fare—they get paid on commission. Students and under-26ers holding

ISIC and IYTC cards (see p. 12), respectively, qualify for big discounts from student travel agencies. Most flights from budget agencies are on major airlines, but in peak season some may sell seats on less reliable chartered aircraft.

usit world (www.usitworld.com). Over 50 **usit campus** branches in the UK (www.usitcampus.co.uk), including 52 Grosvenor Gardens, **London** SW1W 0AG (☎ (0870) 240 1010); **Manchester** (☎ (0161) 273 1721); and **Edinburgh** (☎ (0131) 668 3303). Nearly 20 **usit now** offices in Ireland, including 19-21 Aston Quay, O'Connell Bridge, **Dublin** 2 (☎ (01) 602 1600; www.usitnow.ie), and **Belfast** (☎ (028) 9032 7111; www.usitnow.com). *Let's Go* also lists additional offices in many cities with universities.

Council Travel (www.counciltravel.com), usit's US partner. Offices include: Emory Village, 1561 N. Decatur Rd., **Atlanta,** GA 30307 (☎ (404) 377-9997); 273 Newbury St., **Boston,** MA 02116 (☎ (617) 266-1926); 1160 N. State St., **Chicago,** IL 60610 (☎ (312) 951-0585); 931 Westwood Blvd., Westwood, **Los Angeles,** CA 90024 (☎ (310) 208-3551); 254 Greene St., **New York,** NY 10003 (☎ (212) 254-2525); 530 Bush St., **San Francisco,** CA 94108 (☎ (415) 566-6222); 424 Broadway Ave E., **Seattle,** WA 98102 (☎ (206) 329-4567); 3301 M St. NW, **Washington, D.C.** 20007 (☎ (202) 337-6464). **For US cities not listed,** call ☎ (800) 2-COUNCIL (226-8624). In the **UK,** usit Council, 28A Poland St. (Tube: Oxford Circus), **London,** W1V 3DB (☎ (020) 7437 7767).

STA Travel, head office 6560 Scottsdale Rd. #F100, Scottsdale, AZ 85253, US (☎ (800) 777-0112; fax (602) 922-0793; www.sta-travel.com or www.sta-travel.co.uk). A student and youth travel organization with over 150 offices worldwide. Ticket booking, travel insurance, railpasses, and more. In the **UK,** 11 Goodge St., **London** WIP 1FE (☎ (020) 7436 7779 for North American travel). **US** offices include: 297 Newbury St., **Boston,** MA 02115 (☎ (617) 266-6014); 429 S. Dearborn St., **Chicago,** IL 60605 (☎ (312) 786-9050); 7202 Melrose Ave., **Los Angeles,** CA 90046 (☎ (323) 934-8722); the ministerial 10 Downing St., **New York,** NY 10014 (☎ (212) 627-3111); 4341 University Way NE, **Seattle,** WA 98105 (☎ (206) 633-5000); 2401 Pennsylvania Ave., Ste. G, **Washington, D.C.** 20037 (☎ (202) 887-0912); 51 Grant Ave., **San Francisco,** CA 94108 (☎ (415) 391-8407). In **New Zealand,** 10 High St., **Auckland** (☎ (09) 309 0458). In **Australia,** 366 Lygon St., **Melbourne** Vic 3053 (☎ (03) 9349 4344).

Student Universe (www.studentuniverse.com). An Internet travel agency which doesn't require you to have an ISIC card to purchase student fares.

Travel CUTS (Canadian Universities Travel Services Limited), 187 College St., **Toronto,** ON M5T 1P7 (☎ (416) 979-2406; fax 979-8167; www.travelcuts.com). 40 offices across Canada. Also in the UK, 295-A Regent St., **London** W1R 7YA (☎ (020) 7255 1944).

Wasteels, Platform 2, Victoria Station, London SW1V 1JT (☎ (020) 7834 7066; fax 7630 7628; www.wasteels.dk/uk). A huge chain in Europe, with 203 locations. Sells BIJ tickets, discounted (30-45% off regular fare) 2nd-class international point-to-point train tickets with unlimited stopovers for those under 26 (sold only in Europe).

AIRLINES

MAJOR COMMERCIAL AIRLINES

The main commercial airlines' lowest regular offer is the **APEX** (Advance Purchase Excursion) fare, which provides confirmed reservations and allows "open-jaw" tickets. Generally, reservations must be made 7 to 21 days in advance, with 7- to 14-day minimum and up to 90-day maximum-stay limits, and hefty cancellation and change penalties (fees rise in summer). Book peak-season APEX fares early, since by May you will have a hard time getting the departure date you want. Although APEX fares are probably not the cheapest possible fares, they will give you a sense of the average commercial price, from which to measure other bargains. Specials advertised in newspapers may be cheaper but have more restrictions and fewer available seats. Popular carriers to Britain and Ireland include:

Aer Lingus (Ireland reservations ☎ (01) 886 8888; UK ☎ (08459) 737747; US ☎ (800) 223-6537; www.aerlingus.ie), Ireland's national carrier, flies from Boston, Chicago, Los Angeles, Newark, and New York to Dublin and Shannon.

Air New Zealand (UK reservations ☎ (020) 8741 2299, flight info ☎ (01426) 915500; NZ ☎ (09) 357 3000; www.airnz.com): no prizes for guessing where it flies from.

American Airlines (US ☎ (800) 433-7300; www.americanair.com), flies transatlantic.

British Airways (UK reservations ☎ (08457) 773 3377, flight info ☎ (0990) 444000; US ☎ (800) 247-9297, Australia ☎ (02) 9258 3300, NZ ☎ (09) 356 8690; www.british-airways.com), has extensive direct flights to London from all over the world.

Qantas (UK reservations ☎ (0345) 747767, flight info ☎ (01426) 910020; Australia ☎ 13 1211; NZ ☎ 0800 808 767; www.qantas.com.au) brings those Down Under over.

Singapore Airlines (Australia ☎ 13 10 11; NZ ☎ (09) 379 3886; www.singaporeair.com) offers flights from Australasia to London via Singapore.

United Airlines (UK reservations ☎ (08458) 444777, flight info ☎ (01426) 915500; US ☎ (800) 241-6522; www.ual.com) competes for the transatlantic market.

Virgin Atlantic (UK reservations ☎ (01293) 747747, flight info ☎ (01293) 511581; US ☎ (800) 862-8621; www.fly.virgin.com) flies from many US cities to London, and also runs a popular Johannesburg-London route.

DISCOUNT AIRLINES

If you can book in advance (sometimes *way* in advance) and/or travel at odd hours, the newly popular discount airlines may be the least costly way of making cheap quick jaunts between Britain and Ireland to the continent. Fares change all the time, and a good source of offers are the travel supplements of newspapers or the classifieds in *Time Out*; many of the airlines will also advertise offers (and sell tickets) on the Internet. However, not all the seats on their planes are available at the advertised prices. Remember that saving money often means cutting back on frills—food and drinks don't always come free on these flights, and ground transportation may cost more if you travel to out-of-the-way airports such as Luton.

British Midland (London ☎ (08706) 070555; Dublin ☎ (01) 283 0700; Belfast ☎ (01232) 241188; US ☎ (800) 788-0555; www.britishmidland.com). Service between Aberdeen, Belfast, Dublin, Edinburgh, Glasgow, Leeds, London Heathrow, Manchester, and Teesside (Newcastle).

Debonair (UK ☎ (0541) 500300) offers budget flights between Britain and France, Germany, Spain, Italy, and Ireland.

easyJet (UK ☎ (0870) 600 0000; www.easyjet.com). Luton to Aberdeen, Edinburgh, and Glasgow; Belfast to Luton and Liverpool; and to Britain from many European cities.

Go (UK ☎ (0845) 6054321; from abroad ☎ +44 (1279) 666388; www.go-fly.com). Stansted (3-7 flights a day) to Edinburgh, Denmark, Italy, and Portugal, and more.

Ryanair (UK ☎ (0541) 569569; www.ryanair.ie) flies from Luton and Stansted to Cork, Dublin, Kerry, Knock, and Glasgow, as well as European destinations.

Virgin Express (UK ☎ (020) 7744 0004; Ireland ☎ (061) 704470; www.virginexpress.com). To Shannon and the Continent from Heathrow, Gatwick, and Stansted.

OTHER CHEAP ALTERNATIVES

AIR COURIER FLIGHTS

Couriers help transport cargo on international flights by guaranteeing delivery of the baggage claim slips from the company to a representative overseas. Generally, couriers must travel light (carry-ons only) and deal with complex restrictions on their flight. Most flights are round-trip only with short fixed-length stays (usually one week), and many operate only out of big cities like London or New York. Generally, you must be over 21 (in some cases 18), have a valid passport, and procure your own visa, if necessary. Groups such as the **Air Courier Association** (US ☎ (800) 282-1202; www.aircourier.org) and the **International Association of Air Travel Couriers,** 220 South Dixie Hwy., P.O. Box 1349, Lake Worth, FL 33460, USA (☎ (561) 582-8320; www.courier.org) provide their members with lists of opportunities and courier brokers worldwide for an annual fee. For more information, consult *Air Courier Bargains*, by Kelly Monaghan (The Intrepid Traveler, US$15) or the *Courier Air Travel Handbook* by Mark Field (Perpetual Press, US$10).

CHARTER FLIGHTS

Charters are flights that a tour operator contracts with an airline to fly extra loads of passengers during peak season. Charters can sometimes be cheaper than flights on scheduled airlines, some operate nonstop, and restrictions on minimum advance-purchase and minimum stay are more lenient. However, charter flights fly less frequently than major airlines, make refunds particularly difficult, and are almost always fully booked. Schedules and itineraries may also change or be cancelled at the last moment (as late as 48 hours before the trip without a full refund), and check-in, boarding, and baggage claim are often slower. As always, pay with a credit card if you can, and consider travel insurance against trip interruption.

Discount clubs and **fare brokers** offer members savings on last-minute charter and tour deals. Study their contracts closely; you don't want to end up with an unwanted overnight layover. **Travelers Advantage** (US ☎ (800) 548-1116; www.travelersadvantage.com) specializes in European travel and tour packages (US$60 annual fee includes discounts, newsletters, and cheap flight directories).

STANDBY FLIGHTS

To travel standby, you will need considerable flexibility in the dates and cities of your arrival and departure. Companies that specialize in standby flights don't sell tickets, but rather the promise that you will get to your destination (or near your destination) within a certain window of time (anywhere from 1-5 days). You may only receive a refund if all available flights which depart within your date-range from the specified region are full, but future travel credit is always available.

Carefully read agreements with any company offering standby flights, as tricky fine print can leave you in the lurch. To check on a company's service record, call the Better Business Bureau of New York City (☎ (212) 533-6200). It is difficult to receive refunds, and clients' vouchers will not be honored when an airline fails to receive payment in time. A good company is **Airhitch**, 2641 Broadway, 3rd fl., New York, NY 10025 (☎ (800) 326-2009 or (212) 864-2000; www.airhitch.org) and Los Angeles, CA (☎ (310) 726-5000). In Europe, the flagship office is in Paris (☎ (01) 47 00 16 30) and the other one is in Amsterdam (☎ +31 (20) 626 32 20). Flights from London to Ireland and other European destinations cost US$99 each way; flights from the US to London from the Northeast cost US$159 each way, $239 from the West Coast or Northwest, $209 from the Midwest, and $189 from the Southeast (excluding $16 in taxes when flying east).

TICKET CONSOLIDATORS

Ticket consolidators (**"bucket shops"**) buy unsold tickets in bulk from commercial airlines and sell them at discounted rates. The best place to look is in the Sunday travel section of any major newspaper, where many bucket shops place tiny ads. Call quickly, as availability is extremely limited. Not all bucket shops are reliable, so insist on a receipt that gives full details of restrictions, refunds, and tickets, and pay by credit card. For more info, check the **Consolidators FAQ** (www.travel-library.com/air-travel/consolidators.html) or the book *Consolidators: Air Travel's Bargain Basement*, by Kelly Monaghan (Intrepid Traveler, US$8).

BY CHANNEL TUNNEL

In 1994, the **Channel Tunnel** (Chunnel) was completed, physically connecting England and France (the horror!/*l'horreur!*). In a wry display of humor, the British terminus of the **Eurostar** cross-channel train (☎ (01233) 617575) is London's **Waterloo Station.** Napoleon is not amused. Some trains also stop at **Ashford International,** Kent. Eurostar ticketing operates like an airline with similar discounts, reservations, and restrictions. Return tickets start at US$120, and trains run from London,

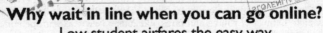

Paris, and Brussels. While BritRail passes, Eurail passes, and such do not include free Eurostar travel, they are tickets to a discount, as is being under 26. Call ☎ (800) 387-6782 to purchase your ticket, or contact Rail Europe (see p. 39).

BY TRAIN. Eurostar, Eurostar House, Waterloo Station, London SE1 8SE (UK ☎ (0990) 186186; US ☎ (800) 387-6782; elsewhere call UK ☎ +44 (1233) 617575; www.eurostar.com; www.raileurope.com) runs a frequent train service between London and the continent. Ten to 28 trains per day run from Paris (3hr., £100-155), Brussels (3hr. 50min., £100-135), and Eurodisney. Prices are cheaper if you purchase your ticket in London or Paris. Routes include stops at Ashford in England, and Calais and Lille in France. Book at major rail stations in the UK, at the office above, by phone, or on the web.

BY CAR. If you're traveling by car, **Eurotunnel** (UK ☎ (08000) 969992; www.euro-tunnel.co.uk) shuttles cars and passengers between Kent and Nord-Pas-de-Calais. Return fares for vehicle and all passengers range from £219-299 with car, £259-598 with campervan, and £119-299 for a trailer/caravan supplement. Same-day return costs £110-150, five-day return £139-195. Book online or via phone. Travelers with cars can also look into sea crossings by ferry (see below).

BY FERRY

Ferry travel is dependable, inexpensive, and slow. Most European ferries are comfortable and well equipped; the cheapest fare class usually includes a reclining chair or couchette where you can sleep. Almost all sailings in June, July, and August are **controlled sailings,** which means that you must book the crossing at least a day in advance. If you're traveling with a **car** in July or August, reserve through a ferry office or travel agency. Advance planning and reserved ticket purchases through a travel agency can spare you days of waiting in dreary ports for the next sailing. Ask ahead where to board the ferry, arrive at the port an hour in advance, and remember your passport. Unlike train or air travel, ferries lack the convenience of location; you often land in odd parts of the country, and must then arrange connections to larger cities at additional cost.

Prices vary greatly by ports, season, and length of stay. In the summer expect to pay at least £25 per foot passenger to cross from France and £60 from Belgium and the Netherlands. Limited-day returns (usually 5-10 nights including travel) are generally not much more expensive than the single fare. Ask for **discounts; ISIC** holders can often get student fares, and **Eurail pass-holders** can get many reductions and free trips (check the brochure that comes with your railpass). Children under 4 usually travel free and bicycles can be carried for a small fee, if any. Some travelers ask car drivers to let them travel as one of the four or five free passengers allotted to a car. This can reduce costs considerably, but consider the risks before getting into a stranger's car. The main ferry companies operating between Britain and France or Northern Europe are listed below; call or write for brochures with complete listings of routes and fares. **A2bEurope** (www.a2beurope.com) details crossing the Channel by ferry or Eurostar, with timetables.

The following fares listed are **one-way** for adult foot passengers unless otherwise noted. Though standard return fares are in most cases simply twice the one-way fare, **fixed-period returns** (usually within five days) are almost invariably cheaper. Ferries run **year-round** unless otherwise noted. **Bikes** are usually free, although you may have to pay up to UK£10 in high-season. For a **camper/trailer** supplement, you will have to add anywhere from UK£20-140 to the "with car" fare. If more than one price is quoted, the quote in UK£ is valid for departures from the UK, etc. A directory of ferries in this region can be found at www.seaview.co.uk/ferries.html.

Brittany Ferries: UK ☎ (08709) 012400; France ☎ 08 03 82 88 28; www.brittany-ferries.com. **Plymouth** from **Roscoff, France** (6hr.; in summer 1-3 per day, off-season 1 per week; UK£20-58 or 140-300F) and **Santander, Spain** (24-30hr., 1-2 per week, return UK£80-145). **Portsmouth** from **St-Malo** (8¾hr., 1-2 per day, 150-320F) and **Caen, France** (6hr., 1-3 per day, 140-290F). **Poole** from **Cherbourg, France** (4¼hr., 1-2 per day, 140-290F). **Cork** from **Roscoff** (13½hr., Apr.-Sept. 1 per week, 340-650F).

Cork-Swansea Ferries: UK ☎ (01792) 456116; Ireland ☎ (021) 271166. **Swansea, Wales,** from **Cork** (10hr.).

DFDS Seaways: UK ☎ (08705) 333000; www.scansea.com. **Harwich** from **Hamburg, Germany** (20hr.) and **Esbjerg, Denmark** (19hr.). **Newcastle** from **Amsterdam, Netherlands** (14hr.); **Kristiansand, Norway** (19hr.); and **Gothenburg, Sweden** (22hr.).

Fjord Line: www.fjordline.no. Norway ☎ 55 54 88 00; UK ☎ (0191) 296 1313. **Newcastle** from **Stavanger** (19hr.) and **Bergen, Norway** (26hr.).

Hoverspeed: UK ☎ (08702) 408070; France ☎ 08 20 00 35 55; www.hover-speed.co.uk. **Dover** from **Calais, France** (35-55min., every hr., UK£24) and **Ostend, Belgium** (2hr., 5-7 per day, UK£28). **Folkestone** from **Boulogne, France** (55min., 3-4 per day, UK£24). **Newhaven** from **Dieppe, France** (2¼-4¼hr., 1-3 per day, UK£28).

Irish Ferries: Ireland ☎ (1890) 31 31 31; UK ☎ (08705) 171717; France ☎ 01 42 66 90 90; www.irishferries.ie. **Rosslare, Ireland** from: **Cherbourg, France** (17hr., IR£45-85); **Roscoff, France** (14½hr., Apr.-Sept. 1-2 per week, 315-650F); and **Pembroke Dock, Wales** (3¾hr.). **Holyhead, Wales** from **Dublin** (2-3¼hr., return IR£35-60, students IR£28-48).

P&O European Ferries: UK ☎ (08702) 424999; France ☎ 01 44 51 00 51; www.poef.com. **Portsmouth** from **Le Havre** and **Cherbourg, France** (both 5½hr., 1-7 per day, UK£18-32) and **Bilbao, Spain** (35hr., 2 per week, UK£75-194). Also **Cairn-ryan** from **Larne** (1-2¼hr.).

P&O North Sea Ferries: UK ☎ (01482) 377177; http://www.ponsf.com. Daily ferries to **Hull** from **Rotterdam, Netherlands** (13½hr.) and **Zeebrugge, Belgium** (14hr.). Both UK£38-48, students UK£24-31, cars UK£63-78. Online bookings.

P&O Stena Line: UK ☎ (08706) 000611; from Europe ☎ +44 (1304) 864003; www.posl.com. **Dover** from **Calais, France** (1¼hr., 30 per day, UK£24).

SeaFrance: UK ☎ (08705) 711711; France ☎ 03 21 46 80 00; www.seafrance.co.uk. **Dover** from **Calais, France** (1½hr., 15 per day, UK£15).

Stena Line: UK ☎ (01233) 646826; www.stenaline.co.uk. **Harwich** from **Hook of Holland** (3¾-8½hr., UK£24-29). **Fishguard, Wales** from **Rosslare, Ireland** (1-3½hr., UK£20-41). **Holyhead, Wales** from **Dublin** (4hr., UK£30-35) and **Dún Laoghaire, Ireland** (1-3½hr., £20-35, students £16-28). **Stranraer, Scotland** from **Belfast** (Mar.-Jan. 1¾-3¼hr., UK£20-27).

GETTING AROUND

BY PLANE

The Irish and British national carriers, **Aer Lingus** (Ireland ☎ (01) 886 8888; UK ☎ (08459) 737747; www.aerlingus.ie) and **British Airways** (☎ (08457) 773 3377; www.british-airways.com), fly regularly between London and Dublin; fares start from £81 (Aer Lingus 1½hr., every hr. 7:40am-10:45pm; British Airways 1½hr., 6 flights per day). **Ryanair** (☎ (0541) 569569) also flies frequently between London and Dublin. The same **discount airlines** (see p. 32) that offer cheap intra-Europe flights also have travel bargains within the Isles, particularly between the London airports (City, Gatwick, Heathrow, Luton, and Stansted) and other large cities in Britain and Ireland; call, or check newspaper travel supplements for offers. If you plan to go to the **Shetland Islands** (see p. 624) or the **Isle of Man** (see p. 343), the time saved may be worth the extra cost of flying.

BY TRAIN

BRITAIN

Britain's train network is extremely well-developed, criss-crossing the length and breadth of the island. Privatization of British Rail, which happened in 1995, seems only to have brought confusion and delays; last year, Transport Minister John Prescott called privatized trains "a national disgrace." In cities which have more than one train station, the city name is given first, followed by the station name (for example, "Manchester Piccadilly" and "Manchester Victoria" are the two major stations in Manchester). In general, traveling by train costs more than by coach/bus. *Let's Go* quotes one-way prices for standard (also known as 2nd-class) seats, unless specified otherwise. Railpasses covering specific regions are sometimes available from local train stations; these may include travel on bus and ferry routes. *Let's Go* lists available passes where appropriate. Prices and schedules often change; find up-to-date information from **National Rail Inquiries** (☎ (08457) 484950), or online at **Railtrack** (www.railtrack.co.uk; schedules only). For information on using the **London Underground,** see p. 92.

TICKET TYPES

The array of available tickets on British trains is bewildering, and prices aren't always set logically—it's entirely possible that buying an unlimited day pass to the region will cost you less than buying a one-way ticket. Instead of just stating a destination, which will get you a single, you might want to ask what the cheapest ticket to the destination is. **Single** or **one-way** tickets are valid for just one trip. There are two types of return (round-trip) tickets: **day return** tickets, which allow a return trip only on the same day and usually cost only slightly more than a single, and **open return** (also known as **period return**) tickets, which allow a return within 30 days but are usually pricier than day returns. Prices for many fares rise on Friday and Saturday; prices before 9:30am are usually more expensive. Always keep your ticket with you, as it will sometimes be inspected on the journey or collected at the station when you arrive. Tickets should be purchased before boarding, except at unstaffed train stations, in which case tickets are bought on the train.

There are five major **discount ticket** types. **APEX** (Advance Purchase Excursion) tickets have to be bought at least seven days in advance; **SuperAPEX** tickets are similar but have to be bought at least 14 (sometimes 21) days in advance. **Saver** tickets are valid any time except before 9:30am; **SuperSaver** ones are not valid before 9:30am or on Fridays and most Saturdays; and **SuperAdvance** tickets are similar to SuperSavers, but you must buy them before 2pm on the day before you travel.

BRITRAIL PASSES

If you plan to travel a great deal on trains within Britain, the **BritRail Pass** can be a good buy. Eurail passes are *not* valid in Britain, but there's often a discount on BritRail passes if you purchase the two simultaneously. BritRail passes are only available outside Britain; **you must buy them before traveling to Britain.** They allow unlimited train travel in England, Wales, and Scotland, regardless of which company is operating the trains, but do not allow free travel in Northern Ireland, or on Eurostar. BritRail pass prices are listed below. **Youth** passes are for travelers under 26, while **senior** ones are for travelers over 60. One child aged 5-15 can travel free with each adult pass, as long as you ask for the **Family Pass** (free). Additional children pay half the standard adult fare, while children under 5 travel free. In deciding which pass to buy, consider what kinds of train journeys you will be making, since first-class seats are not available on short routes. Other varieties of passes (e.g. passes for rail travel including Eurostar) are also available; contact the following distributors for more details.

1st-class Classic: Consecutive days travel: 8 days US$400, 15 days US$600, 22 days US$760, 1 month US$900.

Standard-class Classic: Consecutive days travel: 8 days US$265, 15 days US$400, 22 days US$505, 1 month US$600.

Youth Classic: Standard-class only; consecutive days travel: 8 days US$215, 15 days US$280, 22 days US$355, 1 month US$420.

Senior Classic: 1st-class only; consecutive days travel: 8 days US$340, 15 days US$510, 22 days US$645, 1 month US$765.

Flexipass: Travel within a 2-month period: any 4 days (1st-class US$350, 2nd-class US$235), any 8 days (US$510/US$340), any 15 days (US$770/US$515).

Youth Flexipasses: 2nd-class only; travel within a two-month period: 4 days US$185, 8 days US$240, 15 days US$360.

Senior Flexipasses: 1st-class only; travel within a two-month period: 4 days US$300, 8 days US$435, 15 days US$655.

Britrail Pass Plus Ireland: 2nd-class travel for a limited number of days within a month on all British and Irish (both Northern Ireland and the Republic of Ireland) trains, plus two ferry crossings on Stena Ferries. 5 days US$396, 10 days US$566.

Freedom of Scotland Travelpass: Valid for all trains within Scotland, the Glasgow Underground, and selected ferry and bus routes. 4 out of 8 days US$137, 8 out of 15 days US$189, 12 out of 20 days US$206.

BRITRAIL DISTRIBUTORS

Passes and additional details on discounts are available from most travel agents (see p. 29). The distributors listed below will either sell you passes directly, or tell you the nearest place to buy passes.

Australia: Rail Plus, Level 3, 459 Little Collins St., Melbourne, Victoria 3000 (☎ (09) 9642 8644). **Concorde International Travel** (Rail Tickets), Level 9, 310 King St., Melbourne Victoria 3000 (☎ (03) 9920 3833).

Canada and the US: Rail Europe, 226 Westchester Ave., White Plains, NY 10604 (☎ (800) 438-7245; www.raileurope.com), is the North American distributor of BritRail products. Or try **Rail Pass Express** (☎ (800) 722-7151; www.railpass.com).

Ireland: BritRail Ireland, 123 Lower Baggot St., Dublin 2 (☎ (01) 661 2866).

New Zealand: Holiday Shoppe, (☎ (0800) 729 435). **Budget Travel,** (☎ (0800) 808 040).

South Africa: World Travel Agency, Cape Town (☎ (021) 252470)

RAIL DISCOUNT CARDS

Unlike the passes above, these can be purchased in Britain. The **Young Person's Railcard** (£18, valid for 1 year) offers 33% off most fares and discounts on Holyman Sally Ferries. Buy it at Travel Centres in train stations in the UK. You must prove you're either between 16 and 25 (with a birth certificate or passport), or a full-time student over 25 at a "recognized educational establishment," and submit a passport-sized photo. Those 60 and over can purchase a **Senior Railcard** (£16) from Travel Centres, also taking up to 33% off most fares. There are also Family Railcards, and Railcards for travelers in wheelchairs.

IRELAND

Iarnród Éireann (Irish Rail), is useful only for travel to urban areas, from which you'll need to find another form of transportation to reach Ireland's picturesque villages and wilds. Trains from Dublin's Heuston Station chug towards Cork, Tralee, Limerick, Ennis, Galway, Westport, Ballina, and Waterford; others leave from Dublin's Connolly Station to head for Belfast, Sligo, Wexford and Rosslare. Trains also make various connections between these cities. For schedule information, pick up an *InterCity Rail Travellers Guide* (50p), available at most train stations. The **TravelSave** stamp, available for £8 at any **usit** agency with an ISIC card, cuts fares by 30-50% on national rail. (It also provides 15% discounts on bus fares above £1.) A **Faircard** (£5) can get anyone age 16 to 26 up to 50% off the price of any intercity trip. Those over 26 can get the less potent **Weekender card** (£8; up to a third off, valid F-Tu only). Both are valid through the end of the year. The **Rambler** allows unlimited train travel on five days within a 15-day travel period (£67). Information is available from Irish Rail, 35 Lower Abbey St., Dublin (☎ (01) 836 3333; www.irishrail.ie). Unlike bus tickets, train tickets sometimes allow travelers to break a journey into stages yet still pay the price of a single-phase trip. Bikes may be carried on most trains for a fee of £2-6, depending on weight; check at the station for the restrictions of specific trains.

While the **Eurailpass** is not accepted in Northern Ireland, it *is* accepted on trains (but not buses) in The Republic. A range of youth and family passes are also available, but Eurailpasses are generally cost-effective only if you plan to travel to the Continent as well. The BritRail pass does not cover travel in Northern Ireland, but the month-long **BritRail Plus Ireland** works in both the North and the Republic with rail options and round-trip ferry service between Britain and Ireland (US$408-770). Great value resides in the youth passes for individuals under the age of 26. You'll find it easiest to buy a Eurailpass before you arrive in Europe; contact Council Travel (p. 29), or any of many other travel agents. **Rail Europe** (☎ (800) 438-7245; www.raileurope.com), also sells point-to-point tickets.

Northern Ireland Railways (☎ (01232) 899411; www.nirailways.co.uk) is not extensive but covers the northeastern coastal region well. BritRail passes are not valid here, but Northern Ireland Railways offers its own discounts. A valid **Northern Ireland Travelsave** stamp (UK£6, affixed to back of ISIC) will get you 50% off all trains and 15% discounts on bus fares over UK£1 within Northern Ireland. The **Freedom of Northern Ireland** ticket allows unlimited travel by train and Ulsterbus and can be purchased for seven consecutive days (UK£38), three consecutive days (£25), or a single day (£10).

BY BUS AND COACH

The British and the Irish distinguish between **buses** that cover short local routes, and **coaches** that cover long distances. For practical purposes, *Let's Go* usually uses the term "buses" to refer to both. Regional bus/coach **passes** offer unlimited travel on buses within a certain area for a certain number of days; these are usually known as **Rovers, Ramblers,** and **Explorers;** *Let's Go* lists these where available.

BUSES IN BRITAIN

Long-distance coach travel is more extensive in Britain than most European countries, and is the cheapest option. **National Express** (☎ (08705) 808080; www.goby-coach.co.uk) is the principal operator of long-distance coach services in Britain, although **Scottish Citylink** (☎ (08705) 505050) has extensive coverage in Scotland. National Express tickets can usually be purchased at the bus station; otherwise, *Let's Go* lists a ticket agent in the town. **Discount Coachcards** are available for seniors (over 50), students, and young persons (ages 16-25) for £8 and reduce fares on National Express by about 30%. For those planning a lot of coach travel, the **Tourist Trail Pass** offers unlimited travel for a number of days within a given period. (2 days out of 3 £49, concessions £39; 5 out of 10 £85, £69; 7 out of 21 £120, £94; 14 out of 30 £187, £143.) Tourist information centres often carry timetables for the buses in their regions, and will help befuddled travelers decipher them. Most National Express buses from **London** leave from **Victoria Coach Station** (p. 89).

BUSES IN IRELAND

Ireland's national bus company, **Bus Éireann** (www.buseireann.ie), operates both long-distance **Expressway** buses, which link larger cities, and **Local** buses, which serve the countryside and smaller towns. Find timetables for bus services by visiting local bus stations, or Bus Eireann's website. The invaluable bus timetable book

(£1) should be available for purchase at Busáras Station in Dublin and the occasional tourist information centre. Expressway buses allow passengers to store luggage under the bus, or carry hand-luggage on board. Bicycles may be stored for a £5 fee in the undercarriage, provided there's room. A myriad of **private bus services** are faster and cheaper than Bus Éireann. *Let's Go* lists these private companies in areas they service.

Return tickets are always a great value. For students, purchasing a **TravelSave** stamp (see **Trains in Ireland**, p. 39) along with your ISIC affords huge discounts on bus travel. Bus Éireann's discount **Rambler** tickets, offering unlimited bus travel within Ireland (3 days in 8 £28; 8 days in 15 £68; 15 days in 30 £98; children half-price) aren't usually worth buying; individual tickets often provide better value. A combined **Irish Explorer Rail/Bus** ticket allows unlimited travel on 8 in 15 consecutive days on train and bus lines (£100; child £50). Purchase these tickets from Bus Éireann at their main bus station on Store St. in **Dublin** (☎ (01) 836 6111), or at their Travel Centres in **Cork** (☎ (021) 508188), **Waterford** (☎ (051) 879000), **Galway** (☎ (091) 562000), **Limerick** (☎ (061) 313333), and other transportation hubs.

Ulsterbus, Laganside, Belfast (☎ (01232) 333000; www.ulsterbus.co.uk), runs throughout Northern Ireland, where there are no private bus services. Coverage expands in summer, when several buses run a purely coastal route, and full- and half-day tours leave for key tourist spots from Belfast. Pick up a regional timetable free at any station. Again, the bus discount passes won't save you much money: a **Freedom of Northern Ireland** bus and rail pass offers unlimited travel for one day (UK£10), or several consecutive days (3-day pass £25; 7-day £38).

The **Irish Rover** pass covers Bus Éireann and Ulsterbus services. It sounds ideal for visitors intending to travel in both the Republic and Northern Ireland, but unless you'll be taking lots of bus trips, its true value is debatable. (Unlimited travel on 3 in 8 days £36, children £18; 8 in 15 days £85, children £43; 15 in 30 £130, children £65.) The **Emerald Card** offers unlimited travel on Ulsterbus; Northern Ireland Railways; Bus Éireann Expressway, Local, and City services in Dublin, Cork, Limerick, Galway, and Waterford; and intercity, DART, and suburban rail Iarnród Éireann services. (8 days in 15 £115, children £58; 15 days in 30 days £200, £100.)

BUS TOURS

Staffed with young and energetic guides, these tours cater to backpackers, with minibuses stopping right at the door of hostels. They are a good way to meet other people traveling independently and to get to places that public transport doesn't reach. Some tours are "hop-on, hop-off," which means you can stay for as long as you like in any of the stops. Accommodations are not included in the price, although the companies will usually book beds in hostels.

Britain: Stray Travel, 171 Earl's Court Rd., London SW5 9RF (☎ (020) 7373 7737; www.straytravel.com), sends three coaches a week on a clockwise circuit of London, Bath, Llangollen, the Lake District, Edinburgh, and York, arriving at the door of hostels and stopping at all major sights along the way. £129 buys a ticket, good for four months, so travelers can move at any rate they wish. Also offers other shorter routes.

Wales: Hairy Hog, 22 Conduit Pl., London W2 1HS (☎ (029) 2066 6900 or (020) 7706 1539; www.hairyhog.co.uk). 5-day tours of Wales leaving from Cardiff for £119.

Scotland: HAGGiS, 60 High St., Edinburgh EH1 1NB (☎ (0131) 557 9393; www.radicaltravel.com), runs excellent hop-on, hop-off flexitours from Edinburgh through major sights of Scotland (from £85). They also conduct day trips for £19 and 3- to 6-day tours for £79-139, plus tours of **Britain** (£129) and fully Irish-staffed tours of **Ireland** (3 days UK£75, 6 days UK£129). Lodgings prices not included.

Scotland: MacBackpackers, 105 High St., Edinburgh EH1 1SG (☎ (0131) 558 9900; www.macbackpackers.com), runs terrific tours of Scotland, focusing on Skye, the West Coast, and the Highlands (3-7 days £39-129), as well as £15 day trips from Edinburgh and £55 hop-on hop-off flexitours. Lodgings prices not included.

Ireland: Stray Travel, 6 William St. South, Dublin (☎ (01) 6792684; www.straytravel.com), runs three coaches a week between Dublin, Cork, Schull, Killarney, Galway, Donegal, and Cork, and, like its British counterpart, stops at major sights along the way. UK£129 buys a hop-on hop-off ticket good for four months. For UK£149, the trip extends to Ballycastle and Belfast in Northern Ireland. Shorter routes also available.

BY CAR

Cars offer speed, freedom, access to the countryside, and an escape from the town-to-town mentality of trains. Unfortunately, they insulate you from the *esprit de corps* of rail travel, and introduce the hassle of driving and parking in large cities and the high cost of petrol (gasoline). Although a single traveler won't save by renting a car, four usually will. If you can't decide between train and car travel, you may benefit from a combination of the two; combination rail-and-drive packages can be bought from BritRail pass distributors (p. 39). Remember you may not be used to **driving on the left,** or to driving a **manual transmission** ("stick-shift"; far more common than automatic transmissions in cheap rental cars). Be particularly cautious at **roundabouts** (rotary interchanges) and remember to give way to traffic from the right. Road atlases for the UK are available in any travel bookshop and from many tourist information centres. Petrol is sold by the liter, not the gallon; there are about four liters to the gallon (see **Measurements**, p. 746).

DRIVING IN BRITAIN

You must be 17 and have a license to drive in Britain. The country is covered by a high-speed system of **motorways** ("M-roads"), connecting London with major cities around the country. These are supplemented by a tight web of "A-roads" and "B-roads" that connect towns: A-roads are the main routes between towns, while B-roads are narrower but often more scenic. **Distances** on road signs are in miles (1mi.=1.6km). **Speed limits** are 60mph (97km/h) on single carriageways (non-divided highways), 70mph (113km/h) on motorways (highways) and dual carriageways (divided highways), and usually 30mph (48km/h) in urban areas. Speed limits are always marked at the beginning of town areas; upon leaving, you'll see a circular sign with a slash through it, signaling the end of the restriction. The law requires drivers and front-seat passengers to wear **seat belts,** and rear-seat passengers are also required to buckle up when belts are provided. Driving in **London** is often a nightmare superceded only by parking in London—to maintain sanity, stick to public transport. Copies of the Highway Code, which details Britain's driving regulations, can be purchased at most large bookstores or newsagents.

In the event of a breakdown in Britain, contact the **Automobile Association** (☎ (0800) 887766), **Green Flag** (☎ (0800) 400600), or the **Royal Automobile Club** (☎ (0800) 828282). All three are open 24hr.; however, you may have to be a member to receive breakdown assistance (see below). Membership is sometimes available on the spot. Call ☎ **999** in an emergency. See **Safety on the Road,** p. 21, for more info.

DRIVING IN IRELAND

In the Republic, roads between towns are designated as "N" and "R" roads, though locals refer to them by destination ("the Kerry Road"). Roads numbered below N50 are primary routes that connect all major towns; roads numbered N50 and above are secondary routes, similar to Britain's A-roads; regional R-roads are comparable to Britain's B-roads. Most of these are two-lane. The general **speed limit** is 55mph (90km/h) on the open road and either 30mph (50km/h) or 40mph (65km/h) in town. Signs on roadways are usually in both English and Irish; destinations are sometimes listed only in Irish. Old black-and-white road signs give distances in miles; new green and white signs are in kilometers. Speed limits are signed in miles. For breakdown service, call the **Irish A.A.** (toll-free ☎ (800) 667788).

INTERNATIONAL DRIVING PERMIT (IDP)

If you plan to drive a car while in Britain or Ireland, you must have a valid foreign driver's license and an International Driving Permit (IDP). An IDP, valid for one year, must be issued in your own country before you depart. An application for an IDP needs to include one or two photos, a current local license, an additional form of identification, and a fee. You must be 18 years old to receive the IDP. EU license-holders do not need an IDP to drive in Britain or Ireland.

Australia: Contact your local Royal Automobile Club (RAC) or the National Royal Motorist Association (NRMA) if in NSW or the ACT (☎ (08) 9421 4298; www.rac.com.au/travel). Permits AUS$15.

Canada: Contact any Canadian Automobile Association (CAA) branch office in Canada, or write to CAA, 1145 Hunt Club Rd., Suite 200, K1V 0Y3 Canada. (☎ (613) 247-0117; www.caa.ca/CAAInternet/travelservices). Permits CDN$10.

New Zealand: Contact your local Automobile Association or their main office at Auckland Central, 99 Albert St. (☎ (09) 377 4660; www.nzaa.co.nz). Permits NZ$8.

South Africa: Contact your local Automobile Association of South Africa office or the head office at P.O. Box 596, 2000 Johannesburg (☎ (011) 799 1000). Permits SAR28.50.

US: To buy an IDP, visit any American Automobile Association (AAA) office or write to AAA Travel Related Services, 1000 AAA Drive (mail stop 100), Heathrow, FL 32746 (☎ (407) 444-7000); you do not have to be an AAA member. Offers travel services and auto insurance. Permits US$10.

CAR INSURANCE

Most credit cards cover standard insurance. If you rent, lease, or borrow a car, or use your own, you will need a **green card,** or **International Insurance Certificate,** to prove that you have liability insurance. Obtain it through the car rental agency; most include coverage in their prices. If you lease a car, you can obtain a green card from the dealer. Some travel agents offer the card; it may also be available at border crossings. Verify whether your auto insurance applies abroad; even if it does, you will still need a green card to certify this to foreign officials. If you have a collision abroad, the accident will show up on your domestic records if you report it to your insurance company.

RENTALS

Rentals vary by company, season, and pickup point. Expect to pay UK£130 or IR£100-300 per week for a teensy car. Automatics are generally more expensive than manuals (stick shifts). If possible, reserve well before leaving for Britain or Ireland and pay in advance. It is usually significantly less expensive to reserve a car from overseas than from Britain or Ireland. All plans require sizable deposits (about £100) unless you pay by credit card. Always check if prices quoted include tax, unlimited mileage, and collision insurance; some credit card companies will cover this automatically. Ask about discounts and check the terms of insurance, particularly the size of the deductible. Non-Europeans should check with their national motoring organization (like AAA or CAA) for international coverage. Ask your airline about special fly-and-drive packages; you may get up to a week of free or discounted rental. A special BritRail **Pass 'N' Drive** pass combines rail travel and car rental. At most agencies, all that's needed to rent a car is a driver's license and proof that you've had the license for a year; some will ask for an additional ID confirming your home address. For insurance reasons, renters in Britain are required to be over 21; those 18-21 should consider leasing. In Ireland, those under 23 generally cannot rent. You can rent cars from the following rental agencies:

Auto Europe: 39 Commercial St., P.O. Box 7006, Portland, ME 04101 (☎ (888) 223-5555; www.autoeurope.com). From US$135 per week, automatics from US$197.

Avis: UK ☎ (0990) 900500, Australia ☎ (800) 225533, NZ ☎ (09) 526 2847, US and Canada ☎ (800) 331-1084; www.avis.com. Minimum age 23.

Budget: UK ☎ (0800) 181181, Ireland ☎ (01) 837 9611, Australia ☎ 13 27 27, Canada ☎ (800) 527-0700, NZ ☎ (09) 375 2222, US ☎ (800) 472-3325; www.budget-rentacar.com. From IR£45 per day.

Europe by Car: 1 Rockefeller Plaza, New York, NY 10020 (US ☎ (800) 223-1516 or (212) 581-3040; www.europebycar.com).

Europcar: 30 Woburn Pl., London WC1H 0JR (UK ☎ (0345) 222525, Canada ☎ (800) 227 7368, US ☎ (800) 227-3876; www.europcar.com).

Hertz: UK ☎ (0990) 996699, Australia ☎ 13 30 39, Canada ☎ (800) 263 0600, US ☎ (800) 654-3001; www.hertz.com.

Kemwel Holiday Autos: 106 Calvert St., Harrison, NY 10528 (☎ (800) 678-0678; www.kemwel.com). From £129 per week, automatics from £199.

BY FERRY

Ferry services connecting ports in England, Scotland, Wales, and Ireland are inexpensive and usually the cheapest way of crossing the Irish Sea. Ferry companies advertise special low rates for day returns in local papers; otherwise, expect to pay £20-30 depending on route, season, and length of stay. Ferry companies often offer special discounts in conjunction with bus or train companies; a little advance research can save you and your wallet much angst.

Caledonian MacBrayne, The Ferry Terminal, Gourock, Renfrewshire PA19 1QP (☎ (01475) 650100; www.calmac.co.uk). Cal-Mac's the daddy of Scottish ferries, with routes in the Hebrides and the west coast of Scotland.

Irish Ferries, 2-4 Merrion Row, Dublin 2 (☎ (01) 638 3333; www.irishferries.ie) and Reliance House, Water St., Liverpool L2 8TP (☎ (0990) 171717). Dublin, Ireland to Holyhead, Wales (2hr.; return £35-60, students and seniors £28-48); Rosslare, Ireland to Pembroke, Wales (4hr.; return £35, students and seniors £28).

Isle of Man Steam Packet Company serves the Isle of Man; see p. 343 for details.

P&O Scottish Ferries, P.O. Box 5, P&O Ferries Terminal, Jamieson's Quay, Aberdeen AB11 5NP (☎ (01224) 589111 or 572615; www.poscottishferries.co.uk). Sails between Aberdeen, Lerwick, Stromness, and Scrabster.

SeaCat Scotland, 34 Charlotte St., Stranraer, Wigtownshire DG9 7EF (UK ☎ (0990) 523523; Ireland ☎ (1800) 551743). Belfast, Northern Ireland to Stranraer, Scotland.

Stena Line, Charter House, Park St., Ashford, Kent TN24 8EX (☎ (0990) 707070; www.stenaline.co.uk), and Dún Laoghaire Travel Centre (☎ (01) 204 7777). Dún Laoghaire (near Dublin), Ireland to Holyhead, Wales (£20-35, students and seniors £16-28); Belfast, Northern Ireland to Stranraer, Scotland (£20-42, day return £18, students and seniors £15-32); Rosslare, Ireland to Fishguard, Wales (£20-41, students and seniors £16-40).

Swansea Cork Ferries, Ferry Port, King's Dock, Swansea SA1 8RU (☎ (01792) 456116) and 52 South Mall, Cork (☎ (021) 271166). Swansea, Wales to Cork, Ireland (10hr., £22-32).

BY BICYCLE

Biking is one of the key elements of the classic budget voyage. Much of the British and Irish countryside is well-suited for cycling; many roads are not heavily traveled. Consult tourist offices for local touring routes, and always bring along the appropriate **Ordnance Survey maps.** Keep safety in mind—even well-traveled routes often cover highly uneven terrain (see **Safety on the Road,** p. 21).

GETTING OR TRANSPORTING A BIKE. Many airlines will count a bike as part of your luggage, although a few charge an extra US$60-110 each way. Bikes must be packed in a cardboard box with the pedals and front wheel detached; airlines sell bike boxes at the airport (US$10). If you plan to explore several widely separated regions, you can combine cycling with train travel. Depending upon the route you are traveling, many trains allow you to put your bike in the luggage compartment free (except during rush hour); however, you might need to make an advance reservation for your bike for longer journeys. In addition, bikes often ride free on ferries leaving Britain and Ireland. A better option for some is to buy a bike in Britain and Ireland and sell it before you leave. A bike bought new overseas is subject to customs duties if brought into your home country; used bikes, however, will not be taxed. **Renting** (also called **hiring**) a bike is preferable to bringing your own if your touring will be confined to one or two regions. *Let's Go* lists bike rental stores in many towns. Those who need more details on cycling in Britain should consult the free British Tourist Authority pamphlet *Britain for Cyclists.*

BICYCLE EQUIPMENT. Riding a bike with a frame pack strapped on it or your back is about as safe as pedaling blindfolded over a sheet of ice; panniers are essential. The first thing to buy is a suitable **bike helmet** (US$25-50). U-shaped **Citadel** or **Kryptonite locks** are expensive (starting at US$30), but the companies insure their locks against theft of your bike for one to two years. For mail order equipment, **Bike Nashbar,** 4111 Simon Rd., Youngstown, OH 44512 (☎ 800-627-4227; www.nashbar.com), ships anywhere in the US or Canada. According to British law, your bike must carry a white light at the front of the cycle and a red light and red reflector at the back.

USEFUL ORGANIZATIONS. The **Cyclists' Touring Club,** 69 Meadrow, Godalming, Surrey GU7 3HS (☎ (01483) 417217; www.ctc.org.uk), has everything you wanted to know about cycling in Britain, from routes to cyclists' books. Membership costs £25 (under 26 or over 65 £15, families £40), and includes free touring advice, and a bimonthly magazine. If you are nervous about cycling on your own, **CBT Tours,** 415 W. Fullerton #1003, Chicago, IL 60614 (☎ 800-736-2453; www.cbttours.com), runs one- to seven-week tours for around US$115 per day, including all lodging and breakfasts, one-third off all dinners, airport transfers, and extensive route notes and maps. Tours run May through August. Many local bike rental companies also offer guided bike tours of their region.

BY THUMB

> *Let's Go* strongly urges you to consider seriously the risks before you choose to hitch. We do not recommend hitching as a safe means of transportation, and none of the information presented here is intended to do so.

No one should hitchhike without careful consideration of the risks involved. Not everyone can be an airplane pilot, but any bozo can drive a car. Hitching means entrusting your life to a random person who happens to stop beside you on the road and risking theft, assault, sexual harassment, and unsafe driving. In spite of this, there are gains to hitching. It can allow you to meet local people and get where you're going, especially in rural parts of Scotland, Wales, and Ireland, where public transportation is sketchy. The choice, however, remains yours. Depending on the circumstances, men and women traveling in groups and men traveling alone might consider hitching beyond the range of bus or train routes. If you're a woman traveling alone, don't hitch—it's just too dangerous. A man and a woman are a safer combination, two men will have a hard time, and three will go nowhere.

Where one stands is vital. Experienced hitchers pick a spot outside built-up areas, where drivers can stop, return to the road without causing an accident, and have time to look over potential passengers as they approach. Hitching or even standing on motorways (any road labelled "M," such as the M1) is illegal. Success also depends on what one looks like. Successful hitchers travel light and stack their belongings in a compact but visible cluster. Drivers prefer hitchers who are neat and wholesome. No one stops for anyone wearing sunglasses.

Safety issues are always imperative, even for those not hitching alone. Safety-minded hitchers will not get into a car that they can't get out of again in a hurry (especially the back seat of a two-door car) and never let go of their backpacks. If they feel threatened, they insist on being let off, regardless of where they are. Acting as if they are going to open the car door or vomit on the upholstery usually gets a driver to stop. Hitching at night can be particularly dangerous and difficult; experienced hitchers stand in well-lit places, and expect drivers to be leery.

BY FOOT

BRITAIN. An extensive system of well-marked and well-maintained long-distance paths cover Britain, ranging from the gently rolling paths of the **South Downs Way** (p. 187) to the rugged mountain trails of the **Pennine Way** (p. 369). The Ordnance Survey 1:25,000 maps mark almost every house, barn, standing stone, graveyard, and pub. Less ambitious hikers will want the 1:50,000 scale maps. The **Ramblers' Association,** 1-5 Wandsworth Rd., London SW8 2XX (☎ (020) 7339 8500), publishes a *Yearbook* on walking and places to stay, as well as free newsletters and magazines. (Membership £18, students and seniors £9, couples and families £22.)

IRELAND. There are many long-distance rural paths in the Republic, though they lack the sophisticated infrastructure of England's. **Wicklow Way** (p. 691), a popular trail through mountainous County Wicklow, is an exception, with hostels within a day's walk of each other. Bord Fáilte publishes numerous brochures describing the trails. The best hill-walking maps are the Ordnance Survey series, which cost IR£4.20 each. The **Ulster Way** encircles **Northern Ireland** with 560 mi. of marked trail. For detailed leaflets on various trails, contact **Sports Council for Northern Ireland,** House of Sport, Upper Malone Rd., Belfast BT9 5LA (☎ (028) 9038 1222).

ACCOMMODATIONS

HOSTELS

> **A HOSTELER'S BILL OF RIGHTS** There are certain standard features that we do not include in our hostel listings. Unless we state otherwise, you can expect that every hostel has: no lockout, no curfew, a kitchen, free hot showers, secure luggage storage, and no key deposit.

Hostels generally provide dorm-style accommodations, often in large single-sex rooms with bunks, although some offer private rooms for families and couples. They offer a chance to meet others, and often have kitchens for your use, bike rentals, storage areas, and laundry facilities. There can be drawbacks: some hostels (particularly YHA hostels in rural areas) close during certain daytime "lockout" hours, have a curfew, impose a maximum stay, or, less frequently, require you to do chores. In Britain, a hostel bed will cost around £6 in rural areas, £12 in larger cities, and £13-20 in London; in Ireland, around IR£6 (IR£10 in Dublin).

Youth hostels in the UK and Ireland are run by the **Youth Hostels Association (YHA) of England and Wales,** the **Scottish Youth Hostels Association (SYHA), Hostelling International Northern Ireland (HINI),** and **An Óige** (an OYJ) in the Republic of Ireland. All four are affiliated with **Hostelling International (HI),** and you usually must be a member of an HI-affiliated association (see below for a partial listing) to stay in any of their hostels. Many HI hotels accept reservations via the **International Booking Network** (England and Wales ☎ (01629) 581418; Scotland ☎ (0541) 553255; Northern Ireland ☎ (01232) 324733; Republic of Ireland ☎ (01) 830 1766; Australia ☎ (02) 9261 1111; Canada ☎ (800) 663-5777; New Zealand ☎ (09) 379 4224; US ☎ (800) 909-4776). HI's umbrella organization's web page (www.iyhf.org), which lists the web addresses and phone numbers of all national associations, can be a great place to begin researching hostelling in a specific region. Other comprehensive hostelling websites include **Hostels.com** (www.hostels.com) and **Eurotrip** (www.eurotrip.com/accommodation).

Unless noted as "self-catering," the YHA hostels listed in *Let's Go* offer cooked meals at roughly standard rates—breakfast £3.20, small/standard packed lunch £2.80/£3.65, evening meal £4.15 (£4.80 for a three-course meal in some hostels), and children's meals (breakfast £1.75, lunch or dinner £2.70).

Most HI hostels also honor **guest memberships**—you'll get a blank card with space for six validation stamps. Each night you'll pay a nonmember supplement (one-sixth the membership fee) and earn one guest stamp; get six stamps, and you're a member. Most student travel agencies (see p. 29) sell HI cards, as do all of the national hosteling organizations listed below. All prices listed below are valid for a **one-year membership** unless otherwise noted.

Youth Hostels Association (England and Wales) Ltd., Trevelyan House, 8 St. Stephen's Hill, St. Albans, Hertfordshire AL1 2DY (☎ (01727) 855215; fax 844126; www.yha.org.uk). £12, under 18 £6, families £24. **YHA Book-a-Bed-Ahead** (☎ (01629) 581061). Books beds in hostels along hiking routes for 50p per night.

Scottish Youth Hostels Association (SYHA), 7 Glebe Crescent, Stirling FK8 2JA (☎ (01786) 891400; fax 891333; www.syha.org.uk). £6, under 18 £2.50.

Hostelling International Northern Ireland (HINI), 22-32 Donegall Rd., Belfast BT12 5JN (☎ (01232) 324733; fax 439699; www.hini.org.uk). £7, under 18 £3.

An Óige (Irish Youth Hostel Association), 61 Mountjoy St., Dublin 7 (☎ (1) 830 4555; fax 830 5808; anoige@iol.ie; www.irelandyha.org). IR£10, under 18 IR£4.

Australian Youth Hostels Association (AYHA), 422 Kent St., Sydney NSW 2000 (☎ (02) 9261 1111; fax 9261 1969; www.yha.org.au). AUS$49, under 18 AUS$14.50.

ESSENTIALS

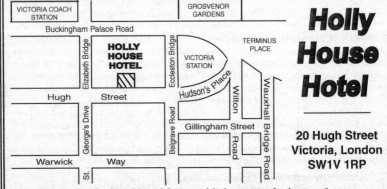

Hostelling International-Canada (HI-C), 400-205 Catherine St., Ottawa, ON K2P 1C3 (☎ (800) 663-5777 or (613) 237-7884; fax (613) 237-7868; info@hostellingintl.ca; www.hostellingintl.ca). CDN$25, under 18 CDN$12.

Youth Hostels Association of New Zealand (YHANZ), P.O. Box 436, 173 Cashel St., Christchurch 1 (☎ (03) 379 9970; fax 365 4476; info@yha.org.nz; www.yha.org.nz). NZ$40, ages 15-17 NZ$12, under 15 free.

Hostels Association of South Africa, 3rd fl. 73 St. George's St. Mall, P.O. Box 4402, Cape Town 8000 (☎ (021) 424 2511; fax 424 4119; info@hisa.org.za; www.hisa.org.za). SAR50, under 18 SAR25, lifetime SAR250.

Hostelling International-American Youth Hostels (HI-AYH), 733 15th St. NW, #840, Washington, D.C. 20005 (☎ (202) 783-6161 ext. 136; fax 783-6171; hiayh-serv@hiayh.org; www.hiayh.org). US$25, under 18 free.

Independent hostels tend to attract younger crowds, be closer to city centers, and be much more relaxed about lockouts or curfews than their YHA or An Óige counterparts. On the other hand, they may not have single-sex rooms, and may not be as family-oriented. **Backpackers Britain** (www.backpack.co.uk) operates a website listing their network of good independent hostels in England and Wales. A number of hostels in Ireland belong to the **IHH (Independent Holiday Hostels)** organization. IHH hostels require no membership card, accept all ages, and usually have no lockout or curfew; all are Bord Fáilte-approved. For a free booklet with complete descriptions of IHH hostels, contact the IHH office at 57 Lower Gardiner St., Dublin (☎ (01) 836 4700). For an extensive list of independent hostels in Britain and Ireland, see *The Independent Hostel Guide: Britain & Europe* (The Backpackers Press, £4.95).

BED AND BREAKFASTS

For a cozier alternative to impersonal hotel rooms, B&Bs and guest houses (often private homes with rooms available to travelers) range from the acceptable to the sublime. The "breakfast" that's included in the price is usually a **full cooked breakfast** (bacon, eggs, sausages, and more), but vegetarian alternatives are sometimes available. A **continental breakfast** is just juice and tea or coffee with cereal, pastries, and bread with jam. B&B owners will sometimes go out of their way to be accommodating, giving personalized tours, or offering home-cooked meals. On the other hand, some B&Bs do not provide private bathrooms (rooms with private bathrooms are often referred to as **ensuite** rooms; *Let's Go* uses the phrase "with bath"), and many do not provide phones. The cheapest rooms in British B&Bs cost £12-£20 for a single—not always easy to find—and £20-40 for a double. London, as always, inhabits a stratospheric price range of its own. In Ireland, expect to pay IR£14-18 for a single and IR£20-36 for a double. A "double" room is one with a large bed for two people; a "twin" room is one with two separate beds; *Let's Go* lists B&B prices by room type (not per person) unless otherwise stated.

You can book B&Bs by calling directly, or by asking the local **tourist information centre** (TIC) to help you find accommodations; most can also book B&Bs in other towns. TICs usually charge a 10% deposit on the first night's price, deductible from the amount you pay the B&B proprietor. Sometimes, especially in big cities, a flat fee is added on. In Wales, a £1 fee is always added to the 10%.

The British tourist boards operate a B&B **rating system,** using a scale of one to five diamonds (in England) or stars (in Scotland and Wales). Rated accommodations get to be part of the tourist board's booking system, but don't treat these ratings as the final word. It costs money to be rated; some perfectly good small B&Bs choose not to participate in ratings. Approval by the **Northern Ireland Tourist Board** is legally required of all Northern Ireland accommodations. In the Republic of Ireland, **Bord Fáilte** approves accommodations. Bord Fáilte's standards are very specific and, in some cases, far higher than budget travelers expect or require.

Most official TICs in Ireland will refer *only* to approved accommodations; some won't even tell you how to get to an unapproved hostel, B&B, or campground.

Bed and Breakfast (GB), 94-96 Bell St., Henley-on-Thames, Oxon, England RG9 1XS (☎ (01491) 578803), is a reservation service which covers England, Scotland, Wales, and Ireland. It books rooms for a minimum deposit of £30, which is not refundable, but can be deducted from the total price of your stay. **Hometours International, Inc.,** P.O. Box 11503, Knoxville, TN 37939 (☎ (800) 367-4668; http://thor.he.net/~hometour), sells a catalog of UK B&B listings ($7), and offers a booking service for a deposit of US$60, also deductible from the total price.

DORMS AND RESIDENCE HALLS

Many universities open their residence halls to travelers when school is not in session (mid-June to mid-October, and sometimes for the Christmas and Easter holidays); some do so even during term-time. These dorms offer the privacy of personal space, are often close to student areas, and are usually clean; however, many do not offer private bathrooms. Getting a room may take a couple of phone calls and require advanced planning, but rates tend to be low. *Let's Go* lists dorm rooms where available, and the **British Universities Accommodation Consortium,** Box No. W00, University Park, Nottingham NG7 2RD (☎ (0115) 846 6444; www.buac.co.uk), has a list of rates and schedules on their website.

YMCAS AND YWCAS

Not all **Young Men's/Women's Christian Association** (YMCA/YWCA) locations offer lodging; those that do are often located in urban downtowns, which can be convenient but a little gritty. In Britain and Ireland, many YMCAs (www.ymca.org.uk) cater more to long-term residents, but they will still accept short-term stays. Rates are usually lower than a hotel's but higher than a hostel's and may include daily housekeeping and 24hr. security. Many YMCAs accept women, while many YWCAs are women-only. Some will not lodge people under 18 without parental permission. For a small fee (US$3 in North America, US$5 elsewhere), **Y's Way International,** 224 E. 47th St., New York, NY 10017 (☎ (2120 308-2899; fax 308-3161) will make reservations for the YMCAs in Britain and in Ireland.

HOME EXCHANGE

Home exchange offers the traveler various types of homes (houses, apartments, condominiums, villas, even castles in some cases), plus the opportunity to live like a native and to cut down on accommodation fees. Home exchanges are ideal for families, or travelers with special dietary needs; you often get your own kitchen, TV, and telephones. Most services have membership fees of £40-£50 to get access to their listings. For more information, contact **HomeExchange.com** (US ☎ (407) 862-7211; www.homeexchange.com), **Intervac International Home Exchange** (UK ☎ (012) 2589 2208; Ireland ☎ (041) 983 0930; www.intervac.com), or **The Invented City: International Home Exchange** (US ☎ (800) 788-2489, elsewhere call US ☎ +1 (415) 252-1141; www.invented-city.com). **Green Theme International** (UK ☎ (012) 0887 3123; www.gti-home-exchange.com), based in Cornwall, also offers exchanges.

CAMPING AND THE OUTDOORS

Britain and Ireland have quite a number of campsites, which sadly tend to be a long hike away from many of the popular sights and cities. Campsites tend to be privately owned, with basic ones costing £3 per person, and posh ones costing up to £10 per person. **It is illegal to camp in national parks,** since much of their land is privately owned. Don't camp without permission: not only is it against the law, but you could receive a midnight visit from cows or sheep.

USEFUL RESOURCES

A variety of publishing companies offer hiking guidebooks to meet the educational needs of novice or expert. For information about camping, hiking, and biking, contact the publishers listed below. Campers heading to Europe should consider buying an **International Camping Carnet.** Similar to a hostel membership card, it's required at a few campgrounds and provides discounts at others. It is available in North America from the Family Campers and RVers Association and in the UK from The Caravan Club (see below). See also *Alan Rogers' Good Camps Guide: Britain and Ireland* (Deneway Guides and Travel, £8).

Automobile Association, A.A. Publishing. Orders and enquiries to: TBS Frating Distribution Centre, Colchester, Essex, CO7 7DW (☎ (01206) 255678; www.theaa.co.uk). Publishes *Camping and Caravanning: Britain & Ireland* (£8).

The Caravan Club, East Grinstead House, East Grinstead, West Sussex, RH19 1UA (☎ (01342) 326944; www.caravanclub.co.uk). For £27.50, members receive equipment discounts, a 700-page directory and handbook, and a monthly magazine. The club publishes *Caravanner's Guide to Scotland* (£2) and *Caravanner's Guide to the North* (£2).

Ordnance Survey (☎ (08456) 050505; www.ordsvy.gov.uk). Britain's national mapping agency (also known as OS) publishes topographical maps of the country. They are available at tourist information centres and from many bookstores. Their excellent *Outdoor Leisure* (£6.50), *Explorer* (£5.50), and *Pathfinder* (£4.50) series of maps cover the whole of Britain in 1:25,000 scale.

CAMPING AND HIKING EQUIPMENT

WHAT TO BUY...

Good camping equipment is both sturdy and light. Camping equipment is generally more expensive in Britain and Ireland than in North America.

Sleeping Bags: Most good sleeping bags are rated by season, or the lowest outdoor temperature at which they will keep you warm ("summer" means 30-40°F/0-5°C at night; "four-season" or "winter" often means below 0°F/-15°C). Sleeping bags are made either of **down** (warmer and lighter, but more expensive, and miserable when wet) or of **synthetic** material (heavier, more durable, and warmer when wet). Prices may range from US$80-210 for a summer synthetic to US$250-300 for a good down winter bag. **Sleeping bag pads,** including foam pads (US$10-20) and air mattresses (US$15-50), cushion your back and neck and insulate you from the ground. Bring a stuff sack to store your bag and keep it dry.

Tents: The best tents are free standing, with their own frames and suspension systems; they set up quickly and only require staking in high winds. Low-profile dome tents are the best all-around since when pitched their internal space is almost entirely usable. Tent sizes can be somewhat misleading: two people *can* fit in a two-person tent, but will find life more pleasant in a four-person. If you're traveling by car, go for the bigger tent, but if you're hiking, stick with a smaller tent that weighs no more than 5-6lbs (2-3kg). Good two-person tents start at US$90, four-person tents at US$300. Seal the seams of your tent with waterproofer, and make sure it has a rain fly. Other tent accessories include a **battery-operated lantern,** a **plastic groundcloth,** and a **nylon tarp.**

Backpacks: If you intend to do a lot of hiking, you should have a frame backpack (sometimes called a **rucksack** in Britain). **Internal-frame packs** mold better to your back, keep a lower center of gravity, and can flex adequately to allow you to hike difficult trails. **External-frame packs** are more comfortable for long hikes over even terrain—including city streets—since they keep the weight higher and distribute it more evenly. Whichever you choose, make sure your pack has a strong, padded hip belt, which transfers the weight from the shoulders to the hips and legs. Any serious backpacking requires a pack of at least 4000 in^3 (16,000cc). Allow an additional 500 in^3 for your sleeping bag in internal-frame packs. Sturdy backpacks cost anywhere from

US$125-500. This is one area where it doesn't pay to economize—cheaper packs may be less comfortable, and the straps are more likely to fray or rip. Before you buy any pack, try it on and imagine carrying it, full, a few miles up a rocky incline. Better yet, fill it up with something heavy and walk around the store to get a sense of how it distributes weight before committing to buy it. A waterproof **backpack cover** will prove invaluable. Otherwise, plan to store all of your belongings in plastic bags inside your backpack.

Boots: Be sure to wear hiking boots with good **ankle support.** They should fit snugly and comfortably over 1-2 pairs of wool socks and thin liner socks. Break in boots over several weeks first in order to spare yourself painful and debilitating blisters.

Other Necessities: Raingear in two pieces, a top and trousers, is far superior to a poncho. **Synthetics,** like polypropylene tops, socks, and long underwear, along with a **pile jacket,** will keep you warm even when wet. When camping in autumn, winter, or spring, bring along a **"space blanket,"** which helps you to retain your body heat and doubles as a groundcloth (US$5-15). Plastic **canteens** or water bottles keep water cooler than metal ones, and are virtually shatter- and leak-proof. Large, collapsible **water sacks** will significantly improve your lot in primitive campgrounds and weigh practically nothing when empty, though they are bulky and heavy when full. Bring **water-purification tablets** for when you can't boil water, unless you are willing to shell out money for a portable water-purification system. For places that forbid fires or the gathering of firewood, which includes most British and Irish campsites, you'll need a **camp stove** (the classic Coleman starts at US$40) and a propane-filled **fuel bottle** to operate it. A **first aid kit, swiss army knife** or **pocketknife, insect repellent, calamine lotion,** and **waterproof matches** or a **lighter** are other essential camping items. And always bring an **Ordnance Survey (OS) map** of the region you're camping or hiking in.

...AND WHERE TO BUY IT

The mail-order/online companies listed below often offer lower prices than many retail stores, but a visit to a local camping or outdoors store will give you a good sense of the look and weight of certain items. Sales reps at outdoor stores often know of a range of **organized adventure tours** (include hiking, biking, canoeing, kayaking, rafting, and climbing), which are another way of exploring the wild. They also often offer training programs for people travelling independently.

YHA Adventure Shop, 14 Southampton St., London, WC2E 7HA (☎ (020) 7836 8541). The main branch of one of Britain's largest outdoor equipment suppliers. 10% off with YHA membership.

Campmor, P.O. Box 700, Upper Saddle River, NJ 07458, USA (US ☎ (888) 226-7667; elsewhere call US ☎ +1 (201) 825-8300; www.campmor.com).

Discount Camping, 880 Main North Rd., Pooraka, South Australia 5095, Australia (☎ (08) 8262 3399; www.discountcamping.com.au).

L.L. Bean, Freeport, ME 04033 (US and Canada ☎ (800) 441-5713; UK ☎ (0800) 962 954; elsewhere, call US ☎ +1 (207) 552-6878; www.llbean.com).

Mountain Designs, P.O. Box 1472, Fortitude Valley, Queensland 4006, Australia (☎ (07) 3252 8894; www.mountaindesign.com.au).

Recreational Equipment, Inc. (REI), Sumner, WA 98352, USA (☎ (800) 426-4840 or ☎ (253) 891-2500; www.rei.com).

CAMPERS, RVS, AND CARAVANS

Renting a camper van (RV in the US) will always be more expensive than tenting or hosteling, but the costs compare favorably with the price of staying in hotels and renting a car. The convenience of bringing along your own bedroom, bathroom, and kitchen sometimes makes it an attractive option, especially for older travelers and families with children. Rates vary widely by region, season (July and

August are the most expensive months), and type of van; contact several companies to compare vehicles and prices. **Auto Europe** (☎ (0800) 899893; US ☎ (800) 223-5555) rents caravans in Britain (four-passenger caravan for a week £1300). For further information, consult publications from the A.A. and the Caravan Club (see **Useful Resources,** p. 51).

WILDERNESS SAFETY

Stay warm, stay dry, and stay hydrated. The vast majority of life-threatening wilderness situations can be avoided by following this simple advice. On any hike, however brief, you should pack enough equipment to keep you alive should disaster befall. This includes **raingear, hat, mittens, first-aid kit, reflector, whistle, high energy food,** and extra **water.** Dress in warm layers of **synthetic materials** designed for the outdoors, or **wool.** Pile fleece jackets and Gore-Tex raingear are excellent choices. Never rely on cotton for warmth, as it is absolutely useless when wet. Check all equipment for any defects before setting out.

Check **weather forecasts** and pay attention to the skies when hiking. Weather patterns can change suddenly. Always let someone know when and where you are going hiking, either a friend, your hostel, a park ranger, or a local hiking organization. Do not attempt a hike beyond your ability—you may be endangering your life. See **Health,** p. 23, for information about outdoor ailments such as heatstroke and hypothermia, as well as basic medical concerns and first-aid. The **emergency number**—for police, ambulance, and, in some areas, mountain rescue—is ☎ 999.

For more information, consult *How to Stay Alive in the Woods,* by Bradford Angier (Macmillan Press, £5.95, US$8).

KEEPING IN TOUCH

BY LETTER

SENDING MAIL TO BRITAIN AND IRELAND

Airmail letters under 1 oz. between North America and Britain or Ireland take 3-5 days and cost US$1 or CDN$0.95. From Australia, airmail takes 5-7 days (AUS$1.20 for small letters up to 20g, AUS$1.50 for large letters up to 20g). Envelopes should be marked "air mail" or "par avion" to avoid having letters sent by sea. Sending mail by sea **(surface mail)** is the cheapest and slowest way, taking one to three months to cross the Atlantic and two to four to cross the Pacific—appropriate for sending large quantities of items you won't need for a while. When ordering items from overseas, always include **International Reply Coupons (IRCs)**—a way of providing the postage to cover delivery. IRCs should be available from your local post office (60p or US$1.05).

POSTAL CODES. The characters before the space in British postal codes refer to the postal district; the characters after identify the exact street or building. *Let's Go* lists the exact postal code for the given post office; most other places in town will share the postal district, but not the last three characters. Big cities such as London and Glasgow often encompass several postal districts. If you need exact postal codes, call ☎ (013) 1550 8999 or check the Royal Mail website (www.royalmail.co.uk). In Ireland, only Dublin has postal codes.

RECEIVING MAIL IN BRITAIN AND IRELAND

There are several ways to arrange pickup of letters sent to you by friends and relatives while you are abroad:

Poste Restante: Mail can be sent through Poste Restante (the international phrase for **General Delivery**) to almost any city or town with a post office in Britain and Ireland.

Address Poste Restante letters to the post office, highlighting the last name (for example Michelle JABULANI, Poste Restante, New Bond St. Post Office, Bath BA1 1A5, United Kingdom). If you don't specify a post office by street address or postal code, the mail will go to a special desk in the central post office. As a rule, it is best to use the largest post office in the area; mail may be sent there regardless of what is written on the envelope. When possible, it is usually safer and quicker to send mail express or registered. However, post offices often will *not* accept FedEx and other non-postal service deliveries. When picking up your mail, bring a form of photo ID, preferably a passport. There is generally no charge, unless the sender has not paid enough postage. If the clerks insist that there is nothing for you, have them check under your first name as well. Post offices usually hold Poste Restante mail for a month. *Let's Go* lists post offices and their postal codes in the **Practical Information** section of our listings.

American Express: AmEx travel offices throughout the world offer a free **Client Letter Service** (mail held up to 30 days and forwarding upon request) for cardholders who contact them in advance. Address the letter in the same way shown above. Some offices will offer these services to non-cardholders (especially AmEx Travelers Cheque holders), but call ahead to make sure. *Let's Go* lists AmEx office locations for most large cities in **Practical Information** sections; for a complete, free list, call (800) 528-4800.

Express Services: Federal Express (in Australia ☎ 13 26 10; Ireland ☎ 800-535-800; New Zealand ☎ (0800) 733 339; UK ☎ (0800) 123800; US and Canada ☎ (800-463-3339) can send a letter from New York to London in two days for a whopping US$40. Express services offered by local post offices bridge the gap in prices and speed between FedEx and regular mail. Post offices will hold letters sent using these services, as long as no signature is required. From the US, **USPS Global Priority Mail** service can send a letter to Britain or Ireland within 3-5 working days for US$5. From Australia, **EMS International Courier** takes 3-4 working days (AUS$32).

SENDING MAIL FROM BRITAIN AND IRELAND

Aerogrammes, printed sheets that fold into envelopes and travel via airmail, are available at post offices (UK 40p). It helps to mark "airmail" if possible, though "par avion" is universally understood. Most post offices will charge exorbitant fees or simply refuse to send aerogrammes with enclosures. **International airmail** from Britain and Ireland averages 5-10 days (faster for North America, slower for Australia), although times are more unpredictable from smaller towns. Within Europe, airmail takes 3-5 days.

To send a **postcard** to another European country costs UK36p or IR45p; to send one to any other international destination via airmail costs UK40p or IR45p. To send a **letter** within Britain costs 27p/19p (1st/2nd-class). To send one via airmail to another European country (including the Republic of Ireland) costs 36p (up to 20g), and to a non-European international destination costs 45p for letters up to 10g, and 65p for letters weighing 10-20g. To send a letter up to 25g via airmail from Ireland to another European country or any other international destination costs IR45p. British stamps are indicated by a profile of the Queen's head, and are the only stamps in the world without the country's name on them; this privilege stems from being the first country in the world to issue prepaid postage stamps, in 1840.

TELEPHONES

CALLING HOME FROM BRITAIN AND IRELAND

A **calling card** is probably your best bet. Calls are billed either collect or to your account. To obtain a calling card before you leave home, contact your national telecommunications service, the first number listed below. **To call home with a calling card,** contact the British or Irish operator for your service provider by dialing the second or third number listed.

PLACING INTERNATIONAL CALLS

To call Britain or Ireland from home or to place an international call from Britain or Ireland, dial:

1. The **international dialing prefix.** To dial out of **Australia,** dial 0011; **Canada** or the **US,** 011; the **Republic of Ireland, New Zealand,** or the **UK,** 00; **South Africa,** 09.

2. The **country code** of the country you want to call. To call **Australia,** dial 61; **Canada** or the **US,** 1; the **Republic of Ireland,** 353; **New Zealand,** 64; **South Africa,** 27; the **UK,** 44.

3.The **city** or **area code.** *Let's Go* lists the phone codes for cities and towns in Britain and Ireland opposite the city or town name. If the first digit is a zero (e.g., 020 for London), omit it when calling from abroad (e.g., dial 011 44 20 from Canada to reach London).

4. The **local number.**

Australia: Telstra **Australia Direct** (☎ 13 22 00). UK ☎ (0800) 890061. Ireland ☎ (1800) 550061.

Canada: Bell Canada **Canada Direct** (☎ (800) 565 4708). UK ☎ (0800) 890016. Ireland ☎ (1800) 555001.

Ireland: Telecom Éireann **Ireland Direct** (☎ (1800) 250250). UK ☎ (0800) 890353.

New Zealand: Telecom New Zealand (☎ (800) 000 000). UK ☎ (0800) 890064. Ireland ☎ (1800) 550064.

South Africa: Telkom South Africa (☎ 09 03). UK ☎ (0800) 890027. Ireland ☎ (1800) 550027.

UK: British Telecom **BT Direct** (☎ (0800) 345144). Ireland ☎ (1800) 550144.

US: AT&T (☎ (888) 288-4685). UK ☎ (0800) 890011. Ireland ☎ (1800) 550000. **MCI Worldphone** (☎ (800) 444-4141). UK ☎ (0800) 890222; Ireland ☎ (1800) 551001. **Sprint** (☎ (800) 877-4646). UK ☎ (0800) 890877; Ireland ☎ (1800) 552001.

Many newsagents in the UK sell **prepaid international phonecards,** such as those offered by Swiftcall. These cards are usually the cheapest way to make long international phone calls, but sometimes carry a minimum charge per call, which make quick calls less cost-effective. Stores such as **Call Shop** offer cheap international calls from their booths, and can be found in parts of cities with large numbers of tourists and/or immigrants.

Calling cards are the next best option for making international phone calls, as international rates are often exorbitant. You can make direct international calls from **payphones,** but if you aren't using a calling card you may need to drop your coins as quickly as your words. **BT phonecards** and occasionally major credit cards can also be used for direct international calls, but they are still less cost-efficient. Although incredibly convenient, in-room **hotel calls** invariably include an arbitrary, sky-high surcharge (as much as £6). B&B in-room phones tend to be less expensive than in hotels, but they are still more costly than calling cards.

If you do **dial direct,** you must first insert the appropriate amount of money or a phonecard (*not* a calling card), then dial 00 (the international access code in both Britain and Ireland), and then the country code and number of your home. **Country codes** include: Australia 61; Canada 1; France 33; Ireland 353; New Zealand 64; South Africa 27; UK 44; US 1. Phone rates tend to be highest in the morning, lower in the evening, and lowest on Sunday and late at night. Many BT phone booths have country codes listed inside.

The expensive alternative to dialing direct or using a calling card is using an international operator to place a **collect call.** The **international operator** in Britain can be reached by dialing 155. Alternatively, dialing the appropriate service provider listed above will connect you to an operator from your home nation, who will usually place a collect call even if you don't possess one of their calling cards.

CALLING WITHIN BRITAIN AND IRELAND

To make a call within a city or town, just dial the number; from outside the region, dial the phone code and the number. For **directory inquiries,** which are free from payphones, call ☎ 192 in the UK or ☎ 1190 in Ireland. *Let's Go* lists phone codes opposite the city or town name, and all phone numbers in that town use that phone code unless specified otherwise. To call Britain from Ireland, or vice versa, you will have to make an international call; dial 00 44 followed by the British phone number, or 00 353 followed by the Irish one; remember to drop the initial 0 of the city code. Northern Ireland is part of the UK phone network, and calls there should be treated like calls to any other part of the UK.

PHONE CODES. Recent changes to British phone codes have produced a system in which the first three numbers of the phone code identify the type of number being called. **Premium rate calls,** costing about 50p per minute, can be identified by their 090x phone code, while **freephone** (toll-free) numbers have a 080x code. Numbers with the 084x code incur the **local call rate,** while calling the 087x code incurs the **national call rate** (the two aren't significantly different for short calls). Your British friends might give you their **mobile phone** (cellphone) number; note that calling a mobile is more expensive than a regular phone call. By 2001, all mobile phone numbers will carry 077, 078 or 079 codes, and pagers will begin with 076.

Note that several regions underwent recent phone code changes. London (020), Cardiff (029), Coventry (024), Portsmouth and Southampton (023), and Northern Ireland (028) began using their new codes in April 2000. *Let's Go* lists all new area codes, but you might see old codes listed in brochures and advertising. For more information on these changes, or to check the status of a number, call the toll-free number change helpline at ☎ (0808) 224 2000 or check www.numberchange.org.

PUBLIC PHONES IN BRITAIN. Public payphones in Britain are mostly run by **British Telecom (BT),** recognizable by the ubiquitous piper logo, although in larger cities you may find some run by upstart competitors such as Mercury. Many public phones in the UK now only accept **phonecards** or credit cards. The BT phonecard, available in denominations from £2-20, is probably a useful purchase, since BT phones tend to be omnipresent. Still, it's a good idea to carry some change in addition to a BT phonecard, since non-BT phones will not accept the phonecards.

Public phones charge a minimum of 10p for calls, and don't accept 1p, 2p, or 5p coins. The dial tone is a continuous purring sound; a repeated double-bell means the line is ringing. A series of harsh beeps will warn you to insert more money when your time is up. For the rest of the call, the digital display ticks off your credit in suspenseful 1p increments. You may use remaining credit on a second call by pressing the "follow on call" button (often marked "FC"). Otherwise, once you hang up, your remaining phonecard credit is rounded down to the nearest 10p, or unused coins are returned. Pay phones do *not* give change—if you use 22p out of a 50p coin, the remaining 28p is gone once you put the receiver down.

PUBLIC PHONES IN IRELAND. Most people in Ireland use **callcards;** they're essential for international calls. When the unit number on the digital display starts flashing, you may push the eject button on the card phone; you can then pull out your expired card and replace it with a fresh one (don't wait for the units to fall to zero or you'll be disconnected). Public coin phones will sometimes make change, but private payphones in hotels and restaurants do not. In any payphone, do not insert money until you are asked to, or until your call goes through. The frightening "pip-pip" noise that the phone makes before it starts ringing is normal and can last up to 10 seconds. Local calls cost 20p for four minutes on standard phones.

EMAIL AND INTERNET

Britain is one of the world's most online countries, and cybercafes can usually be found in larger cities (*Let's Go* lists them under **Internet Access** in the **Practical Information** section of cities). They cost £4-6 an hour, but often you pay only for time used, not for the whole hour. Cybercafes can also be found in the larger cities of Ireland, and cost IR£4-6 per hour. On-line guides to cybercafes in Britain and Ireland that are updated daily include **The Cybercafe Search Engine** (http://cybercaptive.com) and **Cybercafes.com** (www.cybercafes.com). Many hostels are also starting to offer email services to their residents, charging about the same rates. **Libraries** in Britain usually have Internet access, often at lower rates than cybercafes; the downside is that you might have to wait, or even make an advance reservation, to use their computers. **Free web-based email** lets people send you messages while you're on the road. Providers include **Hotmail** (www.hotmail.com), **Rocket-Mail** (www.rocketmail.com), and **Yahoo! Mail** (mail.yahoo.com).

SPECIFIC CONCERNS

 If you need to talk confidentially about emotional problems, the **Samaritans** number in the UK is ☎ (0345) 909090; in Ireland call ☎ (1850) 609090. Both are open 24hr., and can also refer you to the appropriate sources.

WOMEN TRAVELERS

From the Suffragettes on, British and Irish women have fought long and hard to bring about one of the most successful changes to women's status; Britain and Ireland can be counted among the world's best destinations for women travelers. Of course, women exploring the two countries on their own inevitably face some additional safety concerns, particularly in larger cities such as London or Dublin. The following suggestions shouldn't discourage women from traveling alone—it's easy to keep your sense of adventure without taking undue risks.

Stick to **centrally located accommodations** and avoid solitary late-night treks or metro/Tube rides. You might consider staying in places that offer single rooms that lock from the inside. Some hostels offer safer communal showers than others; check them before settling in. If catching a bus at night, wait at a well-populated stop. Choose train or Tube compartments occupied by other women or couples. When traveling, always carry extra money for a phone call, bus, or taxi. **Hitchhiking** is never safe for lone women, or even for two women traveling together.

Carry a **whistle** on your keychain or a **rape alarm** (£9.95 from John Lewis or other department stores), and don't hesitate to use them in an emergency. Mace and pepper sprays are illegal in Britain. The national **emergency** number is ☎ 999. The number for the **London Rape Crisis Centre** is ☎ (020) 7837 1600; the **Dublin Rape Crisis Centre** is ☎ (1800) 778888. *Let's Go* lists other hotlines in the **Practical Information** section of our city write-ups. An **IMPACT Model Mugging** self-defense course can prepare you for a potential attack, as well as raising your level of awareness of your surroundings and your confidence (see **Self Defense**, p. 22). Women also face some specific health concerns when traveling (see **Women's Health**, p. 25).

For **further information,** consult *A Journey of One's Own: Uncommon Advice for the Independent Woman Traveler,* by Thalia Zepatos (Eighth Mountain Press, US$17); *Travelers' Tales: Gutsy Women, Travel Tips and Wisdom for the Road,* by Marybeth Bond (Traveler's Tales; £6); or *A Foxy Old Woman's Guide to Traveling Alone,* by Jay Ben-Lesser (Crossing Press; £9).

TRAVELING ALONE

There are many benefits to traveling alone, among them greater independence and challenge. As a lone traveler, you have greater opportunity to interact with the residents of parts of Britain or Ireland you're visiting. Without distraction, you can write your own great travelogue, in the grand tradition of Samuel Johnson, Jonathan Swift, and Joseph Conrad. On the other hand, any solo traveler is a more vulnerable target of harassment and street theft. Try not to stand out as a tourist.

ESSENTIALS

If questioned, **never admit that you are traveling alone.** Maintain regular contact with someone at home who knows your itinerary.

Backpacker bus tours (see p. 41) are a good way for solo travelers to meet people. A number of organizations supply information for solo travelers, and others find travel companions for those who don't want to go it alone. **Connecting: Solo Traveler Network,** P.O. Box 29088, 1996 W. Broadway, Vancouver, BC V6J 5C2 (☎ 604-737-7791; www.cstn.org) has a bimonthly newsletter featuring going solo tips, single-friendly tips, and travel companion ads; its annual directory lists holiday suppliers that avoid single supplement charges. Connecting also facilitates exchanges of advice and lodging between members. (Membership US$25-35.) **Travel Companion Exchange,** P.O. Box 833, Amityville, NY 11701 (☎ (516) 454-0880 or ☎ (800) 392-1256; www.travelalone.com), publishes *Travel Companions,* a bimonthly newsletter for travelers seeking a travel partner (subscription US$48).

For **further information,** consult *Traveling Solo,* by Eleanor Berman (Globe Pequot Press; £13, US$17), or *The Single Traveler Newsletter,* P.O. Box 682, Ross, CA 94957 (☎ 415-389-0227; 6 issues US$29).

OLDER TRAVELERS

Senior citizens are often eligible for a wide range of discounts on transportation, museums, movies, theaters, restaurants, and accommodations. Discount prices are sometimes listed under "concessions" or "OAPs" (Old Age Pensioners). If you don't see a senior-citizen price listed, ask, and you may be delightfully surprised.

A useful resource while traveling in Britain is the information line of the national pressure group **Age Concern** (☎ (020) 8765 7200). Two of the increasing rack of British magazines targeted to the growing older population are *Yours,* a middle-of-the-road publication brimming with nostalgia, and Richard Ingrams's hilariously dour *The Oldie.* Agencies for senior group travel are growing in enrollment and popularity. These are only a few:

ElderTreks, 597 Markham St., Toronto, Ont. M6G 2L7 (☎ (800) 741-7956 or (416) 588-5000; www.eldertreks.com).

Elderhostel, 75 Federal St., Boston, MA 02110-1941 (☎ 617-426-7788 or 877-426-8056; www.elderhostel.org). Programs at colleges, universities, and other learning centers in Britain and Ireland on varied subjects, as well as walking or bus tours, lasting 1-4 weeks. Must be 55 or over (spouse can be of any age).

Walking the World, P.O. Box 1186, Fort Collins, CO 80522 (☎ 970-498-0500; www.walkingtheworld.com). Runs 2-week trips to Britain and Ireland (US$2000-2500).

For **further information,** consult *No Problem! Worldwise Tips for Mature Adventurers,* by Janice Kenyon (Orca Book Publishers, US$16); *A Senior's Guide to Healthy Travel,* by Donald L. Sullivan (Career Press, US$15); or *Unbelievably Good Deals and Great Adventures That You Absolutely Can't Get Unless You're Over 50,* by Joan Rattner Heilman (Contemporary Books, US$13).

BISEXUAL, GAY, AND LESBIAN TRAVELERS

Britain, the land of W.H. Auden, Noel Coward, Boy George, and Virginia Woolf, has long had an open and accepting gay scene, but even this is far from perfect. As is true elsewhere, people in rural areas of Britain and Ireland may not be as accepting of gay travelers as those in big cities. Public displays of affection in Ireland and most of Britain may bring you verbal harassment. The legal age of consent for homosexual and heterosexual sex is 16 in the UK, and 17 in Ireland.

Large cities, notably London, Dublin, Manchester, and Brighton, are far more open to gay culture than rural Britain, though evidence of bigotry and violence remains. On one hand, the visibility of gay culture is evident in the Gay Listings section of *Time Out* magazine; on the other, queer bashings do occur.

With so many bisexual-, gay-, and lesbian-specific periodicals, it's easy to educate yourself of the current concerns of Britain's gay community. *Capital Gay* (free) mostly caters to men in London and the surroundings. The *Pink Paper* (free) is available in newsagents in larger cities, covering stories of interest to the pink community. Its bimonthly sister publication, *Shebang*, covers all aspects of lesbian life. *Gay Times* (£3) covers political issues; *Diva* (£2) is a monthly lesbian lifestyle magazine with an excellent mix of features and good listings.

Listed below are contact organizations, mail-order bookstores, and publishers which offer materials addressing some specific concerns.

The British Tourist Authority (US ☎ (877) 857-2462) publishes a gay guide to British cities called *You Don't Know The Half Of It!* For a copy, call the number above, contact the BTA (p. 14), or visit www.usagateway.visitbritain.com and click on the rainbow icon.

Gay's the Word, 66 Marchmont St., London WC1N 1AB (☎ (020) 7278 7654; www.gaystheword.co.uk). The largest gay and lesbian bookshop in the UK. Mail-order service available. No catalog of listings, but they will provide a list of titles on a given subject.

Ireland's Pink Pages (http://indigo.ie/~outhouse/). Ireland's web-based bisexual, gay, and lesbian directory. Regional info, including the Republic and the North. Helpful links.

International Gay and Lesbian Travel Association, 4331 N. Federal Hwy., Suite 304, Fort Lauderdale, FL 33308 (☎ (954) 776-2626 or (800) 448-8550; www.iglta.com). An organization of over 1350 companies serving gay and lesbian travelers worldwide. Call for lists of travel agents, accommodations, and events.

London Lesbian and Gay Switchboard, (☎ (020) 7837 7324). Confidential advice and information. Open 24hr.

For **further information,** consult *Spartacus International Gay Guide* by Bruno Gmunder Verlag (£16, US$33), *Damron's Accommodations* and *The Women's Traveller* (Damron Travel Guides; £9), or the *Ferrari Guides* series of gay travel guides (Ferrari Guides; £9-14, US$14-16).

TRAVELERS WITH DISABILITIES

Many transportation companies in Britain are very conscientious about providing facilities and services to meet the needs of travelers with disabilities. It is strongly recommended that you notify a bus or coach company of your plans ahead of time so that they will have staff ready to assist you; trains also require advance notice especially by those using wheelchairs. There's also a discounted railcard for disabled British citizens, with up to 50% discount on train tickets. Not all stations are accessible, though; write for the pamphlet *British Rail and Disabled Travelers.* For travel on the London **Underground,** pick up the free booklet *Access to the Underground* from Tourist Information Centres and London Transport Information Centres, or from the Unit for Disabled Passengers, London Transport, 172 Buckingham Palace Rd., London SW1W 9TN (☎ (020) 7918 3312). Several **car rental agencies,** such as Wheelchair Travel in Surrey (☎ (01483) 233 640) can provide and deliver hand-controlled cars, but at a hefty price.

The British Tourist Boards have begun rating accommodations and attractions using the **National Accessible Scheme** (NAS), which designates three categories of accessibility. Look for the NAS symbols in Tourist Board guidebooks, or ask a site directly for their ranking. Many **theaters** and performance venues have space for wheelchairs; some larger theatrical performances include special facilities for the hearing-impaired. Guide dogs (called "seeing-eye dogs" in the US) fall under the new PETS regulations (see p. 15) concerning bringing animals to the UK; guide dogs coming from EU countries, Australia and New Zealand need to be microchipped, vaccinated, bloodtested, and certified against tapeworm and ticks before entering the UK. Guide dogs from elsewhere need to be quarantined for six months. Call the PETS helpline at (087) 0241 1710 or consult www.maff.gov.uk/animalh/quarantine with questions. The owner must also obtain a veterinary certificate. Check with the nearest British embassy or consulate for details.

ESSENTIALS

The following organizations provide information that might be of assistance, or arrange tours or trips for disabled travelers:

Directions Unlimited, 123 Green Ln., Bedford Hills, NY 10507, USA (☎ (800) 533-5343; www.travel-cruises.com). Specializes in arranging individual and group vacations, tours, and cruises for the physically disabled.

DTour (www.iol.ie/infograf/dtour). A web-based visitors' guide to Ireland for people with disabilities. Index of accommodation and transportation facilities, plus useful links.

The Guided Tour Inc., 7900 Old York Rd., Suite 114B, Elkins Park, PA 19027, USA (☎ (800) 783-5841; www.guidedtour.com). Organizes travel programs for persons with developmental and physical challenges around London and Ireland.

Holiday Care Service, 2nd Fl., Imperial Bldg., Victoria Rd., Horley RH6 7PZ (☎ (01293) 774535; fax (01293) 784647; reservation service ☎ (01293) 773716). Info on site accessibility and books accommodations around the UK for travelers with disabilities.

Society for the Advancement of Travel for the Handicapped (SATH), 347 Fifth Ave., #610, New York, NY 10016 (☎ (212) 447-7284; www.sath.org). An advocacy group that publishes the quarterly travel magazine *OPEN WORLD* (free for members, US$13 for nonmembers). Also publishes a wide range of info sheets on disability travel facilitation and destinations. Annual membership US$45, students and seniors US$30.

Tripscope, The Courtyard, Evelyn Rd., London W4 5JL (☎ (08457) 585641; outside UK ☎ +44 (20) 8580 7021). Provides information for the elderly and disabled on traveling by public transport in London, the UK, and Europe. Helpline open M-F 9am-4:45pm.

FURTHER INFORMATION. Consult **Disability Net** (www.disabilitynet.co.uk/info/transport) or **Global Access** (www.geocities.com/Paris/1502/disabilitylinks.html) for tips for disabled travelers in Britain, or contact the British Tourist Authority for free handbooks and access guides. *Access in London,* by Gordon Couch (Quiller Press, £8; or Cimino Publishing Group, US$12), details wheelchair-accessible locations in the Greater London area.

MINORITY TRAVELERS

In the 1991 census, roughly 5.5% of the British population chose not to categorize themselves as white. The majority of Britain's ethnic communities are centered around London or other English cities. Ireland is only beginning to experience racial diversity, while rural Scotland and Wales remain predominantly white. Minority travelers should steel themselves for reduced anonymity in the latter regions, but this is usually motivated by curiosity rather than ill will, and should not cause you to alter your travel plans. It's hard to look like a minority in London, Manchester, Bradford, and other large English cities. This is not to say that these cities do not have problems with racism, only that as a traveler you probably will not feel its effects. There are few resources specifically oriented toward minority travelers in Britain; in cases of harassment or assault, contact the police or the **Commission for Racial Equality**, Elliot House, 10-12 Allington St., London SW1E 5EH (☎ (020) 7828 7022; www.cre.gov.uk).

TRAVELERS WITH CHILDREN

Family vacations often require that you slow your pace, and always require that you plan ahead. If you pick a B&B or a small hotel, call ahead and make sure it allows children. If you rent a car, make sure the company provides a car seat for younger children. Be sure that your child carries some sort of ID in case of an emergency or in case he or she gets lost. Restaurants in Britain and Ireland often have children's menus, and almost all tourist attractions have a children's rate, usually applicable to those under 16 (those under 5 often get in free). Children under 2 generally fly for 10% of the adult fare—this does not necessarily include a seat. International fares are usually discounted 25% for children aged 2-11.

For **further information,** consult *Backpacking with Babies and Small Children*, by G. Silverman (G.P. Putnam and Sons, £7; or Wilderness Press, US$10); *Take Your Kids to Europe*, by C. Harriman (Globe Pequot, US$17); or *Have Kid, Will Travel: 101 Survival Strategies for Vacationing With Babies and Young Children*, by C. and L. Tristram (Andrews and McMeel; US$9).

DIETARY CONCERNS

Vegetarians should have no problem finding exciting cuisine, with the abundance of ethnic food and the increasing apprehension to meat that followed the BSE crisis. Joy of joys, you can now get a vegetarian fried breakfast (complete with veggie sausage) in most cafes and some B&Bs. Virtually all restaurants have vegetarian selections on their menus, and many cater specifically to vegetarians. *Let's Go* notes restaurants with good vegetarian selections. For more information about vegetarian travel, contact **The Vegetarian Society of the UK,** (☎ (0161) 925 2000; www.vegsoc.org) or the **North American Vegetarian Society** (☎ (518) 568-7970; www.navs-online.org). For **further information,** consult *The Vegan Travel Guide: UK and Southern Ireland* (The Vegan Society, £4.95; Book Publishing Co., US$15), or *The Vegetarian Traveler: Where to Stay if You're Vegetarian*, by Jed Civic (Larson Publications; £13 or US$16).

Travelers who keep **kosher** should contact synagogues in larger cities for information; your own synagogue or college Hillel should have access to lists of Jewish institutions across Britain and Ireland. The significant Orthodox community in North London (in neighborhoods such as **Golders Green** or **Stamford Hill**), Leeds, and Manchester provide a market for kosher restaurants and grocers. Kosher options decrease in rural areas, but most restaurants and B&Bs will be open to your concerns and will try to accommodate them. **The Jewish Travel Guide** lists synagogues, kosher restaurants, and Jewish institutions in over 100 countries including Britain and Ireland. (Available in the UK from Vallentine-Mitchell Publishers, ☎ (020) 8599 8866), or in the US from ISBS, ☎ (800) 944-6190.)

ALTERNATIVES TO TOURISM

Studying or working in Britain or Ireland gives you a chance to experience culture in a way that tourists never do. For an extremely useful guide to making the transition to life in Britain, read *Living and Working in Britain: A Survival Handbook*, by David Hampshire (Survival Books; £12.95 or US$21.95). A more general guide to available options is *The Alternative Travel Directory* (US$19.95), available from **Transitions Abroad** (www.transabroad.com), a website which lists various programs in both Britain and Ireland for work, study, and specialized travel.

STUDY

Britain has a history of welcoming foreign students—education, in fact, is a good source of foreign revenue for the country. Studying abroad in Britain, whether for a summer, a year, or even for the entire period of your undergraduate career, is thus relatively easy, administratively speaking. Space permits us to list only a few of the myriad study abroad programs available; research other programs at your own colleges, or at your local British Council.

Short **study-abroad** programs (less than a year) in Britain often do not require much paperwork. You won't need a visa if you're from the EU, or from most Western countries. Rules, however, often change, and it's a good idea to check at your local embassy. Enrolling as a **full-time student** requires non-EU citizens to get a student visa from your local embassy. If you encounter any troubles while you're in Britain, contact the **UK Council for Overseas Student Affairs,** 9-17 St. Alban's Pl., London N1 0NX (☎ (020) 7354 5210), an organization dedicated to meeting the needs of international students in the country.

THE BRITISH COUNCIL

The British Council is the arm of the government charged with promoting educational opportunities in Britain, among other responsibilities. Its offices are an invaluable source of information for those intending to study in Britain at a secondary or university level, or for those enrolling in language classes in Britain. For their numerous branches in countries not listed here, call the London office or check out their website at www.britishcouncil.org.

London Office: 10 Spring Gdns., London SW1A 2BN (☎ (0161) 957 7755).

Australia: Suite 401, Level 4, Edgecliff Centre, 203-233 New South Head Rd. (P.O. Box 88), Edgecliff, Sydney NSW 2027 (☎ (02) 9326 2022; www.britishcouncil.org.au).

Canada: 80 Elgin St., Ottawa, Ont. K1P 5K7 (☎ (613) 237-1530); www.britcoun-canada.org).

Ireland: Newmount House, 22/24 Lower Mount Street, Dublin 2 (☎ (01) 676 4088).

New Zealand: 44 Hill St., P.O. Box 1812, Wellington (☎ (04) 495 0898; www.british-council.org.nz).

South Africa: 76 Juta St. (P.O. Box 30637), Braamfontein 2017, Johannesburg (☎ (011) 403 3316).

United States: British Embassy, 3100 Massachusetts Ave. NW, Washington, D.C. 20008-3600 (☎ (202) 588-6500; www.britishcouncil-usa.org).

UNIVERSITIES IN BRITAIN

The British higher-education system is almost a thousand years old, and universities dot the island, many offering study abroad programs. Most American undergrads enroll in programs sponsored by US universities. Though receiving academic credit for them may involve more administrative hassle, UK university programs can be cheaper than American ones and allow more interaction with locals. Some organizations that offer study abroad programs in the UK are listed below. Those who wish to undertake a full degree course in Britain should apply through the **Universities and Colleges Admissions Service** (UCAS), Rosehill, New Barn Ln., Cheltenham GL52 3LZ ☎ (01242) 222444; www.ucas.ac.uk); non-EU residents pay full tuition, while EU residents pay the same (minimal) rates as UK students. Further information can be found at your local British Council (see above).

American University Programs:

The American Institute for Foreign Study, College Division, 102 Greenwich Ave., Greenwich, CT 06830 (☎ (800) 727-2437 ext. 6084; www.aifs.com) organizes summer-, semester-, and year-long programs for high-school and college students in Britain and Ireland. Scholarships available.

Beaver College Center for Education Abroad, 450 South Easton Rd., Glenside, PA 19038 (☎ (888) 232-8379; www.beaver.edu/cea), conducts summer, semester, and year-long programs in Britain and Ireland, from US$1900 for a summer to $20,000 for a year. Applicants should have completed three full semesters at an accredited university.

Central College Abroad, Office of International Education, 812 University, Pella, IA 50219 (☎ (800) 831-3629; www.studyabroad.com/central), has semester- and year-long study abroad programs in London, Colchester, and Carmarthen. Scholarships available.

Association of Commonwealth Universities, John Foster House, 36 Gordon Sq., London WC1H OPF (☎ (020) 7387 8572; www.acu.ac.uk). Administers scholarship programs and publishes information about Commonwealth universities.

Council on International Educational Exchange (CIEE), 205 E. 42nd St., New York, NY 10017, US (☎ (888) 268-6245; www.ciee.org); also at The University Centre, Level 8, 210 Clarence St., Sydney 2000, Australia (☎ (02) 9373 2730; www.ciee.org.au). Sponsors work, volunteer, academic, internship, and professional study abroad programs in Britain and Ireland.

University College London, International Office, UCL, Gower St., London WC1E 6BT (☎ (020) 7380 7765; www.ucl.ac.uk). Offers a Junior Year Abroad program, and treats students on study abroad programs just like regular students for better cultural exchange.

Queen's University Belfast, International Liaison Office, Queen's University Belfast, Belfast BT7 1NN (☎ (028) 9033 5415). Has semester- and year-long study abroad programs, and a new 4-week Introduction to Northern Ireland program in January that studies the political, social, and economic questions unique to the North.

UNIVERSITIES IN IRELAND

Irish universities are also open to foreigners; non-EU residents pay full tuition (EU students pay the same rates as Irish students); however, places can be limited.

Irish Studies Summer School, Usit NOW, 19-21 Aston Quay, Dublin 2 (☎ (01) 602 1741; www.usitnow.ie); from North America, contact Irish Studies Summer School, usit, New York Student Centre, 895 Amsterdam Ave., New York, NY 10025 (☎ (212) 663 5435). A 7-week program held at Trinity College Dublin in Irish culture and history. Also administers **Ireland in Europe,** 2 weeks of summer courses about Irish civilization.

Trinity College Dublin, The Office of International Student Affairs, Arts and Social Sciences Bldg., Trinity College, Dublin 2 (☎ (01) 608 1396). Runs a 1-year program of high-quality courses for visiting undergraduates. Graduates can also register as one-year students not reading for a degree.

University College Galway, International Office, Galway (☎ (091) 750304). Semester- and year-abroad opportunities for junior-year students who meet the college's entry requirements. **Summer school** courses between July and August include Irish studies, education, and creative writing.

LANGUAGE STUDY

Many come to Britain and Ireland to improve their English; others to study the various Celtic languages—Irish, Welsh, and Scottish Gaelic—of the Isles. The British Council has a special website dedicated to English language education; check out www.englishinbritain.co.uk. **Oideas Gael,** Glencolmcille, Co. Donegal, Ireland (☎ (073) 30248; www.Oideas-Gael.com). conducts week-long Irish-language and culture courses from Easter until Aug. in various activities including hill walking, dancing, archaeology, and weaving.

WORK

Unless you're an EU citizen, you need a **work permit** to legally work in Britain and Ireland. **EU citizens** can work in both Britain and Ireland, and if your parents were born in an EU country, you may be able to claim dual citizenship or at least the right to a work permit. If your parents were born in Britain, you may be eligible for a British passport, which allows unrestricted employment. If your grandparents are British, you can apply for a Right of Abode visa (£50), which allows you to stay and work for up to four years in Britain without a permit. Citizens of certain **Commonwealth countries** (including Australia, Canada, New Zealand, and South Africa) between 17-27 years' old can apply for a **working holiday visa** at their local British embassy (£33). This allows you to work in Britain during a visit of up to two years if the employment you take is "incidental to your holiday." **American citizens** who are full-time students at American universities and are older than 18 can apply for a **Blue Card Permit** from BUNAC (see **Work/Travel Programs,** below), which allows them to work for up to six months. Non-EU students who are full-time students in the UK may work up to 20 hours per week on their student visas.

Temporary jobs are rarely glamorous or well paid. Still, they're a good way of finding out more about Britain or Ireland beyond the tourist view. Prepare a **c.v.** (curriculum vitae; resume), and bring along proof of your qualifications. Also prepare references. Backpacker magazines such as *TNT* or *Southern Cross* often list classifieds looking for part-time workers. Those intending to work **full-time** in Britain should be sponsored by a UK employer.

JOBS: AU-PAIR AND AGRICULTURE

InterExchange, 161 Sixth Ave., New York, NY 10013 (☎ (212) 924-0446) provides information on international work and au-pair programs in both Britain and Ireland.

Childcare International, Ltd., Trafalgar House, Grenville Pl., London NW7 3SA (☎ (020) 8906 3116; www.childint.demon.co.uk) offers au-pair positions in the UK. Provides info on qualifications required and local language schools. £80 application fee.

Willing Workers on Organic Farms (WWOOF), PO Box 2675, Lewes, East Sussex BN7 1RB (www.phdcc.com/sites/wwoof). Membership (£15) allows you to receive room and board at organic farms throughout Britain and Ireland in exchange for help on the farm. However, unless you're an EU citizen, you'll need to get a valid work visa first.

WORK/TRAVEL PROGRAMS

British Universities North America Club (BUNAC), 16 Bowling Green Ln., London EC1 0BD (☎ (020) 7251 3472, US ☎ (800) 462-8622; www.bunac.org.uk), procures 3-6 month work permits for US college students. Application fee US$225.

International Exchange Programs (IEP), 196 Albert Rd., South Melbourne, Victoria 3205, Australia (☎ (03) 9690 5890), and PO Box 1786, Shortland St., Auckland, New Zealand (☎ (09) 366 6255; www.iepnz.co.nz). Runs work/travel programs in Britain for citizens of Australia and New Zealand.

South Africa Student Travel Services, 8th Fl., J.H. Isaacs House, 5 Heerengracht, Foreshore, Cape Town 8001 (☎ (021) 418 3794; www.sasts.org.za). Their Work and Travel Britain program helps South Africans on the two-year working holiday visa find jobs and meet up with other participants.

For **further information,** consult *International Jobs: Where they Are, How to Get Them,* by Eric Kocher and Nina Segal (Perseus Books; US$16); *How to Get a Job in Europe,* Robert Sanborn (Surrey Books; £16.50 or US$22); *Work Abroad,* by Clayton Hubbs (Transitions Abroad; US$16); or *Overseas Summer Jobs 1999* and *Directory of Jobs and Careers Abroad* (Peterson's; US$17-18 each).

VOLUNTEERING

Volunteer jobs are fairly easy to secure. However, if you receive room and board in exchange for your labor, you are considered a worker and have to get a work visa. You can sometimes avoid the high application fees charged by the organizations that arrange placement by contacting the individual workcamps directly. **Volunteers for Peace,** 1034 Tiffany Rd., Belmont, VT 05730-0202 (☎ (802) 259-2759; www.vfp.org), is a non-profit organization that arranges placement in 2- to 3-week workcamps in Britain and Ireland comprising 10-15 people (registration fee US$200). For more information, see the *International Directory of Voluntary Work,* by Victoria Pybus (Vacation Work Publications; UK£10.99 or US$15.95).

THE WORLD WIDE WEB

Almost every aspect of budget travel (the most notable exception, of course, being experience) is accessible via the web. Even if you don't have internet access at home, seeking it out at a public library or at work is well worth it; within 10 minutes, you can make a reservation at a hostel, get advice on travel hotspots or experiences from other travelers who have just returned from the British Isles, or find out exactly how much a train from Nether Wallop to Shellow Bowells costs.

Listed here are some budget travel sites to start off your surfing; other relevant web sites are listed throughout the book. Because website turnover is high, use search engines (such as **www.google.com**) to strike out on your own. But in doing so, keep in mind that most travel websites simply exist to get your money.

LEARNING THE ART OF BUDGET TRAVEL

How to See the World: www.artoftravel.com. A compendium of great travel tips, from cheap flights to self defense to interacting with local culture.

Rec. Travel Library: www.travel-library.com. A fantastic set of links for general information and personal travelogues.

Shoestring Travel: www.stratpub.com. An e-zine focusing on budget travel.

INFORMATION ON BRITAIN AND IRELAND

CIA World Factbook: www.odci.gov/cia/publications/factbook/index.html. Tons of vital statistics on Britain and Ireland's geography, government, economy, and people.

MyTravelGuide: www.mytravelguide.com. Country overviews, with everything from history to transportation to live web cam coverage of Britain and Ireland.

Geographia: www.geographia.com. Describes the highlights, culture, and people of Britain and Ireland.

Columbus Travel Guides: www.travel-guides.com/navigate/world.asp. Helpful practical information.

TravelPage: www.travelpage.com. Links to official tourist information sites throughout Britain and Ireland.

PlanetRider: www.planetrider.com/Travel_Destinations.cfm. A subjective list of links to the "best" websites covering the culture and tourist attractions of Britain and Ireland.

AND OUR PERSONAL FAVORITE...

Let's Go: www.letsgo.com. Our recently revamped website features video, info about our books, a travel forum buzzing with stories and tips, and links that will help you find everything you could ever want to know about Britain and Ireland.

GREAT BRITAIN

Those who visit Great Britain to seek its past in grand castles and cathedrals, to exult in the vast collections of its museums, or to seek solitude in its beautiful parks will certainly be satisfied—but just as important a part of Britain are its hip clubs, its innovative theater, and the conversations over a pint or three in any one of its several thousand pubs. One of Britain's most alluring features is its size: two hours on a train can take you from large cities to historic towns to breathtaking hiking regions and back. Britain's long history—often glorious, sometimes inglorious, never dull—has profoundly affected most of the world, and the English literary tradition is one of our finest, but Britain does not rest on past achievements—at least, not always. Defying the thatched-cottage-and-bowler-hat stereotypes, modern Britain is an exciting place, hurtling into the new century as progressively as it can, and providing visitors with limitless possibilities for exploration.

While the terms "Great Britain" and "England" are often (incorrectly) used interchangeably, England is in fact only one part—along with Scotland and Wales—of the island of Great Britain, the largest of the British Isles, which together with Northern Ireland forms Her Majesty's United Kingdom of Great Britain and Northern Ireland. Never refer to the Scots or the Welsh as "English"; it is neither accurate nor polite. United in the 9th century, England had by the 17th century conquered Wales and Ireland, and united with Scotland in 1707. Ireland won independence in 1921, and while Scotland and Wales have for centuries been part of a United Kingdom administered primarily from London, they are, like Ireland, separate and distinct lands, with their own languages, cultures, and customs. The following pages on the life and times of Great Britain focus primarily on English history, literature, and culture; Scotland (p. 488) and Wales (p. 415) are treated separately, as are Northern Ireland (p. 629) and the Republic of Ireland (p. 656).

HISTORY

History will be kind to me, for I intend to write it.
—Winston Churchill

EARLY INVADERS

Ages before the Channel Tunnel, foreigners had found their way over water to scatter throughout Britain. The stone circles at **Stonehenge** (see p. 196) and **Avebury** (see p. 197) bear mute witness to the isle's earliest inhabitants, whose peace was shattered by Celtic and then Roman invasions. The Romans occupied southern Britain until AD 410, establishing **Londinium** (now London) and various other forts in the Roman Empire's northernmost colony. Expansion farther northward proved unsuccessful: the Pictish tribes, described fancifully in Roman histories as having blue skin, fought Imperial rule, and their fierce resistance inspired the Romans to construct **Hadrian's Wall**—an edifice 73 mi. long and 12 ft. high—in an effort to diminish the threat of northern invaders (see p. 410). The Picts finally sent the Romans scuttling south in the Picts War of AD 367-8. The 4th century saw the decline of the Roman Empire, leaving Britain vulnerable to raids. Angles and Saxons—Germanic tribes from Denmark and northern Germany—established settlements and kingdoms in the south, pushing the Celts into Wales, Cornwall, and Scotland; the name "England" in fact derives from "Anglaland," land of the Angles.

CHRISTIANS, VIKINGS, AND NORMANS

Christianity, which in Britain had fallen out of favor along with the Romans, returned for good in AD 597 when eager missionary **Augustine** successfully converted King Æthelbert of Kent and founded England's first church, in **Canterbury** (see p. 151). Even though not all English kingdoms or subsequent kings were receptive to the new religion, Christianity was all the rage by the end of the 7th century. Its spread was immortalized by the **Venerable Bede** (see p. 401) in 731 with his *Ecclesiastical History of the English People*, in which he became the first to perceive of an English nation. In the mid-9th century, Danish Vikings, who had been raiding England's east coast, Scotland, and Ireland since 793, conquered much of England and settled north of a border called the Danelaw, which ran roughly from modern Liverpool to the Thames Estuary east of London. Late in the 9th century, King Alfred the Great of Wessex sought to unify the different English kingdoms against the Danes, and also established centers of learning throughout the land. His successor, Edward the Elder, managed to defeat the Danes, although they briefly regained control of England before their final defeat in 1042. In 1066, William I of Normandy (better known as **William the Conqueror**), to whom Edward the Confessor promised the throne in 1051, invaded England upon the death of the old king, won the pivotal **Battle of Hastings** (see p. 161), and slaughtered his rival Harold II (and for good measure, his two brothers).

William promptly set about cataloguing his new English acquisitions in the epic **Domesday Book,** completed in 1088. This compilation of all landholders and their possessions, originally intended to facilitate taxing, has come to serve as the starting point of the written history of most English towns. Norman French became the language of the educated and elite for centuries—Henry IV, crowned in 1399, was the next king whose mother tongue was English. During the intervening years, English was marginalized, developing within 14 dialects, each with its own spelling and grammar. The English people were likewise subjugated by feudalization, which began when William distributed large tracts of land to his followers, galvanizing class division between those who owned and those who worked the land.

PLANTAGENETS AND TUDORS

Henry Plantagenet, Duke of Normandy, ascended the throne as Henry II in 1154 and initiated the conquest of Ireland, proclaiming himself its overlord in 1171. His son **Richard the Lionheart** was more interested in taxing nobles to finance the Crusades and his family's (and thus England's) French holdings than in the well-being of the people, and only spent six months of his ten-year reign on the island. Tired of such royal abuses of authority, noblemen forced his brother and successor King John to sign the **Magna Carta** in 1215 (see Salisbury Cathedral, p. 195). The document, often seen as a battle cry against oppression, has been credited with laying the groundwork for modern English democracy—the first **Parliament** convened 50 years later in 1265. In 1284, Edward I united Wales under the English crown, a move that still rankles in Wales today. While English kings expanded the nation's territory, the **Black Death** ravaged its population, killing more than one third of all Britons between 1348 and 1361. Many more fell in the **100 Years' War** (or the 116 Years' War, to be precise), which started with Edward III's 1337 invasion of France in response to the French invasion of English-ruled Aquitaine; Edward's claim to the French throne had prompted the maneuver by his rival, King Philip VI.

While King Richard II was on an Irish holiday in 1399, his cousin Henry Bolingbroke invaded Britain and usurped the throne. This bold move put the Lancasters in control, and gave Shakespeare something decent to write about. More Shakespearian subject matter was created when Henry V defeated the French in the **Battle of Agincourt** (1415), a victory for the British underdogs that soon became legendary. But his son Henry VI blew it when, failing to stave off French resistance under Joan of Arc, he lost almost all English land in France; Henry continued his losing streak by suffering two bouts of insanity that precipitated the **Wars of the Roses** (1455-85). This lengthy crisis of royal succession culminated in the suspicious death of the boy-king Edward V in the Tower of London at the tender age of 12 and the crowning of his uncle Richard III.

The Lancasters claimed final victory in the Wars of the Roses, when the last of their line, Henry VII, won the throne in 1485 and inaugurated the rule of the **House of Tudor,** a dynasty that survived until 1603. His successor, **Henry VIII,** reinforced England's control over the Irish, proclaiming himself their king in 1542. In his infamous battle with the Pope over multiple marriages, Henry converted Britain from Roman Catholicism to Protestantism, establishing the Anglican Church and placing himself at its head—which is ironic, considering most of his wives lost theirs.

REPUBLICANISM AND RESTORATION

Despite Henry VIII's attempts to solidify the Protestants' grip on power, his sudden death in 1547 did not help the cause. Nine-year-old Edward VI was, not surprisingly, a weak ruler, and gave way to that of his elder sister and staunch Catholic **Bloody Mary,** who earned her gory nickname for persecution of Protestants. In a nice spate of sibling rivalry, **Elizabeth I** reversed the religious convictions imposed by her sister, and cemented the success of the Reformation—under her reign the English defeated the Spanish Armada to become the leading Protestant power in Europe. The union of England, Wales, and Scotland effectively took place in 1603, when **James VI** of Scotland ascended to the throne as **James I** of England. The strength of Protestantism took a blow from James and successive fellow members of the house of Stuart, who began to irk Parliament with their Catholic sympathies and firm belief in the "divine right" of kings.

Tensions erupted in the **English Civil Wars** (1642-51). The Parliamentarians were nicknamed **Roundheads** for their short haircuts, which defied the long-locked tradition of the Royal Court, while Charles's supporters adopted the chivalrous name **Cavaliers.** The monarchy was abolished when Parliament saw to it that Charles I and his head parted ways, and the first British Commonwealth was founded in 1649. **Oliver Cromwell** emerged as a rebellious and adept military leader of this new Commonwealth. His massacre of nearly half of the indigenous Irishmen earned him temporary submission and eternal bitterness from Britain's neighbor. Cromwell's son Richard succeeded him as Lord Protector, but he was unable to cement the institution of the republic. Much to the relief of the masses, Charles II was brought back to power unconditionally in 1660. But the **Restoration** did not signal the end of the troubles: although Charles II was pliant enough to suit Parliament, there was much debate about whether to exclude Charles II's fervently Catholic brother James II from the succession. Debate during the **Exclusion Crisis** established two political parties: the Whigs, who insisted on exclusion, and the Tories, who supported hereditary succession.

PARLIAMENT AND THE CROWN

The relatively bloodless **Glorious Revolution** erupted in 1688 to prevent James II from establishing a Catholic dynasty; James left England when Dutch Protestant William of Orange arrived with an army, at the invitation of several prominent Englishmen. With James gone, the William was offered and accepted the throne, and he and his wife Mary (James's own daughter) wrote the Bill of Rights to ensure the Protestantism of all future kings. The ascension of **William and Mary** marked the end of a century of violent upheaval. Jacobite supporters of the Scot James II remained a distant threat, and became only less so in 1745 when James II's grandson, **Bonnie Prince Charlie,** failed in his attempt to invade and recapture the throne. Parliament's role in the Glorious Revolution had worked a quiet revolution of its own, changing the relationship between Crown and Parliament. Under the ineffectual leadership of the Hanoverian kings (beginning with **George I**), the office of Prime Minister, held at the beginning of the century by the master negotiator **Robert Walpole** and at the end by the astute **William Pitt the Younger,** gradually eclipsed the monarchy as the seat of power in British government.

EMPIRE AND INDUSTRY

During the 18th and 19th centuries, Britain came to rule more than one quarter of the world's population and two fifths of its land. The early impetus for this domination originated from the enterprise of private companies rather than the initiative of the governing powers—the Cape of Good Hope was captured in order to secure shipping routes to the far East, allowing the colonization of southern Africa. Parliament soon realized they were on to a good thing, acquiring all of Australia and New Zealand by 1840, and throwing in the Western Pacific Islands for good measure in 1877. Arch-enemy France actually aided Britain's colonization efforts by focusing on Europe in the Napoleonic Wars—in the meantime, Britain acquired Sri Lanka and parts of Indo-China from comparatively weak French occupying forces. In 1857, Parliament requested that the East India Trading Company cede control of the sub-continent to the Crown, thus making the governmental control of the Empire complete. Given Britain's continuing control of the Canadian colonies, which had gained importance after the loss of the American colonies in 1776, it could rightfully be said in the mid-1800s that "the sun never sets on the British Empire."

The **Industrial Revolution** allowed Britain to attain the military and economic power necessary for colonization. In one of the greatest social changes in British history, massive portions of the rural populace migrated to towns, pushed off the land by restrictive legislation and lured by rapidly growing opportunities in industrial employment. The age-old gulf between workers and landowners was replaced by a wider gap between factory owners and their laborers. British entrepreneurs grew wealthy, as did the British government, giving both groups the means to enlarge the Empire. The **Gold Standard,** which Britain first adhered to in 1821, ensured the pound's value with gold and by 1870 had become an international financial system, thus establishing Britain's economic hegemony. The first hundred years of industrialization irreversibly altered the texture of British and global society as Britain expanded her Empire.

THE VICTORIAN ERA

The stable rule of **Queen Victoria** (1837-1901) dominated the 19th century, in foreign and domestic politics, social changes, and even stylistic mores. She oversaw the beginnings of domestic industrial regulation, spurred by the combined force of class divisions and often frightening workplace conditions. At the same time, Victorian Liberals such as **William Gladstone** picked up where free-traders like **Robert Peel** left off, extending the economic notion of a free market to encompass a more open attitude toward different religions. The **Reform Act** of 1832 provided sweeping changes in working conditions and voting rights for middle-class men. The **Chartist Movement** of the mid-19th century dramatically pressed for universal male suffrage, but voting rights spread gradually over the course of the century in several reform bills. The 1840s brought the **Irish famine,** which killed over a million people and caused twice that many to emigrate.

By the end of the century, trade-union organization had strengthened, assuming its modern form during the 1889 strike of the East London dockers and finding a political voice in the **Labour Party** at the turn of the century. Despite the gains of organized labor, the quality of urban life declined alarmingly. Perched comfortably on divans, the Victorian elite took up aid to the poor, paving the way for a slew of Liberal government welfare programs established in 1910. Meanwhile, pressures to alter the position of different marginalized groups just before the war proved largely ineffectual. The **Suffragettes,** led by **Emmeline Pankhurst,** attempted to win women the right to vote by disrupting Parliament and staging hunger strikes, but their methods unfortunately alienated political support for their cause; women had to wait until after World War I to earn their right to vote. Increasing troubles with Ireland had plagued the nation for half a century, and Prime Minister **William Gladstone**'s 1880 attempt to introduce a Home Rule Bill for Ireland had splintered the Labour Party. Herbert Asquith traded support for Irish Home Rule for the votes of the Home Rule party, only to face the possibility of civil war in Ireland (see p. 661)—a threat interrupted by the explosion of **World War I.**

GREAT BRITAIN

THE WORLD WARS

The **Great War,** as World War I was known until 1939, brought British military action back to the European stage, scarred the British spirit with the loss of a generation of young men, and dashed Victorian dreams of a peaceful, progressive society. The technological explosion of the 19th century was evident in the new weapons introduced during the war, as gas attacks, machine guns, and tanks caused unprecedented massive casualties on both sides. The war demoralized the nation: in a conflict that was originally expected to last for four months and dragged on for four years, almost a million British men died and twice as many were left wounded. The scars of the Great War left Britons determined never to repeat large-scale involvement in international conflict, explaining their reluctant entry into World War II just twenty years later.

With the end of World War I, hope for a new beginning within England was generally lost—though women gained suffrage at this time—as a sense of aimlessness overtook the nation's politics. The 1930s brought **depression** and mass unemployment; during this period, famed social economist **John Maynard Keynes** came to his fore. In December 1936, King Edward VIII shocked the world and brought shame on the Windsor family with the announcement of his abdication of kingship. His decision was prompted by his desire to marry Wallace Simpson, a twice-divorced Baltimore socialite; he left the throne to his brother George. Meanwhile, tensions in Europe were once again escalating with the German reoccupation of the Rhineland. The Prime Minister, Neville "Peace in Our Time" Chamberlain, pushed through a controversial **appeasement** agreement with Hitler.

Appeasement lasted only so long: in response to the German invasion of Poland, Britain declared war on Germany on September 3, 1939, thus precipitating the outbreak of **World War II.** The earlier World War I, with its fighting based in continental Europe, failed to prepare the British Isles for the utter devastation of concerted military attacks. The British were forced to face German air attacks as early as the summer of 1940, when the prolonged **Battle of Britain** began. London, Coventry, and other British cities were demolished by the fiery **"Blitzkriegs"** of the early 40s, destroying military factories and leaving scores of Britons without homes. As soon as war had broken out, the majority of city children were evacuated to host families in the countryside—the devastation of the cities left a generation of children orphaned. The fall of France in 1940 precipitated the end of the Chamberlain government and the creation of a war cabinet led by the determined and eloquent **Winston Churchill.** American forces in Europe augmented the Allied effort in the 1944 **D-Day Invasion** of Normandy; the invasion swung the tide of the war and eventually produced peace in Europe in May 1945.

THE POST-WAR YEARS

The growing affluence and diversity of the post-war era propelled Britain to the center stage of international popular culture. A radical experiment in socialist medicine was initiated by the institution of the **National Health Service** in 1946, guaranteeing government-funded medical care to all Brits. Later, Harold Wilson's Labour government relaxed divorce and homosexuality laws and abolished capital punishment. Under Wilson's successor Edward Heath, Britain joined the **European Community** in 1971, a union that received a rocky welcome from many British MPs and citizens and continues to inflame passions today. Increasing economic problems in the 1970s stemmed from Britain's colonial retreat, which had begun in earnest after World War II. Conservative and Labour governments alike floundered in attempts to curtail unemployment while maintaining a base level of social welfare benefits, and economic unrest culminated in a series of public service strikes in 1979's **"Winter of Discontent."**

It was against this backdrop that Britain grasped for change, electing the Tory **Margaret Thatcher** ("The Iron Lady") as Prime Minister, putting faith in her nationalism and Victorian values. Thatcher's term seemed hexed by painful economic recession, but by 1983, British victory against Argentina in the territorial dispute for the **Falkland Islands** and embarrassing disarray in the Labour Party clinched her second term. Thatcher turned from the war in the Falklands to the state of the British Isles, denationalizing and dismantling the welfare state with legislation and quips like "there is no such thing as society." Unlike her post-war predecessors, Thatcher rejected low unemployment as a policy goal and focused instead on economic growth. Her policies brought dramatic prosperity to many, but sharpened the divide between rich and poor. Thatcher prided herself on "politics of conviction," but her stubbornness was her undoing, as she clung to the unpopular **poll tax** and resisted the European Community. Though still divided on Europe, the Conservative Party conducted a vote of no confidence that led to Thatcher's 1990 resignation and the intra-party election of **John Major** as Prime Minister.

In 1993, the Major government suffered its first embarrassment when the British pound toppled out of the EC's monetary regulation system. In August of the same year, Britain ratified the **Maastricht Treaty** on a closer **European Union (EU),** but only after severe division between Major and anti-treaty rebels within the Conservative Party. Despite these Conservative debacles and a string of scandals, the Tories won the April 1992 election, mostly due to Labour's inability to shed its image of ineffectiveness from the 1970s. Major struggled with unpopularity, and by 1995, his ratings were so low that he resigned as Party leader to force a leadership election. Major won the election, but the Conservatives had lost parliamentary seats and continued to languish in the polls.

BRITAIN TODAY

The Labour Party, under the leadership of charismatic **Tony Blair,** reduced ties with the labor unions, refashioned itself into the alternative for discontented voters, and finally began to rise in popularity. Despite tense relations with unions, the "new" Labour Party claimed a clear victory under Blair in the May 1997 elections, garnering the biggest Labour majority ever. In 1998, Blair nurtured closer relations with the EU, maintained a moderate economic and social position, and was named one of *People Magazine's* 50 Most Beautiful People. All in all, not a bad year for Tony. 1999 was more turbulent, with Britain's stance in the Kosovo crisis gaining Blair the title of "little Clinton" for his blind following of American foreign policy. Under Blair, Britain has held fast to its refusal to adopt the euro, a single European currency that went into operation in January 1999, because Parliament is concerned that it would bring about a decrease in economic independence and national sovereignty. Britain's leaders say they remain prepared to exercise the nation's option of participating in a unified currency early in its next government, which will come into power no later than the spring of 2002.

The Labour government has also tackled various constitutional reforms promised in its platform, beginning with domestic **devolution** in Scotland and Wales. The Scots voted in a 1997 referendum to have their own Parliament, which opened in 1999, paving the way for greater independence (see p. 493), and the Welsh opened the first session of their National Assembly in 1999 (see p. 420). Progress has been more halting in the latest attempts at **Northern Irish** autonomy; the British government suspended the Stormont assembly for several months in 2000 after debilitating squabbles over weapons decommissioning, but restored its powers again after the Irish Republican Army promised to begin disarming. Still, the movement for modernization continued when the Labour government sent over 600 hereditary peers scuttling home from the **House of Lords** in November 1999. A Royal Commission in 2000 unveiled further reform proposals for the Lords, including the introduction of elected peers, but Blair has so far put further action on hold.

A ROYAL MESS?

The royal family has had its share of troubles in recent years. In 1992, over a hundred rooms in Windsor Palace burned on Queen Elizabeth II's wedding anniversary, and in 1993 she started paying income tax. The sad spectacle of royal life took a tragic turn in 1997 as **Princess Diana** died in a car crash in a Paris tunnel. The resultant outpouring of grief, crystallized in photos of Kensington Palace drowned in flowers, has now subsided, but tourists still mourn at the Diana memorial at

Althorp. The immediate fate of the royals will depend on whether the monarchy embraces Diana's fervent populism or retreats with traditional aloofness to the private realm. Royal-watchers are hoping that the 1999 marriage of the youngest royal brother, **Edward,** to Sophie Rhys-Jones will fare better than those of his three divorced siblings. True to their usual form, bookies are offering 5:1 odds that the royal couple will stay married for 20 years. However, it is clearly the young **Prince William** on whom the spotlight shines. After Wills finished his studies at Eton last summer, speculation on his university of choice (he ended up picking St. Andrews in Scotland) and revelations of a pen-pal correspondence with American popster Britney Spears consumed his adoring, often pre-pubescent, public. Whether "His Royal Sighness" will be able to survive the trip to adulthood under the paparazzi's unforgiving lens remains to be seen. The monarchy's official website, www.royal.gov.uk, features public events listings, history, and bios.

GOVERNMENT

Despite being one of the world's most stable constitutional monarchies, Britain has no written constitution. A combination of parliamentary legislation, common law, and convention create the flexible system that runs the British government. While kings once ruled, since the 1700s the monarch has served in a purely symbolic role, leaving real political power to **Parliament**. Consisting of the **House of Commons**, with its elected Members of Parliament (MPs), and the **House of Lords**, most of whom are government-appointed Life Peers, Parliament holds supreme legislative power and may change and even directly contradict its previous laws (flexible, isn't it?). Of Parliament's two houses, power has shifted from the Lords to the Commons over the course of the centuries, and Blair's latest move to abolish hereditary peerage is just one step in this process. All members of the executive, which includes the **Prime Minister** and the **Cabinet**, are also MPs; this fusing of legislative and executive functions, called the "efficient secret" of the British government, ensures the quick passage of the majority party's programs into bills. The Prime Minister is generally the head of the majority party, and he (or she) chooses the members of the Cabinet, who serve as heads of the government's departments. British politics is a group effort; the Cabinet may bicker over policy in private, but their sense of collective responsibility ensures that they present a cohesive program to the public. Political parties also keep their MPs in line on most votes in Parliament and provide a pool of talent and support for the smooth functioning of the executive. The two main parties in UK politics are **Labour** and the **Conservatives,** representing roughly the left and the right, respectively; a smaller third party, the **Liberal Democrats**, tries its best to be the fulcrum on which power balances shift.

SEX SCANDALS, A QUICKIE HISTORY British
attitudes towards sexuality can be baffling: while tabloids sport topless girls, the same papers are also willing to act totally shocked when a Member of Parliament is caught *in flagrante delicto*. Perhaps the most famous of British sex scandals was the **Profumo Affair,** when John Profumo, then Secretary of State for War, had to leave government after he lied about having sex with Christine Keeler, a call-girl who was also having an affair with a Soviet naval attache. More recently, David Mellor, Heritage Secretary, had to resign in 1992 after his affair with actress Antonia de Sancha was disclosed, while the revelation of Piers Merchant's affair with teenager Anna Cox added to voter discontent with the Major government in 1997. Merchant was quoted as saying "my male instinct was far stronger than any immediate thoughts I had for John Major." But if voters thought they'd finally managed to "throw the bums out," the current Labour government proved them wrong, with Ron Davies' need to compete.

LANGUAGE AND LITERATURE

Outdone worldwide only by Mandarin Chinese in sheer number of speakers, the English language mirrors in its own vocabulary the diversity of the hundreds of millions who use it today. Originally a minor Germanic dialect, English was in its formative stages enriched by words and phrases from Danish, French, and Latin, thus giving even its earliest speakers, poets, and wordsmiths a supple and vast vocabulary rivalled by few European languages. In the last few centuries, with English spread to the corners of the world by British colonialism, the language has picked up countless borrowings from other tongues, and serves as the voice literary and popular of people far removed from the British Isles, from Chinua Achebe in Nigeria to Derek Walcott in the Caribbean. With the spread of language went the spread of literature, and Britain's long literary tradition, which remains very much alive and well today, is widely recognized as one of the world's finest. Of course, it is absurd to attempt an overview of the history of English literature in a few pages, but we'll give it a shot. A well-chosen novel or collection of poems will illuminate any sojourn in Britain, and the following survey hopes to give an idea of the diverse range of choices available. Note that the survey is of English literature; Welsh and Scottish literature are treated separately, p. 420 and p. 494 respectively.

OLD ENGLISH AND THE MIDDLE AGES

Most of the earliest poetry in English was part of an oral tradition, of which little survives. The finest piece of Anglo-Saxon (Old English) poetry for which record does exist is *Beowulf*. Dated tenuously at the first half of the 7th century, the anonymously authored poem details the Scandinavian prince Beowulf's struggle against the monster Grendel. **Geoffrey Chaucer,** writing centuries later, tapped into the spirited side of Middle English; his *Canterbury Tales* (c. 1387) remain some of the funniest—and sauciest—stories in the English canon. The anonymously authored *Sir Gawain and the Green Knight*, another Middle English masterwork (c. 1375), is an alliterative romance of chivalry in a mysterious, magical landscape. A more meditative masterpiece is **William Langland's** *Piers Plowman* (c. 1367), which turns the theme of pilgrimage into an intense, tortured allegory.

The need to adapt religious material into a form understood by the masses led **John Wycliffe** to make the first translation of the **Bible** into English in the 1380s, thus enhancing the English language's prestige at a time when French was the language at court. The Biblical translator **William Tyndale** fled to the Continent in 1524 to finish his work, but was martyred there for his pains. His work, however, became the model for future English translations. Calvinist expatriates produced an English edition of the Bible in Geneva in the mid-16th century, prompting King James to set 47 translators to bring forth a Word of God the Protestant King could tolerate. The resulting **King James Version,** completed in 1611, rumbles with magnificent pace and rhetoric, and remains a literary monument to this day.

THE ENGLISH RENAISSANCE

English literature flourished under the reign of Elizabeth I. While **Sir Philip Sidney** wrote sonnet sequences and **Edmund Spenser** composed such epics as *The Faerie Queene*, **John Donne,** the Dean of London's St. Paul's Cathedral, wrote introspective devotional poetry and penned erotic verse on the side. The era's greatest contributions to English literature came in drama, with the appearance of the first professional playwrights. As *Shakespeare in Love* moviegoers know, **Christopher Marlowe** lost his life to a dagger in a pub brawl, fortunately not before he guided *Tamburlaine* (c. 1587) and *Dr. Faustus* (c. 1588) into the world of English letters. Meanwhile, **Ben Jonson,** when he wasn't languishing in jail (for acts as varied as insulting Scotland and killing an actor in a sword-fight), redefined satiric comedy in *Volpone* (1606) and *Bartholemew Fair* (1614). The giant of the day, and still the figure against whom all things literary are measured, was of course **William Shakespeare,** who mixed high and low to create some of the finest comedies, histories, and tragedies ever to grace the world. Those who equate the Bard with a

SHAKESPEARE MADE EASY

Have great sex.	"Put a ducat in her clack-dish" (*Measure for Measure*)
This guy from Iceland's a moron, and I hate him.	"Pish for thee, Iceland dog! Thou prick-ear'd cur of Iceland!" (*Henry V*)
Some guy in a bar is annoying you.	"Thou art a boil, a plague-sore, or embossed carbuncle, in my corrupted blood" (*King Lear*)
You kicked his butt and want to tell your friends.	"I took by the throat the circumcised dog, and smote him, thus." (*Othello*)
Dude, you suck.	"Methink'st thou art a general offense and every man should beat thee." *(All's Well That Ends Well)*
You are the worst human being ever to walk on the planet.	You are "a base, proud, shallow, beggarly, three-suited, hundred-pound, filthy worsted-stocking knave; a lily-livered, action-taking, whoreson, glass-glazing, super-serviceable, finical rogue." *(King Lear)*

schoolroom avalanche of "whithers" and "wherefores" should know that he held one of the filthiest feathers ever to scrawl the English language, and that Shakespeare invented (or used for the first time) a staggering number of words now in everyday use, among them "arouse," "laughable," and "scuffle," as well as such common phrases as "tower of strength," "sleep not one wink," "dead as a doornail," and "foregone conclusion." An entire town bustles year-round in tribute to the man (see **Stratford-upon-Avon**, p. 262), but his plays, from *Hamlet* and *King Lear* to *The Tempest*, remain the truest monuments to his genius.

GODS AND MEN
The British Puritans of the late 16th and early 17th centuries produced a huge volume of obsessive and beautiful literature. In *Paradise Lost* (1667), the epic poem to end all epic poems, the blind **John Milton** gave Satan, Adam, and Eve a complexity the Bible did not grant them. Another Puritan vision came from **John Bunyan,** a self-taught Nonconformist pastor whose *Pilgrim's Progress* (1678) charts the Christian's quest for redemption in a world awaiting the apocalypse. After the monarchy regained full power, writers such as **John Dryden** and **Alexander Pope** led a Neoclassical revival, which yielded a keen satire of English social and political life. The major literary figure and critic of the late 18th century was **Samuel Johnson,** author of *The Lives of the Poets* (1779-81). Dr. Johnson's greatest achievement was spending nine years in Gough Square in London writing the first definitive (and lovably idiosyncratic) English **dictionary.**

THE NOVEL COMES INTO ITS OWN
In 1719, **Daniel Defoe** inaugurated the era of the English novel with his popular island-bound *Robinson Crusoe*. Explorations of the new form continued with **Samuel Richardson**'s *Pamela* (1740) and **Henry Fielding**'s picaresque *Tom Jones* (1749), a novel which shows that traveling could be far more dangerous in those pre-*Let's Go* times. **Jane Austen** brought the novel to new heights, slyly criticizing self-importance in *Pride and Prejudice* (1813) and *Emma* (1815). The harsh industrialization of the Victorian period spawned numerous classic novels: **Charles Dickens's** often biting, sometimes sentimental works, such as *A Christmas Carol* (1843), draw on the bleakness of his childhood (see **Portsmouth,** p. 178) and the severe destitution of much of the British population. From their Haworth home (see p. 376), the **Brontë sisters** composed works of great intensity: in *Wuthering*

Heights (1847), Emily Brontë contrasts the noble but limp Edgar Linton with the exquisitely ferocious Heathcliff. Not to be outdone, her sister Charlotte created madwoman Bertha in *Jane Eyre*. **Thomas Hardy** brought the Victorian age to an end on a dark note in the fate-ridden Wessex landscapes of *Jude the Obscure* (1895) and *Tess of the d'Urbervilles* (1891). It is easy to recognize similarities to real locales in southwest England—"Casterbridge" is Dorchester (see p. 213), for instance. Like Hardy, **George Eliot** (Mary Ann Evans) lost her religious faith; her skepticism drew her to the security of traditional village life. Her *Middlemarch* (1871) depicts the entangled lives of an entire town; the novel is majestic in scope and in its realization of human tragedy.

ROMANTICISM AND THE 19TH CENTURY

Partly in reaction to the rationalism of the preceding century, the early 19th century saw the rise of the Romantic movement, which found its greatest expression in poetry. Painter-poet **William Blake's** *Songs of Innocence and Experience* (1794) was a precursor to the movement in its antimaterialist spirit, but the watershed event launching Romanticism in Britain was the joint publication of *Lyrical Ballads* in 1798 by **William Wordsworth** and **Samuel Taylor Coleridge,** which included such classics as "Lines Composed a Few Miles above Tintern Abbey" (see p. 431) and "The Rime of the Ancient Mariner." The Romantic poets celebrated the transcendent beauty of nature and the power of the imagination to a degree never before seen in English letters; many of their revolutionary ideas—such as childhood experiences having a profound influence on the development of the human being—are accepted as common knowledge today. Wordsworth's immense blank-verse poem *The Prelude* (1805 and 1850), in which he remembers childhood "spots in time," cemented his reputation as Romantic icon. His sonnet sequence *The River Duddon* (1820) is an overlooked gem. Wordsworth's younger colleagues were plagued by early deaths: the great **John Keats** died of tuberculosis at 26—but not before penning the maxim "beauty is truth, truth beauty" and odes full of the richest language since Shakespeare—while **Percy Bysshe Shelley** drowned off the Tuscan coast at 29. **Lord Byron's** *Don Juan* (1819-24) established him as the heartthrob of the age before he was killed in the Greek War of Independence.

The poetry of the Victorian age struggled with the impact of societal changes. **Alfred, Lord Tennyson** spun gorgeous verse about faith and doubt for over a half-century, while **Matthew Arnold** rebelled against the industrialization of literature and the anarchy of mass rule. Combining skepticism and the grotesque, **Robert Browning** eschewed Tennyson's lyricism. **Gerard Manley Hopkins** revolutionized English poetry with his "sprung rhythm" verses, making him the chief forerunner of poetic modernism.

THE MODERN AGE

Willing or not, English audiences experienced the poignant outrage of war poets **Siegfried Sassoon** and **Wilfred Owen.** After World War I, London was the home of artistic movements such as the **Bloomsbury Group,** pulling the world's intellects into its midst. **Virginia Woolf,** a key group member, explored the private yearnings of the individual mind in *To the Lighthouse* (1927). **T.S. Eliot** grew up a Missouri boy but became the "Pope of Russell Square" (see p. 123); *The Waste Land* (1922), one of this century's most important poems, is a picture of a fragmented, motionless, precious world waiting for the end. **D.H. Lawrence** explored tensions in the British working-class family in *Sons and Lovers* (1913) before traveling the other way across the Atlantic. Although he spoke only a few words of English when he arrived in the country aged 21, **Joseph Conrad** proceeded to masterfully employ the language to examine evil in *Heart of Darkness* (1902). Disillusionment also pervades **E.M. Forster**'s half-critical, half-abashedly romantic novels such as *A Passage to India* (1924), which connect repression and class hypocrisy. Writing in the 1930s matched the tumult and depression of the decade: **Evelyn Waugh** turned a satirical eye on society in *Vile Bodies* (1930),

GREAT BRITAIN

while **Graham Greene** studied moral ambiguity in *Brighton Rock* (1938). More optimistically, poets such as **W.H. Auden** saw in Freud and socialism hope for a better future.

LATE 20TH-CENTURY LITERATURE

Fascism and the horrors of the Second World War led to **William Golding's** and **Muriel Spark's** musings on the nature of evil, while in **George Orwell's** *1984* (1949), a ravenous totalitarian state strives to strip the world of memory and words of meaning. Later, the end of Empire and rising affluence splintered British literature in a thousand directions. Nostalgia pervades the poems of **Philip Larkin** and **John Betjeman**, which search for beauty amidst knowledge of mortality, in contrast to the vigorous poems of the Yorkshire-raised **Ted Hughes** and **Tony Harrison** (Andrew Motion succeeded the late Hughes as the country's Poet Laureate in May 1999). Postcolonial voices have also become an important literary force in an increasingly multicultural country. **Timothy Mo** examines British rule in East Asia in *An Insular Possession* (1986), while Nigerian-born-and-educated **Ben Okri** draws on the myths of Africa and Europe. The South Asian writing contingent, including **Hanif Kureishi** and **Vikram Seth,** has been especially strong— **Salman Rushdie's** spellbinding *Midnight's Children* (1981) is a glorious amalgam of Indian myth and modern culture. British playwrights, as always, continue to innovate. **John Osborne** looked back in anger, **Harold Pinter** wrote more than his fair share of tense conversations, and **Tom Stoppard** challenged everything you thought you knew about theater in plays such as *Rosencrantz and Guildenstern are Dead* (1967).

OUTSIDE THE CLASSROOM

Britain has produced a great number of less literary yet still hugely popular writers. **Sir Arthur Conan Doyle** immortalized London's 221B Baker St. (see p. 122) and fired the detective story craze, continued by the elegant mysteries of **Dorothy L. Sayers** and **Agatha Christie.** The espionage novels of **Ian Fleming** and **John Le Carré** provided thrills of another sort. The hilarious work of **P.G. Wodehouse** (featuring Bertie Wooster and his butler Jeeves) affectionately satirizes the idle aristocrat, while **Douglas Adams's** *Hitchhiker's Guide to the Galaxy* series parodies sci-fi. **James Herriot** (Alf Wight), author of *All Creatures Great and Small* (1972), faced a backlash when a flock of steadfastly unanthropomorphized sheep broke his leg.

Britain has also produced volumes of children's literature. **Lewis Carroll's** Alice and **C.S. Lewis's** Narnia continue to enchant generations, and the stories of **Enid Blyton** remain vastly popular despite allegations of stereotyped characters. **Roald Dahl** spun tales of chocolate fantasy for children (and tales of other types of fantasy for adults). Adolescence in Thatcherite Britain found its voice in **Sue Townsend's** *Adrian Mole* series. **Richard Adams's** *Watership Down* (1920) depicts Britain as a wandering nation searching for new myths and heroes, while the engrossing fantasies of **J.R.R. Tolkien** prove that old myths remain vibrant sources.

ROAD BOOKS Besides the works listed above, these books are our picks for further glimpses into British life—and for sheer light-reading entertainment.
Bill Bryson, *Notes from a Small Island*: An American expatriate's acute (and acutely funny) observations about Britain.
Helen Fielding, *Bridget Jones's Diary*: This chronicle of single womanhood in 1990s London was a cult sensation.
Nick Hornby, *Fever Pitch*: If you've ever been a fan of any sport, you'll appreciate this fine novel about the Arsenal Football Club and obsessive fanship.
Geoff Nicholson, *Bleeding London*: A novel for London lovers, the book cleverly connects a man intent on walking every street in London, a woman whose body is turning into a map of the city, and a brutal visitor from Sheffield.

ART AND ARCHITECTURE

FINE ARTS

British art has long been dominated by influences from abroad, first from continental Europe and most recently from America. After the Reformation brought the medieval tradition of religious art to an end, a string of secular foreign portraitists, including **Hans Holbein** the Younger and **Sir Anthony Van Dyck,** dominated the court-sponsored art scene of the 16th and 17th centuries. Even the works of the acclaimed British-born artists of the time, Elizabethan court painter **Nicholas Hilliard** (1547-1619) and Baroque decorative artist **Sir James Thornhill** (1675-1734; see his Painted Hall in Greenwich) exhibit continental influences. The Civil War freed British artists from the constraints of the court, making way for **William Hogarth** (1697-1764) and his narrative engravings of distinctly British "modern moral subjects" in *A Rake's Progress*. Portraiture continued to flourish under the brush of **Sir Joshua Reynolds** (1723-92), the founder of the Royal Academy of Art, whose work incorporated elements of historical painting. The long, feathery strokes of his contemporary **Thomas Gainsborough** (1727-88) produced portraits with prominent settings and, later, Britain's first classical landscapes.

Landscape art reached its pinnacle in the 19th century, when **J.M.W. Turner** (1775-1851) and **John Constable** (1776-1837) glorified the English countryside with their magnificent, light-filled oil paintings. Reacting to the popularity of genre painter **David Wilkie's** (1785-1841) drably-depicted and trivial subject matter, the three young artists **William Holman Hunt** (1827-1910), **Dante Gabriel Rossetti** (1828-82), and **Sir John Everett Millais** (1829-96) founded the Italian-inspired Pre-Raphaelite Brotherhood in 1848. Hunt's *The Hireling Shepard* and Millais' *Ophelia* illuminated their respective moral and romantic subjects with clear, bright colors by painting over a pure white ground. The Pre-Raphaelites in turn inspired **William Morris** (1834-1896) to turn from the lackluster machine-made design of his age and rediscover England's rustic roots in the Arts and Crafts Movement. The art of illustration also flourished in this period, typified by the output of Punch cartoonist **John Leech** (1817-64), the illuminated manuscripts of mystic artist and lyric poet **William Blake** (1757-1827), the bizarre and grotesque imagery of **Aubrey Beardsley** (1872-1898), and the satirical musings of **Sir John Tenniel** (1820-1914), who furnished the whimsical illustrations for Lewis Carroll's *Alice's Adventure in Wonderland*.

The 20th century began with the basically pre-Modern paintings of **Sir Stanley Spencer** (1891-1959). Modernism reached Britain with the sculpture of **Henry Moore** (1898-1986), whose reclining and often abstract nudes express themes of life and fertility. His contemporary **Dame Barbara Hepworth** (1903-1975) used pure abstract forms to explore space and texture in her sculpture. The disturbing, meat-filled portraits of **Frances Bacon** (1909-1992) and the emotionally intense realism of **Lucian Freud** (b. 1922), Sigmund's grandson, have transformed British portraiture, while Pop artist **David Hockney** (b. 1937) infused an American-born movement with British wit. More recently, the multimedia artist **Damien Hirst** (b. 1965) has both fascinated and appalled audiences worldwide with such installations as a shark suspended in a formaldehyde solution. Active conservative art patron **Prince Charles** provides much fodder for postage stamps and continues the English tradition of landscape painting with his bland watercolors.

ARCHITECTURE

The many cathedrals and castles dotting Britain's architectural landscape trace the early history of foreign conquests and cultural invasions. Pre-Christian builders of the Bronze Age left their mark at **Stonehenge** (p. 196), while remnants of the **Roman spa** at Bath (p. 202) testify to the engineering savvy of England's ancient conquerors. Anglo-Saxon architects tried their own hand at building in the 6th century, and **St. Martin's** (p. 152) in Canterbury has the small windows and rectangular body typical of Saxon construction. When the Normans arrived, they built cruciform churches (shaped like a cross) with thick walls and rounded arches, such as **Durham Cathedral** (p. 401). Beginning with the **White Tower** at the Tower of London (p. 107), they also introduced the squat, square towers of England's first stone castles, which both fortified the coastline and became the symbol of feudal life.

Gothic architecture may have originated in France, but beginning around 1175 the English took the style to new heights in three distinct and increasingly elegant stages. In addition to the pointed arches and ribbed stone vaults common to all Gothic buildings, the 13th-century **Wells Cathedral** (p. 209) also has lancet windows that exemplify the Early English stage. Decorated period buildings like the 1334 **Salisbury Cathedral** (p. 195) show off intricately carved windows, and the 80-foot high **King's College Chapel** in Cambridge (p. 303), completed in 1547, demonstrates the Perpendicular style's long windows and strong vertical lines. The late medieval years also saw the declining importance of castles as military strategy began to favor explosive battles over long sieges, but **Harlech Castle** (p. 462) has the concentric layout and rounded towers that signaled sophistication in 1290. Half-timber cottages housed the lower classes and were made from wood frames filled with plaster to overcome the scarcity of strong timber.

The age of the architect dawned with **Inigo Jones** (1573-1652), whose admiration of Italian design can be seen in the symmetry and pillars of his **Queen's House** in Greenwich (p. 125) and the classical **Covent Garden piazza** in London. When the Great Fire of London destroyed most of the city in 1666, **Sir Christopher Wren** (1632-1723) rebuilt 53 churches, including **St. Paul's Cathedral** (p. 107). A wave of random revivals and exotic influences swept through Britain in the 18th and 19th centuries, leaving in its wake the Gothic **Houses of Parliament** (p. 119), an Egyptian-flavored **Marshall's Woollen Mill** in Leeds (the obelisks are really chimneys), and the **British Museum** (p. 128), a Greek revivalist's dream. **John Nash** (1752-1835) worked both classy, in his Regency buildings with stucco fronts, and gaudy, at the **Royal Pavilion** in Brighton (p. 166), which mixes Hindu and Oriental elements in a carnivalesque mess. The second destruction of London during the air raids of World War II allowed architects to replace the city's industrial docklands with the skyscraper **Canary Wharf** (p. 126), and the modernism continued in 1986 with Richard Rodger's metallic **Lloyd's Building** (p. 109). Greenwich's **Millennium Dome** opened for the year 2000, and while the exhibition within will end in December 2000, the futuristic exterior will remain.

FILM

British film has endured an uneven history, marked by cycles of relative independence from Hollywood followed by increasing drains of talent to America. World War II inspired a more nationally orientated state of affairs, as the government commissioned and funded a series of propaganda films, including stage impresario **Laurence Olivier's** glorious *Henry V* (1944). Master of suspense **Alfred Hitchcock** snared audiences with films made on both sides of the Atlantic, including *Dial M for Murder* (1954) and *Psycho* (1960). **David Lean** employed the brilliant **Sir Alec Guinness** as his lead in *Lawrence of Arabia* (1962) and in *Dr. Zhivago* (1965). Guinness, now famous as the original Obi-Wan Kenobi, started his career with a string of wickedly funny films such as *The Man in the White Suit* (1951), and *The Lavender Hill Mob* (1951), both products of the patently British **Ealing Studios**.

The 60s phenomenon of "swingin' London" created new momentum for the British film industry and jump-started international interest in British culture. American Richard Lester made rock stars into film stars in the **Beatles'** *A Hard Day's Night* (1963), and Scot **Sean Connery** drank the first of many martinis, shaken not stirred, as **James Bond** in *Dr. No* (1962). As the hopes of the decade began to look tarnished, elements of British cinema became darker. Adopted Brit **Stanley Kubrick** went beyond the infinite without leaving England in *2001: A Space Odyssey* (1968) and descended into mayhem in *A Clockwork Orange* (1971). Kubrick's work exposes the restless British youths' discontent with society.

Elaborate costume dramas and offbeat independent films have come to represent contemporary British film. The heroic sagas of **Hugh Hudson's** *Chariots of Fire* (1981) and **Richard Attenborough's** *Gandhi* (1982) swept the Oscars in successive years. Director-producer team **Merchant-Ivory** have led the way in adaptations of British novels, ranging from Ishiguro's *The Remains of the Day* (1993) to Forster's *Howard's End* (1992). **Kenneth Branagh** has focused his talents on adapting Shakespeare, with glossy, critically acclaimed works such as *Henry V* (1989). Elements from all these films can be seen in **John Madden's** devastatingly witty *Shakespeare in Love* (1998). The offbeat, low-budget comedy *Four Weddings and a Funeral* (1994) was instantly successful, while hilarious fellow indie flick *Trainspotting* enjoyed equal success but far more drug-fueled controversy in 1996. *The Full Monty* (1997) bared the comedic underbelly of the Sheffield unemployed and, along with *Lock, Stock and Two Smoking Barrels* (1998), tapped into earlier cinematic conventions. East End boy **Peter Greenaway** produced less commercially viable, more esoteric independent films: *Prospero's Books* (1991) is cutting edge and definitely not family fare. **Mike Leigh**'s work is equally disturbing, with his *Secrets and Lies* (1995) making a sizable impression on an international audience. The British Tourist Authority (see p. 13) produces a "Movie Map" listing more than 200 movie locations across the country.

GREAT BRITAIN

MUSIC

CLASSICAL

Britain was long called "a land without music," a tag not entirely deserved. Starting from the monastic chants of the 900s, the past millenium of British classical music has witnessed brilliant composition amongst the dry spells. During the English Renaissance, all published music, by royal decree, came from the printing presses of anthem writer **Thomas Tallis** (1550-1640), "Father of English Cathedral music," and his partner **William Byrd** (1543-1623), who gave the Italians a run for their money by developing motets and psalms in Latin and English. During the same creative period, **Thomas Morley** (1557-1602) created the quintessentially British madrigal, and the melodies for solo voice and lute in **John Dowland's** (1563-1626) collection of airs were as light as, well, air. **Thomas Weelkes** (1575-1623) and **John Wilbye** (1574-1638) continued these motet and madrigal traditions into the 16th and 17th centuries, and later **Henry Purcell** (1659-1695) composed instrumental music as well as England's first great opera, *Dido and Aeneas*.

The 18th century, regarded as Britain's musical Dark Age, welcomed the visits of the foreign geniuses Mozart, Haydn, and **George Frederic Handel,** who enjoyed Britain enough to become a naturalized subject in his later years. British composer **William Boyce** (1710-79) contributed to his country's musical heritage with a 3-volume collection of early English cathedral music. **Sir William Sterndale Bennett** (1816-75) wrote sprightly piano compositions bearing the influence of his friend Mendelssohn, but today's audiences are more familiar with the operettas of **W.S. Gilbert** (1836-1911) and **Arthur Sullivan** (1842-1900); the pair were rumored to hate each other, but they managed to produce gems filled with social satire and farce, such as *The Mikado* and *The Pirates of Penzance*. A second renaissance of more serious music began under **Edward Elgar** (1857-1934), whose pomp is outweighed by circumstances of eloquence in his *Enigma Variations*. **Gustav Holst** (1874-1934), in contrast to his suites for military band, adapted Neoclassical methods and folk materials to Romantic moods in *The Planets*.

Also borrowing elements from folk music's simple melodies, **Ralph Vaughan Williams** (1872-1958) and **John Ireland** (1879-1962) brought musical modernism to the island, while composer **William Walton's** (1902-83) world conducting tours erased the "not for export" stamp so long attached to British music. The world wars provided adequate fodder for this continued musical resurgence, provoking **Benjamin Britten's** (1913-76) heartbreaking *War Requiem* and **Michael Tip-**

pett's (1905-98) spiritually humanitarian oratorio, *A Child of Our Time*. Present stalwarts **Peter Maxwell Davies** (b. 1934), whose symphonies evoke Medieval and Renaissance themes, and **Harrison Birtwistle** (b. 1934), are also valued for sponsoring performances of contemporary compositions. **Richard Rodney Bennett** (b. 1936) has experimented with 12-tone methods of writing, while **Jonathan Harvey** (b. 1939) added electronics to the mix in his choral/instrumental works. On the British stage, **Oliver Knussen** (b. 1952) set Maurice Sendak's *Where the Wild Things Are* to music in his one-act opera, and **Andrew Lloyd Webber** (b. 1948) has transformed musical theater with his blend of opera, popular music, and falling chandeliers. Youngsters **Brian Ferneyhough** (b. 1943), **Anthony Powers** (b. 1953), and **Philip Grange** (b. 1956) also stand poised to carry Britain's classical music into the 21st century.

POPULAR

THE BRITISH ARE COMING

Maybe the smaller size of the music market makes it easier to break into. Maybe it's just something in the water. Whatever it is, Britain has continually been the source of much innovation in popular music in its various incarnations. After World War II, imported American rock and blues provided musical inspiration for the first wave of "British Invasion" rock groups. From Liverpool (see p. 328) and then London, **The Beatles** stood at the fore of every musical and cultural trend, spinning out the classic songs that became part of the international cultural vocabulary. Their Satanic Majesties **The Rolling Stones** were London's harder-edged answer to the Fab Four, while **The Kinks** spurned psychedelia and voiced horror at the American vulgarity that seemed, to them, to have crushed Little England. **The Who** began as Kinks-like popsters, then expanded into "rock operas" like *Quadrophenia*, which chronicled the fights between "rockers" (who liked leather jackets and America) and "mods" (who liked speed, androgyny, and the Who).

Psychedelic drugs and high hopes produced a flurry of great tunes by white British adapters of the blues. **The Yardbirds** spawned guitar heroes **Eric Clapton** and **Jimmy Page**, who went on to dominate mass markets in the 70s through their bands **Cream** and **Led Zeppelin**, respectively. The same period also saw the release of long self-indulgent concept albums by "progressive-rock" groups such as **Yes, Genesis, Pink Floyd,** and **Roxy Music.**

ANARCHY IN THE UK

The theatrical excess of **Queen** and **Elton John** characterized mid-70s rock. While **David Bowie** flitted through personae, "pub rock" groups tried to return rock to the people, leading to the punk movement. In London, Malcolm McLaren organized the **Sex Pistols** to get publicity for his King's Road boutique, "Sex." With "Sex's" clothes and Johnny Rotten's snarl, the Pistols indelibly marked music and culture. **The Clash** made political punk with an idealistic leftist slant, while the sloppy sounds of **The Damned** degenerated into goth posturings. Perhaps the most popular of punk's first-wave bands among the British was **The Jam,** led by Paul Weller's resolutely British lyrics. The fans who sent it up the charts were surprised to learn that **The Buzzcocks'** Pete Shelley wrote "Ever Fallen in Love?" about a man.

Inspired by punk's DIY ethos, but adding synthesizers, **Joy Division** and Factory Records made Manchester echo with gloomily poetic rock, and **The Cure** shook teens everywhere. **Elvis Costello** and **Squeeze** found that punk had cleared the ground for smart pop, which stayed bitingly British even as it took over world charts. From the same anti-establishment impulses as punk came the metal of **Ozzy Osbourne** and **Iron Maiden,** which was much less acclaimed but still attracted a cult following. Sheffield's **Def Leppard** took the hard-rock-big-hair ethic through the 80s.

SYNTH-POP, INDIE, AND DANCE

Alas, punk died an angry death with Sid Vicious, leaving the music scene increasingly receptive to the burgeoning field of electronic music. Prompted by the keyboard swagger of Germans Kraftwerk, a swarm of bubbly New Romantics such as **The Human League** and **Spandau Ballet** took to the English stage in the 80s with their synthesisers. **Duran Duran** and **Eurythmics** may have more successfully crossed the Atlantic to dominate American charts, but **Depeche Mode, Erasure,** and the ever-witty **Pet Shop Boys** refined the synth-pop message and kept the home crowds dancing through the night. The producing machine of **Stock, Aitken, and Waterman** churned out a string of embarrassingly catchy hits by **Rick Astley** and **Bananarama** among others, while **Wham!** managed to be equally embarrassing on their own.

Manchester took on the role of center of musical development throughout the 80s. The melancholy musings of the Morrissey-led **Smiths** were matched by the bittersweet beats of **New Order** (formerly Joy Division). Another Mancunian, Mark E. Smith, founded influential cult band **The Fall.** In the late 80s, a crop of guitar noise bands from the city helped to create the early rave movement. Mop-topped, sweaty youths dropped Ecstasy and danced maniacally to the "Madchester" sounds of **The Stone Roses, The Happy Mondays,** and **The Charlatans.** This evolved in the mid-90s into the sounds of a diverse range of indie bands tenuously held together under the "Britpop" label, including the Beatles-esque **Oasis,** the glam **Suede,** the wry **Blur,** and the campy **Pulp.**

The pop charts have also been subject to the musical stylings of the **Spice Girls** and equally spicy boy-bands like **Take That,** now defunct but survived by the extremely successful **Robbie Williams.** The music of other cultures, including the sitar-tinged Indian sounds of **Cornershop,** continues to influence the direction of British pop, keeping it fresh. Shoppers should note that genre-classifications in music stores may be different from what they're used to. "Swing" refers not to big band music but to the R&B sounds of singers such as **All Saints;** "ska", meanwhile, refers to the original Jamaican musical form, not the American ska-punk hybrid.

The UK has also taken **dance music** to heart, with record stores having to create separate sections for the genres of dance music—house, techno, trance, drum 'n' bass, and others too numerous to include—that rule much of the club scene. The rave scene (and the synthetic drugs that accompanied it) exploded in Britain in the late 80s, and **DJs** like **Carl Cox** and **Tony de Vit** became stars in their own right. While "trip-hop"—the name given to the downtempo Bristol sound of **Massive Attack, Tricky,** and **Portishead**—provided something to chill to, the Big Beat dance-rock sound of **The Chemical Brothers** and **Fatboy Slim** continues to draw the punters into the clubs. In the house music of **Basement Jaxx** and the drum 'n' bass of **Roni Size and Reprazent**, Britain in the new millennium continues to stake its long-standing claim to musical innovation.

GET YER ROCKS OFF If you're looking for road tunes, you could do worse than to pick something from this selection of albums.

British Invasion: The Beatles, *Sergeant Pepper's Lonely Hearts Club Band; Something Else by the Kinks;* and The Rolling Stones, *Beggar's Banquet.*

Punk/post-punk: The Clash, *London Calling;* Joy Division, *Permanent;* and The Sex Pistols, *Never Mind the Bollocks, Here's the Sex Pistols.*

Synth-pop: Depeche Mode, *101;* Duran Duran, *Decade; (The Best of) New Order;* Pet Shop Boys, *Discography;* and Spandau Ballet, *True.*

Indie: The Smiths, *The Queen is Dead; The Stone Roses;* Blur, *Parklife;* Oasis, *What's the Story (Morning Glory);* and Pulp, *Different Class.*

Dance: Basement Jaxx, *Remedy;* Fatboy Slim, *On the Floor at the Boutique;* Massive Attack, *Blue Lines;* and Roni Size vs Reprazent, *New Forms.*

FOOD AND TEA

English cooking, like the English climate, is a training for life's unavoidable hardships.
   —R.P. Lister

British cuisine's deservedly modest reputation redeems itself in the few specialties without which the world's palate would be sadly incomplete. Chances are you may well leave the island addicted to rice pudding, Yorkshire pudding, bread pudding, shortbread, the inestimable Hobnob, and of course, spotted dick.

Britons like to start their day off heartily with the famous **English breakfast,** served in most B&Bs across the country. Meat is the main staple of any British meal, and this cholesterol-filled repast, consisting of fried eggs, fried ham, fried bacon, fried sausage, fried bread, marmalade, grilled tomatoes and mushrooms, and (in winter) porridge, is no exception. You will probably want a "nice cuppa" (tea) to wash it all down; unlike its French and Italian counterparts, British coffee is far from exceptional. The best native dishes for lunch or dinner are **roasts**—beef, lamb, and Wiltshire hams. **Bangers and mash** uses up left-over sausages and potatoes, while **bubble and squeak** does the same for cabbage and potato. Vegetables, often boiled into a flavorless, textureless mass, are generally the weakest part of the meal. Beware the British salad—it often consists of a few limp lettuce leaves mixed with an abundance of sweetened mayonnaise called "salad cream."

The British like their **desserts** exceedingly sweet and gloopy. Fools, sponges, trifles, and puddings in various varieties will satiate even the most severe of sweet teeth. **Fruit trifle** is a misnomer consisting of wondrous combination of all the best things in life—cake, custard, jam, whipped cream, fresh fruit, and sherry. **Treacle tart** and **spotted dick**—a sponge cake with raisins—are a feast unto themselves. For a more delicate end to the meal, **fools** (whipped cream blended with fruit) and light cakes called sponges are delicious. Most desserts are served with large dollops of thick, yellow custard or whipped cream.

Pub grub (food served in pubs) is fast, filling, and a fine option for budget travelers. Hot meals vary from **Cornish pasties** (PAH-stee: meat and vegetable wrapped in pastry) to the warm and filling **steak and kidney pie.** The cold, inexpensive **ploughman's lunch,** found throughout country pubs, is simply cheese, bread, pickled gherkin, chutney, and pickled onion. More cheap culinary options abound at the perennial chippy—deep fried **fish and chips** are served in a cone of paper, dripping with grease, salt, and vinegar. In recent years, **restaurant chains** have sprung up all over the country (or at least its large cities). You can always find a reliable if slightly pricey meal in establishments such as All Bar One, Café Rouge, Pizza Express, or Dôme, while light snacks are for the taking in Prêt-à-Manger. **Outdoor markets** and **supermarkets** (such as Marks & Spencer, Waitrose, and Tesco) provide another source of cheap food, especially for picnics—try Stilton cheese with digestive biscuits and find a suitably picturesque view.

FLAKES AND SMARTIES British food has character (of one sort or another), and the traditional snack menu is a unique hodgepodge of sweets, crisps, and squashes. **Cadbury's chocolate** bars to die for include Flake, Crunchie (made out of honeycombed magic), and the classic Dairy Milk. Get clever with Smarties, especially the orange ones—made of orange chocolate. **Sweets** come in many forms—the fizzy Refreshers, the chewy Wine Gums, or frosted Fruit Pastilles. Potato chips, or **crisps** as they are known in England, are not just salted, but come in a range of flavors, including Prawn Cocktail, Cheese 'n' Onion, and Salt 'n' Vinegar. All this sugar and salt can be washed down with a bottle of Ribena, a blackcurrant manna from heaven. This beverage belongs to a family of drinks known as **squash,** fruit-based syrups watered down to drink.

Britain's extensive imperialism and resultant immigration have resulted in an abundance of excellent ethnic food throughout the country. For a welcome alternative to traditional British food, try Chinese, Greek, and especially Indian cuisines—Britain offers some of the best **tandoori** and **curry** outside of India, particularly in London and the larger northern cities. Ethnic restaurants are widespread and tend to be open late—stopping for a quick *chicken tikka masala* on the way home from a night at the pub has become a common phenomenon, substituted occasionally by a nice *shish kebab*.

British "tea" refers both to a drink and a social ceremony. The ritual refreshment, accompanying almost every meal, is served strong and milky; if you want it any other way, say so when ordering. The standard tea—colloquially known as a nice **cuppa**—is mass produced by PG Tips or Tetleys; more refined cups specify particular blends such as **Earl Grey, Darjeeling,** or **Lapsang Souchong.** The cliched British ritual of afternoon **high tea,** served around 4pm, includes cooked meats, salad, sandwiches, and pastries. Fans of Victorianism will appreciate the dainty **cucumber sandwiches** served at classy tea joints like Fortnum and Mason's or the Savoy Hotel in London. **Cream tea,** a specialty of Cornwall and Devon, includes toast, shortbread, crumpets, scones, and jam, accompanied by clotted cream (a cross between whipped cream and butter). Many Britons take short tea breaks each day, including mornings ("elevenses"), but Sunday takes the cake for best tea day; the indulgent can while away a couple of hours over a pot of Earl Grey, a pile of buttered scones, and the Sunday newspaper supplements.

PUBS AND BEER

O Beer! O Hodgson, Guinness, Allsopp, Bass! Names that should be on every infant's tongue!
—S.C.L. Calverley

"As much of the history of England has been brought about in public houses as in the House of Commons," said Sir William Harcourt. You may not witness history in the making, but you will certainly absorb the spirit of the land with a stop at a local tavern. Smoke-stained ceilings and wood-paneled walls usually contain the obligatory dart board. The routine inspired by the pub is considerable: to stop in for a sharpener at lunchtime and then again after work is not uncommon. Thanks to this established pace, Brits rapidly develop affinities for neighborhood establishments, becoming loyal to their **locals.** Many pubs cater to a regular clientele—student discounts are common near university dorms, while village pubs maintain a sleepier atmosphere. Those seeking more variety head on to a **pub crawl,** the British equivalent of bar hopping. The drinking age is 18, but enforcement is often lax.

Bitter, named for its sharp, hoppy aftertaste, is the standard pub drink, and should be hand-pumped or pulled from the tap at cellar temperature into government-stamped pint glasses (20oz.) or the more modest but socially scorned half-pints. Abbot's, Youngs, and Ruddles are dark and full-bodied southern examples, while worthy northern brews are Tetleys, John Smith, and Samuel Smith. **Real ale,** using top-fermenting yeast and drawn from a barrel, retains a die-hard cult of connoisseurs in the shadow of giant corporate breweries. Brown, pale, and India pale ales—less common varieties—all have a relatively heavy flavor with noticeable hop. **Stout,** the distinctive subspecies of ale, is rich, dark, and creamy; try the Irish Guinness (see p. 666) with its silky foam head, rumored to be a recipe stolen from the older Beamish. Most draught ales and stouts are served at room temperature, so if you can't stand the heat, try a **lager,** the tasty European precursor of American beer. **Cider,** a fermented apple juice served sweet or dry, is one potent, cold, and tasty alternative to beer. Especially succulent brands include Strongbow, Blackthorn, Woodpecker, and the unrefined Scrumpy Jack. Variations on the standard pint include **shandy,** a combination of beer and fizzy lemonade that no respectable drinker would go near; **black velvet,** a mating of stout and champagne; **black and tan,** layers of stout and ale; and **snakebite,** a murky mix of lager and cider with a dash of blackcurrant Ribena.

Visitors will learn to their dismay that government-imposed **closing times** force revelries to end early, especially in England. Drinking hours imposed during World War I to prevent munitions workers from arriving at the factory drunk are still in place; generally, drinks are served 11am-11pm Monday to Saturday, and from noon-3pm and 7-10:30pm on Sundays, though this varies from region to region. A bell 10 minutes or more before closing time signifies "last orders." T.S. Eliot knew the special agony of pub closings: many a drunkard has argued that the most painful words in all of *The Waste Land* come in its second part, with the publican-god's cry, "HURRY UP PLEASE IT'S TIME." Whether or not patrons consider the existential implications of the call, they know that just 15 minutes remain to finish their beers before chairs go up and lights go down.

In recent months, however, the government has been making noise about extending hours, or doing away with restrictions altogether, thus bringing the dream of the 24-hour pub a bit closer to reality. As *Let's Go* went to press, many pubs were planning to apply for longer hours when their current licenses expire. In reality, though, many establishments, particularly in larger towns and cities, find ways around closing times anyway—serving food or having an entertainment licence allows an establishment to serve alcohol later, so late-night wine bars are popular and around pub closing time clubs really start to get going.

SPORT

Many evils may arise which God forbid.
    —King Edward II, banning football in London, 1314

FOOTBALL

The not-entirely-fair stereotype of English athletic performance is that the English are masters of inventing sports but only average players. **Football** (soccer), whose rules were formalized by the English Football Association (F.A.) in 1863, remains Britain's—and the world's—most popular sport. Tiny grounds dot the countryside, and grand, storied stadia attract thousands every weekend like the cathedrals they are. At the top echelon of English football are the 20 clubs (teams) of the **Premier League,** which are populated with world-class players from Britain and abroad. Below the Premiership lie the three divisions of the Nationwide League. At the end of the season, the three clubs with the worst records in the Premiership face relegation to the First Division, whose top three clubs are promoted. The same process affects the teams of the Second Division, Third Division, lower divisions, and non-league clubs. **Scottish** football is organized along similar lines, although the quality of play is weaker. The **F.A. Cup,** held every May on the hallowed turf of Wembley (see **Football,** p. 139), is English football's premier knockout competition, and the ultimate achievement for an English football club is to "do the Double"—to win both the Premier League and the F.A. Cup in one season.

At present, the English Premier League is dominated by **Manchester United** (see p. 338), and **Arsenal** (see p. 139), with Leeds, Chelsea, and Liverpool also doing well, while the Scottish counterpart is dominated almost every year by the "Old Firm," the two Glaswegian clubs Rangers and Celtic. English clubs are well-known worldwide, and Manchester United ("Man U") was able to capture the prestigious European Cup in 1999, defeating the best teams in Europe behind the play of such legends as Danish goalie Peter Schmeichel. Unfortunately, the four British international teams (England, Scotland, Wales, and Northern Ireland compete as separate countries) have not performed as well in World Cups and European Championships—England's 1966 World Cup victory being the glorious exception.

Over half a million fans attend professional matches in Britain every weekend from mid-August to May, and if you can get tickets, a football match is well worth attending for a glimpse of British **football culture.** Fans sporting painted faces and dressed in team colors make themselves heard with uncanny synchronized (and usually rude) singing. Football passion exceeds the level of religious fervor, and intracity club rivalries (Arsenal-Tottenham in London or Everton-Liverpool in Liverpool) have been known to divide families and neighborhoods. Being a true football fan often involves

ALL THE KING'S HORSES In sport, questions of social class are always close at hand. Horse racing's epithet—the "Sport of Kings"—is hardly hyperbolic; the sport has long enjoyed royal patronage. Edward VII liked nothing better than a day spent relishing what he called "the glorious uncertainty of the turf" and watching his famed wonder-horse, Diamond Jubilee. Polo, another horsey sport, is also a favorite of the privileged. Tennis has long been accorded a similar position, with the Duke and Duchess of Kent participating in the winner's ceremony at Wimbledon. The members of the upper-class who frequent such events, sipping Pimms and indulging in strawberries, are known as "toffs," a word of uncertain origin (perhaps derived from the tassels worn by well-to-do students). Sports like football, by contrast, are associated with people known as "yobs." "Yob" refers to a loutish person; the word comes from "boy" spelled backwards, a reversing process known as backslang.

a certain form of masochism, supporting a team across the country despite years of setbacks. Excessive enthusiasm has, however, proved problematic. Violence and vandalism used to dog the game, causing tension between fans and the police trying to control huge crowds in old stadia. Hooligans are usually on their worst behavior when the England national team plays abroad; things are a bit better at home, though far from perfect. The atmosphere in stadia has become safer now that clubs have been forced to convert to seating-only, rather than standing spaces in the once-infamous terraces. As a result, football has become more family-friendly, albeit pricier.

A LOAD OF BALLS

According to legend, **rugby** was born one glorious day in 1823 when William Webb Ellis, an inspired (or perhaps slightly confused) Rugby School student, picked up a soccer ball and ran it into the goal. Since then, rugby has evolved into a complex and subtle game. The first amateur **Rugby Union** was formed in 1871, and play, involving 15-man teams, started in 1895. **Rugby League,** a professional sport using modified rules and played by teams of 13, was soon formed. Although both variants now have professional and amateur teams, the rugby world remains separated into union and league; in Britain, the former is associated with Wales and the south of England, and the latter with northwest England. A *melée* of blood, mud, and drinking songs, rugby is exciting to watch, with no non-injury substitutions and little stoppage of play. An oval shaped ball is carried or passed backward until the team is able to touch the ball down past the goal line (known as a "try" and worth five points) or kick it through the uprights (worth three points). The most striking play in rugby is the **scrum,** a woven knot of sweaty men seething around a ball. The club season runs from September to May, while the culmination of international rugby union is the Rugby World Cup, last played in Cardiff, Wales, in 1999.

While fanatically followed within the Commonwealth, **cricket** remains a confusing spectacle to most outsiders. At first glance, it might seem incomprehensible to those not raised on Marmite, but its rules are actually quite simple. The game is played by two 11-player teams on a 22-yard green, marked by two **wickets** (three vertical stumps and two bails) at each end. In an innings, one team acts as **batsmen** and the other as **fielders.** The batting team sends out two batsmen, and a **bowler** from the fielding side throws the ball so that it bounces towards the wickets. The goal of the fielders is to try to get the batsmen out by **taking** the wickets (hitting the wickets so that the bails fall) or by catching the ball. The batsmen's goal is to make as many runs as they can while protecting their wickets, scoring every time they switch places. The teams switch positions once 11 batsmen are out; usually both sides bat twice. Matches last one to five days, with the biggest crowd-pullers being the one-day internationals of the Cricket World Cup, won by Australia in 1999. International games are known as Test matches; the **Ashes,** named for the remains of a cricket bail, are the prize in England's Test series with Australia. London's **Lords** cricket grounds (see p. 140) is regarded as the spiritual home of the game.

The Scots have not lagged in their contributions to world sport either, introducing **golf** to the world. The spiritual home of the game is **St. Andrews** (see p. 550), which houses the Royal and Ancient Golf Club of St Andrews, the game's rule-setting authority, and its famed **Old Course.** When **tennis,** another individual sport with a long history, was becoming popular at the end of the 15th century, Henry VII played in black velvet. As the game developed, the cooler white became the traditional color for players to wear on the court. Today, the era of wearing exclusively white on the court is over, but the fun continues. For two weeks in late June and early July, tennis buffs all over the world focus their attention on **Wimbledon,** home to the only Grand Slam event played on grass (see p. 139).

HORSES AND COURSES

Prized for their speed and grace, **horses** have pleased riders and observers alike in several arenas. Princess Anne competed in the 1976 Olympics in **equestrian,** which involves three days of competition in dressage, cross-country, and show-jumping. In late June, **polo** devotees flock to the **Royal Windsor Cup.** And even those who aren't too fond of the four-legged beasts agree that watching them clamber down the track gets the adrenaline pumping. The **Royal Gold Cup Meeting** at **Ascot** has occurred in the second half of June for every summer since 1711. An important society event, some see it as essentially an excuse for British people of all strata to indulge in drinking and gambling while wearing silly hats. Top hats also distinguish the famed **Derby** (DAR-bee), which has been run since 1780 on Epsom Racecourse, Surrey, on the first Saturday of June.

Britain remains a force in rowing, and the annual **Henley Royal Regatta** is the most famous series of rowing races in the world. The five-day regatta ends on the first Sunday in July; Saturday is the most popular day, but some of the best races are the Sunday finals. The **Boat Race,** between eights from Oxford (see p. 249) and Cambridge (see p. 297), enacts the traditional rivalry between the schools. Britain is the center of **Formula One** racecar design, and the British Grand Prix is held every July. Meanwhile, the **T.T. races** bring hordes of screeching motorcycles to the Isle of Man in the first two weeks of June (see p. 345).

THE MEDIA

PRINT

In a culture not yet completely addicted to the telly, the influence of newspapers is enormous. The UK's plethora of national newspapers provides a range of political viewpoints. **The Times** (www.the-times.co.uk), long a model of thoughtful discretion and mild infallibility, has turned Tory under the ownership of Rupert "Buy It" Murdoch. **The Daily Telegraph** (www.telegraph.co.uk), dubbed "Torygraph," is fairly conservative and old-fashioned; **The Guardian** (www.guardian.co.uk) leans leftist; while **The Independent** (www.independent.co.uk) lives up to its name. Of the infamous tabloids, **The Sun** (www.the-sun.co.uk), Murdoch-owned and better known for its page-three topless pin-up than for its reporting, is probably the most influential. Among the others, **The Daily Mail, The Daily Express** (www.lineone.net/express), and **The London Evening Standard** (www.thisislondon.com), which is the only evening paper, make serious attempts at popular journalism, although the first two tend to position themselves as the conservative voice of Middle England. **The Daily Mirror** (www.mirror.co.uk), **The News of the World** (www.nowww.co.uk), and **The Star** (www.megastar.co.uk) are as shrill and lewd as the Sun. The best international news is in the *Times,* the *Guardian,* and the *Independent,* while **The Financial Times** (www.financialtimes.com), on pink paper, does more elegantly for the City what the *Wall Street Journal* does for Wall Street.

Although they share close association with their sister dailies, the **Sunday newspapers** are actually separate newspapers, with a subtly distinctive look and style. **The Sunday Times** (www.sunday-times.co.uk), **The Sunday Telegraph, The Independent on Sunday,** and the highly polished **Observer** (www.observer.co.uk), the world's oldest paper and sister to the Guardian, publish multi-section papers with glossy magazines. Sunday editions offer detailed arts, sports, and news coverage, together with more "soft bits" than the dailies. If you're looking for events, *The Independent* publishes a supplement every Thursday, *The Guardian* on Saturday.

A quick glance around any High Street newsagent will show that Britain has no shortage of magazines. World affairs are covered with a refreshing candor and surreptitious wit by **The Economist**. **The New Statesman** on the left and **The Spectator** on the right cover politics and the arts with verve. The satirical **Private Eye** is subversive, hilarious, and overtly political. Some of the best music mags in the world are UK-based. **Melody Maker** and **New Musical Express** (NME) trace the latest trends with wit; check them for concert news. **Q** covers a broader spectrum of rock music in excellent detail, while **Gramophone** focuses on classical music. Club kids should check out **Mixmag** and **Jockey Slut** for listings and dance music reviews, while **The Face** remains the UK's ultimate scene mag. The indispensable London journal **Time Out** is the most comprehensive listings guide to the city and features fascinating pieces on British culture; its website (www.timeout.co.uk) also keeps tabs on events in Dublin, Edinburgh and Glasgow. Recent years have also seen the explosion of "lad's magazines" such as **FHM** and **Loaded,** which feature scantily-clad women and articles on beer, "shagging," and "pulling" (see p. 746). Though meant for female readers, the British edition of **Vogue** also features scantily-clad women; **New Woman** offers more practical fashion tips and relationship advice.

RADIO AND TELEVISION

The **BBC** (British Broadcasting Corporation, sometimes known as the Beeb) established its reputation for fairness and wit with its radio services, and its World Service continues to provide citizens of countries around the world with a glimpse into British life. Within the UK, BBC **Radio 1** (98.8 FM) has ceded responsibilities of news coverage to its cousin **Radio 4** (93.5 FM), but continues to feature rock institution John Peel as well as current pop-rock with such radio personalities as Zoe Ball. Completing the BBC stable, **Radio 2** (89.1 FM) takes on easy listening and non-rock forms of music such as folk and jazz, **Radio 3** (91.3 FM) broadcasts classical music, and **Radio 5 Live** (693 MW/AM) carries mainly sports broadcasts. Each region also has a variety of local commercial broadcasting services.

British television has brought to the world such wonders as *Monty Python's Flying Circus* and *Mr. Bean*, and continues to produce many programs of great quality. A **licence fee** paid by all television owners in Britain ensures that BBC TV, which sent out the world's first broadcast in 1929, remains advertisement-free. National TV listings are slightly modified to fit different regions. A repository of wit and innovation, the BBC broadcasts on two national channels. **BBC1** carries news at 1pm, 6pm, and 9pm as well as various Britcoms. Telecast on **BBC2** are cultural programs and fledgling sitcoms (*Absolutely Fabulous* and the marvelous *Blackadder* both started here), along with the ubiquitous Teletubbies. **ITV**, Britain's first and most established commercial network, carries drama and comedy, along with its own news. **Channel 4** has the hilarious *Big Breakfast* morning show, highly respected arts programming, and imported American shows. **Channel 5,** the newest channel, features late-night sports shows and action movies at 9pm. In the world of satellite broadcasting, Rupert Murdoch's **Sky TV** shows football, futbol, soccer, and any other incarnations of the global game that it can find on its Sky Sports channel, while its Sky One channel features mostly American shows.

SOAPS AND SUDS Addiction to the soaps broadcast over the airwaves could almost be a marker of British identity. Britain pioneered the soap opera on radio with *The Archers*, the longest-running soap in the world. Set in the idyllic fictional village of Ambridge, *The Archers* chronicles the escapades of a farming family in its weekday broadcasts on Radio 4. It is television, however, that has become the preferred purveyor of soaps. The most popular TV soaps, with almost 20 million viewers a week each, are *Eastenders* on BBC1 and *Coronation Street* on ITV, which chronicle the lives of rough-and-tumble working-class neighborhoods in London and Manchester, respectively. Public enthusiasm for these TV soaps has infected even the once-pastoral *Archers*, who now boast their own share of disasters and illicit love-affairs.

GREAT BRITAIN

LONDON

A man who is tired of London is tired of life; for there is in London all that life can afford.
    —Samuel Johnson

Ever an assault on the senses, London defies simple categorization. Those expecting tea-drinking, Royal-loving gardeners will quickly find London equally the province of black-clad slinky young things lounging in Soho bars, Indian takeaway owners in the East End, and pinstriped bankers in the City. While London abounds with remnants of Britain's long history, a trip to one of many futuristic boutiques will eclipse any impression—culled from bobbies, Beefeaters, and Big Ben—that London is chained to bygone days. Many pubs may close early, but London roars on, full throttle, around the clock, with 24-hour cafes and clubs pounding until the first light of the new day. One of the world's greatest centers for the arts, London dazzles with a dizzying array of concert halls, theaters, museums, and bookshops. Trends bloom and die here—buy something in London and six months later you'll see it on the catwalks—and despite the stereotypes about British food, the city has steadily gained status as a culinary center. This is in no small measure due to London's large and diverse multinational population, ever-growing and ever renewing this city of the world with energy and optimism. For more detailed coverage of this great and good city, get thee to a bookstore for a copy of *Let's Go: London 2001.*

HIGHLIGHTS OF LONDON

ALL THE POSTCARD STUFF To catch the London unmissables, start at stately **Westminster Abbey** (p. 117), gaze upward at **St. Paul's Cathedral** (p. 107), watch your head at the imposing **Tower of London** (p. 107), do a spot of shopping and catch a bite in **Covent Garden** (p. 114). Follow up the sights with a night of **clubbing** (p. 142).

MUSEUMS Revel in the magnificent collections of London's museums, some of the finest in the world, including the **British Museum** (p. 128), the **National Gallery** (p. 129), and the quirky **Sir John Soane's Museum** (p. 133), idiosyncratic home of the architect of the Bank of England, replete with sarcophagi and green glass floors.

THEATER Forget the West End and turn your theatrical attention to **Shakespeare's Globe Theatre** (p. 137), where you can stand and jostle with the other "groundlings" or cram onto hard wooden benches while watching Shakespeare as it was meant to be.

FOOTBALL Take in a Premier League **football match** (p. 139) at Highbury (Arsenal FC), Stamford Bridge (Chelsea FC), or White Hart Lane (Tottenham Hotspur), where the fans are as spectacular as the teams. Just don't call it soccer.

◪ GETTING THERE

BY PLANE

For information on international flights to London, see **By Plane,** p. 36.

TO CENTRAL LONDON FROM HEATHROW. With a plane landing every 47 seconds, **Heathrow Airport** (☎ 8759 4321) in Hounslow, on the western edge of the city, is the world's busiest international airport. There are cash **machines** and **bureaux de change,** open 24hr., in each terminal.

Underground: The cheapest way to reach London, by the **Piccadilly line,** with 1 stop for terminals 1-3, another for terminal 4 (50-60min., about £4).

Heathrow Express: The fastest way is by this wheelchair-accessible train to **Paddington Station** (15min.; 4 per hr. 5:10am-11:40pm; £12, return £22, up to four children free with an adult). Buy tickets at Heathrow Express counters, on board, or at platform self-service machines; BritRail passes not accepted.

Airbus: (☎ (08705) 757747). Makes the 1hr. trip to central points in London approximately every 20min. (£7, return £12; student and senior discounts; under 16 free). Faster **Airbus Direct** (same prices) runs to **Victoria Station** only.

Taxis: Fares to central London run at least £30.

TO CENTRAL LONDON FROM GATWICK. Gatwick Airport (☎ (01293) 535353), in West Sussex, is London's second-busiest airport, and is a bit farther out than Heathrow. A number of 24hr. restaurants, **cash machines,** and **bureaux de change** are located in both the North and South Terminals. From Gatwick, the **Gatwick Express** (☎ (0990) 301530) zooms to **Victoria Station** (30-35min.; 4 per hr. 5:50am-midnight, 4 departures midnight-5:50am; £10.20, return £20.40; tickets on board). **Connex** offers marginally slower service to Victoria at a lower price, while **Thameslink** trains run to **London Bridge** and **King's Cross.** Tickets for all rail services can be purchased at the desk immediately after immigration, before the baggage reclaim, or at the Gatwick train station. **Taxis** to central London cost at least £50-60.

TO CENTRAL LONDON FROM STANSTED, LUTON, AND CITY. Some international flights, especially charters and discount airlines, arrive at LoNSndon's less crowded airports: **Stansted Airport** (☎ (01279) 680500), northwest of London in Essex, served by **Stansted Skytrain** to **Liverpool Street Station** (40min., 2 per hr. M-Sa 5am-11pm, £12); **Luton Airport,** with Thameslink to **King's Cross, Farington,** and **Blackfriars Stations** (35min., 1 per hr., £9.60, £16.80 return); and **London City Airport** (☎ 7646 0888), with shuttles to the **Liverpool Street** and **Canning Town Underground Stations,** and buses #69, 473, and 474 to the city center.

BY TRAIN

Trains arrive in London at six major stations (see chart below for details). Call the centralized **National Rail Enquiries information number** (24hr. ☎ (08457) 484950) for information on journey times, frequencies, and prices.

All major stations sell various **Railcards,** which offer regular discounts on train travel (see **By Train,** p. 37); they do *not* sell BritRail passes, which must be purchased abroad. The **Network Card** and **Network Rover** passes allow unlimited travel in the Network Southeast area (London environs and south of London, including Canterbury, Dover, and Brighton; 3 weekend days £47; 7 days £69).

STATION	ARRIVALS FROM:
Euston	North and northwest (including Birmingham, Carlisle, Glasgow, Holyhead, Inverness, Liverpool, and Manchester).
King's Cross	North and northeast (Cambridge, Edinburgh, Leeds, Newcastle, York).
Liverpool St.	East Anglia (Colchester, Ipswich, Norwich); Stansted Airport.
Paddington	West (Oxford); southwest (Bristol, Cornwall); and South Wales (Cardiff).
St. Pancras	The Midlands (Nottingham); northwest (Sheffield).
Victoria	South (Brighton, Canterbury, Dover, Hastings); Gatwick Airport.
Waterloo	South and southwest (Portsmouth, Salisbury); European continent.

BY BUS

Long-distance buses (known as **coaches** in the UK) arrive in London at **Victoria Coach Station,** 164 Buckingham Palace Rd. SW1 (☎ 7730 3466; Tube: Victoria). **National Express** (☎ (08705) 808080; www.gobycoach.co.uk) is the principal operator of long-distance coach services in Britain. **Eurolines** (☎ (01582) 404511) runs coaches into Victoria from Europe.

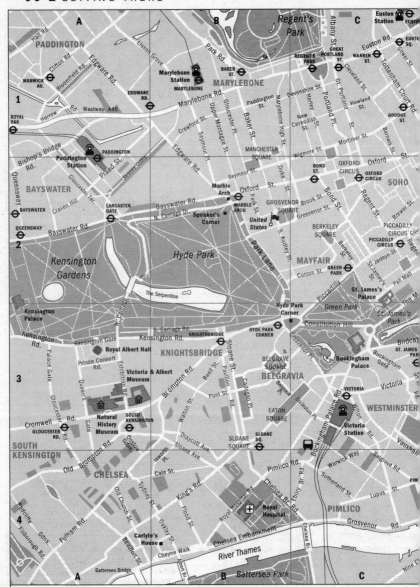

Central London: Major Street Finder

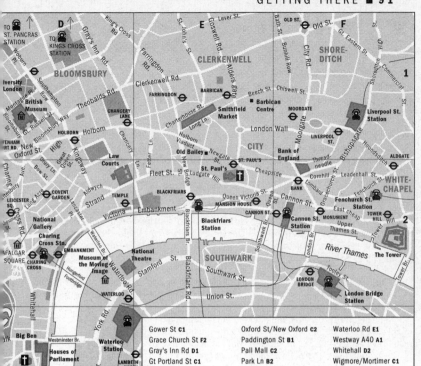

Gower St **C1**
Grace Church St **F2**
Gray's Inn Rd **D1**
Gt Portland St **C1**
Gt Russell St **D1**
Grosvenor Pl **C3**
Grosvenor Rd **C4**
Grosvenor St (Upr) **C2**
Haymarket **C2**
Holborn/High/Viaduct **D1**
Horseferry Rd **C3**
Jermyn St **C2**
Kensington High St/Rd **A3**
King's Cross Rd **D1**
King's Rd **B4**
Kingsway **D2**
Knightsbridge **B3**
Lambeth Palace Rd **D3**
Lisson Grove **A1**
Lombard St **F2**
London Wall **E1**
Long Acre/Grt Queen **D2**
Long Ln **E1**
Ludgate Hill **E2**
Marylebone High St **B1**
Marylebone Rd **B1**
Millbank **D4**
Montague Pl **D1**
Moorgate **F1**
New Bridge St **E2**
New Cavendish **C1**
Newgate St **E1**
Nine Elms Ln **C4**
Oakley St **B4**
Old St **F1**
Old Brompton Rd **A4**
Onslow Sq/St **A3**

Oxford St/New Oxford **C2**
Paddington St **B1**
Pall Mall **C2**
Park Ln **B2**
Park Rd **B1**
Park St **B2**
Piccadilly **C2**
Pont St **B3**
Portland Pl **C1**
Queen St **E2**
Queen Victoria St **E1**
Queen's Gate **A3**
Queensway **A2**
Redcliffe Gdns **A4**
Regent St **C2**
Royal Hospital Rd **B4**
St. James's St **C2**
Seymour Pl **A1**
Seymour St **A2**
Shaftesbury Ave **C2**
Sloane/Lwr Sloane **B3**
Southampton Row **D1**
Southwark Bridge Rd **E2**
Southwark Rd **E2**
St. Margarets/Abingdon **D3**
Stamford St **E2**
Strand **D2**
Sydney St **A4**
Thames St(Upr&Lwr) **F2**
The Mall **C2**
Theobald's Rd **D1**
Threadneedle St **F2**
Tottenham Ct Rd **C1**
Vauxhall Br. Rd **C4**
Victoria Embankment **D2**
Victoria St **C3**
Warwick Way **C4**

Waterloo Rd **E1**
Westway A40 **A1**
Whitehall **D2**
Wigmore/Mortimer **C1**
Woburn Pl **D1**
York Rd **D3**

RAILWAY STATIONS
Blackfriars **E2**
Cannon St **F2**
Charing Cross **D2**
Euston **C1**
Holborn Viaduct **E1**
King's Cross **D1**
Liverpool St **F1**
London Bridge **F2**
Marylebone **B1**
Paddington **A2**
St Pancras **D1**
Victoria **C3**
Waterloo East **E3**
Waterloo **D3**

BRIDGES
Albert **B4**
Battersea **A4**
Blackfriars **E2**
Chelsea **C4**
Hungerford Footbridge **D2**
Lambeth **D3**
London Bridge **F2**
Southwark **E2**
Tower Bridge **F2**
Waterloo **D2**
Westminster **D3**

Edgware Rd **A1**
Euston Rd **C1**
Exhibition Rd **A3**
Farringdon Rd **E1**
Fenchurch/Aldgate **F2**
Fleet St **E2**
Fulham Rd **A4**
Gloucester Pl **B1**
Gloucester Rd **A3**
Goswell Rd **E1**

▣ GETTING AROUND

BY UNDERGROUND

The color-coded **Underground** railway system, or **Tube,** is the easiest way to get around London, with over 260 stations on 11 lines. The **Docklands Light Railway** (DLR) connects the Docklands to the City of London; the lines appear on all Tube maps. For help, call the 24-hour Tube info line (☎ 7222 1234) or the DLR info line (☎ 7363 9700; M-F 8:30am-5:15pm). Small but invaluable "Journey Planner" maps are available at all stations and inside the front cover of this very book.

Fares depend on the number of zones passed through—a journey within Zone 1 will cost much less than a trip to a distant suburb. On Sundays and bank holidays, trains run less frequently. All transfers are free. Most central London trips cost £1.50-£1.80. Return tickets cost exactly double the price of a single. If you plan to make multiple trips in a day, a **Travelcard** will save you money, and also let you ride buses within the zones covered. You might also consider buying a **Carnet** (£11), which is a booklet entitling you to 10 trips within Zone 1, if you'll be using the Tube sporadically. The ticket allows you to go through the automatic gates; **keep your ticket** until you reach your final destination, where the exit gates will collect it. Inspectors strictly enforce the Tube's on-the-spot £10 fine for travel without a valid ticket. Be aware that **"Ticket touts"** sometimes try to harass passengers into buying or selling used Travelcards. Not only is this illegal, it's also the new mayor's pet peeve; remember that entrepreneurship of this kind is a bad idea.

The last trains on most lines leave central London between midnight-12:30am M-Sa and 11-11:30pm Su. Service resumes around 6am. **Night buses** (see **By Bus,** below) bridge the gap in service. Many stations feature labyrinthine tunnels and steep staircases. If you have **mobility problems** or are carrying a lot of **luggage,** you may fare better on a longer route that requires fewer transfers. Elevator access to platforms is still abysmal. The best bet is to call the information number (see above) and ask which stations are accessible. Stand to the right and walk on the left on escalators, or risk a rude tumbling from commuters in full stride.

BY BUS

Gliding through subway tunnels can hardly match the majesty of rolling through London's streets on the top floor of a red double-decker. Not only is a bus ride a great way to orient yourself to the city's layout, but it also provides a fantastic opportunity to soak up London's atmosphere and sights—and buses are cheaper than the Tube. Route #11, beginning at Liverpool Street Station, winds past St. Paul's, Fleet St., the Strand, Trafalgar Sq., Westminster, Sloane Sq., and all of King's Rd. Route #14 originates in Riverside-Putney and coasts down Fulham Rd., past the South Kensington museums, Knightsbridge, Hyde Park Corner, Piccadilly Circus and Leicester Sq., and ends on Tottenham Court Rd. in Soho.

Unfortunately, double-decker Routemaster buses, with their conductors and open rear platforms, are being replaced to save money. On Routemasters, take a seat and wait for the conductor, who will tell you the fare and let you know when to get off. On modern double-deckers and single-deck "hoppa" buses, you pay your fare to the driver as you board. Newer buses, **while not strictly wheelchair accessible**, do have a lower platform that makes it possible to board, and are definitely more **stroller-friendly.** Bus stops are marked with route information; at busy intersections or complicated one-way systems, maps indicate where to board each bus. Each stop is marked with route numbers and only those buses stop there. The signs saying which route stops there also say which zone the stop is in, and in which direction the bus is headed. On stops marked "request," buses stop only if you flag them down to get on or pull the bell cord to get off. Service is notoriously sporadic during the day; waiting 20min. only to be greeted by a succession of three identical buses is not uncommon. Buses run from about 6am to midnight.

The bus network is divided into four zones. Be sure you have change to pay your fare; drivers will not accept bills. Underground **Travelcards** are valid on buses, and allow you to hop on or off as often as you like.

Night buses ("N" routes) run while the Underground and regular bus service is closed. All night buses originate at **Trafalgar Sq.**, with many also making a stop at **Victoria Station**, starting at 11:30pm and running until the early morning. London Transport puts out a free brochure with lists of the last buses and Underground trains. Call London Transport's 24hr. information line (☎ 7222 1234) for fares and schedules. On New Year's Eve, all night bus routes are diverted away from Trafalgar Sq. Travelcards valid for more than 7 days are valid on night buses.

London Transport issues a **free bus map** for London called the *All-London Bus Guide*, available at most tube stations and LRT information offices. The *Central Bus Guide* is more manageable, detailing only routes in Zone 1. If you require more detailed info, there are 35 different local bus guides which will help you navigate specific neighborhoods. The *Visiting London* pamphlet is aimed directly at tourists and may be downloaded from www.londontransport.co.uk. To find out whether buses are running on schedule or whether routes have changed, call ☎ 7222 1200. For free local guides, call ☎ 7371 0247.

Wheelchair-accessible Mobility Bus routes, numbered in the 800s and 900s, service most of outer London. Stationlink (numbered SL1 and SL2) travels hourly between the major train stations (9am-7pm; £1). For information on the route, call ☎ 7918 3312; for further general information, see **Travelers with Disabilities,** p. 59.

BY TRAIN

Most of London is fully served by buses and by the Tube. Some districts, however, notably southeast London, are most easily reached by train. Local surface trains are speedy, run frequently to suburbs and daytrip areas around London, and are often cheaper than the Tube. The North London Link, stretching across north London from **North Woolwich** to **Richmond,** often deposits travelers closer to sights than the Tube. Trains scoot from Hampstead Heath to Kew (25min., every 20min.).

BY TAXI

To earn a license, London **black-cab** drivers must pass a rigorous exam called "The Knowledge," proving that they know the city's streets by heart; the route taken by a cabbie is almost certainly the shortest and quickest. Most of the high-ceilinged cabs are black, although many are plastered bumper-to-bumper in ads of all colors. You are most likely to find taxis at large hotels or at major intersections, but taxis abound throughout central London and are easy to hail (except in rain). A taxi is available if the sign on the roof or blue light in the window is lit. If you want to order a taxi, call a radio dispatcher, but beware that you may be charged extra for ordering by phone (☎7272 0272 or ☎ 7253 5000). Drivers are required to charge according to the meter for trips within London, and there's a surplus charge for extra baggage or passengers. A 10% tip is expected. You can reclaim **lost property** left in a licensed taxi at 15 Penton St., N1. (☎ 833 0996. Tube: Angel. Open M-F 9am-4pm.) Apart from the licensed taxis, there are many **minicab** companies, listed in the Yellow Pages. Confirm the price when you order, because most are not metered. **Freedom Cars,** 52 Wardour St., is a gay and lesbian minicab company. (☎ 7734 1313. Tube: Piccadilly Circus.) **Ladycabs** has only female cabbies and accepts only female passengers. (☎ 7254 3501. Open M-F 8am-12am, Sa 9am-2am, Su 10am-5pm.)

BY BOAT

River boats provide excellent views of many of London's major sights, with a number of services ploughing up and down the Thames. **Thames Leisure** offers an hour-long circular cruise, leaving from Tower Pier and as far west as the Houses of Parliament. (☎ 7623 1805; www.thamesleisure.co.uk. Boats run daily 11am-6pm every 30min. £5.80, ages 5-15 £3.20, families £16.50.) **Westminster Passenger Services Association** offers cruises from Westminster Pier (Tube: Westminster) up the river to

Richmond, Kew, and Hampton Court Palace; schedules and journey times vary with the tides. (☎ 7930 2062; www.wpsa.co.uk. To Kew £7, day return £11, children £3, day return £5; to Richmond £8, £12, £3.50, £6; to Hampton Court £10, £14, £4, £7.) You can also glide down the **Regent's Canal** between Camden Town and Little Venice through Regent's Park; call the **London Waterbus Company** for details. (☎ 7482 2660. Daily service in summer; off-season Sa-Su only.)

▓ ORIENTATION

London is a colossal aggregate of distinct villages and anonymous suburbs, of ancient settlements and modern developments. As London grew, it swallowed adjacent cities and nearby villages, and chewed up parts of the counties of Kent, Surrey, Essex, and Hertfordshire (called the "Home Counties"). London is divided into boroughs and into postal code areas whose letters stand for compass directions. The borough name and postal code appear at the bottom of most street signs. The City (always a capital C) refers to the ancient **City of London,** which covers only one of Greater London's 620 sq. mi., and is today one of the world's great financial centers. Besides the City, the neighborhoods tourists are most likely to visit are: the **West End,** south of Oxford St., which includes **Soho, Leicester Square,** and **Covent Garden; Westminster,** just south of the West End; **Bloomsbury** and **Marylebone**, just north of Oxford St.; **Knightsbridge, Kensington,** and **Chelsea** to the southwest; **Bayswater** and **Notting Hill** to the west; the **East End,** east of the city; and the **South Bank,** south of the Thames. Farther afield, **Camden Town, Islington,** and **Hampstead** are to the north; **Greenwich** and the **Docklands** lie to the east; and **Brixton** stands to the south. The most useful navigational aids are street atlases such as *London A to Z* (the "A to Zed") and Nicholson's *London Streetfinder*.

▓ PRACTICAL INFORMATION

London's phone code is 020.

TOURIST INFORMATION CENTRES

British Travel Centre, 12 Regent St. (☎ 8846 9000). Tube: Piccadilly Circus. Run by the British Tourist Authority and ideal for travelers bound for destinations outside London. £5 surcharge for accommodations booking and a required deposit (1 night or 15% of the total stay; does not book hostels). Open M-F 9am-6:30pm, Sa-Su 10am-4pm.

London Tourist Board Information Centre, Victoria Station Forecourt, SW1 (recorded message ☎ (0839) 123432; 39-49p per min.). Tube: Victoria. Offers information on London and England and credit-card accommodations booking (☎ 7932 2020, fax 7932 2021; £5 booking fee, plus 15% refundable deposit). Open Apr.-Nov. daily 8am-7pm; Dec.-Mar. M-Sa 8am-7pm, Su 8am-5pm. Additional tourist information centres at: **Heathrow Airport** (open daily Apr.-Nov. 9am-6pm; Dec.-Mar. 9am-5pm); **Liverpool St. Underground Station** (open M 8:15am-7pm, Tu-Sa 8:15am-6pm, Su 8:30am-4:45pm); and **Selfridges** (open during store hours; see **Department Stores,** p. 133).

EMERGENCY, SOCIAL, AND LOCAL SERVICES

Emergency (Medical, Police, and Fire): Dial ☎ 999 or ☎ 112; no coins required.

Hospitals: In an emergency, you can be treated at no charge in the Accidents and Emergencies (A&E) ward of a hospital. The following have 24hr. walk-in A&E (also known as casualty) departments: **Royal London Hospital,** Whitechapel Rd., E1 (☎ 7377 7000). Tube: Whitechapel. **Royal Free Hospital,** Pond St., NW3 (☎ 7794 0500). Tube: Belsize Park. Train: Hampstead Heath. **Charing Cross Hospital,** Fulham Palace Rd. (entrance on St. Dunstan's Rd.), W6 (☎ 8846 1234). Tube: Baron's Court or Hammersmith. **St. Thomas' Hospital,** Lambeth Palace Rd., SE1 (☎ 7928 9292). Tube: Westminster. **University College Hospital,** Gower St. (entrance on Grafton Way), WC1 (☎ 7387 9300). Tube: Euston or Warren St.

Dental Care: Eastman Dental Hospital (☎ 7915 1000).

Pharmacies: Every police station keeps a list of emergency doctors and chemists in its area. Listings under "Chemists" in the Yellow Pages. **Bliss Chemists,** 5 Marble Arch, W1 (☎ 7723 6116), is open daily, including public holidays, 9am-midnight.

Samaritans: (☎ 7734 2800 or ☎ (0345) 909090). 24hr. crisis hotline.

Police: Stations in every district of London. **Headquarters,** New Scotland Yard, Broadway, SW1 (☎ 7230 1212). Tube: St. James's Park. **West End Central,** 10 Vine St., W1 (☎ 7437 1212). Tube: Piccadilly Circus. For emergencies, dial 999.

COMMUNICATIONS

Internet Access: Cybercafes are everywhere. Get connected at **easyEverything,** 9-13 Wilson Rd., W1 (☎ 7482 9502), directly opposite Victoria Station. The owners of budget airline easyJet bring you this dirt-cheap (£1 per hour) Internet emporium, with over 400 terminals. Training and help available. Cafe serves coffee (espresso 80p) and sandwiches (chicken tikka £2.25). Open daily 24hr.

Post Office: Post offices are everywhere; call ☎ (0345) 223344 to find the nearest one. When sending mail within the UK, be sure to write the postal code: London has 7: King's Roads, eight Queen's Roads, and two Mandela Streets (there is, however, only one Pablo Neruda Close). The main office is the **Trafalgar Square Post Office,** 24-28 William IV St., WC2N 4DL (☎ 7484 9304; Tube: Charing Cross), which has late hours. All mail sent Poste Restante or general delivery to unspecified post offices ends up here. Open M-Th and Sa 8am-8pm, F 8:30am-8pm.

█ ACCOMMODATIONS

Landing in London with no place to stay is a bit like landing on a bicycle and finding that it has no seat: painful and confusing. Plan ahead to nab one of the more desirable rooms, particularly in July and August. The Tourist Information Centre Accommodations Service is the source for official bureaucratic room-finding (see **Tourist Information Centres,** above).

ACCOMMODATION DISTRICTS

What follows is a thumbnail sketch of the areas in which tourists are most likely to bunk down. Popular hotels fill up weeks in advance; call ahead.

CITY OF LONDON. Places to stay in the City are scarce, with most available space gobbled up by offices. However, many sights are nearby and the region is well served by the Tube and buses, particularly on weekdays.

WESTMINSTER. The area near Victoria Station is full of budget hotels. Play them off each other. Hotels closer to Pimlico are nicer than those around Victoria.

KENSINGTON AND KNIGHTSBRIDGE. Kensington is not the cheapest part of town; still, it's close to the stunning array of museums that line the southwest side of Hyde Park, as well as the huge department stores in Knightsbridge.

EARL'S COURT. West of Kensington, this area feeds on the budget tourist trade, spewing forth travel agencies, souvenir shops, and bureaux de change. Some streets seem solely populated by B&Bs and hostels. The area has a vibrant gay and lesbian population and is also a tremendously popular destination for Aussie travelers cooling their heels in London (in the 1970s, it gained the nickname "Kangaroo Valley"). Be careful at night. Also, beware of over-eager guides willing to lead you from the station to a hostel. Some B&Bs in the area conceal grimy rooms behind fancy lobbies and well-dressed staff; always ask to see a room.

MARYLEBONE AND BLOOMSBURY. A few hotels can be found near Marble Arch, in the sidestreets off the Edgware Road. It's convenient to Oxford St., Regent's Park, and the British Museum, and numerous night buses serve the area.

The quiet residential streets are lined with B&Bs, a few halls of residence, and a few hostels. The closer the neighborhood is to the King's Cross, St. Pancras, and Euston train-station triumvirate, the dodgier it tends to be, especially after dark.

YHA HOSTELS

Staying at Youth Hostel Association hostels is restricted to members of **Hostelling International** and its affiliated **Youth Hostel Association of England and Wales** (☎ (0870) 870 8888; www.yha.org.uk). You can join at YHA London Headquarters or at the hostels themselves for £12, under 18 £6. An **International Guest Pass** (£1.90) permits non-members not resident in England or Wales to stay at hostels, often at slightly higher rates. Buy six guest passes and you automatically become a full member. Hostels are not always able to accommodate every written request for reservations, much less on-the-spot inquiries, but they frequently hold a few beds available—it's always worth checking. To secure a place, show up as early as possible and expect to stand in line, or book in advance with a credit card at the number or website above; you can also write to the warden of the individual hostel.

All hostels are equipped with large **lockers** that require a padlock. Bring your own or purchase one from the hostel for £3. London hostels do not charge for a sheet or sleeping bag. Most have laundry facilities and some kitchen equipment. Theater tickets and discounted attraction tickets are available.

◪ **YHA Hampstead Heath,** 4 Wellgarth Rd., NW11 (☎ 8458 9054; fax 8209 0546; hampstead@yha.org.uk). Tube: Golders Green, then bus #210 or 268 toward Hampstead; or on foot turning left from the station onto North End Rd., then left again onto Wellgarth Rd., a 10min. walk. A beautiful, sprawling hostel. Kitchen and laundry facilities. Restaurant. 24hr. security and reception. Book in advance. Dorms £19.70, under 18 £17.30; doubles £35; triples £51.95; quads £68.95; quints £85.95; 6-bed rooms £100.

◪ **YHA City of London,** 36 Carter Ln., EC4 (☎ 7236 4965; fax 7236 7681). Tube: St. Paul's. Sleep in quiet comfort a stone's throw from St. Paul's. Scrupulously clean, with many services, including secure luggage storage, currency exchange, laundry, Internet access (£5 per hr.), and theater box office. Many rooms feature the less-than-ideal triple-decker bunks common in London hostels. 24hr. security. Reception 7am-11pm. Dorms £20.50-22.95, under 18 £18.70-24.10; singles £26.80, £23.30; doubles and twins (some with TV) £52.10, £44.60. Private rooms £50-135, families £40-120.

◪ **YHA Holland House,** Holland Walk, W8 (☎ 7937 0748; fax 7376 0667; hollandhouse@yha.org.uk). Tube: High St. Kensington or Holland Park. Clean, spacious rooms with lockers—bring a padlock. Full breakfast included. Laundry and kitchen facilities. Free daytime luggage storage. 24hr. access. Dorms £19.95, under 18 £17.95.

YHA King's Cross/St. Pancras, 79-81 Euston Rd. (☎ 7388 9998; fax 7388 6766; stpancras@yha.org.uk). Tube: King's Cross/St. Pancras. Some rooms air-conditioned. Many family rooms. Premium rooms include bathroom, TV, and coffee/tea facilities. Dinner (£4) from 6-9pm. Full English breakfast included. Luggage storage. Laundry, Internet access, and kitchen facilities. Max. stay 1 week. Book way in advance. Dorms £23, under 18 £19.70; doubles £40; premium doubles £53; premium quads £100.

YHA Rotherhithe, 20 Salter Rd. (☎ 7232 2114; fax 7237 2919; rotherhithe@yha.org.uk). Tube: Rotherhithe or Canada Water. Bus #381 from Waterloo stops directly in front. Modern 320-bed hostel. Kitchen. Breakfast (English or continental) included. Laundry. Other facilities: Internet access, currency exchange, restaurant, and bar. All rooms with bath. Bigger rooms have triple bunks. Book ahead. Dorms £23, under 18 £19.70; doubles £25; family bunk room (1 child under 16, at least) doubles £40, quads £80, 6 beds £120. Wheelchair accessible.

PRIVATE HOSTELS

Private hostels don't require HI/YHA membership, serve a youthful clientele, and have usually single-sex rooms. Some have kitchen facilities. Curfews are rare, and the dorms are usually cheaper. Almost all accept major credit cards.

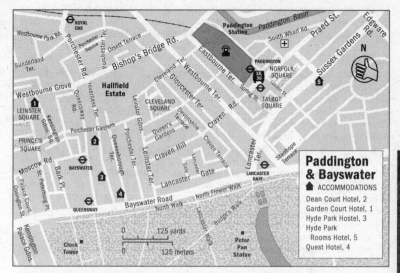

Paddington
& Bayswater

♠ ACCOMMODATIONS

Dean Court Hotel, 2
Garden Court Hotel, 1
Hyde Park Hostel, 3
Hyde Park
 Rooms Hotel, 5
Quest Hotel, 4

LONDON

International Student House, 229 Great Portland St., W1 (☎ 7631 8300; fax 7631 8315). Tube: Great Portland St. At the foot of Regent's Park, across the street from the Tube station's rotunda. Films, concerts, discos, athletic contests, expeditions, and parties. Over 500 beds. Laundry facilities, currency exchange. Continental breakfast. Dorms (without breakfast) £10; singles £31; doubles £22.50; triples £20; quads £17.50. With ISIC card: singles £24.50; doubles £19.50.

Ashlee House, 261-65 Gray's Inn Rd. (☎ 7833 9400; fax 7833 6777; info@ashleehouse.co.uk; www.ashleehouse.co.uk). Tube: King's Cross. Clean, bright rooms within easy walking distance of King's Cross (which is good and bad). Some rooms have skylights; all have washbasins and central heating. No hot water noon-6pm. Generous breakfast included (M-F 7:30-9.30am, Sa-Su 8-10am). Secure luggage room, laundry, kitchens, and Internet access. Linen provided. Reception 24hr. Check-out 10am. Dorms Apr.-Oct. £15-19, Nov.-Mar. £13-17; twins £22, 24 per person.

Central University of Iowa Hostel, 7 Bedford Pl. (☎/fax 7580 1121). Tube: Tottenham Court Rd. or Russell Sq. On a quiet street near the British Museum. Spartan, narrow dorm rooms with bunk beds and washbasins. Continental breakfast included. Laundry facilities, towels and linen, TV lounge. £10 key deposit. Reception 9am-10:30pm. No curfew. Open approximately May 20-Aug. 20. Dorms £20; twins £22.

Astor's Museum Inn, 27 Montague St. (☎ 7580 5360; fax 7636 7948; astorhostels@ msn.com). Tube: Russell Sq. Coed dorms almost inevitable. Kitchen, cable TV. Continental breakfast included. Linens provided. 24hr. reception. No curfew. Book a month ahead. Dorms £14-16; doubles £40; triples £51. Discounts available Oct.-Mar., including a weekly dorm rate of £70.

Tonbridge Club, 120 Cromer St. (☎ 7837 4406). Tube: King's Cross/St. Pancras. Follow Euston Rd. towards the British Library and turn left onto Judd St.; the hostel is 3 blocks down on the left. Students and foreigners only. A clean, no- frills place to sleep and shower. Men sleep in basement gym, women in karate-club hall. Pool tables, TV, video games. Daytime storage space. Blankets and foam pads provided. Lockout 9am-9pm; lights out 11:30pm; midnight curfew. Floor space £5.

HALLS OF RESIDENCE

London's universities rent out rooms in their **halls of residence,** which are generally the cheapest single rooms available, particularly if you have a student ID. Rooms tend to be standard, spartan student digs, but clean. The halls usually offer rooms to individuals for two or three months over the summer, and during the long Easter break in the spring. Some halls reserve a few rooms for travelers year-round. Calling ahead is advisable. The **King's Campus Vacation Bureau,** 127 Stanford St., SE1 (☎7928 3777), controls bookings for a number of University of London residence halls, all available from early June to mid-September.

High Holborn Residence, 178 High Holborn, WC1 (☎ 7379 5589; fax 7379 5640). Tube: Holborn. A comfortable, modern, and extremely well-located place. Rooms come with phones, and each has a kitchen. Laundry facilities. Excellent wheelchair facilities. Full English breakfast included. Open mid-June to Sept. (peak rates in July). Singles £27-34; twins £46-57, with bath £56-67; triples with bath £66-77.

Wellington Hall, 71 Vincent Sq. (☎ 7834 4740; fax 7233 7709; reservations ☎ 7928 3777). Tube: Victoria. An Edwardian building on a beautiful square near Victoria Station. TV lounge, library, and bar. English breakfast included. Laundry. Rooms available around Easter and mid-June to mid-Sept. Singles £26; twins £40. 10% discount for stays over a week.

Queen Alexandra's House, Kensington Gore. (☎ 7589 1120; fax 7589 3177). Tube: South Kensington. **Women only.** Kitchen, laundry, sitting room, and 20 piano-filled music rooms. Common showers/lavatories. No visitors 11pm-10am. Continental breakfast included. 2-night minimum stay. Write weeks in advance for a booking form; fax is best. Cozy singles £25; weekly rates for stays over 2 weeks £150 per week upon availability, including breakfast and dinner. No credit cards.

John Adams Hall, 15-23 Endsleigh St., WC1 (☎ 7387 4086; fax 7383 0164; jah@ioe.ac.uk). Tube: Euston Sq. An elegant Georgian building with small, wrought-iron balconies. Singles are small and simple. TV lounge, pianos. Laundry facilities. English breakfast included. Open July-Sept. and Easter. Singles £24; twins £42; triples £59. Discounts for students, stays of 6 nights or more, and in the off-season.

BED AND BREAKFASTS

All B&Bs listed serve full English breakfasts and accept credit cards unless otherwise noted.

WESTMINSTER

■ **Luna and Simone Hotel,** 47-49 Belgrave Rd. (☎ 7834 5897; fax 7828 2474; lunasimone@talk21.com). Tube: Victoria. Fabulous! Stylish, fun, and immaculate; the area's best option. Yellow and blue rooms all come with TV, phones, hair dryers, and firm mattresses. Luggage storage. Book a month ahead. Singles £28-34; doubles £48-60, with bath £50-75; triples £65-80, with shower £75-95. 10% discount for long-term stays.

■ **Melbourne House,** 79 Belgrave Rd. (☎ 7828 3516; fax 7828 7120; melbourne.househotel@virgin.net). Tube: Pimlico. An extraordinarily clean, well-kept establishment. The rooms are spacious, all non-smoking, and have TV, phone, and hot pot. Breakfast served 7:30-8:45am. Free luggage storage. Book ahead with credit card. 48hr. cancellation fee. Singles £30, with bath £50-55; doubles or twins with bath £70-75; triples with bath £90-95; family quad with bath £100-110. Cash preferred.

Alexander Hotel, 13 Belgrave Rd. (☎ 7834 9738; fax 7630 9630). Tube: Pimlico. Sumptuously carpeted rooms are slightly crunched but attractive and sparkling clean throughout. All with satellite TV, radio, and private bath. TV lounge. Breakfast served 7:30-9am. Check-out 11am. Singles £45; doubles and twins £60-65; triples £75-80; family rooms £80-110. Winter discount.

Dover Hotel, 42/44 Belgrave Rd. (☎ 7821 9085; fax 7834 6425; dover@rooms.demon.co.uk). Tube: Pimlico. All rooms and facilities are clean, in good condition, and have bathrooms. Continental breakfast served 7:30-9:30am. Singles £40-55; doubles and twins £50-70; triples £60-75; quads £70-100; quints £80-110.

Stanley House Hotel, 19-21 Belgrave Rd. (☎ 7834 5042). Tube: Pimlico. Ceilings lower and rooms get smaller as you go up. Test mattresses before you rest to get the best. English breakfast. TV lounge. 24hr. reception. Book 2 weeks in advance. Singles £42, with shower £50; doubles £50, with shower or bath £60; family rooms £25 per person.

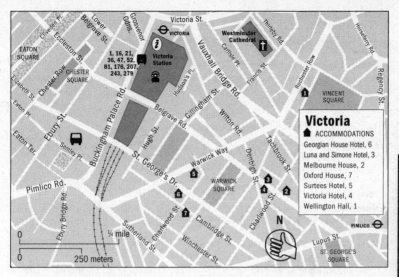

Victoria

ACCOMMODATIONS
Georgian House Hotel, 6
Luna and Simone Hotel, 3
Melbourne House, 2
Oxford House, 7
Surtees Hotel, 5
Victoria Hotel, 4
Wellington Hall, 1

KENSINGTON, KNIGHTSBRIDGE, AND CHELSEA

Abbey House Hotel, 11 Vicarage Gate. (☎ 7727 2594) Tube: High St. Kensington. The elegant black and white marble entrance to this historic house makes you feel like royalty. After you check in, the owners (who live in-house) or an assistant will spend 20min. giving you an introduction to London. The hotel achieves a level of comfort unrivaled at these prices. 24hr. tea, coffee, and ice room. Palatial pastel rooms with color TVs, washbasins, towels and soap, and billowing curtains. Reception 8:30am-10pm. Book far ahead. Singles £43; doubles £68; triples £85; quads £95; quints £105. Weekly rates in winter only. No credit cards.

Vicarage Hotel, 10 Vicarage Gate (☎ 7229 4030; fax 7792 5989; reception@london-vicaragehotel.com). Tube: High St. Kensington. Stately foyer and breakfast room surpassed only by comfortable bedrooms and spotless bathrooms. Singles £45; doubles and twins £74, with bath and TV £98; triples £90; family rooms £98. No credit cards.

Swiss House Hotel, 171 Old Brompton Rd. (☎ 7373 2769; fax 7373 4983; recep@swiss-hh.demon.co.uk). Tube: Gloucester Rd. A beautiful, plant-filled B&B with 16 airy, spacious rooms, most with fireplaces. Cable TV, telephone, and tea-and-coffee-making facilities included. Fax and Internet access. All rooms have showers. Continental breakfast included. English breakfast £6. Reception open M-F 7:30am-11pm, Sa-Su 8am-11pm. Singles £46, with toilet £65; doubles/twins with bath £80-90; triples with bath £104; quads with bath £118. 5% discount for stays over a week in the off-season. 5% discount for cash payments.

MARYLEBONE AND BLOOMSBURY

Arosfa Hotel, 83 Gower St. (☎/fax 7636 2115). Tube: Tottenham Court Rd. Spacious rooms, immaculate facilities, and furnishings. All rooms with TV and sink. No smoking. Singles £35; doubles £48, with bath £63; triples £65, £76; quad with bath £88.

Euro Hotel, 51-53 Cartwright Gdns., WC1 (☎ 7387 4321; fax 7383 5044; reception@euro-hotel.co.uk). Tube: Russell Sq. Large, high-ceilinged rooms with cable TV, radio, kettle, phone, and sink. Sparkling, spacious bathroom facilities. Free email. Singles £46, with bath £68; doubles £65, £85; triples £79, £99; quads £88, £108. Under 13 sharing with adults £10.

Ridgemount Hotel, 65-67 Gower St. (☎ 7636 1141; fax 7636 2558). Tube: Tottenham Court Rd. Charming staff keep the loyal guests happy and the well-kept hotel radiantly clean. Snug singles with TVs. Garden in back, free tea and coffee in the TV lounge. Laundry service £3. Book ahead. Singles £32, with shower £43; doubles £48, £62; triples £63, £75; quads £72, £86; quints £78, £89.

The Langland Hotel, 29-31 Gower St. (☎ 7636 5801; fax 7580 2227; sarah@ langlandhotel.freeserve.co.uk). Tube: Euston. Renovations have added bathrooms to many of the rooms and TVs to all. Cable-TV lounge with comfy blue sofas. Laundry facilities. Winter and long-term student discounts. Singles £40; doubles £50, with bath £70; triples £70; quads £90; quints £110. Rooms with bath range £60-120.

Mentone Hotel, 54-56 Cartwright Gdns. (☎7387 3927; fax 7388 4671; mentonehotel@ compuserve.com). Tube: Russell Sq. Bright, cheery place. Airport shuttle available with advance reservation (from Heathrow £24, Gatwick £40, Luton £34, Stansted £43). Singles £42, with bath £60; doubles with bath £79; triples with bath £90; quads with bath £99. Reduced rates for longer stays in Dec.-Apr.

Cosmo/Bedford House Hotel, 27 Bloomsbury Sq. (☎ 7636 4661; fax 7636 0577; cosmo.bedford.hotel@dial.pipex.com). Tube: Holborn. Location prevails in this family-run establishment with neat, comfortable rooms that come with color TVs and sinks. Continental breakfast. Singles £36, with bath £48; doubles £58, £70; triples £75, £85; quad £85, £90. AmEx, DC, MC, V. 5% credit card surcharge.

Alhambra Hotel, 17-19 Argyle St. (☎7837 9575; fax 7916 2476; postmaster@ alhambrahotel.demon.co.uk). Tube: King's Cross/St. Pancras. Sinks and TVs in all rooms. Not the loveliest neighborhood. Singles £32, with shower £42, with bath £60; doubles £44, with shower £50, with bath £60; triples £62, with bath £77; quads with bath £92.

Jesmond Dene Hotel, 27 Argyle St. (☎7837 4654; fax 7833 1633; JesmondDene-Hotel@msn.com). Tube: King's Cross/St. Pancras. Black-and-white rooms with sinks and large TVs are slightly worn but scrupulously clean. Reserve 2 weeks early. Singles £30; doubles £42, with shower £55; triples £60, £75; quads with bath £90; quints £95.

EARL'S COURT

▓ **Oxford Hotel,** 24 Penywern Rd. (☎ 7370 1161; fax 7373 8256; oxfordhotel@btinter-net.com). Clean rooms installed with new beds and repainted every year. The stylish dining room includes a bar. Breakfast 7:30-9:30am. Luggage storage and safe. 24hr. reception. Singles with shower £34, with bath £47; doubles £53, £63; triples £63, £73; quads with shower £75, with bath £85; quints with shower £95, with bath £105. Winter and weekly rates may be 10-15% lower. Reserve ahead.

▓ **Mowbray Court Hotel,** 28-32 Penywern Rd. (☎ 7373 8285; fax 7370 5693; mowbraycrthot@hotmail.com). Staff this helpful is a rarity in London; wake-up calls, tour arrangements, taxicabs, theater bookings, and dry cleaning. Rooms with firm mattresses, towels, shampoo, hair dryers, TV, radio, trouser press, phone, Bible, and *The Teachings of Buddha.* Internet access. Reserve ahead; no deposit required. In-room safes £2 per day. Singles £45, with bath £52; doubles £56, £67; triples £69, £80; family rooms for 4 £84, £95; for 5 £100, £110; for 6 £115, £125.

Beaver Hotel, 57-59 Philbeach Gdns. (☎ 7373 4553; fax 7373 4555). Warm and wel-coming—plush lounge with polished wood floors and cable TV. Lift access. All rooms with desks, phones, and hair dryers. All bathrooms are a study in cleanliness. Wheel-chair accessible. Parking £5. Singles £38, with bath £55; doubles £45, £80; triples with bath £90. Breakfast 7:30-9:30am. Reserve several weeks ahead.

Philbeach Hotel, 30-31 Philbeach Gdns. (☎ 7373 1244; fax 7244 0149). The largest gay B&B in England, popular with all genders. Jimmy's Bar downstairs is residents-only. Internet access. Continental breakfast included. Book 1 week ahead. Budget single £30, else £35-50, with shower £50-60; doubles £65, with bath £85; triple £75, £90.

Half Moon Hotel, 10 Earl's Ct. Sq., SW5 (☎ 7373 9956; fax 7373 8456). From Earl's Court Tube station, take a right, and Earl's Court Sq. is the second right. Looks like a two-star, charges like a budget. Continental breakfast included. Singles £30, with shower £45; doubles £55, with bath £60; triples £65, £80; quads with shower £100.

◯ FOOD

Savoring the booty of imperialism needn't be a guilty pleasure; imports from former colonies have spiced up London kitchens considerably. The city is perhaps most famous for its **Indian restaurants,** the true British food (the cheapest cluster around Westbourne Grove near Bayswater, Euston Sq., and Brick Ln. in the East End), but food from various corners of the globe can be found everywhere. The wealth of international restaurants shouldn't deter you from sampling Britain's own cuisine. As usual, **pubs** are a solid choice for meat dishes, while **fish-and-chip shops** and **kebab shops** can be found on nearly every corner. They vary little in price but can be miles apart in quality. Look for queues out the door and hop in line. The "New British" label applies to restaurants that blend continental influences with British staples to form a tasty, if sometimes pricey, cuisine.

THE CITY OF LONDON

Futures!, 8 Botolph Alley (☎ 7623 4529). Tube: Monument. Off Botolph Ln. Fresh takeaway vegetarian breakfast and lunch prepared in a petite kitchen open to view. Daily main dishes, like quiche, £3.40. Spinach pizza £1.85. **Branch** in Exchange Sq., behind Liverpool St. Open M-F 7:30-10am and 11:30am-3pm.

The Place Below, in St. Mary-le-Bow crypt, Cheapside (☎ 7329 0789). Tube: St. Paul's. Generous vegetarian dishes served to City executives in an impressive church crypt. The second dining room moonlights as an ecclesiastical court, where the Archbishop of Canterbury still settles cases pertaining to Anglican law and swears in new bishops a few times a year. Quiche and salad £6, takeaway £4.20. £2 discount 11:30am-noon. Significant takeaway discount. Open M-F 7:30am-2:30pm.

Sushi & Sozai, 51a Queen Victoria St. (☎ 7332 0108). Tube: Mansion House. A cheap sushi stand in the City. Medium sushi £4; large sushi £5. Heated Japanese dishes, including deep-fried pork cutlet and egg on rice, £3. Open M-F 11am-3pm.

COVENT GARDEN AND SOHO

Belgo Centraal, 50 Earlham St. (☎ 7813 2233). Tube: Covent Garden. Waiters in monk's cowls and great specials make this one of Covent Garden's most popular restaurants. During "Beat the Clock," (M-F 6-7:30pm) the time you order is the cost of your meal; order at 6:30, your meal costs £6.30. Open M-Sa noon-11:30pm, Su noon-10:30pm. Wheelchair access.

World Food Cafe, 14-15 Neal's Yd. (☎ 7379 0298). Tube: Covent Garden. A bit pricier than similar veggie-loving enclaves, but the food quality explains it all. Features a worldwide array of *meze*, light meals, and appetizing platters (£6-8). Open M-Sa noon-5pm.

Yo!Sushi, 52 Poland St. (☎ 7287 0443). Tube: Oxford Circus. As much an eating experience as a restaurant. Diners sit at an island bar and pick and choose from dishes placed on a central conveyer belt. Plates are color-coded by price (£1.50-3.50). An electronic drink cart makes its way behind diners delivering liquid delights. Great fun. Open daily noon-midnight.

Don Zoko, 15 Kingley St. (☎ 7734 1974). Tube: Oxford Circus. This unassuming sushi bar handwrites the menu on strips of paper attached to the wall. Thankfully, an English translation is available, because the made-as-you-order sushi is some of London's best. *Don Zoko* means "rock bottom," and its prices are just that. Sushi £2-4, dishes £3-6.50, beer £1.60-3.90, saki £3.50-5.50 per glass. Open M-F noon-2:30pm and 6-10:30pm; Sa-Su 6-10:30pm.

Wagamama, 101 Wigmore St. (☎ 7409 0111). Tube: Marble Arch. See p. 104.

Lok Ho Fook, 4-5 Gerrard St. (☎ 7437 2001). Tube: Leicester Sq. Busy place with good prices and a welcoming atmosphere. Extensive selection of seafood, noodles, and vegetarian dishes £4-8. Dim sum (£1.40-1.60) is made to order—not strolled on carts. Helpful staff will aid the novice in selection. Not to be confused with the nearby and more expensive Lee Ho Fook. Dim sum served until 6pm. Open daily noon-11:45pm.

LONDON

Neal's Yard Salad Bar, 2 Neal's Yard (☎ 7836 3233). Tube: Covent Garden. Takeaway or sit outside at this vegetarian's nirvana. Hot vegetable dishes £4.50-5 (takeaway discount 50p). Tempting mix 'n' match salads from £2. Eat-in £5 minimum, but the benches nearby count as takeaway. Open M-Sa 10:30am-6pm.

Neal's Yard Bakery & Tearoom, 6 Neal's Yard (☎ 7836 5199). Tube: Covent Garden. Only organic flour and filtered water are used in the delicious breads. Small, open-air counter offers many vegan and vegetarian dishes. Beanburger £2.20, takeaway £1.80. 50% discount on day-old bread. No smoking. Open M-Sa 10:30am-4:30pm.

Mandeer, 8 Bloomsbury Way (☎ 7242 6202). Tube: Tottenham Court Rd. Some of the best Indian food around and an education about owner Ramesh Patel's Ayurvedic Science of Life. The cuisine is tasty, fresh, organic, and vegetarian. The best deals in the house are the lunch buffet options, from £3.50. Open M-Sa noon-3pm and 5-10pm.

Kowloon Restaurant, 21-22 Gerrard St. (☎ 7437 0148). Tube: Leicester Sq. Meal-sized portions of rice noodles (£3.50-6) are served steaming and cheap. Rice dishes also under £4. Tea service available 11:30am-6pm. Satisfy your sweet tooth in the bakery. Open daily noon-11:45pm.

PICADILLY AND MAYFAIR

■ **Wagamama,** 10a Lexington St. (☎ 7292 0990). Tube: Piccadilly Circus. See p. 104.

Sofra, 18 Shepherd St. (☎ 7493 3320). Tube: Green Park/Hyde Park Corner. The house specialty, mixed *meze*, is £5.45, while other main courses cost £7.45-8.95. Open noon-midnight. **Branches:** 36 Tavistock St. (☎ 7240 3773) and Hyde Park.

WESTMINSTER

Al-Fresco (☎ 7233 8298). Tube: Victoria. Trendy variations on old standbys. Jacket potato with brie £2.75. Fresh melon juice £1.70. Panini sandwiches £2.80. Open M-F 8am-5:30pm, Sa-Su 9am-4:30pm.

Goya, 34 Lupus St. (☎ 7976 5309). Tube: Pimlico. Corner tapas bar popular with locals for sipping drinks and munching Spanish snacks. Outdoor tables filled on summer nights. Tapas £2.50-4.50. Hearty garlic chicken £4.20. Open daily noon-midnight.

KENSINGTON, KNIGHTSBRIDGE, AND CHELSEA

■ **Wagamama,** 26 Kensington High St. (☎ 7376 1717). Tube: High St. Kensington. See Marylebone and Bloomsbury, p. 104.

■ **New Culture Revolution,** 305 King's Rd. (☎ 7352 9281). Tube: Sloane Sq. Take a great leap forward and enjoy delicious north Chinese food, mostly noodles and dumplings. Open daily noon-11pm. **Branches:** 43 Parkway (☎ 7267 2700; Tube: Camden Town); Notting Hill; and 42 Duncan St. (☎ 7833 9083; Tube: Angel).

Café Floris, 5 Harrington Rd. (☎ 7589 3276). Tube: High St. Kensington. A bustling cafe offering large, fresh sandwiches (£1.60-2.90) and filling breakfasts. Colossal all-day breakfast special £3.50. Min. purchase £3 noon-3pm. Open daily 6am-7pm.

Rotisserie Jules, 6-8 Bute St. (☎ 7584 0600). Tube: High St. Kensington. This lively restaurant serves free-range poultry. Dishes from £4.95. Open daily noon-11:30pm. **Branches:** 338 King's Rd. and 133 Notting Hill Gate.

Vingt-Quatre, 325 Fulham Rd. (☎ 7376 7224). Tube: High St. Kensington. Hyper-modern steel decor gives this diner a space age feel. All-day English breakfast; small £4.75, large £6.75. Main courses £6.75-9.95. Alcohol served noon-midnight. Open 24hr.

Lomo, 222 Fulham Rd. (☎7 349 8848). Tube: High St. Kensington. This chic tapas bar, decorated with burnt orange tall tables, opens onto the sidewalk. Hot *chorizo* £3.75, sausages £3.50-5.75. Lunch special £5 for 3 tapas. Happy hour (half price beer and cocktails) 5-7pm. Open M-Sa noon-midnight; Su noon-11:30pm.

Sticky Fingers Cafe, 1a Phillimore Gdns. (☎ 7938 5338). Tube: High St. Kensington. Former Rolling Stone Bill Wyman operates this memorabilia-crammed diner. Those fearing a Hard Rock Cafe experience shouldn't worry; the only cheese here goes on the burgers (£7.95-8.95 with fries). Kids menu: 2 courses and fries £4.95. Open M-Sa noon-11:30pm; Su noon-11pm.

Borshtch 'n' Tears, 46 Beauchamp Pl. (☎ 7589 5003). Tube: Knightsbridge. Here, the atmosphere is more extraordinary than the food. Starters £3-6. Main dishes £7-9. 16 varieties of vodka shots (around £2.50). Live music nightly. Cover £1. Last orders 1am. Open daily 6pm-2am. **Branch: Borshtch 'n' Cheers,** 273 King's Rd., Chelsea.

Arco Bars, 46 Hans Crescent (☎ 7584 6454). Tube: Knightsbridge. The hearty food, while not outstanding, suits the office crowds and shoppers from nearby Harrods who want a quick meal. Pasta £3.70-5.20; sandwiches £4-5.80. 20% takeaway discount. Open M-F 7am-6pm, Sa 8am-6pm.

My Old Dutch Pancake House, 221 King's Rd. (☎ 7376 5650). Tube: Sloane Sq. Gorge on hubcap-sized pancakes. Set lunch menu (served weekdays noon-4pm) offers a pancake with your choice of toppings and tea or coffee (£6). Any crepe £5 from 4-7pm. Open M-Th noon-11:30pm, F-Sa noon-midnight, Su 10am-11pm.

Chelsea Kitchen, 98 King's Rd. (☎ 7589 1330). Tube: Sloane Sq. Super-cheap food: turkey and mushroom pie, spaghetti bolognese and Spanish omelettes £2.80 or less. Menu changes daily. Set menu £4-5. Breakfast served 8-11:25am. Open M-Sa 8am-11:30pm, Su 9am-11:30pm.

NOTTING HILL, BAYSWATER, AND HYDE PARK

▨ **The Grain Shop,** 269a Portobello Rd. (☎ 7229 5571). Tube: Ladbroke Grove. This takeaway sells a surprisingly large array of foods. Organic whole grain breads baked daily on the premises 90p-£1.90 per loaf. Main dishes from £2.40. Vegan brownies £1. Groceries also available, many organic. Open M-Sa 9:30am-6pm.

▨ **Cockney's Pie & Mash,** 314 Portobello Rd. (☎ 8960 9409). Tube: Ladbroke Grove. Cheap, no-nonsense pie and mash (£1.85), with portions of eel (F-Sa only) for a mere £2.70. Open Tu-Sa 11:30am-5:30pm.

▨ **Royal China,** 13 Queensway (☎ 7221 2535). Tube: Bayswater. For the full Cantonese experience, try the steamed duck's tongue (£1.80) or the marinated chicken feet (£1.80). Generous dishes £10-15. Dim sum served M-Sa noon-5pm, Su 11am-5pm. Open M-Th noon-11pm, F-Sa noon-11:30pm, Su 11am-10pm.

▨ **Mandola,** 139 Westbourne Grove (☎ 7229 6391). Tube: Bayswater. Simply put, it rocks. A tiny diner that has rapidly shot into trendy eating notoriety, but hasn't raised its prices to match. Salads £3, main dishes £4-8. To finish, try the date mousse (£2.40) and Sudanese coffee, in a traditional pot (£3.50; serves 2). Takeaway available. Open M-Sa noon-11:30pm, Su noon-10:30pm.

▨ **New Culture Revolution,** 157-159 Notting Hill Gate (☎ 7313 9688). Tube: Notting Hill Gate. See Chelsea, p. 102.

▨ **Khan's,** 13-15 Westbourne Grove (☎ 7727 5240). Tube: Bayswater. Cavernous, noisy, and crowded, Khan's remains a great bargain for Indian food. Though most dishes are under £4, Khan's charges a £6 per person minimum and a 10% service charge. Uses only *halal* meats. Open daily noon-3pm and 6pm-midnight.

Sofra, 1 St. Christopher's Pl. (☎ 7224 4080). Tube: Bond St. See Mayfair, p. 102.

Manzara, 24 Pembridge Rd. (☎ 7727 3062). Tube: Notting Hill Gate. A wonderful place to refuel after a stroll through Portobello Market. Their speciality is Turkish *pide,* a pizza-like pie. In the afternoon, *pides* are £3.50, sandwiches £2. Vegetarians should try the mixed *meze* (£4.25). Takeaway discount. Open daily 7:30am-midnight.

MARYLEBONE AND BLOOMSBURY

▨ **Mandalay,** 444 Edgware Rd. (☎ 7258 3696). Tube: Edgware Rd. This Burmese restaurant is so consistently good it only needs word of mouth to attract customers. Friendly owners. Set lunches include curry and rice £3.50; curry, rice, dessert, and coffee £5.90. Open M-Sa noon-3pm and 6-11pm; last orders 2:30pm and 10:30pm.

■ **Wagamama,** 4A Streatham St. (☎ 7323 9223). Tube: Tottenham Ct. Rd. If a restaurant could be a London must-see on the level of Buckingham Palace, this would be it. The waitstaff radio orders to the kitchen and diners slurp happily from massive bowls of ramen at long tables, like extras from *Tampopo*. Noodles in various combinations and permutations, all obscenely tasty (£5-7.25). Open M-Sa noon-11pm, Su 12:30-10pm. **Branches:** Picadilly, Soho, North London: Camden Town, and Kensington.

■ **Diwana Bhel Poori House,** 121 Drummond St. (☎ 7387 5556). Tube: Warren St. The specialty is *thali* (an assortment of vegetables, rices, sauces, breads, and desserts; £4.50-6.20). The "Chef's Special" is served on weekdays with rice for £4.80. Lunch buffet (served noon-2:30pm, £4.50) includes 4 vegetable dishes, rice, savories, and dessert. Open daily noon-11:30pm.

Ranoush Juice, 43 Edgware Rd. (☎ 7723 5929). Tube: Marble Arch. The best Lebanese takeaway on the Edgware Rd. (and that's some stiff competition). Fortunately, you don't need to spend a fortune to enjoy the fresh meat of their kebabs and shwarmas (£2.50-4). Wash it down with the excellent juices (£1.50). Open daily 9:30am-3am. Cash only.

Seashell, 49-51 Lisson Grove (☎ 7224 9000). Tube: Marylebone. Always a contender in the eternal debate over the best fish and chips in London. Get the same high-quality fish from the takeaway for much less than at the restaurant (cod and chips £3.25). Open M-F noon-2:30pm and 5-10:30pm, Sa noon-10:30pm.

Woolley's Salad Shop and Sandwich Bar, 33 Theobald's Rd. (☎ 7405 3028). Tube: Holborn. Fight the tsunami of suits for healthy picnic fare, mostly vegetarian. Mix and match their 10 fresh salads (70p-£6.30). The adjoining sandwich shop offers everything from chicken *saag* to smoked salmon lovingly swaddled in fresh rolls (£1.70-2.90). Dried fruit, nuts, herbal tea, and *muesli* also for sale. Open M-F 7am-3:30pm.

Buon Appetito, 27 Sicilian Ave. (☎ 7242 7993). Tube: Holborn. Fantastic lunch option near the British Museum. Full breakfast served all day £3.50, sandwiches £1.80-2.90. Open M-Sa 6:15am-4:30pm.

SOUTH LONDON

■ **Tas,** 33 The Cut (☎ 7928 2111). Tube: Waterloo. Tas manages to serve gourmet quality Turkish and Mediterranean food at low prices. Starter and main for a scandalously low £6.45. Rejoice! Open M-Sa noon-11:30pm, Su noon-10:30pm.

EAST LONDON

Arkansas Cafe, Old Spitalfields Market. (☎ 7377 6999). Tube: Aldgate East. This may not give you a taste of jolly old England, but the Brits are flocking here in droves. Schooled in the art of flesh in Louisiana, Bubba uses nothing but free-range, happy-while-it-lasted meat, and the results are to die for. If your arteries block on-site, the Royal London Hospital is nearby. Open M-F noon-2:30pm, Su noon-4pm.

Spitz, 109 Commercial St. (☎ 7 247 9747). Tube: Aldgate East. Inside Spitalfields Market, this elegant bar serves delicious lunches from £5. During the weekend, there is live music upstairs, with an emphasis on folk, jazz, and klezmer. Open daily 11am-midnight.

NORTH LONDON

■ **Tartuf,** 88 Upper St. (☎ 7288 0954). Tube: Angel. A convivial Alsatian place that serves *tartes flambées* (£4.90-6.10), like pizzas on very thin crusts, but much tastier. All-you-can-eat tartes £8.90. £4.90 "lunch express" gets you a savory and a sweet *tarte* before 3pm. Open M-F noon-2:30pm and 5:45-11:30pm, Sa noon-11:30pm, Su noon-11pm.

■ **Le Mercury,** 140a Upper St. (☎ 7354 4088). Tube: Angel. This French restaurant feels like the quintessential Islington gourmet bistro, but with outstandingly low prices. All main courses, including honey-roasted breast of duck, £5.85. Lunch and dinner 3-course *prix fixe* menu changes daily. Kids eat Sunday roast free. Open daily 11am-1am. Reservations recommended for evening. MC, V.

■ **Le Crêperie de Hampstead,** 77 Hampstead High St. Tube: Hampstead. This Hampstead institution is guaranteed nirvana, serving paper-thin Brittany crepes stuffed with fillings both sweet and savory from a tiny van outside the King William IV pub. Crepes £1.55-3.95. Open M-Th 11:45am-11pm, F-Su 11:45am-11:30pm.

Wagamama, 11 Jamestown Rd. (☎ 7428 0800). Tube: Camden Town. See p. 104.

Afghan Kitchen, 35 Islington Green (☎ 7359 8019). Tube: Angel. This small cafe overlooking Islington Green offers cheap, scrumptious food. Everything on the short menu (8 main dishes £4.50-5) tastes fresh and comes in generous portions. The rice (£2) is some of the best in London. Open Tu-Sa noon-3:30pm and 5:30-11pm.

Bar Gansa, 2 Inverness St. (☎ 7267 8909). Tube: Camden Town. A small tapas bar with bright walls, festive Spanish candles, and Mediterranean ornaments. By night, a raucous international crowd enjoys tapas (£2-3.95) bottled beers (£2.25), sangria (£2.25), and throbbing Latin music. Limited outdoor seating. Open daily 10am-late.

Ruby in the Dust, 102 Camden High St. (☎7485 2744). Tube: Camden Town. Bright decor (butterflies hang from every free inch of plaster) and fun cocktails draw in a twentysomething crowd. Bangers and mash £6.85, burgers £6.55. Brunch 10am-6pm. Wide vegetarian selection. Open M-Th and Su 10am-11pm, F-Sa 10am-11:30pm.

Giraffe, 46 Rosslyn Hill (☎ 7435 0343). Tube: Hampstead. The menu runs the gamut from Cajun fish cakes to *meze*. Breakfast served M-F 8am-noon. During "Giraffe time" (M-F 6-7pm) a starter and main course cost the same when you order: order at 6:30, you pay £6.30. Open M-F 8am-midnight, Sa 9am-midnight, Su 9am-11:30pm.

WEST LONDON

Troubador, 265 Old Brompton Rd. (☎ 7370 1434). Tube: Earl's Court. Assorted snacks, soups, and sandwiches (£3-6), and special breakfasts (£4.50-5) draw scores. Vast selection of coffee drinks. Open daily 9am-midnight.

NOTABLE CHAINS

Prêt-à-Manger. This bustling chrome-adorned sandwich chain has become a London institution. And no wonder: everything Prêt serves is made of the fresh, organic ingredients. Sandwiches £1.35-2.90; eat-in prices are slightly more expensive. Many branches are closed for dinner.

Pierre Victoire. Brasserie chain offers inexpensive Parisian fare in expensive London neighborhoods. Staples like seafood *pot au feu* and mackerel pâté. Menu changes daily. 2-course lunch £4.90.

TEA

Quintessentially English, the tradition of **afternoon tea** is a social ritual combining food, conversation, and of course, a pot of tea–served strong and taken with milk. Don't commit a gaffe by pouring the tea first—aficionados always pour the milk first so as not to scald it. Afternoon **high tea** includes cooked meats, salad, sandwiches, and pastries. **Cream tea,** a specialty of Cornwall and Devon, includes pastries accompanied by clotted cream (a cross between whipped cream and butter).

Claridges, Brook St. (☎ 7629 8860). Tube: Bond St. Old-fashioned elegance combined with comfortable sofas and armchairs encourage a long afternoon linger. Smartly dressed waiters pour your tea and present plates of sandwiches and pastries. Tea served daily 3-5:30pm; book in advance for weekends. £19; with champagne £25.

The Orangery Tea Room, Kensington Palace, Kensington Gardens (☎ 7376 0239). Tube: High St. Kensington. Light meals and tea served in the marvelously airy Orangery built for Queen Anne in 1705. Two scones with clotted cream and jam £4. Pot of tea £2.10, set teas from £5.25. Trundle through the gardens afterward. Open daily 10am-6pm.

GROCERIES AND SUPERMARKETS

Tesco and **Sainsbury's** are the two largest supermarket chains. Other chains include **Europa, Spar,** and **Asda.** If you're willing to spend a bit more, then you might consider **Marks and Spencer,** which introduced baby tomatoes, baby potatoes, and other cute produce to Britain. For those who want to splurge, the food halls of **Harrods** and **Fortnum and Mason's** are sights in their own right.

🔲 SIGHTS

London's landmarks annually face an onslaught of around five million visitors. These stampedes thicken from the late morning onwards, so try to get started as early as possible. US sightseers (particularly couples) who don't qualify for student or senior discounts may want to consider the **London for Less** card, issued by Metropolis International (☎ (888) 463 6753), which offers discounts for major attractions, theaters, restaurants, and hotels. The card is endorsed by the British Tourist Authority, and is available at all BTA offices (see p. 13 and p. 94; 2-person, 4-day card £13). *Let's Go* divides sights up by districts within London; however, major museums and galleries are placed in their own separate section (see p. 128).

TOURS. A good city tour lets you familiarize yourself with the eclectic wonders of London. Hostels, B&Bs, and TICs are stacked with leaflets competing for your tourist pound. Many **bus tours** are "hop-on/hop-off," allowing you to stop at the sights you find particularly fascinating before joining later tours. Be sure to ask how often buses circle through the route. **Walking tours** can fill in the specifics that buses zoom past. Among the best are **The Original London Walks** (☎ 7624 3978), which cover specific topic such as Legal London, Jack the Ripper, or Spies and Spycatchers. The two-hour tours are led by well-regarded guides. **Historical Tours of London** also leads popular tours. (☎ 8668 4019. £5, concessions £4.) *Time Out* lists walks in its "Around Town" section. If glancing at London from the top of a bus is unsatisfactory and hoofing it seems daunting, a tour led by **The London Bicycle Tour Company** may be the happy medium. (☎ 7928 6838. Tours £11.90.) A cheaper way to see the city is from the top of an ordinary double-decker bus; you'll miss the commentary, but gain authentic London experience. Bus #11 cruises between main sights, passing Chelsea, Sloane Sq., Victoria, Westminster Abbey, the Houses of Parliament, Whitehall, Trafalgar Sq., St. Paul's, and the City.

THE CITY OF LONDON

Until the 18th century, the City of London *was* London; all other boroughs and neighborhoods now swallowed up by "London" were neighboring towns or outlying villages. Today, the one-square-mile City of London is the financial center of Europe. Each weekday 350,000 people surge in at 9am and rush out again unfailingly at 5pm, leaving behind a resident population of only 6000. Today's City hums with activity during the week, is dead on Saturdays, and seems downright ghostly on Sundays. At the center, the massive **Bank of England** controls the country's finances, and the **Stock Exchange** makes (or breaks) the nation's fortune.

Behind this array of modern chaos rest pieces of another city: old London. Aged churches, friaries, and pubs, many of them still in use, dwell behind small alleys and above the roofs of steel office buildings. St. Paul's Cathedral, the most glorious of these structures, anchors London's memory to its colorful past. The City owes much of its graceful appearance to Sir Christopher Wren, who was the chief architect working after the **Great Fire of 1666** almost completely razed the area. Charles II issued a proclamation after the fire that City buildings should be rebuilt in brick and stone, rather than highly flammable wood and thatch. Wren's studio designed 52 churches to replace the 89 destroyed in the fire, and the surviving 24 churches are some of the only buildings in the City from the period immediately following the Great Fire. All variations on a theme, they gave Wren a chance to work out design problems that would come up as he rebuilt St. Paul's Cathedral.

The City of London information center, St. Paul's Churchyard, provides information on a host of traditional municipal events. One of the largest is the **Lord Mayor's Show,** held each year on the second Saturday of November. Information and street plans are available from mid-Oct. *(Tube: St. Paul's. ☎ 7332 1456. Open Apr.-Sept. daily 9:30am-5pm; Oct.-Mar. M-F 9:30am-5pm, Sa 9:30am-12:30pm.)*

ST. PAUL'S CATHEDRAL

Tube: St. Paul's. Open M-Sa 8:30am-4pm. Dome open M-Sa 9:30am-4pm. Ground floor and crypt wheelchair accessible. 90min. "Supertours" depart at 11am, 11:30am, 1:30pm, and 2pm; £2.50, students and seniors £2, children £1. 45min. audio tours available 8:45am-3:30pm; £3.50, concessions £3. Admission to cathedral, galleries, and crypt £5, students and seniors £4, children £2.50.

St. Paul's, topped by its beautiful Neoclassical dome, is arguably the most stunning architectural sight in London, a physical and spiritual symbol of the city. Sir Christopher Wren's enormous (157m by 76m) creation dominates its surroundings, even as modern usurpers sneak up around it. The current edifice is the 5th cathedral dedicated to St. Paul to stand on the site; the first was founded in AD 604 and destroyed by fire. The 4th and most massive cathedral, now referred to as "Old St. Paul's," was a medieval structure built by the Normans. This was one of the largest in Europe, topped by a spire ascending 150m, a structure taller than the current one, which tops out at 111m. Falling into almost complete neglect in the 16th century, the cathedral became more of a marketplace than a church. Wren had already started drawing up his grand scheme in 1666 when the Great Fire demolished the cathedral, giving him the opportunity to build from scratch.

QUIRE AND ALTAR. The stalls in the Quire narrowly escaped a bomb during World War II, but the old altar did not. It was replaced with the current marble **High Altar,** above which looms the crowning glory, the ceiling mosaic of Christ Seated in Majesty. Farther into the church, the north quire aisle holds *Mother and Child,* a modern sculpture of the Madonna and Child by Henry Moore. Behind the altar you'll find the **American Memorial Chapel,** dedicated to the 28,000 US soldiers based in Britain who died during World War II.

THE DOME. Climbing to any of the three levels within the dome rewards the stout of heart, leg, and soul. Over 250 steps lead to the **Whispering Gallery,** on the inside base of the dome. It's a perfect resounding chamber: whisper into the wall, and your friend on the other side should be able to hear you. The dome displays scenes from the life of St. Paul. A further 119 steps up, the first external view beckons from the **Stone Gallery,** only to be eclipsed 152 steps up by the incomparable panorama from the **Golden Gallery** atop the dome.

CRYPT. In the other vertical direction, the crypt (the largest in Europe) is saturated with tombs of and monuments to great Britons Florence Nightingale, Lawrence of Arabia, and Alexander Fleming, the discoverer of penicillin. The massive tombs of the Duke of Wellington and Horatio Nelson command attention; Nelson was the first national hero to be buried in the crypt (predecessors' tombs were moved here), and his black coffin lies directly beneath the dome. To the right of the crypt entrance, a black slab in the floor marks Wren's grave, with his son's famous epitaph close by: *Lector, si monumentum requiris circumspice* (roughly, "If you seek his monument, just look around you").

EVENSONG. Evensong is performed Monday through Saturday at 5pm. This lovely Anglican ceremony celebrates Christ's assumption of mortal form, and gives visitors a chance to hear the Cathedral's superb choir. Five minutes before the singing begins, worshippers will be allowed to sit in the choir, a few feet from the singers, though this means that you must stay for the duration (about 45min.).

THE TOWER OF LONDON

Tube: Tower Hill or DLR: Tower Gateway. ☎ 7709 0765; www.hrp.org.uk/tol/indextol.htm. Yeoman Warders ("Beefeaters") lead free tours every 30min. starting 9:30am M-Sa, Su 10am, plus 8 daily themed tours. Audio tours available in 7 languages; £2. Frequent exhibitions, ceremonies, and re-enactments of historic events; call for details. For tickets to the Ceremony of the Keys, the the 700-year-old nightly ritual locking of the gates, write 6 weeks in advance to the Ceremony of the Keys, Waterloo Block, HM Tower of London, EC3N 4AB, with the full name of those attending and a choice of dates, enclosing a stamped addressed envelope or international response coupon; free. Tower open Mar.-Oct. M-Sa 9am-5pm, Su 10am-5pm; Nov.-Feb. closes 4pm; closes 1hr. after last admis-

LONDON

sion. Last ticket sold at 4pm. £11, students and seniors £8.30, ages 5-15 £7.30, families £33. Avoid long queues by buying tickets in advance or from Tube stations.

The oldest continuously occupied fortress in Europe, "The Tower" was founded by William the Conqueror in 1066 to provide protection for and from his subjects. Richard the Lionheart began the construction of additional defenses around the original White Tower in 1189, and further work by Henry III and Edward I brought the Tower close to its present condition. Now 20 towers stand behind its walls, all connected by massive walls and gateways, forming fortifications disheartening to visitors even today. The whole castle used to be surrounded by a broad moat, but cholera epidemics led to its draining in 1843. The filled land became a vegetable garden during World War II but has since sprouted a tennis court for the Yeomen of the Guard Extraordinary. These "Beefeaters"—whose nickname is a reference to their daily allowance of beef in former times—still guard the fortress. To be eligible for Beefeaterhood, a candidate must have at least 22 years of service in the armed forces, as well as a strong appetite for flash photography.

Visitors enter the Tower through this tower on the southwest of the **Outer Ward,** which sports a precariously hung portcullis. The password, required for entry here after hours, has been changed every day since 1327. German spies were executed in the Outer Ward during World War II. Along the outer wall, **St. Thomas's Tower** (named after Thomas à Becket) tops the evocative **Traitors' Gate,** through which boats once brought the condemned to the Tower.

WHITE TOWER. Many associate the White Tower with the Tower of London. Completed in 1097, it overpowers all the fortifications that were later built around it. The White Tower houses an expansive display from the **Royal Armouries** and a display of **Instruments of Torture.** The **Bell Tower** squats in the southwest corner of the **Inner Ward.** Since the 1190s, this tower has sounded the curfew bell each night. Henry III lived in the adjacent **Wakefield Tower,** the 2nd largest in the complex.

CROWN JEWELS. For many, a visit to the Tower climaxes with a glimpse of the Crown Jewels. The queue at the **Jewel House** is a miracle of crowd management. Tourists file past room after room of rope barriers while video projections on the walls show larger-than-life depictions of the jewels in action, including footage of Elizabeth II's coronation. Finally, the crowd is ushered into the vault and onto moving walkways that whisk them past the dazzling crowns and insure no awestruck gazers hold up the queue. Cromwell melted down much of the original booty; most now dates from after Charles II's restoration in 1660. The **Imperial State Crown** and the **Sceptre with the Cross** feature the Stars of Africa, cut from the Cullinan Diamond. Scotland Yard mailed the stone third class from the Transvaal in an unmarked brown paper parcel, a scheme they believed was the safest way of getting it to London. **St. Edward's Crown,** made for Charles II in 1661, is only worn during coronation. Look for the **Queen Mother's Crown,** which contains the Koh-I-Noor diamond. Legend claims the diamond brings luck—to women only.

OTHER CITY OF LONDON SIGHTS

TOWER BRIDGE. A granite-and-steel structure reminiscent of a castle with a drawbridge, the bridge is a postcard image of the city. The **Tower Bridge Experience,** an exhibition nearly as technologically elaborate as the bridge itself, explains the bridge's genesis through the eyes of its designers in cute but expensive 75-minute tours. The view from the upper level, hampered by steel bars, is far less panoramic than it seems from below. (☎ 7403 3761. *Experience open Apr.-Oct. daily 10am-6:30pm; Nov.-Mar. 9:30am-6pm. Last entry 1¼hr. before closing. £6.25, concessions £4.25.)*

BANK OF ENGLAND. The massive windowless walls and forbidding doors of England's main bank enclose four full acres. The present building dates from 1925, but the 8 ft. thick outer wall is the same one built by eccentric architect Sir John Soane in 1788. The only part open to the public is the plush **Bank of England Museum** (see p. 131). Its neighbors, the Greek-columned **Royal Exchange,** the **Stock Exchange,** and the Lloyd's financial building (see below), stand as relics of the days when this block stood as the financial capital of the world. *(Tube: Bank.)*

MONUMENT. Before even the most basic rebuilding of the city, Wren designed a tall Doric pillar. Completed in 1677, the simply-named structure lies at the bottom of Monument St. Supposedly, the 202 ft. pillar stands exactly that many feet from where the Great Fire broke out in Pudding Ln. on September 2, 1666, and "rushed devastating through every quarter with astonishing swiftness and worse." If you have the resolve to climb its 311 steps, the column rewards you with an expansive view of London. Upon descending the tower, you'll be given a certificate announcing your feat, signed by the City Secretary. *(Fish Street Hill. Tube: Monument. Open Apr.-Sept. daily 10am-6pm. £1.50, children 50p.)*

LONDON BRIDGE. Spanning the river near the Monument, the current London Bridge succeeds a number of ancestors. The famed version crowded with houses stood from 1176 until it burned in 1758. The most recent predecessor didn't fall down; in 1973 it was sold to an American millionaire for £1.03 million and shipped, block by block, to Lake Havasu City, Arizona.

LLOYD'S. This 1986 building supplies the most startling architectural clash in the City. The ducts, lifts, and chutes of Lloyd's are straight out of the 21st century. As one commentator put it, it is not so much a building as a vertical street. This futuristic setting houses the Lutine Bell, which is still occasionally rung—once for bad insurance news, twice for good. *(Off Leadenhall St. Tube: Monument.)*

BARBICAN CENTRE. Housing some of England's greatest cultural treasures, the Barbican is a maze of apartment buildings, restaurants, gardens, and exhibition halls, described at its 1982 opening as "the City's gift to the nation." The Royal Shakespeare Company, the London Symphony Orchestra, the Museum of London, the Guildhall School for Music and Drama, and the Barbican Art Gallery call this complex home, as do the many politicians and actors who reside in the Barbican's distinctive apartment buildings. *(Tube: Barbican or Moorgate. Library open M and W-F 9:30am-5:30pm, Tu 9:30am-7:30pm, Sa 9:30am-12:30pm.)*

SMITHFIELD MARKET. If you want to visit this ancient meat and poultry market, you'd better be up early or up late: it finishes by noon. Smithfield is really more of a wholesalers' market, but individual customers are usually welcome. Smithfield, or "smoothfield," was the sight of many executions, including those of Scotsman William Wallace (of *Braveheart* fame) and peasant's revolt leader Wat Tyler. It was also one of tolerant Queen Mary's most favorite Protestant-burning sites.

CHURCHES. St. Mary-le-Bow Cheapside, Bow Ln., is a Wren creation, and home to the famous bells of the medieval nursery rhyme, Oranges and Lemons: "I do not know, says the Great Bell of Bow." The range of the Bow bells' toll is supposed to define the extent of true-blue Cockney London. *(Tube: Mansion House. ☎ 7246 5139. Open M-F 6:30am-6pm.)* In order to reach **St. Bartholomew the Great,** exit the Barbican Tube on Long Ln., and turn right on West Smithfield to Little Britain. Enter through a narrow Tudor house to reach this architectural jewel. Parts of the church date from 1123, although 800 years of alteration have much embellished it. *(☎ 7606 5171. Open M-F 8:30am-5pm, Sa 10:30am-1:30pm, Su 8am-1pm and 2-8pm. Closed M in Aug.)* Pepys witnessed the spread of the Great Fire from atop **All Hallows by the Tower,** at the end of Great Tower St. The back of the church's bookshop is an arch from a 7th-century Saxon structure, discovered in 1960. To the left, the baptistry contains a striking wood font cover by Grinling Gibbons. *(Tube: Monument. ☎ 7481 2928. Open daily 9am-6pm.)* Behind Mansion House, the imposing home of the Lord Mayor, stands the elegant **St. Stephen Walbrook,** Walbrook St. Arguably Wren's finest, and his personal favorite, the church combines four styles: the old-fashioned English church with nave and chancel, the Puritan hall church, which lacks any separation between priest and congregation, the Greek Cross, and the domed church, a study for St. Paul's. *(Tube: Mansion House. ☎ 7283 4444. Open M-Th 9am-4pm, F 9am-3pm.)*

HOLBORN AND THE INNS OF COURT

Home to grey buildings and grey flannel, the Holborn area has traditionally been the stomping ground of the legal profession. The historical center of English law lies in an area straddling the precincts of Westminster and the City and surrounding long and litigious precincts of **High Holborn, Chancery Lane,** and **Fleet Street.**

ROYAL COURTS OF JUSTICE. At the Strand entrance there are a helpful set of displays explaining the court system. Security is tight, and the metal detectors are highly sensitive. You can trace the history of the wig in the legal costume exhibit on the first floor. In the Great Hall, you stand upon the largest mosaic floor in Europe. *(Tube: Temple.* ☎ *7947 6000. Courts and galleries open to the public M-F 9am-6pm, last entrance 4:30pm. Court cases start at 10-10:30am, but break for lunch 1-2pm.)*

THE INNS OF COURT. Barristers in the City are affiliated with one of the famous Inns of Court (Middle Temple, Inner Temple, Lincoln's Inn, and Gray's Inn), four ancient legal institutions that provide lectures and apprenticeships for law students and regulate admission to the bar. Today, students may seek their legal training outside of the inns, but to be considered for membership they must "keep term" by dining regularly in one of the halls. *(Most inns are closed to visitors; take the "Legal London" walking tour (☎ 7624 3978), or spend 4 years in law school. 2hr. tours leave M 2pm, W 11am, and F 2pm from Holborn tube. Students £3.50.)*

TEMPLE. South of Fleet St., this labyrinthine structure encloses the prestigious and stately Middle and Inner Temple Inns. They derive their name from the clandestine, Crusading Order of the Knights Templar, who embraced this site as their English seat in the 12th century. *(Tube: Temple.)*

TEMPLE CHURCH. Held in common by both the Middle and Inner Temples, the Temple Church is formed from an older round church (AD 1185) and a newer addition of a rectangular nave (AD 1240). The older portion is the finest of the few round churches left in England, with stained-glass windows, a handsome 12th-century Norman doorway, an altar screen by Wren (1682), and 10 arresting, armor-clad stone effigies of sinister Knights Templar dating from the 12th-14th centuries.

MIDDLE TEMPLE. According to Shakespeare's *Henry VI*, the red and white roses that served as emblems throughout the War of the Roses were plucked from the Middle Temple Garden. On Groundhog Day, 1601, Shakespeare himself starred in a performance of *Twelfth Night* in Middle Temple Hall, an Elizabethan dining room on Middle Temple Lane, just past Brick Ct. *(Closed to the public.)* A large wooden dining table is said to be made from the hatch of Sir Francis Drake's *Golden Hinde.* Nearby, London's last functioning gas lamps illuminate the lane. *(Gardens open May-Sept. M-F noon-3pm.)*

LINCOLN'S INN FIELDS AND ENVIRONS. London's largest square stands to the north of the Law Courts. On its north side is found **Sir John Soane's Museum;** it's the house bedecked with sculptures amidst a row of plain buildings (see p. 133). **New Square** and its cloistered churchyard (to the right as you enter from Lincoln's Inn Fields) appear today much as they did in the 1680s. The **Old Hall,** east of New Sq., dates from 1492; here the Lord High Chancellor presided over the High Court of Chancery from 1733 to 1873. Dickens knew well what he described, having worked as a lawyer's clerk in New Court just across the yard. **Lincoln's Inn,** back across Fleet St., on the other side of the Royal Courts, was the only inn to emerge unscathed from the Blitz. *(Tube: Holborn.)*

GRAY'S INN. Dubbed "that stronghold of melancholy" by Dickens, and reduced to ashes by German bombers in 1941, Gray's Inn was restored during the 1950s. The Hall, to your right past the archway, retains its original stained glass (1580) and most of its ornate screen. Francis Bacon maintained chambers here from 1577 until his death in 1626, and is the purported designer of the gardens. *(The northern end of Fulwood Pl., off High Holborn. Tube: Chancery Ln. Open M-F noon-2:30pm.)*

FLEET STREET AND THE STRAND

Named for the one-time river (now a sewer) that flows from Hampstead to the Thames, **Fleet Street** was until recently the hub of British journalism. Nowadays, Fleet St. is just a celebrated name and a few (vacated) famous buildings. Following a standoff with the printing unions in 1986, *The Times*, under the command of infamous media mogul Rupert Murdoch, moved to cheaper land at Wapping, Docklands, initiating a mass exodus. When looking for addresses of the following sights, beware that Fleet St. is numbered up one side and down the other. *(Tube: Blackfriars or St. Paul's.)* As Fleet St. runs from Holburn toward Covent Garden it changes its name to **the Strand** a third of the way there. As host to two major London universities, it is a center of education, as well as being home to the original **Twining's Tea Shop** (see p. 136)—not only the oldest business in the UK on its original premises, but also London's narrowest shop. *(Tube: Charing Cross or Temple.)*

ST. BRIDE'S. The tiered spire of Wren's 1675 church, near 89 Fleet St., became the inspiration for countless wedding cakes thanks to an ingenious local baker. Dubbed "the printers' cathedral" because the first printing press with moveable type was housed here in 1500, it has long had a connection with newspapermen. Next to St. Bride's stands **Reuters,** one of the last remaining media powerhouses left on Fleet St. *(Open M-F 8am-6pm, Sa 9am-5pm.)*

SAMUEL JOHNSON'S HOUSE. Samuel Johnson, a self-described "shrine to the English language," lived in this abode from 1748 to 1759. Here he completed his Dictionary, the first definitive English lexicon. He compiled this amazing document by reading all the great books of the age and marking the words he wanted included in the dictionary with black pen. The books he used were unreadable by the project's end. *(17 Gough Sq.; an alley leads to the square from opposite #54 Fleet St. ☎ 7353 3745. Open May-Sept. M-Sa 11am-5:30pm; Oct.-Apr. M-Sa 11am-5pm. Guided tours available for groups by reservation; day tours £2 per person; evening tours (after closing) £3, with coffee £5, with wine £6. House also available for private functions; call for details. £4, students and seniors £3, children £1, families £9. Audio tour 50p.)*

SOMERSET HOUSE. A magnificent 1776 Palladian structure built by Sir William Chambers, the house stands on the former site of the palace where Elizabeth I resided during the reign of her sister Bloody Mary. Once the administrative center of the Royal Navy, the building now houses the exquisite **Courtauld Gallery** of Impressionist paintings (see p. 132) and provides impressive views of the Thames.

ST. CLEMENT DANES. Further down the Strand stands this handsome church, whose melodious bells get their 15 seconds of fame in the nursery rhyme "Oranges and lemons, say the bells of St. Clement's." Children get their 15 minutes of fruit when oranges and lemons are distributed in a ceremony near the end of March. Designed by Wren in 1682, the church was built over the ruins of an older Norman structure reputed to be the tomb of Harold Harefoot, leader of a colony of Danes who settled the area in the 9th century. Today it is the official church of the Royal Air Force. *(Tube: Charing Cross. ☎ 7242 8282. Open daily 8am-5pm.)*

STRAND UNIVERSITIES. As you stroll away from the Courts of Justice on Houghton St., two of London's top educational institutions come into view. The first, **King's College,** is an unremarkable concrete building. Straight across the road stands the prestigious **London School of Economics and Political Science** (LSE), the setting for feisty student radicalism in the 1960s and now Tony Blair's favorite source of political ideas.

WIG AND PEN CLUB. The only Strand building to survive the Great Fire stands at 229-230 the Strand. Constructed over Roman ruins in 1625, the club is frequented by the best-known barristers and journalists in London. The club is open to members only, though an overseas traveler dressed in a coat and tie may be able to peek upstairs. If you have the nerve, walk up the ancient, crooked staircase—the only remnant of the original 17th-century house—and take note of the photo of

Prince Charles dining at the club, as well as signed photos of US Presidents Nixon, Reagan, and Bush. Beware—the doorman will reject underdressed travelers. *(Members only upstairs, pricey restaurant open to the public. Open M-Sa 11am-11pm.)*

EMBANKMENT. To the south of the Temple Bar, The Embankment runs along the Thames, parallel to The Strand. The first person to suggest a river embankment green was Sir Christopher Wren after the fire of 1666. The **Victoria Embankment Gardens** sit next to the Embankment tube station. *(☎ 7641 5264. Open 7:30am-dusk.)* Between the Hungerford and Waterloo Bridges stands London's oldest (though not indigenous) landmark, **Cleopatra's Needle,** an Egyptian obelisk from 1450 BC, stolen by the Viceroy of Egypt in 1878. A sister stone stands in Central Park in New York. *(Tube: Charing Cross or Embankment.)*

CHARING CROSS. The original Charing Cross, the last of 13 crosses set up to mark the stages of Queen Eleanor's royal funeral procession in 1291 ("charing" is a corruption of *chère reine,* French for "beloved queen"), was originally located at the top of Whitehall, immediately south of Trafalgar Square. Like many things, it was destroyed by Cromwell, and a replica now stands outside Charing Cross Station. "Fleet Street has a very animated appearance," Samuel Johnson once remarked, "but I think the full tide of human existence is at Charing Cross."

COVENT GARDEN AND SOHO

COVENT GARDEN

The outdoor cafes, upscale shops, and slick crowds animating Covent Garden today belie the square's medieval beginnings as a literal "convent garden" where the monks of Westminster Abbey grew their vegetables. Today, Covent Garden is filled with street performers and lots of pubs, cafes, and trendy shops.

THE THEATRE ROYAL AND THE ROYAL OPERA HOUSE. These venerable venues represent a long tradition of theater in the Covent Garden area. For ticketing info, see **Theater,** p. 137. *(Drury Ln. Tube: Covent Garden. ☎ 7494 5091. Box office open M-Sa 10am-8pm. Tours offered M-Tu, Th, F, and Su 12:30pm, 2:15pm, 4:45pm; W and Sa 11am and 1pm. £7.50, children £5.50.)* The **Royal Opera House** began as a theater for concerts and plays in 1732 and currently houses the Royal Opera and Royal Ballet. For performance details, see **Classical Music,** p. 138. *(Bow St. Tube: Covent Garden. ☎ 7304 4000. Open M-Sa 10am-3pm, box office open M-Sa 10am-8pm. Guided tours £3.)*

ST. PAUL'S CHURCH. Not to be confused with St. Paul's Cathedral, this Inigo Jones church now stands as the sole remnant of the original Covent Garden piazza, although the interior had to be rebuilt after a 1795 fire. Known as "the actor's church," St. Paul's is filled with plaques commemorating the achievements of Boris Karloff, Vivien Leigh, Noel Coward, and Tony Simpson ("inspired player of small parts"), among others. *(Covent Garden Piazza. Tube: Covent Garden. Open M 10am-2:30pm, Tu 9am-4pm, W 9:30am-4pm, Th 8:30am-4pm, F 9:30am-4pm, Su 9am-12:30pm. Frequent weekday concerts 1:30pm. Evensong 2nd Su of the month, 4pm.)*

OTHER COVENT GARDEN SIGHTS. Curious stage design shops cluster near the Opera House, and moss-covered artisans' studios, interspersed with an odd assortment of theater-related businesses, stud the surrounding streets. Rose St. leads to the **Lamb and Flag** (see **Pubs and Bars,** p. 140), supposedly the only timber building left in the West End. At the northern end of St. Martin's Lane, six streets converge at the **Seven Dials** monument; the 7th dial is the monument itself, a sundial.

SOHO

Soho takes its name from a 17th-century hunting cry, although it's hard to fathom, considering the narrow streets and distinct lack of open space that make up the area today, that this was ever a hunting ground. Loosely bounded by Oxford St. to the north, Shaftesbury Ave. to the south, Charing Cross Rd. to the east, and Regent St. to the west, Soho is a vibrant, cheerfully dirty area with streets lined by cafes and classic pubs. Many Londoners agree that some of the city's best eats (espe-

Hmm, call home or eat lunch?
With  ^{SM}
you can do both.

Nathan Lane for YOU^{SM}.

No doubt, traveling on a budget is tough. So tear out this wallet guide and keep it with you during your travels. With YOU, calling home from overseas is affordable and easy.

If the wallet guide is missing, call collect 913-624-5336 or visit www.youcallhome.com for YOU country numbers.

Dialing instructions:
Need help with access numbers while overseas? Call collect, 913-624-5336.

Dial the access number for the country you're in.
Dial 04 or follow the English prompts.
Enter your credit card information to place your call.

Country	Access Number	Country	Access Number	Country	Access Number
Australia **v**	1-800-551-110	Israel **v**	1-800-949-4102	Spain **v**	900-99-0013
Bahamas **+**	1-800-389-2111	Italy **+ v**	172-1877	Switzerland **v**	0800-899-777
Brazil **v**	000-8016	Japan **+ v**	00539-131	Taiwan **v**	0080-14-0877
China **+ ▲ v**	108-13	Mexico **u v**	001-800-877-8000	United Kingdom **v**	0800-890-877
France **v**	0800-99-0087	Netherlands **+ v**	0800-022-9119		
Germany **+ v**	0800-888-0013	New Zealand **▲ v**	000-999		
Hong Kong **v**	800-96-1877	Philippines **T v**	105-16		
India **v**	000-137	Singapore **v**	8000-177-177		
Ireland **v**	1-800-552-001	South Korea **+ v**	00729-16		

Service provided by Sprint

v Call answered by automated Voice Response Unit.   **+** Public phones may require coin or card.
▲ May not be available from all payphones.   **u** Use phones marked with "LADATEL"and no coin or card is required.
T If talk button is available, push it before talking.

Pack the Wallet Guide
and save 25% or more* on calls home to the U.S.

It's lightweight and carries heavy savings of 25% or more*
over AT&T USA Direct and MCI WorldPhone rates. So take this
YOU wallet guide and carry it wherever you go.

To save with YOU:
- Dial the access number of the country you're in (see reverse)
- Dial 04 or follow the English voice prompts
- Enter your credit card info for easy billing

Service provided by Sprint

cially for budgeteers) are to be found here. The area has acquired a significant and visible gay presence; a concentration of gay-owned restaurants and bars has turned **Old Compton Street** into the heart of gay London.

Soho also has a rich literary past: William Blake and Daniel Defoe lived on **Broadwick Street,** and Thomas de Quincey *(Confessions of an English Opium Eater)* did dope in his houses on **Greek Street** and **Tavistock Street.** To the north, a blue plaque at **28 Dean Street** locates the two-room flat where the impoverished Karl Marx lived with his wife, maid, and five children while writing *Das Kapital. Kapital,* however, has almost made Soho too stylish for its own good.

CARNABY STREET. In the 1960s, Carnaby St. was at the heart of Swingin' London. A few denizens (like **Luderwicks,** the oldest pipe-makers in London), have weathered storms of fads and tourists alike, and some newer labels have opened branches. Fashionistas will probably find more interesting diversions in nearby **Foubert's Place.** *(Parallel to Regent St. Tube: Oxford Circus.)*

ST. ANNE'S CHURCH. Only Wren's 1685 tower and the ungainly steeple added by Cockerell in 1803 emerged unscathed from the Blitz; for long timed eerily ruined, a new building was constructed around it in 1991. *(Wardour St. ☎ 7437 5006. Gardens open M-Sa 8am-dusk, Su 9am-dusk.)*

LEICESTER SQUARE. Amusements at this entertainment nexus range from mammoth cinemas, including London's two largest, the **Odeon Leicester Square** and the **Empire** (see **Film,** p. 138) to free performances provided by street entertainers, to the portraitists crowded around the Swiss Centre offering to sketch pictures for more than a few pounds. On the south side, a long queue marks the **Half-Price Ticket Booth;** see **Theater,** p. 137. *(Tube: Leicester Sq.)*

CHINATOWN. Cantonese immigrants first arrived in Britain as cooks on British ships, and London's first Chinese community formed around the docks near Limehouse, in the East End. The area around **Gerrard Street** swelled with immigrants from Hong Kong in the 1950s, becoming the heart of Chinatown. Chinatown is most vibrant during the year's two major festivals: the **Mid-Autumn Festival** at the end of September, and the raucous **Chinese New Year Festival** in February. *(Gerrard St. and Lisle St. form the heart of Chinatown. Tube: Leicester Sq.)*

PICCADILLY AND MAYFAIR

PICCADILLY

PICCADILLY CIRCUS. Five of the West End's major arteries (Piccadilly, Regent St., Shaftesbury Ave., and the Haymarket) merge and swirl around Piccadilly Circus, and at times it seems as though the entire tourist population of London has decided to bask in the lurid neon signs. The central focus of the Circus is the statue of **Eros,** by Lord Shaftesbury; Eros originally pointed his bow and arrow down Shaftesbury Avenue, but recent restoration work has put his aim significantly off. Once ground zero for Victorian popular entertainment, today only the **Criterion Theatre** survives amidst the grand facades of former music halls.

MADAME TUSSAUD'S ROCK CIRCUS. Wax versions of rock stars through the ages, from Elvis to the Beatles to Robbie Williams, plus their handprints, other rock memorabilia, and a creepy "cemetery" commemorating rock's dearly departed. *(London Pavilion, 1 Piccadilly Circus. ☎ (0870) 400 3030. Open Mar.-Aug. Su-M and W-Th 10am-8pm, Tu 11am-8pm, F-Sa 10am-9pm; Sept.-Feb. Su-M and W-Th 10am-5:30pm, Tu 11am-5:30pm, F-Sa 10am-9pm. £8.25, students and seniors £7.25, children £6.25.)*

BURLINGTON HOUSE. One of the remnants of Piccadilly's stately past is this showy mansion, built in 1665 for the Earls of Burlington and redesigned in the 18th century by Colin Campbell to accommodate the burgeoning **Royal Academy of Arts** (see p. 133). Founded in 1768, the Academy comprises 50 academicians and 30 associates who administer exhibitions, galleries, and a massive annual summer show. *(Piccadilly, opposite Fortnum and Mason. ☎ 7300 5959.)*

THE ALBANY. An easily overlooked courtyard next to the Academy opens this 18th-century apartment block renowned as one of London's most prestigious addresses. Built in 1771 and remodeled in 1812, the Albany evolved into an exclusive enclave of literary repute. Lord Byron wrote his epic "Childe Harold" here. Other past residents include Macaulay, Gladstone, Canning, "Monk" Lewis, and J.B. Priestley. *(Albany Court Yard, off Piccadilly next to the Royal Academy.)*

REGENT STREET. Running from Piccadilly Circus to Oxford Circus are the grand facades of (upper) Regent St. John Nash designed the street and its buildings in the early 19th century as part of a processional route for the Prince Regent to his house in Regent's Park. Regent St. has evolved since Nash's time, although **Liberty's** (see **Shopping**, p. 133) makes a false claim to age with a mock-Tudor facade. Today the street has everything from the crisp cuts of Burberry raincoats to the Continental slickness of Zara trousers; those with kids will find it hard to resist the Pied Piper of **Hamley's,** London's largest toy store (see p. 136).

MAYFAIR

Mayfair takes its name from the 17th-century May Fair held on Shepherd's Market near Green Park. While the fair was famously raucous, modern Mayfair is blue-blooded to the core. After all, how many other parts of central London have proper mansions? In the 18th and 19th centuries, the aristocracy kept houses in Mayfair where they lived during "The Season" (winter was the time for opera and balls in the city), retiring to their country estates in the summer. The reigning Queen was born in a house at 17 Bruton St., although that has since been demolished.

SOTHEBY'S. This world-famous auction house displays everything in its honeycomb of galleries. While the 257-year-old institution may seem daunting, they're really quite welcoming, and you can spend a delightful hour perusing the collections that you can't afford (bids for some rare items may start at £1 million). Even though there's no official dress code, you might want to dress smartly to avoid feeling self-conscious. *(34-35 New Bond St. Tube: Bond St. ☎ 7293 5000; www.sothebys.com. Open for viewing M-F 9am-4:30pm, and some Su noon-4pm.)*

GROSVENOR SQUARE. Running west off Bond St., Grosvenor St. ends at Grosvenor Square, one of the largest in central London. The square, occasionally called "little America," has gradually evolved into a US military and political enclave since future American President John Adams lived at #9 while serving as the first American ambassador to England in 1785. Almost two centuries later, General Eisenhower established his wartime headquarters at #20, and memory of his stay persists in the area's postwar nickname, "Eisenhowerplatz."

SHOPPING. Bond St., the traditional address for the oldest and most prestigious shops, art dealers, auction houses, and hair salons in the city, is divided into Old and New. Not surprisingly—in this historically snobby part of London—**Old Bond St.** is the locale of choice for the area's most expensive shops. Alongside these Continental extravagances, long-established homegrown shops, many sporting crests indicating royal patronage, sell everything from handmade shotguns to emerald tiaras to *objets d'art*. On the eastern side of Mayfair, running parallel to New Bond St., runs **Savile Row,** where you can window-shop for the finest in men's threads. The name is synonymous with the elegant and expensive "bespoke" tailoring that has prospered here for centuries.

THE MALL AND ST. JAMES'S

BUCKINGHAM PALACE

I must say, notwithstanding the expense which has been incurred in building the palace, no sovereign in Europe, I may even add, perhaps no private gentleman, is so ill-lodged as the king of this country.
—Duke of Wellington, 1828

Buckingham Palace Rd. Tube: Victoria, Green Park, or St. James's Park. ☎ 7839 1377, recorded info ☎ 7799 2331; www.royal.gov.uk. For tickets before opening dates call ☎ 7321 2233. Open daily Aug.-Sept. 9:30am-4:30pm. £10.50, seniors £8, under 17 £5.

When a freshly crowned Victoria moved from St. James's Palace in 1837, Buckingham Palace, built in 1825 by John Nash, had faulty drains and a host of other difficulties. Improvements were made, and now the monarch calls it home. The 20th-century facade on the Mall is only big, not beautiful—the Palace's best side, the garden front, is seldom seen by ordinary visitors as it is protected by the 40-acre spread where the Queen holds garden parties.

Visitors are allowed in the **Blue Drawing Room,** the **Throne Room,** the **Picture Gallery** (filled with pictures by Rubens, Rembrandt, and Van Dyck), and the **Music Room** (where Mendelsohn played for Queen Victoria), as well as other stately rooms. In the opulent **White Room,** the large mirror fireplace conceals a door used by the Royal Family at formal dinners.

CHANGING OF THE GUARD. Though public support for the royal family has waned considerably in the past years, tourist enthusiasm for the bearskin-capped guards has not. From April to June, the ceremony takes place daily; during the rest of the year, it occurs on odd-numbered dates. The "Old Guard" marches from St. James's Palace down the Mall to Buckingham Palace, leaving at approximately 11:10am. The "New Guard" begins marching as early as 10:20am. When they meet at the central gates of the palace, the officers of the regiments then touch hands, symbolically exchanging keys, *et voilà*, the guard is officially changed. The soldiers gradually split up to relieve the guards currently protecting the palace. The ceremony moves to the beat of royal band music and the menacing clicks of thousands of cameras. In wet weather or on pressing state holidays, the Changing of the Guard does not occur. To witness the spectacle, show up well before 11:30am and stand directly in front of the palace. You can also watch along the routes of the troops prior to their arrival at the palace (10:40-11:25am) between the Victoria Memorial and St. James's Palace or along Birdcage Walk.

OTHER MALL AND ST. JAMES'S SIGHTS

ST. JAMES'S PALACE. A residence of the monarchy from 1660 to 1668 and again from 1715 to 1837, this palace has hosted tens of thousands of the young girls whose families "presented" them at Court. Ambassadors and the elite set of barristers known as "Queen's Counsel" are still received into the Court of St. James's. Today, **Prince Charles** inhabits St. James's, and his grandmother, the **Queen Mum,** bunks next door at Clarence House. The palace is closed to the public, except for Inigo Jones's **Queen's Chapel,** built in 1626, which is open for Sunday services from October to Good Friday at 8:30am and 11am. *(Just north of Buckingham Palace and the Mall, up Stable Yard or Marlborough Rd. Tube: Green Park.)*

ST. JAMES'S PARK. Henry VIII declared this London's first royal park in 1532. **Duck Island,** the fenced-off peninsula at the east end of the pond, is the mating ground for thousands of waterfowl. St. James's is also a good place to discover that lawn chairs in England are not free—chairs have been hired out here since the 18th century. Don't find the attendants; sit and they'll find you. *(Chairs £1 per 4hr.)*

POLITICAL AND LITERARY CLUBS. The Regency storefronts of Jermyn St. rub elbows with a number of famous London clubs. The coffeehouses of the early 18th century, whose political life was painted vividly by Addison and Steele in *The Spectator*, were transformed into exclusive clubs for political and literary men of a particular social station. The chief Tory club, the **Carlton,** 69 St. James's St., was bombed by the IRA not long ago. The chief Liberal club, the **Reform,** 104 Pall Mall, served as a social center of Parliamentary power. In 1823, a prime minister and the presidents of the Royal Academy and the Royal Society founded the **Athenaeum,** on Waterloo Pl., for scientific, literary, and artistic men. Gibbon, Hume, and Garrick belonged to the **Whig Brooks,** 60 St. James's St., founded in 1764.

CHRISTIE'S. The full name is Christie, Manson, and Wodds Fine Art Auctioneers, but even they call themselves Christie's. The galleries display furniture, historical documents, and artwork. Auctions, open to the public, are held at 10:30am or 2:30pm. Don't cough. *(8 King St., off St. James's St. Tube: Green Park. ☎ 7839 9060; www.christies.com. Open M-F 9am-4:30pm; during sales also open Tu 4:30-8pm and Su 2-5pm.)*

TRAFALGAR SQUARE. Unlike many squares in London, Trafalgar Square, which slopes down from the **National Gallery** (see p. 129) into the center of a vicious traffic roundabout, has been public land ever since the razing of several hundred houses made way for its construction in the 1830s. The fluted granite pillar of **Nelson's Column** commands the square, with four majestic, beloved lions guarding the base. The monument and square commemorate Admiral Horatio Nelson, killed during his triumph over Napoleon's navy off Trafalgar—the monument's reliefs were cast from French cannons. *(Tube: Charing Cross.)*

ST. MARTIN-IN-THE-FIELDS. Designer James Gibbs topped the templar classicism of this 18th-century church with a Gothic steeple. The **crypt** has been cleared of all those dreary coffins to make room for a gallery, a book shop, a brass rubbing center, and a cafe. *(Trafalgar Sq. ☎ 7930 0089. Free concerts M-Tu and F 1:05pm. Reserve seats for evening concerts online; by phone M-F 10am-4pm ☎ 7839 8362; or in the bookstore, open M-W 10am-6pm and Th-Sa 10am-7:30pm. Cafe open M-Sa 10am-8pm, Su noon-6pm.)*

WHITEHALL

Whitehall, which stretches from Parliament to Trafalgar Sq., has become the home of and a synonym for the British civil service. Whitehall was originally a residence for the Archbishops of York. Henry VIII later took up residence here in 1530.

10 DOWNING STREET. Conveniently enough, the Prime Minister's headquarters lies just steps up Parliament St. from the Houses of Parliament. Sir George Downing, ex-Ambassador to the Hague, built this house in 1681, and Prime Minister Sir Robert Walpole made it his official residence in 1732. The Chancellor of the Exchequer traditionally resides at #11, and the Chief Whip at #12; however, Tony Blair's family is too big for 10 Downing St., so he's moved to #11. Visitors have long been barred from entering Downing St. by gates and bobbies. *(Tube: Westminster.)*

NEW SCOTLAND YARD. The headquarters of the Metropolitan Police will probably fall short of crime-hounds' expectations. The second of three incarnations of the lair of those unimaginative detectives (fictionally humbled by Sherlock Holmes and Hercule Poirot) is no more than two buildings, connected by an arch and containing government offices. *(6 Derby Gate, just off Whitehall. Tube: Westminster.)*

MINISTRY OF DEFENCE BUILDING. In 1953, the government erected this massive structure (the largest office building in London at the time) over Henry's VIII's wine cellar. Technically, visitors may view the cellar, but permission is dauntingly difficult to obtain (apply in writing to the Department of the Environment or the Ministry of Defence with a compelling story). Near the statue of General Gordon in the gardens behind the Ministry of Defence Building, you'll find the remnants of **Queen Mary's terrace,** built for Queen Mary II. *(Tube: Westminster.)*

BANQUETING HOUSE. This 1622 house is one of the few intact masterpieces by Inigo Jones. James I and Charles I held feasts and staged elaborate masques (thinly-disguised pieces of theatrical propaganda) in the main hall. Charles commissioned the 18m ceiling; the scenes Rubens painted are allegorical representations of the divine strength of James I. The party ended on January 27, 1649, when Charles, draped in black velvet, stepped out of a ground-floor window to the scaffold where he was beheaded. From 1724 to 1890, the Banqueting House served as a Chapel Royal. These days the hall serves state dinners and the occasional concert, not death warrants. *(At the corner of Horse Guards Ave. and Whitehall, opposite Horse Guards Hall. Tube: Westminster. ☎ 7930 4179. Open M-Sa 10am-5pm, last admission 4:30pm. Closed for government functions. £3.80, students and seniors £3, children £2.30.)*

OTHER SIGHTS. At the end of King Charles St., near Horse Guards Rd., lurk the **Cabinet War Rooms,** where a protected Winston Churchill directed operations near the end of World War II. The rooms are now a museum (see p. 131). The formal **Cenotaph,** which honors the war dead, is usually decked with wreaths, and stands where Parliament St. turns into Whitehall. *(Tube: Westminster.)*

WESTMINSTER

WESTMINSTER ABBEY

Parliament Sq. Tube: Westminster or St. James's Park. ☎ 7222 5152; www.westminster-abbey.org. "Supertours" include admission to Abbey and all sights inside (bookings ☎ 7222 7110), offered M-F 10am, 11am, and 2pm, M-Th also 3pm, Sa 10am, 11am, and 12:30pm; Apr.-Oct. also M-F 10:30am and 2:30pm. £10. Audio tour £3. Open M-F 9am-4:45pm, Sa 9am-2:45pm; last admission 1hr. before close. Closes for special events. £5, students and UK seniors £3, ages 11-16 £2, families £10.

The site of every royal coronation since 1066, Westminster Abbey's significance is secular as well as sacred. Controlled by the Crown and not the Church of England, the Abbey is the temple of England's civic religion. Only the Pyx Chamber and the Norman Undercroft (now the Westminster Abbey Undercroft Museum) survive from the original structure, which was consecrated by King Edward the Confessor on December 28, 1065. Most of the present Abbey was erected under Henry III in the 13th century, and the post-1850 North Entrance is the latest addition.

STATESMEN'S AISLE. The north transept is full of memorials to important figures. Prime Ministers Disraeli and Gladstone could not stand each other in life, but in death their figures sit close together. On the left is the tomb of Sir Francis Vere, a 16th-century army commander. In front of his tomb is the imposing monument to James Wolfe, who secured British supremacy in Canada.

SHRINE OF ST. EDWARD AND LADY CHAPEL. Kings' tombs surround the **Shrine of St. Edward,** and following these tombs leads to the **Lady Chapel.** The exquisite ceiling was hand-carved in chunks of stone and set in place after the chapel was erected. Every one of its magnificently carved stalls, reserved for the Knights of the Order of the Bath, features a colorful headpiece bearing the chosen personal statement of its occupant. The chapel walls display representations of 95 saints. Henry VII and his wife Elizabeth lie at the end of the chapel, and nearby is the stone that once marked Cromwell's grave. Protestant Queen Elizabeth I and the Catholic cousin she ordered beheaded, Mary Queen of Scots, are buried on opposite sides of the Henry VII chapel (in the north and south aisles, respectively).

CORONATION CHAIR. At the exit of the Lady Chapel stands the Coronation Chair, which used to rest on the Stone of Scone (see **Stoned,** p. 118). Used in the coronation of ancient Scottish kings, it was taken to London by James I, who was King of Scotland when he inherited the English crown. During World War II, it was hidden from possible German capture—rumor has it that only Churchill, Roosevelt, the Canadian Prime Minister, and the two workers who moved it knew its whereabouts. The chair sits by the 7 ft. State Sword and the shield of Edward III.

CHAPEL. A number of monarchs are interred here, from Henry III (d. 1272) to George II (d. 1760). Edward I (d. 1307) saw himself as a secret weapon—dead or alive. He had himself placed in an unsealed crypt, in case he was needed to fight the Scots; his mummy was used as a standard by the English army in Scotland. An engraving by William Blake commemorates the moment in 1774 when the Royal Society of Antiquaries opened the coffin to assess the body's state of preservation.

POETS' CORNER. The Poets' Corner celebrates those who have died and been anthologized; note that most of the poets are not actually buried here. It begins with Geoffrey Chaucer, who was originally buried in the Abbey in 1400—the short Gothic tomb you see today in the east wall of the transept was not erected until 1556. A modern stained-glass window includes the name of Oscar Wilde, who was honored in 1995, the centenary of his conviction for sodomy. Floor panels com-

memorate Tennyson, T.S. Eliot, Henry James, Lewis Carroll, Lord Byron, and W.H. Auden, all at Chaucer's feet. Each bears a relevant description or image: for example, D.H. Lawrence's publishing mark (a phoenix) and T.S. Eliot's symbol of death.

SOUTH WALL. The south transept is graced with the graves of Samuel Johnson and actor David Garrick, as well as busts of William Wordsworth, Samuel Taylor Coleridge, and Robert Burns. A full-length representation of Shakespeare overshadows the tiny plaques memorializing the Brontë sisters and the ashes of Sir Laurence Olivier. On the west wall of the transept, Handel's massive memorial looms over his grave next to the resting place of Charles Dickens. On this side of the wall, you'll also find the grave of Rudyard Kipling and a memorial to Thomas Hardy. Among the writers and poets lie two outsiders: Old Parr, who reportedly lived to the age of 152, and "Spot" Ward, who healed George II of a thumb injury.

HIGH ALTAR. The High Altar, between the North and South transepts, has long been the scene of coronations, royal weddings, and funerals. The quire contains elaborately decorated stalls and a 1268 mosaic floor. The Queen's stall is just to the left of the High Altar Screen, marked by the royal coat of arms.

SCIENTISTS' CORNER AND MUSICIANS' AISLE. Scientists' Corner holds a memorial to Sir Isaac Newton, which sits next to the grave of Lord Kelvin. Visitors may be surprised to see Charles Darwin here; thanks to his friends in the clergy and his affirmation of faith before his death, his body is interred in a place of worship. Just before the gate to the north aisle of the nave, Musicians' Aisle contains the Abbey's most accomplished organists, John Blow and Henry Purcell, as well as memorials to Elgar, Britten, Vaughan Williams, and William Walton.

CHAPTER HOUSE AND PYX CHAMBER. The Chapter House, east down a passageway off the cloister, has one of the best-preserved medieval tile floors in Europe. The windows in the ceiling depict scenes from the Abbey's history. The King's Great Council used the room as its chamber in 1257 and the House of Commons used it as a meeting place in the 16th century. Even today, the government, and not the Abbey, administers the Chapter House and the adjacent Pyx Chamber, once the Royal Treasury and now a plate museum. *(Chapter House open Apr.-Oct. 10am-5:30pm, Nov.-Mar. 10am-4pm; last admission 30min. before closing. Pyx Chamber and Abbey Museum open daily 10:30am-4pm; last admission 3:45pm. Hours often depend on the light. All three £2.50, concessions £1.30; with Abbey admission £1.)*

STONED On Christmas Day, 1950, daring Scottish patriot Ian Hamilton—posing as a visitor—hid himself in Westminster Abbey until it closed. He meant to steal the 200kg Stone of Scone and return it to Scotland, but as he approached the door near Poet's Corner to let in his three accomplices, he was detected by a watchman. Hamilton (now a prominent Scottish MP) talked fast enough to convince the watchman that he had been locked in involuntarily.

That same night the foursome forcibly entered the Abbey and pulled the stone out of its wooden container, in the process inadvertently breaking the famed rock into two uneven pieces. Hamilton sent his girlfriend driving off to Scotland with the smaller piece, while he returned to deal with the larger piece. The remaining two accomplices had been instructed to drag the larger piece toward the cars, but when he returned Hamilton found only the stone. He lugged the piece to his car, and, while driving out of London, happened across his wayward accomplices. The stone was repaired in a Glasgow workyard, but the patriots were frustrated that they could not display it in a public place. On April 11, 1951, Hamilton and Company carried the stone to the altar at Arbroath Abbey where it was discovered and returned to England.

The final chapter of the story is that now-deceased Glasgow councilor Bertie Gray claimed, before he died, that the stone was copied and the one residing in the Abbey was a fake. The British authorities dispute his claim.

LIBRARY. The library of Westminster Abbey holds a collection of 14,000 books, most dating from before 1801. Among the exquisite books and manuscripts on display is a house lease dated 1399 and granted to Geoffrey Chaucer by the Abbey. *(Open May-Sept., W only 11am-3pm. Admission with Chapter House ticket.)*

GRAVE OF THE UNKNOWN WARRIOR. Past the cloisters, in the Abbey's narrow nave, the highest in England, a slab of black Belgian marble marks the Grave of the Unknown Warrior. Here the body of a World War I soldier is buried in soil from the battlefields of France, with an oration written in letters made from melted bullets. A piece of green marble engraved with "Remember Winston Churchill" sits nearby, where Parliament placed it 25 years after the Battle of Britain.

EVENSONG. Music lovers can catch Evensong and Organ recitals. Evensong is sung at 5pm M-Tu and Th-F, and at 3pm Sa-Su. Organ recitals are given during the summer on Tuesdays at 6:30pm. *(Reservations ☎ 7222 5152, or write to the Concert Secretary, 20 Dean's Yard, SW1P 3PA. £6, concessions £4.)*

THE HOUSES OF PARLIAMENT

Parliament Sq. Tube: Westminster. Public tours offered early Aug. to mid-Sept. M-Sa 9:30am-4:15pm. Tickets, £3.50, go on sale in mid-June and must be booked in advance from Ticketmaster (☎ 7344 9966; www.ticketmaster.co.uk). For foreign-language tours book 4 weeks ahead. At other times of the year, UK residents should contact their MP or a friendly Lord; tours normally available M-Th 9:30am-noon and F 3:30-5:30pm. Overseas visitors can request tours through the Parliamentary Education Unit, Norman Shaw Building (North), London SW1A 2TT (☎ 7219 3000; edunit@parliament.uk); tours, limited to 16 people, offered only F 3:30-5:30pm, so book faaaaaaaar ahead. Government business may lead to cancellation of tours at any time.

For the classic view of the Houses of Parliament, as captured by Claude Monet, walk about halfway over Westminster Bridge, preferably at dusk. Like the government offices along Whitehall, the Houses of Parliament occupy the former site of a royal palace. Only Jewel Tower (see below) and Westminster Hall (to the left of St. Stephen's entrance on St. Margaret St.) survive from the original building, which was destroyed by a fire in 1834. Sir Charles Barry and A.W.N. Pugin won a competition for the design of the new houses. The immense complex blankets eight acres and includes more than 1000 rooms and 100 staircases. Space is nevertheless so scarce that Members of Parliament (MPs) have neither private offices nor staff, and the archives—the originals of every Act of Parliament passed since 1497—are stuffed into **Victoria Tower,** the large tower to the south. A flag flown from the tower indicates that Parliament is in session.

BIG BEN. Big Ben is not the famous northernmost clock tower but rather the 14-ton bell that tolls the hours. Ben is most likely named after the robustly proportioned Sir Benjamin Hall, who served as Commissioner of Works when the bell was cast and hung in 1858. The familiar 16-note tune that precedes the top-of-the-hour toll is a selection from Handel's *Messiah*. On the clock, still wound manually, 14 ft. minute hands point to Roman numerals 2 ft. long.

HOUSE OF COMMONS' GALLERY. After you sign a form promising not to read, use cameras or opera glasses, or otherwise cause disturbances, the guards will show you to the Chambers of the House of Commons. You can watch MPs at work from the House of Commons Gallery for "Distinguished and Ordinary Strangers". If you don't have an advance booking (see below), arrive early and wait at the public entrance at St. Stephen's gate; keep left (the right-hand queue is for the Lords). Weekdays after 6pm and Fridays are the least crowded; afternoon waits can be as long as two hours. MPs set their own hours, so don't be surprised if everyone's packed up and gone home earlier than expected. Places in the gallery during Prime Minister's Question Time (W 3-3:30pm), when the Prime Minister answers questions from MPs, are particularly hard to obtain. *(☎ 7219 4272. Gallery open M-W 2:30-10:30pm, Th 11:30am-7:30pm, F normally 9:30am to around 3pm. For advance tickets, UK residents should contact their MP; overseas visitors must apply for a Card of Introduction from their Embassy or High Commission in London. Book at least a month in advance. Free.)*

HOUSE OF LORDS' GALLERY. To enter the Lords' Gallery, go through the Central Lobby and pass through the Peers' corridor where the MPs have bedecked the passage with scenes of Charles I's downfall. (☎ 7219 3107. *Keep right in the queue at St. Stephen's entrance. Open M-W from 2:30pm-rise, Th from 3pm, occasionally F 11am. Free.*)

OTHER PARLIAMENTARY SIGHTS. The 14th-century **Jewel Tower,** built for Edward III to store personal treasures, stands by the southeastern end of the Abbey, across from the Houses of Parliament. (☎ 7222 219. *Open daily Apr.-Sept. 9:30am-6pm, last admission 5:30pm; Oct.-Mar. 9:30am-5pm, last admission 4:40pm. £1.50, concessions £1.10.*) **St. Stephen's Hall** is the chapel where the House of Commons used to sit. In the floor are four brass markers where the Speaker's Chair stood. **Old Palace Yard,** outside, hosted the executions of Sir Walter Raleigh and Gunpowder Plot conspirator Guy Fawkes (the palace's cellars are still ceremonially searched before every opening of Parliament).

OTHER WESTMINSTER SIGHTS

ST. MARGARET'S WESTMINSTER. Literally in Westminster Abbey's shadow, St. Margaret's is the church that tourists point to and ask "Is that the Abbey?" St. Margaret's has served as the church of the House of Commons since 1614, when Protestant MPs feared the Abbey would become Catholic. John Milton, Samuel Pepys, and Winston Churchill were married here. The window above the main entrance depicts a blind Milton dictating *Paradise Lost* to one of his daughters, while the stunning east window, made in Holland in 1501, honors the marriage of Catherine of Aragon to Prince Arthur. The modern windows to the south provide a marked contrast; entitled "Spring in London," they are appropriately composed in shades of gray. Beside the high altar lies the headless body of Sir Walter Raleigh, who was executed across the street in 1618. The inscription on his memorial asks readers not to "reflect on his errors." Instead, reflect on the four modernist sundials that grace the tower and guess the hour. (*Parliament Sq. Tube: Westminster.* ☎ 7222 6382. *Open daily 9:30am-4:30pm when services are not being held. Free.*)

ST. JOHN OF SMITH SQUARE. Four assertive corner towers distinguish this former church, now a concert hall. Queen Anne, whose imagination was taxed by her role designing 50 new churches, supposedly upended a footstool and told Thomas Archer to build the church in its image. Chamber music, choral, and orchestral concerts take place most evenings; tickets cost £6-20. (*Smith Sq. Tube: Westminster.* ☎ 7222 1061. *For concert info, see Classical Music, p. 138.*)

WESTMINSTER CATHEDRAL. Not to be confused with the Anglican abbey, the Cathedral is the headquarters of the Roman Catholic church in Britain. The architecture is Christian Byzantine, in pointed contrast to the Gothic abbey. The structure, completed in 1903, rests on the former site of a 19th-century prison complex. It has an as-yet-unfinished interior, and the blackened brick of the domes contrasts dramatically with the swirling marble of the lower walls. A lift carries visitors to the top of the rocket-like, striped 273 ft. tall brick bell tower for a decent view of the Houses of Parliament, the river, and Kensington. (*Cathedral Piazza, off Victoria St. Tube: Victoria.* ☎ 7798 9055. *Open daily 7am-7pm. Suggested donation £2. Lift open daily Apr.-Nov. 9am-5pm; Dec.-Mar. Th-Su 9am-5pm. £2, concessions £1, families £5.*)

KENSINGTON, KNIGHTSBRIDGE, AND CHELSEA

KENSINGTON AND KNIGHTSBRIDGE

Kensington, a gracious, sheltered residential area, reposes between multi-ethnic Notting Hill to the north and chic Chelsea to the south. Kensington High St., which pierces the area, has become a locus for shopping and scoping. Specialty shops fill the area along Kensington Church St. to the north, and the area around **Earl's Court** has become something of a tourist colony, yet retains a substantial gay population. To reach the museums of **South Kensington,** take the Tube to South Kensington or bus #49 from Kensington High St. The **Victoria and Albert Museum,** on Cromwell

Rd. (see p. 131), the **Natural History Museum,** also on Cromwell Rd. (see p. 132), and the **Science Museum,** on Exhibition Rd. (see p. 133), all testify on a grand scale to the Victorian mania for collecting and cataloging. Patrician **Knightsbridge,** the former haunt of Princess Di, harbors those for whom luxury shopping is sport. The doyenne of the area, of course, is **Harrod's** (see **Shopping,** p. 134).

HOLLAND PARK. This peacock-peppered swath of green is full of small pleasures. **Holland House,** a Jacobean mansion built in 1607, lies on the grounds. Destroyed in World War II, the house has been restored and turned into a youth hostel (see p. 96). The park also holds rose gardens, an open-air amphitheater, and a number of playgrounds, as well as cricket pitches and the traditional Japanese Kyoto Gardens. *(Tube: High St. Kensington, Notting Hill Gate, or Holland Park. Open daily 7:30am-dusk.)*

LEIGHTON HOUSE. This curious house, devised by the imaginative painter Lord Leighton in the 19th century, is a presumptuous yet pleasant pastiche. The thoroughly blue Arab Hall, with inlaid tiles, a pool, and a dome, is an attempt to recreate the wonders of the Orient in thoroughly Occidental Kensington. Now a center for the arts, Leighton House features concerts, as well as frequent art exhibitions and competitions. *(12 Holland Park Rd. ☎ 7602 3316. Open M-W 11am-5:30pm. Free.)*

CHELSEA

Now quiet and expensive, Chelsea has historically been one of London's flashiest districts—Thomas More, Oscar Wilde, and the Sex Pistols were all residents here at one time or another. On Chelsea's famed **King's Road,** mohawked UB40s (a reference to the unemployed: it's the form they fill out to get benefits) and pearl-necklaced Sloane Rangers (the London equivalent of US preppies) gaze at trendy window displays and at each other.

CHEYNE WALK, CHEYNE ROW, AND TITE STREET. These three thoroughfares formed the heart of Chelsea's artist colony at the turn of the century. J.M.W. Turner moved into a house in Cheyne Walk, and Edgar Allan Poe lived nearby. Mary Ann Evans (a.k.a. George Eliot) moved into #4 just before her death. Today, fashionable artists' and designers' homes line the street, though the area is too expensive to remain a true bastion of bohemian culture. *(Tube: Sloane Sq.)*

CARLYLE'S HOUSE. Just beyond Cheyne Walk stands the former home of historian Thomas Carlyle, where he hung out with Dickens, Thackeray, George Eliot, and Ruskin. *(24 Cheyne Row. Tube: Sloane Sq. ☎ 7352 7087. Open Apr.-Oct. W-Su 11am-5pm. Last admission 4:30pm. £3.50, children £1.75.)*

ROYAL HOSPITAL. Totally immune to the ever-changing world of King's Rd. are the commandingly militaresque buildings of Wren's Royal Hospital, founded in 1691 by Charles II for retired soldiers and still inhabited by 400 ex-army "Chelsea pensioners." The museum features war medals of deceased veterans. The north wing has borne war's scars quite directly in the last century. *(Royal Hospital Rd. Tube: Sloane Sq. or buses # 11, 19, 22, 137. ☎7730 5282. Grounds open daily Apr.-Sept., 10am-8pm. Museum open Apr.-Sept. M-Sa 10am-noon and 2-4pm, Su 2-4pm. Free.)*

SLOANE SQUARE. Mostly just a square, with four sides at 90° angles, Sloane Square takes its name from Sir Hans Sloane (1660-1753), who founded the British Museum. The presence of super-modeling agencies in the square fills many of the boutiques with London's most fashionable/thinnest women. *(Tube: Sloane Sq.)*

NOTTING HILL, BAYSWATER, AND HYDE PARK

NOTTING HILL AND BAYSWATER

Contrary to what Hollywood and children's characters would have you believe, Notting Hill is not a white yuppieville infested with bears looking for marmalade. In the days after World War II, Notting Hill was an undesirable area where waves of poor immigrants (mostly West Indian) lived in dirt-cheap flats. Today, Notting Hill is thoroughly mixed—media types party alongside blue-collar Londoners, espcialy during the Notting Hill Carnival each August (see **Festivals,** p. 145).

LONDON

PORTOBELLO ROAD. This commercial road is the heart of Notting Hill's bustling activity. The name "Portobello" may evoke childhood memories, even if you've never been to London—one of the market's patrons is **Paddington Bear,** whose purchases at the famous **Portobello market** (see p. 136) always landed his paws in a pot of trouble. Antique stores and galleries line the quiet southern end of Portobello near the Notting Hill Gate tube station.

HYDE PARK AND KENSINGTON GARDENS
Tube: Bayswater, High St. Kensington, Hyde Park Corner, Knightsbridge, Marble Arch, or Queensway. Constabulary ☎ 7298 2076. "Liberty Drives" for people with disabilities ☎ (0407) 498 096; available May-Oct. Tu-F 10am-5pm. Hyde Park open daily 5am-midnight; Kensington Gardens open daily dawn-dusk.

Totalling 630 acres, Hyde Park and the contiguous Kensington Gardens constitute the largest open area in the center of the city, thus earning their reputation as the "lungs of London."

KENSINGTON PALACE. At the far west of the Gardens, you can drop your calling card at Kensington Palace, originally the residence of King William III and Queen Mary II. The birthplace of Queen Victoria, and most recently home to the late Princess Diana, the palace has served solely as a museum since Diana's death. The uninhabited royal rooms (the State Apartments) are now home to the stunning **Royal Ceremonial Dress Collection. Orangery Gardens,** an exquisite flower display, lines the eastern side of the palace. Be sure to seek out the cloistered **Sunken Garden** as well. *(Kensington Gardens. Tube: High St. Kensington. ☎ 7937 9561. Open Mar.-Oct. daily 10am-6pm, Nov.-Dec. daily 10am-5pm; last admission 1hr. before closing. Audio tour included. £8.50, students and seniors £6.70, under 16 £6.10, families £26.10.)*

SPEAKERS' CORNER. Nowadays, on summer evenings and Sundays from late morning to dusk, proselytizers, politicos, and flat-out crazies assemble to dispense the fruits of their knowledge to whoever's biting at Speakers' Corner, in the northeast corner of Hyde Park. You can listen to the finest example of free speech in action anywhere in the world. *(Tube: Marble Arch, not Hyde Park Corner.)*

SERPENTINE LAKE. This 41-acre lake, carved in 1730, runs from fountains in the north, near Bayswater Rd., toward Knightsbridge. From the number of people who pay £6.50 per hour to row in the pond, one would think the water was the fountain of youth. Perhaps not—Harriet Westbrook, Percy Bysshe Shelley's first wife, numbers among the famous people who have drowned in this human-made "pond." A statue of **Peter Pan** stands near the **Italian Fountains** on the Serpentine's west bank. The **Serpentine Gallery** also stands to the west (see **Museums and Galleries,** p. 133).

MARYLEBONE AND BLOOMSBURY

MARYLEBONE
Located between Regent's Park and Oxford St., the grid-like district of Marylebone (MAR-lee-bun) is dotted with elegant late-Georgian town houses. There's little to see in this well-kept, well-bred region of residences and office buildings, but **Madame Tussaud's** (p. 132) and the **Wallace Collection** (p. 133) are in this part of town. Marylebone has had its share of notable denizens. Wimpole St. saw the reclusive poet Elizabeth Barrett write the fabulous *Sonnets from the Portuguese* before she eloped and moved in with Robert Browning. At different times, 19 York St. has been the home of John Milton, John Stuart Mill, and William Hazlitt. Harley St. is the address for Britain's pre-eminent medical specialists.

221B BAKER STREET. The area's most fondly remembered resident is Sherlock Holmes who, although fictitious, still receives about 50 letters per week addressed to his 221b Baker St. residence. The **Abbey National Building Society** currently occupies the site and employs a full-time secretary to answer requests for Holmes's assistance in solving mysteries around the world. The official line is that Holmes has retired from detective work and is keeping bees in the country. The **Sherlock Holmes Museum,** 239 Baker St., will thrill Holmes enthusiasts with the meticulous re-creation of the detective's lodgings (see **Museums and Galleries,** p. 133).

REGENT'S PARK. Just to the north of Baker St. and the south of Camden Town, the 500-acre, wide-open Regent's Park is full of lakes, gardens, promenades, and Londoners. One of London's most beautiful spaces, the park contains well-kept lawns, broad walkways (including Broad Walk), playing fields, and scores of sunbathers. It also houses the **London Zoo.** (☎ 7486 7905; constabulary ☎ 7935 1259. Tube: Regent's Park, Great Portland St., Baker St., or Camden Town. Open 6am-dusk.)

BLOOMSBURY

During the first half of the 20th century, Bloomsbury gained its reputation as an intellectual and artistic center, due largely to the presence of the famed Bloomsbury Group, which included biographer Lytton Strachey, novelist E.M. Forster, art critic Roger Fry, painter Vanessa Bell (sister of Virginia Woolf), and hovering on the fringe, T.S. Eliot, the eminent British poet from St. Louis, Missouri. Although very little of the famed intellectual gossip and high modernist argot currently emanates from 51 Gordon Sq. (Virginia Woolf's house and the center of the group), the area maintains an earnestly intellectual atmosphere. Today, the **British Museum** (p. 128), the **British Library** (p. 131), and the University College London guarantee a continued concentration of cerebral, as well as tourist, activities in the area. Bloomsbury's streets are lined with B&Bs and student housing.

RUSSELL SQUARE. Directly northeast of the British Museum, Russell Square squares off as central London's second-largest, after Lincoln's Inn Fields. T.S. Eliot, the "Pope of Russell Square," hid from his emotionally ailing first wife at #24 while he worked as an editor at and later director of Faber and Faber, the famed publishing house. Also of note is the decadently Victorian **Hotel Russell** on the eastern side of the square, a confection of brick and terra-cotta. (Tube: Russell Sq.)

SOUTH LONDON

SOUTH BANK AND SOUTHWARK

OXO TOWER. The most colorful recent changes in the South Bank landscape result from the unflagging efforts of a nonprofit development company, Coin Street Community Builders (CSCB). The CSCB's grandest renovation project, the Oxo Tower, is the Art Deco building notable for its clever subversion of rules prohibiting permanent advertising on buildings—architects built the tower's windows in the shape of the company's name. The nearby **Museum Of...** and the **gallery@oxo** are succeeding in their aim to provide a democratic artistic forum. (Between Waterloo and Blackfriars Bridges on Barge House St. Tube: Blackfriars or Waterloo.)

SOUTH BANK CENTRE. This massive performing-arts center occupies a series of prominent modern buildings overlooking the river. The center is comprised of the **National Film Theatre,** the **Hayward Gallery,** the **Royal Festival Hall,** and the **Royal National Theatre.** The **National Film Theatre,** tucked under Waterloo Bridge directly on the South Bank, operates a continually rotating program of British cinema, as well as classic films from other countries. The **Hayward Gallery** (see p. 132) houses imaginative contemporary art exhibitions, and is visible for miles by the fluorescent weather sculpture that tops the building. The 3000-seat **Royal Festival Hall** (see p. 138) is home to the London Philharmonic Orchestra, while its smaller counterparts, the **Queen Elizabeth Hall** and the **Purcell Room** host chamber concerts and smaller orchestras. There are free foyer concerts in the Festival Hall Wednesday to Sunday lunchtimes and Friday evenings. The **Royal National Theatre** (see p. 137) contains three state-of-the-art theaters, the 1400-seat Olivier, the smaller Lyttleton, and the experimental Cottlesloe. (Tube: Waterloo, then follow signs for York Rd.; or Embankment and cross the Hungerford footbridge.)

ROSE AND GLOBE THEATRES. Southwark's greatest vice has always been theater. Shakespeare's and Marlowe's plays were performed at the Rose, which was built in 1587. Remnants of the Rose, discovered during construction in 1989, are displayed underneath a new office block at Park St. and Rose Alley. The remains of Shakespeare's **Globe Theatre** (see p. 137) were discovered just months after those of the Rose, and soon after, the late actor/director Sam Wanamaker spearheaded the reconstruction of the Globe on the riverbank. The theater held its first full season in 1997. The space itself is not only a wonderful reconstruction, but a unique experience in theater-going. *(New Globe Walk, Bankside. Tube: London Bridge. ☎ 7902 1400. 45min. tours available May-Sept. M 9am-6pm, Tu-Su 9am-noon; Oct.-Apr. daily 10am-5pm. £6, seniors and students £5, children £4.)*

GOLDEN HINDE. Around the corner from the Globe, landlubbers are given the chance to board a rebuilt 16th-century galleon. Attendants clad as pirates lead tours through the vessel geared especially toward the kiddies. Families with children ages six to twelve can spend a night onboard, learning seafaring skills, eating Tudor meals and wearing period clothes. Yar. *(Cathedral St. Tube: London Bridge. ☎ 7403 0123. Open daily 10am-6pm. £2.50, seniors £2.10, under 13 £1.75, families £6.50.)*

LIBERTY OF THE CLINK. Before the "hoose-gow" and the "big house" there was "the Clink," testament to Southwark's less-than-rosy past. The Clink itself, which was in operation for more than six centuries, was the Bishop's private prison for London's criminals. The **Clink Prison Museum** recreates the glory days of the prison with an eerie soundtrack and hands-on restraining and torture devices. *(1 Clink St. Tube: London Bridge. ☎ 7378 1558. Open daily 10am-6pm. £4, concessions £3, families £9.)*

SOUTHWARK CATHEDRAL. The cathedral, an endearing remnant of ecclesiastical power, is probably the city's most striking Gothic church after Westminster Abbey. Mostly rebuilt in the 1890s, only the church's 1207 choir and retro-choir survive. Ed Shakespeare, brother of Will, lies buried beneath a stained-glass window depicting his sibling's characters. *(Montague Close. Tube: London Bridge. ☎ 7367 6712. Open M-F 8am-6pm. Evensong Su 3pm. Free. Photo permit £1, video permit £5.)*

HMS BELFAST. Moored on the south bank of the Thames, just upstream from Tower Bridge, this World War II warship led the bombardment of the French coast during the D-Day landings. The labyrinth of the engine house and the whopping great guns make it a fun place to play sailor. *(Morgan's Lane, Tooley St. Tube: London Bridge. ☎ 7940 6300. Open daily Mar.-Oct. 10am-6pm; Nov.-Feb. 10am-5pm; last admission 45min. before close. £5, students £3.90, children under 16 free.)*

GREENWICH
DLR: Cutty Sark or Rail: Greenwich.

A real town in its own right, Greenwich (GREN-itch) seems a world away from London. The village functioned historically as a point of entry for ships bearing goods, while many of England's best loved heroes, among them Drake, Raleigh, and Cook, departed from her docks. In modern-day minds, Greenwich means time. After Charles II authorized the establishment of a small observatory here in 1675 "for perfecting navigation and astronomy," successive royal astronomers perfected their craft to such a level that an international convention held in Washington, D.C. blessed the village with the **Prime Meridian** in 1884.

The **Greenwich Tourist Information Centre** arranges a variety of afternoon tours. The building also contains a cafe and a slick exhibit on the history of Greenwich. *(Opposite the Cutty Sark. ☎ (0870) 608 2000; www.greenwich.gov.uk. Open daily 10am-5pm. 1-1½hr. tours at 12:15pm and 2:15pm; £4, concessions £3, under 14 free.)*

OLD ROYAL OBSERVATORY AND FLAMSTEED HOUSE. At the top of the hill in the middle of Greenwich Park stands a Wren-designed observatory, cunningly disguised as a freakishly large onion. Wren also designed Flamsteed House, remarkable for its unique octagonal top room. Inside its walls are Britain's largest refracting telescope and an excellent collection of early astronomical instruments displayed with nearly comprehensible explanations. The Prime Meridian is marked by a brass strip in the observatory courtyard and a laser beam inside; play "now I'm west, now I'm east" for as long as you're amused. Greenwich Mean Time, still the standard for international communications and navigation, is displayed on a clock over 120 years old. *(☎ 8312 6565. Open daily 10am-5pm; last admission 4:30pm. Old Royal Observatory, National Maritime Museum, and the Queen's House £10.50, students*

£8.40, families £15, under 16 and seniors who can make it up the hill free. Observatory alone £6, students and seniors £4.80, children free. 45min. observatory audio guide £2. Planetarium shows usually M-Sa afternoon. £2.50, concessions £1.50.)

QUEEN'S HOUSE. At the foot of the hill is the so-called "Queen's House," a 17th-century home that was started for James I's wife, Anne of Denmark, and finished for Henrietta Maria, the wife of Charles I. Designed by the age's master architect, Inigo Jones, it is England's first Palladian villa, celebrated by architects and art historians for its strict purity. The western addition is the highly informative **National Maritime Museum;** see p. 132. *(Romney Rd. ☎ 8858 4422. Open daily 10am-5pm. No separate entry; see observatory prices. Free maps available.)*

CUTTY SARK. One of the last great tea clippers stands anchored in dry dock. The ship carried 1.3 million pounds of tea on each 120-day return trip from China. Its name, which means "short shirt," describes the sailors' costume and comes from Robert Burns's poem "Tam O'Shanter." In the prime of its sea-going days, between 1869 and 1938, it set new records for speed. Those who hanker after the whiff of gunpowder will be glad to learn that the cannon is fired loudly at 1pm every day. *(Waterfront beside Greenwich Pier. ☎ 8858 3445. Open M-Sa 10am-6pm, Su noon-6pm. £3.50, students and seniors £2.50, families £8.50.)*

ROYAL NAVAL COLLEGE. Charles II commissioned Wren to tear down the Royal Palace of Placentia, a favorite home of Henry VIII and daughter Elizabeth, and to construct this college in its place. Because it was situated directly between the Queen's House and the river, the college was constructed in two halves in order to leave the Queen's view unobstructed. James Thornhill's elaborately frescoed ceiling in the Painted Hall, which took 19 years to complete, and Benjamin West's painting of a shipwrecked St. Paul in the chapel provides an excellent opportunity to view breathtaking art in its original location. *(Off King William Walk, directly ahead of the Cutty Sark. ☎ 8269 4744. Open daily 2:30pm-4:30pm. Chapel services Su 8:30am, holy communion; Su 11am, sung eucharist. Free.)*

EAST LONDON

THE EAST END

Tube: Aldgate East. To reach Brick Ln., go left up Whitechapel as you exit the Tube station; turn left onto Osbourne St., which turns into Brick Ln.

A large working-class English population moved into the district during the Industrial Revolution, followed by a wave of Jewish immigrants fleeing persecution in Eastern Europe, who settled around **Whitechapel.** Jewish success in the rag trade drew the attention of the British Union of Fascists, who instigated anti-Semitic violence that culminated in the "Battle of Cable Street" in 1936. A mural on St. George's Town Hall at 236 Cable St. commemorates the victory won in the streets that day. In 1978, a wave of immigration brought a large Bangladeshi community to the East End. Today's East End is a conglomeration of minority groups. The most recent wave of immigrants to join the East End consists of London artists; their work occasionally hangs in the **Whitechapel Art Gallery** (see p. 133). At the heart of the Muslim Bangladeshi community is **Brick Lane,** lined with Indian and Bangladeshi restaurants, colorful textile shops, and grocers. Stalls selling everything from leather jackets to salt beef sandwiches flank Brick Ln. and **Petticoat Lane** (see **Street Markets,** p. 136). Nearby on 82-92 Whitechapel Rd., the **East London Mosque,** London's first, testifies to the size of the Muslim community.

BEVIS MARKS SYNAGOGUE. The city's oldest standing synagogue sits at Bevis Marks and Heneage Ln. The congregation traces its roots back to Spanish and Portuguese Jews who inhabited the area as early as 1657. Rabbi Menashe Ben Israel founded the synagogue in 1701, 435 years after Jews were first expelled from England. *(Tube: Aldgate. From Aldgate High St. turn right onto Houndsditch; Creechurch Ln. on the left leads to Bevis Marks. ☎ 7626 1274. Organized tours Su-W and F noon; call in advance. Open Su-M, W, and F 11:30am-1pm, Tu 10:30am-4pm. Entrance donation £1.)*

DOCKLANDS

London has a long history as a maritime gateway—it was already a prominent port in Roman times—and by the Middle Ages the city's wharfs and quays had crept east from the City. As London grew in importance, the docks grew with it, stretching miles down the Thames, until they had become the powerful trading center of the British Empire. During World War II, the Blitz obliterated much of the dock area. Though the sun had set on the empire, the docks continued to do brisk business until the early 1960s, when the advent of container transport and the move of the Port of London to Tilbury rendered them obsolete. By 1982, all had closed, leaving the Docklands barren. As part of the Thatcher government's privatization program, redevelopment of the area was handed over to the private sector in the form of the **London Docklands Development Corporation (LDDC),** which took helm of what it called "the most significant urban regeneration program in the world."

Docklands proper covers a huge expanse (55 mi. of waterfront to be exact), from the Tower of London to Greenwich. The center of the new 8.5 sq. mi. development is on the **Isle of Dogs,** the spit of land defined by a sharp U-shaped bend in the Thames. To the east lie the **Royal Docks,** once the center of one of history's proudest trading empires. **Canary Wharf,** at a towering 800 ft., is Britain's tallest edifice and the jewel of Docklands, visible from almost anywhere in London. (*DLR: Canary Wharf.*) Getting off at Shadwell station, you'll see **St. George-in-the-East,** an old, working-class community. Drab housing, dusty streets, traditional pubs, cafes, and pie-and-mash shops stand in the throes of a major transformation brought on by an infusion of Bengali immigrants. (☎ *7481 1345. Open daily 9am-5pm.*)

NORTH LONDON

ISLINGTON

Lying in the low hills just north of the City, Islington began as a royal hunting ground. The village was first absorbed into the city by fugitives from the Great Fire of 1666, and later by industrialization and trade along Regent's Canal. Islington became "trendy" during the late 17th century, when its ale houses and cream teas made it popular for wealthy scene-makers. In more recent times it has established a reputation as an academic and artistic haven. Indeed, a clutch of wonderful the-aters—the Almeida, the King's Head, the Little Angel, and nearby Sadler's Wells—continue to serve Islington's increasingly upmarket populace. Previously known as The People's Republic of Islington for its reputation as a socialist hotbed, the area's politics step in time with the Labour Party. The borough is today considered the home territory of New Labour.

CAMDEN TOWN

When the Regent's Canal (which passes through Camden Town) was constructed in the 19th century, Camden was a working-class district. Charles Dickens spent his childhood here, crowded in a four-room tenement with his extended family at 141 Bayham St.; the experience served as the model for the Cratchits in *A Christmas Carol.* Waves of immigrants brought a diversity to the area that persists to this day. Famously bohemian, Camden Town is a stomping ground for all subcultural affiliations. At the raucous **Camden Market** (see p. 136), hundreds of merchants set up stands that draw swarms of bargain-seekers every weekend. Almost anything can be found here, from vintage pornography to antique sewing machines.

HAMPSTEAD

The "village" of Hampstead has captivated London's elite for centuries. Such affluence gives rise to curiosities that make the area worth a visit, though none is particularly earth-shattering on its own. Keats, Dickens, and Freud all worked here, and the villages claim more writers per capita that any other London postcodes.

KEATS HOUSE. One of London's finest literary shrines is the restored house of John Keats. Before dashing off to Italy to breathe his last in true Romantic style, Keats pined here for his next-door fiancée, Fanny Brawne. Not only did he cough up his first consumptive droplet of blood in the house, he also composed "Ode to a Nightingale" under a plum tree here. To get there from the Tube station, head left down High St., turn left down Downshire Hill, and turn right onto Keats Grove. The rail station is much closer. *(Train: Hampstead Heath. Tube: Hampstead. ☎ 7435 2062. Phone ahead as hours are erratic, but generally Apr.-Oct. M-F 10am-1pm and 2-6pm, Sa 10am-1pm and 2-5pm, Su 2-5pm; Nov.-Mar. M-F 1-5pm, Sa 10am-1pm and 2-5pm, Su 2-5pm. Free.)*

HAMPSTEAD HEATH. The most fabulous green space in the metropolis is owned by the Corporation of London, the men in gray who run the City. The Heath is far more rural than the central parks, and the perfect place to get lost in acres of meadow and woodland and forget the hustle and bustle of the city among the carefree picnickers, kite-flyers, and anglers. At night the Heath, particularly West Heath, becomes one of the city's oldest gay cruising areas. On a hot day, take a dip in the murky waters of the **Kenwood Ladies' Pond, Highgate Men's Pond,** or the **Mixed Bathing Pond.** *(Train: Hampstead Heath. Tube: Hampstead, or Kentish Town and then C2 or 214 bus to Parliament Hill. ☎ 7485 4491. Open Easter-Oct. 7-9:30am and 10am-7pm, Nov.-Easter 7-10am. Heath open 24hr.; be extremely careful in the park after dark.)*

WEST LONDON

HAMPTON COURT PALACE

Train to Hampton Court from Waterloo (32min., 2 per hr., day return £4, £3.50 with zone 2-6 Travelcard); or Tube: Richmond and take the R68 bus (70p); or take a Westminster Passenger Association (☎ 7930 4721) boat from Westminster Pier, Tube: Westminster (£10, ages 5-15 £4; day return £14, £7). ☎ 8781 9500. Free audio guides and tours. Wheelchairs and electric buggies available from West Gate; ask a warder. Palace and privy gardens open mid-Mar. to mid-Oct. M 10:15am-6pm, Tu-Su 9:30am-6pm; mid-Oct. to mid-Mar. closes 4:30pm. Last admission 45min. before close. Gardens open daily 7am-dusk. Palace, privy gardens, and maze £10.15, students and seniors £8, ages 5-15 £7, families £31.40; maze only £2.50, ages 5-15 £1.60; gardens free.

Although a monarch hasn't lived here since George II packed it in over 200 years ago, **Hampton Court Palace** continues to ooze regal charm. Located six miles down the Thames from Richmond, the palace housed over 1500 court members at its height. Cardinal Wolsey built it in 1514, showing Henry VIII by his example how to act the part of a splendid and all-powerful ruler. Henry learned the lesson well, confiscating the Court in 1525 when Wolsey fell out of favor, and added new lodgings for each of his numerous wives. To help tourists make sense of the chaotic and schizophrenic arrangement of the palace, it is divided into six "routes" through which visitors may meander. Seeing all six plus the gardens and maze could easily take up the whole day; if you've got less time, the staff at the **information centre,** off **Clock Court,** can help.

Fans of Henry have myriad options for discovering how the king lived, reigned, and ate his way to a 54-inch waist. **Henry VIII's State Apartments,** including the spectacular **Great Hall,** allow would-be sycophants a chance to reenact some Tudor brown-nosing. For those curious as to how Henry acquired his massive girth in the days before deep-fat fryers, the **Tudor Kitchens** provide the answer. Sir Christopher Wren's work can be seen in the opulent **King's and Queen's Apartments,** built for William III and meticulously restored after a catastrophic fire in 1986. In **King's Guard Chamber,** almost 3000 guns and weapons remind visitors that the monarch they were about to see was not to be trifled with. The **Wolsey Rooms,** which housed Cardinal Wolsey before he fell from favor, now house some of the finest treasures of the Royal Collection, including **tapestries** woven from the Raphael cartoons in the Victoria and Albert Museum (see p. 131), and a roomful of *grisaille* work originally by Mantegna but poorly repainted in the 18th century.

🏛 MUSEUMS AND GALLERIES

The main museums and galleries in London are the British Museum, the National Gallery, the National Portrait Gallery, the Tate Britain, the Tate Modern, and the Victoria and Albert. London's collections of museums are distinguished not just by their high quality, but by their (often) free admission. The **London Go See Card** is a discount card that allows unlimited access to 13 participating smaller museums for three or seven days. The card can be purchased at any of the participating museums, but will afford you substantial discounts only if you plan to visit *many* museums, or if you plan to visit a particularly expensive museum more than once. Participating museums are: the V&A, the Science Museum, the Natural History Museum, the Royal Academy of Arts, the Hayward Gallery, the Design Museum, the London Transport Museum, the Museum of London, the Museum of the Moving Image, and the Courtauld Institute. (3-day £16, families £32; 7-day £26, £50.)

BRITISH MUSEUM

Great Russell St., rear entrance on Montague St. ☎ 7323 8299; www.british-museum.ac.uk. Tube: Tottenham Court Rd., Goodge St., Russell Sq., or Holborn. 1½hr. highlights tour M-Sa 10:30am, 11am, 1:30pm, 2:30pm; Su 12:30pm, 1:30pm, 2:30pm, and 4pm; £7, students and under 16 £4. 1hr. focus tours depart M-Sa 1pm from upstairs, 3:30pm and Su 4:30pm downstairs; £5, £3. Visually-impaired travelers should enquire about tactile exhibits and touch-tours. Open M-Sa 10am-5pm, Su noon-6pm. Free; suggested donation £2. Special exhibits £4, concessions £3.

Founded in 1753, the museum began with the personal collection of Sir Hans Sloane. Robert Smirke drew up the design of the current Neoclassical building in 1824; construction took 30 years.

EGYPTIAN AND ASSYRIAN GALLERIES. The outstanding Egyptian collection contains imposing statues of Amenophis III as well as the **Rosetta Stone.** The head of Ramses II dominates the northern section of Room 25. The Egyptian gallery contains papyri such as the *Book of the Dead of Ani,* a comprehensive exhibit on Egyptian funerary archaeology, and a how-to guide on mummification. The Assyrian galleries contain enormous reliefs from Nineveh (704-668 BC). Room 16's entrance is guarded by the giant five-legged, human-headed bulls, made to look stationary from the front, mobile from the side.

GREEK AND ROMAN ANTIQUITIES. The Greek exhibits are dominated by the **Elgin Marbles,** 5th-century BC reliefs from the Parthenon, now residing in the spacious Duveen Gallery. Carved under the direction of classical Athens' greatest sculptor, Phidias, the marbles comprise three main groups: the frieze, which portrays the most important Athenian civic festivals; the metopes, which depict incidents from the battle of the Lapiths and Centaurs (symbolizing the triumph of "civilization" over "barbarism"); and the remains of large statues that stood in the east and west pediments of the building. Recently opened are two new galleries devoted to the Elgin marbles, complete with a miniature model of the Acropolis. Other Hellenic highlights include the complete Ionic facade of the **Nereid Monument,** one of the female caryatid columns from the Acropolis. Frieze slabs and some free-standing sculpture commemorate the second wonder—the **Temple of Artemis,** built to replace the one buried by Herostratus in 356 BC to perpetuate his name. Among the many sculptures of the Roman antiquities, the dark blue glass of the **Portland Vase** stands out. In 1845, it was shattered by a drunken museum-goer; when it was put back together, 37 small chips were left over. Since then, the vase has been beautifully reconstructed twice, with more left-over chips being reincorporated each time—don't touch!

ROMANO-BRITAIN COLLECTION. The Romano-Britain section includes the **Mindenhall Treasure,** a magnificent collection of 4th-century silver tableware. With a diameter of almost two feet and weighing over 18 lb., the aptly named Great Dish impresses with its size and elaborate decorations. Nearby lies **Lindow Man,** an Iron Age Celt apparently sacrificed in a gruesome ritual and preserved in a peat bog. The **Money Gallery** is next door, tracing finance from cowrie shells to credit cards.

MEDIEVAL GALLERIES. The **Sutton Hoo Ship Burial,** an Anglo-Saxon ship buried (and subsequently dug up) in Suffolk complete with an unknown king, is the centerpiece of the Medieval galleries. Other fascinating highlights of these allegedly dark ages include a display of clocks and the elaborately carved 800-year-old ivory **Lewis Chessmen** (see **Check, Mate,** p. 605).

ASIAN COLLECTIONS. The majority of the Asian Collections resides in Gallery 33. The gallery's eastern half is dedicated to the Chinese collection, renowned for its ancient Shang bronzes and fine porcelains, and the western half is filled by Indian and Southeast Asian exhibits, which include the largest collection of Indian religious sculpture outside of India. Upstairs, the collection continues with a series of three galleries displaying Japanese and Korean artifacts, paintings, and calligraphy. Downstairs by the Montague St. entrance, don't miss the **Islamic art gallery** with its tiles, ceramics and other treasures from all over the Muslim world.

NATIONAL GALLERY

Trafalgar Sq. Tube: Charing Cross, Leicester Sq., or Piccadilly Circus. ☎ 7747 2885; www.nationalgallery.org.uk. Mid-May to Sept., a free Art Bus shuttles between the National Gallery, the Tate Britain, and the Tate Modern (2 per hr., 10am-6pm). Tours start from the Sainsbury Wing info desk daily at 11:30am and 2:30pm and W 6:30pm; tours for the visually impaired 3rd Sa of month 11:30am; sign-language tour 1st Sa of month 11:30am. Audioguides covering almost every work available at main entrance and Sainsbury Wing foyer; donation requested. Orange St. and Sainsbury Wing entrances wheelchair accessible. Open Th-Tu 10am-6pm, W 10am-9pm. Free except for some exhibitions.

The National Gallery maintains one of the world's finest collections of Western art from the Middle Ages to the end of the 19th century, divvied up chronologically among four distinct wings. You could spend days ambling through the maze of galleries; if you're pressed for time and know what you want to see, the high-tech **Micro Gallery,** in the Sainsbury wing, will guide you through the collection on-line and print out a personalized tour of the paintings you want to see.

The **Sainsbury Wing,** the newest part of the Gallery, holds the oldest part of the collection. Botticelli's *Venus and Mars*, Raphael's *Crucifixion*, and da Vinci's *Virgin of the Rocks*, number among the more famous works, most of which are devotional works created between 1260 and 1510. Paintings from 1510 to 1600 are found in the **West Wing,** left of the Trafalgar Sq. entrance. The **North Wing** holds 17th-century Italian, Spanish, Flemish, and French paintings, including 12 Rembrandts. The **East Wing,** to the right of the main entrance, is devoted to painting from 1700 to 1900, including a strong English collection. Impressionist works include a number of Monet's near-abstract water lilies and Cézanne's *Old Woman with Roses*.

NATIONAL PORTRAIT GALLERY

St. Martin's Pl., just opposite St.-Martin's-in-the-Fields. Tube: Charing Cross or Leicester Sq. ☎ 7306 0055, recorded info ☎ 7312 2463; www.npg.org.uk. Frequent free daytime lectures. Evening lectures Th 7pm (£3, concessions £2); concerts F 7pm (mostly free). Orange St. entrance is wheelchair accessible. Audioguide available in entrance hall; suggested donation £3, ID or credit card deposit required. Open M-W 10am-6pm, Th-F 10am-9pm, Sa-Su 10am-6pm. Free, excluding temporary exhibits.

This unofficial Who's Who in Britain began in 1856 as "the fulfillment of a patriotic and moral ideal"—namely to showcase Britain's most officially noteworthy citizens. The museum's declared principle of looking "to the celebrity of the person represented, rather than to the merit of the artist" does not seem to have affected the quality of the works displayed. The sleek new Ondaatje wing opened in May 2000, providing a suite of climate-controlled top-floor rooms for the oldest paintings. The Elizabethan portraits hang in a room modeled after a Tudor long gallery; the dark walls and dramatic fiber-optic backlighting highlight pictures such as William Scrot's astonishing distorted-perspective portrait of Edward VI, designed to be viewed from an extreme angle. In the 20th-century display the importance of pop culture makes itself felt. The Gallery normally commissions three new portraits a year; new backs against the wall for 2000 include stage director and physician Jonathan Miller, author Doris Lessing, and tycoon Richard Branson.

TATE BRITAIN

Millbank. Tube: Pimlico. ☎ 7887 8008, recorded info ☎ 7887 8000; www.tate.org.uk. Museum tour M-F 12:30pm, Sa 3pm; Turner collection tour M-F 11:30am. Audio tour £3, concessions £2. Touch tours for visually impaired visitors ☎ 7887 8725. Shop open M-Sa 10:30am-5:40pm, Su 10am-5:40pm. Cafe open daily 10:30am-5:30pm; Espresso Bar daily 10am-5:30pm. Restaurant, a swanky setting for a pricey lunch, open M-Sa noon-3pm and Su noon-4:30pm; AmEx, MC, V. Museum open daily 10am-5:50pm. Free.

With the opening of the new Tate Modern (below), the original Tate has now been renamed the Tate Britain, and holds a superb collection of British works from the 16th century to the present day. The collection starts with a room at the far end of the gallery devoted to 16th- and 17th-century painting. The parade of Constables includes the famous views of Salisbury Cathedral, and a number of Hampstead scenes dotted with red saddle splashes. Don't miss the visionary works of William Blake, or the haunting images of Sir John Everett Millais, a founder of the Pre-Raphaelite Brotherhood. The Tate's chronologically ordered displays have been supplemented by thematic arrangements. "Representing Britain 1500-2000" combines works to explore "Literature & Fantasy," "Public & Private," "Home & Abroad," and "Artists & Models." There are also rooms devoted to individual artists; works by Gainsborough, Hockney, Sickert, and Blake are all highlighted.

CLORE GALLERY. The Tate's 300-work J.M.W. Turner collection, the world's largest, resides in the adjoining gallery. Architect Sir James Stirling designed the annex to allow natural light to illuminate both the serenity of *Peace—Burial at Sea* and the raging brushstrokes of gale-swept ocean scenes. The collection covers all of Turner's career, from early, dreamy landscapes such as *Chevening Park* to the later visionary works. There is also a collection of Constable works.

TATE MODERN

Sumner St., Bankside. Tube: Southwark. ☎ 7887 8000; www.tate.org.uk. Mid-May to Sept., a free Art Bus shuttles between the National Gallery, the Tate Britain, and the Tate Modern (every 30min. 10am-6pm). Daily highlights tours at 10:30, 11:30am, 2:30, 3:30pm; free. Call for schedule of special talks; free. Audioguide £1. Wheelchair access; 6 wheelchairs can be reserved ☎ 7887 8888. Guide dogs welcome. Open Su-Th 10am-6pm, F-Sa 10pm-10pm. Cafe 7 open F-Sa until 11pm. Free; admission charged to some exhibitions.

Some might call it instant karma. Where other millennium projects struggled to pull in the crowds, the Tate became an instant landmark and the crowning glory of the revitalized South Bank area upon its opening in May 2000. Crowds snaked around London's first large-scale museum dedicated entirely to modern art, housed in a stunning converted power station designed by Giles Gilbert Scott. The Swiss firm Herzog and de Meuron renovated the building and have turned the old turbine room into an immense top-lit cavern 155m long and 35m high while preserving the old power station's industrial feel.

Despite the fanfare that greeted its opening, Tate Modern has taken some flak for its controversial curatorial method, which groups works thematically instead of chronologically. The permanent collection is divided into four major sections ("Landscape/Matter/Environment," "Still Life/Object/Real Life," "History/Memory/Society," and "Nude/Action/Body"), spread over floors 3 and 5, with floor 4 dedicated to temporary exhibits. For instance, in the "Desire for Order" room in "Still Life/Object/Real Life," Cezanne's *Still Life with Water Jug* shares the room with Carl Andre's 1970s low-form sculpture *Steel Zinc Plain.* And while Auguste Rodin's *The Kiss* puts on a public display of affection outside Nude/Action/Body section, the room next door contains a series of harsh, flat Nan Goldin photographs. Whatever you think about the way it's arranged, there's no doubt that the Tate now has the space to put more of its collection on display. The third floor alone has Marcel Duchamps's *Fountain*, Roy Lichtenstein's *Bull Profile Series: Bull I-VI*, and Jackson Pollock's hyperactive *Summertime 9a*, while the fifth holds Andy Warhol's *Marilyn Diptych* and Picasso's *Weeping Woman.* And of course, there's a plethora of works that will evoke the usual "is that art?" response.

VICTORIA AND ALBERT

Cromwell Rd. Tube: South Kensington. ☎ *7942 2000; www.vam.ac.uk. Wheelchair access at the side entrance on Exhibition Rd.; call ahead (*☎ *7942 2000). Tours (1hr.) leave hourly from Cromwell St. info desk daily 12:30-3:30pm, Tu-Su also 10:30am and 11:30am. Open M-Su 10am-5:45pm plus W 6:30-9:30pm. £5, seniors £3; free for students, disabled, and under 15; free for everyone daily 4:30-5:45pm. Night openings (select galleries only) £3. Season ticket for all 3 South Kensington museums (the V&A, the Science, and the Natural History) £29, two adults £49.50, students £16.*

Founded in 1852 to encourage excellence in art and design, the original curators were deluged with objects from around the world. The 150-odd galleries arrange items either by time and place or by material and style. The popular **dress collection** traces clothing fashions, focusing mainly on women's wear, from the 16th-century to the present. Persian carpets and Moroccan rugs distinguish the V&A's collection of **Islamic Art,** the largest and most breathtaking piece of which is the Persian Ardabil carpet. The **Asian collections** are particularly formidable. The Gallery of Indian Art contains splendid textiles, painting, Mughal jewelry, and decor. The elegant Gallery of Chinese Art divides 5000 years of Chinese art into six categories—Eating and Drinking, Living, Worship, Ruling, Collecting, and Burial. The Japanese gallery displays elaborate armor and intriguing contemporary sculpture, and the Korean gallery recognizes the depth and longevity of Korean culture.

The **European collections** are just as impressive. The Medieval Treasury, in the center of the ground floor, features vestments, plates, stained glass, and illuminations. Among the upstairs collections you'll find the **silver, stained glass,** and the heavily-protected **jewelry** galleries. Galleries 70-74 exhibit 20th-century **design,** with some emphasis on chairs, and typefaces (including Johnston Sans Serif, the omnipresent London Transport font). The **Frank Lloyd Wright Gallery** shows designs by the architect, including the interior of the Kauffmann Office, originally commissioned for a Pittsburgh department store. On the same floor, the **Gallery of Photography** traces the history of photography and displays famous snapshots.

There are various less conventional ways to see the museum. On Sundays, the New Restaurant hosts a jazz brunch, with live music accompanying either an English breakfast or lunch. **Late View,** late night openings (most summer W and occasional F), feature lectures, live performances, guest DJs, and a bar.

OTHER RECOMMENDED COLLECTIONS

Bank of England Museum, Threadneedle St. (☎ 7601 5545). Tube: Bank. Entrance on Bartholomew Ln., left of Threadneedle St. In the Bank of England itself, this museum traces the Bank's history from its 1964 foundation. Includes notes and gold bars, as well as muskets once used to defend the bank. Open M-F 10am-5pm. Free.

British Library, 96 Euston Rd. (☎ 412 7332). Tube: King's Cross/St. Pancras or Euston. This red brick building beside St. Pancras station is a modern, airy home to Britain's national collection of over 180 million books. While the reading rooms are not open to the public, you can still enjoy the excellent exhibits downstairs. In the manuscript area, the English Literature displays contain parchments of *Beowulf* (c. 1000) and the *Canterbury Tales* (1410), as well as works by Jonson, Jane Austen, Elizabeth Barrett Browning, James Joyce, Virginia Woolf, and Philip Larkin. Tours M, W, F 3pm, Tu 6:30pm, Sa 10:30am and 3pm, and Su 11:30, 4pm; £5, concessions £4. Book in advance. Open M and W-F 9:30am-6pm, Tu 9:30am-8pm, Sa 9:30am-5pm, Su 11am-5pm. Free.

Cabinet War Rooms, Clive Steps, King Charles St. (☎ 7930 6961). Tube: Westminster. Churchill ran a nation at war from these underground rooms. A free audioguide leads you through the room where he made his famous wartime broadcasts and points out the transatlantic hotline disguised as a loo. Open daily Apr.-Sept. 9:30am-6pm; Oct.-Mar. 10am-6pm. Last entrance 5:15pm. £5, students and seniors £3.60, under 16 free, disabled reduced price.

LONDON

132 ■ OTHER RECOMMENDED COLLECTIONS

The Courtauld Gallery, Somerset House, the Strand (☎ 7848 2526). Tube: Temple, Embankment, or Charing Cross. This intimate 11-room gallery in Somerset House is an ideal place to see some world-famous masterpieces, mostly Impressionist and post-Impressionist works. Holds periodic free lectures; call for info. Wheelchair accessible. Open M-Sa 10am-6pm, Su 2-6pm. £4, concessions £2; M half-price.

Design Museum, Butlers Wharf (☎ 7403 6933). Tube: London Bridge. Dedicated to classics of culture and industry, with everything from cars to underwear. Space also devoted to excellent changing exhibitions. Open daily 11:30am-6pm, last entry 5:30pm. £5.50, students £4.50, under 16 and over 60 £4, families £15.

Hayward Gallery, at Hall, Belvedere Rd. (☎ 7960 4242, recorded info ☎ 7261 0127). Tube: Waterloo. Superb temporary exhibitions of 20th-century art. Open daily 10am-6pm, Tu-W until 8pm. Generally around £6, concessions £4, under 12 free with adult.

Imperial War Museum, Lambeth Rd. (☎ 7416 5000). Tube: Lambeth North or Elephant and Castle. Gripping exhibits illuminate aspects of two world wars. The Blitz and Trench Experiences recreate every detail (even smells); veterans and victims speak through telephone handsets. In 2000, the museum opened a new wing dedicated entirely to the Holocaust. Wheelchair accessible. Open daily 10am-6pm. £5.20, students £4.20, ages 16 and under free; free 4:30-6pm.

London Dungeon, 28-34 Tooley St. (☎ 7403 0606). Tube: London Bridge. Plague, decomposition, and anything else remotely connected to horror and Britain thrown in for effect. New in 2000 is "Firestorm! 1666," a look at the Great Fire of London. Reserve at least 2hr. ahead, not including the queue, to get in. Open daily Apr.-Sept. 10am-5:30pm; Nov.-Feb. 10am-5pm; last entrance 1hr. before close. £9.95; students £8.50; under 14, seniors, and disabled £6.50.

London Transport Museum, Covent Garden (☎ 7379 6344, recorded info ☎ 7565 7299). Tube: Covent Garden. Exhibits provide a thought-provoking cultural history: see how expanding the transportation system fed the growth of the suburbs. A fabulous place for kids. Wheelchair accessible. Open M-Th and Sa-Su 10am-6pm, F 11am-6pm, last admission 5:15pm. £4.95, concessions £2.95, families £12.85, under 5 free.

Madame Tussaud's, Marylebone Rd. (☎ (0870) 400 3000). Tube: Baker St. The classic waxwork museum, founded by an *emigré* aristocrat who manufactured life-size models of French nobility who met their demise at the guillotine. To avoid horrific queues, book by phone; form a group with 9 in the line and use the group entrance; or go either when they first open or in the late afternoon. Open summer daily 9am-5:30pm (last admission); rest of year opens 10am. £11.50, seniors £9, children £8; combined entry with Planetarium £13.95, £10.80, £9.30. 50p credit card fee for advance bookings.

Museum of London, 150 London Wall (☎ 7600 3699, 24hr. info ☎ 7600 0807). Tube: St. Paul's or Barbican. This fabulously engrossing museum tells the story of the metropolis from its origins as Londinium up through the present day. Free historical lectures W-F; check for times. Wheelchair accessible. Open Tu-Sa 10am-5:50pm, Su noon-5:50pm, last admission 5:30pm. £5, students and seniors £3, under 17 free.

National Maritime Museum, Romney Rd., Greenwich (☎ 8858 4422). Rail: Greenwich or DLR: Island Gardens and use the pedestrian foot tunnel under the Thames. The museum's loving documentation of the history of British sea power will have even the staunchest land-lubber swearing allegiance to Admiral Nelson. Open daily 10am-5pm, last admission 4:30pm. £7.50, students and seniors £6, children under 16 free.

Natural History Museum, Cromwell Rd. (☎ 7942 5000). Tube: South Kensington. The Natural History Museum displays awe-inspiring fossils in its **Life Galleries.** The **Earth Galleries,** near the Exhibition Rd. entrance, focus on the history of the planet. "The Power Within" simulates being in an earthquake or a volcanic eruption. Wheelchair accessible. Open M-Sa 10am-5:50pm, Su 11am-5:50pm. £7.50, students £4.50, seniors and under 17 free; free for everyone M-F 4:30-5:50pm, Sa-Su 5-5:50pm. Season ticket for all 3 South Kensington museums (the V&A, the Science, and the Natural History) £29, two adults £49.50, students £16.

Royal Academy of Arts, Piccadilly (☎ 7439 7438). Tube: Green Park. The academy hosts traveling exhibits of the highest order. The whopping annual summer exhibition (June-Aug.) is a London institution—the works of established and unknown contemporary artists festoon every square inch of wall space and all pieces are for sale. Open daily M-Sa 10am-6pm, Su 10am-8:30pm. Admission varies by exhibition; average £6, concessions £4; advance tickets often necessary for popular exhibitions.

Royal Air Force Museum, Grahame Park Way (☎ 8205 2266, 24hr. info ☎ 8205 9191). Tube: Colindale. The RAF has converted this former World War I airbase into a hangar full of the country's aeronautic greatest hits. World War I Bristols, Korean War submarine hunters, Falkland War Tornados, and Gulf War footage display the dignified history of the RAF. Wheelchair accessible. Open daily 10am-6pm, last admission 5:30pm. £6.50, students and under 16 £3.25, families £16.60.

Science Museum, Exhibition Rd. (☎ (0870) 870 4868; IMAX bookings ☎ (0870) 870 4771; disabled info ☎7942 4446). Tube: South Kensington. A child's wonderland of planes, trains, and automobiles, with a few spaceships thrown in for good measure. Wheelchair accessible. Open daily 10am-6pm. £6.95, students £3.50; including IMAX £12, £8; including IMAX and "virtual voyages" £15, £10; under 16 free, seniors £5.75, disabled £7.75; family pass (including IMAX, "virtual voyages," and guidebook) £43. Free for everyone 4:30-6pm. Season ticket for all 3 South Kensington museums (the V&A, the Science, and the Natural History) £29, two adults £49.50, students £16.

Serpentine Gallery, Off West Carriage Drive, in Kensington Gardens (☎ 7298 1501). Tube: Lancaster Gate. Londoners often rank the Serpentine among their favorite small galleries. The crisp white walls make the perfect space for the gallery's temporary displays of contemporary works. Open daily 10am-6pm. Free.

Sherlock Holmes Museum, 239 Baker St., marked "221b." (☎ 7738 1269). Tube: Baker St. Students of Holmes's deductive method will be intrigued by the museum's meticulous recreation of his storied lodgings. Upstairs are "artifacts" from the stories and wax replicas of key plot moments. Open daily 9:30am-6pm. £6, children £4.

Sir John Soane's Museum, 13 Lincoln's Inn Fields (☎ 7405 2107). Tube: Holborn. Soane was an architect's architect, but his own self-designed idiosyncratic home will intrigue architecture buffs and laypersons alike. Open Tu-Sa 10am-5pm. Tours (£3; restricted to 22 people) leave Sa 2:30pm; tickets sold from 2pm day of tour. Free.

The Wallace Collection, Hertford House, Manchester Sq. (☎ 7935 0687). Tube: Bond St. This sumptuous collection holds Old Masters as well as 18th-century French painting and furniture. Medieval buffs should note that the collection holds London's largest armor and weaponry collection. Wheelchair accessible. Tours M-Sa 1pm, W 11:30am and 1pm, Th-F 1pm, Sa 11:30am, Su 3pm. Open M-Sa 10am-5pm, Su 2-5pm. Free.

Whitechapel Art Gallery, Whitechapel High St. (☎ 7377 7888). Tube: Aldgate East. The high-ceilinged and sunny galleries of the Whitechapel contain no permanent collection, but host some of Britain's (and Europe's) most daring exhibitions of contemporary art. Wheelchair accessible. Open Tu and Th-Su 11am-5pm, W 11am-8pm. Free.

 # SHOPPING

London Transport's handy *Shoppers' Bus Wheel* instructs Routemaster shoppers on the routes between shopping areas (available free from any London Transport Information Centre). Non-EU tourists who have purchased anything over £50 should ask about getting a refund on the 17.5% VAT (see **Taxes,** p. 20). Each shopping area has a late night of shopping. Kings Rd. and Kensington High St., for example, stay open late on Wednesdays, while shops in the West End open their doors to the night on Thursdays. Many stores may be closed on Sunday.

DEPARTMENT STORES

Fortnum & Mason, 181 Piccadilly (☎ 7734 8040). Tube: Green Park or Piccadilly Circus. Famed for its sumptuous food hall, with liveried clerks, chandeliers, and fountains, occupying the entire ground floor. The upper floors carry clothing, jewelry, and shoes in a posh and sophisticated setting. Open M-Sa 9:30am-6pm. AmEx, DC, MC, V.

Harrods, 87-135 Brompton Rd. (☎ 7730 1234). Tube: Knightsbridge. Simply put, this is *the* store in London, perhaps in the world. The sales (July and January) get so crazy that the police bring out a whole detail to deal with the shoppers. Open M-Tu and Sa 10am-6pm, W-F 10am-7pm. AmEx, DC, MC, V.

Harvey Nichols, 109-125 Knightsbridge (☎ 7235 5000). Tube: Knightsbridge. The trendiest and most expensive of London's department stores. Cell phones ring at "Harvey Nick's" just as often as the registers. Open M, T, and Sa 10am-7pm, W-F 10am-8pm, Su noon-6pm. AmEx, DC, MC, V.

Liberty's of London, 210-220 Regent St. (☎ 7734 1234). Tube: Oxford Circus. Home of the famous Liberty prints, from bolts of fabric to silk ties. Great cosmetics department. Open M-W 10am-6:30pm, Th 10am-8pm, F-Sa 10am-7pm, Su noon-6pm. AmEx, DC, MC, V and most foreign currencies.

Marks & Spencer, 458 Oxford St. (☎ 7935 7954). Tube: Bond St. or Marble Arch. Hundreds of other locations. Brits know it as Marks & Sparks or M&S. Everyone British, including Tony Blair, buys underwear here. Also features a marvelous food department (sandwiches £2; microwaveable meals £3-4). Open M-F 9am-8pm, Sa 9am-7pm, Su noon-6pm (weekend hours vary slightly). AmEx, MC, V.

Selfridges, 400 Oxford St. (☎ 7629 1234). Tube: Bond St. There's a reason their yellow shopping bags are ubiquitous around Oxford St.: Selfridges has *everything*. The neo-classical building's vast cosmetics department features every conceivable makeup brand from Bobbi Brown to Miss Mascara; the fashion departments, while not cheap, are extensive and trendy. Will refund the difference on any item found for less elsewhere. Huge Jan. and mid-July sale. Open M-W 10am-7pm, Th-F 10am-8pm, Sa 9:30am-7pm, Su noon-6pm. AmEx, DC, MC, V.

CLOTHING

◼ **French Connection (fcuk),** 99-103 Long Acre (☎ 7379 6560). Tube: Covent Garden. Numerous other branches. Friendly staff and catchy slogans have let fcuk fill the gap in affordable, trendy urbanwear. Simple designs in dark colors make for a good buy. Huge sales during January and July when clothes are up to 70% off regular prices. Open M-W 10:30am-7pm, Th 11am-8pm, F-Sa 10:30am-7pm, Su 11am-6pm. AmEx, DC, MC, V.

◼ **Top Shop/Top Man,** 214 Oxford St. (☎ 7636 7700). Tube: Oxford Circus. Some other branches. An absolute must for the club kid on a budget. This multi-story megastore offers the trendiest inexpensive fashions with something to suit everyone's flamboyant side. Free Playstations, foosball, and Internet access complete the experience. Open M-W and F 9am-8pm, Th and Sa 9am-9pm, Su noon-6pm. AmEx, MC, V.

Cyberdog, 9 Earlham St. (☎ 7836 7855). Tube: Leicester Sq. Also at Stables Market, Chalk Farm Rd., Camden Town. Clubwear displayed as it's meant to be seen—under UV light. Fluorescent-colored T-shirts (£20). Techno always playing and available for sale downstairs. Open M-Sa 11am-7pm, Su 1-6:30pm. AmEx, MC, V.

Reiss, 78-79 New Bond St. (☎ 7493 4866) Tube: Bond St. Some branches. One of the most influential trendsetters in men's fashions, using classic fabrics and smooth lines to introduce new styles. They'll be wearing what you buy here next season. Open M-W and F-Sa 10am-7pm, Th 10am-8pm, Su noon-6pm. AmEx, MC, V.

Jigsaw, 31 Brompton Rd. (☎ 7584 6226). Tube: Knightsbridge. Numerous other branches. Somewhat pricey, but very stylish men's and women's threads in luscious fabrics (e.g. deliciously soft leather) and muted, subtle colors. Large men's store at Floral St. (Tube: Covent Garden). Open M-Tu and Th-F 10:30am-7pm, W 10:30am-7:30pm, Sa 10am-7pm, Su noon-5pm.

Next, 54-58 Kensington High St. (☎ 7938 4211). Tube: High St. Kensington. Many branches. For a wide age range. Fair prices for basic, sophisticated pieces, from office to beach garb. Open M-W and F-Sa 10am-7pm, Th 10am-8pm, Su 11:30am-6pm.

BOOKSTORES

In London, even the chain bookstores are wonders. An exhaustive selection of bookshops lines Charing Cross Rd. between Tottenham Court Rd. and Leicester Sq., and many vend secondhand paperbacks. Cecil Court, near Leicester Sq., is a treasure trove of tiny shops with specialty bookstores for seemingly any topic. Establishments along Great Russell St. stock esoteric and specialized books on any subject from Adorno to the Zohar.

Blackwells, 100 Charing Cross Rd. (☎ 7292 5100). It's academic (mostly). Go for the postmodern theory, stay for the huge selection of fiction. Open M-Sa 9:30am-8:30pm, Su noon-6pm. Amex, MC, V.

Foyles, 113-119 Charing Cross Rd. (☎ 7437 5660). Tube: Tottenham Court Rd. A giant warehouse—over 4 floors. Open M-W and F-Sa 9am-6pm, Th 9am-7pm. AmEx, MC, V.

Maggs Brothers, 50 Berkeley Sq. (☎ 7493 7160). Tube: Green Park. A bibliophile's paradise in an allegedly haunted 18th-century mansion. Tremendous selection of 19th-century travel narratives, illuminated manuscripts, militaria, and autographs. Open M-F 9am-5pm. MC, V.

The Travel Bookshop, 13-15 Blenheim Crescent (☎ 7229 5260). Yes, it's the tiny specialist bookstore featured in *Notting Hill*. No, the people behind the counter rarely look like Hugh Grant. Yes, they stock *Let's Go*. Open M-Sa 10am-6pm.

Gay's the Word, 66 Marchmont St. (☎ 7278 7654). Tube: Russell Sq. Widest stock of gay and lesbian literature in England; mail order service available. Notice board (including accommodations listings), discussion groups, and readings. Open M-Sa 10am-6:30pm, Su 2-6pm. AmEx, MC, V.

Souls of Black Folk, 407 Coldharbour Lane (☎ 7738 4141). Tube: Brixton. A friendly neighborhood store stocked high with books on Africa and the Caribbean, as well as fiction. Cafe serves huge smoothies (£3). Open M-Th 11am-10pm, F 11am-3am, Sa 11am-1am, Su 10am-8pm. MC, V.

RECORD STORES

As anyone who read *High Fidelity* knows, London crawls with music junkies. Fortunately, the city has a record collection to match. Don't expect any bargains, and remember that when it comes to records, "import" means "rip-off." Vinyl still remains an important part of the London music retail scene. The megastores carry vinyl versions of most major-label releases, but to get those rare promos, white labels, or collectibles, you'll probably have to go to an independent record store. In **Camden Town, Brixton,** and **Ladbroke Grove,** record stores tempt collectors and intimidate browsers with rare vinyl and memorabilia at rock star prices. The best collection of record stores, though, are probably at **Berwick Street** in Soho, and **Hanway Street,** off Tottenham Court Rd.

HMV, 150 Oxford St. (☎ 7631 3423). Tube: Oxford Circus. Jazz, classical, world music, and soundtracks and most everything else. Open M-F 9:30am-8pm, Sa 9am-7:30pm, Su noon-6pm. AmEx, DC, MC, V.

Honest Jon's, 276-278 Portobello Rd. (☎ 8969 9822). Tube: Ladbroke Grove. Still funky after all these years. 276 holds an impressive jazz collection, 278 a wide selection of hip-hop LPs and some decent 12-inch singles, as well as soul and funk holdings. Open M-Sa 10am-6pm, Su 11am-5pm. AmEx, MC, V.

Red Records, 500 Brixton Rd. (☎ 7274 4476). Tube: Brixton. The sign reads "Black Music Specialists"; inside is an impressive collection of reggae, hip-hop, soul, garage, and jazz. Vinyl, CDs, tapes, and DJ equipment. Open M-Sa 9:30am-8pm. AmEx, MC, V.

Rough Trade, 130 Talbot Rd. (☎ 7229 8541). Tube: Ladbroke Grove. **Branch:** 16 Neal's Yard (☎ 7240 0105), Tube: Covent Garden. Birthplace of the legendary independent record label. Open M-Sa 10am-6:30pm, Su 1-5pm. AmEx, MC, V.

LONDON

SPECIALTY STORES

Dr. Marten's Dept. Store Ltd, 1-4 King St. (☎ 7497 1460). Tube: Covent Garden. Tourist-packed 5-tiered megastore; watches, sunglasses, candles, and of course the hard-as-nails shoes. Buy Docs for everyone you know, from baby to granny. Open M-W and F-Sa 10am-7pm, Th 10:30am-8pm, Su noon-6pm. AmEx, MC, V.

Hamley's, 188-189 Regent St. (☎ 7734 3161). Tube: Oxford Circus. Even Santa and his elves do their shopping here, in a place most kids would call heaven. London's largest toy shop spans 6 floors filled with every conceivable toy and game. Open M-W 10am-7:30pm, Th-Sa 10am-8pm, Su noon-6pm. Major credit cards.

Lush, Units 7 and 11, The Piazza, Covent Garden (☎ 7240 4570). Tube: Covent Garden. Branches at 40 Carnaby St. (☎ 7287 5874) and 123 King's Rd. (☎ 7376 8348). A delicious array of freshly made cosmetics. Slabs of fragrant soaps are almost good enough to eat (£1.20-1.90 for 100g). Open M-Sa 10am-7pm, Su noon-6pm. MC, V.

R. Twining & Co, 216 The Strand (☎ 7353 3511). Tube: Charing Cross. This institution of tea honors the leaf that remains the Queen's official brew. A tiny museum in the back traces the tea's lineage. Leaf teas include Earl Grey (£1.45 per 125g), Prince of Wales (£1.50 per 100g), and other regal blends. This may be as close as you get to royalty. Open M-F 9:30am-4:30pm. MC, V.

STREET MARKETS

Brick Lane. Tube: Aldgate East. Filled with South Asian flair: food, rugs, bolts of fabric, and sitar strains. Open Su 6am-1pm.

Brixton Market, Electric Ave., Pope's Rd., Brixton Station Rd., Granville Arcade, and Market Row. Tube: Brixton. Shoppers from all over London browse through the stalls of African crafts and discount clothing. Open M-Tu and Th-Sa 8:30am-5pm, W 8:30am-1pm.

Camden Market, off Camden High St. and Chalk Farm Rd. (☎ 7284 2084, Stables Market ☎ 7485 5511). Tube: Camden Town or Chalk Farm. Popular crowded place to find anything old or funky. Weekends are best. Open W-Su 9:30am-5:30pm.

Camden Passage, Islington High St. Tube: Angel. Right from the Tube, then right on narrow, pedestrian-only Islington High St. Antiques, prints, and drawings. Open W and Sa 8:30am-3pm, but many start to pack up around 2pm.

Petticoat Lane. Tube: Liverpool St., Aldgate, or Aldgate East. Street after street of stalls, mostly cheap clothing and household appliances. The real action begins at about 9:30am. Open Su 9am-2pm; starts shutting down around noon.

Portobello Market, Portobello Rd. Tube: Notting Hill. The market makes this already lively 'hood downright vivacious every Sa. From museum-quality antiques to costume baubles, there's something for every taste and budget (or lack of either). Portobello has hosted freakshows, fortune-tellers, conjurers, and charlatans selling miracle elixirs since the early Victorian age. A look at the tattoo parlors or juice bars hawking Gusto herbal drink today should convince cynics that some things never change. Antique market Sa 7am-5pm. Clothes market F-Sa 8am-3pm. General market open M-W 8am-6pm, Th 9am-1pm, F-Sa 7am-7pm; Sa is the best day.

🎭 ENTERTAINMENT

On any given day or night, Londoners and visitors can choose from the widest range of entertainment options a city can offer. Suffering serious competition only from Broadway, the West End is the world's theater capital, led by a surprisingly experimental, well-financed Royal National Theatre. Music scenes range from the black ties of the Royal Opera House to Wembley mobs and nightclub raves. The work of British filmmakers like Derek Jarman, Sally Potter, and Mike Leigh is shown in cinemas all over the city. Dance, comedy, sports, and countless unclassifiable happenings can leave you in bewildered awe over the listings in *Time Out* ($1.80) and *What's On* ($1.30). **Kidsline** answers queries on children's events. (☎ 7222 8070. Open M-F 4-6pm.) **Artsline** has information about disabled access at entertainment venues across London. (☎ 7388 2227. Open M-F 9:30am-5:30pm.)

THEATER

In theaterspeak, the **West End** refers not only the part of central London where all the big theaters are, but also to all top-class theaters. The **Fringe** is the collective name for the dozens of smaller, less commercial theaters in London: here, you'll find everything from community productions to avant-garde experiments. Fixed between those two extremes are **Off-West End** productions, which may lack West End resources but generally feature high-quality acting and intelligent writing. **Stalls** are seats nearest the stage. **Dress Circle** and **Upper Circle** refer to the balcony seats above the stalls. **Slips** are seats along the top edges of the theater, usually cheapest but with the worst views. The **interval** is the time for gin or the loo.

The **Leicester Square Half-Price Ticket Booth** sells tickets at half price (plus £1.50-2 booking fee) on the day of the performance, but carries them only for the West End, the Barbican, and the National Theatre. Tickets are sold from the top of the pile, which means you can't choose seats, and the priciest seats are sold first. Lines are particularly long on Saturdays. (Open M-Sa noon-6:30pm, Su noon-3pm; cash only.) Your next best bet for low prices is to schlepp to a theater's box office where day seats, standbys, or student-rate tickets are often available. Major **repertory theaters** are listed below; for other venues, especially those with constant repertoires, check *Time Out*. For popular **musicals,** you should book far in advance.

Royal Shakespeare Company, Barbican Centre, Silk St. (box office ☎7638 8891; www.barbican.org.uk). Tube: Barbican or Moorgate. The RSC makes its London home in the two theatres of the Barbican Centre. Forward-leaning balconies in the **Barbicon Theatre** guarantee that none of the 1166 seats sit farther than 65 ft. from center stage, and every seat gives a clear view. **The Pit** provides a more intimate (200-seat) setting. Tickets for the main stage £7.50-24; weekday matinees £6-13; Saturday matinees and previews £8-18. Student and senior standby available in person or by phone from 9am on the day of performance, £8 (1 per person). There are always several sign-language and audio-described performances during each run. Box office open daily 9am-8pm.

Royal National Theatre, South Bank Centre (☎ 7452 3400; www.nt-online.org). Tube: Waterloo. As you might expect from the "National" part of the name, the RNT's brilliant repertory company puts on a bit of everything on its three stages. All seats offer an unobstructed view of the stage. Backstage tours M-Sa £4.75, concessions £3.75. Book in advance; call for times. Box office open M-Sa 10am-8pm.

Olivier and **Lyttelton:** Tickets £10-32, day seats (available from 10am on day of performance) £10-14, general standby seats (available 2hr. before show) £12-16, student standby (available 45min. before show) £8-10, standing £4.50-6. Discounted admission for those in wheelchairs (all seats £15-16) and for other disabled people (£8-16). Discounted seats to matinees for under-18s (all seats £9-10) and seniors (£13-14).

Cottesloe: Tickets £10-22. Discounted admission for those in wheelchairs and the visually impaired (all seats £15) and for other disabled people (£8-15). Discounted entry to matinees for under-18s (£9) and seniors (£13).

Shakespeare's Globe Theatre, New Globe Walk, Bankside (☎ 7401 9919 or Ticketmaster ☎ 7316 4703). Tube: London Bridge. Using this reconstruction of the original Globe (where the Bard himself put on some plays) might have been nothing more than a gimmick, but the company employs the 3-tiered open-air space well. Patrons may either purchase spots on the wooden benches or stand through a performance as "groundlings." However, groundlings should prepare for the possibility of rain: umbrellas are prohibited because they impede sight lines. Shows take place May-Sept. Wheelchair access. Box office open M-Sa 10am-8pm, until 6pm by phone.

Old Vic, Waterloo Rd. (☎ 7928 7616). Tube: Waterloo. One of the most beautiful performance spaces in London. High-brow theater. £7.50-30.

FILM

The degenerate heart of the celluloid monster is **Leicester Square,** where the most recent hits premiere a day before hitting the chains. Many cinemas reduce prices all-day Monday and for matinees Tuesday through Friday. The **Empire** (☎ (0870) 603 4567) and **Odeon Leicester Sq.** are London's biggest cinemas. Outside the main-stream, the following cinemas offer independent, foreign, and classic films:

The Prince Charles, Leicester Pl. (☎ 7734 9127; www.princecharlescinema.com). Tube: Leicester Sq. A Soho institution: 4 shows daily; generally second runs and a few classics for only £2.50-3.50 (M £1.50-2). Originator of hot trend *Sing-a-Long-a-Sound-of-Music,* where von Trappists dress as everything from nuns to "Ray, a drop of golden sun" (F 7:30pm, £12.50; Su 2pm, £10, children always £8). Catch the *Rocky Horror Picture Show,* complete with a live troupe, every F at 11:45pm for £6, concessions £3.

Gate Cinema, 87 Notting Hill Gate (☎ 7727 4043). Tube: Notting Hill Gate. A Victorian-interior 240-seater with an arthouse selection. £6.50, M-F first film before 3pm £3.50, M-F before 6pm and late shows F and Sa, students, and seniors £3.

National Film Theatre (NFT), South Bank Centre (☎ 7928 3232; www.bfi.org.uk). Tube: Waterloo, or Embankment and cross the Hungerford footbridge. One of the world's leading cinemas, with a mind-boggling array of films (mostly arthouse favorites and recent raves) in three auditoriums. Most screenings £6.50, concessions £5.

CLASSICAL MUSIC, OPERA, AND BALLET

London's unparalleled classical resources include five orchestras, two huge arts centers, and countless concert halls. Even so, its world-class orchestras provide only a fraction of the notes that fill its major music centers. Visiting orchestras continually parade through the city, and London has been the professional home of some of the greatest conductors of the century, including Sir Thomas Beecham, Otto Klemperer, and Andre Previn. The major venues for orchestral and chamber music are listed below.

Barbican Hall, Barbican Centre, Silk St. (☎ 7638 8891; 24hr. recorded info ☎ 7382 7272; www.barbican.org.uk). Tube: Barbican or Moorgate. The venerable **London Symphony Orchestra** (www.lso.co.uk) inhabits this modern hall with superb acoustics. LSO concerts £6.50-35, under 16 £3, student and senior standby tickets sold shortly before the performance £6-8. Prices may vary for other concerts. Box office open 9am-8pm.

Royal Albert Hall, Kensington Gore (☎ 7589 8212; www.royalalberthall.com). Tube: South Kensington or Knightsbridge (buses #9, 10, and 52 go by the Hall from either station). London's premier concert hall, seating 5300. The **Proms** (BBC Henry Wood Promenade Concerts) never fail to enliven London summers with concerts every day for 8 weeks from mid-July to mid-Sept. All the Proms are also broadcast live on BBC Radio 3, 90-93 FM. £5-60. Over 1000 standing tickets in the Arena (the floor of the hall) and the Gallery (the very top of the hall) are available 1hr. before each concert for just £3, but be ready to queue for longer. Box office open daily 9am-9pm.

Wigmore Hall, 36 Wigmore St. (☎ 7935 2141). Tube: Bond St. or Oxford Circus. Elegant venue hosts concerts and chamber music. Tickets £6-35. 1hr. standbys at lowest price. In summer, Su morning coffee concerts begin at 11:30am; £8, coffee free. Closed end of July through Aug. Box office open 10am-5pm.

Royal Opera House, at Covent Garden, Box St. (box office ☎ 7304 4000). The newly refurbished stage hosts its resident companies, the Royal Opera and the Royal Ballet. All works at the English National Opera are sung in English. It's best to call the box office, 48 Floral St. (Tube: Covent Garden) for ticket prices. Open M-Sa 10am-7pm.

London Coliseum, St. Martin's Ln. (☎ 7632 8300). Tube: Charing Cross or Leicester Sq. Seats for opera cost £6.50-55. Box office open M-Sa 10am-8pm.

Sadler's Wells, Rosebery Ave. (☎ 7863 8000). Tube: Angel. London's premier space for dance, featuring anything from ballet to contemporary dance. Free bus travel to the theatre; just show your ticket at the ticket office. Tickets £7.50-30; some student and senior tickets £5. Student and senior standbys £7.50-10, available 1hr. before performance. Box office open M-Sa 10am-8:30pm.

ROCK AND POP

Major rock concert venues include the indoor **Wembley Arena,** the huge outdoor **Wembley Stadium,** the **Royal Albert Hall** (see p. 138), and the **Forum.** In the summer, outdoor arenas such as **Finsbury Park** become venues for major concerts and festivals. For details on catching big-name bands, check *Time Out;* the following is a selection of pubs, clubs, and venues with regular live music.

Borderline, Orange Yard, Manette St., off Charing Cross Rd. (☎ 7734 2095; www.borderline.co.uk). Tube: Tottenham Court Rd. British record companies test new rock and pop talent in this basement club. Sometimes the site of secret concerts by famous rockers. Tickets £5-10 in advance, student discount £5. Box office open M-F 4-7:30pm.

Brixton Academy, 211 Stockwell Rd. (☎ 7771 2000). Tube: Brixton. Time-honored venue hosts a variety of music, including rock, reggae, rap, and alternative. 4300 capacity. Box office open M-F 10am-8pm, Sa noon-6pm; phone bookings M-F 10am-6pm, Sa noon-6pm. Tickets £8-25. Cash only at the door.

Dublin Castle, 94 Parkway (☎ 7485 1773). Tube: Camden Town. Irish pub facade hides one of London's most legendary indie clubs. 3-4 bands per night. Tickets £3.50-5. Open daily 11am-midnight; music M-Sa 9pm-midnight, Su 8:30-11pm.

The Garage, 20-22 Highbury Corner (☎ 8963 0940, box office ☎ 7344 0044). Tube: Highbury and Islington. Club/performance space with decent views that attracts big names, but patrons complain about its sound system. Rock, pop, and indie bands most nights. Music starts 8pm. Tickets £4-10.

Rock Garden, The Piazza, Covent Garden (☎ 8836 4052; www.rockgarden.co.uk). Tube: Covent Garden. A variety of one-off new bands play nightly—rock, indie, acid jazz, soul. Happy hour daily 5-8pm, free admission and cheap drinks. Open M-Th 5pm-3am, F-Sa 5pm-4am, Su 7pm-midnight. Tickets £5, concessions £4; F-Sa after 10pm £8-10.

Shepherd's Bush Empire, Shepherds Bush Green (☎ 7771 2000). Tube: Shepherds Bush. Hosts dorky-cool musicians like David Byrne, the Proclaimers, and Boy George. 2000 capacity, with 6 bars. Box office open M-F 10am-6pm, Sa noon-6pm; phones bookings M-F 10am-8pm, Sa noon-6pm. Tickets £5-20.

JAZZ

Ronnie Scott's, 47 Frith St. (☎ 7439 0747). Tube: Leicester Sq. or Piccadilly Circus. The most famous jazz club in London and one of the oldest in the world has seen the likes of Ella Fitzgerald and Dizzy Gillespie. Expensive food (but don't overlook the cheaper starters) and great music. Waiters masterfully keep noisy clients from ruining the music by politely telling them to shut up. Reservations essential. Box office open M-Sa 11am-6pm. Music M-Sa 9:45pm-2:30am. Open M-Sa 8:30pm-3am, Su 7:30-11:30pm. Cover M-Th £15, F-Sa £20; students M-W £9.

100 Club, 100 Oxford St. (☎ 7636 0933). Tube: Tottenham Court Rd. Offerings vary from traditional modern jazz, swing, and blues to indie rock and comedy, all hidden behind a battered doorway. Regular nights include jazz dance parties F, swing jazz Sa, rhythm and blues Su, "Stompin" swing dance M. Open Su-Th 7:30pm-midnight, F-Sa 7:30pm-2am. Cover usually £6-10; free sessions F at lunch.

Pizza Express Jazz Club, 10 Dean St. (☎ 7439 8722). Tube: Tottenham Court Rd. or Leicester Sq. Packed club beneath a pizzeria. Fantastic groups and occasional greats; get there early or reserve ahead. Music nightly 9pm-midnight; doors open 7:45pm. Restaurant open daily 11:30am-12:30am. £10-20.

SPECTATOR SPORTS

FOOTBALL. London has been blessed with 13 of the 92 professional teams in England. The big three are **Arsenal,** Highbury Stadium, Avenell Rd. (☎ 7704 4000; Tube: Arsenal); **Chelsea,** Stamford Bridge, Fulham Rd. (☎ 7386 7799; Tube: Fulham Broadway); and **Tottenham Hotspur,** White Hart Lane, 748 High Rd. (☎ 8365 5000; Rail: White Hart Lane). The football scene is very partisan and favorites vary from neighborhood to neighborhood. England plays occasional international matches at the historic but soon to be redesigned **Wembley Stadium,** usually on Wednesday evenings (☎ 8902 8833; Tube: Wembley Park). On a non-professional level, footy is also played in parks all over London: on Sunday morning, the massive grid of pitches on Hackney Marshes are a sight well worth beholding.

RUGBY. The most significant contests, including the springtime Six Nations championship (featuring England, Scotland, Wales, Ireland, France, and new-comer Italy) are played at **Twickenham** (☎ 8831 6666; Rail: Twickenham). Other venues include **Saracens,** Dale Green Rd. (☎ (01923) 496200; Tube: Oakwood), and **Rosslyn Park,** Priory Ln., Upper Richmond Rd. (☎ 8876 1879; Rail: Barnes).

CRICKET. London's two grounds stage both county and international matches. **Lord's,** St. John's Wood Rd. (☎ 7289 1611; Tube: St. John's Wood), is the home turf of the **Marylebone Cricket Club (MCC),** the established governing body of cricket. Archaic stuffiness pervades the MCC; women have yet to see the pavilion's interior. **Foster's Oval,** Kennington Oval, home to **Surrey Cricket Club,** also fields Test Matches. (☎ 7582 7764. Tube: Oval. Tickets £7-8, internationals £21-36.)

TENNIS. Every year, for two weeks in late June and early July tennis buffs all over the world focus their attention on **Wimbledon.** If you want to get in, arrive early (6am); the gate opens at 10:30am (get off the Tube at Southfields or take buses #39, 93 or 200 from central London, which run frequently during the season). Get a copy of the order of play on each court, printed in most newspapers. Outer courts have first-come, first-served seats or standing room only. If you fail to get Centre or No. 1 Court tickets in the morning, try to find the resale booth (usually in Aorangi Park), which sells tickets handed in by those who leave early (open from 2:30pm; tickets £5 before 5pm, £3 after). Also, on the first Saturday of the championships, 2000 extra Centre Court tickets are put up for sale at the "bargain" price of around £25. Call ☎ 8971 2473 for ticket information.

▉ PUBS AND BARS

The atmosphere and clientele of London's 7000 pubs vary considerably. Avoid pubs within a half-mile radius of a main-line train station (Paddington, Euston, King's Cross/St. Pancras, and Victoria). Some prey upon tourists by charging an extra 20-40p per pint. Stylish, lively pubs cluster around the fringes of the West End, while cheaper pubs proliferate in the East End. Many historic alehouses lend an ancient air to areas swallowed by urban sprawl, such as Hampstead. Some of the oldest pubs cluster in the City. Buy drinks at the bar; a pint should set you back £1.80-3. Just remember—don't tip the bar man!

THE CITY OF LONDON

Ye Olde Cheshire Cheese, Wine Office Ct., by 145 Fleet St. (☎ 7353 6170). Tube: Blackfriars or St. Paul's. Classic pub, dating to the 17th century, where Dr. Johnson and Dickens, as well as Americans Mark Twain and Teddy Roosevelt, hung out. Today it's hot among businesspeople and lawyers. Open M-Sa 11:30am-11pm, Su noon-3pm.

Fuego Bar y Tapas, 1 Pudding Ln. (☎ 7929 3366). Tube: Monument. This snazzy executive watering hole compensates for lack of window space and cavernous basement location with lively evening events. Spanish music M nights, Th-F disco nights. Tapas £2-4. Dinner main course £6.90-10. Open M-F 11:30am-2am.

HOLBORN AND THE INNS OF COURT

Black Friar, 174 Queen Victoria St. (☎ 7236 5650). Tube: Blackfriars. One of London's most exquisite pubs. The edifice's past purpose as a 12th-century Dominican friary is celebrated not only in the pub's name but in the intriguing arches, mosaics, and reliefs that line the pub's walls. Carlsberg £2.35, Tetley's £2.15. Lunch served 11:30am-2:30pm. Open M-F 11:30am-11pm, Sa noon-5pm, Su noon-4:30pm.

COVENT GARDEN AND SOHO

■ **Freud,** 198 Shaftesbury Ave. (☎ 7240 9933). Tube: Covent Garden. Cheaper than an hour on the couch. Open M-Sa 11am-11pm, Su noon-10:30pm. No credit cards.

■ **Crown and Anchor,** 22 Neal St. (☎ 7836 5649). Tube: Covent Garden. One of Covent Garden's most popular pubs. Open M-Sa 11am-11pm, Su noon-10:30pm.

Yo!Below, 52 Poland St. (☎ 7439 3660). Tube: Oxford Circus. Located below Yo!Sushi. Customers sit on cushions on the floor and dispense their own beer from taps at the table. Free massages and tea ceremonies, along with a karaoke-singing staff, make for a great night out. Open M-Su noon-midnight.

KENSINGTON, KNIGHTSBRIDGE, AND CHELSEA

The Social, 5 Little Portland St. (☎ 7636 4992). Tube: Oxford Circus. Raucous crowd, tiny space, great music, ear-debilitating bass. Manages to be both flashy and welcoming. Perhaps it's the comfort food they serve (eggy bread £2). Pints £2.60-2.70. Open M-Sa noon-midnight, Su 5-10:30pm.

The King's Head and Eight Bells, 50 Cheyne Walk (☎ 7352 1820). Tube: Sloane Sq. or South Kensington. Richly textured 16th-century pub close to the Thames where Thomas More would have a jar with his dangerous friend Henry VIII. Wide selection of beers on tap, including a decent Belgian selection (Hoegaarden £3.55). Standard pub grub £5.75-6.50. Open M-Sa 11am-11pm, Su noon-10:30pm.

NOTTING HILL, BAYSWATER, AND HYDE PARK

■ **192,** 192 Kensington Park Rd. (☎ 7229 0482). Tube: Ladbroke Grove. Despite its repeated mentions in the *Bridget Jones* books, this wine bar is worth a visit. Wines £2.60-6 per glass. Open M-Sa 12:30-11:30pm, Su 12:30-11pm.

The Westbourne, 101 Westbourne Park Villas (☎ 7221 1332). Tube: Westbourne Park. A fixture of the Notting Hill scene: funky inside, with a heated terrace packed to the gills outside. Open M 5-11pm, Tu-F noon-11pm, Sa 11am-11pm, Su noon-10:30pm.

SOUTH LONDON

■ **Cubana,** 48 Lower Marsh. (☎ 7928 8778). Tube: Waterloo. Staff keep people happy with spiky cocktails, live salsa music W nights, a cheap and intriguing menu (crab and papaya salad £6.95), and a wide selection of edible cigars. Open M-Sa noon-midnight.

Bread and Roses, 68 Clapham Manor St. (☎ 7498 1779). Tube: Clapham Common. With socialist roots, Bread and Roses has a history of liquoring up the people. Primarily trad pub that has great beers (Smile's Workers' Ale £2) and often hosts theater and music; call for a schedule. Open M-Sa 11am-11pm, Su noon-10:30pm.

EAST LONDON

■ **Shoreditch Electricity Showrooms,** 39a Hoxton Sq. (☎ 7739 6934). Tube: Old St. Where the super-cool go. Cocktails £6, beers from £2.30. Open Tu and W noon-11pm, Th noon-midnight, F-Sa noon-1am, Su noon-10:30pm.

■ **Prospect of Whitby,** 57 Wapping Wall (☎ 7481 1095). Tube: Wapping. Open ceilings and flagstone bar in a building dating from 1520 pale next to the glorious Thamescape. Lunch served noon-2:30pm, dinner 6-9pm daily. Open M-F 11:30am-3pm and 5:30pm-11pm, Sa 11:30am-11pm, Su noon-10:30pm.

The Vibe Bar, The Brewery, 91-95 Brick Ln., E1 (☎ 7377 2899). Tube: Aldgate East. DJs day and night. Plop on a sofa, tackle a Playstation game, or check your email for free. Pints £2.50. Wheelchair access. Open M-Sa 11am-11pm, Su noon-10:30pm.

NORTH LONDON

■ **Filthy MacNasty's Whiskey Café,** 68 Amwell St. (☎ 7837 6067). Tube: Angel. Renowned for traditional Irish music Su, and one of Shane Macgowan's favorite pubs. Live readings and music every M, and W-Th. Guinness £2.20. Wheelchair accessible. Open daily noon-11pm.

The Engineer, 65 Gloucester Ave. (☎ 7722 0950). Tube: Chalk Farm. A thousand miles away from boisterous Camden, join the beautiful Luvvies at this classic pub. A bright atmosphere and a sumptuous back garden makes everybody feel relaxed. Pints £2.50. Wheelchair accessible. Open M-Sa 9am-11pm, Su 9am-10:30pm.

BI, GAY, AND LESBIAN PUBS

▧ **The Candy Bar,** 4 Carlisle St. (☎ 7494 4041). Tube: Tottenham Ct. Rd. Three floors of women (men welcome as guests) at London's first and the UK's original all-week lesbian bar. Bar downstairs becomes dance floor W-Sa. Bar open M-Th 5-midnight, F 5pm-2am, Sa 11am-11pm, Su 5-10:30pm; club open M-Th 8pm-12am, F-Sa 8pm-2am, Su 7-11pm. Cover F and Sa after 10pm £5.

Vespa Lounge, St. Giles High St. (☎ 7240 1860). Tube: Tottenham Court Rd., under the giant skyscraper, on the back. A newcomer to the lipstick-lesbian scene, but definitely a keeper, and always packed at weekends. Men welcome as guests. Open daily 6-11pm.

▧ **Ku Bar,** 75 Charing Cross Rd. (☎ 7437 4303). Tube: Leicester Sq. Attracts well-dressed, younger gay men and those that love them. The crowd frequently spills onto the street, attesting to the popularity of this pre-club venue. Beer £2.25. Open M-Sa 12:30-11pm, Su 12:30-10:30pm.

Admiral Duncan, 54 Old Compton St. (☎ 7437 5300). Tube: Leicester Sq. or Piccadilly Circus. Always a popular hangout, now forever noted as a defiant symbol against intolerance. Since the 1999 bombing here, the pub's been renovated and still pulls in the crowds. Foster's £2.37. Open M-Sa 11am-11pm, Su noon-10:30pm.

Comptons of Soho, 53 Old Compton St. (☎ 7479 7461). Tube: Leicester Sq. or Piccadilly Circus. Soho's "official" gay pub is always busy, with a mostly male crowd of all ages. Horseshoe-shaped bar encourages the exchange of meaningful glances, while upstairs offers a more mellow scene. Open M-Sa 11am-11pm, Su noon-10:30pm.

WINE BARS

▧ **Vinopolis, City of Wine,** 1 Bank End (☎ (0870) 444 4777). Tube: London Bridge. With a ticket to this Dionysian Disneyland guests are treated to an interactive (yes, that means samples) tour of the world's wine history and offerings. £11.50, under 18 £4.50, £1 discount for advance booking. Open daily 10am-5pm; last entry 4:30pm.

▧ **Bleeding Heart Bistro,** Bleeding Heart Yard, off Greville St. (☎ 7242 2056). Tube: Farringdon. A tremendous cellar coupled with tremendous food might give you a coronary; the price tag on the wines at the upper end of the bistro's selection most definitely will. Glass £4-5, bottles £11 on up. Open M-F noon-11pm.

Vats, 51 Lamb's Conduit St. (☎ 7242 8963). Tube: Russell Square. Knowledgeable staff willing to give suggestions for the best wines on a budget. Open M-F noon-11pm.

▧ CLUBS

I like the nightlife. I like to boogie.
—Rumor attributes this to Winston Churchill

Every major DJ in the world either lives in London or makes frequent visits there. While the US may have introduced house music to the world, the UK has taken the lead in developing and experimenting with new types of dance music. Take advantage of your tourist status and party during the week—though there are fewer options, London has enough tourists, slackers, and devoted partyers to pack a few clubs even Sunday through Wednesday. If you want go out with the rest of the city on Friday and Saturday, show up before the pubs close—perverse things happen to cover charges after 11pm. Cover charges are listed after opening hours below.

Planning is important for the discriminating budget clubber. Look before you leap, and especially before you drink. It's best to avoid the bright glitzy clubs in Leicester Square (e.g. Equinox and Hippodrome), which are crowded with out-of-town English youth looking to get lucky. *Time Out* is the undisputed scene cop, and their starred picks of the day are usually a safe bet. Many clubs have after-hours parties called "chill outs," usually 6am-noon. For those who choose not to stay out until the morning hours, remember that the **tube** shuts down shortly after midnight and **black cabs** are especially hard to find when clubs are closing. Some late-night frolickers catch **"minicabs,"** unmarked cars that sometimes wait outside clubs; negotiate a price before you get in, and be wary of riding alone. It's advisable to arrange transportation in advance or acquaint yourself with the extensive network of **night buses** (information ☎ 7222 1234). Listings include some of the night bus routes that connect to venues outside of central London, but routes change and a quick double-check is recommended.

London's gay scene ranges from the flamboyant to the campy to the cruisy to the mainstream. The 24hr. **Lesbian and Gay Switchboard** (☎ 7837 7324) is an excellent source of info. If you can't find what you need here, consult *Gay Times, Capital Gay, Pink Paper, Diva*, and others at **Gay's the Word**, 66 Marchmont St., Britain's largest gay bookstore (see p. 135).

The Africa Centre, 38 King St. (☎ 7836 1973). Tube: Covent Garden. Art center by day, psychedelic, blacklit den of funk by night. Live African and samba music at the "Lompopo Club" most F, some Sa. F and Sa 9pm-3am. £7-8 in advance, £10 at the door.

The Aquarium, 256 Old St. (☎ 7251 6136). Tube: Old Street. Ultra-trendy club comes complete with swimming pool for club kids to take a dip in. Caters to a twentysomething crowd. Open Th 9am-3pm, F (garage) 10pm-4am, Sa (house) 10am-5pm. £5-15.

The Astoria (LA1), 157 Charing Cross Rd. (☎ 7434 0403). Tube: Tottenham Court Rd. From the station, take Charing Cross towards Soho. Megavenue (capacity 2000), hosts frequent live acts as well as Jeremy Joseph's popular *G.A.Y.* In the basement is the **LA2,** whose Sa *Carwash* requires a costume and a love of the 70s. £7-14.

Bagleys, York Way (☎ 7278 2777). Tube: King's Cross. This former movie studio is London's biggest club venue (capacity 3000). Four cavernous rooms with garage, house and old school raves. Open F 10pm-6am, Sa 10pm-8am. £10-14. **Be careful around King's Cross at night.**

Bar Rumba, 35 Shaftesbury Ave. (☎ 7287 2715). Tube: Piccadilly Circus. Brilliant nights out in a cozy underground space. Open M-Tu and Th-F 10pm-3am, W 10pm-3:30am, Sa 10pm-4am, Su 8pm-1:30am. £4-12.

Bug Bar, The Crypt, St. Matthew's Church, Brixton Hill (☎ 7738 3184). Tube: Brixton. Maybe it's become cliché to talk about the "vibe" of a bar, but if any place has vibe, this converted church crypt does. DJs spin on Th-Su. Open M-W 7pm-1am, Th and Su 7pm-2am, F-Sa 7pm-3am. F-Sa £5, £3 before 11pm.

Camden Palace, 1A Camden High St. (☎ 7387 0428). Tube: Morning Crescent. Huge and hugely popular with tourists and locals alike. *Peach* (F) packs 'em in with house and garage, while *Feet First* (Tu) does the same with indie, Britpop, and the occasional live act. Open Tu 10pm-2am, F-Sa 10pm-6am. £2-10.

The Dogstar, 389 Coldharbour Ln. (☎ 7733 7515). Tube: Brixton. A strong emphasis on the "club" part of club-bar, with DJs every night and a large central space to shake it. Open Su-Th noon-2:30am, F-Sa noon-4:30am.

Dust, 27 Clerkenwell Rd. (☎ 7490 5120). Tube: Farringdon. Glittery walls vibrate to house and salsa music at night when this pub morphs into a club. Program changes regularly, so call ahead. Open M-W 11am-11pm, Th 11am-midnight, F 6pm-midnight, Sa noon-2am. Free-£3.

The End, 18A West Central St. (☎ 7419 9199). Tube: Tottenham Court Rd. The End possesses not only the most beautiful sound system of all the London clubs, but also a decidedly stylish interior and a friendly group of staff and patrons. Open Th 9pm-3:30am, F-Su 9pm-6am. £5-20, Th and some other nights free with flyer before 11pm.

The Fridge, Town Hall Parade, Brixton Hill (☎ 7326 5100). Tube: Brixton. From the station, cross the street and walk to the left up Brixton Hill. Look for the long line. Converted cinema hosts some of the most popular nights in London, announcing them on the marquee. Open F-Sa 10pm-6am. £8-12. If you're stumbling out of the club and can't take the sunlight, head next door for the after party at the **Fridge Bar,** with a music policy that leans heavily towards soul and R&B. DJs spin Th-M. Open M-Th 6pm-2:30am, F 6pm-4am, Sa 5:30am-noon and 6pm-4am, Su 5:30am-noon and 6pm-3am. £5 F-Sa after 10pm, Su after 9pm; £3 F-Sa 9-10pm, Sa 5:30am-noon and 9-10pm.

The Hanover Grand, 6 Hanover St. (☎ 7499 7977). Tube: Oxford Circus. Multiple floors crammed full of well-dressed people. Getting in, however, may take ages—plan to go early, even on weekdays. Open W (hiphop and UK garage) 10:30pm-3:30am, F (garage) 10pm-4am, and Sa (house) 10:30pm-5:30am. £3-15.

Ministry of Sound, 103 Gaunt St. (☎ 7378 6528). Tube: Elephant and Castle. Take the exit for South Bank University. The granddaddy of all serious clubbing. Open F 10:30pm-6:30am, Sa midnight-9am. Cover £10-15.

Notting Hill Arts Club, 21 Notting Hill Gate (☎ 7460 4459). Tube: Notting Hill Gate. Hard beats fill the basement dance floor. Soul, Latin, jazz, house. £3-5. Open M-Sa 5pm-1am, Su 4-11pm. £3-5 M-Sa after 8pm, Su after 7pm.

The Office, 3-5 Rathbone Pl. (☎ 7636 1598). Tube: Tottenham Court Rd. By day it's a restaurant/bar, by night a 300-capacity club that pulls in a twentysomething crowd. DJs spin on Th (R&B, house, and garage), F (70s and 80s) and Sa (80s) nights, and on Su "recovery parties," beginning at 6:30am. Cover £4-9 on Th-Sa nights. Open daily noon-3am, some Su from 6:30am.

Salsa!, 96 Charing Cross Rd. (☎ 7379 3277). Tube: Leicester Square. Attracts lovers and looking-for-love-ers alike. Partners not needed, they'll find you. Beware lest the roaming tequila shot ladies lead you to perdition. Open M-Sa 5:30pm-2am, last admission midnight. M-Th £4, students £2; F-Sa £8, before 9pm £4.

Subterania, 12 Acklam Rd. (☎ 8960 4590). Tube: Ladbroke Grove. One of West London's finest clubs, tucked in under the Westway flyover (hence the name). Peek at the well-dressed crowds below from the balcony. *Rotation* (F) is a major crowd-puller. Reggae W, hiphop and garage F, garage and house Sa. Open W 10pm-2am, F-Sa 10pm-3am. £5-10; go early for cheaper cover.

Turnmills, 63B Clerkenwell Rd. (☎ 7250 3409). Tube: Farringdon. Walk up Turnmill St. and turn right onto Clerkenwell Rd. *Trade* gets kickin' at 3am and keeps on kickin' until noon. Get there early or late to avoid long queues, or reserve in advance. Open F-Sa 3am-noon. £10.

The Wag Club, 35 Wardour St. (☎ 7437 5534). Tube: Piccadilly Circus. The Whiskey-a-go-go, name duly abbreviated, continues to go strong, although its location means it can get quite touristy. Tu house, W rock, Th indie, F 70s and 80s, Sa 60s R&B. Open F-Sa 10pm-4am, Tu and Th 10pm-3am, W 10pm-3:30am. £4-10.

BI, GAY, AND LESBIAN NIGHTLIFE

For details about London's gay and lesbian nightlife scene, check out *Boyz* (www.boyz.co.uk) or *QX* (www.qxmag.co.uk), available free at many gay bars.

"Atelier," Thursday at The End, 18 West Central St. (☎ 7419 9199). Tube: Tottenham Court Rd. Dressing up is essential. £5, free with flyer from **Manto,** 30 Old Compton St.

The Black Cap, 171 Camden High St. (☎ 7428 2721). Tube: Camden Town. North London's best-known drag bar. Nightly live shows attract a mixed crowd. When the shows aren't on, a DJ plays Top 40. M "oldies and trash" night is a favorite. Open M-Th 9pm-2am, F-Sa 9pm-3am, Su noon-3pm and 7pm-midnight. Tu-Sa £2-4, free before 11pm.

The Box, Seven Dials, 32-34 Monmouth St. (☎ 7240 5828). Tube: Covent Garden or Leicester Sq. Intimate and stylish gay/mixed bar and brasserie. Menus change to match the season (main courses £6-9). Fun, hip clientele of both genders and all races. The dance floor downstairs makes this an excellent venue for a night of dancing and drinking (lager £2.50). Open M-Sa 11am-11pm, Su 7-10:30pm.

Freedom, 60-66 Wardour St. (☎ 7734 0071). Tube: Piccadilly Circus. A very trendy cafe-bar (look the part!) that draws a mixed crowd for cocktails. DJs and dancing below.

Heaven, Under The Arches, Craven St. (☎ 7930 2020). Tube: Charing Cross or Embankment. The most famous gay disco in Britain, if not the world. On the busiest nights, 5 dance floors are open. Open M, W, F-Sa, some Tu and Th 10pm-5am. £1-12; frequent concessions, some nights half-price or free.

❈ FESTIVALS

City of London Festival (☎ 7638 8891; www.colf.org). An explosion of activity around the city's grandest monuments: music in the livery halls and churches, plays at various venues, opera, art exhibitions, and walks that often allow access to buildings otherwise closed to the public. Box office (Barbican Centre, Silk St. entrance) open daily 9am-8pm. Many events free, most others £10-40. Booking begins early May.

Greenwich and Docklands International Festival (☎ 8305 1818; box office ☎ 8900 0355; www.festival.org.uk). Outdoor concerts, dance and theater from performers across the globe. Closing ceremonies culminate in a spectacular fireworks display. Festival July 6-15, 2001. Free-£20, depending on the event.

Notting Hill Carnival The neighborhood explodes with festivity every summer during the Notting Hill Carnival, Europe's biggest outdoor festival, which is held over the last weekend in August. Around 2 million people line Portobello Rd. to watch and walk in a parade of steel drummers, fantastic costumes, entranced followers, and dancing policemen while Caribbean music reverberates through the streets. A bit of warning: the Notting Hill Carnival attracts huge crowds to come and drink in a small area.

SOUTH ENGLAND

Amidst South England's sprawling pastures unfolds a history that asserts Britain's island heritage and expresses a continental link running deeper than the Channel Tunnel. Early Britons settled the counties of Kent, Sussex, and Hampshire after crossing the English Channel the hard way. The later, modestly-titled European visitor William the Conqueror left his mark upon the downsland in the form of awe-inspiring cathedrals, many built around settlements begun by the Romans. More recently, long-buried evidence of Caesar's invasion was uncovered by the German bombings of World War II. Victorian mansions perching atop seaside cliffs, babbling rivers lapping medieval town walls, and majestic cathedrals towering over graceful skylines summon a chorus of past voices, many of them literary. Geoffrey Chaucer's pilgrims colored the way to Canterbury with tales both spiritual and bawdy. Jane Austen's pen made its masterful strokes in the archipelago of named houses near the southern downs and borders. Charles Dickens drew mammoth novels from his early experiences in Portsmouth. E.M. Forster, Virginia Woolf, and other Bloomsburyites vacationed and lived near the South Downs, where the deeply ingrained local traditions are as timeless as the land itself.

HIGHLIGHTS OF SOUTH ENGLAND

CANTERBURY CATHEDRAL Ride on horseback to the cathedral that has inspired pilgrims since the 12th century. Visit the Altar of the Sword's Point and find purity in ancient enmity (p. 151).

BRIGHTON Stroll through the carnival madness of the beach and take a tour of Brighton's pan-Asian Royal Pavilion (p. 162).

DOVER CLIFFS Don't miss the famous chalk-white cliffs of Dover, one of the first glimpses of England for ferry travelers. Climb the Grand Shaft, carved into the rock in Napoleonic times, and visit Shakespeare Cliff, featured in *King Lear* (p. 156).

SOUTH DOWNS WAY Hike the salty slopes and sleep surrounded by Bronze-Age burial mounds (p. 187).

KENT

CANTERBURY ☎ 01227

And specially from every shires ende
Of engelond to caunterbury they wende.
　　—Geoffrey Chaucer, *Prologue to The Canterbury Tales.*

Flung somewhere between the cathedral and the open road, the soul of Canterbury is as flighty as the city's itinerant visitors. Archbishop Thomas à Becket met his demise in Canterbury Cathedral in 1170 after an irate Henry II asked, "Will no one rid me of this troublesome priest?" and a few of his henchmen took the hint. Since then, the site of one of British history's most gruesome executions has become the focus of many pilgrimages dedicated to the "hooly blisful martir." Geoffrey Chaucer saw enough irony in pilgrim flocks to capture them in his bawdy *Canterbury Tales*. Visitors today can admire the soaring, grand cathedral and discover the city's living charms closer to the ground; amidst Canterbury's rich history dwell friendly spirits and warm welcomes.

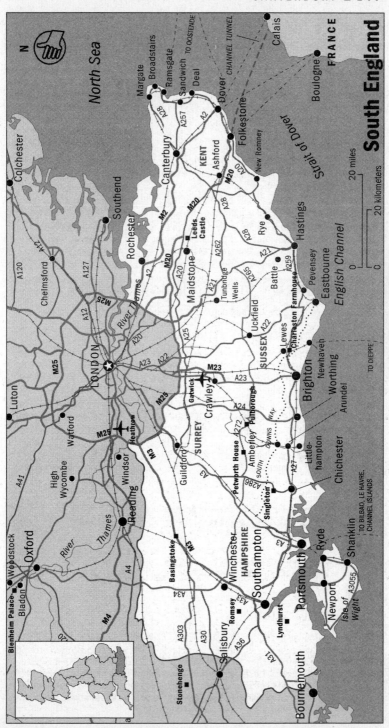

▐ GETTING THERE AND GETTING AROUND

Trains: East Station, Station Rd. East, off Castle St., southwest of town. Open M-Sa 6:10am-8:20pm, Su 6:10am-9:20pm. **Connex South Trains** (☎ (08457) 484950) from **London Victoria** (1½hr., every 30min., £15.30, day return £15.80). **West Station,** Station Rd. West, off St. Dunstan's St. Open M-F 6:15am-8pm, Sa 6:30am-8pm, Su 7:15am-9:30pm. Connex South Trains from **London Charing Cross** and **London Waterloo** to Canterbury West (1½hr., every hr., £15.30, day return £15.80). Ask everyone in your compartment to tell one story each way.

Buses: Bus Station, St. George's Ln., (☎472082). Open M-Sa 8:15am-5:15pm. **National Express** (☎ (08705) 808080) **buses** from **London** (2hr., 1 per hr., £6-8). Book tickets by 5pm. **Explorer** tickets allow passengers to hop on and off buses throughout Kent all day for the price of a single ticket (£6, seniors and children £4, family £12). Canterbury, on the rail and bus lines from Dover and Folkestone, is often a first stop for travelers from the Continent (see **Dover,** p. 156).

Taxis: Longport (☎ 458885). Open daily 7am-2am.

Bike Rental: Byways Bicycle Hire, 2 Admiralty Walk (☎ 277397) Owner delivers from home office; call at any reasonable hour. £10 per day, £50 per week; £50 deposit. Trailer attachments available for children. **Downland Cycle Hire,** West Railway Station (☎ 479543). Reserve in advance. £10 per adult per day, £7 per child. Bike trailers £6 per day. £50 deposit.

✴ ▐ ORIENTATION AND PRACTICAL INFORMATION

Canterbury is roughly circular, as defined by the eroding city wall. An unbroken street crosses the city from northwest to southeast, changing names from **St. Peter's St.** to **High St.** to **The Parade** to **St. George's St.**

Tourist Information Centre: 34 St. Margaret's St. (☎ 766567; fax 459840; canterburyvisitorinformation@compuserve.com). Free mini-guide. Wide range of maps and guides to Canterbury. "Book a bed ahead" service £2.50 and a 10% deposit (☎ 780063). Open daily Apr.-Aug. 9:30am-5:30pm; Sept.-Mar. 9:30am-5pm.

Tours: 1½hr. guided tours of the city from the tourist information centre daily Apr.-Oct. at 2pm; additional tour July-Aug. M-Sa at 11:30am. £3.50, concessions £3, families £8.50, under 14 free. The tourist information centre has info on hot-air balloon tours.

Financial Services: Lloyds TSB, 49 High St. (☎ 451681). Open M-Tu and Th 9am-5pm, W 9:30am-5pm, F 9am-6pm, Sa 9am-12:30pm. **Bureau de change** closes half an hour before the bank. **Thomas Cook,** 14 Mercery Ln. (☎ 767656). Open M-Sa 9am-5:30pm.

Launderettes: 36 St. Peter's St. (☎ 786911), near Westgate Towers. Open M-Sa 8:30am-5:45pm.

Police: Old Dover Rd. (☎ 762055), outside the eastern city wall.

Hospital: Kent and Canterbury Hospital (☎ 766877), off Ethelbert Rd.

Internet Access: Library, 18 High St. (☎ 463608), in the same building as the Royal Museum. Open M and W-Th 9:30am-6pm, Tu and F 9:30am-7pm, Sa 9am-5pm. Free 1hr. bookings. Usually about a 4-day wait, so call ahead.

Post Office: 28 High St. (☎ 473811), across from Best Ln. Open M-Sa 8:30am-5:30pm. **Postal Code:** CT1 2BA.

▌ ACCOMMODATIONS

Canterbury gets busy in the summer, so reserve early or arrive by mid-morning to secure recently vacated rooms. Singles are scarce. B&Bs are concentrated around the lanes stemming from High St., with quite a few scattered near West Station. The more costly B&Bs ($18-20) along **New Dover Rd.,** a half-mile walk from East Station, tend to fill fast. Turn right as you leave the station and continue up the main artery, which becomes Upper Bridge St. At the second roundabout, turn right onto St. George's Pl., which becomes New Dover Rd.

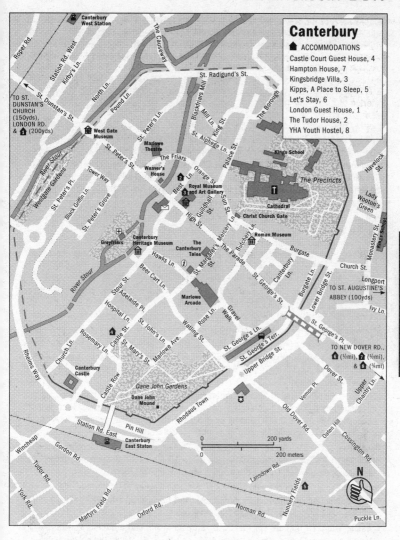

Canterbury

♠ ACCOMMODATIONS

Castle Court Guest House, 4
Hampton House, 7
Kingsbridge Villa, 3
Kipps, A Place to Sleep, 5
Let's Stay, 6
London Guest House, 1
The Tudor House, 2
YHA Youth Hostel, 8

SOUTH ENGLAND

🏠 **Hampton House,** 40 New Dover Rd. (☎ 464912). A luxurious house with comfortable, quiet, Laura Ashley-esque rooms; the orthopedic mattresses are heavenly. Lovely proprietors provide tea and coffee room service and a traditional English breakfast. £20-25 per person. Singles more expensive in summer. Off-season prices vary.

YHA Canterbury, 54 New Dover Rd. (☎ 462911; fax 470752; canterbury@yha.org.uk), ¾ mi. from East Station and ½ mi. southeast of the bus station. 86 beds. Laundry facilities. Lockers £1 plus deposit. Self-catering kitchen; meals also available. Relaxing lounge offers **Internet access** (50p per 6min.). **Bureau de change.** Reception open 7:30-10am and 1-11pm. In summer book a week in advance. Call for off-season openings. Dorms £10.85, under 18 £7.40.

Let's Stay, 26 New Dover Rd. (☎ 463628). Hostel-style accommodation in delightful Irish hostess's immaculate home. Vegetarian breakfast available; engaging conversation included. Ask about the origin of the name! Hours slightly irregular—call before arrival. Beds £10 per person.

Kipps, A Place to Sleep, 40 Nunnery Fields (☎ 786121; fax 766992; kipps@FSB-dial.co.uk). 10min. walk from the city center, 15min. from East Station. Friendly place for a kip, featuring a variety of accommodations and a terrific self-catering kitchen. Towels £1. Washers available. Key deposit £5. Dorms £11-13; singles £15; doubles £28. Weekly rates and family discounts available.

The Tudor House, 6 Best Ln. (☎ 765650), off High St. in the town center. Eat breakfast in front of a Tudor fireplace in this 16th-century house. Guests can rent bikes and boats for £5 per day. Singles £18; doubles £36, with bath £4, family rooms £50.

Castle Court Guest House, 8 Castle St. (☎/fax 463441), a few minutes from Eastgate. Clean and quiet, this pleasant B&B offers a 10% discount to *Let's Go* users. Continental and vegetarian breakfasts available. Singles £22; doubles/twins £36, with bath £42.

Camping: The Camping and Caravaning Club Site, Bekesbourne Ln. (☎ 463216), off the A257 (Sandwich Rd.), 1½ mi. east of city center. Take Longport Rd. from the city wall. Good facilities and 210 pitches for tents. Open year-round. £4.30 pitch fee; £5.30 per person; weekly rates and family discounts available.

FOOD

Bakeries and sweet shops please the palates of weary pilgrims around the cathedral. Pubs, restaurants, and fast-food dens crowd the High St. The **Safeway** supermarket, St. George's Pl., is four minutes from the town center. (☎ 769335. Open M-Th and Sa 8am-8pm, F 8am-9pm, Su 10am-4pm.) Just across the way on St. George's Pl. is another supermarket, **Netto.** (Open M-W 8:30am-7pm, Th-F 8:30am-8pm, Sa 8:30am-6pm, Su 10am-4pm.)

Marlowe's, 55 St. Peter's St. (☎ 462194). An eclectic mix of vegetarian and beefy English, American, and Mexican food in a friendly setting. They pride themselves on their Mexican improvisations. Choose from 8 toppings for 8 oz. burgers (£6.60), or select one of 18 vegetarian dishes (£6.35-8.95). Open daily 11:30am-10:30pm.

Il Pozzo, 15 Best Ln. (☎ 450154). Separates itself from the scads of Italian restaurants in Canterbury by serving traditionally cooked, richly sauced Italian food. Though more expensive than others (main courses around £13), its superlative, aromatic food makes it a real bargain. Open M-Sa noon-2pm and 7-10pm.

Raj Venue, 92 St. Dunstan's St. (☎ 462653). Fairly-portioned Indian food (many dishes £4.50-6.95) will please the gourmet, and the 10% student discount will please the cash-strapped traveler. Open daily noon-2:30pm and 6-11:30pm.

Goodchild's, 10 Butchery Ln (☎ 780333). Satiates queues of Canterbury pilgrims with a wide selection of sandwiches, baguettes, and filled rolls. Soup 40-65p, takeaway sandwiches £1.05-1.95. Open M-Sa 10am-4:30pm.

C'est la Vie, 17b Burgate (☎ 457555). Attracts locals and students who take away inventive sandwiches on freshly baked bread (£1.90-2.20). Open daily 9am-6pm.

PUBS

The White Hart, Worthgate Pl. (☎ 765091), near East Station. A congenial pub with homemade lunch specials (£4.50-6), as well as some of Canterbury's best bitters (£1.80). Open daily 10am-11pm.

Patrick Casey's, Butchery Ln. (☎ 463252). Offering a vast menu of traditional Irish foods, Casey's warms a traveler's stomach, as well as providing amply flowing beverages. Bitter £1.80, other ales and lagers £2. Live folk music Tu, Th, and F nights. Open M-Sa 11am-11pm, Su noon-10:30pm.

Alberry's, 38 St. Margaret's St. (☎ 452378). A snazzy wine bar that pours for students and travelers late into the evening. Happy hour 5:30-7pm. Open M-W noon-11pm, Th noon-1am, F-Sa noon-2am.

SIGHTS

An amazingly quiet and blissful Canterbury greets the early riser; get up and enjoy the city before the daytrippers arrive. The main sight, of course, is Canterbury Cathedral, the can't-miss building towering within the old city walls.

CANTERBURY CATHEDRAL

☎ 762862. www.canterbury-cathedral.org. Cathedral open Easter-Sept. M-Sa 9am-6:30pm, Su 12:30-2:30pm and 4:30-5:30pm; Oct.-Easter M-Sa 9am-5pm, Su 12:30-2:30pm and 4:30-5:30pm. Evensong services M-F 5:30pm, Sa 3:15pm, Su 6:30pm. Precincts open daily 7am-9pm. 75min. tours 4 per day, fewer off-season; £3, students and seniors £2, children £1.20; check the nave or welcome center for times. Self-guided tour booklet £1.25. 25min audio tour £2.50. Admission £3, concessions £2. Visitors are charged at the gate; after hours you may be able to wander into the precincts for free, but not into the building, unless you happen to be an Anglican bishop. Wheelchair accessible.

Money collected from pilgrims built much of Canterbury Cathedral's splendors, including the early Gothic nave, constructed mostly between the 13th and 15th centuries on a site allegedly first consecrated by St. Augustine 700 years earlier. Among the nave's entombed residents are Henry IV, his wife Joan of Navarre, and the Black Prince. A taste for the macabre has drawn the morbidly curious to the cathedral since 1170, when Archbishop Thomas à Becket was beheaded here with a strike so forceful it broke the blade of the axe. The murder site today is closed off by a rail—a kind of permanent police line—around the Altar of the Sword's Point. Travelers with a taste for the gruesome can view a 14-minute audio-visual recreation of the homicide just off the cloisters. (Shown continuously 10am-4pm. £1, students and seniors 70p, children 50p.) In the adjacent **Trinity Chapel**, a solitary candle marks where Becket's body lay until 1538, when Henry VIII burned his remains and destroyed the shrine to show how he dealt with bishops who crossed the king.

In a building beset with fire and rebuilt again and again, the **Norman crypt**, a huge 12th-century chapel, remains intact. The **Corona Tower**, 105 steps above the easternmost apse, recently reopened after renovations. (60p, children 30p.) Under the **Bell Harry Tower**—at the crossing of the nave and western transepts—perpendicular arches support intricate 15th-century fan vaulting. The cathedral's **welcome center**, also a gift shop, dispenses information and pamphlets. (Open M-Sa 9am-4pm.)

OTHER SIGHTS

THE CANTERBURY TALES. After atoning for that night in Brighton with a cathedral pilgrimage, you can be entertained by the gap-toothed Wife of Bath and her waxen companions in an abbreviated Modern English version of the Tales—complete with the smells of sweat, hay, and general grime. The museum simulates the journey of Chaucer's pilgrims all over again, only this time with headsets, and in several different languages. (St. Margaret's St. ☎ 479227. Open daily July-Aug. 9am-5.30pm; Mar.-June and Sept.-Oct. 9:30am-5:30pm; Nov.-Feb. Su-F 10am-4:30pm, Sa 9:30am-5:30pm. £5.50, concessions £4.60.)

WEST GATE MUSEUM. The remainder of medieval Canterbury crowds around the branches of the River Stour near the West Gate, through which pilgrims enter the city. The gate is one of the few medieval fortifications to survive the wartime blitz. Within the gate stands the museum, surrounded by well-tended gardens. Formerly a prison, it now keeps armor, old weapons, and prison relics, and commands broad views of the city. (☎ 452747. Open M-Sa 11am-12:30pm and 1:30-3:30pm. £1, students and seniors 65p, children and disabled 50p, families £2.30.)

GREYFRIARS. England's first Franciscan friary, Greyfriars was built over the River Stour in 1267 by Franciscan monks who arrived in the country in 1224, two years before Francis of Assisi died. A small museum and chapel can be found inside the simple building. For a quiet break, walk over to Greyfriars' riverside gardens. (Stour St. Open in summer M-F 2-4pm. Free.)

CANTERBURY HERITAGE MUSEUM. Housed in the medieval Poor Priests' Hospital, the museum spans Canterbury's history, from medieval times to World War II bomb-ravaging to much loved children's book character Rupert Bear. *(Stour St. ☎ 452747. Open June-Oct. M-Sa 10:30am-5pm, Su 1:30-5pm; Nov.-May M-Sa 10:30am-5pm. £2.40, concessions £1.60, families £5.30. Limited handicap access.)*

ST. AUGUSTINE'S ABBEY. Little remains of the abbey, built in AD 598, but you can view older Roman ruins and the site of St. Augustine's first tomb (AD 605). Exhibits from the site's excavation and the free audio tour reveal the abbey's history as a burial place, a royal palace, and a pleasure garden. *(Outside the city wall near the cathedral. ☎ 767345. Open daily Apr.-Oct. 10am-6pm; Nov.-Mar. 10am-4pm. £2.50, students and seniors £1.90, children £1.30. Handicap accessible.)*

CHURCH OF ST. MARTIN. Just around the corner from St. Augustine's on North Holmes St. stands the oldest parish church in England. Pagan King Æthelbert was married here to the Christian French Princess Bertha in AD 562. Joseph Conrad is buried here, sleeping in darkness. *(☎ 459482. Open M-Su 9am-5pm. Free.)*

BEST OF THE REST. Home of the Huguenots during the 15th century, the **Weaver's House,** 1 St. Peter's St., features an authentic witch-dunking stool swinging above the river. **Weaver's River Tours** runs 30min. cruises leaving from the house several times daily. *(☎ 464660. £4, student and seniors £3.50, children £3.)* The **Roman Museum,** Butchery Ln., houses hairpins, building fragments, and other artifacts from Roman Canterbury in a hands-on exhibit. *(☎ 785575. Open M-Sa 10am-5pm, Su 1:30-5pm. Last admission 4pm. £2.40, students and seniors £1.60, children £1.20. Handicap accessible.)* The **Royal Museum and Art Gallery** showcases new local talents and recounts the history of the "Buffs," one of the oldest regiments of the British Army. *(In the public library on 18 High St. ☎ 452747. Wheelchair accessible. Open M-Sa 10am-5pm. Free.)*

Near the city walls in the southwest lie the **Dane John Mound and Gardens,** now a park, and the massive, solemn remnants of the Norman **Canterbury Castle,** built for William the Conqueror himself. Outside the city walls to the northwest, the vaults of **St. Dunstan's Church,** north of St. Dunstan's St., contain a relic said to be the head of *Utopia* author Sir Thomas More. Legend has it that his daughter bribed the executioner at the Tower of London and buried the head beside the altar.

🎵 ENTERTAINMENT

What, Where, When, published biweekly, describes Canterbury's entertainment in all its urban guises and is free at the tourist information centre. Call ☎ 767744 for the recorded "Leisure Line." Buskers (street musicians) blend in with the crowds, especially along St. Peter's St. and High St. Budding streetside string quartets play Vivaldi while young bands of impromptu players ramble from corner to corner, acting out the most absurd of Chaucer's scenes. The occasional Fool can be found performing juggling tricks.

The task of regaling pilgrims with stories today falls upon the **Marlowe Theatre,** The Friars, which stages touring London productions. *(☎ 787787. Box office open M and W-Sa 10am-8pm, Tu 10:30am-8pm. Tickets £6.50-22. Concessions available.)* The **Gulbenkian Theatre,** at the University of Kent, University Rd., west of town out St. Dunstan's St., past St. Thomas' Hill, stages a range of productions. *(☎ 769075. Box office open M-F 10:30am-5:30pm. Tickets £5-21. Ask about student and senior discounts; unsold tickets available from 7pm on performance evening for £5.)*

For information on summer arts events and the October **Canterbury Festival**— two full weeks (Oct. 13-27) of drama, opera, cabaret, chamber music, dance, and exhibitions inspired by French culture—contact Canterbury Festival, Christ Church Gate, The Precincts, Canterbury, Kent CT1 2EE *(☎ 452853).* The **Chaucer Festival Spring Pilgrimage** *(☎ 470379)* in April ushers in a medieval fair and period-costumed performers. The **Stour Music Festival,** a popular celebration of Renaissance and Baroque music, lasts for 10 days at the end of June in Ashford, five miles southwest of Canterbury. The festival takes place in and around All Saint's Boughton Aluph Church, on the A28 and accessible by rail from West Station. Call the Canterbury bookings office *(☎ 455600)* for tickets (£5-14); reserve a month ahead.

NEAR CANTERBURY: LEEDS CASTLE

☎ (01622) 765400; www.leeds-castle.co.uk. Castle open daily Mar.-Oct. 11am-7:30pm; Nov.-Feb. 10:15am-5:30pm. Grounds open daily Mar.-Oct. 10am-7pm; Nov.-Feb. 10am-5pm. Last admission 2hr. before closing. Castle and grounds £9.50, students and seniors £7.50, children £6, families £26; grounds only £7.50, students and seniors £6, children £4.50, families £20. Wheelchair access, reduced rates for disabled travelers.

Twenty-three miles southwest of Canterbury on the A20 London-Folkestone road near Maidstone, Leeds Castle was named after the fun-loving chief minister of Ethelbert IV. Henry VIII transformed it into a lavish dwelling whose 500 acres of woodlands and gardens host unusual waterfowl, including black swans; lose yourself in a maze of 2400 yew trees. The castle houses an alarming collection of medieval dog collars. From Canterbury, take the train from West Station to Bearsted.

SANDWICH ☎01304

More a light snack than a meal, Sandwich (pop. 5,000) was the northernmost of the Cinque Ports, a defensive system of coastal towns. The town received special privileges from the King in exchange for a pledge to provide ships should war arise on the coast. Eventually, silt encroached, leaving the sea miles away, and making Sandwich useless to the King's Navy. Narrow streets, medieval gateways, and 600-year-old half-timbered houses make Sandwich worth an afternoon's exploration.

GETTING THERE AND PRACTICAL INFORMATION. Sandwich slices in five miles north of Deal and 11 mi. east of Canterbury; trains and buses run regularly among the three. The **train station** lies just off St. George's Rd. To reach the center of town, bear left on Delfside St., turn left on St. George's Rd., then right onto New St. **Trains** (☎ (08457) 484950) depart for Sandwich at least every hour from: **Deal** (6min., £1.90); **Dover** (24min., £4); and **London Charing Cross** (2hr., £19.80). **Buses** stop across from Guildhall on Cattlemarket. **Stagecoach** (☎ 472082) buses make the trip from **Deal** several times daily. **National Express** (☎ (08705) 808080) heads down to Sandwich from **London** once a day (£11).

The **tourist information centre** (TIC), Old Police Waiting Room, Guildhall, New St. (☎ 613565), hands out a free leaflet outlining a self-guided **tour** of town. (Open May-Sept. daily 10am-4pm.) Also available at the TIC is the free packet entitled *Sandwich Historic Town Trails*, which details short, pleasant jaunts about the town and countryside. When the Sandwich TIC is closed, the Deal TIC (☎ (01304) 369576) will answer questions. Services include: **banks** on Market St., **Barclay's** at 2 Cattlemarket (☎ 592000; open M-F 9:30am-4:30pm); free **Internet access** at the **library** (M-T and Th 9:30am-1pm and 2-6pm, F 9:30am-1pm and 2-7pm, Sa 9:30am-1pm); a small **police** station on Cattlemarket—but unless the crime is committed in the morning or early afternoon on a weekday (M-F 10am-noon and 1-3pm), better give nearby Dover a call (☎ 240055); and the **post office,** 16-20 Market St. (☎ 615327; open M-F 8:30am-6pm, Sa 8:30am-5pm). **Postal code:** CT13 9DA.

ACCOMMODATIONS AND FOOD. Sandwich lacks a youth hostel, and executives visiting the nearby Pfizer plant (and the golf courses) have driven up prices. Those with an itch to spend the night should call in advance. Six minutes from the train station is **Mrs. Rogers,** 57 St. George's Rd. Effervescing with geniality, the owners have been known to drive visitors on tours of the town. (☎ 612772. 2 bedrooms. Single £18; double/twin £32). **The B&B Above the Sandwich Golf Shop,** 38 King St., spoils you with bubble bath, down blankets, and chocolate croissants for breakfast in this tiny 700-year-old-house. (☎ 620141. £25 per person, discounts for longer stays.) **New Inn,** 2 Harnet St., near the Guildhall, should rightfully be called a B&B&B—bed, full breakfast, and access to a full bar. ((☎ 612335). £25 per person.) Campers walk along Moat Sole behind Guildhall and across train tracks to the **Sandwich Leisure Park Campsite,** Woodnesborough Rd., ½mi. from town. (☎ 612681. 100 pitches. Electric hook-up. Open Mar-Oct. Sites £7.50-9.50.)

Food hasn't been the same since the Earl of Sandwich munched his master-work. Pick up the makings for your own at the neighborhood **Pioneer,** Moat Sole. (☎ 620004. Open M-Sa 8am-10pm, Su 10am-4pm.) The **Little Cottage Tea Room,** The Quay (☎ 614387), hits the spot with scones, freshly-brewed tea (80p) and made-to-order sandwiches ($1.40-$1.95). Try the sticky toffee cake. (Open May-Sept. Tu-Sa 9:30am-5pm, Su 9:30am-4pm; Oct.-Apr. Tu-F 9:30am-3pm, Sa-Su 9:30am-4pm. 10% discount for *Let's Go* readers.) **Yummies,** Strand St., exceeds the Earl's wildest dreams, concocting truly inventive sandwiches and filled rolls for $2.25. Sample their "Italian stallion" or mix and match to create your own masterpiece. (☎ 614631. Open daily 8.30am-5pm.) Have a hearty pub lunch at **The Red Cow,** 12 Moat Sole, behind the Guildhall Museum. (☎ 613243. Lunch $3.50-6. Meals served M-F 11am-2:30pm and 6-11pm, Sa 11am-3pm and 6-11pm, Su noon-3pm and 7-10:30pm.)

🏛 🎭 **SIGHTS AND ENTERTAINMENT.** The elevated Butts, Rope Walk, and Mill Wall that once provided fortification for the town now make for an enjoyable stroll. The River Stour, dominated by the **Barbican,** was built by Henry VIII as part of his coastal defense scheme and was the site of one of the world's longest-running shakedowns: from 1127 until the early 1900s, tolls were taken to cross the river. A stroll down **Strand Street** will reveal perhaps the largest concentration of half-timbered Tudor buildings in England. The **Guildhall Museum,** beside the TIC on Cattlemarket, contains detailed histories of every possible point of interest in Sandwich's geography and history—except the origins of its culinary offspring. (☎ 617197. Open Apr.-Sept. Tu-W and F 10:30am-12:30pm and 2-4pm, Th and Sa 10:30am-4pm, Su 2-4pm; Oct.-Mar. T-W, F, and Su 2-4pm, Th and Sa 10:30am-4pm. $1, children 50p, family $2.) For an irreverent taste of the town, and one last pun, take a **Bite of Sandwich** theatrical tour, which walks tourists on a riotous trip back to the day when Sandwich was still England's most important port. (July-Aug. 7:30pm. $3 per person. Call the TIC for details.) To get to the **Gazen Salts Nature Reserve** from the Butts, follow signs across Gallows Field, a former execution site. The reserve hosts numerous birds and animals and just borders the marshland which silted over and separated Sandwich from the sea. (☎ 611925. Evenings only. Free.) The town heats up Aug. 23-27, 2001, for the annual **Sandwich Festival,** when jazz musicians and street performers entertain crowds free of charge.

DEAL ☎ 01304

Julius Caesar came ashore with an invasion force at Deal in 55 BC, and the town's three 16th-century castles represent Henry VIII's tardy efforts to prevent similar occurrences. Quiet and serene today, Deal deals in subtle pleasures and reserved charm. Inland visitors will find it almost quiet enough to hear the waves lapping at the pebbly shore.

🚉 ℹ **GETTING THERE AND PRACTICAL INFORMATION.** The **train station** is just west of town off Queen St.; to reach Deal's center, turn left onto Queen St. and follow it until you reach the pedestrian precinct of High St. (Open M-Sa 5:45am-10:10pm, Su 7:10am-6:40pm.) **Trains** arrive at least every hour from: **London** (2¼hr., $18.80); **Canterbury** (1hr., $4.40); **Dover Priory** (15min., $2.90); and **Sandwich** (6min., $1.90). **Buses** congregate on South St., one block south of Broad St. **National Express** (☎ (08705) 808080) runs from **London** (3hr., 3 per day, $9.50). **Three Castles taxi** service is on 54 Queen St. (☎ 374001). Rent bikes at **Hutchings Motor Cycles,** 7 South St. for $5 per day with a $50 deposit. (☎ 364945. Open daily 9am-6pm.)

Deal lies eight miles north of Dover and 12 mi. southeast of Canterbury. The town extends north to south along the coast; main arteries **Beach St., High St.,** and **West St.** are all parallel to the water. Deal's **tourist information centre** (TIC), Town Hall, High St., books accommodations for a 10% deposit and pulls in a good catch of free leaflets, including the indispensable *Deal Historic Town Trails,* which details 10 walks (3-8½mi.) in the area. (☎ 369576. Open M-F 9am-12:30pm and 1:30-5pm; mid-May to mid-Sept. also Sa 9am-2pm.) Services include: **National Westminster Bank,** 31 High St., corner of Queen St. (☎ 372126; open M-Tu and Th-F 9am-

4:30pm, W 9:30am-4:30pm, Sa 9:30am-1pm); a **launderette,** 5 Queens St. (☎ 204592;
load £2.40, change and soap 40p; open M-F 8am-8pm, last wash 6:45pm; Sa-Su 8am-
6pm, last wash 4:45pm); **Internet access** at the **Library,** corner of Middle St. and
Broad St. (☎ 374722; open M-T and Th 9:30am-6pm, W 9:30am-1pm, F 9:30am-7pm,
Sa 9:30am-5pm, Su 10am-4pm), and **PC Integrated,** also corner of Middle St. and
Broad St. (£4 per hr., min. charge £2; open M-F 10am-6pm, Sa 10am-2pm); the
police station (☎ 218017), London Rd.; and the **post office,** 17-19 Queen St. (☎
374216; open M-F 8:30am-5:30pm, Sa 9am-5:30pm). **Postal code:** CT14 6BB.

⌐⌐⌐ ACCOMMODATIONS AND FOOD. B&Bs populate many of the roads jutting near the coast, but affluent golfers playing the channel-side courses have
driven up their prices. Less expensive B&Bs are located closer to the town center.
Cannongate, 26 Gilford Rd., serves a full English or vegetarian breakfast and provides comfortable beds. (☎ 375238. Singles £18, with bath £20; doubles £34.) **The
Malvern,** 5-7 Ranelogh Rd., also provides inexpensive housing with relatively luxurious rooms and an ample breakfast (☎ 372944. £17.50 per person, children ages 5-
11 £12, children under 5 £8.50.)

    Tesco, 2 Queen St., sells the usual supermarket stuff. (Open M-W 8am-7pm, Th-F
8am-7:30pm, Sa 8am-6pm, Su 10am-4pm.) **Sainsbury's** does the same by the train
station. (Open M-Th 8am-8pm, F 8am-9pm, Sa 7:30am-7:30pm, Su 10am-4pm.)
Enjoy the Channel view and photos of motley locals with their catches at the **Lobster Pot,** 81 Beach St. All-day English breakfast is available, as well as takeaway
fish and chips for £3.60 (☎ 374713. Open daily 7am-9:45pm.) **The Sandwich Factory,**
33 High St., deals a menu of fresh sandwiches and cakes—try their crispy bacon
and avocado sandwich for £1.70. (☎ 362111. Open M-F 7:30am-3:30pm, Sa 8am-
3pm.) **Dunkerley's Bistro,** 19 Beach St., overlooking the sea, is slightly more expensive (main courses about £12), but residents from all parts of Kent flood in to dine
on local fish. (☎ 375016. Open Tu-Su noon-2:30pm and 6-10pm.) At **Ronnie's Tea
Rooms,** 1b Stanhope Rd., revel in plush chairs as you enjoy a light snack with tea.
(☎ 374300. Open M-Sa 9am-4pm.) **Corner Parlor,** 27 Beach St., blends the best thick
milkshakes around (£1.50) and serves lunch (£2-£3) while patrons gaze at the deep
blue beyond. (☎ 364564. Open M-Sa 9:30am-4:30pm.)

◨ SIGHTS. Deal Castle, south of town at the corner of Victoria Rd. and Deal Castle Rd., is the largest of Henry VIII's coastal constructions. Meant to serve as an
imposing bulwark against the French, it holds a maze of corridors and cells guaranteed to entangle potential visitors. Check out the medieval subliminal advertising: the castle's six buttresses form the distinctive shape of the Tudor Rose,
Henry's family symbol. (☎ 372762. Free audio tour. Open daily Apr.-Sept. 10am-
6pm; Oct.-Mar. W-Su 10am-4pm. £3, students and seniors £2.30, children £1.50.
Limited wheelchair access.) **Walmer Castle** rests south of Deal on the A258 to
Dover, about half a mile from town. The best preserved and most elegant of Henry
VIII's citadels, Walmer has been gradually transformed into a country estate. Since
the 1700s, it's been the official residence of the Lords Warden of the Cinque Ports,
a defensive system of coastal towns. Notable Lords Wardens include the Duke of
Wellington (whose famed boots are on display) and Winston Churchill. The post is
currently filled by the Queen Mum. (☎ 364288. Open Apr.-Sept. daily 10am-6pm;
Oct. daily 10am-dusk; Nov.-Mar. W-Su 10am-4pm. £4.50, students and seniors
£3.40, children £2.30. Wheelchair access to gardens and courtyard.)

    Along the coast to Deal Pier ticks the **Timeball Tower,** a fascinating contraption
connected to Greenwich Observatory. When ships used the Deal area as a makeshift port before crossing the Channel, the ball atop the tower was lowered at precisely 1pm each day to indicate the time. Today, the ball drops every hour on the
hour. (☎ 201200. Open July-Aug. Tu-Su 10am-5pm. Tours in winter by arrangement. £1.20, seniors and children 80p.) The **Maritime and Local History Museum,** 22
St. George's Rd., behind the TIC, delves into Deal's past with such maritime relics
as figureheads and stern boards. (☎ 372679. Open Apr. to late Sept. M-Sa 2-5pm.
£1.50, students and seniors £1, children 50p.)

SOUTH ENGLAND

A **street theater tour,** the "Deal Trail of Blood," brings to life the town's smuggling past and includes a pinch of pub-crawling in Old Deal. (£3; 1½hr.; reserve tickets at the TIC.) For a more relaxing tour of the town, amble through Deal's old footpaths, along the town streets and over beachfront property. Refer to the TIC's free pamphlet, *Deal Walks.* Late July unleashes the **Deal Summer Music Festival,** with a score of musical acts ranging from classical to modern music. (☎ 612292. Tickets £5-12). **Astor Theater** stages local productions. (☎ 367625. Tickets £2-7.)

DOVER   ☎ 01304

And thence to France shall we convey you safe,
And bring you back, charming the narrow seas.
   —William Shakespeare, *Henry V*

The tranquility and majesty of Shakespearean Dover has flitted furtively away across the English Channel: though the tides still crash against the famed white cliffs, their rhythm is often drowned out by the puttering of ferries and the hum of hovercraft depositing new and temporary Doverians every twenty minutes. The Channel Tunnel, completed in 1994, has altered Dover's identity, moving families *en vacances* in and out of France and England like the smuggled wares of centuries past. Despite the clamor, Dover retains a bit of its dignified maritime identity. The beach often seems a darkling plain of lighthouses and Norman ruins, but on a clear day, you may glimpse the coast of Normandy.

▐ GETTING THERE AND CROSSING THE CHANNEL

Trains: Priory Station, Station Approach Rd. Ticket office open M-Sa 4:15am-11:20pm, Su 6:15am-11:20pm. Trains (☎ (08457) 484950) from **London** stations **Victoria, Waterloo East, London Bridge,** and **Charing Cross** (2hr., every 30min., £19.80) and **Canterbury** (20min., every 30min., £4.40). Many trains branch off en route; check schedules to see which trains split.

Buses: Pencester Rd., between York St. and Maison Dieu Rd. (☎ (01304) 240024). Ticket office open M-F 8:30am-5:30pm, Sa 8:30am-noon. **National Express** (☎ (08705) 808080) from **London,** continuing to the Eastern Docks after stopping at Pencester Rd. (2¾hr., 23 per day, £9). **Stagecoach** (☎ (01227) 472082) from: **Canterbury** (45min., £4); **Deal** (40min., £2.50); and **Sandwich** (50min., £3.40). A bus from **Folkestone,** the actual termination point for the Channel Tunnel trains, runs every half hour (30min., £2.10).

Ferries: Major **ferry** companies operate ships from the Eastern Docks to **Calais** and **Oostend, Belgium,** and the Dover tourist information centre offers a ferry booking service. **P&O Stena** lines (☎ (08706) 000600; www.posl.com) to Calais for £24 (departing 35 times daily); **SeaFrance** (☎ (08705) 711711; www.seafrance.com) for £15 (departing 15 times daily). **Hovercrafts** leave from the Hoverport at the Prince of Wales Pier for Calais, foot passengers £25 one way. Free bus service leaves Priory Station for the docks 45min. to 1hr. before sailing time. (See **By Ferry,** p. 35, for complete ferry and hovercraft information.) The **Channel Tunnel** offers passenger service on Eurostar and car transport on Le Shuttle to and from the continent (see **By Train,** p. 37).

Taxis: **Central Taxi Service** (☎ 2400441), 24hr.

▐ PRACTICAL INFORMATION

Tourist Information Centre: Townwall St., a block from the shore (☎ 205108; fax 245409; tic@dover.gov.uk). Sells ferry and hovercraft tickets; after hours call for a list of accommodations. Open daily 9am-6pm.

Tours: Bus tours depart hourly from Market Sq. (1hr., 10am-4pm).

Financial Services: Several **banks** bump elbows in Market Sq. **National Westminster,** 25 Market Sq. (☎ (01227) 780087) is open M-Tu and Th-F 9am-4:30pm, W 9:30am-

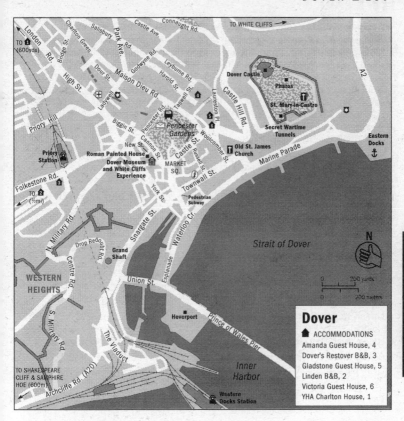

Dover

🏠 ACCOMMODATIONS
Amanda Guest House, 4
Dover's Restover B&B, 3
Gladstone Guest House, 5
Linden B&B, 2
Victoria Guest House, 6
YHA Charlton House, 1

4:30pm. **Thomas Cook,** 3 Cannon St. (☎ 204215), offers foreign exchange. Open M-Tu and Th-Sa 9am-5:30pm, W 10am-5:30pm.

Launderette: Cherry Tree Ave., right off London Rd., beyond the hostel (☎ 242822). Change machine and soap available. Open daily 8am-8pm; last wash 7:15pm. Or get sudsy at **Worthington,** off Your St. Open daily 8am-8pm; soap available.

Police: Ladywell St., right off High St. (☎ 240055).

Hospital: Take bus #D9 or #D5 from outside the post office to the **Buckland Hospital** on Coomb Valley Rd., northwest of town (☎ 201624).

Internet Access: Library, Biggin St. (☎ 204241). Free 1hr. bookings. Open M-T and Th 9:30am-6pm, W 9:30am-1pm, F 9:30am-7pm, Sa 9:30am-5pm.

Post Office: 68 Pencester Rd. (☎ 241747), by the bus station. Open M-F 8.30am-5:30pm, Sa 8:30am-noon. **Postal Code:** CT16 1PB.

ACCOMMODATIONS

At the height of the tourist season, rooms can be difficult to find. Plan ahead—the ferry terminal makes an ugly and unsafe campground. Dover's B&Bs tend to be pricey, and the cheapest places are generally on **Folkestone Rd.** past the train station—quite a walk from the center of town. Several of the Folkestone Rd. B&Bs stay open all night; if the lights are on, ring the bell. During the day, try the B&Bs near the center of town on **Castle St.** Look for "White Cliffs Association" plaques outside homes for quality, moderately-priced rooms. Most B&Bs ask for a deposit.

YHA Charlton House, 306 London Rd. (☎ 201314; fax 202236), with overflow at **14 Goodwyne Rd.** (closer to town center). A ½ mi. walk from the train station; turn left onto Folkestone Rd., then left again at the roundabout onto High St., which becomes London Rd. The hostel is further from the center of Dover than the private B&Bs: expect more barren and unfriendly streets. 69 beds, 2-10 beds per room. Lounge and game room with pool table. Kitchen, forceful showers, and lockers available. Lockout 10am-1pm, curfew 11pm. Overflow building has 60 beds, kitchen and lounge area. You may have to wait a bit after ringing for staff at the overflow hostel; same prices as main hostel, but bring exact change. Dorms £10.85, under 18 £7.40.

Victoria Guest House, 1 Laureston Pl. (☎/fax 205140; WHam101496@aol.com). The well-traveled hosts extend a friendly welcome to their international guests. Think twice about complaining of sore muscles; your neighbor might have just swum the Channel. Gracious Victorian rooms in an excellent location. No singles. Doubles £30-46; family room £50-56. Special 5-day rates available.

Gladstone Guest House, 3 Laurelston Pl. (☎ 208457; kud3gladstone@aol.com). Tastefully decorated pale rooms with cherry finish hand-created by the jovial owner. Ask for a room with views of the lovely rolling hills and fish ponds below. Singles £25-28; doubles £44-48. Children under 10 free. Family rates £15 per person.

Amanda Guest House, 4 Harold St. (☎ 201711; pageant@port-of-dover.com). Hall bathrooms are a small price to pay for the elegant Victorian light fixtures and marble fireplaces in a house built by the former mayor. Twins £34; family room £50.

Linden Bed & Breakfast, 231 Folkestone Rd. (☎ 205449; fax 212499; lindenrog@aol.com). Plush B&B makes every effort to accommodate its guests—ask for courtesy pick-up from the train station and the docks. £24 per person, off-season £20.

Dover's Restover Bed & Breakfast, 69 Folkestone Rd. (☎ 206031; fax 216052), across from the train station. Comfortable B&B offers well-equipped rooms, pleasant service, and a full English breakfast. £20-28 per person, off-season £15-20.

Camping: Harthorn Farm (☎ 852658), at Martin Mill Station off the A258 between Dover and Deal. Close to the railway. 250 pitches. Electricity hook-up £2. Car-and-tent fee June to mid-Sept. £11 for 2 people, mid-Sept.-Oct. and Mar.-May £8.50. £2 per extra person. Without car £3.50 per person.

⬛ FOOD

Despite (or perhaps because of) the proximity of the Continent, Dover's cuisine remains staunchly English. Grease fires rage dawn to dusk in the fish and chip shops on London Rd. and Biggin St., and a decent pub lunch can be had anywhere in the city center. Amateur cooks can pick up raw materials at the local supermarket, **Pioneer,** on the corner of Bridge St. and High St. (Open M-F 8:30am-10pm, Sa 7:30am-10pm, Su 10am-4pm.)

Chaplin's, 2 Church St. (☎ 204870). Pictures of Charlie complement the classic feel of this Dover diner. Shoe leather is (sadly) not on the menu, but you won't miss it with specials like their English kidney pie (£4.75 with vegetables). Try the strawberry sundae. Open daily 8:30am-9pm, off-season until 8.30pm.

The Lighthouse Cafe and Tea Room (☎ 242028), at the end of Prince of Wales Pier. Basic English fish and chips fare, but not a basic location: a view of Dover castle, beaches, and the White Cliffs as you sip tea from ½ mi. off shore. Open daily, only in summer, 10am-5:30pm.

Moonflower, 32-34 High St. (☎ 212198). Chinese takeaway in full spicy splendor, with fish and chips for the less adventurous. Set meals £5.80, chicken dishes £3.30-4.10. Open M-Th noon-2:30pm and 6-11:30pm, F-Sa noon-2:30pm and 5pm-midnight.

◉ SIGHTS

DOVER CASTLE. The view from Castle Hill Rd., on the east side of town, reveals why Dover Castle is famed both for its magnificent setting and for its impregnability. Many have launched assaults on the castle by land, sea, and air. The French tried in 1216, the English themselves during the Civil War in the 17th century, and the Germans in World Wars I and II; all efforts failed. Boulogne, 22 mi. away across the Channel, can (barely) be seen on clear days from the castle's top; it was from that coast that the Germans launched rocket bombs in World War II. These "doodle-bug" missiles destroyed the **Church of St. James,** the ruins of which crumble at the base of Castle Hill. The empty **Pharos,** built in 43 BC, sits alongside **St. Mary-in-Castro's,** a tiled Saxon church. The only Roman lighthouse still in existence and certainly the tallest remaining Roman edifice in Britain, the Pharos's gaping keyhole windows testify to its original purpose. The **Secret Wartime Tunnels** constitute an impressive 3½ mi. labyrinth only recently declassified. Originally built in the late 18th century to defend Britain from attack by Napoleon, the graffiti-covered tunnels served as the base for the evacuation of Allied troops from Dunkirk in World War II. A tour winds its way through the underground hospital and army facilities, but watch out for the ghost of the headless drummer boy said to haunt the tunnels. Tours fill up quickly, and there is usually a long wait, so check in before visiting the rest of Dover Castle. *(Buses from the town center run every hour daily Apr.-Sept. (45p). Open daily Apr.-Sept. 10am-6pm; Oct. 10am-5pm; Nov-Mar 10am-4pm. £6.90, students and seniors £5.20, children £3.50, families £17.30. Partial wheelchair access.)*

THE WHITE CLIFFS EXPERIENCE AND DOVER MUSEUM. This museum/pageant employs costumed Roman soldiers, videos, and a rebuilt ferry deck to illustrate Dover's nearly two millennia of history. On the third floor note the painted figure of Michael Jackson next to Charles II and Richard the Lionheart—all famous channel crossers. *(Market Sq. ☎ 214566. Open daily Apr.-Oct. 10am-5pm; Nov.-Mar. 10am-3pm. £5.95, students and seniors £4.80, children £4.15, families £18.95. Check the brochure, free at the TIC, for discount coupons.)* Tickets purchased at White Cliffs include a tour of the nearby **Dover Museum,** which displays curious bits of Dover history, with a new gallery featuring the Bronze Age Boat, the oldest seafaring boat discovered. At 3600 years, it's older than Moses! *(Market Sq. ☎ 201066. Open daily Apr.-Oct. 10am-6pm; Nov.-Mar. 10am-5:30pm. £1.70, concessions 90p. Wheelchair access.)*

THE WHITE CLIFFS. Covering most of the coastline to the east and west of the port, the white cliffs make a beautifully scenic backdrop for a stroll along the pebbly beach. A few miles west of Dover sprawls the whitest, steepest, and most famous of the cliffs, known as Shakespeare Cliff because it is traditionally identified as the sight of eyeless Gloucester's battle with the brink in *King Lear. (25min. by foot along Snargate St.)*

THE GRAND SHAFT. The 140 ft. triple spiral staircase was shot through the rock in Napoleonic times to link the army on the Western Heights with the city center. The first stairwell was for "officers and their ladies," the second for "sergeants and their wives," the last for "soldiers and their women." *(Snargate St. ☎ 201200. Ascend July-Aug. W-Su 2-5pm; on bank holidays 10am-5pm. £1.25, seniors and children 85p.)*

OTHER SIGHTS. A relatively recent excavation has unearthed a remarkably well-preserved **Roman painted house** off Cannon St. near Market Sq. It's the oldest Roman house in Britain, complete with an under-floor central heating and indoor plumbing—nicer than some modern B&Bs! *(New St. ☎ 203279. Open Apr.-Sept. Tu-Su 10am-5pm. £2, concessions 80p.)* There are dozens of **cliff walks** within a short distance of the center of town; consult the TIC for more information. For more startling views, take the A20 toward Folkestone to **Samphire Hoe,** a well-groomed park planted in the summer of 1997 from material dug from the Channel Tunnel.

SUSSEX

RYE   ☎01797

Settled before the Roman invasion, Rye's status soared with its admission to the elite Membership of the Cinque Ports, a defensive organization initiated by Edward the Confessor. As though Rye were getting too big for its boots, nature interfered and choked the waterways with silt—according to local myth, Rye's name derives from the French *la rie*, the waste spot. Throughout the 18th century, the town was best known for its bands of smugglers, who darted past royal authorities to stash contraband in an elaborate network of cellars and secret passageways. Today's Rye (pop. 4,400) is cloaked in the affluent life of the distant past. Green, rolling hills studded with sheep lie on the outskirts, while in town, cobbled stone streets await visitors looking for a typical English village experience.

⌐ GETTING THERE. Visitors no longer float into Rye from the Channel. Now, **trains** (☎ (08457) 484950) puff in to the station just off Cinque Port St. from: **London Bridge** (1½hr., £17.60); **Brighton** (1¾hr., £11.30); **Eastbourne** (1hr., £6.40); and **Dover** (1¾hr., £9.30). **National Express** (☎ (08705) 808080) runs from **London**, £12. **Buses** (☎ 223343) run all around south England and beyond; schedules flap in the train station's car park, where the buses stop.

⚎⚐ ORIENTATION AND PRACTICAL INFORMATION. Rye sits at the mouth of the River Rother. To get to the tourist information centre (TIC) from the station, steer yourself to Cinque Port St. proper, and turn right; turn left onto the Strand Quay and the TIC is on the left. To reach the oldest part of town, hike 5min. up Market Rd. to High St., Lion St., and Mermaid St.

The **tourist information centre,** Rye Heritage Centre, Strand Quay, distributes the free *Rye: 1066 Country* guide, which lists points of interest, accommodations, and restaurants. (☎ 226696; ryetic@rother.gov.uk. Open mid-Mar. to Oct. daily 9am-5:30pm; Nov.-Feb. M-F 10am-3pm, Sa-Su 10am-4pm.) The TIC also shows a "laser and light film" (a movie, in big-city lingo) about Rye's smuggling past and hands out self-guided audio tours. (£2, concessions £1.50.) Services include: **banks** on High St.; a **launderette,** in Ropewalk Arcade (open daily 8:30am-6pm); the **police** (☎ 222112), Cinque Port St.; **Internet access** at the **library** (☎ 223355; £1.50 per 30min.; open M and W 9:30am-5:30pm, Th 9:30am-12:30pm, F 9:30am-6pm, Sa 9:30am-5pm); and the **post office,** 22-24 Cinque Port St. (☎ 222163; open M-Tu and Th-F 8:30am-5:30pm, W and Sa 9am-5:30pm). **Postal code:** TN31 7AA.

⌐ ACCOMMODATIONS. The area's only **YHA Youth Hostel,** Rye Rd., is a 7mi. trek from Rye, or 5mi. from Hastings. Head down the A259 past Winchelsea and Icklesham (look for the sign on the right). Alternatively, take bus #711 from Rye to the White Hart in Guestling (M-Sa roughly 2 per hr., summer also Su every 2hr., last bus around 7:45pm; £1.85). From the White Hart, the hostel is downhill on the left. You can also take the train to Three Oaks (£1.90) and walk 1½ mi. (☎ 812373; fax 814273. 51 beds with 4-12 per room. Open July-Aug. daily, Mar.-June and Sept.-Oct. 6 days per week—call ahead since the one day it's closed varies; Nov.-Dec. F-Sa. Dorms £9.15, under 18 £6.20.) The hostel also has **camping** (£4.40 per pitch).

Rye's many fine, inexpensive B&Bs are often away from the center (usually about a 10min. walk), but then Rye is a *small* town. Call ahead, and you may get a ride. Most B&Bs are either on the roads past the railroad station or on **Winchelsea Rd.** To reach the B&B at **Glencoe Farms,** West Undercliff, exit right from the train station and turn right on Ferry Rd. across the tracks; after Ferry Rd. becomes Udimore Rd., West Undercliff comes up on the left; follow the signs to the farm. The farm has friendly proprietors, animals to pet, and three airy rooms with bath. (☎ 224347. £16 per person.) The Beatles will always rock at Richard and Jane

McGowan's **Amberley Bed and Breakfast,** 51 Winchelsea Rd. (☎ 225693. £13-19 per person, with breakfast £15-21. Pastoral views free.) **Vine Cottage Bed and Breakfast,** 25a Udimore Rd., offers privacy and comfort, and attends to guests in either English, Spanish, or German. (☎ 222822. Singles £20, doubles £32; reduced rates for students and longer stays.)

⚑📧 **FOOD AND PUBS.** Fresh fruit grocers sprout along High St. For conventional grocery items, visit **Budgens** across from the train station. (Open M-Sa 8am-8pm, Su 10am-4pm.) For standard English grub, several pricey tea rooms and bakeries rise on High St. **Jempson's Coffee House and Bakery,** 45 Cinque Port St., features a mouthwatering assortment of pastries and lunch dishes. (☎ 223986. Open M-Sa 8am-6pm.) In continued obedience to your sweet tooth, climb to **Ye Olde Tuck Shoppe,** 9 Market St., to sample their homemade fudge and heavenly cakes. (☎ 222230. Open M-Sa 9:30am-5:30pm, Su 10am-5:30pm.) Classic tea shop **The Mariners,** 15 High St., offers cream tea for £2.90. (☎ 223480. Open daily 9:30am-5pm.) Buy a drink of whisky at the **Mermaid Inn** (see below) and sit above old smuggling tunnels (restaurant open daily noon-2:30pm and 7-9:30pm). **Ye Olde Bell Inn,** 33 The Mint, serves good pub food, including toasted sandwiches for £1.75-2. (☎ 223323. Open M-Th 11am-11pm, F-Sa 11am-midnight, Su 11am-10:30pm.)

📷🎭 **SIGHTS AND ENTERTAINMENT.** Well-preserved half-timbered homes cover the hill on which much of the town sits, recalling the days when smugglers stole through a sleepy Rye. At the top of the hill, for a further turn of the screw, Henry James wrote his later novels while living in **Lamb House,** at the corner of West St. and Mermaid St. (Open Apr.-Oct. W and Sa 2-6pm. £2.50, children £1.25.) Before descending the hill, check out **St. Mary's Church,** at the top of Lion St., a huge 12th-century parish church that houses one of the oldest functioning clocks in the country. A climb up the tower steps reveals a terrific view of the river valley, but avoid the ascent when the bell is about to ring—your ears may never forgive you. (☎ 222430. Open M-W and F 9am-6pm, Th 10:40am-6pm, Sa 9am-5:30pm, Su 11:40am-5:30pm. £2, students and seniors £1.) Around the corner from the church rises the **Ypres Tower** (EE-pres), built in 1350. Intended to fortify the town against invaders from the sea, the tower has served as a jail, and now contains the **Rye Museum.** (☎ 226728. Open Apr.-June and Oct. Th-M 10:30am-5:30pm, July-Sept. M-Su 10:30am-5:30pm; Nov.-Mar. Sa-Su 10:30am-3:30pm. £2, students and seniors £1.50, children £1, families £4.50.) A walk down Mermaid St. leads you to the famed **Mermaid Inn,** where smugglers once cavorted until dawn. (☎ 223065. Open M-Sa 11am-11pm, Su noon-10:30pm.) You can watch potters mold the famous Rye pottery at the many shops sprinkled through the town.

At **Horizon,** 48 Ferry Rd., Rye's only nightclub, ordinary dance beats reign (☎ 222343. Cover about £3.50.) Some cavort during the **festival** of art, theater, and music for two weeks at the start of September. (☎ 227338. Tickets £2-12.)

NEAR RYE

HASTINGS. Having given up its name and identity to a decisive battle (see p. 67), Hastings has produced little of notoriety since, though it provides a useful transport hub for exploring the region around Rye. The fragmentary remains of **Hastings Castle** include the **1066 Story,** an interactive display of the famous spat between William the Conqueror and Harold. (☎ (01424) 781111. £3, students and seniors £2.45, children £1.95.) **Trains** arrive from Rye daily (20min., every 45min.).

BATTLE. Appropriately renamed after the little tiff between Normans and Anglo-Saxons that took place in 1066, the town of Battle makes a fine expedition from Rye. To commemorate his victory in the Battle of Hastings, William the Conqueror had **Battle Abbey** built in 1094, spitefully positioning its high altar upon the very spot where Harold was felled by an arrow in the eye (see p. 67). The town grew prosperous enough to survive Henry VIII's closing the abbey in 1538. Little remains of the abbey apart from the gate and a handsome series of 13th-century common quarters. (☎ (01424) 773792. Open daily Apr.-Sept. 10am-6pm; Oct. 10am-5pm; Nov.-Mar. 10am-4pm. £4, students and seniors £3, children £2, families £10.) The battlefield where Harold's troops were taken by surprise is now a pasture trampled only by sheep. In summer, you can take an audio tour of the abbey and walk the **battlefield trail**, a one-mile jaunt up and down the green hillside.

Bus #5 runs directly to the Abbey from Hastings, near the bank buildings (20min.; M-Sa every hr., Su every 2hr.; £4.40). **B&Bs** in Battle charge £15-20 and can be booked through the **tourist information centre**, 88 High St., opposite Battle Abbey. (☎ (01424) 773721; fax 773436; battletic@rother.gov.uk. Open Apr.-Sept. daily 10am-6pm; Oct.-Mar. M-Sa 10am-4pm.)

PEVENSEY. William the Conqueror's march to Battle began from **Pevensey Castle**, originally a Roman fortress named Anderita. Will then gave it to his brother, who added a keep. The castle now lies at the center of town. (☎ (01323) 762604. Open Apr.-Sept. daily 10am-6pm; Oct. 10am-5pm; Nov.-Mar. W-Su 10am-4pm. £2.50, students and seniors £1.90, children £1.30.) The best part of Pevensey owes its origins to commerce rather than conquest. The **Mint House**, on the High St., begun as a mint under the Normans, was transformed by Henry VIII's physician into a country retreat, and eventually became a smugglers' den, complete with sliding ceiling panels. It now teems with Victorian miscellany, stuffed birds, and other fascinating oddities worth the price of admission in themselves. (☎ (01323) 762337. Open M-F 9am-5pm, Sa 10:30am-4:30pm. £1, children 25p.) **Trains** run from Rye and Hastings to Pevensey (every hr., £5.60). Pevensey's **tourist information centre** recently closed—to get info about the town, call the TIC in nearby Boship (☎ 442667).

BRIGHTON   ☎01273

In Lydia's imagination, a visit to Brighton comprised every possibility of earthly happiness.
   —Jane Austen, *Pride and Prejudice*

The undisputed home of the dirty weekend, Brighton (pop. 180,000) sparkles with a risqué, tawdry luster. According to legend, the future King George IV sidled into Brighton around 1784 for some hanky-panky. Having staged a fake wedding with a certain "Mrs. Jones" (Maria Fitzherbert), he headed off to the farmhouse known today as the Royal Pavilion, and the royal rumpus began. Since then, Brighton has turned a blind eye to some of the more outrageous activities that occur along its shores; holiday-goers and locals alike peel it off—all off—at England's first bathing beach. Kemp Town (jokingly called Camp Town), among other areas of Brighton, has a thriving gay and lesbian population, while the immense student crowd, augmented by flocks of foreign youth purportedly learning English, feeds Brighton's decadent clubbing scene. The ancient, narrow streets that make up the Lanes district provide an anarchic setting for Brighton's wild behavior. Lovingly known as "London-by-the-Sea," Brighton's open demeanor and youthful spirit make for a memorable sojourn for adventurous travelers.

▌ GETTING THERE AND GETTING AROUND

Trains: Brighton Station lies at the northern end of Queen's Rd. Ticket office open 24hr. Travel center open M-Sa 8:15am-6pm. Trains (☎ (08457) 484950) from: **London** (1¼hr., at least 6 per hr., £9.90); **Arundel** (50min., 3 per hr., £6.10, day return £6.20); **Portsmouth** (1½hr., 1 per hr., £11.70, day return £12.30); and **Rye** (1½hr., 1 per hr., £11.30, day return £11.50).

Buses: Stop at Pool Valley, at the southern angle of Old Steine. Tickets and info at **One Stop Travel**, 16 Old Steine (☎ 700406). Open M-F 8:30am-5:45pm, Sa 9am-5pm; June-Sept. also Su 11am-4:30pm. **National Express** (☎ (08705) 808080) buses come from **London** (2hr., 15 per day, £8 return).

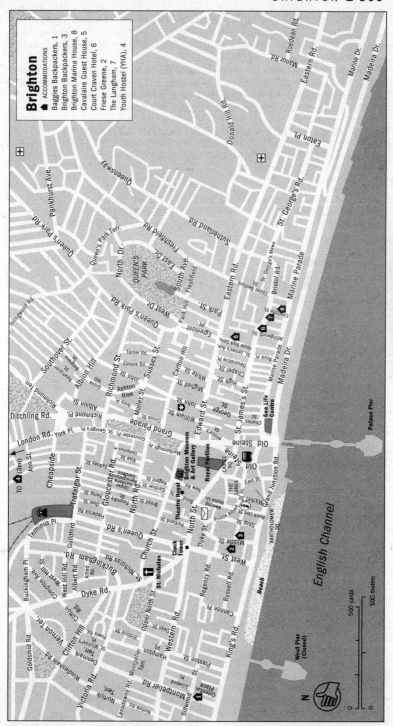

Brighton

▲ ACCOMMODATIONS
Baggies Backpackers, 1
Brighton Backpackers, 3
Brighton Marina House, 8
Cavalaire Guest House, 5
Court Craven Hotel, 6
Friese Greene, 2
The Langham, 7
Youth Hostel (YHA), 4

SOUTH ENGLAND

English Channel

Palace Pier

West Pier (Closed)

Sea Life Centre

Brighton Museum & Art Gallery

Royal Pavilion

Theatre Royal

Clock Tower

St. Nicholas

QUEEN'S PARK

N

500 yards
500 meters

Public Transportation: Local buses operated by **Brighton and Hove** (☎ 886200) congregate around Old Steine. The tourist information centre can give route and price information for most buses, though all carriers charge 70p in the central area.

Taxis: Brighton Taxis (☎ 202020), 24hr.

Bike Rental: Freedom Bikes, 108 St. James's St. (☎ 681698). £10 per day for a snazzy mountain bike, £50 per week; £50 deposit. Open Oct.-May M-Sa 9:30am-5:30pm. Vendors on the **waterfront** also rent small watercraft, bikes, and in-line skates, but the prices are higher and the quality somewhat lower.

✦❼ ORIENTATION AND PRACTICAL INFORMATION

Stumble into **the Lanes,** a pedestrian shopping area, by turning left off **Prince Albert St.** before arriving at the TIC. **Old Steine,** a road and a square, runs in front of the **Royal Pavilion,** while **King's Rd.** runs along the waterfront.

TOURIST, FINANCIAL, AND LOCAL SERVICES

Tourist Information Centre: 10 Bartholomew Sq. (☎ (0906) 711 2255; http://tourism.brighton.co.uk). Enthusiastic staff vends materials on practically any subject, books National Express tickets, and reserves rooms at B&Bs for £1 plus 10% deposit. Open M-Tu and Th-F 9am-5pm, W and Sa 10am-5pm, Su 10am-4pm.

Tours: Walking tours leave from the TIC June-Aug. Th 11am; £3. **Guide Friday** (☎ 746205) gives 1hr. bus tours departing Palace Pier, the train station, and a few other sites every 30min. £6.50, students and seniors £5.50, children £2.50, families £15.50.

Budget Travel: Campus Travel, 61 Ditchling Rd. (☎ 570226). Open M and W-F 9:30am-6pm, Tu 10am-6pm, Sa 10am-5pm. **STA Travel,** 38 North St. (☎ 728282). Open M-W and F 9:30am-5:30pm, Th 10am-5:30pm, Sa 11am-5pm.

Financial Services: Banks line North St., near Old Steine. **Thomas Cook,** 58 North St. (☎ 325711). Open M-Tu and Th-Sa 9am-5:30pm, W 10am-5:30pm.

American Express: 82 North St. (☎ 321242). Open M-Tu and Th-Sa 9am-5pm, W 9:30am-5pm.

Launderette: 5 Palace Rd. (☎ 327972). Open daily 8am-8pm.

Women's Center: 10 St. George's Mews (☎ 600526). Services include pregnancy testing. Open M and W-Th 10:30am-3:30pm, Sa 11:30am-1:30pm.

Disabled Information: Snowdon House, 3 Rutland Gdns., Hove (☎ 203016). Open M-F 10am-4pm. The **TIC,** above, has a phenomenal printout detailing local services.

EMERGENCY AND COMMUNICATIONS

Police: (☎ 606744), John St.

Hospital: Royal Sussex County (☎ 696955), Eastern Rd., parallel to Marine Parade.

Internet Access: VGZ The Arena, 36 Preston St. (☎ 710730). £3.50 per hr., min. 80p; after 6pm £2 per hr. Open M-Su 10am-10pm. Also at the **Library,** Church St. (☎ 296971), across from the Brighton Museum. £1.50 per 30min. Open M and Th-F 9:30am-5pm, T 9:30am-7pm, Sa 9:30am-4pm.

Post Office: 51 Ship St. (☎ 573209), off Prince Albert St., in the Lanes. **Bureau de Change.** Open M-F 9am-5:30pm, Sa 9am-12:30pm. **Postal Code:** BN1 1BA.

▌ ACCOMMODATIONS

Brighton's best budget beds are in its four hostels. B&Bs and cheaper hotels begin at £18; many mid-range B&Bs line **Madeira Pl.,** and the shabbier B&Bs and hotels collect west of **West Pier** and east of **Palace Pier.** There is a huge number of B&Bs in **Kemp Town,** the neighborhood east of Palace Pier that runs perpendicular to the sea. Test the beds and smell for dust before signing your night away. Frequent conventions make rooms scarce—book early or consult the TIC upon arrival. Luckily, the high concentration of accommodations means that a little legwork can go a long way. The TIC keeps a list of guest houses owned and operated by gays or lesbians. Rooms may be cheaper in the **Hove** area, just west of Brighton.

Brighton Backpackers Hostel, 75-76 Middle St. (☎ 777717; fax 887778; stay@bright-onbackpackers.com). Lively independent hostel that bubbles with international flavor. *The* place to meet other backpackers in Brighton, although outgoing atmosphere may not suit reclusive travelers. Great location; many clean rooms overlook the ocean. Innovative artwork—courtesy of previous guests—graces the walls. Gregarious owner Miles offers advice and melodies from his guitar against the chirp of resident parakeets. Pool table, Internet access (£1.50 per 30min.), and TV lounge for Sunday-night *Simpsons* rituals. The quieter **annex** faces the ocean. 4- to 8-bed coed and single-sex dorms. Inexpensive breakfast and dinner. Kitchen and laundry. No curfew. Email reservations encouraged. Dorms £10-11, weekly £55-£60; doubles £25.

YHA Brighton (☎ 556196), Patcham Pl. 4 mi. north on the main London Rd; take Patcham bus #5 or 5A (stop E) from Old Steine to the Black Lion Hotel (£1.25). Georgian-style country house filled with friendly staff. 6-16 beds rooms look new, although they're 400 yrs. old. Good jumping-off point for the South Downs Way (see p. 187), but not the place if you want to party late. Laundry facilities. Reception closed 10am-1pm. Curfew 11pm. Often full; call ahead July-Aug. Closed Jan. Dorms £10.15, under 18 £6.85.

Baggies Backpackers, 33 Oriental Pl. (☎ 733740). Go west of West Pier along King's Rd.; Oriental Pl. will be on your right. Jazz, exquisite murals, and a mosaic floor set the tone for this mellow international hostel. Spacious and clean. Vast video collection. 50 beds in coed and single-sex dorms, some doubles. Kitchen and laundry. Key deposit £5. No lockout or curfew. Dorms £10, weekly £45; doubles £23.

Friese Greene, 20 Middle St. (☎ 74755). Bohemian, family-run hostel situated in the heart of Brighton's nightlife. Great location attracts serious partiers and seasoned travelers looking for a cheap place to crash after a night of clubbing, but it's not very clean. £5 deposit for key and linen. Laundry, kitchen, pool, and TV. Dorms £10, weekly £50; doubles £13-15 per person.

Brighton Marina House Hotel, 8 Charlotte St., Marine Parade (☎ 605349; fax 679484; rooms@jungs.co.uk). Gracious, clean guest house decorated in Swedish or Tudor style; many rooms with bath. Phones for incoming calls, convenient location, and elaborate breakfasts with vegetarian and vegan items. Singles £25-39; twins £45.

Cavalaire Guest House, 34 Upper Rock Gdns. (☎ 696899; fax 600504). TV and assorted electrical appliances in each room. Wonderful breakfast choices, from tropical to vegetarian; clean and tidy rooms. Internet £5 per hr. Singles £25; doubles £42-55.

The Langham, 16-17 Charlotte St. (☎/fax 682843). Nine tidy, inexpensive rooms with cheerful pink walls. £22-27.50 per person.

Court Craven Hotel, 2 Atlingworth St. (☎ 607710). A guest house in Kemp Town for gays. Clean, elegant, and with a bar for thirsty guests. Singles £19-21; doubles £36-38; prices depend on season and time of the week.

FOOD

The area around the Lanes is full of trendy and expensive places waiting to gobble up tourists' cash. For cheaper fare, try the fish-and-chip shops along the beach or north of the Lanes. As always, the best deal is to cook for yourself. Brighton has several supermarkets, including **Safeway,** 6 St. James's St. (☎ 570363. Open M-W 8am-8pm, Th-Sa 8am-9pm, Su 10am-4pm.)

Food for Friends, 17a-18 Prince Albert St. (☎ 202310). Cheap, well-cooked, well-seasoned vegetarian food in a breezy, easy atmosphere. Daily salad specials (£2.25-3.55) send taste buds straight to heaven. The "Taster" (£5.20) offers a bit of all the day's main courses. 20% student discount. Open M-Sa 8am-10pm, Su 9:15am-10pm.

Donatello, 1-3 Brighton Pl. (☎ 775477; fax 734001). This open-air Italian restaurant on the fringe of the Lanes makes a hot people-watching spot. Gain a few pounds sampling the 3-course lunch special (£6.40). Delicious pizza £4-6. Reservations advised. Open daily 11:30am-11:30pm.

Crepe Dentelle, 65 Preston St. (☎ 323224). A delicious taste of French cuisine, Crepe Dentelle cooks up sweet and savory crepes (£2.30-4.60) and galettes (£4.35-6.95). 20% off takeaway items. Open M-F 10am-3pm and 6-10pm, Sa-Su noon-10pm.

Piccolo, 56 Ship St. (☎ 203701). *Benvenuti a* Piccolo, home of great pizzas and even better dough. An expansive menu lists 17 pizza choices (£3.30-4.90). Wheelchair access. Open daily noon-midnight.

Bombay Aloo, 39 Ship St. (☎ 776038). Pure buffet and purely vegetarian in this inventive Indian restaurant. £4.95 all-you-can-eat from 20 items (£3.50 between 3:15-5:15pm). Open Su-Th noon-11pm, F-Sa noon-midnight.

Regency Restaurant, 131 Kings Rd. (☎ 325014). A restaurant that reels in the locals with tasty fish (£4.40-11.95) and seafront views. Also serves English breakfast all day. Open daily 9am-11pm.

Terre à Terre, 71 East St. (☎ 729051). If you want to splurge, this is the place to do it. If not, just sample the tapas before heading out for the evening. Well-prepared vegetarian dishes cheerfully dispensed along with organic wine and beer. Main courses from £9. Open M 6-10:30pm, Tu-F noon-10:30pm, Sa-Su 11am-10:30pm.

👁 🗺 SIGHTS AND BEACHES

In 1750, Dr. Richard Russell wrote a treatise on the merits of drinking and bathing in sea water to treat glandular disease. Before then, sea-swimming was thought nearly suicidal. The treatment received universal acclaim, and seaside towns soon prospered. Thus began the transformation of the sleepy village of Brighthelmstone into England's center of fame and fashion, a town with a decidedly hedonistic bent. Although an early-90s recession hit Brighton hard, the town has nearly completed a revitalization of the waterfront, and tourism is bouncing back.

ROYAL PAVILION. Perhaps it's wrong to reduce an entire city to one of its parts, but the proudly extravagant Royal Pavilion seems to have created much of Brighton's present brand of gaudiness. George IV, then Prince of Wales, enlisted the help of architect John Nash to turn an ordinary farm villa into the Oriental/Indian/Gothic/Georgian palace visible today. Rumor has it that George wept tears of joy upon entering it, proving that wealth does not give one taste. Enjoy the pavilion from the surrounding large, shady parks by renting a deck chair (£1), or take in a view of the parks and a sandwich at **Queen Adelaide's Tea Room,** inside the pavilion. (☎ 290900. Open daily June-Sept. 10am-6pm; Oct.-May 10am-5pm. Partial wheelchair access. Guided tours at 11:30am and 2:30pm, £1.25. Audio tour £1. Admission £4.90, concessions £3.55, families £12.80. Tea Room open daily 10:30am-5pm.)

SUN OF A BEACH. The main attraction in Brighton is, of course, the **beach.** Those who associate the word "beach" with visions of sand and sun may be sorely disappointed—the weather can be quite nippy even in June and July, and the closest thing to sand on the beach are the fist-sized brown rocks. At least, as one optimistic guest-house owner observes, no one tracks sand into her room at night. Even in 70°F (21°C) weather with overcast skies, beach-goers gamely strip to bikinis and lifeguards don sunglasses. During the peak of the summer, visitors have to fight for a spot on the beach. To visit **Telescombe Beach,** nearly 4½ mi. to the east of Palace Pier, look for a sign before Telescombe Tavern marked "Telescombe Cliffs." Numerous **sailing** opportunities crop up in summer; check at the TIC.

PALACE PIER AND OTHER PIERS. The Pavilion's gaudiness permeates to the beachfront, where the relatively new Palace Pier, the fourth largest tourist attraction in England, operates as a mecca of slot machines and video games. The pier's toilets have prolific condom machines dispensing a vast array of colors, shapes and flavors, just in case, and the deck chairs are free. **Volk's Railway,** Britain's first 3 ft. gauge electric train, shuttles along the waterfront. (☎ 681061. Apr.-Sept. daily 11am-6pm. Rides £1.10, children 60p.) The **Grand Hotel,** on the front on King's Rd., home to many political conventions, has been rebuilt since a 1984 IRA bombing that killed five but left then-Prime Minister Margaret Thatcher unscathed. Farther along, the once lavish but now decrepit **West Pier** lies abandoned out in the sea. Full-scale renovation was set to begin in the spring of 1999, but the abrupt collapse of part of the pier put a wrinkle in the plans, delaying the project indefinitely. A short walk along the coast past West Pier leads to **Hove.**

BRIGHTON MUSEUM AND ART GALLERY. More edifying than most of the town's other attractions, this gallery features paintings, English pottery, and Art Deco and Art Nouveau collections wild enough to make viewers spontaneously dance the Charleston. Recently under renovation, the museum should completely reopen in early 2001, allowing visitors once again to leer at Salavador Dalí's incredibly sexy, red, pursing sofa, *Mae West's Lips.* At the fine **Willett Collection of Pottery,** inside the museum, avant-garde art and antique Brighton relics simultaneously reflect the varied faces of this seaside escape. *(Church St., around the corner from the Pavilion. ☎ 290900. Open M-Tu and Th-Sa 10am-5pm, Su 2-5pm. Limited wheelchair access. Free.)*

THE LANES. Small fishermen's cottages once thrived in the Lanes, a jumble of 17th-century streets south of North St.—some no wider than 3 ft.—constituting the heart of Old Brighton. Now filled with overpriced antique jewelry shops, the Lanes are losing some of their age-old charm, though many worthy stores still sparkle. Those looking for fresher shopping opportunities should head towards North Laine, where alternative merchandise and colorful cafes still dominate.

BRIGHTON SEA LIFE CENTRE. Although England's largest aquarium has freed its dolphins, Missie and Silver, many other sea creatures remain trapped in large glass tanks for your viewing pleasure. *(Marine Parade, near Palace Pier. ☎ 604234. Open daily in summer 10am-7pm; in winter 10am-6pm. Last admission 1hr. before close. Wheelchair access. £5.50, seniors £4.25, children £3.95.)*

OTHER SIGHTS. To escape Brighton's frivolity, head to **St. Nicholas' Church,** on Dyke Rd., which dates from 1370 and treasures a 12th-century baptismal font considered to be the most beautiful Norman carving in Sussex. **St. Bartholomew's Church,** on Ann St., was originally called "The Barn" or "Noah's Ark." This little-known spurt of Victorian genius rises higher than Westminster Abbey, to 135 ft. To get there, take bus #5, 5A, or 5B from Old Steine. **Queens Park,** north of Kemp Town, and other green spots around Brighton, provide tranquil locations for nature-lovers and picnickers. Casual walkers will find many examples of Regency architecture in **Brunswick Square,** in discreet contrast to Brighton's ostentations.

PUBS

J.B. Priestly once wisely noted that Brighton was "a fine place either to restore your health, or…to ruin it again." Indeed, the sea of alcohol flowing through the city presents ample opportunities to demonstrate Priestly's latter point. Brighton is a student town, and where there are students there are cheap drinks. Many pubs offer fantastic drink specials during the week—some budget-minded travelers find no reason to go out on weekends, when places get crowded and expensive. Pub-crawling in the Lanes is a good bet on any night. Revelers congregate in front of pubs on the beach between West Pier and Palace Pier.

Fortune of War, 157 King's Road Arches (☎ 205065). Always a lucky choice. Open M-Sa 10:30am-11pm, Su 11am-10:30pm.

Mash Tun, 1 Church St. (☎ 684951). Attracts an eclectic crowd with "friendly food and tasty waitstaff"; sample their hot chocolate and dark rum concoction (£2.50). Open M-Sa noon-11pm, Su noon-10:30pm.

Squid, 78 Middle St. (☎ 727114). Next door to the Backpackers hostel and linked to Zap Club. Bright walls and a vodka mural make this pub a popular place to begin an evening. Open M-F 5-11pm, Sa 3-11pm, Su 3-10:30pm.

Smugglers, 10 Ship St. Bedsteads, two dance floors, and vodka bottle chandeliers make this pub a raucous place to drink. Pints £1.60. Happy hour M-F noon-8pm. Open M-Sa 11am-11pm, Su noon-10:30pm.

Ye Olde King and Queen (☎ 607207), Marlborough Pl. Serves cheap food and drink all day to its thirsty peasants. Open M-Sa 11am-11pm, Su noon-10:30pm.

♪ ENTERTAINMENT

Brighton's dizzying array of nighttime choices has helped it become one of England's most popular seaside resorts. And, as surely as the tide turns, venues go in and out of fashion. *The Punter*, a local monthly found at pubs, newsagents, and record stores, details evening events. *What's On*, a poster-sized flysheet found at record stores and pubs, points the hedonist toward hot-and-happening scenes. Gay and lesbian venues can be found in the latest issues of *Gay Times* (£2.50) or *Capital Gay* (free), available at newsstands.

Summer brings outdoor concerts and assorted entertainment, including mimes and jugglers, to the pavilion lawn, the beach deck, and around the Lanes. Although the Lanes are the most vibrant part of town at night, they are not necessarily the safest. The City Council spent £5 million installing surveillance equipment along the seafront and major streets to ensure safety during late-night partying, but it's still a good idea to avoid walking alone late at night through Brighton's spaghetti-style streets. **Night buses** #N97, N98, and N99 run infrequently but reliably in the early morning, picking up passengers at Old Steine and in front of many clubs, and 24 hour cab companies are always an option, albeit an expensive one.

CLUBS

Brighton is the hometown of Norman Cook, better known as Fatboy Slim, and major dance record label Skint Records, so these Brightonians know a thing or two about dance music. Most clubs are open M-Sa 10pm-2am. Like pubs, many offer student discounts on weeknights and then push the prices up at weekends.

☒ The Beach, 171-181 King's Road Arches (☎ 722272). Adds monstrous big beat to the music on the shore. Fatboy Slim still mixes his beats here on some Friday nights, when the club is known as The Boutique. For a club with big-name resident DJs, it's still refreshingly unpretentious.

Paradox (☎ 321628), West St. Paradox gets a bit dressy towards the end of the week. The monthly "Wild Fruit" gay night is popular among people of all persuasions.

Event II (☎ 732627), West St. Among the most technically armed and massively populated, Event II spent over £1 million adding all of the electric trimmings to its already immense dance floor.

Zap Club (☎ 202407), King's Road Arches. The arches of old World War II tunnels turned into a club provide space for dark rendezvous and dirty dancing; come here for hard-core grinding to rave and house music.

Casablanca (☎ 321817), Middle St. Plays live jazz to a largely student crowd. Get ready to sweat it again, Sam. Discount for Backpackers hostelers (see p. 165).

Zanzibar, 129 St. James's St. (☎ 622100). Gay clubbers flock to this zany club.

Queen's Arms, 8 George St. (☎ 696873). Packs an enthusiastic gay and lesbian crowd into its Saturday night cabaret, and serves relatively inexpensive pints (£2.30).

MUSIC, THEATER, AND FESTIVALS

Brighton Centre, King's Rd., and **The Dome,** 29 New Rd., host Brighton's biggest rock and jazz concerts and events ranging from Chippendales shows to youth orchestra concerts. The Dome is currently being refurbished, but the common box office remains open for events at the Brighton Centre. (☎ 290131. Open M-Sa 10am-5:30pm.) The TIC also sells tickets. Local plays and touring London productions take the stage at the **Theatre Royal** on New Rd., a Victorian beauty with red plush interior. (☎ 328488; fax 765507. Tickets £6-20. Open M-Sa 10am-8pm.) **Komedia,** on

Gardner St., houses a cafe, bar, theater, comedy club, and cabaret. (☎ 647100; www.komedia.co.uk. Tickets £5-8; discounts available. Standby tickets 15min. before curtain. Box office open M-Sa 11am and Su 10am to start of the last show.)

The **Brighton Festival** (☎ 292950, box office ☎ 709709), held each May, is one of the largest festivals in England, celebrating music, film, and other art forms. Gays and lesbians celebrate the concurrent **Brighton Pride Festival** (☎ 730562).

DAYTRIPS FROM BRIGHTON

LEWES
Trains leave for Lewes from Brighton's Queen's Rd. Station (10min., return £1.90).

If you are inclined to leave the urban attractions and distractions of Brighton in search of more relaxed pursuits, escape to the historic town of Lewes, hometown of Thomas Paine, author of *Rights of Man*. The views from the Norman **Lewes Castle,** High St., five minutes northwest of the train station, merit as much of a visit as the remains do. (☎ (01273) 486290. Open M-Sa 10am-5:30pm or dusk, Su 11am-5:30pm or dusk. £3.50, students and seniors £3, children £1.80, families £10.) The 15th-century **Anne of Cleves House Museum,** Southover High St., nearly 15 minutes from the castle, celebrates the clever woman who got the house in her divorce from Henry VIII without losing her head. (☎ (01273) 474610. Open Feb.-Oct. M-Sa 10am-5pm, Su noon-5pm; Nov.-Feb. Tu, Th, and Sa 10am-5pm. £2.30, students and seniors £2.10, children £1.10, families £6.20.)

THE CHARLESTON FARMHOUSE
South of Lewes, off the A27. Call bus information (☎ (01273) 474747) for departures from Lewes to Charleston. Farmhouse ☎ (01323) 811265. Open July-Aug. W-Sa 11:30am-6pm, Su 2-6pm; Apr.-June and Sept.-Oct. W-Su 2-6pm. Last admission 5pm. £5.50, concessions £3.50.

The Charleston Farmhouse was the country home of the Bloomsbury Group. Though originally lacking amenities such as electricity and a telephone, Charleston soon became a center for literary, artistic, and intellectual life in Britain. Frequent guests included economist John Maynard Keynes, art theorist Clive Bell, and Virginia Woolf. Today the farmhouse highlights the domestic decorative art of Vanessa Bell and Duncan Grant.

ARUNDEL   ☎01903
Arundel (pop. 3200) sits in the shadow of towers and cathedral spires, but the town refuses to let those stone landmarks overshadow its character. Yes, the romantic castle does draw most visitors (with good reason), and wearisome antique shops do clutter the streets. Careful observers, however, will find the town's relaxed spirit ambling through the roads and rippling down the River Arun. From Arundel's hillside spot, the treasures embedded in the beautiful surrounding countryside are easily explored.

TRANSPORTATION AND PRACTICAL INFORMATION

Trains (☎ (08457) 484950) come into Arundel from: **London Victoria** (1½hr., 2 per hr., £11.50, day return £16.10); **Chichester** (20min., 2 per hr., £3.40, day return £3.90); **Portsmouth** (50min., 1 per hr., £7.40, day return £7.80); and **Brighton** (1 hr., 3 per hr., £6.10, day return £6.20). Many routes require connections at **Littlehampton** to the south or **Barnham** to the west. **Buses** stop across from the Norfolk Arms on High St., and come from **Littlehampton** (#702; M-Sa 2 per hr., Su 1 per hr.). Arundel doesn't have any local bike stores, but two-wheelers can be hired for £12.50 per day at **Wests,** in nearby Angmering (☎ (01903) 770649). Hail a cab from **Castle Taxi.** (☎ 884444. Open daily 24hr.)

The **tourist information centre** (TIC), 61 High St., hands out the free *Town Guide*. (☎ 882268. Open Oct.-Easter daily 10am-3pm; Easter-Oct. M 9:30am-5pm, Tu-Su 9am-5pm.) **Banks** in town include **Lloyds TSB,** 14 High St. (☎ 717221. Open M-F 9:30am-4:30pm.) Services include the **post office,** 2-4 High St. (☎ 882113. Open M-F 9am-5:30pm, Sa 9am-12:30pm.) **Postal code:** BN18 9AA.

⚑ ACCOMMODATIONS

A glut of tourists takes its toll on accommodations during summer; savvy travelers plan ahead to avoid anxiety and a severe gouging of the wallet. The TIC maintains an up-to-date list of vacancies in town just outside its entrance; make it your first stop if you haven't booked ahead. B&Bs are consistent with Arundel's elegance, and are priced accordingly (singles £20-25).

Arundel House, 11 High St. (☎ 882136; arundelhouse@btinternet.com). Moderately priced accommodations with immoderate luxuries, including 400-year-old architecture and an adjacent cake shop (see **Food,** below). Singles, doubles, and twins all have bathrooms and TVs. £20 per person.

YHA Warningcamp (☎ 882204; fax 870615), half a mile out of town. Turn left from the train station and right at the "Public Footpath" sign, making another right onto the path. Follow the trail and the River Arun until you cross the railroad tracks, then go through the gate, and make a left to the hostel. The hostel is a Georgian house with aqua-green interior. Single-sex and coed showers with private changing booths. Huge kitchen and laundry facilities. Lockout 10am-5pm. Curfew 11pm. Open July-Aug. daily; Apr.-June M-Sa; Sept.-Oct. Tu-Sa; Nov.-Dec. F-Sa. Dorms £9.15, under 18 £6.20, camping £3.85.

Arden House, 4 Queens Ln. (☎ 882544). Eight immaculate rooms, some with wood-beamed ceilings, are convenient to town center and station. Doubles or twins £35, with bath £40. Singles available off-season and occasionally during the summer for £20.

Camping: Ship and Anchor Site (☎ (01243) 551262), 2 mi. from Arundel on Ford Rd. along the River Arun. Pub and shops nearby. Showers. Open Apr.-Sept. £3.50 per person, children £1.75. £1.50 per vehicle.

◓ FOOD

Arundel's pubs and tea shops are generally a bit expensive, as are the new wine bars. A few fruit and bread peddlers line High and Tarrant St. For picnics and late-night snacks, **Alldays,** 17 Queen St., honors its name, selling food practically all day. (Open M-Sa 6:30am-11pm, Su 7:30am-11pm.)

White Hart, 12 Queen St. (☎ 882374), serves pub grub and local ales (£2.20 per pint). The whose main courses, though slightly pricey (£6-7), are tasty; seek out the summer homemade specials and vegetarian selections. Open M-F 11am-3pm and 5:30-11pm, Sa-Su 11am-11pm.

WHAT A SCHISM Many people can define the word "schism"—a division within a church; few could describe what one looks like. Those few must have visited Arundel's **Parish Church of St. Nicholas** (☎ 882262, open dawn-dusk), across from the Cathedral of Our Lady and St. Philip Howard. The church, built in 1380, straddles a property line such that when the Anglican Church broke from the Roman Catholic Church, the western portion of the parish fell under the Church of England's control, while the eastern portion remained property of the Catholic Duke of Norfolk. Therefore, though the western portion still operates as an Anglican place of worship, the eastern portion, called the Fitzalan Chapel (access from castle grounds), serves as a Catholic burial chamber. Today, a glass wall separates the two spiritually diverse areas, making the building the only example in England of two faiths operating under one roof.

Belinda's, 13 Tarrant St. (☎ 882977). Locals frequent this 16th-century tea room with a large selection of traditional English fare. Linger over cream teas (£3.50) and delicious homemade jam. Open Tu-Sa 9am-5pm, Su 11am-5:30pm.

Castle Tandoori, 3 Mill Ln. (☎ 884224), dishes out an all-you-can-eat buffet of spicy Indian cuisine for £9.95 (Th-Su 6-11pm). Many dishes go for £3.5-£6. Open daily noon-2:30pm and 6pm-midnight.

Country Life Café, Tarrant Sq. (☎ 883456), will awaken your taste buds with a variety of vegetarian, vegan, and other options for around £4. Open M-W and F-Sa 10:30am-5pm, Su 11am-5pm.

SIGHTS AND FESTIVALS

Poised above the town like the backdrop of a fairy-tale, ⊠ **Arundel Castle** is lord of the skyline. The castle, seat of the Duke of Norfolk, was built in the 11th century but heavily damaged during the Civil War because the Duke was, like his successors, the highest-ranking Catholic in all British aristocracy. The castle was restored piecemeal by the dukes who called it home in the 18th and 19th centuries. Portraits by Van Dyck, Overbech, and others stare from the **Barons' Hall.** The many photographs of the current Duke and his family lend the place a comfortable air of home-sweet-castle. The 122 ft. library, meticulously carved in the late 18th century, and the family chapel will make you want to marry nobility. Don't overlook the graphically defined death warrant served against one of the Duke's ancestors by agreeable Elizabeth I. (☎ 883136. Castle open Apr.-Oct. Su-F noon-5pm, last entry 4pm. £7 and worth it, seniors £6, children £4.50, families £19.)

Along the River Arun, across from the castle, are the remains of **Blackfriars,** a Dominican priory. A nearby placard recounts the troubled past of the monks who lived there. Atop the same hill as Arundel Castle sits the **Cathedral of Our Lady and St. Philip Howard.** A Catholic cathedral, the French Gothic building was designed by Joseph Hansom, inventor of the hansom cab, and is decidedly more impressive from the outside than within. Though executed for cheering on the Spanish Armada in 1588, St. Philip occupies an honored place in the north transept. (☎ 882297. Open daily in summer 9am-6pm; in winter 9am-dusk. Free.)

The **Arundel Museum and Heritage Center,** 61 High St., chronicles over two millennia of the town in a collection highlighted by a history of the castle. The "Do Not Touch" signs outnumber the things you'd want to grab. (☎ 882344. Open Apr.-Sept. M-Sa 10:30am-5pm, Su 2-5pm. £1, concessions 50p.) Concealed observation enclosures at the **Wildfowl and Wetlands Trust Centre,** less than 1 mi. past the castle on Mill Rd., permit visitors to "come nose to beak with nature"—just make sure nature doesn't nip back. Over 12,000 birds roost on 60 acres. (☎ 883355. Open daily in summer 9:30am-5pm; in winter 9:30am-4:30pm; last admission 1hr. before closing. £4.75, students and seniors £3.75, children £2.75.)

In late August, Arundel castle is the glorious centerpiece of the **Arundel Festival,** which consists of 10 days of symphonic concerts, Shakespeare performances, and art exhibitions. The **Festival Fringe** simultaneously offers free or inexpensive concerts and events. Tickets for both go on sale 6-8 weeks before the festivals begin. (☎ 883690; box office ☎ 883474. Tickets up to £20.) The annual **Corpus Christi Carpet of Flowers** will be held in the Cathedral of Our Lady and St. Philip Howard on June 13-14, during which thousands of flowers will be laid in a pattern stretching 93 ft. down the center aisle.

DAYTRIP FROM ARUNDEL: PETWORTH HOUSE

Ten miles from Arundel, Petworth showcases the talents of Capability Brown and J.M.W. Turner, among other artists. Brown landscaped the gardens; Turner painted the landscape. Some of Turner's best works hang in the library of the Third Earl of Egremont, an early 19th-century patron of arts and letters. Petworth now retains the artwork produced 1802-1812 and 1827-1831; the ground floor vsitors' gallery contains 71 other sculptures and 59 paintings, including works by William Blake and Anthony Van Dyck. *(Take the train to Pulborough (10min.) and walk the remaining 2 mi. to the house or catch bus #1 or 1A. Ask for directions at the TIC. House ☎ (01798) 343929. House open Apr.-Oct. Su-W 1-5:30pm, last admission 4:30pm; extra rooms shown M-W. Grounds open daily July-Aug. 11am-6pm; Apr.-June and Sept.-Oct. noon-6pm. Ground-floor wheelchair access. House and grounds £5.50, under 17 £2.50, families £13.50.)*

CHICHESTER   ☎01243

Despite centuries of confinement within eroding Roman walls and a culture revolving around a cathedral's conventions, the citizens of Chichester (pop. 30,000) seem content with their lot. The town still thrives on its markets (cattle, corn, and others), and its roads all still lead to the ornate Market Cross, a gift of kindly Bishop Storey in 1501 to "help the poore people of the cityе." Today, Chichester hosts one of the country's best theaters, a summer arts festival, a host of gallery exhibits, and a nearby summer motor racing spectacular.

▐ GETTING THERE AND GETTING AROUND

Chichester is 45 mi. southwest of London and 15 mi. east of Portsmouth. **Trains** (☎ (08457) 484950) run into the **Southgate station** from: **London Victoria** (1½hr., 3 per hr., £16.50, day return £16.60); **Portsmouth** (40min., 2-3 per hr., £4.80, day return £4.90); and **Brighton** (50min., 2-3 per hr., £7.80, day return £8.10). The **bus station** (☎ (01903) 237661) also lies on Southgate. **National Express** (☎ (08705) 808080) **buses** come from **London** (1 per day, return £9). **Stagecoach Coastline** buses connect Chichester with **Portsmouth** (#700 and 701, 1hr., 2 per hr., £3.90) and **Brighton** (#702, 3hr., 2 per hr., £4.60). If you plan forays into the local area, ask about the **Explorer** ticket, which gives a day's unlimited travel on buses servicing southern England from Kent to Salisbury (£4.80, seniors £3.50, children £2.50, families £10). **Central Cars of Chichester,** 30 South St. (☎ (0800) 789432), provides reliable taxi service.

▐ ORIENTATION AND PRACTICAL INFORMATION

Four Roman streets named for their compass directions divide Chichester into quadrants that converge at **Market Cross.** To reach the **tourist information centre** (TIC), 29a South St., from the train station, turn left as you exit onto Southgate, which turns into South St. (☎ 775888; fax 539449; www.sussexlive.co.uk. Open July-Aug. M-Sa 9:15am-5:15pm, last booking 5pm; Su 10am-4pm; Sept.-June M-Sa 9:15am-5:15pm; 24hr. computer info.) **Guided tours** of the city depart from the TIC. (June-Sept. M-Sa 10:30am; £2.) Several **banks** reside on East St., as does **Thomas Cook,** 40 East St. (☎ 536733. Open M and W-Sa 9am-5:30pm, Tu 10am-5:30pm.) Wednesday and Saturday bring a **market** to the parking lot off Market Ave. Surf the **Internet** from **Junction Club,** 2 Southgate, for £1.50 per 30min., £2.50 per hr. (☎ 776644. Open M-F 10am-10pm, Sa 10am-8pm, Su 11am-4pm.) Other services include: the **launderette,** 11 Eastgate (open daily 8am-8pm, last wash 7pm); the **police,** Kingsham Rd (☎ (0845) 607 0999); and the **post office,** 10 West St. (☎ 771736, open M-W and F-Sa 8:30am-5:30pm, Th 8:30am-5:45pm). **Postal code:** PO19 1AB.

▐ ACCOMMODATIONS AND FOOD

B&Bs are abundant, but cheap rooms are rare, especially on big racecourse weekends; plan on paying £16-20, and expect a 15min. walk to the town center. **Hedgehogs,** 45 Whyke Ln., close to the town center, offers cozy rooms, a cheerful black labrador, and happy hedgehog paraphernalia. (☎ 780022. No smoking. Singles £23-24; doubles £36-38.) **Bayleaf,** 16 Whyke Rd., welcomes guests with colorful geraniums, freshly squeezed orange juice, and sugared grapefruits. (☎ 774330. No smoking. £23 per person.) **Campsites** lie at **Southern Leisure Centre,** Vinnetrow Rd., a 15min. walk southeast of town. (☎ 787715. Showers and laundry. Open Apr.-Oct. £2 per person; pitch fee £8-10.)

The hot scent of yeast flows from **bakeries** on North St., while groceries await at **Iceland,** 55 South St. (Open M-Th and Sa 8:30am-7pm, F 8:30am-8pm, Su 10am-4pm.) The town's best eateries congregate around the cathedral and tend to gouge the pocket. Twentysomethings mingle with the pre-theater crowd at **Woodies Wine Bar and Brasserie,** 10 St. Pancras, the oldest wine bar in Sussex. Sandwich and a glass of wine (or pint of ale) £4.50, main courses £6.95-£10. (☎ 779895. Open M-Sa noon-2:30pm and 6-11pm, Su 6-11pm.) **The Crypt,** 12a South St., is actually housed in an 800-year-old undercroft. It's a bit dear for dinner (£10-14), but has excellent lunch specials and salads, like mozzarella and tomato or chicken liver (£4.75). Tapas £2.95-4.95. (☎ 537033. Open daily noon-3pm and 6-10pm.) The **Pasta Factory,** 6 South St. (☎ 785764), rolls out fresh pasta twice daily; its *cannelloni* will give you pleasant dreams for weeks (£7.50). **Maison Blanc Boulangerie and Patisserie,** 56 South St., bakes cakes, fills pastries ranging from eclairs to exotic passionata (*Pain au chocolat;* 80p), and builds sandwiches on organic bread for £3.95. (☎ 539292. Open M-F 8:45am-5:30pm, Sa 8:45am-6pm; June-Sept. also Su 9am-5pm.)

👁 SIGHTS

Begun in 1091, **Chichester Cathedral** stands just west of the town's 15th-century market cross. It is a hybrid of Norman remains and later additions. A glorious Marc Chagall stained-glass depiction of Psalm 150 ("let everything that hath breath praise the Lord") brings all walks of the animal kingdom into one coherent pattern. The carved effigy of 14th-century Earl Richard Fitzalan inspired Larkin's "An Arundel Tomb," now displayed on a nearby pillar. Restorations to the west front should be completed by early 2001. Free lunchtime concerts are featured on Tuesdays. (☎ 782595. Open daily in summer 7:30am-7pm; in winter 7:30am-5pm. Tours from the West Door Apr.-Oct. M-Sa 11am and 2:15pm. Evensong M-Sa 5:30pm, Su 3:30pm. Wheelchair access. £2 donation encouraged.)

Chichester's other attractions include the **Pallants,** a quiet area with elegant 18th- and 19th-century houses in the southeast quadrant. **The Pallant House,** 9 North Pallant, a restored Queen Anne building complete with period furniture, has been optimistically attributed to Sir Christopher Wren and contains a small gallery of mainly 20th-century British art. Familiar foreign faces in the crowd include Picasso and Cézanne, though displays rotate. (☎ 774557. Open Tu-Sa 10am-5:45pm, last admission 4:45pm. £4, students £2.50, seniors £3, children free.)

🎵 🌺 ENTERTAINMENT AND FESTIVALS

Unexpectedly located in a residential neighborhood north of town, the **Chichester Festival Theatre** (☎ 781312; www.cft.org.uk) is the cultural center of Chichester. Founded by Sir Laurence Olivier, the venue has attracted such artists as Dame Maggie Smith, Peter Ustinov, Kathleen Turner, and Julie Christie. The newer **Minerva Studio Theatre** is a smaller space for more intimate productions, including theater in the round. Call to make special arrangements for the visually and hearing impaired. The **Theatre Restaurant and Café** caters to patrons from 12:30pm on matinee days and from 5:30pm for evening shows. (Box office open M-Sa 9am-8pm, or until 6pm non-performance days. Wheelchair access. Tickets £15-20, 60 seats available at box office at 10am on day of show £6-8, max. 2 tickets per person.)

During the first two weeks in July, the **Chichester Festivities** enliven the quiet town. Artists and musicians collaborate to produce one of the finest spells of concentrated creativity in England. A full program is published in April. (☎ 780192; www.chifest.org.uk. Tickets from £2. Box office open mid-May until the end of the festival M-Sa 10am-5:30pm.)

🅓 DAYTRIPS FROM CHICHESTER

FISHBOURNE ROMAN PALACE. Built around AD 80, possibly as the home of a local king, the palace is the largest domestic Roman building found in Britain. The remains include many mosaic floors, among them the famous *Cupid on a Dolphin*, and a formal garden replanted according to the original excavated plans. *(2 mi. from Ave. de Chartres roundabout in Chichester; walk west along Westgate, which becomes Fishbourne Rd. (the A259) for 1½ mi., or take bus #11, 56, or 700 from Chichester center. Buses stop at Salthill Rd., 5min. from the palace. Fishbourne rail station is also 5min. from the palace. ☎ (01243) 785859. Open Aug. daily 10am-6pm; Mar.-July and Sept.-Oct. daily 10am-5pm; Feb. and Nov.-Dec. daily 10am-4pm, Jan. Su 10am-4pm. £4.40, students and seniors £3.70, children £2.30, families £11.50.)*

GOODWOOD HOUSE. Three miles northeast of Chichester stands the ancestral home of the Duke of Richmond. Splendid Canalettos, Reynoldses, and Stubbs vie for attention in the 18th-century country abode. *(Take bus #268 from Chichester, then 1 mi. and follow signs to the house. ☎ (01243) 755048. Open Aug. Su-Th 1-5pm; Apr.-July and Sept. Su-M 1-5pm. £6, children 12-18 £3.)*

WEALD AND DOWNLAND OPEN AIR MUSEUM. For a leisurely stroll through a village unlike any other you'll find in England, head to this 50 acre museum in Singleton. Over the past 25 years, 40 buildings representing different eras in British history have been removed from their original sites and reconstructed here. Visitors can time travel from a medieval farmstead to a Tudor market hall to a Victorian rural school. *(7 mi. north of Chichester off the A286. ☎ (01243) 811348; www.wealddown.co.uk. Open Mar.-Oct. daily 10:30am-6pm, last admission 5pm; Nov.-Feb. W and Sa-Su 10:30am-4pm. £6, seniors £5.50, children £3, families £15).*

HAMPSHIRE

PORTSMOUTH   ☎023

> Don't talk to me about the naval tradition. It's nothing but rum, sodomy, and the lash.
> —Winston Churchill

Set Victorian prudery against prostitutes, drunkards, and a lot of bloody cursing sailors, and an image of the 900-year history Portsmouth (pop. 190,500) will emerge. Henry VIII's *Mary Rose*, which sank in 1545 and was raised 437 years later, epitomizes an incomparable naval heritage in a city that will appeal most to those fascinated by the storied history of the Royal Navy. On the seafront, older visitors relive D-Day while fresh faces explore the warships and learn of the days when Britannia truly ruled the waves.

🄵 GETTING THERE AND GETTING AROUND

Trains: Portsmouth and Southsea Station, Commercial Rd. Travel Center open M-F 8:40am-6pm, Sa 8:40am-4:30pm. Office open M-Sa 5:40am-8:30pm, Su 6:40am-8:40pm. **Portsmouth Harbour Station,** The Hard, ¾ mi. away at the end of the line. Office open M-F 5:50am-7:30pm, Sa 6am-7:30pm, Su 6:40am-8:10pm. Trains (☎ (08457) 484950) go to stations from **London Waterloo** (1½hr., 3 per hr., £19, day return £19.10) and **Chichester** (40min., 2 per hr., £4, day return £4.90).

Buses: The Hard Interchange, The Hard, next to the Harbour station. **National Express** (☎ (08705) 808080) rumbles from **London** (2½hr., 1 per hr., £10.50) and **Salisbury** (2hr., 1 per hr., £8.25). Office open M-F 7:45am-5pm, Sa 7:45am-4pm.

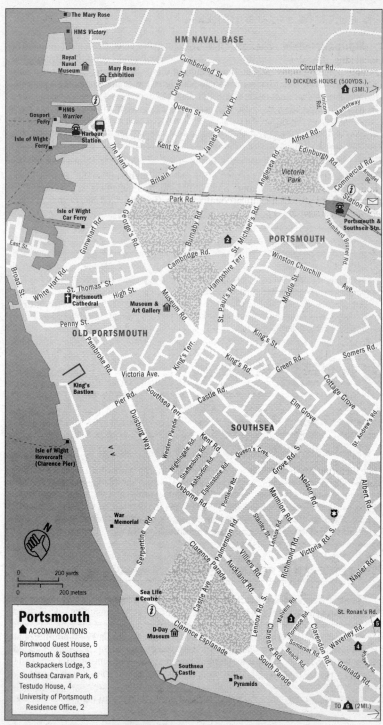

HM NAVAL BASE

■ The Mary Rose

■ HMS *Victory*

Royal
Naval
Museum

Mary Rose
Exhibition

Circular Rd.

TO DICKENS HOUSE (500YDS.),
(3MI.)

Cumberland St.

Cross St.

Queen St.

York Pl.

Gosport
Ferry

HMS
Warrior

Harbour
Station

Kent St.

St. James St.

Alfred Rd.

Edinburgh Rd.

Anglesea Rd.

Commercial Rd.

Isle of Wight
Ferry

The Hard

Britain St.

Victoria
Park

Union Rd.

Marketway

Arundel St.

Station St.

Park Rd.

Isambard Brunel Rd.

Portsmouth &
Southsea Stn.

Isle of Wight
Car Ferry

Gunwharf Rd.

St. George's Rd.

Burnaby Rd.

Cambridge Rd.

2

St. Michael's Rd.

PORTSMOUTH

Winston Churchill

Ave.

East St.

White Hart Rd.

Hampshire Terr.

Middle St.

Somers Rd.

Broad St.

St. Thomas St.

Portsmouth
Cathedral

High St.

Museum &
Art Gallery

Museum Rd.

St. Paul's Rd.

King's St.

Green Rd.

Cottage Grove

Penny St.

OLD PORTSMOUTH

Pembroke Rd.

King's Terr.

King's Rd.

St. Andrew's Rd.

Victoria Ave.

King's
Bastion

Pier Rd.

Southsea Terr.

Castle Rd.

Elm Grove

Western Parade

Duisburg Way

SOUTHSEA

Isle of Wight
Hovercraft
(Clarence Pier)

Nightingale Rd.

Kent Rd.

Queen's Cres.

Grove Rd.

Nelson Rd.

Albert Rd.

Shaftesbury Rd.

Ashburton Rd.

Elphinstone Rd.

Portland Rd.

Marmion Rd.

Osborne Rd.

Serpentine Rd.

War
Memorial

Stanley St.

Lennox Rd.

Richmond Rd.

Victoria Rd. S.

Napier Rd.

Clarence Parade

Palmerston Rd.

Villiers Rd.

Auckland Rd.

Lennox Rd.

Clarence Rd.

South Parade

Malvern Rd.

Florence Rd.

Clarendon Rd.

St. Ronan's Rd.

5

Sea Life
Centre

Castle Ave.

3

Somerset Rd.

Beach Rd.

Waverley Rd.

Granada Rd.

Whitwell Rd.

4

D-Day
Museum

Clarence Esplanade

South Rd.

Southsea
Castle

The
Pyramids

TO 6 (2MI.)

0   200 yards
0   200 meters

Portsmouth

▲ ACCOMMODATIONS

Birchwood Guest House, 5
Portsmouth & Southsea
  Backpackers Lodge, 3
Southsea Caravan Park, 6
Testudo House, 4
University of Portsmouth
  Residence Office, 2

SOUTH ENGLAND

Ferries: Ferries (☎ 9282 7744) chug to the Isle of Wight from the harbor (15-20min., in summer 2 per hr., in winter 1 per hr.; half day return £5.80, day return £7). **Isle of Wight Hovercraft** (☎ 9281 1000) departs from Clarence Esplanade (9min., 2 per hr., return £7.10, children £3.60). For services to the **Continent,** consult **By Ferry,** p. 35.

Public Transportation: A reliable and comprehensive bus system connects the out-stretches of the city. The **local bus** company **First Provincial** (☎ 9286 2412) runs throughout the city; daily pass £2, weekly pass £10.

Taxis: Aqua Cars (☎ 9281 8123). **Streamline Taxis** (☎ 9281 1111).

ORIENTATION AND PRACTICAL INFORMATION

Portsmouth sprawls along the coast for miles—Portsmouth, Old Portsmouth, and the resort community of Southsea can seem like altogether different cities. Major sights in Portsmouth cluster at **The Hard, Old Portsmouth** (near the Portsmouth and Southsea train station), and **Southsea Esplanade.**

Tourist Information Centre: (☎ 9282 6722), The Hard, by the historic ships. Open daily 9:30am-5:45pm. **Branch,** 102 Commercial Rd. (☎ 9283 8382), next to the train station. Open M-Sa 9:30am-5:30pm. **Bureau de change** in branch. Free accommodations booking service. **Seasonal offices** (☎ 832464) near the Sea Life Centre and Clarence Esplanade. Open daily Apr.-Sept. 9:30am-1:30pm and 2:30-5:45pm.

Tours: Guide Friday buses stop every half hour at many major areas of the city. A ticket entitles you to get on and off as you please for one full day, 10am-6pm. £6, students and seniors £5, children £2. **Waterbus** (☎ 9282 2584) offers 50min. guided rides in Portsmouth Harbour. Waterbuses run 10:30am-5pm from The Hard. £3.50, seniors and students £3, children £2.

Budget Travel: Travel Shop (☎ 9281 6645), University of Portsmouth Union, Alexandra House, Museum Rd. Bus, train, and plane tickets. Open during term M and Th 9:30am-6pm, Tu-W 9:30am-5pm, F 10:30am-5pm.

Financial Services: Major banks clump around the Commercial Rd. shopping precinct, just north of Portsmouth and Southsea Station, including **Lloyds TSB,** open M-Tu and Th-F 9am-5pm, W 9:30am-5pm, Sa 9:30am-12:30pm.

American Express: 110 Commercial Rd. (☎ 9286 5865). Open M-Sa 9am-5:30pm.

Police: (☎ 9283 9333), Winston Churchill Ave.

Hospital: QA Hospital (☎ 9228 6000) handles emergencies. Also **St. Mary's Hospital** (☎ 9282 2331), Milton Rd.

Internet Access: The Cyber Café (☎ 9266 4158), corner of Victoria Rd. South and Albert Rd. £2 first 30min., £1.75 next 30min.; £2.50 per hr. 1-5pm. Open M-F 10:30am-8pm, Sa 10:30am-9pm, Su noon-4pm.

Post Office: (☎ 9283 5201), Slindon St., near the train station. Open M and Th 8:45am-5:30pm, Tu-W and F-Sa 9am-5:30pm. **Postal Code:** PO1 1AA.

 PHONE CODE Portsmouth's phone code recently changed to 023. If you see Portsmouth's old code of 01705 on brochures, just add "92" in front of the local number. For further details on phone code changes, see Phone Codes, p. 56.

ACCOMMODATIONS

Moderately priced B&Bs (hovering near £20) clutter **Southsea,** Portsmouth's con-tiguous resort town, 1½ mi. east of The Hard along the coast. Many are located along Waverly Rd., Clarendon Rd., and South Parade, all within blocks of the coast. If you're arriving via the Portsmouth and Southsea Station, catch one of the many buses that wind around Commercial Rd. (#16 and #5 are good choices). If your ferry or train arrives at Portsmouth Harbor, hop aboard one of the several buses that make the pilgrimage from The Hard to South Parade (#5 is one option). Cheaper lodgings lie two or three blocks inland—Whitwell Rd., Granada Rd., St. Roman's Rd., and Malvern Rd. all have a fair sprinkling.

Birchwood Guest House, 44 Waverly Rd. (☎ 9281 1337). Bright, spacious rooms with bath, recently refurbished with a dash of aboriginal art. Friendly dog and friendlier hosts invite guests to unwind with a drink in the lounge. Ample breakfast included. £16-25 per person, children half price.

YHA Portsmouth (☎ 9237 5661), Wymering Manor, Old Wymering Ln., Medina Rd., Cosham. Take any bus to Cosham (#1, 3, 40, and others) to police station and follow the signs. By train, make a right and walk up High St. from Cosham Station; turn left on Wayte St. and cross the roundabout to Medina Rd. After 6 blocks, Old Wymering Ln. is on your right; the hostel is across from the church. The former home of Catherine Parr, sixth wife of Henry VIII, the hostel features exquisitely detailed woodwork and architecture. Sleep in a Tudor drawing room. 58 beds. Lockout 10am-5pm. Curfew 11pm. Open Feb.-Aug. daily; Sept.-Nov. F-Sa. Dorms £9.15, under 18 £6.20.

Portsmouth and Southsea Backpackers Lodge, 4 Florence Rd. (☎/fax 9283 2495). Take any Southsea bus and get off at The Strand. Very clean rooms spreading over a 4-story home. Pan-European crowd and energetic owners. Comfy lounge, wooden bunks, satellite TV, and Internet access (£2.50 per 30min.). 2 kitchens and well-stocked grocery counter. Laundry facilities (£2). Dorms £10; doubles £22, with bath £25.

Testudo House, 19 Whitwell Rd., Southsea (☎ 9282 4324). The Padfields, enthusiastic offspring and all, provide beds for families. No smoking. Singles £17.50; doubles £34.

University of Portsmouth Halls of Residence (☎ 9284 3178), Nuffield Centre, St. Michael's Rd., overlooking Southsea Common, 15min. from The Hard. Small, modern rooms in **Burrel House, Rees Hall,** or **Harry Law Hall,** all reasonably convenient. Booking ahead is highly recommended, but last minute arrivals should contact Rees Hall directly. Singles and twins available mid-July through Sept. Rooms £22.25 with full English breakfast (cheaper with self-catering).

Camping: Southsea Caravan Park, Melville Rd., Southsea (☎ 9273 5070). At the eastern end of seafront, 5-6mi. from The Hard. Toilets, showers, laundry facilities, shop, restaurant-bar, and pool. Open year-round; no reservations, but call ahead for availability. 2-person tent £8-9 per night; after Sept. from £7.

FOOD AND PUBS

Good restaurants reside along Osborne Rd., Palmerston Rd., and Clarendon Rd. in the Southsea shopping district. There is no drought of pubs in Portsmouth to provide the weary sailor with galley fare and a bottle of gin, especially near **The Hard** or along **Palmerston.** Ethnic food spices up the scene on Albert Rd. The **Tesco** supermarket awaits on Craswell St., just off the town center, and has a habit of cutting prices to ridiculous levels just before closing. (☎ 839222. Open M-Th 8am-8pm, F 8am-9pm, Sa 8am-7pm, Su 10am-4pm.)

Country Kitchen, 59a Marmion Rd. (☎ 9232 1148). Pampers eaters with its delectable menu of vegetarian and vegan dishes, plus the genuine genial service. Savory dishes (around £4.50) and un-decadent desserts score big points. Open daily 9:30am-5pm.

Fabio's, 108 Palmerston Rd. (☎ 9281 1139). Pizzas and pasta romance the air. Meals £5, with a 25% discount for takeaway. Open daily 5pm-midnight, Sa also 10am-3pm.

Brown's, 9 Clarendon Rd. (☎ 9282 2617). The coffee will keep you wide-eyed for days at Brown's, which serves solid fresh English food in relaxed surroundings. Omelettes £3-4. Open daily in summer 9:30am-9:30pm, in winter 9:30am-5pm.

The Outback Bar (☎ 9282 3497), Ashley Pl., off Clarendon Rd. in Southsea. Jumping with Aussie energy, this is the place to be if you develop a hankering for a kangaroo steak. Happy "hour" all day Tu for women and Su for everyone. Open daily noon-11pm.

👁 🎵 SIGHTS AND ENTERTAINMENT

Portsmouth overflows with magnificent ships and seafaring relics. The bulk of sights worth seeing anchor near The Hard, delighting war buffs, intriguing historians, and looking like some pretty big boats to the rest of the world.

🚢 NAVAL HERITAGE CENTRE

In the Naval Yard. ☎ 9286 1512 or 9286 1533. Entrance next to the TIC on The Hard—follow the signs to Portsmouth Historic Ships. Ships open daily Mar.-Oct. 10am-5:30pm, Nov.-Feb. 10am-5pm; last entry to many sights 4:45pm. Each sight £5.95, students and seniors £5.20, children £4.45. If you plan to see more than two sights, the Passport ticket offers unlimited touring for £14.90, students and seniors £12.90, children £10.90.

War buffs and historians will want to plunge head first into the unparalleled Naval Heritage Centre, which brings together a virtual armada of Britain's most storied ships and nautical artifacts. Resurrect the past with these floating monuments to Britain's former majesty of the seas—even the staunchest Army man can't help but be awed by the history within these hulls. The five galleries of the **Royal Naval Museum** fill in the historical gaps between the three ships.

MARY ROSE. The center includes one of England's warships, Henry VIII's Mary Rose. Henry was particularly fond of her, but like many other women Henry associated with, the *Mary Rose* died before her time—she sank after setting sail from Portsmouth in July 1545. Not until 1982 was she raised from her watery grave. The eerie, skeletal hulk is now being continuously sprayed with a waxy preservative mixture designed to slowly dry the timber over the next 20 years.

HMS VICTORY. Napoleon must be rolling around in his tiny coffin to know that the HMS Victory is still afloat. Cinching Britain's reputation as king of the waves with its defeat of Napoleon's forces at Trafalgar in 1805, the *Victory* embodies the order and invincible regimentation of Admiral Nelson's Navy. It vividly portrays the dismal, cramped conditions for press-ganged recruits and contains Nelson's death-bed—now a veritable shrine for members of the Royal Navy. Only on view via a guided tour—be sure to check your admission ticket for your time slot.

HMS WARRIOR. Eclipsed by its neighbor, the HMS Warrior provides an intriguing companion to the *Victory*. The pride of Queen Victoria's navy and the first ironclad battleship in the world, *Warrior* never saw battle. Nonetheless, a respectful Napoleon III called it "The Black Snake among the Rabbits in the Channel."

OTHER NAVAL SIGHTS

Not surprisingly, Portsmouth's collection of museums rarely deal with more than the sea and its inhabitants. **Spitbank Fort** has protected Portsmouth through two World Wars and remains relatively unscathed. Boats depart from the Historic Dockyard. *(25min. crossing. Runs Easter-Oct. W and Sa 1:30pm, Su 2pm. Trips £6.50, concessions £5.)* The **Royal Navy Submarine Museum** surfaces Britain's only walk-on submarine, the **HMS Alliance,** and provides tours of this underwater village. A passenger ferry crosses from the Harbour train station continuously, or take bus #9 to Haslar Hospital. *(☎ 9252 9217. £3.75, concessions £2.50, families £10.)* The **Royal Marines Museum** chronicles various battles and includes a prodigious display of medals, a jungle room, and a marine in drag. *(☎ 9281 9385. Open daily Sept.-May 10am-4:30pm; June-Aug. 10am-5pm. £3.75, seniors and students £2.75, children £2.)*

BEST OF THE REST

CHARLES DICKENS BIRTHPLACE MUSEUM. Charles Dickens was born in Portsmouth, returning later to derive inspiration for *Nicholas Nickleby*. His birthplace is today an uninspired museum. The only authentic Dickens artifacts in the Regency-style house are the couch on which he died and a lock of his precious hair. *(393 Old Commercial Rd., ¾ mi. north of Portsmouth and Southsea station. ☎ 9282 7261. Open daily Apr.-Oct. 10am-5:30pm; Nov.-Dec. and Feb. 7, Dickens's Birthday, 10am-5pm. £2, seniors £1.50, students and children £1.20, families £5.20.)*

SOUTHSEA. Don't let the garish exterior of the **Sea Life Centre** fool you—the insides reveal a finful of verve. "Don't touch the catfish. They bite!" (☎ 9287 5222. *Open daily in summer 10am-7pm; in winter 10am-5pm. £5.50, seniors £4.50, students £4, children £3.50.)* The **D-Day Museum,** on Clarence Esplanade, houses the impressive Overlord Embroidery commissioned in 1968 and finished in the early 70s. Like a latter-day Bayeux Tapestry (but 41 ft. longer), the work recounts the invasion of France. (☎ 9282 7261. *Open Apr.-Sept. daily 10am-5:30pm; Oct.-Mar. daily 10am-5pm. Wheelchair access. £4.75, seniors £3.60, students and children £2.85, families £12.35. Audio guide to embroidery 50p.)* **Southsea Castle,** situated along Clarence Esplanade, recounts Portsmouth's military history from the perspective of this seaside fortress. (*Open Apr.-Sept. daily 10am-5:30pm. £2, senior £1.80, student and children £1.20, families £5.20.)* **The City Museum,** Museum Road, fills in the details of Portsmouth's past and also features the occasional art exhibit. (☎ 9282 7261. *Open daily Apr.-Sept. 10am-5:30pm, Oct-Mar 10am-5pm. Free.)*

Several annual festivals heat up Portsmouth during the summer. In early June, see the **Southsea Carnival** (☎ 9242 7873). Late August brings both the **Southsea Show** (☎ 9283 4158) and the **Kite Festival** (☎ 9283 4158). But, even in the absence of a lively event, the Southsea shoreline, dotted with parks, flower beds, and war memorials, makes for a wonderfully peaceful stroll.

ISLE OF WIGHT ☎ 01983

She thinks of nothing but the Isle of Wight and she calls it the Island, as if there were no other island in the world.
—Jane Austen, *Mansfield Park*

Far more tranquil and sun-splashed than its mother island to the north, the Isle of Wight offers travelers dramatic scenery, beautiful sandy beaches, and relaxing family holidays. The quiet life of the Isle has softened the hardest of hearts through the centuries, from Queen Victoria, who reportedly found much amusement here (and little elsewhere), to Karl Marx, who exclaimed that "the island is a little paradise!" Best known for its lovely shores of stone and sand, the Isle of Wight also shelters much inland beauty.

▐ GETTING THERE AND GETTING AROUND

Ferries: Several companies whisk travelers from the mainland. **Wight Link** (☎ (0870) 582 7744; www.wightlink.co.uk) ferry services include: **Lymington** to **Yarmouth** (return £8.20, children £4.10); **Portsmouth Harbour** to **Fishbourne** (return £8.20, children £4.10); and **Portsmouth Harbour** to **Ryde** (return £10.30, children £5.20). **Red Funnel** ferries (☎ (023) 8033 4010) steam from **Southampton** to **East Cowes** (1 per hr., return £7.80, children £3.90). **Hovertravel** (☎ (023) 9281 1000) sails from **Southsea** to **Ryde** (9min., 34 per day, return £10.20, children £5.10).

Public Transportation: Trains and buses run throughout the island. The **Island Line** train service (☎ 562492) is limited to the eastern end of the island, including Ryde, Shanklin, Sandown, Brading, and a few points in between. **Southern Vectis** buses (☎ 827005) cover the entire island; **Travel Centres** (☎ 827005) in Cowes, Shanklin, Ryde, and Newport sell the complete service timetable (50p). Buy tickets on board. The **Island Rover** ticket gives you unlimited travel on bus and rail services. (1 day £6.25, children £3.15; 2 days £9.95, £5; week £25.50, £12.75.)

Car Rental: Self-Drive Minibus and Car Hire, 10 Osborne Rd. (☎ 864263), in Shanklin, offers free pick-up and drop-off service. Rentals from £22.50 per day. Open daily 8:30am-5:30pm. **Solent Self Drive** (☎ 282050 or (0800) 724734), Marghams Garage, Crocker St., Newport, as well as Red Funnel Terminal, West Cowes, has rates from £27.50 per day, £48 per weekend, £165 per week.

Bike Rental: Solent Self Drive (see above). £9 per day, £40 deposit. **Island Cycle Hire,** 17 Beachfield Rd. (☎ 407030), in Sandown. £8-12 per day, £30-40 per week; ID plus £25 deposit. Open Apr.-Sept. daily 9am-5pm; Oct.-Mar. 5-6 days a week 9am-5pm.

SOUTH ENGLAND

✳🛈 ORIENTATION AND PRACTICAL INFORMATION

The Isle of Wight is 23 mi. by 13 mi. and shaped like a diamond, with towns clustered along its sparkling edges. **Ryde, Cowes, Sandown, Shanklin, Ventnor, Yarmouth,** and, in the center (at the origin of the River Medina), **Newport,** are the best places to find tourist information centres (TICs), accommodations, and bus service.

Tourist Information Centres: Each offers an individual town map as well as the free Isle of Wight "Official Pocket Guide." A **general inquiry service** (☎ 862942; fax 863047; www.islandbreaks.co.uk) directs questions to one of the seven regional offices listed below—call this number first. All books accommodations (☎ 813813).

Cowes: (☎ 291914), Fountain Quay. In the alleyway next to the ferry terminal for RedJet (to Southampton). Open July-Aug. daily 9am-6pm; Apr.-June Tu-Su 9am-5:30pm; Jan.-Feb. Tu-Sa 10am-4pm; Cowes week (1st week in Aug.) daily 8am-8pm.

Newport: (☎ 525450), South St., near the bus station. Open Apr.-Oct. M-Sa 9am-5:30pm, Su 9am-5pm. Call the central line for winter hours.

Ryde: (☎ 562905), at the corner of Western Esplanade and Union St., opposite Ryde Pier. Open July-Aug. daily 9am-7pm; Easter-June and Sept.-Oct. daily 9am-6pm; Nov.-Easter W and F-M 10am-4pm.

Sandown: 8 High St. (☎ 403886), across from Boots Pharmacy. Open Apr.-Oct. M-Sa 9am-5:30pm, Su 9am-5pm; Nov.-Mar. daily 9am-5pm.

Shanklin: 67 High St. (☎ 862942). Open Apr.-Oct. M-Sa 9am-5:30pm, Su 9am-5pm; Nov.-Mar. daily 9am-5pm.

Ventnor: 34 High St. (☎ 853625). Open Apr.-Oct., M-Tu and Th-Sa 10am-3pm. Call the central line for winter hours.

Yarmouth: (☎ 813818), The Quay. Follow the signs from the ferry stop. Open Easter-Oct. daily 9:30am-6pm; Nov.-Dec. Th-Su 10am-4pm; Jan.-Easter F-M 10am-4pm.

Financial Services: Banks can be found in all major town centers. Make sure you stock up on cash, as cash machines are rare in the smaller towns.

Police: ☎ 528000.

Medical Services: St. Mary's Hospital (☎ 524081), in Newport. Disabled travelers can seek assistance from **Dial Office** (☎ 522823).

Internet Access: The Internet has reached the island at the **Lord Louis Library** (☎ 823800) in Newport and the **Ryde Library** (☎ 562170) in Ryde. Both offer access for £3 per 30min. or £5 per hr.; book sessions in advance.

Post Office: Post offices are found in every town center.

▌ ACCOMMODATIONS

Accommodations on the Isle of Wight tend to require a two-night-minimum stay. Prices range from decent to absurd, often depending on proximity to the shore. Budget travelers should try one of the **YHA Youth Hostels** on either end of the island or look into less-visited areas. Lodgings are also occasionally offered above **pubs.**

YHA Sandown (☎ 402651; fax 403565), The Firs, Fitzroy St. Sandown Offers clean, spanking new rooms, a pleasant respite from a hard day's sunbathing. Extensive menu comes with a friendly welcome. Luggage storage. Lockout 10am-5pm. Open mid Apr.-Sept. daily; mid Feb.-mid Apr. and Sept. W-Su. Dorms £10.85, under 18 £7.40.

YHA Totland Bay (☎ 752165; fax 756443), Hurst Hill, Totland Bay, on the west end of the island. Take Southern Vectis buses #7 or 7A to Totland War Memorial; turn left up Weston Rd., and take the 2nd left onto Hurst Hill. Hostel is on the left. Comfortable hostel in a fantastic location. Cliffs, walking trails, and Alum Bay are all close by. Open Mar.-June M-Sa; July-Aug. daily; Sept.-Oct. F-Sa. Dorms £10.85, under 18 £7.40.

Seaward Guest House, 14 George St., Ryde (☎ 563168; seaward@FSBDial.co.uk). Spacious rooms and a hearty breakfast, near the hovercraft and train stations. Singles £18-£20; doubles £30-44.

Union Inn (☎ 293163), Watch House Ln., Cowes. Very reasonable rates, for rooms and only rooms. No breakfast, but evening meals (£4-8) available. £20 per person.

Camping: Check the free Isle of Wight *Camping and Touring Guide*, available from all TICs; sites are plentiful. **Beaper Farm Camping Site** (☎ 615210), in Ryde, has shower and laundry facilities. £7 per tent and 2 people.

FOOD

Hungry travelers in towns throughout the Isle of Wight can begin their hunt for food on the local High St. or Esplanade; these commonly named roads often feature uncommonly excellent restaurants. Locally caught fresh fish is a typical specialty. *The Official Guide to Eating Out,* distributed by TICs, offers additional dining options. Supermarkets can be found in most large cities, and thirsty vacationers need not look far for a pub, since the island harbors nearly one public house for every square mile. When using **Ryde** as a center for island exploration, feast on exquisite gourmet baguettes and pastries (£1.30-£3.30) from the **Baguette Factory,** 24 Cross St. (☎ 611115. Open M-Sa 8:30am-4pm.) Visitors descend upon **Michelangelo,** 30 St. Thomas St., for homemade Italian delights (£6.50-£12) and a seafront location. (☎ 811966. Open daily noon-3pm and 6-11pm.)

SIGHTS AND ENTERTAINMENT

The image of Queen Victoria as a stern, aging monarch, perpetually in mourning, is shattered by the airy splendor and romantic dreams that still fill **Osborne House,** featured in the 1997 film *Mrs. Brown.* Completed in 1846, the house was meant to serve as a "modest" country home providing a family refuge from affairs of the state. Victoria used it as a long-term retreat after Albert's death in 1861. Visitors are able to see the bedroom where she died in 1901. The house and grounds are filled with Italian sculptures and paintings, many of which portray Victoria and Albert's nine children and numerous grandchildren. Take a turn on the grounds that lead to the sea. A free **horse-and-carriage ride** takes you to the children's **Swiss Cottage.** To reach Osborne House, take Southern Vectis bus #4 or 5 from Ryde or Newport. (☎ 200022. Open Apr.-Sept. daily 10am-6pm; Oct. daily 10am-5pm; Feb.-Mar. and Nov. to mid-Dec. by booked tours only. House and grounds £6.90, students and seniors £5.20, children £3.50. Grounds £3.50, £2.60, £1.80.)

In Newport, **Carisbrooke Castle,** a former Norman fortress, harkens back to the Civil War period. The castle was the 1647 prison of Charles I, where the lonely king awaited his fate in the ancient chapel. Now the only permanent tenants are the donkeys operating the well house. The castle museum includes the **Tennyson Room,** which contains the poet's hat, desk, cloak, and—for the morbid—his funeral pall. (☎ 522107. Open daily Apr.-Sept. 10am-6pm; Oct. 10am-5pm; Nov.-Mar. 10am-4pm. £4.50, students and seniors £3.40, children £2.30, families £11.30.)

Some of the Isle of Wight's most charming sights predate both Victorians and Normans. On the western tip of the island, the white chalk **Needles** jut into the dark blue sea. The third rock sports a lighthouse that was manned until 1997. A good view of the Needles can be had from **Alum Bay;** check for local cruises to see the chalk cliffs around the bay. The **Pleasure Park** may distract you from the natural beauty of the bay, but a chairlift runs down to the base of the cliffs and back. The famous colored sands, used by Victorians as pigment for painting, can now be yours in cheesy, but cute, glass ornaments. Walkers and cyclists will enjoy the **coastal path** stretching from nearby Totland, past lighthouses both modern and medieval at St. Catherine's Point, to St. Lawrence at the southern end of the island.

Explore the island's 500 mi. of well-maintained footpaths during the annual **Walking Festival** (May 5-20, 2001) and **Cycling Festival** (June 9-24, 2001), when participants pace along scenic routes or race over strenuous courses. Visit the TIC for more details. Racing ships speed past the coastline in the regatta that takes place during **Cowes Week** in early August.

WINCHESTER   ☎01962

Best known for its dramatic cathedral, Winchester (pop. 32,800) traces its origins back to Roman times, when it was a walled city known as Venta Belgarum. Both William the Conqueror and Alfred the Great deemed the town the center of their kingdoms, and monks painstakingly prepared the *Domesday Book* for William here (see **Christianity, Vikings, and Normans,** p. 67). During the Great Plague of 1665, Charles II moved his court to Winchester, where he checked up frequently on the well-being of his London properties and less often on that of his dying subjects. In the more recent past, Jane Austen and John Keats both lived and wrote in town, and Winchester inspired Keats's much-adored "To Autumn." While its grandest days may have passed, Winchester has managed to polish some luster back into its old walls. Locals meander through quiet gardens along the River Itchen, and the pedestrian area bustles with students and shoppers. Weekends splash some hedonism on the celestial Cathedral Close, enlivening the nights of visitors hoping to relive the romance and intrigue of a century past at Austen sights during the day.

▐ GETTING THERE AND GETTING AROUND

Just north of Southampton, Winchester makes an excellent daytrip from **Salisbury,** 25 mi. away, or **Portsmouth,** 27 mi. away.

Trains: Winchester Station, Station Hill, northwest of the city center. Travel center open M-F 9am-6pm, Sa 9am-5pm, Su 9am-4pm. Ticket counter open M-F 6am-8:30pm, Sa 6am-7:30pm, Su 7am-8:30pm. Trains (☎ (08457) 484950) from: **London Waterloo** (1hr., 2 per hr., £16.60); **Portsmouth** (1hr., 1 per hr., £7); and **Brighton** (1½hr., 1 per hr., £16.10). Be prepared to change trains at Basingstoke or Fareham.

Buses: National Express (☎ (08705) 808080) stops at Alfred's statue, down the street from the hostel. Open M 7:30am-5:30pm, Tu-F 8:30am-5:30pm, Sa 8:30am-12:30pm. Buses from **London** via **Heathrow** (1½hr., 7 per day, £12) and **Oxford** (2½hr., 2 per day, £6.75). **Hampshire Stagecoach** (☎ (01256) 464501) heads to: **Southampton** (#47, 50min., 2 per hr., return £2.90); **Salisbury** (#68, 1½hr., 7 per day, return £4.45); and **Portsmouth** (#69, 1½hr., 12 per day, return £4.45). **Explorer** tickets are available for bus travel in Hampshire and Wiltshire for £4.80, seniors £3.50, children £2.50, families £10.

Local Transportation: Local buses (☎ (01256) 464501) stop at Broadway, across from the Guildhall.

Taxis: Francis Taxis (☎ 884343) collect by the market.

▐ ORIENTATION AND PRACTICAL INFORMATION

Winchester's major axis, **High St.,** spans the length of the town's commerce, stretching from a statue of Alfred the Great at one end to the arch of **West Gate** at the other. The city's bigger roads stem off High St., which transforms into **Broadway** as you approach Alfred. The tourist information centre (TIC) faces the bus station on Broadway.

Tourist Information Centre: The Guildhall (☎ 840500; fax 850348; www.winchester.gov.uk), Broadway, near King Alfred. Stocks free maps, seasonal *What's On* guides, guides to wheelchair accessible city attractions, and city guides (£1). **Walking tours** £2.50, children free. Helpful multilingual staff book accommodations for £3 plus a 10% deposit. Open June-Sept. M-Sa 10am-6pm, Su 11am-2pm; Oct.-May M-Sa 10am-5pm.

Financial Services: Major banks, including **Barclays** and **Lloyds TSB,** cluster around the junction of Jewry St. and High St. **Thomas Cook,** 30 High St. (☎ 841661 for travel information). Open M-Tu and Th-Sa 9am-5:30pm, W 10am-5:30pm.

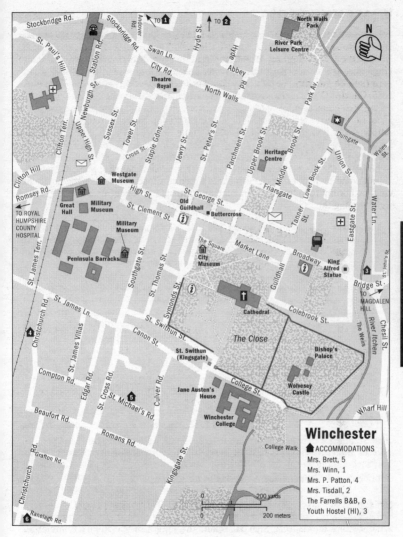

Winchester

▲ ACCOMMODATIONS

Mrs. Brett, 5
Mrs. Winn, 1
Mrs. P. Patton, 4
Mrs. Tisdall, 2
The Farrells B&B, 6
Youth Hostel (HI), 3

0   200 yards
0   200 meters

SOUTH ENGLAND

Launderette: 27 Garbett Rd., Winnall (☎ 840658). Climb Magdalen Hill, and continue straight as it changes to Alresford Rd. Turn left on Winnall Manor Rd., and follow until reaching Garbett Rd. on your left. 25p for soap, £2 per load. Open M-F 8am-8pm, Sa 8am-6pm, Su 10am-4pm. Last wash 1 hr. before close.

Police: North Walls (☎ 868100), near the intersection with Middle Brook St.

Hospital: St. Paul's Hospital, St. Paul's Hill. **Royal Hampshire County** (☎ 863535), Romsey Rd., at St. James Ln.

Internet Access: Mailboxes Etc., 80 High St. (☎ 622133). £3 per 30min. Reservations suggested. Open M-F 8:30am-6pm, Sa 10am-4pm.

Post Office: (☎ 854004), Middle Brook St. Turn off High St. at Marks and Spencer. Open M-Sa 9am-5:30pm. **Postal Code:** SO23 8WA.

 ACCOMMODATIONS

Winchester's B&Bs cluster half a mile southwest of the TIC, near **Ranelagh Rd.**, on the corner of Christchurch Rd. and St. Cross Rd. Buses #29 and 47 make the journey from the town center to Ranelagh Rd. twice every hour; bus #69 runs the same route once per hour. Many pubs also offer accommodations, but try to book early, especially in the summer. A steady stream of Londoners drives up prices all over town, making Winchester's youth hostel particularly attractive.

Mrs. P. Patton, 12 Christchurch Rd. (☎ 854272), between St. James Ln. and Beaufort Rd., 5min. from the cathedral on a silent street of stately houses. Graceful doubles, recently repainted and refurbished. Look for the partridge-in-a-pear-tree curtains in the bedroom on the right. Singles £22-25; doubles £30-35.

YHA Winchester, 1 Water Ln. (☎ 853723). Located in an 18th-century watermill perched atop rushing water of the River Itchen. Unfortunately, its historic high ceilings are less appealing once you feel the draft blow in. All single-sex rooms. Kitchen available. Lockout 10am-5pm. Stringent 11pm curfew. Open July-Aug. daily; mid-Feb. to June and Sept.-Oct. Tu-Sa. Dorms £8.80, under 18 £6.

The Farrells B&B, 5 Ranelagh Rd. (☎ 869555), 10min. walk from town off Christchurch Rd. Furniture a mother would rave over in a well-kept home. Feels instantly welcoming with the decades of family photos on the wall. Three doubles are let out as singles in the off-season (or after 6pm). £20 per person, £22 with bath.

Mrs. Winn, 2 North Hill Close (☎ 864926). Comfortable, cheap rooms just up the road from the train station. The price of proximity is the dull rumble of coaches lumbering by. Still, it's tended by two warm hosts with an affection for backpackers and other budget travelers. Mind the teddy bears as you climb the stairs. £13 per person.

Mrs. Brett, 3 St. Michael's Rd. (☎ 861450). Large, comfortable rooms, and plenty of Dick Francis mysteries to choose from. Singles £22; doubles £40; reduced prices for week-long stays.

Mrs. Tisdall, 32 Hyde St. (☎ 851621), a 5min. walk from town on Jewry St., which becomes Hyde St. Conveniently located between the train station and the town center. Large, comfortable rooms. Singles £20; doubles £32. 10% discount for *Let's Go* users.

FOOD AND PUBS

High St. and **St. George's St.** are home to several food markets, fast food venues, and tea and coffee houses. **Jewry St.** serves up more substantial restaurants. **Sainsbury's,** at Middle Brook St. off High St., hawks groceries. (☎ 861792. Open M-Th 8am-6:30pm, F 8am-9pm, Sa 7:30am-6pm.) If you're looking for a **market,** vegetables and fruits are sold by vendors on Middle Brook St., behind Marks and Spencer and across from the town library. (Open W-Sa 8am-6pm.)

The Eclipse Inn (☎ 865676), The Square. Winchester's smallest pub, in a 16th-century rectory that the claustrophobic should avoid. Pub grub from £3.50 attracts many regulars and, supposedly, a ghost or two. Open M-Sa 11am-11pm, Su 10:30am-noon; food served M-Sa noon-2:30pm and 6-9pm, Su 12:30-3pm.

Le Matelot, 8 High St. (☎ 866668). Women cancan on the painted walls in this tremendously popular sandwich shop, where you can't-can't go wrong. Scrumptious baguettes (£1.40-3.20), pastries, pizzas, and designer milkshakes. Open M-Sa 8:30am-6:30pm.

Royal Oak (☎ 842701), Royal Oak Passage, next to the Godbegot House off High St. Despite its refurbished gleam, this is another one of the English pubs that claims to be the kingdom's oldest. Descend into the 900-year-old subterranean foundations and enjoy the locally brewed hogshead cask ale (£1.75) and English cuisine (£3-6). Open daily 11am-11pm; food served noon-5pm.

The Exchange, 9 Southgate St. (☎ 854718). A wild menu, with crocodile, vegan nut, and (for the truly adventurous) beef burgers. Discounts for students and seniors. Open M-Sa 10am-11pm, Su noon-11pm.

SIGHTS

WINCHESTER CATHEDRAL. Duck through the archway (note the stones from William the Conqueror's palace), pass through the square, and behold the 900-year-old cathedral, famed for its nave. At a length of 556 ft., it's the longest medieval building in Europe. Magnificent tiles, roped off for preservation, cover much of the floor near the chancel. Jane Austen's tomb rests in the northern aisle of the nave; while staring at her memorial plaque, don't walk past (or over) Jane herself buried in the floor. The stained glass window in the rear seems oddly Cubist—Cromwell's soldiers smashed the original window in the 17th century, and though the original glass pieces have been reinserted, the pattern got lost in the shuffle. *(5 The Close. ☎ 857225. Open daily 7:15am-5:30pm; visiting encouraged after 8:30am. East End closes at 5pm. Free tours of cathedral, 50min. 10am-3pm, water level permitting; meet at West end of Nave. Tower tours (75min.) also available. Wheelchair access. Voluntary donation £3, students £2.)*

The **Norman crypt,** supposedly the oldest, and definitely one of the finest in England, can only be viewed in the summer by guided tour. The crypt contains the statues of two of Winchester's most famous figures: Bishop William of Wykeham, founder of Winchester College, and St. Swithun, patron saint of weather. St. Swithun was interred inside the cathedral against his will; in retaliation, the saint brought torrents down on the culprits for 40 days. Supposedly, if it rains on July 15 (St. Swithun's Day), it will rain for the next 40 days. Considering this is England, it might anyway. The 12th-century *Winchester Bible* resides in the library. The **Triforium Gallery** at the south transept contains several relics, including 14th-century altar-screen figures. *(Free 20min. crypt tours depart from crypt door. Gallery open Easter-Oct. M 2-4pm, Tu-Sa 10am-noon and 2-4pm; Nov.-Feb. W 11am-2:30pm and Sa 11am-3:30pm. Book before arriving—gallery subject to closures. £1, students 50p, families £2.)*

NEAR THE CATHEDRAL. Though some may find the walk along the river to **Wolvesey Castle** more enjoyable than the site itself, its ruins provide a glimpse into the historic relationship of church and state. The Norman bishop used to live here, exerting influence on the surrounding area. You can see most of the ruins from the entrance without paying, although the guides inside the site are informative. *(☎ 854766. Open daily Apr.-Oct. 10am-6pm. £1.80, students and seniors £1.40, children 90p.)* Southward, tiny **St. Swithun's Chapel,** rebuilt in the 16th century, nestles above **King's Gate,** one of two surviving city gates (the other is West Gate).

WINCHESTER COLLEGE. Kingsgate St. leads to England's first public (read: private) school, founded in 1382 and still active today. Most of the 14th-century buildings remain intact and can only be seen by a guided tour. *(Tour booking ☎ 621217. Tours M-Sa 11am, 2pm, 3:15pm and Su 2pm, 3:15pm. Tours £2.50, seniors and children £2.)*

GREAT HALL. Henry III built his castle on the remains of an earlier fortress sponsored by William the Conqueror. The fortress was a haunt for royals, including Henry V, who lodged here with his happy few en route to Agincourt. What remains is the Great Hall, which contains a Round Table modeled after King Arthur's and dated six centuries after his legendary reign. Henry VIII tried to pass the table off as authentic to Holy Roman Emperor Charles V and had it painted with an "Arthur" resembling Henry himself. *(At the end of High St. atop Castle Hill. Open daily Mar.-Oct. 10am-5pm. Free, but donations encouraged.)*

MILITARY MUSEUMS. Just through **Queen Eleanor's Garden,** in the Peninsula Barracks, five military museums detail the story of the city and the country's military power. The **Royal Greenjackets Museum** features a 276 sq. ft. diorama of the Battle of Waterloo, containing 21,500 tiny soldiers and their 9600 steeds; for 10p, fire a couple more shots into the fray. *(☎ 863846. Open M-Sa 10am-1pm and 2-5pm, Su noon-4pm; hours for the other four museums vary. £2, seniors and children £1, families £6.)*

WALKS. The Buttercross, 12 High St., is a good starting point for a walking tour of the town. This statue of St. John, William of Wykeham, and King Alfred derives its name from the shadow it cast over the 15th-century markets to keep the butter cool. Another beautiful walk is the along the **River Itchen,** the same taken by poet John Keats; directions and his poem *To Autumn* are available at the TIC for 50p.

🎵 🎇 ENTERTAINMENT AND FESTIVALS

Weekend nights attract hordes of artists and teenagers to bars along Broadway and High St. **Muswell's,** 8-9 Jewry St., draws the 18- to 30-year-old crowd on Fridays and Saturdays; Sundays see an all-day Happy Hour. (☎ 842414. Open M-Sa 11am-11pm, Su noon-10:30pm.) **Mash Tun,** 60 Eastgate St., packs in the wacky youngsters with funky music and discounts on Carlsberg and bitters for students. (☎ 861440. Open daily noon-11pm.) **Old Monk,** 1 High St. across from the hostel, filters hundreds of students indoors and onto a riverside patio. (☎ 855111. Open M-Sa 11am-midnight, Su noon-10:30pm.) For a different type of fun, and since the weather won't let you stay dry anyway, go aquatic at **River Park Leisure Centre** (☎ 869525). The park contains a huge pool, as well as Twister the Water Slide, included in the price of a swim. (Open daily 6:30am-11pm. £1.80, concessions 95p.)

With its Edwardian glory, the **Theatre Royal,** Jewry St., hosts regional theatrical companies and concerts. In early July, the **Hat Fair** (☎ 849841; cat@hatfair.global-net.co.uk), the longest running street festival in Britain, fills a weekend with free theater, street performances, and peculiar headgear. Late May features the **Homelands Music Festival,** and though the venue is smaller than Glastonbury's summer music orgy, bands still play to sell-out crowds. Acquire tickets from the TIC.

🅿 DAYTRIPS FROM WINCHESTER

▓ AUSTEN'S COTTAGE. Jane Austen lived in the meek village of **Chawton,** 15 mi. northeast of Winchester, from 1809 to 1817. The number of visitors to her cottage has supposedly quadrupled since the recent release of film versions of several of her novels. It was here that she penned *Pride and Prejudice, Emma, Northanger Abbey,* and *Persuasion,* and some of her manuscripts, as well as other personal belongings, are on display. The door was deliberately left creaky to warn Austen so she could hide her manuscript in her needlework basket. *(Take Hampshire bus #X64 (M-Sa 11 per day, return £4.50), or London and Country bus #65 on Sundays, from the bus station. Ask to be let off at Chawton roundabout and follow the brown signs. ☎/fax (01420) 83262. Open Mar.-Dec. daily 11am-4:30pm; Jan.-Feb. Sa-Su 11am-4:30pm. Wheelchair access. £3, concessions £2.50, under 18 50p.)*

BROADLANDS. Just outside **Romsey,** southwest of Winchester along the A31, lies Broadlands. The Palladian mansion was once home to the Victorian Prime Minister Lord Palmerston and the late Lord Mountbatten—the last Viceroy of India and uncle of Prince Philip. You can experience the uncanny sensation of being inside a piece of china in the Wedgewood room. *(☎ (01794) 505010. Open mid-June to mid-Sept. noon-5:30pm; last admission 4pm. £5.50, students and seniors £4.70, under 12 £3.85.)*

THE NEW FOREST. The New Forest, 20 mi. southwest of Winchester in **Lyndhurst,** was William the Conqueror's 145 sq. mi. personal hunting ground. The **Rufus Stone** (near Brook and Cadnam) marks the spot where his son was accidentally slain. Today, ponies, donkeys, cows, and deer frolic freely. A **Museum and Visitor Centre** has a list of campsites. *(Take bus #66 to Romsey (1 per hr.) and transfer to a Lyndhurst bus; Su take bus #X66 (mid-May to mid-Sept., 3 per day, return £4.10). Or take a train to Southampton and then a bus to Lyndhurst. High St., Lyndhurst. Visitor Centre ☎ (023) 8028 2269. Open daily 10am-6pm. Wheelchair access. £2.50, seniors £2, children £1.50, families £6.50.)*

SOUTH DOWNS WAY   ☎01323

The South Downs Way stretches from Eastbourne west towards Portsmouth and Winchester, never far from coastal towns yet rarely crossing into civilization's domain. Robbed of some of its pastoral innocence during the air raids of World War II, the Way nonetheless remains a ribbon of salt-sprayed, sheep-watched timelessness. The windswept slopes and chalk cliffs of the Downs hide the footprints of millennia. Once stretching through to the Continent, its sparse soil and light vegetation provided land that prehistoric tribes could cultivate. Forts and settlements dot the paths of Bronze and Iron Age tribes, who were followed by Romans, Saxons, and Normans. This is fertile ground for legend; from *The Domesday Book* to A.A. Milne, the Downs have borne words as prodigiously as flowers.

▐ GETTING THERE AND GETTING AROUND

Trains (☎ (08457) 484950) run to **Eastbourne** from **London Victoria** (1½hr., 2 per hr., £16.60) and to **Petersfield** from **London Waterloo** (1hr., 3 per hr., £16.60). From the west, take a train to **Amberly** (via **Horsham**), where the Way greets the River Arun. Eastbourne's helpful **Bus Stop Shop,** Arndale Centre, dispenses info on local bus services that travel to the Way. From the train station, turn left onto Terminus Rd.; Arndale Centre is on the left. (☎ 416416. Open M-Sa 9am-5pm.)

Walking the entire path takes about 10 days, but public transportation makes it possible to walk just a segment of the trail. **Trains** connect **Lewes** to **Southease** (3 per hr.), while **County Bus** #1232 heads from Lewes to **Kingston** (20min., 6 per day) and **Rodmell** (15min., 1 per day). Bus #126 runs 5 times per day from **Eastbourne** to **Alfriston** (40min.) and **Wilmington** (30min.). For bus schedules, call Eastbourne Buses (☎ 416416) or East Sussex County Busline (☎ (01273) 474747).

Cycling has long been a popular alternative means of seeing the downlands: D.H. Lawrence cycled the Way in 1909, visiting his friend Rudyard Kipling. Except for a brief section of the Way stretching from Alfriston to Eastbourne, and the western section between Brighton and Winchester, cycling and **horse riding** are permitted. **Cuckmore Cycle Company** has four locations in the Way. (☎ 870310. Bikes £3.50 per hr., £20 per day.) **Audiburn Riding Stables,** Ashcombe Ln., conducts guided one-hour horseback tours. (☎ (01273) 474398. £10 per person.)

✳▐ ORIENTATION AND PRACTICAL INFORMATION

Serious hikers will want to begin their exploration of the Way in **Eastbourne,** the official start of the Way, which offers accommodations and local services. Travelers looking for a shorter excursion along the Way may choose to base themselves in the larger cities of **Brighton** (see p. 162) and **Chichester** (see p. 172).

Tourist Information Centres:

Eastbourne: Cornfield Rd. (☎ 411400). Provides vague maps (free) and detailed Ordnance Survey Landranger 1:50,000 maps (#185, 197, 198, and 199 are the most useful; around £5). Also sells a number of guides (see below). Open M-Sa 9am-6pm, Su 10am-1pm.

Lewes: 187 High St. (☎ (01273) 483448). Books rooms and sells Ordnance Survey maps. Open M-F 9am-5pm, Sa 10am-5pm; summer also Su 10am-2pm.

Financial Services: All major banks are located in Eastbourne town center. Be sure to pick up your sterling before hitting the trail. **Thomas Cook,** 101 Terminus Rd. (☎ 725431). Open M-Tu and Th-Sa 9am-5:30pm, W 10am-5:30pm.

Guidebooks and Outdoor Supplies: Eastbourne Tourist Information Centre provides *On Foot in East Sussex* (£3.20) and *Along the South Downs Way* (£5), useful for trekkers; *Exploring East Sussex* (£2) lists various guided walks and cycle rides; *The South Downs Way* photocopied edition (£2) offers info on accommodations. **Millets Leisure,** 146 Terminus Rd., Eastbourne (☎ 723840), stocks camping supplies and Ordnance Survey Maps. Open M-Sa 9am-5:30pm, Su 10:30am-4pm.

ACCOMMODATIONS

There are few towns along the Way, and B&Bs fill quickly, especially in the summer. Consider making daytrips along parts of the Way, especially from Brighton. If you're looking for **B&Bs** in one of the larger towns, try Brighton (p. 162) or Southcliff Ave. in Eastbourne. **Camping** on the Way is permitted with the landowner's permission. Fortunately, the following four **YHA youth hostels** lie along or near the Way, each within a day's walk of the next. Be sure to call at least a week ahead; the hostels are often full at the same time. Unless noted, all the hostels listed here have a 10am-5pm lockout and an 11pm curfew. For other hostels near the Way, check the **Accommodations** sections in Brighton (p. 164) or Arundel (p. 170).

> **YHA Eastbourne:** East Dean Rd., Eastbourne, East Sussex (☎/fax 721081). Converted golf clubhouse on the A259 between South Downs Way and the Seven Sisters, about 3 mi. from Beachy Head. From Eastbourne Station, turn right and follow the A259 (marked Seaford/Brighton) for 1½ mi.; even pro cyclists gasp at the steep hill leading to the hostel. Buses #711 and 712 depart from Shelter H on Terminus Rd., just left of the station (95p). Spare, clean rooms with bunks. Breakfast £3.20. Open July-Sept. daily; Apr.-June Th-M; closed Oct.-Mar. Dorms £9.80, under 18 £6.75.

> **YHA Alfriston:** Frog Firle, Alfriston, Polegate, East Sussex (☎ 870423; fax 870615; alfriston@yha.org.uk). 1½ mi. from the Way and from Alfriston, 8 mi. from Eastbourne. At the market cross, turn left at the sign marking "South Downs Way" and pass the village green toward the White Bridge. Follow the overgrown riverside path to Litlington footbridge and turn right along the path; the hostel is at the end of the path in a stone house with bovine neighbors. Authentic Tudor wood. Open July-Aug. daily; Feb.-June and Sept.-Oct. M-Sa; Nov.-Dec. F-Sa. Dorms £9.80, under 18 £6.75.

> **YHA Telescombe:** Bank Cottages, Telescombe, Lewes, East Sussex (☎/fax (01273) 301357). 2 mi. from Way, 12 mi. from Alfriston. 18th-century house. Open July-Aug. daily; Easter-June W-M, closed Sept.-Easter. Dorms £9, under 18 £6.20.

> **YHA Truleigh Hill:** Tottington Barn, Truleigh Hill, Shoreham-by-Sea, West Sussex (☎ (01903) 813419; fax 812016). At the center of the Way, 10 mi. from Brighton. Modern building on 4½ acres. No lockout. Open June-Sept. daily; Apr.-May and Sept.-Oct. Tu-Sa. Dorms £9.80, under 18 £6.75.

HIKING THE SOUTH DOWNS WAY

EASTBOURNE TO ALFRISTON

The best place to begin walking the Way is the Victorian seaside city of **Eastbourne,** which lives in the shelter of **Beachy Head,** the official starting point of the path. If you plan to start hiking immediately, the open-topped bus #3, from Terminus Rd. in Eastbourne, will bring you to the top of **Beachy Head** (Su-F 9 per day, £1.80). You can save money and gain scenic vistas by asking to be let off at the bottom of Beachy Head and climbing it yourself. (No beach here: *beau chef* means "fine headland.") Make the strenuous ascent and follow the fields ever upward past some inquisitively bent trees and an inordinate amount of bunny doo-doo to reach the cliffs. Beachy Head itself, 543 ft. above the sea, is reputed by mountaineers to have the same vertiginous effects as Alpine ridges. Whatever breath you have left after the climb will certainly be taken away by the view. Visible from Beachy Head is the westward coterie of the **Seven Sisters,** a series of chalk ridges carved by centuries of receding waters and surpassing the Head in majesty. The queenly sisters hold court about 4½ mi. away, over a windswept series of hills. The path winds past a number of *tumuli*—the burial mounds of Bronze Age peoples constructed around 1500 BC—but the overgrown bush makes them impossible to distinguish. To reach **Alfriston,** follow the Way four miles over a path reputedly used by smugglers who docked among the cliffs. You can also take bus #711 or 712 from Terminus Rd. in Eastbourne (35min., M-Sa 6 per day, 95p).

Another option is the shorter **bridleway path** to Alfriston (8 mi., as opposed to the 11 mi. coastal jaunt). The bridleway can be joined from a path just below the YHA hostel and passes through the village of **Wilmington** and by its famous **Long Man,** a 260 ft. earth sculpture of mysterious origins. Varyingly attributed to prehistoric peoples, Romans, 14th-century monks, and aliens, the Long Man is best viewed from a distance and is almost invisible when you first come over his hillside on the Way. It is rumored that Victorian prudes robbed the fellow of male attributes that might have elucidated his name. Proceeding back through the Long Man's gate and onto the South Downs Way path over Windover Hill will lead you to **Alfriston,** a sleepy one-road village called "the last of the old towns."

ALFRISTON TO FORTY ACRE LANE

From Alfriston town center you can pick up the Way behind the Star Inn, on High St. (the *only* street), and continue 7 mi. to **Southease** among hills so green and vast, one might fear Julie Andrews lurks tunefully over the next ridge. The Way directly crosses **Firle Beacon,** with a mound at the top said to contain a giant's silver coffin. Reaching Southease, proceed north ¾ mi. to **Rodmell.** A Merchant-Ivory set of a town, Rodmell's single street contains **Monk's House,** home of Leonard and Virginia Woolf from 1919 until each of their deaths. Thanks to the National Trust, the house retains its intimacy and most of the original furnishings. Virginia's bedroom contains a fireplace with tiles painted by Vanessa Bell. The faithful can retrace the writer's last steps to the River Ouse (1 mi.), where she committed "the one experience I shall never describe"; her ashes nourish a fig tree in the garden. (Open Apr.-Oct. W and Sa 2-5:30pm. £2.50, children £1.25, families £15.) For information, call the regional **National Trust** office (☎ (01892) 890651). The **Telescombe** YHA hostel (see above) lies 1 mi. south of Rodmell.

The closest that the Way actually comes to **Lewes** (LEW-is) is at the village of **Kingston** to the southwest. A stone at the parish boundary, called **Nan Kemp's Corner,** feeds one of the more macabre Downs legends: townspeople whisper that a woman named Nan Kemp, jealous of her husband's affection for their newborn, roasted it for him to eat, then killed herself at the site of the present stone. From here, continue on an 8 mi. stretch of the Way from Kingston to **Pyecombe,** which will bring you to **Ditchling Beacon,** the highest point in East Sussex's Downs. The hill was one in a series that relayed the message of the defeat of the Spanish Armada to Elizabeth I. Ambling from Pyecombe to **Upper Beeding** (another 8 mi.) brings you to **Devil's Dyke,** a dramatic chalk cliff that looks like a cross-section cut out of a hillside. Local legend says that the Dyke was built by Lucifer himself to let the sea into the Weald and float away all Christian churches. The Prince of Darkness was interrupted by the light of an old woman's candle, which, in a moment of diabolic weakness, he thought was the sun. On the path from Upper Beeding to **Washington** lies the grove of **Chanctonbury Ring**—trees planted in the 18th century around a 3rd-century Roman template, built on a previous Celtic one.

Completing the 6½ mi. trek from Washington to **Amberly** brings you to a path leading to **Burpham,** from which the **YHA Warningcamp** (see **Accommodations,** p. 170) is accessible by a 3 mi. walk. The 19 mi. of orchids and spiked rampion fields from Amberly to **Buriton,** passing through **Cocking,** complete the Way to the northwest. Southward, across the River Arun to **Littleton Down,** are views of the Weald and occasionally the North Downs. The spire of Chichester Cathedral (p. 173) marks the beginning of **Forty Acre Lane,** the final arm of the Way, which reaches out to touch the West Sussex/Hampshire border.

SOUTHWEST ENGLAND

Chiefly agricultural, the southwest's lazily rolling hills and salty sea air provide a refreshing change from city rhythms. In England's West Country, mists of legend shroud the counties of Dorset, Devon, and Cornwall almost as densely as the fog rolling in from the Atlantic. King Arthur was allegedly born at Tintagel on Cornwall's northern coast and is said to have battled Mordred on Bodmin Moor. One hamlet purports to be the site of Camelot, another claims to be the resting place of the Holy Grail, and no fewer than three small lakes are identified as the final resting place of Arthur's sword, Excalibur. In a more modern myth, the ghost of Sherlock Holmes still pursues the Hound of the Baskervilles across Dartmoor.

Legends aside, the southwest has been a place of refuge for several distinct peoples, all of whom left their mark on land and culture. Cornwall was the last holdout of the Celts in England, while stone circles and the excavated remnants of even older Neolithic communities reveal only shards, leaving volumes to the imagination. Farther northeast, the counties of Somerset, Avon, and Wiltshire hold markers of various historical eras, from Salisbury's medieval cathedral to Bath's Roman baths to forever-mysterious Stonehenge.

HIGHLIGHTS OF SOUTHWEST ENGLAND

STONEHENGE Puzzle over the ancient rocks at one of the greatest engineering feats of the 2nd millennium BC, also one of the world's great mysteries (p. 196).

BATH Revisit the world of eighteenth-century pleasure-seekers who paved this old Roman spa town with their glorious buildings and uproarious behavior (p. 198).

TINTAGEL Tackle the steep, slippery cliffs leading to Merlin's Cave in the reputed birthplace of King Arthur (p. 235).

ST. IVES Ride the surf or ponder modernist sculpture in Cornwall's sophisticated coastal beacon (p. 245).

▐ GETTING AROUND SOUTHWEST ENGLAND

It's usually easier to get to Somerset, Avon, and Wiltshire than to regions farther southwest. **Trains** (☎ (08457) 484950) offer fast and frequent service from London and the North. The region's primary east-west line from **London Paddington** passes through **Taunton, Exeter,** and **Plymouth,** ending at **Penzance.** Frequent trains connect London to Bath, Bristol, and Salisbury. Trains from the north pass through **Bristol,** although it may sometimes be easier to travel through London. Branch lines connect **St. Ives, Newquay, Falmouth,** and **Barnstaple** to the network. As elsewhere in Britain, day return fares are often only slightly more expensive than single fares.

A variety of **Rail Rover passes** (☎ (0345) 125625) can be used in the region: the **Freedom of the Southwest Rover** is covers in the area from Bristol Parkway through Salisbury and down to Weymouth, covering all of Cornwall, Devon, Somerset, and parts of Avon and Dorset. (8 days in 15 £59). The **Devon Rail Rover** is bounded by and includes travel on the Taunton-Exmouth line on the east and the Gunnislake-Plymouth line in the west. (3 days in 7 £23, 8 in 15 £38.) The **Cornish Rail Rover** is bounded by the Gunnislake-Plymouth line. (3 days in 7 £17.50, 8 in 15 £32.)

Buses can be few and far between; plan carefully. **National Express** (☎ (08705) 808080) runs to major points along the north coast via **Bristol** and to points along the south coast (including **Penzance**) via **Exeter** and **Plymouth.** For journeys within the region, local

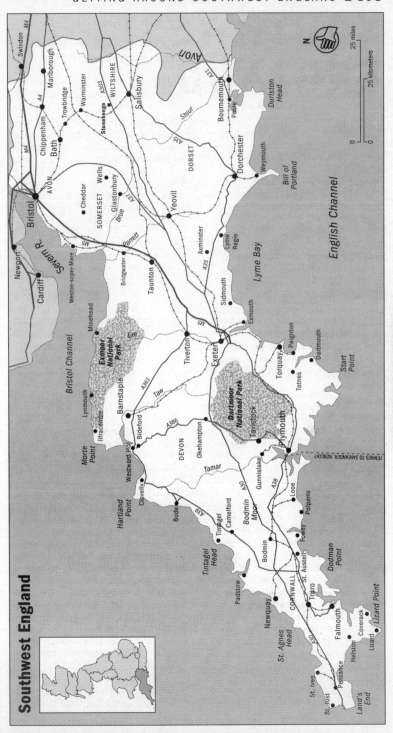

SOUTHWEST ENGLAND

bus services are usually less expensive and more extensive than trains. All the large regional bus companies—**Western National** in Cornwall and south Devon (☎ (01752) 222666), **Southern National** in Somerset and West Dorset, **Devon General,** and **Badgerline** in Somerset and Avon (☎ (0117) 955 3231)—sell **Explorer** or **Day Rambler** tickets, which allow a full day's travel on any bus within their region for £4-6. The aptly named **Key West** ticket is good on all Devon and Cornwall routes (3 days £13.40, 7 days £22.65).

Train or bus passes may not cover all of the worthwhile spots in the southwest, and at times you may find yourself renting a bike or walking to a spot of interest. Phone ahead in the off-season; branch-line **train** service on Sundays shuts down for the winter, and many bus lines don't run between September and March.

⚠ HIKING AND BIKING AROUND THE REGION

Distances between towns in southwestern England are so short that you can travel through the region on your own steam. The narrow roads and hilly landscape can make biking difficult, but hardy cyclists will find the quiet lanes and countryside rewarding terrain. If you're walking or cycling, on- or off-road, bring along a large-scale **Ordnance Survey** map and an impregnable windbreaker to shield you from foul weather. When hiking through countryside, respect the property of local residents, whose livelihood depends on the land you're crossing.

The **South-West Peninsula Coast Path,** the longest coastal path in England, originates in Dorset and passes through South Devon, Cornwall, and North Devon, ending in Somerset. Winding past cliffs, caves, beaches, and resort colonies, it takes several months to walk in its entirety. However, journeys of any length are possible, as buses serve most points along the route, and hostels and B&Bs are spaced at 5-25-mi. intervals. Many rivers intersect the path, so you will have to take a ferry or wade through the crossings. Check times carefully to avoid being stranded. Some sections of the trail are difficult enough to dissuade all but the most ambitious; check with tourist officials before you set out to make sure that the area you want to visit is well-marked. Most TICs sell guides and Ordnance Survey maps covering appropriate sections of the path. Most of the path is smooth enough to cover on a bike; bike rental shops will often suggest 3-7 day routes along the coast.

The path is divided into four parts. The **Dorset Coast Path,** stretching from Lyme Regis to Poole Harbor, can be negotiated in a few days; the *Purbeck Outdoor Leisure Map* or Ordnance Survey Landranger series maps 193, 194, and 195 (1:50,000 scale) will help planning. The **South Devon Coast Path** picks up near Paignton and continues through Plymouth, winding around spectacular cliffs, wide estuaries, and remote bays set off by lush vegetation and wildflowers. The **Cornwall Coast Path,** with some of the most rugged stretches, starts in Plymouth (a ferry takes you on to Cremyll), rounds the southwestern tip of Britain, and continues up the northern Atlantic coast to Bude. The magnificent Cornish cliffs here harbor a vast range of birds and sea life. The final section, the **Somerset and North Devon Coastal Path,** extends from Bude through Exmoor National Park to Minehead. The least arduous of the four, it features the highest seaside cliffs in southwestern England. On the way, the path passes Culbone and England's smallest church, the 100 ft. dunes of Saunton Sands, and the steep cobbled streets of Clovelly Village on Hartland Point, with pubs dating back to the 1500s.

WILTSHIRE

SALISBURY ☎ 01722

That all roads in Salisbury (pop. 37,000) seem to lead to its cathedral gates is no accident. Salisbury's small grid of streets (five running north to south and six east to west) was carefully charted by Bishop Poore in the early 13th century. The cathedral is the geographic center of town and the Salisbury Stake is the highest spire in England. Salisbury's proximity to Stonehenge draws many of its visitors.

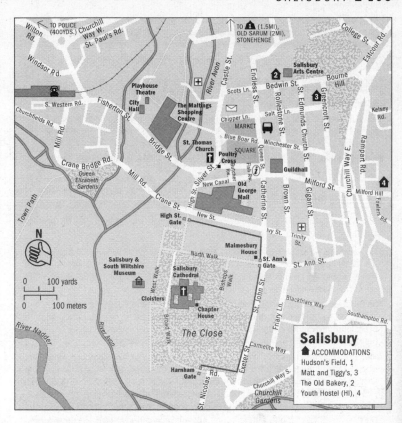

Salisbury
ACCOMMODATIONS
Hudson's Field, 1
Matt and Tiggy's, 3
The Old Bakery, 2
Youth Hostel (HI), 4

GETTING THERE AND GETTING AROUND

Trains: South Western Rd., west of town across the river. Ticket office open M-Sa 5:30am-8pm, Su 7:30am-8:45pm. Trains (☎ (08457) 484950) from most major towns, including: **London Waterloo** (1½hr., 1 per hr., £22-30); **Southampton** (40min., 2 per hr., £7.10); **Winchester** (1½hr., 1 per hr., £10.60); and **Portsmouth and Southsea** (1½hr., 1 per hr., £11-13).

Buses: Bus Station, 8 Endless St. (☎ 336855). Open M-F 8:15am-5:30pm, Sa 8:15am-5:15pm. **National Express** (☎ (08705) 808080) runs from **London** (2¾hr., 4 per day, £11.50, return £12.50) Buy tickets at the TIC. **Wilts and Dorset** (☎ (01722) 336855) from **Bath** (#X4, 2hr., 6 per day, £3). An **Explorer** ticket is good for a day's worth of travel on **Wilts and Dorset** buses and some **Hampshire, Provincial,** and **Solent Blue** buses (£4.80, seniors £3.50, children £2.40, families £9.80).

Taxis: Taxis cruise by the train station and New Canal. **A and B Taxis** (☎ 744744). Wheelchair facilities. **505050 Value Cars** (☎ 505050) run 24hr.

Bike Rental: Hayball Cycles, 26-30 Winchester St. (☎ 411378). £9 per day, £2.50 overnight, £55 per week; cash deposit £25. Open M-Sa 9am-5:30pm.

PRACTICAL INFORMATION

Tourist Information Centre: (☎ 334956; fax 422059), Fish Row, in the Guildhall in Market Sq. Extremely helpful staff. **National Express** ticket service. Books rooms with a

10% deposit. Open July-Aug. M-Sa 9:30am-7pm, Su 10:30am-5pm; June and Sept. M-Sa 9:30am-6pm, Su 10:30am-4:30pm; Oct.-May M-Sa 9:30am-5pm. 1½hr. **city tours** leave Apr.-Oct. 11am and 6pm; £2, children £1.

Financial Services: Banks are easily found. **Thomas Cook,** 18-19 Queen St. (☎ 313500). Open M-Tu and Th-Sa 9am-5:30pm, W 10am-5:30pm.

Launderette: Washing Well, 28 Chipper Ln. (☎ 421874). Open daily 8am-9pm.

Police: (☎ 411444), Wilton Rd.

Internet Access: ICafé, 30 Milford St. (☎ 320050). Funky music and decor, 8 terminals. Go surfing on the web for £2 per 30min.; watch fish go surfing in the tank for free. Ask about the 20% student discount. Open M-Sa 9am-11pm, Su 10am-11pm.

Post Office: 24 Castle St. (☎ 421174), at Chipper Ln. **Bureau de change.** Open M-Sa 9am-5:30pm. **Postal Code:** SP1 1AB.

■ ACCOMMODATIONS

Salisbury's proximity to much-frequented Stonehenge breeds many B&Bs, mostly comfortable and reasonably priced (around £18-20).

YHA Salisbury, Milford Hill House, Milford Hill (☎ 327572; fax 330446). 74 beds. Smell the cedar from your window or tent. Lockout 10am-1pm. Curfew 11:30pm. Phone ahead, especially in peak season. Dorms £10.85, under 18 £7.40; annex £9.85, under 18 £6.75. **Camping** £4.70 per person.

The Old Bakery, 35 Bedwin St. (☎ 320100). The Bunces share their love of history and architecture with guests in this 15th-century building. Rooms to match the needs of every kind of traveler. Rooms £15-20 per person; with full English breakfast £18-25. Backpackers' cottage £15 per person; with continental breakfast £17.

Matt and Tiggy's, 51 Salt Ln. (☎ 327443), just up from the bus station. A welcoming 450-year-old house with warped floors and ceiling beams and an overflow house located nearby; both are remarkably convenient. Mellow, hostel-style, 2-, 3-, and 4-person rooms; no bunk beds. Breakfast £2. Sheets 80p. Dorms £9-10.

Camping: Hudson's Field of the **Camping Club of Great Britain** (☎ 320713), Castle Rd. On the way to Old Sarum, with showers, 100 pitches, and scattered electrical points. Vehicle curfew 11pm. Pitches £5 per night, higher July-Aug. £5 per person, May-June £4, Mar.-Apr. and Sept. £3.50.

◐▨ FOOD AND PUBS

Whatever the mysterious Neolithic architects of Stonehenge had, they certainly didn't have Salisbury's ample assemblage of restaurants to tide them over. Even the most jaded pub dweller will find a pleasing venue among Salisbury's 60-odd watering holes. Most serve cheap food (£3-5), and live music is common. **Market Sq.** in the town center resounds on Tuesdays and Saturdays with vendors hawking everything from peaches to posters. (Open 7am-4pm.) A **Sainsbury's** supermarket is at The Maltings. (☎ 332282. Open M-Th 8am-8pm, F 8am-9pm, Sa 7:30am-7pm, Su 10am-4pm.) Stocking a wide variety of health foods, **Salisbury Health Foods,** Queen St., is near the TIC. (Open M-Sa 9am-5:30pm.)

▨ **Harper's "Upstairs Restaurant"** (☎ 333118), Market Sq. Their slogan is "real food is our speciality," but their true speciality is really good food. Inventive English and international dishes (£6-10) make a hearty meal, and the "8B48" (2 generous courses for £8 before 8pm) buys a lot of bang for your buck. Open M-Sa noon-2pm and 6-9:30pm.

The Asia Restaurant, 90 Fisherton St. (☎ 327628), overwhelms guests with a vast menu of generously-spiced Indian dishes. Open Su-F noon-3pm and 5:30pm-midnight, Sa noon-midnight.

The Old Mill (☎ 327517), Town Path, atop the river at the end of a 10min. scenic stroll along Town Path. A fun pub, and *the* setting for an outdoor drink on a summer's evening. Real ales from Salisbury's Hopback Brewery on tap for your drinking pleasure. Open M-Sa 11am-11pm, Su noon-10:30pm.

Coach & Horses (☎ 336254), Winchester St. Meals and drinks flow all day in what could be Salisbury's oldest pub—open since 1382. Open M-Sa 11am-11pm.

The New Inn, 41-47 New St. (☎ 327679). Forged the way for non-smoking pubs in Britain and offers a warm atmosphere. Sip your brew with a view in the garden, facing the cathedral. Open M-Sa 11am-3pm and 6-11pm, Su 11am-3pm and 7-10:30pm.

🔊 SIGHTS

📖 SALISBURY CATHEDRAL

☎ 555120; www.salisburycathedral.org.uk. Open June-Aug. M-Sa 7am-8:15pm, Su 7am-6:15pm; Sept.-May daily 7am-6:15pm. Free tours May-Oct. M-Sa 9:30am-4:45pm, Nov.-Feb. M-Sa 10am-4pm, May-Sept. Su 4-6:15pm; more in summer. Roof and tower tours, 90min.; May-Sept. M-Sa 11am, 2pm, 3pm, Su 4:30pm; June-Aug. M-Sa also 6:30pm; winter hours vary. £3, concessions £2. Call ahead. Evensong M-Sa 5:30pm, Su 3pm. Suggested donation £3, students and seniors £2, children £1, families £6.

Salisbury Cathedral rises from its grassy close to a neck-breaking height of 404 ft. In 1320, architects clung to the idea that the higher a building climbed into the sky, the closer it came to God. Built in just 38 years, rather than the usual centuries required to construct cathedrals, Salisbury Cathedral has a singular design. The bases of the marble pillars literally bend inward under the strain of 6400 tons of limestone; if a pillar rings when you knock on it, you should probably move away. Nearly 700 years have left the cathedral in need of structural and aesthetic repair; scaffolding shrouds parts of the spire, tower, and west front of the cathedral, but the work is almost done. Once inside, head to the wooden tomb of William Longespee, Earl of Salisbury (d. 1226), rare in a universe of stone sarcophagi. The chapel houses the oldest functioning mechanical clock, a strange collection of wheels and ropes that has ticked 500 million times over the last 600 years. A tiny stone figure rests in the nave. Legend has it either that a boy bishop is entombed on the spot or that it covers the heart of Richard Poore, founder of the cathedral. The incongruously abstract window at the eastern end, gleaming in rich jewel-like hues, is dedicated to prisoners of conscience, for whom a prayer is said each day.

Much to King John's chagrin, one of four surviving copies of the *Magna Carta* rests in the **Chapter House.** Named for the practice of reading a chapter of the Bible at meetings there, the Chapter House is surrounded by detailed medieval friezes. On one favorite, Noah fills his ark and releases the dove while Cain bludgeons his fair brother's head with what looks like a pick axe. Ask a guide for a complete list of the figures in relief. *(Open June-Aug. M-Sa 9:30am-7:45pm, Su 9:30am-5:30pm; daily Sept.-May 9:30am-5:30pm. Free.)* The **cloisters** adjoining the cathedral somehow grew to be the largest in England, even though the cathedral never housed any monks.

OTHER SIGHTS

MALMESBURY HOUSE. The open lawns of the cathedral close flank some beautifully preserved old homes, including Malmesbury House, where Handel once lived and which the ghost of a cavalier now haunts forever. And ever. Hallelujah. But not even Handel shall reign eternally—the house is now a private residence. Tours every 30min. by arrangement. *(☎ 327027. Open Apr.-Sept. Tu-Th noon-5:30pm. Tours £4.)*

SALISBURY AND SOUTH WILTSHIRE MUSEUM. The museum houses a potpourri of artwork (including Turner's exquisite watercolors of the cathedral) and random oddities. Exhibits trace the history of Salisbury and display Stonehenge artifacts. *(West Walk near the cathedral close. ☎ 332151. Open July-Aug. M-Sa 10am-5pm, Su 2-5pm; Sept.-June M-Sa 10am-5pm. £3, students and seniors £2, children 75p.)*

🎵 🎭 ENTERTAINMENT AND FESTIVALS

See shows by Salisbury's repertory theater company at the **Playhouse,** Malthouse Ln., over the bridge off Fisherton St. (☎ 320333. Box office open daily 10am-6pm. Wheelchair access. £8.50-14, concessions £2 less. Half-price tickets available same day.) **The Salisbury Arts Centre,** Bedwin St., offers music, theater, and exhibitions throughout the year. (☎ 321744; www.sac.dircon.co.uk. Box office open Tu-Sa 10am-4pm. From £5.) In the summer there are free Sunday concerts in various parks; call the TIC for info. The **Salisbury Festival** features dance exhibitions, music, and wine-tasting for two weeks in mid- to late May. Contact the Festival Box Office at the Playhouse. (☎ 320333; www.salisburyfestival.co.uk. From £2.50.)

🗺 DAYTRIPS FROM SALISBURY

OLD SARUM. At Old Sarum, the prehistoric precursor to Salisbury, an Iron Age fort evolved into a Saxon town, and then a Norman fortress. In the 13th century, church officials moved the settlement into the neighboring valley, where they built Salisbury Cathedral. Old Sarum was the most notorious of the "rotten boroughs" eliminated by the Reform Act of 1832. Now a lonely windswept mound strewn with stone ruins, it is still an atmospheric place to visit. Look for the crop circle, a detailed wheatfield imprint supposedly left by celestial visitors that appears annually. *(Off the A345, 2 mi. north of town. Buses #3 and 5-9 run every 15min. from Salisbury. ☎ (01722) 335398. Open July-Aug. M-Sa 10am-5pm, Su 2-5pm; Apr.-June and Sept.-Oct. M-Sa 10am-5pm; Nov.-Mar. M-Sa 10am-4pm. £2, students and seniors £1.50, children £1.)*

WILTON HOUSE. Declared by James I to be "the finest house in the land," the home of the Earl of Pembroke showcases paintings by Van Dyck, Rembrandt, and Rubens. Its impressive, almost outrageous, interior was designed partly by Inigo Jones. The Tudor kitchen and Victorian laundry shed a new light on the domestic arts. *(3 mi. west of Salisbury on the A30. Catch bus #60 or 61 (M-Sa every 10min., Su 1 per hr.) outside Marks and Spencer in Salisbury. ☎ (01722) 746720; www.wiltonhouse.com. Open Apr.-Oct. daily 10:30am-5:30pm; last admission 4:30pm. House and grounds £6.75, students and seniors £5.75, children £4, families £17.50; grounds only £3.75, children £2.50.)*

STONEHENGE

You may put a hundred questions to these rough-hewn giants as they bend in grim contemplation of their fellow companions; but your curiosity falls dead in the vast sunny stillness that shrouds them and the strange monument, with all its unspoken memories, becomes simply a heart-stirring picture in a land of pictures.
   —Henry James

Perhaps the gentle giants on Salisbury's windswept plain will remain fascinating for millennia to come, both for their mystery and their sheer longevity. A submerged colossus amid swaying grass and indifferent sheep, Stonehenge stands unperturbed by 50mph whipping winds and the legions of people who have been by its side for over 5000 years. The present stones—22 ft. high—comprise the fifth temple constructed on the site. The first probably consisted of an arch and circular earthwork furrowed in 3050 BC, and was in use for about 500 years. Its relics are the **Aubrey Holes** (white patches in the earth) and the **Heel Stone** (the isolated, rough block standing outside the circle). The next monument consisted of about 60 stones imported up the River Avon from Wales around 2100 BC, used to mark astronomical directions. This may once have been composed of two concentric circles and two horseshoes of megaliths, both enclosed by earthworks. The present shape, once a complete circle, dates from about 1500 BC; Stonehenge must have seemed old even to the Celts and Romans.

The monument is even more impressive considering that its stones—some of which weigh 45 tons—are thought to have been erected by an infinitely tedious process of rope-and-log leverage. The most famous Stonehenge legend holds that the circle was built of Irish stones magically transported by Merlin. Other stories alternately attribute the monument to giants, Phoenicians, Mycenaean Greeks, Druids, Romans, Danes, and aliens. In any case, whether they traveled by land, water, or flying saucer, the Bronze Age builders seem to have possessed more technology than we can explain. The giants keep their ageless secret from archaeologists and supermarket tabloids alike.

Many peoples have worshipped at the Stonehenge site, from late Neolithic and early Bronze Age chieftains to contemporary mystics. Religious devotees in many different eras persevered to complete temples at this spot, leaving us to marvel at the religious dedication inspired by the site. In 300 BC, Druids arrived from the Continent and claimed Stonehenge as their shrine. Each year, Druids are permitted to enter Stonehenge on the Summer Solstice to perform their ceremonial exercises. In the last two years, however, new-age mystics beat them to the spot and invaded the circle; in 1999 this lead to conflicts with the police and eventual arrests, but 2000's celebration proved to be considerably more peaceful.

📠 GETTING THERE. Getting to Stonehenge, 8 mi. northwest of Salisbury, doesn't require much effort—as long as you don't have a 45-ton rock in tow. **Wilts & Dorset** (☎ (01722) 336855) runs several **buses,** including daily service from the Salisbury train station (#3, 40min., return £4.80). The first bus leaves Salisbury at 8:45am (Su 10:35am), and the last leaves Stonehenge at 6:30pm (Su 5:45pm). For the same price as a Salisbury-Stonehenge return, get an **Explorer** ticket that allows you to travel all day on any bus, including those stopping by **Avebury,** Stonehenge's less-crowded cousin (see below). **Guide Friday,** with Wilts and Dorset, runs a **tour bus** from Salisbury (3 per day, £6-12.50).

The most scenic walking or cycling route from Salisbury is the **Woodford Valley Route** through Woodford and Wilsford. Go north on Castle Rd., bear left just before Victoria Park onto Stratford Rd., and follow the road over the bridge through Lower, Middle, and Upper Woodford. After about 9 mi., turn left onto the A303 for the last mile. If Stonehenge isn't enough rock for you, keep your eyes peeled when you reach Wilsford for the Jacobean mansion that belongs to singer Sting, on the right-hand side. Don't go inside or you'll meet the police, not the Police.

🔘 ON THE ROCKS? NEAT! Admission to Stonehenge includes a 40-minute English Heritage audio tour that makes use of handsets resembling cellular telephones. The effect may be more haunting than Stonehenge itself—a bizarre march of tourists who seem to be engaged in business calls. Nonetheless, the tour is helpful, and includes arguments between a shepherd and his mother about the stones' origins. English Heritage also offers free guided personal tours (30min.) throughout the day. If you'd rather not get stoned by the price of admission, admire the rocks from the roadside or from Amesbury Hill, 1½ mi. up the A303. Even if you do see Stonehenge up close, it's worth the walk to view the coterie of giants looming in the distance. *(☎ (01980) 625368. Open daily June-Aug. 9am-7pm; mid-Mar. to May and Sept. to mid-Oct. 9:30am-6pm; mid-Oct. to mid-Mar. 9:30am-4pm. Wheelchair access. £4, students and seniors £3, children £2, families £10.)*

NEAR STONEHENGE: AVEBURY

The little village that has sprouted within the **stone circle** at Avebury is evidence of the more personal nature of this sight compared to Stonehenge, 18½ mi. south. People can wander among these silent stones or even picnic in their midst. With stones that date from 2500 BC, Avebury's sprawling titans are 500 years older than their favored cousin at Stonehenge. Taking perhaps hundreds of years to build, the circle remains in its form from the past, permanently marking the civilization that created it. Archaeologists, mathematicians, and astronomers have all studied the circle, but its meaning rests stubbornly with the dead. Just outside the circle, **Silbury Hill,** built in 2660 BC, rises curiously out of the ground. Europe's largest manmade mound has baffled archaeologists, and its date was only determined by the serendipitous excavation of a flying ant from the mound. The **Alexander Keillor Museum** details the history of the stone circle, as well as of nearby sights. (☎ (01672) 539250. Open daily Apr.-Oct. 10am-6pm; Nov.-Mar. 10am-4pm. £2.50.)

To reach Avebury, take bus #5 or 6 from **Salisbury** (1½hr., 6 per day, £3.90). To get to the Avebury **tourist information centre,** head to the car park near the stone circle and follow the signs. (☎ (01672) 539425. Open W-Sa 10am-5pm, Su 10am-4pm.)

SOMERSET AND AVON

BATH   ☎01225

A visit to the elegant spa city of Bath (pop. 83,000) remains *de rigeur*, even if it is now more of a museum—or perhaps a museum's gift shop—than a resort. But expensive trinkets can't conceal Bath's underlying sophistication. Early in their occupation of Britain, the Romans built an elaborate complex of baths to house the curative waters at the town they called Aquae Sulis, and the excavated remains of that complex draw visitors today. In 1701, Queen Anne's visit to the hot springs reestablished the city's prominence, making it a meeting place for artists, politicians, and intellectuals. More than highbrow talk was exchanged, though, as Bath became the social capital of England, second only to London. Its sometimes eyebrow-raising role in social history was immortalized by authors as diverse as Fielding, Austen, and Dickens. Bath's Georgian architecture, heavily bombed in World War II, has been painstakingly restored so that today every thoroughfare remains fashionable, even if more hair salons than literary salons grace its fair streets.

▐ GETTING THERE AND GETTING AROUND

Trains: Railway Pl., at the south end of Manvers St. Booking office open M-F 5:30am-8:30pm, Sa 6am-8:30pm, Su 7:45am-8:30pm. Travel center open M-F 8am-7pm, Sa 9am-6pm, Su 9:30am-6pm. Trains (☎ (08457) 484950) from: **London Paddington** (1½hr., 2 per hr., £34); **London Waterloo** (2¼hr., 4 per day, £21); **Bristol** (15min., 3 per hr., £4.60;) and **Exeter** (1¼hr., 1 per hr., £21.50).

Buses: Station at Manvers St. (☎464446). Ticket office open M-F 8:30am-5:30pm, Sa 8:30am-4:30pm; Information Centre M-Sa 9am-5:30pm; National Express office M-Sa 8:30am-5pm. **Luggage storage** available during ticket office hours (£2 per 2 days). **National Express** (☎ (08705) 808080) from: **London** (3hr., 9 per day, £11.50) and **Oxford** (2hr., 6 per day, £12). **Badgerline** buses sell a **Day Rambler** ticket for unlimited bus travel in the region (£5.30, seniors and children £3.75).

Taxis: Abbey Radio (☎ 444446) or **Orange Grove Taxis** (☎ 447777).

Bike Rental: Avon Valley Bike Hire (☎ 461880), behind the train station. £9 per half-day, £14 per day; steep £350 deposit by credit card. Open Apr.-Oct. daily 9am-5:30pm; Nov.-Mar. M-Sa 9am-5:30pm, Su 10am-5pm.

Boat Rental: Bath Boating Station (☎ 466407), at the end of Forester Rd., about ½ mi. north of town. Punts and canoes £5 per person per hr., £1.50 each additional hr. Open daily in summer 9am-9pm, winter 9am-5:30pm.

◆▐ ORIENTATION AND PRACTICAL INFORMATION

The beautiful **Pulteney Bridge** and **North Parade Bridge** span the River Avon, which bends around the city. The **Roman Baths,** the **Pump Room,** and **Bath Abbey** cluster in the city center, while the **Royal Crescent** and **The Circus** lie to the northwest.

Bath

▲ ACCOMMODATIONS
Camping, 2
Lynn Shearn, 1
International Backpackers Hostel, 4
Mrs. Rowe, 5
Toad Hall Guest House, 6
White Guest House, 7
YHA Youth Hostel, 8
YMCA International House, 3

North Rd.

Sham Castle Ln.

Oakwood Walk

TO 8 (200yds)

George St.

Sydney Buildings

Beckford Rd.

Sydney Gardens

Holburne Museum

Sydney Pl.

Bathwick

Lime Grove Gdns.

6

Pulteney Gdns.

7

Pulteney Rd.

Broadway

Bathwick St.

Sutton St.

Great Pulteney St.

Henrietta Gardens

Henrietta Park

Garden for the Blind

Henrietta Mews

County Cricket Grounds

North Parade Rd.

Ferry Ln.

Rossiter Rd.

Henrietta Rd.

La Laura Pl.

St. Pierre Argyle St.

Victoria Art Gallery

Orange Grove

Pierrepont St.

South Parade

Manvers St.

Book Museum

Dorchester St.

Claverton St.

St. John's Rd.

River Avon

The Building of Bath Museum

The Paragon

Walcot St.

Royal Photographic Society Octagon

Broad St.

Guildhall

Abbey

High St.

Pump Room & Roman Baths

Stall St.

No. Parade Passage

York St.

Cheap St.

Newark St.

Southgate St.

Manvers St.

TO 5 (¼mi)

Lansdown Rd.

Assembly Rooms & Museum of Costume

Bartlett

George St.

Bennett St.

Milsom St.

New Bond St.

Upper Borough Walls

Union St.

Green St.

Westgate St.

St. James Parade

Corn St.

St. James's Parade

Broad Quay

Julian Rd.

Museum of East Asian Art

Alfred St.

Queen St.

Barton St.

Gay St.

QUEEN SQUARE

Prince's St.

Theatre Royal

Monmouth St.

James St. West

River Avon

Green Park Rd.

THE CIRCUS

Brock St.

Charlotte St.

Charles St.

Herschel House and Museum

Upper Bristol Rd.

Green Park

Lower Bristol Rd.

Wells Rd.

Crescent Ln.

One Royal Crescent

Royal Crescent

Royal Ave.

Royal Victoria Park

Bridge Rd.

Midland Rd.

Lower Oldfield Park

Marlborough buildings

Marlborough Ln.

1

Royal Victoria Park

N

TO A4

TO A36, (2Ml)

2

2 (2Ml)

0   200 yards
0   200 meters

Tourist Information Centre: Abbey Chambers (☎ 477101; fax 477787; tourism@bathnes.co.uk). Books accommodations for £2.50 plus 10% deposit. Town map and mini-guide 50p. Pick up *This Month in Bath* (free) for event listings. Open May-Sept. M-Sa 9:30am-6pm, Su 10am-4pm; Oct.-Apr. M-Sa 9:30am-5pm, Su 10am-4pm.

Tours: The Mayor's Honorary Guides lead free **walking tours** from the Abbey Churchyard daily at 10:30am and 2pm. The **Bizarre Bath Walking Tour** (☎ 335124) begins at the Huntsman Inn at North Parade Passage nightly at 8pm (1¼hr). Tours vary from mildly amusing to hysterically funny and include absolutely no historical content. Tours £4.50, students £4. **Guide Friday** (☎ 444102) runs narrated 1hr. hop-on hop-off bus tours, departing from the bus station every 12min. 9:15am-5:30pm; £8.50, students and seniors £6.50, children £3.50. **Mad Max Tours** (☎ 465674) send young people on daytrips to Wiltshire, including Stonehenge and the Cotswolds. Departs 8:45am from the statue on Cheap St., stops at the YHA hostel at 8:50am. Book ahead. Tours £14.

Financial Services: Banks are ubiquitous; try **Lloyds TSB**, 47 Milsom St. (☎ 310256). Open M-Tu and Th-F 9am-5pm, W 9:30am-5pm, Sa 9:30am-12:30pm. **Thomas Cook**, 20 New Bond St. (☎ 492000). Open M-Tu and Th-Sa 9am-5:30pm, W 10am-5:30pm.

American Express: 5 Bridge St. (☎ 444757), just before Pulteney Bridge. Open M-Sa 9am-5:30pm. **Branch** (☎ 424416) in the tourist information centre.

Launderette: Spruce Goose, Margaret's Buildings, off Brock St. Small load £2, large load £3, soap 60p. Open daily 8am-9pm, last wash 8pm.

Police: (☎ 444343), Manvers St., just up from the train and bus stations.

Hospital: Royal United Hospital, Coombe Park, in Weston (☎ 428331). Take bus #14, 16, or 17 from the train or bus stations.

Internet Access: Click Internet Cafe, 19 Broad St. (☎ 337711). £2.50 per 30min. Open daily 10am-10pm. Also at the **Midnight Express Café** (☎ 446787) at the International Backpackers Hostel. £2.50 per 30min., £4.50 per hr. Open daily 8am-1am; see below.

Post Office: 21-25 New Bond St. (☎ 445358), across from the Podium Shopping Centre. **Bureau de change.** Open M-Sa 9am-5:30pm. **Postal Code:** BA1 1A5.

ACCOMMODATIONS

Bath's well-to-do visitors drive up **B&B** prices—don't try to find a bargain basement room, since some are quite frightening. Instead, expect to pay £18 and up, and enjoy Bath's gracious style. B&Bs cluster on **Pulteney Rd.** and **Pulteney Gdns.** From the stations, walk up Manvers St., which becomes Pierrepont St., right onto North Parade Rd. and past the cricket ground to Pulteney Rd. For a more relaxed setting, continue past Pulteney Gdns. (or take the footpath from behind the rail station) to **Widcombe Hill.** The steep climb has prices to match (from £17). A walk west toward Royal Victoria Park on **Crescent Gdns.** reveals another front of B&Bs.

Lynn Shearn, Prior House, 3 Marlborough Ln. (☎ 313587; fax 443543; keith@shearns.freeserve.co.uk). Convenient location on the west side of town beside the arbor of Royal Victoria Park. Easy 12min. walk, or take bus #14 from the station (6 per hr.) and get off at Hinton Garage. Look for the *Let's Go* sticker in the window. Among Bath's best values; warm proprietors welcome you as friends. No smoking. Doubles/twins from £40, doubles with bath £45.

YHA Bath, Bathwick Hill (☎ 465674; fax 482947; bath@yha.org.uk). From North Parade Rd., turn left onto Pulteney Rd., then right onto Bathwick Hill. A footpath takes the hardy up the ever-ascending hill to the hostel (a steep 20min. walk). Save your energy for the city: Badgerline "University" bus #18 (6 per hr. until midnight; return £1) runs to the hostel from the bus station or the Orange Grove roundabout. Secluded Italianate mansion overlooking the city. 124 beds. TV, laundry, lockers. No lockout or curfew. In summer reserve a week in advance. Dorms £11, under 18 £7.75.

International Backpackers Hostel, 13 Pierrepont St. (☎ 446787; fax 446305; info@backpackers-uk.demon.co.uk). Extremely convenient location, up the street from the stations and 3 blocks from the baths. A self-proclaimed "totally fun-packed mad place to stay." Each room and bed is identified by a music genre and artist ("I'm sleeping in Rap"). A pool table, game room, and bar reside in the even more manic basement. Internet access in attached cafe (see above). Breakfast £1. Laundry £3. Dorms £12; doubles and triples £30.

Mrs. Rowe, 7 Widcombe Crescent (☎ 422726). Go up Widcombe Hill and turn right. In the southeast, uphill from the stations and 10min. from town center. The height of elegance with a view to match. Singles £26; twins £44; doubles with bath £46.

The White Guest House, 23 Pulteney Gdns. (☎ 426075). A homey B&B with a patio filled with flowers. All rooms have TVs and bath. Kind proprietors will knock £2 off if you tell them *Let's Go* sent you, 10% off if you stay 3 or more nights. Singles £25-30; doubles £45-50. Prices lower Nov.-Apr.

Toad Hall Guest House, 6 Lime Grove (☎/fax 423254). A florid, friendly B&B with 3 comfortable doubles (one can be let as a single) and hearty breakfasts. Single £20-25; doubles £38-42; discount for stay of 2 nights or more.

YMCA International House, Broad Street Pl. (☎ 460471). Men and women accepted. Central location (3min. from tourist information centre). Sheet rental £1.50 in dorms; sheets included in private rooms. 210 beds. Continental breakfast included. Heavily booked in summer. Dorms £11; singles £15 for one night, £14 per night for 2 nights or more; doubles £28 for one night, £26 per night for 2 nights or more; triples £39.

Camping: Newton Mill Camping, Newton Rd. (☎ 333909; fax 461556), 2½ mi. west of city center off the A36. Take bus #5 from bus station (5 per hr.; £1.60 return) to Twerton and ask to be let off at the campsite. 105 car and caravan sites in an idyllic streamside setting. Shop, laundry, restaurant, and free showers. No reservation necessary for individual campers; drivers should book a week ahead. July-Aug. £4.75 per person, Sept.-June £4.25. Tent, car, and 2 people £11.95 July-Aug., £9.95 Sept.-June.

◘ FOOD

Although many restaurants in Bath are expensive and elegant, several decently priced cafes and restaurants populate the city. Pub food is always an option, especially on Sundays, when many offer three-course lunches at bargain prices. For fruits and vegetables, visit the **Guildhall Market**, between High St. and Grand Parade. (Open M-Sa 8am-5:30pm.) Grab picnic fare from the excellent salad bar at **Waitrose Supermarket** in the Podium on High St. across from the post office. (Open M-F 8:30am-8pm, Sa 8:30am-7pm, Su 11am-5pm.)

▨ Tilleys Bistro, 3 North Parade Passage (☎ 484200). Salivate over Tilleys' impressive French creations and large selection of English and vegetarian fare. Mushroom crepes under £5. Open M-Sa noon-2:30pm and 6:30-11pm, Su 6:30-10:30pm.

Demuths Restaurant, 2 North Parade Passage (☎ 446059), off Abbey Green. Creative vegetarian and vegan dishes even the most devoted carnivore would enjoy. Fresh, colorful veggies to match the bright paintings; the lemon yellow walls may inspire you to try the luscious lemon sponge (£2.50). Main courses around £8. Open daily 10am-10pm.

Sally Lunn's, 4 North Parade Passage (☎ 461634). Reputedly the oldest house in Bath; Sally Lunn began baking buns here in 1680. On the expensive side, but worth the £2.78 afternoon tea for history's sake. Open daily 10am-10pm.

Adventure Cafe, 5 Princes Buildings, George St. (☎ 462038). The oversized paragraphs of exotic locales aren't really from paradise, but the sandwiches (£2.50-3.75) will certainly send your tastebuds there. Casual atmosphere and satisfying fare take the worry out of any lunching adventure. Open M-F 9am-5pm, Sa 8am-5pm, Su 11am-4pm.

Café Retro, 18 York St. (☎ 339347). Not that retro, but compensates with delicious dishes and lunch specials. Swing in at lunch for one of their towering club sandwiches (£4.95)—after 6pm, prices rise as steeply as Bathwick Hill. Open daily 10am-11pm.

The Pump Room, Abbey Churchyard (☎ 444477). Exercises its monopoly over Bath Spa drinking water (45p per glass) in a palatial Victorian ballroom. Cream tea (£6.75) is served from 2:30pm until closing; weekend reservations are essential. Handel plays in

SOUTHWEST ENGLAND

the background, and once you've paid the check you may be Baroque as well. Open daily Apr.-Sept. 9am-6pm; Oct.-Mar. 9:30am-5pm.

The Walrus and the Carpenter, 28 Barton St. (☎ 314864). Lewis Carroll's characters watch over this trendy poster-plastered bistro. No talking oysters here, but the steak kebabs and ample salad options are popular lunch choices. Main courses £5-12. Open M-Sa noon-2:30pm and 6-11pm, Su noon-11pm.

Itchy Feet Café, 4 Bartlett St. (☎ 337987). This cybercafe-adventure travel shop purveys sandwiches and smoothies to an exuberant clientele. Huge stacked sandwiches for slim prices (salad and sandwich £2.95). Open M-Sa 10am-6pm, Su 11am-5pm.

◉ SIGHTS

THE ROMAN BATHS. Once the spot for naughty sightings, the baths are now a must-see for all. In 1880, sewer diggers inadvertently uncovered the first glimpse of what excavation has shown to be a splendid model of advanced Roman engineering. Most of the outside complex, however, is not Roman, but a Georgian dream of what Romans might have built. Penny-pinching travelers can view one of the baths in the complex for free by entering through the **Pump Room** (see p. 198).

Underneath the baths, the ▨ **museum** makes the entrance price worth it, with its display of the complexity of Roman engineering, including central heating and internal plumbing. Bath flourished for nearly 400 years as a Roman spa city, and walkways wind visitors through the remains of their sprawling bath complex. Attentive eyes will connect the strands of recovered artifacts and structural remnants to imagine the society that spawned them. Read the various recovered curses that Romans cast into Minerva's spring. Tradition said that if the written curse floated on the water, it would be visited back upon the curser. The Romans neatly avoided this by writing their ill wishes on lead. *(Stall St. ☎ 477759; www.roman-baths.co.uk. Open daily Apr.-July and Sept. 9am-6pm; Aug. 9am-6pm and 8-10pm; Oct.-Mar. 9:30am-5pm; last admission 30min. before closing. Partial wheelchair access. Hourly guided tours and audio tours included. £6.70, seniors £6, children £4, families £17; joint ticket to the Baths and the Museum of Costume £8.70, seniors £7.80, children £5.20, families £22.60.)*

BATH ABBEY. On a site that once contained a Saxon cathedral three times as large, the 15th-century abbey still towers over its neighbors. An anomaly among the city's Roman and 18th-century Georgian sights, the abbey saw the crowning of King Edgar, "first king of all England," in AD 973. The whimsical west facade sports angels climbing ladders up to heaven and two angels climbing down. Tombstones cover every possible surface in the church save the sanctuary and ceiling. Peruse the protruding markers—they reveal the eerie and often mysterious ways various Brits and Yanks met their ends. Play "Trivial Pursuit: New Testament Edition," with the 56 stained-glass scenes of Jesus' life at the east end. *(Next to the Baths. ☎ 477752. Open M-Sa 9am-4:30pm, Su 1-2:30pm and 4:30-5:30pm. Requested donation £1.50.)* Below the Abbey, the **Heritage Vaults** detail the abbey's history and its importance to Bath. Among the exhibits are statues from the original facade and a fascinating disappearing diorama. *(☎ 422462. Open M-Sa 10am-4pm; last admission 3:30pm. Wheelchair access. £2, students and seniors £1, children free.)*

THE MUSEUM OF COSTUME AND ASSEMBLY ROOMS. This museum houses a dazzling fashion parade of 400 years of catwalks, with everything from silver tissue garments to Queen Victoria's "generously cut" wedding gown. The museum's phenomenal wardrobe is so vast that only a tenth of the items can be displayed at any one time. *(Bennett St. ☎ 477752. Open daily 10am-5pm. Wheelchair access. £3.90, seniors £3.50, children £2.70; for info on joint ticket with the Roman Baths, see above.)* The museum is in the basement of the **Assembly Rooms,** which staged fashionable events in the 18th century. Although World War II ravaged the rooms, renovations duplicate the originals in fine detail. *(☎ 477789. Open daily 10am-5pm. Free.)*

JANE AUSTEN CENTRE. Austen lived in Bath from 1801 to 1806 (at 13 Queen Sq.) and thought it a "dismal sight," although she still managed to write *Northanger Abbey* and *Persuasion* here. The center organizes Austen's references to Bath, and invites dilettantes and devotees alike to visit 1806 Bath. *(40 Gay St. ☎ 443000. Open Apr.-Sept. M-Sa 10am-5:30pm, Su 10:30am-5:30pm; Oct.-Mar. M-Sa 10am-5pm, Su 10:30am-5pm. £3.95, seniors and students £2.95, children £1.95, families £9.95.)* **Tours** of the sights in her novels run three days a week from the center, depending on demand. *(£3.50, seniors and students £2.50, children £2, families £8.)*

HISTORIC BUILDINGS. In the city's residential northwest corner, Beau Nash's contemporaries John Wood, father and son, made the Georgian rowhouse a design to be reckoned with. Walk up Gay St. to **The Circus,** which has attracted illustrious residents for two centuries. Blue plaques mark the houses of Thomas Gainsborough, William Pitt the Elder (who was MP for Bath), and Dr. Livingstone. Proceed from there up Brock St. to Royal Crescent, a half-moon of Georgian townhouses, stopping at the oasis of book, art, and antique stores at **Margaret's Building** on the way. The interior of **One Royal Crescent** has been painstakingly restored to a near-perfect replica of a 1770 townhouse, authentic to the last teacup and butter knife. *(1 Royal Crescent. ☎ 428126. Open mid-Feb. to Oct. Tu-Su 10:30am-5pm; Nov. Tu-Su 10:30am-4pm. £4, concessions £3.50, families £10.)* Climb the 156 steps of **Beckford's Tower** for stupendous views. *(Lansdowne Rd. ☎ 338727. £2, concessions £1.)*

THE AMERICAN MUSEUM. Homesick Yankees and those who want to visit the States vicariously (but haven't yet found a McDonald's) will find a series of furnished rooms transplanted from historically significant American homes, including a cozy Revolutionary War-era kitchen with a working beehive oven. *(Climb Bathwick Hill, or let bus #18 (£1.20) save you the steep 2 mi. trudge. Claverton Manor. ☎ 460503. Museum open late Mar. to late Oct. Tu-Su 2-5pm. Gardens open Tu-F 1-6pm, Sa-Su noon-6pm; also M in Aug. Limited wheelchair access. House, grounds, and galleries £5.50, students and seniors £5, children £3. Grounds, Folk Art, and New Galleries only £3, children £2.)*

OTHER MUSEUMS AND GALLERIES. The **Victoria Art Gallery,** Bridge St., next to the Pulteney Bridge, will please those with a discerning eye. The permanent gallery holds a diverse collection of works including Old Masters and British art, such as Thomas Barker's "The Bride of Death"—Victorian melodrama at its sappiest. The "Cabinets of Curiosities" feature unusual and amusing artifacts. *(☎ 477772. Open Tu-F 10am-5:30pm, Sa 10am-5pm, Su 2-5pm. Wheelchair access. Free.)* Away from the tourist-trafficked abbey and baths, the **Royal Photographic Society Octagon Galleries,** Milsom St., lets visitors view well-executed contemporary exhibits and trace the history of photography, from daguerreotypes to holograms. *(☎ 462841. Open daily 9:30am-5:30pm; last admission 4:45pm. Wheelchair access. £4, concessions £2, families £8.)* **The Museum of East Asian Art,** 12 Bennett St., displays objects dating as far back as 5000 BC, and holds amazing collections of jade and rhino horn carvings. *(☎ 464640. Open Tu-Sa 10am-5pm, Su noon-5pm; last admission 4:30pm. £3.50, students £2.50, seniors £3, children £1, under 6 free, families £8.)* The **Building of Bath Museum,** on the Paragon, recounts in precise, scale-model detail how the city's masterful Georgian architecture progressed from the drawing board to the drawing room. *(☎ 333895. Open mid-Feb. to Nov. Tu-Su 10:30am-5pm. £3.50, students and seniors £2.50, children £1.50.)*

GARDENS AND PARKS. Throughout the city lie stretches of green cultivated to comfort weary limbs (consult a map or enquire at the tourist information centre for the *Borders, Beds, and Shrubberies* brochure). Next to Royal Crescent, **Royal Victoria Park** contains one of the finest collections of trees in the country, and its botanical gardens nurture 5000 species of plants from all over the globe. For bird aficionados, there's also an aviary. *(Open M-Sa 9am-dusk, Su 10am-dusk. Free.)* **Henrietta Park,** laid out in 1897 to celebrate Queen Victoria's Diamond Jubilee, was later redesigned as a garden for the blind—only the most olfactory pleasing flowers and shrubs were chosen for its tranquil grounds. Walk a few blocks beyond the Pulteney Bridge to Henrietta Rd. *(Free.)*

SOUTHWEST ENGLAND

⬛ PUBS AND CLUBS

The ⬛ **Paragon Wine Bar,** 1a The Paragon (☎ 466212), holds an eclectic set of laid-back drinkers and talkers, while **The Garrick's Head,** St. John's Pl. (☎ 448819), is a scoping ground for the stage door of the Theatre Royal. Still, it's not all luvvies, y'know. Luring in the backpacker contingent, **The Pig and Fiddle,** on the corner of Saracen St. and Broad St., brings in a young crowd for pints around its large patio. **The Boater,** 9 Argyle St. (☎ 464211), overlooks the river with outdoor seating and a view of the lit-up Pulteney Bridge. Its basement has become a shrine to the vodka-Red Bull combination. (All pubs open M-Sa 11am-11pm, Su noon-10:30pm.)

Bath nights wake up at **The Bell,** 103 Walcot St., an artsy pub which challenges its clientele to talk over the live jazz, blues, funk, and reggae. (☎ 460426. Open daily 11am-11pm.) For clubs, try **Cadillacs** on Walcot St. for the standard chart music (located just below The Bell). At 14 George St., **Moles** burrows underground and pounds out techno and house music. Dress sharp. The club is "members only," but you might get in...if you can find it. (☎ 404445. Cover £5. Open M-Sa 9pm-2am.)

♫ ▒ ENTERTAINMENT AND FESTIVALS

In summer, buskers (street musicians) perform in the Abbey Churchyard, and a brass band often graces the Parade Gardens. The magnificent **Theatre Royal,** Saw-close, Beau Nash's old haunt at the south end of Barton St., showcases opera and theater. (☎ 448844. Box office open M-Sa 10am-8pm, Su noon-8pm. Tickets £8-22; standby tickets £5; discounts for seniors and students M-Th.)

The renowned **Bath International Festival of the Arts** (☎ 463362) induces merriment all over town over two weeks of concerts and exhibits in May and June. Book well in advance for the **Bath International Music Festival,** with world-class symphony orchestras, choruses, and jazz. (Box office ☎ 463362. Open M-Sa 9:30am-5:30pm.) The **Contemporary Art Fair** opens the festival by bringing together the work of over 700 British artists. For a brochure or reservations, write to the Bath Festivals Office, 2 Church St., Abbey Green, Bath BA1 1NL. The concurrent **Fringe Festival** (☎ 480097) celebrates music, dance, and liberal politics. The **Litera-ture Festival** in late February, the **Balloon Fiesta** in mid-May, and the **Film Festival** in October are all popular events. Stay abreast of current entertainment news by picking up *Venue* or *The Bath Chronicle*, available at the TIC and around town.

BRISTOL   ☎ 0117

Bristol's wealth and one-time status as a "second city" to London grew mostly from its once-bustling slave and sugar cane trade with the West Indies and the Americas. Still the southwest's largest city, Bristol (pop. 401,000) hums along as a working business center by day and jumps into energetic revelry by night. Local pubs, clubs (this is the city that spawned dance music pioneers Massive Attack and Portishead), and late-night eateries cluster near the educational and commercial districts. Although much of Bristol's architectural might was felled by the bombs of World War II, some spectacular locations remain, most notably Clifton Suspension Bridge; others, such as the newly erected science center, add the glitter and glory of modernity. Despite a rebuilt city center and lavish quay front, Bristol remains largely undiscovered by tourists, allowing bold travelers to enjoy the lack of pretension in one of Britain's best-kept secrets.

▣ GETTING THERE

Trains: Bristol Temple Meads Station (☎ 929 4255). Ticket office open M-Sa 5:30am-9:30pm, Su 6:45am-9:30pm. **Luggage storage** £2 per item. Open M-Sa 8:30am-9:30pm, Su 9:30am-9:30pm. Trains (☎ (08457) 484950) from: **London Paddington** (1½hr., 2 per hr., £36); **Bath** (15min., 3 per hr., £4.60); **Cardiff** (50min., 2 per hr.,

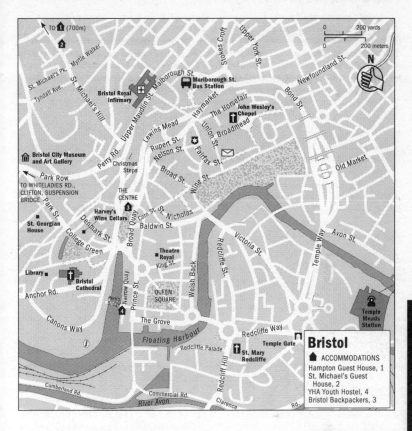

Bristol

ACCOMMODATIONS
Hampton Guest House, 1
St. Michael's Guest House, 2
YHA Youth Hostel, 4
Bristol Backpackers, 3

£8.90); and **Manchester** (3½hr., 1 per hr., £41). Another station, **Bristol Parkway,** is far, far away; make sure to get off at Temple Meads.

Buses: Marlborough St. Bus Station (☎ 955 3231). Information shop open M-F 7:30am-6pm and Sa 10am-5:30pm. Travel center open M-F 8:30am-6pm, Sa 8:30am-5pm. **National Express** (☎ (08705) 808080) from: **London** (2½hr., 21 per hr., £10); **Cardiff** (1¼hr., 11 per day, £4.50); **Birmingham** (2hr., every 2hr., £14); and **Manchester** (5hr. via Birmingham, 8 per day, £22).

Public Transportation: Badgerline (☎ 955 3231) buses run through Bristol and environs. A **Rambler** ticket gives unlimited travel on their buses for one day if your travel plans are especially ambitious (£5.30, seniors and children £3.75, families £10.60).

Taxis: Yellow Cab Company (☎ 963 1414).

ORIENTATION AND PRACTICAL INFORMATION

Bristol is a sprawling mass of neighborhoods. The shopping and commerce center is the **Broadmead** district, while **Corn St., Baldwin St., Quay St., St. Augustine's Parade,** and **Broad St.** run through the oldest part of the city. To get to **Cotham,** take St. Michael's Hill. **Park St.** (which becomes **Queens Rd.**) offers nighttime entertainment and takes you into the tiny **Clifton** neighborhood. Wander northwest of Broadmead in the direction of the **St. Pauls** neighborhood to find more nightlife options.

Tourist Information Centre: The Annexe, Wildscreen Walk, Harbourside (☎ 926 0767; fax 929 7703; http://visitbristol.co.uk), next to Explore@Bristol. Books accommodations for £3 and a 10% deposit. Sells tickets for local attractions and a wide selection of city maps and books. Guided walking **tours** (1hr.) Apr.-Oct.; £3, children £2. Open July-Aug. M-W and Sa-Su 10am-6pm, Th-F 10am-8pm; Sept.-July daily 10am-6pm.

Financial Services: Banks can be found in the Broadmead area as well as closer to the city center, including **HSBC**, 11a Broadmead. Open M and W-F 9am-5pm, Th 9am-7pm, and Sa 9:30am-3:30pm.

American Express: 31 Union St. (☎ 927 7788). Open M-F 9am-5:30pm, Sa 9am-5pm. Also at 74 Queens Rd. (☎ 975 1751). Open M-F 9am-5:30pm, Sa 9am-5pm.

Police: (☎ 927 7777), Nelson St.

Hospital: Bristol Royal Infirmary (☎ 923 0000), Upper Maudlin St.

Internet Access: Internet Exchange, 23-25 Queens Rd. (☎ 929 8026). 10p per minute for non-members; lower prices with free membership. Open M-F 8am-10pm, Sa 9am-9pm, Su 10am-6pm. Access is free at the **Library,** St. George's Rd., next to Bristol Cathedral. Open M-Tu and Th 9:30am-7:30pm, W and F-Sa 9:30am-5pm, Su 1-4pm.

Post Office: The Galleries, Wine St. (☎ 925 2322), inside the shopping center. Open M-Sa 9am-5:30pm. **Postal Code:** BS1 3XX.

▌ ACCOMMODATIONS

Budget B&Bs are nearly impossible to find in Bristol; travelers may have to hop over to nearby Bath for cheaper accommodations. Pricier accommodations can be found in **Clifton** and nearby **Cliftonwode,** as well as **Cotham.** While there are a few B&Bs in the **St. Paul's** neighborhood, travelers should note that the area is difficult to navigate and potentially unsafe.

Bristol Backpackers, 17 St. Stephen's St. (☎ 925 7900; info@bristolbackpackers.co.uk; www.bristolbackpackers.co.uk). Hot off the presses, this new independent hostel in an old newspaper building is making headlines. Thoughtful owners provide every comfort a backpacker could desire. Sociable dorms off street level are equipped with window seats; each room is creatively named after an international newspaper. Two lounges, one featuring medieval city walls and a basement bar. Internet access. Dorms £12.50 per person.

YHA Bristol, Hayman House, 14 Narrow Quay (☎ 922 1659; fax 927 3789; bristol@yha.org.uk). An 88-bed hostel inhabiting a beautifully renovated warehouse in the city center. Bureau de change, free luggage storage (bring a padlock), laundry and games facilities. If you plan to return after midnight, arrange late-night entry beforehand. Book ahead, especially in summer. Dorms £12.15, under 18 £8.35.

Hampton Guest House, 124 Hampton Rd. (☎ 973 6392). 1½ mi. from the city center. Large, clean rooms in a plush B&B. Singles £21; doubles £34.

St. Michael's Guest House, 145 St. Michael's Hill (☎ 907 7820), above St. Michael's Café. A 10min. walk from the city center. Cable TV and fairly spacious rooms are your reward for that walk. Book in advance. Singles £25; doubles £35; triples £45.

University of Bristol (☎ 926 5698). Accommodations in the heart of the city, during the summer months and at Easter. Around £21 per person.

◖ FOOD

Boston Tea Party, 75 Park St. (☎ 929 8601). Keeps Bristol buzzing with its exquisite selection of coffees and lattes. The Thai chicken sandwich (£3.25) seduces you for lunch, while the evening menu owns your taste buds (and your wallet) for dinner (£13 for two courses, £15 for three). Open M 7am-6pm, Tu-Sa 7am-10pm, Su 9am-7pm.

San Carlo, 44 Corn St. (☎ 922 6586). The owners stir springtime into their dishes, with a diverse menu of meat, pasta, and pizza. Meals range from the bargain (£5) to the budget-busting (£20). Open M-F noon-2:30pm and 5:30-11pm, Sa noon-11pm.

Tequila Worm, 64 Park St. (☎ 921 0373). Mexican food at its searing best, with great enchiladas (£8-10.95). The bar upstairs has tequila and a salsa DJ for the partiers. Two meals for the price of one M-F 5-7pm. Restaurant open M-Sa 5pm-midnight, Su 5pm-11:30pm; bar open Th-Sa until 2am.

St. Michael's Café, 145 St. Michael's Hill (☎ 907 7804). Murals of Elvis serenade you as you devour the huge breakfasts (£3.50-5), veggie meals (most under £4), or tasty milkshakes. Open M-F 7:30am-7:30pm, Sa 8am-4pm, and Su 9am-3pm.

Three Sugar Loaves, 2 Christmas Steps (☎ 929 2431). Samuel Pepys did his drinking in this friendly pub, among low ceilings and dislocated wooden beams. Main courses £2-4.50. Meals served M-F noon-2:30pm; pub open M-Sa 11am-11pm.

▣ SIGHTS

▧ CLIFTON SUSPENSION BRIDGE. Isambard Kingdom Brunel had a prodigious career as engineer-architect—his works include Paddington Station in London. His famous bridge, an architectural masterpiece spanning the Avon Gorge, can be reached via a pleasant walk through the Clifton neighborhood. The genius of the bridge becomes more apparent to the architecturally clueless after visiting the Bridge House Visitor's Centre, close by on Sion Pl. The museum documents the history of the bridge and gives an abridged course in bridge engineering. *(☎ 974 4664. Open daily Apr.-Sept. 10am-5pm; Oct.-Mar. M-F 11am-4pm, Sa-Su 11am-5pm. £1.50, seniors £1.30, under 16 £1, families £3.80.)*

@BRISTOL. Bristol's newest attraction, a grouping of three related complexes, has been enlightening wide-eyed visitors since July of 2000. **Explore** educates students of all ages with hands-on exhibits about the mysteries of subjects as diverse as flight and emotions, while interactive art and virtual volleyball intrigue the kid in everyone. **Wildscreen** traces the history of evolution and emphasizes the importance of biodiversity by presenting live animals and plants, augmented with participatory multimedia presentations and a thematic soundtrack. The **IMAX theater** astonishes viewers with enveloping, informative films. *(Explore Lane, Harbourside. ☎ 915 5000; www.at-bristol.org.uk. Explore open daily 10am-6pm; Wildscreen 10am-6pm; IMAX 10am-9pm. Single sight £6.50, children £4.50; 2 sights £11, £8; all 3 sights £15.50, £11.)*

CHURCHES. John Wesley's Chapel, the world's oldest Methodist building, sits incongruously opposite The Galleries, Bristol's shopping shrine. Marvel at anomalies such as the He Bible—a misprint replaces "she" with "he," not exactly making matters clear—and a chair fashioned from an inverted elm trunk. *(☎ 926 4740. Open M-Sa 10am-4pm.)* **Bristol Cathedral,** on the College Green, was begun in 1298, and in 1542 was named the Cathedral Church of the Holy and Undivided Trinity. Remnants of both Saxon and Norman architecture linger in the South Transept and chapter house. The surrounding College Green receives swarms of students, skateboarders, and suntanners. *(☎ 926 4879. Open daily 8am-6pm. Evensong 5:15pm. Suggested donation £2.)* Elizabeth I termed the medieval church of **St. Mary Redcliffe,** 10 Redcliffe Parade West, the "fairest, goodliest, and most famous Parish Church in England." It sits above the once-bustling "floating harbour" and is the burial site of Admiral William Penn (father of the founder of Pennsylvania). Samuel Johnson got stuck in one of the spiral staircases. *(☎ 929 1487. Open in summer M-Sa 8am-8pm, Su 7:30am-8pm; in winter M-Sa 8am-5.30pm, Su 7:30am-8pm. Donations requested.)*

CITY MUSEUM AND ART GALLERY. Covering all the bases, the impressive museum displays everything from minerals to mummies to a dinosaur. The art gallery also exceeds expectations, sampling many styles and periods, including local modern art. Summer 2001 sees an exhibition from the museum's collection of 1500 drawings of Bristol. *(Queens Rd. ☎ 922 3571. Open daily 10am-5pm. Free.)*

BRANDON HILL. A turn left off of Park Street onto Great George Street leads to Brandon Hill, one of the most peaceful, secluded sights in Bristol. Snaking pathways climb through the flower beds up to **Cabot Tower,** a monument commemorating the 400th anniversary of explorer John Cabot's arrival in North America. The tower offers a bird's eye view of local sights to anyone willing to ascend the steep stairs, and bronze etchings also point toward not so local sights, such as Helsinki, only 1250 miles away. *(☎ 922 3719. Open daily until dusk. Free.)*

OTHER SIGHTS. In the Great Western Dockyard, south of the city center, rests Brunel's **S.S. Great Britain,** the first iron-hulled ocean-going liner ever built. It made its maiden voyage in 1845, from Bristol to New York. *(☎ 926 0680. Open daily Apr.-Oct. 10am-5:30pm; Nov.-Mar. 10am-4:30pm. £4.50, seniors £3.50, children £3.)* If city walking has worn you out, try **Harvey's Wine Cellars,** 12 Denmark St., where the famous Bristol Cream sherry was born. *(☎ 927 5036. Open M-Sa 10am-5pm. Group bookings only. £4, students and seniors £3. Tasting tour £6.50.)*

🎵🎭 ENTERTAINMENT AND NIGHTLIFE

Britain's oldest theater, the **Theatre Royal,** King St. (☎ 987 7877), was rebuked for encouraging wickedness until King George III finally approved of the actors' antics. The Old Vic, the famous London repertory company, takes the stage regularly. Backstage tours are available. The **Hippodrome,** St. Augustine's Parade, presents the latest plays and concerts. (☎ 0870 607 7500. Box office open M-F 8:30am-10pm, Sa 8:30am-9:30pm, Su 10am-8pm.) In July, the amazingly popular **Bristol Community Festival** explodes with a wide range of musical performances. The event raises money for charity, so while entrance officially is free, a £2 "voluntary" donation is strongly encouraged. Contact the tourist information centre for details.

Home to thousands of university students, Bristol offers its own fair share of nightlife. The massive **Lakota,** 6 Upper York St., is the hippest place for a hefty dose of dancing and people-watching, with a cover charge to match. (☎ 942 6208. Open F-Sa nights.) **The Sedan Chair,** 4-11 Broad Quay, is usually filled with students and twentysomethings. (☎ 926 4676. F-Sa £3 after 10pm. Open M and Th-Sa noon-2am.) Travel toward St. Paul's neighborhood and stop at **Powerhouse,** on Stokes Croft, for big beat music. (☎ (0585) 68216. £1 before midnight, £5 after. Open 10pm-3am.)

WELLS   ☎ 01749

The town of Wells (pop. 10,000), named for the natural springs at its center, bows humbly before its magnificent cathedral, its main streets drawn toward the colossal church. Lined with petite Tudor buildings and golden sandstone shops, the streets of Wells fade elegantly (if expensively) into the Somerset meadows.

◾ GETTING THERE AND GETTING AROUND

Trains leave Wells enough alone, but **buses** stop at the **Princes Rd. Depot.** (☎ 673084. Office open M-Tu and Th-F 9am-5pm, W and Sa 9:30am-1pm.) **Badgerline** (Bath ☎ (01225) 464446, Bristol ☎ (0117) 955 3231) runs from **Bath** (#173; 1¼hr.; M-Sa 1 per hr., Su every 3hr.; £3) and **Bristol** (#376 and 676; 1hr.; M-Sa 1 per hr., Su every 3hr.; £3). If you'll be skipping around in the area, buy a **Day Rambler** (£5.30, seniors and children £3.75). **Bakers Dolphin** (☎ 679000) runs fast buses from **London** (2hr., 1 per day, £15.95). **Wookey Taxis** (☎ 678039) and **A Taxis** (☎ 670200) scurry through Wells's cramped streets. Rent bicycles at **Bike City,** 31 Broad St. (☎ 671711. £6.95 per half-day, £8.95 per day, £39.95 per week; deposit £50. Open M-Sa 9am-5:30pm.)

✳🔢 ORIENTATION AND PRACTICAL INFORMATION

To reach the tourist information centre from the bus station, turn left onto Priory Rd., which becomes Broad St. and eventually merges with High St. At the top of High St. rests Market Place.

The **tourist information centre** (TIC), in the Town Hall on Market Pl., to the right as you face the cathedral grounds, books rooms for a 10% deposit and has free bus timetables. (☎ 672552; fax 670869; wells.tic@ukonline.co.uk. Open daily Apr.-Oct. 9:30am-5:30pm; Nov.-Mar. 10am-4pm.) Services include: **banks** clustering on High St. and Market Pl., including **HSBC,** 1 Market Pl. (☎ 316700; open M-F 9:15am-4:45pm); **Thomas Cook,** 8 High St., near the entrance to the cathedral (☎ 313000; open M-Sa 9am-5:30pm); **Wells Launderette,** 39 St. Cuthbert St. (☎ (01458) 835804; open daily 7am-8pm; last wash 7pm); the **police,** Glastonbury Rd. (☎ (01934) 635252); **Wells and District Cottage Hospital,** St. Thomas St. (☎ 673154); **Internet access** at **d'e.c@fe,** South St., in the YMCA building (☎ 679757; 50p per 30min.; open M 1-3pm, Tu-F 1-3pm and 4-6pm); and the **post office,** Market Pl. (☎ 677825; open M and W-F 9am-5:30pm, Tu 9:30am-5:30pm, Sa 9am-12:30pm). **Postal code:** BA5 2RA.

▌ ACCOMMODATIONS

B&Bs in Wells are lovely but expensive; most offer only doubles and prefer longer stays, so you may have to daytrip from Bath. The closest **YHA Youth Hostels** and **campgrounds** are 10 mi. away in Wookey Hole and Cheddar (see **Near Wells,** p. 210).

▨ **Richmond House,** 2 Chamberlain St. (☎ 676438). Brass mirrors and an antique fire-place—and that's just the bathroom. Large rooms a breath away from the town. Vegetarian breakfast available, including bubble and squeak. Flexible proprietors help travelers organize their treks through the area. £20 per person.

  Number Nine, 9 Chamberlain St. (☎ 672270; number9@ukf.net). Immaculate Georgian house with a rose garden. Enormous airy rooms with TVs and baths. Serves up a true "full" English breakfast, which will fill even the most voracious of eaters. Ask Mrs. Elliott to show you her artwork. Singles £22, sometimes less in off-season; doubles £38.

  The Old Poor House, 7a St. Andrew St. (☎ 675052, mobile ☎ (0831) 811070). No need to be a pauper to stay here. Miss Helen Bowley has resumed where charming former proprietress Mrs. Wood left off, keeping tidy rooms right up the street from the cathedral. From £20 per person.

  Bay Tree House, 85 Portway (☎ 677933). On the quiet outskirts of town, this new B&B's proprietor blends discreetly decorated rooms with pleasant conversation in a comfortable, homey atmosphere. Singles £25; doubles £36, £10 extra for 3rd person.

▌ FOOD

Assemble a picnic at the **market** behind the bus stops (open W and Sa 8:30am-4pm), or purchase tasty breads, cheeses, and other provisions at **Laurelbank Dairy Co.,** 14 Queens St. (☎ 679803; open M-Sa 9am-5:30pm). A **Tesco** supermarket is at Princes Rd. (Open M-W 8:30am-8pm, Th-F 8:30am-9pm, Sa 8am-8pm, Su 10am-4pm.) **Boxer's Restaurant** and **The Fountain,** 1 St. Thomas St., behind the cathedral, are a restaurant-pub dynamic duo. The Fountain will quench your thirst, but a meal upstairs at the renowned Boxer's Restaurant will pamper your taste buds. Some dishes approach stratospheric prices (£11) but their warm chicken salad will send your mouth to the stars for less at £6.75. (☎ 672317. Open M-Sa 6-10pm, Su 7-9:30pm.) Find great home-cooked pizzas (£1.85 per slice) and quiches (£1.70) at **The Good Earth,** 4 Priory Rd. There's an adjoining takeaway as well, selling soups for £1-1.65, and salads for £1.55-2.75. (☎ 678600. Open M-Sa 9:30am-5:30pm.)

▌ SIGHTS

CATHEDRAL CHURCH OF ST. ANDREW. The 13th-century church in the center of town anchors a fantastically preserved cathedral complex, with a bishop's palace, vicar's close, and chapter house. Atop the 14th-century astronomical clock in the north transept, a pair of jousting, mechanical knights spur on their chargers and strike at each other every 15 minutes—the same unfortunate rider is unseated every time. Walter Raleigh, Dean of Wells and nephew to the Sir, was murdered in the deanery where he had been imprisoned for his Royalist ways. M.C. Escher would be inspired by the swerving steps to the Chapter House, though the house itself is a Gothic dream of symmetry. The **Wells Cathedral School Choir**—one of the best in the country—sings services from September to April; visiting choirs assume the honor through summer break. Pick up the leaflet *Music in Wells Cathedral* at the cathedral or TIC for concert details and ticket information; many of the lunchtime performances are free. *(☎ 674483. Open in summer daily 7:15am-8:30pm if there's no concert; until 6pm in winter. Free guided tours 10:15am, 11:15am, 12:15pm, 2:15pm, and 3:15pm. Evensong M-Sa 5:15pm, Su 3pm. Suggested donation £4, students and seniors £2.50, children £1.)*

BISHOP'S PALACE. A humble parish priest's abode, the palace was built in the 13th century. Ralph of Shrewsbury (1329-63) was alarmed by village riots a little later and built the moat and walls to protect himself. The mute swans in the moat are trained to pull a bell-rope when they want to be fed; visitors are encouraged to feed them brown and wholemeal bread (but not white—they get sick). The palace **gardens** offer Arcadian ecstasy, with lush springs that give the city its name—the ideal setting for a champagne picnic. *(Near the cathedral. ☎ 678691. Open Aug. daily 10:30am-6pm; Easter-July and Sept.-Oct. Tu-F 10am-6pm, Su 2-6pm. Palace and gardens £3, students £1.50, seniors £2, children free.)* **Vicar's Close,** behind the cathedral, is reputedly the oldest street of houses in Europe; the houses date from 1363, their chimneys from 1470. **St. Andrew's Well,** bubbling up in the palace grounds, produces 40 gallons of spring water per second. Bishop Beckynton controlled the flow in the 15th century, harnessing the water and power for use. Today the spring water trickles down channels along High Street on its way to the River Sheppey.

WELLS MUSEUM. North of the cathedral green and left of the cathedral's entrance, the refurbished museum enshrines an above-average collection, including cathedral statuary. The statues look ill-proportioned but are designed to appear normal when viewed from below. Also on display are an alabaster "crystal ball" and the bones of an elderly woman, found in nearby Wookey Hole Caves, supposedly those of the legendary "Witch of Wookey Hole." *(8 Cathedral Green. ☎ 673477. Open daily July-Aug. 10am-8pm; Easter-Oct. 10am-5:30pm; Nov.-Easter W-Su only 11am-4pm. £2, students and seniors £1.50, children and disabled £1, families £5.)*

NEAR WELLS: WOOKEY HOLE AND CHEDDAR

A short journey from Wells brings you to a vale of cheese, in every sense of the word. If you plan to see both Wookey Hole and Cheddar, buy a **Day Rambler** in Wells (see p. 208). The **Wookey Hole Caves and Papermill,** only two miles northwest of Wells, hold some odd prehistoric animal mutations and a collection of wooden carousel animals. Admission includes the subterranean caves and a tour of the working paper mill. *(☎ 672243. Open daily 10am-5pm. £7.20, children £4.20.)* You can **camp** nearby at **Homestead Park,** beside a brook. *(☎ (01749) 673022. £9 per tent, car, and 2 people; £3 per additional person.)*

The **Cheddar Gorge,** formed by the River Yeo (YO!) in the hills just northeast of town of **Cheddar,** may be worth a daytrip, depending on your sensibilities and toleration for an overcrowded melange of touristy tea shops. Take bus #126 from Wells (20min., M-Sa 1 per hr., £1.60) and follow the signs to **Jacob's Ladder,** a 322-step stairwell to the top. A view of the hills to the north and the broad expansive plain to the south rewards the intrepid climber. *(£2.50, children £2.)* At the foot of the cliffs huddle the **Cheddar Showcaves,** England's finest. Feast your eyes on the stalactites and stalagmites, and on Cheddar Man, a 9000-year-old skeleton typical of the Stone Agers who settled in the Gorge. *(☎ (01934) 742343. Caves open daily May to mid-Sept. 10am-5pm; mid-Sept. to Apr. 10:30am-4:30pm. Caves, Jacob's Ladder, and open-top bus ride around the Gorge £7.50, children £5, families £20; discount tickets available from Wells TIC.)*

Cheddar's **tourist information centre** is located at the base of Cheddar Gorge. (☎ (01934) 744071. Open daily Feb.-Nov. 10am-5pm; Dec.-Jan. Su 10am-5pm.) The town's **YHA Youth Hostel,** Hillfield, is in a stone Victorian house off the Hayes, 3 blocks from the bus stop up Tweentown Rd., and half a mile from Cheddar Gorge. (☎ (01934) 742494. No lockout if staying more than one night. Curfew 11pm. Open July-Aug. daily; May-June and Sept.-Oct. M-Sa; Feb.-Mar. and Nov.-Dec. Sa-Su. Dorms £9.80, under 18 £6.75.) The hostel is served by frequent buses from Wells (#126 and 826; M-Sa 1 per hr. until 5:40pm; £1.20). Camp at **Bucklegrove Caravan and Camping Park,** in Rodney Stoke, near Cheddar. (☎ (01934) 870261. Open Mar.-Oct. daily; from £5 for tent and 2 people.)

In 1170, Henry II declared Cheddar cheese the best in England. Today, cheese enthusiasts nibble away at **Chewton Cheese Dairy,** just north of Wells on the A39. Take bus #126 toward Bristol and get off at Cheddar Rd., just outside Wells. (☎ (01761) 241666. Open Apr.-Sept. daily 9am-5pm; Oct.-Mar. daily 9am-4pm. Best time to view cheese-making 11:30am-2pm. No cheese-making Th and Su. Free.)

GLASTONBURY   ☎01458

The reputed birthplace of Christianity in England and a seat of Arthurian myth, Glastonbury (pop. 6900) has evolved into an intersection of religion and mysticism. People pilgrimage here to the stark **Glastonbury Tor,** where the Messiah is purportedly slated to return. According to legend, Jesus, Joseph of Arimathea, and Saints Augustine and Patrick all came here. Other myths hold that the area is the resting place of the Holy Grail, that the Tor is the Isle of Avalon, where King Arthur sleeps, and that the Tor contains a passage to the underworld. Glastonbury's streets bustle in the morning with old women buying curative herbs and Osiris candles, not milk and vegetables. Grow your hair, suspend your disbelief, and join hands with Glastonbury's subculture of hippies, spiritualists, and mystics.

■ GETTING THERE. Glastonbury has no train station; most **buses** stop in front of the town hall. **Baker's Dolphin** (☎ (01934) 616000) buses swim speedily from **London** (3¼hr., 1 per day, £5). **Badgerline** bus #376 runs from **Bristol** (1½hr.; 1 per hr., Su every 3hr.; £4.50), and #163, 167, 168, 378, and 379 come in from **Wells** (£2.70). From **Bath,** change at Wells (£3.90). For information on other Badgerline services, call their Bristol (☎ (0117) 955 3231), Bath (☎ (01225) 464446), or Wells (☎ (01749) 673084) offices. **Explorer Passes** let you travel a full day on Badgerline buses (£5.30, seniors and children £3.75). **Southern National** (☎ (01823) 272033) buses take travelers to points south, such as **Lyme Regis** and **Weymouth.**

◼◪ ORIENTATION AND PRACTICAL INFORMATION. Glastonbury is six miles southwest of Wells on the A39 and 22 mi. northeast of Taunton on the A361. The compact town is bounded by **High St.** in the north, **Bere Ln.** in the south, **Magdalene St.** in the west, and **Wells Rd.** in the east. To get to the **tourist information centre** (TIC), The Tribunal, 9 High St., from the bus stop, turn right onto High St.; the TIC is on the left through the alleyway. They'll book rooms for a 10% deposit; after hours find the B&B list behind the building in St. John's carpark. (☎ 832954; fax 832949; glastonbury.tic@ukonline.co.uk. Open Apr.-Sept. Su-Th 10am-5pm, F-Sa 10am-5:30pm; Oct.-Mar. S-Th 10am-4pm, F-Sa 10am-4:30pm.) Services include: numerous **banks** on High St., including **Barclays,** 21-23 High St. (☎ 582200; open M-F 9:30am-4:30pm); the **police** in the nearby town of **Street** at 1 West End (☎ (01823) 337911); **Internet access** at Glastonbury Backpackers and Café Galatea (see below); and the **post office** at 35-37 High St. (☎ 831536; Open M-F 9:30am-5pm, Sa 9am-1pm). **Postal code:** BA6 9HG.

▦ ACCOMMODATIONS. Single rooms are rare in Glastonbury. The nearest youth hostel is the **YHA Street,** The Chalet, Ivythorn Hill St., off the B3151 in the town of Street. Take Badgerline bus #376 to Loythorn Rd., and walk one mile. The hostel is a Swiss-style chalet with views of Glastonbury Tor, Sedgemoor, and the

Mendip Hills. (☎ 442961. Lookout 10am-5pm. Curfew 11pm. Open July-Aug. daily; mid-Apr. to May W-M; June Tu-Su. Dorms £9.35, under 18 £6.40.) **Glastonbury Backpackers,** in the Crown Hotel, Market Pl., contributes its own splashes of color to Glastonbury's tie-dye. The attached restaurant and bar and friendly staff only improve the hostel's great location. Check out the "Bridal Suite" with jungle-print sheets and ceiling mirror. (☎ 833353. Internet access £3 per 30min., £5 per hr., £1 minimum charge. Dorms £10; doubles £26-30.) For glorious private bathrooms, lovely gardens, and lovelier proprietors, call upon Mr. and Mrs. Hankins at **Blake House,** 3 Bove Town. Chat about your travels and immortalize your visit with a pin on their world map. (☎ 831680. Substantial continental breakfast included. From £19 per person.) You'll find clean, bright rooms with TVs at **The Bolt Hole,** 32 Chilkwell St., opposite the Chalice Well, a 12min. walk from the town center. Sit at breakfast with Mrs. Eastoe, a Glastonbury resident all her life, and gaze out on the rolling hills. (☎ 832800. £18 per person.) **Tamarac,** 8 Wells Rd., Mrs. Talbot's modern house on a central residential street, has biscuits in every room and plenty of novels to peruse. (☎ 834327. Singles £25; doubles £38; triples £57.)

◱ **FOOD.** The **Truckle of Cheese** deli, 33 High St., lets you grab food for a picnic. (☎ 832116. Open M-Sa 9am-5:30pm.) So does **Heritage Fine Foods,** 34 High St. (Open M-Sa 7am-9pm, Su 8am-9pm.) ◪ **Rainbow's End,** 17a High St., serves vegetarian and wholefood specials. The menu changes depending on the availability of vegetables and the chef's creative whims; try her £1.95 broccoli and cheddar quiche. (☎ 833896. Open daily 9am-4pm.) The age of Aquarius meets the age of technology at **Café Galatea,** 8 High St., a wholefood vegetarian-vegan cafe and cyberspace station. Mmm, pita with a side of slow 'net access. (☎ 834284. Internet access £1 per 10min., £5 per hr. Open M 11am-6pm, W-Th 11am-9pm, F 11am-10pm, Sa 10:30am-10pm, Su 10:30am-9pm.) **Abbey Tea Room,** 16 Magdalene St., serves lovely cream teas with scones and jam for £3.50. (☎ 832852. Open daily 10am-5pm.)

▣ **SIGHTS.** The ruins of **Glastonbury Abbey** lurk behind the archway on Magdalene St. The oldest Christian foundation and once the most important abbey in England was constructed "so as to entice even the dullest minds to prayer." Let your travel-worn mind marvel at the model of the Abbey as it looked in 1539 when Henry VIII commenced his antics. Modern new-age religion finds an outlet in the open-air masses that are periodically held among the ruins—inquire at the TIC. (☎ 832267. Open daily June-Aug. 9am-6pm; Sept.-May 9:30am-6pm. £3, students and seniors £2.50, children £1, families £6.50.)

Present-day pagan pilgrimage site **Glastonbury Tor** towers over Somerset's flatlands. Visible miles away, the Tor was known in its earlier incarnation as St. Michael's Chapel, and is supposedly the site of the mystical Isle of Avalon, where King Arthur sleeps but will reappear when his country needs him most. Once surrounded by water, the Tor at times resumes its island appearance, rising supernaturally from the morning fog. From the top of the hill, you can survey the Wiltshire

ABBEY ROAD Glastonbury has served as a backdrop to almost 2000 years of Christian history and legend. Joseph of Arimathea supposedly built the original wattle-and-daub church on this site in AD 63; larger churches were successively raised (and razed), until the current abbey was erected in 1184. Its sixth and final abbot, Richard Whiting, refused to obey Henry VIII's order that all Catholic churches be dissolved. Displaying his characteristic religious tolerance, Henry had Whiting hanged, drawn, and quartered on Glastonbury Tor. Two national patron saints, St. Patrick of Ireland and St. George of England, have been claimed by the abbey—St. Patrick is said to be buried here and St. George to have slain his dragon just around the corner. St. Dunstan hails from Glastonbury, where he served the diocese. In 1191, the remains of King Arthur and Queen Guinevere were supposedly discovered just in time for an abbey rebuilding campaign; their bones were reinterred in the church in 1276.

Downs and the Mendips. To reach the Tor, turn right at the top of High St. and continue up to Chilkwell St., turning left onto Wellhouse Ln.; take the first right up the hill. Magicians get their kicks by burning incense in the remaining tower. In summer, the **Glastonbury Tor Bus** takes weary pilgrims around for 50p.

On the way down from the Tor, visit the **Chalice Well** on the corner of Wellhouse Ln., the supposed resting place of the Holy Grail. Legend once held that the well ran with Christ's blood; in these post-Nietzsche days, rust deposits at the source turn the water red. Ancient mystics, in their propensity to find symbolism everywhere, saw the iron-red water mingling with white water from a nearby well and giggled at the sexual imagery. Water gurgles from the well down through a tiered garden of hollyhocks, climbing vines, and dark yew trees. (Open daily Easter-Oct. 10am-6pm; Nov.-Feb. 1-4pm. £1.50, children and seniors 75p.)

Head down Bere Ln. to Hill Head to reach **Wearyall Hill,** where legend has it that the staff of early Christian St. Joseph of Arimathea bloomed and became the **Glastonbury Thorn.** The Thorn has grown on Wearyall Hill since Saxon times, and blooms each year at Christmas and Easter. Legend says that the Thorn should flower in the presence of royalty, and horticulturists here and abroad (where offshoots of the Thorn are planted) have wasted considerable time making the trees bloom each time the Queen comes to visit. Five miles east stands Worthy Farm, the site of the annual **Glastonbury Festival** (www.glastonburyfestivals.co.uk), Britain's largest summer music festival.

THE DORSET COAST

DORCHESTER ☎01305

Every city has its favorite children, but in Dorchester, Thomas Hardy is an only son. Those who live here indulge his spirit, perhaps to the point of spoiling it. Before draining a pint, gray-haired men in pubs will tell you handed-down stories about the author whose statue soberly overlooks the town's main street. It seems every business here—from inns to shoe stores—manages to incorporate "Hardy" into its name. Those travelers not Hardy-hooked will hardly be hooked on Dorchester. The inspiration for the novelist's "Casterbridge" is a sleepy city that has seen more prosperous times. But Dorchester *is* far from the madding crowd; enjoy the sloping hills and the Neolithic and Roman oddities outside of town.

▌ GETTING THERE AND GETTING AROUND

The county seat of Dorset, Dorchester is 120 mi. southwest of London. Most **trains** (☎ (08457) 484950) come into **Dorchester South,** off Weymouth Ave., which runs southwest from the bottom of South St. (Ticket office open M-F 6:05am-8pm, Sa 6:40am-8pm, Su 8:40am-7pm.) Trains run from **London Waterloo** (2½hr., 14 per day, £32.40). Some trains arrive at the unstaffed **Dorchester West,** also off Weymouth Ave., including from **Weymouth** (15min., 20 per day, £2.50). Dorchester is easily accessible by **bus,** even though it lacks a bus station. **National Express** (☎ (08705) 808080) travels from **London** (3¾hr., 1 per day, £13) and **Exeter** (2hr., 1 per day, £10.50); tickets are sold at the tourist information centre. **Southern National** (☎ (01392) 382800) #X53 is a better bargain from **Exeter** (M-Sa 4 per day, return £3.20). The **Wilts & Dorset bus** (☎ 673555) comes from **Salisbury** via **Blandsford** (4 per day, first at 8:50am; £4.50). **Dorchester Coachways** (☎ 262992), Grove Trading Estate, provides local service and makes daily trips to **London** (return £17.50). **Dorchester Cycles,** 31a Great Western Rd., rents **bikes.** (☎ 268787. £5 per half-day, £10 per day, £50 per week. Credit card deposit. Open M-Sa 9am-5:30pm.)

■✦ ❼ ORIENTATION AND PRACTICAL INFORMATION

The intersection of **High West** with **South St.** (which eventually becomes **Cornhill St.**) serves as the unofficial center of town. The main **shopping district** extends southward along South St. To get to the tourist information centre (TIC) from South Station, follow the brown signs or walk out of the station onto Weymouth Ave. Cross Great Western Rd. onto South St. and continue up almost until the top of the street, where you'll see a statue of a leaping antelope. Turn left onto Antelope Walk; the office is at the end of the arcade on the left. To reach the TIC from West Station, turn right onto Great Western Rd. and then left onto South St.

The **tourist information centre**, 11 Antelope Walk, sells helpful maps and walking tour pamphlets (10p-£5), as well as tickets for local and regional buses. (☎ 267992. Open Apr.-Oct. M-Sa 9am-5pm, Su 10am-3pm; Nov.-Mar. M-Sa 9am-4pm.) **Walking tours** leave from the TIC (mid-June to mid-Sept. M, W, and Su 2pm, Th 6:30pm; £3, students and seniors £2.75, under 16 free). The **Thomas Hardy Experience,** booked through the TIC, guides visitors to every piece of the town remotely connected with the author (M and W 10:30am, Tu 2:30; £10). Services include: **Barclays bank,** 10 South St. (☎ 326700; open M-Tu and Th-F 9am-5pm, W 10am-5pm); a **market,** in the parking lot near South Station (open W 8am-3pm); a **launderette,** 16c High East St. (£3 for large load, £2.60 small; open daily 8am-7pm); the **police** (☎ 251212), Weymouth Ave.; **West Dorset Hospital** (☎ 251150), Dames Rd.; free **Internet access** at the **library,** Colliton Park, off The Grove (☎ 224448; open M 10am-7pm, Tu-W and F 9:30am-7pm, Th 9:30am-5pm, Sa 9am-4pm); and the **post office,** 43 South St., with a **bureau de change** (☎ 251093; open M-Sa 9am-5:30pm). **Postal code:** DT1 1DH.

⌐ ACCOMMODATIONS

The nearest **YHA Youth Hostel** is several miles away at **Litton Cheney.** (☎ (01308) 482340. Open Jan.-Sept. Tu-Su. Dorms £9.80, under 18 £6.75.) Lodging in Dorchester is pricey (£15-18) at the town's scattered boarding houses and pubs. No B&Bs are especially plush, and most have only two rooms for rent. Call ahead, especially for the town's scarce singles.

> **Maumbury Cottage,** 9 Maumbury Rd. (☎ 266726). Close to Dorchester West station and 5min. from Dorchester South station, kind Mrs. Wade keeps 1 single, 1 double, and 1 twin. Lucky guests will hear Hardy stories and get a free tour of town. Jolly good English breakfast included. Rooms £17 per person.

> **Barbara Broadway,** 11 Sydenham Way (☎ 260248). The Broadways open their home to visitors, enthusiastically accommodating guests in this tiny B&B with singles, 1 double and 1 twin. Singles £18; double and twin £26.

> **Mountain Ash,** 30 Mountain Ash Rd. (☎ 264811). Head up High West St. through the roundabout, turn right onto St. Thomas Rd. at the Sidney Arms, and take the first left onto Mountain Ash Rd.; it's on the left. Mrs. Priddle owns a well-kept home with recently refurbished rooms. 1 single and 2 doubles £18-20 per person.

> **The White House,** 9 Queens Ave. (☎ 266714), right off Maumbury Rd. Quite possibly the largest guest rooms you'll find in southern England; unfortunately there are only two of them, with bath and TV. £18 per person.

> **Camping: Giant's Head Caravan and Camping Park** (☎ (01300) 341242; giantshead@westcountry.net), Old Sherborne Rd., Cerne Abbas, 8 mi. north of Dorchester. Head out of town on The Grove, and bear right onto Old Sherborne Rd. Open Apr.-Oct. 2 people and tent £5-7, depending on the season.

◖▧ FOOD AND PUBS

The eateries along **High West St.** and **High East St.** provide a range of options, and an inordinately large number of **bakeries** lurk in the alleys off **South St.** For groceries, **Waitrose** rests in the Tudor Arcade off South St. (Open M-W and Sa 8:30am-6pm,

Th-F 8:30am-8pm; in summer also Su 10am-4pm.) **Mount Stevens,** 8 Cornwall St., bakes shelves of pastries and Belgian buns for under £1. (Open M-Sa 8am-5pm.) The **Potter In,** 19 Durngate St., puts whole orchards into their apple cake (£1.20) and serves towering sandwiches and homemade ice cream on a sunny, secluded patio. (☎ 260312. Open M-Sa 9:30am-5pm; July-Aug. also Su 11am-4pm.)

Dorchester barely dabbles in nightlife, but there are some decent pubs. **The Sun Inn,** at the junction of Old Sherbourne Rd. and Lower Burton, has wonderful pub grub. (☎ 250445. Open M-Sa 11am-3pm and 5:30-11pm; food served M-Sa noon-2pm and 6:30-10pm, Su noon-2pm and 6:30-10:30pm.) Heed the warning to "duck or grouse" when entering the **King's Arms,** 30 High East St., then have a pint in this historic inn, featured in Hardy's *Mayor of Casterbridge.* (☎ 265353. Open M-F 11am-3pm and 5:30-11pm, Sa 11am-11pm, Su 11am-3pm and 7-10:30pm.)

👁 SIGHTS

Dorchester's half-dozen Hardy attractions can't quite compete with the compelling sights in the hills just outside of town. Two vastly different periods collide in the countryside, Roman Britain and Hardy's Wessex. The traveler with a taste for adventure, and preferably in possession of a bike, can negotiate both in a day. In town, at the **Dorset County Museum,** 66 High West St., a replica of Hardy's study shines among the relics of Dorchester's other keepers—the Druids, Saxons, and Romans. (☎ 262735. Open M-Sa 10am-5pm, May-Oct. also Su 10am-5pm. £3.30, students and seniors £2.20, children £1.60, families £8.20.) Before hitting the high road to visit the pastoral sites of Hardy's youth, take a walk to **Max Gate,** the home that Hardy, who studied architecture, designed at Arlington Ave. and Syward Rd. He wrote *Tess of the D'Urbervilles* and *Jude the Obscure* here. (☎ 262538. Drawing room and garden open Apr.-Sept. Su-M and W 2-5pm. £2, children £1.)

The next stop on the Hardy adventure is the ever-so-small **Stinsford Church,** to the northeast of town in Stinsford Village. Follow the London Rd., which eventually becomes Stinsford Hill. At the roundabout, proceed straight ahead onto the continuation of Stinsford Hill, take the first right on Church Ln. The churchyard will be over the hill, straight ahead. Hardy was christened in the church and his family plot can be found in the yard. His desire to be entombed in the shadow of the tiny church was satisfied only in part—his heart alone is buried there, for his ashes rest in Westminster Abbey (see p. 117). Alongside the Hardy heart rests the classicist Cecil Day Lewis (Daniel's dad), who asked to be buried near the author.

Scattered ruins outside of town testify to Dorchester's status as a former Roman stronghold. Just past the entrance to South Station on Weymouth Ave. sprawl the **Maumbury Rings,** a Bronze Age monument with a gaping, grassy maw used as an amphitheater by the Romans. The complete foundation and mosaic floor of a **Roman Town House** are at the back of the County Hall complex, near the Top o' Town roundabout. (Enter the parking lot and walk all the way back; the gate—marked by black signs—is unlocked during daylight hours.) The only remaining fragment of the **Roman Wall** is on Albert Rd., a short walk to the south. Look carefully, or you'll walk right by. The most significant of Dorchester's ancient ruins is **Maiden Castle,** a fortification dating from 3000 BC that was seized by the Romans in AD 44. The "castle" is really a fortified hilltop patrolled by sheep. There is no bus transport, but the local shuttle to Vespasian Way goes halfway (every 15min. from Trinity St.). Alternatively, take a scenic two-mile hike from the center of town down Maiden Castle Rd.

Neither Roman nor Hardy-related, the **Keep Military Museum of Devon and Dorset,** Bridport Rd., holds its own volumes of history, collecting uniforms, weapons, and memorabilia from the Devon and Dorset regiments' participation in wars since the 1600s. See the desk swiped from Hitler's study. (☎ 264066. Open M-Sa 9:30am-5pm, also July-Aug. Su 10am-4pm. £2.50, concessions £1.50, families £7.50.)

BOURNEMOUTH
☎01202

At only 190 years old, Bournemouth (pop. 150,000) is an infant among English cities. Founded as a seaside resort and made popular by its healing pine scents and curative seabaths, visitors still clamor for the town's natural treasures. Today, day-trippers and active retirees enjoy the city's clean, expansive beach and coastal ravines, while clubbers and students fuel Bournemouth's growing nightlife.

⌐ GETTING THERE AND GETTING AROUND. Bournemouth enjoys sun and surf along the coast 104 mi. southwest of London; the Isle of Wight, 15 mi. to the west, helps shelter the city from the usual dismal English weather. The **train station** lies on Holdenhurst Rd. (Travel center open M-F 8am-5pm, Sa 9am-6pm, Su 9am-5:30pm.) Trains (☎ (08457) 484950) bring vacationers from: **London Waterloo** (1¾hr., 3 per hr., £27.20); **Dorchester** (40min., 1 per hr., £7); and **Bristol** (2½hr., 1 per hr., £20.60). Purchase **National Express** (☎ (08705) 808080) **bus** tickets at the tourist information centre; buses pull up near The Square from: **London** (2½hr., 1 per hr., £12); **Dorchester** (1¼hr., 3 per day, £4.50); and **Bristol** (3¼hr., 1 per day, £11.75). **Central Taxis** (☎ 394455) is open 24 hours.

🚹 PRACTICAL INFORMATION. The **tourist information centre** (TIC), Westover Rd., books rooms for a 10% deposit. (☎ (0906) 802 0234, premium rate; fax (01273) 696933. Open July-Aug. M-Sa 9:30am-7pm, Su 10:30am-4pm; Sept.-June M-Sa 9:30am-5:30pm.) The TIC also leads free guided **walks** (90min.; May-Sept. M-F 10:30am, Su 2:30pm). Many **banks** lie in The Square; **Thomas Cook** serves travelers from Richmond Hill. (Open M-Sa 9am-5:30pm.) Other services include: **American Express,** in the pedestrian area of Christchurch Rd. (open M-F 9:30am-5:30pm, Sa 9am-5pm); a **launderette,** 172 Commercial Rd. (wash £2.40 per load; open daily 8am-9pm); the **police** (☎ 552099), Madeira Rd.; **Bournemouth Hospital** (☎ 303626), Castle Land East, Littledown; **Internet access** at **Click 'n' Link**, 248 Old Christchurch Rd. (☎ 780444; £2 per hr.); and the **post office,** Post Office Rd., off Richmond Hill (open M-Sa 9am-5:30pm). **Postal Code:** BH1 2BU.

▮▮ ACCOMMODATIONS AND FOOD. In true seaside-resort fashion, most quality Bournemouth **B&Bs** range from mildly pricey to ludicrously expensive. **Boscombe** (a 20min. walk from the city center) features family villas converted into affordable B&Bs. The most reasonable rates are found at **Bournemouth Backpackers,** 3 Frances Rd. This small but friendly independent hostel can help guests obtain cheap bus passes to surrounding sights. (☎ 299491; bournemouth.backpackers@virgin.net. £8-15 per person.) **Campers** enjoy the facilities at **Merley Court Park,** Merley, Wimborne, 8 mi. north of town on the A341. (☎ 881488; fax 881484. £12 per couple.)

Bournemouth dishes out a smorgasbord of restaurants; **Christchurch Rd.** is particularly rich in diversity and quality. The cacti may be fake at **Coriander,** 22 Richmond Hill, but the Mexican cuisine is as authentic as it comes. Spice up your meal with sizzling fajitas (£5-8), or sample the green coriander soup. (☎ 552202. Open daily noon-10:30pm.) You don't have to be a scientist to understand the chemistry of **CH2,** 37 Exeter Rd.: modern decor, inexpensive lunch specials, and fusion cuisine are a reactive combination. (Open daily noon-2:30pm and 6-10:30pm.) Those with a sweet tooth shouldn't pass up **Shake Away,** 7 Post Office Rd., which serves over 100 flavors of milkshakes (£1.95), from the conservative marshmallow to the outrageous pecan popcorn. (☎ 310105. Open daily 9am-5:30pm.)

▮▮ SIGHTS AND BEACHES. The **Russell-Cotes Art Gallery and Museum,** East Cliff, houses a remarkable collection of Victorian art and sculpture, and the building is a fine sample of Victorian architecture itself. (☎ 451800. Open Tu-Su 10am-5pm. Free.) The **Shelley Rooms,** Beechwood Avenue, Boscombe, contain a small collection of Percy Bysshe Shelley memorabilia that only the poet's die-hard fans will appreciate. (☎ 451500. Open Tu-Su 2-5pm. Free.) For more of the Shelley clan, the remains of Mary Shelley, author of *Frankenstein*, rest in **St. Peter's** parish church, on the corner of Hilton Rd.

Careful city planning left one-sixth of Bournemouth's total area dedicated as **public gardens** ideal for a stroll or a picnic. Though not free, the internationally themed gardens of **Compton Acres,** Canford Cliffs Rd., Poole, are reputedly the finest in England. (Open Mar.-Oct. daily 10am-5pm. £4.95, seniors £3.95, children £2.45.) Many prefer to pursue their outdoor activities along the seven miles of clean, sandy shoreline known as **Bournemouth Beach.** The area surrounding **Bournemouth Pier** (☎ 451781) has been spoiled by cheap amusements, but a short walk will take sunbathers to relatively uncrowded spots where they can rent bungalows and deck chairs for the afternoon.

🎭🎆 ENTERTAINMENT AND FESTIVALS. Bournemouth's nightlife has received a revitalizing boost from swarms of foreign-language students and young vacationers. A large number of clubs and bars line **Christchurch Rd.** For mainstream club beats with a sprinkling of soul, local kiddies visit **The Zoo** and **The Cage,** both under the same roof on Firvale Rd., off Christchurch Rd. (Open M, W, and F-Sa.) A little remodeling has transformed a theater into **The Opera House,** 57 Christchurch Rd. Prepare to pay £2-10 to dance with the fashionable clientele. Every summer Wednesday since 1896, 15,000 candles have lit up the Lower Gardens during the **Flowers by Candlelight Festival.** Bournemouth's **music festival** (☎ 451702), in late June, is another popular way to spend a lazy summer day.

LYME REGIS ☎01297

Known as the "Pearl of Dorset," Lyme Regis (pop. 3500) perches precariously on the face of a hillside on the Dorset coast. Steep climbs, startling views, and stunning natural beauty entice both budget travelers and would-be beach bums to this quiet hamlet, where you can hear the sigh of waves from the main road. The stark coast, with its waves receding into infinity, and the echoes of the Cobb have inspired intellectuals over the years. It was here that Jane Austen worked and vacationed and Whistler painted *The Master Smith* and *The Little Rose.* More recently, native John Fowles set his neo-Victorian novel *The French Lieutenant's Woman* in Lyme Regis, and part of the movie was filmed on location.

🚉📋 GETTING THERE AND PRACTICAL INFORMATION. Lyme Regis makes a fine daytrip from Exeter, and is also accessible from Weymouth. To reach Lyme by **train** (☎ (08457) 484950), stop at **Axminster** (5 mi. north of Lyme on the A35) and transfer to **Southern National** (☎ (01305) 783645) bus #31 or X31 (1 per hr., £1.50). Southern National bus #X53 goes directly to Lyme from **Exeter** (£4.40).

The **tourist information centre** sits on Church St. at Guildhall St., and helps you look for a bed. Walk down the hill from the bus stop, turn left onto Bridge St. and walk straight ahead. (☎ 442138. Open M-F 10am-6pm; in summer also Sa-Su 10am-5pm.) Services include: **banks** on Broad St., including **Lloyds TSB,** 54 Broad St. (open M-Tu and Th-F 9am-4:30pm, W 9:30am-4:30pm); **Internet access** at **LymeNet,** Church St. (☎ 444570; M-F £3 per 30min., Sa free; open M-Th 9am-8pm, F 9am-4pm, Sa 10am-1pm); a **launderette,** Lyme Close (☎ 443461; wash £2, soap 20p; open daily 8am-9pm); the **police** (☎ 442603), Hill Rd.; **Axminster Hospital** (☎ 32071), Chard Rd., Axminster; and the **post office,** 37 Broad St. (☎ 442836; open M-F 8:30am-5:30pm, Sa 8:30am-6pm). **Postal code:** DT7 3QF.

🏠🍴 ACCOMMODATIONS AND FOOD. The **Newhaven Hotel,** at the start of Pound St., has ocean glimpses, a cheerful hostess, and impressive breakfasts, including omelettes and smoked mackerel fillet. (☎ 442499. £19.50 per person in summer; £17 in winter.) **Camp** at **Hook Farm,** a 25-minute walk along the River Exe footpath. (☎ 442801. £2 per person, additional £1 each for tent and car.)

Coffee shops and greengrocers line **Broad St.,** the town's main strip, and fish and chips sizzle where the **Cobb** meets **Marine Parade.** Pubs along Broad St. offer generous portions of food in dark-wooded decor; try **The Volunteer Inn,** 31 Broad St. (☎ 442214), or the **Royal Lion,** 60 Broad St. (☎ 445622). For excellent seafood (fresh cooked crab £6.50) and a view, stroll down to the **Cobb Arms** pub on Marine Parade. (☎ 443242. Open daily 7am-11pm, food served until around 9pm.) Wholefoods abound at **Lyme Green,** 57-58 Ground Floor, Broad St., where their Lyme green pie (£2.95) pays homage to both the town and the tart green fruit. (☎ 444936. Open M-Th 9:30am-5:30pm, F-Sa 9am-6pm.)

◨⬛ SIGHTS AND ENTERTAINMENT. Lyme's stone **Cobb,** a large rock seawall, curves out from the land to cradle the small harbor. In Jane Austen's *Persuasion,* Louisa Musgrove suffered an unfortunate fall here and brightened Anne Elliot's prospects. A few years ago, a man who fell off the Cobb evoked a national scandal by suing the government for £96,000, presumably charging that the rocks were negligent for getting wet. Footpaths wind along the coast towards Seaton and over clifftops to Charmouth. Navigate down to the beach itself to enjoy the abundant rock pools. The **Marine Aquarium** on the Cobb features local catches such as luminescent, frighteningly magnified models of plankton. Ask them to show you the sea mice. (☎ 443678. Open May-Oct. daily 10am-5pm; later in July-Aug. Wheelchair access. £1.40, students and seniors £1.10, children 90p, under 5 free.) Chalkboard notices on the Cobb advertise **fishing trips.** Call the *Predator* (☎ 442397) or the *Neptune* (☎ 443606) for details (3hr. trips £10). History buff Richard J. Fox, former world-champion town crier, conducts **tours** dressed in 17th-century military regalia on Tuesdays in July and August at 3pm. Inquire at Country Stocks, 53 Broad St., or meet at the Guildhall. (☎ 443568. 1½hr. tours £1.50, children £1.20.) The **Philpot Museum,** Bridge St., a museum recently refurbished under Sir David Attenborough's auspices, houses local fossils and chronicles Lyme Regis's geological and cultural histories. (☎ 443370. Open Apr.-Oct. M-Sa 10am-5pm, Su 10am-noon and 2:30-5pm. £1.20, students and seniors £1, children 50p.)

The green expanse of **Langmoor Gardens,** accessible from Pound St., looks down upon the ocean and includes lonely palm trees, standing like exiles from across the sea. Follow the signs and turn off Coombe St. to the left to reach the **Riverside Walk,** a short path with lovely garden views and the Lym hurrying past on both sides. A small stone memorial marks where the Lepers' Hospital once stood. In the summer, several **festivals** visit Lyme Regis. Popular among these are the **Jazz Festival** (early July) and the **Regatta Carnival** (early August).

DEVON

EXETER   ☎01392

Exeter (pop. 110,000) has had a much-beleaguered history. In 1068, the inhabitants of Exeter earned the respect of William the Conqueror, holding their own against his forces for 18 days. When the wells within the city ran dry, the Exonians used wine for cooking, bathing, and (of course) drinking, which might explain why the city finally fell. As the years went by, Exeter's cathedral (built in 1133) made it the religious center of the southwest, and it gradually developed into a major city and the county seat of Devon, only to be flattened in a few days of Nazi bombing in 1942. Frantic rebuilding has made Exeter an odd mixture of the venerable and the banal: Roman and Norman ruins poke from parking lots, and the cash registers of a bustling department store stand atop a medieval catacomb.

▐ GETTING THERE AND GETTING AROUND

Trains and buses travel to Exeter from London and Bristol and transfer here for trips to the rest of Devon and Cornwall.

Trains: Exeter St. David's Station, St. David's Hill. Ticket office open M-F 5:45am-8:40pm, Sa 6:15am-8pm, Su 8am-8:40pm. Trains (☎ (08457) 484950) from **London**

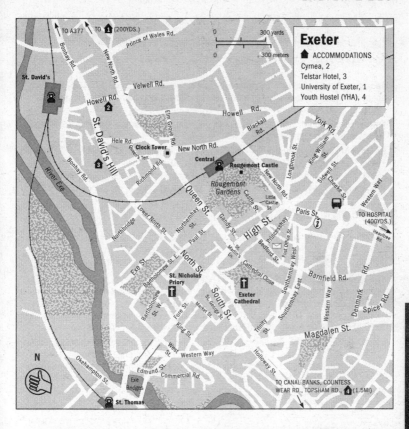

Exeter

🏠 ACCOMMODATIONS
Cyrnea, 2
Telstar Hotel, 3
University of Exeter, 1
Youth Hostel (YHA), 4

Paddington (2½hr., 2 per hr., £39) and **Bristol** (1½hr., 1 per hr., £13.60). **Exeter Central Station,** Queen St., next to Northernhay Gardens. Office open daily 8am-6pm. From **London Waterloo** (3hr., 6 per day, £38.30).

Buses: Paris St. (☎ 256231), off High St. Open M-Sa 8:30am-6pm, Su 9am-5pm. 24hr. lockers (50p-£2). **National Express** (☎ (08705) 808080) comes in from: **London Victoria** (4hr., every 90min., return £16); **Bristol** (2¾hr., 7 per day, £10.50); and **Bath** (2¾hr., 3 per day, £13).

Public Transportation: Minibuses shuttle between city areas. An **Exeter Freedom Ticket** allows unlimited travel (£2.50 per day, £8.25 per week; 2 passport-sized photos needed for week passes).

Taxis: Capital (☎ 433453) and **City Central** (☎ 434343).

🚹 PRACTICAL INFORMATION

Tourist Information Centre: At the Civic Centre in the City Council Building, Paris St. (☎ 265700), across the street from the rear of the bus station. Books accommodations for a 10% deposit. Wheelchair access. Open M-Sa 9am-5pm; summer also Su 10am-4pm.

Tours: An institution for over a decade, the Exeter City Council's 1½hr. themed **walking tours** (☎ 265203) are frequented as often by locals as tourists and are the best way to explore this idiosyncratic city. Most walks leave from the front of the Royal Clarence Hotel on High St.; the "Port of Exeter" tour departs from the Quay House Visitor Centre on the Quay. Apr.-Oct. 4-5 per day; Nov.-Mar. 11am and 2pm. Free.

Financial Services: Banks are easy to find, including **Barclays**, 20 High St. (☎ 602200). Open M-W and F 9am-5pm, Th 10am-5pm, Sa 9:30am-noon. **Thomas Cook,** 9 Princesshay (☎ 601300). Open M-W and F 9am-5:30pm, Th 10am-5:30pm.

American Express: 21-23 Princesshay (☎ 493222). Open M-W and F 9am-5:30pm, Th 9:30am-5:30pm, Sa 9am-5pm.

Launderette: St. David's Launderette, 24 St. David's Hill (☎ 274459), halfway between the town center and the train station. Bring soap and 20p coins. Open daily 8am-9pm, last wash 8pm.

Police: Heavitree Rd. (☎ (0990) 777444), three blocks past the junction of Heavitree Rd., Western Way, and Paris St.

Internet Access: Hyperactive (☎ 201544), Castle Street, off High Street, in the Central Train Station building. £2.50 per 30min., students £2.25. Open M-F 10:30am-7:30pm, Sa 10am-6pm, Su noon-6pm. The **library** books free 20min. slots on the computer.

Post Office: Bedford St. (☎ 423401). Open M-Sa 9am-5:30pm. **Postal Code:** EX1 1AA.

■ ACCOMMODATIONS

Exeter's less expensive B&Bs flourish on **St. David's Hill,** between the train station and the center of town, as well as on **Howell Rd.,** closer to the Central Station. There are also limited accommodations at the **University of Exeter** (☎ 211500).

YHA Exeter, 47 Countess Wear Rd. (☎ 873329; fax 876939), 2 mi. southeast of the city center off Topsham Rd. Take minibus #K or T from High St. to the Countess Wear Post Office (97p). Follow Exe Vale Rd. to the end and turn left. Spacious, cheery hostel. Reception open 8-10am and 5-10pm. No curfew, but ask for the door code. Dorms £10.15, under 18 £6.85. About 10 **campsites** at half the price of dorm beds.

Telstar Hotel, 77 St. David's Hill (☎ 272466; telstar_hotel@compuserve.com). Eager-to-please owners (and their friendly black dog) usher you into large, comfortable rooms. Their full breakfast includes a fresh fruit salad. Book a week ahead in summer. Singles £17 in summer, less offseason; doubles from £32.

Cyrnea, 73 Howell Rd. (☎/fax 438386). Central location and friendly atmosphere. If Mr. Budge is home when you call, he may pick you up from the station. £15-17 per person.

■ FOOD AND PUBS

St. George's Market, 91 High St., holds several stalls selling produce and meats. (Most stalls open M-Tu and Th-Sa 8am-5pm, W 8am-3pm.) A small **Sainsbury's** stands in the Guildhall Shopping Centre off High St. (☎ 217129. Open M-W and F 8am-6:30pm, Th 8am-7pm, Sa 7:30am-6pm, Su 10:30am-4:30pm.)

Exeter has a dearth of cheap restaurants, though there are a few outside the town center near Central Station along **Queen St.** At **Herbies** (as in herbivorous), 15 North St., you'll find leafy delights for £3 to £4. (☎ 258473. Open M 11am-2:30pm, Tu-F 11am-2:30pm and 6-9:30pm, Sa 10:30am-4pm and 6-9:30pm.) To escape the crowds on High St., duck into **Cripes!,** 21 Gandy St., for crepes (from £4) and lunchtime specials. (☎ 491411. Open daily noon-11pm.) **Christie's Patisserie,** 29 Gandy St., serves hefty, made-to-order sandwiches (£1.35-1.60) and savories (most under £1) with a vegetarian spin. (☎ 423003. Open M-F 8am-5pm, Sa 8am-5:30pm.)

Pubs abound in Exeter—many hide in the alleys off **High St.** A skeleton guards the medieval well in the basement of the **Well House Tavern,** on Cathedral Close (an annex of the ancient and blue-blood-haunted Royal Clarence Hotel), while hearty ale flows upstairs. (☎ 319953. Open M-Sa 11am-11pm, Su noon-10:30pm; food served noon-2pm.) When Sir Francis Drake wasn't aboard his own ship, he preferred no place to the **Ship Inn,** 1-3 St. Martin's Ln., off High St. Burgers cost less in the pub and snack bar downstairs; upstairs is plush and more expensive. Look for their many promotions. (☎ 272040. Open M-Sa 11am-11pm, Su noon-10:30pm.) Duck into **Coolings,** 11 Gandy St., for a relaxed atmosphere and a young local crowd. (☎ 434184. Open daily 9:30am-11pm; food served until 5:30pm.)

SIGHTS

EXETER CATHEDRAL. The west front holds hundreds of stone figures in various states of mutilation, crowned by a statue of St. Peter as a virile naked fisherman. Inside, effigy tombs, including cadavers, line the walls, and shattered flagstones mark the chapel where a German bomb landed in 1942. When the intricate 15th-century clock strikes one, look for the tiny hole in the wooden door beneath, where the bishop's cat once ran in after mice (hence, perhaps, "Hickory Dickory Dock"). The building has been extensively (and expensively) restored, thanks to a staunch campaign by locals and the patronage of Prince Charles. The 60 ft. **Bishop's Throne,** made without nails, was disassembled in 1640 and again during World War II to save it from destruction. A collection of manuscripts, donated to the cathedral in the 11th century by the munificent Bishop Leofric and known to modern scholars as the **Exeter Book,** is the richest treasury of early Anglo-Saxon poetry in the world. The book is on display in the cathedral library. Ask at the information desk about the shortcut. (☎ 255573. Cathedral open daily 7am-6:30pm; library open M-F 2-5pm. Evensong services M-F 5:30pm, Sa-Su 3pm. Free guided tours Apr.-Oct. M-F 11:30am and 2:30pm, Sa 11am. Requested donation £2.50, seniors £1, families £5.)

ST. NICHOLAS PRIORY. The 900-year-old building used to enclose much of today's High St. in its walls. It has a medieval guest hall and kitchen, along with a timeworn toilet seat young Arthur himself couldn't lift. (Take the alleyway next to The Mint at 154 Fore St. ☎ 665870. Open Easter-Oct. M, W, and Sa 2:30-4:30pm. 50p.)

THE ROYAL ALBERT MUSEUM. To piece together what reduced the St. Nicholas Abbey to its remaining priory, explore the museum's thorough reconstruction of Exeter and Devon through epochs. The museum also houses a large elephant from Kenya and an impressive collection of exotic butterflies. (Queen St. ☎ 265858. Open M-Sa 10am-5pm. Free.)

THE UNDERGROUND PASSAGES. Six hundred years ago, the church built underground passages to deliver clean water to the church community. Not to be outdone, wealthy merchants built their own subterranean piping network. Access to the passages has since become easier for the common man. Although the pipes were pilfered a few hundred years ago, you can still explore the passages, which are two by six feet and contain doors built by Cavaliers from 1642 to 1646 to keep out besieging Roundheads—not for the claustrophobic. (Accessible from Romangate Passage next to Boots on High St. ☎ 265887. Open July-Sept. M-Sa 10am-5:30pm; Oct.-June Tu-F 2-5pm, Sa 10am-5pm. 2 tours per hr.; last tour 4:30pm. Book tickets in person by noon during July and Aug. Tours £3.50, concessions £2.50, families £10.)

OTHER SIGHTS. After his siege, William the Conqueror built **Rougemont Castle** on Castle St. to keep the locals in check. The ruins between High St. and Central Station include a gatehouse dating from 1070. The immaculate flower beds of the Regency-era **Rougemont Gardens** surround the remaining castle walls. Due to security at the adjacent court building, tourists can only view the ruins from a non-photogenic angle below; there are no good views unless you're on trial. (Free. Crime does not pay.) The expansive 17th-century **Northernhay Gardens** unfold just beyond the castle and the preserved **Roman city walls.**

♫ ⚘ ENTERTAINMENT AND FESTIVALS

The Cavern, in a brick cellar at 83-84 Queen St., hosts up-and-coming bands every night; check the kiosks plastered in fluorescent paper on High St. for details. (☎ 495370. Open Su-Th 8:30pm-1am, F-Sa 8:30pm-2am; cafe open M-Sa 11am-2:30pm.) Exeter's students hang at the **Double Locks,** on Canal Banks towards Topsham from the Exe Bridges. A boat leaves every hr. from the Quay during the day. (☎ 256947. Open M-Sa 11am-11pm, Su noon-10:30pm.) The professional **Northcott Theatre** company, based on Stocker Rd. at the University of Exeter, performs throughout the year. (☎ 493493. Tickets £7-15, student standbys £6.) The **Arts Booking and Information Centre** (☎ 211080), opposite Boots just off High St., supplies monthly listings of cultural events in the city. The **Exeter Festival** features concerts, opera, talks, and an explosion of theater for three weeks in July (call the Arts Centre for details). Pick up your spirits at the 3-day **Blues Festival** during the second May bank holiday; contact the TIC for details.

EXMOOR NATIONAL PARK

Once a royal hunting preserve, Exmoor is among the smallest of Britain's national parks, covering 265 sq. mi. on the north coast of England's southwestern peninsula. Dramatic sea-swept cliffs fringe moors cloaked in purple heather where sheep and cattle graze. Wild ponies still roam, and England's last herds of red deer graze in woodlands between the river valleys. Although over 80% of Exmoor is privately owned (as in most British national parks), the territory is accommodating to respectful hikers and bikers.

▐ GETTING THERE

You'll get to Exmoor with fewer gray hairs if you grab a copy of the *Exmoor and West Somerset Public Transportation Guide*, free from tourist information centres (TICs). The guide provides bus timetables as well as vague but well-meaning walking maps. Exmoor's western gateway, **Barnstaple**, is a good hiking base. **Trains** (☎ (08457) 484950) arrive in town from **Exeter St. David's** (1hr., 1 per hr., £10.10). **National Express** (☎ (08705) 808080) **buses** chug from **London** (5hr., 3 per day, £27) and **Bristol** (2½hr., 2 per day, £18.60). Catch **Western National** (☎ (01208) 79898) bus #86 to Barnstaple from **Plymouth** (2½hr., 2 per day, £4.10). **Stagecoach** bus #315 rolls from **Exeter** to **Ilfracombe** (2¼hr., M-Sa 2 per day, £6). For more information, call the bus station in Plymouth (☎ (01752) 222666) or Exeter (☎ (01392) 256231).

You can reach **Minehead**, Exmoor's eastern gateway, by **Southern National** (☎ (01935) 476233) **bus** #600 from **Porlock** (7 per day, £1.45) and #928 from **Taunton** (1¼hr.; M-Sa 1 per hr., Su 4 per day, £3.20). To get to Taunton, take the train from **Exeter** (25min., £7). **West Somerset Railway** (☎ (01643) 704996), a private line, runs to **Minehead** from **Bishops Lydeard**, 4 mi. from Taunton (1¼hr.; July-Aug. 4-7 per day, May-June and Sept.-Oct. 4 per day; £5.40). Buses shuttle to Bishops Lydeard from the Taunton train station.

▐ GETTING AROUND

Although getting to the outskirts of Exmoor by public transportation is relatively easy, bus service within the park is erratic. Again, the *Exmoor and West Somerset Public Transportation Guide*, found at all TICs near Exmoor, is invaluable. Buses from **Minehead** run to: **Ilfracombe** (Devon Bus #300, 2hr., M-F 2 per day, £4.70); **Williton** (Bryants Coaches #305-7, 30min., M-Sa 1 per hr., £1.10); and **Dunster** (Southern National #34, M-Sa 1 per hr., 65p). **North Devon Bus** (☎ (01271) 45444) runs from **Barnstaple** to **Ilfracombe** (M-Sa 2 per hr., £1.60) and from **Ilfracombe** to **Combe Martin** (1 per day, 80p). *Accessible Exmoor*, free from National Park Information Centres, provides a thorough guide to the park for disabled visitors.

Exmoor is best toured on **foot** or by **bike**; Exmoor is relatively flat, and large parts of the park are reserved for cyclists. Two long-distance paths are the **Somerset and North Devon Coast Path** for hikers and the **coastal path**, which follows the ghost of the Barnstaple railroad, for bikers. Both routes pass through or near the towns of (west to east) Ilfracombe, Combe Martin, Lynton, Porlock, Minehead, and Williton. The **Tarka Trail** traces a 180 mi. figure-eight (starting in Barnstaple), 31 mi. of which are bicycle-friendly.

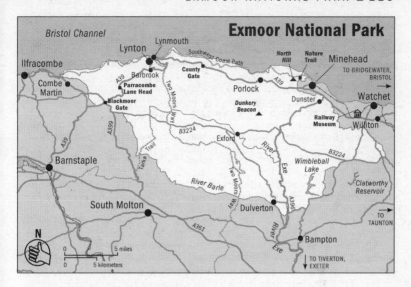

Exmoor National Park

🛈 PRACTICAL INFORMATION

The National Park Information Centres listed below supply detailed large-scale Ordnance Survey maps of the region (£5.25), bus timetables, and the invaluable *Exmoor Visitor*. The centers offer themed guided walks of 1½-10 mi. Always be prepared for a sudden rainstorm. Sea winds create volatile weather, and thunderstorms blow up without warning. Be sure to stock up on food and equipment in the larger towns, as stores in coastal villages have smaller selections.

NATIONAL PARK INFORMATION CENTRES

Combe Martin: Seacot, Cross St. (☎/fax (01271) 883319), 3 mi. east of Ilfracombe. Open Easter-Sept. daily 10am-5pm; open until 7pm in peak season.

County Gate: A39, Countisbury (☎ (01598) 741321), 7 mi. east of Lynton. Open daily Apr.-Sept. 10am-5pm; Oct. 10am-4pm.

Dulverton: Dulverton Heritage Centre, The Guildhall, Fore St. (☎ (01398) 323841). Open daily Apr.-Oct. 10am-5pm; limited winter opening.

Dunster: Dunster Steep Car Park (☎ (01643) 821835), 2 mi. east of Minehead. Open Apr.-Oct. daily 10am-5pm; limited winter opening.

Lynmouth: The Esplanade (☎ (01598) 752509). Open daily Apr.-Jul. and Sept.-Oct. 10am-5pm; Aug. 10am-6pm; limited winter opening.

TOURIST INFORMATION CENTRES

Barnstaple: 36 Boutport St. (☎ (01271) 375000). Open Apr.-Oct. M-Sa 9:30am-5pm.

Ilfracombe (Il-fra-COOM): The Landmark Seafront, in the Landmark Theatre (☎ (01271) 863001). Open Easter-Sept. M 9:30am-showtime, Tu-F 10am-showtime, Sa 11am-7pm, Su 10am-8:15pm; Nov.-Easter M-F 10am-5pm.

Lynton and Hunmouth: Town Hall, Lynton (☎ (01598) 752225). Also has info on Lynmouth. Open Easter-Oct. daily 9:30am-6pm; Nov.-Mar. M-Sa 9:30am-1:30pm.

Minehead: 17 Friday St. (☎ (01643) 702624). Open July-Aug. M-Sa 9:30am-5:30pm; Apr.-June and Sept.-Oct. 9:30am-5pm; Nov.-Mar. M-Sa 10am-4pm.

ACCOMMODATIONS

Rain or shine, hostels and B&Bs ($14-16) fill up quickly; check listings and the *Exmoor Visitor* at the TIC. At busy times, **camping** may be the easiest way to see the park. The *Exmoor Visitor* lists several caravan parks that accept tents, but campsites that don't advertise are easy to find, especially near coastal towns. Most land is private; before pitching a tent, ask the owner's permission. The quality of Exmoor's **YHA Youth Hostels** varies widely according to proprietor and location. In general, you can expect small accommodations with a kitchen, a day lockout (usually 10am-5pm), a curfew (around 11pm-midnight), and no laundry facilities.

YHA Crowcombe: (☎/fax (01984) 667249), Crowcombe Heathfield. A large house in the woods on the Taunton-Minehead Rd., 2 mi. from Crowcombe Heathfield below Quantock Hills. Turn onto the road marked "Crowcombe Station & Lydeard St. Lawrence." The hostel is 1 mi. down the road, on the left. Open mid-Apr. to early May and July-Aug. daily; early May to June F-W. Dorms £9, under 18 £6.20.

YHA Elmscott: (☎ (01237) 441367; fax 441910), 4 mi. southwest of Hartland village by footpath. Extremely difficult to find—get a map before you go. On weekends bus #199 goes to Hartland. Call for off-season times. Dorms £9, under 18 £6.20.

YHA Exford: (☎ (01643) 831288; fax 831650), Withypoole Rd., Exe Mead, Exford. The superior hostel is next to the River Exe bridge, the first road on the left. In the center of the moorland. Laundry facilities. Open July-Aug. daily; mid-Feb. to June and Sept.-Oct. M-Sa. Dorms £9.80, under 18 £6.75.

YHA Ilfracombe: 1 Hillsborough Terr., Ilfracombe (☎ (01271) 865337; fax 862652). Take Red bus #3, 30, or 123 from Barnstaple, just off the main road. Georgian house with a view of the Welsh coast. Family rooms available. Open Mar.-Oct. daily. Dorms £9.80, under 18 £6.75.

YHA Lynton: (☎ (01598) 753237; fax 753305), Lynbridge, Lynton. Take Red bus #309 or 310 from Barnstaple to Castle Hill Car Park. A former Lyn West valley hotel. Open daily July-Aug.; Sept.-Oct. Th-M; mid-Feb. to June W-M. Dorms £9.80, under 18 £6.75.

YHA Minehead: (☎ (01643) 702595; fax 703016), Alcombe Combe, Minehead, 2 mi. from the town center. Follow Friday St. as it becomes Alcombe Rd., turn right on Brook St. and follow to Manor Rd. From Taunton, take the Minehead bus to Alcombe; the bus stops 1 mi. from the hostel. Spacious grounds. Open July-Aug. daily; mid-Apr. to June M-Sa. Dorms £9.80, under 18 £6.75.

YHA Quantock Hills: (☎/fax (01278) 741224), Sevenacres, Holford, Bridgwater, 1½ mi. past the Alfoxton Park Hotel in Holford—keep right after passing through the gate by the hotel stables. From Kilze, take Pardlestone Ln. by the post office for 1 mi., then follow signs. Country house overlooking Bridgwater Bay. Open daily mid-July to. Aug. Dorms £8.10, under 18 £5.65.

BARNSTAPLE   ☎01271

Although Barnstaple, just outside the park, isn't the only suitable hiking base for the coastal path or the Tarka Trail, it is the largest town in the region, a transport center, and the best place to get camping and hiking gear and a hearty pre-trip meal. The town holds a **tourist information centre** (TIC; see above). There are daily markets at the **Pannier Market,** while **Giovanni's,** 35 Boutport St. (☎ 321274), next to the TIC, serves up Italian fare. **Tarka Trail,** conveniently located at the head of the coastal bike path, **rents bikes.** From the center of town, cross the bridge and take the second left after the bridge at the roundabout; Tarka is by the train station. (☎ 324202. $6.50-8.50 per day. Open daily 9:30am-5pm.) The coastal path provides level cycling for 15 mi., where the old Barnstaple rail tracks used to run.

Two good places to begin traipsing into the forest close to Barnstaple are **Blackmoor Gate,** nine miles northwest of Barnstaple, and **Parracombe,** two miles farther northwest along the road. Both are on Filer's Barnstaple-Lynton bus line.

MINEHEAD AND DUNSTER ☎01643

Only a mile from the park's eastern boundary, **Minehead** boasts a **nature trail** that winds past labeled vegetation and offers wheelchair access. Other well-marked paths weave through North Hill, an easy walk from the town center. The **South-West Peninsula Coast Path,** Britain's longest National Trail, ends in Minehead.

The village of **Dunster** lies three miles east of Minehead, and buses from Minehead stop at its base every hour in the summer. **Dunster Castle** towers over the former 17th-century yarn market. Home to the Luttrell family for six centuries, the castle has seen its share of battles. The elaborate interior includes a not-to-be-missed 16th-century portrait of Sir John Luttrell wading buck-naked through the surf. (☎ 821314. Open Apr.-Sept. Sa-W 11am-5pm; Oct. Sa-W 11am-4pm. Subtropical gardens open daily Apr.-Sept. 10am-5pm; Oct.-Mar. 11am-4pm. £5.40, children £2.80; grounds only £2.90, children £1.30, families £6.90.)

DARTMOOR NATIONAL PARK

Much of Dartmoor National Park, south of Exmoor and ten miles west of Exeter, is scattered with remnants of the past, from oddly balanced granite tors to Neolithic rock formations. Ramblers among the standing stones and chambered tombs littered across the 367 sq. mi. park may also come across the skeleton of a once-flourishing tin-mining industry and the heavily guarded Princetown prison. Because of its rough terrain and harsh climate, Dartmoor has remained largely untouched for centuries, except by sheep and native wild ponies. Today, many spirits linger in Dartmoor's almost mystical bleakness, the most famous being the canine immortalized in Sir Arthur Conan Doyle's *Hound of the Baskervilles.*

⌐ GETTING THERE AND GETTING AROUND

Buses are infrequent and often erratic: plan well ahead, using the schedules available at every tourist information centre (TIC). The best day to travel is Sunday, when frequencies increase and the **Sunday Rover** allows unlimited bus travel (£5, seniors and students £4.50, children £3). The **Transmoor Link,** a.k.a. **Stagecoach Devon** bus #82 (late May to Sept.; M-Sa 3 per day, Su 5 per day; £5) cuts through the middle of the park on its southwest-northeast route between **Plymouth** and **Exeter,** passing through **Yelverton** at the southwest corner of the park, and **Princetown, Postbridge, Moretonhampstead,** and **Steps Bridge** at the northeast. Stagecoach Devon bus #X38 also binds **Exeter** and **Plymouth,** stopping in **Buckfastleigh** and **Ashburton** along the park's southern edge (M-Sa 8 per day, Su 6 per day; £4.85). Sit on the right-hand side for the views. **Plymouth Buses** #X80 and **Western National** #88 and X88 run from **Ivybridge** (30min.; 3 per hr.). Plymouth Buses also run from **Tavistock,** north of Yelverton on the park's western edge (#83, 84, or 86; 1hr.; 4 per hr.); and **Okehampton,** on the northern edge (#86, M-F 9 per day, Su 2 per day).

For more information, contact the **Exeter bus station** (☎ (01392) 256231), the **Devon County Council's Public Transportation Helpline** (☎ (01392) 382800 or (01271) 382800; open M-F 8:30am-5pm), or any National Park Information Centre (see below). The invaluable *Dartmoor Public Transportation Guide,* in any nearby bus station or TIC, contains listings of relevant bus routes and useful phone numbers, and suggests walking routes. Once you've reached the park's perimeter, make your way on bike or foot, as bus connections require careful planning. A 30 mi. drive across the park takes three hours; the bus stops every time a sheep crosses its path. In winter, snow often renders the park and its tortuous roads virtually impassable. **Hitchhikers** report that rides are frequent; *Let's Go* does not recommend hitchhiking, though, as a safe mode of transport.

⚡ PRACTICAL INFORMATION

The National Park Authority conducts walks (2-6hr.; £2-4) from many locations in the park. Check the *Dartmoor Visitor*, available at the following **National Park Information Centres:**

Hantor: (☎ (01364) 661520), near Leonard's Bridge. In the bottom end of a car park just off the B3387. Open in summer daily 10am-5pm.

Ivybridge: (☎ (01752) 897035). Books accommodations within 10 mi. for a 10% deposit, beyond 10 mi. for an additional £3 fee. Open July-Aug. M-F 9am-5pm, Sa 10am-4pm, Su 10am-2pm; Sept.-June M-Sa 9am-5pm.

Okehampton: 3 West St. (☎ (01837) 53020), in the courtyard adjacent to the White Hart Hotel. Books beds for a £3 fee (you must be there in person). Open June-Aug. daily 10am-5pm; Apr. and Sept.-Oct. M-Sa 10am-5pm.

Newbridge: (☎ (01364) 631303), in the Riverside car park. Books accommodations for £2 deposit. Open Easter-Oct. daily 10am-5pm.

Postbridge: (☎ (01822) 880272), in a car park off the B3212 Moretonhampstead-Yelverton Rd. Open roughly Apr.-Oct. daily 10am-5pm; Nov.-Mar. Sa-Su 10am-4pm.

Princetown (High Moorland Visitor Centre): (☎ (01822) 890414), in the former Duchy Hotel. Wheelchair access. Open in summer daily 10am-5pm; in winter daily 10am-4pm.

Tavistock: Town Hall, Bedford Sq. (☎ (01822) 612938). Books accommodations for a £3-3.50 fee. Open Easter-Oct. M-Sa 10am-5pm; Nov.-Easter M-Tu and F-Sa 10am-4pm.

⚠ HIKING AND OTHER ACTIVITIES

Visitors should not underestimate Dartmoor's moody weather or treacherous terrain. An Ordnance Survey Outdoor Leisure 28 map (1:25,000; £6.50), a compass, and waterproof garb are essential; mists come down without warning, and there is no shelter away from the roads. Stick to the marked paths. However, since footpaths marked on the map are usually not signposted on the high moor, the terrain markings on the Outdoor Leisure map make it a better choice than the Landranger 191 or 202 maps that also cover the region (1:50,000; £5.25). The *Dartmoor Visitor*, free at TICs, is almost as indispensable as bus schedules, providing maps and information on accommodations and food. TICs also offer very detailed guides to walks, some with map supplements (50p to £9). The official **Dartmoor Rescue Group** is on call at ☎ 999. See **Wilderness Safety,** p. 53, for more information.

Most of Dartmoor's roads are hilly but good for cycling. Fishing, canoeing, and climbing are also popular. For canoeing arrangements, contact Mr. K. Chamberlain, **Mountain Stream Activities,** Hexworthy (☎ (01364) 646000). For **horse riding,** contact **Sherberton Stables,** Hexworthy (☎ (01364) 631276; £7.50 per hr.), or **Moorland Riding Stables,** Will Farm, Peter Tavy, Tavistock (☎ (01822) 810293; £6 per hr, £10 per 2hr., £18 per day).

WARNING. The Ministry of Defense uses much of the northern moor for target practice; consult the *Dartmoor Visitor* or an Ordnance Survey map for the boundaries of the danger area, and check the weekly firing timetable, available in National Park Information Centres and tourist information centres, hostels and campsites, police stations, local pubs, and the Friday papers. Danger areas change yearly, so be sure your information is up-to-date.

⛺ ACCOMMODATIONS

B&BS AND HOSTELS. B&B signs are often displayed on pubs and farmhouses along the roads. All the National Park Information Centres will give you a free accommodations list, and the Tavistock, Ivybridge, and Okehampton centres all book rooms. The YHA hostels in the park are:

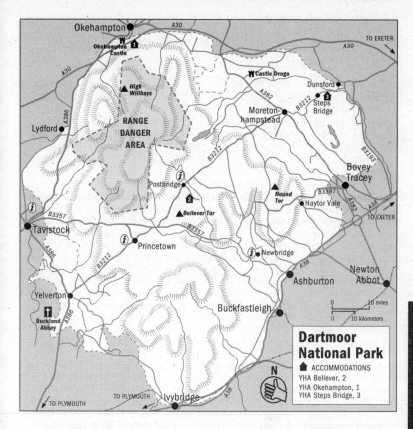

Dartmoor National Park
🏠 ACCOMMODATIONS
YHA Bellever, 2
YHA Okehampton, 1
YHA Steps Bridge, 3

YHA Bellever: (☎ (01822) 880227; fax 880302), one mile southeast of Postbridge village on bus #82 from Plymouth or Exeter to Postbridge. Ask to be let off as close to the hostel as possible. In the heart of the park and very popular. Open July-Aug. daily; Apr.-June M-Sa; Sept.-Oct. Tu-Sa. Dorms £9.80, under 18 £6.75.

YHA Okehampton: Klondyke Rd. (☎ (01837) 53916; fax 53965; okehampton@yha.org.uk). From the TIC, turn onto George St., right onto Station Rd., and continue under the bridge. Offers occasional rock-climbing trips. Open Feb.-Nov. Dorms £11, under 18 £7.50; doubles £24.50.

YHA Steps Bridge: (☎ (01647) 252435; fax 252948), one mile southwest of Dunsford on the B3212, near the eastern edge of the park. Take bus #359 from Exeter, get off at Steps Bridge, and hike up the steep drive. The warden creates vegetarian delights in this cabin in the woods. Open mid-Apr. to Aug. Dorms £8.10, under 18 £5.15.

CAMPING. Although official campsites exist, many travelers camp on the open moor. Dartmoor land is privately owned, so ask permission before crossing or camping on land. Backpack camping is permitted on non-enclosed moor land more than 100 yd. away from the road or out of sight of inhabited areas and farmhouses. Pitching is prohibited in common areas used for recreation. Campers may only stay for one night in a single spot. Don't build fires in the moors or climb fences or walls unless posted signs say you may do so. If using the official campsites below, call ahead for reservations, especially in the summer.

SOUTHWEST ENGLAND

Ashburton Caravan Park (☎ (01364) 652552), Waterleat, Ashburton: 1½ mi. from town; head north on North St. and follow the signs. July-Aug. £10 per 2-person tent, £6 per single; Easter-June and Sept.-Oct. £4 per single, £7.50 per 2-person tent.

Higher Longford Farm (☎ (01822) 613360), Moorshop, Tavistock. 2 mi. from Tavistock toward Princetown on B3357. Office open daily 10am-5pm. Open year-round. £7.50 for first adult, £2 per additional adults.

River Dart Country Park (☎ (01364) 652511), Holne Park, Ashburton. Open Apr.-Sept. £6.50 per adult, £5.15 per child.

Yertiz Caravan and Camping Park (☎ (01837) 52281), Exeter Rd., Okehampton. ¾ mi. east of Okehampton, off the A30, on the brow of a hill near the Esso garage. Open year-round. July-Aug. £2.75 per person; Sept.-June £2.25; 50p per additional camper.

⛰ SIGHTS

Postbridge and **Princetown** hover at the southern edge of the park's north-central plateau. Dartmoor's forbidding maximum-security **prison** looms over Princetown, the larger of the two towns. A walking tour with a view of the prison is available. Frenchmen from the Napoleonic Wars and Americans who fought to annex Canada in 1812 once languished within its walls. Princetown and its prison stand isolated by miles of bleak moors. The moors are the setting for one of the most famous of the Sherlock Holmes tales, *The Hound of the Baskervilles*, which emerged from an ancient Dartmoor legend of a gigantic, glowing pooch. Several peaks crown the northern moor, the highest of which is **High Willhays** at 2038 ft. **Merrivale** lies four miles outside Princetown, holding knee-high Neolithic stone circles; to get there, take bus #172 (M-Sa 2 per day, Su 3 per day; return £1.25).

The rugged eastern part of the park gathers around **Hay Tor** village. Two miles north lie Dartmoor's celebrated medieval ruins at **Hound Tor,** where excavations unearthed the remains of 13th-century huts and longhouses. Check the *Dartmoor Visitor* for guided walks on the mound and bus routes. Sir Francis Drake was born west of Hay Tor at **Tavistock.** South of Hay Tor, 2¾ mi. outside **Yelverton,** is **Buckland Abbey,** off Milton Combe Rd. Cisterian monks built the abbey in 1273; Drake later bought the abbey and transformed it into his private palace. The exterior and grounds, including the huge **Tithe Barn,** make for an interesting wander, but you may not want to bother with the lusterless interior. (☎ (01822) 853607. Open Apr.-Oct. M-W and F-Su 10:30am-5:30pm; Nov.-Mar. Sa-Su 2-5pm. Wheelchair access. £4.40, students and seniors £2.30. Grounds only £2.10, students and seniors £1.10.) The last castle built in England isn't Norman or Tudor. It's **Castle Drogo,** built between 1910 and 1930 by tea baron Julius Drewe. Convinced that he was a direct descendant of a Norman baron who had arrived in the 11th century with William the Conqueror, Drewe constructed this granite fortress in the style of his supposed ancestor. (☎ (01647) 433306. Open Apr.-Oct. Sa-Th 11am-5:30pm; grounds open daily 10:30am-5:30pm. £5.40; grounds only £2.60.)

TORQUAY   ☎01803

The largest city in the Torbay resort region, the self-proclaimed "English Riviera," Torquay isn't quite as glamorous as the French original, but still provides friendly beaches, abundant palm trees, and stimulating nightlife. Super sleuth and local resident Agatha Christie plotted many of her schemes here, and although Basil Fawlty was fictional, it was in Torquay that he ran his madcap hotel into the ground, limbs flailing wildly. Semitropical when it doesn't rain, Torquay serves as a fine base for exploring the sunnier parts of the southwestern English coast.

🗗 GETTING THERE AND GETTING AROUND. Torquay's **train station** is off Rathmore Rd., near the Torre Abbey gardens. **Trains** (☎ (08457) 484950) arrive from: **London Paddington** (3½hr., 3 per day, £52.50); **London Waterloo** (4hr., 5 per day, £52.50); **Exeter** (45min., 2 per hr., £6.60); **Plymouth** (1hr., 2 per day, £7.30); and **Bristol** (2hr., 4 per day, £21). **Buses** depart from the Pavilion; the nearby resort towns of **Paignton** and **Brixham** are accessible by the #12 bus. Call ☎ 213213, for a **taxi** 24hr.

🛈 PRACTICAL INFORMATION. The **tourist information centre** (TIC), Vaughan Parade, arranges theater bookings, discounted tickets for nearby attractions, and accommodations bookings for a 10% deposit. (☎ (0906) 680 1268; fax 214885; torquay.tic@torbay.gov.uk. Open summer M-Sa 9:30am-6pm, Su 10am-6pm; winter M-Sa 9:30am-5pm.) Services include: **banks** on Fleet St., including **Barclays** (open M-Sa 9am-4:30pm); **Thomas Cook,** Union St. (☎ 352140. Open M-Sa 9am-5:30pm); a **launderette**, 63 Princes Rd., off Market St. (£2 per load, soap 40p; open M-F 9am-7pm, Sa 9am-6pm, Su 9am-3pm); the **police** (☎ (0990) 777444), South St.; **Torbay Hospital** (☎ 614567), Newton Rd.; **Internet access** at **Cyberpoint,** 240 Union St. (☎ 297675; £2.50 per 30min.; open M and W 9:15am-5:30pm, Tu and Th 9:15am-7pm, F 9:15am-6:30pm, Sa 10am-6:30pm); and the **post office** (open M-Sa 9am-5:30pm). **Postal Code:** TQ2 5JG.

🛏🍴 ACCOMMODATIONS AND FOOD. Though the fictitious hotel in *Fawlty Towers* was in Torquay, most accommodations today promise budget-busting prices rather than side-splitting humor. Both reasonable and extravagant **B&Bs** are scattered throughout the surrounding residential areas, but most are a good 10-15min. walk from the waterfront. Since Torquay is a resort town, book well in advance for July and August. For a cheap bed, there's always **Torquay Backpackers,** 119 Abbey Rd. (☎ 299924. Dorms £8 the first night, £7 thereafter; weekly rates available.)

Buy groceries at **Somerfield,** Union Square. (Open M-Sa 8:30am-8pm, Su 10am-4pm.) Many pubs, including **Hole in the Wall,** near Park Lane, serve surprisingly good meals in a youthful atmosphere. The waterfront is lined with cheap cafes and restaurants perfect for the beacher on the go; of these, **Breezes,** Torbay Rd., by the Princess Theatre, has wonderful sandwiches. (Open daily noon-late.) If you want to splurge for dinner, **🍴 Number Seven,** Beacon Terrace, is the restaurant where you should take the plunge. This fish-obsessed bistro dishes up superb seafood in a simple setting. (☎ 295055. Open W-Sa 12:45-1:45pm and 6-10pm.)

📷 SIGHTS. To get out of the sun, head for **Torre Abbey,** Kings Drive. Founded in 1196 as a monastery and converted into a private mansion in the 16th century, the building now serves as a museum. Check out the recreation of Torquay resident Agatha Christie's study. (☎ 293593. Open daily Easter-Oct. 9:30am-6pm, last admission 5pm. £3, students and seniors £2.50, children £1.50, families £7.25.) For more on Agatha's and Torquay's history, visit the **Torquay Museum,** Museum Rd. (☎ 293975. Open M-F 10am-4:45pm; Easter-Oct. also Sa 10am-4:45pm and Su 1:30pm-4:45pm. £2.) Horticulturists will enjoy a tour around the surrounding residential areas; the **gardens** are filled with palm trees and other subtropical plants not normally associated with (or found in) the British Isles.

🏖 BEACHES AND ENTERTAINMENT. The name of **Torre Abbey Sands,** Torquay's main beach, is slightly misleading: from a distance the area looks more like a muddy strip than a sand-filled paradise. Even so, the slightest hint of blue sky sends the crowds swarming, and the beach is often saturated with more tanning bodies than grains of sand. Deck chairs can be rented (75p, 9:30am-6pm). The beaches are better north of town, where **Oddicombe, Maidencombe,** and **Watcombe** are peaceful and sandy. When the sun goes down and the beaches empty, Torquay's nightlife awakens. **Princess Theatre,** Torbay Rd. (☎ 290290), hosts a variety of productions. Among Torquay's nightclubs, **Claires,** Torwood St., stands out, with popular house music. (Open Th-Sa. Cover £2-5.) Or try the **Monastery,** Torwood Gardens Rd.

PLYMOUTH   ☎ 01752

Massive air raids during World War II left Plymouth (pop. 250,000) a cracked shell of a city. In the spaces once occupied by ancient streets and buildings, a new urban plan emerged—identical, rectilinear rows of buildings and awkward thoroughfares. Plymouth is famed for being a port city—the English fleet set off from here to defeat the Spanish Armada in 1588. But while sailors still start and finish voyages at the historic Barbican, Plymouth's transformations have left it with only patches of that past. Sir Francis Drake, Captain Cook, the Pilgrims, Lord Nelson, and millions of emigrants to the United States and New Zealand immortalized Plymouth's name in their haste to sail away from it. But don't be so quick to follow their lead; before heeding the age-old message to flee town, pause long enough to stroll along the seaside ramparts and soak up the bits of history left standing.

▐ GETTING THERE, GETTING AROUND, AND SAILING AWAY

Plymouth lies on the southern coast between Dartmoor National Park and the Cornwall peninsula, on the London-Penzance train line.

Trains: Plymouth Station, North Rd. Ticket office open M-F 5:30am-8:30pm, Sa 5:30am-7pm, Su 9:30am-8:30pm. Western National bus #14, 16B, 72, 83, and 84 to the city center. (It's a long walk—take a bus.) Trains (☎ (08457) 484950) from: **London Paddington** (4hr., 17 per day, £60); **Penzance** (2hr., 21 per day, £10.30); and **Bristol** (3hr., 18 per day, £44).

Buses: Bretonside Station, Western National Office (☎ 222666). **Lockers** on the downstairs platform 50p-£2. Information office open M-Sa 7am-7pm, Su 9am-5pm. **National Express** (☎ (08705) 808080) from **London** (4½hr., £20) and **Bristol** (2½hr., £18.50). **Stagecoach Devon** bus #X38 from **Exeter** runs through **Dartmoor** (1¼hr.; M-Sa 8 per day, Su 6 per day; £4.85).

Ferries: Millbay Docks. City bus #33 and 34 go to the docks (to the west of the city center at the mouth of the River Tamar). Follow signs to the ferry stand, a 15min. walk from the bus stop. Taxi to the terminal £3. Buy tickets at least 24hr. in advance, though foot passengers may need to come only 2hr. ahead. Check in 1hr. before departure, 2hr. for disabled travelers. **Brittany Ferries** (☎ (0990) 360360) to **Roscoff, France** (6hr., 12 per week, £20-58) and **Santander, Spain** (24hr., 1-2 per week, return £80-145).

Public Transportation: Hoppa and **Citybus** buses from Royal Parade (70p-£1.80).

Taxis: Plymouth Taxis (☎ 606060).

Bike Rental: Caramba! 8-9 Quay Rd., The Barbican (☎ 201544). Bikes! £10 per day, £60 per week. Credit card deposit £150! Open M-Sa 10am-5pm, Su 10am-4pm.

✦ ⁊ ORIENTATION AND PRACTICAL INFORMATION

Plymouth's center, wedged between the River Tamar and Plymouth Sound, combines lush grass and bleak buildings. Almost all the attractions and shops are scattered in a rough semicircle around the city's crown jewel, the **Hoe** (or "High Place"), the area along the coastal road and overlooking the harbor. The Hoe stretches from the rim of the blocky, metropolitan corridors of the **Royal Parade** and **Armada Way,** is home to a wide, grassy park topped by twin monuments. The city center and cobbled streets of the **Barbican** quake with tourists and shoppers.

Tourist Information Centre: Island House, 9 The Barbican (☎ 304849; fax 257955), Sutton Harbour. In a building said to have housed the Pilgrims just before their departure on the *Mayflower* (look for a list of those on the boat). Books accommodations. Free map. Open M-Sa 9am-5pm, Su 10am-4pm.

Tours: Guide Friday bus tours (☎ 222221) leave every 20min. from stations near the Barbican and the Hoe. £5.50, students and seniors £4.50, children £1.50, families £9. **Boat cruises** around the harbor depart sporadically from spots near the *Mayflower* shrine on the Barbican; check boards there for times and prices.

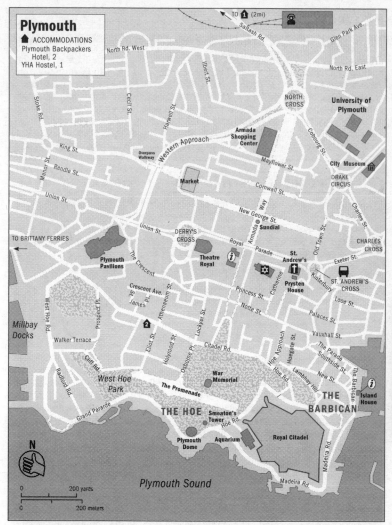

Plymouth

🏠 ACCOMMODATIONS
Plymouth Backpackers
   Hotel, 2
YHA Hostel, 1

Financial Services: Banks are plentiful along Royal Parade and Armada Way. **Thomas Cook,** 9 Old Town St. (☎ 667245), opposite the post office. Open M-Sa 9am-5:30pm.

American Express: 139 Armada Way (☎ 228708), in the plaza formed by New George St. and Armada Way. Open M-Sa 9am-5pm.

Launderette: Hoegate Laundromat, 55 Notte St. (☎ 223031). Open M-Th 8am-8pm, F-Su 8am-7pm. Last wash 1hr. before closing. Small loads £2; soap 70p.

Police: (☎ (0990) 777444), Charles St., near Charles Cross bus station.

Hospital: Derriford Hospital, Derriford (☎ 777111). About 5 mi. north of the city center. Take bus #10, 11, or 15 from Royal Parade in front of Dingles.

Internet Access: Cyber Cafe, 15-17 PTCI House, Union St. (☎ 201830). Rub elbows with the university masses. Make reservations. £2.50 per 30min.; 20% student discount. Open M-Th 9am-8pm, F-Sa 9am-4pm.

Post Office: 5 St. Andrew's Cross. Open M-Sa 9am-5:30pm. **Postal Code:** PL1 1AB.

ACCOMMODATIONS

Inexpensive B&Bs grace **Citadel Rd.** and **Athenaeum St.** between the west end of Royal Parade and the Hoe. Rooms tend to be small but cheap ($12-15 per person).

YHA Plymouth, Belmont House, Belmont Pl., Stoke (☎ 562189; fax 605360; plymouth@yha.org.uk), 2 mi. from the city center. Take bus #15 or 81 from the train station or Royal Parade to Stoke; it's on your left. Space and elegance in a mansion with beautiful two-acre grounds. Lockout 10am-5pm. Curfew 11pm, but a door code allows later access. Book in advance. Dorms £10.85, under 18 £7.40.

Plymouth Backpackers Hotel, 172 Citadel Rd. (☎ 225158; fax 207847), 2 blocks from the west end of the Hoe. Basic dorms, laid-back atmosphere in a hostel that attracts a mix of travelers from backpackers to their grandparents. Free showers; baths £1.50. Laundry service. No curfew. Smoking allowed downstairs. Dorms £8.50, 3 days £22, £50 weekly; singles £10; triples £27.

The Caledonia, 27 Athenaeum St. (☎ 229052). Comfortably furnished, well-kept bedrooms in a central location. Ample breakfast included. Singles £17; twins from £30.

Camping: Riverside Caravan Park, Longbridge Rd., Marsh Mills (☎ 344122). Take bus #21 or 51 from the city center toward Exeter. July-Aug. £3 per person, £4 per pitch; Sept.-June £3 per person, £3.50 per pitch, £7 per car.

 ## FOOD AND PUBS

The largest supermarket in town is **Sainsbury's,** in the Armada Shopping Centre, at the top of Armada Way. (☎ 674767. Open M-Sa 8am-8pm, Su 10am-4pm.) Pick up picnic fixings at **Plymouth Market,** an indoor bazaar at the west end of New George St. (☎ 264904. Open M-Tu and Th-Sa 8am-5:30pm, W 8am-4:30pm.)

Platters, 12 The Barbican (☎ 227262). The fish around the harbor swim with terror on the faces / 'Cos they know the hordes at Platters will eat them by the pla-tes. You didn't think we'd forget to include a chippy in a port town, did you? Grab a great fish and chips for £2.95. Open daily 11:30am-11pm.

Art Garden Cafe, Parade Quay Rd. Standing out among the seaside cafes, this refreshing restaurant offers filling sandwiches and baps (£1.90-2.25). Grab a seat on the patio or enjoy the artwork inside. Open M-F 9am-5pm, Sa 9am-6pm, Su 9:30am-6pm.

Cap'n Jaspers, a stand by the Barbican side of the Harbor. Sells local catch to schools of tourists. Gobble sandwiches on picnic tables guarded by seagulls. Burgers from £1.10; half-yard hot dog £2.95. Open M-Sa 6:30am-11:45pm, Su 10am-11:45pm.

Crawl through pubs on Southside St. on the way to the Barbican; **The Ship** and **The Navy,** almost at the end of Southside St., serve seaside spirits with some fishing nets hanging about. A thirtysomething crowd frequents the **Queen's Arms** on Southside St. at Friar's Ln., while the younger set sips at **The Bank** near the cinema.

 ## SIGHTS

THE HOE. Having overseen battles with the Spanish Armada, the Hoe nonetheless creates a visual impression of its own. Climb the spiral steps and leaning ladders to the balcony of **Smeaton's Tower** for ferocious blasts of wind from the Channel and a magnificent view of Plymouth and the Royal Citadel. Originally a lighthouse 14 mi. offshore, the 72 ft. tower was moved to its present site in 1882. Legend has it that Sir Francis Drake was playing bowls on the Hoe in 1588 when he heard that the Armada had entered the Channel. English through and through, Drake finished his game before hoisting sail. *(Tower open Easter-Sept. 10:30am-5pm. 75p, seniors 55p, children 40p, free with admission ticket to the Plymouth Dome.)*

MAYFLOWER STEPS. A plaque and a not-too-weathered American flag mark the spot on the Barbican where the **Pilgrims** set off in 1620 for their historic voyage to America. Subsequent departures have been marked as well, including Sir Humphrey Gilbert's voyage to Newfoundland, Sir Walter Raleigh's attempt to colonize North Carolina, and Captain Cook's voyage to Australia and New Zealand.

PRYSTEN HOUSE. Standing behind the 13th-century **St. Andrews Church,** which was bombed in 1941, this 15th-century house contains an 11th-century tapestry and the **New World Tapestry,** which narrates the story of North American settlement and which, when finished, will be the longest in the world. Add your own stitch for £1. (*Open Apr.-Oct. M-Sa 10am-3:30pm. 50p, seniors and children 25p.*)

CHARLES CHURCH. The blackened shell of Charles Church, destroyed by a bomb in 1941, stands in the middle of the Charles Cross traffic circle half a block east of the bus station. The roofless walls are Plymouth's memorial to her citizens killed in the Blitz; grass grows where the altar used to stand. Keys to the ruin are available from the chief inspector's office at the Bretonside Bus Station.

OTHER SIGHTS. The **National Marine Aquarium,** The Barbican, offers elaborate, attractive marine-life exhibits such as a tank of sharks and an immense recreation of a coral reef. (☎ 220084. *Open Apr.-Oct. 10am-6pm; Nov.-Mar. 10am-4pm. £6.50, students and seniors £5, children £4, families £19.*) **Plymouth Gin,** Southside St., is England's oldest active gin brewery, having been at it since 1793. 40min. tours depart through the still-active distillery and give historical tidbits. (☎ 665292. *Open Easter-Dec. M-Sa 10:30am-4pm. £2.75, concessions £2.25, families £7; 50p discounts off bottles of gin with ticket.*) In 1762, the local Jewish community built a **synagogue** on Catherine St. behind St. Andrew's Church. Still active, it is the oldest Ashkenazi synagogue in the English-speaking world. The building isn't clearly labeled; from the church, turn right into the alley behind the Eyeland Express store.

🎵 🎇 ENTERTAINMENT AND FESTIVALS

The **Theatre Royal,** on Royal Parade, offers perhaps the best stage in the West Country, featuring ballet, opera and West End touring companies, including the Royal National Theatre. Discount tickets available for limited shows, usually midweek performances. (☎ 267222. From £12, student standby 30min. before curtain from £10.) Plymouth's festivals revolve around its harbour, from the **August Navy Days,** a celebration of Plymouth's great ships, to the myriad boat rallies and regattas throughout the summer months. The **British National Fireworks Championship** explodes in early August.

CORNWALL

With Cornwall's lush vegetation stretching out into the Atlantic, a look at the terrain will alert you to the fact that you're no longer quite in England. Cornwall's isolation made it a favored place for Celtic migration in the face of Saxon conquest. While there are no longer any native speakers of the Cornish language, the area remains fiercely Cornish and only tepidly English. Westward movement continues today: every year hundreds of thousands of British and foreign tourists jockey for rays on the beaches of Penzance, St. Ives, and Newquay. England's southwest tip has some of the broadest, sandiest beaches in northern Europe, and the surf is up year-round whether or not the sun decides to break through. Cornwall is also home to a rich collection of Stone Age and Iron Age monuments and stone circles, and to the pasty (PAH-stee), the region's frighteningly ubiquitous stuffed turnover.

⌐⊐🏃 GETTING AROUND

By far the best base for exploring the region is Penzance, the southwestern terminus of Britain's **trains** (☎ (08457) 484950). The main rail line from **Plymouth** to **Penzance** bypasses the coastal towns, but there is connecting rail service to **Newquay,
Falmouth,** and **St. Ives.** Trains are frequent and distances short enough that you can
easily make even Newquay a daytrip. **Rail Rover** tickets make it even easier (3 days
unlimited travel within a 7-day span £24.50, 8 out of 15 days £39).

The **Western National bus** network is similarly thorough, although the interior is
not served as well as the coast. Buses run frequently from **Penzance** to **Land's End**
and **St. Ives,** and from **St. Ives** to **Newquay,** stopping in the smaller towns along these
routes. Pick up a set of timetables at any Cornwall bus station (20p). Many buses
don't run on Sundays, and many run only May-Sept.; call the Camborne bus station
(☎ (01209) 719988) to check. **Explorer tickets** are an excellent value for those making long-distance trips or hopping from town to town (£6 per day, seniors £4). Also
potentially money-saving are 3- and 7-day **Key West** tickets (£13.90 and £23.50;
seniors £10.30 and £17.50). Cyclists may not relish the narrow roads, but the cliff
paths, with their evenly spaced hostels, make for easy hiking. For serious hikers,
the famous **Land's End-John O' Groats** cross-Britain walking route begins here.

 The Cornwall **police** are at ☎ (0990) 777444. Region-wide **helplines** include
the **Samaritans** crisis line (☎ (01872) 77277; open 24hr.); the **Cornwall AIDS
Helpline** (☎ (01872) 42520; open M-F 10am-4pm); the **Gay and Lesbian
Switchboard Cornwall** (☎ (01209) 314449; open M and F 7:30-10:30pm);
and **Women's Aid** (☎ (01736) 350319; open M-F 10am-4pm).

BODMIN MOOR

Like Dartmoor and Exmoor to the east, Bodmin Moor is high country, containing
Cornwall's loftiest points—Rough Tor (1311 ft.) and Brown Willy (1377 ft.). The
region is rich with ancient remains; for instance, Bronze Age Cornishmen littered
stone hut circles at the base of Rough Tor. Some maintain that Camelford, at the
moor's northern edge, is the site of King Arthur's Camelot, and that Arthur and his
illegitimate son Mordred fought each other at Slaughter Bridge, a mile north of
town. Keep to designated paths and the sheep won't prosecute.

⌐⊐ GETTING THERE AND GETTING AROUND

Bodmin Moor spreads north of **Bodmin** town towards **Tintagel** on the coast, and
Camelford and **Launceston,** both inland. Bodmin is the park's point of entry, accessible from all directions; however, it is not a good place to start hiking. **Trains** (☎
(08457) 484950) stop at **Bodmin Parkway** from **London Paddington** (4hr., 1 per hr.,
£61.50) and **Plymouth** (35min., 2 per hr., £6.80). **National Express** (☎ (08705) 808080)
buses arrive from **Plymouth** (1½hr., 3 per day, £3.75). The town is served directly by
buses from **Padstow** on the north coast (M-Sa 10 per day) and **St. Austell** to the
south (M-Sa 12 per day). **Western National** (☎ (01208) 79898) #X4 service arrives at
the Mt. Folly bus stop by the Bodmin post office from **Tintagel** via **Camelford** (1hr.,
1 per hr., £2.70).

Since Bodmin is not a national park, it lacks National Park Visitor Centres dedicated to the area; visit local tourist information centres (TICs) instead. **Hiking** is
convenient, especially from Camelford, and is the only way to reach the tors,
which give grand views of the boulder-strewn expanse. **Bikes** can be hired in surrounding towns. **Hitchhiking** is dangerous, especially on the A roads: the roads are
narrow, leaving drivers with only six inches of road shoulder space in some
places—hardly enough to stand. Don't hitchhike.

ACCOMMODATIONS

B&Bs may be booked through the Bodmin TIC (☎ (01208) 76616). **Colliford Tavern,** Colliford Lake, St. Neot, Liskeard, in the middle of the moorland, offers B&B. (☎ (01208) 821335. Open Easter-Dec. From £26 per person; room only from £20 per person.) The nearest youth hostels are on the beautiful, rugged northern coast of Cornwall, a few miles northwest of the moor; both have a 10am-5pm lockout and an 11pm curfew. **YHA Boscastle Harbour,** Palace Stables, Boscastle Harbor, is beautifully set among steep green hills and flowery riverbanks, and has all single beds. Take bus #X9 from Exeter, #125 from Bodmin or Wadebridge, or #X4 from Bude. (☎ (01840) 250287; fax 250615. Open June-Aug. daily; Sept.-Oct. and mid-Apr. to May W-Su. Dorms £10, under 18 £6.90.) For directions to **YHA Tintagel,** see p. 236.

BODMIN ☎01208

The unremarkable town of Bodmin (pop. 14,500) is the last supply stop before venturing onto Arthurian stomping grounds. Hidden in the quiet forests and farmlands that surround Bodmin is the stately mansion **Lanhydrock,** 17th-century Gothic on the outside and plush Victorian on the inside. Built in the 1600s and gutted by fire in 1881, the mansion retains few original features except the magnificent gallery ceiling, decorated with scenes from the Old Testament in delicate plasterwork. The estate's elaborate gardens make for pleasant picnics. To get to Lanhydrock from Bodmin, take Western National bus #55 (return £1.70) or walk 2½ mi. southeast on the A38. (☎ 73320. Open Apr.-Oct. Tu-Su 11am-5:30pm. £6.40, children £3.20, families £16; grounds only £3.20, children £1.60.)

To get to the center of town from the **Bodmin Parkway Station,** five miles out of town on the A38, hop on Western National bus #55 (£1.20). If you miss the bus, call **ABTaxis.** (☎ 75000. £4.50 between station and town.) The helpful **tourist information centre** (TIC), at the Mount Folly Car Park, sells Ordnance Survey maps of the area for £5. (☎ 76616. Open M-Sa 10am-5pm.) Services include: major **banks** on Fore St.; the **police** (☎ (0990) 777444), up Priory Rd., past the ATS car parks; and the **post office,** St. Nicholas St., just beyond the TIC up Crinnicks Hill (☎ 72638; open M-F 9am-5:30pm, Sa 9am-12:30pm). **Postal code:** PL3 1AA.

Camp a mile north of town at the **Camping and Caravanning Club,** Old Callywith Rd., with laundry, showers, and a shop. (☎ 73834. Open Mar.-Oct. Electricity £1.60. £2.75-4.05 per person, depending on season; non-members £4.30 per pitch.) At Fore St., grocers hawk edibles. **Pots Coffee Shop and Restaurant,** 55 Fore St., sells a plethora of sandwiches and jacket potatoes, and makes blackcurrant milkshakes as thick as honey. (☎ 74601. Open June-Aug. M-Sa 9am-8pm, Su 11am-2pm; Sept.-May M-Sa 9am-5:30pm, Su 11am-2pm.)

CAMELFORD ☎01840

Thirteen miles north of Bodmin, Camelford seems not to have grown much since the days when it was Arthur's Camelot (if the legend is to be believed). Tiny **Slaughter Bridge,** a mile north of town, crudely inlaid with hunks of petrified wood, marks the site where Arthur supposedly fell. Folks at the Camelford **tourist information centre,** in the North Cornwall Museum, can tell you how to find the inscribed stone marking his alleged grave. (☎ 212954. Open Apr.-Sept. M-Sa 10am-5pm.) From the center of town, **Rough Tor** is a 1¼hr. walk through mist and nervous sheep. Take Rough Tor Rd. to the end. The climb is not arduous until the 300 ft. ascent at the top, where stacked granite boulders form steps and passageways, offering a wind-ravaged lookout above the moor. To get to Camelford from **Bodmin,** take **Western National** bus #X4 (1hr.; M, W, and F 2 per day; £2.70), or #55 to Wadebridge bus station (40min., 7-8 per day, £1.70) and transfer to #22 to Camelford (1hr., 7-8 per day, £2).

TINTAGEL   ☎01840

Tintagel, six miles northwest of Camelford, is both the name of a village and of the ▨ **fortress** of Arthurian legend. Roman and medieval ruins cling to a headland besieged by the Atlantic; some have already collapsed into the sea. If you want to climb through the debris to Merlin's cave below, check for low-tide times and be careful on the steep cliffs. Though the site is a bit bludgeoned by the King Arthur's Castle Hotel and the attached Excali-Bar (ouch!), looming on a neighboring cliff, it's still possible to imagine a mythical figure stepping forth from this brittle castle hacked into the hillside. And even if you don't buy into the legends, the views are haunting. (Castle open daily July-Aug. 10am-7pm; Apr.-June and Sept. 10am-6pm; Oct. 10am-5pm, Nov.-Mar. 10am-4pm. £2.90, students and seniors £2.20, children £1.50.)

Inland lies the one-road village, lined with gift shops. In **King Arthur's Great Hall of Chivalry,** Fore St., an antechamber tells Arthur's story with spotlights and a "mist of time" laid down by a humidifier. The great hall houses not one, not two, but *three* Round Tables. (☎ 770526. Open daily in summer 10am-5pm, in winter 10am-dusk. £2.75, children £2.) The **Tintagel Visitor Centre,** Bossiney Rd., affords glimpses into the village's geological and mythical roots (☎ 779084. Open M-Sa 9am-5pm, Su 10am-4pm. Free.) Escape the gaudy Arthur homages by taking a glorious 1½ mi. walk through ▨ **St. Nectan's Glen** to its cascading 60 ft. waterfall. To go chasing waterfalls, go past the Visitor Centre out of town to Bossiney. About ¾ mi. later, take the footpath on your right across from the Ocean Cove caravan park, and follow signs through the woods. (Open daily 10am-6:30pm.)

Tintagel has no tourist information centre; for **B&Bs,** try Bossiney Rd. To get from town to **YHA Tintagel,** at Dunderhole Point, walk ¼ mi. past the 900-year-old St. Materiana's Church, then bear left through the cemetery and keep close to the shore. After 250 yd., look for the hostel's chimney, located in a hollow by the sea. Kitchen, spectacular sea views, and one happy owner. (☎ 770334; fax 770733. Open Jun.-Aug. daily; Apr.-May and Sept. Th-Tu. Dorms £9.80, under 18 £6.75.)

FALMOUTH   ☎01326

Seven rivers flow into the port of Falmouth (pop. 18,300), guarded by two spectacular castles. In the 16th and 17th centuries, Falmouth's ruthless Killigrews built a name on piracy and murder. The Killigrews were loyal to none but themselves; a particularly faithless one sold Pendennis Castle to the Spanish. Though only souvenir shops now skirmish in Falmouth, the 450-year-old fortresses of Pendennis and St. Mawes still eye each other across the narrow harbor, like two retired soldiers in seafront beach chairs, occasionally awakening to welcome modern-day armadas sailing sedately through one of the world's deepest natural harbors.

▌ GETTING THERE AND GETTING AROUND

Falmouth is about 60 mi. west of Plymouth along England's southern coast.

Trains: Three small **stations,** all stops on the Truro-Falmouth line. **Penmere Halt** is a 10min. walk northwest from town, though it's the closest stop to the tourist information centre (TIC); **Dell-Falmouth Town** is east of the center and close to budget B&B-land; and **Falmouth Docks** is nearest the hostel and Pendennis Castle. None of the stations sell tickets; instead, head for **Newell's Travel Agency,** 26 Killigrew St., The Moor, next to the TIC. (☎ 315066. Open M-F 9am-5:30pm, Sa 9am-4pm.) Trains (☎ (08457) 484950) from: **London Paddington** (5½hr., 1 per hr., £64); **Truro** (track 1; 22min., 1 per hr., £2.60); **Plymouth** (2hr.; M-Sa 17 per day, in summer Su 9 per day; £9.70); and **Exeter** (3½hr., 6 per day, £24).

Buses: Out-of-town and local **Hoppa buses** stop opposite the TIC at **The Moor,** a large traffic island on Killigrew St., perpendicular to the harbor. **National Express** (☎ (08705) 808080) from **London** (6½hr., 2 per day, £34.50) and **Plymouth** (2¼hr., 2 per day, £5.25). **Western National** (☎ (01209) 719 9880) from **Truro** (#88A, 89,

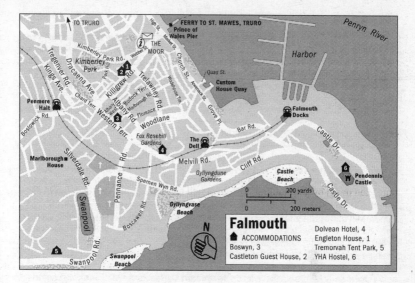

Falmouth

⌂ ACCOMMODATIONS
Boswyn, 3
Castleton Guest House, 2

Dolvean Hotel, 4
Engleton House, 1
Tremorvah Tent Park, 5
YHA Hostel, 6

X89, and X90; M-Sa 2 per hr., Su 1 per hr.; £2.20) and **Helston** (#2 and 2A, 7 per day, £3.50). **National Express** schedules and tickets at Newell's Travel Agency (see above).

Ferries: Check signs on Prince of Wales Pier and Custom House Quay for boats and ferries; several make runs around the bay, most charging £4.30.

Taxis: Falmouth & Penryn Radio Taxi (☎ 315194).

Hitchhiking: Hitchhikers report good conditions 1½ mi. out of town at Dracaena Ave., where the streets are wider; *Let's Go* does not recommend hitchhiking, even where the streets are veritable avenues.

ORIENTATION AND PRACTICAL INFORMATION

The exceptional **tourist information centre**, 28 Killigrew St., The Moor, books accommodations for a 10% deposit and has information on the Lizard Peninsula. From inland, follow signs to Killigrew Rd. or Kimberley Park Rd., then go downhill toward the river. (☎ (08700) 110018; fax (08700) 110019. Open Apr.-Sept. M-Sa 9:30am-5:30pm, July-Aug. also Su 10am-2pm; Oct.-Mar. M-F 9am-5:30pm.) **Banks** line Killigrew St., including **Lloyds TSB**, 11-12 Killigrew St. (☎ 212600. Open M-Tu and Th-F 9am-5pm, W 9:30am-5pm.) The nearest **police station** (☎ 213432) is in the nearby town of Penryn; the **Falmouth Hospital** (☎ 434700) is on Trescobeas Rd. **Internet access** is available at the **Seaview Inn**, Woodhouse Terr. Cyberpubs—whatever will they think of next? (£2 per 30min. Open M-F 11:30am-3pm and 6-11pm, Sa 11am-11pm, Su noon-10:30pm.) Internet access can also be had at the **library,** The Moor. (☎ 314901. £2 per hr. Open M-Tu and Th-F 9:30am-6pm, Sa 9:30am-12:30pm.) The **post office** is on The Moor. (☎ 312525. Open M-F 9am-5:30pm, Sa 9am-12:30pm.) **Postal code:** TR11 3RB.

ACCOMMODATIONS

The **B&Bs** on Cliff Rd. and Castle Dr. have spectacular views of the cliffs; reserve ahead and expect to pay for the thrill (£25 and up). B&Bs closer to town are cheaper, but lack beach access and views. **Dolvean Hotel,** 50 Melvill Rd., features a luxurious view of the beach and a short walk to the shore. Paul makes sure you have everything you need, including biscuits and chocolates by your bedside in the morning. (☎ 313658; fax 313995; reservation@dolvean.freeserve.co.uk. All rooms with bathroom. £25 per person.) Find comfortable accommodations with TVs in **Castleton Guest House,** 68 Killigrew St., in a 200-year-old house. Vegetarians may request alternatives to the English breakfast; everyone may request umbrellas for the English weather. (☎ 311072. From £18 per person.) **Boswyn,** Western Terr., is a plush set-up only a block or two from the beach. Comfortable rooms, all with bath, and a gregarious owner welcome you. (☎ 314667. £18.50 per person.) If you're **camping,** try **Tremorvah Tent Park,** Swanpool Rd., just past Swanpool Beach and reachable by Hoppa bus #6 (every 30min.), a lovely hillside spot with laundry and showers. (☎ 318311. £3 per night, car 50p extra; £18 per week, July-Aug. £20.)

☐ FOOD

You won't escape Falmouth without picking up the ubiquitous Cornish pasty at any bakery, coffeehouse, or barbershop on the waterfront. ("Welcome to the bank. Pasty?") The local **W.C. Rowe** and **Pengenna** bakeries vie for the title of best pasty-makers in the city. Look on the blackboard menus of the various bistros and small restaurants that line Church St. for deals. A **Tesco** supermarket is on The Moor. (Open M-Tu and Sa 8:30am-5:30pm, W-F 8am-8pm, Su 10am-4pm.) The ☒ **Citrus Café Gallery,** 6 Arwenack St., serves up refreshing milkshakes (90p), homemade doughnuts, and filling lunches (£3) with flair. (☎ 318585. Open M-W 10am-6pm, Th-Sa 10am-10pm, Su noon-4pm.) The ☒ **Warehouse Bistro** is slightly pricier, with 3-course "value meals" going for £9.45-12.75, but it's a good spot for treating your-self. (Open daily 6-10pm). **De Wynn's 19th Century Coffee House,** 55 Church St., deliv-ers exotic teas and exquisite cakes (£2) in a dainty antique-shop setting. (☎ 319259. Open M-Sa 10am-5pm, Su 11am-4pm.)

☐☐ SIGHTS AND BEACHES

Pendennis Castle, built by Henry VIII to keep French frigates out of Falmouth, now features a walk-through diorama that assaults the senses with waxen gunners bel-lowing incoherently through artificial fog. Better views and ventilation are to be found on the battlements. (☎ 316594. Open daily July-Aug. 9am-6pm; Apr.-June and Sept. 10am-6pm; Oct. 10am-5pm; Nov.-Mar. 10am-4pm. £3.80, students and seniors £2.90, children £1.90.) An occasionally wet 20-minute ferry ride across the channel ends among the thatched roofs and aspiring tropical gardens of **St. Mawes** village. (☎ 313201. Ferries depart from Town Pier and the Quay every 30min. in summer, less often in winter. £3.50 return.) On St. Mawes stands the magnificently preserved **St. Mawes Castle,** built by Henry VIII to blow holes through any Frenchman that the gunners of Pendennis spared. Henry's stone minion is now a six-story playset where schoolboys try to froth enough spit to make scary cannon sound effects. The tower is worth climbing, but Pendennis wins the battle for superior views. (Open daily Apr.-Sept. 10am-6pm; Oct. 10am-5pm; Nov.-Mar. F-Tu 10am-1pm and 2-4pm. Regardless of what the brochure might say, there is not a whit of wheelchair access. 1hr. audio tour included. £2.50, students and seniors £1.90, children £1.30.)

THE PASTY'S PAST You've watched them being baked. You've read the recipes. Maybe you've even tried them for lunch. But what the devil are past-ies? Besides being a concoction of savories and sweets stuffed into a pastry turnover pocket, pasties are a rich part of Cornwall's history. Pasties were a source of crucial sustenance in Cornwall's mining towns, providing a complete balanced meal for the miners—and the original pasties were so rock-hard that they wouldn't break if dropped down a mine shaft. Furthermore, their ridged crusts gave the perfect grip for the miners' dirty fingers, allowing workers to eat a soot-free lunch and toss the crust later. Pasties also played their part in ensuring Cornwall's safety; according to legend, the devil refused to cross into Cornwall for fear of being diced up and baked into wholesome pasties by the local housewives. Talk about paranoia!

To taste the surf, head to one of the three beaches on Falmouth's southern shore. If the skies look gray in the morning, hold a sun vigil until noon, and the Cornish weather might surprise you. **Castle Beach,** on Pendennis Head, is too pebbly for swimming or sunbathing, but low tide reveals a labyrinth of seaweed and tidepools writhing with life. **Gyllyngvase Beach** is the sandiest and has the best facilities, making it popular with windsurfers and families.

PUBS AND ENTERTAINMENT

For a fairly small town, Falmouth has a surprisingly vibrant social scene. Swill your rum and sail for booty at the **Pirate Inn** on Grove Pl., opposite the Killigrew Monument and the Quay, where local bands perform live every night. (Open M-Th 7pm-midnight, F-Sa 7pm-1am, Su 7-10:30pm.) Falmouth's hottest club, **Paradox,** on The Moor, puts in a few good hours spinning rock and chart music before heading off to bed. (☎ 314453. Cover £3. Open daily 9pm-1am.) On Friday and Saturday nights, the crowd at **The Cork and Bottle,** 67 Church St. (☎ 316909), vies to match that of **The Grapes Inn** (☎ 314704), directly across the road at 64 Church St. (both open M-Sa 11am-11pm, Su noon-10:30pm). The **Falmouth Arts Centre,** Church St., hosts art exhibitions, concerts, theater, and films. (☎ 212300. Theater tickets around £5.) The town itself throws a tizzy over the first two weeks of August with **Carnival** and **Regatta Weeks.**

NEAR FALMOUTH: THE LIZARD PENINSULA

Once a leper colony, the Lizard Peninsula between Falmouth and Penzance sits in relative isolation, untrampled by tourists. Although the peninsula's name isn't helping the tourist information centre corner the herpephobic market, visitors will probably not encounter reptilia. "Lizard" is a corruption of Old Cornish "Lys ardh," meaning "the high place." A scaly line of cliffs and caves striped with serpentine paths leads to **Lizard Point,** the southernmost prong of England, where the Atlantic becomes the English Channel. Inland, the heath of **Goonhilly Downs** is riven by slices of purple rock: the Lizard's rare minerals produce soil that yields exotic flora. Pay a visit to **Earth Station Goonhilly,** the world's largest satellite station. Exhibits, films, and a shuttle tour through the satellites' perimeter are offered, as well as a free "Internet Zone." (☎ (0800) 679593. Open daily 10am-6pm. £4, seniors £3, children £2.50.) 1½ mi. from Mullion, a village on the west coast of the Lizard, waves swirl around rocks at **Mullion Cove,** lined with steep but grassy and climbable cliffs. Hundreds of seabirds nest on **Mullion Island,** 250 yd. off the cove.

Access to the peninsula is tedious; take **Western National bus** #2 or 2A from **Falmouth** or **Penzance** to **Helston** (1hr., 2 per hr., £3), then one of the **Truronian** (☎ (01872) 273453) lines down to Mullion and the Lizard (1hr., 6 per day, £2.25 and £2.45 respectively). **Bus tours** (£5.70, children £3.80) of the peninsula leave **Penzance** (Tu 11am) and **St. Ives** (Tu 11:30am). For information on bus service into the peninsula, call Camborne (☎ (01209) 719988). **Driving** access is via the A30383 from the A394. The tiny town of **The Lizard** has capitalized handily on its unique claim to fame, enjoying a roaring (or at least hissing) trade in "serpentine sales and gifts." Snaking out of the town is the path to ⬛ **Lizard Point,** where perilous cliffside paths slither past wildflowers. A small information booth near the car park vends walking maps for a small fee. Don't waste your trip to The Lizard stuck with an inflexible tour guide; take short walks down coastal paths to the visual epiphanies of the imperious Atlantic, or skip stones amidst colossal rock caverns.

Contact the **Helston tourist information centre,** in front of the Coinagehall bus stop, if you'd like to stay the night. Pick up the free *Guide to the Lizard Peninsula* while you're there. (☎ 565431. Open M-F 10am-1pm and 2-5pm, Sa 10am-1pm and 2-4:45pm.) Stock up on cash in Helston if you need it—**banks** and **cash machines** are rare in the peninsula. **YHA Coverack,** to the southeast, is the only hostel on the peninsula; take Truronian bus #T3 from Helston to Coverack Village. (☎ 280687; fax 280119. Open July-Aug. daily; Apr.-June F-W. £9.80, under 18 £6.75.) At **Henry's Campsite,** Shetland ponies share their digs with campers. (☎ 290596. £3 per 1-person tent, £5 per 2-person, each additional person 50p.)

PENZANCE ☎ 01736

Penzance is the very model of an ancient English pirate town: water-logged, stealthy, and unabashed. The city holds an armada of ship-in-a-bottle booty raids on tourist doubloons, and the countless souvenir shops can make Penzance feel as authentic as the wooden pirates on a Disney ride. The city's most valuable treasures lie elsewhere—in its glorious sun, and in the strands of glib and mildly bawdy conversation that still float out of pubs.

▐ GETTING THERE

Trains: Wharf Rd., at the head of Albert Pier. Ticket office open M-F 6:15am-6:15pm, Sa 6:15am-6:10pm, Su 8:15am-6pm. Trains (☎ (08457) 484950) from: **London** (5½hr., 1 per hr., £54); **Plymouth** (2hr., 1 per hr., £10); and **Exeter** (3hr., 1 per hr., £19), and on another line from **Newquay** (2hr., 6 per day via Par, £11.40) and **St. Ives** (25min., 3-4 per day, £4.30). Other St. Ives trains change at **St. Erth** (25min., 1 per hr., £4.30).

Buses: Wharf Rd. (Camborne, ☎ (01209) 719988), at the head of Albert Pier. Information and ticket office open M-F 8:30am-4:45pm, Sa 8:15am-3pm, Su 9:30am-12:30pm. **National Express** (☎ (08705) 808080) from: **London** via **Heathrow** (8hr., 8 per day, £27) and **Plymouth** via **Truro** (3hr., 2 per hr., £6).

✦❼ ORIENTATION AND PRACTICAL INFORMATION

Penzance's train station, bus station, and tourist information centre (TIC) stand conveniently together on **Wharf Rd.** in the same square, adjacent to both the harbor and the town. **Market Jew St.** rises from the harbor, laden with well-stocked bakeries and ill-stacked bookstores (the street's name is a corruption of the Cornish "Marghas Yow," meaning "Market Thursday"). It mutates into **Alverton St.**, then **Alverton Rd.**, then changes face again as it turns into the A30, the road to Land's End. **Chapel St.**, the cobblestone row of antique shops and pubs, descends from the town center into a welter of alleys near the algaed docks.

Tourist Information Centre: (☎ 362207), Station Rd., between the train and bus stations. Books beds for a 10% deposit. Free map of Penzance. Open in summer M-F 9am-5pm, Sa 9am-4pm, Su 10am-1pm; in winter M-F 9am-5pm, Sa 10am-1pm.

Tours: The TIC arranges minibus tours of attractions in west Cornwall, led by the mirthful **Harry Safari** (see p. 242). **National Express, Western National,** and **Cornwall** buses offer guided tours of the area. **Western National** (☎ (01209) 719988) tours include weekly trips from Penzance to King Arthur's Country (Boscastle and Tintagel; Th 9:30am; £7.20, children £4.80), fishing villages (W 9:30am; £6, children £4), and the Lizard Peninsula (M 11am; £6, children £4).

Financial Services: Barclays, 8-9 Market Jew St. (☎ 362271). Open M-Tu and Th-F 9am-5pm, W 10am-5pm, Sa 9:30am-noon.

Launderette: Polyclean, on the corner of Leskinnick St. and Market Jew St. Soap available. Open daily 8am-8pm.

Police: (☎ (0990) 777444), Penalverne Dr., off Alverton St.

Hospital: West Cornwall Hospital (☎ 874000), St. Clare St. Take bus #10, 10A, 11, 11A, or 11D.

Internet Access: Penzance Public Library, Morrab Rd. Email 50p per 15min., net surfing £2.50 per 30min. **The Internet Place,** 28 Market Jew St. (☎ 363284). £1 per 10min., £5 per hr. Open M-Sa 10am-6pm.

Post Office: 113 Market Jew St. (☎ 363284). Open M-F 9am-5:30pm, Sa 9am-12:30pm. **Postal Code:** TR18 2LB.

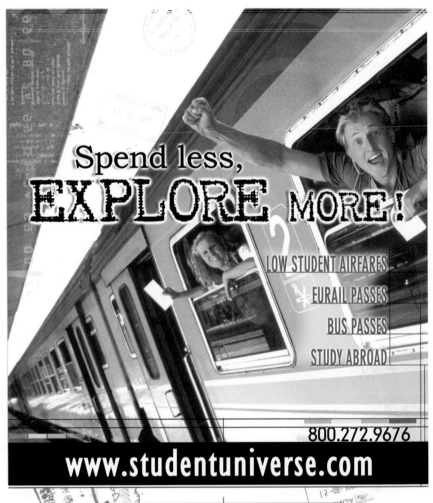

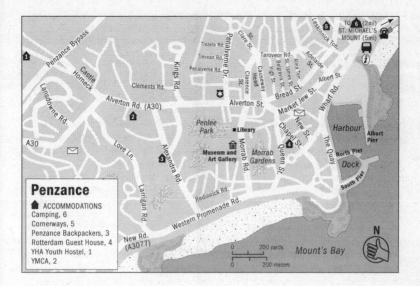

Penzance

♠ ACCOMMODATIONS
Camping, 6
Cornerways, 5
Penzance Backpackers, 3
Rotterdam Guest House, 4
YHA Youth Hostel, 1
YMCA, 2

ACCOMMODATIONS

Penzance's fleet of B&Bs (£13-16) occupies the hills above the Esplanade and beach, primarily **Morrab Rd.** between Alverton St. and Western Promenade Rd. Also check out the side streets off **Chapel St.** and, further out, **Alexandra Rd.** Camping areas blanket the west Cornwall peninsula.

YHA Penzance, Castle Horneck (☎ 362666; fax 362663; penzance@yha.org.uk). A 30min. walk, or take Hoppa bus #B and hop off at Pirate Inn, or Albert's Taxi from the train or bus stations (£2.30). An 18th-century mansion restored to its former glory amidst rich foliage. The effusive staff and the chit-chat and charm of Paul the warden keeps the place lively and colorful. Great cafeteria pizza. Classy lounge, kitchen, and laundry facilities. Reception open daily 3-11pm. Lockout 10am-1pm. No curfew. Open year-round. Dorms £10.85, students £9.85, under 18 £7.40. **Campsites** in the backyard for £5, including use of hostel facilities.

Penzance Backpackers, Blue Dolphin, Alexandra Rd. (☎ 363836; fax 363844; pzbackpack@ndirect.co.uk). A relaxed, comfortable place to take a load off. 29 beds. Internet access (8p per min.) and ample lounge. Laundry and kitchen facilities. No curfew. Dorms £8-9; doubles £18-22.

Cornerways, 5 Leskinnick St. (☎ 364645), a block from the train station. You're in luck—you'll get a warm B&B welcome from the entire royal family, past and present, and on porcelain. Friendly proprietress offers vegetarian breakfast. Book weeks ahead. Singles for £15; twins £28; triples with bath £50.

Rotterdam House, 27 Chapel St. (☎/fax 332362). Comfortable rooms and congenial proprietors—what else do you need? How about smoked haddock for breakfast and a night in a room built by Grandpa Brontë? £15 per person.

Camping: Bone Valley, Heamoor, Penzance (☎ 360313). Family-run site two miles from the city center. July-Aug. £5 per person; Sept.-June £4.50 per person; £1 per car.

FOOD AND PUBS

Expect to pay at least £7 for Penzance's excellent seafood dinners along **The Quay. Market Jew St.** fare is unexciting and expensive. The best buys are in coffee shops and local eateries on smaller streets and alleys, far from the hustle of town.

■ **The Turk's Head,** 49 Chapel St. (☎ 363093). A 13th-century pub (Penzance's oldest), sacked by Spanish pirates in 1595. A smuggler's tunnel allegedly wound here from the harbor in the 17th century. Locals drift in to sample great meats (main courses around £6). Food served M-Sa 11am-2:30pm and 6-10pm, Su noon-2:30pm and 6-10pm.

The Hungry Horse (☎ 363446), Old Bakehouse Ln., in an alley off Chapel St. Pizzas from £4, chargrilled specialties from £8.50; it's worth the splurge. Open M-Sa 7-10pm.

Snatch-a-Bite, 45 New St. (☎ 366866), off Market Jew St. at the Lloyds TSB bank. Great booty to swipe—you'll find sumptuous salads (under £3.50), sandwiches (under £2), and that rarity in Britain, a *mug* of coffee (60p). Open M-Sa 9am-5pm.

Chocolate House, 44 Chapel St. (☎ 368243). An Eden for chocoholics: forget your dentist for 10 minutes. A box of their Cornish chocs is £1.99-14. Open M-Sa 10am-5pm.

The Dolphin Tavern (☎ 364106), The Quay. Supposedly haunted by an old sea captain's ghost, this pub was the first place tobacco was smoked in Britain.

👁 SIGHTS

Penzance's attractions are enjoyable but scant. Most museums reside on or near Chapel St. Follow in the swashbuckling steps of the pirates of Penzance and use the city as a port for sailing out to Cornwall's scenic landscapes.

THE MARITIME MUSEUM. A life-like stone sailor greets visitors to this museum, which bears a resemblance to a 17th-century galleon, complete with low ceilings and plastic cannons. The museum holds shelves of corroded coins, plates, spoons, and other wreckage recovered in the 1960s from the *Association* and the *Colossus,* ships that sank off the Isles of Scilly in the 18th century. *(19 Chapel St. Open M-Tu and Th-F 11am-4pm and W 11am-2pm. £2, seniors £1.50, children £1, families £5.)*

ST. MICHAEL'S MOUNT. In AD 495, the archangel St. Michael supposedly appeared to some fishermen on Marazion, a small island across the bay from Penzance. A Benedictine monastery was built on the spot, and today St. Michael's Mount sits offshore, with a church and castle at its peak and a village at its base. The Mount is essentially a smaller and squatter version of the more celebrated Mont St. Michel, across the English Channel in Normandy. The castle's interior is unspectacular (see if you can spot Oliver Cromwell's bib); however, the grounds are pleasant, and the 30-story views captivating. Joachim von Ribbentrop, Hitler's foreign minister, had it picked out as his personal residence after the conquest of England. *(Take bus #2 or 2A to Marazion, and turn right at the post office, toward the harbor (M-Sa 3 per hr., return 80p). Access to the mount is by the painfully uneven, seaweed-strewn causeway to the island, or by ferry (return £1, children 50p, goats and sheep 50p) during high tide. ☎ 710507. Open Apr.-Oct. M-F 10:30am-5:30pm, in summer also most weekends; Nov.-Mar. in good weather. Last admission 4:45pm. £4.40, children £2.20; families £12.)*

OTHER SIGHTS. The **Penlee House Gallery and Museum,** on Morrab Rd., rotates new exhibits through elegantly sparse galleries every few months. Look for the 18th-century Scold's Bridle, a menacing discouragement for loose lips. *(☎ 363625. Open M-Sa 10:30am-4:30pm. £2, students and seniors £1, children free.)* The bizarre and gaudily painted facade of the **Egyptian House,** near the top of Chapel St., pokes fun at itself and at the 1830s craze for Egyptian ornamentation. In the wasteland of B&Bs near Morrab Rd., **Morrab Gardens** is a mirage of grassy lawns on which to rest.

🎵 🌾 ENTERTAINMENT AND FESTIVAL

It's almost compulsory for people with an interest in 1) Cornish history, 2) touring in a folk band, or 3) making jokes about Neolithic man to take a tour with ■ **Harry Safari.** It's a riotous trip through the Cornish wilds, stone circles, and Neolithic community, and easily superior to those soporific bus rides on the A30. (☎ 711427. Tours 4hr., Su-F 1 per day. $12.50, $10 for YHA hostelers.)

For seven weeks during the summer, natives and tourists flock to the open-air **Minack Theatre,** nine miles from Penzance, which puts on performances from Shakespeare to the inevitable *Pirates of Penzance.* Hacked into a cliffside at Porthcurno, the theater reportedly appeared in a dream of Rowena Cade, a Victorian who enlisted the help of sympathetic souls and constructed the amphitheater "with her own hands." A bus runs from the TIC on Wednesdays (£9.50, children £6, including show tickets). For other buses, call Western National (☎ (01209) 719988), Mount's Bay Coaches (☎ 363320), or Oates Travel (☎ 795343). Access by car is via the B3283. (Visitor center ☎ 381081. Ticket office open M-F 9:30am-8pm, Sa-Su 9:30am-5:30pm; closed noon-4:30pm during matinees. Performances £5-6, children £2.50-3; matinees £2, seniors £1.50, under 18 £1, under 12 free.)

Bacchus visits the city in June during the pagan **Golowan Festival,** featuring bonfires, fireworks, and the election of the mock Mayor of the Quay.

NEWQUAY ☎01637

At the Newquay (NEW-key; pop. 30,000) station, a range of hair-styles disembark: bald, bleached-blond, even blue. Sheathed surfboards strapped to their back, the travelers run straight for the beaches to hit the waves. Others, the imposter surfers in Airwalks, run to the pubs, tongues lapping. That's Newquay: partiers here, families there, tackiness everywhere. In summer, the population swells to 100,000, as holidaymakers seek golden beaches and tumbling waters. The surf *is* great—among Europe's best—and the parties *do* throb late into the night; just watch your step around the jaws of treacherous tourist traps.

▐ GETTING THERE AND GETTING AROUND

Trains: Cliff Rd. **Luggage** storage. (£1 per item; open daily 8:30am-3pm). Buy train tickets from **LSA Travel** at the station. (☎ 877180. Open M-F 9am-5pm, Sa 9am-4pm.) Getting to Newquay from the main London-Penzance line requires a quick stopover in the small town of **Par; trains** (☎ (08457) 484950) barrel in from: Par (50min., 1 per hr., £4.30); **Plymouth** (2hr., 1 per hr., £8.10); and **Penzance** (2hr., 1 per hr., £10.30).

Buses: 1 East St. Western National ticket office open M-F 9am-8pm, Sa 8:30am-5:30pm, Su 9am-1pm and 2-8pm. **National Express** (☎ (08705) 808080) from **London** (5¾hr., 3 per day, £26.50). **Western National** (☎ (01208) 798798) from **St. Austell** (45min.; 2 per hr., off-season M-Sa only; £2.95); **Bodmin** (2hr., 3 per day, £3.50); and **St. Ives** (2hr., June-Sept. 1 per day, £4.90). Call Jody at **Roadland Trip Overland Tours** (☎ (0800) 056 0505) for £25 trips to London—his whimsical bus ride will make the trip pass in a second.

Bike Rental: Newquay International Backpackers, 69-73 Tower Rd. (☎ 879366). £2.50 per hr., £10 per day, £50 per week.

▐ PRACTICAL INFORMATION

The **tourist information centre** (TIC) is on Marcus Hill; facing the street from the train station, turn left and go four blocks. It sells street maps for 50p and "What's On in Newquay" for £1. (☎ 854022; fax 854030; info@newquay.co.uk. Open M-Sa 9am-6pm, Su 9am-4pm; closed earlier in winter.) Get a board at **Fistral Surf,** 1 Beacon Rd., which rents all the surf paraphernalia one needs to bust the rippingest British tubes, mate. (☎ 850520. Board £5 per day, £25 per week; wetsuit £5 per day, £20 per week. Open daily 9am-6pm, until 10pm in summer.) Up-to-the-minute **surf condition updates** (☎ (0891) 360360) cost 50p per min. Services include: **Newquay Hospital** (☎ 893600), St. Thomas Rd.; **Internet access** at **Newquay International Backpackers** (10p per min.) and **Emoceanl Surf,** 2 Grover Ln. (☎ 851121; £1.50 per 15min.; open daily 9am-6pm); and the **post office,** 31-33 East St. (☎ 873364; open M-F 9am-5:30pm, Sa 9am-12:30pm). **Postal code:** TR7 1BU.

ACCOMMODATIONS

The local YHA Youth Hostel closed a few years ago, partly because its curfew was incompatible with the town's nocturnal habits, but Newquay's surfer subculture has led to loads of **independent hostels** springing up. Be wary of choosing a place to stay based solely on proximity to the beach: while some hostels are well-kept and offer initiation into the ways of the wetsuited, others are dark, dirty, and do not welcome those not already into the scene. Many advertise £5 beds to seduce surfers into staying, but that often translates into a 6-by-1 ft. rectangle of mattress-less, grimy floor space. Hordes of **B&Bs** (around £14 per night) manifest themselves near Fistral Beach, and closer to town in the avenues near the bus station, bounded by East St. and Mount Wise.

Newquay International Backpackers, 69-73 Tower Rd. (☎ 879366; back-packer@dial.pipex.com). Welcomes heaps of surf bunnies and hydrophobes alike. A fun international crowd gives the place energy to last the whole night long. Guests get clean showers; discounts on area pubs, clubs, and restaurants; and free shuttle service to and from its sister hostel in St. Ives. Internet access 10p per min. Dorms £10 in season, less in winter.

Seagull Cottage, 98 Fore St. (☎ 875648). Rooms close to Fistral Beach, a scone's throw from town. Breakfast with a jungle of parrots. £16 per person, off-season £10.

Quebec Hotel, 34 Grosvenor Ave. (☎ 874430). Simple rooms close to the bus and train stations. No singles. £12-14 per person.

Camping: Trevelque Caravan and Camping Park (☎ 851851), in Porth. Sites £4.80-5.50 per person. Or try **Hendra Tourist Park** (☎ 875778), 2 mi. east of town on the A392 beyond the Lane Theatre. From Trenance Gdns., go under the viaduct and past the boating lake, then turn left. Bus #58 runs directly from the town center every 30min. Families and couples only. Electricity £2.75. Sites £3-5 per person.

FOOD

The restaurants in Newquay pour tea and squish pasties into tourists who clamor for a quick, bland, and costly fill-up. For a cheap alternative, head for pubs with dinner specials between 5-7pm, or craft something from **Somerfield** supermarket, off Fore St. (☎ 876006. Open M-Sa 8am-11pm, Su 11am-5pm.)

Ye Olde Dolphin, 39-47 Fore St. (☎ 874262). Newquay's abysmal diet of restaurants has at least one jewel. Meals can get a bit dear here, but take advantage of their 6-8pm specials, including a 3-course meal for £8.45. Open daily 6-11pm.

Food for Thought, 33b Beachfield Ave. (☎ 871717), at the corner of Bank St. and Beachfield Ave., grills up burgers, stuffs sandwiches, and cultivates salads for £2-3. Open daily 8:30am-1:30am.

Boston's, 28-30 East St. (☎ 852626). Fires up its ovens to create tasty pizzas from £3. Open Su-Th 8:30am-11:30pm, F-Sa 8:30am-1:30am.

Wilbur's Cafe (☎ 877805), Fore St. If you're feeling a bit sodden with grease, head here for something light and homemade. Their fresh sandwiches (£1.75) and irresistible cakes (£1-1.60) pack in the crowds.

The Red Lion, North Quay Hill (☎ 872195). Pub grub at its most transcendent heights. Most homemade specials less than £6. Food served daily noon-9pm.

BEACHES AND ENTERTAINMENT

After a 3000 mi. trip across the Atlantic, winds descend on **Fistral Beach** with a vengeance, creating what most consider the best surfing conditions in Europe. The shores are less cluttered than the sea, where throngs of wetsuited surfers pile in between the troughs and crests all year. Ominous skies often forecast the liveliest surf, which can tumble from heights of 12 ft. on the best of days. Just in case the waters get too fierce, lifeguards roam the white sands May-Sept. 10am-6pm. On the bay side, **Towan Beach** and **Great Western Beach** are overcrowded with throngs of families, lured by the tamer waters. Nearby, enticing **Lusty Glaze Beach** attracts beachgoers of all ages.

If surfing and clubbing wear you out, **The Lane Theatre,** the stage for the Newquay Dramatic Society, presents a midsummer night's drama. (☎ 876945. Book tickets M-W 9:30am-2:30pm. £5-6.) Comedians and musicians also often entertain by the beach.

◤ NIGHTLIFE

The party beast stirs at about 9pm and reigns uncontested through the wee hours of the morning. The pilgrimage trail of surfer bars begins on North Quary Hill at the corner of Tower Rd. and Fore St. All the spots listed below exceed critical density at the end of July and the beginning of August.

The Red Lion (☎ 872195), on North Quay Hill at Tower Rd. and Fore St. Surfers and a young international crowd jam at this traditional first stop on the clubbing tour.

Sailors, next to the Red Lion. Features two levels, four bars, 24 video screens, a disco night on Thursday, and no dearth of tanned flesh. Dress is smarter, but still casual, like everything in Newquay. Cover £4-6 before 11pm, but up to £10 on busy nights.

Bertie's (☎ 872255), East. St. Take in some more club madness. Go on and shake what your momma gave you. Open until 1am.

San Francisco Rock Cafe (☎ 878800), Grover Ln. Newquay's newest club. Dance off what you have left of your legs to old classics. Cover around £2. Open M-W 11am-12:30am, Th-Su 11am-1:30am, Su noon-10:30pm.)

ST. IVES ☎ 01736

As I was going to St. Ives, I met a man with seven wives.
Each wife had seven sacks, each sack had seven cats,
Each cat had seven kits. Kittens, cats, sacks, and wives,
How many were going to St. Ives?

Only one, of course! But plenty of people nowadays are attracted to St. Ives (pop. 11,100), perched 10 mi. north of Penzance on a spit of land lined by pastel beaches and azure waters. The town's cobbled medieval alleyways, splashed with the color of overflowing flowerpots, have drawn visitors for more than a century. In the 1920s, a colony of painters and sculptors moved here; today, their legacy fills the windows of the countless local art galleries, including a branch of the Tate Gallery. Virginia Woolf too was bewitched by the energy of the Atlantic at St. Ives: *To the Lighthouse,* one of her masterpieces, is thought to refer to the Godrevy Lighthouse in the distance, disappearing and reappearing in the morning fog. Whether you seek the perfect muse or just the perfect strip of sand, St. Ives has it, even if it's hidden beneath a veneer of postcards and ice cream cones.

⚏ GETTING THERE AND PRACTICAL INFORMATION. Trains (☎ (08457) 484950) on the Plymouth-Penzance line run the 10min. ride from **St. Erth** (10min., 2 per hr., £3); St. Erth connects to both **Penzance** and **Truro.** Intermittent trains run directly from **Penzance** (M-F 6 per day, Sa-Su 3-4 per day). **National Express** (☎ (08705) 808080) **buses** stop in St. Ives on their way between **Plymouth** and **Penzance** (6 per day). **Western National** (☎ (01208) 798798) runs from **Penzance** (#16; 3 per hr., off-season M-Sa only; £2.50) and **Newquay** (#57 or X2).

The **tourist information centre** (TIC) is in the Guildhall on Street-an-Pol. From the bus and train stations, walk to the foot of Tregenna Hill and turn right on Street-an-Pol. The staff books beds for a 10% deposit on the first night's stay and sells 10p maps of the medieval maze that is St. Ives—trust us, you'll need one. (☎ 796297. Open M-Sa 9:30am-6pm, Su 10am-1pm; closed Sa-Su in winter.) Wednesday evenings at 6pm (July-Aug. only), weave up one alley and down another on a **walking tour** leaving from the bus station. (☎ 796389; 90min.; £3.) **Luggage** can be stored at the **St. Ives Travel Agency** (£1-1.50; open M-F 9am-5:30pm, Sa 9am-5pm), or at the **Western National Office,** at the Malakoff (£1-2; open M-Sa 9am-5pm, Su 9am-2pm).

Bikes and surfboards can be hired or repaired at **Windansea Surf Shop,** 25 Fore St. (☎ 794830. Surfboards and wetsuits £5 per day, £25 per week; £5 deposit. Open daily 9:30am-9:30pm.) Services include: **Barclays bank,** High St., across from the post office (☎ 362261; open M-Tu and Th-F 9:30am-4:30pm, W 10am-4:30pm); **Internet access** at **TEK**, 3-4 Treganna Hill (☎ 799416; £1 per 10min., £5 per hour; open daily 9am-9pm in summer, 10am-7pm in winter), and at **St. Ives International Backpackers** (10p per min., £5 per hr.; see below); and the **post office**, 1 Tregenna Pl. (☎ 795004; open M-F 9am-5:30pm, Sa 9am-1pm). **Postal code:** TR26 1AA.

⌐ ACCOMMODATIONS. B&Bs await on **Park Ave.** and **Tregenna Terr.**; for fine sea views, try **Clodgy View** and **West Pl.** Prices usually dip for rooms farther from the water and higher up on the gusty hillside. **St. Ives International Backpackers,** The Stenmack, fills a renovated 19th-century Methodist church. There's a free shuttle service for those staying at its sister Backpackers in Newquay. (☎/fax 799444. Dorms £12 peak-season, £8 off-season; £40-45 per week.) **Harbour Lights,** Court Cocking, Fore St., occupies a 536-year-old building just 30 ft. from the sea on one of the oldest streets in St. Ives, and features canopies above the beds and TVs. (☎ 795525. Rooms £18 per person, 10% student discount.) In a more tranquil setting is **Downlong Cottage,** 95 Backroad East. Ask for an upstairs room for glimpses of the glimmering sea. (☎ 798107. Rooms £15-18 per person.) If you can't find a room, seek one of the £15 B&Bs in **Carbis Bay** (a 20min. coastal walk or a 3min. train ride on the St. Ives-Penzance line; return £1). Places to **camp** abound in nearby **Hayle;** try **Trevalgan Camping Park** (☎ 796433), with laundry and cooking facilities, and access to the coastal path, or **Ayr Holiday Park** (☎ 795855), at the top of Bullans Ln.

◨▩ FOOD AND PUBS. Stock up on groceries at **Spar**, Tregenna Pl. (Open daily 7am-10pm.) **Fore St.** is packed with small bakeries, each hawking its own interpretation of the pasty. Many places also sell Cornish cream teas (a pot of tea with scones, jam, and Cornish clotted cream); try one for £2.60 at **Bumble's Tea Room,** Digey Sq., near the Tate. (☎ 797977. Open M-Sa 10am-5pm, summer also Su 11am-4pm.) Minuscule **Ferrell's Bakery**, 64 Fore St., bakes a delicious pasty as well as a lovely saffron bun (40p) rumored to be Cornwall's best. (☎ 797703. Open daily 9am-5:30pm.) Earning the scorn of pasty purists, the iconoclastic chocolate and banana pasty (£1.40) at **Granny's Pasties,** 9 Fore St., does for pasties what color did for TV. (☎ 793470. Open daily 9am-5:30pm; in summer 9am-9pm.) For the pasty-weary, **The Café,** Island Sq., has vegetarian meals such as spinach and feta pasta for around £7. (☎ 793621. Open daily 11am-3pm and 7-10pm.) Beer has flowed at **The Sloop,** on the corner of Fish St. and The Wharf, since 1312. (☎ 796584. Open daily 11am-11pm; food served noon-3pm and 6-8:45pm.)

◨◪ SIGHTS AND BEACHES. The modernist fruits of this art colony by the sea are on display at the **Tate Gallery,** on Porthmeor Beach. Like its sister, the new Tate Modern in London (see p. 130), the gallery focuses on abstract art (mainly local, in constantly shifting displays); its seafront location is fairly successful at integrating art and the environment that inspired it. (☎ 796226. Open Tu-Su 10:30am-5:30pm; July-Aug. also M 10:30am-5:30pm. Free tours M-F 2:30pm. Wheelchair access. £3.95, students, seniors, and disabled £2.50, children free.) Under the protective wing of the Tate is the nearby **Barbara Hepworth Museum and Sculpture Garden,** where Hepworth's works, which helped set the standard for 20th-century abstract sculpture, are set within her former studio and lush garden. (Open same times as the Tate. £3.50, students and seniors £1.80, children free. Same-day admission to both museums £6, students and seniors £3.30.) For information on the town's innumerable other galleries, check the TIC's *Arts Guide* (£1).

The sun god accepts burnt offerings of British skin at a number of beaches. Follow the hill down from the train station to **Porthmaster Beach,** a white, sandy expanse with tamer waves perfect for the families that crowd it on warm days. Some people enjoy tanning around the harbor, but the tourists wandering Wharf Rd. make it less intimate than **Porthguidden Beach,** hugged by the jutting arms of the island. On **Porthmeor Beach,** right below the Tate, the raging waves attract surfing lads and lasses. For quiet, find a perch on the shore, stare out at the bewitching Godrevy Lighthouse, and lose yourself in its shrouded solitude. **Boats** occasionally head out from The Wharf: check with the TIC or look at the blackboards sprawled across the pier. (To the lighthouse £6, children £4.)

SOUTHWEST ENGLAND

FROM ST. IVES TO LAND'S END

The Penwith Peninsula scrolls into the Celtic Sea at **Land's End,** Britain's south-westernmost point. Unfortunately, protective efforts could not prevent the area from being transformed into a zone of outlandish commercial booty. Land's End is now a tourist park of rides and plastic phenomena, but a look out to the dramatic granite cliffs and sea will remind you why you came. **Western National** (☎ (01208) 798798) **buses** run to Land's End from **Penzance** (1hr., 1 per hr., £3) and **St. Ives** (35min., 3 per day, £2). For those unafraid of hills and hell-bent drivers, **biking** is the best way to tour the region, affording glimpses of sparkling coastlines. If the Atlantic winds are chill, the water's-edge **First and Last Inn** (☎ (01736) 871680), on the A30 five minutes outside Land's End, will sell you a 60p cup of coffee.

ST. JUST. Just north of Land's End on Cape Cornwall, the remarkably beautiful, craggy coast of St. Just (pop. 2700) remains untouched by tourism. Derelict copper and tin mines abound in this former mining center, while the ever-present Neolithic stone circles find their way unobtrusively into the landscape. 2-4 mi. day hikes are outlined in leaflets in most tourist information centres, but the dramatic cliff path winding around the entire coast unveils the best of Cornwall. The **YHA Land's End,** at Letcha Vean, is set on three pristine acres with a view of the sea from many rooms. From the bus station's rear exit, turn left and follow the lane to its end, past the chapel and farm. (☎ (01736) 788437; fax 787337. Daytime bedroom lockout. Open Mar.-Oct. daily. Dorms £9.80, under 18 £6.75.) **Buses** #10, 10A, 10B, or 11 run from the **Penzance** bus station.

SENNEN. Just 1½ mi. from Land's End, or nine miles from Penzance on the A30, in the tiny hamlet of Sennen, **Land's End Backpackers and Guest House,** White Sands Lodge, dazzles with its Crayola-bright walls and communal spirit. Their adjoining **restaurant** whips up an array of meals that brings in a drive-by trade of young and old eaters tired of pub grub. (☎/fax (01736) 871776. Restaurant open 8am-10pm. English or vegetarian breakfast £4. Dorms £10; private guest house singles £14.50; doubles with bath £35. Camping £6.) Give 'em a ring and they may pick you up from the Penzance bus or train station; or take Western National #1 or 1A from **Penzance** or **Land's End** (1hr., 12 per day) or #15 from **Land's End** (5min., 1 per day).

ZENNOR. Legend has it that at the tiny village of Zennor (accessible by bus from St. Ives), a mermaid, drawn by the singing of a young man, happily returned to the sea with him in tow. On misty evenings, locals claim to see and hear the happy pair. A mermaid is carved on one of the benches of the local church. Zennor contains **The Old Chapel Backpackers Hostel,** a beautiful and immaculate independent hostel, close to hiking and four miles from the beaches at St. Ives's. Rest your weary soul with a meal at the cafe. (☎ (01736) 798307. Dorms £10.)

ANCIENT MONUMENTS. Inland on the Penwith Peninsula, some of the best-preserved Stone and Iron Age monuments in England lie along the Land's End-St. Ives bus route. Once covered by mounds of earth, the quoits (also called cromlechs or dolmens) are thought to be burial chambers from 2500 BC. The **Zennor Quoit** is named for the village. The **Lanyon Quoit,** off the Morvah-Penzance road about three miles from each town, is one of the area's best-preserved megaliths.

The famous stone near Morvah (on the Land's End-St. Ives bus route) with a hole through the middle, has the Cornish name **Mên-an-Tol,** or "stone with a hole through the middle." The big donut is allegedly endowed with curative powers. Climbing through the aperture supposedly remedies backaches, assures easy childbirth, or induces any alteration in physiology your heart desires. The best-preserved Iron Age village in Britain is at **Chysauster,** about 4 mi. from both Penzance and Zennor. Take Western National bus #16 (4 per day, £1.60) or the 2½ mi. footpath off the B3311 near Gulval. (☎ (0831) 757934. Open daily Apr.-Oct. 10am-6pm. £1.60, students and seniors £1.20, children 80p.)

THE MIDLANDS

"The Midlands" often evokes images of industrial cities, but the heart of England contains a fair share of the "must-sees" in England. Even Birmingham, the much-maligned industrial center of the Midlands, has its saving graces, not least of which are its fantastic nightlife and the hub of the Cadbury chocolate empire. Saved from industrialization by Shakespeare's preeminence, the tranquil country scenery of Stratford-upon-Avon peeks out from under crowds of tourists. The colleges of Oxford, England's oldest university town, and the castle at Warwick lay claim to grandeur, as do the region's grand cathedrals at Hereford, Worcester, and Lincoln. To the west, the light yellow stones of the Cotswolds brighten the region. Spend more than a day in these towns, and roam free from the glut of daytrippers. Only an overnight can provide the wonder of twilight at an English river's edge.

HIGHLIGHTS OF THE MIDLANDS

OXFORD Bask in eight centuries of brilliance at a university layered with architectural fantasies, historical relics, and bizarre traditions (p. 249).

STRATFORD-UPON-AVON Strut into Shakespeare's hometown, where historic buildings try to honor the Bard's footsteps and the world-renowned Royal Shakespeare Company venerates his every syllable (p. 262).

THE COTSWOLDS Tread footpaths past yew hedges and mind the sheep when traveling between England's most colorfully named villages (p. 272).

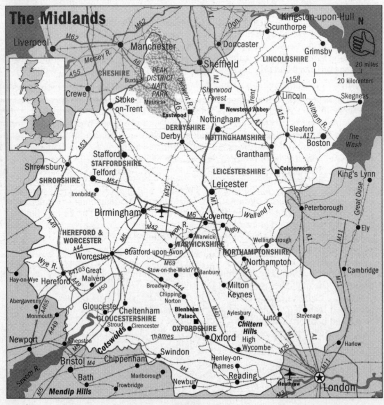

The Midlands

OXFORDSHIRE AND BERKSHIRE

OXFORD   ☎01865

Almost a millennium of scholarship has taken place at Oxford—22 British Prime Ministers were educated here, as were numerous other world leaders. Some form of teaching had existed here in the 11th century, but it was in 1167 that Henry II founded the actual university, Britain's first. After his tiff with Thomas à Becket Henry ordered the return of English students in Paris, so that "there may never be wanting a succession of persons duly qualified for the service of God in church and state." There is no want of a succession of persons today, as trucks rumble, bus brakes screech, and bicycles crush the toes of pedestrians shoving past each other in Oxford's streets. Despite the tourists, however, Oxford has an irrepressible grandeur, and there are pockets of respite to charm and edify the academic pilgrim: the basement room of Blackwell's Bookshop, the impeccable galleries of the Ashmolean, and the perfectly maintained quadrangles of Oxford's 39 colleges.

▐ GETTING THERE AND GETTING AROUND

Trains: Botley Rd. (☎ 794422), down Park End. Ticket office open M-F 6am-8pm, Sa 6:45am-8pm, Su 7:45am-8pm. Trains (☎ (08457) 484950) from **London Paddington** (1hr., 2-4 per hr., day return £14.80).

Buses: Bus Station, Gloucester Green. **Stagecoach Express** (☎ (01604) 620077) from **Cambridge** (2¾hr., 1 per hr., day return £8.75, concessions £6.50). **Stagecoach Oxford** (☎ 772250) operates the **Oxford Tube** to **London** (1½hr.; 1-6 per hr.; next-day return £7.50, concessions £6.50; return £9.50). **Oxford CityLink** (☎ 785400) from: **London** (1¾hr., 1-4 per hr., next-day return £7.50, concessions £6.50); **Gatwick** (2hr.; 1 per hr. daytime, every 2hr. at night; next-day return £19, children £9.50); and **Heathrow** (2 per hr., day return £12, children £6). **National Express** (☎ (08705) 808080) from **London** (1¾hr., every 30min., £7) and **Cambridge** (3¼hr., 1 per hr., £8).

Public Transportation: Most local services board on the streets around Carfax. The **Oxford Bus Company** (☎ 785400) and **Stagecoach Oxford** (☎ 772250) have swift and frequent service. The Oxford Bus Company operates **Park & Ride** (mostly for commuters) and **Cityline.** Cityline buses #4, 4A, 4B, and 4C go down Iffley Rd.; 13A, 13B, and 13C go up Marston Rd.; 2A, 2B, 2C, 2D go up Banbury Rd.; 16 and 35 go down Abingdon Rd.; and 5, 5A, and 5F go down Cowley Rd. Fares are low (most 70p). Day and week passes available from bus drivers or at the bus station.

Taxis: Radio Taxi (☎ 242424). **ABC** (☎ 770681).

▐ ORIENTATION AND PRACTICAL INFORMATION

Queen St., High St., St. Aldates, and **Cornmarket St.** meet at right angles at **Carfax,** the town center. The easiest way to orientate yourself in Oxford is to locate the colossal Carfax Tower. Oxford extends some three miles around Carfax, but the colleges are all within a mile of each other, lying mainly to the east of Carfax along High St. and Broad St. The bus and train stations and tourist information centre (TIC) are to the northwest. Past the east end of High St. over Magdalen Bridge, the neighborhoods of East Oxford stretch along Cowley Rd. and Iffley Rd. Abingdon Rd. leads off to South Oxford, while more upscale residential areas surround Woodstock Rd. and Banbury Rd. to the north.

When walking around Oxford, especially near Carfax, enjoy the pedestrian zone; beware, however, that from 6pm to 10am, bikes are allowed to intrude. College parks and quads remain sacrosanct. For cyclists, the *Cycle into Oxford* pamphlet, with excellent cycling maps of the city and its hinterland, is free at the TIC.

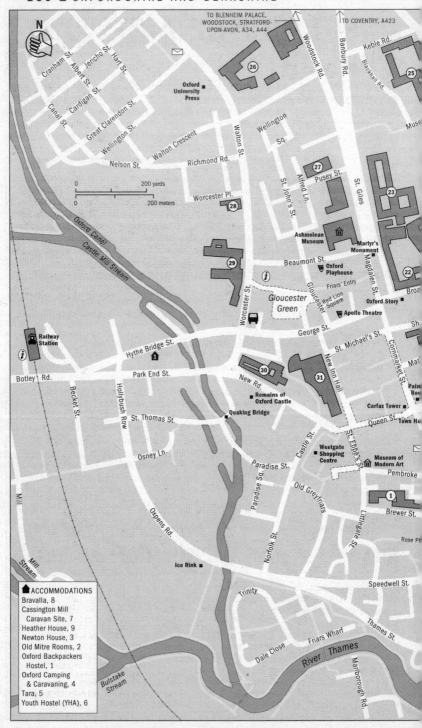

N

TO BLENHEIM PALACE,
WOODSTOCK, STRATFORD-
UPON-AVON, A34, A44

TO COVENTRY, A423

Keble Rd.

Banbury Rd.

Blackhall Rd.

Woodstock Rd.

25

26

Cranham St.

Albert St.

Jericho St.

Hart St.

Cardigan St.

Great Clarendon St.

Canal St.

Wellington St.

Oxford
University
Press

Walton St.

Wellington
Sq.

Muse

Nelson St.

Walton Crescent

Richmond Rd.

Alfred Ln.

St. John's St.

27 Pusey St.

St. Giles

23

Oxford Canal

0   200 yards
0   200 meters

Worcester Pl.

28

Ashmolean
Museum

Martyr's
Monument

Beaumont St.

Magdalen St.

22

Castle Mill Stream

29

Oxford
Playhouse

i

Friars' Entry

Gloucester St.

Worcester St.

Gloucester
Green

Red Lion
Square

Oxford Story

Broa

Apollo Theatre

Railway
Station

i

George St.

St. Michael's St.

Cornmarket St.

Sh

Hythe Bridge St.

New Inn Hall

Mar

Botley Rd.

Park End St.

Becket St.

Hollybush Row

New Rd.

30

31

Pain
Roo

St. Thomas St.

Remains of
Oxford Castle

Carfax Tower

Quaking Bridge

Queen St.

Town Ha

Osney Ln.

Castle St.

St. Ebbe's

Westgate
Shopping
Centre

Museum of
Modern Art

Paradise St.

Pembroke

Paradise Sq.

Old Greyfriars

1

Brewer St.

Oxpens Rd.

Norfolk St.

Littlegate St.

Rose Pl

Mill
Stream

Ice Rink

Speedwell St.

Trinity

Dale Close

Friars Wharf

Thames St.

River Thames

Marlborough Rd.

Bulstake
Stream

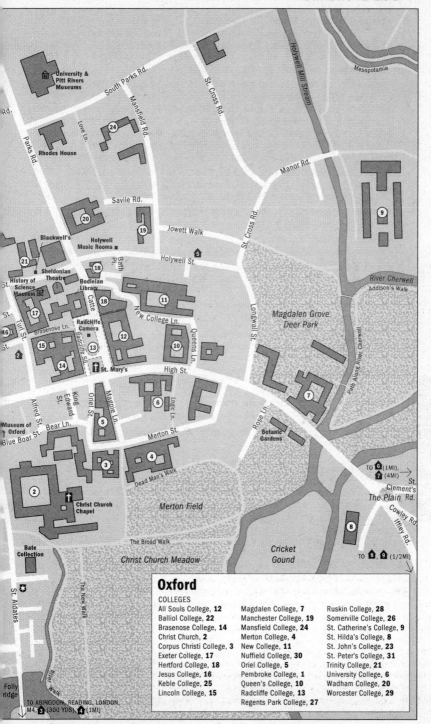

Oxford

COLLEGES

All Souls College, **12**
Balliol College, **22**
Brasenose College, **14**
Christ Church, **2**
Corpus Christi College, **3**
Exeter College, **17**
Hertford College, **18**
Jesus College, **16**
Keble College, **25**
Lincoln College, **15**

Magdalen College, **7**
Manchester College, **19**
Mansfield College, **24**
Merton College, **4**
New College, **11**
Nuffield College, **30**
Oriel College, **5**
Pembroke College, **1**
Queen's College, **10**
Radcliffe College, **13**
Regents Park College, **27**

Ruskin College, **28**
Somerville College, **26**
St. Catherine's College, **9**
St. Hilda's College, **8**
St. John's College, **23**
St. Peter's College, **31**
Trinity College, **21**
University College, **6**
Wadham College, **20**
Worcester College, **29**

Tourist Information Centre: The Old School, Gloucester Green (☎ 726871; fax 240261), beside the bus station. A pamphleteer's paradise. The extremely busy staff books rooms for £2.50 and a refundable 10% deposit over the entire stay. Accommodations list 60p. The £1 street map and guide includes a valuable index. Open M-Sa 9:30am-5pm; Easter-Oct. also Su 10am-3:30pm.

Tours: A 2hr. **walking tour** on the history of Oxford University leaves daily from the TIC, providing access to some colleges that are otherwise closed to visitors. 2-5 per day, 10:30am-2pm. £4.50, children £3. **Guide Friday** (☎ 790522) runs bus tours from the train station. Tours every 15min. 9:30am-6pm. £8.50, students and seniors £7, children £2.50. **The Oxford Classic Tour** (☎ (01235) 819393), another bus service, charges less and will hand you earphones in the language of your choice. £7, students and seniors £5, children £2. Both bus tours allow hop on/hop off access all day.

Budget Travel: STA Travel, 36 George St. (☎ 792800). Open M-W and F 9am-5:30pm, Th 10am-5:30pm, Sa 11am-5pm. **UC Campus,** 105 St. Aldates (☎ 242067). Open M-Tu and Th-F 9am-5:30pm, W 10am-5:30pm, Sa 10am-5pm.

Financial Services: Many banks line Carfax. **Barclays** is on 54 Cornmarket St. Open M-Tu and Th-F 9am-5pm, W 9:30am-5pm, Sa 9:30am-noon.

American Express: 4 Queen St. (☎ 207101). Open M-Tu and Th-F 9am-5:30pm, W 9:30am-5:30pm, Sa 9am-5pm, call for Su hours. **Bureau de change** open July-Aug.

Luggage Storage: Pensioners' Club in Gloucester Green (☎ 242237), by the bus station. Luggage can be left from several hours to several weeks. £1-2 donation requested. Open M-Sa 9am-4:45pm.

Launderette: Clean-o-Fine, North Parade (☎ 553631). Open daily 7:30am-10pm, last wash 9:30pm. Washer load £2.20 or £3, soap £1 or 20p per scoop.

Public Toilets: Gloucester Green Bus Station. Changing room and disabled access. (Open 24hr. Free.) Also by the intersection of St. Giles St. and Magdalen St., along Castle St. at the Westgate Shopping Centre, and along Market St. at the Covered Market.

Police: St. Aldates and Speedwell St. (☎ 266000).

Hospital: John Radcliffe Hospital, Headley Way (☎ 741166). Bus #13B or 14A.

Internet Access: Pickwick Papers, 90 Gloucester Green (☎ 793149). Conveniently located next to the bus station. £1 per 15min. Open daily 4:30am-6:30pm.

Post Office: 102-104 St. Aldates (☎ 202863). Open M-F 9am-5:30pm, Sa 9am-6pm. **Bureau de change. Postal Code:** OX1.

▄ ACCOMMODATIONS

Oxford's abundant accommodations completely fill up in the summer. Book at least a week ahead from June to September, especially for singles, and be prepared to mail in a deposit or give a credit card number. **B&Bs** line the main roads out of town and are reachable by Cityline buses (or a 15-45min. walk for the energetic). The 300s on **Banbury Rd.** stand north of town and are reachable by buses #2A, 2C, and 2D. Cheaper B&Bs lie in the 200s and 300s on **Iffley Rd.** (bus #4), between 250 and 350 **Cowley Rd.** (buses #51 or 52), and on **Abingdon Rd.** in South Oxford (bus #16). Wherever you go, expect to pay £20-25 per person. If it's late and you're homeless, call the **Oxford Association of Hotels and Guest Houses** at one of the following numbers: 721561 (East Oxford), 862138 (West Oxford), 554374 (North Oxford), or 244268 (South Oxford).

YHA Youth Hostel, 32 Jack Straw's Ln., Headington (☎ 762997; fax 769402). Catch bus #13 heading away from Carfax on High St. and ask the driver to stop at Jack Straw's Ln. (4 per hr., last bus 11:10pm, 70p, return £1.10). The hostel is a further 8min. walk up the hill. Large (105 beds), with generous facilities to match: kitchen, laundry, and lockers. Most rooms have 6-8 bunks. Close quarters and large lounges promote multilingual chatter. June-Aug. book 2 weeks ahead and expect to send a deposit or give a credit card number. Dorms £10.85, under 18 £7.45, students £1 off.

Oxford Backpackers Hotel, 9a Hythe Bridge St. (☎ 721761). Right between the bus and train stations, this independent hostel combines good prices and a great location. Non-stop music enlivens the common room, hallways, and bathroom; make friends in an extremely social atmosphere. As for the decor, the colors are *not* meant to go together. Guests must show passport. Laundry facilities (£2.50) and kitchen, plus full Internet access (£1.50 per 15min.). Linens provided, but no towels. Dorms £11-12 per night.

Bravalla, 242 Iffley Rd. (☎ 241326; fax 250511). Six sunny rooms with soothing floral patterns and pastels, all with bath and TV. Breakfast in a conservatory, with good vegetarian options. Guests sign breakfast board the previous night. Reserve several weeks ahead. Singles £35; doubles/twins £50.

Old Mitre Rooms, 4b Turl St. (☎ 279821; fax 279963). Lincoln College dorms with shaggy green carpet. Some Lincoln Quad views. Open July to early Sept. Singles £25, with bath £32; twins £46, with bath £50.50; triples/family rooms £60, with bath £65.

Heather House, 192 Iffley Rd. (☎/fax 249757). Walk 20min. or take the bus marked "Rose Hill" from the bus station, train station, or Carfax Tower (70p). Vivian, the vibrant Australian proprietress, keeps the modern rooms sparkling, and her matchless repository of advice and information will remind you why you love to travel. Singles £28; doubles with bath £48. Cheaper for longer stays.

Tara, 10 Holywell St. (call *Typetalk* ☎ (0800) 515152 or ☎ (0151) 494 2022; give the operator Tara's number ☎ (01865) 202953). A lark-charmed dream on Oxford's oldest street. Framed paperback covers, including *Gone with the Wind.* Kind, hearing-impaired proprietors Mr. and Mrs. Godwin lip-read well and speak clearly. Many rooms overlook a college. Basin and TVs in each room. Guest kitchen. Refurbished in 2000, call for opening dates. Reserve at least 2 weeks ahead. Singles £20; doubles £38.

Newton House, 82-84 Abingdon Rd. (☎ 240561), ½mi. from town; take any Abingdon bus across Folly Bridge. Affable proprietor, TVs in all rooms, and dark wardrobes await Narnia fans; don't get lost. Doubles £44, with bath £58; varies with season.

Camping: Oxford Camping and Caravaning, 426 Abingdon Rd. (☎ 244088, call 8am-8pm), behind the Touchwoods camping store. 84 sites. £4.90-£6.25 per tent, depending on the season. 2-night max. stay for non-members. Toilet and laundry facilities. Showers free. **Cassington Mill Caravan Site,** Eynsham Rd., Cassington (☎ 881081), about 4mi. northwest on the A40. 87 pitches and hot showers. £8 for large tents, £6.50 for small tents. The **YHA Hostel** may also offer limited camping; call ahead.

☕ FOOD

The proprietors of Oxford's swank, bulging eateries know they have a captive market: students fed up with fetid college food are easily seduced by a bevy of budget options. If you're cooking for yourself, the **Covered Market** between Market St. and Carfax has fresh produce, deli goods, breads, and even shoe leather. (Open M-Sa 8am-5:30pm.) Keep an eye out for the **kebab vans** that fuel students after hours—usually at Broad St., High St., Queen St., and St. Aldates.

For those staying across Magdalen Bridge, there are a number of cheap and tasty restaurants along the first four blocks of Cowley Rd., including the funky **Hi-Lo Jamaican Eating House,** 70 Cowley Rd. (☎ 725984); the Bangladesh cuisine of **Dhaka,** 186 Cowley Rd. (☎ 202011); and **The Pak Fook,** 100 Cowley Rd. (☎ 247958). Those near Somerville College should seek **Jamal's Tandoori Restaurant,** 108 Walton St. (☎ 310102).

Café CoCo, 23 Cowley Rd. (☎ 200232). Lively atmosphere and a great Mediterranean menu. Populated by students and thirtysomethings, CoCo's is a bargain not to be missed. Try the Merguez (lamb and beef spiced sausages with veggies, salad, and tzatziki) for £7.50. Main courses £5.95-8.50. Open daily 10am-11pm.

The Nosebag, 6-8 St. Michael's St. (☎ 721033). A different gourmet-grade menu each night, served cafeteria-style. Good vegetarian items. Lunch under £6.50, dinner under £8. Open M 9:30am-5:30pm, Tu-Th 9:30am-10pm, F-Sa 9:30am-10:30pm, Su 9:30am-9pm. **The Saddlebag Café** downstairs sells sandwiches, salads, and cakes during the day. Open M-Su 9:30am-5:30pm, sandwiches served until 5pm.

Chiang Mai, 130a High St. (☎ 202233), tucked down an alley. Wide selection of Thai food in half-timbered surroundings. Extensive vegetarian menu; main courses £5.50-9. Those with a taste for adventure should try the jungle curry with wild rabbit (£6.95). Open M-Sa noon-2:30pm and 6-11pm, Su noon-3pm and 6-10pm.

Harvey's of Oxford, 58 High St. (☎ 723152), near Magdalen College. Eat and run at one of Oxford's better takeaways, recognizable by the line out the door. Cherry-apple flapjacks 85p, mighty sandwiches £1.60-2.90, and a great variety of coffee. The staff recommends the Gourmet Chicken. Open M-F 8am-7pm, Sa 8am-6pm, Su 8:30am-6pm.

Heroes, 8 Ship St. (☎ 723459). Where students dine on sandwiches, freshly baked breads, and a plethora of meat and cheese fillings (£1.80-3.65). A popular takeout, but there's a small eat-in area. Open M-F 8am-7pm, Sa 8:30am-5pm, Su 10am-5pm.

PUBS

Pubs far outnumber colleges in Oxford; many even consider them the city's prime attraction. Most pubs open by noon, begin to fill up around 5pm, and close at 11pm (10:30pm on Sundays). Food is sometimes served only during lunch and dinner hours (roughly noon-2pm and 6-8pm). Be ready to pub crawl—some pubs are so small that a single band of merry students will squeeze out other patrons, while just around the corner, others have several spacious rooms.

■ **Turf Tavern,** 4 Bath Pl. (☎ 243235), off Holywell St. Arguably the most popular student bar in Oxford (they call it "the Turf"), this sprawling, cavernous 13th-century pub is tucked into an alleyway against the ruins of the city wall. Features a maze of rooms and two secluded terraces. Intimate and relaxed until the student crowd arrives. Many, many drinks: beers, punches, ciders, and country wines. Open M-Sa 11am-11pm, Su noon-10:30pm. Hot food served in back room noon-8pm.

The Eagle and Child, 49 St. Giles (☎ 310154). One of Oxford's most historic pubs, this archipelago of paneled alcoves moistened the tongues of C.S. Lewis and J.R.R. Tolkien. As the many photos of the Inklings Club testify, *The Chronicles of Narnia* and *The Hobbit* were first read aloud here. Settle into a dim alcove and observe distinguished dons and students still roll in. The front has more flavor than the newer back conservatory. Open M-Sa 11am-11pm, Su 11:00am-10:30pm. Food served noon-2:30pm and 5-7:30pm.

The Kings Arms, Holywell St. (☎ 242369). Oxford's unofficial student union draws in a huge young crowd. The coffee room at the front of the bar lets quieter folks retreat from the merry masses at the back. Open M-Sa 10:30am-11pm, Su 10:30am-10:30pm; coffee bar closes at 5:30pm.

The Bear, Alfred St. (☎ 721783). Over 5000 ties from Oxford students and other famous people cover every flat surface but the floor of this tiny pub, established in 1242. During the day, the clients are older than the neckwear, and the young sit out back. Open M-Sa noon-11pm, Su noon-10:30pm.

The Jolly Farmers, 20 Paradise St. (☎ 793759). Take Queen St. from Carfax, turn left on Castle St., then right on Paradise St. One of Oxfordshire's first gay and lesbian pubs, featuring occasional comedy, female impersonators, and male strippers. Crowded with students and twentysomethings, especially on the weekends; significantly more sedate in the student-free summer. Open M-Sa noon-11pm, Su 12:30-10:30pm.

SIGHTS

Oxford was originally named as the place where oxen could ford the Thames, and three of **Oxford University**'s most famous sons—Lewis Carroll, C.S. Lewis, and J.R.R. Tolkien—sat near the stone-bridged waters of the Isis (as the Thames is known here) dreaming of crossings through mirrors, wardrobes, and mountain passes. The university has traditionally been a breeding ground for the country's leaders. Christ Church College alone has produced 13 prime ministers, while St. John's College alumni may have been surprised when their fellow undergraduate, the long-haired rock-band member Tony Blair, was elected to govern Britain.

OXFORD MADE EASY Oxford undergraduates study for three years, each year consisting of three eight-week terms; more time is spent on holiday than at school. The university itself has no official, central campus. Though central facilities—libraries, laboratories, and faculties—are established and maintained by the university, Oxford's independent colleges, where students live and learn simultaneously (at least in theory), are scattered throughout the city. Students must dress in formal wear called **sub fusc** for all official University events, including exams; carnations are obligatory. At the end of their last academic year, students from all the colleges assemble for degree examinations, a gruelling three-week ordeal that takes place in the Examination Schools on High Street in late June and early July. Each year, university authorities do their best to quell the vigorous post-examination celebrations in the street. Each year they fail. The authorities, that is.

During summer, hordes of international students arrive for programs on the University's campus, and the chatter is a thousand-tongued Babel of anything but British English. The TIC sells a map (£1) and the *Welcome to Oxford* guide (£1), which lists the colleges' public visiting hours—usually for a few hours in the afternoon, but these are often curtailed without explanation or prior notice. Some colleges charge admission (often only during peak tourist times). Don't bother trying to sneak into Christ Church outside opening hours (even after cleverly hiding your backpack and *Let's Go*): elderly bouncers sporting bowler hats and stationed 50 ft. apart will squint at you and kick you out. Other colleges have been known to be less vigilant near the back gates. Coddle the porters or you will get nowhere.

CHRIST CHURCH COLLEGE
Just down St. Aldates St. from Carfax. ☎ *276492. Open M-Sa 9:30am-5:30pm, Su 11:30am-5:30pm; closed Christmas. Services Su 8am, 10am, 11:15am, and 6pm; weekdays 7:30am and 6pm. £2.50, concessions £1.50, families £6.*

An intimidating pile of stone dwarfing the other colleges, "The House" has Oxford's grandest quad and its most socially distinguished students. In June, (you'd bloody well better) hush while navigating the narrow strip open to tourists lest you be rebuked by irritable undergrads prepping for exams. Charles I made Christ Church his capital for three and a half years during the Civil War, escaping dressed as a servant when the city was besieged.

CHRIST CHURCH CHAPEL. Also Oxford's cathedral, it's the smallest in England. In AD 730, Oxford's patron saint, St. Frideswide, built a nunnery on this site in honor of two miracles: the blinding of an annoying suitor, and his subsequent recovery. The cathedral contains a stained glass window (c. 1320) depicting Thomas à Becket kneeling in supplication just before being hacked apart in Canterbury Cathedral. A rather incongruous toilet floats in the background of an 1870 stained glass window depicting St. Frideswide's death. The Reverend Charles Dodgson (better known as Lewis Carroll) was friendly with Dean Liddell of Christ Church—and friendlier with his daughter Alice—and used to visit the family in the gardens of the Dean's house. From the largest tree in the garden (which is private but visible from the cathedral), the Cheshire Cat first grinned and vanished; the White Rabbit can be spotted fretting in the stained glass of the hall.

QUADRANGLES. The site of undergraduate lily-pond-dunking, Tom Quad adjoins the Chapel grounds. The quad takes its name from Great Tom, the seven-ton bell in Tom Tower, which has faithfully rung 101 strokes (the original number of students) at 9:05pm (the original undergraduate curfew) every evening since 1682. Sixty coats of arms preside over the ceiling under the tower. Nearby, the fan-vaulted college hall bears imposing portraits of some of Christ Church's most famous alums— Sir Philip Sidney, William Penn, John Ruskin, John Locke, and a bored-looking W.H. Auden in the corner by the kitchen.

OTHER SIGHTS. Through an archway (to your left as you face the cathedral) lies **Peckwater Quad,** encircled by the most elegant Palladian building in Oxford. Look here for faded rowing standings chalked on the walls and for Christ Church's library, which unfortunately is closed to visitors. Spreading east and south from the main entrance, **Christ Church Meadow** compensates for Oxford's lack of "backs" (the riverside gardens in Cambridge). A fenced portion of the meadow contains a herd of American longhorn cattle, given by Bill Clinton on a visit to the city.

Housed in the Canterbury Quad, the **Christ Church Picture Gallery** is a fine collection of Italian, Dutch, and Flemish paintings, starring Tintoretto and Vermeer. Leonardo and Michelangelo come out of hiding on occasion. *(Enter on Oriel Sq. and at Canterbury Gate; visitors to the gallery only should enter through Canterbury Gate off Oriel St.* ☎ *202429. Open Apr.-Sept. M-Sa 10:30am-1pm and 2-5:30pm, Su 2-5:30pm; Oct.-Mar. closes at 4:30pm. £1, students and seniors 50p.)*

OTHER COLLEGES

MERTON COLLEGE. Merton features a fine garden and a 14th-century library holding the first printed Welsh Bible. J.R.R. Tolkien lectured here, inventing the language of Elvish in his spare time. The college is also home to **Mob Quad,** Oxford's oldest and least impressive, dating from the 14th century. Nearby **St. Alban's Quad** has some of the University's best gargoyles. Residents of Crown Prince Narahito's native Japan visit daily and try to identify the rooms he inhabited in his Merton days. *(Merton St.* ☎ *276310. Open M-F 2-4pm, Sa-Su 10am-4pm. Closed around Easter and Christmas, and on certain Saturdays. Free.)*

UNIVERSITY COLLEGE. The soot-blackened college dates from 1249 and vies with Merton for the title of oldest college, claiming Alfred the Great as its founder. Percy Bysshe Shelley was expelled from University for writing the pamphlet *The Necessity of Atheism,* but has since been immortalized in a prominent monument inside the college (to the right as you enter). Bill Clinton spent his Rhodes days here; his rooms at 46 Leckford Rd. are a tour guide's endless source of smoked-but-didn't-inhale jokes. *(High St.* ☎ *276619.)*

ORIEL AND CORPUS CHRISTI COLLEGES. Oriel College (a.k.a. "The House of the Blessed Mary the Virgin in Oxford") is wedged between High St. and Merton St. and was once the turf of Sir Walter Raleigh. *(*☎ *276555. Open daily 2-5pm. Free.)* Just south of Oriel, **Corpus Christi College** surrounds a quad with a sundial in the center, crowned by a golden pelican. The garden wall contains a gate built to facilitate visits between Charles I and his queen, residents at adjacent Christ Church and Merton during the Civil War. *(*☎ *276700. Open daily 1:30-4:30pm. Free.)*

ALL SOULS COLLEGE. A graduate college with a prodigious endowment, All Souls is reputed to have the most heavenly wine cellar in Oxford. Candidates who survive the difficult admission exams get invited to dinner, where it is ensured that they are "well-born, well-bred, and only moderately learned." **The Great Quad,** with its fastidious lawn and two spare spires, may be Oxford's most serene. *(Corner of High St. and Catte St.* ☎ *279379. Open M-F 2-4:30pm; closed Aug. Free.)*

QUEEN'S COLLEGE. A statue of Queen Caroline (wife of George II) crowns the college's front gate. Around since 1341, Queen's was rebuilt by Wren and Hawksmoor in the 17th and 18th centuries with a distinctive Queen Anne style, in glorious orange, white, and gold. A trumpet call summons students to dinner; a boar's head graces the Christmas table. The latter tradition supposedly commemorates an early student of the college who, attacked by a boar on the outskirts of Oxford, choked his assailant to death with a volume of Aristotle. Alumni include starry-eyed Edmund Halley and the more earthly Jeremy Bentham. *(High St.* ☎ *279121. Closed to the public, except for those on authorized tours from the TIC.)*

MAGDALEN COLLEGE. Extensive grounds surround the flower-laced quads of Magdalen (MAUD-lin), traditionally considered Oxford's most handsome college. The college also boasts a deer park with the river watering its flank, and Addison's

THE MIDLANDS

Walk (a circular path) framing a meadow at one edge. A cowled monk allegedly paces through Magdalen's oft-photographed cloisters. The college's spiritual patron is alumnus Oscar Wilde—the place has always walked on the flamboyant side. Marking a personal decline, Edward Gibbon declared the 14 months he spent here "the most idle and unprofitable of my whole career." *(On High St. near the River Cherwell. ☎ 276000. Open July-Sept. M-F noon-6pm, Sa-Su 2-6pm; Oct.-June 2-5pm. Apr.-Sept. £2, concessions £1; Oct.-Mar. free.)*

TRINITY COLLEGE. Founded in 1555, Trinity has a splendid Baroque chapel with a limewood altarpiece, cedar lattices, and pediments with cherubim everywhere. The college's series of eccentric presidents includes Ralph Kettell, who would come to dinner with a pair of scissors and chop anyone's hair that he deemed too long. *(Broad St. ☎ 279900. Open daily 10:30am-noon and 2-4pm. £2, concessions £1.)*

BALLIOL COLLEGE. Students at Balliol preserve a semblance of tradition by hurling bricks over the wall at their conservative Trinity College rivals. The interior gates of the college still bear scorch marks from the immolations of 16th-century Protestant martyrs (the pyres were built a few yards from the college, where a small cross set into Broad St. rattles cyclists today). A mulberry tree planted by Elizabeth I still shades slumbering students. Matthew Arnold, Gerard Manley Hopkins, Aldous Huxley, and Adam Smith were all sons of Balliol's spires. *(Broad St. ☎ 277777. Open daily 2-5pm (term only). £1, students and children free.)*

NEW COLLEGE. Named because it was founded by William of Wykeham "only" in 1379, this is one of Oxford's most prestigious colleges. The layers of the front quad—compare the different stones of the first and second stories—reveal the architectural history of the college. A croquet garden is encircled by part of the **old city wall**, and every three years the City of Oxford's mayor visits for a ceremonial inspection to ascertain the wall's state of repair. The bell tower has Seven Deadly Sins gargoyles on one side, and Seven Virtues on the other, all equally grotesque. A former warden, Rev. William Spooner, is now remembered as the unintentional inventor of "spoonerisms"; he allegedly rebuked a student who had "hissed all the mystery lectures" and "tasted the whole worm." *(New College Ln. From Carfax, head down High St. and turn onto Catte St.; New College Ln. is to the right. ☎ 279555. Open daily Easter-Oct. 11am-5pm; Nov.-Easter 2-4pm, use the Holywell St. Gate. £1.50 in the summer.)*

SOMERVILLE COLLEGE. Somerville is Oxford's most famous women's college, with alumnae including Indira Gandhi and Margaret Thatcher. Women were not granted degrees until 1920—Cambridge held out until 1948. Today, all of Oxford's colleges are coed except St. Hilda's, which remains women-only. *(Woodstock Rd. From Carfax, head down Cornmarket St. which becomes Magdalen St., St. Giles, and finally Woodstock Rd. ☎ 270600. Open daily 2-5:30pm. Free.)*

KEBLE COLLEGE. Designed by architect William Butterfield to stand out from the Ashmolean Museum's sandstone background, the intricate, multi-patterned red brick, known as "The Fair Isle Sweater," was deemed "actively ugly" by architecture guru Sir Nikolaus Pevsner. Through a passageway to the left, the **Hayward** and **deBreyne Buildings** squat on the tarmac like black plexiglass spaceships. *(Corner of Keble and Park St. ☎ 272727. Open M-Sa 2-5pm. Free.)*

OTHER SIGHTS

■ASHMOLEAN MUSEUM. The imposing Ashmolean, the finest classical collection outside London, was Britain's first public museum when it opened in 1683. Leonardo, Monet, Manet, Van Gogh, Michelangelo, Rodin, and Matisse convene for the permanent collection. While the museum is being renovated, the entire collection is on display. The **Cast Gallery**, behind the museum, has over 250 casts of Greek sculptures. *(Beaumont St. From Carfax, head up Cornmarket St., which becomes Magdalen St.; Beaumont St. is on the left. ☎ 278000. Open Tu-Sa 10am-5pm, Su 2-5pm. Extended summer hours; call for details. Free.)*

THE MIDLANDS

BODLEIAN LIBRARY. Oxford's principal reading and research library has over five million books and 50,000 manuscripts. Sir Thomas Bodley endowed the library's first wing in 1602 on a site that had housed university libraries since 1488; the institution has since grown to fill the immense **Old Library** complex, the round **Radcliffe Camera** next door, and two newer buildings on Broad St. As a copyright library, the Bodleian receives a copy of every book printed in Great Britain. Admission to the reading rooms is by ticket only. If you can prove you're a scholar (a student ID may be sufficient, but a letter of introduction from your college is encouraged), present two passport photos (or have two shot on the spot), and promise not to light any fires, the Admissions Office will issue a two-day pass for £3. No one has ever been permitted to take out a book, not even Cromwell. Well, especially not Cromwell. *(Catte St. Take High St. and turn left on Catte. ☎ 277224. Library open M-F 9am-6pm, Sa 9am-1pm. Tours leave from the Divinity School, across the street; in summer M-F 4 per day, Sa-Su 2 per day; in winter 2 per day. Tours £3.50.)*

SHELDONIAN THEATRE. This Roman-style auditorium was designed by Christopher Wren as a teenager. Graduation ceremonies, conducted in Latin, take place in the Sheldonian and can be witnessed with permission from one of the "bulldogs" (bowler-hatted university officers). The cupola affords an inspiring view of the spires of Oxford. The ivy-crowned stone heads on the fence behind the Sheldonian do not represent emperors; they are a 20th-century study of beards. *(Broad St. ☎ 277299. Open M-Sa 10am-12:30pm and 2-4:30pm, subject to change. £1.50, children £1.)*

BLACKWELL'S BOOKSTORE. Guinness lists it as the largest room devoted to bookselling anywhere in the world. The basement room dwarfs the building and underpins the foundations of Trinity College next door. *(48-50 Broad St. ☎ 792792; www.bookshop.blackwell.co.uk. Open M and W-Sa 9am-6pm, Tu 9:30am-6pm, Su 11am-5pm.)*

CARFAX TOWER. A hike up this tower's 99 spiral stairs gives a grand view of the city from the only present reminder of the medieval St. Martin's Church. Admire the bell-ringing chamber as you climb. *(Corner of Queen St. and Cornmarket St. ☎ 792653. Open daily Apr.-Oct. 10am-5:30pm; Nov.-Mar. 10am-3:30pm. £1.20, under 16 60p.)*

THE MUSEUM OF OXFORD. The museum has perhaps the most comprehensive local history collection in Britain. The exhibit is staid, save for the skeleton of a murderer dissected at Christ Church, which is simply stale. *(St. Aldates, across from the post office. ☎ 815559. Open Tu-F 10am-4pm, Sa 10am-5pm. £2, students and seniors £1.50, children 50p, families £5; audio tour £1.)*

THE OXFORD STORY. A combination history lesson and amusement park ride, The Oxford Story hauls visitors around on medieval-style "desks" through dioramas recreating Oxford's past. Share the pleasures of a 13th-century student making merry with a wench. It's a bit excessive when you can stay outside and see real stone quads instead of fiberglass imitations. *(6 Broad St. ☎ 790055. Open daily. July-Aug. 9am-6pm; Apr.-June and Sept.-Oct. 9:30am-5pm; Nov.-Mar. M-F 10am-4:30pm, Sa-Su 10am-5pm. Closed Christmas. £5.70, concessions £4.70.)*

THE BOTANIC GARDEN. The garden cultivates a sumptuous array of plants that have flourished for three centuries. The path connecting the Botanic Garden to the Christ Church Meadow provides a beautiful view of the Thames as well as the cricket and tennis courts on the opposite bank. *(From Carfax, head down High St.; the Garden is on the right. Open daily Apr.-Sept. 9am-5pm; Oct.-Mar. 9am-4:30pm; glasshouses open daily 2-4pm. Late June to early Sept. £2, children free; free the rest of the year.)*

BEST OF THE REST. Although the **Museum of Modern Art,** 30 Pembroke St., has no permanent collection, it constantly showcases new works by different artists. *(☎ 722733. Open Tu-W and F-Su 11am-6pm, Th 11am-9pm. Wheelchair access. £2.50, students and seniors £1.50, children free. Free for all on W 11am-1pm and Th 6-9pm.)* Right before Folly Bridge, in the Faculty of Music on St. Aldates St., stands the **Bate Collection of Historical Instruments.** *(☎ 276139. Open M-F 2-5pm. Free.)* The **Museum of the History of Science,** on Broad St., was recently renovated and holds a radiant collection of sundials and countless clocks. (☎ 277280. Call for hours. Free.) Across Parks Rd. from Keble College stands the iron and stone temple of the **University Museum,** Parks Rd. (☎ 272950. Open daily noon-5pm. Free.) At the attached **Pitt Rivers Museum,** behold an eclectic ethnography and natural history collection that includes shrunken heads and rare butterflies. (☎ 270949. Open M-Sa 1-4:30pm, Su 2-4:30pm. Free.)

🎵 ENTERTAINMENT

Like pubs, public transit in Oxford shuts down sometime after 11pm, but nightlife can last until 3am. See *This Month in Oxford* (free from the TIC) for upcoming events, or check out the posters plastered around town. *Daily Information,* posted in the TIC, most colleges, and some hostels, provides some pointers, and pubs often have their own brochures.

Music: Centuries of tradition give Oxford a quality music scene; attend a concert or an Evensong service at one of the colleges—**New College Choir** is one of the best boy choirs around—or a performance at the **Holywell Music Rooms** (on Holywell St.), the oldest in the country. The **City of Oxford Orchestra** (☎ 744457), the city's professional symphony orchestra, plays a subscription series in the Sheldonian and in college chapels during summer. Concerts once a month; tickets £10-15; 25% student discount. The **Apollo Theatre,** George St. (☎ (0870) 6063500), presents a wide range of performances, ranging from lounge-lizard jazz to the Welsh National Opera, which visits in late Mar., late June, and Oct. Open M-Sa 10am-6pm on non-performance days, until 8pm on show days. Tickets from £10; discounts for students and seniors.

Theaters: The **Oxford Playhouse,** 11-12 Beaumont St. (☎ 798600), hosts bands, dance troupes, and the Oxford Stage Company. Tickets from £6; standby tickets for seniors (matinees only) and students (any show time) on day of show with cash. The **Oxford Union,** St. Michael's St. (☎ (01865) 778119), puts up solid theater productions. Tickets £8, concessions £5. The university itself offers marvelous entertainment; college theatre groups often stage productions in gardens or in cloisters.

Clubs: Head up **Walton St.** or down **Cowley Rd.,** by far the most self-indulgent of Oxford's neighborhoods—both areas provide late-night clubs, as well as a fascinating jumble of ethnic restaurants, exotic shops, used bookstores, and unusual lifestyles. The **Zodiac,** 193 Cowley Rd. (☎ 726336), has crazy themes every night and the best bands around, for a hefty cover of £5 and up. **Freud's,** 119 Walton St. (☎ 311171), in the former St. Paul's Parish Church (stained-glass windows included), is cafe by day and club by night. Expensive cocktails (£3.25-4.95), but then how often do you party in a church? Open until M-Tu 11pm, W-Th 1am, F-Sa 2am, Su 10:30pm.

Punting and Cruises: A more traditional pastime in Oxford is **punting** on the River Thames (known in Oxford as the Isis) or on the River Cherwell (CHAR-wul). Before venturing out, punters receive a tall pole, a small oar, and an advisory against falling into the river. Try to avoid creating an obstacle course for irate rowers. (Another water safety tip: don't jump into one of the canals—you could wind up with a tetanus shot and stitches.) Don't be surprised if you come upon **Parson's Pleasure,** a small riverside area where men sometimes sunbathe nude. **Magdalen Bridge Boat Co.,** Magdalen Bridge (☎ 202643), east of Carfax along High St., rents from March to November. (M-F £9 per hr., Sa-Su £10 per hr., deposit £20 plus ID; open daily 10am-9pm.)

Festivals: The university celebrates **Eights Week** at the end of May, when all the colleges enter crews in the bumping races and beautiful people nibble strawberries and sip champagne on the banks. In early September, **St. Giles Fair** invades one of Oxford's main streets with an old-fashioned carnival, complete with Victorian roundabout and whirligigs. Daybreak on **May Day** (May 1) brings one of Oxford's loveliest moments: the Magdalen College Choir greets the summer by singing madrigals from the top of the tower to a crowd below, and the town indulges in morris dancing, beating the bounds, and other age-old rituals of merrymaking—pubs open at 7am.

THE MIDLANDS

⚡ DAYTRIP FROM OXFORD: BLENHEIM PALACE

In the town of Woodstock, 8mi. north of Oxford on the A44. Stagecoach Express (☎ (01865) 772250) runs to Blenheim Palace from Gloucester Green bus station (20min., return £3.50). ☎ (01993) 811091. Open daily mid-Mar. to Oct. 10:30am-5:30pm; grounds open year-round 9am-9pm. Last admission 4:45pm. £9, students and seniors £7, children £4.50.

The largest private home in England (and one of the loveliest), Blenheim Palace (BLEN-em) was built in appreciation of the Duke of Marlborough's victory over Louis XIV at the Battle of Blenheim in 1704, and as a token of Queen Anne's friendship with the Duke's wife, Sarah. The 11th Duke of Marlborough now calls the palace home. His rent is a single French franc, payable each year to the Crown—not a bad deal for 187 furnished rooms. High archways and marble floors accentuate the beautiful artwork inside, including wall-size tapestries of 17th- and 18th-century battle scenes. **Winston Churchill**, a member of the Marlborough family, spent his early years here before his family packed him off to boarding school; his baby curls are on display. The 2100 gorgeous acres include fantastic gardens, roaming goats, and a lake, all designed by landscaper **"Capability" Brown** (well, except the goats—he wasn't *that* capable). Blenheim's full glory is on display in Kenneth Branagh's four-hour film of *Hamlet* (1996). Geoffrey Chaucer once lived in Woodstock, and Winston Churchill rests in the nearby village churchyard of **Bladon.**

WINDSOR ☎ 01753

The town of Windsor, and the attached village of Eton, are completely overshadowed by its two bastions of the British class system, Windsor Castle and Eton College. Windsor itself was built up around the castle during the Middle Ages, and is now filled with specialty shops, tea houses, and pubs, all of which are charming enough but worth overlooking for the stupendous sights nearby.

⬛ GETTING THERE

Windsor is probably best seen as a daytrip from London. Two train stations are near Windsor Castle; signs point the way into town. **Trains** (☎ (08457) 484950) pull into **Windsor and Eton Central** from **London Victoria** and **London Paddington** via **Slough** (50min., 2 per hr., day return £5.70). Trains arrive at **Windsor and Eton Riverside** from **London Waterloo** (50min., 2 per hr., day return £5.70). **Green Line** (☎ 8668 7261) **buses** #700 and 702 make the trip from **London,** leaving from Eccleston Bridge, behind Victoria station (1-1½hr., day return £4.35-5.50).

⬛ ACCOMMODATIONS AND FOOD

If you intend to spend the night, the **YHA Windsor,** Edgeworth House, Mill Ln., doesn't have a lockout. (☎ 861710; fax 832100. £10.85, under 18 £7.40.) **The Waterman's Arms** is just over the bridge into Eton and to the left at Brocas St., next to the Eton College Boat House. Founded in 1542, it's still a local favorite. Cod an chips cost £4.15. (☎ 861001. Open M-Sa noon-2:30pm and 6-11pm, Su noon-3pm and 7-10pm.) **Michael's The Eton Bakery,** 43 Eton High St., Eton, over the bridge from Windsor, is an old-time bakery. You can buy stale for the ducks for 10p. (☎ 864725. Takeaway only. Open M-F 7:30am-5pm, Sa 7:30am-4:30pm, Su 11am-4:30pm.)

⬛ SIGHTS

WINDSOR CASTLE

☎ 868286, 24hr. info ☎ 831118. Mostly wheelchair accessible—call ☎ 868286 ext. 2235 for details. Open daily Apr.-Oct. 10am-5:30pm, last entry 4pm; Nov.-Mar. 10am-4pm, last entry 3pm. £10, over 60 £7.50, under 17 £5, families £22.50.

Within these ancient stone walls lie some of the most sumptuous rooms in Europe and some of the rarest artwork in the Western world. But beyond the velvet and fine art, this castle's charm lies in its location high above the Thames and the thousands of arms that bedeck its walls. Built by William the Conqueror as a fortress rather than as a residence, it has grown over nine centuries into the world's largest inhabited castle. Be aware that Windsor is a working castle, which may sound a little strange in this age, but only means that various members of the Royal Family reside here on weekends and for various special ceremonies. The practical consequence of the Royals' residence is that large areas of the castle will be unavailable to visitors, often without warning. The steep admission prices will be lowered, but it is wise to call before visiting to check that the areas you want to see are open. Visitors can watch the **Changing of the Guard** take place in front of the Guard Room at 11am (summer M-Sa; winter alternate days M-Sa).

UPPER WARD. On passing through the Norman Tower and Gate (built by Edward III from 1359-60) you enter the upper ward. Many of its rooms are open to the public, including the elegantly furnished **state apartments,** used mostly for ceremonial occasions and official entertainment. The rooms are richly decorated with art from the massive Royal Collection, including works by Holbein, Rubens, Rembrandt, and Van Dyck. In the same wing is **Queen Mary's Doll House,** an exact replica of a grand house on a 1:12 scale, with classic books in the tiny library handwritten by their original authors, as well as a fully working plumbing system.

MIDDLE AND LOWER WARD. The middle ward is dominated by the **Round Tower** and its surrounding moat-cum-rose garden. A stroll to the lower ward brings you to **St. George's Chapel,** a sumptuous 15th-century building with delicate fan vaulting and an amazing wall of stained glass dedicated to the Order of the Garter. Most recently used for the marriage of Sophie and Prince Edward, the chapel's intimate atmosphere is born from its role as the repository of the bones of Edward's ancestors. Ten sovereigns rest here in all, including George V, Queen Mary, Edward IV, Charles I, and Henry VI. Henry VIII rests below a remarkably humble stone.

OTHER SIGHTS

ETON COLLEGE. Eton College, founded by Henry VI in 1440 as a college for paupers, is England's preeminent public (which is to say, private) school—Prince Harry is a current student. The Queen is the sole (honorary) female Old Etonian. Eton boys still wear tailcoats to every class and solemnly raise one finger in greeting to any teacher on the street. Despite its position at the apex of the British class system, Eton has molded some notable dissidents and revolutionaries, including Aldous Huxley, George Orwell, and former Liberal Party leader Jeremy Thorpe. Wander around the schoolyard, a central quad where Eton boys have frolicked for centuries, complete with a statue of Henry VI. The central area is surrounded by 25 houses that shelter approximately 1250 students. King's Scholars, students selected for full scholarship based on their exam scores, live in the house known as "College," in the courtyard of College Chapel. *(10min. down Thames St. from the town center, across the river.* ☎ *671177. Tours depart daily 2:15pm and 3:15pm; £3.60, under 16 £3. Open daily July-Aug. and late Mar. to mid-Apr. 10:30am-4:30pm; other times 2-4:30pm. £2.60, under 16 £2.)*

LEGOLAND WINDSOR. A recent (1996), whimsical, and expensive addition to the town, this high-class amusement park, beautifully landscaped and wonderfully staffed, will thrill the 11-and-under set with its rides, playgrounds, and circuses. Adults will be amazed by **Miniland,** which took 100 workers three years and 25 million blocks to make. The replica of the City of London includes a 6 ft. St. Paul's, as well as every other major building and landmark in the city. The Lego buses that motor along the city's streets without hitting a car or building are a marvel. *(☎ (0990) 040404. Open daily July 18-Aug. 31 10am-8pm; mid-Mar. to Oct. weekends 10am-6pm. £16.50, children £13.50, seniors £10.50; £1 for the shuttle from the train stations.)*

WARWICKSHIRE

STRATFORD-UPON-AVON   ☎ 01789

The remarkable thing about Shakespeare is that he is really very good—in spite of
all the people who say he is very good.
    —Robert Graves, British poet and novelist

Shakespeare lived here. This fluke of fate has made Stratford-upon-Avon a town
more visited than most. Knick-knack huts hawk "Will Power" T-shirts, while proprietors tout the dozen-odd properties linked, however tenuously, to Shakespeare
and his extended family. But behind the tourist industry lurks Stratford-besides-
Shakespeare, concealed in the nooks of the weeping Avon and the crannies of the
Teddy Bear Museum. Of course, all the perfumes of Arabia will not sweeten the
exhaust from tour buses, but the ghosts of true Stratford are here: ducking into
groves in the Forest of Arden, guzzling sack in 16th-century inns, and appearing in
the pin-drop silence before a soliloquy in the Royal Shakespeare Theatre.

▐ JOURNEY'S END

Trains: Station Rd., off Alcester Rd. Ticket office open M-Sa 6am-10:55pm, Su 9:45am-
6:30pm. **Thames Trains** (☎ (08457) 484950) from: **London Paddington** (2¼hr., 7-10
per day, return £22.50); **Warwick** (25 min., £2.60); and **Birmingham** (1hr., £3.60).

Buses: Riverside Car Park, off Bridgeway Rd. near the Leisure Centre, receives **National
Express** (☎ (08705) 808080) buses from **London** (3hr., 3-4 per day, £11). Buy
National Express tickets at the tourist information centre (TIC). **Stagecoach** runs buses
into Gloucester Green Station from **Oxford** (day return £5.25).

Public Transportation: Local **Stratford Blue** bus services stop on Wood St.

Taxis: Main Taxis (☎ 415111) or **Taxiline** (☎ 266100). Both open 24hr.

Bike Rental: Clarke's Cycle Rental (☎ 205057), the corner of Guild St. and Union St.
£10 per day, £40 per week; deposit £75 or credit card. Open M-Sa 9am-5pm.

Boat Rental: Stratford Marina, (☎ 269669), Clopton Bridge. Rowboats £8 per hr.; 6-
seater motorboats £12 per hr. **Behind the RST.** Rowboats £6 per hr.

▐ HERE CEASE MORE QUESTIONS

Tourist Information Centre: Bridgefoot (☎ 293127, bed booking hotline ☎ 415061).
Maps, guidebooks, and tickets for attractions. Free accommodations guide. Books
rooms for £3 plus 10% deposit of entire stay. Open Apr.-Oct. M-Sa 9am-6pm, Su 11am-
5pm; Nov.-Mar. M-Sa 9am-5pm.

Tours: Guide Friday, Civic Hall, 14 Rother St. (☎ 294466). Transport to all of Shakespeare's houses. 4-5 tours per hr. depart daily from shrines around town. £8.50, students and seniors £7, children under 12 £2.50. They also go to the **Cotswolds**
(£17.50, students and seniors £15, children £8) and **Warwick Castle** (£17.50, £15,
£8; castle admission included). Office open daily 9am-5:30pm.

American Express: (☎ 415856; fax 262411). In the TIC. Open same hours.

Market: At the intersection of Rother St. and Wood St. Open F 8:30am-4:30pm.

Launderette: Sparklean (☎ 269075), the corner of Bull St. and College Ln. Near B&Bs.
Bring change. Wash £2.50, dry 20p per 4min. Open daily 8am-9pm, last wash 8pm.

Police: Rother St. (☎ 414111).

Hospital: Stratford-upon-Avon Hospital, Arden St. (☎ 205831), off Alcester Rd.

Internet Access: Java Café, 28 Greenhill St. (☎ 263400). £3 per 30min., £5 per hr.;
students and seniors £2.50 and £4. Also cheap international phone calls. Open M and
W 10am-5:30pm, Tu 11am-5:30pm, Th 10am-6pm, F 10am-7pm, Sa 11am-6pm.

Post Office: 2-3 Henley St. (☎ 414939). **Bureau de change.** Open M-F 8:30am-
5:30pm, Sa 8:30am-6pm; June-Aug. also Su 10am-3pm. **Postal Code:** CV37 6PU.

▌ TO SLEEP, PERCHANCE TO DREAM

To B&B or not to B&B? This hamlet has tons of them, but singles are hard to find. In summer, 'tis nobler to make advance reservations. B&Bs in the £15-26 range line **Grove Rd., Evesham Pl.,** and **Evesham Rd.** Or try **Shipston Rd.** and **Banbury Rd.** across the river, 15min. from the station.

YHA Stratford, Hemmingford House (☎ 297093; stratford@yha.org.uk), Wellesbourne Rd., Alveston, 2 mi. from Stratford. Follow the B4086, or take bus #X18 from the Bridge St. stop (1 per hr., £1.70). Large, attractive grounds and a 200-year-old building with RSC photos on the wall. Friendly staff offers Shakespearean wisdom and full English breakfasts. With return bus fare, this may cost as much as some B&Bs. 130 beds in rooms of 2-14. Kitchen. Reception 24hr. £14.90, students £13.90, children £11.20.

Stratford Backpackers Hotel, 33 Greenhill St. (☎/fax 263838). Clean and comfortable, with 6-8 beds per room. The dining area is a recently converted cafe with bright blue walls. Kitchen, small common room, storage area. Photo ID required to stay. Dorms £12, £1 off if you come directly from the Oxford Backpackers Hotel.

Bradbourne Guest House, 44 Shipston Rd. (☎ 204178), 8min. walk from the center. Recently redecorated Tudor-style home with a pleasant conservatory. Breakfast includes veggie dishes. Cable TV in every room. Singles £30; doubles £50. Rates lower Oct.-Apr.

The Hollies, 16 Evesham Pl. (☎ 266857). Warm and attentive proprietors for whom the guest house has become a labor of love. From the mint walls to the ivy scaling the outside, green prevails. Spacious and well decorated, with big mirrors adorning some rooms. Doubles £35, with bath £45.

Clodagh's B&B, 34 Banbury Rd. (☎ 269714; clodagh@lycosmail.com). One of Stratford's best values. Once Clodagh takes you into her home you'll be tempted to stay longer than planned. Superb showers in shared bathrooms. Singles £16; doubles £32.

Field View Guest House, 35 Banbury Rd. (☎ 292694). Quiet, peaceful rooms with a welcoming owner. Vegetarian menu at breakfast. Singles £16; doubles £32.

Nando's, 18 Evesham Pl. (☎/fax 204907). Friendly owners. Comfortable rooms all have TVs; most have private bathrooms. Singles £22; doubles £48. Rates lower in winter.

Ashley Court, 55 Shipston Rd. (☎ 297278). Spacious rooms with private bathrooms, remote control TVs, radios, and private phones—but you pay for such luxury. Half-acre garden in back. Only a 5min. walk across a footbridge to all the sights. Bar open most nights from 5-11pm. Doubles and twins £48, £53 on weekends.

Camping: Riverside Caravan Park, Tiddington Rd. (☎ 292312), 1 mi. east of Stratford on the B4086. Sunset views on the Avon, but can get crowded. Village pub is a 3-4min. walk. Showers. Open Easter-Oct. Tent and two people £7, each additional person £1.

OFF YER ROCKER 1999 marked the passing of David Sutch, founder of one of Britain's most dynamic political parties, the **Official Monster Raving Loony Party (OMRLP).** Perhaps the most bizarre if not the most ridiculous of Britain's political leaders, Screaming Lord Sutch, as David Sutch was known, began his political career as the National Teenage Party's candidate for Stratford-upon-Avon. After brief membership in both the Young Ideas Party and the Go To Blazes Party, Sutch founded the OMRLP in 1980. Though initially dismissed as a "Shakespearean antic for the TV age," the OMRLP enjoyed surprising success in the 1990 by-election, beating the Social Democrats in one constituency.

The Loonies will fight on, despite the death of their leader—Alan "Howling Lord" Hope fought for a seat in parliament in a 1999 by-election, while Baron Von Thunderclap, previously the party's spokesman for transport/saving the dodo/decimal time, has assumed temporary leadership. Meanwhile, 13-year-old Oliver Hewitt has been asked to become the junior party chairman after chaining himself to the railings of Downing Street, protesting that children should not be made to study algebra. Hewitt is being groomed to take over the party leadership in 2010.

THE MIDLANDS

⚉ FOOD OF LOVE

Faux Tudor fast food and pub grub clogs Stratford. Baguette stores and bakeries are scattered like itinerant minstrels throughout the town, and a **Safeway** super-market beckons on Alcester Rd., just across the bridge past the train station. (Open M-Th and Sa 8am-9pm, F 8am-10pm, Su 10am-4pm.)

Hussain's Indian Cuisine, 6a Chapel St. (☎ 267506). Probably Stratford's best Indian cuisine, with a slew of tandoori prepared as you like it. A favorite of Ben Kingsley. The chicken tikka masala is fabulous. Three-course lunch £6. Main courses £6 and up. 15% discount for takeaway. Open Th-Su 12:30-2:30pm and daily 5pm-midnight.

ASK Pizza and Pasta, Old Red Lion Court (☎ 262440), off Bridge St. Enjoy heaping por-tions of Italian food in simple surroundings. Many pizza and pasta options at this chain restaurant; main courses £5-7. Open daily 10am-11pm.

De:alto, 13 Waterside (☎ 298326). Very trendy for this historical town, De:alto's blue lighting, light wood, and metal decor will make the New Yorker in you feel at home. Sur-prisingly well-priced. Pizza £5.50-6, salad £5.50-7, calzones £6.15. Open M-Th noon-10pm, F-Sa noon-11pm, Su 2-9:30pm.

Le Petit Croissant, 17 Wood St. (☎ 292333). A great place for breakfast or lunch, with delicious baked treats such as tarts, baguettes, and quiches. Open M-Sa 8am-6pm.

Stratford Health Foods, 10 Greenhill St. (☎ 292353). The "Whole Food Takeaway" sec-tion of this store includes sausage rolls (45p), veggie samosas (57p), pita bread pizza (79p), and healthy desserts. Open M and W-Sa 9am-5:30pm, Tu 9:30am-5:30pm.

⊔ DRINK DEEP ERE YOU DEPART

Dirty Duck Pub, Waterside (☎ 297312). River view outside, huge bust of Shakespeare within. Theater crowds abound, and the actors themselves make frequent entrances—look for the room with pictures of the regulars. Traditional pub lunch £3-9; dinner £6-20. Open M-Sa 11am-11pm, Su noon-10:30pm.

Bar M, 1 Arden St. (☎ 297641). Bright inviting colors highlight the pub by day; by night, the blue and silver spiral staircase leads you to the club's dance area. Promotions throughout the week. Open M and Th noon-1am, Tu-W noon-midnight, F-Sa noon-2am, Su noon-10:30pm.

The Cross Keys, Ely St. (☎ 293909). Order food at the bar and snuggle into a booth in one of three rooms. Large covered patio has a big screen TV for major sporting events. Open M-Sa 11am-11pm, Su 11am-10:30pm. Food served noon-3pm and 5-8pm.

Chicago Rock Cafe, 8 Greenhill St. (☎ 293344). Modern bar with special nights almost all week: M 2-for-1 drinks, Tu karaoke, W live bands, Th half-price cocktails, F-Sa party nights. Open M-Th 11:30am-11:30pm, F-Sa 11:30am-12:30am, Su noon-10:30pm.

Cox's Yard, Bridgefoot (☎ 404600). Food and fun for all ages. Features a microbrewery as well as a tea shop. Live bands on Su. Open daily 11am-11pm.

⊙ THE GILDED MONUMENTS

TO BE

Stratford's mostly Will-centered sights are best seen before 11am, when the herds of daytrippers have not yet arrived, or after 4pm, when the hurly-burly's done. Bar-dolatry peaks at 2pm. Five official **Shakespeare properties** (☎ 204016) grace the town: Shakespeare's Birthplace, Hall's Croft, Nash's House and New Place, Anne Hathaway's Cottage, and Mary Arden's House. Diehard fans should buy the **combi-nation ticket,** which offers savings of £8 if you make it to every shrine. (£12, stu-dents and seniors £11, children £6.) If you don't want to visit them all (dark-timbered roof beams and floors begin to look the same no matter who lived between them), buy a **Shakespeare's Town Heritage Trail** ticket, which covers only the sights in town—the Birthplace, Hall's Croft, and Nash's House and New Place. (£8.50, students and seniors £7.50, children £4.20.)

SHAKESPEARE'S BIRTHPLACE. Half period re-creation and half Shakespeare life-and-work exhibition, this includes an exhibit on the glove-making career of Will's father. Sign the guestbook and enter the company of such distinguished pilgrims as Charles Dickens. *(Henley St. ☎ 204016. Open Mar. 20-Oct. 19 M-Sa 9am-5pm, Su 9:30am-5pm; Oct. 20-Mar. 19 M-Sa 9:30am-4pm, Su 10am-4pm. Partial wheelchair access. £5.50, students and seniors £5, children £2.50, families £14.)*

HALL'S CROFT. Dr. John Hall married Shakespeare's oldest daughter Susanna. Aside from that link to the Bard, Dr. Hall garnered fame in his own right by being one of the first doctors to keep detailed records of his patients, and the Croft features an exhibit of his work, and of medicine in Shakespeare's time. *(Old Town. Open Mar. 20-Oct. 19 M-Sa 9:30am-5pm, Su 10am-5pm; Oct. 20-Mar. 19 M-Sa 10am-4pm, Su 10:30am-4pm. £3.50, students and seniors £3, children £1.70, families £8.50.)*

NASH'S HOUSE AND NEW PLACE. Tenuous Shakespeare Connection Alert: Thomas Nash was the first husband of Shakespeare's granddaughter Elizabeth, who was the last of the playwright's descendants. Nash's House contains Tudor furnishings and a local history collection. The adjacent **New Place** was Stratford's hippest home when Shakespeare bought it in 1597 after writing some hits in London. Only the foundation remains after a disgruntled 19th-century owner tore the house down in a tax dispute. Admission to Nash's House allows you to view the plot and foundation remains of the New Place. *(Chapel St. Open Mar. 20-Oct. 19 M-Sa 9:30am-5pm, Su 10am-5pm; Oct. 20-Mar. 19 M-Sa 10am-4pm, Su 10:30am-4pm. £3.50, students and seniors £3, children £1.70, families £8.50.)*

Down Chapel St. from Nash's House, the sculpted bushes, manicured lawn, and abundant flowers of the **Great Garden of New Place** offer a peaceful retreat from Stratford's streets. Bring a picnic lunch, and enjoy one of Stratford's most tourist-free areas. *(Open M-Sa 9am-dusk, Su 10am-dusk. Free.)*

SHAKESPEARE'S GRAVE. The least crowded way to pay homage to the institution himself is to visit his little, little grave in **Holy Trinity Church,** though groups still pack the arched door at peak hours. The church also holds the graves of his wife and his daughter Susanna. The lush grounds are shady, and benches can be found amidst the headstones. *(Trinity St. £1, students and children 50p.)*

AROUND THE ROYAL SHAKESPEARE THEATRE. The violets have not withered in the free **Royal Shakespeare Theatre Gardens,** south of the theater. In the gardens, the **RST Summer House** holds a **brass-rubbing studio,** an alternative to plastic Shakespeare memorabilia. *(☎ 297671. Open daily Apr.-Sept. 10am-6pm; Oct.-Mar. 11am-4pm. Prices of rubbing plates 95p-£4 and higher; materials included.)* The riverbank between the RST and Clopton Bridge is a sight in itself. Gazing out at the serene rowers, you'd never guess that about six million buses are behind you.

ANNE HATHAWAY'S COTTAGE. The birthplace of Shakespeare's wife lies about one mile from Stratford in **Shottery;** take the ill-marked footpaths north. This is probably the thatched-roof cottage you saw on the travel agent's poster. Entrance entitles you to sit on a bench Will may or may not have sat on; view from outside if you've seen the birthplace. *(☎ 292100. Open Mar.-Oct. daily 9am-5pm; Nov.-Feb. daily 9:30am-4:30pm. £4.20, students and seniors £3.70, children £1.70.)*

MARY ARDEN'S HOUSE. This farmhouse, restored in the style a 19th-century entrepreneur determined to be precisely that of Shakespeare's mother, stands four miles from Stratford in Wilmcote. A footpath connects it to Anne Hathaway's Cottage. *(☎ 293455. Open Mar.-Oct. M-Sa 9:30am-5pm, Su 10am-5pm; Nov.-Feb. M-Sa 10am-4pm, Su 10:30am-4pm. £5, students and seniors £4.50, children £2.50, families £12.50.)*

NOT TO BE

If you're bored of the Bard, fear not—non-Shakespearean sights *are* available (if not particularly exciting) in Stratford.

TEDDY BEAR MUSEUM. The museum hosts a collection of thousands of stuffed, ceramic, painted, and handmade bears. Though most of them went to children in Yugoslavia, 12 of the "Diana bears" (left in front of Kensington Palace), take up residence alongside the original Fozzie Bear, who was given to the museum by Jim Henson and now waves goodbye. *(Exit, pursued by a bear. 19 Greenhill St. ☎ 293160. Open daily 9:30am-6pm. £2.25, students and seniors £1.75, children £1.)*

HARVARD HOUSE. Period pieces and pewter punctuate this authentic Tudor building, vaguely connected with the man who lends his name to the American college that owns it (his mother lived here). The "Harvard-Only" guestbook contains the names of such notables as Teresa Crockett. *(High St. ☎ 204507. Open May-Sept. M-Sa 10am-4:30pm, Su 10:30am-4:30pm. Free.)*

STRATFORD-UPON-AVON BUTTERFLY FARM. This collection of exotic butterflies and insects is located at Tramway Walk, across the river from the TIC. *(Off Swan's Nest Ln. ☎ 299288. Open daily summer 10am-6pm; winter 10am-dusk. £3.75, students and seniors £3.25, children £2.75.)*

RAGLEY HALL. Eight miles from Stratford on Evesham Rd. (the A435), Ragley Hall houses the Earl and Countess of Yarmouth. Set in a 400-acre park, the estate holds a collection of paintings and a captivating maze. *(Take a bus to Alcester (M-Sa 5 per day), walk 1 mi. to the gates, then ½ mi. up the drive. ☎ 762090. Open July-Aug. daily 11am-5pm; Apr.-Oct. Th-Su 11am-5pm. £5, students and seniors £4.50, children £3.50.)*

 ## THE PLAY'S THE THING

THE ROYAL SHAKESPEARE COMPANY
The box office in the foyer of the Royal Shakespeare Theatre handles ticketing for all three theaters. ☎ 403403, 24hr. recording ☎ 403404; www.rsc.org.uk. Open M-Sa 9am-8pm. Tickets for RST £5-40; Swan £5-36; Other Place £10-20. RST and Swan have £5 standing room tickets; under 25 get half-price same-day tickets; and £8-12 student and senior same-day standbys exist in principle—be ready to pounce.

One of the world's most acclaimed repertories, the Royal Shakespeare Company sells well over one million tickets each year, and claims Kenneth Branagh and Ralph Fiennes as recent sons. In Stratford, it performs in three theaters: the Royal Shakespeare, the Swan, and The Other Place. A group gathers outside about 20 minutes before opening for same-day sales (it's easier to get same-day tickets for matinees). A happy few get customer returns and standing-room tickets for evening shows; queue 1-2 hours before curtain. **Disabled travelers** should call in advance to advise the box office of their needs—certain seats are wheelchair accessible, while some performances feature sign language interpretation or audio description. The RSC also conducts **backstage tours** that cram camera-happy groups into the wooden "O"s of the RST and the Swan. *(☎ 412602. Tours daily 1:30pm, 5:30pm, and after performances. £4, students and seniors £3.)*

Royal Shakespeare Theatre, Waterside, across from Chapel Ln. He was born on Henley St., died at New Place, and lives on at the RST, which towers eloquently over the slanting willows on Waterside. The boards of the RST are graced only by the great man's plays: lesser playwrights are relegated to the other stages.

The Swan Theatre, Waterside, across from Chapel Ln. Tastefully mixing two historical milieus, the RSC took the shell of the burnt-out Memorial Theatre and renovated it to resemble Shakespeare's Globe. The venue showcases RSC productions of Renaissance and Restoration plays. Smaller and more intimate than the RST.

The Other Place. The RSC's newest branch, on Southern Ln., produces avant-garde premieres, and modern, rarely performed plays in an experimental black-box theater.

FESTIVALS
Astonishingly, for two weeks in July the **Stratford Festival** celebrates artistic achievement other than Shakespeare's, from music to poetry. Tickets (when required) can be purchased from the Festival box office (☎ 414513), on Rother St. The modern, well-respected **Shakespeare Centre**, Henley St., hosts an annual **Poetry Festival** every Sunday evening in July and August. Over the past few years, Seamus Heaney, Ted Hughes, and Derek Walcott have put in appearances. (☎ 204016. Open M-F 9am-5pm. Tickets £7.) The center also has a library and a bookshop.

WARWICK ☎01926

Most of the tourists that reach Warwick (WAR-rick) come only by day to visit the castle, and indeed it makes a good daytrip from Birmingham or Stratford. However, the unique architectural heritage of the town, created by rebuilding after the Great Fire of 1694, makes it well worth the overnight stay.

🖥🔁 GETTING THERE AND PRACTICAL INFORMATION. The Warwick **train station** sits on Coventry Rd. (Ticket office open M-Sa 6am-10:30pm, Su 8:30am-10pm.) Several **trains** (☎ (08457) 484950) run daily from: **London Marylebone** (2½hr., 2 per hr., £24.50, day return £19.50); **Stratford** (20min., 1 per hr., £2.50); and **Birmingham** (40min., 1 per hr., £3.50). **National Express** (☎ (08705) 808080) **buses** stop in Old Square from **London** (3hr., 3 per day., £11); buy tickets at **Coop Travel,** Market St.(☎ 410709). **Stagecoach Midland Red** (☎ (01788) 535555) buses stop at Market Place from **Stratford** (#X16, 30min., 1 per hr.) and **Coventry** (#X18, 1 hr.; 1 per hr.). **Warwickshire Traveline** (☎ 562036) has local bus info. For cabs, try **Tudor Taxi** (☎ 495000).

The **tourist information centre** (TIC), Court House, Jury St., books rooms for £2.50 plus a 10% deposit, and stocks a 30p guided map and a free town map. (☎ 492212; fax 494837; www.warwick-uk.co.uk. Open daily 9:30am-4:30pm.) **Tours** leave from the TIC on Sunday at 10:45am and some Mondays at 2:30pm. Services include: **Barclays,** 5 High St. (☎ 303000; open M-F 9am-5pm); **Warwick Hospital** (☎ 495321), Lakin Rd.; the **police station** (☎ 410111), Priory Rd.; and the **post office,** Westgate House, 45 Brook St. (☎ 491061). **Postal code:** CV34 4BL.

🍴🛏 ACCOMMODATIONS AND FOOD. Trying to stay near the castle can be pricey, but **Emscote Rd.** has cheaper places. From the train station, turn right onto Coventry Rd. and left at the Crown's Hotel onto Cotton End, which becomes Emscote Rd. (10min. walk). **Avon Guest House,** 7 Emscote Rd., has standard singles and spacious doubles across the street from the beautiful green of St. Nicholas Park. (☎ 491367. Singles £20; doubles £22, some with bath.) The humorous, young proprietor of **Westham Guest House,** 76 Emscote Rd., maintains a laid-back atmosphere and a breakfast menu with vegetarian choices. (☎ 491756; westhamhouse@aol.com. Singles £18; doubles £32, with bath £36-40.) **Ashburton Guest House,** 74 Emscote Rd., is bright and modern, with a comforting dining room. (☎ 401082. Singles £20; doubles with bath £40.) At **Park House Guest Host,** 17 Emscote Rd., all rooms have attached baths. (☎ 494359. Singles £20-25; doubles £36-40.)

As in most English towns, there are numerous takeaways scattered throughout the town center. For a sit-down meal, the **Crown Hotel Pub,** 4-6 Coventry Rd., down St. Nicholas St. from the castle, offers cheap lunch specials (sandwich and chips £2) and dinners (burger £4.50) in a traditional pub. (☎ 492087. Open M-Sa 11am-11pm, Su noon-10:30pm.) **The Roebuck,** Smith St. (☎ 494900), offers cheap "quick serve dishes" (£3.75-4.75) and desserts, in addition to a traditional menu. For **medieval banquets** call Warwick Castle (☎ 495421).

🏰 SIGHTS. Many historians, architects, and P.R. hacks regard ⚔ **Warwick Castle,** visible throughout town, as England's finest medieval castle. Climb the 530 steps to the top of the towers and see the countryside unfold like a fairytale kingdom of hobbits and elves. The dungeons are filled with life-size wax figures of people preparing for battle, while "knights" and "craftsmen" talk about their trades. (☎ 495421, 24hr. recording ☎ 406600; www.warwick-castle.co.uk. Open daily Apr.-Oct. 10am-6pm; Nov.-Mar. 10am-5pm. Limited wheelchair access; lockers £1. £10.95, students and seniors £7.85, children £6.50.)

Warwick's other sights are not as impressive as the castle, but not as expensive either. Stroll by **St. Mary's Church,** Church St., to see stained-glass windows and the grave of Fulke Greville, who's said to haunt the castle's Watergate Tower. In 1571, Lord Leycester acquired the buildings of the **Lord Leycester Hospital,** 60 High St., to house 12 old soldiers who had fought with him in the Netherlands; today, seven retired veterans still live inside. (☎ 491422. Open Easter-Oct. Tu-Su 10am-5pm, Oct.-Easter 10am-4pm. £2.75, students and seniors £2, children £1.50.) The **War-**

wickshire Museum, in the Shirehall, holds displays on archaeology and natural history. (☎ 410410. Open M-Sa 10am-5:30pm. Free.) **St. John's Museum,** on St. John's St., houses Victorian costumes and musical instruments. (☎ 410410. Open Tu-Sa 10am-12:30pm and 1:30-5:30pm; also Su 2:30-5pm May-Sept. Free.)

NEAR WARWICK: COVENTRY   ☎024

Twelve miles northeast of Warwick burgeons the city of Coventry. Bombed during World War II, Coventry has rebuilt itself into a modern city and a major transportation hub, with not always pretty results. The phrase "sent to Coventry" means the silent treatment, a term which arose from the Royalist/Puritan antagonism during the Civil War. Now Coventry is united around its two **cathedrals**—the destroyed and the resurrected. The shards of the old cathedral are visible through the glass "west wall" (actually the south wall) of the new, which was dedicated in 1962 to the strains of Benjamin Britten's *War Requiem*. A small bell in the cathedral is inscribed "Peace, *Friede*," a theme which resounds throughout the building. (☎ 7622 7597; www.coventrycathedral.org. Open daily 9:30am-6:30pm. Requested donation £2. Visitor center £2, children and seniors £1.) The city's other benefactor, the Daimler Company, is honored in the **Museum of British Road Transport,** St. Agnes Ln., Hales St. (☎ 7683 2425. Open daily 10am-5pm. Free.)

Besides the cathedral, Coventry has a pedestrian-only downtown area that resembles a shopping mall, littered with fast-food shops. Those staying in Coventry can visit the **tourist information centre,** Bayley Ln., and pick up *Your Where to Stay Guide.* (☎ 7683 2303; fax 7683 2370. Open Easter-Oct. M-F 9:30am-5pm, Sa-Su 10am-4:30pm; Nov.-Easter M-F 9:30am-4:30pm, Sa-Su 10am-4:30pm.) Once home to **Lady Godiva,** the city honors her memory with a week-long June festival featuring a (fully clothed) parade.

GLOUCESTERSHIRE

CHELTENHAM   ☎01242

A spa town second only to Bath, Cheltenham (pop. 107,000) exudes a carefree sophistication. Manicured gardens of bursting red adorn expensive shops and tree-lined lanes. Cheltenham's Laura Ashley-esque quality is a break from the heavily touristed centers of Bath and Stratford and the gloomy industrial megaliths of the Midlands. A useful launching pad into the Cotswolds, this city also has a large student population that brings the pubs and clubs to life at night.

▐ GETTING THERE AND GETTING AROUND

Cheltenham lies 43 mi. south of Birmingham. Daytrips from Oxford and other locales are possible, and Cheltenham makes an excellent stopover for cyclists and walkers traveling the Cotswolds. The tourist information center (TIC) stocks a free *Getting There* pamphlet with detailed information on area travel.

Trains: Cheltenham Spa Station, on Queen's Rd. at Gloucester Rd. Ticket office open M-F 5:45am-8:15pm, Sa 5:45am-7:15pm, Su 8:15am-8:15pm. Trains (☎ (08457) 484950) from: **London** (2½hr., 1 per hr., £31.50); **Birmingham** (30min., 2 per hr., £12.60); **Bath** (1½hr., 1 per hr., £11.10); and **Exeter** (2hr., every 2hr., £28.50).

Buses: Royal Well, Royal Well Rd. National Express office open M-Sa 9am-5:30pm. **Luggage lockers** £1-2. **National Express** (☎ (08705) 808080) from: **London** (3hr., 1 per hr., £10.50); **Bristol** (1¼hr., every 2hr., £6.50); and **Exeter** (3½hr., every 2hr., £18). **Swanbrook Coaches** (☎ (01452) 712386) from **Oxford** (1½hr., return £8).

Taxis: Central Taxi (☎ 228877). **Associated Taxis** (☎ (01452) 311700). Taxis wait outside the bus station all day, while there's a free phone in the train station.

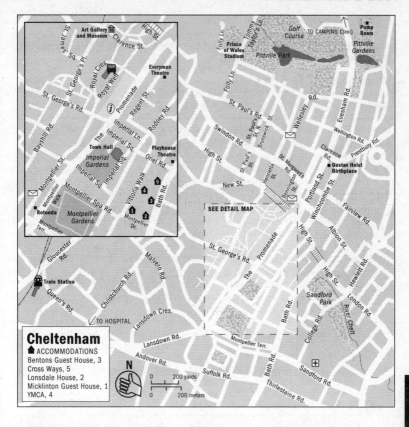

Cheltenham

⬥ ACCOMMODATIONS
Bentons Guest House, 3
Cross Ways, 5
Lonsdale House, 2
Micklinton Guest House, 1
YMCA, 4

ORIENTATION AND PRACTICAL INFORMATION

The majority of attractions in Cheltenham are within walking distance of the town's center. **The Promenade,** a pedestrian-only walkway one block east of the bus station, is home to the tourist information centre. To get there from the train station, walk down Queen's Rd. and bear left onto Lansdown Rd. Head left again at the Rotunda onto Montpellier Walk, which leads to The Promenade. Or save yourself the 15min. walk and jump on one of the frequent F or G buses (8 per hr., 75p). A free city-center bus service is available from the Royal Well station.

Tourist Information Centre: Municipal Offices, 77 The Promenade (☎ 522878; accommodations booking ☎ 517110; fax. 515535; www.visitcheltenham.gov.uk). Well-organized staff sells National Express tickets and books accomodations for refundable 10% deposit. B&B vacancies posted outside after hours. Open M-Sa 9:30am-5:15pm. **Tours** leave from the office late June to mid-Sept. M-F 2:15pm; 1¼hr., £2.50.

Finanical Services: Banks are everywhere; try **Lloyds TSB,** 130 High St. (☎ 518169). Open M-Tu and Th-F 9am-5pm, W 9:30am-5pm, Sa 9am-12:30pm.

Launderette: Soap-n-Suds, 312 High St. Soap and change available. Open daily 8am-8pm; last wash 7pm.

Police: Holland House, 840 Lansdown Rd. (☎ 521321). From the town center follow The Promenade until it becomes Montpellier Walk; Lansdown Rd. is on the right.

Hospital: Cheltenham General, Sandford Rd. (☎ 222222). Follow the Bath Rd. southwest from town and turn left onto Sandford Rd. Emergency entrance on College Rd.

THE MIDLANDS

Internet Access: Rendezvous Cyber Café, 16 Portland St. (☎ 577893). £1 per 15min. Open M-Sa 9am-5:30pm, Tu and Th also 6-9pm.

Post Office: 225-227 High St. (☎ 526056). Open M-Sa 9am-5:30pm. **Bureau de change. Postal Code:** GL50.

ACCOMMODATIONS

Standards in Cheltenham's B&Bs tend to be high, but so do the prices. A handful of B&Bs can be found in the **Montpellier** area and along **Bath Rd.,** a five-minute walk from the town center. The TIC publishes a thick accommodations booklet.

Cross Ways, 57 Bath Rd. (☎ 527683; fax 577226; crossways@btinternet.com). The flowers that line the walkway outside are as warm and inviting as the proprietress. The floral decorations inside are amazing—she made the bedding and curtains herself. TVs in rooms, and tasty breakfast with veggie items. £22-25 per person.

Bentons Guest House, 71 Bath Rd. (☎ 517417; fax 577744). Floral patterns everywhere, from the exuberant gardens to the well-kept rooms with TVs. Platter-sized plates can barely hold the breakfast. £25-35 per person, depending on season and facilities.

Lonsdale House, 16 Montpellier Dr. (☎ 232379; lonsdale-house@hotmail.com). Large home with a bounty of singles. The Mallinsons offer comfortable, spacious rooms with TVs, and shelves full of English literary classics. Singles £21; doubles with bath £49.

Micklinton Guest House, 12 Montpellier Dr. (☎ 520000; fax 704056; dobeid@cableinet.co). Reminiscent of an American country home, with unstained wood and green decoration. They even have menus at breakfast. The rooms are comfortable, and all have TVs. Singles £20-24, doubles £40-44.

YMCA, Vittoria Walk (☎ 524024; fax 232365). At the town hall, turn left onto the Promenade and walk three blocks; Vittoria Walk is on the right. Men and women accepted. Well located, with clean rooms. Many long-term tenants. Booming loudspeaker informs guests of phone calls. Continental breakfast included. Limited parking available. Office open 24hr., but if you want B&B, arrive before 9:30pm. Porter lets in guests after 11pm. Singles £15, £13.80 after first night.

FOOD AND PUBS

Fruit stands, butchers, and bakeries dot the **High St.,** while down the road, **Tesco** supermarket has it all under one roof. (☎ 847400. Open M-Tu and Sa 7:30am-7pm, W-F 7:30am-8pm, Su 11am-5pm.) A **market** takes place on Henrietta St. on Thursday mornings.

Pepper's Café Bar (☎ 573488), on Regent St., across from the Slug and Lettuce. A popular local hangout that combines the atmosphere of an English pub with a trendy Californian cafe. Salsa dancing Friday nights until 1am. Creative sandwiches start at £4, and salads are around £5. Open M-Sa 8am-11pm, Su 9am-10:30pm.

Choirs Restaurant, 5-6 Well Walk (☎ 235578). The French owner serves lunch (under £7) in an atmosphere as dainty as the delicious food; sadly, prices rise after 7pm.

The Orange Tree, 317 High St. (☎ 234232). Pampers vegetarians. Follow a hummus sandwich with organic beer. Main courses £8. Weekend reservations recommended. Open M 9:30am-4pm, Tu-Th 9:30am-9pm, F-Sa 9:30am-10pm, Su 11am-3pm.

Moon Under Water, 16-28 Bath Rd. (☎ 583945). Satisfy your craving for a plate of nachos and a great burger. Dine on their outdoor patio, which overlooks Sandford Park. The running waterfall in the background will make you crave their cask ales. Open daily 11am-11pm, food served until 10pm.

Downtown Eats, 293 High St. (☎ 516388). Has takeaway sandwiches (80p-£1.65) that are perfect for a picnic in the marvelous Montpellier or Imperial Gardens. Open M-Sa 8am-3:30pm.

Frog and Fiddle, 315 High St. (☎ 701156; fax 701157). Chill on the big blue couches, relax on the patio, or examine the artwork in the upstairs gallery. A large student clientele fills the pub's cavernous back rooms. Open M-Sa 11am-11pm, Su noon-10:30pm.

Dobell's, 24 The Promenade (☎ 525537). Perfect for a relaxing pint, good conversation, and quirky decor. Open M-Sa 11am-11pm, Su noon-10:30pm.

◉ SIGHTS

Cheltenham proudly possesses the only naturally **alkaline water** in Britain. Crazy George III took the waters in 1788; in the 19th century the Duke of Wellington claimed that the spring cured his "disordered liver." You don't need an illness to enjoy the diuretic and laxative effects of the waters at the **town hall.** (Open M-F 9:30am-5:30pm. Water tasting free.) Two blocks from the bus station, the **Cheltenham Art Gallery and Museum** houses an impressive collection of pottery, mementos of the Arts and Crafts movement, and a giant beer bottle. Special exhibits are changed every month. (Clarence St. ☎ 237431. Open M-Sa 10am-5:20pm. Wheelchair access. Free.) The **Gustav Holst Birthplace Museum,** 4 Clarence Rd. (*not* Clarence St.), portrays the composer's early life. Follow the signs to the bus station, then walk one block to Clarence Rd. (☎ 524846. Open Tu-Sa 10am-4:20pm. £2.25, concessions 75p.) A walk down Clarence St. and a left at St. James Sq. will bring you to the house in which **Tennyson** wrote *In Memoriam.* No museum here—the house is in disrepair, with windows thickly crusted, one and all. Bouffants and bikers sunbathe amidst the exquisite blooms of the **Imperial Gardens,** just past the Promenade away from the center of town.

❈ FESTIVALS

The indispensable *What's On* poster, displayed on kiosks and at the TIC, lists many concerts, plays, tours, sporting events, and evening hot-spots. The **Cheltenham International Festival of Music** in July celebrates modern classical works, as well as opera. The Fringe branch of the Festival features jazz, rock, and world premieres; many performances are free. Full details are available in March from the box office, Town Hall, Imperial Sq., Cheltenham GL50 1QA. (☎ 227979. Tickets £2-19.) The **Cheltenham Cricket Festival,** the oldest in the country, commences in mid-July. Purchase tickets at the gate and inquire about game times at the TIC. October heralds the **Cheltenham Festival of Literature,** which runs a fortnight. Recent guests have included Seamus Heaney, P.D. James, and Stephen Spender. For a full program of events, write to the Town Hall or call the 24-hour Festival Box Office. (☎ 237979. Advance tickets £1.50-4.) The **National Hunt,** a horse-racing event, starts in the winter and culminates in March, when the population of Cheltenham nearly doubles—you can find over 50,000 people per day at the race course.

NEAR CHELTENHAM: TEWKESBURY
☎ 01684

Ten miles northwest of Cheltenham, at the confluence of the Rivers Avon and Severn, lies Tewkesbury, site of stately **Tewkesbury Abbey.** Consecrated in 1121, the abbey captures the beautiful power of Norman (or "English Romanesque") architecture and is illuminated by 14th-century stained glass. During the Battle of Tewkesbury, some Lancastrians tried to seek refuge in the abbey. The monks attempted to protect them, but the Yorks killed the monks as well, and the abbey had to be reconsecrated. The abbey stands today only because townsfolk raised £453 to save it from the dissolution planned by Henry VIII. (☎ 850959. Open in summer M-Sa 7:30am-6:30pm, Su 7:30am-7pm; in winter daily 7:30am-5:30pm. Services Su at 8am, 9:15am, 11am, and 6pm. Requested donation £2.) Small museums dot the village, including the **Tewkesbury Town Museum,** 64 Barton St., which has an exhibit on the 1471 Battle of Tewkesbury. (☎ 295027. Open daily 10am-4pm. 75p, seniors 50p, children 25p.) The **Little Museum,** Church St., is a merchant's cottage built in 1450 and restored five centuries later. (☎ 297174. Open Apr.-Oct. Tu-Sa 10am-5pm. Free.) Once an Iron Age fort, the **Country Park,** Crickley Hill, offers ethereal views and artifacts of archaeological interest.

  Tewkesbury makes a leisurely day trip from Cheltenham and can be adequately visited in a few hours. **Cheltenham District** (☎ (01242) 522021) bus #41 departs from Cheltenham (M-F every hour until 7pm, Sa every 30min., return £2.15). The town's **tourist information centre** nests in the Town Museum. It sells a 10p town map and a 20p pamphlet outlining walks through Tewkesbury's alley-like streets. (☎ 295027.

Open daily 9am-5pm, Su 10am-4pm.) **Banks** line High St. The **post office** is at 99-100 High St. (☎ 293232. Open M-F 9am-5:30pm, Sa 9am-4pm.) **Postal code:** GL20.

Hanbury Guest House, Barton Rd., five minutes from the town center on the left, has comfortable rooms, with washbasins, TVs, and comfy quilts. (☎ 299911. Doubles £36, with bath £40.) The **Crescent Guest House,** 30 Church St., is next to the Abbey. Comfortable, pleasant rooms with lovely window views all have TVs and washbasins. (☎ 293395. Doubles £38.)

THE COTSWOLDS

The Cotswolds have deviated little from their etymological roots—"Cotswolds" means "sheep enclosure in rolling hillsides." These verdant, vivid hills enclose small towns with names longer than their main streets (Bourton-on-the-Water, Stow-on-the-Wold, Moreton-in-Marsh), which are barely touched by modern life, save periodic strings of antique shops and summer tourists. Saxon villages and Roman settlements, hewn straight from the famed Cotswold Stone, link a series of trails accessible to walkers and cyclists. The Cotswolds are not just for outdoors enthusiasts, however; anyone with an interest in rural England will find something here. The towns seem like scenes from a rustic past, and brilliant greens, golds, and purples color the entire area with natural beauty.

▐ GETTING THERE AND GETTING AROUND

If you like to travel spontaneously, a bike or a car is a must in the Cotswolds, since there's a paucity of public transport. Decide beforehand which villages you aim to hit, as those in the so-called "Northern" Cotswolds (Stow-on-the-Wold, Bourton-on-the-Water, Moreton-in-Marsh) are more easily reached via Cheltenham, while the "Southern" Cotswolds (notably Slimbridge and Painswick) are served more frequently by Gloucester. The Gloucester tourist information centre (TIC) has transport information, and the Cheltenham TIC provides the invaluable *Getting There from Cheltenham* pamphlet.

Trains frequent the area's major gateways (Cheltenham, Bath, and Gloucester), but Moreton-in-Marsh and Charlbury are the only villages with train stations. **Trains** (☎ (08457) 484950) depart from **Oxford** for **Moreton-in-Marsh** (30min., 1 per hr., £7.40) and **Charlbury** (20min., 1 per hr., £3.70). Several **bus** companies operating under the auspices of the county government cover the Gloucestershire Cotswolds, which includes most of the range, though many buses run only one or two days a week. Two regular services are **Pulham's Coaches** (☎ (01451) 820369) from **Cheltenham** to **Moreton-in-Marsh** (1hr., M-Sa 7 per day, £1.50) via **Bourton-on-the-Water** and **Stow-on-the-Wold,** and **Castleway's Coaches** (☎ (01242) 602949) from **Cheltenham** to **Broadway** (50min., M-Sa 4 per day, £1.80) via **Winchcombe.** The indispensable *Connection* timetable is free at bus stations and TICs. Various **coach tours** run to the Cotswolds from Cheltenham, Cirencester, Gloucester, and Tewkesbury.

If you want your own wheels, **Country Lanes Cycle Center** rents bikes at the Moreton-in-Marsh train station. Phone ahead—bikes are popular in these rolling hills. (☎ (01608) 650065. £14 per day, plus two pieces of ID and refundable deposit; gear and maps included. Open daily 9:30am-5:30pm.) **Stow Cycle Hire** delivers bikes for no additional charge. (☎ (01451) 832291. £8 per half-day, £12.50 per day.)

✦❷ ORIENTATION AND PRACTICAL INFORMATION

The Cotswolds lie mostly in Gloucestershire, bounded by **Banbury** in the northeast, **Bradford-on-Avon** in the southwest, **Cheltenham** in the north, and **Malmesbury** in the south. The range hardly towers; a few areas in the north and west rise above 1000 ft., but the average Cotswold hill reaches only 600 ft. A 52 mi. long unbroken ridge, **The Edge,** dominates the western reaches of the Cotswolds. The best bases to use to explore the region are **Cheltenham, Cirencester,** and **Moreton-in-Marsh.**

Tourist Information Centres: There are many in the area, all of which provide maps and pamphlets of the area and book accomodations (usually for a 10% deposit).

Bath: Abbey Chambers (☎ (01225) 477101). Open June-Sept. M-Tu and F-Sa 9:30am-6pm, W-Th 9:45am-6pm, Su 10am-4pm; Oct.-May M-Sa 9am-5pm, Su 10am-4pm.

Bourton-on-the-Water: 5 Station Rd. (☎ (01451) 810597). Open M-Sa 10am-1pm and 2-5:30pm.

Broadway: 1 Cotswold Court (☎ (01386) 852937). Open Mar.-Oct. M-Sa 10am-1pm and 2-5pm.

Cheltenham: 77 Promenade (☎ (01242) 522878; accomodations booking ☎ (01242) 517110; www.visitcheltenham.gov.uk). Open M-Sa 9:30am-5:15pm.

Chipping Campden: Rosary Court, High St. (☎ (01386) 841206). Open daily 10am-5:30pm.

Cirencester: Corn Hall, Market Pl. (☎ (01285) 654180; fax 641182). Open Apr.-Oct. M 9:45am-5:30pm, Tu-Sa 9:30am-5:30pm; Nov.-Mar. daily 9:30am-5pm.

Gloucester: 28 Southgate St. (☎ (01452) 421188). Open M-Sa 10am-5pm.

Stow-on-the-Wold: Hollis House, The Square (☎ (01451) 831082). Open Easter-Oct. M-Sa 9:30am-5:30pm, Su 10:30am-4pm; Nov.-Easter M-Sa 9:30am-4:30pm.

Winchcombe: Town Hall (☎ (01242) 602925). Open Apr.-Oct. M-Sa 10am-1pm and 2-5pm, Su 10am-1:30pm and 2-4pm.

ACCOMMODATIONS AND FOOD

The *Cotswold Way Handbook and Accommodation List* (£2) lists many **B&Bs.** They are usually spaced in villages three miles apart and offer friendly lodgings to trekkers. If you're not hiking, pick up the cheaper *Cotswolds Accommodation Guide* (50p). Savvy backpackers stay outside the larger towns to enjoy the silence and the prices. **Campsites** congregate close to Cheltenham; Bourton-on-the-Water, Stow-on-the-Wold, and Moreton-in-Marsh also provide convenient places to rough it. When in doubt, consult the *Gloucestershire Caravan and Camping Guide* (free at local TICs). The **YHA** has a number of **youth hostels** in the area, all of which serve meals and have an 11am-5pm lockout:

Charlbury: The Laurels, The Slade, Charlbury (☎/fax (01608) 810202). On the River Evenlode, 1 mi. north of Charlbury, 13 mi. northwest of Oxford; off the Oxford-Worcester rail line. From town, follow road sign-posted "Enstone." At the crossroads with the B4022, go straight across; the hostel is 50 yd. on left. Open Feb. 9-Feb. 28 T-Sa, Mar.-Aug. daily; Sept. T-Sa. Call for exact dates. Dorms £9.80, under 18 £6.75.

Slimbridge: Shepherd's Patch, Slimbridge (☎ (01453) 890275; fax 890625), across from the Tudor Arms Pub, next to the swing bridge. Off the A38 and the M5, 4 mi. from the Cotswold Way and ½ mi. from the Wild Fowl Trust Reserve and Wetlands Centre. The nearest train station (Cam and Dursley) is 3½ mi. away; it's easier to take a bus from Gloucester. Comes complete with its own ponds and wildfowl. 56 beds, small store. Open Feb.-Oct. F-Sa; also Feb. 9-24, Apr. 6-21, May 6, May 25-June 2, Jul. 20-Sept. 8, Oct. 19-Nov. 3, Dec. 28, and Jan. 2, 2002. Dorms £10.10, under 18 £6.95.

Stow-on-the-Wold: The Square (☎ (01451) 830497). In the center of Stow, between the White Hart Hotel and the Old Stocks. On the A424 highway; Pulham's bus stops every hour from Cheltenham (17 mi.), Moreton-in-Marsh (4 mi.), and Bourton-on-the-Water. 49 beds in bright rooms with wooden bunks, most with attached bathrooms. Helpful warden. Kitchen. Lockout 10am-5pm. Open Mar. M-Sa, Apr.-Oct. daily; Nov. and Feb. F-Sa. Dorms £10.85, students £9.85, under 18 £7.40.

Supermarkets, takeaways, and full-fledged restaurants call larger towns like Cirencester home, while smaller towns have "if-we-don't-have-it-you-don't-need-it" general stores, as well as numerous tea shops catering to tourists. Country pubs crop up in villages along the way.

HIKING THROUGH COTSWOLD VILLAGES

Experience the Cotswolds as the English have for centuries—by treading well-worn footpaths from village to village. Speed-walking will enable you to see several settlements in a day, which proves especially convenient for day trippers. TICs shelves strain with the weight of various walking guides. Bear in mind that the Northern Cotswolds have a decidedly different feel from the South; many think the former are the more picturesque, while the latter suffer from less congestion. Look for spring festivities such as cheese rolling or wool-sack races, where participants dash up and down hills laden with 60 lb. TICs sell the *Cotswold Map and Guidebook in One* (£5), and give out *Guided Walks and Events in the Cotswolds.* Ordnance Survey Outdoor Leisure map 45 covers the Cotswolds (1:25,000; £6.50). The Cotswolds Voluntary Warden Service conducts **guided walks** through the Cotswolds, some with an historical bent. (1½-7½hr. Free.)

Those in search of **long-distance hiking routes** have a choice among a handful of carefully marked trails. B&Bs and pubs rest conveniently within reach of both the **Cotswold Way** and the **Oxfordshire Way.** The more extensive of the two, the **Cotswold Way,** spans just over 100 mi. from Bath to Chipping Campden. The entire walk can be done in about a week at a pace of about 15 mi. per day. Due to pockmarks and gravel, certain sections of the path are not suitable for biking or horseback riding. What's more, many sections cross pasture land; try not to disturb Cotswold sheep and cattle. Consult the **Cotswold Voluntary Warden Service** (☎ (01452) 425674) for details. The **Oxfordshire Way** (65 mi.) runs between the popular hyphen-havens of Bourton-on-the-Water and Henley-on-Thames, site of the famed annual regatta (p. 86). A comprehensive *Walker's Guide* can be found in TICs. Plod over cowpats to wend your way from Bourton-on-the-Water to Lower and Upper Slaughter along the **Warden's Way** (a half-day). Most adventurous souls can continue on to Winch-combe for a total of about 14 mi.

Local roads are perfect for biking, and the rolling hills welcome casual and hardy cyclers alike; the closely spaced, tiny villages make ideal watering holes. TICs sell trail guides specially designed for the cyclist. Parts of the footpaths of the Oxfordshire Way are hospitable to cyclists, if slightly rut-ridden.

CHIPPING CAMPDEN. Years ago, quiet Chipping Campden was the capital of the Cotswold wool trade. Later, the village became a market center ("chipping" means "market"). The town is currently famous for its **Cotswold Olympic Games** at **Dovers Hill,** highlighted by the obscure "sport" of shin-kicking. This sadistic activity was prohibited from 1852 to 1952, but has since been enthusiastically revived in late May and early June to the glee of local bone-setters (buy tickets on game day).

BROADWAY. Only 3 mi. west of Chipping Campden, restored Tudor, Jacobean, and Georgian buildings, with thatch or Cotswold-tile roofs, give the Broadway a museum-like air. **Broadway Tower** enchanted the likes of decorator-designer-poet William Morris and his pre-Raphaelite comrade Dante Gabriel Rossetti. Built in the late 1700s in a superfluous attempt to intensify the beauty of the landscape, the tower affords a view of 12 counties. (☎ (01386) 852390. Open early Apr. to late Oct. daily 10:30am-5pm. £4, students and seniors £3, children £2.30, families £11.50.)

STOW-ON-THE-WOLD. Stow-on-the-Wold hides languidly in the hills. Despite a reluctant concession to progress—a Tesco supermarket opened recently amidst ardent local objections—its fine views of the surrounding countryside mean it will never be confused for anything but the tiny Cotswold village it is. Stow will con-firm your suspicion that Cotswold settlers looked no farther than their backyards for building materials. Stick your feet into the village's authentic stocks and snap a photo (everybody else does anyway). Stow holds one antique shop for every 33 residents. Near the stocks stands a **YHA Youth Hostel** (see p. 273). If the hostel's full, head to the B&B of **Rosemary Quinn,** 22 Glebe Close, to find a warm welcome and cushy rooms with fluffy quilts and pillows. (☎ (01451) 830042; ro@quinn.freeserve.co.uk. £18.50 per person). You can find rugged simplicity at **Pear Tree Cottage,** on High St., in an old stone house with comfortable rooms. (☎ (01451) 831210. Doubles with bath £40). Replenish glucose at **The Organic Shop** across from the hostel, or down a pint at **The King's Arms** across the way.

THE SLAUGHTERS. Like the proverbial lamb, you can travel a few miles south-west to the Slaughters (Upper and Lower), a pair of tranquil villages connected by footpaths. Fortunately, your visit will be heralded by a host of lively sheep, not an unhinged butcher. The **Old Mill** at Lower Slaughter scoops and skims water from the placid river that flows through the Slaughters.

BOURTON-ON-THE-WATER. Rather inexplicably touted as the "Venice of the Cotswolds" (no gondolas, just a picturesque stream and a series of footbridges), Bourton hosts its share of affluent tourists. Many of the larger trails, including the Cotswold and Oxfordshire Ways, converge here. Between the olfactory heaven and hell of rose-laden gates and fields strewn with sheep dung lies **The Cotswold Perfumery,** on Victoria St., which houses a theater equipped with "Smelly Vision," a system that releases actual scents into the theater as they're mentioned on screen. (☎ (01451) 820698. Open M-Sa 9:30am-5:30pm, Su 10:30am-5:30pm; sometimes later in summer. Wheelchair access. £1.75, concessions £1.50, families £6.50.)

CIRENCESTER. One of the larger villages, and sometimes regarded as the capital of the region, Cirencester (SI-ruhn-ses-ter) is the site of Corinium, a Roman town founded in AD 49 and second in importance only to Londinium, which has continued to be the more successful sister. Cirencester today caters to its older population; younger travelers should stay elsewhere and make it a daytrip. Although only scraps of the amphitheater still exist, the **Corinium Museum,** on Park St., has culled a formidable collection of Roman paraphernalia, including a hare mosaic. (☎ (01285) 655611. Open Apr.-Oct. M-Sa 10am-5pm, Su 2-5pm; Nov.-Mar. Tu-Sa 10am-5pm, Su 2-5pm. £2.50, students £1, seniors £2, children 80p, families £5.) The second longest yew hedge in England bounds Lord Bathwist's mansion in the center of town; the garden is scattered with Roman ruins.

The **Cirencester Parish Church,** is Gloucestershire's largest parish church. A "wool church," the money to build it came from the wealthy wool merchants in the surrounding area. (Open daily 10am-5pm. Morning Prayer before opening, Evening Prayer around 4:45pm. Donation requested.) On Fridays, the entire town turns into a frenetic antique market; a smaller craft fair appears on Saturdays inside Corn Hall, near the **tourist information centre** at Market Pl. Pricey **B&Bs** cluster a few minutes from town along Victoria Rd. Stop by the **Golden Cross** on Black Jack St. or the **Crown** at West Market Pl. near the Abbey for a pint.

CHEDWORTH. Tucked away in the Chedworth hills southwest of Cheltenham, Chedworth contains the well-preserved **Chedworth Roman Villa,** equidistant from Cirencester and Northleach off the A429. The famed Roman mosaics in the villa were discovered in 1864 when a gamekeeper noticed fragments of tile revealed by clever rabbits. The site now displays a water shrine and two bathhouses just above the River Coln. (☎ (01242) 890256; recorded info ☎ (01684) 855371. Open Mar.-Nov. Tu-Su and bank holidays 10am-5pm. Partial wheelchair access. £3.40, children £1.70, families £8.50.)

SLIMBRIDGE. Fowl deeds occur at Slimbridge, 12½ mi. southwest of Gloucester off the A38 and the site of the largest of the seven **Wildfowl Trust** centers in Britain. Sir Peter Scott has developed the world's largest collection of wildfowl here, with over 180 different species. All six varieties of flamingos nest here, and white-fronted geese visit from Siberia. In the tropical house, hummingbirds skim through jungle foliage. The visitor center has exhibits and food—just don't ask for duck. (☎ (01453) 890333. Open daily in summer 9:30am-5pm; in winter 9:30am-4pm. £5.75, students and seniors, £4.75, children £3.50, families £15.) **YHA Slimbridge** (p. 273) benefits from Sir Peter's ornithological efforts as well, hosting its own flocks.

Just south of Slimbridge on the A38 rises the massive **Berkeley Castle** (BARK-lay), ancestral home of the Berkeley family, founders of the university in California. This stone fortress has impressive towers, a dungeon, and the timber-vaulted Great Hall, where barons of the West Country met before forcing King John to sign the *Magna Carta.* (☎ (01453) 810332. Open July-Aug. M-Sa 11am-5pm, Su 1-5pm; June and Sept. Tu-Sa 11am-5pm, Su 2-5pm; Apr.-May Tu-Su 1-5pm; Oct. Su 1-4:30pm. £5.40, students and seniors £4.40, children £2.90, families £14.50.)

THE MIDLANDS

LIKE A ROLLING STONE According to legend, the curious group of stones that comprise the Rollright Stones near Chipping Norton were created when an evil witch told an ambitious king, "seven long strides shalt thou take / If Long Compton thou canst see, then King of England thou shalt be. / If Long Compton thou cannot see, then King of England thou shalt not be." The king bounded up the hill, but found a large stone blocking his view. To ensure the accuracy of her prophecy, the witch turned all the king's party, including the poor king himself, into stone. Today the king stone, an 8 ft. loner, is still surrounded by his circle of men, 77 stones 100 ft. in diameter. The group of stones a quarter-mile west, known as the Whispering Knights, are said to have been a group of knights who were plotting treason. Too bad the beleaguered king couldn't just climb the Broadway Tower.

SUDELEY CASTLE. West of Stow-on-the-Wold and six miles north of Cheltenham on the A46 lies **Sudeley Castle,** neighboring the town of Winchcombe. Once the manor estate of King Ethelred the Unready, the castle was a prized possession in the Middle Ages, with lush woodland, a royal deer park, and later Charles I's gloriously carved four-poster bed. The Queen's Garden is streamlined by a pair of yew-hedge corridors leading to rose and herb beds, while the newly planted Knot Garden was inspired by a pattern on a gown worn by Queen Elizabeth. **St. Mary's Chapel** contains the tomb of Henry VIII's Queen Katherine Parr. Present occupants Lord and Lady Ashcombe welcome you and your admission fee into their home. (☎ (01242) 602308. Open Mar.-Oct. daily 10:30am-5:30pm. £6.20, seniors £5.20, children £3.20; grounds only £4.70, seniors £3.70, children £2.50, families £17.)

PREHISTORIC REMAINS. Archaeologists have unearthed some 70 ancient habitation sites in the Cotswolds. **Belas Knap,** a 4000-year-old burial mound, stands about 1½ mi. southwest of Sudeley Castle, accessible from the Cotswold Way. The **Rollright Stones,** off the A34 between Chipping Norton and Long Compton (a 4½ mi. walk from Chipping Norton), are a 100 ft. wide ring of 11 stones (see below). Consult Ordnance Survey Tourist Map 8 (£4.50) for locations of other sites.

WEST MIDLANDS

HEREFORD ☎01432

A square of activity in the bucolic patchwork of the Wye River region, Hereford (HAIR-uh-fuhd; pop. 60,000) was for centuries an important market town. Today the town still incorporates its rural wares into its busy center, from the cider pressed in its orchards to the white-faced Hereford cattle and sheep that congregate on the livestock market every Wednesday. A pedestrian city center and narrow streets make Hereford a town best seen on foot, while Hereford's excellent bus and rail connections make it a fine springboard westward into the Wye Valley on the Welsh-English border (see p. 429).

⊟ GETTING THERE. The **train** and **bus stations** are both located on Commercial Rd. Trains (☎ (08457) 484950) arrive from: **London Paddington** (2¾hr., 1 per hr., £33); **Abergavenny** (25min., 2 per hr., £5.60); **Shrewsbury** (1hr., 1 per hr., £11.20); **Cardiff** (1hr., 1 per hr., £11.70); and **Chepstow** via **Newport** (1½hr., every 2hr., £13.20). **National Express** (☎ (08705) 808080) runs buses from **London** (4hr., 3 per day, £13.50) and **Birmingham** (2hr., 1 per day, £6.25). A few steps past the tourist information centre (TIC) along Broad St. is the **bus stop** for local services. **Stagecoach Red and White** (☎ (01633) 266336) bus #20 connects Hereford from **Newport** and the **Wye Valley** (M-Sa 4 per day). Bus #39 comes in from **Brecon** via **Hay-on-Wye** (1¾hr., M-Sa 5 per day, £5). On Sundays, **Yeoman's** bus #40 takes over (2 per day). For bus info, pick up the free *Hereford and Worcester County Public Transport Map and Guide* at the TIC.

⁊ PRACTICAL INFORMATION. The **tourist information centre,** 1 King St., in front of the cathedral, books beds for a 10% deposit of the first night's stay. (☎ 268430; fax 342662. Open M-Sa 9am-5pm, May-Sept. also Su 10am-4pm.) **Walking tours** (90min.) leave from the TIC. (Mid-May to mid-Sept. M-Sa 10:30am, Su 2:30pm. £2, seniors and children over 12 £1, under 12 free.) **Cathedral Cruises** offers 40min. **river tours.** (☎ 358957. Mar.-Oct. Subject to weather.) Services include: **Barclays bank,** Broad St. (open M and W-F 9am-5pm, Tu 10am-5pm, Sa 9:30am-noon); **Thomas Cook,** St. Peter's St., near the Old House (☎ 422540; open M-W and F-Sa 9am-5:30pm, Th 10am-5:30pm); the **Coin-op Launder Centre,** 136 Eign St. (☎ 269610; open daily 6am-7pm); **Internet access** at the **Pi Shop,** 17 King St. (☎ 377444; non-members £2 per 30min., members £1 per 30min.; open M and W-Sa 9am-9pm, T 9am-10pm, Su 10am-5pm); the **County Hospital,** Union Walk (☎ 355444), and the **post office,** 20 Broad St., next to the bus stop (☎ 273611; open M-Th 9am-5:30pm, F 9:30am-5:30pm, Sa 9am-12:30pm). **Postal code:** HR4 9HQ.

⌂ B&BS AND FOOD. Cheap lodgings in Hereford are scarce; your best bet is to walk to the B&Bs (£16 per person) at the T-junction at the end of **Bodenham Rd.** At the **Holly Tree,** 19-21 Barton Rd., TVs await you in every room. (☎ 357845. Singles £20; doubles £40. Non-smoking.) For local flavor eat at the **Black Lion Inn,** 31 Bridge St., a friendly pub with a generous menu. Scampi with peas and chips goes for £4.25, and the bar flows generously for under £2 a pint. (☎ 354016. Open M-Sa 11am-11pm, Su noon-10:30pm; food served noon-8pm.) The **Cafe@All Saints,** in the still-in-use All Saints' Church on High St., puts local ingredients to work. Down leek and potato soup for £1.90, or cider tart for £1.95. (☎ 370415. Open M-Sa 8:30am-5:30pm, hot food served noon-2:30pm.)

◪ SIGHTS. Rising above surrounding greens, the heavy rose walls of the 11th-century **Hereford Cathedral** enclose a light and airy sanctuary and museum. Most visitors flock to see the **Mappa Mundi,** a map of the world drawn on animal skin around 1290. Sodom and Gomorrah lie drowned in the Dead Sea, a tipsy polar bear staggers about Norway, and the Bonnacon, a mythical bull-horse, discharges flaming dung, literally laying waste to large parts of Syria. In the **Chained Library,** 1500 rare books are linked to their shelves by slender chains. (☎ 359880. Cathedral open daily until Evensong. Mappa Mundi and Chained Library open May-Sept. M-Sa 10am-4:15pm, Su 11am-3:15pm; Oct.-Apr. M-Sa 11am-3:15pm. Cathedral admission free; Mappa Mundi and library £4, concessions £3, families £10.)

The steeples of St. Peter's Church and All Saints' Church act as bookends to the pedestrian **High Town,** which occupies the triangular site of the medieval market. Half-timber Tudor buildings once lined High Town, but only the 17th-century **Old House** remains fully intact. A former butcher's shop, the Old House's creaky wooden floors now support loads of 17th- and 18th-century furniture. (☎ 260694. Open Apr.-Sept. Tu-Sa 10am-5pm, Su 10am-4pm; Oct.-Mar. Tu-Sa 10am-5pm. Free.) "Cheers!", written in several languages, greets visitors to the **Cider Museum** on Pomona Pl., where you can learn about traditional cider-making. (☎ 354207. Open Apr.-Oct. daily 10am-5:30pm; Nov.-Mar. Tu-Sa 1-3pm. £2.30, concessions £1.80.)

♫ ENTERTAINMENT. Those looking for a night out on the town will find that Hereford offers decent if unspectacular options. **Booth Hall** on East St., where St. Peter's St. meets High Town, is large, loud, and jumping. (☎ 344487. Open M-Sa 11am-11:30pm, Su 7:30-10:30pm.) **Eros,** 100 Commercial Rd., has a Wednesday student night and cheap drinks to 80s rock Thursdays; the crowd is in general youngish. (☎ 353868. Open W-Th 9pm-1am, F-Sa 9pm-2am.)

WORCESTER ☎ 01905

The city of Worcester (WOO-ster) crouches by the Severn River halfway between Cheltenham and Birmingham, but lacks both the gentility of the former and the frenetic pace of the latter. The name of the city (pop. 95,000) has been made famous by Worcestershire sauce and Worcester porcelain, but beyond the beautiful cathedral, Worcester's sights are lackluster; the city hoards such crumbs of fame as the site of the Civil War's final battle and makes great pomp of its circumstantial role as the birthplace of the composer Elgar.

▣ GETTING THERE AND GETTING AROUND

The city's main **train station** sits at the edge of the town center on Foregate St. (Ticket window open M-Sa 6am-11:20pm, Su 6:30am-11:05pm. Travel center open M-Sa 9am-4pm.) Trains also pull into the **Shrub Hill Station** (mainly serving the southwest) just outside town. To get to town from Shrub Hill (a 15min. walk), turn right onto Shrub Hill Rd., then left onto Tolladine Rd., which becomes Lowesmoor; follow Lowesmoor to St. Nicholas St., which intersects The Foregate, the town's main drag. (Ticket window open M-Sa 5:30am-7pm, Su 7am-7pm. Travel center open M-Sa 9am-4pm.) **Trains** (☎ (08457) 484950) travel to Worcester from: **London** (2½hr., 1 per hr., £22.80, return £38.90); **Birmingham** (2 per hr. 9am-6pm, day return £5.40); and **Cheltenham** (30min., every 2hr., £5.50).

The **bus station** is at Angel Pl. near the Crowngate Shopping Centre. **National Express** (☎ (08705) 808080) **buses** run from: **London Paddington** (4hr., 1 per day, £14.50); **Birmingham** (1hr., 1 per hr., £3, return £3.50); and **Bristol** (1½hr., 2 per day, £8.10, return £10). **Midland Red West** (☎ 763888) is the regional bus company; their **Day Rover** allows unlimited one-day travel within Worcestershire (£4.60, seniors £3.60, children £3.10, families £9.20). **Associated Radio Taxis** is at ☎ 763939. **Peddlers,** 46-48 Barbourne Rd. rents **bikes.** (☎ 24238. £8 per day, £30 per week; mountain bikes £15, £60; £50 deposit. Open M-Sa 9:30am-5:45pm, Su 9:30am-4:30pm.)

▨ ❼ ORIENTATION AND PRACTICAL INFORMATION

The city center is bounded by the train station in the north and the cathedral in the south. A fickle street runs between the two, switching names along the way from **Barbourne Rd.** to **The Tything** to **Foregate St.** to **The Foregate** to **The Cross** to **High St.** To reach the tourist information centre (TIC) from the rail station, turn left onto **Foregate St.** From the bus station, turn left onto **Broad St.** and right onto **The Cross.**

The helpful **tourist information centre,** The Guildhall, High St., is packed with free maps and pamphlets; it also sells the *Worcester Visitor* guide for 75p and books beds for a 10% deposit. (☎ 726311; fax 722481. Open M-Sa 10am-5:30pm.) 1½hr. **tours** leave from the TIC. (May-Sept. W 11am and 2:30pm. £3, children £1.50.) **Barclays** is on 54 High St. (☎ 684828. Open M-Tu and Th-F 9am-5pm, W 9:30am-5pm, Sa 9:30am-12:30pm.) **Severn Laun-Dri** is on 22 Barbourne Rd. (Wash £2-3, dry £1 or more, bring 20p coins. Open daily 9am-8pm; last wash 7pm.) Other services include: the **police** (☎ (0845) 744 4888), Deansway, behind the Guildhall, across from St. Andrew's Park; **Ronkswood Hospital** (☎ 763333), Newtown Rd., take bus #29D and #31A; and the **post office,** 8-10 Foregate St., next to the train station, with a **bureau de change** (☎ (0845) 722 3344; open M-Sa 9am-5:30pm). **Postal code:** WR1.

▤ ACCOMMODATIONS

B&B prices in Worcester are high, as proprietors cater to businessmen or to Londoners looking for a weekend in the country; the beginning and end of summer tend to be the busiest times. Try your luck on **Barbourne Rd.,** the fifth manifestation of High St. about a 15- to 20-minute walk from the city center. The nearest **YHA Youth Hostel** is 7 mi. away in the town of Malvern, 12min. by train (p. 280). **Osbourne House,** 17 Chestnut Walk in a convenient and quiet location, offers TVs and electronic, touch-operated showers in every bedroom, three types of cookies on your nightstand, and brilliant marmalade. (☎/fax 22296. Wheelchair access. Singles £20; doubles £36, with bath £40.) Monty Python fans will appreciate the name of the **Shrubbery Guest House,** 38 Barbourne Rd. Everyone else will appreciate Mrs. Law's laying down of comfortable beds and TVs. (☎ 24871; fax 23620. Singles £20; doubles £40, with bath £45.) Campers can try **Ketch Caravan Park,** Bath Rd. on the banks of the Severn, with an onsite restaurant, phones, toilets, and showers. (☎ 820430. £6-8 per tent, £8 per caravan. Electricity hook-up £1.75; Open Easter-Oct. Take the A38 2 mi. south of Worcester or take local bus #32, every 10min.)

FOOD AND PUBS

For run-of-the-mill groceries, try **Sainsbury's,** tucked into the Lynchgate Shopping Centre off High St. (☎ 21731. Open M-Th 8am-6pm, F 8am-7pm, Sa 8am-6pm.) Those wanting to eat out should head to **Mealcheapen St.** for food deals, plus bonus fun with street name puns; or try one of the Indian restaurants on **The Tything.** At **Clockwatchers,** 20 Mealcheapen St. farm-fresh sandwiches start at £1.60 takeaway (eat-in £2.50-3), and bagels are only 70p. (☎611662. Open M-Sa 8:30am-5pm). **Natural Break** off Foregate St. at The Hopmarket, offers organic respite in the form of sandwiches and quiches from £2.75. (☎ 26654. Open M-Sa 9am-5pm.) **The Cardinal's Hat,** 31 Friar St. is Worcester's oldest pub, dating from 1482. Sit in front of open fires sipping ales (£1.60-2) brewed on-site. (☎ 22423. Open daily 11am-11pm.) They'll put another shrimp on the barbie for you at **Bushwacker's,** a gargantuan Australian pub-turned-nightclub at the end of The Avenue off The Cross. Ladies drink free Monday nights. (☎ 26878. Open M-Sa 11am-1am.)

SIGHTS

Worcester Cathedral, founded AD 680, towers majestically by the River Severn at the southern end of High St., cloaking a frail internal structure. The buttresses supporting the central nave have deteriorated and the central tower is in danger of collapsing. Renovation attempts are underway; the steel rods set into the tower's base, however, do not detract from the awe-inspiring Norman detail of the nave and quire. To the delight of schoolchildren and *Let's Go* researchers, one of the tombs in the south wall is that of Bishop Freake (1516-91). In the quire are intricately detailed 14th-century misericords and the tomb of King John; copies of the *Magna Carta* stand outside. Steps lead down to Wulston's Crypt, an entire underground level with its own chapel. (☎ 28854. Cathedral open daily 7:30am-6:30pm; choral Evensong M-F 5:30pm, Su 4pm. Free tours May-Sept.; tower tours Sa, late July also M-Th. Touch and Hearing Centre for the visually impaired. Wheelchair access. Suggested donation £2, tower tours £2.)

Retrace the 1651 Battle of Worcester at the **Commandery,** Sidbury Rd., occupying the vast buildings of the former Royalist headquarters. Sit in on the trial of Charles I and choose whether to sign the king's death warrant. Your vote counts. (☎ 36182. Open M-Sa 10am-5pm, Su 1:30-5pm. £3.70, seniors and children £2.60, families £9.90.) The **Worcester City Museum and Art Gallery,** on Foregate St., near the post office, evokes the city's military past in an exhibit that includes Hitler's clock (frozen at 5:51), found in his office when it was captured by the Worcester Regiment in 1945. The art gallery has a good Victorian collection, with temporary exhibits of contemporary work. (☎ 25371. Open M-W and F 9:30am-5:30pm, Sa 9:30am-5pm. Free.) The **Royal Worcester Porcelain Company,** southeast of the cathedral on Severn St., manufacturer of the famous blue-red-and-gold-patterned bone china, has serviced the royal family since George III visited in 1788. Porcelain junkies can visit the adjacent **Worcester Museum of Porcelain,** which has the largest collection in England. (☎ 23221. Open M-Sa 9am-5:30pm. Wheelchair access. Tours M-F at regular intervals; £5, no children under 11. Museum £3, students £2.25, children under 5 free. Museum and tour £8, seniors and students £6.75.)

Behind the Guildhall, all that remains of St. Andrew's Church is a magnificent 245 ft. spire, known locally as the **Glover's Needle** because of its shape and the area's ties with glove-making. Among the half-timbered buildings on **Friar Street** stands the **Museum of Local Life,** which showcases the Worcester lifestyle during the past few centuries. (☎ 722349. Open M-W and F-Sa 10:30am-5pm. Free.)

Three miles south of town lies **Elgar's Birthplace Museum,** filled with manuscripts and memorabilia of the composer. Midland Red West bus #419/420 makes the journey (10min., return £1.80). From the Crown East Church bus stop walk 15 minutes to the museum. Otherwise, cycle six miles along the Elgar trail. (☎ 333224. Open May-Sept. Th-Tu 10:30am-6pm; Oct. to mid-Jan. and mid-Feb. to Apr. Th-Tu 1:30-4:30pm. £3, students £1, seniors £2, children 50p.)

THE MIDLANDS

NEAR WORCESTER: MALVERN ☎01684

The name Malvern refers collectively to the contiguous towns of Great Malvern, West Malvern, Malvern Link, Malvern Wells, and Little Malvern, all of which hug the base and the eastern side of the Malvern Hills. The tops of the Malvern Hills peek over the A4108 southwest of Worcester and offer the hiker eight miles of accessible trails and quasi-divine visions of greenery. **Great Malvern,** a Victorian spa town, was built around the 11th-century **church** on Abbey Rd. Benedictine monks completely rebuilt the structure in the 15th century, adding stained glass windows. (Suggested donation £1.) On the steep hillside above town, **St. Ann's Well** supplies the famous restorative "Malvern waters" that fueled Great Malvern's halcyon days as a spa town. The beautifully redone **Malvern Theatres** on Grange Rd. host plays, including a season of top-quality London theatre by the Almeida Company in August. (☎ 892277. Box office open M-Sa 9:30am-8pm. Wheelchair access.)

The **Worcestershire Way** slips through the Malverns for 36 mi. to Kingsford County Park in the north. The **Countryside Service** (☎ (01905) 766493), in the County Hall in Worcester, will tell you about hiking in the area. **Trains** (25min., 10 per day) and **Midland Red West** (M-Sa every 30min., hourly on Su) come from **Worcester.** The **tourist information centre,** 21 Church St., by the post office, assists in hill navigation. (☎ 892289; fax 892872. Short-distance walk pamphlets 30p. Open daily 10am-5pm.) The **YHA Hatherly Youth Hostel,** 18 Peachfield Rd., in Malvern Wells, holds 59 beds and a TV lounge. Take Citibus #42 from Great Malvern or walk 20min. from the train station. (☎ 569131; fax 565205. Lockout 10am-5pm. Curfew 11pm. Open mid-Feb. to Oct. daily; Nov.-Dec. F-Sa. £9.15, under 18 £6.20.)

BIRMINGHAM ☎0121

Castle-scouring, monument-seeking history buffs, move on—no great battles were fought in Birmingham, and no medieval landmarks are situated here. Birmingham, industrial heart of the Midlands, is resolutely modern in its style, packing its city center with convention-goers, cell phones, and three-piece suits. Britain's second-largest city proper is a huge transport hub surrounded by ugly ring roads, but efforts at civic renovation have improved things somewhat. Witness the elegant statues and fountain of Victoria Sq. or the chi-chi cafes bordering the redeveloped canal banks. Cadbury World offers some daytime diversion, but it isn't until night that the city—fueled by world-class entertainers, a young crowd from the universities, and some of Britain's best clubs—comes alive.

▐ GETTING THERE AND GETTING AROUND

Birmingham snares a clutch of train and bus lines between London, central Wales, southwest England, and points north.

Flights: Birmingham International Airport (☎ 767 5511). Free transfer to the nearby Birmingham International train station for connections to New St. Station and London.

Trains: New St. Station, Britain's busiest. Trains (☎ (08457) 484950) from: **London Euston** (2hr., 2 per hr., £22.50); **Nottingham** (1¼hr., 2-4 per hr., £8.20); **Oxford** (1¼hr., 1-2 per hr., £14.20); **Liverpool Lime St.** (1½hr., 1-2 per hr., £18.50); and **Manchester Piccadilly** (2½hr., 1 per hr., £14.20). Some trains pull into **Moor St.** and **Snow Hill** stations. A red line on the pavement guides travelers changing trains between New St. and Moor St. (10min. walk).

Buses: Digbeth Station, Digbeth. Open 24hr. **Luggage storage** £1-3. National Express office open M-Sa 7:15am-7pm, Su 8:15am-7pm. **National Express** (☎ (08705) 808080) from: **London** (3¼hr., 1 per hr., return £15); **Cardiff** (2¼hr., 4 per day, return £18.75); **Liverpool** (2½hr., 15per day, return £11); and **Manchester** (2½hr., every 2hr., return £12.50). Buses also stop at Colmore Row and Bull Ring.

Public Transportation: Information at **Centro** (☎ 200 2700), in New St. Station. Stocks local transit map and bus schedules. Bus and train day pass £5; bus only £2.50, children £1.70. Open daily 7:30am-10:30pm.

✦ 🛈 ORIENTATION AND PRACTICAL INFORMATION

Streets beyond the central district can be dangerous. As always, take care at night.

Tourist Information Centre: 2 City Arcade (☎ 643 2514; fax 616 1038). Books rooms for 10% deposit of first night for accommodations listed with the English tourist board, £2 fee for other accommodations. Sells theater and National Express tickets. Open M-Sa 9:30am-5:30pm. **Branch,** Victoria Sq. (☎ 693 6300; fax 693 9600). Open M-Sa 9:30am-6pm, Su 10am-4pm.

Tours: Guide Friday (☎ 693 6300) runs 90min. hop-on hop-off bus tours, departing from Waterloo St. daily every hr. 10am-4pm. £7.50, students and seniors £6.50, under 14 £2.50, under 5 free.

Financial Services: Barclays, 56 New St. (☎ 480 2351). Open M-Tu and Th-F 9:30am-4:30pm, W 10am-4:30pm.

American Express: Bank House, 8 Cherry St. (☎ 644 5533). Open M-F 8:30am-5:30pm, Sa 9am-5pm.

Police: Lloyd House (☎ 626 5000), Colmore Circus, Queensway.

Internet Access: NetAdventure Cyber Café, 68-70 Dalton St. (☎ 693 6655), off Newton St. £3 per hr., £1 minimum. Also **Input Output Centres,** Central Library, Chamberlain Sq. (☎ 233 2230), near Colmore Row. Fast connections. £1 per 15min. Open M-F 9am-8pm, Sa 10am-5pm.

Post Office: 1 Pinfold St., Victoria Sq. (☎ 643 5542). **Bureau de change.** Open M-F 8:30am-5:30pm, Sa 8:30am-6pm. **Postal Code:** B2 4AA.

ACCOMMODATIONS

Despite its size, Birmingham has no hostels. Hotels cater to convention-goers, and inexpensive B&Bs are rare; the tourist information centre (TIC) has good listings. B&Bs line **Hagley Rd.;** buses that go there include #9, 109, or 139. Hagley Rd. is a major thoroughfare, so be prepared to sleep to the sounds of passing traffic. Call to reserve a place at the YMCAs or YWCAs; they are often booked solid.

Lyby, 14-16 Barnsley Rd., Edgbaston (☎ 429 4487), off Hagley Rd. Take bus #9 or 127 from Corporation St. to Quantum Pub, walk 50m back, and turn left at the New Talbot. Large rooms with TVs. Grab a late-night kebab nearby. Singles £15; doubles £27.

Grasmere Guest House, 37 Serpentine Rd., Harborne (☎/fax 427 4546). Take bus #22, 23, or 103 from Colmore Row to the Duke of York pub. Turn right off Harborne Rd. onto Serpentine Rd. A bit far out, but the chatty proprietor offers tidy rooms and a lovely back garden. Board games in lounge, and tea and biscuits every night at 9:30pm. No smoking. £15 per person, with bath additional £10 per room.

Woodville House, 39 Portland Rd., Edgbaston (☎ 454 0274). Take bus #128 or 129 from Colmore Row in the city center (10min.) Comfortable, affordable and well located. TVs in rooms. Singles £18; doubles £30, with bath £35.

YMCA: 200 Bunburg Rd. (☎ 475 6218); bus #61, 62 or 63 to Church Rd., Northfield; and 300 Reservoir Rd. (☎ 373 1937); bus #104 to Six Ways in Erdington. Basic rooms in decent areas. Both men and women accepted, must be over 18 and a member (£1). Breakfast included; dinner £3.50. Singles £15.50; weekly with dinner £116.91.

YWCA: Alexandra Residential Centre, 27 Norfolk Rd. (☎ 454 8134). Take bus #9, 126, 140, or 258 from Broad St. or Corporation St. and get off outside Liberty's nightclub; Norfolk Rd. is the first street on your left. Singles £10; weekly small room £52.55, large room £56.95. Also at 5 Stone Rd. (☎ 440 5345). Take bus #61, 62, or 63 to Bristol Rd., by the McDonald's. Ask the bus driver to announce the stop if possible; it's not clearly marked. Be wary in the neighborhood, especially after dark. Women and men accepted. Weekly only, £56.15.

FOOD

Brum's eateries conjure up expensive delights, as well as the requisite cheap cod and kebabs (*Let's Go* does not recommend eating cod and kebabs together). What Birmingham is most proud of is balti, a Kashmiri-Pakistani cuisine invented here by immigrants from the subcontinent and cooked in a special pan. Brochures at the TIC map out the city's numerous balti restaurants. Most of the best are southeast of the city center in Birmingham's "Balti Triangle."

Warehouse Café, 54 Allison St. (☎ 633 0261), off Digbeth above the Friends of the Earth office. Vegetarians in the area partake of the veggie burgers at lunch for £2. Bowl of soup and (organic) roll £1.95. Vegan items. Open M-F 11am-3pm, Sa 11am-4pm.

Al Frash, 186 Ladypool Rd. (☎ 753 3120). One of Brum's Balti Triangle restaurants. Tasty, generous portions of Balti chicken for £3.90. Open daily 5pm-1am.

Wine Republic, Centenary Square (☎ 644 6464), next to Symphony Hall and the Repertory Theatre. Down a drink amidst the wavy, bright blue decor or get free tapas in the outdoor dining area between 5:30 and 9:30pm. Paninis £4.50, pasta £6.50; over 40 wines available. Open M-Sa 11am-11pm, also Su when there's a show.

SIGHTS

Twelve minutes south of town by rail lies ◪ **Cadbury World,** an unabashed celebration of the chocolate firm and its enlightened treatment of workers. Hear the story of chocolate's roots in the Mayan rainforests and smell the unmistakable scent of chocolate production, but be prepared to fend off hordes of schoolchildren. Bring back a 400g chocolate bar ($1.97) and indulge. Take a train from New St. to Bournville, or buses #83, 84, or 85 from the city center. (☎ 451 4180. Open daily 10am-3pm; closed certain days Nov.-Feb. Wheelchair access. $8, students and seniors $6.50, children $6, families $24. Includes about 3 free bars of chocolate.)

The **City Museum and Art Gallery,** Chamberlain Sq. off Colmore Row, supports **Big Brum,** a northern cousin to London's Big Ben. The museum houses eclectic collections of costumes, pre-Raphaelite paintings, and William Blake illustrations of Dante's *Inferno.* The interactive *Light on Science* makes science fun for kids and adults alike; check out the skeleton riding a bike. (☎ 303 2834. Open M-Th and Sa 10am-5pm, F 10:30am-5pm, Su 12:30-5pm. Wheelchair access. Free.) Further afield, the **Barber Institute of Fine Arts,** in the University of Birmingham on Edgbaston Park Rd., displays works by artists as diverse as Rubens, Gainsborough, and Magritte. Take bus #61, 62, or 63 from the city center. (☎ 414 7333. Open M-Sa 10am-5pm, Su 2-5pm. Wheelchair access. Free.)

The more than 100 jewelry shops that line the **Jewellery Quarter** hammer out almost all of Britain's jewelry. The **Museum of Jewellery Quarter,** 77-79 Vyse St., Hockley (signposted from the city center), lets jewelry buffs tour an old factory, watch skilled jewelers, and interact with a series of audiovisual displays. (☎ 554 3598. Open M-F 10am-4pm, Sa 11am-5pm. Wheelchair access. £2.50, concessions £2.) The **National Sea Life Centre,** The Waters Edge, Brindleyplace, overlooks the city's canal network, and has 55 displays, including the world's first completely transparent 360-degree underwater tunnel. (☎ 633 4700; www.sealife.co.uk. Open daily from 10am. £8, seniors £5.95, children £5.)

🎵 🎆 ENTERTAINMENT AND FESTIVALS

BARS AND CLUBS

Forget run-of-the-mill chart hits; Birmingham's club scene is on the cutting edge of dance music in Britain. Pick up a copy of the bimonthly *What's On* or the monthly *Leap* to discover the latest hotspots, or head down **Broad St.** and let the big beat lead you. Hordes of yuppies gather in the bars along the canal bank that parallels **Gas St.** Clubbers on a budget should grab a guide to public transport's Night Network from the Centro office in New St. Station—**night buses** generally run every hour until 3:30am on Friday and Saturday nights.

Stoodibakers, 192 Broad St. (☎ 643 5100). Half club, half bar. Uplifting music, although sometimes cheesily commercial, draws a lively crowd of socialites into its neon interior. Cover £4 after 9:30pm F-Sa.

Ministry of Sound, 55 Broad St. (☎ 632 5501), across from the Chamberlain Towers. The Ministry has extended from London to set up its new Birmingham bar, with dance and soul in a refurbished interior. Cover £7-12.

Bakers, 162 Broad St. (☎ 633 3839; www.bakerstheclub.co.uk). Hosts *B1* (uplifting house) on Wednesday, *Horny* (female DJs) on Friday, and the packed *Republica* (hard house) on Saturday. Cover £3 W after 10:30, £7-10 F-Sa; look for discounts in flyers.

Brannigan's, 196-209 Broad St. (☎ 616 1888). Huge dance floor, three bars, big couches, video games, and live bands several nights a week. Packed on weekends. Tu Student Night (£1 pints), W-Th 2-for-1 night, Su select drinks half price. Cover £2 W-Sa.

MUSIC, THEATER, AND FESTIVALS

City of Birmingham Symphony Orchestra, (☎ 7803333; www.cbso.co.uk), plays in the superb acoustics of Symphony Hall at the Convention Centre on Broad St. Box office open M-F 10am-8pm, Sa 10am-10pm; Su hours dependent on showtimes. Wheelchair access; facilities for hearing-impaired. Tickets £5-32; some concessions and group discounts; student standbys £7.50 after 1pm on concert days.

Hippodrome Theatre, Hurst St. (☎ 622 7486). The Hippodrome continues Birmingham's rich theatrical tradition. Originally a variety music hall featuring big-name vaudeville artists, the theater now stages musicals transferred from the West End, as well as quality opera. Undergoing renovations, but will reopen by spring 2001; call for hours and ticket prices.

Birmingham Repertory Theatre, Centenary Sq. (☎ 236 4455; www.birmingham-rep.co.uk), on Broad St. One of Brum's less grandiose, but still celebrated, theaters. Open M-Sa 9:30am-8pm, Su 4-8pm on performance days. Tickets £7-20, some half-price standby tickets for students and UB40 cardholders.

The **Birmingham Jazz Festival** (☎ 454 7020) brings over 200 jazz bands, singers, and instrumentalists to town during the first two weeks of July; book through the TIC.

IRONBRIDGE   ☎01952

One day in 1709, when he was mucking about in his furnace workshop, a Coalbrookdale man discovered a way to smelt iron ore using cheap and abundant coke (coal residue) instead of expensive charcoal. Realizing that mass production of iron was now possible, Abraham Darby bought his workers an extra case of beer. Before long, the wooded hills became smoke-belching infernos of iron production, and the Industrial Revolution was born. From this Shropshire valley came the world's first iron rails, and, in 1779, the first cast-iron bridge, over a deep gorge of the River Severn. No industry remains, but the mines and ironworks are now museums collectively designated a World Heritage Site.

▤ **GETTING THERE.** The best (well, only) way to reach Ironbridge is by **bus.** The nearest **train** station is at **Telford,** 20 minutes from Shrewsbury on the Birmingham-Shrewsbury-Chester line. **Arriva Midlands North** (☎ 223766) bus #96 stops at Ironbridge from **Telford** (20min.; M-Sa 6 per day, no Su service; £2.20) and **Shrewsbury** (30min.; M-Sa 6 per day, Su 5 per day; £2.20). The Sunday bus from Shrewsbury also stops at **Coalbrookdale, Blists Hill,** and **Coalport.** Arriva buses #6 and 99 run on the Wellington-Bridgnorth route, stopping at **Ironbridge** and **Coalbrookdale** from **Telford** (25min., M-Sa 16 per day, £2.20). On Sundays, Arriva bus #899 between **Telford** and **Wellington** swings through the area, stopping at **Coalport, Ironbridge,** and **Coalbrookdale** (20min., 8 per day each way, £2.20).

▰▱ **ORIENTATION AND PRACTICAL INFORMATION.** Ironbridge is both the collective name for the cluster of villages and factories-turned-museums, and the name of the village at the center. The nine **Ironbridge Gorge Museums** huddle on the steep banks of the Severn valley in an area covering six square miles; some are difficult to reach without a car, since buses stop only at selected points and bike rental stores are conspicuously absent. The museums cluster in three main areas. Central **Ironbridge** is home to the tourist information centre and the **Iron Bridge & Tollhouse;** the **Museum of the Gorge** is about half a mile to the west. Some two miles northwest of the bridge is **Coalbrookdale,** where you'll find the **Coalbrookdale Museum of Iron** and the **Darby Houses.** Two miles east of the bridge, past the **Jackfield Tile Museum,** is the village of **Coalport,** home to the **Coalport China Museum** and the **Tar Tunnel.** A mile north of Coalport is **Blists Hill Victorian Town.**

The helpful and incredibly friendly staff at the **tourist information centre** (TIC), the Wharfage, in Ironbridge, will give you a free copy of the 74-page tome *Ironbridge Gorge Visitor Guide,* book accommodations for a 10% deposit of the first night, and **exchange currency.** (☎ 432166 or toll-free (0800) 590258; fax 432204; www.ironbridge.org.uk. Open M-F 9am-5pm, Sa-Su 10am-5pm.) There are **no banks** or **cash machines** anywhere in Ironbridge. The **post office** is on The Square in Ironbridge. (Open M-Tu and Th-F 9am-1pm and 2-5:30pm, W 9am-1pm, Sa 9am-12:30pm.) **Postal code:** TF8 7AW.

▰▱ **ACCOMMODATIONS AND FOOD.** Two **YHA Youth Hostels** grace each end of the valley, three miles apart. **YHA Ironbridge Gorge** in Coalbrookdale is more accessible; **YHA Coalport** is visited by buses only on Sundays. The Ironbridge Gorge hostel offers comfortable and recently renovated interiors; the Coalport hostel, next to the Coalport China Museum, is equipped with a laundry room, reading lights, handicapped facilities, and an all-day restaurant. (Both ☎ 588755; fax 588722; ironbridge@yha.org.uk. Dorms £10.85, children £7.40). Besides the hostels, budget accommodations are practically non-existent. One of the cheaper B&Bs is **Coalbrookdale Villa,** an elegant Gothic house with well tended gardens about ten minutes from Ironbridge in the side of town called Paradise. The kind proprietress strives to supply every cereal you could desire. (☎/fax 433450. £24 per person.) If sleeping under the stars is your thing, the nearest campsite is the **Severn Gorge Caravan Park,** one mile north of the Blists Hill Victorian Town on Bridgnorth Rd. in Tweedale. (☎ 684789. Showers and electric hookup. £6.)

Oliver's Vegetarian Bistro, 33 High St., serves a wide selection of vegetarian fare (main courses £4-7) in a cozy setting. (☎ 433086. Open Tu-F 7-11pm, Sa noon-3pm and 7-11pm, Su 11am-5pm.) The **Horse and Jockey** pub, 15 Jockey Bank, is said to serve the best steak-and-kidney pie in Britain. (☎ 433798. Open daily noon-2:30pm and 7-11pm; food served until 9:30pm.)

🏛 MUSEUMS. There's not much more to Ironbridge than the **Ironbridge Gorge Museums,** but you'd be hard pressed to find a better portrayal of Britain's unique industrial heritage. Count on spending at least two days to cover the lot. If you plan to visit each of the nine museums, buy an **Ironbridge Passport** from any one of the museums, which admits you once to each of the museums on any dates you choose (£10, seniors £9, students and children £6, families £30; YHA members 10% discount). The major museums are open daily 10am-5pm, while smaller museums such as the Darby Houses, the Iron Bridge Tollhouse, and the Broseley Pipeworks are open only limited hours November-March; call the TIC for more information.

The **Iron Bridge,** built in 1779 by Abraham Darby III, crosses a deep gorge of the River Severn; it attracted worldwide attention when it opened. At its southern end is a little exhibit in the **Tollhouse.** (Free.) Ten minutes to the west of Ironbridge, the **Museum of the Gorge** provides a fine audio-visual introduction to the area's history. (£2, students and children £1, seniors £1.50.) In Coalbrookdale to the northwest, the **Coalbrookdale Museum of Iron,** once a great warehouse, recreates the fiery furnace of Abraham Darby I where the whole brouhaha started, traces the history of iron use through the millennia, and exhibits iron products beyond your wildest imagination. (£4.60, seniors £3.90, students and children £2.90.) Nearby, the **Darby Houses** model the pleasant quarters of a 19th-century ironmaster. (£2.65, seniors £2, students and children £1.50.) In Coalport to the west, the **Coalport China Museum** and **Jackfield Tile Museum** show the products of the porcelain and tile industries that moved in when iron production tailed off. (Each museum £3.90, students and children £2.25, seniors £3.60.) Don a hard hat at the eerie **Tar Tunnel** and descend deep underground in a tunnel constructed to connect the Blists Hill mines to the Severn. (£1, seniors 80p, students and children 50p.) After staring at a lot of iron, which, quite frankly, tends not to hold up its end of the conversation, make haste to the open-air **Blists Hill Victorian Town,** where you can chat with real actors going about their make-believe business, as well as exchange your silly 20th-century money for serious Victorian shillings and brass farthings with which to buy ale. (£7.50, seniors £7, students and children £5.)

SHREWSBURY   ☎ 01743

A town "islanded in Severn stream," in the words of poet A.E. Housman, Shrewsbury (SHROWS-bree; pop. 59,000) has been occupied by many peoples. The horseshoe-shaped patch of land was first settled by pugnacious Saxons, who decided to call it Scrobbesbyrig, and then by Roger de Montgomery, second-in-command to William the Conqueror, who sashayed up from Hastings in the 11th century. By the 16th century, wool-rich Shrewsburyites had redecorated, raising distinctive timber houses later made accessible by the railways that grew like weeds over Victorian England. Taking a bit of a breather today, Shrewsbury continues to attract architectural buffs and travelers in transit.

◪ GETTING THERE AND GETTING AROUND

Shrewsbury is a whirlpool of rail links. The **train station,** a splendid neo-Gothic building, is at the end of Castle St. (Ticket office open M-Sa 5:30am-10pm, Su 7:30am-8:30pm.) Trains (☎ (08457) 484950) run from: **London** (3hr., 1 per hr., £31.60); **Wolverhampton** (50min., every 2hr., £5.20); **Aberystwyth** (2hr.; M-Sa 7 per day, Su 5 per day; £10.50); **Swansea,** on the Heart of Wales Line (4hr., 1 per hr., £15.20); and most of North Wales via **Wrexham General** and **Chester** (1hr.; M-Sa 9 per day, Su 4 per day; £5.80). The **bus station** is at Raven Meadows, parallel to Pride Hill. (☎ 244496. Office open M-F

8:30am-5:30pm, Sa 8:30am-4pm.) **National Express** (☎ (08705) 808080) **buses** arrive from: **London** (5hr., 4 per day, £12.50); **Llangollen** (1hr., 1 per day, £3); and **Birmingham** (2hr., 3-4 per day, £3.75). Train and bus schedules are listed in the *Shrewsbury Public Transport Guide*, free at the bus station and the tourist information centre (TIC). **Taxis** queue in front of the train station, or call **Access Taxis** at ☎ 360606.

✦ ORIENTATION

The **River Severn** encircles Shrewsbury's town center in a horseshoe shape, with the curve pointing south. Running from the train station in the northeast to Quarry Park in the southwest is the town's central axis, which undergoes various name changes: starting as **Castle Gates** and then **Castle St.** near the station, the road becomes the pedestrian-only **Pride Hill**, and then **Shoplatch** and **St. John's Hill. Raven Meadows**, where the bus station is located, runs parallel to this axis, separated by the Darwin Shopping Centre. One end of High St. joins the bottom of Pride Hill at right angles; at its other end, it becomes **Wyle Cop,** then crosses the river via the **English Bridge,** and becomes **Abbey Foregate. Princess St.** runs parallel to High St.; the two streets are connected by **The Square.** Also perpendicular to the axis, but in an opposite direction from High St., is **Mardol,** which heads northwest towards the **Welsh Bridge.** Signposts help travelers navigate.

⚡ PRACTICAL INFORMATION

Tourist Information Centre: Music Hall, The Square (☎ 281200; fax 281213; www.shrewsburytourism.co.uk), across from the Market Bldg. Free town maps; accommodations booking service for £1 and a 10% deposit of the first night's stay. Oversized town trail leaflets (95p), the new *Shrewsbury Guide* (£2.50), and piles of brochures. Open May-Sept. M-Sa 10am-6pm, Su 10am-4pm; Oct.-Apr. M-Sa 10am-5pm.

Tours: Get an insight into historic Shrewsbury by passing through Shrewsbury's "shuts" (lanes that could be shut), and ask about the origins of Grope Lane's name, on 1½hr. walking tours starting at 2:30pm from the TIC. May-Sept. daily; Oct. M-Sa; Nov.-Apr. Sa only. £2, children £1.

Financial Services: Barclays, corner of Castle St. and St. Mary's St. Open M-F 9am-5pm, Sa 9:30am-1pm. **HSBC,** 33 High St. Open M-F 9am-5pm, Sa 9am-3pm. **Thomas Cook,** corner of Pride Hill and Butcher Row. Open M-Tu and Th-Sa 9am-5:30pm, W 10am-5:30pm.

American Express: 27 Claremont St. (☎ 357204), off Mardol St. Open M-W and F 9am-5:30pm, Th 9:30am-5:30pm, Sa 9am-5pm.

Launderette: Stidgers Wishy Washy, Monkmoor Rd. (☎ 355151), off Abbey Foregate. No soap, and proud of it. £3 per wash. Open M-F 7:30am-5pm; Sa 10am-4pm; Su 10am-2pm; last wishy washy 1hr. before closing.

Police: Raven Meadows. Open M-Sa 9am-5pm. Also at Clive Rd. (☎ 232888), in Monkmoor. Open 24hr.

Hospital: Shrewsbury Hospital (☎ 261138), Mytton Oak Rd.

Internet Access: Megabyte, 5-6 St. Austin's St. (☎ 233605). £6 per hr.

Post Office: (☎ 362925), St. Mary's St., just off Pride Hill. **Bureau de change.** Open M-Sa 9am-5:30pm. **Postal Code:** SY1 1ED.

🏠 ACCOMMODATIONS AND FOOD

YHA Shrewsbury, The Woodlands, Abbey Foregate, lies about 1½ mi. from the city center. From town, cross the English Bridge, pass the abbey, and head straight down Abbey Foregate; the hostel is opposite the Lord Hill monument. Or catch bus #8 or 26 from the town center and get off at Shirehall just before the Lord Hill's Column roundabout. This Victorian house holds laundry facilities and a pool table. (☎ 360179; fax 357423; shrewsbury@yha.org.uk. Lockout 10am-5pm. Curfew

11pm. Laundry £1, dry 20p, soap free. Open Feb.-Oct. daily. Dorms £8.35, under 18 £5.65.) **B&Bs** (£17-20) cluster on Abbey Foregate and Monkmoor Rd. across the English Bridge. Comely **Glyndene,** Park Terr., has an elaborate bell pull and lovely, comfortable rooms with TVs. From the bridge, follow the road to the left of the Abbey. (☎ 352488. £18-20 per person.) Two doors down, **Allandale** hangs its walls with prints of wide-eyed babies and cityscapes. (☎ 240173. £18 per person.) **Abbey Lodge,** 68 Abbey Foregate, will put you to sleep (so to speak) in flowery-scented, spacious rooms with TVs. (☎/fax 235832. Singles £18; doubles with bath £42.50.)

The Good Life Wholefood Restaurant, Barracks Passage, off Wyle Cop, offers tasty vegetarian dishes (all under £2.50) in a restored 14th-century building in an alley by the Lion Hotel. (☎ 350455. Open M-Sa 9:30am-4:30pm.) Crayon-in the crazy-happy cat logo in the **Blue Cat Café,** 1 Fish St., as you munch on sandwiches and bagels for £2.60-3.10. (☎ 232236. Open M-Sa 10am-4pm.) Lunch crowds queue up at **Subs,** Wyle Cop, which prepares excellent hot panini (£2.50) and a wide range of sandwiches and pasta dishes in the £2 range. (☎ 241620. Open M-Sa 9am-4:30pm.) The **King's Head** pub, Mardol St. (☎ 362843), displays a medieval wall painting of the Last Supper uncovered during renovation and serves great specials such as the £3.50 full roast dinner. (☎ 241620. Open M-Sa 10:30am-11pm, Su noon-11pm.)

⊙ SIGHTS

Shrewsbury's biggest attraction is undoubtedly its architecture. Tudoresque houses dot the central shopping district and rally in full force at the **Bear Steps,** which start in the alley on High St. across from the Square. At the end of Castle St., the riverside acres of **Quarry Park** explode with bright flowers. According to local law, sheep can graze anywhere; a number infiltrate the churchyard at **St. Mary's.** Shrewsbury also makes a habit of honoring its native sons, and memorials pepper the city. Check out **Darwin's statue** opposite the castle, the colossal **Lord Hill Column** at the end of Abbey Foregate, and the **Clive of India** outside Market Sq.

The original earth and timber version of **Shrewsbury Castle,** just up from the train station, was constructed in 1083 by William the Conqueror's buddy Roger de Montgomery, who demolished 50 Saxon houses to make way for it. Climb **Laura's Tower** for a grand view of town. (☎ 358516. Castle and tower open Tu-Su 10am-4:30pm. £2, seniors £1, under 18 free. Grounds open 9am-5pm. Free.) **Rowley's House Museum,** Barker St., off Shoplatch, displays Iron Age log boats, a silver mirror from AD 130, and a recreation of King Arthur's sword Excalibur. (☎ 361196. Open Easter-Sept. Tu-Sa 10am-5pm, Su 10am-4pm; Oct.-Easter Tu-Sa 10am-5pm. Free.)

Beyond the English Bridge, the red **Shrewsbury Abbey** holds a shrine to St. Winefride, a 7th-century princess who was beheaded, then miraculously re-capitated to become an abbess and patroness of North Wales and Shrewsbury. In the abbey garden rests a memorial to local boy and World War I poet Wilfred Owen. (☎ 232723. Open daily Easter-Oct. 9:30am-5:30pm; Nov.-Easter 10:30am-3pm.)

EAST MIDLANDS

NOTTINGHAM ☎ 0115

Nottingham (pop. 261,500) maintains its age-old tradition, created by the mythical Robin Hood and his band of merry men, of taking from the rich and giving to the poor. The modern-day city uses Robin Hood as an economic tool, luring visitors to a tourism industry based on little substance and plenty of thrill. But don't be fooled: Nottinghamshire has produced more famed residents than its socially-conscious outlaws, including Lord Byron, D.H. Lawrence, and Jesse Boot, whose name appears on pharmacies England-wide. Walking through Nottingham today, however, you'll more likely see savvy urban youths than either merry men or club-footed poets, since the city is also home to 20,000 university students.

THE MIDLANDS

⌐ GETTING THERE AND GETTING AROUND

Trains: Nottingham Station, Carrington St., in the south of the city, across the canal. Trains (☎ (08457) 484950) arrive in Nottingham from: **London St. Pancras** (2hr., 1 per hr., £35.50); **Sheffield** (50min., 1 per hr., £7); and **Lincoln** (1hr.; M-Sa 32 per day, Su 7 per day; £6.10).

Buses: Broad Marsh Bus Station (☎ 950 3665), between Collin St. and Canal St. Ticket and information booth open M-F 9am-5:30pm. **Victoria Bus Station,** at the corner of York St. and Cairn St. **National Express** (☎ (08705) 808080) speeds to Broad Marsh from **London** (3hr., 7 per day, £14) and **Sheffield** (1¼hr., 1 per hr., £8.50). **Nottinghamshire County Council Buses** connect to points throughout the county.

Public Transportation: For short urban journeys, hop on a **Nottingham City Transport** bus (70p). All-day local bus passes £2.20. For public transit info call **Nottinghamshire Buses Hotline** (☎ 924 0000). Open daily 7am-8pm.

■✴❷ ORIENTATION AND PRACTICAL INFORMATION

Nottingham is a busy city and its streets are confusing. Its hub is **Old Market Sq.,** a paved, fountain-filled plaza near the Council House (beware of the pigeons). The train and bus stations lie at the extreme south of the city. The trendy neighborhood of **Hockley** is east of the city center.

Tourist Information Centre: 1-4 Smithy Row (☎ 915 5330), just off Old Market Sq. Many reference guides, a free city map, and the free *City Lights* nightlife guide. Open M-F 9am-5:30pm, Sa 9am-5pm; Aug.-Sept. also Su 10am-3pm.

Tours: The Nottingham Experience Theme Tour Company (☎ (0410) 293348) leads a 30min. tour by car, leaving from the Castle gatehouse. Tours Easter-Oct. daily 10am-4pm; £4, concessions £3.50.

Budget Travel: STA Travel, Byron House, Shakespeare St. (☎ 952 8802), near Nottingham Trent University. Open M-F 10am-5pm.

Financial Services: Barclays, 2 High St. Open M-Tu and Th-F 9am-5pm, W 10am-5:30pm, Sa 9:30am-3:30pm. **Thomas Cook,** 4 Long Row (☎ 909 3000). Offers budget travel services. Open M-Tu and Th-Sa 9am-5pm, W 9:30am-5:30pm.

American Express: 2 Victoria St. (☎ (08706) 001060). Open M-Tu and Th-F 9am-5:30pm, W 9:30am-5:30pm, Sa 9am-5pm.

Launderette: Brights, 150 Mansfield Rd. (☎ 948 3670), near the Igloo hostel. Open M-F 8:30am-7pm, Sa 8:30am-6pm, Su 9:30am-5pm. Last wash 1hr. before closing.

Police: North Church St. (☎ 948 2999).

Hospital: Queen's Medical Center (☎ 924 9924), Derby Rd.

Internet Access: Mailboxes Etc., 48 Derby Rd. (☎ 955 9400). 3 terminals. £5 per 1hr. Open M-F 8:30am-6:15pm, Sa 10am-2pm.

Post Office: Queen St. (☎ 947 4311). Open M-Sa 9am-5:30pm. **Bureau de change. Postal Code:** NG1 2BN.

⌐ ACCOMMODATIONS

B&Bs are scattered throughout the central city and also in neighboring areas to the north and south. The tourist information centre (TIC) books rooms for a £2.50 deposit plus 10% of your first night's stay (daily 9am-4:30pm). A number of guesthouses cluster along **Goldsmith St.** (near Nottingham Trent University) and run £16-20 per person.

Igloo, 110 Mansfield Rd. (☎ 947 5250; reception@igloohostel.co.uk), on the north side of town. From the train station, take bus #90 to Mansfield Rd. From the TIC, walk right to Clumber St., then take a left and walk straight for 10min. Well-kept, homey hostel operated by an experienced, affable backpacker. Dorm-style accommodation offered within lively orange and green walls. Info-stocked lounge with TV, kitchen, and two black cats. Sleepsacks available. Curfew 3am. £9.50 per person.

Nottingham

🏠 ACCOMMODATIONS
Bentinck Hotel, 4
Castle Rock Guesthouse, 3
Igloo, 1
YMCA, 2

Castle Rock Guest House, 79 Castle Blvd. (☎ 948 2116). 5min. walk from the train station. Clean double and family rooms with TVs. Attentive hostess. £17-25 per person.

Bentinck Hotel (☎ 958 0285), Station St., directly across from the train station. Great location makes up for worn carpets. Clean rooms with TVs. £17-21 per person.

YMCA, 4 Shakespeare St. (☎ 956 7600; fax 956 7601; admin@notting-ham.ymca.org.uk). Large building with bland decor on a busy street. Breakfast included. Key deposit £5. Dorms £11; singles £16.

🍴 FOOD

Quick, inexpensive bites are easily found, especially on **Milton St.** and **Mansfield Rd.** Gaggles of sandwich shops, trendy cafes, and ethnic eateries line **Goosegate.** There is a **Tesco** supermarket in the Victoria Shopping Centre. (Open M-T and Th-Sa 8am-7pm, W 8am-8pm, Su 11am-5pm.)

Ye Olde Trip to Jerusalem, 1 Brewhouse Yard (☎ 947 3171). Claiming the title "Oldest Inn in England," the pub pulled its first drink in 1189 and added a "new" section in the 17th century. Soldiers stopped here en route to the Crusades. Locally known as "The Trip," the pub is carved into Nottingham Castle's sandstone base. Watch your head on the 6 ft. ceiling. Open M-Sa 11am-11pm, Su noon-10:30pm; food served noon-6pm.

Casa, 12-18 Friar Ln. Attentive service in expansive surroundings. Scan stylish patrons and passers-by as you munch fresh sandwiches (£4-6). Finish with dessert for £3-5. Open daily noon-10:30pm.

Balti House, 35 Heathcote St. (☎ 947 2871). This tandoori treasure trove offers the cuisine of modern Britain. Try a £6.65 chickpea starter, followed by a sizzling Balti dish with *chapati* and *naan* bread. Open daily 6-10pm.

◉ SIGHTS

THE GALLERIES OF JUSTICE. An innovative museum experience at its interactive best. The Crime and Punishment Galleries drag the unsuspecting visitor before a merciless court, throw them behind unforgiving bars, and let them see the English prison system through the eyes of the convicted. Tourists are regularly sentenced to Australia; Australians may not use this as a free return ticket. You can then switch sides and discover how criminals are caught in the Police Galleries. *(High Pavement. ☎ 952 0558. Open Tu-Su 10am-5pm, last admission to Crime and Punishment 3pm, Police Galleries 4pm. £7.95, students and seniors £5.95, children £4.95, families £23.95. Family tickets purchased in advance £20.95, call 952 0555.)*

NOTTINGHAM CASTLE. Originally constructed in 1068 by William the Conqueror, the remains of the castle top a sandstone rise in the south of the city. In 1642, Charles I raised his standard against Parliament here, kicking off the Civil War. For his troubles, the king was beheaded and the castle destroyed. It now houses the **Castle Museum,** featuring historical exhibits, Victorian art, a silver collection, and the regimental memorabilia of the Sherwood Foresters, as well as temporary exhibits. *(☎ 915 3700. Open Mar.-Oct. daily 10am-5pm; Nov.-Feb. Sa-Th 10am-5pm. Admission M-Th free; Sa-Su £2, concessions £1, free for disabled visitors.)* While you're there, check out **Mortimer's Hole,** the 100m long underground passageway that leads from the base of the cliff to the castle. After Mortimer and Queen Isabella murdered Edward II, they retreated to Nottingham Castle. Edward III created the passageway to sneak up on the castle and capture his father's assassin. *(☎ 915 3700. 50min. tours at 2pm and 3pm daily from the Castle Museum entrance. £2, concessions £1.)*

THE UNDERGROUND SCENE. Beneath Nottingham lie hundreds of ancient caves. As early as the 10th century, Nottingham dwellers dug homes out of the soft and porous "Sherwood sandstones" on which the city rests. Even in medieval times, the caves were often preferred to more conventional housing—they required no building materials and incurred lower taxes. While cave residency dwindled during the Industrial Revolution, Nottingham citizens (and pub owners) continued to use some for storage, and during World War II many caves were converted to air raid shelters. Visitors can tour one cave complex, surreally sited beneath the Broad Marsh Shopping Centre. The 40-minute audio tour of the "Tigguo Cobauc," or "city of caves," includes a trip through Britain's only underground medieval tannery—authentic smells included. *(☎ 924 1424. Open M-Sa 10am-5pm, Su 11am-5pm. £3.25, concessions £2.25, families £9.50.)*

TALES OF ROBIN HOOD. Well, there had to be something in Nottingham commemorating the man. Cable cars will carry you and your five-year-old through Robin's "Sherwood Forest." *(30-38 Maid Marion Way. ☎ 948 3284; www.robinhood.uk.com. Open daily 10am-6pm, last admission 4:30pm. £4.95, students and seniors £4.50, children £3.95, families from £15.75.)*

THE LACE INDUSTRY. A local myth holds that there are five women for every Nottingham man. This unlikely ratio gained credibility from Nottingham's lace industry, which employed thousands of young women in the city during the mid-19th century. The **Museum of Costumes and Textiles,** 51 Castle Gate, recreates scenes to demonstrate how clothes have changed over time. *(☎ 915 3500. Open W-Su 10am-4pm. Free.)* Showing a different side of the industry, the **Museum of Nottingham Lace,** 3-5 High Pavement, uses a working 1850s spinning machine to explain how the material is woven into the social fabric of the city. Demonstrations take place daily from 11am to 1pm and 1:30 to 3:30pm. *(☎ 989 7365. Open daily 10am-5pm. £2.95, students and seniors £2.50, children £1.95. 50min. audio tour requires £1.95 deposit.)*

🎵 ENTERTAINMENT

Nottingham presents a wide range of entertainment and nightlife options, from high culture to clubs, drinking, and dancing. The **Theatre Royal** (☎ 989 5555), at Theatre Sq., and the **Nottingham Playhouse** (☎ 941 9419), at Wellington Circus, offer musicals, dramas, and comedies (tickets from £6).

Clubs and pubs blanket the city. Nights, covers, and crowds vary tremendously, but students can be found everywhere. Despite its tame name, the **County Tavern & Angel Yard,** at the Lace Market, hosts weekend dance parties and Tuesday student nights. On Thursdays, "Anything Can Happen." Sunday salsa parties fill the **Market Bar,** 16-22 Goosegate, Hockley (☎ 924 1780), when most other clubs are closed. **Rock City,** 8 Talbot St., entertains with local bands and mainstream rock. "Damaging" Thursday nights offer metal appreciation, and Saturdays are alternative. (☎ 950 0102. Open 8:30pm-2am. Cover £3-4.) **The Hippo,** 45 Bridlesmith Gate, carries up to 270 loyalists on its royal ship of funk, dance, and garage music. (☎ 950 6667. Open 10:30pm-2am; disabled access by arrangement.)

🏛 DAYTRIPS FROM NOTTINGHAM

🏛 NEWSTEAD ABBEY

Bus #757 travels from Victoria Bus Station, Nottingham to the Abbey gates (35min., 2 per hr., return £3). House and gardens lie 1 mi. from gates. ☎ (01623) 793557. House open Apr.-Sept. daily noon-5pm; grounds open year-round daily 9am-dusk. House and grounds £4, students and seniors £2, under 16 £1.50. Grounds only £2, concessions £1.

North of Nottingham, in the village of **Linby,** stands Newstead Abbey, the gorgeous ancestral estate of Romantic poet Lord Byron. Byron took residence as a 10-year-old and remained here until forced to sell. Many of his personal objects stayed behind, including a replica of "Byron's skullcap," an ancient human cranium unearthed at Newstead in 1806, which Byron had coated in silver, inscribed with verse, and filled with wine before its mysterious re-interment in 1863. Several lively peacocks now hold full reign over the gracious gardens, and a cheerfully well-informed staff stands ready to enlighten those who step indoors.

SHERWOOD FOREST

Buses #33 and 36 leave Victoria Bus Station in Nottingham for the Sherwood Forest Visitors Centre (1hr., every 2hr., £4). Forest open daily dawn-dusk.

To the north spreads famed Sherwood Forest, considerably thinned since the 13th century. The **Sherwood Forest Visitor Centre** holds a small museum, but beware of the multitude of children circling with mini-archery sets. (☎ (01623) 823202. Open daily Apr.-Oct. 10:30am-5pm; Nov.-Mar. 10:30am-4:30pm. Free.) To escape the crowds and rediscover the forest, take the 3½ mi. walk from the center deep into the wilderness. The medieval-style **Robin Hood Festival** (☎ (01623) 823202) centers around a jousting tournament each August. You can stay at the **YHA Sherwood Forest** at Forest Corner, Edwinstowe. Forty beds and laundry facilities grace this abode. (☎ (01629) 825850. Dorms £10.15-11.75, under 18 £6.85.)

EASTWOOD

Six miles west of Nottingham. Rainbow bus #1 leaves from Victoria Bus Station for Eastwood (40min., every 10min. 7am-6pm, every half hour 6-11:30pm).

D.H. Lawrence was an Eastwood native and schoolteacher who went on to write blessedly dirty books of poetry and prose. Once he was banned from the bookshelves; now he's buried in Westminster Abbey. The **D.H. Lawrence Birthplace Museum** fills his childhood home at 8A Victoria St., near Mansfield Rd. (☎ (01773) 717353. Open daily Apr.-Oct. 10am-5pm; Nov.-Mar. 10am-4pm. £2, concessions £1.20.) The **Sons and Lovers Cottage,** 28 Garden Rd. (☎ (0151) 653 8710), where young Lawrence lived from 1887 to 1891, is free and open by appointment.

LINCOLN   ☎01522

Lincoln's imposing hilltop cathedral dominates the view from the surrounding countryside for miles. Medieval streets climb their cobbled way past half-timbered Tudor houses to the 12th-century cathedral, itself a relative newcomer in a town built for retired Roman legionnaires. Lincoln (pop. 90,000), often thought of as a cold industrial town, does not draw in hordes of tourists, but those who do make the trip and the steep uphill climb to the city's peak will consider it worthwhile.

▐ GETTING THERE AND GETTING AROUND

Trains: Central Station, St. Mary's St. Ticket office open M-Sa 5:45am-7:30pm, Su 10:30am-9:20pm. Travel center open M-Sa 9am-5pm. Trains (☎ (08457) 484950) on the Doncaster-London rail route from: **London King's Cross** (2½hr.; M-Sa 1 per hr., Su every 2hr.; return £39); **Nottingham** (1hr.; M-Sa 2 per hr., Su 7 per day; return £5.60); and **Leeds** (2hr., 1 every 2½hr., return £17.50).

Buses: City Bus Station, Melville St. off St. Mary's St., opposite the train station. Open M-F 8:30am-5pm, Sa 9am-1:45pm. **National Express** (☎ (08705) 808080) from: **London** (5hr., 2 per day, £18). For information on rural Lincolnshire bus services, contact the **Lincolnshire Roadcar** station on St. Mark St. (☎ 522255). Open M-F 8:30am-5pm, Sa 8:30am-4:30pm.

Travel Hotline: ☎ 553135. Open M-Th 8am-5:15pm, F 8am-4:45pm.

✦ ▐ ORIENTATION AND PRACTICAL INFORMATION

Roman and Norman military engineers were attracted to the summit of **Castle Hill;** later railway engineers preferred its base. As a result, Lincoln is divided into the affluent acropolis to the north and the cottage-filled lower town near the rail tracks. The TIC and major sights lie at the junction of Steep Hill and Castle Hill.

Tourist Information Centre: 9 Castle Hill (☎ 529828; fax 579055). Books rooms for 10% of the first night. Pick up the free map and glossy city *Holiday Guide* (50p). Open M-Th 9:30am-5:30pm, F 9:30am-5pm, Sa-Su 10am-5pm. Another **branch** (☎ 579056), is on the corner of Cornhill and High St. Same hours on M-Sa, closed Su.

Tours: 1hr. tours depart from the TIC July-Aug. daily 11am and 2pm; Sept.-Oct. and Apr.-June only Sa-Su. £2, children £1. **Guide Friday** (☎ 522255) runs bus tours all around the city, at least 1 per hr. during the summer. Hop on at any one of the many stops. Tours 50min. £5.50, students and seniors £4, children £2.

Financial Services: Barclays Bank, 316 High St. (☎ 343555). Open M-Tu and Th-F 9am-5pm, W 10am-5pm, Sa 9:30am-12:30pm. **Thomas Cook,** 4 Cornhill Pavement (☎ 346400). Open M-Tu and Th-Sa 9am-5:30pm, W 10am-5:30pm.

Launderette: Burton Laundries, 8 Burton Rd. (☎ 543498), at Westgate near the cathedral. Dry cleaning too. Open daily at 8:30am; M-F last wash 7pm, Sa-Su last wash 4pm.

Police: (☎ 882222), West Parade, near the town hall.

Hospital: Lincoln County Hospital (☎ 512512), Greenwell Rd..

Internet Access: Central Library, Free School Ln. (☎ 510800), between Saltergate and Silver St. Three terminals; one you must call ahead and reserve (£3 per hr.), two you just drop in and use (£1 per 15min.). Open M-F 9:30am-7pm, Sa 9:30am-4pm. **Sun Café,** 7a St. Mary (☎ 579067), across from the train station. Two gateways to the Net. £2.50 per 30min. Open M-Sa 9am-6pm, Su noon-5pm.

Post Office: (☎ 532288), Cornhill, just off High St. **Bureau de change** on request. Open M-F 9am-5:30pm, Sa 9am-5pm. **Postal Code:** LN5 7XX.

▐ ACCOMMODATIONS

B&Bs line Carline and Yarborough Rd., west of the castle. Most can be had for £17-20 a person. Call ahead in summer, as rooms fill quickly. For more information, see the free *Friends and Holiday* or *Holiday Guide* leaflets from the TIC.

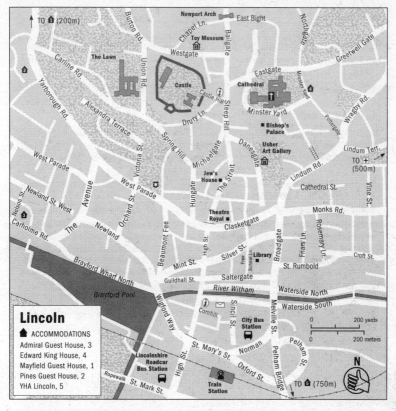

Lincoln

🏠 ACCOMMODATIONS

Admiral Guest House, 3
Edward King House, 4
Mayfield Guest House, 1
Pines Guest House, 2
YHA Lincoln, 5

YHA Lincoln, 77 South Park Ave. (☎ 522076; fax 567424), opposite South Common at the end of Canwick Rd. Veer right from the station, turn right onto Pelham Bridge (which becomes Canwick Rd.), and turn right after the traffic lights at South Park Ave. 47-bed Victorian villa with a solarium and a wonderful view of meandering ponies. Lockout 10am-5pm. Curfew 11pm. Open Feb.-Oct. Dorms £9.80, under 18 £6.75.

Mayfield Guest House, 213 Yarborough Rd. (☎/fax 533732). Entrance behind house on Mill Rd., a 20min. walk from train station and near the Ellis Mill, a working windmill. If you have a backpack, spare yourself and take bus #7 or 8 (50p). A bright Victorian mansion with large rooms, almost all with bath, and gigantic fluffy quilts. Panoramic breakfast view of the countryside. No smoking. Singles £19-25; doubles £38-40.

Edward King House (☎ 528778), Minster Yard, next to the Bishop's Palace. The diocese runs this place, so bibles replace TVs in the rooms. The views out the windows are divine, the breakfast room and building immaculate, and the city center location miraculous. Continental breakfast included, English breakfast £2. £19 per person.

Admiral Guest House, 18 Nelson St. (☎/fax 544467), in the lower part of town. From the railway station, take Wigford Way across the canal, then take the immediate steps down to the canal and walk along Brayford Wharf North; turn left onto Carholme Rd., then right onto Nelson St. Mrs. Robertson's decor is so nautical, if it wasn't for the cable TV in every room, you'd think you were at sea. Singles £17; doubles £35.

Pines Guest House, 104 Yarborough Rd. (☎/fax 532985). Take bus #7 or 8, or a 15min. walk from the station. Large, thickly carpeted B&B. All rooms have TV, but you'll probably spend your time hanging out in the game room stocked with a pool table and full bar. Singles from £16; twins and doubles £32, with bath £36.

THE MIDLANDS

🍴 FOOD

The **market,** at Sincil St. outside Astoria shopping center, sells sundries. (Open M-F 9am-4pm, Sa 9am-4:30pm.) A variety of restaurants, tearooms, and takeaways grace **High St.,** tempting those trekking up the hill to take a break. Or hold out for the pubs that abound on **Bailgate St.,** on the other side of the hill.

The Ice Cream Parlour, at the base of Bailgate. This tiny, traditional shop scoops out first-rate homemade ice cream and sorbets. A cone of coconut costs a modest 90p. Open M-Th 10:30am-6pm, F-Su 9:30am-sunset.

The Spinning Wheel, 39 Steep Hill (☎ 522463), one block south of the TIC in a leaning, half-timbered building. Tea (80-90p) and vegetarian dishes (£4-5) are nicely priced; others are a bit steeper, but filling (from £6). Open daily 11:30am-10pm.

Stokes High Bridge Café, 207 High St. (☎ 513825). Busy tearoom in a Tudor-style house-cum-bridge, displayed on many a postcard. Sit by a window, watch swans float by on the green canal, and munch steak pie (£4.50). 2-course lunch (£5.40) served 11:30am-2pm; tea served 9:30am-5pm. Coffee shop downstairs, open daily 9am-5pm.

The Mediterranean, 14 Bailgate St. (☎ 546464). Snappy decor, candy-colored wrought-iron tables, and fresh flowers accompany inventive dishes from around the world. Starters and lunch run £3-5, and a daily two-course set menu is £7.95. Open M-T noon-2:30pm and 6-9:30pm, W-Th noon-2:30pm and 6-10pm, F noon-2:30pm and 6-10:30pm, Sa noon-3pm and 6-10:30pm, Su noon-4pm and 6-9:30pm.

Lion and Snake, 79 Bailgate St. (☎ 523770), up by the cathedral. An alluring pub setting with picnic tables out back for a restorative pint and 3-course meal (£6.50). Two one-course meals for £6 between 3-7pm. Open M-Sa 11am-11pm, Su noon-10:30pm; food served M-F noon-7pm, Sa-Su noon-3pm.

👁 SIGHTS

LINCOLN CATHEDRAL. While the rest of Lincoln endured a millennium of rumblings and crumblings in which Roman barricades, bishops' palaces, and conquerors' castles were all erected and destroyed, the undefeated king of the hill is the magnificent Lincoln Cathedral. Although construction began in 1072, the cathedral wasn't completed until three centuries later, when it towered over Europe as the continent's tallest building. The cathedral's many alluring features include the legendary imp in the Angel Choir, who turned to stone while attempting to chat with angels. A treasury room displays ancient sacred silver and a shrine to child martyr Sir Hugh, mentioned in Chaucer's *Prioress's Tale* and Marlowe's *The Jew of Malta.* Other exhibits reside in a library designed by Christopher Wren. (☎ 544544. Open June-Aug. M-Sa 7:15am-8pm, Su 7:15am-6pm; Sept.-May. M-Sa 7:15am-6pm, Su 7:15am-5pm. Free tours depart May-Aug. daily 11am, 1pm, 3pm; Sept.-Apr. Sa only, same times. Roof tours W and Sa £2; book in advance. Cathedral £3.50. Library £1, children free.)

LINCOLN CASTLE. Home to one of the four surviving copies of the *Magna Carta,* the grandiloquent ancestor of all modern constitutions and civil liberties, this 1068 castle was also the house of pain for the inmates of the Victorian Castle Prison. A cheerful tour guide leads the "Prison Experience," among other walks. (☎ 511068. Open Apr.-Oct. M-Sa 9:30am-5:30pm, Su 11am-5:30pm; Nov.-Mar. M-Sa 9:30am-4pm, Su 11am-4pm. Tours Apr.-Oct. 11am-2pm. £2.50, seniors £1.50, children £1, families £6.50.)

BISHOP'S PALACE. Rather than destroy the leftovers of Lincoln's ancient imperial settlers, the pragmatic Lincolnites of the Middle Ages put them to good use. The medieval Bishop's Palace was originally wedged between the walls of the upper and lower Roman Cities. Thanks to 12th-century cleric Bishop Chesney, a passageway through the upper city wall links the palace remains to Lincoln Cathedral at the top of the hill. The palace itself, in Chesney's time the seat of England's largest diocese, is now an English Heritage sight with peaceful ruins, vineyards, and long views over greater Lincoln. *(☎ 527468. Open Apr.-Oct. daily 10am-6pm; Nov.-Mar. Sa-Su 10am-4pm. £1.50, students and seniors £1.10, children 80p.)*

TOY MUSEUM. The perfect setting for either a child's fantasy or a horror movie, the museum houses a fantastic collection of antique toys. Exhibits change every year—the latest glorified robots and mechanical gadgets. *(26 Westgate. ☎ 520534. Open Apr.-Sept. Tu-Sa 11am-5pm; Oct.-Dec. Sa 11am-5pm, Su noon-4pm. £2.20, students and seniors £1.80, children £1.20.)*

🎵 ENTERTAINMENT

Lincoln's nightlife is respectable. Head for **High St.,** where the nightlife will make itself known; watch for **The Barracuda Club,** 780-781 High St., (☎ 525828). On the corner of Silver St. and Flaxengate, **Mustang Sally's** offers a variety of theme nights, including karaoke. Next door, **Ritzy** (☎ 522314) is one of the more popular clubs.

For less strenuous entertainment, pick up the monthly *What's On In Lincoln* pamphlet at the tourist office, or ask at the Cathedral about choral and organ performances. The **Theatre Royal,** Clasketgate at the corner of High St. (☎ 525555), stages all sorts of dramas and musicals year-round. (Box office open M-Sa 10am-6pm. Wheelchair access. Tickets $7-16.50, some student discounts.) **The Lawn,** on Union Rd. by the castle, hosts regular outdoor music and dance events. (☎ 560306. Open Apr.-Sept. M-F 9am-5pm, Sa-Su 10am-5pm; Oct.-Mar. M-F 9am-4:30pm, Sa-Su 10am-4pm. Free.) Late July brings **Medieval Weekend** and August supports the relatively new **Lincoln Early Music Festival.**

🗺 DAYTRIPS FROM LINCOLN

GRANTHAM. It was in Grantham that Sir Isaac Newton attended the **King's School,** on Brook St., and left a carving of his schoolboy signature in a windowsill. (☎ (01476) 563180. Open by appointment only. Free, but donations accepted.) The **Grantham Museum,** on St. Peter's Hill by the tourist office, features exhibits on Newton's life and work, as well as a video exhibit on another Grantham progeny, Margaret Thatcher. *(25 mi. south of Lincoln. Trains reach Grantham from Lincoln (45min., 1 per hr., day return £2.30). Lincolnshire Roadcar (☎ 522255) buses run from Lincoln's St. Mark St. bus station (#601; 1¼hr.; M-Sa 1 per hr., Su less frequent; day return £4). ☎ (01476) 568783. Open M-Sa 10am-5pm. Free).*

COLSTERWORTH. Within Colsterworth rests **Woolsthorpe Manor,** birthplace of Sir Isaac Newton. It was here, under an apple tree, that the scientist conceptualized gravity and dreamt up calculus, the bane of students everywhere. *(7 mi. south of Grantham. Trains run from Grantham (15min, about 1 per hr., day return £3). Lincolnsire Roadcar also services Colsterworth from Grantham (20min., every 2-3hr., day return £2.30). ☎ (01476) 860338. Open Apr.-Oct. W-Su 1-5pm. £2.50, children £1.30, families £5.70.)*

EAST ANGLIA

The plush green farmland and delicate watery flatness of East Anglia stretch northeast from London, cloaking the counties of Cambridgeshire, Norfolk, and Suffolk, as well as parts of Essex. Literally England's newest landscape, the vast fields and plains of the Fens were drained as late as the 1820s. From Norwich east to the English Channel, the water that long ago drenched enormous areas of medieval peat bogs was channeled into the maze of waterways known as the Norfolk Broads, now a National Park. Continental-style windmills helped ensure the Fens stayed drained; some survivors of the towery clan still perch in the marshes. Farther inland and 800 years earlier, Norman invaders had made their way to the elevated mound at Ely, and built a stunning cathedral from stone transported by boat across the then-flooded fenland. In the 15th century, in a minor village to the south, renegade scholars from Oxford set up shop along the River Cam. Eventually granted a royal imprimatur, they built a university. Farther northeast, the imposing houses and magnificent "wool churches" of small towns in Norfolk and Suffolk stand as a testament to their past as thriving wool centers. But despite the obvious impact humans have made on this region, much of the rustic beauty that inspired the landscape paintings of natives Constable and Gainsborough remains.

HIGHLIGHTS OF EAST ANGLIA

CAMBRIDGE Stroll through the colleges (but keep off the grass!) in this university city, one of the world's best-known reserves of learning (p. 297). Don't miss punting on the Cam, or attending Evensong at the exquisite King's College Chapel.

ELY CATHEDRAL Gaze skyward at this medieval masterpiece, still breathtaking as it rises out of former fenland like an oasis of civilization (p. 309).

NORWICH Don't get lost in this wool-trading town, once the largest in Anglo-Saxon England, in which churches, markets, and festivals have endured for centuries (p. 311).

GETTING AROUND EAST ANGLIA

A **combined Anglia Plus Pass** (about £60, discount with Railcard), available only at stations within East Anglia, entitles you to a week's unlimited travel on all **train** routes in the region. A **regular Anglia Plus Pass** allows a week of unlimited travel within either Norfolk or Suffolk (£27.50). Both zones are also covered by one- and three-day passes (£8.50 and £18). All Anglia Plus passes also allow free travel on various lines of the Norwich, Ipswich, and Great Yarmouth local **bus** services. The **Out 'n' About** ticket allows unlimited day travel on the Stagecoach Cambuses (£4.20, students £3.30, children £2.80). You might end up paying with your time; buses run infrequently.

East Anglia's flat terrain and relatively low annual rainfall please bikers and hikers, although rental bikes can be difficult to find outside of Cambridge and Norwich. The area's two longest and most popular walking trails, together covering 200 mi., are the **Peddar's Way,** which runs from Knettishall Heath to Holme and includes the Norfolk coast path, and the **Weaver's Way,** an extended trail that traverses the north coast from Cromer to Great Yarmouth. Both cross a town with a bus or train station every 10 miles or so. Tourist information centres in Norwich, Bury St. Edmunds, and several Suffolk villages issue guides for the Weaver's Way. For the Peddar's Way, pick up *Peddar's Way and Norfolk Coast Path* at tourist information centres.

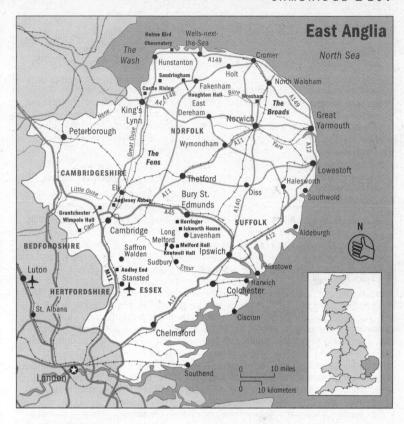

East Anglia

CAMBRIDGESHIRE AND ESSEX

CAMBRIDGE ☎ 01223

Cambridge (pop. 105,000) has weathered many winds of change. Once inhabited by Romans, this trading town endured a series of nasty Viking raids before the Normans arrived in the 11th century. The 13th century brought Oxford's refugees to the banks of the Cam, an influx that would permanently alter the city more than any military conquest. Cambridge is feistily determined to remain under its pastoral academic robes, in contrast to museum-oriented metropolitan Oxford. The tourist information centre will tell you that they manage, not encourage, visitors. In recent decades, the **University of Cambridge** has ceased to be an exclusive preserve of upper-class sons, bringing the student ratios for state school pupils and women to more just levels. Some of the old upper-crust traditions are slipping: students only bedeck themselves with gown and cravat for meal times about once a week now, for instance. At exams' end, Cambridge explodes with Pimms-soaked glee, and **May Week** (in mid-June, naturally) launches a dizzying schedule of cocktail parties and balls in celebration of pending graduation ceremonies.

▐ GETTING THERE AND GETTING AROUND

Trains: Station Rd. Purchase tickets daily 5am-11pm. **Trains** (☎ (08457) 484950) run from **London King's Cross** (¾hr., 2 per hr., £14.50) and **London Liverpool St.** (1¼hr., 2 per hr., £18.80).

Bus Station: Drummer St. Station—more a street than a station. Ticket booth open daily 8:45am-5:30pm; tickets also often available on boarding. **National Express** (☎ (08705) 808080) arrives from **London** (2hr., 17 per day, from £8). **Jetlink** coach service runs hourly shuttles to Drummer St. from: **Heathrow Airport** (2hr., £18); **Gatwick Airport** (3hr., £20); and **Stansted Airport** (45min., £8). **Stagecoach Express** (☎ (01604) 620077) runs from **Oxford** (2¾hr., 10-12 per day, £7).

Public Transportation: Cambus (☎ 423554) runs a free city center shuttle, a 6min. shuttle from the train station, and area service (65p-£1.60). **Whippet Coaches** (☎ (01480) 463792) runs daytrips from town.

Taxis: Cabco (☎ 312444). **Camtax** (☎ 313131). Both open 24hr.

Bike Rental: Mike's Bikes, 28 Mill Rd. (☎ 312591). £5 per day, £8 per week, £25 deposit; lock, light, and basket included. Open M-Sa 9am-6pm, Su 10am-4pm. The tourist information centre has a full list of bike shops.

▟▐ ORIENTATION AND PRACTICAL INFORMATION

About 60 mi. north of London, Cambridge is an old city; streets twist at will. The city has two main avenues, both of which suffer from multiple personality disorder. The main shopping street starts at **Magdalene Bridge** and becomes **Bridge St., Sidney St., St. Andrew's St., Regent St.,** and finally **Hills Rd.** The other—alternately **St. John's St., Trinity St., King's Parade,** and **Trumpington St.**—is the academic thoroughfare, with several colleges lying between it and the River Cam. The two streets cross at **St. John's College.** From the bus station at **Drummer St.,** a hop, skip, and a jump down **Emmanuel St.** will land you right in the shopping district near the tourist information centre (TIC). To get to the heart of things from the train station on **Station Rd.,** turn right onto Hills Rd. and continue straight ahead.

The primary mode of transport in Cambridge is the **bicycle.** This city claims to have more bikes per person than any other place in Britain. A confusing series of one-way streets and an armada of foreign teenagers used to riding on the wrong side of the road make summer transport more difficult. If you plan to ride, use hand signals and heed road signs. Pedestrians should look both ways—as well as behind, above, and under—twice before crossing.

Tourist Information Centre: Wheeler St. (☎ 322640; fax 457588; www.cambridge.gov.uk/leisure/tourism), a block south of Market Sq. Mini-guide 40p, maps 20p. *Cambridge: The Official Guide* gives a clear map of the town center as well as suggested walks and commercial listings (£3.95). Maps of cycling tours around the area £4. Books rooms for £3 and a 10% deposit of the first night's stay. Advance booking hotline (5 days or more in advance; ☎ 457581; M-F 9:30am-4pm). Open Apr.-Oct. M-F 10am-5:30pm, Sa 10am-5pm, Su 11am-4pm; Nov.-Mar. M-F 10am-5:30pm, Sa 10am-5pm.

Tours: Informative 2hr. walking tours of the city and some colleges leave from the TIC. Call for times. Tours are well narrated but usually enter only one college—usually King's. £7, children £4. Special **Drama Tour** in July and Aug. led by guides in period dress (Tu 6:30pm; £4.20). **Guide Friday** (☎ 362444) runs its familiar 1hr. **bus tours** every 15-30min. You can jump on at any stop. Apr.-Oct. £8.50, students and seniors £7, children £2.50, families £19.50.

Budget Travel: STA Travel, 38 Sidney St. (☎ 366966). Open M-W and F 9am-5:30pm, Th 10am-5:30pm, Sa 11am-5pm.

Financial Services: Numerous **banks** line Market Sq. and Trinity St. **Lloyds TSB,** 3 Sidney St. Open M-Tu and Th-F 9am-5pm, W 9:30am-5pm, Sa 10am-1pm. **Thomas Cook,** 8 Andrews St. (☎ 366141). Open M-Tu and Th-Sa 9am-5:30pm, W 10am-5:30pm.

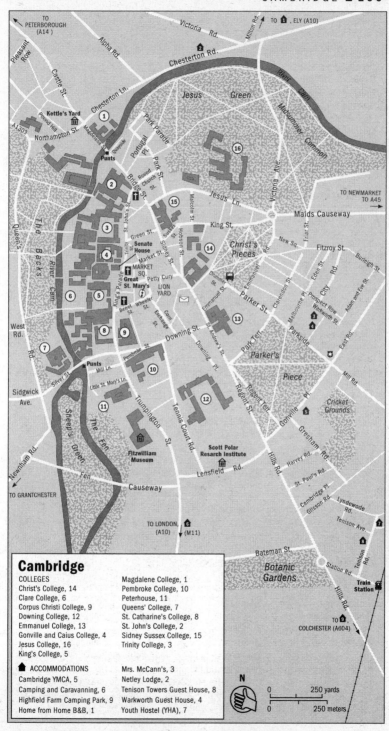

Cambridge

COLLEGES

Christ's College, 14
Clare College, 6
Corpus Christi College, 9
Downing College, 12
Emmanuel College, 13
Gonville and Caius College, 4
Jesus College, 16
King's College, 5

Magdalene College, 1
Pembroke College, 10
Peterhouse, 11
Queens' College, 7
St. Catharine's College, 8
St. John's College, 2
Sidney Sussex College, 15
Trinity College, 3

♠ ACCOMMODATIONS

Cambridge YMCA, 5
Camping and Caravanning, 6
Highfield Farm Camping Park, 9
Home from Home B&B, 1

Mrs. McCann's, 3
Netley Lodge, 2
Tenison Towers Guest House, 8
Warkworth Guest House, 4
Youth Hostel (YHA), 7

EAST ANGLIA

American Express: 25 Sidney St. (☎ (08706) 001060). Open M-Tu and Th-F 9am-5:30pm, W 9:30am-5:30pm, Sa 9am-5pm.

Launderette: Clean Machine, 22 Burleigh St. (☎ 578009). Open daily 7am-8:30pm.

Police: Parkside (☎ 358966).

Hospital: Addenbrookes, Hills Rd. (☎ 245151). Catch Cambus #4, 5, or 5a from Emmanuel St. (£1), and get off where Hills Rd. intersects Long Rd.

Internet Access: International Telecom Centre, 2 Wheeler St. (☎ 357358). Across from the TIC and painted bright yellow—impossible to miss! £1 for first 33min., 3p per min. thereafter 9am-noon, 6p thereafter noon-10pm. £1 min. charge. Open daily 9am-10pm. **CB1,** 32 Mill Rd. (☎ 576306), near the hostel. 5p per min. Open daily 10am-8pm.

Post Office: 9-11 St. Andrew's St. (☎ 323325). Open M-Sa 9am-5:30pm. **Postal Code:** CB2 3AA.

◤ ACCOMMODATIONS

The lesson Cambridge teaches budget travelers is to book ahead, especially in summer. Rooms are scarce, which makes prices high and quality low. Most B&Bs aren't in the town center; many around **Portugal St.** and **Tenison Rd.** house students during the academic year and are open to visitors in July and August. If a house is full, ask about others in the neighborhood—B&Bs are often not labeled. Pick up a guide from the TIC (50p), or check the comprehensive list in the window after it closes. The TIC also has a campsite list (30p). Cheaper accommodations in nearby **Ely** (see p. 309) make it a good base for exploring Cambridge.

▨ **Tenison Towers Guest House,** 148 Tenison Rd. (☎ 566511). Fresh flowers grace airy rooms 2 blocks from the train station; Mrs. Chance keeps an impeccable house. Singles £22; doubles £38, with shower £42.

YHA Cambridge, 97 Tenison Rd. (☎ 354601; fax 312780; cambridge@yha.org.uk). Friendly staff fosters a relaxed, welcoming atmosphere, although more showers wouldn't hurt. 100 beds, mostly 3-4 beds to a room; a few doubles. Rock music filters through a well-equipped kitchen. Laundry facilities. TV lounge. Small lockers in some rooms. Bureau de change. Cafeteria could pass as a restaurant in its own right. Breakfast £3.20, packed lunch £2.80-3.65. No curfew or lockout. Crowded Mar.-Oct.; in the summer, call a week ahead. Dorms £15.10, under 18 £11.40.

Home from Home B&B, 39 Milton Rd. (☎ 323555). A 20min. walk from the city center. Pricey but worthwhile. Sparkling, spotless rooms, wicker chairs, and a pleasant hostess in Liz Fasano. 6 rooms, variable occupancy; rooms include TVs and showers. Full English breakfast with fresh fruit, cereal, and croissants. Yum. Biscuits and hot chocolate in every room. Yum. Call ahead with a credit card for reservations. Yum. Singles from £35; doubles from £48; discounts for longer stays.

Mrs. McCann, 40 Warkworth St. (☎ 314098). A jolly hostess with comfortably lived-in TV-equipped rooms, in a quiet neighborhood near the bus station. 3 singles, 1 twin. £16-18 per person; discount after 3 nights.

Cambridge YMCA, Gonville Pl. (☎ 356998; fax 312749; bleech@camymca.org.uk). Good location between the train station and town center. Large, clean rooms, even if they feel slightly industrial. Breakfast included. Singles £22.65; doubles £37.

Netley Lodge, 112 Chesterton Rd. (☎ 363845). Plush red carpets and a conservatory lush with greenery welcome you to sunny rooms. Roses inside and out—hostess Mrs. Mikolajczyk is a study in elegance. Singles £22; doubles £40.

Warkworth Guest House, Warkworth Terr. (☎ 363682). Sunny rooms near the bus station. Packed lunch on request. Singles £25, with bath £30; twins £50, with bath £55.

Highfield Farm Camping Park, Long Rd., Comberton (☎ 262308). Head west on the A603 3 mi., then turn right on the B1046 to Comberton for 1 mi.; or take Cambus #118 from the Drummer St. bus station (every 45min.). Flush toilets, showers, and laundry. Open Apr.-Oct. Call ahead. £7 per tent, with car £8.75; off season £6.25, £7.25.

Camping and Caravanning Club Site, 19 Cabbage Moor, Great Shelford (☎ 841185). Head 3 mi. south on the M11, then left onto the A1301 for three quarters of a mile, or take Cambus #102 or 103 and ask for Westfield Rd. Flush toilets, showers, and facilities for the disabled. Open Mar.-Oct.; call ahead in July. £5.30 per person for members, children £1.60; £4.30 non-member pitch fee.

⬤ FOOD

Cooking for yourself or buying pub grub are both good budget options in Cambridge. **Market Sq.** has bright pyramids of fruit and vegetables, cheaper than those in supermarkets, for the budget shopper. (Market open M-Sa usually 9:30am-4:30pm.) Students buy beer and cornflakes at **Sainsbury's,** 44 Sidney St., the only supermarket in the middle of town. (☎ 366891. Open M-F 8am-9pm, Sa 7:30am-9pm, Su 11am-5pm.) Indian and Greek restaurants sate the curious tastebuds of hungry students (make sure that you don't meet the Christ's College football club on their ritual curry night out). South of town, Hills Rd. and Mill Rd. brim with good, cheap restaurants.

▧ **Nadia's,** 11 St. John's St. (☎ 460961). An uncommonly good bakery with reasonable prices and a divine smell. Wonderful flapjacks and quiches (65p-£1). You'll get smiles from the chocolate-chocolate-chip cookie. Sandwiches (£1.75) and muffins (75p) that are a brunch unto themselves. Takeaway only. Open daily 8:30am-5pm. Also at 16 Silver St. and 20 King's Parade.

▧ **Hobbs' Pavillion,** Parker's Piece (☎ 367480), off Park Terr. Renowned for imaginative, overpowering, thin, rectangular pancakes. Hobbs' feels like a stylishly comfortable living room, with a view across Parker's Piece, jaunty jazz music...and a Mars Bar and ice cream pancake for £3.95—you won't need to eat again for two weeks. Open Tu-Sa noon-2:15pm and 6-9:45pm. No credit cards.

Clown's, 54 King St. (☎ 355711). Stunningly cheerful staff add the final dash of color to this humming spot—children's painted renderings of clowns plaster the walls, as do adoring odes by local regulars. Everything from cakes to toasties to lasagna £1.20-5.95, plus some of the best coffee in Cambridge. Open daily 7:30am-midnight.

The Little Tea Room, 1 All Saints' Passage (☎ 366033), off Trinity St. As hopelessly precious as it sounds. Heroic waitstaff navigate two tightly-packed rooms to serve tip-top teas. "Traditional English cream tea" £3.95 (pot of tea, scone, clotted cream, jam). Open M-Sa 10am-5:30pm, Su 1-5:30pm.

Tatties, 11 Sussex St. (☎ 323399). The jacket potatoes make up for the fast-food ambiance. Fillings range from the butter (£1.95) to Philly cheese and smoked salmon (£5.75). Open M-Sa 8:30am-7pm, Su 10am-5pm.

Chopsticks, 22a Magdalene St. (☎ 556510). A quiet, dim exterior makes way for tasty Chinese dishes inside. Two-course lunch with tea £5.95. Open M 5:30-11pm, Tu-Su noon-2:30pm and 5:30-11pm.

Trattoria Pasta Fresca, 66 Mill Rd. (☎ 352836). Filling, basic Italian food at reasonable prices. Spaghetti with garlic bread £7.95, pizza £4.45-7.25. Open M-F noon-3pm and 6-10:30pm, Sa noon-4:30pm and 6-10:30pm, Su 1-4:30pm and 6-10pm.

Rainbow's Vegetarian Bistro, 9a King's Parade (☎ 321551). Duck under the rainbow sign on King's Parade. A tiny, creative burrow featuring delicious international vegan and vegetarian fare, all for £6.25. Open M-Sa 11am-11pm.

⬛ PUBS

Cantabrigian hangouts offer good pub crawling year-round, though they lose some of their character as well as their best customers in summer. **King St.** has always been home to a diverse collection of pubs, and used to host the King St. Run, a race in which contestants ran the length of the street stopping at each of the 13 pubs to down a pint. The winner was the first to cross the finish line on his own two feet. Most pubs stay open from 11am to 11pm, Sundays noon to 10:30pm. The local brewery, Greene King, supplies many of the pubs with the popular bitters IPA (India Pale Ale) and Abbott.

The Eagle, Benet St. (☎ 505020). Have a pint in the oldest pub in Cambridge. This was where Watson and Crick first rushed in breathless to announce their discovery of the DNA double helix. The barmaid insisted they settle their 4-shilling tab before she'd serve them a toast. During World War II, British and American pilots stood on each other's shoulders to burn their initials into the ceiling of the RAF room with Zippos. Open 11am-11pm, Su noon-10:30pm.

The Mill, Mill Ln. (☎ 357026), off Silver St. Bridge. Claims the riverside park as its own on spring nights for punt- and people-watching. In summer, it fills with the odd remaining student and hordes of international youth. The mix becomes even stranger once you add the cows that roam the riverbanks. Open M-Sa noon-11pm, Su noon-10:30pm.

The Anchor, Silver St. (☎ 353554). Another undergraduate watering hole, the Anchor allows you to get one in while watching students pour their pints onto the Silver St. Bridge, weather permitting. Open M-Sa 11am-11pm, Su 1-10:30pm.

The Maypole, Portugal Pl. (☎ 352999), between Bridge St. and New Park St. Celebrates a lengthy Happy Hour (5-11pm) and cherishes its reputation for the best cocktails in town. Hearty pub food and Italian dishes £2-7. Open 11am-11pm, Su noon-10:30pm.

The Rattle and Hum, 4 King St. (☎ 505015). A prerequisite before hitting the clubs, with a DJ spinning dance tunes 7 nights a week. Open 11am-11pm, Su noon-10:30pm.

The Champion of the Thames, 68 King St. (☎ 352043). About the size of a broom closet, and filled with regulars; the bartender tells the customer personally when a phone call comes in. Bring your own food. Open 11am-11pm, Su noon-10:30pm.

The Free Press, Prospect Row (☎ 368337), behind the police station. Named after an Abolitionist newspaper, it now sponsors a local boat club in the Amateur Rowing Association. Mostly a local haunt. Non-smoking! Open 11am-11pm, Su noon-10:30pm.

The Town and Gown, Poundhill (☎ 353791), just off Northampton St. Gay men gather to have a pint. Strong community feel. Open M-F 11am-3pm and 7-11pm, Sa 11am-11pm, Su noon-10:30pm.

Five Bells, 126-128 Newmarket Rd. (☎ 314019). Primarily gay clientele gathers in the beer garden. Open M-F 11am-3pm and 7-11pm, Sa 11am-11pm, Su noon-10:30pm.

👁 COLLEGES AND OTHER SIGHTS

Cambridge is an architect's fantasia, packing some of England's most breathtaking monuments into less than one square mile. The soaring grandeur of **King's College Chapel** and the postcard-familiar St. John's **Bridge of Sighs** are sightseeing staples, while more obscure college courts veil undiscovered delicacies. Most historic buildings are on the east bank of the Cam between Magdalene Bridge and Silver St. The gardens, meadows, and cows of the **Backs** lend a pastoral air to the west bank.

The **University of Cambridge** has three eight-week terms: Michaelmas (Oct.-Dec.), Lent (Jan.-Mar.), and Easter (Apr.-June). Visitors can gain access to most of the college grounds daily from 9am to 5:30pm, though many close to sightseers during the Easter term, and virtually all are closed during exam period (mid-May to mid-June); your safest bet is to call ahead (☎ 331100) for hours. Some buildings shut down during vacations. If you have time for only a few colleges, **King's, Trinity, Queens', Christ's, St. John's,** and **Jesus** should top your list, though the Britain-in-a-week traveler could trample through 12 or 14 colleges in a few hours—most cluster around the center of town. Porters (plump bowler-bedecked ex-servicemen) maintain security. Those who look and act like Cambridge undergrads (i.e. no traveler's backpack, no camera, and definitely no Cambridge sweatshirt) are often able to wander freely through most college grounds even after hours. For maximum camouflage carry a plastic bag from the local Sainsbury's and wear your rucksack over one shoulder—in the scoffing words of one student: "only the French wear it over two." In summer, a few undergrads stay to work or study, but most skip town, leaving it to 5000 PhD students and mobs of foreign teenagers.

KING'S COLLEGE

King's Parade. ☎ 331100. Chapel and grounds open M-Sa 9:30am-4:30pm, Su 9:30am-2:30pm. Listing of services and musical events available at porter's lodge, £1. Evensong 5:30pm most nights. Contact TIC for tours. £3.50, concessions £2.50, under 12 free.

King's College was founded by Henry VI in 1441 as a partner to a small school for paupers he had founded near Windsor; it wasn't until 1861 that students from schools other than Eton were allowed to compete for scholarships. Despite this history, or perhaps because of it, King's is now the most socially liberal of all the Cambridge colleges, drawing more of its students from state schools than any other; the college was also the site of the student riots of 1968. As a result, Cambridge's best-known college is also its least traditional—there are no formal dinners or black-tie balls, and interior corridors are covered in lurid graffiti.

Little of this is noticeable to most visitors to Cambridge, who descend in droves on what is now the UK's biggest tourist attraction outside London—the magnificent **King's College Chapel,** a spectacular Gothic monument. One of England's more pious monarchs, Henry VI cleared away much of the center of medieval Cambridge for the foundation of the College, and he intended this chapel to be England's finest. If you stand at the southwest corner of the courtyard, you can see where Henry's master mason left off and where work under the Tudors began—the earlier stone is off-white, the later dark. The elaborate stone wall that separates the college grounds from King's Parade was not part of the original plans—it's a neo-Gothic 19th-century addition; originally the chapel and grounds were hidden behind a row of shops and houses. The chapel's interior is one enormous chamber cleft by a carved wooden choir screen. Crowned by trumpeting angels, the screen is one of the purest examples of the early Renaissance style in England; its designs were destroyed by their Italian creators, who didn't want their work replicated. The heralding angels flit about against the backdrop of the world's largest fan-vaulted ceiling, described by Wordsworth as a "branching roof self-poised, and scooped into ten thousand cells where light and shade repose." Tudor roses, symbols of Henry VIII's reign, abound. The chapel also houses a few works of sacrilege—look for the 15th century graffiti on the wall to the right of the altar and the devilish portrait of a craftsman's estranged wife on the choir screen.

Behind the altar hangs Rubens's magnificent *Adoration of the Magi* (1639), a gift to the college and the most expensive painting ever auctioned at the time of its purchase. The canvas has been protected by an electronic alarm since a crazed attack by a man with a chisel several years ago. Free musical recitals often play at the chapel—pick up a schedule at the entrance. Enjoy the classic view of the chapel and of the adjacent **Gibbs Building** from the river. As you picnic by the water, think of those who have gone before you: John Maynard Keynes kept watch over the college finances, Alan Turing invented the digital computer, and E.M. Forster used his undergraduate experiences as fuel for *The Longest Journey* and *Maurice*; Salman Rushdie also felt the college's grounds beneath his feet. In early June the university posts the names and final grades of every student in the Georgian **Senate House** opposite the King's College chapel, designed by Gibbs and built in the 1720s; about a week later, degree ceremonies are held there.

M.A.? B.S.! Cambridge graduates are eligible for the world's easiest master's degrees: after spending three and one-third years out in the Real World, a graduate sends £15 to the university. Provided that said graduate is not in the custody of one of Her Majesty's Prisons, the grad receives an M.A. without further ado, making Cambridge the world's easiest correspondence school.

TRINITY COLLEGE

Trinity St. ☎ 338400. Chapel and courtyard open daily 10am-5pm. Wren Library open M-F noon-2pm, Sa 10:30am-12:30pm. Easter-Oct. £1.75, otherwise free.

Henry VIII, not a man to be outdone by Henry VI, intended the College of the Holy and Undivided Trinity to be the largest and richest of all the Cambridge colleges. Founded in 1546 shortly before Henry VIII's death, the college has amply fulfilled his wish, being today the third largest landowner in Britain (after the Queen and the Church of England); legend holds that it is possible to walk from Cambridge and Oxford without stepping off Trinity land. Having two recent Nobel-prize winning economists in residence hasn't hurt the college's finances, either.

The alma mater of Sir Isaac Newton, who lived in E staircase for 30 years, the college boasts an illustrious list of alumni: literati include John Dryden, Lord Byron, Alfred, Lord Tennyson, A.E. Housman, and Vladimir Nabokov; while James Clerk Maxwell, who discovered the laws of electromagnetism, atom-splitter Ernest Rutherford, philosopher Ludwig Wittgenstein, and Indian statesman Jawaharlal Nehru also studied here.

The heart of the college is the aptly named **Great Court,** the largest enclosed courtyard in the world. Great Court is reached from Trinity St. through **Great Gate,** a castle-like gateway fronted by a statue of Henry VIII grasping a wooden chair leg—the original scepter was stolen years ago as a student prank, and never recovered. If you want to be taken as a student (and skip the entrance fee), hide your camera and enter confidently through the smaller door on the right—only tourists use the main gate. Newton's room in E staircase is now part of the Porters Lodge; nearby on the west side of the court stands the dour **chapel,** whose interior is festooned with plaques naming famous alums and a large statue of Newton, and the **King's Gate** tower. The tower is home to what William Wordsworth called the "loquacious clock that speaks with male and female voice"; try to run around the court during the 24 strikes of midday—Great Court is the site of the original race against the clock made famous in the movie *Chariots of Fire.* The finely carved **fountain** (1602) in the center of the court is the only one in Cambridge; Lord Byron used to bath nude in it. The eccentric poet also kept a bear as a pet—college rules only forbade cats and dogs—and claimed it would take his fellowship examinations for him. The south side of the court is home to the palatial **Master's Lodge** and the cathedral-like **Great Hall** (another original name), where students and dons dine under the gaze of Henry VIII and hundreds of grotesque carved faces.

On the other side of the Hall is the exquisite Renaissance facade of **Nevile's Court.** Newton measured the speed of sound by timing the echo in the cloisters—stamp your feet to make your own estimate. The cloisters lead down towards Sir Christopher's **Wren Library** (1695). While the college's collection has long outgrown the building, it is still used to house old books and precious manuscripts; those on view include alumnus **A.A. Milne's** original handwritten copies of *Winnie-the-Pooh* and Newton's own copy of his *Principia,* as well as many of his personal effects. To cap it all, the library is dominated by a large stained-glass window of who else but Newton being presented to George III. Adjacent to Nevile's Court, pass through the drab, neo-Gothic **New Court** (Prince Charles lived in E staircase) to get to the Backs where you can rent **punts** or just enjoy the view of the Wren Library and St. John's college from **Trinity Bridge.**

> # DUCKING AND DINING
> While you're wondering at the height of the ceiling in Trinity's Great Hall, take the time to search for a fake duck hanging from the rafters. While no one is sure how the tradition started, it has become a challenge for undergraduates to try and scale the ceiling and move the duck around. Success is rewarded with membership in the ultra-secretive Mallard Society; failure (if you're caught in the act), with immediate expulsion from the college. While the College disapproves of this risky pastime, student lore claims that the president of the society is none other than the Dean—the very man who expels those caught in the act.

OTHER COLLEGES

ST. JOHN'S COLLEGE. Established in 1511 by Lady Margaret Beaufort, mother of Henry VIII, St. John's is one of seven Cambridge colleges founded by women (but *for* men). The striking brick-and-stone gatehouse bears Lady Margaret's heraldic emblem. St. John's centers around a paved plaza rather than a grassy courtyard, and its two most interesting buildings stand across the river from the other colleges. The **Bridge of Sighs** (nothing like the one in Venice) connects the older part of the college to the towering neo-Gothic extravagance of **New Court,** which is likened by some to a wedding cake in silhouette. The **School of Pythagoras,** a 12th-century pile of wood and stone supposedly the oldest complete building in Cambridge, hides in St. John's Gardens. *(St. John's St. ☎ 338600. Chapel and grounds open daily 10am-4:45pm. Evensong 6:30pm most nights. £1.75, seniors and children £1, families £3.50.)*

QUEEN'S COLLEGE. Founded not once, but twice—by painted Queen Margaret of Anjou in 1448 and again by Elizabeth Woodville in 1465—Queen's College has the only unaltered Tudor courtyard in Cambridge, housing the half-timbered President's Gallery. The **Mathematical Bridge,** just past Cloister Court, was built in 1749 without a single bolt or nail, relying on mathematical principle. A meddling Victorian took apart the bridge to see how it worked and the inevitable occurred—he couldn't put it back together without using steel rivets every two inches. *(Silver St. ☎ 335511. College open Mar.-Oct. daily 10am-4:30pm. Closed during exams. £1.)*

CLARE COLLEGE. Clare's coat-of-arms, golden teardrops ringing a black border, conveniently symbolizes the circumstances of the college's founding in 1326 by the thrice-widowed, 29-year-old Lady Elizabeth de Clare. Misery has not shrouded the college indefinitely, though—Clare has some of the most frolicsome gardens in Cambridge. The gardens lie across the elegant Clare Bridge. Walk through Clare's **Old Court,** designed by Wren, for a view of the University Library, where 82 mi. of shelves hold books arranged according to size rather than subject. George V called it "the greatest erection in Cambridge." *(Trinity Ln. ☎ 333200. College open daily 10am-5pm. Old Court open during exams after 4:45pm to groups of 3 or fewer. £1.80, under 10 free.)*

CHRIST'S COLLEGE. Founded as "God's-house" in 1448 and renamed in 1505, Christ's has since won fame for its association with John Milton and for its gardens. Charles Darwin dilly-dallied through Christ's before dealing a blow to its religious origins—his rooms (unmarked and closed to visitors) were on G staircase in First Court. **New Court,** on King St., is one of the most modern structures in Cambridge; its symmetrical, gray concrete walls and black-curtained windows make it look like the amalgam of an Egyptian pyramid, a Polaroid camera, and a typewriter. Bowing to pressure from aesthetically-offended Cantabrigians, a new wall was built to block the view of the building from all sides except the inner courtyard of the college. Like most other colleges, Christ's closes during exams, save for access to the chapel—inquire at the porter's desk. *(St. Andrews St. ☎ 334900. Gardens open in summer M-F 9:30am-noon; term-time M-F 9am-4:30pm. Free.)*

JESUS COLLEGE. Spacious Jesus has preserved an enormous amount of unaltered medieval work from as far back as 1496. Beyond the long, high-walled walk called the "Chimny" lies a three-sided court fringed with colorful gardens. Through the archway on the right sit the remains of a gloomy medieval nunnery. The Pre-Raphaelite stained glass of Edward Burne-Jones and ceiling decorations by William Morris festoon the chapel. *(Jesus Ln. ☎ 339339. Courtyard open 9am-6pm; closed during exams to groups of 3 or more.)*

MAGDALENE COLLEGE. Inhabiting buildings from a 15th-century Benedictine hostel, Magdalene (MAUD-lin), sometime teaching home of Christian allegorist C.S. Lewis when he wasn't at Oxford, has retained its religious emphasis. Don't forget to take a peek at the **Pepys Library,** in the second court; the library displays the noted statesman and prolific diarist's collection in their original cases. *(Magdalene St. ☎ 332100. Library open Easter-Aug. 11:30am-12:30pm and 2:30-3:30pm; Sept.-Easter M-Sa 11:30am-12:30pm. Courtyards closed during exams. Free.)*

SMALLER COLLEGES. Thomas Gray wrote his *Elegy in a Country Churchyard* while staying in **Peterhouse**, on Trumpington St., the oldest and smallest college, founded in 1294. (☎ *338200. Call for opening hours.)* In contrast, **Robinson College,** across the river on Grange Rd., is the university's newest. Founded in 1977, this modern-medieval brick pastiche sits just behind the university library. Bronze plants writhe about the door of the college chapel, which features some fascinating stained glass. (☎ *339100. Call for opening hours.)* **Corpus Christi College,** Trumpington St., founded in 1352 by the common people, contains the dreariest and oldest courtyard in Cambridge, forthrightly called Old Court and unaltered since its enclosure. The library, on the other hand, maintains the snazziest collection of Anglo-Saxon manuscripts in England, including the Parker Manuscript of the *Anglo-Saxon Chronicle.* Alums include Sir Francis Drake and Christopher Marlowe. (☎ *338000. Courtyard open until 6pm; closed during exams.)*

The 1347 **Pembroke College,** next to Corpus Christi, harbors the earliest architectural effort of Sir Christopher Wren and counts Edmund Spenser, Ted Hughes, and Eric Idle among its grads. (☎ *338100. Courtyard open until 6pm; closed during exams. Call ahead for hours.)* **Downing College,** Regent St., was founded in 1807, and is pleasantly isolated. Downing's austere Neoclassical buildings flank an immense lawn. (☎ *334800. Courtyard open until 6pm.)* A chapel designed by Sir Christopher Wren dominates the front court of the 1584 **Emmanuel College,** St. Andrews St., known fondly to its residents as "Emma." John Harvard, benefactor of the New England university, attended Emmanuel. A stained-glass panel depicting Harvard graces the college chapel. Among alumni with more tangible accomplishments is John Cleese. (☎ *334200. Courtyard open until 6pm.)*

MUSEUMS AND CHURCHES

FITZWILLIAM MUSEUM. A welcome break from the academia of the colleges, the Fitzwilliam Museum dwells within an immense Neoclassical building, built in 1875 to house Viscount Fitzwilliam's collection. The mosaic tile floors could be a display of their own, while the grand entrance hall, lined with marble busts and austere columns, impresses. A goulash of Egyptian, Chinese, Japanese, and Greek antiquities bides its time downstairs, coupled with an extensive collection of 16th-century German armor. The **Founder's Library** is a must-see, housing an intimate collection of French Impressionists. The drawing room displays William Blake's books and woodcuts. Call to inquire about lunchtime and evening concerts. *(Trumpington St. ☎ 332900. Open Tu-Sa 10am-5pm, Su 2:15-5pm. Guided tours Sa 2:30pm. Free, but suggested donation £3. Tours £3.)*

OTHER MUSEUMS. ▨ **Kettle's Yard,** at the corner of Castle St. and Northampton St., houses early 20th-century art. The gallery rotates its showings, but the house, created in 1956 by Tate Museum curator Jim Ede as "a refuge of peace and order," is a relaxed and quiet constant. Local students perform free Friday lunchtime concerts. (☎ *352124. House open Apr.-Sept. Tu-Sa 1:30-4:30pm, Su 2-4:30pm; Oct.-Mar. Tu-Su 2-4pm; gallery open year-round Tu-Su 11:30am-5pm. Free.)* The **Scott Polar Research Institute,** Lensfield Rd., commemorates icy expeditions with photographic and artistic accounts and memorabilia. (☎ *336540. Open M-Sa 2:30-4pm. Free.)*

CHURCHES. The **Round Church (Holy Sepulchre),** where Bridge St. meets St. John's St., is one of five circular churches surviving in England, built in 1130 (and later rebuilt) on the pattern of the Church of the Holy Sepulchre in Jerusalem. (☎ *311602. Free.)* It merits comparison with **St. Benet's,** a rough Saxon church on Benet St. The tower, built in 1050, is the oldest structure in Cambridge. The tower once had a spire, but spire-building was a technology the Normans lacked, so they spitefully knocked it down. (☎ *353903. Free.)* The tower of **Great St. Mary's Church,** off King's Parade, asserts the best view of the broad greens and the colleges. Pray that the bell doesn't ring while you're ascending the 123 tightly packed spiral steps! *(Tower open M-Sa 9:30am-5pm, Su 12:30-5pm. £1.75, children 60p, families £4.20.)*

♪ ENTERTAINMENT

PUNTING. Punts (flat-bottomed boats propelled by a pole) are a favored form of hands-on entertainment in Cambridge. Punters take two routes—one from Magdalene Bridge to Silver St., and the other from Silver St. to Grantchester. On the first route—the shorter, busier, and more interesting of the two—you'll pass the colleges and the Backs. Beware of students stealing your pole as you go under a bridge. **Tyrell's,** Magdalene Bridge (☎ (01480) 413517), has punts and rowboats for £8 per hr. plus a £40 deposit. At **Scudamore's,** Silver St. Bridge (☎ 359750), punts are £10 per hr. plus a £50 deposit. Student-punted **guided tours** (about £20), are another option for those unwilling to risk a capsizing mishap. Inquire at the TIC for a complete list of companies; Trinity College also rents punts.

THEATRE. The Arts Box Office (☎ 504444) handles ticket sales for the newly reopened **Arts Theatre,** around the corner from the TIC, which stages traveling productions, and the **ADC Theatre** (Amateur Dramatic Club; ☎ 503333), Park St., which offers lively performances of student-produced plays as well as movies during the term and the Folk Festival. The **Cambridge Shakespeare Festival,** in association with the festival at that other university, features four plays in open-air repertory throughout July and August. Tickets are available from the Arts Box Office or at the Corn Exchange. (£9, concessions £6.) You can get an earful of concerts at the **Corn Exchange,** at the corner of Wheeler St. and Corn Exchange St. across from the TIC, a venue for band, jazz, and classical concerts. The box office also has info about other local events. (☎ 357851; fax 329074; boxoffice@cambridge.gov.uk. Open M-Sa 10am-6pm, till 9pm on performance evenings; Su 6-9pm on performance days only. £7.50-24; some student standbys 50% off on day of show.)

NIGHTLIFE. Just as the sun begins to fall, **Evensong** begins at King's College Chapel, a breathtaking treat for day-worn spirits—not to mention a good way to sneak into the college grounds free of charge! (M-Sa 5:30pm, Su 3:30pm. Free. Also look into Evensong at other colleges, notably St. John's, Caius, and Clare.) The night will wear on, and **live music** will start up at a choice of pubs. The **Boat Race,** 170 East Rd., a packed and popular joint near the police station, features a variety of live music every evening. (☎ 508533. Usually free, but call ahead.) **Bar Coast,** Quayside (☎ 556961), offers free, frequent and variably-themed dance nights, from disco to "uplifting house and garage." Students, bartenders, and the latest issue of the term-time *Varsity* (20p) will be your best sources of information on where it's really at. The TIC also stocks useful brochures.

MAY WEEK. During the first two weeks of June, students celebrate the end of the term with May Week (a May of the mind), crammed with concerts, plays, and elaborate balls followed by recuperative breakfasts by the river. Along the Cam, the college boat clubs compete in an eyebrow-raising series of races known as the **bumps.** Crews line up along the river (rather than across it) and attempt to ram the boat in front before being bumped from behind. May Week's artistic repertoire stars the famous **Footlights Revue,** a collection of comedy skits; performers have gone on to join such troupes as Beyond the Fringe, and its graduates include Monty Python members John Cleese, Eric Idle, and Graham Chapman.

FESTIVALS. Midsummer Fair, which dates from the early 16th century, appropriates the Midsummer Common for about five days in the third week of June. The free **Strawberry Fair** (☎ 560160), on the first Saturday in June, attracts the hard-core crowd to Cambridge for food, music, dreads, and body piercing. Address inquiries to the TIC. During the rest of the summer, Cambridge caters more to tourists than to students. **Summer in the City** and **Camfest** brighten the last two weeks of July with a series of concerts and special exhibits culminating in a huge weekend celebration, the **Cambridge Folk Festival** (☎ 357851). Book tickets for well in advance (about £38); camping on the grounds is £5-18 extra.

◪ DAYTRIPS FROM CAMBRIDGE

GRANTCHESTER

To reach Grantchester Meadows from Cambridge, take the path that follows the River Cam. Grantchester itself lies about a mile from the meadows; ask the way at one of the neighborhood shops, or follow the bikepath signs. (About 45min. by foot.) If you have the energy to pole or paddle your way, rent a punt or canoe from Scudamore's Boatyards (see p. 307). Or hop aboard Stagecoach Cambus #118 (9-11 per day from Drummer St., £1.10).

In 1912, Rupert Brooke wrote "Grantchester! Ah Grantchester! There's peace and holy quiet there." His words from "The Old Vicarage" still hold true today, as idyllic Granchester is a mecca for Cambridge literary types. The gentle flow of the Cam and the swaying seas of grain offer rejuvenation after bustling Cambridge. You can see Grantchester's **church clock tower** next to Brooke's home at the **Old Vicarage,** now owned by novelist and erstwhile London-mayor-wannabe Jeffrey Archer, and closed to the public. The weathered 14th-century **Parish Church of St. Andrew and St. Mary,** on Millway, is beautifully intimate and not be missed. The main village pub, the **Rupert Brooke,** 2 Broadway, will reward the famished and parched for their efforts. (☎ 840295. Open M-F 11am-3pm, Sa 11am-11pm, Su noon-10:30pm.) Or wander farther down the road to the idyllic ▨ **Orchard** on Mill Way, once the leisurely Sunday afternoon haunt of the "neo-Pagans," a Grantchester offshoot of the famous Bloomsbury Group, including Brooke, Wittgenstein, and Keynes. Outdoor plays are occasionally performed on summer evenings; ask at the Cambridge TIC. (☎ 845788. Open daily 10am-7pm; year-round indoor and outdoor seating.)

ANGLESEY ABBEY

6 mi. from Cambridge on the B1102 (off the A1303). Buses #111 or 122 run from Drummer St. (25min., 1 per hr.); ask to be let off at Lode Crossroads. ☎ 811200. House open Easter to mid-Oct. W-Su and bank holidays 1-5:30pm. Gardens open Easter to mid-Oct. W-Su and bank holidays 10:30am-5:30pm. Last admission 4:30pm. Wheelchair access. Admission W-F £6.10, children £3.05, Sa-Su £7.10, children £3.55.

Northeast of Cambridge, 12th-century Anglesey Abbey has been remodeled to house the priceless exotica of the first Lord Fairhaven. One of the niftiest clocks in the universe sits inconspicuously on the bookcase beyond the fireplace in the library, but don't worry if you miss it—there are 55 other clocks to enjoy. In the 100-acre gardens, trees punctuate lines of clipped hedges and manicured lawns.

OTHER DAYTRIPS

WIMPOLE HALL. Cambridgeshire's most spectacular mansion, built in elegant 18th-century style, lies 10 mi. southwest of Cambridge. The hall holds works by Gibbs, Flitcroft, and Joane, and gardens sculpted by Capability Brown. *(Whippet Bus #175 from Drummer St. (35min., £2). ☎ 207257. Open Apr.-Nov. T-Th and Sa-Su 1-5pm. £5.90, children £2.70.)* **Wimpole's Home Farm** brims with Longhorn and Gloucester cattle, Soay sheep, and Tamworth pigs. *(☎ 208987. Open Apr.-Nov. Tu-Th and Sa-Su 10:30am-5pm. Farm £4.70, children £2.70. Gardens £2.50.)*

AUDLEY END. Trains leave Cambridge about every hour for nearby Audley End, a magnificent Jacobean hall set on grounds designed by Capability Brown. Watch for the Little Drawing Room: one lady of the manor altered it to suit her own taste—in clothes, that is: the room had to be modified to fit her voluminous evening dresses. *(☎ (01799) 522842. House open Apr.-Sept. W-Su and bank holidays 1-5pm, grounds 11am-5pm. Wheelchair access. £6.50, students and seniors £4.90, children £3.30; grounds only £4.50, students and seniors £3.40, children £2.30.)*

SAFFRON WALDEN. Dating from the Saxon invasions and possibly the Neolithic and Bronze Ages, the market town of Saffron Walden (pop. 15,000), 15 mi. south of Cambridge in Essex (take Cambus #102), was named after the saffron that used to be sold here and the Anglo-Saxon word for "wooded valley." The town is best known for the "pargetting" (plaster moulding) that adorns its Tudor buildings, and its **tourist information centre,** 1 Market Pl., Market Sq., stocks a free map. (☎ (01799)

510444. Open Apr.-Oct. M-Sa 9:30am-5:30pm; Nov.-Mar. 10am-5pm.) The **YHA Youth Hostel**, 1 Myddylton Pl., in the north part of town, occupies one of the town's oldest buildings. (☎ (01799) 523117. Lockout 10am-5pm. Curfew 11pm. Open July-Aug. daily; Apr.-June and mid-Sept. to Oct. Tu-Sa; Mar. F-Sa. £9, under 18 £6.20.)

ELY
☎ 01353

The ancient town of Ely (EEL-ee) was an island until its surrounding fens were drained in the 17th century. Legend has it that St. Dunstan saw fit to turn the local monks into eels as punishment for their lack of piety, a transformation that earned Ely its name. A more likely story is that "Elig" (eel island) was named for the eels that lived in the fens. Here, brave Hereward the Wake defended himself against Norman invaders, earning the title "the last of all the English." One of the most spectacular structures in England, **Ely Cathedral** rules over the far-reaching flatlands; the breathtaking colossus is reason enough for a quick visit.

GETTING THERE. Ely serves as the junction for **trains** (☎ (08457) 484950) between London and various points in East Anglia, including **Cambridge** (20min., 1 per hr., day return £3) and **Norwich** (1½hr., 1 per hr., £10.80). **Cambus** (☎ (01223) 423554) #X9 arrives at Market St. from **Cambridge** (30min., 1 per hr., £3).

ORIENTATION AND PRACTICAL INFORMATION. Ely's two major streets run parallel to the cathedral; the town's sights and businesses line **High St.** and **Market St.**, with Cromwell's House and some shops trailing behind on **St. Mary's St.** To reach the cathedral and **tourist information centre** (TIC) from the train station, walk up Station Rd. and continue on Back Hill. The TIC shares and operates the Cromwell House, 29 St. Mary's St. Its dedicated staff offers free maps. (☎ 662062. Open Apr.-Sept. daily 10am-5:30pm; Oct.-Mar. M-Sa 10am-5pm.) The TIC also operates **tours** of the city for groups of 7 or more in July and August (about £3.20, concessions £1.40), but schedules are irregular. They also sell a combination admission ticket, the **Passport to Ely**, that lets you into Ely Cathedral, Cromwell House, Ely Museum, and the Stained Glass Museum. (£9, students and children £7.) Services include: the **police** (☎ (01223) 358966), Nutholt Ln.; **Internet access** at **Ely Computer Supplies**, 17 Broad St. (☎ 668863; £2.50 per 30min.) and the **Library**, 6 The Cloisters, just off Market Pl. (☎ 662350; free, but often a long wait); and the **post office**, in Lloyd's Chemist on 19 High St. (☎ 669946). **Postal code:** CB7 4HF.

ACCOMMODATIONS AND FOOD. Cheaper accommodations make Ely a good base for exploring Cambridge. Check the TIC for accommodations listings and for their booking service (10% of first night's stay and a £1 fee; call at least two days in advance). B&B options include **The Post House**, 12a Egremont St. (☎ 667184), which offers rooms with TVs from £19; **Jane's B&B**, 82 Broad St. (☎ 667609), £18 per person; and **Mr. and Mrs. Friend-Smith's**, 31 Egremont St. (☎ 663118), with garden views, from £23—all close to the train station and the river. Camp among spuds and sugarbeet, with a view of the cathedral, at **Braham Farm**, Cambridge Rd., off the A10, one mile from city center. (☎ 662386. Toilets and cold water available; electricity hook-up £1 per night. £2.50 per tent.)

Tea houses—and seemingly only tea houses—abound in Ely. Most shops in the town close down on Tuesday afternoons in winter. On Thursdays and Saturdays 8am-4pm, stock up on provisions at the **market** in Market Pl. **Waitrose Supermarket**, Brays Ln., awaits behind a Georgian facade. (☎ 668800. Open M-Tu and Sa 8:30am-6pm, W-Th 8:30am-8pm, F 8:30am-9pm, Su 10am-4pm.) The **Minster Tavern**, Minster Pl., opposite the cathedral, is popular for lunches. (£2-5. Open M-Sa 11am-11pm, noon-10:30pm.) The **Steeplegate**, 16-18 High St., serves tea and snacks in two rooms built over a medieval undercroft; fall into a romantic reverie over a pot of Earl Grey (85p) and then visit the medieval exhibition below. (Open M-Sa 10am-4:30pm. Non-smoking.) The action in Ely centers around the cathedral, so you might want to stay nearby for lunch. **The Almonry**, just off the corner of High St. and Brays Ln., serves up well-heeled basics for £6-7; eat outside, weather permitting, for a stunning garden and cathedral vista. (Open M-Sa 10am-5pm, Su 11am-5pm.)

🔆 **SIGHTS.** The towers of massive ⬛ **Ely Cathedral** are impossible to miss for miles around. The cathedral was founded in 1081 on the spot where St. Ethelreda had formed a religious community four centuries before, and was redecorated in the 19th century, when the elaborate ceiling above the nave and many of the stained-glass windows were completed. The space now greets visitors with a breathtaking combination of light and color. In 1322, the original Norman tower collapsed and the present **Octagon Altar,** topped by the **lantern tower,** replaced it. The eight-sided cupola appears to burst into mid-air, but is in fact held up by eight stone pillars (total weight 400 tons). To the north, headless figures in the Lady Chapel and empty grottoes throughout mark visits by Reformation iconoclasts. In the south transept lies the tomb of Dean of Ely, Humphrey Tyndall, an eternal P.R. boost for the monarchy: heir to the throne of Bohemia, Humphrey refused the kingdom, saying he'd "rather be Queen Elizabeth's subject than a foreign prince." Incongruous but beautifully rendered stained glass windows depict pilots and planes from both World Wars. Though Ely's population is only 12,000, it is the cathedral that gives Ely its city status. (☎ 667735. Open Easter-Sept. daily 7am-7pm; Oct.-Easter M-F 7:30am-6:30pm, Su 7:30am-5pm. Evensong M-Sa 5:30pm, Su 3:45pm. Tours of the Octagon May-Sept. about 3 per day, £2.50. Free tours of the West Tower July-Aug. 4 per day. Ground floor tours £2, seniors £1.40. Wheelchair access. £4, students and seniors £2.50.)

The **Stained Glass Museum** overlooks the nave of the cathedral. (Open M-F 10:30am-5pm, Sa 10:30am-5:30pm, Su noon-6pm. £3.50, concessions £2.50, families £7.) The brass-rubbing center is free, but you pay for the materials you use in your frottage. (Open July-Aug. daily 10:30am-4pm, Su noon-3pm. Materials £1.70-8.70.) The monastic buildings surrounding the cathedral are still in use: the **infirmary** now houses one of the resident canons, and the **bishop's palace** is a home for children with disabilities. The rest of the buildings are used by the **King's School,** one of the older public (read: private) schools in England. Get great external views of the Cathedral from Dean's Meadow, between the monastic buildings and Back Hill St.

For an architectural tour of Ely, follow the path outlined by the TIC's detailed and free *Town Trail* pamphlet. **Ely Museum,** at the Old Gaol on the corner of Market St. and Lynn Rd., tells the story of the fenland city and its people in a chronological tour, highlighting the intriguing saga of the swamp-draining project that created the land around Ely. (☎ 666655. Open in summer 10:30am-5:30pm; in winter 10:30am-4:30pm. £2, concessions £1.25.) Perturbing Royalists everywhere, **Oliver Cromwell's House,** 29 St. Mary's St., has been immortalized with wax figures, 17th-century decor, and a "haunted" bedroom, replete with fake ghost—it's more entertainment than hard-hitting history. (☎ 662062. Open Apr.-Sept. daily 10am-5:30pm; Oct.-Mar. M-Sa 10am-5pm, Su 11am-3pm. £3, concessions £2.70.)

COLCHESTER ☎ 01206

England's oldest recorded town, Colchester (pop. 89,000) has been so thoroughly beaten on so many different occasions it's a wonder everyone hasn't packed up and left. The Trinovantes tribe, the town's first inhabitants, were conquered by the Romans, who were in turn slaughtered by the Iceni (led by Queen Boadicea), who were pillaged by the Saxons, who were finally flogged by the Normans. However, the most recent invader to rush down from the hills has been the modern consumer. A pedestrian-only shopping center now sits on what was once Trinovantean farmland, a Roman market, and a Norman stronghold. Fine evidence of the past does remain; resilient as ever, Colchester has fantastic Roman ruins, a crumbling castle and England's largest castle keep, ruptured walls, and musketball-ridden pubs.

🖪🖪 **GETTING THERE AND PRACTICAL INFORMATION.** Colchester makes a good daytrip from London. **Trains** (☎ (08457) 484950) run from **London Liverpool St.** (45min., every 15min. £13.90) and **Cambridge** (2hr., 2 per hr., £27.30). **Buses** run from **London** (2¼hr., 4 per day, £7.90) and **Cambridge** (2hr., 1 per day, £7).

The **tourist information centre** (TIC), 1 Queen St., right across the street from the castle, books rooms 2 days in advance for a 10% deposit of the first night's stay and leads 2hr. **tours** of the city. (June-Sept. 11am. £2.50, students and seniors £2, children £1.25.)

Pick up a free map and copies of local magazines *The Sticks* and *The Grapevine*, which list music in pubs. (☎ 282920. Open Easter-Nov. M-Tu and Th-Sa 9:30am-6pm, W 10am-6pm, Su 10am-5pm; Dec.-Easter M-Sa 10am-5pm.) Services include: the **police,** 10 Southway (☎ 762212); **Internet access** at **Webs Netcafé,** two blocks from the TIC (☎ 560400; £4 per hr.) and at the **Library,** just off Trinity St. (☎ 245900; free, but book ahead; open M-T and F 9am-7:30pm, W 10am-7:30pm, Th and Sa 9am-5pm, Su 1-4pm); and the **post office,** 68-70 North Hill (☎ 549807). **Postal code:** CO1 1AA.

◨◨ ACCOMMODATIONS AND FOOD. Ever since the YHA Youth Hostel packed up and left town five years ago, Colchester has provided no substitute for the penny-pinching budget traveler. The TIC can help to find a room that fits your budget. One of the cheapest places to stay in town is the **Scheregate Hotel,** 36 Osborne St., which offers large, spotless, TV-equipped rooms with showers and bath down the hall. (☎ 573034. Singles £20-25, breakfast included.)

Sainsbury's supermarket stakes its claim on Priory Walk, just off Queen St. (Open M-W 8am-6:30pm, Th-F 8am-7pm, Sa 7:30am-6:30pm.) **Jackpots,** along Red Lion Walk off High St., dishes out jacket potatoes (£2.50-4) and a £4 "classic dish" of lasagna, vegetarian chili, or macaroni and cheese with a side potato. (☎ 549990. Open M-Sa 8am-5pm.) **The Thai Dragon,** 35 East Hill, has a full lunch for only £5.50. Dinner is a bit more pricey (main courses £4-8), but the traditional dishes are quite tasty. (☎ 863414. Open M-Sa noon-2:30pm and 6-11pm, Su noon-2:30pm and 6-10:30pm.) A little bit farther down the road, **Siege House,** 75 East St. (☎ 867121), serves up pints with a twist of history. Established in the late 15th century, the building has survived a few plagues and the English Civil War of 1648—check out the musketball holes in the wall. Nearby, the **Goat and Boot** serves up friendly pints under the careful watch of the resident parrot.

◨ SIGHTS. In Colchester, an archaeologist's dream, one civilization's buildings became the foundation for the next. **Colchester Castle** embodies this layering of civilization: the Norman fortress was built by William the Conqueror upon the ruins of the Roman temple of Claudius that stood over a thousand years earlier. But don't expect to find mildewed walls and musty towers today, as now the Norman stronghold houses the **Castle Museum,** where you can see, touch, and hear history, thanks to an interactive display. Act out a short scene behind Roman theater masks, try on Roman battle gear, and experience a chilling witch confession in the dungeon. A tour takes you to the depths of the Roman foundations and the heights of the Norman towers. (☎ 828 2931. Castle open M-Sa 10am-5pm Su 11am-5pm. 5 tours per day. £3.70, concessions £2.50, families £10.20. Tours £1, children 60p.)

The castle is flanked by two lesser museums. In a Georgian townhouse built in 1718, the **Hollytrees Museum,** next to the castle, displays a cache of 18th-century knick-knacks from toys and games to musical instruments and scientific equipment. (Reopens in July 2001. Free.) Marveling at a fine collection of 18th-century grandfather clocks in **Tymperleys Clock Museum,** off Trinity St., is a great way to pass the time. Tick. That is, unless constant ticking drives you mad. Tock. (Open M-Sa 10am-5pm, Su 11am-5pm. Free.)

NORFOLK AND SUFFOLK

NORWICH ☎ 01603

In the mood for getting lost? Try navigating the dizzying medieval streets of Norwich (NOR-rich) as they wind outwards from the Norman castle, past the cathedral, and to the scattered fragments of the 14th-century city wall. Even though Norwich retains the hallmarks of an ancient city, a university and active art community ensure that it is also thoroughly modern. One sign of the times: Norwich once had a church for every Sunday and a pub for every day of the year, but now only 36 churches coexist with 380 pubs. Though the wool trade has long since fallen by the wayside, a daily market thrives alongside the pulsing nightlife, proof that the hum of "England's city in the country" has not yet abated.

EAST ANGLIA

⌐ GETTING THERE AND GETTING AROUND

Easily accessible by bus, coach, or train, Norwich makes a decent base for touring both urban and rural East Anglia, particularly the Norfolk Broads.

Trains: Corner of Riverside and Thorpe Rd., 15min. from town center. Buses (40p) run to the city center. Ticket window open M-Sa 4:45am-8:45pm, Su 6:45am-8:45pm. Information open M-Sa 9am-7pm, Su 10:15am-5:30pm. **Regional Railways** (☎ (08457) 484950) from: **Great Yarmouth** (30min.; M-Sa 12 per day, Su 6 per day; return £4.30); **Peterborough** (1½hr.; M-Sa 15 per day, Su 8 per day; return £11.30); **Cambridge** (1½hr., 12 per day, £10.60); and **London Liverpool St.** (2hr., M-Sa 30 per day, £34.50). Those under 16 ride at half-price.

Buses: Station (☎ 660553), on Surrey St. off St. Stephen St., southwest of the castle. **Luggage storage** in the cafeteria £1-3. Information center and ticket desk open M-F 8am-5:30pm, Sa 9am-5:15pm. **National Express** (☎ (08705) 808080) from **Cambridge** (2hr., 1 per day, day return £10) and **London** (3hr., 7 per day, £13.80). **Cambridge Coach Services** (☎ (01223) 423900) from **Cambridge** (#74, 2hr., 4 per day, £9, students and seniors £6.75, children £4.50). **First Eastern Counties** (☎ (08456) 020121) travels to King's Lynn, Peterborough, and other Norfolk towns; **Ranger tickets** offer 1 day of unlimited travel (£6, seniors £4.70, children £4, families £11.50).

Norfolk Bus Information Centre (NORBIC), Castle Meadow, behind the TIC (☎ (0845) 3006116). Open M-Sa 8:30am-5pm.

Taxis: Express Taxis (☎ 767626), open 24hr. One wheelchair taxi, limited hours (☎ 300300). **Canary Taxis** (☎ 414243) has a 24hr. wheelchair taxi.

✴❷ ORIENTATION AND PRACTICAL INFORMATION

Want to find your way around Norwich? Get a map, and pray. The city's planner must have had a wobbly hand, for although all the sights are fairly close together and walking is an efficient way to get around, the twisty streets are guaranteed to confuse you. Take care in the center of town after dark.

Tourist Information Centre: Guildhall, Gaol Hill (☎ 666071). Stocks brochures about the region and a 30p city guide map. Books rooms for £2.50 and a 10% deposit. **Luggage storage** £2.50 plus £2.50 key deposit. Open June-Sept. M-Sa 9:30am-5pm; Oct.-May M-F 9:30am-4:30pm, Sa 9:30am-1pm and 1:30-4:30pm. **Walking tours** (1½hr.) leave Apr.-Oct.; £2.50, children £1.

Financial Services: Banks line **London St.** and **Bank Plain,** including **Barclays,** 36 Bank Plain (☎ 244500). Open M-Tu and Th-F 9am-4:30pm, W 10am-4:30pm.

Launderette: Laundromat, 179a Dereham Rd. (☎ 626685). Change and soap available. Open M-Sa 8am-8pm, Su 10am-7pm; last wash 1½hr. before closing.

Police: (☎ 768769), Bethel St.

Hospital: Norfolk and Norwich Hospital (☎ 286286), corner of Brunswick Rd. and St. Stephen's Rd.

Internet Access: Play It Buy 'Ere, 121 Ber St. (☎ 630223). Perhaps the coolest place in Norwich, it sells records and spins techno in addition to providing Internet access. Groove down Ber St. and take a right into Jolly Butchers Yard. £6 per hr. Open Tu-Sa 10am-7pm. **Ukcybercafes Ltd.,** 46 Magdalen St. (☎ 612643). A few minutes up Tombland from the Cathedral. Open M-F 9am-9pm, Sa 10am-5pm, Su 10am-4pm.

Post Office: Castle Mall, 84-85 Castle Meadow Walk (☎ 761635). **Bureau de change.** Open M-F 9am-5:30pm, Sa 9am-6pm. **Branches** at Queen St. (☎ 220278) and 13-17 Bank Plain (☎ 220228). Open M-F 9am-5:30pm, Sa 9am-12:30pm. **Postal Code:** NR1 3DD.

⌐ ACCOMMODATIONS

Cheap (£17-20) and convenient lodgings are located on **Stracey Rd.** about a five-minute walk from the train station. Instead of taking a left onto Prince of Wales Rd., turn left onto Thorpe Rd., walk two blocks up (away from the bridge), and go

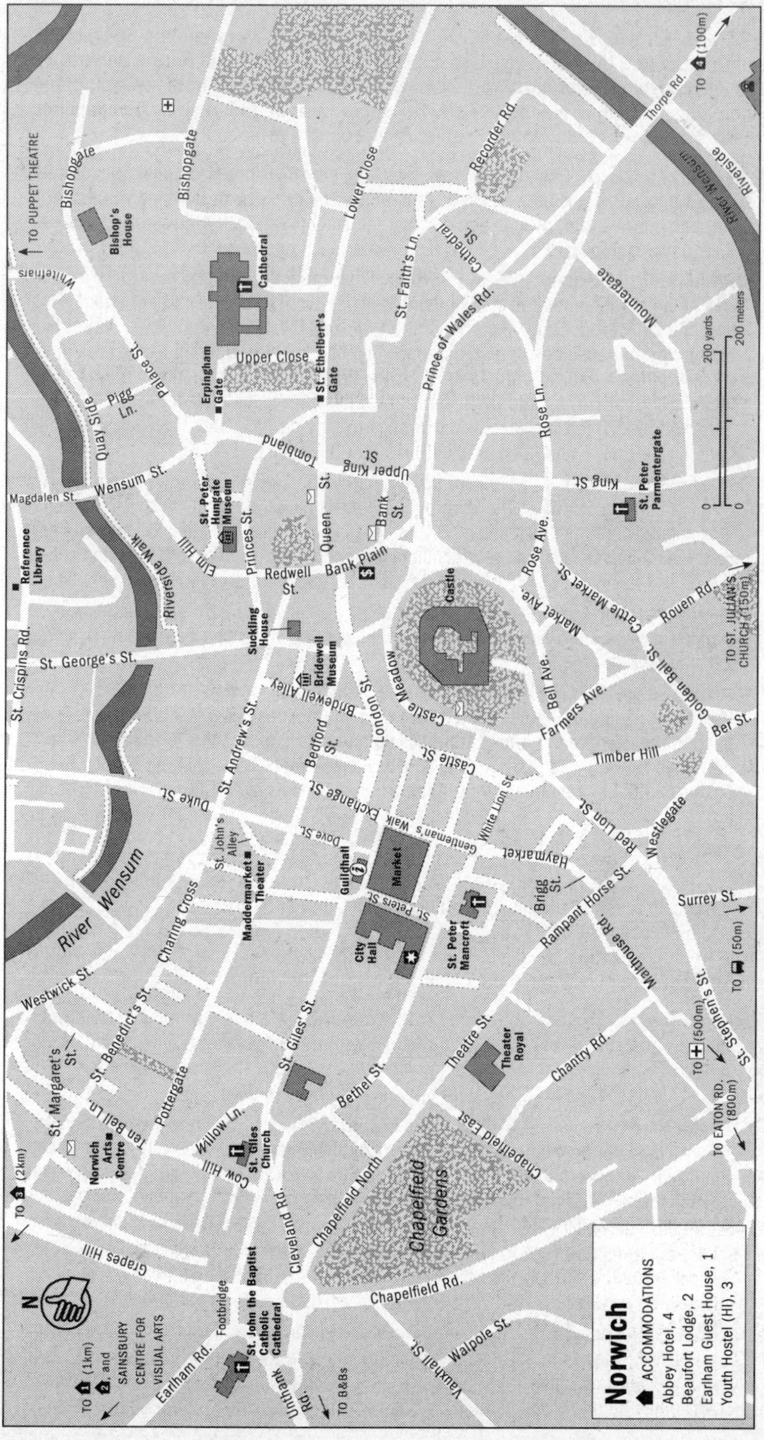

Norwich
ACCOMMODATIONS
Abbey Hotel, 4
Beaufort Lodge, 2
Earlham Guest House, 1
Youth Hostel (HI), 3
200 yards
200 meters
TO PUPPET THEATRE
TO ST. JULIAN'S CHURCH (150m)
TO EATON RD. (800m)
TO B&Bs
SAINSBURY CENTRE FOR VISUAL ARTS
Cathedral
Bishop's House
Erpingham Gate
St. Ethelbert's Gate
Upper Close
St. Peter Hungate Museum
Reference Library
Suckling House
Bridewell Museum
Castle
Guildhall
Market
City Hall
St. Peter Mancroft
Maddermarket Theater
St. John's Alley
Theater Royal
St. Peter Parmentergate
Norwich Arts Centre
St. Giles Church
St. John the Baptist Catholic Cathedral
Chapelfield Gardens
River Wensum
Bishopgate
Whitefriars
Palace St.
Quay Side
Pigg Ln.
Wensum St.
Magdalen St.
Tombland
Lower Close
St. Faith's Ln.
Cathedral St.
Recorder Rd.
Thorpe Rd.
Riverside
Prince of Wales Rd.
Mountergate
Rose Ln.
King St.
Upper King St.
Queen St.
Bank St.
Bank Plain
Redwell St.
Princes St.
Elm Hill
Riverside Walk
St. Crispins Rd.
St. George's St.
Bridewell Alley
St. Andrew's St.
Bedford St.
London St.
Castle Meadow
Castle St.
Exchange St.
Gentleman's Walk
Dove St.
Duke St.
White Lion St.
Haymarket
Brigg St.
Red Lion St.
Timber Hill
Farmers Ave.
Bell Ave.
Market Ave.
Rose Ave.
Cattle Market St.
Rouen Rd.
Golden Ball St.
Ber St.
Westlegate
Rampant Horse St.
Malthouse Rd.
Surrey St.
St. Stephen's St.
St. Peters St.
Charing Cross
Westwick St.
St. Benedict's St.
St. Margaret's St.
Pottergate
Ten Bell Ln.
St. Giles' St.
Bethel St.
Theatre St.
Chantry Rd.
Chapelfield East
Chapelfield North
Chapelfield Rd.
Willow Ln.
Cow Hill
Cleveland Rd.
Grapes Hill
Earlham Rd.
Footbridge
Unthank Rd.
Vauxhall St.
Walpole St.

EAST ANGLIA

right onto Stracey Rd. Many pleasant B&Bs in the £18-24 range line **Earlham Rd.** and **Unthank Rd.**, but they are at least a 20-minute westward hike from downtown and even farther from the train station. Most guest houses on both streets appear when house numbers reach the 100s. B&Bs may also be found along **Dereham Rd.**: follow St. Benedict's St., which eventually becomes Dereham Rd.

🏠 **Beaufort Lodge,** 62 Earlham Rd. This spanking new B&B promises plushly-carpeted, wide-windowed rooms at gently indulgent prices. The lovely hosts will feed you tea, coffee, and cookies after picking you up from the station. Color TV. Non-smoking. Singles £35; doubles from £50.

YHA Norwich, 112 Turner Rd. (☎ 627647). From the train station, cross the river and wait at the shelter in front of the Furniture Store for bus #19 or 20 (85p), or walk 1½mi. from the city center. Drag your bones along Prince of Wales Rd. until Bank Plain, then take a right and continue as the road becomes Dereham Rd. Upon reaching the Earl of Leicester Pub, turn right onto Turner Rd.; the hostel is the last building on your right. Clean rooms of varying sizes (2-8 bunks per room). Luggage storage. Lockout 10am-1pm. Curfew 11pm, but guests can arrange to stay out late. Often full July-Aug.; call ahead. Open Jan. to mid-Dec. daily. Dorms £9.80, under 18 £6.75.

Earlham Guest House, 147 Earlham Rd. (☎ 459469). Take bus #26 or 27 from the city center and ask to get off at The Mitre pub. The guest house of friendly hosts Mr. and Mrs. Wright stands out from surrounding B&B's because of its cozy lounge and refreshing garden. The rooms, tastefully done in gentle blues and pastels, each have TV, tea and coffee maker, and wash basin. Non-smoking. Singles £22; doubles and twins £20-23 per person.

The Abbey Hotel, 16 Stracey Rd. (☎ 612915). A 5min. walk from the train station up Thorpe Rd. A TV and wash basin await you in every room of this clean, yellow building. £18 per person.

Camping: Closest is the **Lakenham** campsite, Martineau Ln. (☎ 620060; no calls after 8pm), 1 mi. south of the city center. First Eastern Counties buses #9, 29, and 32 stop nearby. Cars can't enter after 11pm. Toilets and showers; facilities for disabled travelers. Sites July-Aug. £3.90, children £1.50; Easter-June £3.55, children £1.50; Sept.-Easter £2.60, children free. £3.50 pitch fee; family deals available.

🍴📷 FOOD AND PUBS

In the heart of the city and just a stone's throw from the castle spreads one of England's largest and oldest **open-air markets.** (Open M-Sa roughly 8:30am-4:30pm.) Feast your eyes on it from the steps of the TIC, then feast your gut on everything from fresh fruits and cheeses to ice cream. Or, visit the **Tesco,** alongside the square on St. Andrew's St. (Open M-Sa 7:30am-8pm, Su 11am-5pm.)

🍴 **The Treehouse,** 14 Dove St. (☎ 763258). Eat fresh vegetarian cuisine on earthenware plates while stuffed parrots eye you hungrily from their perches. Daily menu £4.65-6.10; bowl of assorted salads and wholebread £3.60. The store downstairs sells healthy vittles. Open M-W 11:30am-5pm, Th-Sa 11:30am-9pm.

🍴 **The Waffle House,** 39 St. Giles St. (☎ 612790). A family restaurant with wicker galore. Astounding Belgian waffles (wholemeal or white) made with organic ingredients and fillings from ham, cheese, and mushrooms to tuna and bean sprouts (£2.15-5.75). Fruity milkshakes wash down your waffle. £4.95 fixed price lunch, served weekdays 11am-4pm, includes one savory and one sweet waffle. Open M-Th 10am-10pm, F-Sa 10am-11pm, Su 11am-9pm.

Bar Tapas, 16-20 Exchange St. (☎ 764077). Experience the rhythm of South America and the spirit of Spain. This flag-adorned eatery serves authentic Spanish dishes, from *Tortilla Española* to *Brochetta da Gambas* (£3-5). Open M-W 10:30am-5:30pm, Th-Sa 10:30am-11pm.

The Maid's Head Hotel (☎ 209955), Tombland. A perennial reminder not to judge a book by its cover. One of the poshest hotels in Norwich serves one of the best lunch deals in town. The "Best of British Menu" (affectionately called BOB), a two-course meal served in a luminated atrium, costs only £5.95. Open daily noon-2pm and 6:30-9:45pm.

Pizza One and Pancakes Too, 24 Tombland (☎ 621583), by the cathedral. Creative pizza and crepe dishes. Have the 4-cheese "charity pizza" (£5) and 50p goes to charity; order the banana-dog (£2) and ask questions later. Ingest any meal and get free admission to neighboring clubs Boswell's and Hy's (see p. 316). Students get 20% off main course. Open M-W noon-10pm, Th noon-10:30pm, F-Sa noon-11pm, Su noon-9pm.

The Adam and Eve (☎ 667423), Bishopgate, behind the cathedral at the Palace St. end of Riverside Walk. Norwich's first pub (est. 1249) is older than sin and still one of its most pleasing watering holes. Half-pint of cider £1.05. Cheese-drenched jacket potatoes and other treats served noon to 7pm. Open M-Sa 11am-11pm, Su noon-10:30pm.

Take 5 (☎ 763099), St. Andrews St., in the old Suckling House. One of the best spots for an evening drink in town isn't even a pub—it's a cafe, restaurant, and exhibition center in a fantastic 14th-century building with a hidden cobblestone courtyard. Open M-Sa 10:30am-11pm; Su 6-10:30pm, bar only.

🔍 SIGHTS

NORWICH CASTLE. The original Norwich Castle was built in 1089 by a Norman monarchy intent on subduing the Saxon city. Its current exterior dates from an 1830s restoration. It was here that English nobles forced King John to sign the Magna Carta in 1215, curbing the power of the monarchy. The Castle Museum occupies the castle keep. Unfortunately, the castle will be closed until spring 2001 for renovations. Call 493642 for further information.

NORWICH CATHEDRAL AND TOMBLAND. The castle and the Norman Norwich Cathedral dominate the skyline. The cathedral, built by an 11th-century bishop as penance for having bought his episcopacy, features unusual two-story cloisters (the only ones of their kind in England) and flying buttresses that help support the second tallest spire in the country (315ft.; the Salisbury Stake is the tallest). Use the mirror in the nave to examine the overhead bosses carved with biblical scenes. Though it sounds like a macabre amusement park, **Tombland,** which runs in front of the Cathedral Park, is the burial site of thousands of victims of the Great Plague. In the summer, the cathedral frequently hosts orchestral concerts and art exhibitions. (☎ 764385. Open daily mid-May to mid-Sept. 7:30am-7pm; mid-Sept. to mid-May 7:30am-6pm. Free tours May-Oct. 2-3 per day. Evensong M-F 5:15pm, Sa-Su 3:30pm. Wheelchair access. Free.)

BRIDEWELL MUSEUM. This museum displays the history of local industry, turning back time by recreating an early 19th century pharmacy, public bar, and tap room, among other common locales of the past. The enchanting medieval building has its own storied history, serving at various times as a merchant's house, mayor's mansion, factory, warehouse, and prison: still visible are dates and initials carved in the courtyard. (Bridewell Alley, off St. Andrew's St. ☎ 667228. Open Apr.-Sept. M-Sa 10am-5pm, Su 2-5pm. £2, students and seniors £1.50, children £1, families £5.)

ST. JULIAN'S CHURCH. Long before Aphra Behn held a pen, a 14th-century nun named Juliana of Norwich took up a cell of her own here and became the first known woman to write a book in English. Her 20-year work, Revelations of Divine Love, is based on her mystic experiences as an anchoress at this church, where you can visit her lonely cell and shrine. (Between King St. and Rouen Rd. ☎ 767380. Open daily May-Sept. 8am-5:30pm; Oct.-Apr. 8am-4pm. Free.)

SAINSBURY CENTRE FOR VISUAL ARTS. Standing at the **University of East Anglia,** 3mi. west of town on Earlham Rd, this center was destroyed during the English Reformation and restored after World War II. Sir Sainsbury (of the supermarket chain) donated his superb collection of art, including works by Picasso, Moore, Degas, and other modern artists, to the university in 1973. Many buses journey from Norwich city center; ask for the Constable Terr. stop. Check at the bus station (☎ 660553) for the frequently changing route numbers. (☎ 456060. Open Tu-Su 11am-5pm. Wheelchair access. £2, concessions £1.)

♫ ENTERTAINMENT

Norwich offers a rich array of cultural activities, especially in summer. Information on all things vaguely entertaining, as well as tickets for virtually all venues in Norwich, are kept by **The Ticket Shop,** Guildhall (☎ 764764), next door to the TIC. Next to the Assembly House on Theatre St., the Art Deco **Theatre Royal** houses opera and ballet touring companies, as well as London-based theater troupes such as the Royal Shakespeare Company and Royal National Theatre. (☎ 630000; www.theatreroyalnorwich.co.uk. Tickets £3-17, some concessions. Box office open M-Sa 9:30am-8pm, until 6pm on non-performance days.) The home of the Norwich Players, **Maddermarket Theatre,** has revived high-quality amateur drama, performed in an Elizabethan-style theater. Adhering to a bizarre tradition, all actors remain anonymous, adding new meaning to "Who's Who in the Cast." (☎ 620917; www.maddermarket.freeserve.co.uk. 1 St. John's Alley. Box office open M-Sa 10am-9pm; on non-performance days, open M-F 10am-5pm, Sa 10am-1pm. Wheelchair access. Tickets £7, under 25 and seniors £5.) The **Norwich Arts Centre** provides the city's most versatile venue, hosting folk and world music, ballet, and comedy. (☎ 660352; www.norwichartscentre.co.uk. Box office open M-Sa 9am-10pm. Wheelchair access. Tickets £2-10, concessions available.) The **Norwich Puppet Theatre,** St. James, Whitefriars, comes in handy with shows for all ages. (☎ 629921. Box office open M-F 9:30am-5pm, Sa 1hr. prior to show. Tickets £5, children £3.75.) Also look for the City Council's free summer presentations of **Theatre in the Parks** (☎ 212137).

A few pubs and clubs offer live music, including **Boswells,** 24 Tombland, near the cathedral. (☎ 626099. Tu-Sa cover £1-3 after 9pm; open M-Sa noon-2am, Su noon-6pm.) Slide (electrically) to **Hy's,** next door, where theme nights bring anything from salsa rhythms to disco beats. (☎ 621155. Cover £1-4; open Tu-Sa 9pm-2am.) **The Loft,** on Rose St., features live music downstairs while soul and funk waft from its loft. **Ikon,** on Tombland across from the Maid's Head Hotel, and **Manhattan Nightclub** on Dove St. (with its Sunday night "Exclusive Chilled-out Zone") are other hotspots. On **Prince of Wales Rd.,** near the city center, five more clubs within two blocks jockey for social position.

The **Norfolk and Norwich Festival**—featuring theater, dance, music, and visual arts—explodes in mid-October. **Picture This,** in mid-June, offers two weeks of open artists' studios around the county. Pick up leaflets at the TIC or call 764764 for information and tickets. July welcomes the **LEAP Dance Festival** (mostly contemporary dance). Norwich's outdoor parks also host a stream of other **festivals** and **folk fairs** in the summer.

⚐ DAYTRIPS FROM NORWICH

NORFOLK BROADS NATIONAL PARK

To reach the Broads, take a train from Norwich, Lowestoft, or Great Yarmouth to the smaller towns of Beccles, Cantley, Lingwood, Oulton Broad, Salhouse, or Wroxham. From Norwich, First Eastern Counties buses leave from the corner of St. Stephen's St. and Surrey St. to: Wroxham (#723-726, 30min., 4 per day, return £2); Horning (#723 or 726, 45min., 4 per day, £3); Potter Heigham (#723-726, 1hr., 4 per day, return £3.10); and other Broads towns (#705, M-F 1 per day in the evening).

The ports along the northeast East Anglian coast yielded to the iron fists of London and other towns to the south, which pirated away much of their trade. Despite the loss, folk around here still engage in seafaring adventures. Birds, beasts, and humans alike flock to the national parkland of the **Norfolk Broads,** a watery maze of navigable marshlands, where traffic in narrow waterways hidden by hedgerows creates the surreal effect of sailboats floating through flowery fields. The broads didn't occur naturally, but were formed in medieval times when peat was dug out to use for fuel. Over the centuries, water levels rose and the shallow lakes or "broads" were born. The marshes and the hills looming nearby beckon nature enthusiasts traveling by foot, cycle, or boat. Exercise care when walking about the

Broads, a designated environmentally sensitive area; continual abuse by humans has damaged the area tremendously. Among the many **nature trails** that pass through the Broads, **Cockshoot Broad** lets you birdwatch, a circular walk around **Ranworth** points out the Broads' various flora, and **Upton Fen** is popular for its bugs. Hikers can challenge themselves with the 56 mi. long **Weaver's Way** between Cromer and Great Yarmouth. By collecting stamps along the trek, the hardy receive an exclusive woven patch upon completion. Girl scouts eat your heart out.

Numerous companies offer **cruises** around the Broads. **Broads Tours** depart from Wroxham (see below) and from **Potter Heigham** (☎ (01692) 670711). **Southern River Steamers,** 65 Trafford Rd., gives cruises from Norwich to Surlingham Broad, leaving from quays near the cathedral and train station. (☎ (01603) 624051. 30min. to 3¼hr excursions leaving periodically May-Sept. 11am-5:30pm. Wheelchair access. £1.63-6.70, children 80p-£4.30.)

The small village of **Strumpshaw,** with its bird reserve, is especially popular among birdwatchers. (☎ (01603) 715191. Open daily 9am-9pm or dusk. Wheelchair accessible trails. £3.) From Norwich take buses #30-33 to Strumpshaw (30min., M-Sa 8 per day, return £2.)

WROXHAM

Seven miles northeast of Norwich. From Norwich, take First Eastern Counties bus #54 (40 min.; M-Sa 1 per hr., Su every 1½hr.; return £2.40).

Wroxham provides a good point of departure for exploring the more remote areas of the Broads. To reach the **Hoveton tourist information centre** from the bus stop, take a right down Station Rd. and walk about 90 yards. The office also has lists of boat rentals and of campsites scattered through the area. (☎ (01603) 782281. Open Easter-Oct. M-Sa 9am-1pm and 2-5pm.) The sheer number of guesthouses and hotels (which may be booked through the TIC) within Wroxham proper and just outside attests to the popularity of the waterways and byways. While in the TIC, pick up free copies of *The Broadcaster*, which outlines local happenings, and *The Broad Miniguide*, which recommends certain sights and includes a map. *Broads Bike Hire* lists cycle rentals—certain areas of the Broads are accessible only by car or by bike. The closest place to rent a bike is **Camelot Craft,** though it's best to call ahead; follow Station Rd. to the river and take a left onto The Rhond. (☎ (01603) 783096. £8 per day, £5 per half-day. Open 9am-5pm daily.) **Broads Tours,** on the right-hand side before the bridge, runs cruises (1-2hr.) through the Broads. (☎ (01603) 782207; www.broads.co.uk. Office open daily 9am-5:30pm. Tours July-Aug. 7 per day, Sept.-June 11:30am and 2pm. £4.60-6.25, children £3.40-5.)

KING'S LYNN ☎01553

King's Lynn (pop. 36,000) was one of England's foremost 16th-century ports, awash in wealth and power and bathing in the limelight of a thriving social scene. Four hundred years later, the once mighty flow of the Great Ouse (OOze) river has slowed to a leisurely current, and the town has slowed its pace in step. This dockside city borrows its Germanic look from trading partners such as Hamburg and Bremen; the earth tones of the flat East Anglian countryside meet with a somber red-brick facade. The town slumbers early and heavily and the sights can be quite dry, but King's Lynn makes a perfect stopover for cyclists exploring the region and those seeking rest and relaxation.

▐▌ GETTING THERE AND PRACTICAL INFORMATION

The **train station** is on Blackfriars Rd; to get to the tourist information centre, walk down Waterloo St. until you reach the bus station, then veer left onto New Conduit St., which turns into Purfleet. **Trains** (☎ (08457) 484950) steam in from: **London King's Cross** (1½hr., 19 per day, day return £21.50); **Cambridge** (1hr., 20 per day, return £7.50); and **Peterborough** (1hr., 6 per day, return £8.30). **Buses** arrive at the **Vancouver Centre** (☎ 772343; office open M-F 8:30am-5pm, Sa 8:30am-noon and 1-5pm). **First Eastern Counties** (☎ (01603) 660553) buses travel from: **Norwich** (#X94, 1½hr., 8 per day, £5) and **Peterborough** (1¼hr., 11 per day, £5.50). **National Express** (☎ (08705) 808080) runs once daily from **London** (£11).

The **tourist information centre,** in the Custom House, on the corner of King St. and Purfleet, books rooms for a 10% deposit and provides bus and train info. Pick up a free miniguide. (☎ 763044. Open M-Sa 9:15am-5pm, Su 10:15am-5pm.) Buy National Express tickets from **West Norfolk Travel,** 2 King St. (☎ 772910). Other services include: the **police** (☎ 691211), at the corner of St. James and London Rd.; the **hospital** (☎ 613613), located on Gayton Rd.; and the **post office,** at Baxter's Plain on the corner of Broad St. and New Conduit St. **Postal code:** PE30 1YB.

ACCOMMODATIONS AND FOOD

A quayside **YHA King's Lynn** (☎ 772461; fax 764312), a short walk from the train and bus stations and right in the town center, occupies part of the 16th-century Thoresby College, on College Ln., opposite the Old Gaol House. Its location, wonderful view of the river, clean and tasteful decoration, and friendly staff make the hostel your best bet. It often fills, so call ahead. Keep your eyes peeled; it's easy to miss. (Lockout 10am-5pm. Curfew 11pm. Open May-Aug. daily; Apr. and Sept.-Oct. W-Su. £9, under 18 £6.20.) **B&Bs** are a hike from the city center; the less expensive ones span **Gaywood Rd.** and **Tennyson Ave.** Reasonable accommodations can be found at the **Maranatha Guest House,** 115 Gaywood Rd. (☎ 774596; £14-20 per person), or the **Fairlight Lodge,** 79 Goodwins Rd. (☎ 762234; £17-24 per person).

King's Lynn restaurants operate on their own sweet time, and many close on Sunday. A **Sainsbury's** supermarket is one of several located at St. Dominic's Sq., Vancouver Centre. (☎ 772104. Open M-W 8am-8pm, Th-F 8am-9pm, Sa 7:30am-8pm, Su 10am-4pm.) For fresh fruits and vegetables, visit the **markets** (open Tu and Sa roughly 8:30am-4pm) held at the larger Tuesday Market Pl. on the north end of High St., or at the Saturday Market Pl. If you're craving a sit-down meal, try **Antonio's** on Baxter's Plain, off Tower St., where inexpensive and tasty Italian meals, including a 3-course lunch (£6.20), await the weary traveler. (☎ 772324. Open M-Sa noon-2pm and 6-10pm.) **Archers,** just a few steps up Purfleet from the TIC, offers tasty lunches and teas (£1-4) in a quietly stylish cafe setting. (Open M-Sa 9am-5pm.) The **Seven Sisters** pub presides at the top of Extons Rd. and feels nicely out of the way after a stroll from the town center through The Walks (see below).

SIGHTS AND ENTERTAINMENT

The sights of King's Lynn pale in comparison to neighboring Norwich, but a walking tour (guide 30p from the TIC) can be quite rewarding on a nice day. The huge 15th-century **Guildhall of St. George,** 27-29 King St., near the Tuesday Market, is said to be the last surviving building where Shakespeare appeared in his own play, and the oldest surviving medieval guildhall in England; it now hosts the **King's Lynn Arts Centre.** There are no tours or plaques; just wander around yourself. (☎ 774725. Open M-F 10am-2pm. Free. Arts Centre ☎ 764864.)

The **Tales of the Old Gaol House,** Saturday Market Pl., occupies the Regalia Room, where the priceless 14th-century "King John Cup" and other treasures from King's Lynn's past are displayed. Next door, an audio guide leads you through the town's old jail, spinning stories of Lynn's murderers, robbers, and witches in gory detail. (☎ 774297. Open Apr.-Oct. daily 10am-5pm; Nov.-Mar. F-Tu 10am-5pm. £2.50, concessions £1.80.) **St. Margaret's Church,** across from the Gaol House on Saturday Market Pl., was built in 1101. Most of what stands today was added later, but bits date back to the 12th century. The peaceful **Tower Gardens** ensconce Greyfriars Tower on one side of St. James' St., while on the other side, **The Walks** stretch away from the town center in shady expanses.

The **Corn Exchange** at Tuesday Market Pl. sells tickets for a variety of music, dance and theater events. (☎ 764864. Open M-Sa 10am-6pm and at evening showtimes, Su 1hr. prior to show.) During the last half of July, the Guildhall hosts the **King's Lynn Festival,** an orgy of classical and jazz music, along with ballet, puppet

shows, and films. Get schedules at the Festival Office, 27 King St., PE30 1HA. (Info
☎ 767557, tickets ☎ 764864. Tickets £3-10. Box office open M-F 10am-5pm, Sa
10am-1pm and 2-4pm.)

DAYTRIPS FROM KING'S LYNN

The stomping grounds of the wealthy, punctuated by huge mansions, give way to
wilder country as the road leading north from King's Lynn bends east to flank the
Norfolk coast.

SANDRINGHAM. If you want to see how royalty lives, journey to Sandringham,
which has been a royal home since 1862. The beautiful house shows off halls lined
with weaponry, high ornate ceilings, and detailed Spanish tapestries; the grounds
contain flowing lawns, neat gardens, and a breathtaking lake; and the museum
touts the big-game trophies of King George V and the royal cars from King Edward
VII in 1900 to Prince Charles in 1990. George once described the place as "dear old
Sandringham, the place I love better than anywhere else in the world." Its 600
acres are open to the public when not in use by the royals. It's usually closed in
June; ask at the King's Lynn TIC. The best time to visit, though, is during the **flower
show** in the last week of July. *(10 mi. north of King's Lynn. First Eastern Counties buses
#411 and 414 arrive from King's Lynn (25 min.; M-Sa 8 per day, last return 6pm; Su 5 per day,
last return 8:30pm; £2). ☎ (01553) 772675. Open Apr.-Sept. 11am-4:45pm. Admission to
house, grounds, and museum £5.50, seniors and students £4.50, children £3.50; museum and
grounds only £4.50, seniors and students £4, children £3.)*

CASTLE RISING. Closer to King's Lynn, this intimidating solid keep set atop massive earthworks was home to Queen Isabella, "She-Wolf of France," after she plotted the murder of her husband, Edward II. The beautiful view, well preserved and
navigable ruins, and personal and informative tour make the easy trip worthwhile.
*(First Eastern Counties buses run from King's Lynn (#410 and 411, 15min., M-Sa 16 per day, last
return 8:45pm; #415, Su 11 per day, £1.50). Open Apr.-Oct. daily 10am-6pm; Nov.-Mar. W-Su
10am-4pm. Admission and audio tour £3.25, students and seniors £2.50, children £1.60.)*

HOUGHTON HALL. Built in the mid-18th century for Sir Robert Walpole, the first
prime minister of England, Houghton Hall is a magnificent example of Palladian
architecture, with paintings, tapestries, and "the most sublime bed ever designed."
*(14 miles northeast of King's Lynn. Take First Eastern Counties bus #411 (45 min., M-Sa 2 per
day). ☎ (01485) 528569. Open Easter to late Sept. Th, Su, and bank holidays 2-5:30pm; gate
closes 5pm. Admission to house and grounds £6, children £2.)*

NEAR KING'S LYNN: THE NORTHERN NORFOLK COAST

The northern **Norfolk Coast,** with its expanses of beach, sand dunes, and salt marsh,
stretches from **Hunstanton,** 16 mi. north of King's Lynn, to **Wells-next-the-Sea** and
beyond. Bird sanctuaries and nature preserves abound; the **Scolt Head Island Reserve**
and the **Holme Bird Observatory** are superb. Buses #410 and 411 run from Vancouver
Centre in King's Lynn to Hunstanton (2hr., M-Sa 2 per hr., Su every 2hr., £2.40). A **YHA
Youth Hostel,** 15 Avenue Rd., perches in the center of Hunstanton near the Wash. (☎
(01485) 532061. Open July-Aug. daily; Easter-June M-Sa.; Sept.-Oct. Tu-Sa. Dorms
£10, under 18 £6.85.) Holme is 3 mi. to the east; buses run from Hunstanton to
Holme's Crossing in the summer only (Tu-Th and Su). To visit **Scolt Head Island** go via
Brancaster Staithe (an Anglo-Saxon word meaning "pier"), 10 mi. east along the A149.

BURY ST. EDMUNDS ☎ 01284

In AD 869, Viking invaders tied the Saxon monarch King Edmund to a tree, used
him for target practice, and then beheaded him. Approximately 350 years later, 25
barons met in the Abbey of St. Edmund to sow the seeds of democracy, swearing
to force King John to sign the *Magna Carta*. From these two defining moments in
English history, Bury St. Edmunds came to be known as "shrine of a king, cradle of
the law," and is now a charmingly intimate small English town.

📠 GETTING THERE AND GETTING AROUND. Suffolk enjoys prolific train and bus service. Commuter buses run between Bury St. Edmunds and London, two hours away. Bury makes a good daytrip from either Norwich or Cambridge, especially if you include a jaunt to Lavenham, Sudbury, Long Melford, or any of the other historic villages scattered throughout Western Suffolk. **Trains** (☎ (08457) 484950) arrive from: **London Liverpool St.** (2hr., 1 per hr., return £26.40); **Colchester** (1 hr., every 90min., return £11); and **Felixstowe** (1¼hr., 2 per hr., return £9.30). **National Express** (☎ (08705) 808080) **buses** come in from **London** (2hr., 2 per day, £11). **R.W. Chenery** (☎ (01379) 741221) runs an express bus from **London Victoria** once each day (£13). **Cambus** (☎ (01223) 423554) #X11 runs from Drummer St. in **Cambridge** (55min.; M-Sa every 2hr., Su every 4hr.; return £4). The area around Bury is also explorable by bike, but rentals are difficult to come by. Try **Barton's Bicycles,** 5 Marrio's Walk, Stowmarket, but call a few days in advance. (☎ (01449) 677195. Bikes £8 per day, £30 per week. Open M-Sa 9am-5:30pm.)

🔧🛈 ORIENTATION AND PRACTICAL INFORMATION. Laid out according to the original 12th-century plan, Bury's streets are easier to untangle than those of neighboring towns. The enthusiastic folks at the **tourist information centre,** 6 Angel Hill, will happily supply you with maps, an accommodations list, and a copy of *What's On.* (☎ 764667; fax 757084. Open Easter-Oct. M-Sa 9:30am-5:30pm, Su 10am-3pm; Nov.-Easter M-F 10am-4pm, Sa 10am-1pm.) To reach the TIC from the train station, follow Outnorthgate St. past the roundabout onto Northgate St.; turn right onto Mustow St. and walk up to Angel Hill. From the bus station, follow St. Andrew's St. to Brentgovel St., turn right at Lower Baxtel St. and then left onto Abbeygate St. The TIC also runs 1½hr. guided **walking tours** of the city (June-Sept. Su-F 2:30pm; £2.50). Banks in town include **Lloyds,** on Buttermarket St., half a block from the marketplace. (☎ (0845) 303 0105. Open M-Tu and Th-F 9am-5pm, W 9:30am-5pm, Sa 9:30am-12:30pm.) **Thomas Cook** is at 43b Cornhill St. (☎ 752184. Open M and W-Sa 9am-5:30pm, Tu 10am-5:30pm.) The **post office** is at 17-18 Cornhill St. (☎ 701095. Open M-F 9am-5:30pm, Sa 9am-12:30pm.) **Postal code:** IP33 1AA.

🛏️🍴 ACCOMMODATIONS AND FOOD. The TIC books B&Bs in town or on a nearby farm (£16-20). The most central B&B is Mrs. Williams's 📱 **The Garden House,** whose delightful rooms and cheerful presence will have moved to St. Andrew's St. South as of January. (☎ 703880. £15 per person.) Or call **Mrs. Norton,** 16 Cannon St., for a warm welcome on a quiet street. (☎ 761776. Singles £18; twins £32.)

For groceries, head down Cornhill St. from the post office to the **Iceland** supermarket. (Open M-W and Sa 8:30am-6pm, Th-F 8:30am-7pm.) Pints go for £1.80 at the pint-sized **Nutshell,** Abbeygate at the Traverse (☎ 764867), the world's smallest pub. The hostess speaks with reverence about her entry in the pages of the *Guinness Book of World Records,* created when the 15 by 17 ft. pub squeezed 102 people and one dog into its tiny depths. A crowd of locals lead the budget eater into **The Baker's Oven,** 11 Abbeygate St. (☎ 754001), where you can munch on scrumptious toasties filled with tomatoes, ham, and eggs, and a side salad for under £2.50.

📷🎭 SIGHTS AND ENTERTAINMENT. A few hours of whimsical wandering reveal Bury's prized charms. Along Crown St., across from the TIC on the soggy banks of the River Lark, lie the beautiful ruins of the 📱 **Abbey of St. Edmund,** 11th-century home to cadres of foraging ducks. The weathered, massive pillars look like stone refugees from Easter Island. It was here that the 25 *Magna Carta* barons met in 1214 to discuss their letter to the king. The formal gardens next to the remains won the 1999 Britain in Bloom and Nations in Bloom competitions; go in late June when the flowers blossom. Be sure to see the aviary and the Olde English Rose Garden of Frances Hodgson Burnett's dreams. (Ruins and garden open M-Sa 7am-sunset, Su 9am-sunset. Free.) The **Abbey Visitor Centre,** Samson's Tower, on Crown St., a block south of the Abbey Gate, dwells in the Norman ruins, featuring three plaster-of-paris statues and abbey artifacts strategically placed throughout a gift shop. Don earphones and take an audio tour of the ruins to hear a 12th-century monk named Jocelin tell stories of executions with slightly too much glee. (☎ 763110. Open Easter-Oct. daily 10am-5pm. 45min. tour £1.50, concessions £1.)

Next door lies the delightful 16th-century **St. Edmundsbury Cathedral,** its welcoming interior bathed in magnificent color. The cherub overhanging the entrance, allegedly pilfered years before, was serendipitously rediscovered by a Bury businessman in a Belgian antique shop. Spend a quiet few moments on one of the benches in the light-filled courtyard before you leave. (☎ 754933. Cathedral open daily June-Aug. 8:30am-8pm; Sept.-May 8:30am-6pm. Choral Evensong services W-Sa 5:30 pm, Su 3:30pm. Suggested donation £2.)

The **Manor House Museum** borders the abbey gardens to the south. This elegant Georgian house is a must-see if you're cuckoo for clocks, containing dozens of synchronized timepieces, including a replica of the first rolling-ball clock. The museum also houses an impressive collection of Victorian and 1920s costumes. (☎ 757076. Open Su-W noon-5pm. Wheelchair access. £2.50, concessions £1.50.) The **Moyses' Hall Museum,** Corn Hill in the marketplace, houses a wonderful collection of historical junk, including a mummified cat and a violin made out of a horse's skull. The museum also contains artifacts from the 1828 murder of local Maria Marten, such as a book covered with the murderer's skin. Afraid that an evil criminal might slip unnoticed into heaven, the people of the time were convinced that skinning the murderer would expose his soul so that no one would mistake him. (☎ 757488. Open M-Sa 10am-5pm, Su 2-5pm. £1.70, concessions £1.10, families £5.20, free after 4pm.) Bury bustles on **market** days. (W and Sa 9am-4pm.) To put some spark into your stay, visit in mid-May, when a **festival** brings three weeks of music and street entertainment, all culminating in a firework finale.

🖪 **DAYTRIPS FROM BURY ST. EDMUNDS.** Just 3 mi. southwest of Bury in the village of **Horringer** is **Ickworth,** the massive home of the Marquis of Bristol. Dominated by a 106 ft. rotunda, the opulent state rooms are filled with 18th-century French furniture and more portraits than you could possibly absorb, including some by Reynolds and Gainsborough. The classical Italian garden is splendid, and the manor's sheep quite cordial. **First Eastern Counties** (☎ (01284) 766171) **buses** #141 through 144 leave St. Andrew's Station in Bury for Horringer and Ickworth (M-Sa 9 per day, last return from Horringer 6pm, return £2.20). (☎ (01284) 735270. House open Apr.-Oct. Tu-W, F-Su, and bank holidays 1-5pm. Gardens open Apr.-Oct. daily 10am-5pm, Nov.-Mar. M-F 10am-4pm. Park open year-round daily 7am-7pm. Wheelchair access. £5.30, children £2.40; park and gardens only £2.40, 80p.)

Turrets and moats await those who visit **Long Melford,** a mile-long Suffolk village, graced by two Tudor mansions. **Melford Hall** displays well manicured lawns and colorful gardens. (☎ (01787) 880286. Open May-Sept. W-Th and Sa-Su 2-5:30pm; Apr. and Oct. Sa-Su 2-5:30pm. £4.20.) **Kentwell Hall** is filled with authentically costumed guides; visitors too are sometimes asked to come in Tudor costume. (☎ (01787) 310207. Open Mar.-May and Sept.-Oct. Su noon-5pm; July-Aug. daily noon-5pm. £5.25, students £3.20, seniors £4.50.) While in the area, stop by the **Long Melford Church,** between the two mansions, erected in 1484 by funding from opulent wool merchants. Long Melford is accessible from **Bury** by **H.C. Chambers bus** #753 (☎ (01787) 227233). Hitchhikers report that the trip from Bury to Melford is feasible, although *Let's Go* does not recommend hitchhiking.

HARWICH AND FELIXSTOWE

Continent-bound travelers head south to **Harwich** (HAR-idge), a ferry depot for trips to Holland, Germany, and Scandinavia, and to **Felixstowe,** where boats sail to Belgium (see **By Ferry,** p. 35). Call the **Harwich tourist information centre,** Iconfield Park, Parkeston for details about ferries. (☎ (01255) 506139. Open Apr.-Sept. daily 9am-7pm; Oct.-Mar. M-Sa 9am-4pm.) The **Felixstowe tourist information centre** is on the seafront. (☎ (01394) 276770. Open M-F 9am-5:30pm, Sa-Su 9:30 am-5:30pm.)f

NORTHWEST ENGLAND

The 19th century swept into Northwest England in an industrial coal cloud, revolutionizing quiet village life. By the end of the 1800s, the "dark satanic mills" that horrified William Blake had overrun the region's cities, and, as D.H. Lawrence put it, mines were "like black studs on the countryside, linked by a loop of fine chain, the railway." Even now, great cables still criss-cross the land in incomprehensible patterns of progress. Prosperity followed these smokestacks and coal mines, as the cities of the northwest became the workshops of the world's wool and linen textiles. The later decline of heavy industry affected Merseyside, Lancashire, and Manchester as it did urban areas elsewhere in Britain, if not more so. Still, urban life and a strong youth culture inspired creativity, and today the region possesses one of the most innovative music and arts scenes in Britain: Liverpool and Manchester alone produced four of Q magazine's top ten biggest rock stars of the century. Add to that a large student population in the region and through-the-roof nightlife, and you'll begin to understand the reinvigorated northwest. But if you need a break from frenetic activity, the Peak District to the east provides respite, as does Cumbria to the north, where the Lake District possesses the stunning crags and lakes that sent the Romantic poets into pensive meditation.

HIGHLIGHTS OF NORTHWEST ENGLAND

LIVERPOOL Don't miss Liverpool, **Beatles** fans: virtually every pub, restaurant, and corner claims some connection to the Fab Four (p. 328).

MANCHESTER Revel in the wealth of Manchester's nightlife; many of the trendy cafe-bars morph into late-night venues for dancing and drinking (p. 339).

BLACKPOOL Ride the highest, fastest, steepest rollercoaster in the world—known as the Big One—at Blackpool's **Pleasure Beach** (p. 341).

LAKE DISTRICT Explore the dramatic peaks and sparkling waters of this National Park, one of the most beautiful regions in the country, and the landscape that inspired the poetry of Wordsworth, Coleridge, and other Romantic poets (p. 356).

NORTHWEST CITIES

CHESTER ☎01244

With fashionable chain stores tucked in Victorian mock medieval houses, tour guides in Roman armor, a town crier in full uniform, and a Barclays bank occupying a wing of the cathedral, Chester at times resembles an American theme park pastiche of Ye Olde English Towne. Originally built by frontier-forging Romans, Chester later became a base for Plantagenet campaigns against the Welsh—an old town law states that Welshmen wandering the streets after 9pm can be beheaded—and established a web of trading connections throughout continental Europe. As silt blocked the River Dee in the 17th century, Chester was left to turn its archaism into a selling point. Crowded but lovely, commercial but lively, the city now hosts shoppers jockeying through town at a pace to rival the horses at Chester's world-famous race track.

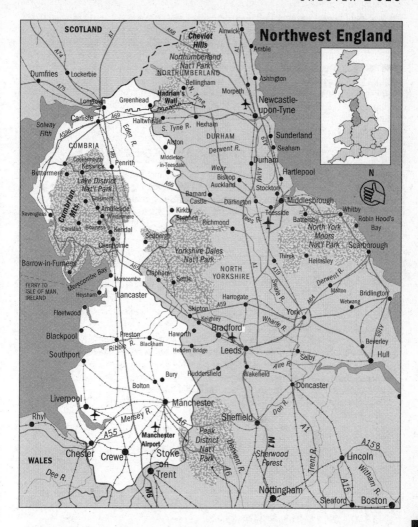

Northwest England

GETTING THERE AND GETTING AROUND

Chester serves as a rail gateway to Wales through the north Wales train line. The train and bus stations both lie 15min. to the north, outside the walls. Save your legs the walk and take bus #20 from the train station to **Foregate St.,** free with a rail ticket. From Foregate St., enter the city walls onto **Eastgate St.,** and turn right onto **Northgate St.** to reach the main tourist information centre (TIC). From the bus station, turn left onto **Upper Northgate St.** and head through **Northgate** to the TIC.

Trains: City Rd. Office open M-Sa 5:30am-12:30am, Su 8am-midnight. Trains (☎ (08457) 484950) from: **London Euston** (4hr.; M-Sa 7 per day, Su 4 per day; £44); **Manchester Piccadilly** (1hr.; M-Sa 1 per hr., Su 5 per day; £8.50); **Holyhead** in Wales (1½hr., 1 per hr., £16.15); and **Birmingham** (1¾hr.; M-Sa 7 per day, Su 4 per day; £10.30). Frequent **Merseyrail** service makes Chester an easy daytrip from **Liverpool** (45min., 1 per hr., £3).

Buses: Delamere St. (☎ 381515), north of the city wall off Northgate St. Office open M-Sa 8:30am-5pm. **National Express** (☎ (08705) 808080) from: **London** (5½hr., 5 per day, £15); **Manchester** (1hr., 3 per day, £4.50); **Birmingham** (2½hr., 5 per day, £8.25); and **Blackpool** (3½hr., 3 per day, £8.70). **Huxley Coaches** (☎ (01948) 770661) #C56 to Foregate St. from **Wrexham** (M-F 2 per hr., Sa 1 per hr.; £2.35).

Public Transportation: Call ☎ 602666 for local bus service info, M-F 8am-6pm, Sa 9am-1pm. Buses run from Delamere St. to the **bus exchange** in Market Sq. around the corner from the Town Hall (6 per hr., 75p). Pick up the hefty *Chester Public Transport Guide* at the bus station or tourist information centres.

Taxis: Radio Taxis (☎ 372372).

◼️🔢 ORIENTATION AND PRACTICAL INFORMATION

Chester's center is encircled by a medieval **city wall,** which is breached by seven gates. **St. Peter Cross** is formed by **Eastgate St., Northgate St.,** and **Watergate St.** to the west, and **Bridge St.,** which passes under the wall as it reaches and crosses over the River Dee. **The Groves,** a left just before the bridge, hugs the river for a mile.

Tourist Information Centre: Town Hall, Northgate St. (☎ 402111; www.chestercc.gov.uk). **Chester Visitor Centre,** Vicars Ln. (☎ 402111; fax 403188), opposite the Roman amphitheater. Both open May-Oct. M-Sa 9am-6pm, Su 10am-4pm; Nov.-Apr. M-Sa 9am-5:30pm, Su 10am-5:30pm. Both book accommodations for a £3 fee and sell city maps for £1.

Tours: Chester has more tours than intact Roman columns. A legionnaire sweating in full armor leads the **Roman Tour** (June-Sept. Th-Sa 2pm from the TIC; £2, concessions £1.25, families £6). The open-top **Guide Friday** (☎ 347457) buses do their usual schtick (4 per hr.; £6.50, students and seniors £5, children £2). Beings ghoulish and ghastly lurk on the **Ghost Hunter Trail** (June-Sept. Th-Sa 7:30pm from the TIC; £3, students and seniors £2.50, families £7). Let us know if you see any. **Boats** (☎ 342694) embark from The Groves, a tree-lined riverside street to the left of Lower Bridge St.; a 2½ mi. trip down the River Dee lasts 1hr. and costs £3.50 (children £2.50).

Financial Services: Barclays, 35 Eastgate St. Open M-Tu and Th-F 9am-5pm, Tu 10am-5pm, W 10am-5pm, Sa 9:30am-3:30pm. **Thomas Cook** has two branches on Bridge St. alone. One opens M-Tu and Th-Sa 9am-5:30pm, W 10am-5:30pm, Su 11am-4pm. The other opens M and W-Sa 9am-5:30pm, Tu 10am-5:30pm.

American Express: 12 Watergate St. (☎ 404401). Open M-Tu and Th-Sa 9am-5:30pm, W 9:30am-5:30pm.

Launderette: 56 Garden Ln. (☎ 371406). Turn left off Northgate St., then right off Canal St. Open daily 9am-6pm; last wash 4:30pm.

Police: (☎ 350222), Grosvenor Rd.

Hotlines: Samaritans, 36 Upper Northgate St. (☎ 377999). Open 24hr. **Lesbian and Gay Switchboard** (☎ (01743) 232393). Open Tu-W and F 8-10pm. **Rape Crisis** (☎ 317922). Open W 7-8pm, Sa 11am-noon.

Hospital: Countess of Chester (West Chester) Hospital, Liverpool Rd. (☎ 365000). Take bus #40A from the station or #3 from the bus exchange.

Internet Access: i-station, Rufus Court (☎ 394203). Open 8am-10pm. £2 per 30min.; many discount offers.

Post Office: 2 St. John St. (☎ 348315), off Foregate St. just before the wall. Open M-Sa 9am-5:30pm. **Bureau de change** and photo booth. **Postal Code:** CH1 1AA.

◤ ACCOMMODATIONS

Concentrations of B&Bs (£15 and up) are at **Hoole Rd.,** a five-minute walk from the train station (turn right from the exit, climb the steps to Hoole Rd., and turn right over the railroad tracks), and **Brook St.** (right from the train station exit, then the first left). Buses #21, 53, and C30 run to the area from the city center.

YHA Chester, Hough Green House, 40 Hough Green (☎ 680056; fax 681204; chester@yha.org.uk), 1½ mi. from the city center. Cross the river on Grosvenor Rd. and turn

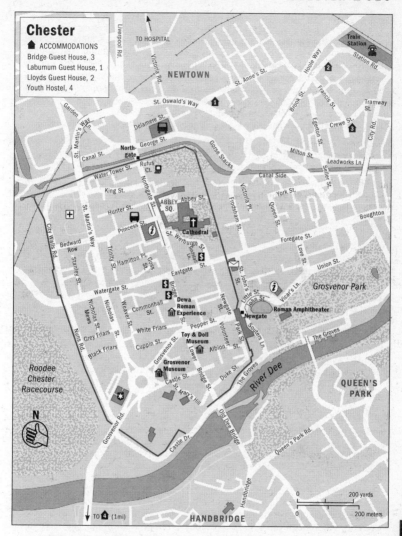

Chester

▲ ACCOMMODATIONS
Bridge Guest House, 3
Laburnum Guest House, 1
Lloyds Guest House, 2
Youth Hostel, 4

right at the roundabout (40min.), or take bus #7 or 16 and ask for the hostel. Beautiful, renovated Victorian house, with luggage storage, a laundry room (wash £2, powder 60p), Internet access (£2.50 per 30min.), and nightlights to read by. Thunderous showers restore lost youth and vitality. Reception open 7am-10:30pm. Curfew 11pm; security code access after curfew. Open mid-Jan. to mid-Dec. Dorms £11, under 18 £7.75.

Laburnum Guest House, 2 St. Anne St. (☎/fax 380313), across from the bus station. Four sparkling rooms, all stocked with TV and bath, rest about as close to the town center as you can get without facing legions of shoppers. £20 per person.

Bridge Guest House, 18-20 Crewe St. (☎ 340438). From the train station, take the first right off City Rd. The exceptionally thick wooden door and sturdy whitewashed walls were erected for railway workers, but now shelter weary train passengers. Comfy TV lounge downstairs. Singles £17; doubles £30.

Lloyds Guest House, 108 Brook St. (☎ 325838; fax 317491), near the train station. Colorful rooms with TVs. £17.50 per person; singles £20.

◖ FOOD

Beware the rustic restaurants lurking behind faux-Tudor facades along Chester's distinctive rows; their prices are decidedly up-to-date. **Tesco** supermarket, hidden at the end of an alley off Frodsham St., has cheaper eats. (Open M-F 8am-9pm, Sa 7:30am-9pm, Su 11am-5pm.) The town's **market**, beside the bus exchange on Princess St., numbers fruit and vegetables among its array of bargains. (Open M-Sa 8am-5pm.) Picnic in the shade of lovely **Grosvenor Park**—its sloping, flowered acres contain neither Roman artifacts nor tourists. From Bridge St., turn left onto Pepper St., cross under Newgate, pass the amphitheater, and enter on your right.

Philpotts, 2 Goss St. (☎ 345123), off Watergate St. Stuffs spectacular sandwiches, including tuna with sweet corn and Somerset brie, into slices or baguettes (£1.85-2.20). Pastas and desserts also stock the shining shelves. Open M-Sa 8am-2:30pm.

Off the Wall, 12 St. John's St. (☎ 348964). A typical pub exterior shelters a remarkably good menu.Lunch on a lime and chili chicken sandwich (£2.45-3.95) and dine on lasagne (£4.75) or great grills (£4.75-5.25). Open for food Su-Th noon-7pm, F-Sa noon-5pm.

Hattie's Tea Shop, 5 Rufus Court (☎ 345173), off Northgate St. Scrumptious home-made cakes and inexpensive lunchtime snacks. The £4 "giant topless" ham salad sandwich turns on porcine fetishists. Wheelchair access. Open July-Aug. M-Sa 9:30am-5pm, Su 11am-4pm; Sept.-June M-F 10am-4pm, Sa 10am-5pm, Su 11am-4pm.

The Kalldra Tearooms, 49 Watergate St. (☎ 323003). A filling selection of lunches (£3-3.50), sandwiches (£1.40-1.75), and salads (£2.95). Open M-Sa 8:30am-4pm.

◉ SIGHTS

ARCHITECTURE. Chester's faux-medieval architecture is its main attraction, and the utter domination of street scenes by wannabe Tudor buildings effectively masks the fact that the city center is really one vast outdoor shopping mall. A few of the buildings are actually from the Tudor age, but the black-and-white paint, like most of the buildings, is a strictly Victorian phenomenon. On summer Saturdays, the already thick crowds coagulate, and a bizarre variety of street musicians, from cowpoke trios to accordion-wielding matrons, set up shop. The famous **city walls** encircle the town, and you can walk on them for free. Also free, unless you give in to the relentless pressures of bourgeois capitalism, are the **rows** of Bridge St., Watergate St., and Eastgate St., where walkways give access to another tier of storefronts above street-level. Some historians theorize that Edward I imported the idea from Constantinople, which he visited while crusading.

A number of pathways slither over and under the walls and pass through unimaginatively named gates. **Northgate,** one such gate with a fine view of the Welsh hills, was rebuilt in 1808 to house the city's jail 30 ft. below ground. The bridge outside the gate is dubbed the Bridge of Sighs; it carried soon-to-be executed convicts from the jail to the chapel for their last mass, although a good number jumped into the canal below and swam for it before railings were installed.

CHESTER CATHEDRAL. Fight your way through the throngs for an awe-inspiring visit. In 1092, Hugh Lupus, the newly named Earl of Chester, founded a Benedictine Abbey here on the site of a church (built AD 907) dedicated to St. Werburgh, a Mercian princess who passed up royal comfort for the austerity of a nunnery, and who resurrected geese as a hobby. A Gothic facelift in 1250 set off a flurry of decorative makeovers, transforming the Romanesque cathedral into a stunning architectural hodgepodge. Intersecting stone arches named "The Crown of Stone" support the tower, and brilliant stained-glass windows sparkle throughout. The choir showcases an enormous pipe organ and ledges along the back walls, carved with aged monks. To learn what a miserichord is, look under the choir seats. *(Just off Northgate St. ☎ 324756. Open 7:30am-6:30pm. Suggested donation £2.)*

ROMAN SIGHTS. In 43 AD, all Britannia was conquered by the Romans. All? No! Oh wait, yes. Well, almost. Apart from Scotland. Just outside Newgate sits the unimpressive base of the largest **Roman amphitheater** in Britain. Excavated in 1960, it once accommodated the legion at Dewa (Chester) for gladiatorial bouts, but now you'll have to bring along your own tigers to fight away a yawn at its utterly ruined state. *(Open Apr.-Sept. 10am-6pm; Oct.-Mar. 10am-1pm and 2-4pm. Free.)* Next door, the **Roman Garden and Hypocaust** offers picnic space on a shaded, narrow strip of grass lined with stunted Roman columns. The **Grosvenor Museum,** 27 Grosvenor St., flaunts Chester's archaeological history with an extensive collection of Roman artifacts. *(☎ 402008. Open M-Sa 10:30am-5pm, Su 2-5pm. Free.)* In a final stop on your whirlwind Roman tour, wander through a half-hearted re-creation at the **Dewa Roman Experience,** Pierpoint Ln., off Bridge St. The experience sits on the sight of Roman ruins, and its highlights include exposed archaeological digs. *(☎ 343407. Open 9am-5pm. £3.95, seniors and students £3.50, under 16 £2.25, families £11.)*

OTHER SIGHTS. Baby giraffes wobble, lemurs leap, and orangutans beat their chests at the █ **Chester Zoo,** two miles north of town on the A41. One of the largest in Europe, the zoo recently opened a Twilight Zone where discombobulated bats whoosh about your ears. *(Take Crosville bus #8 or 8X from the Bus Exchange behind the town hall (£1.95 return). ☎ 380280. Open 10am to 3:30-5:30pm, depending on season. £9.50, seniors £7.50, children £7, YHA members £8.50.)* The **Toy and Doll Museum** holds the largest collection of matchbox cars in the world, as well as the bug-eyed monsters on a 1964 series of "revolting bubble-gum cards." *(13a Lower Bridge Street Row. ☎ 346297. Open M-Sa 10am-5pm, Su 11am-5pm. £2, concessions £1, families £4; YHA members 10% off.)*

▼ PUBS AND NIGHTLIFE

Chester has some 30 pubs to assuage thirst (and hunger); many parrot Ye Olde English decor, and almost all are open M-Sa 11am-11pm, Su noon-10:30pm. Watering holes group on Lower Bridge and Watergate St. Decidedly non-traditional in decor is **Claverton's Café Bar,** on Lower Bridge St., whose cozy couches attract a chic, female-strong crowd. *(☎ 319760. Pints £1.80.)* Traditionalists cross the road into **Ye Olde King's Head,** 48-50 Lower Bridge St. *(☎ 324855),* where an assortment of steins hangs from beams in a restored 17th-century house, or have a pint in the tranquil 16th-century upstairs room at **The Falcon,** 6 Lower Bridge St., whose black-and-white timber seems to tilt precariously. The **Boat House** *(☎ 328719),* at the end of a pleasant walk along the River Dee at the end of The Groves, lets the sun shine in the glass window that runs the entire length of the pub; for a great view of the Dee, be prepared to fight off couples to get a window seat.

A twentyish crowd lines up to enter **Rosie's,** a club which takes up three floors of the Northgate Row. At ground level is a pub littered with Route 66 signs and other bits of Americana. Commercial dance and chart music envelopes the floor above, while funk-soul brothers check it out on the top floor. Fridays feature 80s nights, while Saturdays are all about the three-floor party. *(☎ 327141. Males must wear collared shirts. Cover £3-5. F-Sa over 21 only. Pub open Tu-Sa 8pm-1am, club open Th-Sa 9:30pm-2am.)* **Alexander's Jazz Bar,** Rufus Court, off Northgate St., hosts jazz and blues bands at least three nights a week; Saturday is comedy night. *(☎ 340005. Open M-Th 11am-midnight, F-Sa 11am-12:30am, Su 11am-10:30pm.)*

♫ ▓ ENTERTAINMENT AND FESTIVALS

On sporadic spring and summer weekends, England's oldest horse races are held on the **Roodee,** formerly the Roman harbor. Lodgings fill up quickly on these weekends; write or call the TIC for schedules and advance booking. *(☎ 323170. Entrance £3-20 and up.)* The **Chester Summer Music Festival** draws classical musicians from across Britain into the cathedral during the third and fourth weeks of July. (Box office ☎ 320700. Tickets £22.) During the last week in June and the first week of July, Chester hosts a **Sports Festival** *(☎ 348365).* Celebrations center around a river carnival and raft race down the winding Dee. Check the TIC's free monthly *What's On in Chester* for other events.

LIVERPOOL
☎ 0151

On the banks of the Mersey, Liverpool (pop. 520,000) was on its way to becoming an important port as early as 1715, when it opened England's first commercial docks. Much of its early wealth was amassed through the slave trade, but it was the successful Lancashire cotton industry that bolstered the city's growth. The city's docks also served as the departure point for many an emigrant bound for North America or the Antipodes. However, Liverpool's shipping dominance drew unfortunate attention in World War II as it became Britain's second most heavily bombed city, and the decline of the Empire and the advent of cheap air travel dealt further blows to the industry. In the 1980s, high unemployment and government scandals inhibited the revival of prosperity and enthusiasm. Despite the enduring poverty of some of the city's outlying suburbs, central Liverpool is increasingly vibrant. A transformed Albert Dock studded with restaurants and museums, two enormous cathedrals, and a wild nightlife scene make Liverpool a great destination for travelers. Scousers—as Liverpudlians are colloquially known—are usually happy to introduce you to their dialect and humor, and to discuss the relative merits of Liverpool's two football teams. Oh, yeah—and the Beatles.

▣ TICKET TO RIDE

Trains: Lime St. Station. Ticket office open M-Sa 5:15am-12:30am, Su 7:15am-12:30pm. Luggage storage (☎ 702 2477) open daily 7am-10pm; £2. Trains (☎ (08457) 484950) from: **London Euston** (2hr., 1 per hr., £44, £19 Virgin Value fare available if purchased by 6pm previous day); **Chester** (45min., 2 per hr., £3); **Manchester** (1½hr., 2 per hr., £6.95); and **Birmingham** (2hr., 1 per hr., £18.50). The smaller **Moorfields, James St.,** and **Central** train stations serve mainly as transfer points to local **Merseyrail** trains (including service to Chester and Crewe).

Buses: Norton St. Coach Station services **National Express** (☎ (08705) 808080) from: **London** (4-5hr., 6 per day, day return £15, return £24); **Manchester** (1hr., 1 per hr., £4); and **Birmingham** (2½hr., 6 per day, return £12.50). Other buses stop at the **Queen Sq.** and **Paradise St.** stations.

Ferries: Liverpool Sea Terminal, Pier Head, just north of Albert Dock. Open daily 9am-5pm. The **Isle of Man Steam Packet Company** (☎ (08705) 523523) runs ferries to and from the Isle of Man and Dublin (see **Isle of Man: Getting There**).

Local Transportation: Private buses blanket the city and the surrounding Merseyside area. Consult the transport mavens at **Mersey Travel** (☎ 236 7676), in the tourist information centre. Open daily 8am-8pm.

Taxis: Local taxis are cheap and efficient. Try **Mersey Cabs** (☎ 298 2222).

Bike Rental: The **Hub Café Bar** (p. 331) has an attached cycle store (☎ 708 8819). £8 per day. Deposit of passport or driver's license. Open M-Sa 10am-6pm.

✳ ▣ HELP!

Although Liverpool is part of a vast metropolitan area sprawling across the River Mersey, its central district is pedestrian-friendly. The city has two clusters of museums: those on **William Brown St.,** near the main train station at Lime St., and those at **Albert Dock,** on the river. These flank the central shopping district, whose central axis comprises **Bold St., Church St.,** and **Lord St.** Most sights are within a 20-minute walk of the Lime St. station.

TOURIST, FINANCIAL, AND LOCAL SERVICES

Tourist Information Centre: Merseyside Welcome Centre (☎ 709 3631; fax 708 0204; www.merseyside.org.uk), in Queen Sq. Sells the handy *Visitor Guide to Liverpool and Merseyside* (£1), which contains lists of sights in the city and county and a city map. Books beds for a 10% deposit. Open M-Sa 10am-5:30pm, Su 10am-4:30pm. **Branch,** Atlantic Pavilion, Albert Dock (☎ 708 8854). Same hours.

Liverpool

▲ ACCOMMODATIONS
Belvadere Hotel,
Embassie Youth Hostel,
Feathers Hotel,
Lord Nelson Hotel,
Mulberry Court,
YHA Youth Hostel,
YWCA,

● FOOD
Café Tabac,
Hole in the Wall,
Hub Café-Bar,
Metz Café-Bar,

■ SHOPPING
News from Nowhere,
Quiggins,
The Palace,

📛 PUBS
Baa Bar,
Slatey Bar,
The Jacaranda,
The Philharmonic,
Ye Creek,

♪ CLUBS
Cream,
Heebiejeebees,
Le Bateau.

TO LAUNDERETTE,
ROYAL LIVERPOOL UNIV. HOSPITAL (0.5mi)

Kensington St.
Prescot St.
Sandon St.
FALKNER SQ.
Huskisson St.
Falkner St.
Myrtle St.
Canning St.
Catharine St.
Oxford St.
Percy St.
Hope St.
Pembroke Pl.
Brownlow Hill
Great Newton St.
Duckinfield St.
Daulby St.
Ariel St.
Hardman St.
Rice St.
Roscoe St.
Rodney St.
Upper Duke St.
Washington St.
Alfred St.
Hope St.
Seymour St.
Russell St.
St. Vincent St.
Norton St.
Mount Pleasant
Leece St.
Berry St.
Gt. George St.
Nelson St.
St. James St.
St. James Rd.
Jamaica St.
Copperas Hill
Hawke St.
Brownlow Hill
Renshaw St.
Grenville St. South
Bridgewater St.
Duncan St.
London Rd.
Lord Nelson St.
Lime St.
Ranelagh St.
Bold St.
Slater St.
Fleet St.
Concert St.
Duke St.
Kent St.
Park Ln.
Sparling St.
Chaloner St.
Elliot St.
Roe St.
QUEEN SQ.
Williamson St.
Church St.
Seel St.
Hanover St.
Seymour St.
Parr St.
Paradise St.
Canning Pl.
Canning Pl.
Liver St.
Wapping
North John St.
Lord St.
Dale St.
Victoria St.
Whitechapel
Mathew St.
South Castle St.
Castle St.
James St.
Water St.
Strand St.
Chapel St.
Rumford St.
Covent Garden
Exchange St. East

Metropolitan Cathedral
Everyman Theatre
Philharmonic Hall
Liverpool Cathedral
Lime St. Station
Norton St. Bus Station
Walker Art Gallery
Liverpool Museum
Wm. Brown St.
Empire Theatre
Conservation Centre
Queen Sq. Bus Station
St. John's Ln.
Central Train Station
Open Eye Gallery
The Bluecoat Centre
Beatles Shop
Cavern Club
American Express
Paradise St. Bus Station
Moorsfields Train Station
Exchange St. East
Pier Head (Ferries)
James St. Station
Museum of Liverpool Life
Merseyside Maritime Museum and Customs and Excise Museum
Tate Gallery
Albert Dock
Beatles Story
Queensway Tunnel

TO ANFIELD PARK, GORDON PARK,
ORMSKIRK (A59), & ABBEY FARM

tunnel entrance

River Mersey

300 yards
300 meters

N

Tours: Roll up for the big yellow and blue bus of the **Magical Mystery Tour** (☎ 236 9091), which leaves for the city's Beatles sites daily at 2:30pm from Albert Dock and the Welcome Centre. (2hr., £10.95; book ahead.) **Phil Hughes** (☎ 228 4565) runs an excellent Beatles tour, taking you *everywhere* that's connected with Liverpool's favorite sons in an 8-seat minivan (2hr., call for times, £9). Numerous other bus tours (from £4) and walking tours (£1) rotate throughout the summer; the TIC has the leaflets if you have the feet. Ferry 'cross the Mersey with the river cruises of **Mersey Ferries.** (☎ 333 1444. 50min., £3.50, concessions £2.50.)

Budget Travel: Campus Travel, 25 Bold St. (☎ 709 9200), in the YHA Adventure Shop. Open M-W and F 9:30am-5:30pm, Th and Sa 9:30am-6pm.

Financial Services: The city has many banks, including **Barclays,** 9-11 Whitechapel (☎ 801 3500). Open M-Tu and Th-F 9am-5pm, W 10am-5pm, Sa 9:30am-5pm.

American Express: 54 Lord St. (☎ 702 4501). Members' mail held. Open M-F 9am-5:30pm, Sa 9am-5pm.

Launderette: Fabricare Dry Cleaners, 104 Prescot Rd. (☎ 263 7451). Take bus #9 or 10. Change and soap available. Open M-F 9am-5:30pm.

EMERGENCY AND COMMUNICATIONS

Police: Canning Pl. (☎ 709 6010).

Hotlines: The Samaritans (☎ 708 8888). Open 24hr. **Gay/Lesbian Friend** (☎ 708 9552). Open daily 7-10pm.

Hospital: Royal Liverpool Hospital, Prescot St. (☎ 706 2000).

Internet Access: Central Library, William Brown St. The computer room is up the stairs on the left. Friendly staff, several computers. £1 per 30min. Open M-Sa 9am-5:30pm. Also **Planet Electra,** 36 London Rd. (☎ 708 0303). Serves sandwiches and offers Internet access for £2.50 per 30min. 20% student discount and reduced morning rates. Open M-W and Sa 10am-5:30pm, Th 10am-7:30pm, F 10am-6pm.

Post Office: 42-44 Houghton Way (☎ 708 4165), in St. John's Shopping Centre. **Branch** in the splendid Lyceum building on Bold St. Both open M-F 9am-5:30pm, Sa 9am-7pm. **Postal Code:** L1 1AA.

▌ A HARD DAY'S NIGHT

Your best bet for cheap accommodations lies east of the city center. **Lord Nelson St.,** adjacent to the train station, is lined with modest hotels, and similar establishments are found along **Mount Pleasant,** one block from Brownlow Hill and the bus stop. Stay only at places approved by the tourist information centre (TIC). Both of Liverpool's hostels are full of young music-loving travelers, making for great roomand pub-mates. Demand for rooms is highest in summer, as well as in early April when jockeys and gamblers gallop into town for the Grand National Race.

▨ **Embassie Youth Hostel,** 1 Falkner Sq. (☎ 707 1089). 15-20min. walk from the bus or train stations or a £2 taxi ride. Feels like a laid-back student's flat, with laundry, TV lounge, pool table, and kitchen, as well as all the toast and jam you can eat, all day, every day. One of England's friendliest hostels—ask the energetic staff for pub-crawling tips, or ask Kevin to tell you about the time his band outplaced John Lennon's in a talent competition. No lockout, curfew, or checkout time. Dorms £12.50 first night, £11.50 each additional night.

YHA Liverpool, 24 Tabley St., The Wapping (☎ 709 8888; fax 709 0417; liverpool@yha.org.uk). Spanking new, with comfortable, large, and clean rooms and friendly staff. Ideal location next to Albert Dock. Laundry and kitchen facilities. No lockout. Dorms £17.40, under 18 £13.10.

YWCA, 1 Rodney St. (☎ 709 7791), just off Mt. Pleasant. For both men and women. Renovated rooms are sparkling clean, attractively decorated, and surprisingly spacious, with firm beds. Kitchen, limited laundry facilities (no soap or change available), and hot showers. Key deposit £15 for stays longer than 5 nights. No lockout or curfew. £12 per person; discounted weekly rates.

Belvedere Hotel, 83 Mt. Pleasant (☎ 709 2356). This family-run guest house in the city center has small, comfortable rooms with TVs. Singles £18.50; doubles £37.

University of Liverpool: Mulberry Court, Oxford St. (☎ 794 3298). Clean but spartan self-catering accommodations for £16 per person. The university-wide conference office (☎ 794 6440) has information on other halls open to travelers (£15 including continental breakfast). All university accommodations open mid-July to mid-Sept.

Camping: Abbey Farm, Dark Ln., Ormskirk (☎ (01695) 572686), on the northern rail line from Lime St. station. A £2.50 taxi ride from Ormskirk station. Free showers. Wheelchair access. £4 for 1-person tent; £7 for 2-person tent.

SAVOY TRUFFLE

Trendy vegetarian cafes and reasonably priced Indian restaurants line **Bold St.** and **Hardman St.,** while cheap takeouts crowd **Hardnon St.** and **Berry St.** Liverpool parties late, and many restaurants stay open until 3am. Self-caterers should try **St. John's Market,** sprawled across the top of St. John's shopping mall, for fresh produce and local color.

Metz Café-Bar, Rainford Gdns. (☎ 227 2282), off Mathew St. "Don't discriminate, integrate," they proclaim. At this gay-friendly candlelit underground establishment, everyone's welcome to taste their esoteric and tasty lunch sandwich and soup combos (£4.25; served noon-7pm). Dinner's delightful too, but more expensive (*starigrad* lamb £9.50). Open M-Th noon-11pm, F-Sa noon-midnight, Su noon-10:30pm.

not sushi, Exchange St. East (☎ 709 8894), near Dale St. Opposite the town hall. Watch chefs prepare the primarily Japanese dishes (main courses £5.95-6.95) through huge glass windows as you slurp your noodles. Open M-Sa 11am-11:30pm.

Hub Café Bar, Berry St. (☎ 707 9495). Furniture made out of bicycle parts in a cafe that dishes out light veggie and vegan meals (£1.50-3); the quality of the food spokes for itself. Open M-Sa 10am-6pm.

Hole in the Wall, School Ln. This self-described "coffee lounge" serves scrumptious sandwiches and sweets (£3-5) on two light-filled floors. Open daily noon-6pm.

Café Tabac, 126 Bold St. (☎ 707 3735). Plan your evening by perusing the postered primary-colored walls. An inexpensive and tasty, if traditional, menu (£2-5) and eclectic wines. Open M-Sa 9:30am-11pm, Su 10am-5pm.

MAGICAL MYSTERY TOUR

With classy museums, awe-inspiring cathedrals, and the twin religions of football and the Beatles, Liverpool encourages the tourist to fall in love with the North. **Hope Street,** southeast of the city center, connects Liverpool's two 20th-century cathedrals. Most other sights are located on **Albert Dock,** an open rectangle of Victorian warehouses recently transformed into a cluster of offices, restaurants, and museums. Many museums on Albert Dock and William Brown St. come under the **Eight-Museum Pass** (£3, students and seniors £1.50, children under 16 free); paying for entry into any one museum lets you into all the museums for a year. Visitors intending to visit only the attractions on the dock can purchase a **Waterfront Pass** from the Atlantic Pavilion branch of the TIC (£9.99, concessions £6). It includes admission to the Beatles Story, the Merseyside Maritime Museum, the Museum of Liverpool Life, and a Mersey Ferries cruise.

TATE GALLERY. The intimate Liverpool branch of the London institution contains a select and impressive range of 20th-century artwork. British artists such as Lucian Freud, Damien Hirst, and Francis Bacon dominate the ground floor, while the floor above shows an annually-shifting exhibition from the Gallery's archives. By prior arrangement, the staff will fit the visually impaired with special gloves and allow them to touch some of the art. (*Albert Dock.* ☎ *709 3223. Open Tu-Su 10am-6pm. Wheelchair access. Free; some special exhibits £3, concessions £1.*)

NORTHWEST ENGLAND

MERSEYSIDE MARITIME MUSEUM. Liverpool's heyday as a major port has passed, but the six floors of this museum, which recreates something of the horror of the slave trade and the bomb-induced carnage of the Battle of Britain, continue to impress. Wander through the cramped hull of a slave trader's ship or down a dimly lit dockside street to the voices of desperate emigrants waiting to leave to the New World. A floor above, fans of a certain movie starring Leonardo DiCaprio can check items recovered from the "unsinkable" ship. Attached to the Maritime Museum is the **H.M. Customs and Excise Museum,** with an intriguing array of confiscated goods from would-be smugglers, including throwing stars, a fountain pen that shoots chili powder, and a teddy bear full of cocaine. *(Albert Dock.* ☎ *478 4499. Open daily 10am-5pm, last admission 4pm. Admission with Eight-Museum Pass.)*

METROPOLITAN CATHEDRAL OF CHRIST THE KING. Dubbed "Paddy's Wigwam" by locals, the city's Roman Catholic cathedral looks more like a rocket launcher than a house of worship. Inside, long strips of neon blue stained glass cast a warm, soothing glow on the circular interior. Modern sculptures fill niches and chapels, but despite its *Star Trek* look, the cathedral sticks to some traditions—the organists weren't allowed to play pop music until a 1981 memorial service for John Lennon. *(Mt. Pleasant.* ☎ *709 9222. Open daily in summer 8am-6pm; in winter M-Sa 8am-6pm, Su 8am-5pm. Wheelchair access. Free.)*

THE BEATLES STORY. This exhibit includes recreations of Hamburg, the Cavern Club (complete with "basement smells"), and a shiny Yellow Submarine. Shed a tear on John Lennon's white piano before you leave. *(Albert Dock.* ☎ *709 1963. Open daily Apr.-Oct. 10am-6pm; Nov.-Mar. 10am-5pm. £6.95, concessions £4.95, families £17.)*

For other Beatles-themed locales, pick up the **Beatles Map** for £2.50 at the TIC: it takes you down to Strawberry Fields and Penny Lane. Souvenir hunters can raid the **Beatles Shop,** stuffed with memorabilia. *(31 Mathew St.* ☎ *236 9091. Open M-Sa 9:30am-5:30pm, Su 11am-4pm.)*

LIVERPOOL CATHEDRAL. Begun in 1904 and completed in 1978, this Anglican cathedral is *vast*, featuring the highest Gothic arches ever built (107 ft.), the largest vault and organ (9704 pipes), and the highest and heaviest bells in the world. Take two lifts and climb the final 108 stairs to the top of the tower for a view stretching to Wales. *(Upper Duke St.* ☎ *709 6271. Cathedral open daily 9am-6pm; tower open daily 11am-4pm, weather permitting. Cathedral free. Tower admission £2, children £1.)*

WALKER ART GALLERY. This stately gallery houses a huge collection containing works that date from 1300 and including a variety of impressive post-Impressionist and pre-Raphaelite paintings. *(William Brown St.* ☎ *478 4199. Open M-Sa 10am-5pm, Su noon-5pm. Admission with Eight-Museum Pass.)*

CONSERVATION CENTRE. A small interactive museum on the ground floor of the conservation studios and labs for the National Museum and Galleries of Merseyside, the Centre allows insight into the decisions and processes of art conservation, restoration, and preservation. The hands-on exhibits are particularly engaging for children. *(Whitechapel.* ☎ *478 4999. Open M-Sa 10am-5pm, Su noon-5pm. Admission with Eight-Museum Pass. Tours W and Sa 2pm and 3pm for extra charge.)*

THE MUSEUM OF LIVERPOOL LIFE. This museum traces Liverpool's history of stormy labor struggles and race relations, as well as the city's sporting heritage. A TV runs footage of legendary football matches between Liverpool and Everton, while a plaque marks out Grand National-winning horses. *(Albert Dock.* ☎ *478 4080. Open daily 10am-5pm, last admission 4pm. Admission with Eight-Museum Pass.)*

LIVERPOOL MUSEUM. A natural history exhibit with a carved narwhal horn, a vivarium with live animals including fire-bellied toads, and a planetarium fill this museum, near the Walker Art Gallery. It's still open despite renovations. *(*☎ *478 4399. Open same hours as the Walker. Admission with Eight-Museum Pass.)*

LIVERPOOL AND EVERTON FOOTBALL CLUBS. If you're not here for the Beatles, you're probably here for the football. The rivalry between the city's two main clubs is one of the country's deepest and most passionate. **Liverpool** and **Everton** both offer tours of their grounds (Goodison Park and Anfield respectively) as well as match tickets when available. *(Both stadiums can be reached by bus #26 from the city center. Liverpool ☎ 260 6677. Everton ☎ 330 2266. Tours from £5. Tickets from £14.)*

◪ COME TOGETHER

Pubs teem in almost every street in Liverpool. Two of the city's most notable products—football fans and rock musicians—were born in the pub culture. Liverpool has continued to incorporate these traditions into its present pub renaissance. **Slater St.** in particular brims with £1 pints.

The Jacaranda, 21-23 Slater St. (☎ 708 0233). The site of the first paid Beatles gig, the Jacaranda has a basement where the Beatles did the original paintwork. Live bands still play, and a small dance floor lets you kick loose. Open M-Sa noon-2am.

The Philharmonic, 36 Hope St. (☎ 709 1163). John Lennon once said that the worst thing about being famous was "not being able to get a quiet pint at the Phil." The non-celebrities among us can still get that silent beer, and at reasonable prices (draughts £1.60). Worth going into just to see some of Britain's most ornate bathrooms. Open M-Sa 11:30am-11pm, Su 7-10:30pm.

Slaters Bar, Slater St. Cheap shots and a young crowd jamming by the jukebox. Open M-Sa 11am-2am, Su noon-10:30pm.

Baa Bar, 43-45 Fleet St. (☎ 707 0610), off Bold St. Attracts a lesbian, gay, and trendy crowd for cappuccino during the day and cheap beer at night. Open M-Sa 10am-2am.

Ye Crack, 13 Rice St. (☎ 709 4171). Where John Lennon used to finish off lathery pints, sometimes with then-girlfriend Cynthia. Closes 11pm.

♫ ❀ PLEASE PLEASE ME

Liverpool has a thriving arts and nightlife scene. The free monthly *Ink* (http://talk.to/ink), available at the TIC and many cafes, offers the most up-to-date arts information, as does the *Liverpool Echo*, an evening paper sold by street corner vendors that also includes local news (30p). The emporia of **Quiggins,** 12-16 School Ln. (☎ 709 2462), and the **Palace,** 6-10 Slater St., both sell hipster paraphernalia and have tons of flyers detailing the club scene. For alternative events, check the bulletin board in the **Everyman Bistro,** 9-11 Hope St., where bohemian happenings often occur in the attached **Third Room.** (☎ 708 9545. Open M-Sa noon-midnight.) Read about events at gay and lesbian clubs in **News From Nowhere,** 96 Bold St., a feminist bookshop run by a women's cooperative. (☎ 708 7270. Open M-Sa 10am-5:45pm.)

CLUBS

▨ Cream (☎ 709 1693), in Wolstonholme Sq., off Parr St. In a word, *brilliant*. The queue goes on forever, because people travel from all over Britain (and the world) to come to this nationally-renowned superclub. Steep prices, but it's an amazing party. Cover £11. Open Sa, plus last F of the month, 10pm-4am.

The Cavern Club, 10 Mathew St. (☎ 236 9091). Regular club music on the site where the Fab Four gained prominence, and with the same decor. Club open M and Th-Sa 9pm-2am, pub open from noon. Free admission before 10pm. Live music Sa 2-6pm.

Heebiejebees, 80-82 Seel St. (☎ 709 2666). Billed as "the house that jazz built," this gritty club also plays everything from French pop to Jungle. No cover. Open M and W-Sa.

Le Bateau, 62 Duke St. (☎ 709 6508), swings with 60s music upstairs at **Uptight,** and loosens up with a mellow club downstairs. Cover £5. F-Sa 9pm-3am, hours may vary.

Garland's, 8-10 Eberle St. (☎ 236 3307), off Dale St., is a lesbian and gay club which prides itself on being tolerant of all. House music, plus off-the-wall special events. Cover £5-10. Open F-Sa 10:30pm-4am, open until 6:30am last F of the month.

MUSIC, THEATER, AND FESTIVALS

■ **Bluecoat Centre** (☎ 708 8877; box office ☎ 709 5297), off School Ln., began in 1717 as a charity school and now functions as Liverpool's performing arts center. An art school atmosphere permeates the exhibition spaces. Offers workshops in art, dance, and music; linger in the cafe and second-hand bookstore. Open M-Sa 10am-5pm; box office open M-F 11am-4pm; gallery open Tu-Sa 10:30am-5pm.

Philharmonic Hall, Hope St. (☎ 709 3789). One of the better English orchestras, the **Royal Liverpool Philharmonic,** performs at the hall. Also featured are an array of concerts by other groups, including jazz and funk bands. Box office open M-Sa 10:30am-5:30pm, Su noon-5pm. Wheelchair access. Philharmonic tickets from £8; 25% student and disabled discount; half-price on day of show W and Sa.

Liverpool Empire Theatre, Lime St. (☎ 709 1555), hosts a variety of dramatic performances, welcoming such famous troupes as the Royal Shakespeare Company. Box office open M-Sa 10am-8pm on performance days, else M-Sa 10am-6pm. Wheelchair access. Tickets from £6, with some student and senior discounts.

Everyman Theatre (☎ 709 4776), at the corner of Hope St. and Oxford St., provides space for adventurous contemporary theatrical productions. Box office open M-F 10am-6pm, Sa noon-6pm. Tickets from £7, some concessions.

Festivals: Liverpool hosts many conventions and festivals throughout the year, ranging from the **International Street Theatre Festival** (early Aug.) to the **Mersey River Festival** (mid-June). At the end of August, a week-long **Beatles Convention** draws pop fans and bewildered entomologists from around the world.

MANCHESTER   ☎0161

The Industrial Revolution transformed the once unremarkable village of Manchester into a northern hub, now Britain's second-largest urban conglomeration. A center of industrial innovation, Manchester also spawned a hotbed of liberal politics, feeding the thoughts of Engels, among others. The city stays loose today, savoring its reputation as one of the hippest spots in England. Derided by Ruskin as a "devil's darkness," parts of the semi-gentrified city are still somewhat dodgy; a more dimly lit city would be hard to find, and assiduous street cleaners must pick their battles. With few comely corners and fewer budget accommodations in the city center, Manchester proves that it's not just the pretty who are popular, attracting thousands with its pulsing nightlife and vibrant arts scene.

⌐ GETTING THERE AND GETTING AROUND

Flights: Manchester International Airport (☎ 489 3000; international arrivals ☎ (0839) 888747, domestic arrivals ☎ (0839) 888757, both 50p per min.). Trains (25min.; 4 per hr., 24hr. a day; £2.50) and buses #44 and 105 head to Piccadilly.

Trains: Manchester Piccadilly, London Rd., serves mostly trains from the south, east, and Scotland. Travel center open M-Sa 8am-8:30pm, Su 11am-7pm. Trains (☎ (08457) 484950) from: **London Euston** (2½hr., at least 1 per hr., £84.50); **York** (40min., 2 per hr., £15.80); **Chester** (1hr., 1 per hr., £8.50); **Birmingham** (1¾hr., 2 per hr., £14.20); and **Edinburgh** (4hr., 12 per day, £41.60 via Carlisle, £51.50 via York). **Manchester Victoria,** Victoria St., serves mostly trains from the west and north. Travel center open M-Sa 8:30am-6pm. From **Liverpool** (50min., 2 per hr., £6.95). Both stations open 24hr. and connected by Metrolink.

Buses: Chorlton St Coach Station, Chorlton St. Office open M-F 7:15am-7pm, Sa-Su 7:15am-6:15pm. Luggage storage £2; open 9am-6pm. **National Express** (☎ (08705) 808080) from: **London** (4-5hr., 7 per day, £15); **Liverpool** (50min., 1 per hr., £4); **Leeds** (1hr., 1 per hr., £5.50); and **Sheffield** (1½hr., 6 per day, £5.75).

Public Transportation: Piccadilly Gardens is home to about 50 **bus** stops. Pick up a free route map from the TIC. Buses generally run until 11:30pm, weekends until 2:30am. Office open M-Sa 7am-6pm, Su 10am-6pm. All-day ticket £3. **Metrolink** trams

(☎ 205 2000) link 8 stops in the city center with Altrincham in the southwest, Bury in the northeast, and Eccles in the west (every 5-15min., £1-5). Combined bus and tram ticket £5. **GMPTE information line:** ☎ 228 7811; www.gmpte.gov.uk. Open 8am-8pm.

Taxis: Mantax (☎ 236 5133).

✳❷ ORIENTATION AND PRACTICAL INFORMATION

The city center lies mostly within the rather odd polygon formed by **Victoria Station** to the north, **Piccadilly Station** to the east, **G-Mex** and the canals to the south, and the **River Irwell** to the west. Although the area is fairly compact, and several pedestrian streets makes it easy to get around on foot, the many by-ways and side streets require a good map. Fortunately, many streets bear very clear, illuminated, poster-sized maps, and Manchester residents are generally helpful.

Tourist Information Centre: Manchester Visitor Centre, Town Hall Extension, Lloyd St. (☎ 234 3157, 24hr. info ☎ (0891) 715533). Helpful staff books accommodations (£2.50 plus 10% deposit). Free literature includes a city map, the *Manchester Pocket Guide*, the *Greater Manchester Network Map,* and *What's On*, which lists local events. City **tour** information also available. Open M-Sa 10am-5:30pm, Su 11am-4pm.

Financial Services: Banks include: **Barclays,** 51 Mosley St. (☎ 228 3322). Open M-Tu and Th-F 9:30am-4:30pm, W 10am-4:30pm. **Thomas Cook,** 2 Oxford St. (☎ 236 8575), and 23 Market St. Open M-W and F-Sa 9am-5:30pm, Th 10am-5:30pm.

American Express: 10-12 St. Mary's Gate (☎ 833 0121). Open M-F 9am-5:30pm, Sa 9am-4pm.

Launderette: Mr. Bubbles, 246 Wilmslow Rd. (☎ 257 2640). Change and soap available. Open daily 8am-8pm; last wash 7pm.

Police: Chester House, Bootle St. (☎ 872 5050 or ☎ 273 2081).

Hotlines: Samaritans, 72-74 Oxford St. (☎ 236 8000).

Hospital: Manchester Royal Infirmary (☎ 276 1234), Oxford Rd.

Internet Access: interc@fe (☎ 832 8666), Piccadilly Sq., on the 1st floor of Debenhams department store. £1.50 per 30min., first 30min. free with food purchase. Open M and W-F 9:30am-5:30pm, Tu 10am-5:30pm, Sa 9am-5:30pm, Su 11am-4:30pm. Also **Cyberia** (see p. 339) and **YHA Manchester** (see below).

Post Office: 26 Spring Gdns. (☎ 839 0687). Open M-Tu and Th-F 8:30am-6pm, W 9am-6pm, Sa 8:30am-7pm. Poste Restante has a separate entrance (☎ 834 8605). Open M-F 6am-5:30pm, Sa 6am-12:30pm. **Postal Code:** M2 2AA.

▌ ACCOMMODATIONS

Manchester is only slowly awakening to the demand for budget accommodations, and cheap stays in the city center are still hard to find. Summer offers the possibility of **student housing,** a decently priced option. The highest concentration of budget lodgings is found two to three miles south of the city center in the suburbs of **Fallowfield, Withington,** and **Didsbury;** take bus #40, 42, or 157 to reach any of the small hotels, B&Bs, and university residence halls inhabiting these areas. Browse the listings in *Where to Stay,* available at the tourist information centre (TIC). The TIC staff can scour the town for places within your price range, sometimes getting better rates and special prices, but don't forget the £2.50 fee and 10% deposit.

YHA Manchester, Potato Wharf, Castlefield (☎ 839 9960; fax 835 2054; manchester@yha.org.uk). Take bus #33 from Piccadilly Gardens towards Wigan. Raising hosteling to swanky heights, the sleek reception area with black leather couches leads to spacious rooms with showers. Breakfast included. Laundry £1.50 per load. Lockers £1-2. Members' kitchen and restaurant. Internet access £2.50 for 30min. Currency exchange. Reception open 7am-11:30pm. Wheelchair access. Dorms £17.40, under 18 £13.10; £1 student discount.

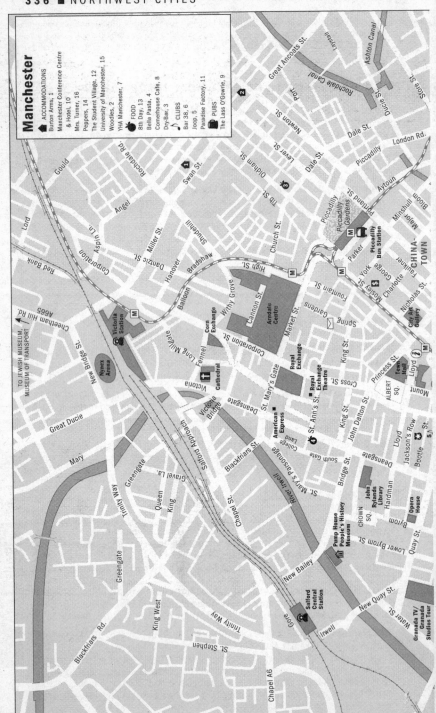

Manchester

▲ ACCOMMODATIONS
Burton Arms, 1
Manchester Conference Centre & Hotel, 10
Mrs. Turner, 16
Peppers, 14
The Student Village, 12
University of Manchester, 15
YHA Manchester, 7
Woodies, 2

♥ FOOD
8th Day, 13
Bella Pasta, 4
Cornerhouse Cafe, 8
Dry-Bar, 3

♪ CLUBS
Bar 38, 6
Joop, 5
Paradise Factory, 11

PUBS
The Lass O'Gowrie, 9

Woodies Backpackers Hostel, 19 Blossom St., Ancoats (☎/fax 228 3456; backpackers@woodiesuk.freeserve.co.uk). The hostel is just beyond the Duke of Edinburgh pub on Blossom St., in a ghost-like part of town. Comfortable dorm accommodations, with TV lounge, kitchen, laundry, free luggage storage, and a friendly, well-traveled staff. Good security. No lockout or curfew. Dorms £12 per night, £60 per week.

Manchester Conference Centre and Hotel (☎/fax 955 8000), Sackville St. Part of this center is a pricey hotel, but the center also offers student halls in a convenient location from mid-June to Sept. Singles £25; £19 through the TIC, including booking fee.

The Student Village (☎ 236 1776; www.thestudentvillage.com), Lower Chatham St. 1039 summer rooms available. A 10min. walk from St. Peter's Sq. Singles £17.

University of Manchester: St. Gabriels Hall, 1-3 Oxford Pl., Victoria Park (☎ 224 7061). Self-catering dorms during school vacations. Reserve a week or more in advance with deposit. 3-day min. stay. Singles £12, students £7; twins £20, students £12. If full, try **Woolton Hall** (☎ 224 7244), Whitworth Ln., Fallowfield. £12 per person, subject to additional VAT. For info on these and other residence halls, contact the **University Accommodation Office** (☎ 275 2888). Open M-F 9:30am-5pm.

Peppers, 17 Great Stone Rd., Stretford (☎/fax 848 9770). Take the Metrolink to Old Trafford (12min.), walk past the cricket ground and turn left, then take the first right onto Great Stone Rd. Simple hostel accommodations. Internet access. £3 key deposit. Dorms £8; twins £10 per person; singles £14.

Burton Arms, 31 Swan St. (☎/fax 834 3455). Basic rooms above a pub on a busy street. A 15min. walk from both train stations and St. Peter's Sq. Full English breakfast included. £19.50 per person, with bath £25.

◖ FOOD

Downtown Manchester offers numerous fast food places and cheap, charmless cafes. Outwit the pricey Chinatown restaurants by eating the multi-course "Businessman's Lunch" offered by most (served M-F noon-2pm; $4-8, with or without the briefcase and masculine gender). Hip youths and yuppies wine and dine in the cafe-bars (see p. 341). For nocturnal appetites, kebab/burger/fish and chips joints on **Whitworth St. West** are open until 4am. A **Tesco** supermarket awaits on Market St. (☎ 835 3339. Open M-Sa 8am-8pm, Su 11am-5pm.)

Cornerhouse Café, 70 Oxford St. (☎ 228 7621). Part of the Cornerhouse Arts Centre, it features a bar, 3 galleries, 3 arthouse cinemas, and trendy crowds. Salads £2.50, main courses from £3.50, desserts from 70p. Open daily 11am-8:30pm; hot meals served noon-2:30pm and 5-7pm; bar open M-Sa noon-11pm, Su noon-10:30pm.

On the 8th Day, 107-111 Oxford Rd. (☎ 273 1850.) An eclectic, dynamic menu of vegetarian and vegan fare. The prices are as appetizing as the flavors, with most meals under £4. Student discounts sweeten the pot. Open M-F 9am-7pm, Sa 10am-4:30pm.

Green Room Theatre Café, 54-56 Whitworth St. West (☎ 950 5777). The minimalist metal and wood interiors are as hip as you'd expect from a cafe next to a theater. Menu includes "leafy herby salad" and no red meat. Snacks £1.50-4.25. Delectable main courses from £5. Food served M-Sa noon-3pm and 6-7:45pm.

Bella Pasta (☎ 832 4332), Deansgate and St. Mary's St. While meals can be budget stretchers (£5-9), portions are large and delicious, and with many cheaper starters and side orders (£1.25-5). Open M-Th 11am-11pm, F 11am-midnight, Su noon-11pm.

◖ SIGHTS

Few of Manchester's buildings are notable—postcards mostly portray the front of trams—but an exception is the neo-Gothic **Manchester Town Hall,** at St. Peter's Sq. Behind the Town Hall Extension is the city's real jewel, the **Central Library.** One of the largest municipal libraries in Europe, the domed building has a music and theater library, an excellent language and literature library, and the UK's second-largest Judaica collection. The Library Theatre Company puts on several shows a year;

2001 productions include *Aladdin* and *Death of a Salesman*. (Library ☎ 234 1900, theater ☎ 236 7110. Open M-Th 10am-8pm, F-Sa 10am-5pm.) The **John Rylands Library,** 150 Deansgate, holds rare books and nifty exhibits in a neo-Gothic fortress. (☎ 834 5343. Open M-F 10am-5:30pm, Sa 10am-1pm. Free. Tours W at noon; £1.)

The **City Art Galleries** (☎ 236 5244) are closed for renovations for the foreseeable future. In the **Museum of Science and Industry,** Liverpool Rd. in Castlefield, working steam engines and looms provide a dramatic vision of the awesome power, danger, and noise of Britain's industrialization. (☎ 832 1830. Open daily 10am-5pm. Wheelchair access. £5, concessions £3.) The Spanish and Portuguese Synagogue-turned-**Jewish Museum,** 190 Cheetham Hill Rd. north of Victoria Station, traces the history of the city's sizeable Jewish community and offers city tours. (☎ 834 9879. Open M-Th 10:30am-4pm, Su 10:30am-5pm. Wheelchair access to ground floor. £3.25, concessions £2.50, families £8.) Loved and reviled, Manchester United is England's best-known football team. The **Manchester United Museum and Tour Centre,** Sir Matt Busby Way, at the Old Trafford football stadium (follow the signs up Warwick Rd. from the Old Trafford Metrolink stop), displays memorabilia commemorating the club from its inception in 1878 to its recent trophy-hogging success. (☎ 877 4002. Museum open daily 9am-5pm. Tours run every 10min., 9:40am-4:30pm. Museum £4.50, seniors and children £3. Museum and tour £7.50, £5.)

 ## MUSIC AND THEATER

One of Manchester's biggest draws is its artistic community, most notably the energetic theater and music scenes. Besides those listed below, Manchester's other major concert venue is the **Nynex Arena** (☎ 950 8000), behind Victoria Station.

Royal Exchange Theatre (☎ 833 9833), has returned to St. Ann's Sq., a few years after an IRA bomb destroyed the original building. The theater regularly puts on Shakespeare and world premieres of original works. Box office open M-Sa 9:30am-7:30pm. M-Th and Sa tickets £7-23, concessions £5 when booked 3 days in advance; separate concession rates apply to W and Sa matinees.

G-Mex (☎ 832 9000), Lower Mosley St. The Greater Manchester Exhibition and Event Centre hosts pop, jazz, and classical concerts in its renovated train station; the front side closely resembles the head of space villain Darth Vader.

Bridgewater Hall (☎ 907 9000), across from the G-Mex. The new home for the superb Hallé Orchestra, directed by Kent Nagano, proves that glass and metal can make for stunning architecture.

Palace Theatre (☎ 242 2503), Oxford St. Caters to more classical tastes in theater, opera, and ballet. Box office open M-Sa 10am-6pm, until 8pm on performance days; Su 2hr. before performance. Some student discounts.

 ## FESTIVALS

Manchester offers many festivals to further entertain the weary traveler. **The Boddington Manchester Festival of the Arts and Television** takes place in September and October. **The Manchester Festival** (www.the-manchester-festival.org.uk) runs all summer long, with dramatic, musical, and multi-media events. Call the Central Library (☎ 234 1944) for information on both events. The Gay Village also hosts a number of festivals, most notably **Mardi Gras** (☎ 237 3237), in late August, which raises money for AIDS relief. The **Independence Festival** (☎ 234 3160) brings in millions of disabled people for a giant celebration in early September.

 ## NIGHTLIFE

CAFE-BARS
Manchester's *très chic* cafe-bar scene defies categorization. Excellent lunchtime chatting spots with reasonable food prices, the bars morph into perfect pre-club drinking venues—or even become clubs themselves. Classifications are murky: in

the **Clubs** section, Generation X and Joop both have good cafe-bars; in the **Food** section, the Cornerhouse and Green Room Cafés both offer stylish locales for the chic to drink, not just eat. Below are our picks for the hippest spots.

▨**The Lass O'Gowrie,** 36 Charles St. (☎ 273 6932). Traditional pubs aren't passé when the late evening crowd is this lively. In the afternoon, BBC personalities trickle in from the neighboring studio, and students trickle in between classes. Good food at amazing prices (£1-3). Open M-Sa 11am-11pm, Su 11:30am-10:30pm. Food served 9am-7pm.

Cyberia, 12 Oxford St. (☎ 950 2233). Not your average cybercafe, Cyberia's metallic decor aptly fits the digerati filling it at night. Internet access £3 per 30min., £5 per hr.; students £2.40 per 30min., £4 per hr. Open M-F 9am-10pm, Sa-Su 11am-10pm.

Temple of Convenience, 100 Great Bridgewater St. (☎ 288 9834), just off Oxford St. A subterranean location creates an intimate atmosphere that draws a bohemian crowd. The name refers to the place's former life as a restroom. Open daily 11am-11pm.

Dry Bar, 28-30 Oldham St. (☎ 236 9840). Founded by Factory Records and the band New Order, this sleek super-long bar draws in the beautiful people after dark. Happy hour M-F 4-8pm, Su all day. Open M-Th noon-1am, F-Sa noon-2am, Su noon-10:30pm.

CLUBS

Manchester's clubbing and live music scene remains a national trendsetter, although the loss of the Hacienda has left the city without any truly large-scale club. Those in the know hang around **Oldham St.** during the day to get a whiff of what's on for the evening. Don't forget to collect flyers—they often get you a discount. **Afflecks Palace,** 52 Church St., supplies groovesters with paraphernalia—from punk to funk—for their exploits; the walls of the stairway are postered with flyers advertising the evening's events. (☎ 834 2039. Open M-F 10am-5:30pm, Sa 10am-6pm.) Just up Oldham St., **Fat City** sells drum 'n' bass and hip-hop records, as well as passes to hip events. (☎ 237 1181. Open M-Sa 10am-5:30pm.)

The revitalization of the derelict **Northern Quarter** is slowly cranking into gear; however, night-time streets are dimly lit. If you're crossing from Piccadilly to Swan St. or Great Ancoats St., use Oldham St., where the bright lights of late-night clubs (and the presence of their bouncers) provide reassurance. There's also no shame in short taxi trips at night in this town.

▨**Generation X,** 11-13 New Wakefield St. (☎ 236 4899). If you're "mad for it," house and breakbeat play on the roof terrace; the cafe-bar below features more conventional music. Mellow out at **Regeneration,** its *après*-clubbing Sunday chill-down. Cover £2 after 11pm. Open F-Sa until 2am, Su noon-10:30pm.

Joop, 47 Peter St. (☎ 839 6263). Attracts a massive 18-25 crowd. House and garage on weekends, 70s music on Wednesdays, anything-goes mix on Thursdays. Just don't wear trainers. No cover. Open W-Sa noon-2am.

The Boardwalk (☎ 228 3555), Little Peter St. Take a break from cutting-edge club music and indulge in your taste for commercial dance—funk on Fridays, and an eclectic Molotov Pop night on Saturday. Plastic cups for drinks are a bit of a put-off. Cover £3-4. Open W-Th 10pm-midnight, F 10pm-2am, Sa 11pm-3am.

Velvet Underground, 111 Deansgate (☎ 834 9975), under the enormous "V". Speed garage and underground house play to the twentysomething, women-strong crowd. Chill out on the plush red sofas. Cover £8, students £4. Open F-Sa 10pm-3am.

THE GAY VILLAGE

Gay and lesbian clubbers will want to check out The Gay Village, northeast of Princess St. Evening crowds fill the bars lining **Canal St.,** in the heart of the area, which is also a lovely, lively place during the day. When weather cooperates, the bars are busy but empty, with patrons flooding the sidewalk tables.

Manto's, 46 Canal St. (☎ 236 2667). Fills its purple interior with all ages, genders, and orientations. Saturday night/Sunday morning "Breakfast Club" 2-6am. Cover £5.

Bar 38, 10 Canal St. (☎ 236 6005). Swooping balconies nest in the mod deco interior that serves as a daytime cafe-bar and transcends into a nighttime dance club. No cover. Open M-W 10am-midnight, Th-Sa 10am-2am, clubbish from 9pm on weekends.

Paradise Factory, 114-116 Princess St. (☎ 228 2966). The site for 2 of the biggest nights in Manchester's gay scene—**Chocolate Factory** (F) and **Paramount Paradise** (Sa)—plays a mix of house, commercial dance, and more. Look for the shiny purple tiles around the entrance. Occasional student promotions. Cover varies £3-10.

BLACKPOOL ☎01253

At the end of the 18th century, Blackpool was a quiet resort town that catered to a small number of well-to-do holiday-makers. Things have changed considerably, earning Blackpool its current title of King of Tack. The present era of raucous gaudiness grew from the railways built in the 1840s, and the introduction of open-air dancing (1870) and electric street lighting (1879). By the end of the 19th century, droves of working class Brits from Lancashire and Yorkshire were pouring in. Today, the resort town's amusements are mind-numbingly numerous—seven miles of hyperactive promenade containing giant dinosaurs, roller-coasters, palm-readers, fruit machines, donkey rides, fun palaces, 24-hour cabarets, and even the occasional beach. Blackpool, for all its unabashed tackiness (or, more likely, because of it), is unrivaled worldwide, with the possible exception of Las Vegas, as a tasteless dispenser of uninhibited fun of the piss drunk, lounge act variety.

☐ GETTING THERE AND GETTING AROUND

Trains: Blackpool North Station (☎ 620385), 4 blocks down Talbot Rd. from North Pier. Travel center open daily 8am-8pm. **Trains** (☎ (08457) 484950) arrive from: **London Euston** (change at Preston, 4hr., 1 per hr., £43, return £44); **Manchester** (1¼hr., 2 per hr., £9.50); and **Liverpool** (1½hr., 1 per hr., £10.65).

Buses: Talbot Rd. station dispenses National Express information. Open M-Sa 8:15am-midnight, Su 10am-6pm. **National Express** (☎ (08705) 808080) **buses** arrive from: **London** (6½hr., 6 per day, £18.75); **Liverpool** (1½hr., 4 per day, £5.50); **Manchester** (2hr., 5 per day, £6); and **Chester** (4hr., 3 per day, £8).

Public Transportation: Local trains utilize Blackpool South and Pleasure Beach stations. **Local bus** info is available at Talbot Rd. station. Single from the Tower to Pleasure Beach 90p. Bus #1 covers the Promenade every 8 min. A 1-day **Travelcard** buys unlimited travel on local buses and **vintage trams.** £4.25, seniors and children £3.75.

☐ PRACTICAL INFORMATION

Tourist Information Centre: 1 Clifton St. (☎ 478222; fax 478210). Books beds for £2 plus 10% deposit. Smoking dragon sculpture and free street maps. Open May-Nov. M-Sa 9am-5pm, Su 10am-4pm. **Branches** on the Promenade, near the Tower (☎ 478222), and 87a Coronation St. (☎ 403223), across from Pleasure Beach, open May-Nov. M-Sa 9:15am-5pm, Su 10:15am-3:30pm.

Financial Services: Banks are easy to find, especially along **Corporation St.**

Launderette: Corner of Albert Rd. and Regent Rd. Open M-F 9am-4pm, Sa 10am-2pm.

Internet Access: Blackpool Public Library (☎ 478111), on the corner of Queen St. and Abingdon St. £1 per 30min. Open M, W, and F-Sa 10am-5pm, Tu and Th 10am-7pm. **CaféNet,** 16 Deansgate (☎ 625003), off Abingdon St. 75p per 15min. Open Su-W 10am-5pm, Th-Sa 10am-7pm.

Post Office: 26-30 Abingdon St. (☎ 622888). Accepts Poste Restante for letters only. Open M-Sa 9am-5:30pm. **Postal code:** FY1 1AA.

▐▞▐ ACCOMMODATIONS AND FOOD

With over 3500 hotel and guest houses, and 120,000 beds, you won't have trouble finding a room—except on weekends during the Illuminations (see p. 343), when advance bookings are essential and prices rise. Budget-friendly **B&Bs** dominate the blocks behind the Promenade between the North and Central Piers (£10-14). Pick up the free Bible-sized *Blackpool Have the Time of Your Life* at the tourist information centre (TIC) for an impressive list.

Clarron House, 22 Leopold Grove (☎ 623748). From the bus or train station, head toward the sea on Talbot Rd., turn left on Topping St., and turn right on Church St.; Leopold Grove is 1 block down on the left. Your chip-heavy, dance-weary body will thank you for the comfy beds. TV in every room. Apr.-June £14 per person, July-Aug. £15, Sept.-Nov. £16-18, Jan.-Mar. £13.

Silver Birch Hotel, 39 Hull Rd. (☎ 622125). Run by a maternal proprietress who has spoiled guests with warm hospitality for 23 years. From the bus and train stations, head down Talbot Rd. toward the ocean, take a left onto Market St., pass the Tower and a bend in the road, and turn left. You can also enter from Albert Rd. TV in every room. Breakfast £3. £10 per person, with bath £13.

York House, 30 South King St. (☎ 624200). Bay windows, tall ceilings, and an aristocratic red decor—all redone by the new owner—fill this cheery B&B. Follow the Clarron House directions, but turn left on Church St.; South King St. is 1 block down on the right. £16.50 per person, all with TVs and bath.

You know you're in Blackpool when McDonald's starts looking like class. Blackpool's hundreds of plastic-faced restaurants are uniform in their oily indulgence. The **Iceland** supermarket, 1 Dickson Rd., is across from the bus station. (☎ 293051. Open M-F 8:30am-8pm, Sa 8:30am-5:30pm, Su 10am-4pm.) Loaves from **Sayers the Baker,** 1 Birley St., make for lovely picnics in the 256 acres of **Stanley Park,** a mile east of the Tower. (☎ 624913. Open M-Sa 8:30am-5pm.) Blackpool's branch of **Harry Ramsden's,** on the corner of the Promenade and Church St., is a step up from most fast-food fare: the fish and chips aren't floating in grease. (☎ 294386. Open daily M-Th and Su 11:30am-7:30pm, F-Sa 11:30am-9pm.)

▐◉▐ ▐♪▐ SIGHTS AND ENTERTAINMENT

No fewer than 36 nightclubs, 38,000 nightly theater seats, several circuses, and still more rollercoasters squat along the 7 mi. long **Promenade,** served by Britain's first, and still active, electric tram line. Even the three 19th-century piers are smothered by amusement centers, ferris wheels, and greasy chip shops. About the only thing the hedonistic hordes don't come for is the ocean.

PLEASURE BEACH. Around 7.1 million people visit the sprawling 40-acre amusement park annually, second in Europe only to its more refined, though mousier, competitor outside Paris. Pleasure Beach is known for its historic wooden rollercoasters—the twin-track **Grand National** (c. 1935) is something of a mecca for coaster enthusiasts, and the **Big Dipper** was invented here. However, thousands of thrill-seekers line up for the aptly-named **Big One,** and aren't disappointed. Their screams vie with the seagulls' cries as they enter orbit. The 235 ft. high steel behemoth, tall enough to merit aircraft warning lights, sends you down a heartstopping 65° slope at 87 mph—the highest, steepest, and fastest in the world. The vertical drop of the **PlayStation** is equally terrifying. Although admission to the gritty themeless park is free, the rides themselves aren't—kiddy rides go for £1, most coasters cost £2.10, and the Big One is a whopping £4.20. On the good side, the pay-as-you-ride system means queues are shorter than at other amusement parks, and discount books of tickets are available. Pleasure Beach entertains at night with illusion shows, as well as family-oriented acts in a "Las Vegas style theatre." *(Across from South Pier. ☎ (0870) 444 5566; www.blackpoolpleasurebeach.co.uk. A book of £20 Ride Tickets gets you about £25 worth of rides. Opens daily at 10-11am; closing time varies, call ahead or check the posted time at the entrance.)*

BLACKPOOL TOWER. When a London businessman visited the 1890 Paris World Exposition, he returned determined to erect Eiffel Tower imitations throughout

Britain. Only Blackpool embraced his enthusiasm, and in 1894 the 560 ft. Tower graced the city's skyline. **Towerworld** at its base is a bizarre seven-floor hotel-like building that's a microcosm of Blackpool's eclectic tackiness. It holds a motley crew of attractions: a black-lit aquarium, a motorized dinosaur ride, an insanely large jungle gym, a daily circus show, and arcade games mixed in with a casino. Couples (mostly senior citizens) dance sedately and somewhat surreally amidst all this pandemonium in the ornate Victorian ballroom, complete with a Wurlitzer organ. (☎ 622242. Open June-Oct. daily 10am-11pm; Nov.-May daily 10am-6pm. £10 Easter-Nov., seniors and children £5; Nov.-Easter £5, children £2.95. Circus open Easter-Oct. only. Tower only Easter to mid-July £6.50, children £4.95; mid-July to Nov. £7.50, £5.95.)

THE ILLUMINATIONS. Blackpool, the first electric town in Britain, consummates its crazed love affair with bright lights in the orgiastic **Illuminations.** The display takes place over five miles of the Promenade, from September to early November. In a colossal waste of electricity, 72 mi. of cables light up the tower, promenade, star-encased faces of Hollywood actors, corporate emblems, and gaudy placards.

NIGHTLIFE. Stretching between North and Central Piers, Blackpool's famous **Golden Mile** shines with more neon than gold, hosting scores of sultry theaters, cabaret bars, and bingo halls. Criss-crossed by laser beams, the multi-tiered dance-floors of the UK's largest nightclub, **The Palace,** Central Promenade, pulsate with bodies. Up to 3000 revelers pack it in for 70s night on Thursday. (☎ 626281. Cover £1-9. Open Th-Sa 9pm-2am.) The more upscale **Main Entrance,** directly below the Palace, only holds 1000. (☎ 292335. Frequent theme nights. Cover £2-12. Open M-Tu and Th-Sa 9pm-2am, second Su of the month 9pm-midnight.)

ISLE OF MAN

The Isle of Man is a speck of land in the middle of the frothy Irish Sea. While the 75,000 Manx swear allegiance to Queen Elizabeth, they aren't fully a part of the UK, and the small island (33 by 13 mi.) has its own parliament, flag, currency, and language. The Vikings landed on Man in the 9th century and established the **Tynwald Court,** the Isle's parliament. When the last Viking king died in 1266, Scottish and English lords fought one another for power and ruled alongside a weakened version of the Court. In 1405, home rule ended altogether and the English "Lords of Man" gained control of the island. Smugglers contributed to this period's booming economy until England's Isle of Man Purchase Act (1765) sent the island spinning into poverty. Man's rejuvenation began in 1828, when self-government was restored, and today Man controls its own internal affairs and finances, but remains a crown possession and

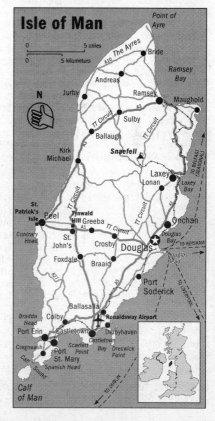

follows British foreign policy. Manx home rule has created the lax tax laws that have lured hundreds of British tycoons to the island.

Ringed by cliffs, sliced by valleys, and crossed by antique railways, Man is small enough to be explored in three or four days. While the island caters more to family-oriented tourists than young backpackers, it draws all types when thousands of motorcycle enthusiasts arrive en masse for the famous **T.T. Races.** Much of the fauna is unique, including the terrifying four- to six-horned **Manx Loghtan sheep** and the tail-less **Manx cats.** Man's most famous delicacy is its **kippers,** herring smoked over oak chips. The **Manx language,** a cousin of Irish and Scots Gaelic, petered out at the beginning of the century but is experiencing a revival, and is now heard when the Manx legislature's laws are annually proclaimed on July 5. The **three-legs-of-Man** emblem appears on every available surface, asserting the independent identity that has come to be a considerable source of pride.

⚔ GETTING THERE

Flights: Ronaldsway Airport (☎ 826000), 8 mi. southwest of Douglas on the coast road. Buses run from Douglas to Port St. Mary, near the airport (25min.; M-Sa 27 per day 6:20am-10:50pm, Su 12 per day 8:40am-10:50pm; £1.50). **Manx Airlines** (☎ 824313, UK ☎ (0345) 256256, Ireland ☎ (01) 260 1588; www.manx-airlines.com) flies from London, Dublin, Glasgow, Manchester, and other airports in Britain and Ireland. **Jersey European** (UK ☎ (0990) 676676; Northern Ireland ☎ (01232) 457200) and **Emerald Airways** (☎ 823173, UK ☎ (0500) 600748) also serve the isle.

Ferries: Douglas Sea Terminal. Travel Shop open Nov.-Mar. M-Sa 6:30am-8pm, Apr.-Oct. daily 6:30am-8pm; stays open 1hr. prior to later departures. The **Isle of Man Steam Packet Company** (☎ 676676 or ☎ (08705) 523523) runs the only ferries to the isle, sailing from: **Belfast** (2¾hr., Apr.-Sept. 2 per week, usually W and Su); **Liverpool** (2½-4hr., Apr.-Oct. 1-3 per day, Nov.-Mar. 3 per week); **Dublin** (2¾-4¾hr., Apr.-Dec. 3 per week, usually Tu, Th, and Sa); and **Heysham,** Lancashire (3½hr., 2 per day year-round). Many ferries travel early in the morning. **Fares** are higher in summer and on weekends (£25-51, students and seniors £19-51, ages 5-15 £12-25). Book 4 weeks ahead for discounts, and call for summertime specials. Combination tickets can save money on round trips; purchase **Sail & Rail** tickets from train stations or the Isle of Man Steam Packet, and **Sail & Coach** tickets from National Express bus stations.

▐ GETTING AROUND

The Isle of Man may have more cars per person than anywhere else in the world except Los Angeles, but it also has an extensive system of public transportation managed by **Isle of Man Transport** (trains ☎ 663366, buses ☎ 662525), in Douglas, which takes you to every sight. Their **Travel Shop,** on Lord St. next to the Douglas bus station, has information on all of the government-run transportation, including free bus and train maps and schedules, as well as discount tickets. (Open July-Aug. M-Sa 8am-5:40pm, Su 9:35am-1pm and 2-5:45pm; Sept.-June M-Sa 8am-5:40pm.) During the summer months, the **branch** at the end of Harris Promenade in Douglas also offers the same services. (Open daily 9am-5pm.) Both locations sell the **7-day Rover,** which provides unlimited passage on all buses, railways, and horse trams (£29.40, under 15 £14.70, under 5 free).

The island's small size makes it easy to get around by **bike.** The southern three-quarters of the island are covered in challenging hills—manageable, but difficult enough that the island is a venue for professional bicycle races. Tourist information centres (TICs) provide a free map of six one-day cycle trails. Locals claim that the Isle of Man is one of the safer places for **hitching,** although *Let's Go* does not recommend it anywhere.

Trains: Isle of Man Railways (☎ 663366) runs along the east coast from Port Erin to Ramsey (Easter-Oct., limited service in the winter). The 1873 **Steam Railway** runs from Douglas to Port Erin via Castletown. The 1893 **Electric Railway** runs from Douglas to

Ramsey. The **MER (Manx Electric Railway)** runs to **Snaefell,** the island's highest peak; the #1 and 2 trains are the oldest in the world. Buses and horse-drawn trams ("toasties") cover the 2 mi. between the Steam and Electric Railway Stations. **Rail Rover passes** allow unlimited train and tram travel. 1-day pass £10.40, children £5.20; 3-day pass valid for 3 out of 7 days £15.40, children £7.70.

Buses: Frequent buses connect every tiny hamlet on the island, including **Peel, Douglas,** and **Port Erin** (1 per hr., day return £2.75). A **1-day Bus Rover** discount ticket allows unlimited bus travel (£5.50, children £2.75); the **3-day Bus Rover** can be used 3 days out of 7 (£12.50, children £6.25). Both are available at the Travel Shop or the outlet off Harris Promenade.

Tours: Isle of Man Bus Tour Company, Central Promenade (☎ 674301), in Douglas, provides several tours, including the popular "Round the Island" departing from Douglas W and F 10:15am and returning at 5pm (£10, children £5). Office open daily 8:30am-2:30pm, also until 4:45pm if there's an evening tour.

⚡ PRACTICAL INFORMATION

Manx **currency** is equivalent in value to currency from Britain but not accepted outside the Isle, though notes and coins from England, Scotland, and Northern Ireland can be used in Man. Manx coins are reissued each year with different bizarre designs. When preparing to leave the island, you can ask for your change in UK tender and usually get it. **Manx stamps** are also unusual, depicting everything from motorcycles to sailboats; UK stamps won't do you much good here. The eagle-eyed will notice that the Queen's head bears no crown on Manx stamps. BT phonecards do not work on Manx **payphones;** post offices and newsagents sell Manx Telecom phonecards instead. The Isle shares Britain's **international dialing code,** 44. **Phone code** for the entire Isle of Man: **01624.**

⚡ HIKING AND WALKING ON THE ISLE OF MAN

Since distances between towns and sights are so short, walking is a feasible means of transport. The government maintains three long-distance trails, marked by the three-legs-of-Man symbol. **Raad ny Foillan** ("Road of the Gull") is a 90 mi. path around the island marked with seagull signs, which can easily be broken up into smaller segments. The ⬛ **Port Erin to Castletown route** is a particularly spectacular hike (12 mi.) offering the very best of the island's south: sandy beaches, cliffs, and splashing surf. **Bayr ny Skeddan** ("The Herring Road"), an old route used by Manx fishermen, covers the less spectacular 14 mi. between Peel in the west and Castletown in the east. It overlaps the **Millennium Way,** which goes from Castletown to Ramsey along the course of the 14th-century Royal Highway for 28 mi., ending a mile from Ramsey's Parliament Sq. For a shorter walk, follow the signs in **Port Erin** to the nature trail that leads you to a peak right on the coast—this easy climb offers one of the best views of the island as well as the **Calf of Man,** the small land mass and bird sanctuary off the isle's southern tip. The Douglas TIC has maps and the free *Visitor's Pocket Guide to Walks and Wildlife on the Isle of Man.*

⚜ EVENTS

The island's economy relies heavily on tourism, so there are always festivals celebrating everything from jazz to angling. The TIC stocks a calendar of events; ask for the bimonthly *What's on the Isle of Man* or the monthly *Events 2001.* By far the most popular events are motor races. Each year, the first two weeks of June transform peaceful Man into a merry, leather-clad motorcycling beast for the **T.T. (Tourist Trophy) Races.** The population doubles, the Steam Packet Co. schedules extra ferries, and Manx Radio is replaced by its evil twin, "Radio T.T." The races originated in 1904 when the tourist-hungry government passed the **Road Closure Act,** under which roads could be closed and speed-limits lifted for a motor race. Today there are 600 racers and 40,000 fans. The circuit consists of 38 mi. of hairpin turns and mountain climbs, and the winner gets his name (no "her" yet) and make

346 ■ ISLE OF MAN

of motorcycle engraved on the same silver "tourist trophy" that has been used since 1907. The T.T. season is a nonstop two-week party, embraced by locals as part of their national identity.

The **Isle of Man International Cycling Week** follows the T.T. Race weeks and uses the same tracks. Established in 1936, it is now the most respected bicycle race on the British Isles. **Southern "100" Motorcycle Races** (☎ 822546) take place over three days in mid-July: more bikers, more fun, this time based in Castletown. Even after the races end, this self-proclaimed "Road Racing Capital of the World" is buzzing with bikes, and pictures and stories of famous races. The Isle also celebrates other festivals: **Tynwald Fair** sees the pronouncement of new laws on July 5, Manx National Day. Representatives don British wigs and robes to read the new laws but do so in the Manx tongue upon a remote hill of ancient significance in the middle of the island. The holiday is followed by the week-long **Manx Heritage Festival.**

DOUGLAS   ☎01624

Recent capital of an ancient island, Douglas (pop. 22,000) has leveled the natural Manx landscape under a square mile of concrete promenades and tall, narrow Victorian townhouses. In the last century, Douglas bloomed as a Victorian seaside resort, but today it profits most from the savvy, tax-evading businessmen who hurry down the promenade from 9 to 5. It's a good spot from which to explore the island, but its own coast view is comparatively mediocre. Escape the worn tackiness of its promenade and retreat to the quieter, more scenic parts of the island.

▐ GETTING AROUND. Ferries arrive at **Victoria Pier**, at the southern end of town near the bus station. **Isle of Man Transport,** Strathallan Crescent (trains ☎ 663366, buses ☎ 662525), runs local trains and buses (see **Getting Around,** p. 344). Slow but inexpensive horse-drawn **trams** run down The Promenade between the bus and Electric Railway station in summer. Stops are posted every 200 yd. or so. (☎ 675522. Continuous service daily June-Aug. 9:10am-8:50pm; Sept.-May 9:10am-6:30pm.) Motorized **buses** also run along The Promenade, connecting the bus and Steam Railway stations with the Electric Railway (65p). For taxis, call **A-1 Taxis** (☎ 674488) or **Castle Cabs** (☎ 621111), both open 24hr. Rent cars at **St. Bernard's Car Rental,** Castle Mona (☎ 613878), off the Central Promenade. They deliver to Ronaldsway Airport. **Eurocycles,** 8a Victoria Rd., off Broadway, rents out regular and mountain bikes. (☎ 624909. Call ahead in summer. Open M-Sa 9am-6pm.)

▚▊ ORIENTATION AND PRACTICAL INFORMATION. Douglas stretches for two miles along the seafront, from **Douglas Head** in the south to the **Electric Railway** terminal in the north. Douglas Head is separated from the rest of town by the River Douglas, which flows into the harbor. The ferry and bus terminals lie just north of the river. **The Promenade,** which changes names frequently, bends from the ferry terminal to the Electric Railway terminal along the crescent of beach; it's lined on one side with grand though sometimes tattered Victorian terrace houses and souvenir shops. **Nobles Park** is the site of recreation facilities and the start of the T.T. course. The shopping district spreads out around pedestrianized **Strand St.**

The **tourist information centre** (TIC), in the Sea Terminal Bldg., books accommodations on a walk-in basis only. (☎ 686766; www.manxisle.com. Open Easter-Sept. daily 9:15am-7pm; Oct.-Easter M-Th 9am-5:30pm, F 9am-5pm.) A **Lloyds TSB** bank is at 78 Strand St. (☎ 673755. Open M-F 9am-5pm.) Also **Thomas Cook,** 1 Regent St. (☎ 623330. Open M-W and F 9am-5:30pm, Sa 10am-5:30pm.) The **police** (☎ 631212) are in Douglas Station, Glencrutchery Rd. **Nobles Isle of Man Hospital** (☎ 642642) is on Westmoreland Rd. **Internet Café,** Duke St., off Lord St. near the bus station, provides **Internet access** for £5 per hr. (Open M-Sa 9am-7pm, Su 10am-4pm.) A **post office** is on Regent St. (☎ 686141. Open M and W-F 9am-5:30pm, Tu 9:30am-5:30pm, Sa 9am-12:30pm.) **Postal Code:** IM1 2EA.

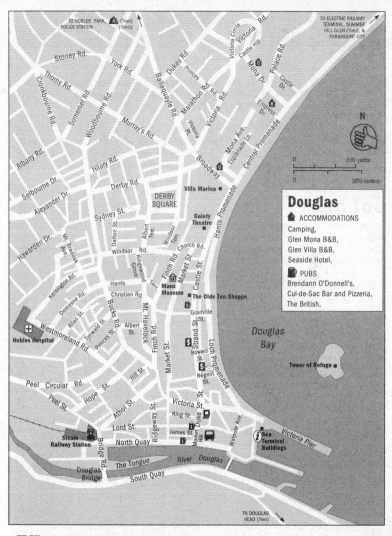

Douglas

⌂ ACCOMMODATIONS
Camping,
Glen Mona B&B,
Glen Villa B&B,
Seaside Hotel,

▮ PUBS
Brendann O'Donnell's,
Cul-de-Sac Bar and Pizzeria,
The British,

▐▐ **ACCOMMODATIONS AND FOOD.** Cheap rooms abound in nearly every house along The Promenade, except during T.T. race weeks, when B&Bs raise their rates and fill up a year in advance. **Glen Villa,** 5 Broadway, is near the grassy lawns of the Villa Marina Gardens, but it's the lively proprietors and private bar that guests love. (☎ 673394. £16 per person, with bath £18.) The **Glen Mona,** 6 Mona Drive, is a family-run hotel with a cheerful bar. (☎ 676755. £17 per person.) **Seaside Hotel,** 9 Empress Dr., is just a minute's walk from The Promenade. (☎ 674765; fax 619242. Open Apr.-Oct. £14 per person.) Another option is **camping,** which must be at a campsite or on the "common land" near the northern tip of the island; consult the TIC. **Nobles Park Grandstand Campsite,** behind the grandstand on the site of the T.T. races' start and finish line, is the only campsite in Douglas. (☎ 621132; office open M-F 9am-5pm. Showers £1; laundry £2. Open mid-June to mid-Aug. and Sept. £6 per site.) It's closed during the T.T. races and Grand Prix week, but other campsites open then—again, check at the TIC.

Cheap grill and chip shops proliferate along The Promenade, Duke St., Strand St., and Castle St. If you just want groceries, **Safeway** supermarket is on Chester St. (☎ 673039. Open M-Tu and Sa 8:30am-8pm, W 8:30am-9pm, Th-F 8:30am-10pm, Su 9am-5pm.) The **Cul-de-Sac Bar and Pizzeria,** 3 Market Hill, by North Quay, has every imaginable pizza topping (Hawaiian pizza £6), over 127 flavors of vodka (toffee vodka £1.75), and the largest selection of beer on the island. (☎ 623737. Free live music F-Su. Open M-Sa 11am-2pm and 5:30-11pm.) At **Brendann O'Donnell's,** 16-18 Strand St. (☎ 621566), Guinness posters and traditional music quickly remind you of the owner's loyalty and the Isle's proximity to Ireland.

⬛🎵 SIGHTS AND ENTERTAINMENT. From the shopping district, signs point to the Chester St. parking garage, where an elevator leads to the fascinating **Manx Museum.** This extensive museum chronicles the history of the island from the Ice Age to the present with geological, historical, and taxidermic displays. Board a real double-decker horse tram to learn about the island's transport history. (☎ 648000. Open M-Sa 10am-5pm. Free.) Just past the Villa Marina Gardens on Harris Promenade, north of the Manx Museum, sits the **Gaiety Theatre.** Designed in 1900 and recently restored, the theater was lush in Douglas's Victorian seaside resort days. To see the fascinating antique machinery you'll have to take a guided **tour.** (☎ 625001. Tours Sa 10:15am; July-Aug. also Tu and Th 1:45pm; 1½hr. Donation encouraged; advance booking recommended. Performances Mar.-Dec. Box office open M-Sa 10am-4:30pm and 1hr. before performances. Tickets for shows £15-18; discounts for seniors and children.) The distant sand castle-like structure sitting in Douglas Bay is the **Tower of Refuge,** closed to the public. The southern end of Douglas is marked by **Douglas Head,** with lovely views of the town.

Most of the late-night **clubs** in Douglas are 21+ and free until 10 or 11pm, with a £2-5 cover afterwards. Paramount City houses two nightclubs: the **Director's Bar,** Queens Promenade (☎ 622447), upstairs plays favorites from the 50s to the 90s, while the **Dark Room** downstairs plays chart and dance music. (21+. No jeans, t-shirts, or sportswear. Cover £3-4. Open F-Sa 8pm-2:15am.)

PEEL   ☎01624

Considered the "cradle of Manx heritage" and headquarters of the Manx kipper industry, Peel is a beautiful fishing town on the west coast of Man. Twisting streets and salt-soaked stone buildings remain practically unchanged since the days fishermen sailed from here to the Hebrides. Romantic ▧ **Peel Castle,** situated atop the gentle height of **St. Patrick's Isle,** is easily reached from the mainland by pedestrian causeway. Not quite as grand as its British counterparts, the castle was home to the Kings and Lords of Man for many centuries. Footpaths ring the ruins before dipping down to a stretch of beach and scaling the cliffs of **Peel Hill.** The damp, eerie **Bishop's Dungeon** was used for hundreds of years to punish sinners for such terrible offenses as missing church. (Open Easter-Oct. daily 10am-5pm, winter hours vary. £3, children £1.50, families £7; includes audio guide.) **Moore's Traditional Curers,** on Mill Rd. off East Quay, is one of Peel's two **kipper factories,** and gives tours if you can bear the smell. (☎ 843622. Tours run June to mid-Sept. at 2pm, 3pm, and 4pm; £1.50, children 50p.)

Buses (☎ 662525) come to the station on Atholl St. from **Douglas** (30min., 1-2 per hr., return £2.70) and **Port Erin** (55min., 2-4 per day; return £3.25). Some buses leave from the town hall on Derby Rd. The **tourist information centre** is in the Town Hall, Derby Rd. (☎ 842341. Open M-Th 8:45am-5pm, F 8:45am-4:30pm.)

Seabourne House, Mt. Morrison, offers nine rooms with TVs and stupendous views of the Irish sea. (☎ 842571. May-Sept. £14.50 per person; Oct.-Apr. £15.) The nearby **Haven Guest House,** 10 Peveril Ave., off Peveril Rd., has three rooms with TVs and delightful mountain views. (☎/fax 842585. £19.50-21 per person.) **Peel Camping Park,** Derby Rd., has laundry and a wheelchair-accessible bathroom. (☎ 842341; fax 844010. Open May-Sept. £3.75 per person.) The town's two **Shoprite** grocery stores are on Derby Rd. and in the center of town. Have a hearty Manx meal at the dainty **Harbour Lights Café and Tearoom,** Shore Rd., which provides a chance to try a Peel kipper. (☎ 897216. Main courses £4-6; open M-Sa 9am-5pm.)

PEAK DISTRICT

Named in 1951 as Britain's first national park, Peak can boast only 555 sq. mi. of ambitious hills; devoid of mountains, the area derives its name from the Old English *peac*, meaning "hill." In the **Dark Peak** area to the north, deep groughs (gullies) gouge the hard peat moorland below gloomy cliffs, while friendlier footpaths wicker the rocky hillsides and village clusters of the **Northern Peak** area. The rolls of the southern **White Peak** cradle abandoned millstones, cringe under derelict lead mines, and swell under its stately country homes.

A green cushion between the hard industrial giants of Manchester, Sheffield, and Nottingham, the park serves as a playground to its millions of urban neighbors. Trampled trails attest to the park's popularity; of the world's national parks, only Mt. Fuji can top the Peak's 26 million annual visitors. The park's southern regions accommodate hikers with gentler terrain and better transport links, but travelers seeking solitude should point their compasses toward the bleaker northern moors, beyond the fingers of commuter rail lines.

▐ GETTING THERE AND GETTING AROUND

Trains (☎ (08457) 484950) seem intimidated by the rustic splendor of the park; only three lines enter its boundaries, and only one dares to cross. One line goes from **Nottingham** and **Derby** north to **Matlock**, on the park's edge. From the west, a train runs from **Manchester** to **Buxton** (1hr., 1 per hr., £5.30). The Hope Valley line (1½hr.; 15 per day) runs from **Manchester** across the park via **Edale** (£6.30), **Hope** (near Castleton), and **Hathersage**, terminating in **Sheffield** (£10.40). Both lines from Manchester enter the park at **New Mills**—the Buxton line at Newtown Station and the Hope Valley line at Central Station. A 20-minute signposted walk separates the stations.

A sturdy pair of legs, grumble veteran hikers, are more than sufficient for inter-village journeys, but if you must depend upon the rare train or the infrequent bus, Derbyshire County Council's *Peak District Timetable* (60p, available in all Peak tourist information centres and some train stations) is invaluable. The timetable includes all bus and train routes as well as a large map and information on cycle hire, youth hostels, tourist information centres (TICs), and hospitals.

Buses make a noble effort to connect the scattered towns of the Peak District. The **bus information line** (☎ (01298) 23098; open daily 7am-8pm) offers solutions and sympathy. Coverage of many routes actually improves on Sundays, especially in summer. **Trent** (☎ (01298) 23098) bus TP, the "Transpeak," winds for three hours through the park between **Manchester** and **Nottingham**, stopping at **Buxton, Bakewell, Matlock, Derby,** and other towns in between. **PMT** (☎ (01782) 207999) runs from **Sheffield** to **Buxton** (#X18, 1hr., M-Sa 5 per day) via **Bakewell** (40min., M-Sa 5 per day). **Mainline** (☎ (01709) 515151) #272 and **Stagecoach East Midland** (☎ (01246) 211007) #273 and 274 both reach **Castleton** (1hr., 14 per day, £2.30, return £3.80). Stagecoach East Midland also runs between **Sheffield** and **Buxton** via **Eyam** (#65/66; 40min.; M-Sa 5 per day, Su 3 per day; £2.90, return £4.40); and from **Bakewell** to **Castleton** (#173, 45min., 3 per day, £2.10, return £3.50).

If you're going to use public transport, make sure to get a bargain. The best deal is the **Wayfarer** (£6.60, seniors and children £3.30), which gives unlimited travel for a day within Greater Manchester and the Peak District as far east as Matlock (including Buxton, Bakewell, Castleton, Edale, and Eyam). The **Derbyshire Wayfarer** (£7.75, seniors and children £3.65), available from Peak TICs or train stations, lets you use the trains and buses all the way through the Peak District north to Sheffield and south to Derby for one day. Both passes are sold at Manchester rail stations and National Park Information Centres.

PRACTICAL INFORMATION

Daytime facilities in the Peak District generally stay open through the winter, due to the proximity of large cities. Some B&Bs and youth hostels stay open until December. TICs will usually book accommodations for free, but 10% of the first night goes to the offices.

NATIONAL PARK INFORMATION CENTRES

These centers display the park's symbol of a circle resting atop a rectangle. All carry detailed walking guides and other park fun-facts.

Bakewell: Old Market Hall (☎ (01629) 813227; fax 816201), at Bridge St. From the bus stop, walk past the right flank of Sandringham Fabrics. Doubles as the TIC. Has a good selection of maps and guides, along with an accommodations booking service (10% deposit). Open Mar.-Oct. daily 9am-5:30pm; Nov.-Feb. daily 10am-5pm.

Castleton: (☎/fax (01433) 620679), Castle St., near the church. From the bus stop, follow the road into town, and turn left at the youth hostel sign. Open daily Apr.-Oct. 10am-1pm and 2-5:30pm; Nov.-Mar. Sa-Su closes at 5pm.

Edale: (☎ (01433) 670207; fax 670216), Fieldhead, between the rail station and village. Open daily Apr.-Oct. 9am-1pm and 2:30-5:30pm; Nov.-Mar. closes at 5pm.

Fairholmes: (☎ (01433) 650953), Upper Derwent Valley, near Derwent Dam. Open Apr.-Oct. daily 9:30am-5pm; Nov.-Mar. Sa-Su 9am-4:30pm.

Langsett Barn: (☎/fax (01226) 370770), near Penistone. Open Easter-Sept. Sa-Su 10:30am-5pm.

Torside: In Longdendale Valley (no phone). Open Easter-Sept. F-Sa and bank holidays 10:30am-5pm; Oct. Su only 10:30am-5pm.

TOURIST INFORMATION CENTRES

Ashbourne: 13 The Market Pl. (☎ (01335) 343666; fax 300638). Open Mar.-Oct. daily 9:30am-5:30pm; Nov.-Feb. M-Sa 10am-4pm.

Buxton: (☎ (01298) 25106), The Crescent. Open Mar.-Oct. daily 9:30am-5pm; Nov.-Feb. daily 10am-4pm.

Matlock: (☎ (01629) 583388), Crown Sq. Open Mar.-Oct. daily 9:30am-5pm; Nov.-Feb. daily 10am-4pm.

Matlock Bath: (☎ (01629) 55082), The Pavilion, along the main road. Open Mar.-Oct. daily 9:30am-5pm; Nov.-Feb. M and W-Su 10am-4pm.

ACCOMMODATIONS

National Park Information Centres and TICs distribute free park-wide and regional accommodations guides; a camping guide costs 30p. **B&Bs** are plentiful and cheap (from £14), as are **youth hostels** (around £8). Most hostels are not open every day of the week. **Buxton** and **Matlock Bath** are particularly well stocked with inexpensive B&Bs. Many farmers allow **camping** on their land, sometimes for a small fee; remember to leave the site exactly as you found it.

YHA YOUTH HOSTELS

The Peak District has almost 20 hostels, many of which are listed below, but don't let numbers fool you—most fill quickly with enthusiastic school groups, so call ahead to reserve a space. Hostels lie within a day's hike of one another, and each sells maps detailing routes to neighboring hostels. Unless noted, they serve meals, and have a 10am-5pm lockout and 11pm curfew. Most offer a £1 **student discount**.

Bakewell: (☎/fax (01629) 812313), Fly Hill. A 5min. walk from the town center. Surrounded by bountiful pots of flowers, this 28-bed hostel delivers huge meals. Open Mar.-Oct. M-Sa; Nov.-Feb. daily 10am-5pm. Dorms £7.50, under 18 £5.15.

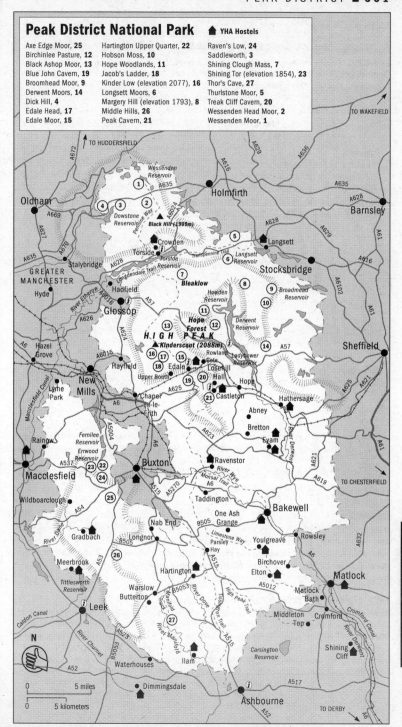

Peak District National Park

🔺 YHA Hostels

Axe Edge Moor, **25**
Birchinlee Pasture, **12**
Black Ashop Moor, **13**
Blue John Cavern, **19**
Broomhead Moor, **9**
Derwent Moors, **14**
Dick Hill, **4**
Edale Head, **17**
Edale Moor, **15**

Hartington Upper Quarter, **22**
Hobson Moss, **10**
Hope Woodlands, **11**
Jacob's Ladder, **18**
Kinder Low (elevation 2077), **16**
Longsett Moors, **6**
Margery Hill (elevation 1793), **8**
Middle Hills, **26**
Peak Cavern, **21**

Raven's Low, **24**
Saddleworth, **3**
Shining Clough Mass, **7**
Shining Tor (elevation 1854), **23**
Thor's Cave, **27**
Thurlstone Moor, **5**
Treak Cliff Cavern, **20**
Wessenden Head Moor, **2**
Wessenden Moor, **1**

Bretton: Self-catering hostel 2 mi. from Eyam atop Eyam Edge (1250 ft.). A heck of a view—rolling hills stretch for miles. For bookings call the central YHA office (☎ (01629) 825898). Open July-Aug. daily; Sept.-Dec. F-Sa. Dorms £8.10, under 18 £5.65.

Buxton: Sherbrook Lodge (☎/fax (01298) 22287), Harpur Hill Rd. The sloped 25min. walk from the train station is rewarded with a charming stone hostel surrounded by a brook and dense woodland. If your pack's too heavy, take bus #105 or 106 from the train station. Open Apr.-Oct. M-Sa; Nov.-Dec. M and Th-Su; Feb.-Mar. F-Sa. Dorms £8.50, under 18 £5.75.

☒ **Castleton:** Castleton Hall (☎ (01433) 620235). Pretty country house and attached old vicarage in the heart of town at the base of the menacing Peveril Castle ruins. The vicarage has a bath, and no curfew. Book *way* in advance. Open Feb. to late Dec. daily. Beds £10.85, under 18 £7.40; vicarage dorms £12.95, under 18 £9.

Crowden-in-Longdendale: (☎/fax (01457) 852135), Crowden, Hadfield, Hyde. Open Apr.-Sept. Th-Tu; Oct. F-M; Nov. F-Sa. Dorms £8.20, under 18 £5.65.

Edale: (☎ (01433) 670302; fax 670243), Rowland Cote, Nether Booth, Edale, 2 mi. from Edale village. This feature-packed 139-bed fortress of a hostel caters mostly to groups who come for "adventure trail" courses, but individuals are welcome. Includes a climbing wall. Travelers arriving at the train station between 4-8pm can arrange to be picked up. No lockout. Open year-round daily. Dorms £10.85, under 18 £7.40.

Elton: Elton Old Hall (☎ (01629) 650394), Main St. Self-catering only. Open mid-Feb. to Oct. M-Sa. Dorms £8.10, under 18 £5.65.

Eyam: (☎/fax (01433) 630335), Hawkhill Rd. With a turret and imposing oak door, this is more castle than hostel. Inside, 60 beds await in newly refurbished rooms. Open Apr.-Oct. daily; Nov. F-Sa; Feb.-Mar. M-Sa. Dorms £10.85, under 18 £7.40.

Hartington Hall: (☎ (01298) 84223; fax 84415), Hartington. 128 beds in a 17th-century manor house with oak paneling. Bonnie Prince Charlie once slept here, *sans* YHA membership. Open mid-Feb. to late Dec. daily. Dorms £9.80, under 18 £6.95.

Hathersage: (☎ (01433) 650493), Castleton Rd. Greystone building with white-framed windows and ivy creeping up the sides. Open mid-Apr. to Oct. M-Sa; mid-Mar. to mid-Apr. F-Sa. Dorms £9.80, under 18 £6.75.

Langsett: Near Penistone. Book through central office (☎ (01629) 825893). Self-catering. Open Jun.-Aug. daily; Sept.-Oct. and Jan.-May F-Sa. Beds £8.10, under 18 £5.65.

Matlock: 40 Bank Rd. (☎ (01629) 582983; fax 583484). Conveniently located hostel with rooms named after countries. Lockout 10am-1pm. Open Mar.-Sept. daily; Nov.-Feb. Tu-Sa. Dorms £10.85, under 18 £7.40.

Ravenstor: (☎ (01298) 871826; fax 871275; ravenstor@yha.org.uk), Millers Dale. In a National Trust-owned house. Open Feb., Apr.-May, Aug., and Oct. daily. Beds £10.85, under 18 £7.40.

Shining Cliff: (☎/fax (01629) 760827), Shining Cliff Woods, near Ambergate. Book through 1 Devonshire Villas, Upperwood Rd., Matlock Bath, Derbyshire DE4 3PD. Self-catering. Open mid-Apr. and Aug. daily. Dorms £7.35, under 18 £5.15.

Youlgreave: (☎/fax (01629) 636518), Fountain Sq. Open Apr.-Oct. M-Sa; Nov. to mid-Dec. and Feb.-Mar. F-Sa. Dorms £10.85, under 18 £7.40.

CAMPING BARNS

The 13 YHA-operated **camping barns** are simple night shelters, providing a sleeping platform, water tap, and toilet (£3.50 per person). Bring a sleeping bag and the usual camping equipment. You must book and pay ahead with the **Camping Barns Reservation Office,** 6 King St., Clitheroe, Lancashire BB7 2EP (☎ (01200) 420102; fax 420103; campbarnsyha@enterprise.net). Camping barns can be found in: **Abney,** between Eyam and Castleton; **Alstonefield,** between Dovedale and Manifold Valley; **Birchover,** near Matlock off the B5056; **Butterton,** near the southern end of the park, along the Manifold track; **Edale; Losehill,** near Castleton; **Middleton-By-Youlgreave; Nab End,** in Hollinsclough; **One Ash Grange,** in Monyash; **Taddington,** on Main Rd.; **Underbank,** in Wildboarclough; and **Upper Booth,** near Eyam.

⚠ HIKING AND BIKING

The central park is marvelous territory for rambling. Settlement is more sparse and buses are fewer north of Edale, in the land of the Kinder Scout plateau, the great Derwent reservoirs, and the gritty cliffs and peat moorlands. From Edale, the **Pennine Way** (see p. 369) runs north to Kirk Yetholm, across the Scottish border. Be advised that warm clothing and the customary supplies and precautions should be taken (see **Wilderness Safety**, p. 53). Also, the land is privately owned, so be respectful and stay on designated paths. Ramblers' guidebooks and the park's invaluable (and free!) newspaper, the *Peakland Post*, are available at National Park Information Centres. Contact the **Peak District National Park Office,** Aldern House, Barlow Rd., Bakewell DE45 1AE (☎ (01629) 816200; www.peakdistrict-npa.gov.uk), for information and a list of publications.

The park authority operates six **Cycle Hire Centres.** They can be found in the towns of **Ashbourne** (☎ (01335) 343156), on Mapleton Ln.; **Derwent** (☎ (01433) 651261), near the Fairholmes Information Centre; **Hayfield** (☎ (01663) 746222), near New Mills on Station Rd. in the Sett Valley; **Middleton Top** (☎ (01629) 823204), near Matlock on the High Peak Trail; **Parsley Hay** (☎ (01298) 84493), in Buxton at the meeting of Tissington and High Peak Trails; and **Waterhouses** (☎ (01538) 308609), in the Old Station Car Park between Ashbourne and Leek on the A523 near the southern end of the Manifold Truck. (Most open Apr.-Sept. daily 9:30am-6pm; Oct.-Mar. call for open days. £6.50 per 3hr., £9 per day; helmet included. £20 deposit. 10% discount for YHA members, seniors, and Wayfarer ticket holders. Children under 15 must have adult accompaniment.)

EDALE AND THE NORTHERN DARK PEAK AREA ☎ 01433

The deep dale of the River Noe cradles a collection of hamlets known as **Edale.** The area offers little in the way of civilization other than a church, railway stop, cafe, pub, school, and nearby youth hostel. Its environs, however, are arguably the most spectacular in northern England. The northern Dark Peak area contains some of the wildest, most rugged hill country in England, with vast moorlands like **Kinder Scout** and **Bleaklow** left undisturbed by motor traffic. In these desolate mazes of black peat hags and deep groughs, paths are scarce and weather-worn. Sparse towns and villages huddle in valleys, offering provisions and shelter for weary hikers. Less experienced hikers should stick to Edale and the southern paths.

On summer weekends Edale brims with hikers and campers preparing to tackle the **Pennine Way** (which passes out of the Peak District and into the Yorkshire Dales after a 3- to 4-day hike; see p. 369), or to trek on one of the shorter (1½-8½ mi.) trails closer to Edale detailed in the National Park Authority's *8 Walks Around Edale* (£1.20). The fairly undemanding 3½ mi. **path** to **Castleton** leaves begins 70 yd. down the road from the TIC towards the town, and affords a breathtaking view of both the Edale Valley (Dark Peak) and the Hope Valley (White Peak). A flagstone detour, offering even more spectacular views, runs along the ridge between these valleys to **Mam Tor,** a decaying Iron-Age hillside fort that receives over 250,000 annual visitors. The hill is known locally as the "shivering mountain" for its shale sides; one such shiver left the road below permanently blocked. Cliffs on three sides beckon fearless hang-gliders from near and far.

Edale lies on the Hope Valley rail line between Manchester and Sheffield, and is served by **trains** every two hours (from Manchester 50min.; Sheffield 35min., £3.50). Stop at the huge **National Park Information Centre** (see p. 350), near the train station, for weather forecasts and training with a map and compass. Unless you reserve centuries ahead, your tent could be your best friend in this town, where the popular 139-bed **YHA Edale** offers the only accommodations (see p. 350). Take a right 70 yd. up the road from the National Park Information Centre towards the town and follow the path to the hostel. Campers can try **Fieldhead,** behind the TIC. (☎ 670386. Shower 50p. £3.40 per person, under 14 £2.40, cars £1.20.)

CASTLETON   ☎01433

Two miles southeast of Edale, the tourist-friendly village of Castleton (pop. 705) winds through mazes of perennial-decked cottages to the natural wonders hidden in its hollow hills. A series of natural caverns carved by ice-age rivers were once mined for lead and later for Blue John, a semi-precious mineral found uniquely in these hills. Today they are the town's main and worthy attractions.

You can ogle at the geological wonders in the multi-chambered belly of ▓ **Treak Cliff Cavern,** a mile west of town on the A625, where Blue John seams course through ceilings and massive pillars in the fantastical chambers of stalagmites and stalagtites. As the excellent tour points out, it was the Harrison family's 1935 decision to open the mines to tourism that preserved these features, for continued blasting and mining would have invariably led to their collapse. (☎ 620571. Tours 40min., every 12min. £5, students and YHA members £4, seniors £4.50, children £3.) Gargantuan **Peak Cavern,** just behind the village at the end of a steep-walled gorge, features the largest aperture in Britain. Decorously known in the 18th century as the "Devil's Arse," the cavern now features tours by guides, pale and wry-humored from long days in Old Harry's Sphincter, who tell stories of cavern-based ropemaking communities. (☎ 620285. Open Easter-Oct. daily 10am-5pm; Nov.-Easter Sa-Su 10am-5pm; last tour 4pm. £4.75, students and seniors £3.75, children £2.75, families £13.)

At **Speedwell Cavern,** out of town on the A625, relentless miners carved a half-flooded route to a huge natural complex of caves and underground streams in pursuit of lead ore and a facile way to transport it. Eerie boat trips retrace the first half-mile of their journey, stopping at a subterranean lake, Bottomless Pit, with an interesting mix of geology and superstition in its story. (☎ 620512. Open Easter-Oct. 9:30am-5pm; Nov.-Easter 9:30am-4pm. £5.25, students and seniors £4.25, children £3.25.) In the depths of **Blue John Cavern,** 1½ mi. west of town on the A625, a small passageway winds downward, finally exploding into a spectacular 170 ft. dome arching over a crystalline chamber. (☎ 620638. Open year-round 10am-5pm. Tours 50min., every 20min. £5, students and seniors £4, children £3.) Be advised that all caverns are the temperature of an average refrigerator, and Speedwell and Blue John in particular involve very steep stair-climbs.

William Peveril, son of William the Conqueror, chose a visually arresting and defensively ideal setting in which to build **Peveril Castle.** Not much of the 11th- and 12th-century castle remains, but the ruins, including a hollowed keep, crown a dramatic peak overlooking the town. Bounded by a 230 ft. gorge, the limestone cliffs of Cave Dale, and a stubbornly steep hill facing town, the ruins make for a tiring climb. Have fun storming the castle. (☎ 620613. Open Apr.-Oct. daily 10am-6pm; Nov.-Mar. W-Su 10am-4pm. £2.20, students and seniors £1.70, children £1.10.)

Castleton lies two miles west of the **Hope** train station (don't ask for Castleton train station, or you'll end up in a suburb of Manchester), and **buses** arrive from Sheffield, Buxton, and Bakewell (see p. 349). Hikers looking for a challenge can set off southward from Castleton on the 26 mi. **Limestone Way Trail** to Matlock. There's a **National Park Information Centre** in town (see p. 350), but the nearest **bank** and **cash machine** lie six miles east in **Hathersage.** Ramblers preparing to assault the moorlands should visit the **Peveril Outdoor Shop,** off the market place by the hostel. (☎ 620320. Open M-F 9:30am-5:30pm, Sa-Su 9:30am-6pm.) The **post office,** How Ln., near the bus stop, is in a convenience store. (☎ 620241. Open M-Tu and Th-F 7am-1pm and 2-5:30pm, W 7am-12:30pm, Sa 7:30am-12:30pm.) **Postal code:** S33 8WJ.

The super **YHA Castleton** and its torrential showers wait by the castle entrance. (see p. 350). Those seeking B&B privacy can try the ivy-walled **Cryer House,** Castle St., where Mr. and Mrs. Skelton keep two lovely rooms and a blooming tea shop. (☎/fax 620244; FleeSkel@aol.com. Doubles with bath £42.)

BAKEWELL   ☎01629

Fifteen miles southwest of Sheffield and 30 mi. southeast of Manchester, Bakewell makes the best spot from which to explore this region and transfer to more elaborate bus trips. Located near several scenic walks through the White Peaks, the

NORTHWEST ENGLAND

town itself is best known as the birthplace of Bakewell pudding. The pudding was created in the 1860s when a flustered cook at the Rutland Arms Hotel tried, in spite of his town's name, to make a tart by pouring an egg mixture over strawberry jam instead of mixing it into the dough. Some have suggested that Jane Austen stayed in the Rutland Arms, and based the town in *Pride and Prejudice* on Bakewell. Bakewell's stone buildings are huddled around a handful of narrow streets and a central square bursting with flowers, wrapped by a lazy bend in the River Wye. Ducks float under the graceful five arches of the **medieval bridge** (c. 1300). On the hill above town, **All Saints Church** lies in a crowded park of gravestones and carved cross fragments. In the south transept, three very curious human gargoyles guard the remains of Anglo-Saxon and Norman headstones. Nearby, a 16th-century timber-frame house encased in stone shelters the **Old House Museum,** which displays a very modest collection of 19th-century toys, blacksmith equipment, and early 20th-century cameras. (☎ 813165. Open daily July-Aug. 11am-4pm; Apr.-June and Sept.-Oct. 1:30-4pm. ₤2.50, children ₤1, under 5 free.)

Buses arrive in Rutland Sq. from: **Sheffield** (#X18 and 240; 1hr.; M-Sa 14 per day, Su 11 per day); **Manchester** via **Buxton** (#TP, 7 per day, ₤2.90); and **Matlock**, site of the nearest train station (#172, R61, TP). Bakewell has a **National Park Information Centre** that doubles as a **tourist information centre,** at the intersection of Bridge St. and Market St. (see p. 350). Services include: **The Royal Bank of Scotland,** Rutland Sq. (open M-Tu and Th-F 9:15am-4:45pm, W 10am-4:45pm); **camping supplies** at Yeoman's, 1 Royal Oak Pl., off Matlock St. (☎ 815371; open M-Sa 9am-5:30pm, Su 11am-5pm); **Bakewell Launderama,** Water St., off Rutland Sq. (open daily 7:30am-7pm, last wash 6pm); the **police,** Granby Rd. (☎ 812504; open M-Th 8:30am-12:30pm and 1:30-5pm, F 8:30am-12:30pm and 1:30-8:30pm, Sa 9am-1pm and 1:30-5:30pm; Apr.-Sept. also open Su 10am-2pm); and the **post office,** Unit 1 Granby Croft, in the **Spar** supermarket on Granby Rd. (☎ 815112; open M-F 8:30am-6pm, Sa 8:30am-3pm). **Postal code:** DE45 1EF.

The comfy **YHA Bakewell,** on Fly Hill, is a short walk from the tourist information centre (see p. 350). **B&Bs** here are more costly than in Matlock Bath; many lie on or near Haddon Rd., the continuation of Matlock St. Entire villages pour into Bakewell's **market,** held since 1330 off Bridge St. (Open M 9am-4pm; follow the doomed mooing of 3000 cows.) Cafes aim to cash in on Bakewell's confectionery reputation. **The Old Original Bakewell Pudding Shop,** Rutland Sq., sells sinful desserts in a wood-paneled restaurant with a vaulted ceiling. Skip lunch and order the ₤3.60 cream tea, which includes sandwiches, two fruit scones with jam and cream, a Bakewell pudding, and tea. (☎ 812193. Open July-Aug. daily 8:30am-9pm; Sept.-June M-Th 9am-6pm, F-Sa 8:30am-9pm.) The **Extra Foodstore** is on the corner of Granby Rd. and Market St. (Open M-Sa 8am-10pm, Su 10am-4pm.) **The Australian,** Granby Rd., off Matlock St., draws a lively, grizzled crowd and serves Outback Bruce Burgers (₤3.95), Billy Can Soup (₤2.20), and other Aussie-themed meals. (☎ 814909. Open daily 11am-11pm.)

NOT FROM NOTTINGHAM Robin Hood fans may have thought that Kevin Costner's portrayal of the Prince of Thieves as some sort of American prospector was a unique travesty, but Kevin isn't the only one confused about the origin of Robin and his merry men. The bandits didn't come from Nottingham, as is often supposed, but from the Peak District, the more plebeian base from which they made sporadic and fruitful inroads on the wealth of nearby Nottingham. "Little John" (examinations of his remains have established that he was actually a giant) is buried in Hathersage, where a corner pub is now emblazoned with his name. It was also in tiny Hathersage that Charlotte Brontë saw another formidable band of men: the twelve apostles eerily painted on a cupboard at the home of one of her acquaintances, Thomas Eyre. Charlotte's mind bore both cupboard and surname back to Haworth where she recreated them in *Jane Eyre.*

NEAR BAKEWELL

CHATSWORTH HOUSE. Near Bakewell are the 100 breathtaking acres of Chatsworth House, home of the Duke and Duchess of Devonshire. The property includes an 80m cascade fountain, each step designed to make a different sound; a hedge maze; a lagoon with waterfalls and boulders; 26 ornate rooms—you'll be pinching yourself to make sure it's all real. Take bus #179 directly to the house (2 per day), or ask the tourist information centre about other buses that go close. (☎ (01246) 582204. Open daily mid-Mar. to Oct. 11am-5:30pm, last admission 4:30pm. £6.75, students and seniors £5.50, children £3, families £16.75.)

HADDON HALL. Two miles southwest of Bakewell (go down Matlock St. as it becomes Haddon Rd. and then the A6), the Duke of Rutland's Haddon Hall may be recognizable to visitors as the setting for Franco Zefferelli's 1996 *Jane Eyre*, as well as *The Princess Bride*. The house lends itself to cinematic romance and glitz because it has been so little altered since the reign of Henry VIII, preserving its antler-lined great hall and frescoed chapel. (☎ 812855. Open Apr.-Sept. daily 10:30am-5pm; Oct. M-Th 10:30am-5pm. No wheelchair access. £5.75, seniors £4.75, children £3, families £15; discounts for YHA members.)

EYAM

Just five miles north of Bakewell, the hamlet of Eyam (Ee-yum) underwent a self-imposed quarantine when the plague spread here from London in 1665, during which 259 of its 350 residents died a bubonic death. Plaques on old houses tally the numbers that died in each, and makeshift graves lie in strangely vibrant gardens (victims were buried quickly to prevent the spread of the disease). The first three victims perished in the flower-ringed stones of the **Plague Cottages,** Edgeview Rd. The tiny **Eyam Museum,** on Hawkhill Rd., commemorates all the grisly details, including touching final letters and heroic stories. (☎ (01433) 631371. Open Apr.-Oct. Tu-Su 10am-4:30pm. £1.50, seniors and children £1, families £4.25.) **Eyam Hall,** on Edgeview Rd., a hundred yards west of the church., traces the owner's family history in a 17th-century manor house. The hall boasts a wall-to-wall tapestry room, an eight-line love stanza carved into the library window, and a 1675 pop-up human anatomy textbook. (☎ (01433) 631976. Open W-Th and Su 11am-4:30pm. £4, students and seniors £3.50, children £3, families £12.50.) To reach Eyam, take **bus** #175 from Bakewell, stand D (20min., 4 per day, £1.45), or #65/66 from Buxton (40min., M-Sa 9 per day, £2.13). Eyam's **YHA Youth Hostel** plants its flag 800m above the town on Hawkhill Rd. (see p. 350).

CUMBRIA

LAKE DISTRICT NATIONAL PARK

Quite possibly the most beautiful place in England, the Lake District enchants. Dramatic mountainsides plummet to shores gently embraced by lapping waves, jagged peaks and windswept fells stand in desolate splendor, and water wends its way in every direction, from glistening hillside torrents to gurgling peat-filled rivers and on into the tranquil, stately lakes. The shores are often busy, but they're less packed than one would expect for a region where tourism employs 85% of the local population. As the Lake District is a national park, little ugly development blights the landscape, and on only one lake, Windermere, can visitors zoom around in their noisy motorboats. In summer, hikers, bikers, and boaters almost equal sheep in number (and there are four million sheep, so it's quite a feat), but there is always in this northwestern corner of the realm some lonely upland fell or quiet cove where your footprints seem the first for generations.

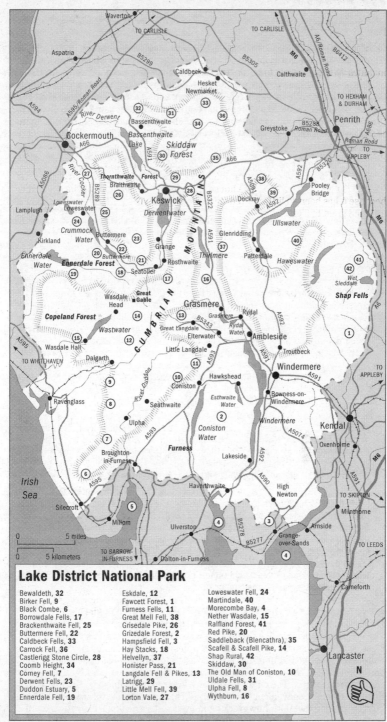

Lake District National Park

Bewaldeth, **32**
Birker Fell, **9**
Black Combe, **6**
Borrowdale Fells, **17**
Brackenthwaite Fell, **25**
Buttermere Fell, **22**
Caldbeck Fells, **33**
Carrock Fell, **36**
Castlerigg Stone Circle, **28**
Coomb Height, **34**
Corney Fell, **7**
Derwent Fells, **23**
Duddon Estuary, **5**
Ennerdale Fell, **19**

Eskdale, **12**
Fawcett Forest, **1**
Furness Fells, **11**
Great Mell Fell, **38**
Grisedale Pike, **26**
Grizedale Forest, **2**
Hampsfield Fell, **3**
Hay Stacks, **18**
Helvellyn, **37**
Honister Pass, **21**
Langdale Fell & Pikes, **13**
Latrigg, **29**
Little Mell Fell, **39**
Lorton Vale, **27**

Loweswater Fell, **24**
Martindale, **40**
Morecombe Bay, **4**
Nether Wasdale, **15**
Ralfland Forest, **41**
Red Pike, **20**
Saddleback (Blencathra), **35**
Scafell & Scafell Pike, **14**
Shap Rural, **42**
Skiddaw, **30**
The Old Man of Coniston, **10**
Uldale Fells, **31**
Ulpha Fell, **8**
Wythburn, **16**

NORTHWEST ENGLAND

GETTING THERE

Trains: Two rail lines flank the park: the **Preston-Lancaster-Carlisle** line (trains connect with **Leeds** at Lancaster) runs south to north along the eastern edge of the park as part of the line to Scotland, while the **Barrow-Carlisle** line serves the western coast. If your first destination is the remote western or southern area, hiking from one of the stations along the Barrow-Carlisle line might be your best bet. Otherwise, catch the Preston-Carlisle line to either **Oxenholme,** just south of the Lake District, or **Penrith.** Trains (☎ (08457) 484950) to **Oxenholme** from: **London Euston** (4-5hr.; M-Sa 16 per day, Su 11 per day; £58.30); **Manchester Piccadilly** (2hr.; M-F 6 per day, Sa 5 per day, Su 7 per day; £11.40); **Edinburgh** (2½-3hr., 6 per day, £31.50); and **Birmingham** (2½hr., 1-2 per hr., £36). A short branch line covers the 10 mi. to **Windermere** from Oxenholme (20min., 1 per hr., £3.20); there is also the occasional train direct to Windermere from **Manchester Piccadilly** (2½hr., 3-4 per day, £11.20, return £11.30).

Buses: National Express (☎ (08705) 808080) arrives in **Windermere** from: **London** (7½hr., 1 per day, £24); **Manchester** (3hr., 1per day, £14); and **Birmingham** (4½hr., 1 per day, £22.50). The buses continue north through **Ambleside** and **Grasmere** to **Keswick.** Call the Windermere tourist information centre (TIC) at ☎ (015394) 46499 for more info.

⫶ GETTING AROUND

Buses: Stagecoach Cumberland (☎ (01946) 63222) serves over 25 towns and villages. The essential *Lakeland Explorer* magazine, free from TICs, presents wonderful up-to-date timetables, clear maps, and walking routes. **"Lakeslink"** bus #555 travels the area from **Kendal** to **Keswick,** stopping at **Windermere, Ambleside,** and **Grasmere** (M-Sa 11 per day, Su 5 per day). If you dig the wind in your hair, Stagecoach's open-top double-decker "Lakeland Experience," bus #599 between **Bowness** and **Grasmere,** should not be missed. For wider-ranging transport, consult *Getting Around Cumbria and the Lake District* (free from TICs). An **Explorer** ticket offers unlimited travel on all area Stagecoach buses. (Exceptional value at £5.75 for one day, seniors and children £4, families £12; 4-day pass £13.60, seniors and children £9.50.)

YHA Minibus: The YHA hostel at **Ambleside** offers a convenient minibus service (☎ (015394) 32304) between hostels. For £2.50 you can travel between hostels in **Windermere, Ambleside, Hawkshead, Coniston Holly How, Elterwater, Langdale,** and **Grasmere** (2 per day; get a schedule from a hostel). Or send your backpack ahead so you can enjoy the inter-hostel walk burden-free. The minibus also takes you from the Windermere train station to the Windermere and Ambleside hostels for free.

Tours: For those who wish to explore the park with minimal effort, **Mountain Goat,** downhill from the TIC in Windermere, does the climbing for you in a series of friendly, off-the-beaten-track, themed minibus and bus tours. (☎ (015394) 45161. £13.50-25.) **Lakes Supertours,** 1 High St., Windermere, just across the road from Mountain Goat in the lobby of the Lakes Hotel, runs similar half- and full-day minibus tours, with superbly knowledgeable and witty local drivers at the wheel. (☎ (015394) 42751. £15-16.50 per half day, £24 per day. Free pickup in the Bowness-Ambleside area. Call for more info 8am-9pm daily.) The **Lakeside and Haverthwaite Railway** (☎ (015395) 31594) runs a sightseeing trip by steam train.

✴❷ ORIENTATION AND PRACTICAL INFORMATION

The major lakes diverge like spokes of a wheel from Wordsworth's village of Grasmere, south of Keswick and north of Ambleside on the A591. Derwentwater is among the most beautiful of the lakes, Wastwater is the most bewitchingly wild, and Windermere, the largest, remains supremely popular, if a bit bludgeoned by condos and marinas. The larger towns of Windermere, Ambleside, Grasmere, and Keswick all make convenient touring bases. The farther west you go from the busy bus route along the A591, however, the more countryside you'll have to yourself.

The following **National Park Information Centres** dispense free information and town maps on the camping-barn network and book accommodations. (10% deposit for local bookings; non-local bookings an additional £3 fee.) *Lake District Holidays 2001* lists accommodations, sights, and entertainment, while *Best of Lakeland* gives the lowdown on the best sights to visit (both free).

National Park Visitor Centre: (☎ (015394) 46601). In Brockhole, halfway between Windermere and Ambleside. Most buses stop at the site. For an introduction to the Lake District, including exhibits, talks, films, and special events, visit this recently renovated house and its beautifully landscaped lakeside grounds. Open Easter-Oct. 10am-5pm, plus most weekends in winter.

Ambleside (Waterhead): (☎ (015394) 32729; fax 31728). Walk south on Lake Rd. or Borrans Rd. from town to the pier. Open Easter-Oct. daily 9:30am-5:30pm.

Bowness Bay: Glebe Rd. (☎ (015394) 42895). Open July-Aug. daily 9:30am-6pm; Apr.-June and Sept.-Oct. daily 9am-5:30pm; Nov.-Mar. F-Su 10am-4pm.

Coniston: Ruskin Ave. (☎ (015394) 41533; fax 41802), behind the Tilberthwaite Ave. bus stop. Open Easter-Oct. daily 9:30am-5:30pm; Nov.-Easter Sa-Su 10am-3:30pm.

Grasmere: Redbank Rd. (☎ (015394) 35245; fax 35057). Open Easter-Oct. daily 9:30am-5:30pm; Nov.-Easter Sa-Su 10am-4pm.

Hawkshead: Main Car Park (☎ (015394) 36525; fax 36349). Open July-Aug. daily 9:30am-6pm; Easter-June and Sept.-Oct. daily 9:30am-5:30pm; Nov.-Easter Sa-Su 10am-3:30pm.

Keswick: Moot Hall, Market Sq. (☎ (017687) 72645). Open Aug. daily 9:30am-6pm; Sept.-July 9:30am-5:30pm.

Pooley Bridge: The Square (☎ (017684) 86530). Open Easter-Oct. daily 10am-1pm, 1:30-5pm.

Seatoller Barn: Borrowdale (☎ (017687) 77294), at the foot of Honister Pass. Open Easter.-Oct. daily 10am-5pm.

Ullswater: Main Car Park, Glenridding, Penrith (☎ (017684) 82414), on the main road through town. Open Apr.-Oct. daily 9am-6pm; Nov.-Mar. Sa-Su 9:30am-4pm.

▞ HIKING, BIKING, AND CLIMBING

Outdoor enthusiasts outnumber water molecules in the Lake District. Park information centres have guidebooks for all occasions—mountain-bike trails, pleasant family walks, tough climbs, and hikes ending at pubs. Among the many available pamphlets is *Countryside Access for People with Limited Mobility* (75p). Hostels are also an excellent source of information, with large maps and posters on the walls and free advice from experienced staff.

If you plan to go on a long or difficult outing, check first with the Park Service, call **weather information** (24hr. ☎ (017687) 75757; YHAs also post daily forecasts), and leave a route plan with your B&B proprietor or hostel warden before setting out. Steep slopes and reliably unreliable weather can quickly reduce visibility to five feet. A good **map**, compass, and the ability to use them are necessities. The 1:25,000 Ordnance Survey Outdoor Leisure Maps #4, 5, 6, and 7 provide good detail of the four quadrants of the Lake District (£6.50), while the 1:50,000 Ordnance Survey Landranger Maps #89, 90, 91, and 96-98 chart every hillock and bend in the road (£5.25). A public right-of-way does not always mean a path, and vice versa.

Any **cyclist** planning an extensive stay in the Lake District should consider investing in the gripping *Ordnance Survey Cycle Tours* (£10), which provides detailed maps of on- and off-trail routes. A selection of bicycle shops is listed below, but any TIC will provide listings. Consider touring some of Cumbria's less-traveled areas via the circular **Cumbria Cycle Way.** The 259 mi. route runs from Carlisle in the north around the outskirts of the Lake District. Pick up *The Cumbria Cycle Way* (£6) from a TIC for details.

Every town has stores that can describe the best climbs, advise on the necessary precautions, and give current weather reports; a few establishments also rent boots and backpacks. In Ambleside, **The Climber's Shop,** on the corner of Rydal Rd. and Compston Rd., rents boots. (☎ (015394) 32297. £2 per day, £10 per week; deposit £20. Open daily 9am-5:30pm.) **Keswick Mountain Sports,** 73 Main St., stocks all the requisite paraphernalia. (☎ (017687) 73843. Open daily 9am-5:30pm). In Grasmere, try **Outdoor World,** Red Lion Sq. (☎ (015394) 35614. Open M-Sa 9am-6pm, Su 9:30am-5:30pm.)

ACCOMMODATIONS

Despite the fact that **B&Bs** line every street in every town (£15-20) and that the Lakes have the highest concentration of youth hostels in the world, lodgings in the Lake District do fill up in July and August; book far ahead. TICs and National Park Centres will book local rooms for a 10% deposit. **Campers** should pick up the YHA's *Camping Barns in England* (free), and call or write ahead to reserve space at the Lake District's 12 **camping barns.** (Lakeland Barns Booking Office, Moot Hall, Market Sq., Keswick CA12 4JR. ☎ (017687) 72645; fax 75043. Prices start at £3.50.) Twenty-six **YHA Youth Hostels** provide accommodations in the park. Reception is usually closed 10am-5pm, but public areas and restrooms are accessible through the day. The YHA **minibus** gets you between the bigger hostels (see **Getting Around,** p. 358). The hostel at Ambleside provides a free Lake District-wide booking service; you can find out which places have beds left. (☎ (015394) 31117. Open daily 9am-6pm; credit card required to reserve a bed.) The following lists a selection of the hostels in the park; see the YHA handbook for others.

▓ Ambleside: Waterhead, Ambleside (☎ (015394) 32304; fax 34408; ambleside@yha.org.uk), 1 mi. south of Ambleside on Windermere Rd. (the A591), 3 mi. north of Windermere on the Lake's northern shores. Bus #555 stops in front of this mother of all hostels. 245 beds in a superbly refurbished old hotel. Distinctive country-club feel—you can even swim off the pier. Books tours, rents mountain bikes, exchanges currency, and operates the YHA shuttle. Internet access £2.50 per 30min. Open year-round. Mar.-Oct. no curfew; Nov.-Feb. midnight. Dorms £11.15, under 18 £7.60.

Black Sail: Black Sail Hut, Ennerdale, Cleator (☎ (0411) 108450). Splendidly set in the hills. Take CMS bus #79 from Keswick to Seatoller and walk 3½ mi. from there. 18 beds. Chilly outdoor showers. No heat or electricity in the bedrooms. Open July-Aug. daily; Apr.-June and Sept.-Oct. Tu-Sa. Dorms £8.10, under 18 £5.65.

Buttermere: King George VI Memorial Hostel, Buttermere (☎ (017687) 70245; fax 70231). ¼ mi. south of the village on the B5289. 70 beds. Lockout 10am-1pm. Open Apr.-Aug. daily; Sept.-Dec. Tu-Sa; Jan.-Feb. F-Sa; Feb.-Mar. Tu-Sa. Dorms £11, under 18 £7.75.

Cockermouth: Double Mills, Cockermouth (☎/fax (01900) 822561), in the town center off Fern Bank at Parkside Ave. Converted 17th-century water mill. 28 beds. Open Apr.-Oct. daily. Dorms £8.10, under 18 £5.65.

Coniston (Holly How): Far End (☎ (015394) 41323; fax 41803; conistonhh@yha.org.uk), just north of Coniston village at the junction of Hawkshead Rd. and Ambleside Rd. A modernized country house. 60 beds. Curfew 11pm. Open Apr. and July-Sept. daily; May-June and Oct.-Nov. and mid-Jan. to Mar. F-Su. Dorms £9.80, under 18 £6.75.

Coniston Coppermines: Coppermines House (☎/fax (015394) 41261), northwest along the Churchbeck River, 1¼ mi. from Coniston. No need to venture into the hills; the rugged journey to the hostel is itself a scenic challenge. 28-bed hostel in the mine manager's house, overlooking the water. Open June-Aug. daily; Apr.-May and Sept.-Oct. Tu-Sa. Dorms £9, under 18 £6.20.

▓ Derwentwater: Barrow House, Borrowdale (☎ (017687) 77246; fax 77396), 2 mi. south of Keswick on the B5289. Take bus #79 to Seatoller, or take the Keswick-bound ferry. It's worth the inconvenience to stay in this 90-bed, 200-year-old house with its own waterfall. Open Jan. to early Dec. daily. Dorms £10.85, under 18 £7.40.

Eskdale: (☎ (019467) 23219; fax 23163). In a quiet valley 1½ mi. east of Boot on the Ravenglass-Eskdale railway. 50 beds. Laundry, kitchen, showers. Open Mar.-Oct. daily. Dorms £9.80, under 18 £6.75.

Grasmere: (☎ (015394) 35316; fax 35798; grasmerebh@yha.org.uk). Two buildings. **Butterlip How,** Easedale Rd. Follow road to Easedale 150 yd. and turn right down sign-posted drive. 80-bed Victorian house north of Grasmere village. No lockout. Open Apr.-Oct. daily; Nov.-Jan. F-Sa; Feb.-Mar Tu-Sa. Dorms £11.90, under 18 £8.20. **Thorney How.** Follow Easedale Rd. ½ mi. and turn right at the fork; hostel is ¼ mi. down on the left. 48-bed farmhouse with a kindly staff. Open Apr.-Sept. daily; mid-Feb. to Mar. and Oct.-Dec. Th-M. Dorms £9.80, under 18 £6.75.

Hawkshead: Esthwaite Lodge (☎ (015394) 36293; fax 36720; hawkshead@yha.org.uk), 1 mi. south of Hawkshead village. Bus #505 from Ambleside stops at the village center. 115 beds. Lockout 10am-noon. Open Apr.-Oct. daily; mid-Feb. to Mar. Tu-Sa; Nov. to mid-Dec. F-Sa. Dorms £10.85, under 18 £7.40.

Honister Hause: (☎/fax (017687) 77267), near Seatoller. A gray building at the summit of imposing **Honister Pass,** 9 mi. north of Keswick. May-Oct. bus #77 takes you there from Keswick; #79 stops within 1½ mi. 26 beds. Open Apr.-Aug. daily. Dorms £9, under 18 £6.20.

Keswick: Station Rd. (☎ (017687) 72484; fax 74129; keswick@yha.org.uk). From the TIC, bear left down Station Rd.; look for the YHA sign on the left. 91 beds in a former hotel with balconies over a river, clean rooms, and a decent kitchen. 6 showers, laundry facilities, TV, and game room. Lockout 10am-1pm. Curfew 11pm. Open daily year-round. Dorms £10.85, under 18 £7.40.

Wastwater: Wasdale Hall, Wasdale (☎ (019467) 26222; fax 26056), ½ mi. east of Nether Wasdale. A 50-bed half-timbered house on the water. Climber's paradise. Bus #6 from Whitehaven to Seascale stops 5 mi. away in the Viking village of Gosforth. Open Apr.-Oct. daily; Nov.-Dec. F-Sa; Jan.-Mar. Th-M. Dorms £9.80, under 18 £6.75.

Windermere: High Cross, Bridge Ln., Troutbeck (☎ (015394) 43543; fax 47165; windermere@yha.org.uk), 1 mi. north of Windermere off the A591. Ambleside bus stops in Troutbeck Bridge; walk ¾ mi. uphill to the hostel, or catch the YHA shuttle from the train station. Spacious, 73-bed house with panoramic views, but few showers. Mountain bikes for rent. Internet access £6 per hr. Open mid-Feb. to Oct. daily. Dorms £10.85, under 18 £7.40.

WINDERMERE AND BOWNESS   ☎015394

Windermere and its sidekick, Bowness-on-Windermere (combined pop. 8500), fill to the gills with vacationers in July and August when sailboats and water-skiers swarm over the lake. The only major sight in the towns is **Bowness Pier,** a mile to the south, which is overpopulated by belligerent swans. The downhill walk from Windermere's station is easy; turn left onto High St., then right on Main St.; walk through downtown to New Rd., which becomes Lake Rd., leading pierward.

🛈 **PRACTICAL INFORMATION.** For information on getting to Windermere, see **Getting There,** p. 358. Windermere's **train station** also serves as the town's primary **bus depot. Lakeland Experience** bus #599 runs to Bowness from the train station (3 per hr., £1). For information, visit the **Windermere tourist information centre** (TIC), next door to the train station. It stocks guides to lake walks (30p), books **National Express** tickets, sells Stageland Explorer passes, books accommodations (10% deposit for local lodgings, £3 fee for beds outside Cumbria), and exchanges currency for a £2.50 commission. (☎ 46499. Open daily July-Aug. 9am-7:30pm; Easter-June and Sept.-Oct. 9am-6pm; Nov.-Easter 9am-5pm. Wheelchair access.) The **National Park Information Centre** beside Bowness Pier is also a fount of knowledge (see p. 359). Fast funds flow from **banks** in both towns—stock up before heading out. Windermere's **NatWest** is across from the TIC. (Open M-Tu and Th-F 9am-4:30pm, W 9:30am-4:30pm.) **Luggage storage** is available at **Darryl's Café,** 14 Church St. (☎ 42894. £1 per bag. Open W-M 8am-7pm.) **Country Lanes Cycle Hire,** at the train station, has nice new bikes. (☎ (015394) 44544. £9 per half-day, £14 per day; £2 discount with train ticket. Open Easter-Oct. daily 9am-5:30pm.) Services include: **Internet access** at **Triarom,** Birch St., near the post office (☎ 44639; £1 per 10min., £5 per hr.; open M-Sa 9:30am-5:30pm); **launderette** on Main Rd. (wash £2, dry 20p per 4min.; open M-F 9am-6pm, Sa 9am-5pm); **Windermere Taxis** (☎ 42355); the **police,** Lake Rd. (☎ (01539) 722611); and the **post office,** 21 Crescent Rd. (☎ 43245.; open M-F 9am-5:30pm, Sa 9am-12:30pm). **Postal code:** LA23 1AA.

⌐⌐⌐ ACCOMMODATIONS AND FOOD. Windermere and Bowness have more **B&Bs** than the hills have sheep. Nevertheless, those who neglect to book ahead risk sleeping in cold, lonely fields amid cowpats and wool tufts. Windermere's YHA Youth Hostel is one mile north of town; see p. 361. To reach the social **Lake District Backpackers Hostel,** on High St., walk from the train station and look for the sign on the right as you descend the hill. (☎ 46374. Reception 9am-1pm and 5-9pm. Dorms £10-12.50.) **Brendan Chase,** 1-3 College Rd., has attractive rooms in two converted Victorian townhouses with an efficient, lively proprietress. (☎ 45638. £15-20 per person.) Other fine B&Bs include **The Village House,** 5 Victoria St. (☎ 46041; £16 per person); **The Haven,** 10 Birch St. (☎ 44017; £19-21 per person); **Dalecote,** 13 Upper Oak St. (☎ 45121; £15-18 per person); and **Greenriggs,** 8 Upper Oak St. (☎ 42265; singles £17-18; doubles £36-50). The nearest **campground, Limefitt Park,** lies 4½ mi. north of Bowness on the A592 just below the Kirkstone path, and has most amenities, except for public transport. However, only couples may stay at the campground, with or without children. (☎ 32300. 2-person tent and car £12.)

All groceries great and small can easily be found in the area. **Booths Supermarket** is housed in Windermere's Old Station at the end of Cross St., by the new train station. (☎ 46114. Open M-F 8:30am-8pm, Sa 8:30am-7pm, Su 10am-4pm.) **Booker's,** on Lake Rd. in Bowness, holds a selection fit for a Bacchanalian revel—bountiful fresh fruit and loads of liquor. (☎ 88798. Open daily 8am-10pm.) In Windermere, vegetarians are catered for in the bright blue and yellow **Wild Oats** cafe on Main Rd. Sandwiches with salad are only £1.85, main courses such as chicken curry only £4, and breakfast is served all day. (☎ 43583. Open daily 10am-9pm.)

◙ SIGHTS. A number of boating companies are located at Bowness Pier. **Windermere Lake Cruises** runs its own **Lake Information Centre** (☎ 43360; fax 43468) at the north end of the pier that vends maps and accommodation guides, and rents rowboats or motorboats. The center also books passage on popular lake cruises. From Easter to October, boats sail north to Waterhead Pier in Ambleside (30min., about 2 per hr. 9am-6pm; return £5.80, ages 5-15 £2.90) and south to Lakeside (40min., 1 per hr. 9am-5pm; return £6, ages 5-15 £3). "Freedom of the Lake" all-day passes are also available. (£10, children £5, families £26.) In town, **The World of Beatrix Potter,** in the Old Laundry Theatre complex, Crag Bow, solicits with fresh scents and smarmy-cutesy displays. Unless you are five, feel as if you're five, or are inextricably bound to a five-year-old, explore other sights. (☎ 88444. Open daily Easter-Sept. 10am-5:30pm; Oct.-Easter 10am-4:30pm. £3.50, children £2.) If bunnies aren't your thing, spend a couple of hours trekking to **Orrest Head,** one of Windermere's most popular walks. Two and a half miles long, the walk affords one of the best views in the Lake District. A guide to the walk is available at the TIC (30p).

AMBLESIDE ☎ 015394

Just under a mile north of the tip of Windermere lake, Ambleside has adapted to the tourist influx without selling its soul to the industry. Oft-times dubbed "anorak capital of England" in recognition of the numerous outdoors stores (14 at last count), Ambleside is geared towards helping you enjoy the Lake District rather than milking your last pound for a rustic hat.

⌐⌐⌐ GETTING THERE AND PRACTICAL INFORMATION. For information on how to get to Ambleside, see **Getting Around,** p. 358. **Buses** stop on Kelsick Rd. (☎ 32231. Open M-W and F-Sa 10am-6pm.) **Lakeslink** bus #555 runs from Grasmere, **Windermere,** and **Keswick** (1 per hr.). Buses #505 and 506 join the town to **Hawkshead** and **Coniston** (M-Sa 10 per day, Su 3 per day). The **tourist information centre** is on Church St. (☎ 32582. Open daily 9am-5:30pm.) The **National Park Information Centre** at Waterhead also has a **bureau de change.** (£3 per transaction. Open daily Easter-Oct. 9:30am-5:30pm.) **Barclays bank** is on Market Pl. (Open M-W and F 9:30am-4:30pm, Th 10am-4:30pm.) The **launderette** is across from the bus station on Kelsick Rd. The energetic can rent bikes from **Ghyllside Cycles,** The Slack. (☎

(015394) 33592. £12.50 per day, £50 per week. ID deposit. Discounts for rentals
longer than 3 days. Open Apr.-Oct. daily 9am-5:30pm; Nov.-Apr. closed Tu.) The
post office, Market Pl., **exchanges money** for £2.50. (☎ 32267. Open M-F 9am-5:30pm,
Sa 9am-12:30pm.) **Postal code:** LA22 9BU.

☐☐ ACCOMMODATIONS AND FOOD. There are almost as many **B&Bs** and
guesthouses here as private residences. Most B&Bs cost £14.50-16 and fill up
quickly in summer. Some cluster on Church St. and Compston Rd.; others line the
busier Lake Rd. leading in from Windermere. Ambleside's **☒ YHA Youth Hostel**
resides near the steamer pier at Waterhead, a pleasant one mile walk from the
town center (see p. 360). **Shirland, Linda's B&B,** on Compston Rd., has four rooms
(doubles, triples, and quads) with TV, cramped attic space for three, and a private,
hostel-style bunkhouse. (☎ 32999. £12-13 per person, without breakfast £9.) Hospitable Mr. and Mrs. Richardson run **3 Cambridge Villas,** on Church St. next to the
TIC, and will make vegetarian breakfasts on request. (☎ 32307. £16 per person,
with bath £20.) Across the street, the Irelands offer crisp, clean rooms with TV at
Melrose Hotel, Church St. (☎ 32500. £18-20 per person.) **Camp** at **Hawkshead Hall
Farm,** five miles south of Ambleside off the B5286. (☎ 36221. Open Mar.-Nov. £1
per person, £1 per tent, £1 per car.)

Ambleside specializes in trail food, from the omnipresent **mint cakes** to gourmet
sandwiches. Assemble your own picnic at the Wednesday **market** on King St. or at
the **Co-op Village Store,** Compston Rd. (☎ 33124. Open M-Sa 8:30am-6pm, Su 10am-
4pm.) The **Golden Rule** (☎ 32257), on Smithy Brow, does unto residents with good
local beer (£1.75).

☒☒ SIGHTS AND HIKES. Ambleside's only noteworthy sight is the tiny **House
on the Bridge,** off Rydal Rd.; actually, house and bridge are one and the same.
About four paces long and one pace wide, it was once inhabited by a basket
weaver, his wife, and six children; it now houses one lone representative of the
National Trust, and even he looks cramped. (☎ 32617. Open Apr.-Oct. daily 10am-
5pm. Free.) If you're feeling a bit homesick for the city, head for the **Homes of Football Photographic Gallery,** 100 Lake Rd., where a great many panoramic photos of
urban soccer shrines grace the walls. (☎ 34440. Open daily 10am-6pm. £1, children
50p.) You can view the surrounding landscape most vividly from the middle of the
lake; rent a rowboat at the Waterhead pier, and float by the splendor of the **Horseshoe Falls.** (Boat rental £3 per hr., each additional person £1.50.)

Great **hikes** extend in all directions from Ambleside. Hidden trail markings, steep
slopes, and weather-sensitive visibility all make a good map and a compass necessary. The mountain rescue service averages two to three crises a day in this area;
don't let yourself be one. For an introduction to the area, you might try one of the
excellent warden-guided **walks** which leave from Ambleside and Grasmere's National
Park Information Centres and TICs. Bring a sweater, rain gear, sturdy walking shoes
or boots, lunch, and water to fuel you for the four- to six-hour rambles of varying
degrees of difficulty. From the oft-trodden top of **Loughrigg,** you can lift your eyes up
to the other, higher surrounding fells—it's only a 2½ mi. hike from Ambleside, with a
3½ mi. circuit descent. For gentler, shorter hikes, buy the *Ambleside Walks in the
Countryside* (30p), which lists three easy walks from the town's center.

CONISTON ☎015394

With fells to the north and a lake to the south, Coniston makes a phenomenal base for hikers and cyclists. On rainy days, admire the sketches, photographs, and geological hammers of the writer-artist-philosopher-critic-social-reformer John Ruskin at the **John Ruskin Museum,** on Yewdale Rd. (☎ 41164. Open daily Easter-Nov. 10am-5:30pm. £3, children £1.75, families £8.50.) The **gravestone** of the writer-etc.-etc. is in St. Andrew's Churchyard. **Brantwood,** Ruskin's manor from 1872, looks across the lake at Coniston and the Old Man; it holds Ruskin's art, as well as prose works by Tolstoy, Proust, and Gandhi. (☎ 41396. Open mid-Mar. to mid-Nov. daily 11am-5:30pm; mid-Nov. to mid-Mar. W-Su 11am-4pm. £4, students £2.10, under 18 £1; gardens only £2.) The easiest way to reach Brantwood is by water: the **Coniston Launch** travels to and from Brantwood. (☎ 36216. Apr.-Oct. 6-8 per day. Return £3.60; combined £6.90 ticket for ferry and admission, students £5.70, children £2.70, families £18.50.) In the hamlet of Hawkshead, four miles east of Coniston, imagine pulling Wordsworth's hair and passing him notes at the **Hawkshead Grammar School,** on Main St., where the poet studied from 1779 to 1787. (Open Easter-Oct. M-Sa 10am-12:30pm and 1:30-5pm, Su 1-5pm. £2, children 50p.)

Coniston serves as the base for a variety of outdoor activities. Ambitious hikers tackle the steep **Old Man** (5 mi. round-trip) or the less lofty but equally vertical **Yewdale Fells.** For a more moderate hike, explore the Coppermines area and search for the "American's stope"—an old copper mine shaft named in honor of an American who leapt over it twice successfully and survived a 160 ft. fall the third time (*Let's Go* does not recommend 160 ft. falls). Cyclists roll down the 40 mi. of forest tracks criss-crossing though **Grizedale Forest,** while climbers tackle **Dow Crag.**

Coniston is accessible by **bus** #505 or 506 (the "Coniston Rambler"), which begins in Kendal and turns, twists, stops, and starts between Windermere, Bowness Pier, Ambleside, and sometimes Hawkshead on its way to Coniston and the lake (from Ambleside 45min., M-Sa 10 per day, Su 3-6 per day). Buses stop at the corner of Tilberthwaite and Ruskin Ave. Coniston's **tourist information centre,** on Ruskin Ave., poses as a **National Park Information Centre.** (☎ 41533. Open Easter-Oct. daily 9:30am-5:30pm; Nov.-Easter Sa-Su 10am-3:30pm.) A **Barclays bank** bereft of cash machine sits at Bridge End. (☎ 41249. Open M-F 9:30am-3:30pm.) Rent bikes from **Summitreks,** 14 Yewdale Rd. (☎ 41212. £9 per half-day, £13 per day.) The **post office** is on Yewdale Rd. (☎ 41259. Open M-F 9am-12:30pm and 1:30-5:30pm, W closes at 5pm, Sa 9am-noon.) **Postal code:** LA21 8DU.

Accommodations are available at **YHA Holly How** (see p. 360) or the delightful **YHA Coppermines** (see p. 360). Hikers and climbers will find their ideal hosts in the ice-, rock-, and mineshaft-climbing proprietors of **Holmthwaite,** on Tilberthwaite Ave. Large rooms and lots of advice make for excellent resting and hiking. (☎ 41231. £18.50 per person; discounts for stays over 3 nights.) For **groceries,** head to the **Coop** on Yewdale St. (☎ 41247. Open M-Sa 9am-9pm, Su 10am-8pm.)

GRASMERE ☎015394

The attractive village of Grasmere, with a lake and a poet all to itself, has its fair share of camera-clicking tourists. The sightseers crowd in at midday to visit the Wordsworth home, grave, and museum, but in the quiet mornings and evenings the peace that the poet so enjoyed returns for a brief appearance. The early 17th-century ▓ **Dove Cottage,** where Wordsworth lived with his wife and his sister Dorothy from 1799 to 1808, is almost exactly as Wordsworth left it. A multitude of guides provide 20-minute tours. Next door, the outstanding **Wordsworth Museum** includes pages of his handwritten poetry and info on his Romantic contemporaries. The cottage is 10 minutes from the center of Grasmere. Bus #555 stops here hourly en route to Ambleside or Keswick, and open-top bus #599 stops every 20min. (☎ 35544. Open mid-Feb. to mid-Jan. daily 9:30am-5pm. Admission to cottage and museum £5, students and YHA members £4.20, seniors £4.70, children £2.50; museum alone £2.50, children £1.25.) A 40-minute hike, starting at Dove Cottage, up the **Old Coffin Trail** towards Ambleside (or one bus stop nearer to Ambleside on bus #555) leads to ⬛ **Rydal Mount,** the poet's home from 1813 until his death in 1850. A stroll across the garden terrace, designed by Wordsworth himself, leads to the small hut where he frequently composed verses. (☎ 33002. Open Mar.-Oct. daily 9:30am-5pm; Nov.-Feb. W-M 10am-4pm. £3.75, students and seniors £3.25, children £1.75.) Hydrophiles can walk down Grasmere's Redbank Rd. and hire a boat to row on the deep green lake. (Open summer daily 10am-5pm. £2-4 per person depending on number of people; deposit £10.) Or you can purchase a pot of tea (80p) at the same port and direct a Romantic gaze across the water at the fells.

As Wordsworth well knew, Grasmere is a good base for walkers. A steep two-hour scramble (up Easedale Rd. until it ends, then follow the signs) leads to the top of **Helm Cragg,** dubbed by locals "the lion and the lamb." Can you find that magic angle? Hint: the lion is lying beside the lamb. Walk to the other side and it's supposed to look like a woman playing an organ. The six-mile **Wordsworth Walk** circumnavigates the two lakes of the Rothay River, passing the poet's grave, Dove Cottage, and Rydal Mount along the way. Star-seeking fell-climbers can tackle the path from Rydal to Legburthwaite (near Keswick) in an athletic day, passing the towering Great Rigg and Helvellyn on the way. Bus #555 will bring you back to Ambleside.

The combined **tourist information centre** and **National Park Information Centre** lies in town on Redbank Rd. The staff of experienced hikers frequently hosts free guided walks on summer Sundays; details are in the *Events 2001* magazine. It also **exchanges currency** for £3 per transaction. (☎ 35245; fax 35057. Open Easter-Oct. daily 9:30am-5:30pm; Nov.-Easter Sa-Su 12:30-5:30pm.)

There are two **Grasmere YHA Youth Hostel** buildings within an eight-minute walk: **Butterlip How** and **Thorney How** (see p. 361). All B&Bs in town cost at least £17 and fill up quickly, so pray that the **Glenthorne Quaker Guest House,** a quarter mile up Easedale Rd. and past the Butterlip How hostel, has a place for thee. Most rooms are clean, spacious singles. (☎ 35389. Optional 15min. Quaker meeting each morning. Wheelchair access. B&B £19, full board £39.) **Newby's Deli,** Red Lion Sq., can pack up superb sandwiches from £1.25. (☎ 35248. Open M-Sa 9am-5:30pm.) Sarah Nelson's famous Grasmere Gingerbread, a staple since 1854, is a bargain at 22p in **Church Cottage,** outside St. Oswald's Church. (☎ 35428. Open Easter-Nov. M-Sa 9:15am-5:30pm, Su 12:30-5:30pm; Nov.-Easter M-Sa 9:15am-5pm, Su 12:30-5:30pm.)

KESWICK   ☎017687

Sandwiched between towering Skiddaw peak and the northern edge of Derwent-water, Keswick (KEZ-ick) rivals Windermere as the Lake District's tourist capital, but far surpasses it in charm.

🛈 PRACTICAL INFORMATION. For information on how to get to Keswick, see **Getting Around,** p. 358. The **National Park Information Centre,** Moot Hall, behind the clock tower in Market Sq., sells a lodgings booklet (£1), hands out town maps for free, and will book you B&B for a 10% deposit. They'll also **exchange currency** for £3. (☎ 72645. Open daily Aug. 9:30am-6pm; Sept.-July 9:30am-5:30pm.) A variety of **guided walks** leave from the information centre, including the popular "Keswick Ramble" that leaves daily at 10:15am and lasts about seven hours. (Bring lunch and rain gear. £5, children £2.) Serious climbers should inquire about taking special trips. Book a tour of the area at the **Mountain Goat Office,** in the car park. (☎ 73962. Open Apr.-Oct. M-F 9am-5pm, Sa-Su 9am-4:30pm; Nov.-Mar. M-F 9am-4:30pm). **Keswick Mountain Bikes,** just out of town in Southey Hill Industrial Estate, rents 2-wheelers. (☎ (017687) 75202. £13 per day, £10 per half-day. Open daily 9am-5:30pm.) **Barclays bank** is on Market Sq. (☎ 864221. Open M-Tu and Th-F 9:30am-4:30pm, W 10am-4:30pm.) Services include: the **launderette,** Main St., just west of the mini-roundabout (wash £1.60; dry £1.50-1.60; open daily from 7:30am, last wash 7pm); the **police** (☎ (01900) 602422), Bank St.; and the multitasking **post office,** 48 Main St., at the corner of Bank St. and Market Pl., where you can reserve **National Express** tickets or get **Internet access** (☎ 72269; Internet access £1.50 for the first 10min., 15p per min. after that; open May-Oct. M-Sa 8:30am-8pm, Su 10:30am-4pm; Nov.-Apr. M-Sa 8:30am-5:30pm). **Postal code:** CA12 5JJ.

⌐⌐ ACCOMMODATIONS AND FOOD. The **Keswick** and **Derwentwater YHA Youth Hostels** grace this small town (see p. 360). Vast quantities of **B&Bs** nestle between Station St., St. John St.-Ambleside Rd., and Penrith Rd. No-frills **Elmtree Lodge,** 16 Leonard St., at Church St., promises quiet slumber. (☎ 74710. £17 per person; £14 without breakfast.) **Century House,** 17 Church St., has bright peaches-and-cream bedrooms in a Victorian-style house. (☎ 72843. £19.50 per person.) **Dorchester Guest House,** 17 Southey St., has lacy curtains and floral decor. (☎ 73256. £17 per person, with bath £24.) **Campers** can pitch a tent at **Castlerigg Hall,** a mile southeast of Keswick on the Windermere bus route, equipped with phones, toilets, and showers. (☎ 72437. Open Apr.-Nov. £3.70 per person, children £2, £1.50 per car.)

Sundance Wholefoods, 33 Main St., sells nature-friendly groceries at Market Pl. (☎ 74712. Open daily in summer 9am-6pm; winter roughly 9am-5pm.) For meatless treats, grab excellent sandwiches for £3 at **Lakeland Pedlar,** in an alley off Main St. (☎ 74492. Open July-Sept. daily 9am-8pm; Apr.-June M-F 10am-4pm, Sa-Su 9am-4:30pm; Sept.-Apr. daily 10am-4pm.) Or duck into a little alley and join the Lost Generation at **Ye Olde Queen's Head,** behind the Queen's Hotel on Main St. (☎ 73333. Open M-Sa 11am-11pm, Su 11am-10:30pm; happy hour 6-7pm.) Those in the know, however, frequent the lively **Dog & Gun** just past Moot Hall on Market Pl. The menu includes veggie treats, but no chips or fried foods. (☎ 73463. Open M-Sa 11am-11pm, Su noon-10:30pm; food served noon-9pm.)

⚠ ACTIVITIES. One of the best ridge hikes in the Lake District begins only one mile from Keswick. Ascend the **Cat Bells** from the west shore of Derwentwater at Hawes End and stroll a gentle three miles atop the ridge, passing **Maiden Moor** and **Eel Crags** on the way to **Dale Head,** one of the highest peaks in the area. Descend via the saddle-shaped Honister Pass to reach Seatoller (total distance 10-12 mi.). For another excellent daytrip, walk southwest through the village of **Portinscale** ("harlot's hut"), over the rugged Derwent Fells, and eventually descend into **Buttermere.** The easy three-mile **Castlehead Walk** from Keswick's Lake Rd. leads to spellbinding **Friar's Crag,** praised by Ruskin, Wordsworth, and *Let's Go.* For another gentle amble, visit the **Castlerigg Stone Circle,** in a sheep-laden field a half-hour walk east of Keswick (take Penrith Rd.).

WESTERN LAKE DISTRICT

With comparatively few visitors and spectacular, windswept scenery, the Western Lake District is delightful. Getting there is not, unless you have a car or like to climb steep hills while carrying a heavy pack. Approach the remote southern villages of **Eskdale** and **Wasdale** from Ravenglass (or less easily from Coniston). The Ravenglass-Eskdale railway (☎ (01229) 717171) stops in Boot, 1½ mi. from **YHA Eskdale** (see p. 360). There are a few B&Bs at Wasdale Head. Facing the famous and forbidding Wastwater Screes is the fetching but oh-so-remote **YHA Wastwater** (see p. 361). Climb the nearby **Whin Rigg** or venture over to the many waterfalls of **Greendale Valley.**

While the fell (mountain) blockade across the Western Lake District can be attacked from the south, the best approach is from the north. From Keswick, take bus #79 eight miles to Seatoller, hike 1¼ mi. south to **Seathwaite,** and pick your mountain. To climb craggy **Great Gable** (2949 ft.) and its sidekick **Green Gable** (2628 ft.; no pigtailed redheads in sight) follow the trail on your left, which climbs steeply along the side of a waterfall (2¼ mi. up from Seathwaite to the summit). Bus #79 also goes 1½ mi. beyond Seatoller to the harrowing **Honister Pass,** which holds **YHA Honister Hause** on its summit (see p. 361).

Set in a splendid valley between two mountain lakes on the other side of Honister Pass, **Buttermere** is a ripping town and a remote fishing hole, reachable by bus #77 from Keswick (2 per day). Nearby, **Sour Milk Gill Falls** curdles from the slopes of Red Pike. The hike up **Hay Stacks** is tough, but the summit delivers bone-chilling views of surrounding mountains. **Red Pike** (2479 ft.), **High Stile** (2644 ft.), and **High Cragg** are the three main challenges for ambitious hikers in the area. Those more sensible might take a constitutional up **Ranndale Knotts.** The **YHA Buttermere** grants a hiker's reprieve (see p. 360). **Sike Farm** in the village offers B&B and camping. (☎ (017687) 70222. £18 per person, discount for longer stays. Camping £4.50 per person; showers 20p.) **Crag Foot Cottage** is a wonderfully friendly B&B. (☎ (017687) 70220. £18 per person, discount for longer stays). Just south of Buttermere, **Ennerdale Forest** shades a valley between the mountains and, at its southeastern edge, 1½ mi. from Great Gable, the remote **YHA Black Sail** (see p. 360).

CARLISLE ☎01228

Nicknamed "The Key of England" for its strategic position in the Borderlands between England and Scotland, Carlisle (pop. 72,000) has undergone a bloody and turbulent history. Over 2000 years of conquests and battles, graced by such historic figures as Emperor Hadrian, Mary, Queen of Scots, Robert the Bruce, and Bonnie Prince Charlie, have shaped Cumbria's principal city, and it remains an ideal stopover for more peaceful border crossings, as well as a good base for examining Hadrian's Wall (see p. 410).

█ GETTING THERE AND GETTING AROUND. Carlisle's **train station** lies on Botchergate, diagonally across from the citadel. (Ticket office open M-Sa 5am-11:30pm, Su 9:30am-11:30pm.) **Trains** (☎ (08457) 484950) arrive from: **London Euston** (4hr., 1 per hr., £67.20); **Newcastle** (1½hr.; M-Sa 1 per hr., Su 9 per day; £9.90); **Edinburgh** (2hr., 1 per hr., £30); **Glasgow** (2½hr., 1 per hr, £20.50); and **Leeds** (2¾hr., 5-6 per day, £20.90). The **bus station,** on the corner of Lowther St. and Lonsdale St., books National Express or local tickets. (Open M-Sa 8:30am-6:30pm, Su 9:45am-5:30pm.) **National Express** (☎ (08705) 808080) **buses** arrive from **London** (1 per day, £22). **Stagecoach Cumberland** (☎ (01946) 63222) bus #555 drives in from **Keswick** in the Lake District (1¼hr.; M-Sa 3 per day, Su 2 per day; £4); the company also offers **bus excursions** to the **Lake District, Northumberland,** and **Scotland.** The 150 mi. **Cumbria Cycle Way** runs along the outskirts of the Lake District through Carlisle (see p. 359). **Bike rental** is available at **Scotby Cycles,** 30 Bridge St. (☎ (0800) 783 2312. £12 per day, £5 for an extra day, £20 deposit. Open M-Sa 9am-5:30pm.

█🛉 ORIENTATION AND PRACTICAL INFORMATION. Carlisle's city center is a pedestrian zone formed by **English St., Scotch St.,** and **Bank St.** The multitasking **tourist information centre** (TIC) lies in the middle of this triangle, at Old Town Hall, Green Market. To get there from the train station, turn left and walk about three blocks; Botchergate becomes English St., then cross the Old Town Square. To get to the TIC from the bus station, cross Lowther St., walk through the shopping center, and go right. The TIC **exchanges currency** and offers day-long **luggage storage** for 75p a bag; it also has fax/photocopy facilities. Booking a room there, for a 10% deposit of the entire stay (plus £3 fee for booking outside Cumbria), gets you a free coupon book for discounts at restaurants and entertainment venues. (☎ 625600;

fax 625604. Open July-Aug. M-Sa 9:30am-6pm, Su 10:30am-4pm; May-June and Sept. M-Sa 9:30am-5pm, Su 10:30am-4pm; Mar.-Apr. and Oct. M-Sa 9:30am-5pm; Nov.-Feb. M-Sa 10am-4pm.) **Barclays bank** lies on 33 English St. (☎ 604400. Open M-Tu and Th-F 9:30am-5pm, W 10am-5pm, Sa 9:30am-noon.) **Internet access** is available at Carlisle Library, 11 Globe Ln., off Scotch St. (☎ 607310. £2 per 30min. Open M-F 9:30am-7pm, Sa 9:30am-4pm.) The **post office,** 20-34 Warwick Rd., has a **bureau de change.** (☎ 512410. Open M-Sa 9am-5:30pm.) **Postal code:** CA1 1AB.

▐▟█ ACCOMMODATIONS AND FOOD. Warwick Rd., running east out of the city, is the primary site for Carlisle's many B&Bs. **Cornerways Guest House,** 107 Warwick Rd., sports a graceful, sky-lit staircase and three floors of big rooms with patterned carpets and astoundingly high ceilings. (☎ 521733. £15-16 per person, with bath £18.) At the nearby **Calreena Guest House,** 123 Warwick Rd., you can walk downstairs on crimson carpets to an excellent breakfast. (☎ 525020. Singles £16; doubles £30.) The **Howard House,** 27 Howard Pl., off Warwick Rd., also has clean rooms and friendly service. (☎/fax 529159. £17 per person, with bath £21). Textured walls and glorious curtains await you in the large, comfortable rooms of **Chatsworth Guest House,** 22 Chatsworth Sq., left off Chiswick St. from the bus station. (☎ 524023. Singles £25; doubles and families £38.)

The fairground interior of the **Market Hall,** off Scotch St., holds fresh fruit, vegetables, and baked goods. (Open M-Sa 8am-5pm.) **Zorba Greek Restaurant,** 68 Warwick Rd., offers a range of dishes including an excellent Greek salad for only £2.50. (☎ 592227. Open daily 5:30-10:30pm, also Tu-Sa noon-2pm.) The **Crown & Mitre Hotel,** English St. (☎ 525491), sells a healthy portion of their dish of the day for only £3.50 during lunch hours (noon-2pm). In the evening, students, regulars and tourists mix in the plush blue and maroon interior of **The Boardroom,** Paternoster Row, near the cathedral. Non-stop jukebox tunes and the occasional live music make for a lively atmosphere, and there's a different special every week. (☎ 527695. Open M-Sa 11am-11pm, Su noon-10:30pm; food served 11am-8pm.)

▣ SIGHTS. The **Tullie House** museum and art gallery on Castle St. houses exciting exhibits on Hadrian's Wall and other areas of local history, plus a large enough collection of old shoes to make Imelda Marcos jealous. (☎ 534781. Open M-Sa 10am-5pm, Su noon-5pm; Nov.-Mar. M-Sa 10am-4pm, Su noon-4pm. £3.75, seniors and children £2.75, students £2.25.) Built in 1092 by William II with stones from Hadrian's Wall, **Carlisle Castle** stands in the northwest corner of the city. Mary, Queen of Scots was imprisoned here until Elizabeth I wanted her a wee bit farther from the border. Hundreds incarcerated in the dungeons of the castle after the 1745 Jacobite rebellion stayed alive by slurping water that collected in the trenches of the dark stone walls. Observe these "licking stones" as you learn about forms of torture employed against the Scots. (☎ 591922. Open daily Apr.-Sept. 9:30am-6pm; Oct. 10am-6pm; Nov.-Mar. 10am-4pm. Guided tours July Su at 11am, 12:30pm, and 2pm; June and Sept. 12:30pm and 2pm. £1.40, children 70p. £3, students and seniors £2.30, children £1.50.)

Carlisle's **cathedral,** founded in 1122, houses some fine 14th-century stained glass and the Brougham Triptych, a beautifully carved Flemish altarpiece. Sir Walter Scott married his French sweetheart on Christmas Eve, 1797, in what is now called the Border Regiment Chapel. (☎ 548151. Open M-Sa 7:30am-6:15pm, Su 7:30am-5pm. Evensong during school year M-F 5:30pm. Suggested donation £2.)

ALPS   ASPEN

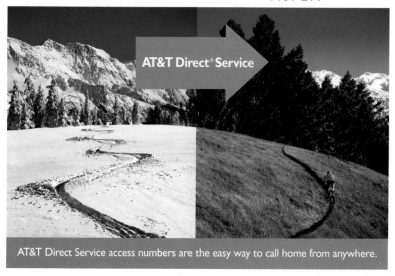

AT&T Direct Service access numbers are the easy way to call home from anywhere.

Global
connection
with the AT&T
Network

AT&T
direct
service

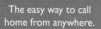

AT&T Direct®Service

The easy way to call
home from anywhere.

AT&T Access Numbers

Austria ●	0800-200-288	France	0800-99-00-11
Belarus ×	........8♦800-101	Gambia ●	00111
Belgium ●	0-800-100-10	Germany 0800-2255-288
Bosnia ▲	00-800-0010	Ghana	0191
Bulgaria ▲	00-800-0010	Gibraltar	8800
Cyprus ●	080-900-10	Greece ●	00-800-1311
Czech Rep. ▲ 00-42-000-101	Hungary ●	...06-800-01111
Denmark	 8001-0010	Iceland ●	800-9001
Egypt ● (Cairo) ✦...510-0200	Ireland ✓......1-800-550-000
Finland ●	0800-110-015	Israel 1-800-94-94-949

AT&T Direct®Service

The easy way to call
home from anywhere.

AT&T Access Numbers

Austria ●	0800-200-288	France	0800-99-00-11
Belarus ×	........8♦800-101	Gambia ●	00111
Belgium ●	0-800-100-10	Germany 0800-2255-288
Bosnia ▲	00-800-0010	Ghana	0191
Bulgaria ▲	00-800-0010	Gibraltar	8800
Cyprus ●	080-900-10	Greece ●	00-800-1311
Czech Rep. ▲ 00-42-000-101	Hungary ●	...06-800-01111
Denmark	 8001-0010	Iceland ●	800-9001
Egypt ● (Cairo) ✦...510-0200	Ireland ✓......1-800-550-000
Finland ●	0800-110-015	Israel 1-800-94-94-949

The best way to keep in touch when you're traveling overseas is with **AT&T Direct®** Service. It's the easy way to call your loved ones back home from just about anywhere in the world. Just cut out the wallet guide below and use it wherever your travels take you.

For a list of AT&T Access Numbers, tear out the attached wallet guide.

Italy ● 172-1011	Russia (Moscow) ▶▲●755-5042
Luxembourg ✦ ..800-2-0111	(St. Petersbg.) ▶▲● ..325-5042
Macedonia ● ..99-800-4288	Slovakia ▲ ..00-42-100-101
Malta 0800-890-110	South Africa ..0800-99-0123
Monaco ● 800-90-288	Spain 900-99-00-11
Morocco 002-11-0011	Sweden 020-799-111
Netherlands ● ...0800-022-9111	Switzerland ● 0800-89-0011
Norway 800-190-11	Turkey ● 00-800-12277
Poland ▲● ..00-800-111-1111	Ukraine ▲ ....8✦100-11
Portugal ▲ 800-800-128	U.A. Emirates ● 800-121
Romania ●.....01-800-4288	U.K..............0800-89-0011

FOR EASY CALLING WORLDWIDE
1. Just dial the AT&T Access Number for the country you are calling from.
2. Dial the phone number you're calling. *3.* Dial your card number.

For access numbers not listed ask any operator for **AT&T Direct®** Service.
In the U.S. call 1-800-331-1140 for a wallet guide listing all worldwide AT&T
Access Numbers.
Visit our Web site at: **www.att.com/traveler**
Bold-faced countries permit country-to-country calling outside the U.S.
- ● Public phones require coin or card deposit to place call.
- ▲ May not be available from every phone/payphone.
- ✦ Public phones and select hotels.
- ◆ Await second dial tone.
- ▶ Additional charges apply when calling from outside the city.
- † Outside of Cairo, dial "02" first.
- ✖ Not available from public phones or all areas.
- ✔ Use U.K. access number in N. Ireland.

When placing an international call *from* the U.S., dial 1 800 CALL ATT.

EMEA   © 8/00 AT&T

Italy ● 172-1011	Russia (Moscow) ▶▲●755-5042
Luxembourg ✦ ..800-2-0111	(St. Petersbg.) ▶▲● ..325-5042
Macedonia ● ..99-800-4288	Slovakia ▲ ..00-42-100-101
Malta 0800-890-110	South Africa ..0800-99-0123
Monaco ● 800-90-288	Spain 900-99-00-11
Morocco 002-11-0011	Sweden 020-799-111
Netherlands ● ...0800-022-9111	Switzerland ● 0800-89-0011
Norway 800-190-11	Turkey ● 00-800-12277
Poland ▲● ..00-800-111-1111	Ukraine ▲ ....8✦100-11
Portugal ▲ 800-800-128	U.A. Emirates ● 800-121
Romania ●.....01-800-4288	U.K..............0800-89-0011

FOR EASY CALLING WORLDWIDE
1. Just dial the AT&T Access Number for the country you are calling from.
2. Dial the phone number you're calling. *3.* Dial your card number.

For access numbers not listed ask any operator for **AT&T Direct®** Service.
In the U.S. call 1-800-331-1140 for a wallet guide listing all worldwide AT&T
Access Numbers.
Visit our Web site at: **www.att.com/traveler**
Bold-faced countries permit country-to-country calling outside the U.S.
- ● Public phones require coin or card deposit to place call.
- ▲ May not be available from every phone/payphone.
- ✦ Public phones and select hotels.
- ◆ Await second dial tone.
- ▶ Additional charges apply when calling from outside the city.
- † Outside of Cairo, dial "02" first.
- ✖ Not available from public phones or all areas.
- ✔ Use U.K. access number in N. Ireland.

When placing an international call *from* the U.S., dial 1 800 CALL ATT.

EMEA   © 8/00 AT&T

NORTHEAST ENGLAND

Fitted between the Pennines to the west and the North Sea to the east, the attractions of the northeast lie primarily in the calm coastal vistas of the North York Moors and the long views of the Yorkshire Dales and Northumberland National Parks, all three of which include some of the most removed areas in England. The far northeast has always been border country: Hadrian's Wall is the prominent marker of skirmishes with tribes farther north, and the isolated countryside still exudes frontier ruggedness. Walkers and ramblers flock here, and no trail tests their stamina more than the Pennine Way, Britain's first and longest official long-distance path. Extensive systems of shorter paths cross the heather-flecked moors that captured the imagination of the Brontës and the rolling dales that figure so prominently in the stories of James Herriot. The isolation of the dales and villages of the northeast bears testament to the region's primarily agricultural bent. Even the area's inclusion in the Industrial Revolution sprang from its fields, as the extensive presence of sheep made it a logical locus for textile manufacturers. But while the principal urban areas of Yorkshire and Tyne and Wear (including Leeds, York, and Newcastle) may have grown out of the wool and coal industries, and bear the scars of industrialization to prove it, today their refurbished city centers accommodate visitors graciously. Windswept Northeast England continues to hang onto both its wilderness and its sense of humor.

HIGHLIGHTS OF NORTHEAST ENGLAND

YORK MINSTER Don't miss the splendid Minster, Britain's largest Gothic cathedral, which contains half of all the medieval stained glass in England, and the largest single medieval glass window in the world (p. 385).

NATIONAL PARKS Wander through the emerald valleys and stone walls of the **Yorkshire Dales** (p. 379), or brave the winds and haunting desolation of the **North York Moors** (p. 391).

NEWCASTLE Sample the pubs and clubs of this gritty city, home of the famed brown ale, where crowded dance floors and lively locals make the nightlife legendary (p. 403).

HADRIAN'S WALL Admire the remains of Hadrian's massive construction, which once stretched from coast to coast and delineated the northernmost border of the Roman Empire (p. 410).

PENNINE WAY

The Pennine peaks form England's spine, arching up the center of Britain from the Peak District National Park to the Scottish border. The 268 mi. Pennine Way, England's first long-distance trail, crowns the central ridge of the watershed. Beginning at Edale, it traverses the massive, boggy plateau atop **Kinder Scout** in the south, then passes into the craggy **Yorkshire Dales** at Malham to reemerge at the formidable 2273 ft. Pen-y-Ghent peak. The northern section crosses the **High Pennines**, a 20 mi. stretch from below Barnard Castle to

Hadrian's Wall and Northumberland National Park, terminating at Kirk Yetholm, just across the Scottish border. The heather-clad moorland and arbored slopes left in the rivers' wake are dotted with stone villages and abandoned textile factories. This grim, often desolate landscape has fostered a gritty, often rebellious population. They erected modest chapels in defiance of Canterbury, shook their fists at textile barons as they embraced socialism, and broke the will of private-property absolutists in winning public right-of-way access for these very trails. The 1949 National Parks and Access to Countryside Act brought about greater access to the region's open spaces, and the Pennine Way was opened in 1965.

◢ HIKING

Hikers have completed the way in as few as 10 days, but most spend three weeks on the long, often remote trail. The less ambitious can make brief but rewarding forays into the landscape on well-traveled walkways leading from the major towns. The unusual limestone formations in the Yorkshire Dales and the lonely moor of Kinder Scout are especially captivating, though any two wayfarers could probably recommend five completely different stretches.

Wainwright's *Pennine Way Companion* (£10), a pocket-sized volume available from bookstores, is a worthwhile supplement to Ordnance Survey maps (£6), available from National Park Information Centres and tourist information centres. Sudden storms can reduce visibility to under 20 ft., leave low-level paths boggy, and sink you knee-deep (or worse) in peat. At some points (especially in the Yorkshire Dales), and in ominous weather, you should stay on the narrow roads that run nearby. Those in the know recommend staying away from the Pennines in the winter unless you are, in truth, a Hiker. Whatever the weather, bring a good map and compass and know how to use them. Rain gear, warm clothing, and extra food are also essential. Consult **Wilderness Safety,** p. 53, for more advice.

▐ ACCOMMODATIONS

YHA Youth Hostels are spaced within a day's hike (7-29 mi.) of one another; note which ones are closed on certain nights. The YHA offers a handy **Pennine Way Package:** you can book a route of 18 or more hostels along the walk (booking 50p per-stamped hostel) and obtain useful advice on paths and equipment. Send a self-addressed, envelope to YHA Northern Region, P.O. Box 11, Matlock, Derbyshire DE4 2XA (☎ (01629) 825850). Any **National Park Information Centre** or **tourist information centre** can supply details on trails and alternate accommodations. The *Pennine Way Accommodations Guide* (90p) is invaluable.

YHA YOUTH HOSTELS
The following hostels are arranged alphabetically by town, with the distance from the nearest southerly hostel listed. Lockout for all is 10am-5pm, curfew is 11pm, and breakfast and evening meals are served, unless otherwise noted.

Alston: The Firs, Alston (☎/fax (01434) 381509), 22 mi. from Dufton. Open Apr.-Aug. daily, Sept.-Oct. Tu-Sa. Dorms £9.15, under 18 £6.10.

Baldersdale: Blackton, Baldersdale (☎/fax (01833) 650629), 15 mi. from Keld in a converted stone farmhouse overlooking Blackton Reservoir. Open Apr.-Aug. daily, Sept.-Oct. F-Tu. Dorms £8.15, under 18 £5.65.

Bellingham: 14 mi. from Once Brewed in Northumberland. See p. 409.

Byrness: 15 mi. from Bellingham, Northumberland. See p. 409.

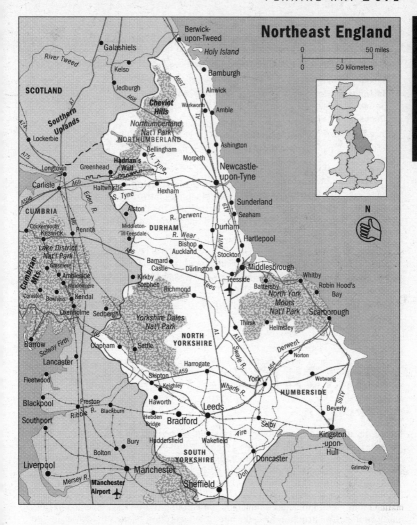

Northeast England

Crowden-in-Longdendale: 15 mi. from Edale in the Peak District. See p. 352.

Dufton: Redstones, Dufton, Appleby (☎ (017683) 51236; fax 53798), 12 mi. from Langdon Beck. Shop in hostel. Open July-Aug. daily; May-June Th-M; Apr. and Sept.-Oct. F-Tu. Dorms £9.15, under 18 £6.10.

Earby: 9-13 Birch Hall Ln. (☎/fax (01282) 842349), 15 mi. from Haworth. Open July-Aug. daily, Apr.-June and Sept.-Oct. M-W and F-Su. Dorms £8.15, under 18 £5.65.

Edale: (☎ (01433) 670302), in the Peak District. See p. 352.

Greenhead: 17 mi. from Alston. See p. 411.

Hawes: 19 mi. from Stainforth in the Yorkshire Dales. See p. 380.

Haworth: 1 mi. from town. See p. 376.

Keld: 9 mi. from Hawes in the Yorkshire Dales. See p. 380.

Kirk Yetholm (SYHA): (☎ (01573) 420631), 27 mi. from Byrness. See p. 517.

Langdon Beck: Forest-in-Teesdale (☎ (01833) 622228; fax 622372), 15 mi. from Baldersdale. Shop in hostel. Open mid-July to Aug. daily, Apr. to mid-July M-Sa, mid-Feb. to Mar. and Sept.-Oct. Tu-Sa, Nov. F-Sa. Dorms £9.80, under 18 £6.75.

Malham: 15 mi. from Earby in the Yorkshire Dales. See p. 380.

Mankinholes: Todmorden (☎/fax (01706) 812340), 24 mi. from Crowden. Shop in hostel. Open mid-Mar. to Aug. M-Sa, Sept.-Oct. Tu-Sa, Feb. to mid-Mar. and Nov. F-Sa. Dorms £8.15, under 18 £5.65.

Once Brewed: 7 mi. east of Greenhead. See p. 411.

Stainforth: 8 mi. from Malham in the Yorkshire Dales. See p. 380.

CAMPING BARNS

In the High Pennines, the YHA operates three **camping barns,** hollow stone buildings on private farms with wooden sleeping platforms, (very) cold water, and a toilet. The telephone numbers below are for confirming arrival times *only;* book with YHA Camping Barns, 16 Shawbridge St., Clitheroe, BB7 1LZ (☎ 01200) 428366).

Holwick Barn: Mr. and Mrs. Scott, Low Way Farm, Holwick (☎ (01833) 640506), 3 mi. north of Middleton-in-Teesdale. Sleeps 20. £4.50 per person.

Wearhead Barn: Mr. Walton, Blackcleugh Farm, Wearhead (☎ (01388) 537395), 1 mi. from Cowshill. No electric lights. Sleeps 12. £3.50 per person.

Witton Barn: Witton Estate, Witton-le-Wear (☎ (01388) 488322), just off the Weardale Way. Sleeps 15. £3.50 per person.

YORKSHIRE

SHEFFIELD   ☎ 0114

In a flurry of chopping, scooping, carving, and spreading, Sheffield (pop. 530,000) rose to fame on the handles of its cutlery. While Manchester was clothing the world, Sheffield was setting its table, first with hand-crafted flatware, then with mass-produced goods, and eventually with stainless steel, invented here. However, 20th-century industry went elsewhere, resulting in the devastating economic depression made familiar by *The Full Monty.* Now, at the onset of the new millennium, Sheffield seeks a new look with a burst of building, leveling, paving, and pruning. Construction has alleviated the laceration of the city center by the ring roads that once made walking tortuous. The reinvigorated city center is seen in three new town squares, two new public gardens, and the mesmerizing National Centre for Popular Music. A dearth of city-center accommodations foils any overnight aspirations of the budget traveler, but Sheffield nonetheless remains the last bastion of nightlife, shopping, and urbanity before the Peak District to the west.

🖂 ☎ GETTING THERE AND PRACTICAL INFORMATION

Sheffield lies on the M1 motorway, about 30 mi. east of Manchester and 25 mi. south of Leeds. The **train station** is on Sheaf St., near Sheaf Sq. (Lockers £1-3.) **Trains** (☎ (08457) 484950) arrive from: **London St. Pancras** (2-3hr., M-Sa 1-2 per hr., £47.50); **Manchester** (1hr., 1 per hr., £10.40); **York** (1¼hr., 1 per hr., £11.90); **Birmingham** (1½hr., 1-2 per hr., £17); and **Liverpool** via **Stockpool** (1¾hr., 1 per hr., £13.45).

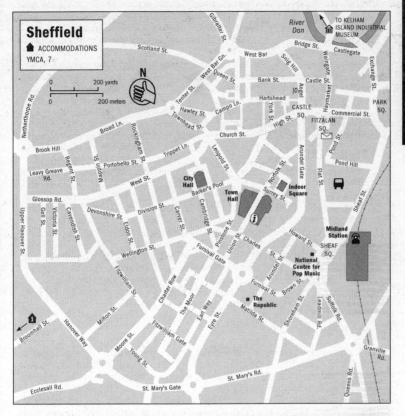

The major **bus station** in town is the **Interchange,** between Pond St. and Sheaf St. (☎ 275 4905. Open M-F 8am-5:30pm. Lockers £1-2.) **National Express** (☎ (08705) 808080) travels from: **London** (3½hr., 8 per day, £12); **Nottingham** (1¼hr., 1 per hr., £6.25); and **Birmingham** (2½hr., 6 per day, £12.25). The **Super-tram,** Sheffield's modern transport system, trundles all around town (all-day ticket £1.80).

Sheffield's **tourist information centre** (TIC), 1 Tudor Sq., off Surrey St., books rooms for a 10% deposit. (☎ 221 1900, bookings ☎ 201 1011; fax 201 1020; www.sheffieldcity.co.uk. Open M-Th 9:30am-5:15pm, F 10:30am-5:15pm, Sa 9:30am-4:15pm.) Services include: **American Express,** 20 Charles St. (☎ 275 1144; open M and W-F 9am-5:30pm, Tu 9:30am-5:30pm, Sa 9am-5pm); **Internet access** at **Havana Bistro** (below); and the **post office,** Fitzalan Sq., uphill from the Interchange (☎ 733525; open M 9am-5:30pm, Tu-Sa 8:30am-5:30pm). **Postal code:** S1 1AB.

ACCOMMODATIONS AND FOOD

Sheffield doesn't exactly roll out the red carpet, or even a worn-out welcome mat, for the budget traveler. A good option, if you don't mind the 30-minute commute by train, is the **youth hostel** in **Hathersage** (see p. 352). A thorough listing of accommodations fills seven pages of *It's Happening in Sheffield,* a free booklet offered by the TIC. The **B&Bs** scattered around town cost at least £16 per night. Unless you opt to nest above a pub, expect a hilly westward hike from the city center. Most places fill up quickly, especially in summer; as always, call in advance.

The **YMCA,** 20 Victoria Rd., between Broomhall Rd. and Victoria Rd., has clean rooms on a quiet street a few blocks from the university. Men and women, 18 and older, are accepted. Take bus #60 to Hallamshire Hospital, bear left on Clarke-house Rd. to Park Ln., turn left again and then right onto the unmarked Victoria Rd. (☎ 268 4807. Continental breakfast. Singles £16; weekly £70.) **Rutland Arms,** 86 Brown St., near the train and bus stations, offers clean rooms above a pub, all with bath. (☎ 272 9003; fax 273 1425. Breakfast included. Singles £23.50; doubles £37; family room £47.) A decently-priced good bed can be found in the city at the **House of Elliott,** 465 Manchester Rd. Feel at home with plush carpets and free rides on the rocking horse. Take bus #51 from the City Hall or Leopold St. to Crosspool. (☎ 268 1677. Continental breakfast. £20 for first night, £18 for subsequent nights.)

Cheap, tasty nourishment in the city center is hard to come by; instead, head for the student haunts on **Ecclesall Rd.,** or the ubiquitous cafe-bars on **Division St.** and **Devonshire St.,** where pre-clubbers prepare for the night ahead. Supermarkets include **Somerfield,** on Pinstone St. (open M-F 7:30am-7pm, Sa 7:30am-6pm); and **Spar,** at the intersection of Holly St. and Division St. (open 24hr.). **Havana Bistro,** 32-34 Division St., dishes up out-of-the-ordinary cybercafe fare, such as chicken gou-jons and melted brie (£3.50), to accompany your net surfing. (☎ 249 5452. £2.50 per 30min., £4 per hr. Open M-Th 10am-10pm, F-Sa 10am-7pm, Su 11am-6pm.) **The Showroom Café-Bar,** 7 Paternoster Row, draws sophists into its minimalist interior. Loll on the couch and think deep thoughts over the large and tasty chicken dishes, burgers, and stir-fry (£5.95-7.25) before watching one of the arthouse films next door. (☎ 275 3588. Open M-Sa 11am-11pm, Su noon-10:30pm.)

👁 SIGHTS

If you think four energetic galleries exhibiting and enhancing your favorite songs in a spaceship shaped like a drum set sounds like a good time, follow your instinct and visit 🏛 **The National Center for Popular Music** on Paternoster Row. The gleaming metallic exterior is impossible to miss, and hints at the innovative approach the center takes to acoustics inside. A 3-D sound chamber adds another dimension to surround sound, and an interactive room lets you tickle electric strings, mix tracks, edit videos, and rediscover your inner rock star. Hurl yourself into the whirlwind of dance, hip-hop, rock, or shameless pop for a few hours and let bleak industrial zones fade away. (☎ 296 2626. Open M-Sa 10am-6pm, last admission 3:30pm. £5.95, students and seniors £4.75, children £4, families £18.)

The **Kelham Island Industrial Museum,** Alma St., studies both the strong hand and the dirty glove of Sheffield's industrial movement. Exhibiting the proletarian and culinary products of the steel industry, it also laments the social repercussions of such international industrial prowess. Take bus #53 from the Interchange to Nurs-ery St.; turn left on Corporation St., right on Alma St., and wind 200 yd. through an industrial park to the museum on the right. (☎ 272 2106. Open M-Th 10am-4pm, last admission 3pm; Su 11am-4:45pm, last admission 3:45pm. Wheelchair access. £3.50, students, and seniors £2.50, children £2, families £8, disabled free.)

A handful of free museums with small collections are scattered around Shef-field. The **Site Gallery,** 1 Brown St., has superb digital exhibitions of media art and photography. (☎ 281 2077. Open Tu-F 11am-6pm, Sa 11am-5:30pm, Su 1-5pm. Free.) In 1875, Victorian critic and artist John Ruskin established a museum to show the working class that "life without industry is guilt, and industry without art is brutality." What emerged was the **Ruskin Gallery,** 101 Norfolk St., which displays the miscellany of the Guild of St. George Collection, including works by Audubon and Turner, and illuminated manuscripts. (☎ 203 9416. Open Tu-Sa 10am-5pm; summer also M 10am-5pm. Free.) The tiny **Graves Gallery,** on Surrey St., in the pub-lic library, dedicates a room to postwar British art and another to Chinese jade and ivory. (☎ 273 5158. Open M-Sa 10am-5pm; off-season closed M. Free.)

🎵 ENTERTAINMENT

At night, the **Crucible** and **Lyceum Theatres,** both in Tudor Sq. and sharing a box office on Norfolk St., stage musicals, plays, and dance performances, many of which are West End transfers. Shows in 2001 include the Rambert Dance Company, Arthur Miller's *The Man Who Had All the Luck*, Marlowe's *Edward II*, and Andrea Dunbar's *The Arbor*. (☎ 249 6000. 20% concessions discount; same-day tickets £4.) Most **clubs** are in the southeastern section of the city, around Matilda St.; *It's Happening in Sheffield* has current nightclub listings. Groove is in the heart of **The Republic,** 112 Arundel St. "Gatecrasher," its Saturday night bash, is Sheffield's largest party. Other nights are healthier for the wallet and body; but no matter when you go, expect crowds. (☎ 249 2210. Cover M and Th £2-3, F £3-5, Sa £10-15 after 10:30pm. Open M and Th-F 10pm-2am, Sa 10pm-6am.)

SOUTH PENNINES

Expecting the sense of isolation and bleakness portrayed in *Wuthering Heights*, visitors to the South Pennines may be surprised at the domesticated feel of this landscape. The villages of Haworth and Hebden Bridge have made substantive inroads into the gorse-strewn moorlands, and the deserted, heathery slopes unfolding quietly between the towns are patterned into well-cultivated fields.

▉ GETTING THERE AND GETTING AROUND

The proximity of the South Pennines to Leeds and Bradford makes transport fairly easy. Two **train** lines (☎ (08457) 484950) chug frequently through the region; the free pocket-sized *West Yorkshire Train Times* lists routes. The Claverdale Line reaches **Hebden Bridge** and **Mytholmroyd** on its way between **Leeds** and **Manchester** or **Blackpool.** Transpennine Express reaches **Hebden Bridge** from **Newcastle-upon-Tyne, Manchester,** and **Liverpool** (every hr. 7am-9pm, fewer on Su). The Airedale Line, from Leeds, stops at **Keighley** (KEETH-lee), 5 mi. north of Haworth, en route to Carlisle or Morecambe. The private steam-hauled trains of the **Keighley and Worth Valley Railway** (☎ (01535) 645214) run a special route from **Keighley** to **Oxenhope,** passing through **Haworth** on the way.

Local **bus** questions are answered by the **Metro Travel Centre.** (☎ (0113) 245 7676. Open M-Sa 8am-7pm, Su 9am-5:30pm.) **West Yorkshire Buses** #663, 664, and 665 go to **Haworth** from **Keighley** and **Bradford. Keighley and District Travel** (☎ (01535) 603284) **bus** #500 travels from **Hebden Bridge** to **Haworth** (30min., 4-5 per day).

Tourist information centres (TICs) hold a wide selection of trail guides. One trail, the **Worth Way,** traces the 5½ mi. route from Keighley to Oxenhope; ride the steam train back to your starting point. From Haworth to Hebden Bridge, choose a trail from the TIC's *Two Walks Linking Haworth and Hebden Bridge* (30p).

HEBDEN BRIDGE   ☎01422

A historic gritstone village built on the side of a hill, Hebden Bridge lies close to the Pennine Way and the circular 50 mi. Calderdale Way. Originally a three-farm cluster, the hamlet stitched its way to rapid growth in the booming textile years of the 18th and 19th centuries. Many of the trademark "double-decker" houses embedded in the hills during this period are still standing. Today, Hebden Bridge has few sights; most visitors use it as a starting point for day (or longer) hikes.

Calder Valley Cruising gives horse-drawn boat trips along the recently restored Rochdale Canal. (☎ 845557. Office open M-F 10am-noon, Easter-Oct. also Sa-Su 11am-5pm. 2-3 trips per day in summer; call in advance. £6, students and seniors £5, children £3, families £14.) From Hebden Bridge, you can make day hikes to the villages of **Blackshaw Head, Cragg Vale,** or **Hepstonstall.** Hepstonstall holds the remains of Sylvia Plath (after her death, husband Ted Hughes moved to nearby Mytholmroyd), and the ruins of a 13th-century church and a 1764 chapel, the oldest Methodist house of worship in the world. Trails also wind to the National Trust's **Harcastle Crags** (☎ 844518), a ravine-crossed wooded valley known locally as Little Switzerland, 1½ mi. northwest along the A6033. Pick up *Walks Around Hebden Bridge* (40p) from the TIC for scenic half-day hikes.

Hebden Bridge lies about halfway along the Manchester-Leeds line, with hourly **train** service in both directions. **Buses** stop at the train station and on New Rd. The **tourist information centre**, 1 Bridge Gate, distributes 40p walking guides. (☎ 843831; www.hebdenbridge.co.uk/tourist-info. Open Easter-Sept. M-Sa 10am-5pm, Su 11am-5pm; Oct.-Easter daily 10am-4pm.) The **post office** is on Holme St. (☎ 842366. Open M-F 9am-5:30pm, Sa 9am-12:30pm.) **Postal code:** HX7 8AA.

Weary travelers rejuvenate in the B&B of photographer **Claire McNamee**, 1 Primrose Terr., and her artistic husband. The simply furnished rooms are adorned with their own works of art. (☎ 844747. £14 per person.) **Mrs. Naish**, 35 Royd Terr., offers spacious rooms and a beautiful stepped garden. (☎ 845304. £16 per person.) The food's fit for a president at the **Watergate Tea Shop**, 9 Bridge Gate. Meals cost around £4. (☎ 842978. Open Su-F 10:30am-5pm, Sa 7am-9:30pm.) Purchase groceries at **Spar**, Crown St. (Open M-Sa 8am-11pm, Su 8am-10:30pm.)

HAWORTH   ☎01535

> I can hardly tell you how the time gets on at Haworth. There is no event whatever to mark its progress. One day resembles another...
> —Charlotte Brontë

Haworth's (HAH-wuth) *raison d'être* stands at the top of its hill—the parsonage at the pinnacle of Brontë-land. Haworth's cobbled main street capitalizes on the town's association with the Brontës; tea rooms and souvenir shops fall over themselves to solicit the crowds in their ascent to the wuthering heights of the Brontë home, even though the village is devoid of heroines wandering windswept moors.

█▓ GETTING THERE AND PRACTICAL INFORMATION. The **train station** (☎ (01535) 645214) only runs the private steam-hauled trains of the Keighley and Worth Valley Railway. **Trains** come in from **Keighley** (20min.; daily mid-Jun. to Aug., call for other times; return £6). **West Yorkshire** (☎ (0113) 245 7676) **buses** provide service to Haworth, stopping at the base of Main St., on routes #663, 664, and 665 from **Keighley** and **Bradford**. **Keighley and District Travel** (☎ (01535) 603284) bus #500 comes from **Hebden Bridge** (30min., 4-5 per day).

The **tourist information centre** (TIC), 2-4 West Ln., at the summit of Main St., provides the useful *Three Walks from the Centre of Haworth* (30p) and the town's mini-guide (35p). The TIC offers a free map and accommodations list, and books rooms for 10% of the first night's stay. (☎ 642329; fax 647721. Open Easter-Oct. daily 9:30am-5:30pm; Nov.-Easter 9:30am-5pm.) The **post office**, 98 Main St., is the only place in bankless Haworth to **change money**. (☎ 644589. Open M and W-F 9am-1pm and 2-5:30pm, Tu 9am-1pm, Sa 9am-12:30pm.) **Postal code:** BD22 8DP.

▐▒ ACCOMMODATIONS AND FOOD. The elegant **YHA Haworth**, Longlands Dr., Lees Ln., is 1 mi. from the TIC in a Victorian mansion. (☎ 642234; fax 643023. No lockout. Open mid-Feb. to Oct. daily; Nov. to mid-Dec. M-Sa. Dorms £9.20, under 18 £6.20.) **B&Bs** (£15-17) await at Main St., all downhill from the TIC. Sweeping views will please at the luxurious ▨ **Ashmount**, Mytholmes Ln., in a house built by the doctor who attended Charlotte Brontë's death. (☎ 645726. Singles £25; doubles £39; triples £45.) The 1850 **Ebor House**, Lees Ln., was built for the owner of the nearby mill. Walk from the steam railway station down Mill Hey, which becomes Lees Ln. (☎ 645869. Singles £16; doubles £30.)

Combined, **Snowden's**, 98 Main St. (☎ 643214), and **Southams**, 123 Main St. (☎ 643196), form an almost adequate grocery store. **The Black Bull**, a pub once frequented by the errant Branwell Brontë, is near the TIC. For reasonably priced restaurants, skip Main St. and head to **Mill Hey**, near the steam-railway station.

SIGHTS. Behind the village church down a tiny lane, the Brontë Society has created a tasteful, low-key museum in the ■ **Brontë Parsonage.** Quiet rooms detailing the lives of Charlotte, Emily, Anne and Branwell provide relief from the tourists outside. The rooms, including the dining room where the sisters penned their classics *Wuthering Heights* and *Jane Eyre*, hold original furnishings and fragments of their daily life. Other artifacts occupy glass cases; Charlotte's minuscule boots and mittens are displayed alongside one of her extraordinarily tiny dresses. Branwell's mediocre oil paintings are (luckily) confined to one room. The exhibition room traces the Brontës' humble origins in Ireland—their real name was either Brunty or Prunty but was changed out of veneration for Lord Nelson, the Duke of Brontë. (☎ 642323. Open Apr.-Sept. daily 10am-5:30pm; Oct.-Mar. 11am-5pm. Closed Jan. 8-Feb. 2, 2001. £4.50, students and seniors £3.30, under 16 £1.40, families £10.) A footpath behind the church leads up the hill toward the pleasant (if untempestuous) **Brontë Falls,** a 2½ mi. hike over the moor.

LEEDS ☎ 0113

Leeds (pop. 700,000) bloomed with textile-based prosperity in the ornate Victorian period, and its building facades feature a curious cast of stone lions, griffins, and cherubs. Even though most textile jobs have moved overseas, Britain's fourth-largest city has experienced a recent economic revival. The birthplace of Marks & Spencer now sports blocks of shops (including the north's sole branch of Harvey Nichols) and a number of new clubs. While the Royal Armouries do make for a fascinating daytrip, most visitors come on business; budget travelers will find nightlife the only significant reason to stay.

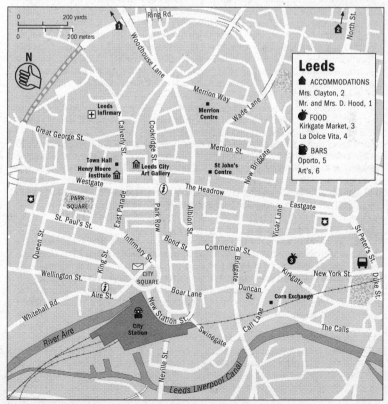

Leeds

🏠 ACCOMMODATIONS
Mrs. Clayton, 2
Mr. and Mrs. D. Hood, 1

🍎 FOOD
Kirkgate Market, 3
La Dolce Vita, 4

🍷 BARS
Oporto, 5
Art's, 6

⌐? GETTING THERE AND PRACTICAL INFORMATION

Leeds is about 50 mi. northeast of Manchester and 10 mi. east of Bradford, midway between the South Pennines and the Yorkshire Dales. The **train station** is on City Sq. (Office open M-Sa 8am-8pm, Su 9am-6pm. Luggage storage.) **Trains** (☎ (08457) 484950) arrive from: **London King's Cross** (2½hr., 1 per hr., £56); **Bradford** (20min., 4 per hr., £2.15); **Manchester** (1½hr., 2 per hr., £10); and **York** (2hr., 2 per hr., £6.50). The **bus station** lies behind Kirkgate Market on York St. (Office open M-F 8:30am-5:30pm, Sa 8:30am-4:30pm. Luggage storage.) **National Express** (☎ (08705) 808080) serves Leeds from most major cities. For local bus info, call **Metroline** at 245 7676.

The **tourist information centre** (TIC), "Gateway Yorkshire," at the train station, offers shelves of schedules and books beds for £1.25 and a 10% deposit. (☎ 242 5242; fax 246 8246. Open M-Sa 9:30am-6pm, Su 10am-4pm.) A second TIC greets travellers at the bus station. (Open M-F 9:45am-5:30pm, Sa 9am-4:30pm.) Every conceivable **bank** lies on Park Row. Services include: the **police** (☎ (0845) 606 0606), at Millgarth; **Internet access** at **The Mouse House,** 3 Wellfield Pl., Headingley, opposite the Headingley Library (£5 per hr., student discount); and the main **post office,** on City Sq. (☎ 372853, open M-Sa 9am-5:30pm). **Postal code:** LS1 2UH.

⌐◌ ACCOMMODATIONS AND FOOD

YHA Leeds, Block H, Clarence Dock Flats, opened in 2000 on Clarence Rd. next to the Royal Armouries. All rooms are singles with bath, in flats of five sharing a kitchen. Call for dates. (☎ (01904) 653147. Laundry facilities. No lockout. Singles with bath £15.50.) **Mr. and Mrs. D. Hood,** 17 Cottage Rd., Headingly, will charm you with conversation over coffee. Cooked breakfast includes homemade bread and marmalade. Take bus #93 or 96 from Infirmary St. (☎ 275 5575. Singles £18; doubles £36.) Mrs. Newby runs the **Holme Leigh Guest House,** 19 Pinfold Ln., Halton, in a Victorian house on a quiet street. Bus #40 picks up at Boar Lane across from the train station; stop at Temple Walk and continue along Pinfold Ln. (☎ 260 7889. Singles from £23; doubles from £35.) TVs await in every room at **Fairbairn House,** 71-75 Clarendon Rd., a sprawling Victorian in the city center, owned by the University of Leeds. (☎ 233 6913; fax 233 6914. TV. Singles from £25.)

At the south end of town, **Kirkgate Market** is Europe's largest indoor market; shoppers can build their own meals from the various butchers and bakers. (Open M-Sa 9am-5:30pm, W 9am-1pm.) **La Dolce Vita,** 130-134 Vicar Ln., serves three-course lunches for £5.55. (☎ 242 0565. Open M-Th noon-2:30pm and 5:30-11pm, F-Sa noon-2:30pm and 5:30-11:30pm, Su 6-11pm.) A posh atmosphere awaits at **Ruskins Tea Room,** 26-28 County Arcade Shopping Centre. Enjoy traditional tea and lunch fare (£2-4) before dashing off to Harvey Nichols around the corner. (Open daily 9am-6pm). **Pubs** line Vicar Ln. and Boar Ln.; the **Whip Inn,** Bowers Yard (☎245 7571), off Duncan St., is singularly atmospheric.

▨♫ SIGHTS AND ENTERTAINMENT

The biggest draw in Leeds is the ▨ **Royal Armouries,** on Armouries Dr. along the waterfront, which rightfully claims to be one of the world's best collections of arms and armor. With galleries devoted to hunting, tournaments, wars, self-defense, and oriental weaponry, the museum eloquently enlightens through disturbing life-size recreations of battle scenes, battle simulations where you're in command, and demonstrations by staff in period dress. (☎ 220 1999. Open Apr.-Oct. daily 10:30am-5:30pm; Nov.-Mar. M-F 10:30am-4:30pm, Sa-Su 10:30am-5:30pm. £4.90, students and seniors £3.90. Book ahead with the TIC for discounts.)

The softer side of life can be found at Leeds's art galleries, clustered conveniently on the Headrow, across Calverly St. from the massive Victorian **Town Hall.** The **Leeds City Art Gallery,** on the corner of the Headrow and East Parade, features one of the best permanent collections of 20th-century British art outside London.

(☎ 247 8248. Open M-Tu and Th-Sa 10am-5pm, W 10am-8pm, Su 1-5pm. Free.) The adjacent **Henry Moore Institute,** 74 Headrow, holds traveling sculpture exhibitions in a solemn building. (☎ 234 3158. Open M-Tu and Th-Sa 10am-5:30pm, W 10am-9pm, Su 1-5pm. Free.) The well-maintained ruins of the 12th-century **Kirkstall Abbey,** Kirkstall Rd., along the River Aire, 3 mi. west of the city center, inspired artists such as J.M.W. Turner. (☎ 275 5821. Open daily dusk-dawn. Free.)

Like other major English cities, Leeds has succumbed to the lure of cafe-bar culture. **Call Lane,** near the Corn Exchange, is particularly saturated with them. **Nato,** 66-69 Boar Ln., packs 'em in with guest and solid resident DJs over the weekend. (☎ 244 5144. Cover £5-10. Open F-Sa 10pm-3am.) **The Cockpit** and **The Rocket,** Swinegate, dominate the live indie music scene. (☎ 244 3446. Cover varies.) Dance with the best-dressed clubbers in Britain at the **Warehouse,** Park Ln., during gay-friendly "Speed Queen" Saturday nights. (☎ 246 1033. Open 10pm-4am. Cover £10.) Up-to-date club listings are in the monthly *Absolute Leeds*, available at the TIC.

YORKSHIRE DALES NATIONAL PARK

A sea of emerald hills and valleys, the Yorkshire Dales National Park is liberally laced with sparkling rivers, subterranean caverns, and innumerable stone walls. The beauty of the dales, valleys formed by a swift river or a lazy glacial flow, is enhanced by traces of earlier residents: abandoned castles, stone farm houses, and tiny villages are scattered throughout. Bronze- and Iron-Age tribes blazed winding "green lanes," footpaths that remain upon the moorland tops; Romans built straight roads and stout hill-forts; and 18th-century workers pieced together the countless stone walls. While the Yorkshire Dales are a National Park, visitors should be aware that the land is not purely recreational—99% is privately owned and used for farming or other purposes. However, most property owners are willing to share the wealth of some of England's most marvelous countryside.

▐ GETTING THERE AND GETTING AROUND

The most convenient way to enter the park is through Skipton, from where buses venture into the smaller villages. **Trains** (☎ (08457) 484950) run to **Skipton** from: **Bradford** (40min., 2 per hr., £3.15, day return £3.70); **Leeds** (50min., 2 per hr., £4.35, day return £4.60); **Carlisle** (2hr., every 2hr., £10.70); and **Morecambe** (2hr., 6-10 per day, £9.90). The **Settle-Carlisle Railway** (☎ (01729) 822007), one of England's most scenic train routes, slices through several towns in the park, including **Skipton, Garsdale,** and **Kirkby Stephen** (Settle to Carlisle 1¾hr., £15.80). **National Express** (☎ (08705) 808080) **buses** run to **Skipton** from **London** (1 per day, £12). **First Leeds** (☎ (0113) 242 0922) #84 travels from **Leeds** (1¼hr., 1 per hr., £1.60).

Those relying on public transport to get around the Dales should procure the *Dales Connection* timetable, free at any tourist information centre or National Park Information Centre. You should get this in advance and plan your journey accordingly, since many **inter-village buses** only run a few times per week and tend to hibernate in winter. **Pride of the Dales** (☎ (01756) 753123) bus #72 connects **Skipton** to **Grassington,** some continuing to **Kettlewell** (M-Sa about 1 per hr., Su 3 per day; return £3.80). **Pennine Bus** (☎ (01756) 749215) connects **Skipton** to **Settle** (#580; M-F 1 per hr., Sa every 2hr.; return £6.40) and **Malham** (#210; M-Sa 4 per day, in summer also Su; return £5.60). Other villages are served less regularly, but **post buses** run once a day to scheduled towns. If you miss your bus, you may be stuck walking. **Hitchhikers** complain that pickups are infrequent and settle for rides that carry them only part way; *Let's Go* does not reccomend hitchhiking.

✦⁊ ORIENTATION AND PRACTICAL INFORMATION

Sampling the many parts of the Dales requires several days, a pair of sturdy feet, and careful planning if you want to use public transport (or a sturdy vehicle). In the south of the park, **Skipton** serves as a transport hub and provides goods and services not available in the smaller villages. **Grassington** and **Linton**, just north, are scenic bases for exploring southern Wharfedale. **Malham** is a sensible starting point for forays into western Wharfedale and Eastern Ribblesdale. To explore Wensleydale and Swaledale in the north, move out from **Hawes** or **Leyburn.**

The following **National Park Information Centres** are staffed by well-informed Dales devotees. Be sure to pick up the invaluable annual park guide, *The Visitor* (free), along with the numerous other maps and walking guides. *Out and About 2001* highlights the various guided walks and events sponsored by the National Park. Centers that remain open in the winter have opening hours noted below. In addition, most towns have tourist information centres (TICs).

Aysgarth Falls: (☎ (01969) 663424), in Wensleydale, less than 1 mi. east of the village. Open Apr.-Oct. daily 10am-5pm; Nov.-Mar. Sa-Su 10am-5pm.

Clapham: (☎ (015242) 51419), in the village center. Open Apr.-Oct. daily 10am-5pm.

Grassington: Hebden Rd., Wharfedale (☎ (01756) 752774). Open Apr.-Oct. daily 10am-5pm; off-season hours vary.

Hawes: Station Yard, Wensleydale (☎ (01969) 667450). Open Apr.-Oct. daily 10am-5pm, some winter weekends.

Malham: Malhamdale (☎ (01729) 830363), at the southern end of the village. Open Apr.-Oct. daily 10am-5pm; Nov.-Mar. Sa-Su 10am-4pm.

Reeth: (☎ (01748) 850252), in the Green. Open Apr.-Oct. daily 10am-5pm, also winter weekends with reduced hours.

Sedbergh: 72 Main St. (☎ (01539) 620125). Open Apr.-Oct. daily 10am-5pm; Nov.-Mar F-Sa 10am-4pm.

⌐ ACCOMMODATIONS

Hostels, converted barns, tents, and B&Bs are all good options in the Dales. The free *Yorkshire Dales Accommodation Guide* is available at National Park Information Centres and at the York TIC. Ask TICs for their lists of area caravan and camping sites.

Twelve **YHA Youth Hostels** play host in the Yorkshire Dales area. Hawes, Keld, and Malham lie on the Pennine Way (see p. 370 for more information). Ingleton, on the western edge of the park, is a good jumping-off point to the Lake District. Linton, Stainforth, Kettlewell, Dentdale, Aysgarth Falls, and Grinton Lodge all sit a few miles off the Pennine Way. Ellingstring, near Ripon, and Kirkby Stephen, north of Hawes, are both served by rail, but are set a little further away from the hiking trail. The hostels tend to fill up in the summer, so booking ahead is strongly advised; if you're planning day by day, hostel employees are usually happy to call other YHA hostels to help you find a bed for the next night.

Aysgarth Falls: (☎ (01969) 663260; fax 663110), ½ mi. east of Aysgarth on the A684 to Leyburn. Lockout 10am-1pm. Open Apr.-Oct. daily; Nov.-Mar. Tu-Sa. Dorms £9, under 18 £6.20.

Dentdale: (☎ (015396) 25251; fax 25068), Cowgill, on Dentdale Rd. 6 mi. east of Dent, 2 mi. from the Hawes-Ingleton Rd. On the River Dee. Open July-Aug. daily; Apr.-June F-W; Sept.-Oct. and Mar. F-Tu; Nov.-Feb. F-Sa. Dorms £9, under 18 £6.20.

Ellingstring: Lilac Cottage (☎ (01677) 460216), in the village. No smoking. Self-catering only. Lockout 10am-5pm. 18 beds. Open July-Aug. daily; Apr.-June and Sept.-Oct. F-Tu. Dorms £6.65, under 18 £4.65.

Grinton: Grinton Lodge (☎ (01748) 884206; fax 884876), on the "Herriot Way," ¾ mi. south of Grinton on the Reeth-Leyburn Rd. Reception opens 5pm. Lockout 10am-1pm. Open Apr.-Sept. daily; Oct. M-Sa; Nov.-Mar. F-Sa. Dorms £9, under 18 £6.20.

NORTHEAST ENGLAND

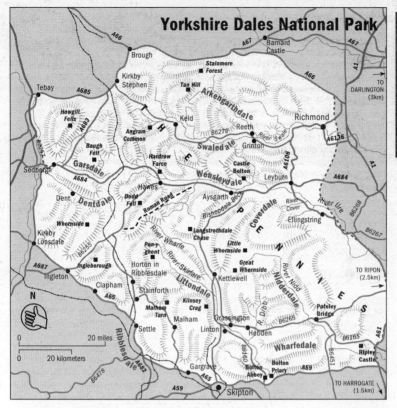

Hawes: (☎ (01969) 667368; fax 667723), Lancaster Terr., west of Hawes on Ingleton Rd., up the hill from town. 58 beds. Open July-Aug. daily; Apr.-June and Sept.-Oct. M-Sa; Mar. and Nov.-Dec. F-Tu. Dorms £9.80, under 18 £6.75.

Ingleton: Greta Tower (☎ (015242) 41444; fax 41854), down the hill from Market Sq. Reception closed noon-5pm. 58 beds. Open Apr.-Aug. daily; Sept.-Oct. M-Sa; Nov.-Dec. F-Su; Feb.-Mar. Tu-Sa. Dorms £10.85, under 18 £7.40.

Keld: Keld Lodge (☎ (01748) 886259; fax 886013), Upper Swaledale, Richmond, west of Keld village. 40 beds. Open Apr.-Aug. daily; Sept.-Oct. W-Su; Jan.-Mar. and Nov. F-M. Dorms £9, under 18 £6.20.

Kettlewell: Whernside House (☎ (01756) 760232; fax 760402), in the village center. 54 beds. Open Apr.-Sept. daily; Oct.-Mar. F-Tu. Dorms £9.80, under 18 £6.75.

Kirkby Stephen: (☎/fax (017683) 71793), Fletcher Hill, Market St. In a former chapel. Kitchen. Laundry. 44 beds. Open July-Aug. daily; Apr.-June and Sept.-Oct. Th-M. Dorms £9, under 18 £6.20.

Linton: The Old Rectory, (☎/fax (01756) 752400), Linton-in-Craven, next to the village green. Skipton-Grassington buses #71 and 72 pass near the hostel, a 17th-century stone rectory. Friendly staff. Lockout 10am-5pm. Open June-Aug. daily; Apr.-May and Sept.-Oct. M-Sa; Jan.-Feb. and Nov. to mid-Dec. M-Th. Dorms £9.80, under 18 £6.75.

Malham: John Dower Memorial Hostel (☎ (01729) 830321; fax 830551), at Malham Tarn. 2 lounges, a classroom, and storage lockers. 82 beds. Open year-round. Wheelchair access. Dorms £10.85, under 18 £7.40.

Stainforth: "Taitlands" (☎ (01729) 823577; fax 825404), 2 mi. north of Settle, ¼ mi. south of Stainforth. Georgian house with walled garden. 50 beds. Open Apr.-Oct. daily; Feb.-Mar. and Nov. F-Sa. Dorms £10.85, under 18 £7.40.

Numerous **Dales Barns** offer cheap accommodations: £5-7 per night for dorm rooms in converted barns split up hostel-style into smaller bunk rooms; most have showers, kitchens, and drying rooms. For lists of barns, ask at a TIC. The barns cater to small groups but are also ideal for hikers exploring the Dales Way. Book weeks in advance with individual barns, and get specific directions and locations on the trails when you call to book. **Airton Quaker Hostel** (☎ (01729) 830263; £5.50, under 16 £3), **Barden Bunk Barn** (☎ (01756) 720330; £5), and **Grange Farm Barn** (☎ (01756) 760259; £6.50, under 18 £5.50) are all a few miles from Skipton. **Dub Cote** (☎ (01729) 860238; £6.75) is in Horton Village, near Settle; **Hill Top Farm** (☎ (01729) 830320; £7) in Malham; and **Skirfare Bridge** (☎ (01756) 752465; £7) in Northcote Farm, Kilnsey, north of Grassington on the B6265. **Craken House Farm** (☎ (01969) 622204; £5) stands ½ mi. south of Leyburn.

Campgrounds are difficult to reach on foot, but farmers may let you sleep on their stretch of dale if you ask politely. In **Grassington**, try **Wood Nook.** (☎ (01756) 752412. Showers free. 2-person tent £8.) In **Hawes**, try **Bainbridge Ings**, half a mile out of town on the Old Gale back road. (☎ (01969) 667354. Showers 20p. Open Apr.-Oct. 2-person tent and car £5.90, additional person 50p.) In **Richmond**, try **Brompton-on-Swale Caravan Park.** (☎ (01748) 824629. Open Apr.-Oct. 2-person tent £5.50, with car £7.25.) In **Aysgarth**, try **Street Head Caravan Park.** (☎ (01969) 663472. Showers included. 2-person tent and car £8.)

 # HIKING

SHAKE YER BOOTY. Be aware that all the Dales are filled with **shake holes**, small depressions similar to grassy potholes that indicate underground caverns. *Don't step on them*—they can give way, and may kill you if the cavern is large. Ordnance Survey maps and a compass are essential, especially on the smaller, unmarked trails. See **Wilderness Safety**, p. 53, for other important tips.

Since buses are infrequent and the scenery is breathtaking, hiking remains the best way to see the Dales. The park's seven National Park Information Centres can help you prepare for a trek along one of three long-distance footpaths: make sure to get a decent map from them before setting out. The challenging 270 mi. **Pennine Way** (p. 369) curls from Gargrave in the south to Tan Hill in the north, passing Malham, Pen-y-ghent, Hawes, Keld, and most of the major attractions in the Dales. The more manageable 84 mi. **Dales Way** runs from Bradford and Leeds past Ilkley, through Wharfedale via Grassington and Whernside, and by Sedbergh on its way to the Lake District; it crosses the Pennine Way near Dodd Fell. The 190 mi. **Coast-to-Coast Walk** stretches from Richmond to Kirkby Stephen.

For those less inclined towards monumental journeys, the National Park Information Centres details walks only a few miles long, and trail guides describe less crowded routes of varying lengths. The park authority encourages visitors to keep to designated walks to protect grasslands and to avoid falling into hidden mineshafts. Definitely take a **map** and **trail guide;** stone walls and hills all look similar after a while, and you'll need some way of retracing your steps. The centers sell leaflets (70p) covering over 30 of these short routes, beginning at Ingleton, Longstone Common, Malham, Aysgarth Falls, Grassington's Centre, Clapham's Centre, and other points. The YHA produces a series of leaflets detailing day-long walks between hostels (available from hostels for 20p). Many hostel employees are also avid walkers, so ask for suggestions. For those wishing to cycle, National Park Information Centres list rental stores and sell route cards plotting the **Yorkshire Dales Cycleway,** a series of six 20 mi. routes connecting the dales (£2.50). **Ordnance Survey** maps are available for most smaller paths; purchase them at any center or hiking supply store (£4.50-8). If you're worried your pack may hold you back, the **Pennine Way/Dales Way Baggage Courier** will lighten your load as you trek through the Dales. (☎ (01729) 830463, mobile ☎ (0411) 835322. £4.70-£8 per bag.)

SKIPTON   ☎01756

Skipton (pop. 13,000) shines as a transfer or sleeping point; once you've gathered
your gear, skip town and head for the Dales. Empty **Skipton Castle** is the main sight,
and a modest one at that, but it's also one of the most complete medieval castles in
England. (☎ 792442. Open Mar.-Sept. M-Sa 10am-6pm, Su noon-6pm; Oct.-Feb.
closes 4pm. £4.20, seniors £3.60, ages 5-18 £2.10.) **Pennine Boat Trips** makes daily
forays from the Canal Basin on Coach St., cruising the Leeds and Liverpool Canal.
(☎ 790829. Cruises depart 1:30pm and 3pm. £3, children £1.50.)

Skipton's **train station** is ¼ mi. west of the city center on Broughton Rd. **Buses**
stop on Keighley St. between Hirds Yard and Waller Hill, behind Sunwin House.
For mountain **bike rental** and repairs, try **Dave Ferguson Cycles,** 1 Brook St., off Gargrave Rd. (☎ 795367. £7.50 per half-day, £12 per day. £40 deposit. Open daily 9am-
5:30pm.) The **tourist information centre,** Unit 12, in the Craven Court Shopping Centre, off High St., books accommodations for £2.50 plus a 10% deposit, and sells
National Express tickets and much-needed maps. (☎ 792809; fax 797528. Open M-
F 10am-5pm, Sa 9am-5pm.) **HSBC,** 61 High St., offers banking. (Open M-F 9:30am-
4:30pm.) Stock up on camping and hiking supplies at **George Fisher's,** at the south
end of Coach St. (☎ 794305. Open M and W-Sa 9am-5:30pm, Tu 10am-5:30pm, Su
10am-4pm.) Skipton's **post office** resides with a **supermarket** in Sunwin House, 8
Swadford St. (☎ 792724. Open M-F 9am-6pm, Sa 9am-4pm.) **Postal Code:** B23 1JH.

Cravendale Guest House, 57 Keighley Rd., offers large rooms and an extensive
breakfast, as well as a TV lounge and bar. (☎ 795129. Singles £17.50-21.50; doubles
£35-44.) The **Alton House,** 5 Salisbury St., features books, brochures, beds, benevo-
lent proprietors, and, of course, TVs. (☎ 794780. Singles £17.50-20; doubles £35-40;
discounts on longer stays.) Or ring up **Ringwood House,** 1 Salisbury St. Complete
with bathtub and bidet, the mauve bathroom is as luxurious as the gracefully cur-
tained bedrooms. (☎/fax 791135; mark@ringwoodskipton.freeserve.co.uk. Singles
£20; doubles £35, with bath £45.) Load up on fresh gooseberries and cheese at the
market, which floods High St. (Open M, W, and F-Sa.) **Healthy Life,** 10 High St., near
the church, peddles revitalizing snacks, including vegetarian haggis; the cafe
upstairs, **Herbs,** serves peanut butter and apple sandwiches for £1.85. (☎ 790619.
Store open M and W-Sa 8:30am-5:30pm, Tu 10am-5pm; cafe open M and W-Sa
9:30am-4:45pm.) **Hatter's Sandwich Emporium,** 17 Otley Rd. (☎ 791534), offers a
selection of takeaway sandwiches (under £1.20) and delicious almond slice cake.

WHARFEDALE AND GRASSINGTON   ☎01756

Wharfedale, created by the river Wharfe, is best explored using the gorgeous riverside town of Grassington, as a base. Spectacular **Kilnsey Crag** lies 3½ mi. from
Grassington toward Kettlewell; *Wharfedale Walk #8* guides you there through a
deep gorge, Bronze Age burial mounds, and views of Wharfedale. The **Stump Cross
Caverns,** adorned with beautiful stalagmite columns and glistening curtains of
rock, are five miles east of Grassington toward Pateley Bridge; some travelers
choose to hitch on the B6265. Dress warmly; it gets chilly down under. (☎ 752780.
Open Mar.-Oct. daily 10am-4pm. £3.90, under 13 £2.) The second half of June
brings in the art and music of the annual **Grassington Festival** (☎ 753068).

Grassington receives Pride of the Dales **bus** service from Skipton (#72; M-Sa
about 1 per hr., Su 4 per day; day return £3.80). The **National Park Information Centre,** Hebden Rd. stocks the useful *Grassington Footpath Map* (£1.30) and gives
occasional guided walks. (☎ 752774. Open May-Aug. daily 9:30am-5:15pm; call for
winter hours. Walks Mar.-Oct.; £1.80-2.50, children 70p-£1.) **Barclays bank** is at the
corner of Main St. and Hebden Rd. (Open M-Tu and Th-F 9:30am-3:30pm, W 10am-
3:30pm.) **The Mountaineer,** Pletts Barn Centre, at the top of Main St., sells outdoor
gear. (☎ 752266. Open daily 10am-5pm.) The **post office** is at 15 Main St. (☎ 752226.
Open M-F 9am-5:30pm, Sa 9am-12:30pm.) **Postal Code:** BD23 5AD.

Florrie Whitehead, 16 Wood Ln., supplies excellent B&B and legendary hospitality. (☎ 752841. £15 per person.) **Burtree,** a few steps from the National Park Information Centre on the corner of Hebden Rd. and Sedber Ln., is a stone cottage with

a glorious garden. (☎ 752442. £16 per person.) Pubs and tea shops abound on Main St., including **Picnic's Café,** 10 Main St., which serves traditional hot meals for £1.25 to £4.45. (☎ 753342. Open daily in summer 10am-5:30pm; in winter 10am-3:30pm.)

MALHAMDALE   ☎01729

Limestone cliffs and gorges slice through the pastoral valley of Malhamdale, creating several spectacular natural sights within easy walking distance of one another. A four-hour hike will take you past the stunning pavement of **Malham Cove,** a massive limestone cliff, to **Malham Tarn,** Yorkshire's second-largest natural lake. Two miles from Malham is the equally impressive **Gordale Scar,** cut in the last Ice Age by a rampaging glacier. Catch all of these beauties in *A Walk in Malhamdale* (leaflet #1), available from Malham's **National Park Information Centre** (☎ 830363) or the superior-grade **YHA Youth Hostel,** thronged by Pennine Way followers (see p. 380). **Townhead Farm,** the last farm before Malham Cove, provides tent sites with showers (50p) and toilets. (☎ 830287. £2.50 per person, £1 per tent, £1 per car.)

INGLETON   ☎015242

North of Malham, the high peaks and cliffs of **Ingleborough, Pen-y-ghent,** and **Whernside** form the Alpes Penninae. The 24 mi. **Three Peaks Walk** connecting the Alpes begins and ends in **Horton-in-Ribblesdale** at the clock of the **Pen-y-ghent Café,** a hiker's haunt with mammoth mugs of tea. The best place to break your journey is **Ingleton** (pop. 2000), where the local **tourist information centre,** in the community center car park, books rooms. (☎ 41049. Open Apr.-Oct. daily 10am-4:30pm.) The 4½ mi. walk through the Ingleton Waterfalls is one of the park's most popular routes. A **YHA Youth Hostel,** Greta Tower, sits in Ingleton (see p. 380). Several small **B&Bs** on Main St. charge around £15, or a mile walk brings one to **Stacksteads Farm,** Butterthorne Rd., which offers B&B and also a bunk barn with 22 beds. (☎ 41386. Rooms £16; barn £8, self-catering.)

WENSLEYDALE AND HAWES   ☎01969

The northerly Wensleydale landscape of potholes, caves, clints, and grikes melts into a broad swath of fertile dairyland. Base your ventures in **Hawes,** which has a **National Park Information Centre** (☎ 667450). Spit out 20p at the Green Dragon Pub to see the overrated **Hardrow Force** waterfall (1 mi. north along the Pennine Way). If you're tired of natural landscapes, the **Dales Countryside Museum,** in the same building as the National Park Information Centre, chronicles the history of "real Dalespeople." (☎ 667494. Open Apr.-Oct. daily 10am-5pm; winter 10am-4pm. £2, concessions £1.) Cruise the museum and cheese factory viewing gallery at the **Wensleydale Creamery,** Gayle Ln., with great free samples at the end. (☎ 667664. Open M-Sa 9:30am-5pm, Su 10am-4:30pm. £2, children £1.50.) ▓ **Cumbria Classic Coaches** (☎ (01539) 623254) runs various trips around the Dales in a vintage 1934 bus. The solid form of **Castle Bolton** graces Wensleydale—explore it from dungeon to 100 ft. battlements. It's a nice day's walk from YHA Aysgarth. (☎ 623981. Open Mar.-Nov. daily 10am-5pm. £4, concessions £3.) Pubs, takeaways, and a **Barclays bank** (open M, W, and F 9:30am-3:30pm, Tu 9:30am-4:30pm, Th 10am-4:30pm) are on Hawes's Main St. A **YHA Youth Hostel** (see p. 380) is in town, and **B&Bs** (£15-20) line Main St.; check the list posted outside the town hall every afternoon.

Farther north, **Swaledale** is known for picture-perfect barns and meadows. Also worthwhile are the **Aysgarth Falls** to the east—rolling in successive tiers down the craggy Yoredale Rocks—and the natural terrace of the **Shawl of Leyburn.** A **National Park Information Centre** (☎ 663424) idles in the car park above Aysgarth Falls. There is a **tourist information centre** in **Leyburn.** (☎ 623069. Open Easter-Sept. daily 9:30am-5:30pm; Oct.-Easter M-Sa 9:30am-noon and 1-4pm.) Both Aysgarth and Leyburn are serviced by **United buses** #156 and 157 from **Hawes** to **Richmond.** The **YHA Youth Hostel** sits ½ mi. east of the village (see p. 380).

YORK   ☎01904

The history of York is the history of England.
—King George VI, then Duke of York

With a pace suitable for ambling and its tallest building a cathedral, York is as different from nearby Leeds as it is from its new American namesake. Although its well-preserved city walls have foiled many, York fails to impede its present-day hordes of visitors. In AD 71, the Romans founded Eboracum as a military and administrative base for Northern England; the town remained important as Anglo-Saxon "Eoforwic" and Viking "Jorvik." William the Conqueror permitted York's Archbishop to officiate at his consecration. In 1069, York thanked him by joining with the Danes to massacre 3000 men in the Conqueror's garrison, producing just some of the ghosts in the self-proclaimed "most haunted city in the world." While earlier invaders came seeking wealth and power, it's no surprise what the current marauders, brandishing zoom cameras, are after—York holds a compact collection of historical sights in England within her walls, including medieval streets and Britain's largest Gothic cathedral. Somehow, though, the city manages to roll out the red carpet without sacrificing the authentic aura of a rich heritage.

◤ GETTING THERE AND GETTING AROUND

Trains: Station Rd. Travel center and information office open M-Sa 8am-7:45pm, Su 9am-7:45pm. Ticket office open M-Sa 5:45am-10:15pm, Su 7:30am-10:10pm. **Luggage storage** £2-4; open M-Sa 8:30am-8:30pm, Su 9:10am-8:30pm. Trains (☎ (08457) 484950) from: **London King's Cross** (2hr., 2 per hr., £56); **Scarborough** (50min., 2 per hr., £9.60); **Newcastle** (1hr., 2 per hr., £14.90); **Manchester Piccadilly** (1½hr., 2 per hr., £16.20); and **Edinburgh** (2-3hr., 2 per hr., £48).

Buses: (☎ 551400), **bus stations** at Rougier St., Exhibition Sq., the train station, and on Piccadilly. **National Express** (☎ (08705) 808080) from: **London** (4½hr., 6 per day, £16.50); **Manchester** (3hr., 6 per day, £7.75); and **Edinburgh** (5hr., 2 per day, £21).

Local Transportation: Call **Rider York** (☎ 435609) for information. Ticket office open M-Sa 9am-5pm. **Yorkshire Coastliner** (☎ (0113) 244 8976 or ☎ (01653) 692556) runs buses to Castle Howard (see p. 390) that board at the train station.

Boats: Several companies along the River Ouse near Lendal, Ouse, and Skeldergate Bridges offer 1hr. cruises. **Yorkboat**, Lendal Bridge (☎ 628324). Easter-Oct. trips depart every 30min.; Feb.-Mar. and Nov. at least 2 trips per day at 11am and 12:30pm, call ahead. £4.50, seniors £4, children £2. Office opens 10:30am.

Taxis: Station Taxis (☎ 623332 or ☎ 628197), open 24hr.

Bike Rental: Bob Trotter, 13 Lord Mayor's Walk (☎ 622868). From £7.50 per day plus £50 deposit. Open M-Sa 9am-5:30pm, Su 10am-4pm. The tourist information centre's free *York Cycle Route Map* is helpful.

◣◥ ORIENTATION AND PRACTICAL INFORMATION

York's streets now present a greater obstacle than the ancient walls ever did. They're winding, short, rarely labeled, and the longer ones change names every block or so. Fortunately, most attractions lie within the city walls, so you can't get too lost, and the **Minster,** visible from seemingly every point, provides an easy marker. The River Ouse (OOZE) cuts through the city, curving west to south. The city center lies between the Ouse and the Minster; **Coney St., Parliament St.,** and **Stonegate** are the main thoroughfares.

Tourist Information Centre: De Grey Rooms, Exhibition Sq. (☎ 621756; www.york-tourism.co.uk). Books rooms for £3 plus a 10% deposit. The *York Visitor Guide* (50p) includes "Where to Stay" and "What to See" sections, and a detailed map. *Snickelways of York* (£5) is an offbeat self-tour guide. Open daily June-Oct. 9am-6pm; Nov.-May 9am-5pm. **Branch,** in the train station, has a **bureau de change.** Open June-Oct. M-Sa 9am-8pm, Su 9am-5pm; Nov.-May daily 9am-5pm. **York Visitor and Conference**

Bureau, 20 George Hudson St., offers similar services. Room booking £4 plus a 10% deposit. Open M-Sa 9am-5:30pm, in summer also Su 10am-4pm.

Tours: A free 2hr. **walking tour,** offered daily by the Association of Voluntary Guides (☎ 630284). Meet in front of the York City Art Gallery, across from the TIC, at 10:15am or 2:15pm. A bewildering array of **ghost tours** all offer similar experiences. Brave **The Ghost Hunt of York** (☎ 608700), which meets on Shambles daily at 7:30pm. 1hr.; £3, children £2. **York Pullman** (☎ 622992) runs a variety of regional half- and full-day tours of the Yorkshire Dales and Moors (£7-20). **Guide Friday** (☎ 640896) leads its familiar open-roof bus tours; hop on at places throughout town. £8, students and seniors £6.50, under 12 £2.50, families £16.

Financial Services: Banks are ubiquitous on Coney St. **Thomas Cook,** 4 Nessgate (☎ 653626). Open M-W and F-Sa 9am-5:30pm, Th 10am-5:30pm, Su 11am-5pm.

American Express: 6 Stonegate (☎ 670030). Open M-F 9am-5:30pm, Sa 9am-5pm; in summer currency exchange also open Su 10:30am-4:30pm.

Launderette: Haxby Road Washeteria, 124 Haxby Rd. (☎ 623379). Open M-F 8am-6pm, Sa 8am-5:30pm, Su 8am-4:30pm. Last wash 2hr. before close.

Police: (☎ 631321), Fulford Rd.

Hospital: York District Hospital (☎ 631313), off Wigginton Rd. Take bus #1, 2, 3, or 18 from Exhibition Sq.

Internet Access: The Gateway Internet Cafe, 26 Swinegate (☎ 646446). Open M-Sa 10am-8pm, Su noon-4pm; 50p quick check, £1.50 per 15min., £4 per hr. 20% student discount. **Branch,** in the basement of City Screen on Coney St. Open daily 11am-11pm.

Post Office: 22 Lendal (☎ 617285). **Bureau de change.** Open M-T 8:30am-5:30pm, W-Sa 9am-5:30pm. **Postal Code:** YO1 2DA.

▌ ACCOMMODATIONS

Competition for inexpensive B&Bs (from £16) can be fierce during the summer. The tourist information centres (TICs) and the York Visitor and Conference Bureau can be helpful. B&Bs are concentrated on the sidestreets along **Bootham** and **Clifton,** in the **Mount** area down Blossom St., and on **Bishopsthorpe Rd.,** due south of town. Book weeks ahead in the summer, even for hostels and campsites.

▨ **Avenue Guest House,** 6 The Avenue (☎ 620575; allen@avenuegh.fsnet.co.uk), off Clifton on a quiet, residential side street. A river footpath from the train station leads to the bottom of The Avenue. Enthusiastic hosts provide 7 immaculate rooms surrounding an impressive spiral staircase. Soft beds and plush towels make it a step up without being pricey. Some family rooms with baths. All rooms with TVs. Singles £15-17; doubles £28-32, with bath £30-40; these prices for those who mention *Let's Go* in advance.

YHA York (☎ 653147), Water End, Clifton, 1 mi. from town center. From Exhibition Sq., walk about ¾ mi. on Bootham, and take a left at Water End; or take a bus to Clifton Green and walk ¼ mi. down Water End. Excellent facilities (kitchen, TV room, laundry, Internet access), but pricey. 156 beds. Reception open 7am-10:30pm. Bedroom lockout 10am-1pm. Open mid-Jan. to mid-Dec. Dorms £16, under 18 £12; singles £18.50; twins £37; family rooms £52 or £78.

York Backpackers Hostel, 88-90 Micklegate (☎/fax 627720; yorkbackpackers@cwcom.net). Fresh and bubbling over with ideas, this hostel occupies a stately, 18th-century urban mansion. Kitchen and laundry facilities. Internet access (£2.50 per 30min.). TV lounge. "Dungeon Bar" open 3 nights a week, long after the pubs close. Dorms £9-12 depending on size of room; doubles £30.

York Youth Hotel, 11-15 Bishophill Senior (☎ 625904). A well-located hostel, but picky travelers beware: the open shower takes you back to your gym class days. Coed 20-bed Room 12 is an excellent place to meet fellow travelers; the rest of the building, including some single-sex rooms, is often booked by youth groups. Sleeps 120. Continental breakfast £2, English breakfast £3. Sheets £1. Laundry facilities. Key deposit £2. 24hr. reception. Bar open 9pm-1am. Dorms £9.50-11; singles £13-14; twins £24-33.

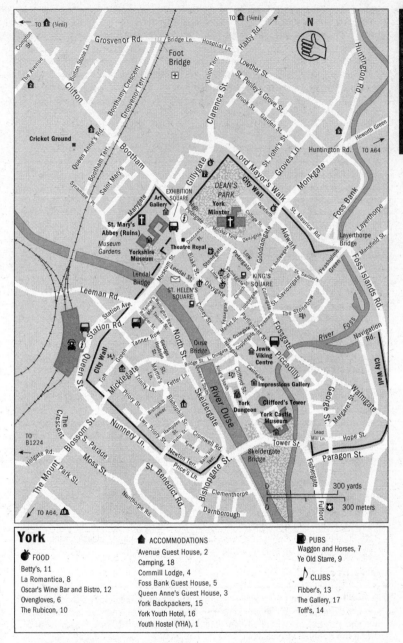

York

 FOOD

Betty's, 11
La Romantica, 8
Oscar's Wine Bar and Bistro, 12
Ovengloves, 6
The Rubicon, 10

 ACCOMMODATIONS

Avenue Guest House, 2
Camping, 18
Cornmill Lodge, 4
Foss Bank Guest House, 5
Queen Anne's Guest House, 3
York Backpackers, 15
York Youth Hotel, 16
Youth Hostel (YHA), 1

 PUBS

Waggon and Horses, 7
Ye Old Starre, 9

 CLUBS

Fibber's, 13
The Gallery, 17
Toff's, 14

Foss Bank Guest House, 16 Huntington Rd. (☎ 635548). Walk, or take bus #B5 or B6 from the train station. A cheery garden and the River Foss welcome the weary traveler. Comfortable beds and wooden desks in clean rooms. Doubles are particularly luxurious. All rooms have showers and sinks. Some with bathtubs, some with TVs. No smoking. Singles £17-19: doubles £37-44.

Queen Anne's Guest House, 24 Queen Anne's Rd. (☎ 629389), a short walk out Bootham from Exhibition Sq. Spotless single and double rooms with TVs; some doubles with baths. Large breakfasts. Singles from £16; doubles from £32.

Cornmill Lodge, 120 Haxby Rd. (☎ 620566; cornmill_lodge@hotmail.com). From Exhibition Sq. go up Gillygate to Clarence St. and then Haxby Rd., or take bus #A1 from the station. Vegetarian B&B with clean rooms with TV. Singles from £20; doubles from £40.

Camping: Riverside Caravan and Camping Park (☎ 705812), York Marine Services, Ferry Ln., Bishopthorpe, 2 mi. south of York off the A64. Take bus #23 from the bus station, and ask the driver to let you off at the campsite (every 30min., return £1.30). Riverside site. July-Aug. £7 for 2 people and a tent; Sept.-June £6.

FOOD AND PUBS

Expensive tea rooms, medium-range bistros, and cheap eateries rub elbows in York. Green grocers peddle at the **Newgate market** between Parliament St. and Shambles. (Open M-Sa 9am-5pm; Apr.-Dec. also Su 9am-4:30pm.) There are more **pubs** in the center of York than gargoyles on the east wall of the Minster. Whether Tudor, Victorian, or in-between, most are packed on weekend nights, and all serve bar meals during the day.

Oscar's Wine Bar and Bistro, 8 Little Stonegate (☎ 652002), off Stonegate. Hearty pub grub in massive portions (£5-7) will keep you going for a week. This popular and classy pub has a swank courtyard, varied menu, and lively mood. Live jazz and blues M nights. Open daily 11am-11pm; happy hour Su-M 4pm-close, Tu-F 5-7pm.

Ovengloves, 74 Gillygate (☎ 625184). Get a sandwich on the go for an itsy-bitsy price at this excellent takeaway bakery and delicatessen. Pies and pasties 65p, filled rolls made to order 95p-£1.20. Open M-Sa 8am-5:30pm.

Betty's, 6-8 St. Helens Sq. Traditional cream tea (pot of tea and 2 scones £4.95) is served in a terrifically refined atmosphere. Also serves lunch and dinner (£3-8). Live piano music daily 6-9pm.Open daily 9am-9pm.

La Romantica, 14 Goodramgate (☎ 626236). Candles dripping over wine bottles and Italian music in the background create a sensuous setting, but the friendly staff at La Romantica realize that the quickest way to a traveler's heart is through his stomach. Generous and delicious servings of pasta and pizza (£5) or a large portion of both together (£7) will reinvigorate after a long day of sightseeing. Open M-Sa noon-2:30pm and 5:30-11pm, Su 5:30-10:30pm.

The Rubicon, 5 Little Stonegate (☎ 676076), off Stonegate. Upscale vegetarian restaurant has creative lunches (£3-5.50), such as butterbean and hazelnut pâté, as well as sandwiches (£3.50). Dinner is more expensive (£6-8; after 6:30pm). Vegan and gluten-free options. Open daily 11am-10pm.

Ye Old Starre, 40 Stonegate (☎ 623063). The city's oldest pub, with a license that dates back to 1644. The best pub meals (£4-5), with sumptuous *chili con carne*, bursting Guinness pie, and giant Yorkshire puddings for lunch, plus a pleasant inner courtyard. Open M-Sa 11am-11pm, Su noon-3pm and 7-10:30pm.

SIGHTS

The best introduction to York is a 2½ mi. walk along its **medieval walls.** Beware of the tourist stampede, which weakens only in the early morning and just before the walls and gates close at dusk. At the TIC, ask for the useful *York Visitor Guide*, then hit the cobbled streets.

■ YORK MINSTER

To the north—you can't miss it. ☎ 639347. *Open in summer daily 7am-8:30pm; off-season 7am-6pm. Evensong services M-F 5pm, Sa-Su 4pm. Tours usually run between 9:30am-3:30pm. Requested donation £3.*

Everyone and everything in York converges at York Minster, the largest Gothic cathedral in Britain. The present structure, erected between 1220 and 1470, was preceded by the Roman fortress where Constantine the Great was hailed emperor in 306 and the Saxon church where King Edwin converted to Christianity in 627. Within this Minster, Miles Coverdale translated and published the first complete printed English Bible in 1535. An estimated half of all the medieval stained glass in England glitters as it holds the walls together. The **Great East Window,** constructed from 1405 to 1408 and depicting both the beginning and the end of the world in over a hundred small scenes, is the largest single medieval glass window in the world. The choral **evensong** is a mind-blowing meeting of organ and choir.

CENTRAL TOWER. It's a mere 275 steps up to the top of the tower, from which you can stare down at the red roofs of York. There's only a 5min. period every 30 minutes during which you may ascend, as the stairs don't allow two people to pass. *(Open daily June-Sept. 9:30am-6:30pm; Mar. and Nov. 10am-4:30pm; Apr. and Oct. 10am-5:30pm; May 10am-6pm. £2.50, children £1.)*

THE FOUNDATIONS AND TREASURY. Displays tell the incredible story of how the central tower began to crack apart in 1967. You can tour the huge concrete and steel foundations inserted by engineers, the remnants of the previous buildings they unearthed, and treasured items of the cathedral. *(Open daily June-Sept. 9:30am-6:30pm; Mar. and Nov. 10am-4:30pm; Apr. and Oct. 10am-5:30pm; May 10am-6pm. £2, students and seniors £1.50, children £1.)*

CRYPT, CHAPTER HOUSE, AND LIBRARY. Also worth a look are the crypt and chapter house. The Minster Library guards books at the far corner of the grounds. *(Chapter house open daily June-Sept. 9:30am-6:30pm; Mar. and Nov. 10am-4:30pm; Apr. and Oct. 10am-5:30pm; May 10am-6pm. Crypt open June-Sept. M-F 9:30am-4:30pm, Sa 9:30am-3:30pm, Su 1-3:30pm; Oct.-May. M-F 10am-4:30pm, Sa 10am-3:30pm, Su 12:30-3:30pm. Admission to both 70p, children 30p. Library open M-Th 10am-4pm, F 10am-noon. Free.)*

OTHER SIGHTS

■YORK CASTLE MUSEUM. Housed in a former debtor's prison, the huge York Castle Museum lives up to its billing as Britain's premier museum dedicated to everyday life. The tormented brainchild of eccentric collector Dr. John Kirk, who began collecting items during his housecalls from the 1890s to the 1920s, the museum now puts objects from the past into context. It contains **Kirkgate,** an intricately reconstructed Victorian shopping street complete with carriage, and **Half Moon Court,** its Edwardian counterpart. *(The Eye of York. ☎ 653611. Open daily Apr.-Oct. 9:30am-5pm; Nov.-Mar. 9:30am-4:30pm. £5.95, concessions £4.25, families £15.50.)*

JORVIK VIKING CENTRE. The Viking Centre is one of the busiest places in York; visit early or late to avoid lines, or book at least 24hr. in advance. Visitors ride through the York of AD 948, with authentic artifacts and painfully accurate smells, to discover Norse truths. No, the Vikings did not wear horns. *(Coppergate. ☎ 643211; advance booking ☎ 543403, M-F 9am-5pm. Open Apr.-Oct. daily 9am-5:30pm; Nov.-Dec. daily 10am-4:30pm; Jan.-Mar. Su-F 9am-3:30pm, Sa 9am-4:30pm; last admission 1hr. before closing. £5.50, students and seniors £4.75, children £3.99, families £17.50.)*

YORKSHIRE MUSEUM. Hidden within the 10 gorgeous acres of the museum **gardens,** the Yorkshire Museum presents Roman, Anglo-Saxon, and Viking artifacts, as well as the £2.5 million **Middleham Jewel** (c. 1450), a gold amulet engraved with the Trinity and the nativity, and set with an enormous sapphire. In the gardens, children chase pigeons into reclining lovers among the haunting ruins of **St. Mary's Abbey,** once the most influential Benedictine monastery in northern England. Visit the basement to get the lowdown on abbey life. *(Enter from Museum St. or Marygate. ☎ 629745. Open daily 10am-5pm. Wheelchair access. £3.75, concessions £2.20; families £10.50; 50p-£1 higher during temporary exhibitions. Gardens and abbey ruins free.)*

CLIFFORD'S TOWER. This tower is one of the last remaining pieces of York Castle, and a chilling reminder of the worst outbreak of anti-Semitic violence in English history. In 1190, Christian merchants tried to erase their debts to Jewish bankers by destroying York's Jewish community. On the last Sabbath before Passover, 150 Jews took refuge in a tower that previously stood on this site and, faced with the prospect of starvation or butchery, committed suicide. Visitors can read informative billboards along a wall walk with panoramic views. *(Tower St. ☎ 646940. Open daily July-Aug 9:30am-7pm; Apr.-June and Sept. 10am-6pm; Oct. 10am-5pm; Nov.-Mar. 10am-4pm. £1.80, students and seniors £1.40, children 90p.)*

BEST OF THE REST. The **York City Art Gallery,** on Exhibition Sq. across from the TIC, has an uneven collection of Continental work, a better selection of English painters (including William Etty, York native and pioneer of the English painted nude), and a sprinkling of pottery. *(☎ 551861. Open M-Sa 10am-5pm; last admission 4:30pm. Wheelchair access. £2, concessions £1.50.)* Another capably curated space, the **Impressions Gallery,** Castlegate, serves as a small contemporary gallery. *(☎ 654724. Open M-Sa 9:30am-5:30pm, Su 11am-5pm.)* The morbidly inclined should try **York Dungeon,** 12 Clifford St. Learn the story of Guy Fawkes and Dick Turpin, and stare at sore-ridden bodies in the Plague exhibit and mangled wax figures in the Torture exhibit—who's ready for lunch? *(☎ 632599. Open daily Apr.-Sept. 10am-5:30pm; Oct.-Mar. 10am-4:30pm. £5.95, students and seniors £4.50, children £3.95.)*

🎵 🎎 ENTERTAINMENT AND FESTIVALS

The weekly *What's On* and *Artscene* guides, available at the TIC, have listings on live music, theater, cinema, and exhibitions. A **Ghost Tour of York** makes a lively start to the evening (see p. 386). In **King's Square** and on **Stonegate,** barbershop quartets share the pavement with jugglers, magicians, and politicians.Next to the TIC on St. Leonards Pl., the **Theatre Royal** stages productions. *(☎ 623568; 24hr. info ☎ 610041.* Box office open M-Sa 10am-8pm, except for one month in spring when open M-Sa 10am-6pm. Wheelchair access. Tickets £6-30, student standbys day of show £3.) York's dressy new club, **The Gallery,** 12 Clifford St., offers plenty of eye candy on two dance floors and at six bars. (Open F-W 9:30pm-2am, Th 10pm-2am. Cover varies.) The excellent **Toff's,** 3-5 Toft Green, plays mainly dance and house music. *(☎ 620203.* No trainers. Open M-Sa 9pm-2am. Cover £3.50, free F before 10:30pm.) **Fibber's** *(☎ 651250),* Stonebow House, the Stonebow, doesn't lie about the quality of the live music playing every night at 8pm.

The Minster and local churches host a series of **summer concerts.** Celebrate Purcell and friends in July at the **York Early Music Festival** *(☎ 658338).* York recently revived a tradition of many centuries past, performing the **York Mystery Plays** in the nave of the minster during June and July every fourth year. The next performances will be in 2004. *(☎ 635444* for more information.)

📌 DAYTRIPS FROM YORK

🏰 CASTLE HOWARD

Fifteen miles northeast of York. Yorkshire Coastliner bus #842 runs half-day excursions to the castle (1 per day, £4); your bus ticket gets you reduced admission. ☎ (01653) 648333. Open mid-Mar. to Nov. 5 daily 11am-4:30pm; gardens mid-Mar. to Nov. 5 daily 10am-6:30pm. Chapel services Sa-Su 5:15pm, 10min. Wheelchair access. £7.50, students and seniors £6.75, children £4.50. Gardens only £4.50, children £2.50.

Castle Howard, still inhabited by the Howard family, made its TV debut as the home of the Marchmains in the BBC adaptation of Evelyn Waugh's *Brideshead Revisited.* Grand halls (including a spectacular entrance with marble floors) and stairways are festooned with portraits of the Howard ancestors in full regalia and cluttered with Roman busts checking each other out. The **long gallery** provides a dazzling and dwarfing promenade between enormous windows and shelves stuffed with books. Head to the **chapel** for the kaleidoscopic stained glass. More stunning than the castle itself are its 999 acres of glorious grounds, including luxurious rose gardens, fountains, and lakes, all roamed by raucous peacocks. Be sure to see the white and gold domed **Temple of the Four Winds,** whose hilltop perch offers views of rolling hills, still waters, and lazy cows.

NORTH YORK MOORS NATIONAL PARK

Atop Yorkshire's windy moors, imagining Heathcliffe and Dracula requires no suspension of disbelief. The moors have changed little since inspiring the Brontë sisters (see p. 74) and Bram Stoker: heathered hills and cliff-lined coasts lend themselves easily to images of passionate men and bloodthirsty immortals. Wayfarers can pace the flagstone "trods" (once used by journeying monks), or guide themselves by the famous stone crosses. Lilla Cross, on Fylingdales Moor, stands in tribute to the servant Lilla, who used his own body to shield King Edwin from an assassin's dagger in AD 626.

The kidney-shaped park, about 30 mi. north of York, encompasses the Vale of Pickering in the south, the Vales of York and Mowbray in the west, the flat Cleveland and Teeside Plains in the north, and the rugged North Sea coastline in the east. Some of the highest cliffs in England line the park's coastal border, interspersed with tiny harbors such as Staithes and Robin Hood's Bay. The seaside towns of Whitby and Scarborough are bigger and busier, and you'll rub shoulders with hordes of beach-bound vacationers. Smaller and quieter, the inland towns of Pickering and Helmsley retain more of the spirit of the moors.

▐ GETTING THERE AND GETTING AROUND

No single town serves as an obvious transport hub—Malton, Helmsley, and Pickering near the southern edge of the park, Whitby and Scarborough in the east, and Middlesbrough to the north all have adequate connections. The essential document for transport within the park is the *Moors Connections* pamphlet, a life-saver which covers both bus and rail service in glorious detail (free at tourist information centres and National Park Information Centres). Pick it up early and plan ahead—service varies by season and is minimal in the winter. The North York Moors public transport information line has up-to-date times and schedules (☎ (0870) 608 2608; 3-8p per min.).

Train (☎ (08457) 484950) service is limited but efficient; two railway lines enter the park. The **Northern Spirit** cuts through the North, running from **Newcastle** to **Whitby,** via **Castleton, Danby,** and **Grosmont** (3hr., 4 per day, £8). The **Transpennine Express** provides access from the south, connecting **York** and **Scarborough** (45min., every 30min., £9.30). More tourist attraction than budget transportation, the steam-hauled **North York Moors Railway** (☎ (01751) 472508) links the north and the south, chugging from **Pickering** to **Grosmont** (1hr., 5 per day, all-day pass £10).

Buses cover more turf and run more frequently than trains. **Yorkshire Coastliner** (☎ (0113) 244 8976) offers a number of useful routes: pick up the free *Yorkshire Coastliner Timetable* at tourist information centres (TICs), National Park Information Centres, and bus stations for a thorough listing. Bus #840 travels between **Leeds, York,** and **Whitby,** with many stops at villages along the way (3hr., 5 per day), while bus #843 runs between **Leeds, York,** and **Scarborough** (3hr., 1 per hr.). **Arriva** bus #93 journeys between **Middlesborough, Whitby,** and **Scarborough** (2hr., 2 per hr.). The Scarborough and District bus #128 covers **Scarborough, Pickering,** and **Helmsley** (1½hr., 1 per hr.). On Sundays from April to September, additional **Moorsbus** services crawl like ants all over the Moors; these buses go everywhere you could want (£2 for an all-day ticket).

The Moors are steep, and **cycling** around them a challenge, but the paths on the plateaus are pleasant. TICs and National Park Information Centres offer several guides to cycling in the Moors (£1.80-7). Stores that rent bikes can be found in most of the towns surrounding the park. Biking on footpaths is both destructive and dangerous; cycles should be used on roads and bridleways only.

🔢 PRACTICAL INFORMATION

Along with the free *Moors Connections*, the *North York Moors Visitor* (50p) is as crucial as sturdy shoes for exploring the park. Available at all TICs and National Park Information Centres, it contains useful advice and lists attractions, events, and accommodations throughout the Moors. In general, TICs in the area are outstandingly helpful, and they've got the awards to prove it. Visitors should bear in mind that many shops are only open daily in the summer.

NATIONAL PARK INFORMATION CENTRES

Danby: The Moors Centre (☎ (01287) 660654). The largest National Park Information Centre in the area, with a colossal amount of information, a sleek cafe, and a huge garden. From the train station, turn right as you leave the platform, left after you pass the gate, and right at the crossroads before the Duke of Wellington Pub; the center is a ½ mi. ahead on the right (20min.). Northern Spirit North East's Middlesbrough-Whitby connection stops off at Danby. Open Apr.-July and Sept.-Oct. daily 10am-5pm; Aug. daily 10am-5:30pm; Nov.-Dec. and Mar. daily 11am-4pm; Jan.-Feb. Sa-Su 11am-4pm.

Sutton Bank: (☎ (01845) 597426), 6 mi. east of Thirsk on the A170. Open Apr.-Oct. daily 10am-5pm; Mar. and Nov.-Dec. daily 11am-4pm; Jan.-Feb. Sa-Su 11am-4pm.

TOURIST INFORMATION CENTRES

Goathland: The Village Store and Outdoor Centre (☎ (01947) 896207). Open Easter-Oct. daily 10am-5pm; Nov.-Easter M-W and F-Su 10am-4pm.

Great Ayton: High Green Car Park (☎ (01642) 722835). Open Apr.-Oct. M-Sa 10am-4pm, Su 1-4pm.

Guisborough: Priory Grounds, Church St. (☎ (01287) 633801). Open Apr.-Sept. Tu-Su 9am-5pm; Oct.-Mar. W-Su 9am-5pm. Closed daily noon-12:30pm (F noon-1pm).

Helmsley: Town Hall, Market Pl. (☎ (01439) 770173). Open daily Mar.-Sept. 9:30am-6pm; Oct. 9:30am-5:30pm; Nov.-Feb. F-Su 10am-4pm. Books rooms fo a 10% deposit.

Malton: Old Town Hall, Market Pl. (☎ (01653) 600048). Open Mar.-Oct. M-Sa 9:30am-5:30pm, Su 10am-4:30pm; Nov.-Feb. M-W and F-Sa 10am-1pm and 1:30-4:30pm.

Pickering: The Ropery (☎ (01751) 473791). Accommodations list posted in window. Books rooms for 10% deposit. Open Mar.-Oct. M-Sa 9:30am-6pm, Su 9:30am-5:30pm; Nov.-Feb. M-Sa 10am-4:30pm.

Scarborough: Unit 3, Pavilion House, Valley Bridge Rd. (☎ (01723) 373333). Open May-Sept. daily 9:30am-6pm; Oct.-Apr. 10am-4:30pm.

Whitby: Station Sq., Langborne Rd. (☎ (01947) 602674). Open daily May-Sept. 9:30am-6pm; Oct.-Apr. 10am-12:30pm and 1-4:30pm. Books rooms for 10% deposit.

🏠 ACCOMMODATIONS

Local TICs will book beds for a small fee plus a 10% deposit. **B&Bs** in the National Park are listed under the appropriate towns. The following **YHA Youth Hostels** provide lodging in the Moors; reservations are recommended. Most offer meals at fixed prices (breakfast £2.85, packed lunch £2.50-3.25, evening meal £4.25).

Boggle Hole: (☎ (01947) 880352; fax 880987), Mill Beck, Fylingthorpe. Easy access to Cleveland Way and Coast-to-Coast trails. 19th-century mill in a ravine on Robin Hood's Bay. Curfew 11pm. Open daily Feb. to mid-Nov. Dorms £10, under 18 £6.80.

Helmsley: (☎/fax (01439) 770433). From Market Pl. walk along Bondgate Rd., turn left onto Carlton Rd., and left again at Carlton Ln.; hostel is on the left. Open daily Apr.-Aug.; Sept.-Oct. M-Sa. Dorms £9.50, under 18 £6.15.

Lockton: The Old School (☎ (01751) 460376), just off the Pickering-Whitby Rd. Take Coastlines bus #840 from Whitby. Fresh, self-catering hostel. Open July-Aug. daily; June and Sept. M-Sa. Dorms £7, under 18 £4.80.

Osmotherley: (☎ (01609) 883575; fax 883715), Cote Ghyll, Northallerton. Between Stockton and Thirsk, just northeast of Osmotherley. Dorms £10, under 18 £6.80.

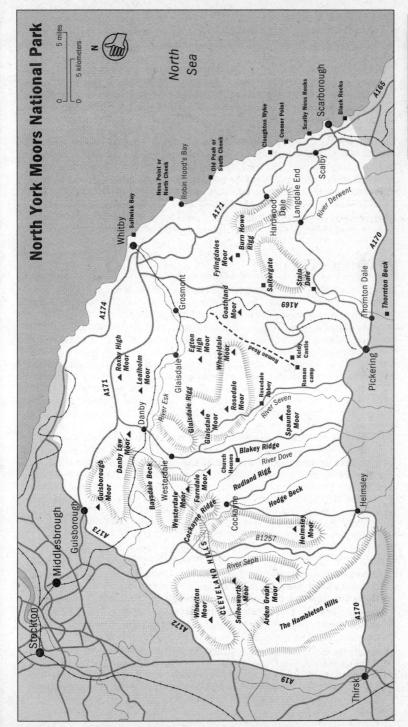

North York Moors National Park

Scarborough: The White House (☎ (01723) 361176; fax 500054), Burniston Rd., 2 mi. from Scarborough. In a former mill on a river, 10min. from the sea. Take bus #3 from the train station. Open Mar.-Aug. daily; Sept.-Oct. M-Sa. Dorms £8.15, under 18 £5.90.

Whitby: (☎ (01947) 602878; fax 825146). 12th-century stone building next to the abbey, atop 199 loathsome steps. Lockout 10am-5pm. Curfew 11pm. Moor-bound school groups often fill the place until mid-July, so call ahead. Family rooms available. Open Apr.-Oct. daily; Feb.-Mar. and Nov. to mid-Dec. F-Sa; closed mid-Dec. to Jan. Dorms £9.50, under 18 £6.15.

The YHA operates four **camping barns** in the Moors, in **Farndale**, Oakhouse farmyard; **Kildale,** on the Cleveland Way; **Sinnington,** on the edge of the Park between Pickering and Helmsley; and **Westerdale,** in Broadgate Farm. These "stone tents" provide a roof, water, and toilets. A good sleeping bag, flashlight, and cooking equipment are essential. For listings, pick up the free *Stay in a Camping Barn* leaflet from information centers or contact the **YHA Northern Region,** P.O. Box 11, Matlock, Derbyshire DE4 2XA (☎ (01629) 825850). Reservations must be made in advance. The barns all cost £3.25-4.75 per person. Barns sleep 12, are open for arrival at 4pm, and must be vacated by 10am.

⚠ HIKING AND BIKING

Hiking is the best way to travel these vast tracts of moor. Wrapping fully around the national park, the 93 mi. **Cleveland Way** is the yellow brick road of the North York Moors. A particularly well-marked and breathtaking portion of the Way is the 20 mi. trail between Whitby and Scarborough, perhaps the perfect day hike: wavering hills on one side, tranquil sea on the other, and miles of shoreline cliffs stretching ahead and falling behind. Ambitious hikers might consider tackling one of the other long-distance footpaths in the park: the 79 mi. **Wolds Way,** the famous (and hence eroding) **Lyke Wake Walk,** or the shorter and unofficial 37 mi. **White Rose** and **Crosses Walks.** The 35 mi. **Esk Valley Trail** hugs the lowlands near the railway track. Not all of the trails are well marked or even visible; hikers should always carry a detailed map and a compass (see **Wilderness Safety,** p. 53).

The amount of tourist literature on the North York Moors is astounding; TICs stock reams of guidebooks. The *Waymark* guides (30-40p), produced by the National Park authority, detail short (up to half-day) walks starting from villages or points of interest. The Ordnance Survey Tourist Map 2 ($4.25) covers the whole park, but may be too general for hikers; the 1:25,000 Outdoor Leisure sheets 26 and 27 ($6) are more precise. Before hitting the trails, purchase a few *Waymark* guides, consult more expensive books ($3-6), and get good advice ($0) from tourist officials. **Disabled travelers** should call the Disablement Action Group (☎ (01947) 821001) for guidance.

Cyclists roll gleefully through the **North Riding Forest Park,** located in the middle of the Moors between Pickering, Scarborough, and Sleights. The park holds mountain-bike paths for riders of all skill levels and short walking trails; the beginning of some of these are accessible by train. For details, inquire at the **Forest District Office,** Crossgates Ln., Pickering. (☎ (01751) 472295. Open M-F July-Aug. 10am-5:30pm; Easter-June and Sept.-Oct. 10am-4:30pm.) Pick up a list of cycle hire stores from an information centre, or check *The Moors Visitor.*

The Moors can be horribly hot or bitterly cold in the summer, and sudden changes in weather can make or break a hike or bike ride. Call the Danby National Park Information Centre (☎ (02187) 660654) for the **weather forecast** before setting out, but be aware that it reports on all of northeast England; the weather can vary dramatically even within the park. Bring raingear.

WHITBY
☎01947

Straddling a harbor between two desolate headlands, the seaside resort town of Whitby (pop. 14,000) has been the muse for many a struggling oddball. Here Caedmon sang the first English hymns, Bram Stoker conjured up evil, and Lewis Carroll wrote *The Walrus and the Carpenter* while eating oysters. One of two English ports where the midsummer sun can be seen both rising and setting over the sea, this former whaling port also inspired Captain Cook to set sail for Australia in the 18th century. The strip of slot-machines, gift shops, and fish-and-chips huts now lends a circus-like atmosphere to Whitby, giving the town an inexplicable charm.

▲▶ ORIENTATION AND PRACTICAL INFORMATION. Trains and **buses** deposit their passengers at **Station Sq.** on **Endeavour Wharf** on the west side of the River Esk, which runs through town. The **train station** has a one-track mind, while **buses** tend to shun the station and stop along Longhorne Rd. The ticket and information desk for both resides in the train station in Station Sq. The friendly folks here will **hold luggage** for you during office hours for £1. (☎ 602146. Open daily 9am-5pm.) Whitby's **tourist information centre** (TIC) is also at Station Sq. across Longhorne Rd. (☎ 602674; see p. 392). Banks are plentiful; **National Westminster Bank,** 79 Baxtergate, has a cash machine that's convenient. (☎ (0845) 609 0001. Open M-F 9am-4:30pm.) Services include: the **police** (☎ 603443), Spring Hill; **Internet access** at **New Tech Computer Systems,** off Flowergate through the stone archway beside the Lloyds TSB bank (☎ 602825; £1 per 10min.; open daily 10am-5:30pm), and at **Java,** Flowergate (£3 per 30min., £5 per hr.; open daily 7:30am-10pm); and the **post office** at the back of the **Whitby Northeastern Superstore** on Endeavour Wharf (post office ☎ 602327; open M-Sa 8:30am-5:30pm; store ☎ 600710; open M-Sa 8am-8pm, Su 10am-4pm). **Postal code:** YO21 1DN.

▶◀▶ ACCOMMODATIONS AND FOOD. The hilltop **YHA Whitby** (☎ (01947) 602878) provides incredible views (see p. 392). Another hostel, **Harbour Grange,** is off Spital Bridge about seven minutes from Station Sq. Walk south on Church St. and look right just after Green Ln. The 24-bed hostel holds a riverside patio, a kitchen, a quiet atmosphere, and velveteen decor at a great price. (☎ 600817; backpackers@harbourgrange.onyxnet.co.uk. Curfew 11:30pm. Dorms £8, with sheets £9.) **B&Bs** mass on the western cliff, along **Bellevue Terr.** and adjacent roads; confusingly, each side of those roads has a different name. Try **Jaydee Guest House,** 15 John St., where the friendly Nicholsons offer pleasant conversation and a nautically-inclined dining room. (☎ 605422. £16.50-19.50 per person.) Campers should look for the **Northcliffe Caravan Park,** three miles south of town in High Hawsker. Take bus #93 or 93A from the bus station (£1), or head down the A171 and turn onto the B1447. (☎ 880477. Showers included. Laundry facilities. Electricity hook-up £2. July-Aug. £10.50 for tent and car, Apr.-June and Sept. £7; Oct.-Mar. £6.)

On the east side of the river, turn left at either Sandgate or Church St. to find the **market** (Tu and Sa 9am-4pm). Cafes and fish-and-chips stores are abundant. **◼ Shepherd's Purse,** 95 Church St., serves a wealth of tasty vegetarian morsels in the charmingly funky cafe and tea garden in back. Hearty homemade soups and bountiful baguette sandwiches go for £2.50-3.75. Dinners are more expensive at £8-9. (☎ 820228. Open daily 10am-5pm and 6:30-10:30pm.) For superb food in a relaxed, elegant atmosphere, **The Vintner** awaits at 42a Flowergate. Specials go for £8-9; try the leek and roquefort canneloni. (☎ 601166. Open M-Tu 5:30-9:30pm, W-Sa noon-2:30pm and 5:30-9:30pm, Su noon-8:30pm. Fewer hours Nov.-Mar.)

▣▶ SIGHTS AND ENTERTAINMENT. Atop a hill buffeted by shrieking winds and with marvelous views of Whitby and the bay below stand skeletal **Whitby Abbey** and the leaning, salt-rubbed headstones of **St. Mary's Churchyard.** Bram Stoker was a frequent visitor to Whitby, and several scenes in *Dracula* occur in the churchyard, the haunting Abbey mentioned in the background. The nonfictional history of the Abbey begins in AD 675 when St. Hilda founded a monastery in Whitby that was burned by the Vikings in 867. The present structure dates back to 1078. (☎

603568. Open daily Apr.-Sept. 10am-6pm; Oct.-Mar. 10am-4pm. £1.70, students and seniors £1.30, children 90p.) Next door to the abbey, atop 199 steps, **St. Mary's Church** holds vigil. The church was built around 1110; its peculiar box pews and clifftop graveyard merit a visit. (☎ 603421. Open July-Aug. daily 10am-5pm; in winter closes at 2pm. Recommended donation £1.)

Proceeding westward from Station Sq. on Bagdale, you will arrive at **Pannett Park,** most easily accessible via Union Rd. on the right. The heady smell of roses (in season) is followed by the visual pleasures of the **Pannett Art Gallery and Whitby Museum.** You'll find an impressive collection of model ships, stuffed birds, and "domestic bygones," but the fossils—including a 20 ft. *Ichthyosaurus Crassimanus*—put this place on the map. The gallery specializes in views of the area. (Both open May-Sept. M-Sa 9:30am-5:30pm, Su 2-5pm; Oct.-Apr. Tu 10am-1pm, W-Sa 10am-4pm, Su 2-4pm. Gallery free. Museum £2, children £1, families £5.)

At East Terr., overlooking the harbor, stands **Captain Cook** himself in substantial bronze. Charts in his left hand, sextant in his right, he squints toward Australia, the continent he charted. You can visit his memorial **museum,** on Grape Ln. across the river, which contains original letters and drawings, native artifacts, European scientific instruments, and a precise model ship and its carefully detailed cargo all carved by hand. (☎ 601900. Open daily Apr.-Oct. 9:45am-5pm. £2.80, seniors £2.30, children £1.80, families £7.80.) Nearby, the self-explanatory **Whalebone Arch** pays tribute to the 17th-century whaling industry.

The western cliffs cradle the **Whitby Pavilion Theatre.** The outdoor pavilion presents family-oriented entertainment, while the indoor theater stages amateur productions from late July to August. (☎ 604855. Box office open M-Sa 10am-4:30pm; tickets £2.60-6.50.) Whitby takes pride in its annual August **Folk Festival** (☎ 708424), which offers 200 hours of dance, concerts, and workshops. The *What's On* brochure at the TIC describes events around town.

NEAR WHITBY: DANBY AND CASTLETON

To the west of Whitby, villages like Grosmont, Danby, Castleton, and Kildale are accessible by the Northern Spirit Middlesbrough-Whitby connection. At **Danby,** pay a visit to the Moors Centre, the mother of all National Park Information Centres (see p. 392). You can also ascend the 1400 ft. **Danby Rigg** to the top of **Danby High Moor,** or stroll to **Danby Castle,** a jumble of roofless 14th-century stones attached to a working farm. (Free, information pamphlet £1.) Despite the castle's current state of disrepair, the easy hour-long walk across the valley and back will inspire you to romp through the fields and sing to attentive sheep. In the area, try the walks up **Castleton** and **Glaisdale Riggs,** which are also accessible from the train station at Castleton, Glaisdale, and Lealholme. Farther afield, walk from the Little Ayton rail station (on the Esk Valley line) or from Newton-under-Roseberry to the summit of **Roseberry Topping** (not a dessert, but deserted).

SCARBOROUGH   ☎ 01723

It all started in 1626 when Mrs. Tanyzin Farrer stumbled upon natural springs under a cliff near town. The bitter tasting stuff seemed to cure minor ailments, and soon "taking the water" became a popularly and medically accepted prescription, thus giving birth to one of England's first seaside resorts. Nearly four centuries later, English families still flock to Scarborough, recreating that all-too-familiar chill and wind-whipped English beach scene.

🖪 **PRACTICAL INFORMATION.** The **tourist information centre** is on Valley Bridge Rd., across from the train station. (☎ 373333. Open daily May-Sept. 9:30am-6pm; Oct.-Apr. 10am-4:30pm.) The major **banks** crowd St. Nicholas St. Services include: the **police** (☎ 500300), at the corner of Northway and Victoria Rd.; **Internet access** at **Complete Computing,** 14 Northway (☎ 500501; £3 per 30min., £5 per hr.; open M-F 9am-5:30pm, Sa 9am-5pm); and the **post office,** 11-15 Aberdeen Walk (☎ 381311; open M-F 9am-5:30pm, Sa 9am-12:30pm). **Postal code:** YO11 1AB.

NORTHEAST ENGLAND

ACCOMMODATIONS AND FOOD. YHA Scarborough is 2 mi. from town (see p. 394). Scarborough's **B&Bs** are quite reasonable (£14-17). The **Avenwood Hotel,** 129 Castle Rd., ideally located between North and South Bays near the castle, will give you those sea views so sought after. (☎ 374640. July-Aug. £15 per person; Sept.-June £14.) The friendly folks at the **Terrace Hotel,** 69 Westborough, offer clean rooms with TVs and a hearty breakfast only two blocks from the train station. (☎ 374937. £17 per person for one night, £15 per night for multiple nights.)

Cheap meals await at the **Public Market Hall,** an indoor market between Friargate and Cross St. (open roughly 9am-5pm). Locals say **Mother Hubbards,** 43 Westborough, is the place to go for fish and chips—a portion of the British delicacy, along with bread and butter, and tea or coffee, can be yours for £4.25, or £3.25 after 3pm. (☎ 376109. Open M-Sa 11am-6:45pm.) The wrought-iron garden chairs face the sea at the bright **Gala Coffee Bar,** 5 Museum Terr., where homebaked goodies, such as a banana toastie for £1, can be had. (Open daily 10am-5:30pm.)

SIGHTS AND ENTERTAINMENT. A glimpse at the cliffs separating North and South Bay makes clear why Scarborough was long a strategic stronghold. On a site once home to a Roman signal station and a Viking fort stands **Scarborough Castle,** built by Henry II around 1160. The castle's fascinating history of stubborn sieges and defiant defenses is more than matched by tremendous views over town and sea. Bring a picnic and a good book while you're at it. (☎ 372451. Open Apr.-Sept. daily 10am-6pm; Oct. daily 10am-5pm; Nov.-Mar. W-Su 10am-4pm. £2.30, students and seniors £1.70, under 16 £1.20; includes 40min. audio tour.) Just down the hill on Castle Rd. rests the 12th-century **St. Mary's Parish Church.** The cemetery, across Church Ln., holds the grave of Anne Brontë, who passed away in Scarborough in 1849. (☎ 500541. Open May-Sept. M-F 10am-4pm, Su 1-4pm.)

On the beach promenade, mini-golf, waterslides, and a sealife center await your leisure. The **Stephen Joseph Theatre** (☎ 370541), on the corner of Westborough and Northway, is known for premiering much of the work of playwright Alan Ayckbourn, including *How the Other Half Loves*. Ayckbourn began his acting career at this theater; when he complained about the parts he was given, the director told him to write a better play. Ayckbourn often did, and the company put them on .

PICKERING   ☎01751

Pickering (pop. 6200), beyond the park's southern border, is a popular jumping-off point for jaunts to the park and the nearby coast. Originally built in fear of invasion from the North, **Pickering Castle** soon became a favorite hunting spot among the royals who jealously guarded their game. A short hunting exhibition will explain harsh measures such as the Forest Law: "Whosoever should slay hart or hind should be blinded..." Remnants of the Norman castle still command an inspiring view from the hill in the center of town. (☎ 474989. Open daily Apr.-Sept. 10am-1pm and 2-6pm; Oct.-Mar. W-Su 10am-1pm and 2-4pm. £2.30, students and seniors £1.70, children £1.20, under 5 free.) Pickering also serves as the southern terminus of the touristy **North York Moors Railway.** Nicknamed the "Heartbeat" Railway, the steam-hauled train travels into the center of the Moors with scenic walks waiting at every stop; pick up *Walks from the Train* (80p) at the tourist information centre. (☎ 472508. £9.50 for an all day pass; BritRail passes not accepted.)

Pickering's **tourist information centre** (TIC) is at The Ropery (see p. 392). Services include: **bike rental** at **Pickering Cycle Centre,** 2 Market Pl. (☎ 472581; open M-Tu and Th-Sa 9am-5pm, summer also Su 10am-4pm; £9 per day; £25 deposit; helmets and locks free); **Barclays bank,** 41 Market Pl. (☎ (0345) 550088; open M-W and F 9:30am-4:30pm, Th 10am-4:30pm); **Internet access** at the library, next to the TIC (open M-T and Th 9:30am-5pm, F 9:30am-7:30pm, Sa 9:30am-12:30pm; book ahead); and the **post office,** 7 Market Pl., inside Morland's Newsagents and with a **bureau de change** (☎ (0345) 223344; open M-F 9am-5:30pm, Sa 9am-12:30pm). **Postal code:** YO18 7AA.

The TIC stocks a free accommodations listing, including **farmhouses.** Stay with delightful and attentive ▨ **Mrs. Kelleher,** Lingfield, Middleton Rd., just off Swansea Ln., for a warm family setting on a quiet street. (☎ 473456. Singles £16; doubles £32.) **Wayside Caravan Park,** Wrelton, 2½ mi. down the Pickering-Helmsley Rd., will let you and a friend camp in your tent for £5. (☎ 472608. Extra person £1.25.)

On the road to the castle, you can enjoy tea, baguettes (£1.50-2.25), and desserts (£1.25-2) in a busy oversized dollhouse called the **Forget-Me-Not Tea Room,** 37 Burgate. (☎ 476747. Open Apr.-Oct. daily 10:15am-5pm; sporadically rest of year.) The smart-casual **White Swan** offers candlelit, gourmet meals, but if you order from the bar you get the same food for less. (Main meals £7-10; dinner served daily 7-9pm.)

HELMSLEY ☎01439

To the south of Pickering lies Helmsley, surrounded by plentiful walks and sights. The big draw in town is **Helmsley Castle,** built around 1120 in case the Scots ever got restless. They did, but the only military action the castle saw was during the Civil War, when the Parliamentarians blew the place in half (which explains its present-day appearance). The well-preserved skeleton of a 16th-century Elizabethan house also shares the grounds. (☎ 770442. Open Apr.-Sept. daily 10am-1pm and 2-6pm; Oct. daily 10am-1pm and 2-5pm; Nov.-Mar. 10am-1pm and 2-4pm. £2.30, students and seniors £1.70, children £1.20.) Unlike the pristine gardens of grand estates, the **Walled Garden** behind the castle is a working patch with 2 acres of fruit and vegetables, 2 acres of ornamental plantings, and over a hundred varieties of clematis, flowering wall-climbing vines which, statistically, are England's favorite flower. (☎ 771427. Open Apr.-Oct. daily 10:30am-5pm, Nov.-Mar. F-Su noon-4pm. £2, students and seniors £1, under 16 free.) **Duncombe Park** features a Baroque mansion and 100 acres of green gardens. It is now a national nature reserve due to its rare beetle population. (☎ 770213. Open Apr.-Oct. M-Th and Su 10:30am-6pm, May-Sept. also F 10:30am-6pm. £5.75; gardens only £3.75, children £1.75.)

A 3½ mi. walk out of town leads to the stunning 12th-century **Rievaulx Abbey** (REE-vo). Established by monks from Burgundy, the abbey was an aesthetic masterpiece until Thomas Mannus, first Earl of Rutland, initiated a swift decay, stripping it of valuables, including the roof. It is now one of the most spectacular ruins in the country. Pick up Weymark Walk #20 guide (40p) at the TIC for more info. (☎ 798228. Open July-Aug. daily 9:30am-7pm; Apr.-June and Sept. daily 10am-6pm; Oct. daily 10am-5pm; Nov.-Mar. daily 10am-4pm. Wheelchair access. £3, students and seniors £2.30, children £1.50.) In late July and early August, music, drama, and literary talks take center stage at the **Reydale Festival** (☎ 771518).

The town centers around Market Pl., where buses stop and shops and eateries abound. The **tourist information centre** is also at Market Pl. (see p. 392). Services include: **Barclays bank,** at the corner of Bandgate and Bridge St. (open M-W and F 9:30am-3:30pm, Th 10am-3:30pm); the **police station,** at the corner of Ashdale Rd. and The Crescent (☎ (01653) 692424; open 9-10am and 6-7pm); and the **post office,** Bridge St., across from Borgate (open M-Tu and Th-F 9am-12:30pm, 1:30-5:30pm; W and Sa 9am-12:30pm). **Postal code:** YO6 5BG

Helmsley is graced by a **YHA Youth Hostel** (☎/fax 770433; see p. 380), small hotels, and B&Bs. Try **Mrs. Wood's,** Buckingham House, 33 Bridge St., which has rooms with basins and TVs. (☎ 770613. £17 per person.) Those exploring the fern-lined **Newtondale Gorge** and the lush **Newtondale Forest** (via the scenic North York Moors Railway from the Newtondale or Levisham stations) can lodge at **YHA Lockton** (☎ (01751) 460376; see p. 380). Take York City District (☎ (01904) 624161) bus #840 or 842 from Pickering or Whitby. The name says it all at **Nice Things,** 10 Market Pl., where a homemade quiche, a jacket potato, and a side salad come for the kind price of £3.95. (☎ 771997. Open M-F 9:15am-5:30pm, Sa-Su 9:15am-6:30pm.)

COUNTY DURHAM

DURHAM ☎ 0191

The commanding presence of England's greatest Norman cathedral lends grandeur to small-town Durham (pop. 26,000). For 800 years, the Bishops of Durham ruled County Durham from this town, with their own currency, army, and courts. In the 1830s, new rulers, otherwise known as students of Durham University, took over the hilltop city encircled by the River Wear. Durham slows down during summer recess, but the town is by no means a sleepy haven—tourists and festival-goers flow steadily into the narrow, winding streets that spiral up toward the cathedral and maintain the lively atmosphere.

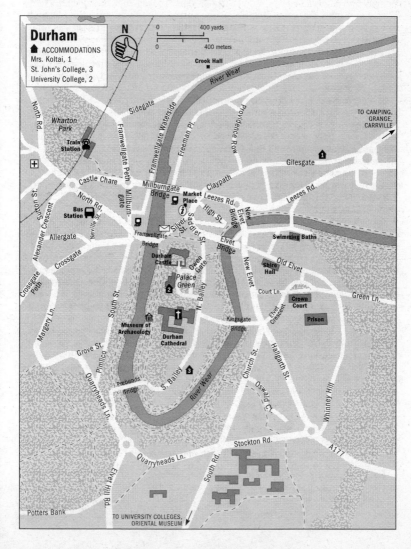

Durham

N

0   400 yards
0   400 meters

♦ ACCOMMODATIONS
Mrs. Koltai, 1
St. John's College, 3
University College, 2

GETTING THERE AND GETTING AROUND

Durham lies 20 mi. south of Newcastle on the A167 and an equal distance north of Darlington. The **train station** is on a steep hill just west of town. (☎ 232 6262. Ticket office open M-F 6am-9pm, Sa 6am-8pm, Su 7:30am-9pm. Advance ticket sales M-Sa 8:30am-5:45pm, Su 10am-5:45pm.) **Trains** (☎ (08457) 484950) arrive from: **London King's Cross** (3hr., 1 per hr., £63); **Newcastle** (20min., at least 2 per hr., £3.60, day return £7.15); and **York** (1hr., roughly 2 per hr., £17, return £25). The **bus station** is on North Rd., across Framwellgate Bridge from the city center. (☎ 384 3323. Office open M-F 9am-5pm, Sa 9am-4pm.) **National Express** (☎ (08705) 808080) runs from: **London** (5½hr., 5-6 per day, £18); **Leeds** (2½hr., 3 per day, £14.50); and **Edinburgh** (4½hr., 1 per day, £17). **Go Northern** and **United** run a joint bus service #722/723 from the Eldon Sq. station in **Newcastle** (1hr., every 10min., £2). Many **bus** companies serve local routes. **Bicycles** can be rented at the bright yellow **Cycle Force,** 29 Claypath. (☎ 384 0319. £12 per day; £35 deposit. Open M-W and F 9am-5:30pm, Tu 9am-7pm, Sa 9am-5pm.)

ORIENTATION AND PRACTICAL INFORMATION

The **River Wear** coils around Durham, creating a partial moat on three sides that is crossed by a handful of footbridges. With its cobblestone medieval streets and restricted vehicle access, Durham is generally pedestrian-friendly, although hills create difficulties for the disabled and those hauling heavy packs.

To reach the **tourist information centre** (TIC), Market Pl., from the train station, descend the hill on Station Approach and take the steps on the left down to the Millburngate Bridge roundabout; cross the bridge and turn right at the first intersection into Market Pl. (☎ 384 3720; fax 386 3015; tic@durhamtic.demon.co.uk. Open July-Aug. M-Sa 10am-5:30pm, Su 11am-4pm; June and Sept. M-Sa 10am-5:30pm; Oct.-May M-Sa 10am-5pm.) **Banks** aplenty in **Market Pl.** support spending urges. Services include: the **police,** New Elvet (☎ 386 4222); **Internet access** at **Reality-X Durham,** 1 Framwellgate Bridge (☎ 384 5700; £3 per 30min., £5 per hr.; open daily 10am-8pm), and at **Saints,** Back Silver St. behind the TIC on the river bank (☎ 386 7700; £2.50 for 30min., £4.50 per hr.; open 10am-6pm daily); and the **post office,** 33 Silver St., with a **bureau de change** (open M-Sa 9am-5:30pm). **Postal code:** DH1 3RE.

ACCOMMODATIONS AND FOOD

Durham is without hostels, but the large supply of inexpensive and often beautiful **dormitory rooms** around the cathedral and south of town is a boon for summer travelers. (☎ 374 3454. Available roughly July-Sept. and around Easter and Christmas; breakfast included.) Others merely tour it, but you can pretend to be the lord or lady of the **University College** dorms in Durham Castle as you consume breakfast in the massive dining hall. (☎ 374 3863; fax 374 7470. Singles from £20.50 per person; doubles from £41.) On a quiet cobbled street behind Durham Cathedral, **St. John's College,** 3 South Bailey, offers B&B in single and twin dorm rooms—vie for a room in the spacious theology students' section or in riverside Cruddas House. (☎ 374 3566; fax 374 3573. Singles £19.25; doubles £38.50.) Bilingual **Mrs. Koltai,** 10 Gilesgate, can explain breakfast options in English and Spanish. Her B&B, with comfy rooms with TVs, is a steep uphill walk from the TIC. (☎/fax 386 2026. Singles £16; doubles £32.) **Belle Vue Guest House,** 4 Belle Vue Terr., a five-minute ride from the city on bus #220, has small, comfortable rooms. (☎ 386 4800. Singles £17.50; doubles £34.) The **camping** is fine at the **Grange,** Meadow Ln., Carrville, on the A690 off the A1, 2½ mi. away. (☎ 384 4778; fax 383 9161. Office open daily 8:30am-8pm. Showers included. Laundry. No electricity. £4.20 per person, £1.25 per child.)

Eat your fill of scones and cakes from the bakeries in the town center. In the **Indoor Market** off Market Pl., you'll find even more fruit and vegetable stands, as well as the butcher, baker, and candle-stick maker. (Open M-Sa 9am-5pm.) For a local specialty, try Lindisfarne mead, made on Holy Island to the north. Students congregate in **Vennel's** 16th-century courtyard over sandwiches or pastas for £2.35-

3.65. (Next to Waterstone's in Saddler's Yard. Open daily 9:30am-5pm.) The bright, crowded **Almshouses Café and Restaurant,** 10 Palace Green, next to the cathedral, serves delicious specials for £4-6. (☎ 361 1054. Open daily in high season 9am-8pm; in low season 9am-5:30pm; meals served noon-2:30pm and 5:30-8pm.)

👁 SIGHTS

▓ DURHAM CATHEDRAL

Crowning the hill in the middle of the city. ☎ 386 4266. Open June-Sept. M-Sa 9:30am-8pm, Su 12:30-8pm; Oct.-May M-Sa 9:30am-6pm, Su 12:30-5pm. Wheelchair access. Tours daily 10:30am and 2:30pm; Aug. also 11:30am. Suggested donation £2.50.

Built in 1093, the extraordinary Durham Cathedral stands, in the words of Sir Walter Scott, as "half church of God, half castle 'gainst the Scot." The pamphlet on the layout, history, and architecture of the cathedral (50p) is invaluable. Behind the choir is the **Tomb of Saint Cuthbert.** St. Cuthbert died in 687, and was buried on Holy Island; Danish raiders in the 9th century sent the island's monks packing, and they carried the saint's body with them in their flight. After wandering to various towns for 120 years, a vision in 995 led the monks to Durham, where the cathedral was built to shelter the saint's shrine. At the other end of the church lies the tomb of the **Venerable Bede,** author of the 8th-century *Ecclesiastical History of the English People,* the first history of England. Note the strip of black marble that separates Bede's tomb and the eastern side from the main part of the church; women had to stay behind this strip during the time the church was used as a monastery. The spectacular view from the top of the **Tower** is well worth the 325-step climb it takes to get there. *(Open mid-Apr. to Sept. 9:30am-4pm; Oct. to mid-Apr. M-Sa 10am-3pm weather permitting. £2, under 16 £1, families £5.)* The **Monks' Dormitory** off the cloister houses pre-Conquest stones and casts of crosses dating back to the 8th century under an enormous 600-year-old timber roof that took over 21 oak trees to build. *(Open Apr.-Sept. M-Sa 10am-3:30pm, Su 12:30-3:30pm. 80p, children 20p, families £1.50.)* The **Treasures of St. Cuthbert** holds the relics of St. Cuthbert, holy manuscripts dating back 1300 years, and the rings and seals of the all-powerful Bishops. *(Open year-round M-Sa 10am-4:30pm, Su 2-4:30pm. £2, students and seniors £1.50, children 50p, families £5.)*

OTHER SIGHTS

DURHAM CASTLE. For centuries a key fortress of the county's Prince Bishops, the castle is today a splendid residence for students at the university or summer sojourners; see **Accommodations,** p. 356. *(Next to the cathedral. ☎ 374 3800. Admission by tour only; call ahead for specific times. Tours Mar.-Sept. daily 10am-12:30pm and 2-4pm; Oct.-Feb. M, W, and Sa-Su 2-4pm. £3, children £2, families £6.50.)*

BEST OF THE REST. The cathedral and castle are the main sights, but there are three other small spots worth a look if you have a specific interest in the material. On the river bank between the Framwellgate Bridge and Prebends Bridge, finds from the prehistoric period to the present day stand alongside an impressive collection of Roman stone altars at the **Museum of Archaeology.** *(☎ 374 3623. Open Apr.-Oct. daily 11am-4pm; Nov.-Mar. M and Th-F 12:30-3pm, Sa-Su 11:30am-3:30pm. £1, concessions 50p, families £2.50.)* Across the river and off South Rd. on Elvet Hill lies the **Oriental Museum,** the only museum in Britain dedicated to Oriental art and archaeology, with an impressive collection of Chinese ceramics and Tibetan tangkas. *(☎ 374 7911. Open M-F 10am-5pm, Sa-Su noon-5pm. £1.50, seniors and children 75p, students free.)* A stroll along Framwellgate Waterside will take you to **Crook Hall,** Frankland Ln. Built in the 13th century, this medieval manor promises an intimate encounter with history as you wander through the many small enchanting gardens and the refreshingly humble rooms of the house. *(☎ 384 8023. Open May-Sept. Su 1-5pm; late July to early Sept. Su-F 1-5pm. £3.60, concessions £2.60, families £9.75.)* Finally, perhaps the best way to truly experience Durham is by a rejuvenating **walk** along the River Wear. Tranquil shade, ambling waters, and uplifting views of the cathedral and castle will bring peace of mind.

♫ ENTERTAINMENT AND FESTIVALS

Brown's Boathouse Centres, Elvet Bridge, rents rowboats, in which you can wind around the horseshoe curve of the River Wear, dodging scullers and ducks. (☎ 386 3779 or ☎ 386 9525. £2.50 per hr., children £1.25; deposit £5.) For a less arduous journey, the center runs a 1hr. cruise on the **Prince Bishop River Cruiser.** (Runs Easter-Sept. daily; call ahead for specific times. £3.50, children £2.50.)

After-hours entertainment in Durham is closely tied to university life; when students depart for the holidays, most nightlife follows suit. The intersection of Crossgate and North Rd., just across Framwellgate Bridge, is a good place to be at 10pm. Many pubs and clubs wait with open doors around here; just follow your fancy. A young crowd fills the popular **Hogshead** pub, 58 Saddler St., which has a fine selection of wines and a wall filled with the theatrical history of Durham. (☎ 386 4134. Open M-Sa 11am-11pm, Su noon-10:30pm.) The sporty riverside **Coach and Eight,** Bridge House, Framwellgate Bridge, is enormous and has a giant-screen TV to match. (☎ 386 3284. Disco W and F-Su. Open M-Sa noon-11pm, Su noon-10:30pm.) The small **Traveller's Rest,** 72 Claypath, offers a sanctuary of quiet with an attractive selection of ales. (☎ 386 5370. Open daily noon-3pm and 6-11pm.)

Durham holds a **folk festival** in August with singing, clog dancing, musicians, and general frolicking. Many events are free; others cost £2-7. Get a leaflet at the TIC. **Camping** is free along the river during festival weekends (F-Su). Other major town events include the **Durham Regatta** in the middle of June, held since 1834, and a massive, sodden **beer festival** (the second largest in the country) in early September. Call the TIC for details on all festivals.

HIGH PENNINES

The area known as the High Pennines stretches north to south about 20 miles west of Durham City, from below Barnard Castle to Hadrian's Wall. This vast landscape straddles the counties of Cumbria, Durham, and Northumbria and gives rise to the great northern rivers: the Tees, Tyne, D erwent, and Wear, whose sources perch high in the moorlands. Unlike the neighboring Yorkshire Dales, access to this region is limited, and it remains largely untouched by the frenetic tourist trade. Open moorland, tree-lined slopes, quiet stone villages, brisk rivers, and waterfalls greet the visitor in the Derwent Valley and the region's other dales—Teesdale, Weardale, and Allendale. The Pennine Way walking path crosses each dale as it winds up to Hadrian's Wall and the Scottish border.

⬚ GETTING THERE AND GETTING AROUND

Given the livestock-laden pastures and relatively level roads that greet the explorer here, the area is best suited to **hiking** and **biking.** Cars can successfully navigate the roads, but buses tackle the region with distressing hesitancy. Four motorways bound the region: the A66 along Darlington's latitude in the south; the A6 or M6 from Penrith to Carlisle in the west; the A69 from Carlisle to Newcastle to the north; and in the east the A167 from Newcastle through Durham and Darlington. The B6277 cuts a diagonal through the area, running northwest from Barnard Castle through Middleton-in-Teesdale to Alston. **Arriva** (☎ (0345) 124125) **buses** #75 and 76 run from **Darlington** to **Barnard Castle** (2 per hr.); **Primrose** bus #352 connects **Durham** and **Barnard Castle** via **Bishop Auckland** (40min.-1hr., 1 per day). The **Explorer North East** pass, available on any bus service, gives unlimited rides for one day from **Berwick-upon-Tweed** and **Newcastle** down to **Whitby,** and from **Barnard Castle** across to **Sunderland** (£5.25, seniors and children £4.25, families £10.50).

BARNARD CASTLE ☎ 01833

Twenty miles southwest of Durham along the River Tees, Barnard Castle, the name of both the peaceful market town and its English Heritage ruins, is the best base for exploring the castles of Teesdale and the peaks and waterfalls of the

North Pennine Hills. Along the river, the ruins of the 12th-century Norman **castle** sprawl over six acres. The castle keep was divided into four different wards that both fortified the defenses and enforced social distinctions. (☎ 638212. Open Apr.-Sept. daily 10am-1pm and 2-6pm; Oct. daily 10am-1pm and 2-5pm; Nov.-Mar. M-Sa 10am-1pm and 2-4pm. Audio tour included. £2.30, students £1.70, under 16 £1.20.)

Past Newgate stands the impressive ▨ **Bowes Museum,** which houses a remarkable collection of European painting and decorative art to match many of London's offerings. Built in the 19th century by John and Josephine Bowes to bring continental culture to England, the gallery houses the couple's extensive and often curious private collection, including the largest collection of Spanish paintings in Britain. Two works alone make the entry worthwhile—El Greco's *Tears of St. Peter* and a life-size mechanized silver swan, mentioned in Mark Twain's *Innocents Abroad.* (☎ 690606. Open daily 11am-5pm. Tours May-Aug. Tu-Sa 2 per day, Sept.-Oct. Sa-Su 1 per day. £3.90, concessions £2.90, families £12.) Dickens fans can follow the author's footsteps by car on **Dickens Drive,** a 25 mi. circular path that traces the route Dickens took in 1838 while researching *Nicholas Nickleby.* Pick up the free *In the Footsteps of Charles Dickens* from the tourist information centre and hit the road. Northeast of Barnard Castle on the A688 looms **Raby Castle** (RAY-bee), an imposing 14th-century fortress with a superb kitchen and gardens. (☎ 660202. Open July-Sept. M-F and Su 1-5pm; May-June W and Su 1-5pm; park and gardens open same days 11am-5:30pm. £4, seniors £3, children £1.50, families £10; park and gardens only £1.50, seniors and children £1.)

Five gracious and witty women manage the small but well-stocked **tourist information centre** (TIC), Woodleigh, Flatts Rd. (☎ 630262; fax 690909. Open daily Apr.-Oct. 10am-6pm; Nov.-Mar. 11am-4pm.) **Guided walks** of town leave from here. (1½hr.; late July to early Sept. Th 2:30pm. £1.50, seniors and children 75p.) **Banks** line Market Pl. The **post office,** 2 Galgate, has a **bureau de change.** (☎ 638247. Open M-F 9am-5:30pm, Sa 9am-12:30pm.) **Postal code:** DL12 8BE.

Barnard Castle has no youth hostel, but is blessed with superb B&Bs, many of which line Galgate. **Mrs. Williamson,** 85 Galgate, rents comfortable rooms with TVs and pay phones. (☎ 638757. Singles £18, with bath £25; doubles with bath £42.) **Mrs. Kilgarrif,** 98 Galgate, offers satellite TV, an exercise room, sauna, and an impressive knick-knack collection in her B&B. (☎ 637493. £19 per person, with bath £25.) Most pubs and restaurants along The Bank and Market Pl. serve lunch and dinner. The **Hayloft,** 27 Horsemarket, is a small eclectic indoor market, with fruit and vegetables, plants and paintings, and a couple of cafes. In the Hayloft sits the **Stables Restaurant,** which satisfies with sandwiches and salads (£2.95), along with other meals for under £4. (☎ 690670. Open daily 8:30am-5:30pm.)

NEAR BARNARD CASTLE: BISHOP AUCKLAND. The town of Bishop Auckland is often the connection point for buses between Durham and Barnard Castle; while you're waiting to change buses, stroll down to **Auckland Castle,** presently the home of the county's Prince Bishops and of the world's largest private chapels. (☎ (01388) 601627. Open mid-July to Sept. Su-F 2-5pm; May to mid-July F and Su 2-5pm. £3, students and seniors £2, under 12 free.) The **tourist information centre** stands in the town hall on Market Pl. (☎ 604922; fax 604960. Open M-F 10am-5pm, Sa 9am-4pm; May-Oct. also Su 1-4pm.)

TYNE AND WEAR

NEWCASTLE-UPON-TYNE   ☎0191

Unequivocally urban Newcastle (pop. 284,000) bills itself a city of firsts. Beyond such constructive contributions as the hydraulic crane and the steam locomotive, this gritty, industrial capital also brought us the world's first beauty contest and first dog show, not to mention Sting (the first person to invoke Nabokov in a pop song). You won't find dreamy spires or evening hush here, but Newcastle has much to offer the motivated pleasure-seeker. What may look worn by day becomes captivating by night. Locals, students, and tourists (many of them British) flock to Newcastle's pubs and clubs, and a good time is had by all. Newcastle Geordies (see below) are proud of their accent, very proud of their football club, very, very proud of their brown ale, and usually happy to show you around.

⌐ GETTING THERE AND GETTING AROUND

Newcastle is the last English stronghold before the Scottish border. The city lies 1½ hours north of York on the A19 and 1½ hours east of Carlisle on the A69. Edinburgh is a straight run up the coast along the A1, or through pastures and mountains via the A68.

Trains: Central Station, Neville St. (☎ (0345) 225225). Travel center sells same-day tickets daily 5:40am-9:15pm and advance tickets M-F 7am-7:50pm, Sa 7am-6:50pm, Su 8:40am-7:50pm. **Luggage storage** £2-4. Open daily 8am-6pm. Trains (☎ (08457) 484950) from: **London King's Cross** (3hr., 1 per hr., £72); **Edinburgh** (1½hr.; M-Sa 23 per day, Su 16 per day; £31); and **Carlisle** (1½hr.; M-Sa 15 per day, Su 9 per day; £8.65).

Buses: Gallowgate Coach Station (☎ 232 7021), off Percy St. Ticket office open M-Sa 8am-6pm. **National Express** (☎ (08705) 808080) from **London** (6hr., 6 per day, return £29.50) and **Edinburgh** (3hr., 3 per day, return £18.50). **Haymarket,** by the Metro stop, for local and regional service. Ticket office open M-F 8:30am-5:30pm, Sa 9am-4pm. **Northumbria** (☎ 212 3000) buses #505, 515, and 525 from **Berwick-upon-Tweed** (2½hr.; M-Sa roughly every 2hr., Su 5 per day; £4).

Ferries: International Ferry Terminal, Royal Quays. For ferry listings, see p. 35. Bus #327 serves all departures, leaving Central Station 2½hr. and 1¼hr. before each sailing. Take the Metro to Percy Main (£1.10) and walk 20min. to the quay, or take a taxi (£10).

Public Transportation: The **Metro** (☎ 232 5325) runs from the city center to the coast and the airport. There are only a few stops in the city center. "Day Saver" allows unlimited travel for one day (£2.80). First train around 6am; last train around 11:30pm.

Travel Information: Nexus Travel Line (☎ 232 5325) will keep you updated on local bus, train, and Metro information. Open M-Sa 8am-8pm, Su 9am-5pm.

Bike Rental: Newcastle Cycle Centre, 11 Westmorland Rd. (☎ 230 3022). £10 per day, £35 per week; £50 deposit. Open M-Sa 9am-5:30pm.

✴🛈 ORIENTATION AND PRACTICAL INFORMATION

The free, full-color map of Newcastle available at the tourist information centre (TIC) is essential—streets shift direction and name without batting an eye. Don't be afraid to ask locals for directions; they're a friendly lot. When in doubt, remember that the waterfront is at the bottom of every hill. The center of town is **Grey's Monument,** an 80 ft. stone pillar in **Monument Mall,** directly opposite **Eldon Sq.** The monument is dedicated to Charles, Earl of Grey, who nudged the steep 1832 Reform Bill through Parliament and mixed bergamot into Britain's tea.

Tourist Information Centre: Newcastle Information Centre, Central Exchange Buildings, 132 Grainger St. (☎ 277 8000; fax 277 8010), facing Grey's Monument. Open M-W and F-Sa 9:30am-5:30pm, Th 9:30am-7:30pm; June-Sept. also Su 10am-4pm. **Branch** at Central Station. Open June-Sept. M-F 10am-8pm, Sa 9am-5pm; Oct.-May M-F 10am-5pm, Sa 9am-5pm.

Tours: Various themed city tours leave from the TIC generally W 6:45pm and Su 2:30pm, though times vary; check to be sure. £2, students and children £1.

Budget Travel: Campus Travel, Newcastle University Student Union Bldg., Kings Walk (☎ 232 1798). Open in term M and W-F 9:30am-5pm, Tu 10am-5pm; closes 4pm during vacations.

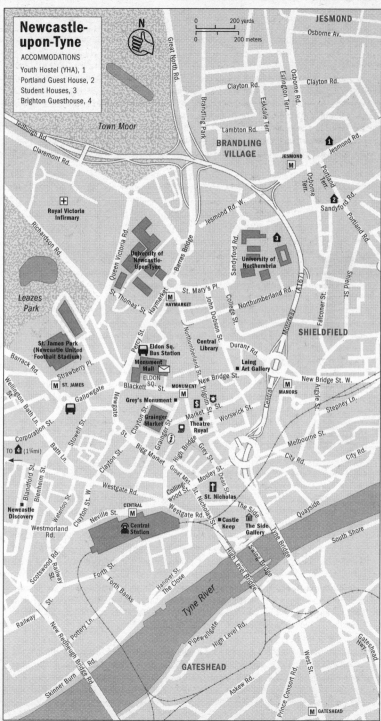

Newcastle-upon-Tyne

ACCOMMODATIONS

Youth Hostel (YHA), 1
Portland Guest House, 2
Student Houses, 3
Brighton Guesthouse, 4

THE GEORDIES What exactly is a Geordie (JOR-die)? Anyone born in the counties of Northumberland, Durham, or Tyne and Wear can claim Geordie status; but possessive as these sturdy Northerners are of their nickname, its origins are debatable. Try one of these:
1. During the Jacobite Rebellion of 1745, Newcastle's denizens supported George I, the reigning king, and were deemed "for George" by the Jacobites.
2. In 1815, George Stephenson invented the miner's lamp, which quickly gained favor among Northumberland miners. The lamp, and eventually the miners, became known as Geordies.
3. In 1826, Stephenson spoke before the Parliamentary Commission of Railways, and his dialect amused the snooty southerners, who began to call all keelmen carrying coal to the Thames "Geordies."

Financial Services: Barclays, 7 Market St. (☎ 200 2000). Open M-Tu and Th-F 9am-5:30pm, W 10am-5:30pm, Sa 9:30am-12:30pm. **Thomas Cook,** 6 Northumberland St. (☎ 219 8000). Open M-Tu and F-Sa 9am-5:30pm, W 10am-5:30pm, Th 9am-8pm.

Launderette: Clayton Rd. Launderette, 4 Clayton Rd. (☎ 281 5055), Jesmond, near the YHA Youth Hostel. Open M-Sa 8am-6pm, Su 8am-1pm.

Police: (☎ 214 6555), on the corner of Market St. and Pilgrim St.

Hospital: Royal Victoria Infirmary (☎ 232 5131), Queen Victoria Rd.

Internet Access: McNulty's Internet Cafe, 26-30 Market St. (☎ 232 0922). £2.50 per 30min.; Tu-W and F 9-11:30am free. Open M-Th 9am-7:30pm, F-Sa 9am-6pm.

Post Office: 24-26 Sidgate (☎ (0345) 223344), in the Eldon Sq. Shopping Centre; either enter by the monument and walk to the other end or enter at Blackett St. and take a right. Open M-Sa 9am-5:30pm. **Bureau de change. Postal Code:** NE1 7AB.

▰ ACCOMMODATIONS

The B&B scene is gasping for breath in Newcastle, which has plenty of dorm-style accommodations but few guest houses. Costlier lodgings neighbor the YHA Youth Hostel and YWCA in residential **Jesmond,** just northeast of town via a 3-minute Metro ride (50p). Slightly less expensive alternatives are scattered a few blocks to the north of Jesmond on Osborne Rd. The cheapest B&Bs run about £15 per person (more for singles); call in advance to secure a room.

YHA Newcastle, 107 Jesmond Rd. (☎ 281 2570; fax 281 8779). Metro: Jesmond. Turn left onto Jesmond Rd. and walk past the traffic lights—it's on the left. This funky townhouse makes a good sightseeing base. Lockout 10am-5pm. Curfew 11pm, but there's a late entry code. Overrun by ferry traffic; call several days in advance. Open Feb.-Dec. Dorms £10.85, students £9.75, under 18 £7.15.

The Brighton Guest House, 47-51 Brighton Grove (☎ 273 3600; fax 226 0563), Fenham, near the General Hospital. Either take a cheap taxi, a frequent bus (#10, 34-36, or 38) from the train station, or make the grueling 1½ mi. walk on Westgate Rd. and then left on Brighton Grove. The cheapest, cheeriest rooms in town, all with TV and wash basin, are worth the trip. Singles from £16; doubles from £32.

Portland Guest House, 134 Sandyford Rd. (☎ 232 7868). From Jesmond Metro stop, turn left onto Jesmond Rd., then right onto Portland Terr.; the guesthouse is at the end. Clean, basic rooms with parking and bike storage. TVs in some rooms. Continental breakfast included. Singles from £18; doubles £37.

University of Northumbria, Coach Ln. (☎ 227 4024; fax 227 3197). From the city center, go up Northumberland St. and take a right onto St. Mary's Pl., which leads into the University Library. The accommodations office is in Student Services in the library. Ideal location, but the dorms are what you'd expect—the standard bed-basin-desk found in universities around the world. No TVs; shared bathrooms. Open late Mar. to mid-Apr. and June to mid-Sept. Breakfast included. Singles £18.75; doubles £35.

FOOD

Every other restaurant in Newcastle has inexpensive pasta and pizza, and those in between serve everything from tandoori chicken to veggie burgers; prices are generally £2-5. Chinese eateries form a small Chinatown along **Stowell St.** near Gallowgate; many offer all-you-can-eat specials for £4 to £6. Many of the restaurants that line **Dean St.** offer cheap lunch specials. For fresh vegetables, duck into the **Grainger Indoor Market,** between Grainger St. and Grey St. near the monument. (Open M and W 7am-5pm, Tu and Th-Su 7am-5:30pm.)

Don Vito's, 82 Pilgrim St. (☎ 232 8923). Stands out among Italian eateries. With generous pizzas and pastas for £4.50, replete with glorious toppings and inventive sauces, the don makes you an offer you can't refuse. Try the *gnocchi.* Open M-F 11:45am-2pm and 5-10pm, Sa 11:45am-10:30pm.

Marco's Supernatural Vegetarian Restaurant, 2 Princess Sq. (☎ 261 2730). Facing the Central Library main entrance, take a left and go up the ramp; it's on your left. Expect more cheap delicious food than paranormal activity. They offer main courses for £2.30-3.75; the quiche and two side salads are a bargain at £2.80. Vegan fare available. 10% student discount. Open daily 10:30am-10:30pm.

Fox Talbot, 46 Dean St. (☎ 230 2229). The earth tones and sheet-metal art may make the place look too chi-chi for your budget, but it has terrific lunch deals. Go for the lunch special: two courses *and* a glass of wine for under £5. Open M-Sa 11am-11pm.

Bob Trollop, 35 Sandhill, Quayside (☎ 261 1037; ask for Bob Trollop), opposite the Guildhall. This pub offers tasty vegetarian dishes (£2.50-5); it shares the building with the **Red House** pub, which serves up meat. Both, of course, serve beer. Open daily 11am-11pm; food served M-Sa 11am-7pm, Su noon-7pm.

SIGHTS

Newcastle's monuments rear their hoary heads right in the midst of chain stores and rushing traffic. Between Central Station and the architectural masterpiece that is **Tyne Bridge** lingers the **Castle Keep.** The keep, at the foot of Dean St., is all that is left of the New Castle, erected in the 12th century on the site of a castle built in 1080 by Robert Curthose, bastard son of William the Conqueror. Oddly enough, the "New Castle" from which the city derives its name is in fact the older Curthose structure, not the 12th-century one. (☎ 232 7938. Open Apr.-Sept. Tu-Su 9:30am-5:30pm; Oct.-Mar. daily 9:30am-4:30pm. £1.50, concessions 50p.) Uphill on Mosley St., the most elegant tower in Newcastle crowns the **Cathedral Church of St. Nicholas.** This set of small towers around a double arch, called "The Lantern," are meant to resemble Jesus' crown of thorns. (Open M-F 7am-6pm, Sa 8am-4pm, Su 7am-noon and 4-7pm. Free.) The ■ **Laing Art Gallery,** on New Bridge St., showcases an excellent collection of local art and a selection of fresh temporary exhibitions. (☎ 232 7734. Open M-Sa 10am-5pm, Su 2-5pm. Wheelchair access. Free.) The **Side Gallery,** perched above the bookstore at 5 Side, features a thoughtful catalogue of documentary photographic exhibitions by local, national, and international artists. (☎ 261 5380. Open Tu-Sa 10am-5pm, Su 11am-3pm. Free.) Opened with millennial fanfare last spring, the extensively interactive **International Centre for Life** sprawls along Scotswood Rd. by the train station in Newcastle's own Times Square. Record your image at a photo caption station and watch yourself (d)evolve into a monkey or a jawed fish, among other prehistoric creatures. The Centre for Life also offers regular live and film presentations. (☎ 243 8223, booking hotline ☎ 243 8201. Open daily 10am-6pm. £6.95, seniors and students £5.50, children £4.50, families £19.95.) Daytrips from Newcastle include the castles at **Alnwick** and **Warkworth,** 20 mi. north by bus #518 (see p. 413), and **Hadrian's Wall** (see p. 410).

🖼️🎵 PUBS, NIGHTLIFE, AND ENTERTAINMENT

Home of the nectar known as brown ale, Newcastle's pub and club scene is legendary throughout England and, increasingly, the world-at-large. Nightlife is divided into two distinct areas: **Bigg Market,** a rowdy Geordie haven, and **Quayside** (KEYside), which is slightly more relaxed and attracts local students. Be cautious at Bigg Market—this is where stocky footballer Paul "Gazza" Gascoigne got beaten up *twice* for deserting Newcastle, and underdressed student-types are frowned upon. Most pubs offer happy hours 4-8pm (Su 7-8pm). You're less likely to stand out if you dress up a bit. *The Crack,* an offbeat magazine available for free at the TIC, has a compact and indispensable calendar of live music and club events. Milder pubs include **Blackie Boy,** 11 Groat Market (☎ 232 0730), and **Macey's,** 31 Groat Market (☎ 261 0924). Down at the Quayside visit **The Red House,** 32 Sandhill, opposite the Guildhall. (All three open daily 11am-11pm.) In the heart of the city, **Legends,** 77 Grey St., is a particular sparkler among Newcastle's many club gems. Music varies from soul to grunge, depending on the night. (☎ 232 0430. Cover £1-7. Open M-Tu and Th-Sa from 9:30pm.) Under the Tyne Bridge floats the **Tuxedo Royale.** As if dancing on a boat weren't disorienting enough, one of this huge club's two dance floors actually rotates. (☎ 477 8899. Open M and W-Sa 7:30pm-2am.) The gay and lesbian crowd flocks to the corner of Waterloo St. and Sunderland St. in the southwest part of the city, where you can find the relaxed atmosphere of **The Village** (a pub) and **Powerhouse** (a nightclub) in the same building. (☎ 261 8874. Pub open daily noon-11pm. Club open M and Th 10pm-2am, Tu-W 11pm-1am, F-Sa 10am-3pm.) Finish the evening in true Newcastle style with a kebab with extra chili sauce.

If you fancy entertainment of the seated variety, treat yourself to an evening at the lush gilt-and-velvet **Theatre Royal,** 100 Grey St. **The Royal Shakespeare Company** makes a month-long stop here, beginning the last week in September. (☎ 232 2061. Box office open M-Sa 10am-8pm. Tickets from £6; occasional discounts—call for details.) In the last full week of June, Newcastle hosts **The Hoppings,** the largest seasonal fair in the world, with 28-30 acres of traveling showmen and general craziness. Call the TIC for more information.

NORTHUMBERLAND

NORTHUMBERLAND NATIONAL PARK

Northumberland is somewhat like Northumberland Avenue on the London version of Monopoly—tucked in the corner, not particularly sought after, and occasionally stocked with tiny houses. Perched at the edge of the Scottish frontier, it was once the site of skirmishes involving territorial Romans or Anglo-Saxons. Today, the 400 sq. mi. Northumberland National Park stretches south from the grassy Cheviot Hills near the border to the dolomitic crags of Whin Sill, where it includes part of Hadrian's Wall. Visitors are guaranteed a struggle with its poor public transport network, but free from tourist legions, the least populated of all England's National Parks retains its frontier character, and its desolate hills shoulder a rough-edged splendor.

▐ GETTING THERE AND GETTING AROUND

As buses run more frequently up the coast than between the towns on the inland borders of the park, **Newcastle, Alnwick,** and **Berwick-upon-Tweed** (known as plain Berwick) make the best bases for park exploration. On the park's border, **Rothbury** (southwest of Alnwick) and **Wooler** (northwest of Alnwick) enjoy the most frequent connections, halfway between "slightly accessible" and "left for dead" on the Access Meter. Postbuses creep like snails on somewhat erratic schedules; contact a post office for timetables.

Trains (☎ (08457) 484950) run to Berwick from: **Newcastle** (1hr., 13 per day, £10); **York** (2hr.; M-F and Su 13 per day, Sa 16 per day; £29); and **Edinburgh** (45min.; M-Sa 25 per day, Su 18 per day; £11.10). **Buses** are cheaper, if less comfortable. Buses #505 and 515 go from **Newcastle** to **Berwick** via **Alnwick** (2hr., every 2hr.). From Alnwick, #501 leaves for **Craster,** going up the coast to Dunstanburgh Castle, Seahouses, and Bamburgh Castle (2hr., every 2hr.). Bus #464 connects **Wooler** and **Berwick** (3-4 per day); #469, 470, and 473 connect **Alnwick** and **Wooler** (45min., 1 per hr.). Bus #416 runs from **Newcastle** to **Morpeth** and **Rothbury** (M-Sa 8 per day, Su 2 per day). Smart ramblers will invest in a **Northeast Explorer** ticket (£5, seniors and under 14 £3.85, families £10), good for unlimited one-day use on most local buses.

The major obstacle to area transport is the large military training area smack dab in the middle of the park, forcing all traffic to endure a significant detour. Hikers and bikers should be aware of this area and stay away. If you don't have a car or bicycle, staying overnight in **Berwick,** with its full train and bus service, is your best bet. From there buses depart to most coastal hotspots. If you plan to village-hop, obtain the essential 256-page tome *Northumberland Public Transport Guide* (£1), available at any tourist information centre (TIC) or bus station, or by sending £1.75 to the Public Transport Office, County Hall, Morpeth, Northumberland NE61 2EF (☎ (0191) 212 3000; open M-F 8am-5:15pm, Sa 8:30am-3pm).

🔼 THE PARK

THE SOUTH PARK

The south park embraces Hadrian's Wall (p. 410), Wark Forest, and strings of low hills. The main **National Park Information Centre** is in **Hexham,** at the south end of town (☎ (01434) 605225; see p. 412). The Pennine Way penetrates the park at **Greenhead,** a meek village on Hadrian's Wall 25 mi. east of Carlisle and 40 mi. west of Newcastle, which possesses a **YHA Youth Hostel** (☎ (016977) 47401; see p. 370). The path winds 7 mi. east to **Once Brewed,** home of the **YHA Once Brewed** (☎ (01434) 344360; see p. 411).

From Once Brewed, the path continues 14 mi. northeast to Bellingham (BELLing-um), due west of Morpeth. In town rests the **YHA Bellingham,** Woodburn Rd. (☎/ fax (01434) 220313. No smoking. Open July to Aug. daily; June and Sept.-Oct. M-Sa. Dorms £6.80, under 18 £4.65.) The Bellingham **tourist information centre,** Fountain Cottage, on Main St., details nearby walks, including a 2 mi. stroll through a woodland ravine to the **Hareshaw Linn Waterfall.** (☎ (01434) 220616. Open June-Sept. M-Sa 10am-1pm and 2-6pm, Su 1-5pm; off-season hours reduced.)

Just outside the west boundary of the park lies **Kielder Water,** the largest manmade lake in Europe. From Bellingham, bus #814 (30min.; M-F 3-5 per day, Sa 2 per day) and postbus #815 run west to **Kielder,** on the northern tip of Kielder Water. **Water Cruises** run from docks on the lake. (☎ (01434) 240436. Tours 4 per day, July-Aug. 10am-6pm; off-season hours reduced. £4, seniors £3.20, children £2.45, families £11.50-£13.50.) Built in 1775 by the Earl Percy, Duke of Northumberland, **Kielder Castle** now houses the **Kielder Castle Visitor Centre,** which glorifies the park's flora and fauna. (☎ (01434) 250209. Open Aug. daily 10am-6pm; off-season hours reduced.) The **tourist information centre** at Tower Knowe, ¾ mi. from the village of **Falstone** on the southeastern shore, knows all about the lay of the lake. (☎ (01434) 240398; fax 250130. Open daily July-Aug. 10am-6pm; May-June and Sept.-Oct. 10am-5pm; call for winter hours.)

High hills to the east and dense forests to the west accompany the 15 mi. Pennine stretch from Bellingham northwest to **Byrness,** home to a **YHA Youth Hostel,** 7 Otterburn Green, with a god-given drying room, cafe, and shop nearby. (☎ (01830) 520425. Open July-Aug. daily; Apr.-June and Sept. W-M. Dorms £6.80, under 18 £4.65.) Bus #915 runs from **Bellingham** (45min., M-F 2 per day). From Byrness, the Pennine Way finishes with a boggy 27 mi. stretch through the Cheviots, bereft of hostels until it ends at **Kirk Yetholm,** Scotland (☎ (01573) 420631; see p. 517).

THE NORTH PARK

At the northern boundary of the park, miles from the Pennine Way and semi-decent bus service, Wooler provides access to less strenuous daytrips into the **Cheviots**—a picturesque range of long dormant volcanos along the English-Scottish border—especially around the Glendale and Kyloe areas. Barring possession of a cycle or car, serious hikers can speed by taxi to trailheads at **Dunsdale, Mounthooly,** and **Hethpool,** each over 8 mi. away. Inquire at the TIC about taxis, or call **Glendale Taxis** (☎ (01668) 282292). The revamped **YHA Wooler,** 30 Cheviot St., has full wheelchair access, enviable bathrooms, and comfortable dormitories 300 yd. uphill from the bus station. (☎ (01668) 281365; fax 282368. Open Apr.-Aug. daily; Sept.-Oct. M-Sa; Mar. F-Sa. Dorms £8.35, under 18 £5.65.) **Camp** at **Highburn House.** (☎ (01668) 281344. Electricity £1.50; showers 20p; laundry facilities. £4 per adult, 50p per child.) The **tourist information centre,** 11 Market Pl., offers details on climbs in the Cheviots and gentler walks through the Happy and College Valleys. (☎ (01668) 282123. Open Apr.-Oct. M-Sa 10am-1pm, 2-5pm, Su 10am-2pm.)

Roughly five miles southeast of Wooler, the quirky little town of **Chillingham** struts its strange stuff. Here lies **Chillingham Castle,** where King Edward I stayed while charting his campaign against William Wallace's rebellion. Among its present occupants is a collection of 15-ft.-wide antlers from the now-extinct Irish Elk and a lovingly restored 19th-century garden. (☎ (01668) 215359. Open May-June and Sept. W-M noon-5pm; July-Aug. daily noon-5pm. Oct.-Apr. groups welcome by appointment. £4.30, seniors £3.80.) Directly next door to the castle graze the 60-so **Wild White Cattle,** the total world endowment of entirely purebred cattle. Originally enclosed in 1235, the cattle have been inbred for over seven centuries; not a single heifer has been introduced from the outside in all that time. Sleek and broad-shouldered, they don't look very different from normal cows, but they cannot be herded, will attack humans, and will even kill one of their own if he or she is touched by human hands. (☎ (01668) 215250. Tours led by warden; 1-1½hr. Open Apr.-Oct. M and W-Sa 10am-noon and 2-5pm, Su 2-5pm. £3, students and seniors £2.50, children £1.) To get to Chillingham take a cab (£6.50) or bus #470, 473, or 871 from Wooler or Alnwick (20min., 3 per day).

The nearest **National Park Visitor Centre** is seven miles south in **Ingram.** (☎/fax (01665) 578248. Open daily July-Aug. 10am-6pm; Mar.-June and Sept. 10am-5pm.) A **Gold Leaf Travel bus** runs between Wooler and Ingram every 1½ hours. 25 mi. farther south of Wooler off the A697 on the B6341, the village of **Rothbury** sits in a densely wooded valley carved by the River Coquet, and has another **National Park Visitor Centre** networked with a **tourist information centre,** Church St. (☎/fax (01669) 620887. Open daily July-Aug. 10am-6pm, Apr.-June and Sept.-Oct. 10am-5pm.)

◐ FESTIVALS

In July, Northumberland comes alive with pomp and pageantry. The **common ridings** are week-long festivals occurring in each town at different times throughout the month. Locals dressed in their finest clothes parade on horseback through the town and surrounding area accompanied by traditional marching bands and the symbol of community spirit, the Burgh Flag. The celebration commemorates the tradition of riding through the town's land holdings to establish and preserve boundaries and burgh rights.

HADRIAN'S WALL

When Roman Emperor Hadrian ordered his magnificent wall built in AD 122, official word went out that he wanted to mark his boundaries, but everyone knew he was just scared of the barbarians to the north (see **Early Invaders,** p. 66). Hadrian's unease created a permanent monument to the Roman frontier—first a V-shaped ditch 27 ft. wide, then a stone barrier 15 ft. high and 8-9 ft. across. Eight years, 17 milecastles (forts), 5500 cavalrymen, and 13,000 infantrymen later, Hadrian's Wall stretched unbroken for 73 mi. from modern-day Carlisle to Newcastle. The years have not been kind to Hadrian's project. Most of the wall's stones have been carted off and recycled into the surrounding structures, and the portions that remain stand at only half their original height. The highest concentration of remains scatters along the western part of the original wall, at the southern edge of Northumberland National Park (see p. 408).

E GETTING THERE AND GETTING AROUND. The wall is best accessed by car; failing that, buses are available. Between May and September, **Stagecoach Cumberland** (☎ (01946) 63222) sends the **Hadrian's Wall Bus,** a.k.a. #682, from English St. in **Carlisle** to **Hexham,** stopping at all the major sights on the wall (2hr., 4 per day, 65p-£3.65). From **Newcastle,** bus #685 runs to **Carlisle** via **Hexham, Haltwhistle, Greenhead,** and other wall-related towns (2hr., 12 per day). A **Hadrian's Wall Bus Whole Day Rover ticket,** available from tourist information centres or from bus drivers, is a good idea for those planning to make numerous journeys within one day (£5, under 14 £3, families £10). Another option is the **Hadrian's Wall Rover,** a 2-out-of-3-day ticket valid between Sunderland and Carlisle on the Tyne Valley train line, on the Hadrian's Wall Bus, and on the Tyne & Wear Metro (£12.50, children £6.25).

Trains (☎ (08457) 484950) run frequently between **Carlisle** and **Newcastle,** but stations all lie 1½-4 mi. from the actual wall. If you do rail it, be prepared to hike to the nearest stones. Trains depart from **Carlisle** to: **Brampton,** 2 miles from Lanercost and 5 miles from Birdoswald (20min.; M-Sa 7 per day, Su 5 per day; £2.60, return £4.10); **Haltwhistle,** 2 miles from Cawfields (35min.; M-Sa 12 per day, Su 7 per day; £3.55); **Bardon Mill,** 2 miles from Vindolanda and 4½ mi. from Housesteads (40min.; M-Sa 7 per day, Su 5 per day; £4.10, return £7.50); and **Hexham** (50min.; M-Sa every 30min., Su 9 per day; £5.80, return £10.60). Call **Northumberland Transport Enquiries** (☎ (01670) 533128) or **Cumbria Journey Planner** (☎ (01228) 606000) for more information.

▦⚗ ORIENTATION AND PRACTICAL INFORMATION. Hadrian's Wall stands between the urban centers of Carlisle to the west and Newcastle to the east. The towns of **Greenhead, Haltwhistle, Once Brewed, Bardon Mill, Haydon Bridge, Hexham** (the hub of Hadrian's Wall transportation), and **Corbridge** lie somewhat parallel to the wall from west to east. The **Hexham tourist information centre** (TIC), on Hallgate, offers accommodations booking and information, as well as the useful pamphlets *The Essential Guide to Hadrian's Wall* (30p) and the free *Hadrian's Wall: Where to Stay for Walkers* (see p. 412). The **Northumberland National Park Information Centre** in **Once Brewed,** on Military Rd., is also helpful. (☎ (01434) 344396 or 344777. Open daily Mar.-Oct. daily 9:30am-5:30pm.)

▐ ACCOMMODATIONS. Both **Carlisle** and **Hexham** have abundant B&Bs and make good bases for day journeys to the wall. Two youth hostels lie close to the wall, on the route of the Hadrian's Wall Bus. The **YHA Greenhead Youth Hostel** stands in a converted chapel 16 mi. east of Carlisle and steps away from Hadrian's Wall. (☎/fax (016977) 47401. Lockout 10am-5pm. Open July-Aug. daily; Apr. to June M-Sa; Sept.-Oct. F-Tu. Dorms £8.10, under 18 £5.80.) The **YHA Once Brewed Youth Hostel,** Military Rd., Bardon Mill, lies seven miles east of Greenhead. It has a central location, 2½ mi. northwest of the Bardon Mill train station, three miles from Housesteads Fort, one mile from Vindolanda, and a half a mile from the wall itself. Binocular rental after 1pm. (☎ (01434) 344360; fax 344045. Lockout 10am-1pm. Open Apr.-Aug. daily; Mar. F-Sa; Sept.-Oct. M-Sa. Wheelchair access. Dorms £10.85, under 18 £7.50.) An independent hostel, the **Hadrian Lodge,** is convenient for serious walkers; take a train to Haydon Bridge, then follow the main road uphill for 2½ mi. (☎ (01434) 688688. Breakfast £1.50-3.50. Kitchen and laundry facilities. Dorms £10; singles £23-28; doubles £42-45.)

▣ SIGHTS. Pick up the free *Visitors' Guide to Hadrian's Wall* from a TIC; **Supersaver tickets** are good for admission to both Vindolanda and the Roman Army Museum. (£5.75, students and seniors £4.70, children £4.10, families £17.50.) The most popular sight, and the one you should go to if you have limited money or time, is **Housesteads,** the most complete Roman fort in Britain, five miles northeast of Bardon Mill on the B6318. The well-preserved waist-high ruins are freckled with informative billboards, and the site itself keeps watch over a good length of unbroken wall stretching to the west away from the crowds. Sheep, in a sad display of illiteracy, ignore the "Please keep off the walls" signs, but you shouldn't: walking on the wall is as dangerous for you as it is damaging to the wall. (☎ (01434) 344363. Open daily Apr.-Sept. 10am-6pm; Oct. daily 10am-5pm; Nov.-Mar. 10am-4pm. £2.80, students and seniors £2.10, under 16 £1.40.)

Built out of stones permanently "borrowed" from the wall, the **Roman Army Museum** at Carvoran, ¾ mi. northeast of Greenhead, presents stockpiles of artifacts, interactive stations, and a faux Roman Army recruiting video. (☎ (016977) 47485. Open Apr.-Sept. daily 10am-6pm; Mar. and Oct. 10am-5pm; Nov.-Feb. 10am-4pm. Wheelchair access. £3, students and seniors £2.60, children £2.10.) Several well-preserved milecastles and bridges lie between Greenhead and **Birdoswald Roman Fort.** The fort itself, 15 mi. east of Carlisle, is the site of recent excavations. (☎ (016977) 47602. Open Mar.-Nov. daily 10am-5:30pm; reduced hours in Nov. Museum and wall £2.50, students and seniors £2, children £1.50, families £6.50; wall only £1, children 50p, placed in an "honesty box".) At **Vindolanda** (1½ mi. north of Bardon Mill and 1 mi. southeast of Once Brewed), a fort and civilian settlement that predates the wall, extensive excavations have revealed hundreds of inscribed wooden tablets that illuminate details of Roman life. Ongoing excavation sites, a charming garden, and a small reconstructed Roman Temple circle the object-crammed museum. (☎ (01434) 344277. Open same hours as the Roman Army Museum. £3.80, students and seniors £3.20, children £2.80.)

HEXHAM ☎01434

West of Newcastle on the A69, the well-heeled market town of Hexham makes a fine base for exploring Hadrian's Wall, but also charms with its own sights. The cobbled town center coils around its impressively kept abbey, the **Priory Church of St. Andrew,** which stands along the Market Place. Built by Augustinian canons, the Abbey, as it's familiarly known, also houses the 7th-century bishop's throne of St. Wilfrid and hosts frequent musical performances. (☎ 602031. Open May-Sept. daily 9am-7pm; Oct.-Apr. daily 9am-5pm; hours dependent on services. Suggested donation £2.) Facing the Abbey is the substantial 14th-century **Gatehouse Tower.**

The **train station** presides along Station Rd., a 5min. walk from Market Place. **Trains** (☎ (08457) 484950) stop frequently (M-Sa 15 per day, Su 9 per day) on their way between **Carlisle** (50min., £5.80, return £10.70) and **Newcastle** (40min., £3.20, return £4.80). The **bus station** is on Priestpopple Rd., just south of the Market Place. From May to September, **Stagecoach Cumberland** (☎ (01946) 63222) bus #682, a.k.a. the **Hadrian's Wall Bus,** runs from English St. in **Carlisle** along the major sights on the wall and ends up in Hexham (2hr., 4 per day, 65p-£3.65). Bus #685 runs from **Newcastle** (2hr., 12 per day). See **Getting There and Getting Around,** p. 411.

Pass through the liberal arch of the Gatehouse Tower to reach the combined **tourist information centre** (TIC) and **Northumberland National Park Information Centre** in the Old Gaol House on Hallgate. It provides up-to-date information on visits to the wall, books accommodations for the Hexham area, and runs free guided walking tours from June to mid-September. (☎ 605225; fax 600325. Open mid-May to Sept. M-Sa 9am-6pm, Su 10am-5pm; Oct. to mid-May M-Sa 9am-5pm.) Services include: **banks** along Battle Hill and Priestpopple Rd.; **Thomas Cook,** 12 Battle Hill (☎ 605233; open M and W-Sa 9am-5:30pm, Tu 10am-5:30pm); the **police** (☎ 604111), Shaftoe Leages, west of the town center; the **General Hospital** (☎ 655655), Corbridge Rd., east of the town center; **Internet access** at **NBS The Computer Shop,** 10b Hencotes (☎ 600022; £1 per 10min., open M-F 9:30am-5:30pm, Sa 9:30am-4:30pm); and the **post office,** hidden within Robbs of Hexham department store, Priestpopple Rd. (☎ 602001; open M-Tu, Th, and Sa 8:30am-5:30pm, W 9am-5:30pm, F 8:30am-6pm). **Postal code:** NE46 1NA.

For a delightful stay, make your way up a fragrant, flower-filled front path to the antique-stuffed interior of Mrs. Boaden's **Number 18 B&B**, 18 Hexham Terr. (☎ 602265. Singles £17; doubles £34.) **Bunters Café**, 10 Hallgate, directly across from the TIC, serves a traditional English menu during the day (£2-5), plus a handful of Greek dishes (£3-4.50); by night, the cafe becomes **Athena's Mediterranean Restaurant**, with fewer of the English standards and slightly higher prices. (Cafe open M-Sa 10am-4:30pm, Su 10:45am-4:30pm; restaurant open Tu-Sa 6:30-9:30pm.) Mounds of glowing fruits and vegetables are available from **Stafford's Fruiterer and Florist**, at the top of Fore St. (☎ 602632. Open M-Sa 8am-5pm, Su 10am-4pm.) Across the Market Place, take in a quiet pint at the **Heart of All England** pub, Market St. (Open M-Sa 11am-11pm, Su 11am-10pm.)

ALNWICK AND WARKWORTH   ☎ 01665

About 31 mi. north of Newcastle off the A1, the tiny town of **Alnwick** (AHN-ick; pop. 7200) oozes charm beside the magnificently preserved ◧ **Alnwick Castle**, another former Percy family stronghold and now home to the Duke and Duchess of Northumberland. This rugged Norman-fortification-turned-stately-home, featured in the recent movie *Elizabeth*, gives way to an ornate Italian Renaissance interior and is circled by three small museums on the grounds. (☎ (01665) 510777. Open Easter-Sept. daily 11am-5pm, last admission 4:15pm. £6.25, students and seniors £5.25, children £3.50, families £15.) Alnwick's well-supplied **tourist information centre**, 2 The Shambles, Market Pl., rests at the town's vortex. (☎ 510665; fax 510477. Open July-Aug. M-Sa 9am-6:30pm, Su 9am-5pm, off-season hours reduced.) The hippest place in town is **Barter Books**, one of Britain's largest secondhand bookshops, which also provides **Internet access** under a model train circling overhead. (☎ 604888. £1.50 per 15min. Open Jul.-Aug. daily 9am-7pm; Sept.-June M-W and F-Su 9am-5pm, Th 9am-7pm.) By the **bus station**, 10 Clayport St. (☎ 602182; open M-Sa 9am-5pm) is a **launderette**, 5 Clayport St. (☎ 604398; open M-F 8am-7pm, Sa-Su 9am-5pm). The **post office** is at 19 Market St. **Postal code:** NE66 155.

Stay with delightful Mrs. Givens and her affectionate mutt at **The Tea Pot**, 8 Bondgate Without, and yes, that's a street name. (☎ 604473. £17-18 per person; £1 off if you mention *Let's Go*.) At ◧ **The Town House** vegetarian restaurant, 15 Narrowgate, baguettes (£2.15), jacket potatoes (£2.35), and other creative meals (£4-7) are served in a heart-warming atmosphere decorated with colorful collages and wine-bottle candles. (☎ 606336. Open M-F 10:30am-3pm, Sa 10am-4pm, Su from noon, F-Sa also from 6:30pm.) Pick up food supplies at the **Safeway**, next to the bus station. (☎ 510126. Open M-Th 8:30am-10pm, F 8am-10pm, Sa 8am-9pm, Su 9am-5pm.)

Seven miles southeast of Alnwick is **Warkworth** (pop. 1300), where the evocative ruins of 12th-century **Warkworth Castle** guard the mouth of the River Coquet. The extraordinary 15th-century keep, foundation rubble, and largely intact curtain wall come to life in an excellent audio tour. (☎ 711423. Open daily Apr.-Sept. 10am-6pm; Oct. 10am-5pm; Nov.-Mar. 10am-1pm and 2-4pm. £2.40, students and seniors £1.80, children £1.60. 40min. audio tour £1.50, two adults £2.50, students and seniors £1.10, children 75p.) Shakespeare set much of *Henry IV Part I* in Warkworth; the 14th-century **hermitage** carved from the Coquet cliffs is the reputed site of Harry Hotspur's baptism. The staff at the castle will row you there. (Open Apr.-Sept. W and Su 11am-5pm. £1.60, students and seniors £1.20, children 80p.)

BERWICK-UPON-TWEED   ☎ 01289

Just south of the Scottish border, Berwick-upon-Tweed (BARE-ick) has changed hands more often than any town in Britain—14 times between 1100 and 1500 alone. The battle blood in town flows so hot that a popular local legend claims Berwick was at war with Russia for over 50 years. Supposedly Queen Victoria used her full title in the 1854 declaration of war, "Queen of Great Britain, Ireland, Berwick-upon-Tweed, and the British dominions beyond the sea," but forgot to include Berwick in the peace treaty. Most of Berwick's **castle** is now buried beneath the present railway station, although the 13th-century Breakneck Stairs still absorb sun rays. (Open M-Sa 6:30am-7:50pm, Su 10:15am-7:30pm.) For a sense of Berwick and its turbulent history on the border, walk along the astounding 16th-century **Elizabethan Walls,** built to encircle the Old Town; the amazing view of Berwick and the River Tweed from **Meg's Mount** is even better now that the arrows have stopped flying. The expansive grass knolls almost merit a visit in themselves. The town's most substantial sight is the tongue-twisting **Berwick Barracks** on the corner of Parade and Ravensdowne. The early 18th-century structures now contain a museum on military life, a crowded and curious exhibition on Berwick's history, and a terrific contemporary art gallery, the **Berwick Gymnasium.** (☎ 304493. Open Apr.-Sept. daily 10am-6pm, Oct. daily 10am-4pm, Nov.-Mar. W-Su 10am-4pm. £2.60, students and seniors £2, children £1.30.) Berwick also makes a good base for exploration of the Scottish Borders; many of the fine houses and abbeys are a short bus ride away. Berwick is the end of **St. Cuthbert's Way,** a hike that begins in Melrose (see p. 518).

The **Bus Information Shop** is at the uphill end of Marygate, providing timetables and selling National Express tickets. (☎ 307283. Open M-F 9am-5pm.) Buses stop at the train station, Golden Sq., Chapel St., or across from the bus shop. The **tourist information centre** lives in a new building on 106 Marygate, and books rooms for a 10% deposit. (☎ 330733; fax 330448. Open M-Sa 10am-6pm, Su 11am-4pm.) Not to be outdone, the **post office** (☎ 307596) shows off its spiffy new home at 103 Marygate. **Postal code:** TD15 1BH.

Overnight visitors can rest up at **Miranda's Guest House,** 43 Church St. From the train station, walk into town on Castlegate; once you've passed the clock tower, turn left, and the B&B is two blocks ahead on the left. (☎ 306483. £15.50-16.50 per person.) Stock up at the **Co-op,** 15 Marygate. (☎ 302596. Open M-Sa 9am-5:30pm.)

NEAR BERWICK-UPON-TWEED: HOLY ISLAND

Just off the coast—halfway between Bamburgh Castle and Berwick-upon-Tweed—lies the idyllically wind-swept █ **Holy Island,** connected to the coast at low tide by a causeway. Awash in religious history and drowning in a strikingly peculiar landscape, the island makes an ideal daytrip for the romantically inclined.

Seven years after Northumberland's King Edwin converted in AD 627, the missionary Aidan came here from the Scottish island of Iona to found England's first Christian monastery, **Lindisfarne Priory,** the ruins of which still stand. (☎ (01289) 389200. Open daily Apr.-Oct. 10am-6pm, Nov.-Mar. 10am-4pm. £2.80, students and seniors £2, children £1.40.) Wily travelers seeking to preserve those precious pounds can climb the hill directly beyond the priory for a good view of the remains. **Lindisfarne Castle,** also on the island, is a fort built in the mid-16th century and converted into a private residence in the early 19th. The castle's hilltop perch is spectacular from the outside, but its interior contains only a plain display of 19th century furnishings. (☎ (01289) 389244. Open Apr.-Oct. M-Th and Sa-Su noon-3pm, sometimes also 1½hr. earlier or later depending on tides. £4, families £10.) The island's most serene and remote spot is also completely free: tiny **Saint Cuthbert's Island,** marked by a wooden cross 220 yd. off the coast of the priory, is where the famed saint took his hermitage when even the monastery proved too distracting.

Check tide tables at a tourist information centre before you go. Bring a jacket; the wind can be so strong that birds fly as if intoxicated. You can cross the 2¾ mi. causeway only at low tide. Don't try swimming; the tidal currents are strong. Bus #477 (☎ (0191) 212 3000) runs from Berwick to Holy Island Feb.-Aug. 2-3 times a week in summer; schedules vary with the tides.

WALES (CYMRU)

This nation, O King, may now as in former times, be harassed, and in a great
measure weakened and destroyed by your and other Powers...but it can never be
totally subdued through the wrath of man, unless the wrath of God shall concur.
    —an Old Man of Pencader to Henry II, quoted by Giraldus Cambrensis

Wales borders England, but if many of the 2.9 million Welsh people had their way, it would be floating miles away. Since England solidified its control over the country with the murder of Prince Llywelyn ap Gruffydd (also known as Llywelyn the Last) in 1282, relations between the two have been marked by a powerful unease (do not refer to the Welsh as "English"). Until late in the 19th century, schoolchildren were forbidden to speak Welsh in the classroom. Those who did were made to wear a "Welsh Knot" around their necks, which was passed around to the next child who dared speak Welsh; whoever was wearing the knot at the end of the day would get some form of punishment. Despite this dominating presence, Wales clings steadfastly to its Celtic heritage, continuing a centuries-old struggle for independence. The mellifluous Welsh language endures in conversations, commerce, and literature, both oral and written. As churning coal, steel, and slate mines fell victim to Britain's faltering economy, Wales turned its economic eye from heavy industry to tourism. Travelers from near and far come for the miles of sandy beaches, grassy cliffs, and dramatic mountains that typify the rich landscape of this corner of Britain, or to scan the numerous castles that dot the towns, remnants of centuries of warfare with England. Against this stunning backdrop, Welsh nationalists have expressed their dissatisfaction mostly in the peace of the voting booths and in a celebration of the distinctive Welsh culture and language at events like the Royal National Eisteddfod.

▛ GETTING AROUND

TRAINS

Britrail passes are accepted on all trains through Wales except narrow-gauge railways. Those traveling solely within Wales can purchase region-specific passes, such as the **Freedom of Wales Flexipass** (any 8 days in 15-day period June-Sept. £92, Oct.-May £75; any 4 days in 8-day period June-Sept. £49, Oct.-May £39), good on the entire Welsh network plus Chester to Abergavenny via Crewe, and also good on all buses (see below). The **Cambrian Coast Day Ranger** (£6.40; £3.50 after 4:30pm) earns a day's rail travel from Aberystwyth north to Pwllheli on the Llŷn Peninsula. The **Freedom of South Wales 7-Day Flexi Rover** and **North and Mid Wales 7-Day Flexi Rover** cover both train and bus travel; see **Buses,** below. Call **National Rail Enquiries** (☎ (08457) 484950) for train information.

   Narrow-gauge railways tend to be attractions in themselves, rather than actual means of transport. Trainspotters can purchase a **Great Little Trains of Wales Wanderer** ticket, which gives unlimited travel on the Ffestiniog, the Welsh Highland, the Bala Lake, Brecon Mountain, Talyllyn, Llanberis Lake, and Vale of Rheidol lines. (4 days out of 8 £33, children £17; 8 days out of 15 £43, children £22.)

BUSES

Pronouncing your destination properly will probably be the least of your problems as you navigate the overlapping routes of Wales's 65 bus operators. Most of these are local services; almost every region is dominated by one or two companies. Life-saving regional public transport guides, available free in tourist information centres (TICs), exist for most places, but for some areas you'll have to consult an array of small brochures. The free and very useful *Wales Bus, Rail, and Tourist*

Map and Guide provides information on bus routes, but not on timetables. Take all bus schedules with a grain of salt—buses sometimes run late. Many local buses don't run on Sunday, but some special tourist buses run *only* on summer Sundays.

TrawsCambria (☎ (08706) 082608) bus #701 is the main north-south bus line. On it, you can travel from Cardiff or Swansea north to Machynlleth, Bangor, and Holyhead. BritRail and Freedom of Wales rail passes are valid on the bus. Within South Wales, **Cardiff Bus** (☎ (029) 2039 6521) blankets the area around Cardiff, while **Stagecoach Red and White** (☎ (01633) 266336) buses serve the routes from Gloucester and Hereford in England west through the Wye Valley, past Abergavenny and Brecon. **First Cymru** (☎ (08706) 082608) covers the Gower Peninsula and the rest of southwest Wales, including the Pembrokeshire Coast National Park.

Passes simplify bus fares. Cardiff Bus offers the **City Rider** day pass (£2.50, children £1.50) and one-week **Multiride** passes (£9.95, children £5; available at their office near the bus station). From Hereford south to Swansea and as far west as Carmarthen, one-day **Roverbus** tickets cover all bus travel on Stagecoach Red and White, First Cymru, and Phil Anslow buses, and can be purchased from bus drivers (£5, children £4). Long-distance and shuttle services such as TrawsCambria, National Express, and First Cymru Shuttles do not honor any rover tickets. The **Freedom of South Wales 7-Day Flexi Rover** offers bus and train travel throughout South Wales (7 days bus and any 3 days train, June-Sept. £32, Oct.-May £27).

In north Wales, **Arriva Cymru** (☎ (08706) 082608) provides excellent service throughout most of the area. Buy the **One Day Explorer** (£5, under 16 £3.50), valid north of Aberystwyth and as far east as Chester. If your travel is confined to the county of Gwynedd, extending from Machynlleth north to Holyhead and Llandudno, the Gwynedd **Red Rover** offers a cheaper deal (£4.60, children £2.30). The **North and Mid Wales 7-Day Flexi Rover** offers bus and train travel throughout most of Wales above the imaginary Aberystwyth-Shrewsbury line, including free travel on the Ffestiniog Railway (3 days in 7, £26.30).

HIKING, BIKING, AND HITCHHIKING

Wales has hundreds of well-marked footpaths. *Walking in Wales*, at TICs, highlights interesting walks with sights and accommodations along the way. Long-distance **hikers** should buy 1:50,000 Ordnance Survey maps and bring along proper equipment (see **Wilderness Safety,** p. 53). The **Offa's Dyke Path** (see p. 430) and the **Pembrokeshire Coast Path** (see p. 448) are popular long-distance walks. For more information, write to the **Countryside Council Wales,** 43 The Parade, Roth, Cardiff DF2 3UH. **Bikers** in north Wales should obtain a copy of *Cyclists' Guide to North Wales* at TICs. *Let's Go* does not recommend **hitchhiking,** but many people choose this form of transport, especially in the summer. Cars stop most readily for hitchhikers who stand in lay-by (pull-off) areas along narrow roads.

LIFE AND TIMES

HISTORY

CELTS, ROMANS, AND NORMANS

As the western terminus of many waves of emigration, Wales has been influenced by a wide array of peoples since prehistoric times. Inhabitants from the Stone, Bronze, and Iron Ages left their mark on the Welsh landscape in the form of stone villages, forts covered in earth, *cromlechs* (standing stones also known as menhirs and dolmens), and partially subterranean burial chambers. It is the early **Celts** about whom we know the most, however, and who make Wales most distinct from her neighbors today—before the Anglo-Saxons arrived in Britain, though, there was no Wales (or England), just Celtic Britain. In the 4th and 3rd centuries BC, modern-day Wales witnessed two waves of Celtic immigration, the first from northern Europe and the second from the Iberian peninsula. By the time the

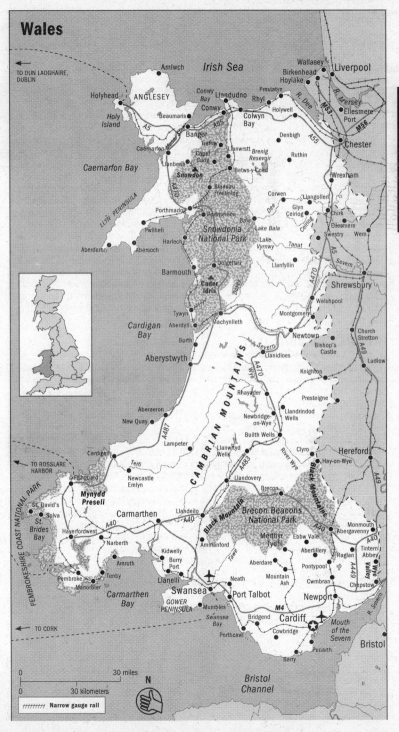

Wales

Romans arrived in AD 50, the Celts had consolidated into four main tribes, with links to each other and to Celts in Ireland and Brittany. By AD 59, the Romans had invaded and established a fortress at Segontium (present-day Caernarfon), across the Menai Straits from Ynys Môn (Anglesey), the center of druidic, bardic, and warrior life in northern modern-day Wales. Crossing the water, the Romans were faced with the bedlam of a Celtic attack, but having conquered Celts in France, Italy, and Spain, they weren't too impressed, and proceeded to kill or capture all the residents. Though the Romans symbolically conquered the Celts, their domination was never fully consolidated, and Celtic resistance compelled the Romans to station two of their four legions in Britain along the modern-day Welsh border.

When the Romans finally departed in the early 5th century AD, they left not only towns, amphitheaters, roads, and mines, but also the Latin language and the first seeds of Christianity, both of which heavily influenced further development of Welsh scholarship and society. For the next 700 years, the Celts ruled themselves, doing their best to hold at bay invading Saxons, Irish, and Vikings, their efforts perhaps spearheaded by the legendary **King Arthur,** whose exploits were detailed by Geoffrey of Monmouth. Yet they were not, in the end, successful, for in the 8th century, King Offa of Mercia and his troops pushed the Celts out of England and into various western corners of Britain, such as Cornwall, Scotland, and Wales. To make sure the Celts stayed put, Offa built **Offa's Dyke,** a 150 mi. earthwork that still roughly marks the border between England and Wales. (The Welsh say it's there to keep the English out.) The newly contained Wales consisted of many Celtic kingdoms united by a single language, a uniform system of customary law, a shared social system based on kinship ties, and a ruling aristocracy linked by common ancestry and marriage, but the kingdoms did not achieve political unity until the time of Gruffydd ap Llywelyn in the 11th century.

THE ENGLISH CONQUEST

Within 50 years of William the Conqueror's invasion of England, one quarter of Wales had been subjugated by the Normans. The newcomers built a series of castles and market towns, introduced the feudal social system, and brought with them a variety of Continental monastic orders. Though the Welsh greeted the rule of the Christian Norman barons with less resistance than they had directed toward previous heathen invaders, conflict never subsided, and the Normans were unable to enter the heart of north Wales.

The English **Plantagenet** Kings invaded Wales throughout the 12th century, but it was not until 1282, when a soldier of **Edward I** (the Longshanks, of *Braveheart* fame) killed Prince **Llywelyn ap Gruffydd,** that independence symbolically ended. Llywelyn's head was taken to London, paraded through the streets wearing a crown of ivy, and displayed at the Tower of London, lest anyone dare imagine the Welsh still had a leader. Edward then appointed his son Prince of Wales, and in 1284 dubbed the Welsh **English subjects.** He would go on to use Welsh expertise with the longbow in his campaigns in Scotland and France. To keep the perennially unruly Welsh in check, Edward constructed a series of massive castles at strategic spots throughout Wales. The magnificent surviving fortresses at Conwy, Caernarfon, Harlech, and Beaumaris stand testament to his efforts.

In the early 15th century, the bold insurgent warfare of **Owain Glyndŵr** (Owen Glendower) temporarily freed Wales from English rule. Reigniting Welsh nationalism and rousing his compatriots to arms, Glyndŵr and his followers captured the castles at Conwy and Harlech, threatened the stronghold of Caenarfon, and convened a national parliament in Wales. While poverty, the Black Plague, and warfare ravaged the country, Glyndŵr created the ideal of a "unified" Wales that has captured the country's collective imagination ever since. But despite support from Ireland, Scotland, and France, by 1409 the rebellion had been reduced to a series of guerrilla raids. By 1417 Glyndŵr had disappeared into the mountains a fugitive, leaving only legend to guide his people. Though Wales had placed her hope in the Welsh-born **Henry VII** of the House of Tudor, who ascended the English throne in 1485, alliance with the Tudors did not bring independence.

Full integration with England came during Henry VIII's reign with the **Act of Union** of 1536, which granted the Welsh the same rights as English citizens and returned the administration of Wales to the local gentry. However, the price of power was assimilation. The act banished the distinctive Welsh legal and administrative system, officially "united and annexed" Wales, and sought to "extirpate all and singular the sinister usages and customs differing." Thus began the rise of the English language in Wales, which quickly became the language of the courts and government as well as the language of the gentry.

METHODISM AND THE INDUSTRIAL REVOLUTION

In the 18th and 19th centuries, religious shifts in Wales changed the nature of society. As the church in Wales became more anglicized and tithes grew more burdensome, the Welsh were ripe for the appeal of new Protestant sects. Nonconformists, Baptists, and Quakers all gained a foothold in Wales as early as the 17th century, but it was the 18th-century Methodist revolution, with its fiery preachers and austere lifestyle, that was most influential. Life in Wales centered on the chapel, not the church, where people created tight local communities through shared religion, heritage, and language. Chapel life remains one of the most distinctive features of Welsh society; the Sabbath closure of stores in parts of Wales (particularly in the north) is but one of the lasting effects.

The 19th century brought the **Industrial Revolution** to Wales, as industrialists from within and without sought to exploit coal veins in the south and iron and slate deposits in the north. New roads, canals, and—most importantly—steam railways were built throughout Wales to transport these raw materials, and the Welsh population grew from 450,000 to 1.16 million between 1750 and 1851. Especially in the south, pastoral landscapes were transformed into grim mining wastelands, and the workers who braved these dangerous workplaces faced lives of taxing work, poverty, and despair. Early attempts at unionism failed and workers turned to violence to improve conditions. Welsh discontent was channeled into the **Chartist Movement,** which asked for political representation for all male members of society; its highest point was an uprising in Newport in 1839. Welsh society became characterized by two forces: a strongly leftist political consciousness—aided by the rise of organized labor—and large-scale emigration. Welsh miners and religious outgroups emigrated to America (founding particularly vibrant settlements in Pennsylvania) and in 1865 a group of Welsh men and women founded **Y Wladfa** (The Colony) in the Patagonia region of Argentina. Rural society was hardly more idyllic, and tenant farmers led the **Rebecca Riots** between 1839 and 1843.

The strength of the Liberal Party in Wales bolstered the career of **David Lloyd George,** who rose from being a rabble-rousing Welshman to Britain's Prime Minister (1916-22). Of the many Welshmen sent to fight the Great War on the Continent, over 35,000 never returned. This loss of a generation, combined with Prime Minister Winston Churchill's violent quelling of a Welsh **coal-miners' strike** and the economic depression of the 1930s (which spurred further emigration, and from which Welsh industry has never truly recovered), led to growing dissatisfaction.

MODERN POLITICS

Politics in Wales in the late 20th century have been especially characterized by nationalism and a vigorous campaign to retain one of Europe's oldest living modern languages. The establishment of Welsh language classes, publications, radio stations, and even a Welsh television channel (known as Sianel Pedwar Cymru, "Channel 4 Wales," or S4C for short), clearly indicates the energy invested in the Welsh language, the binding feature of the Welsh people today. In 1967, the **Welsh Language Act** established the right to use Welsh in the courts, while the 1988 **Education Reform Act** ensured that all children aged 5 to 16 in Wales would be introduced to the Welsh language in school.

Welsh nationalism has typically found its expression in the political realm: **Plaid Cymru,** the Welsh Nationalist Party, was founded in 1925 and has performed increasingly well since its founding, consistently garnering seats in Parliament. In the 1950s, a **Minister for Welsh Affairs** was made part of the national Cabinet, but

WALES

Tory rule in the 1980s, despite the fact that most of the Welsh seats were held by Labour and Plaid Cymru, brought the legitimacy of rule from London into question. On Sept. 18, 1997, the Welsh voted in favor of devolution, but unlike their Scottish counterparts support for the idea was tepid, with only 50.3% voting 'yes' despite major governmental backing. Still, this was enough to lead to elections for the 60-seat Welsh Assembly (held in May 1999), which now has control over Wales's budget. A meager 46% voter turnout saw Labour take home a 28-seat plurality, and Plaid Cymru doing unexpectedly well with 17 seats.

LLITERATURE

The Welsh prefer philosophy to philology; music and poetry to both.
    —T. Charles Williams

In Wales, as in other Celtic countries, much of the national literature stems from a vibrant bardic tradition. The earliest extant poetry in Welsh comes to us from 6th-century northern England, where the **cynfeirdd** (early poets), including the influential poet **Taliesin,** orally composed verse of praise for their patron lords. The *Gododdin*, a series of heroic lays totalling over 1000 lines and attributed to the poet **Aneirin,** is the most noted celebration of valor and heroism from this period. The 9th through 11th centuries brought emotional and often melancholy poetic sagas focusing on pseudo-historical figures such as the poet **Llywarch Hen, King Arthur,** and **Myrddin** (Merlin). Ushering in the most prolific period in Welsh literature, 12th-century monastic scribes compiled manuscripts in the Middle Welsh language. Most notable from this period is the collection of prose tales known as the **Mabinogion** (after a later translation by Lady Charlotte Guest). Under this title are the *Four Branches of the Mabinogi*, four loosely connected and highly dramatic tales of legendary Welsh figures, and seven other tales, including one of the earliest Arthurian stories in European literature, *Culwch ac Olwen*.

In the 14th century, Wales saw the development of the flexible poetic form *Cywydd* by **Dafydd ap Gwilym.** Often called the greatest Welsh poet, he combined playfulness, irony, and emotional depth in his verse, and continued to influence the works of later poets such as **Dafydd Nanmor** and **Iolo Goch** well through the 17th century. Yet a growing anglicizing of the Welsh gentry in the 18th century led to a decline in the tradition of courtly bards. Active composers of verse found their venue mainly at *eisteddfodau*, local poetry competitions, and the Royal National Eisteddfod (see **Ffestivals,** p. 422).

Modern Welsh literature has been influenced heavily in its use of language by Bishop William Morgan's 1588 **Welsh translation** of the Bible, which helped standardize Welsh and provided the foundation for literacy throughout Wales. A circle of Welsh romantic poets, **Y Beridd Newydd** (the New Poets), developed in the 19th century, including T. Gwynn Jones and W.J. Gruffydd. The horrors of World War I touched Wales as much as England and produced an anti-romantic poetic voice typified in the work of **Hedd Wyn,** who won the chief prize at the 1917 National Eisteddfod but was killed on the fields of France before accepting the honor.

The work of 20th-century Welsh writers (in both Welsh and English) features a compelling self-consciousness in addressing problematic questions of identity and national ideals. The incisive poetry of **R.S. Thomas** treads a fine line between a fierce defense of his proud heritage and a bitter rant against its claustrophobic provincialism. **Kate Roberts**'s short stories and novels, such as *Feet in Chains*, dramatize Welsh fortitude in the face of dire poverty. The best-known Welsh writer is, of course, Swansea's **Dylan Thomas,** who has become something of a national industry. His emotionally powerful poetry, as well as popular works like *A Child's Christmas in Wales* and the radio play *Under Milk Wood* (a microcosm of Wales told through a day in the life of a seaside town), describe his homeland with nostalgia, humor, and a tinge of bitterness. Wales's literary heritage is preserved in the **National Library of Wales** in Aberystwyth (p. 459), which receives (by law) a copy of every book published in Welsh in the UK.

MUSIC

Music in "the land of song" has always occupied an important place in cultural life. Not much is known about early Welsh music, but the fact that the Welsh word **canu** means both "to sing" and "to recite poetry" suggests an intimate historical connection between the spoken and the sung word. There is little extant Welsh music dating prior to the 17th century; nonetheless, historians know of three traditional instruments in medieval Wales: the harp, the pipe (hornpipe or bagpipe), and the **crwth**, a six-stringed oblong instrument played with a bow. Wales began to lose its indigenous music tradition when Welsh harpists were incorporated into England's 16th-century Tudor court; traditional playing died out by the 17th century. In the 18th century, the rise of chapels led to an energetic singing culture, as Welsh folk tunes were adapted to sacred songs of praise to God, and hymn-writers such as **Ann Griffiths** made their mark. Their works, sung in unison in the 18th century, became the basis for the harmony **choral singing** of the 19th and 20th centuries that is now Wales's best-known musical tradition. While many associate the all-male choir with Wales, both single-sex and mixed choirs are an integral part of social life, and singing festivals like the **cymanfa ganu** are found throughout Wales.

Today Welsh musical life includes much more than the chorus. Cardiff's **St. David's Hall** (opened in 1983 and regarded as one of the finest venues in Britain) regularly hosts both Welsh and international orchestras, and the **Welsh National Opera** has established a worldwide reputation, with the internationally renowned tenor **Bryn Terfel** as its star performer. Modern Welsh composers of orchestral and vocal works such as **Alun Hoddinott** and **William Mathias** have won respect in the classical genre; Mathias composed an anthem for the wedding of Prince Charles and the late Lady Diana.

Rock music (in both English and Welsh), as elsewhere, has been the voice of youth, although the two most famous Welsh pop music exports are the no longer youthful **Tom** "What's New Pussycat" **Jones** and **Shirley Bassey.** The 1990s has seen the rise of bands from Wales which combine Brit-pop sounds with a sometimes fierce nationalism, led by the **Manic Street Preachers.** Other bands with their share of hits include **Catatonia** (led by the dynamic Cerys Mathews), **Stereophonics,** and the **Super Furry Animals.** Good examples of the Welsh rock sound include the Manics' *Everything Must Go* and Catatonia's *International Velvet.*

FFOOD

Traditional Welsh cooking relies heavily on leeks (the national symbol), potatoes, onions, dairy products, lamb (considered the best in the world), pork, fish, and seaweed. Soups and stews are ubiquitous and often good. **Cawl** is a complex broth, generally accompanied by bread; most soups brim with leeks and generous helpings of lamb or beef. **Welsh rarebit** (also called "Welsh rabbit") is buttered toast topped with a thick, cheesy mustard-beer sauce. It's the baked goods that tempt most. Wales abounds with unique, tasty **breads. Crempogen** (griddle cakes), resembling miniature pancakes, are made with sour cream, studded with currants, and topped with butter. The adventurous should sample **laverbread,** not really bread at all but a cake-like slab made of seaweed. Those with a sweet tooth will love **bara brith,** a fruit and nut bread served with butter, or **teisennau hufen** (cream cakes), fluffy doughnut-like cakes filled with freshly whipped cream. **Cwrw** (beer) is another Welsh staple; **Brains S.A.** (p. 428) is the major brewer.

LLANGUAGE

The word "Welsh" comes from the Old English *wealh,* or "foreigner," and the language does seem alien to most English speakers. Though modern Welsh borrows significantly from English for vocabulary, as a member of the Celtic family of languages, *Cymraeg* is based on a grammatical system more closely related to Cornish and Breton. Out of a total population of three million, more than 500,000

THE ROYAL NATIONAL EISTEDDFOD The Royal National Eisteddfod of Wales was established in 1568 by Elizabeth I to address her concern over the "intolerable multitude of vagrant and idle persons calling themselves minstrels, rhymers, and bards." Today the National Eisteddfod is a grand festival held the first week of August, alternating each year between a different location in North and South Wales. Its present incarnation owes much to the fancy of Iolo Morgannwg, poet and writer, who "invented" a tradition reaching back into the Druidic past of Wales. He created the *Gorsedd Beirdd*—a honorary group of great poets—who parade in white, green, and blue robes at two ceremonies, officiated by the "Archdruid," at which the winners of the crown and the chair (the two main poetry prizes) are introduced to the crowd amid much pomp. In recent years Eisteddfod events, which are conducted in Welsh, have made headsets available with translations for non-Welsh speakers. For information, write to the Eisteddfod Office, 40 Parc Ty Glas, Llanisien, Cardiff CF4 5WU.

people in Wales speak Welsh, and just over half are native speakers. Increasingly, Welsh is becoming the language of everyday life, especially north of Aberystwyth, but almost all Welsh speakers are bilingual.

Though English suffices nearly everywhere in Wales, it's a good idea to familiarize yourself with the language. Mastering Welsh pronunciation takes time. Welsh shares with German the deep, guttural **ch** heard in "Bach" or "loch." **Ll**—the oddest Welsh consonant—is produced by placing your tongue against the top of your mouth, as if you were going to say "l," and blowing. If this technique proves baffling, try saying "hl" (Hlan-GO-hlen for "Llangollen"). **Dd** is said either like the "th" in "there" or the "th" in "think" (hence the county of Gwynedd is pronounced the same way as Gwyneth Paltrow's first name). C and g are always hard. W is generally used as a vowel and sounds either like the "oo" in "drool" or "good." U is pronounced like the "e" in "he." Y trickily changes its sound with its placement in the word, sounding either like the "u" in "ugly" or the "i" in "ignoramus." F is spoken as a "v," as in "vertigo," and ff sounds exactly like the English "f." Emphasis nearly always falls on the penultimate syllable, and there are (happily) no silent letters.

Most Welsh place names are derived from prominent features of the landscape. *Afon* means river, *bedd* grave, *betws* or *llan* church or enclosure, *bryn* hill, *caer* fort, *ffordd* road, *glyn* glen or valley, *llyn* lake, *môr* sea, *mynydd* mountain, *pen* top or end, *pont* bridge, *tref* or *tre* town, and *ynys* island. *Mawr* is big, *bach* is little. The Welsh call their land *Cymru* (KUM-ree) and themselves *Cymry* ("compatriots"). Because of the Welsh system of letter mutation, many of these words will appear in usage with different initial consonants. **Welsh Words and Phrases,** p. 748, provides more information to aid you in your travels.

FFESTIVALS

The most significant of Welsh festivals is the **eisteddfod** (ice-TETH-vod), which literally means a sitting together or session. In practice, an eisteddfod is a competition of Welsh literature (chiefly poetry), music, and arts and crafts. Hundreds of local *eisteddfodau* (the plural) are held in Wales each year, generally lasting one to three days. The most important of these is the *Eisteddfod Genedlaethol Frenhinol Cymru*, or the **Royal National Eisteddfod** (see below). Every July (July 2-7 in 2001), Wales turns its attention to the **International Musical Eisteddfod,** held in the small town of Llangollen (see p. 486) in north Wales. This draws folk dancers, singers, and choirs from around the world for performance and competition. Though not focused on all things Welsh as is the Royal National Eisteddfod, the festival still epitomizes both Welsh hospitality and the Welsh love of music.

SOUTH WALES

South Wales is a master craftsman of natural landscapes. Its rivers carve out lush green valleys, its pastures quilt together patches gold and green, its peaks paint wild, dark silhouettes, and its coastline hews rugged cliffs over rocky waters and sandy beaches. With its proximity and accessibility to England, the Celtic history of this region has been diluted by foreign influences, but Welsh nationalism here grows stronger, and the native language is gradually slipping back into the mainstream. Although the region has suffered with the passing of the mining industry over the past thirty years, recent tourism has begun to revitalize the clustered market towns and romantically gritty harbors. Ancient legends, towering castles, fine beaches, cliff-hanging chapels, and spectacular walking trails link the cities, towns, and hidden treasures of South Wales. Along with sheep. Lots of sheep.

HIGHLIGHTS OF SOUTH WALES

CARDIFF Plunge into the vibrant cultural scene of one of Europe's youngest capitals, then scale the battlements of the majestic castles north of the city (p. 423).

VALES AND HILLS Hike through the Wye Valley for a fine view of silently majestic **Tintern Abbey** (p. 431), and proceed north to the land of wild ponies in **Brecon Beacons National Park** (p. 437).

HAY-ON-WYE Peruse the books in a literary wonderland that boasts the largest secondhand bookstore in the world (p. 435).

TENBY Sunbathe on the white beaches of the "Welsh Riviera," and climb the Coastal Path to St. Govan's Chapel (p. 445).

ST. DAVID'S Savor the soft light in Britain's holiest city, at the wild end of an ancient peninsula in cliff-mad **Pembrokeshire Coast National Park** (p. 452).

CARDIFF (CAERDYDD)   ☎029

Formerly a sleepy provincial town, Cardiff (pop. 340,000) burst on the scene in the late 19th century as the main shipping port for Welsh coal. At its height, the seaport was the world's busiest, with coal from 300 mines being shipped all over the world; the influx of sailors and merchants made the Tiger Bay neighborhood one of Britain's most cosmopolitan. The first settlers from abroad had arrived much earlier—stones from the 2000-year-old Roman town are still incorporated into the walls of Cardiff Castle. Today, Cardiff is the buzzing capital of a Welsh nation and culture very much on the rise. The city center brims with theaters and clubs while ancient Welsh artifacts stand proudly in the National Museum. Home to the National Assembly, site of a vibrant university community, and host of the 1999 Rugby World Cup, the city is growing up quickly to meet the changing needs of its proud populace and to secure a place among international cities.

▇ GETTING THERE AND GETTING AROUND

Trains: Central Station, Central Sq., south of the city center, behind the bus station. Ticket office open M-Sa 5:45am-9:30pm, Su 6:45am-9:30pm. Trains (☎ (08457) 484950) from: **Bristol** (45min., 3 per hr., £7); **Swansea** (1hr., 2 per hr., £8); **Bath** (1-1½hr., 3 per hr., £11.90); **London Paddington** (2hr., 1 per hr., £37); **Birmingham** (2¼hr., 4 per hr., £26.50); and **Edinburgh** (7hr., 7 per day, £100.80).

Buses: Central Station, on Wood St. **National Express** booking office and travel center. Show up at least 15min. before closing to book a ticket. Open M-Sa 7am-5:45pm, Su 9am-5:45pm. **National Express** (☎ (08705) 808080) from: **Birmingham** (2¼hr., 11 per day, £15.25); **Heathrow Airport** (3 hr., 11 per day, £28); **London** (3¼hr., 12 per day, £14); **Gatwick Airport** (4hr., 11 per day, £22); and **Manchester** (5½hr., 11 per day, £25). Check the invaluable *Wales Bus, Rail and Tourist Map and Guide* for further-information. Competing regional bus lines offer an array of day and week passes.

Local Transportation: Cardiff Bus (Bws Caerdydd; ☎ 2039 6521), in St. David's House on Wood St., runs an extensive 5-zone network of orange buses in Cardiff and the surrounding area. If you're far from the city center, show up 5min. early at the bus stop; schedules can be unreliable. Bus service ends M-Sa at 11:20pm, Su at 11pm. Fares 55p-£1.40; reduced fares for seniors and children; fares 5-25p cheaper M-F between 9:15am and 3:45pm. Week-long **Multiride Passes** available (£9.95, children £5). **City Rider** tickets, which allow one-day unlimited travel in the greater Cardiff area, can be purchased from drivers (£2.50, children £1.50, family £5). Open M and F 8am-5:30pm, Tu-Th and Sa 8:30am-5:30pm.

Taxi: Metro Cabs (☎ 2046 4646), and **Supatax** (☎ 2022 6644), both 24hr. Taxi stands in front of the train station and in front of the bus station on Wood St.

✴❷ ORIENTATION AND PRACTICAL INFORMATION

Cardiff Castle stands triumphantly in the city center, with verdant **Bute Park** stretching out behind it along the River Taff. To the east, along Park Pl., are the Civic Centre, university buildings, and the National Museum. Shops, pedestrian walks, and indoor arcades cluster between **St. Mary St.** and **Queen St.**, southeast of the castle. The bus and train stations lie south of the city center, by the River Taff. Farther south lie the waterfront developments of **Cardiff Bay.**

TOURIST, FINANCIAL, AND LOCAL SERVICES

Tourist Information Centre: 16 Wood St., opposite the bus station (☎ 2022 7281; www.cardiffmarketing.co.uk). Free accommodations list and detailed map. Open Jul.-Aug. M-Sa 9am-6pm, Su 10am-4pm; Sept.-Jun. M-Sa 9am-5pm, Su 10am-4pm.

Tours: Leisurelink (☎ 2052 2202). 19-site, 1hr. bus tour, departing every 20min., starting from the main gate of Cardiff Castle. Sept.-Jun. 10am-4pm; Jul.-Aug. 10am-4:40pm. Ticket holders get discounts at Cardiff Castle and Cardiff Cats. Purchase from driver or National Express window at bus station. £7, concessions £5.50, families £16.50, children under 5 free. **Cardiff Cats** (☎ 2071 2693) water buses tour Cardiff Bay, the River Taff, and the River Ely year-round. Call for schedules.

Financial Services: Numerous banks, including **Nationwide,** 26-27 St. Mary's St. (☎ 2042 0200). Open M-F 9am-5pm, Sa 9am-noon. Wheelchair accessible. **Thomas Cook,** 16 Queen St. (☎ 2042 2500). Open M-Th and Sa 9am-5:30pm, F 10am-5:30pm. **American Express,** 3 Queen St. (☎ (0870) 6001 0601). £2 commission for currency exchange. Open M and W-F 9am-5:30pm, Tu 9:30am-5:30pm, Sa 9am-5pm.

Launderette: Launderama, 60 Lower Cathedral Rd. (☎ 2022 8326). Open Th-Tu 9:30am-5:30pm.

EMERGENCY AND COMMUNICATIONS

Police: King Edward VIII Ave. (☎ 2022 2111).

Hospital: University Hospital of Wales, Heath Park, North Cardiff (☎ 2074 7747).

Internet Access: Cardiff Internet Café, 15-17 Wyndham Arcade (☎ 2023 2313), off St. Mary's St. 8am-11pm £1.50 for first 15min.; 11pm-8am £1; rate drops each consecutive 15min. All night deal £9. Discounts with YHA or ISIC cards. Open 24hr. **Cardiff Cybercafé,** 9 Duke St. (☎ 2023 5757), 1st staircase on the left in Crown Court alley. £2.50 per 30min., £4.50 per hr. Open M-F 10am-7pm, Sa 10am-6pm, Su 11am-5pm. **Ecocentrig,** Wood St. by the bus station (☎ 2064 0908). £2 per 30min.

Post Office: 2-4 Hill's St. (☎ 2022 7305), off The Hayes. Open M-Sa 9am-5:30pm. **Bureau de change.** Money Gram wiring service. **Postal Code:** CF10.

Phone Information: If you see Cardiff's old code of 01222 listed, just add "20" in front of the number (for example, (01222) 333333 would become (029) 2033 3333).

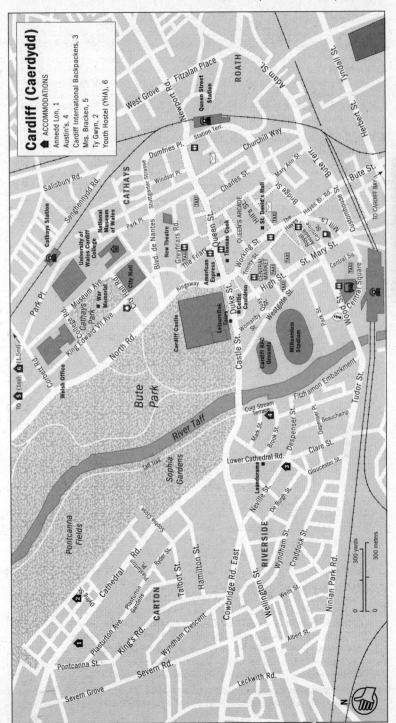

Cardiff (Caerdydd)

▲ ACCOMMODATIONS

Anned Lon, 1
Austin's, 4
Cardiff International Backpackers, 3
Mrs. Bracken, 5
Ty Gwyn, 2
Youth Hostel (YHA), 6

SOUTH WALES

ACCOMMODATIONS

Few budget accommodations lie in the center of Cardiff, but the tourist information centre (TIC) lists reasonably priced **B&Bs** (£16-18) on the outskirts and books
rooms for £1 and a 10% deposit on the entire stay. Many of the B&Bs line the lovely
Victorian **Cathedral Rd.** (a short ride on bus #32 or a 15min. walk from the castle)
are expensive (£20-25), but better bargains await on the side streets. Between June
and September, **Cardiff University Student Housing** (☎ 2087 4027; fax 2087 4990) lets
out dorm rooms (from £11).

Cardiff International Backpacker, 98 Neville St. (☎ 2034 5577; fax 2023 0404).
From Central Station, go down Wood St. and across the river, and turn right onto
Fitzham Embankment. Turn left at the end of the road onto Despenser St. This central
hostel has everything a backpacker could want—kitchen, a cable-TV lounge with pool
table, a bar where you can drink late into the night with the locals, and the occasional
summer barbecue on the roof garden. Internet access £1.50 for 15min., £2.50 for
30min., £4.50 per hr. After dark, take a cab or call for pickup from the station. Toast
and tea included (7:30-10am). Locker deposit £5. Curfew Su-Th 2:30am, F-Sa open
24hr. 4- to 8-bed single-sex dorms £13.50, 3 nights £35; doubles £35; triples £41.

YHA Cardiff, 2 Wedal Rd., Roath Park (☎ 2046 2303; fax 2046 4571), 20min. from city
center on bus #80, 80B, or 82 from Central Station stand D3. Cross the roundabout;
the hostel is next to the highway. Security code access after 11pm. Reception 7:30am-
11pm. Check-out 10am. Lockout 10-11am. Full breakfast included after March 2001.
Open Jan.-Nov. £14.05, under 18 £10.60, non-members £2 extra, students £1 off.

Annedd Lon, 157-159 Cathedral Rd. (☎ 2022 3349; fax 2064 0885). Proprietress
Maria Tucker expanded these Victorian houses to cater to budget travelers. The name
(pronounced ANN-eth LOHN) means "happy dwelling," which the cheerful mood and
comfortably elegant interiors confirm. All rooms have color TVs and sinks. £18 per person, or £20 with bath and continental breakfast. £1 discount for *Let's Go* users.

Ty Gwyn, 5 Dyfrig St. (☎/fax 2041 1988), off Cathedral Rd. "Ty Gwyn" means "White
House" in Welsh. Some of the enormous and well-sunned rooms have TVs. A gate at the
end of Dyfrig St. leads onto the gorgeous Taff Trail, where you can stroll along the rambling River Taff on your way to the castle. Breakfast £2.50, rooms £12.50 per person.

Mrs. Bracken, 302 Whitchurch Rd. (☎ 2062 1557). Take bus #35 from Wood St. opposite the Central Station and ask to be let off at McJohn's (an auto shop). The generous
Irish proprietress makes guests feel at home with a colorful garden, comfortable rooms,
and full breakfast. £16 per person.

Austin's, 11 Cold Stream Terr. (☎ 2037 7148; fax 2037 7158; stephen.hopkins1@vir-
gin.net). Off Castle St., a 5min. walk from the castle, opposite the stadium on the River
Taff. All rooms have color TV, tea service, and sinks. Singles £20; doubles with shower
£35, with bath £39.

Camping: Acorn Camping and Caravanning, Rosedew Farm, Ham Ln. South, Llantwit
Major (☎ (01446) 794024). Take a 1hr. ride on bus #X91 from Central Station; it's a
15min. walk from the stop at Ham Ln. South. Showers and laundry. May-Sept. £6 per
night; Oct.-Apr. £7 per night. Electricity £2. No extra charge for cars.

FOOD AND PUBS

Cardiff offers a reasonable variety of tasty options. Budget travelers gleefully
scour the many stalls of the Victorian **Central Market,** in an arcade between St.
Mary St. and Trinity St., where you can purchase anything from peaches to octopi.
(Open M-Sa 9am-5pm.) For late-night fish and chips and kebabs, head to **Dorothy's**
(open into the wee hours), or a host of similar shops on Caroline St. Pub grub is
another good option; "two for a fiver" deals get you two meals for £5.

The Prince of Wales, corner of St. Mary's St. and Wood St. (☎ 2064 4449). While the
sweeping spiral staircase and balconied second floor remind patrons of the building's

previous incarnation as an elegant theater, the recently renovated and sprawling Prince of Wales offers all the amenities one could hope for in a pub. Grab a Guinness (£1.79) from the enormous bar, call for a bap burger (£2.50) or a steak and mushroom pie (£4.99), or find a friend with whom to split the 2-meals-for-£6 deal. Blinking arcade games and enthusiastic rugby fans make for a lively evening scene. Handicap accessible. Open M-Sa 11am-11pm, Su noon-10:30pm. Food served until 1hr. before closing.

■ **Celtic Cauldron Wholefoods,** 47-49 Castle Arcade (☎ 2038 7185), across from the castle on Castle St. Traditional Welsh food, including faggots (unfortunately named but tasty meatballs dunked in gravy), rarebit (£4-5), and a good selection of vegetarian fare (£3.50-4.50). Finish the £9.50 Mighty Vegetarian For Two yourself and earn the title. The spicy fruit punch is just the thing for a rainy Welsh day (£1.10). Open June-Aug. M-Sa 8:30am-9pm, Su 10am-4pm; Sept.-May M-Sa 8:30am-6pm, Su 11am-4pm.

The Old Arcade, Church St. The post-game hangout for rugby players and fans alike, this pub offers brunch all day for £3.95. Or try the beef and Brains curry (£4.95)—that's Brains the beer, not the cerebral cortex. Open F-Sa 11am-1am, Su-Th 11am-11pm.

Bistro One, 4 Quay St. (☎ 2038 2914). Serves ffast ffood, Welsh style, over a small deli counter with a home-kitchen atmosphere. From jacket potatoes (£1.05) to a salty bacon sandwich (£1.60) to a sweet fruit and custard pie (99p), all orders have the option of takeaway. Open M-Sa 9am-4pm.

Crumbs, 33 David Morgan Arcade (☎ 2039 5007). Tucked away between St. Mary St. and The Hayes, this vegetarian restaurant has great salads (£2-3) and deliciously healthy curry and brown rice (£3.80). Open M-F 10am-3pm, Sa 10am-4pm.

SIGHTS

■ **CARDIFF CASTLE.** The interior of Cardiff Castle is no less flamboyant than the strutting peacocks inside the gates. The third Marquess of Bute employed William Burges, the most lavish of Victorian architect-designers, to restore the castle in a pretentious mock-medieval style. Each room is done in a different theme, from the Victorian nursery to the Arab room. At the back, the Norman keep presides over the grounds; climb the stairs for a sweeping view of Cardiff. The castle also contains the museums of the **1st Queen's Dragon Guards** and the **Welsh Regiment.** (Castle St. ☎ 2087 8100. Open daily Mar.-Oct. 9:30am-6pm; Nov.-Feb. 9:30am-4:30pm. Last entry 1hr. before closing. Tours Mar.-Oct. every 20min., last tour 5pm; Nov.-Feb. 5 tours daily, last tour 3:15pm. £5, students £4, seniors and children £3, families £14 including tours.)

CIVIC CENTRE. Across North Rd. from the castle, the stately white buildings of Cardiff's Civic Centre are set against the grassy lawns of Cathays Park. The giant leek in the sky is the belfry of Cardiff's **City Hall,** which contains a "Hall of Welsh Heroes," marble statues of Welsh historical figures: St. David, the patron saint of Wales, is at center stage, flanked by Owain Glyndwr, the Welsh rebel leader who somewhat unfortunately razed Cardiff in 1404. (Open M-Th 9am-5pm, F 9am-4:30pm.)

NATIONAL MUSEUM AND GALLERY OF WALES. experience the startling audio-visual display of "The Evolution of Wales," which speeds you through millennia of geological transformation. The museum also has a fine collection of European art, especially Impressionist works, and a good assortment of ancient stone crosses. (☎ 2039 7951. Open Tu-Su 10am-5pm. £4.50, concessions free.)

CARDIFF BAY. Formerly the world's busiest seaport, Cardiff Bay (bus #8 from Central Station stand W3) lay derelict for decades before massive waterfront development replaced coal docks with plans for high-tech futuristic buildings such as the National Assembly of Wales and the Millennium Centre, future home of the Welsh National Opera. The **Visitor Centre** has free advice and a fine view of the bay from inside its squished-cigar shape. (☎ 2046 3833. Open May-Sept. M-F 9:30am-5pm, Sa 10:30am-5pm; Oct.-Apr. M-F 9:30am-5pm, Sa 10:30am-5pm. Free.) The beautiful timber edifice of the **Norwegian Church Arts Centre,** built by Norwegian sailors in the 19th century, now hosts concerts and exhibitions. (Open daily 10am-

4pm and for evening events. Free.) Hordes of rambunctious children crowd into **Techniquest,** Britain's largest hands-on science discovery museum. *(☎ 2047 5475. Open M-F 9:30am-4:30pm, Sa-Su 10:30am-5pm. £5.50, concessions £3.80, families £15.75.)*

BRAINS BREWERY. Cardiff's signature Thursday odor emanates from here. Its specialty is Brains S.A. (Special Ale), known to locals as "Brains Skull Attack," and served proudly by many a pub in the city. Call and ask for the marketing department to inquire about tours. *(On Crawshay St. by the railway station. ☎ 2039 9022.)*

🎵 ENTERTAINMENT

CLUBS

Cardiff's club scene centers on the compact downtown area, so there's never much of a walk between clubs. Check out *Buzz!*, the free South Wales entertainment listing guide, to see what music clubs are playing, or take the local advice, head to St. Mary's St., and just follow the crowd. "Student night" often means good deals with hordes taking advantage of cheap cover and £1 drinks. After dark, don't hesitate to hail a cab, and avoid the docks and wharfs.

Clwb Ifor Bach (a.k.a. the **Welsh Club**), 11 Womanby St. (☎ 2023 2199). This manic, 3-tiered club hosts live bands three nights a week, a "rock inferno" on Tuesdays, and pop/jazz on Wednesdays. Bands like Catatonia got their start here, one of the city's major dance venues. Cover £2-8. Open M-Th until 2am, F until 3am, Sa until 3am.

Zeus, Greyfriars Rd. (☎ 2037 7014). A cavernous deco club with a smart casual dress code (no trainers). The party pulses around 6 bars, with 70s and 80s music Th, party music F, and club classics Sa. Cover £2.50-6, free before 10:30pm with flier. Open Tu-Th 9pm-2am, F-Sa 9pm-3am.

Philharmonic, 76-77 St. Mary St. (☎ 2023 0678). Mild-mannered pub by day, hopping club by night, the "Philly" blends wood panels with game machines and your basic disco music. Cover £2-4. Open M-W until 11pm as a pub; Th-Sa until 2am as a club.

Exit Club, 48 Charles St. (☎ 2064 9891). Where Cardiff's gay crowd dances and drinks the night away to chart and commercial favorites. Free before 9:30pm, £1.50 cover after. Open M-Su 6pm-2am.

ARTS

Cardiff's art scene spreads to all corners of the city. The elegant **Chapter Arts Centre,** on Market Rd. in Canton, features an eclectic program of dance, drama, gallery exhibitions, and film. Take bus #17, 18, or 19 from Castle St. up Cowbridge Rd. and get off opposite the Canton police station. (☎ 2030 4400. Box office open M-F 11am-8:30pm, Sa 1-8:30pm, Su 2-8:30pm. Cinema prices £4.20, students and seniors £2.90; discounts on early evening shows and W-Th matinees.) All types of music and dancing, including the **BBC National Orchestra of Wales,** are found in the modern **St. David's Hall,** The Hayes (☎ 2087 8444), considered one of Britain's finest concert venues (prices vary). Contemporary plays and dance are featured at the **Sherman Theatre** (☎ 2064 6900), on Senghennydd Rd., which also serves as the home for a high-quality young people's theater group. **The New Theatre,** Park Pl. (☎ 2087 8889), off Queen St., is home venue to the **Welsh National Opera,** but also features musicals, plays, dance, and children's theater on its classic turn-of-the-century stage. (Box office open M-Sa 10am-8pm).

SPORTS

The variety of adornments gracing the **John Bachelor Statue,** corner of Hill's St. and The Hayes, is a good gauge of the festive atmosphere in Cardiff. Scarves and hats signify rugby or football matches, and a clumsily held can of Brains S.A. is often a sign of sport-induced bacchanalia. **Rugby** games are played at the spectacular **Millennium Stadium** at Cardiff Arms Park; the 73,000 seater with a retractable roof hosted the Rugby World Cup final in November 1999. (☎ 2023 2661 for tour info.) If you're lucky enough to catch the city in the fervor of a local match, call the Welsh Rugby Union (☎ 2039 0111) for ticket info.

▶ DAYTRIPS FROM CARDIFF

Cardiff Bus whisks travelers to nearby **Barry Island** to visit the fairgrounds and bask on sandy beaches (bus #354, 30min. boat to the island, 1 per hr., £2 return). For those seeking the pastoral diversion, the 55 mi. **Taff Trail** winds from Cardiff Bay through the Taff Valley to the heart of the Brecon Beacons National Park (see p. 435). The Cardiff TIC has a free pamphlet on the route.

◪ CAERPHILLY CASTLE. Eight miles north of Cardiff, this largest of Welsh castles floats above its moats and mossy grove. Begun in 1268 by Norman warlord Gilbert de Clare, its water systems, concentric stone walls, catapults, and pivoting drawbridges made it the most technologically advanced fortification of its time. Today its main tower leans a precarious 10 degrees from the vertical, and ducks and kingfishers besiege the grounds. (*Take the train (20min., M-Sa 2 per hr., £2.50), or hourly bus #26, 71, or 72 from Central Station stand B3, and step off in the shadow of a massive curtain wall across the moat. ☎ 2088 3143. Open June-Sept. daily 9:30am-6pm; Apr.-May and Oct. daily 9:30am-5pm; Nov.-Mar. M-Sa 9:30am-4pm, Su 11am-4pm. £2.50, concessions £2, families £7.*)

MUSEUM OF WELSH LIFE. Four miles west of Cardiff and spread across **St. Fagan's Park,** the museum (called Amgueddfa Werin Cymru in Welsh) is home to 30 authentic buildings from all corners of Wales, reassembled into an interactive telling of the Welsh story. The iron-workers' cottages, Victorian schoolhouse, mills, saddlery, and other sites arranged across the 100 green acres of St. Fagan's Park are busily tended by traditionally-garbed craftspeople. The quieter St. Fagan's Castle also graces the grounds, surrounded by gardens and reflecting pools. (*Bus #32 runs to the museum hourly from Central Station stand B1. ☎ 2057 3500. Open daily June-Sept. 10am-6pm; Oct.-May 10am-5pm. June-Sept. £5.50, students and seniors £3.90, children £3.20, families £14; Oct.-May £4.50, concessions £2.65, families £10.25.*)

LLANDAFF CATHEDRAL. Two miles northwest of the city center near the River Taff, the cathedral stands unassumingly amid stone paths and natural wildflower hedges. Built by the Normans, used by Cromwell as an alehouse, restored by the Victorians, and gutted by a German bomb in 1941, the cathedral is now an architectural mince pie—a stern and solid Norman arch behind the altar is overshadowed by an intrusive reinforced-concrete arch from 1957. Worth a longer gaze is the oft-overlooked **Rosetti triptych** (to the left as you step in), and the nearby garden within the ivy-covered ruins of the **Castle of the Bishops of Llandaff.** (*Take bus #25 from Castle St. or bus #33, 62A, or 133 15min. from Central Station, or walk down Cathedral Rd. and through Llandaff Fields; turn left onto Western Ave., right onto Cardiff Rd., and right onto Llandaff High St. ☎ 2056 4554. Open M-Sa 7am-7pm, Su 7am-8pm.*)

CASTELL COCH. Like its cousin in Cardiff, this 13th century castle wears the signature ornate style of Lord Bute and his Victorian renovator Burgess, with morphing birds, butterflies, and stars decorating one ceiling, lascivious monkeys another, and scenes from *Aesop's Fables* a third. Unlike the other Cardiff castles, Castell Coch peers down from a secluded forest hillside, and connections to the Taff Trail lend themselves to a bit of hiking in the area. (*Take bus #26 (25min., 1 per hr.) from the Central Station to the village of Tongwynlais, where a brisk 15min. walk up Mill St. brings you to the castle, or bus #126 (M-F 5 per day), which unloads directly at the castle gate. ☎ 2081 0101. Open Apr.-Sept. daily 9:30am-6pm; Oct. daily 9:30am-5pm; Nov.-Mar. M-Sa 9:30am-4pm, Su 11am-4pm. £2.50, concessions £2, families £7; audio tour 50p extra.*)

WYE VALLEY

Stitching back and forth across the Welsh-English border, the Wye River (Afon Gwy) carves a valley long sought out for its fertile tranquility. Cistercian monks found seclusion from the world's impurities in the lap of the mountains, and Wordsworth escaped the "fever of the world" in its "steep cliffs," "orchard tufts," and "pastoral farms." Today visitors hike, peddle, paddle, and motor through green lands yet unsullied by growing tourism. With legend-rich castles, abbeys, and trails tracing the sylvan Wye from its spring in central Wales to its confluence with the Severn south of Chepstow, the valley merits inclusion in any itinerary.

◪ GETTING THERE AND GETTING AROUND

The valley is best entered from the south, at Chepstow. **Trains** (☎ (08457) 484950) chug to Chepstow from **Cardiff** and **Newport** (40min.; M-Sa 8 per day, Su 7 per day; £5.20). **National Express** (☎ (08705) 808080) **buses** ride to Chepstow from: **Newport** (30min., 6 per day, £2.25); **Cardiff** (50min., 5 per day, £3.25); and **London** (2¼hr., 10 per day, £16.50). **Stagecoach Red and White** bus #69 loops between **Chepstow, Tintern,** and **Monmouth** (M-F 7 per day, Sa 8 per day, Su 4 per day). **Phil Anslow Travel** (☎ (01495) 767999) bus #83 careens from **Monmouth** to **Abergavenny** (6 per day, 40min.). One-day **Roverbus** passes (£5, concessions £4), available on Stagecoach buses, might save you money. There is little Sunday bus service in the valley. Consult the indispensable *Wales Bus, Rail and Tourist Map and Guide* or the even more indispensable *Discover the Wye Valley on Foot and by Bus* in area tourist information centres (TICs) for schedules. **Hitchhiking** is said to be possible on the A466 in the summer; some stand near the entrance to Tintern Abbey or by the Wye Bridge in Monmouth. *Let's Go* does not recommend hitchhiking.

◪ HIKING IN THE WYE VALLEY

The region rewards travellers who follow the Wye's example and go wandering through the woods, thus gaining the most stunning vistas of the valley. Two main trails follow the river on either side, the Wye Valley Walk and the Offa's Dyke Path. TICs disperse trail pamphlets and the *Walking Wales* guide (free) with good walk suggestions, and an Ordnance Survey Landranger 162 map (1:25,000; £6) provides specific details of the terrain in the lower Wye Valley and Royal Forest of Dean.

WYE VALLEY WALK. To the west of the river, the walk treks north from Chepstow via Hay-on-Wye to Prestatyn along wooded cliffs and farmland. At **Symond's Yat,** 25km north of Chepstow, the hills drop away to a panorama of the Wye's horseshoe bends, seven counties, and a white-faced cliff where peregrine falcons make their eyrie every spring. *(Bus #W73 from Coleford Square DIY Shop, 6 per day.)* **Eagle's Nest Lookout,** 3 mi. north of Chepstow, also has a sweeping valley view, and from here 365 steps descend steeply to the bank.

OFFA'S DYKE PATH. To the east of the river, the path winds 177 mi. along the entire length of the Welsh-English border, and is said to have originally been a trench dug to keep the English out. All trails have walks of varying length and difficulty; trail maps should be consulted before setting out, as some paths change grade suddenly and without warning. For info on the path, consult the **Offa's Dyke Association** (☎ (01547) 528753).

ROYAL FOREST OF DEAN. This 20,000-acre forest, once the hunting grounds of Edward the Confessor and Williams I and II, lies just east across the English border. For forest information, contact **Forest Enterprise** on Bank St. in Coleford, England, across the river from Monmouth. (☎ (01549) 833057. Open M-Th 8:30am-5pm, F 8:30am-4pm.) Or try the **Coleford tourist information centre,** High St. (☎ (01594) 812388. Open M-Sa 10am-5pm.) If you're hiking between towns, some B&B owners will send your luggage on to the next B&B.

CHEPSTOW (CAS-GWENT)   ☎01291

Chepstow's strategic position at the mouth of the River Wye and the base of the Welsh-English border made it an important fortification in Norman times and a frontier town during the English Civil War. **Chepstow Castle,** Britain's oldest stone castle, was built by Earl William, a Norman companion of William the Conqueror who undoubtedly had too much pocket money. Its craggy face grows seamlessly

LET THEM EAT CHEESE Don't be alarmed if you wake from an afternoon nap at St. Briavel's youth hostel to a rhythmic chant. The villagers gathered across the street leaping at flying chunks of cheese aren't preparing to storm the castle, but rather engaging in a mysterious ceremony unique to this tiny village.

In the 17th century, the English Earl of Hereford withdrew the local villagers' right to gather wood, but when his compassionate wife protested, the Earl backed down. As a gesture of thanks, his wife suggested that each villager contribute a penny to feed the poor. The ritual has since evolved from its charitable roots, and now residents from all social strata feast on the hurled cheese. Every Whitsunday, bread and cheese are distributed outside the Roman church to this chant: "St. Briavel's water and Whyrl's wheat are the best bread and water King John ever eat."

from the cliff it stands on, staring sternly across the Wye to England. The old **town wall,** in some places as thick as 7 ft. and as high as 15 ft., was designed as an extension of the castle. (☎ 624065. Open Apr.-May and Oct. daily 9:30am-5pm; Jun.-Sept. daily 9:30am-6pm; Nov.-Mar. M-Sa 9:30am-5pm, Su 11am-4pm. £3, concessions £2, families £18.) The second highest rising tide in the world leaves boats stranded on the muddy banks under the **Wye Bridge** at the end of Bridge St. It was from these banks, at the **Wye Knot,** that Welsh emigrants and criminals set sail (or were shipped off) for Australia and America. The **Chepstow Festival,** held throughout July every other year, features open-air Shakespeare and musical events punctuated by fully armored battles in the castle. Smaller exhibitions make up the odd years.

Chepstow's **train station** lies on Station Rd., and **buses** stop above the town gate in front of the Somerfield supermarket. Both stations are unstaffed. The **tourist information centre** faces the castle from Bridge St. (☎ 623772; www.chepstow.co.uk. Open daily Apr.-Sept. 10am-5:15pm; Oct.-Mar. 10:30am-3:30pm.) **The Travel House,** 9 Moor St., sells National Express tickets. (☎ 623031. Open M-F 9am-5:30pm, Sa 9am-4pm.) Services include: **Barclays bank,** Beaufort Sq. (open M-Tu and Th-F 9am-4:30pm, W 10am-4:30pm); **Launder,** 36 Steep St., just up the hill from the train station (self-serve washers 80p per load, driers £2.80; ☎ 626372; open M-F 8:30am-7pm, Sa 9:15am-5:30pm, Su 10am-4pm); the **police** (☎ 623993), on Moor St. across from the post office; the **Community Hospital** (24hr. ☎ 638800), west of town on Mounton Road, and the **post office,** Albion Sq. (☎ 622607; open M-F 9am-5:30pm, Sa 9am-12:30pm). **Postal code:** NP16.

The nearest **YHA Youth Hostel** is at **St. Briavel's Castle,** in England (see p. 432). In Chepstow, be welcomed at ▨ **Lower Hardwick House,** 300 yd. up Mt. Pleasant from the bus station, by the charismatic Eileen Grassby. Her lemon-yellow Georgian mansion delights in its arboreal back gardens, peppered with peeping sculptures. Inside, large windows overlook the gardens and the vista across the river from every comfortable room. (☎ 622162. Singles £18, doubles £30-36. Campers may pitch in the gardens for £5 per tent, with continental breakfast £7.50.) Or visit **Langcroft,** 71 St. Kingsmark Ave., by the Castle Dell, where the Langsleys will make you at home in their peaceful neighborhood, and you can relax in the conservatory and peer at lurking fish or your own TV. (☎/fax 625569. £17 per person.)

TINTERN ☎01291

Five miles north of Chepstow on the A466, the haunting arches of ▨ **Tintern Abbey** "connect the landscape with the quiet of the sky," as Wordsworth wrote in his famous poem composed a few miles north. Built by white-robed Cistercian monks in the 12th and 13th centuries as a center for religious austerity, the abbey became the richest in Wales, until Henry VIII dissolved it and it fell into romantic, ivy-clad ruin. Gaze up through the vast yet delicately detailed windows; their stained glass long since vanished, the windows provide an immediate connection with the nearby hills and dense trees that makes the abbey seem much bigger than it actually is. Arrive in the morning to avoid hordes of tourists and Wordsworth devotees. (☎ 689251. Open June-Sept. daily 9:30am-6pm; Apr.-May and Oct. daily 9:30am-

5pm; Nov.-Mar. M-Sa 9:30am-4pm, Su 11am-4pm. £2.40, concessions £1.90, families £6.70.) If crowds overwhelm, cross the iron footbridge and head for the hills. Marked paths lead to **Offa's Dyke** (45min.) and to **Devil's Pulpit** (1hr.), a huge stone from which Satan is said to have tempted the monks as they worked in the fields.

A mile north of the abbey on the A466 lies Tintern's **Old Station.** Once a stop on the Wye Valley Line, the out-of-service train station now holds a series of train carriages, one of which holds the **tourist information centre.** (☎/fax 689566. Open Apr.-Oct. daily 10:30am-5:30pm.) The nearest **YHA Youth Hostel** is **St. Briavel's Castle,** 4 mi. northeast of Tintern across the English border. Once King John's hunting lodge, later a fortress against the marauding Welsh, the 12th-century castle maintains its medieval character. Historic flooring spans the TV lounge, 15th-century graffiti marks one dorm's walls, and ancient stone walls line the gardens. From the A466 (bus #69 from Chepstow) or Offa's Dyke, follow signs for two miles from Bigsweir Bridge to St. Briavel's. (☎ (01594) 530272; fax 530849. Lockout 10am-5pm. Curfew 11:30pm. Open daily year-round. Breakfast £3.20, pack lunch £2.80, dinner £4.80. Dorms £10.85, under 18 £7.40) The Wye courses just beyond the front hedge of the 400-year-old **Wye Barn Bed and Breakfast,** 200 yd. north of the abbey along a dirt road. All the newly renovated rooms have a river view. (☎ 689456. Singles £22.50, £25 with bath; doubles with bath £50.) Off the A466 at the village, next to the Moon and Sixpence Pub, **The Old Rectory** has a magnificent brick fireplace and water from its own spring. (☎ 689519; fax 689939. Singles £17.50, with bath £20; lower rates for longer stays.) **Campers** can use the field opposite the train station. (Toilets and water, no shower. £1.50 per person. Parking 50p per 3hr.)

HAY-ON-WYE (Y GELLI)   ☎01497

Left to its own devices, Hay-on-Wye might still be just a pretty freckle on the scenic toes of the Black Mountains. In the ambitious mind of Richard Booth, however, there were bigger plans on the books for this tiny town. After establishing his own secondhand bookstore in 1961 on one of Hay's ancient, narrow streets, Booth set about transforming Hay into the world-renowned Town of Books. From Hay Castle he now reigns as king over the 40 secondhand and antiquarian bookshops attracting browsers to the busy stone alleyways, where books literally spill out of tiny shops. This smallest of towns holds the largest of literary festivals every May, when book fervor threatens to ignite the grassy farmlands on its outskirts.

◪⊿ GETTING THERE AND PRACTICAL INFORMATION. The closest **train station** is in Hereford, England (see p. 276). **Stagecoach Red and White** (☎ (01633) 266336) **bus** #39 stops at Hay as it travels between **Hereford** and **Brecon** (1hr., M-Sa 5 per day, £2.80-4.10). On Sundays, **Yeoman's** (☎ (01432) 356202) bus #40 runs the same route twice (£4-5). The **tourist information centre,** on Oxford Rd. next to the bus stop books beds for £2. (☎ 820144; www.hay-on-wye.co.uk. Open daily Apr.-Oct. 10am-1pm and 2-5pm; Nov.-Mar. 11am-1pm and 2-4pm.) A **Barclays bank** stands on Broad St. (☎ 820543. Open M-F 10am-4pm.) **Celtic Canoes,** Newport St., rents and gives canoe instruction. (☎ 847422, mobile ☎ (0966) 505286. £20 per day, £13 per half-day.) The **post office** is at 3 High Town. (Open M and W-F 9am-1pm and 2-5:30pm, Tu 9am-1pm, Sa 9am-12:30pm.) **Postal code:** HR3 5AE.

◪◩ ACCOMMODATIONS AND FOOD. The **YHA Youth Hostel** nearest to Hay-on-Wye lies eight miles out of town at Capel-y-Ffin (see p. 438). Originally a 16th-century coaching inn, **The Bear,** Bear St., upholds tradition with inglenook fireplaces, serving crempog las (Welsh pancakes) with the home-cooked breakfast. (☎ 821302; fax 820506; http://home.clara.net/jonfield/thebear. Singles £22; doubles with bath £27.) Or try sleeping under the solid beams of 16th-century **Brookfield,** Brook St., where each room gets its own Welsh name. (☎ 820518. Singles £19; doubles £32.) If you're willing to walk, head straight for the beautifully restored **Old Post Office,** two miles away in the sleepy village of Llanigon. Take Brecon Rd. (the B4350) out of Hay, turn left after 1½ mi. at the Llanigon sign, follow the road for a

HAY'S DAY Hay-on-Wye stands on the England-Wales border. This indeterminate status, and the compelling logic that the independent city-states of Ancient Greece and Renaissance Italy were the world's greatest civilizations ever, led to Richard Booth's grand April Fool's joke: a declaration of Hay's independence on April 1, 1977. Booth, owner of the largest secondhand bookstore in the world (Booth's Books brings in more books than every university and public library in Wales combined), made his proclamation as an attack on bureaucracy and big government and managed to draw national notice. Now Booth and his wife reign as King and Queen of Hay Castle. Turn up in Hay around April 1 and join in the Independence Day celebrations.

half-mile, and turn left just before you reach the primary school; the former Royal Mail outpost is opposite the church. You'll be rewarded with rustic Welsh furniture and delicious English and vegetarian breakfasts. (☎ 820008; www.hay-on-wye.co.uk/oldpost. Doubles £34, with bath £50.) It's easy to **camp** near Hay along the **Wye Valley Walk** or **Offa's Dyke** (see p. 430). **Radnor's End Campsite**, on a tiny valley plateau, is the closest to town; cross Bridge St. and go 500 yd. to the right towards Clyro. (☎ 820780. £3 per person.)

If you're hungry, sit outside **The Granary,** Broad St., and enjoy generous portions of homecooked food. (☎ 820790. Main courses £4.50-7.50. Open daily June-Aug. 9:30am-10pm, Sept.-May 10am-5:30pm.) **Oscars,** High Town (☎ 821193), specializes in scones, but also serves tasty meals, with especially good vegetarian fare (£2.50-5.20). Shoot pool as you wait for your grub (£2.40-6) at the **Wheatsheaf Inn,** Lion St. (☎ 820186. Open for food daily noon-2:30pm, M-F 6-9pm, Sa 6-8pm.)

🖾 **SIGHTS.** After weathering eight centuries of wars, fires, and neglect, Hay's **Norman castle** has finally been conquered by mobs of unruly first editions, courtesy of another branch of Richard Booth's bookshops (see above). The town's myriad other bookshops are a browser's paradise. Some specialize, like the **Poetry Bookshop,** Brook St., while others *specialize*, notably B&K Books and its shelves dedicated to beekeeping. Others vend a motley general collection of used books. Fortunately, the **Acedia Booksearch** service, 46 Lion St., promises to help readers with specific missions. To remind outsiders that they *really like books*, the townspeople throw a 10-day **literary festival** each year at the end of May (May 25-June 3 in 2001), during which members of the literati such as Harold Pinter and Toni Morrison give readings. Literary buffs, be forewarned: festival crowds strain accommodations, and many readings charge hefty admission prices (£4-10).

ABERGAVENNY (Y FENNI) ☎01873

The market town of Abergavenny (pop. 10,000) styles itself as the traditional gateway to Wales. Many visitors take this literally and dash right through the gateway on their way to the hills; the Black Mountains in the eastern third of Brecon Beacons National Park and the Seven Hills of Abergavenny invite hikers to romp. In 1175, the Norman Lord William de Braose invited the Welsh chieftains to his table at Abergavenny Castle, and then killed them once they were well-sated. Dining out in Abergavenny hasn't been the same since.

🄴 **GETTING THERE. Trains** (☎ (08457) 484950) run from: **London** (2½hr., every 2hr., Sa-Th £33, F £39.50); **Newport** (25min., 22 per day; £4.80); **Chepstow** (30min., every 2hr., £8.30); **Hereford** (30min., 1 per hr., £5.60); **Cardiff** (40min., 19 per day, £7.30); and **Bristol** (1¼hr., every 2hr., £7.60). From the train station, turn right at the end of Station Rd., and walk 15min. along Monmouth Rd. to get to town. The **bus station** sits on Monmouth Rd., by the tourist information centre. **Stagecoach Red and White** (☎ (01633) 266336) **buses** roll in from: **Hereford** (#20, 1hr., M-Sa 5 per day, £3.39); **Newport** (#20, 1hr., 12 per day, £3.23); **Brecon** (#21, 1hr., 6 per day, £3.06); and **Cardiff** (#X4, 2¼hr., 13 per day, £3.92). **Gwent Travel,** 55a Frogmore St., sells **National Express** tickets. (☎ 857666. Open M-F 9am-5pm, Sa 9am-4pm.)

⚑ PRACTICAL INFORMATION. The well-stocked **tourist information centre** (TIC; ☎ 857588; fax 850217; www.abergavenny.co.uk; open daily Apr.-Oct. 10am-5:30pm; Nov.-Mar. 9:30am-4:30pm) shares space with the **National Park Information Centre** on Lower Cross St., by the bus station. (☎ 853254; open Mar.-Oct. daily 9:30am-5:30pm.) Purchase camping supplies at **Crickhowell Adventure Gear,** 14 High St. (☎ 856581. Open M-Sa 9am-5:30pm.) Services include: **Barclays bank,** 57 Frogmore St. (open M-Tu and Th-F 9am-4:30pm, W 10am-4:30pm); the **police** (☎ 852273), Tudor St.; the **hospital,** Nevill Hall on Brecon Rd. (☎ 852091); **Internet access** at **Celtic Computer Systems,** 20 Monk St. (☎ 858111; £4 per hr.; open M-Sa 9am-5:30pm); and the **post office,** with a **bureau de change,** St. John's Sq., where Tudor St. abuts Castle St. (open M-F 9am-5:30pm, Sa 9am-12:30pm). **Postal code:** NP7 5EB.

⚑⚑ ACCOMMODATIONS AND FOOD. Expensive **B&Bs** (£18-20 per person) wait on **Monmouth Rd.;** you're better off trying **Hereford Rd.,** 15min. from town. From the TIC, approach town and turn right at the Great George pub, continue on Monk St., and keep walking. The **Ivy Villa Guest House,** 43 Hereford Rd., provides TVs in rooms and English breakfast. (☎ 852473; ivy.villaguest-house@btinternet.com. Singles £16; doubles £30.) Musical **Mrs. Bradley,** 10 Merthyr Rd., where Frogmore St. becomes Brecon Rd., keeps a house with a TV in every room. (☎ 852206. £10 per person with continental breakfast, £13 with cooked breakfast.)

On Tuesday, Friday, and Saturday mornings, the bustling **market** in Market Hall on Cross St. offers fresh fruit and vegetables, baked goods, and livestock trading. To sample the market wares' cooked incarnations, drop by **Harry's Carvery** on St. John's St., which loads crusty baguettes with fillings like honey-baked gammon and Stilton cheese for £1-3.25. (☎ 852766. Open M-Sa 8:30am-4pm.) For a traditional pub with surprisingly good grub, head for **The Greyhound Vaults,** Market St., and let the smell of cheese ploughman lunches (£5.95) and black pudding fritters (£3.85) draw you in. (☎ 858549. Food served W-M 11:30am-2pm and 7-9pm.) At **Pinch the Baker's,** 16 Frogmore St., you can enjoy freshly baked Welsh cakes (20p) and filled sandwiches (£1.50-2) on soft bread. (☎ 853139. Open M-Sa 8am-5pm.)

◉⚑ SIGHTS AND HIKING. Abergavenny's **castle** is a ruin, with views of the valley and mountains looming in the gaps between its walls. A 19th-century hunting lodge on the grounds houses the **Abergavenny Museum,** where you can traipse through a Victorian Welsh farmhouse kitchen. (☎ 854282. Museum open Mar.-Oct. M-Sa 11am-1pm and 2-5pm, Su 2-5pm; Nov.-Feb. M-Sa 11am-1pm and 2-4pm. Grounds open daily 8am-dusk. £1, seniors and students 75p, children free.)

Abergavenny's real attractions lie in the hills that ring it; the excellent *Walks from Abergavenny* pamphlet (£2), available from the park information centre, details mountain climbs. **Blorenge** (1833 ft., 559m), 2½ mi. southwest of town and the only thing that rhymes with orange, is by far the most massive of the hills. A path begins off the B4246, traversing valley woodlands to the upland area; it climbs the remaining 1500 ft. in 4½ miles. Climbers adore **Sugar Loaf** (1955 ft., 596m) 2½ mi. northwest; the trailhead to the top starts about a mile west of town on the A40. Many report that hitching a ride to the car park and starting the hike from there is a way to save energy for the hike to the summit. *Let's Go* does not recommend hitchhiking. The path to **Skirrid Fawr** (or the Holy Mountain; 1595 ft., 486m) lies northeast of town and starts about 2 mi. down the B4521. The tourist information centre provides information about **pony trekking,** popular around Abergavenny, in the comprehensive *Activity Wales* guide. Reputable local establishments include **Grange Trekking Centre** (☎ 890215; £15 per half-day for beginners, including instruction; £22.50 per day), **Werr Riding Center** (☎ 810899), and **Llanthony Riding and Trekking** (☎ 890359; £10 per half-day, no experience necessary).

DAYTRIPS FROM ABERGAVENNY

If traveling to the sights near Abergavenny by bus, a **network rider pass** ($4.50 per day for travel on all Stagecoach Red and White, Phil Anslow, and Cardiff buses) is often even cheaper than return tickets.

■BIG PIT MINING MUSEUM. The silent hillsides of Blaenavon, 5 mi. southwest of Abergavenny, oversee a green valley scarred by fields of black. Here, this museum remembers the industrial age that so changed the face of these hills and of Wales. Descend a 300 ft. shaft to the subterranean workshops of a 19th-century coal mine operative until 1980, where ex-miners guide you through with stories as grim as the mine. Dress warmly and wear sensible shoes. *(Take bus #X4 (13 per day) to Bryn Mawr then #30 to Blaenavon; #42 also directly from Abergavenny (Tu and F-Sa 3 per day, M and W-Th 1 per day in the morning).* ☎ *(01495) 790311. Open daily Mar.-Nov. 9:30am-5pm. Last guided tour 3:30pm. £5.75, seniors £5.50, children £3.95, families £17; under 5 admitted free to surface facilities, not admitted underground.)*

LLANTHONY PRIORY. All the megaliths in the Black Mountains are believed to point toward the ruined 12th-century Llanthony Priory, perhaps to help errant friars find their way home. Founder William de Lacy laid aside both hunting gear and aristocratic title upon finding the site, retiring to a life of religious contemplation amidst its humbling natural beauty. The **YHA Capel-y-Ffin** (see p. 438) is another 4 mi. *(Take Stagecoach Red and White bus #20 or follow the A465 to Llanfihangel Crucorney, where the B4423 begins. Most walk and some hitch the last 6 mi. to the priory (Let's Go does not recommend hitchhiking). Always open. Free.)*

RAGLAN CASTLE. About halfway between Abergavenny and Monmouth on the A40 lies Raglan Castle, a baby among Welsh castles—it's only 565 years old. Raglan was designed more for residential living than actual defense, as the absence of arrow slits suggests. *(Take Phil Anslow bus #83 from Abergavenny or Monmouth (20min., M-Sa 6 per day, Su 4 per day), or #60 from Monmouth or Newport (40min. from Newport, 4 per day, £3-4.20).* ☎ *(01291) 690228. Open June-Sept. daily 9:30am-6pm; Apr.-May daily 9:30am-5pm; Oct.-Mar. M-Sa 9:30am-4pm, Su 11am-4pm. £2.40, concessions £1.90, families £6.70.)*

BRECON (ABERHONDDU) ☎01874

Just north of the mountains, Brecon (pop. 8000) is the best base for hiking through the craggy Brecon Beacons. This quiet market town takes on a temporary vibrancy with an exceptional **jazz festival** during the second weekend in August, attracting such luminaries as Branford Marsalis, Keb' Mo', and Van Morrison.

▐ GETTING THERE. Brecon has no bus or train station, but **buses** arrive regularly at **The Bulwark,** the central square, from spots in the area. Ask for bus schedules at the tourist information centre. **National Express** (☎ (08705) 808080) **bus** #509 runs once a day from **London** (5hr., $17.50) via Cardiff (1¼hr., $2.75). **Stagecoach Red and White** (☎ (01633) 266336) **buses** come into Brecon from: **Swansea** (#63, 1½hr., M-Sa 3 per day, Su 4 per day, $3.66); **Merthyr Tydfil** (#43, 35min., M-Sa 6 per day, $2.40); and **Abergavenny** and **Newport** (#21, M-Sa 6 per day, $2-4). To reach Brecon from **Cardiff**, take the #X4 to Merthyr Tydfil and transfer to #43 (2 per hr., $3.32). Bus #39 comes in from **Hereford** via **Hay-on-Wye** (M-Sa 5 per day, $2.80-4.10); on Sundays, **Yeomans** (☎ (01432) 356202) follows the same route (#40, 2 per day, $4-5). Along the A40 from Abergavenny or the A470 from Merthyr Tydfil, **hitchhikers** stay near intersections (*Let's Go* does not recommend hitchhiking).

▟ PRACTICAL INFORMATION. The **tourist information centre** (TIC) is located in the Cattle Market Car Park; walk through Bethel Sq. off Lion St. to the car park. (☎ 622485; fax 625256. Open daily Easter-Oct. 10am-6pm, Nov.-Easter 9:30am-5:30pm.) The TIC stocks an abundance of pamphlets, but none as, er, interesting as *Aircraft Crash Sites in the National Park* ($2), available at the **Brecon Beacons National Park Information Centre** in the same building. (☎/fax 623156. Open

SOUTH WALES

Apr.-Sept. daily 9:30am-5:30pm.) **Brecon Bicycle Centre,** High St., rents mountain bikes. (☎ 622651. £15 per day, £25 per weekend.) **Millets,** 31-32 High St., has all the camping supplies you'll need. (☎ 623462. Open M-Sa 9am-5:30pm.) Services include: **Barclays bank,** at the corner of St. Mary's St. and High St. (open M-Tu and Th-F 9am-4:30pm, W 10am-4:30pm); **Internet access** at **123 Computers,** 11 Watergate (☎ 611929; 99p per 30min.); **Mel's Laundry Bin,** St. Mary's St. (☎ 610099; open M-Tu and Th-Sa 9am-6:30pm, W 1-6:30pm); the **police** (☎ 622331), Lion St.; and the **post office,** 6 Church Ln., off St. Mary St. (☎ 611113; open M-Tu and Th-F 8:30am-5:30pm, W and Sa 8:30am-2:30pm). **Postal code:** LD3 7AS.

▌ ACCOMMODATIONS. Only 3min. from town, **The Watton** is lined with B&Bs (£14-17). If you plan to visit during mid-August, book far in advance—the Jazz Festival claims every pillow in town. The nearest hostel is **YHA Ty'n-y-Caeau** (tin-uh-KAY-uh), 3 mi. from Brecon. From the town center, walk down The Watton and continue until you reach the A40-A470 roundabout. Follow the branch leading to Abergavenny on the A40. Just after the roundabout, follow the footpath tucked away to the left to the hamlet of **Groesffordd** (grohs-FORTH); then turn left onto the main road. Continue for 10-15min., bearing left at the fork; the hostel is the second house on the right. The Brecon-Abergavenny bus will stop at a footpath that leads to Groesffordd if you ask the driver. (☎ 665270. Open July-Aug. daily; mid-Feb. to June and Sept.-Nov. M-Sa. Dorms £9, under 18 £6.20.) Itinerants can seek respite in the spacious interiors of **Walker's Rest,** 18 Bridge St. Warm yourself by the fireplace in the bathroom and by the warm glow of TVs in each room. (☎ 625993. Singles £15; doubles £30.) **Mrs. J. Thomas's** signless B&B, 13 Alexandra Rd., rests behind the TIC. The warm proprietress has traveled to 27 countries, lived in 18, and collected exotic memorabilia from each. (☎ 624551. Open Feb.-Nov. £17 per person; lower group rates available.) For **camping** try **Brynich Caravan Park,** 1½ mi. east of town on the A40, signposted from the A40-A470 roundabout. (☎ 623325. Showers and laundry. Open Mar.-Oct. £6.50-7.50 per person with car, £4 per person walkin.) During the Jazz Festival, additional campsites open on farms.

◖ FOOD. Top Drawer Two, on High St. Superior, has everything you'd want for filling a pack (☎ 622601; open M-Tu and Th-Sa 9am-5pm, W 9am-1pm), as does the **Cooperative Pioneer,** Lion St. (☎ 625257; open M-Sa 8am-9pm, Su 10am-4pm). **St. Mary's Bakery,** 4 St. Mary St., offers enormous puffy breads (£1.60 per loaf) and slammin' meat pasties for 75p. (☎ 624311. Open M-F 7am-5pm, Sa 7am-2pm.) When the sun sets over the Beacons, set out for ▧ **The Camden Arms,** 21 The Watton, for drinks and grub in the pub or a more sedate repast in the lounge. Be it a chip butty bap (£1.90) or a 10 oz. rumpsteak (£8.25), the food here deserves a hearty bottoms-up. (☎ 625845. Open M-Sa 8am-11pm, Su 9am-10:30pm.)

▣▥ SIGHTS AND ENTERTAINMENT. Gracefully wearing 900 years of changing architectural fashion, **Brecon Cathedral** squats in a grove above the River Honddu. A nearby 16th-century tithe barn houses the **Heritage Centre,** which uses multimedia to describe the cathedral's history. (☎ 625222. Cathedral open daily 10am-Evensong, around 5:30pm. Heritage Centre open May-Sept. Tu-Sa 10:30am-4:30pm; Apr. and Oct. Tu-Sa 10:30am-2:30pm.) **Theatr Brycheiniog,** on the canal off Canal St., features exhibitions by day and surprisingly big-name performances by night. (☎ 611622. Gallery open M-Sa 10am-6pm. Free. Box office open M-Sa 10am-6pm and 2hr. before every performance. Tickets £5-15.) Brecon draws crowds to its **antique fairs** (last Sa of the month Feb.-Nov.), and craftspeople from all over south Wales congregate in Market Hall on High St. for the **craft fairs** (third Sa of the month Mar.-Dec.). The **Brecon Jazz Gallery,** The Watton, traces the history of jazz from its African roots to the annual Brecon frenzy. (☎ 625557. Open M-F 10am-4pm.) Set to be held August 10-12, the **Brecon Jazz Festival** dubs itself "the only festival in Britain bigger than the town itself." For info, contact the Festival Office, Watton Chambers (☎ 625557), or visit www.breconjazz.co.uk.

BRECON BEACONS NATIONAL PARK

Brecon Beacons National Park (Parc Cenedlaethol Bannau Brycheiniog) encompasses 519 dramatic square miles of barren peaks, well-watered forests, and windswept moorlands. The park divides into four regions: the barren **Brecon Beacon** peaks, where King Arthur's mountain fortress is thought to have stood; **Fforest Fawr,** containing the spectacular waterfalls of Ystradfellte; the **Black Mountains** to the east; and the rugged country around the remote western **Black Mountain** (singular). The market towns on the fringe of the park, particularly Brecon and Abergavenny, make pleasant touring bases, but hostels allow for easier access to the park's inner regions. Since crowds in the Brecon Beacons are less dense than in other Welsh parks, public transport is all the scarcer.

⌷ GETTING THERE AND GETTING AROUND

The **train** line (☎ (08457) 484950) from **London Paddington** to South Wales runs via Cardiff to **Abergavenny** at the park's southeastern corner and to **Merthyr Tydfil** on the southern edge. The **Heart of Wales** rail line passes through the towns of **Llandeilo** and **Llandovery** in the more remote Black Mountain region.

National Express (☎ (08705) 808080) **bus** #509 runs once a day to Brecon, on the northern side of the park, from London and Cardiff. **Stagecoach Red and White** (☎ (01633) 266336) **buses** regularly cross the park en route to **Brecon** from: **Cardiff** via **Merthyr Tydfil** (#43 changing to #X4, 1½hr., M-Sa 5 per day, £5-7); **Swansea** (#63, 1½hr., M-Sa 3 per day, Su 4 per day operated by Sixty Sixty Coaches, £3.66); **Abergavenny** (#20 and 21, 1hr., M-Sa 5 per day, bus #29; Su 2 per day, £3-4.10); and **Hay-on-Wye** (#39, 45min., M-Sa 5 per day, £2.80-4.10). **Yeomans** (☎ (01432) 356202) #40 runs from Hay-on-Wye on Sundays (2 per day, £4-5). **Brecon Bus Service** #760 runs twice on summer Sundays, making it easier to reach certain areas (such as the Ystradfellte Falls). The indispensable *Explore the Brecon Beacons National Park*, free at park information centres, details the infrequent bus coverage and describes a number of walks accessible by public transport. **Brecon Bicycle Centre,** High St., rents mountain bikes. (☎ (01874) 622651. £15 per day, £25 per weekend.) **Hitchhikers** say the going is tougher on the A470 than on minor roads, where drivers often stop to enjoy the view; *Let's Go* does not recommend hitchhiking.

> ❗ The mountains are unprotected and in places difficult to scale. Cloud banks slam down over the Beacons, breeding storms within minutes. In violent weather, do not shelter in caves or under isolated trees, which tend to draw lightning. A compass is essential: much of the park is trackless, and landmarks get lost in sudden mists. Never hike alone. If you're in trouble and can reach a telephone, dial **999**. Otherwise, the standard six blasts on your whistle should summon help (three are the reply); a constant long blast will also indicate distress. See **Wilderness Safety,** p. 53.

⁊ PRACTICAL INFORMATION

Stop at a **National Park Information Centre** before venturing forth. While tourist information centres (TICs) are helpful in planning a route by car or bus, the Park Centres provide pamphlets and advice on hiking as well as updated weather reports. Free maps of the park are available, but the 1:25,000 scale Ordnance Survey Outdoor Leisure maps #12 and 13 (£6.50) are indispensable for both serious exploring and for reaching safety in bad weather. Consider registering with the police before setting out. The National Park staff usually conducts guided walks of varying difficulties between April and November. Centres also stock leaflets detailing several activities from lovespoon carving (see **Love Your Cutlery,** p. 463) to sheepdog demonstrations.

SOUTH WALES

NATIONAL PARK INFORMATION CENTRES

Libanus National Mountain Park Visitor Centre (Mountain Centre), Brecon Beacons (☎ (01874) 623366; fax 624515). Catch the Stagecoach Red and White Brecon-Merthyr bus #43 to Libanus, 5 mi. southwest of Brecon (8min., M-Sa 6 per day), and walk the remaining 1½ mi. uphill, or if you're traveling on a summer Sunday, take the shuttle from Brecon right to the front door (15min., June to mid-Sept. Su 6 per day) or Beacons Bus Service #760 from Brecon (15min., July to mid-Sept. Su 2 per day). Wheelchair access. Open daily July-Aug. 9:30am-6pm; Apr.-June and Sept. 9:30am-5:30pm; Mar. and Oct. 9:30am-5pm; Nov.-Feb. 9:30am-4:30pm.

Abergavenny: see p. 434.

Brecon: see p. 435.

Craig-y-nos: At the Country Park, Pen-y-cae (☎ (01639) 730395). Open May-Aug. M-F 10am-6pm, Sa-Su 10am-7pm; Mar.-Apr. and Sept.-Oct. M-F 10am-5pm, Sa-Su 10am-6pm; Nov.-Feb. M-F 10am-4pm, Sa-Su 10am-4:30pm.

Llandovery: Kings Rd. (☎ (01550) 720693). Open Easter-Sept. M-Sa 10am-1pm and 1:45pm-5:30pm, Su 2-5:30pm; Oct.-Easter M-Sa 10am-1pm and 1:45-4pm, Su 2-4pm. Near the Black Mountain; take either the Heart of Wales train or bus #279 or 280 from Carmarthen in the west.

▌ ACCOMMODATIONS

B&Bs are sparse; the Brecon TIC's free *Where to Stay in Brecknockshire and Brecon Beacons National Park* lists a few. Scattered about the park are five **YHA Youth Hostels,** including **Ty'n-y-Caeau,** near Brecon (see p. 436). The other four are:

Capel-y-ffin (kap-EL-uh-fin; ☎ (01873) 890650), near the River Honddu at the eastern edge of the Black Mountains along Offa's Dyke Path, 8 mi. from Hay-on-Wye. Take Stagecoach Red and White bus #39 (M-Sa 5 per day, £2.80-4.10) or Yeomans bus #40 (Su 2 per day, £4-5) from Hereford to Brecon, stop before Hay and walk uphill; or take a taxi from Hay (Border Taxis, ☎ (01497) 821266; £12). Ideal for hikers and bikers of the Path or of the Brecons, the road to the hostel climbs up Gospel Pass. Horseback riding trips leave from here in conjunction with Black Mountain Holidays. Lockout 10am-5pm, but daytime access to toilets and shelter from bad weather. Open July-Sept. daily; Oct. F-Tu; Nov. and Mar.-June F-Sa. Dorms £7.35, students £6.35, under 18 £5.15. **Camping** allowed on grounds if hostel is full (£3.67 per person).

Llanddeusant (HLAN-thew-sont; ☎ (01550) 74028). At the foot of the isolated Black Mountain near Llangadog village; take the Trecastle-Llangadog road for 9 mi. off the A40. Open mid-Apr. to Aug. daily. Dorms £6.50, under 18 £4.45.

Llwyn-y-Celyn (HLEWN-uh-kel-in; ☎ (01874) 624261; fax 625916), 7 mi. south of Brecon, 2 mi. south of Libanus, and 2 mi. north of the Storey Arms car park on the A470. Take Stagecoach Red and White bus #43 from Brecon or Merthyr Tydfil (M-Sa 7 per day, Su 4 per day). Close to Pen-y-Fan and the rest of the Beacons range. A traditional Welsh farmhouse, near a nature trail, brooks, and grazing sheep. Lockout 10am-5pm, but a rain shed keeps you dry. Curfew 11pm. Open Easter-Aug. daily; Feb.-Easter Th-M; Nov. F-Sa. Dorms £9, under 18 £6.20, student discount £1.

Ystradfellte (uh-strahd-FELTH-tuh; ☎ (01639) 720301), south of the woods and waterfall district, 3 mi. from the A4059 along a paved road; 4 mi. from the village of Penderyn; a 5min. walk from the Porth-yr-Ogof cave. Hard to reach by public transport except on summer Sundays. Two small 17th-century cottages. Kitchen. Open mid-July to Aug. daily.; Apr. to mid-July and Sept.-Oct. F-Tu. Dorms £8.10, under 18 £5.65.

Commercial **campsites** are plentiful and fairly evenly dispersed, but often difficult to reach without a car. *Where to Stay in Brecknockshire and Brecon Beacons National Park* details 14 sites in the park. Many offer laundry and grocery facilities, and all have parking and showers (£3-6 per tent). Farmers may let you camp on their land if you ask first and promise to leave the site as you found it; be prepared to make a donation toward feeding the sheep.

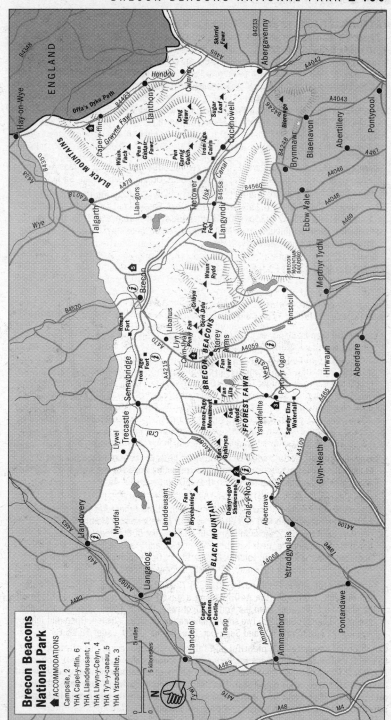

Brecon Beacons National Park

▲ ACCOMMODATIONS
Campsite, 2
YHA Capel-y-ffin, 6
YHA Llanddeusant, 1
YHA Llwyn-y-Celyn, 4
YHA Ty'n-y-caeau, 5
YHA Ystradfellte, 3

N

0   5 miles
0   5 kilometers

⚊ REGIONS OF THE NATIONAL PARK

THE BRECON BEACONS

At the center of the park, the Brecon Beacons lure hikers with pastoral slopes and barren peaks. A splendid view of the range complements an exhibit on its history at the **Mountain Centre** outside Libanus (see **National Park Information Centres,** p. 438); a pamphlet on walks around the center costs 50p. From the Mountain Centre, a one-hour stroll among daredevil sheep and extraordinary views leads to the scant remains of an **Iron Age fort.** The most convenient route to the top of **Pen-y-Fan** (pen-uh-van), the highest mountain in southern Wales at 2907 ft., begins at **Storey Arms,** a large parking lot and bus stop 5 mi. south of Libanus on the A470. Unfortunately, the paths to the peak are so popular that they have been eroded; scree (loose rocks) often shakes underfoot.

A far more pleasant hiking route starts in nearby **Llanfaes,** a western suburb of Brecon, and follows leafy roads past streams and waterfalls. Walk the first 3 mi. from Llanfaes down Ffrwdgrech Rd. to the car park (take the middle fork after the first bridge). From the car park a trail to the peak passes **Llyn Cwm Llwch** (HLIN koom hlooch), a 2000 ft. glacial pool in the shadow of **Corn Ddu** (CORN thee) peak. An arduous ridge path leads from Pen-y-Fan to other peaks in the Beacons.

The touristy **Brecon Mountain Railway,** Pant Station, Merthyr Tydfil, allows a glimpse of the south side of the Beacons as the narrow-gauge train runs north to Pontsticill. (☎ (01685) 722988. Runs June-Aug. daily 10:45am-3:45pm; Apr.-May and Sept. Tu-Th and Sa-Su; Oct. Tu-Th and Su. £6.20, seniors £5.60, children £3.10.)

THE WATERFALL DISTRICT (FFOREST FAWR)

Forest rivers tumble through rapids, gorges, and spectacular falls near **Ystradfellte,** about 7 mi. southwest of the Beacons. At **Porth-yr-Ogof** ("mouth of the cave"), less than 1 mi. from the YHA Ystradfellte (see p. 438), the River Mellte ducks into a cave at the base of the cliff and emerges as an icy pool. Swimming is decidedly *not* recommended: the stones are slippery, the pool deepens alarmingly in the middle, and dipping here has proved fatal in the past. Porth-yr-Ogof provides no solitude, and rubbish crowds the banks. Remote but worth the sweat is the **Sgwdyr Eira** waterfall (on the River Hepste one-third of a mile from its confluence with the Mellte); you can stand behind the thundering water in a hollow in the cliff-face and keep dry. Follow the marked paths to the falls from Gwann Hepste. Hikers can reach the waterfall district from the Beacons by crossing the A470 near the Llwyny-Celyn hostel, climbing Craig Cerrig-gleisaid cliff and Fan Frynych peak, and descending by way of a rocky Roman road. The route crosses a nature reserve as well as some of the park's most trackless heath. Just north of the falls the village of Ystradfellte is rumored to have a pub that will renew your vigor.

Near **Abercrave,** midway between Swansea and Brecon off the A4067, the **Dan-yr-Ogof Showcaves** (☎ (01639) 730284, 24hr. info 730801) are huge and impressive, with enormous stalagmites. From YHA Ystradfellte, 10 mi. of trails pass Fforest Fawr (the headlands of the Waterfall District) on their way to the caves. Walk along the cemented pathways inside the caves or slalom down the dry ski slope outside. (Tours every 20min. Open Apr.-Oct. 10:30am-3pm, slightly later in summer. Tours £7.50, children £4, under 3 free.) A large **campsite** near the caves has full facilities (camping £4 per night; caravans £9 per night; electricity £1). Relax from your adventures at the **Craig-y-nos Country Park,** ½ mi. away. (☎ (01639) 730395. Open daily June-Aug. 10am-6pm; Sept.-Oct. and Mar.-Apr. 10am-5pm; Nov.-Feb. 10am-4pm; May 10am-6pm, with extended hours on the weekend. Free.) **Stagecoach Red and White** bus #63 (1½hr.; M-Sa 3 per day, Su 4 per day) pauses at the hostel, caves, and country park en route from Brecon to Swansea.

THE BLACK MOUNTAINS

Located in the easternmost section of the park, the Black Mountains are a group of long, lofty ridges offering 80 sq. mi. of solitude. Summits like **Waun Fach,** the highest point (2660 ft.), may seem dull and boggy, but the ridge-walks are unsurpassed. The 1:25,000 Ordnance Survey Outdoor Leisure map #13 (£6.50) is essential.

Crickhowell, on the A40 and the Stagecoach Red and White bus #21 route between Brecon and Abergavenny (M-Sa every 2-3hr.), is the best starting point for forays into the area. You can also explore by bus: Stagecoach Red and White bus #39 linking Brecon and Hay-on-Wye (**Getting There and Getting Around,** p. 437) descends the north side of the Black Mountains. **Gospel Pass,** the highest mountain pass in the park, often reveals sunshine above the cloud cover. Nearby, **Offa's Dyke Path** (see **Hiking,** p. 430) sprints down the park's eastern boundary. The ridge valleys are dotted with a handful of impressive churches, castles, and other ruins. There is almost no public transportation along valley routes.

SWANSEA (ABERTAWE)   ☎01792

Like most good paradoxes, native son Dylan Thomas's assessment of Wales's second city as "this ugly lovely town" is both logically impossible and very true. The first sights greeting travelers are the endless rows of box houses that creep up the hills, and parts of the downtown area are sadly bereft of trees and interesting architecture; yet Swansea (pop. 182,000) also has a lovely castle square, a pedestrian-friendly set of walking streets, and a wide and sandy beach that stretches for miles down the bay. A haven for consumers, night-owls, and Dylan Thomas aficionados, Swansea also serves as a transport hub for voyagers to the Gower and seafarers bound for Ireland. Take a walk in the Maritime Quarter, and you'll sense the wave of renewal in the city. Better yet, brave the bracing seafront of Swansea Bay.

SOUTH WALES

⏚ GETTING THERE AND SAILING TO IRELAND. Swansea has direct connections to most major cities in Britain. At the **train station,** 35 High St., trains (☎ (08457) 484950) arrive from: **Cardiff** (1hr., 1-2 per hr., £7.80); **London** (3hr., 1 per hr., £54); and **Birmingham** (4hr., 1 per hr., £31.40). The **Quadrant Bus Station** (☎ 475511) is near the Quadrant Shopping Centre. **National Express** (☎ (08705) 808080) buses come in from: **London,** (4hr., every 2hr., £16); **Cardiff** (1¼hr., 12 per day, £5); and **Birmingham** (4hr., 3 per day, £18.50). **First Cymru** (☎ (08706) 082608) buses cover the Gower Peninsula and the rest of southwest Wales; Monday to Friday a shuttle runs every hour to **Cardiff** (1hr., £6.50). A First Cymru **Day Saver** ticket (£4.80, concessions £3.50, families £9) allows unlimited travel for a day in the area; the 5-day version costs £16. **Local buses** #4 and 4A run between the train and bus stations (5min., departs every 10min., 50p). **Taxis** zip around town and down the bay to Mumbles courtesy of **Cab Charge** (☎ 474747) and **A.A. Taxis** (☎ 360600).

Cork-Swansea ferries (☎ 456116) leave for **Cork, Ireland** from King's Dock (see **By Ferry,** p. 35). **Cruises** (☎ (01446) 720656) leave from Swansea to **Ilfracombe** (£17.95) and other spots on the Bristol Channel from July to September.

⏺ PRACTICAL INFORMATION. On the north side of the bus station, the **tourist information centre** (TIC) books rooms and fills racks with free entertainment booklets, events calendars, and an excellent city map. (☎ 468321; fax 464602; swanstrsm@cableol.co.uk. Open M-Sa 9am-5:30pm.) Services include: **Barclays bank** on the Kingsway (open M-Tu and Th-F 9am-5pm, W 10am-5pm, Sa 9:30am-noon); **Foreign Express Services,** offering services similar to American Express, 28 The Kingsway (☎ 455188; open M-F 9am-5pm, Sa 9am-4pm); the **police** (☎ 456999,) at the corner of Orchard St. and Alexandra Rd.; **Internet access** for a very cheap £1 per 30min. at the YMCA's **Cyber-Café,** 1 The Kingsway (☎ 652032; open M-Tu and F 10am-6pm, W-Th noon-6pm, Sa 9am-2pm); and the **post office,** 35 The Kingsway (open M-Sa 9am-5:30pm). **Postal code:** SA1 5LF.

⏚⏚ ACCOMMODATIONS AND FOOD. Finding quality accommodations can be quite a challenge. Cheaper prices than TIC-recommended B&Bs are found at non-registered B&Bs such as those that line **Oystermouth Rd.** along the bay. Or dash over to the **Harlton Guest House,** 89 King Edward's Rd. (☎ 466938), whose TV-stocked rooms are a bargain at £10. Take bus #37 from the bus station (1 per hr.). The closest hostel is the popular **YHA Port Eynon,** about an hour out of town by bus (see p. 444). In high season, many travelers **camp** along the Gower Peninsula.

Harboring flavors from all seven seas, the city by the bay abounds with places to eat. Indian and Chinese takeaways proliferate along **St. Helen's Rd.,** cafes line the pedestrian zone along **Oxford St.,** and convenience stores line **Bryn-y-Mor.** The city waxes agricultural at the **Swansea Market,** on the other side of the Quadrant Shopping Centre from the bus station. A maze of fruits, cheeses, eggs, meats, and the Welsh laverbread and brith awaits the adventurous. Large portions of Italian fare at **Topo Gigio,** 55 St. Helen's Rd., include *bianchetti* (£3.80), *pasta e fagioli* (£4.90), or fish, chicken, and veal dinners for £10-12. (☎ 467888. Open Tu-Sa 7-11pm, F also noon-2pm.) Those under 18 will find the doors of many traditional pubs closed, but **The Olde Cross Keys,** 12 St. Mary's St., lets kids in for meals. (☎ 630921. Open M-Sa 11am-11pm, Su noon-10:30pm; food served until 8pm.)

🎥 **SIGHTS.** As in Cardiff (Swansea's rival city), the last few years rebuilders have transformed the **maritime quarter** from a decaying dockland into a colorful array of upscale apartment blocks, touristy shops, and outdoor cafes, all set against hundreds of white sails fluttering in the ocean breezes. The **Maritime and Industrial Museum's** gleaming vintage cars and grainy photos of stout little tugboats share space with an exhibit on the world's first passenger railway, which chugged merrily along from Swansea to Oystermouth and into the history books in prehistoric 1807. Climb aboard the lightship **Helwick** docked outside and admire the plush but pint-sized stained-wood bunks. (☎ 650351. Museum open Tu-Su 10am-5pm. Boat open Apr.-Sept. Th-Su 10am-5pm. Both free.)

A pensive and bulbous-nosed **Dylan Thomas** sits at the end of the marina in the square bearing his name, looking up to the city that so looks up to him. A full page of the *Swansea Bay* guide is devoted to guiding poetry junkies along the **Dylan Thomas Uplands Trail** and the new **Dylan Thomas City Centre Trail** past the poet's favorite haunts. The **castle,** reduced to humble ruins by Welsh rebel Owain Glyndwr, lies between Wind St. and The Strand, overshadowed by brash young office buildings. Near the castle in the Parc Tawe complex off The Strand, the jutting glass-and-steel pyramid **Plantasia** incubates over 1000 exotic species of plants and animals, some of them extinct in the wild, in a tropical environment. Piranhas guard the gift shop while Venus flytraps eagerly await careless and unsuspecting visitors. (☎ 474555. Open Tu-Su 10am-5pm. Wheelchair access. £2.50, concessions £1.25.)

🎭 **ENTERTAINMENT.** Evenings in Swansea are lively affairs, with the downtown pedestrian area packed with theater-goers and eager clubbers. The mural-covered **Dylan Thomas Theatre,** along the marina, stages dramas and musicals. (☎ 473238. Tickets £5-7.) Close by at Somerset Pl. is the **Dylan Thomas Centre,** home to dramatic, cinematic, and literary performances. A video in the permanent exhibit on Dylan proclaims that the poet was not at all the world-class drinker and ladies' man that he liked people to think he was. Peruse his annotations of *Spoon River Anthology* by Edgar Lee Masters, a major influence on Dylan's masterpiece *Under Milk Wood.* (☎ 463980; box office ☎ 463892. Open Tu-Su 10:30am-4:30pm. Free.) And while we're on the subject, Swansea hosts an annual **Dylan Thomas celebration,** Oct. 27-Nov. 9 in 2001, with readings, shows, and lectures. The **Grand Theatre,** on Singleton St., puts on operas, ballets, and concerts. (☎ 475715. Box office open 9:30am-8pm. Tickets £6-40, with student discounts sometimes available on day of show.) The **Taliesin Arts Centre,** University College, hosts films, dramatics, visual arts, and dances. (☎ 296883. Open Sept.-July.) For the entire month of October, the **Swansea Festival** (☎ 205318, bookings ☎ 475715) presents a variety of classical concerts. In mid-August, the village of Pontardawe, 8 mi. north of Swansea (take bus #120 or 125), is deluged by folk and rock musicians from all over the world attending the **Pontardawe International Music Festival** (☎ 830200). The monthly *What's On,* free at the TIC, lists arts performances around town.

Nightlife in Swansea centers around the Kingsway and Mumbles (see below). The enormous **Icon** and **Ritzy's** clubs, 72 The Kingsway, jointly occupy the former Odeon Cinema, creating an enormous space that's quite popular on Monday student nights and unabashedly "commercial dance night" Saturdays. (☎ 653142. Cover M and Th-F £1-3, Sa £5-6. Open M and Th 8pm-2:30am, F-Sa 8pm-4am.)

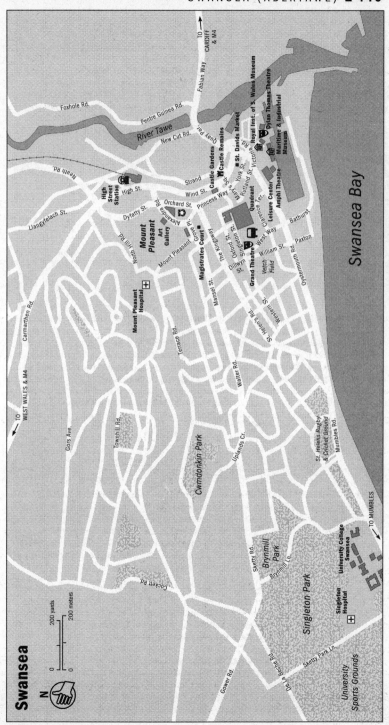

Swansea

N

0 ___ 200 yards
0 ___ 200 meters

TO CARDIFF & M4

Foxhole Rd.

Pentre Guinea Rd.

River Tawe

New Cut Rd.

Neath Rd.

Quay Parade

Fabian Way

Llangyfelach St.

Carmarthen Rd.

Gors Ave.

WEST WALES & M4

Cocket Rd.

Gower Rd.

De la Beche Rd.

Sketty Park Ln.

Sketty Rd.

Uplands Cr.

Towhill Rd.

Terrace Rd.

Walter Rd.

Mansel St.

The Kingsway

North Hill Rd.

Dyfatty St.

High St.

High Street Station

Strand

Wind St.

Orchard St.

Alexandra Rd.

Art Gallery

Mount Pleasant

Mount Pleasant Hospital

Princess Way

Grove Pl.

Magistrates Court

Dillwyn St.

Singleton St.

Oxford St.

Grand Theatre

Castle Gardens

Castle Remains

St. Davids Market

York St.

St. Mary St.

Rutland St.

Victoria Rd.

Royal Inst. of S. Wales Museum

St. Wales Museum

Dylan Thomas Theatre

Maritime & Industrial Museum

Quadrant

Clarence Ter.

West Way

William St.

Leisure Center

Amph Theatre

Bathurst

Oystermouth Rd.

Paxton

St. Helen's Rd.

Western St.

Vetch Field

Brynmill Ln.

Brynmill Park

Cwmdonkin Park

St. Helen's Rugby & Cricket Ground

Mumbles Rd.

University College Swansea

Singleton Park

Singleton Hospital

University Sports Grounds

TO MUMBLES

Swansea Bay

DYLAN'S WORD-WEAVING Son of Swansea, child of Cwmdonkin Drive, Dylan Thomas learned early that he could play with words. Walking to Aplans School every morning with his mates, Dylan passed Mr. Brown's Butcher Shop, Mr. Green's Market, and Mrs. White's Bakery, and convinced the others that to own a shop on this street, your name had to be a color. The rhyme scheme of "Prologue" in *Collected Poems 1934-1952* divides the 102-line poem into two mirror-image verses: line one rhymes with line 102, line two rhymes with line 101, and so on. In *Under Milk Wood*, though, Dylan took his trickery too far for the refined tastes of the BBC. Originally written for radio presentation, the script was set in a fictitious Welsh town that Dylan intended to be "strangely simple and simply strange." The name he gave his town, Llareggub, certainly looked simply Welsh—and the BBC would have none it! When the work was first published in 1954, the spelling was changed to Llaryggub to disguise the fact that, when read backwards, Dylan's famous town says Buggerall.

THE GOWER PENINSULA   ☎01792

With Mumbles, a popular pub crawl destination, connecting it to Swansea at its east end, the 18 mi. Gower Peninsula stretches out into the sea, its limestone cliffs, headlands, and expansive beaches framed against often sparkling waters. Crumbling castles and ancient burial sites lurk among the greenery and the Cefn Bryn hills; the peninsula is rife with unexpected finds. Best of all, its proximity to Swansea means you'll be spared a leg-breaking hike to get there.

▐ GETTING THERE AND GETTING AROUND. Buses overrun the peninsula from Swansea's **Quadrant Station. First Cymru** (☎ (08706) 082608) buses #2, 2A, 3, and 3A leave **Swansea** for Oystermouth Sq. in **Mumbles** (20min., 20 per hr., £1.55). Bus #18 runs to **Oxwich** (40min., every 2hr., return £3), while #18A lurches through the hills to **Rhossili** via **Port Eynon** (1hr., every 2hr., return £2.30). Bus #14 makes its way to **Pennard** hourly. Bus #16 covers **North Gower.** On Sundays, only bus #18D crosses the peninsula, joined by #48 June through August. The First Cymru **Day Saver** is valid through the Gower and beyond (£4.80, concessions £3.50, families £9); the 5-day version is £16. **Network Rider** passes are also accepted (see **Buses,** p. 415). **Hitchhiking** is reported to be quicker than public transport and allows hikers to see more of the coast, since most buses follow inland routes. *Let's Go* does not recommend hitchhiking. The pleasant 4½ mi. **Swansea Bikepath and Promenade** traces the coast to Mumbles pier. **Clyne Valley Cycles,** Dunvant Village Green, Dunvant, on the main cycle path, **rents bikes.** (☎ 208889. £3.50 per 2hr., £7 per day.)

▐ PRACTICAL INFORMATION. Most useful services on the Gower can be found in **Mumbles.** The **tourist information centre** (TIC) stands in a portacabin in the car park near the bus station. (☎ 361302; fax 363392. Open Easter-Oct. M-Sa 9:30am-5:30pm, Su 10am-4pm.) Services include: **Barclays bank,** Newton Rd. (open M-Tu and Th-F 9am-4:30pm, W 10am-4:30pm); **A.A. Taxis** (☎ 360600); the **police** (☎ 456999), Newton Rd. near Castle St.; and the **post office,** 522 Mumbles Rd. (☎ 366821; open M-F 9am-5:30pm, Sa 9am-12:30pm). **Postal code:** SA3 4HH.

▐▐ ACCOMMODATIONS AND FOOD. The farther west you go on the Gower, the more likely you are to find campsites free of tents and caravans. B&Bs in Mumbles charge upwards of £16 and cluster on Mumbles Rd. and in the South End area; singles can be hard to find. Walk down the halls of **Rock Villa,** 1 George Bank, to bay-fresh rooms with TVs and views of the sea. (☎ 366794. 10min. down Mumbles Rd. Singles £20; doubles £38-40.) You may also want to consider taking bus #14 to nearby **Bishopston. Three Cliffs Bay Caravan Park,** North Hills Farm, Penmaen, has showers and overlooks the Bay. (Bus #18 from Swansea. ☎ 371218. Camping sites £4.50 per single adult; £8 per couple; £1 per family.) Port Eynon, west of Mumbles, hosts the no-frills but busy **YHA Port Eynon,** a former lifeboat house on the beach; take bus #18A from Swansea. (☎/fax 390706. Lockout 10am-5pm. Security-code entry after 11pm. Open July-Aug. daily; Apr.-June M-Sa; Sept.-Oct. Tu-Sa. £8.10, under 18 £5.65.) Beachside **camping** is also possible in Port Eynon.

In Mumbles, you can stuff your pack at the **Somerfield** supermarket, 512 Mumbles Rd. (Open M-F 8am-10pm, Sa 8am-8pm, Su 10am-4pm.) Various **bakeries** also dot the streets. For a great view of the tides, take the Bay Footpath or Rotherslade Rd. to ◪ **Brother's Tor Cafe and Restaurant,** where you can eat delicious sandwiches (£3) and jacket potatoes (£4) or take coffee (£1) on rocky cliffs and watch boats cross to the lands blue on the horizon. (Open daily June-Aug. 10am-9pm, Sept.-May 10am-5pm.) Or try the lamb tikka (£5.95) or vegetable biriani (£4.95) at **Seaview Tandoori Restaurant,** 728 Mumbles Rd. (☎ 367071. Open M-Th 6pm-12:30am, F-Sa 6pm-1:30am.) **Hightide Café,** 61 Newton Rd., serves snacks, such as bagels with Welsh smoked salmon and cheese (£4.10) and daily lunch specials. (☎ 363462. Open M-Tu 9am-4pm, W-Sa 9am-10pm, Su 11am-10pm.)

◪ **SIGHTS.** Perched high above Mumbles, the serene 13th-century **Oystermouth Castle,** on Castel Ave. off Newton Rd., hosts birds and tiny flowers that have overrun the battlements. (☎ 368732. Open Apr. to mid-Sept. daily 11am-5pm. £1, concessions 80p.) Picnickers should attempt the heart-stopping ascent to the 56-acre **Mumbles Hill Nature Reserve,** an urban oasis of scrub, wildflowers, and rocky crags overlooking Mumbles and the sea. The endless staircase begins by the George Hotel, 10min. walk from the bus station on Mumbles Rd. The people at the **Lovespoon Gallery,** 492 Mumbles Rd., will give you advice on what to do when a wild-eyed Welshman comes lurching after you with a wooden spoon in his fist (see **Love Your Cutlery,** p. 463). Lovespoons cost £5-50. (☎ 360132. Open M-Sa 10am-5:30pm.)

On the Gower Peninsula proper, spectacular **beaches** are a dime a dozen. From Southgate and Pennard, a half-hour walk along the Coast Path brings you to **Three Cliffs,** a secluded, cave-ridden, and incredibly beautiful beach that is almost completely submerged at high tide. **Caswell Bay, Langland Bay, Port Eynon Bay,** and **Oxwich Bay** are all massively popular, and accessible by a 45min. walk along the Bays Footpath that begins off Plunch Lane, around the point of Mumbles Head. On the peninsula's western tip, green cliffs clutch the sexy curve of ◪ **Rhossili Beach,** whose dramatic expanse makes overcrowding unlikely. At low tide, a causeway of tortured rock gives foot-breaking access to **Worm's Head,** a series of craggy rocks that looks like Nessie's Welsh cousin lumbering out to sea. **Llangennith Beach,** north of Rhossili, draws surfers from all over Wales with its wild waves.

◪◪ **ENTERTAINMENT AND FESTIVALS.** A quiet fishing village by day, **Mumbles** turns into a raving Gomorrah of student indulgence by night. The short stretch of **Mumbles Rd.** at Mumbles Head is lined with pubs, some of them former haunts of the area's most famous dipsomaniac, Dylan Thomas. To hang out on Mumbles Rd. is, in University of Swansea parlance, to "go mumbling"; to start at one end and have a pint at each pub is to "do the Mumbles Mile." Flower's, Usher's, Buckley's, and Felin Foel are the local real ales. The **Gower Festival** fills the peninsula's churches with the sounds of string quartets and Bach chorales during the last two weeks of July. Check the *What's On* guide, free at the Mumbles TIC, for details. (☎ 468321; box office ☎ 475715.)

TENBY (DINBYCH-Y-PYSGOD)   ☎01834

Touted as "fair and fashionable" and nicknamed the Welsh Riviera, Tenby lives up to the good and bad implicit in its reputation. The town is full of animated characters and holiday cheer, and its narrow streets crouch along a rugged peninsula softened by cliffside gardens, pastel houses, and the shadows of brazen seagulls overhead. While beautiful, the soft-sanded beaches can be very crowded—Tenby is largely a summer resort town, after all. But slip away to the leafy, shadowy sidewalk by the town wall, ride across the water to an off-shore island, or just enjoy the vitality of this youthful and ancient town, and Tenby will reward you with history, ghost stories, and that perfect patch of sand.

▐ GETTING THERE AND GETTING AROUND

The *Public Transport Timetables for South Pembrokeshire*, available at tourist information centres, lists bus, rail, and ferry schedules for the area, including Tenby, Pembroke, Saundersfoot, and Manorbier.

Trains: At the bottom of Warren St. Unstaffed. **Tenby Travel** (☎ 843214), in the Tenby Indoor Market between High St. and Upper Frog St., books trains. Open M-Tu and Th-F 9am-5pm, W and Sa 9am-4pm. Trains (☎ (08457) 484950), all M-F 8 per day, Sa 10 per day, Su 5 per day, from: **Pembroke** (30min., £3); **Carmarthen** (45min., £5.20); **Swansea** (1½hr., £8.10); and **Cardiff** (2½hr., £13.90).

Buses: Buses leave from a traffic island on Upper Park Rd., across from the Somerfield supermarket. There are upper and lower bays for boarding. **First Cymru** (☎ (08706) 082608) from **Haverfordwest** via **Pembroke** (#349, 1 per hr. M-Sa until 5:30pm, £4) and **Swansea** (#302; 1½hr.; M-Sa 2 per day, in summer also Su 2 per day; £5.25). Or from **Swansea** to **Carmarthen** (#X11 or X30, M-Sa 1 per hr., £3.60) and transfer to **Silcox Coaches** bus #333 (2½hr., M-Sa 4 per day). The Silcox Coaches (☎ 842189) office is in the arcade between South Parade and Upper Frog St., across from the market hall. A First Cymru **Day Saver** (£4.80) or a **Cleddau Rider** (£11.90) can be purchased for unlimited daily or weekly travel west of Carmarthen.

Taxis: Tenby Taxis (☎ 843678), 24hr. Taxis also congregate by the bus station.

◢▐ ORIENTATION AND PRACTICAL INFORMATION

The old town is in the shape of a triangle pointing into the bay, with **North Beach** along the top edge, **Castle Beach** and **South Beach** along the bottom, and the train station on the back edge. From the station, **Warren St.** approaches town. At the post office, Warren St. becomes **White Lion** and continues to North Beach. Like tines of a fork off of White Lion, **South Parade, Upper Frog St., Crackwell St.,** and **High St.** all lead towards South Beach. **The Croft** runs along North Beach, and the **Old Wall** runs along South Parade.

Tourist Information Centre: The Croft (☎ 842404; fax 845439), overlooking North Beach. Free accommodations list. Town maps 20p. Open mid-July to Aug. daily 10am-9pm; June to mid-July daily 10am-5:30pm, Sept.-May M-Sa 10am-4pm.

Financial Services: Barclays, 18 High St. (☎ 765521). 24hr. cash machine on Upper Frog St., at the back of the bank. Open M-W and F 9am-4:30pm, Th 10am-4:30pm.

Launderette: Secci's (☎ 842484), Lower Frog St. Change machine. Wash £1.60, dry 5p per 5min., soap 20p. Open daily June-Aug. 8:30am-9pm, last wash 8:30pm; Sept.-May 10am-6pm, last wash 5:30pm.

Police: (☎ 842303), Warren St., near the church off White Lion St.

Hospital: Tenby Cottage Hospital (☎ 842040), Church Park.

Post Office: (☎ 843213), Warren St. at South Parade. Open M-Sa 8:30am-5:30pm. **Postal Code:** SA70 7JR.

▌ ACCOMMODATIONS

Warren St., just outside the town wall near the train station, has loads of B&Bs for £14-18; the sidestreets of **Greenhill Ave.,** as well as the streets off Esplanade and Trafalgar Rd., are almost as well endowed. Should these areas fail you, take a short bus ride to **Saundersfoot.**

⊠ **Somerville,** 12 Warren St. (☎ 843158). The world's funkiest carpeting. Singles £12, with cooked breakfast £14, with continental breakfast £13; doubles £28.

Hazlemere, 13 Warren St. (☎ 844691). They work to please with comfortable double rooms and full breakfasts. June-Aug. £16 per person, £4 extra for singles.

Langdon Guest House (☎ 843923), Warren St. The family energy will recharge your battery as you sit in front of a color TV. Easter-Aug. £16 per person, Sept.-Easter £12.50.

Camping: Meadow Farm (☎ 844829), at the top of The Croft and overlooking North Beach. £4, accompanied children £1.50; showers available.

FOOD

Tenby has plenty of restaurants, but many are so expensive you'll be tempted to drink the ketchup just to get your money's worth. Lunch specials can soften the blow. Buy meat, vegetables, and bread for a picnic at the **Tenby Market Hall** between High St. and Upper Frog St. (Open M-Sa 8:30am-5:30pm.) The **Somerfield** supermarket, across from the bus station on Upper Park Rd., will fill your pack. (Open M-Th and Sa 8am-8pm, F 8am-9pm, Su 10am-4pm.)

The Plantagenet, Quay Hill (☎ 842350). Hidden in an alley connecting Bridge St. and St. Julians St. (although its hiding place is betrayed in the warmer months by a jolly jungle of bright flowers). Serves excellent Welsh and continental cuisine as well as a daily fish menu. Try to get a seat under the towering 800-year-old, 40 ft. Flemish stone chimney of this gorgeous house. Main courses are pricey at £9-14, but lunch sandwiches cost £3.50-4.50. Kids eat free before 7pm. Open Easter-Oct. daily 9:30am-12:30am; Nov.-Easter F-Su 9:30am-12:30am.

Candy (☎ 842052), Crackwell St., on the corner of High St., leans like a captain's cabin over the sea. Go for salads and omelettes, or enjoy the traditional steak and kidney pie (£4.60-7). Open Apr.-Oct. daily 9am-8:30pm.

Pam Pam, 2 Tudor Sq. (☎ 842946), satiates with hearty plates and brunch until 5pm. Main courses £5-12, vegetarian dishes £6-7. Open daily Easter-Oct. 10am-10:30pm; Nov.-Easter 10am-9pm.

Balti Cellar (☎ 845045), below the Hilton pub just beyond the B&Bs on Warren St. Great Indian food (£4-10, takeaway 10% discount) with menu options for both the meek and the adventurous. Open Su-Th 5pm-12:30am, F-Sa noon-2pm and 5pm-1am.

BEACHES AND SIGHTS

Promenades and benches on the cliffs high above the beaches afford marvelous views, but most visitors zip straight down to the sand. On a sunny day, **North Beach,** by the Croft, and **South Beach,** beyond the Esplanade, swarm with pensioners and naked toddlers. At the eastern tip of Tenby, **Castle Beach** reaches into cliffs and caves that taunt the lithe and curious explorer, but only by evading the crowds and heading for the rockier, less groomed beaches will you find the treasure troves of Tenby sea shells. For off-shore adventures, **Dragonfly Water Sports,** Castle Slipway on Castle Beach, caters to parasailing, waterskiing, and scuba diving. (☎ 843553. Open daily Easter to late Sept. 9am-late.) A variety of trips leave from the harbor; check the kiosk at Castle Beach. **Coastal and Island Cruises** runs boat trips. (☎ 843545. Open Apr.-Oct. Trips £6, students and seniors £5, children £3.)

Enter lifestyles of the middle-class and merchant at the **Tudor Merchant's House,** on Quay Hill off Bridge Street. Its three floors step up historical display to the highest level, detailing the fun, fascinating superstitions and customs of a 16th-century Welsh household. Learn how cutlery-care attracted murderers, or why lefties were forbidden to stir the stew. (☎ 842279. Open Apr.-Sept. M-Tu and Th-Sa 10am-5pm, Su 1-5pm; Oct. M-Tu and Th-F 10am-3pm, Su noon-3pm. £1.80, children 90p.) The ruins of Tenby's **castle**—no more than patches of crumbled, mossy stone—rest atop the summit of Castle Hill, almost completely surrounded by ocean. Atop the hill, you can see across sparkling Carmarthen Bay to Worm's Head on the Gower Peninsula and sometimes all the way to Devon. At night, Tenby's spooks and ghouls share the streets with resort revelers; see if you can spot them on the **Ghost Walk of Tenby,** which departs from outside the Lifeboat Tavern in Tudor Sq. at 8pm. Buy tickets at Dales Music Shop, High St. (☎ 845841, last-minute booking ☎ (07970) 420734. Runs June-Sept. daily, advance booking suggested; Oct.-May M-Sa, advance booking required. £3.25, children £2.25, families £10.)

SOUTH WALES

DAYTRIPS FROM TENBY

CALDEY ISLAND. Three perfume-drenched miles south of Tenby lies this saffron-sanded island. Site of an active **monastery** founded in the 6th century, the current building is the dogged third coming of the monastery after the Vikings and Henry VIII sacked the first two. The land hosts a community of seabirds, seals, and 20 enterprising Cistercian monks, who produce perfume and chocolate for sale at **The Caldey Shop** on Quay Hill in Tenby. The island's **post office** dispenses information and fake stamps. (*Caldey Boats sail to the island from Tenby harbor.* ☎ 842296. Runs June-Aug. 9:45am-5:30pm. Cruises 20min. 4 per hr. Return £7, children £3.)

CAREW CASTLE. Sstrange, handsome Carew Castle is 5 mi. northwest of Tenby and is an odd mix of Norman fortress and Elizabethan manor, where ruins of mighty stone mingle with pretty windows of delicate glass. Nearby, one of Britain's three **tidal mills,** dating to 1558, turns by a medieval bridge and an 11th-century cross. (*Take Silcox bus #361 from Tenby (M-Sa 5 per day). Castle* ☎ *(01646) 651782. Open Easter-Oct. daily 10am-5pm. Tours run at 11am, 2pm, and 3pm. Mill and castle £2.75, seniors and children £1.80; castle only £1.90, seniors and children £1.40, families £7.30.)*

MANORBIER CASTLE. Halfway between Tenby and Pembroke stands the superbly preserved Manorbier Castle, a 13th-century Norman baron's palace where mood music strains from the ceilings and wax figures populate the halls. A garden in the keep and a beach below the ramparts lend to the castle's fresh feeling. (*Trains from Tenby and Pembroke run 10 per day. First Cymru bus #349 shuttles between Tenby, Manorbier, Pembroke, and Haverfordwest (M-Sa 1 per hr.; in summer also Su 4 per day). Castle* ☎ *(01646) 871394. Open Easter-Sept. daily 10:30am-5:30pm. £2, seniors £1.50, children £1.)* Manorbier also holds a **YHA Youth Hostel** (☎ 871803; see p. 450). The National Park authorities organize guided walks in the area, outlined in their free seasonal publication *Coast to Coast.*

DYLAN THOMAS BOAT HOUSE. Dylan Thomas spent his last four years in the Boat House in **Laugharne** (LARN) at the mouth of the River Taff, about 15 mi. northeast of Tenby. The boat house, now fairly commercialized, displays Thomas's photographs, art, and books, and the shed where he wrote is exactly how he left it. (*Take First Cymru bus #351 to Pendine (7 per day), then switch to First Cymru bus #222 from St. Clear's. House* ☎ *(01994) 427420. Open daily May-Oct. 10am-5pm; Nov.-Apr. 10:30am-3pm. £2.75, children £1, seniors £1.75, under 7 free.)*

PEMBROKESHIRE COAST NATIONAL PARK

The 225 square miles of The Pembrokeshire Coast National Park (Parc Cenedlaethol Arfordir Penfro), best known for craggy peninsular coasts and madly dramatic scenery, also feature the wooded Gwaun Valley and prehistoric Celtic remnants hidden away deep in the Preseli Hills. But the coastline is the area's supreme drawing card; hikers from near and far follow the 186 mi. of the Coastal Path past secluded inlets, towering rocks overrun by birds, tiny chapels, squat cathedrals, and sheer cliffs rising high out of the crashing Atlantic surf.

GETTING THERE AND GETTING AROUND

The best place to enter the region is centrally located **Haverfordwest.** Buses offer more frequent and wide-ranging service than trains. The Dale Peninsula, southwest of Haverfordwest, is not served by public transport at all. While *Let's Go* does not recommend hitching, **hitchers** rave about the area. Mountain **bikes** are excellent means of transport on the park's one-lane roads, many of which lead to secluded beaches. Do not, however, ride on the coastal path itself; it is illegal and extraordinarily dangerous, in that you might plummet over a cliff.

Trains: (☎ (08457) 484950). To **Haverfordwest** from **London Paddington** (4hr., 1 per hr., M-Th £44, F £61) and **Cardiff** (7 per day, £13.90). To **Fishguard** on the north coast (change at Clarbeston Rd., 4 per day, £4.90) and **Tenby** and **Pembroke Dock,** both on the south coast (change at Whitland).

Buses: Richards Brothers (☎ (08706) 082608) from **Haverfordwest** to **St. David's** (#411, 45min., 1 per hr., £2) and **Fishguard** (1½hr., 4 per day, £4). **First Cymru** (☎ (08706) 082608) from **Haverfordwest** to **Broad Haven** (#311, 15min., M-Sa 6 per day, £1.45) and **Milford Haven** (#302, 20min., M-Sa 2 per hr., Su 1 per hr., £1.90). A **West Wales Rover Ticket** (£4.60 per day, children £3.40) gets you virtually unlimited travel in **Pembrokeshire** and neighboring **Carmarthenshire** and **Ceredigion.** Find bus schedules in *Public Transport Timetables for Pembrokeshire.*

Bike Rentals: Mr. Codd, Cross Inn Garage, (☎ (01834) 813266), Broadmoor, in Saundersfoot, rents bikes for £6 per day plus £30 deposit. Open M-Sa 8am-6pm; July-Aug. book ahead. **Preseli Venture** (☎ (01348) 837709), on the coast between Fishguard and St. David's. Bikes £15 per half-day, £20 per day.

Boat Rentals: Preseli Venture (see above) also has kayaks (£30 per half-day, £59 per day; call in advance) or the whole shebang: kayaking, coasteering, and mountain biking for 2 days and nights (£139, food and accommodations included; book ahead). The park is also a-flutter with **Outdoor Activity Centres,** which rent canoes, kayaks, ponies, bicycles, and other archaic means of transport (£10-20 per day). Check the *Coast to Coast* pamphlet available at Park Information Centres for locations.

🛈 PRACTICAL INFORMATION

The **National Park Information Centres** listed below sell 10 annotated maps covering the coastal path (from 35p each). Brian John's *The Pembrokeshire Coast Path* (£11) is a methodically thorough option. Helpful National Park officers will aid your planning for free; ask them about the guided walks offered by the park. Write for brochures to National Park Information Services, Pembrokeshire Coast National Park Head Office, Winch Ln., Haverfordwest, Pembrokeshire, Wales SA61 1PY (☎ (01437) 764636; www.pembrokeshirecoast.org). For **weather info,** call any park office; in emergency, contact **rescue rangers** by dialing 999 or 112.

NATIONAL PARK INFORMATION CENTRES
Haverfordwest: 40 High St. (☎ (01437) 760136, 24hr. info ☎ 771455; fax 775140). Open Easter-Sept. M-Sa 10am-1pm and 1:45-5:30pm.

Newport, Pembrokeshire: Bank Cottages, Long St. (☎/fax (01239) 820912). Open Easter-Oct. M-Sa 10am-5:30pm.

St. David's: The Grove (☎ (01437) 720392, fax 720099). Doubles as the town tourist information centre. Open Easter-Oct. daily 9:30am-5:30pm; Nov.-Easter M-Sa 10am-4pm. Closed for two weeks in January.

TOURIST INFORMATION CENTRES
Fishguard: Town Hall, The Square (☎ (01348) 873484; fax 875246). Open Easter-Oct. 10am-5:30pm, Nov.-Easter 10am-4pm.

Haverfordwest: 19 Old Bridge (☎ (01437) 763110; fax 767738). Open M-Sa 10am-5:30pm.

Milford Haven: 94 Charles St. (☎ (01646) 690866; fax 690655). Open Easter-Oct. M-Sa 10am-5pm.

Saundersfoot: The Barbecue, Harbour Car Park (☎ (01834) 813672; fax 813673). Open Easter-Sept. daily 10am-5:30pm.

Tenby: The Croft (☎ (01834) 842404; fax 845439). Open mid-July to Aug. daily 10am-9pm; June to mid-July daily 10am-5:30pm; Sept.-May M-Sa 10am-4pm.

ACCOMMODATIONS

Conveniently spaced along the coastal path, the park's **YHA Youth Hostels** are all within a reasonable day's walk of one another. Reserve in advance in July and August. If you plan your route ahead, you can book at all of the hostels at least 14 days beforehand for a £2.50 fee through the **West Wales Booking Bureau,** Anna Davis, YHA St. David's, Pembrokeshire SA62 6PR (early 2001 ☎ (01437) 720345, after mid-year ☎ (01629) 51061). The roads between Tenby, Pembroke, and St. David's teem with **B&Bs** (£14-23). Despite the quantity, B&Bs can be hard to secure, especially in the summer. The coast is lined with **campsites,** as many farmers convert fallow fields into summer sites (about £4 per tent); enquire before pitching. The Manorbier, Poppit Sands, and Pwll Deri hostels also allow camping.

> **YHA Broad Haven:** (☎ (01437) 781688; fax 781100), on St. Bride's Bay off the B4341. Easily accessible; take the #311 bus from Haverfordwest. 75 beds and some of the best facilities on the Walk. Laundry facilities. Wheelchair access. Lockout 10am-5pm. Curfew 11pm. Open mid-Feb. to Oct. daily. Dorms £10.85, under 18 £7.40.

> **YHA Manorbier:** Skrinkle Haven (☎ (01834) 871803; fax 871101), near Manorbier Castle. From Manorbier train station, walk up past the A4139 to the castle, make a left onto the B4585, a right up to the army camp, and follow the signs. Vigorously hot showers and laundry facilities. Wheelchair access. Lockout 10am-5pm. Curfew 11pm. Open mid-Feb. to Oct. daily. Dorms £10.85, under 18 £7.40; camping £5.40.

> **YHA Marloes Sands:** (☎/fax (01646) 636667), near the Dale Peninsula. A cluster of farm buildings on National Trust Property. Difficult to reach by public transportation; hiking's your best bet. No laundry. Lockout 10am-5pm. Curfew 11pm. Open Apr.-Oct. daily. Dorms £7.35, under 18 £5.15.

> **YHA Pwll Deri:** (☎ (01348) 891233), on breathtaking cliffs just around Strumble Head near Fishguard. Lockout 10am-5pm. Curfew 5pm. Open July-Aug. daily; Apr.-June and Sept.-Oct. W-Su. Dorms £8.10, under 18 £5.65, camping £4.

> **YHA St. David's:** (☎ (01437) 720345; fax 721831), near St. David's Head at the foot of a mountain. Take the path past the bishop's palace and follow signs to the hostel, or walk White Sands Road to the golf course and follow the signs from there (about 2 mi. either way). Tony's Taxis (☎ (0860) 967058) will deliver you to the door for £4-5. Beds in a converted stable. Lockout 10am-5pm, but daytime access to dining hall. Curfew 11pm. Open mid-July to Aug. daily; Apr. to mid-July and Sept.-Oct. W-Su. Dorms £8.10, under 18 £5.65.

> **YHA Trevine:** (☎ (01348) 831414), between St. David's and Fishguard. Bus #411 will stop at the hostel upon request. Lockout 10am-5pm. Curfew 11pm. Open July-Aug. daily; Apr.-June and Sept.-Oct. Tu-Sa. Dorms £8.10, under 18 £5.65.

HIKING

For short hikes, stick to the more accessible **St. David's Peninsula,** in the northwest. Otherwise, set out on the 186 mi. **Coastal Path,** which is marked with acorn symbols and covers mostly manageable terrain. The path begins in the southeast at Amroth and continues west through Tenby to St. Govan's Head, where steep, worn steps down a cliffside lead to ◪ **St. Govan's Chapel,** clinging to a tiny patch of cliff over crashing ocean. Many myths surround the chapel, one being that Arthurian knight Sir Gawain retreated here after the fall of Camelot. In folklore, its well waters heal ills and grant wishes, and no mortal can count its steps.

From here to the impressive **Elegug Stacks,** towering rock pinnacles a bit offshore, birds cling to the rocks and the high cliffs. The path passes natural sea arches such as the Green Bridge of Wales, mile-wide lily pools at Bosherston, and limestone stacks. Unfortunately, the six-mile stretch from St. Govan's Head to the Stacks is sometimes closed to hikers for use as an artillery range. Call **Pembroke National Park Office** (☎ (01646) 682148) for open times, or check postings at the tourist information centre in Tenby. For approximately 10 mi. west of the Stacks, the coast is permanently off-limits, and the path veers inland until **Freshwater West.**

From Freshwater West to **Angle Bay,** the coastline walk covers mild and exceptionally pretty terrain. The path breaks slightly at Milford Haven, where it is crossed by a channel running over 25 mi. inland. Geologists call it a "ria," or drowned river valley. From the Dale Peninsula, the path passes by the long, clean beaches of St. Bride's Bay, turns up to Newgale, and arrives at the ancient **St. David's Head,** the site of pre-Cambrian formations and the oldest named feature on the coast of Wales. The ocean has carved away caves and secluded inlets; the surrounding jagged terrain is awe-inspiring.

▓ ISLANDS OFF THE PEMBROKESHIRE COAST

GRASSHOLM. On Grassholm, farthest from the shore, 35,000 pairs of gannets nest and raise their young. **Dale Sailing Company** (☎ (01646) 601636) runs trips around, but not to, the island from Martin's Haven on the Dale Peninsula, often encountering Manx shearwaters and storm petrels along the way. (May-Sept. M and F at 10am and noon. Guided trips Th 5pm. £20. Reservations required.)

The company also sails to the island of **Skomer,** a marine reserve and breeding ground for auks, seals, and puffins. (Apr.-Oct. Tu-Su. £6, children £4; landing fee £6, students £3, seniors £5, under 16 free.)

SKOKHOLM ISLAND. Serious bird enthusiasts sing the praises of Skokholm Island, accessible on Mondays via cruises run by the National Park, June to mid-August. Contact any National Park Information Centre or the Wildlife Trust West Wales at Lockley Lodge; reservations are required. (☎ (01646) 636234. Departs 10am. £6.50, children £5; landing fee £9, children £3.50, includes guide and walk.)

RAMSEY ISLAND. Seals and rare seabirds live on Ramsey Island, off St. David's farther up the coast. On the east side of the island lurk the **Bitches,** a chain of offshore rocks where sailors have come to grief. **Thousand Islands Expeditions** (☎ (01437) 721686, ☎ (0800) 163621), Cross Sq. in St. David's, sail from Whitesands Bay or St. Justinians for a tour around Ramsey Island. (2hr., Easter-Nov. daily, weather permitting. £10, children £6.) They also offer landing trips to the island from St. Justinians (Easter-Oct. W-M twice a day; £10, children £5), and occasionally trips with both landing and a tour around the island (£18, children £9). The adventurous will brave the frothy passages between the Bitches on a white-water jetboat trip (1hr., £20; adults only), or on a trip through the island's sea-caves, the longest in Wales (2hr., £20, children under 14 £10). **Ramsey Island Cruises,** Cross Sq., St. David's, also runs tours around the island. (☎ (01437) 721911, after hours ☎ (01437) 721802. Tours in normal boats £10, seniors £8, children £6; in super-speedy inflatable boats £12, children £7.)

PEMBROKE (PENFRO) AND PEMBROKE DOCK   ☎01646

Bounded by a towering Norman castle and 14th-century walls, Pembroke is not the military stronghold it once was. This former bastion of anti-Cromwell resistance now invites visitors to stroll down Main St., above the surrounding houses. Nearby Pembroke Dock lacks the ancestry of its neighbor—the ferry to Rosslare, Ireland, is its greatest attraction today. Both towns are stepping stones to the Pembrokeshire Coast National Park, but Pembroke is the more popular place to stay.

Ⅲ GETTING THERE. Pembroke's unstaffed **train station** rests on Lower Lamphey Rd. **Trains** (☎ (08457) 484950) run to Pembroke and Pembroke Dock from **Tenby, Swansea,** and points farther east (Su-F 5 per day, Sa 9 per day). In Pembroke, **buses** going east stop outside the Somerfield supermarket; those going north stop at the castle. **National Express** (☎ (08705) 808080) arrives from **London** (#508, 6hr., 3 per day, £19.50) and **Cardiff** via **Swansea** (3½hr., 3 per day, £10.75). In Pembroke Dock, buses stop at the **Silcox Garage** (☎ 683143; open M-F 8:30am-5:30pm). Be sure to clearly signal your stop to the bus driver. **First Cymru** (☎ (0870) 6082608) stops in Pembroke and Pembroke Dock between **Tenby** and **Haverfordwest** (#349, M-Sa 12 per day, Su 5 per day). **Irish Ferries** (☎ (0990) 171717) and **Stena Sealink** (☎ (0990) 707070) send ferries and catamarans from Pembroke Dock to **Rosslare, Ireland** (walk-on single £16, vehicle 5-day return £189). See **By Ferry**, p. 35.

■⌧ ORIENTATION AND PRACTICAL INFORMATION. Pembroke Castle lies up the hill on the western end of **Main St.;** the street's other end fans into five streets from a roundabout. The **tourist information centre** (TIC) occupies a former slaughterhouse on Commons Rd. below the elevated heights of the town center, and displays an exhibit on the town's history. The staff books ferries and accommodations and carries decent town maps. (☎ 622388; fax 621396. Open Easter-Oct. daily 10am-5:30pm; Nov. and Feb.-Easter Tu, Th, and Sa 10am-4pm.) **Barclays bank** is on 35 Main St. (☎ 684996. Open M and W-F 9am-4:30pm, Tu 10am-4:30pm.) Services include the **police** (☎ 682121), Water St., Pembroke Dock; and the **post office,** 49 Main St., Pembroke (☎ 682737; open M-F 9am-5:30pm, Sa 9am-1pm). **Postal code:** SA71 4JT.

⌧⌧ ACCOMMODATIONS AND FOOD. The nearest **YHA Youth Hostel** is in Manorbier on the bus line between Tenby and Pembroke (see p. 450). The few B&Bs in Pembroke are scattered about. Originally a Victorian merchant's house, **Merton Place House,** 3 East Back, off Main St., holds a walled rose garden. (☎ 684796. £17.50 per person.) Restaurants in Pembroke know well that hungry tourists will gobble up anything within reach. Gather a bargain feast at **Somerfield** on Main St. (Open M-Sa 8am-8pm, Su 10am-4pm.) **Mallard's,** 16 Main St., sells sandwiches and baguettes (£1.75-3.25), and selections of fudge and truffles. (☎ 682889. Open M-Sa 10am-5pm.) Across the Northgate St. Bridge on your right is the **Watermans Arms** pub, where you can sit by Mill Pond with a view of swans and the occasional carousing otter. (Open M-Sa 11am-3pm and 6-11pm, Su 7-10:30pm.)

⌧ SIGHTS. ⌧ Pembroke Castle, at the head of Main St., is a mighty fortress, authentically restored and a feast for the imagination. Imagine racing down snail shell staircases and high guard walks in the heat of battle; imagine hearing the first cries of baby Henry VII and the Tudor dynasty in one of the seven massive towers; imagine camera crews hauling across the immaculate inner courtyard while filming C.S. Lewis's Chronicles of Narnia; imagine a five-story stone-cold latrine tower. Whoa. Climbing the 100 steps of Britain's most imposing Norman keep results in a fine view of rolling hills and a not-so-fine view of Pembroke Dock's smokestacks. The gatehouse runs a thorough exhibit on the castle's history. (☎ 684585. Open daily Apr.-Sept. 9:30am-6pm; Mar. and Oct. 10am-5pm; Nov.-Feb. 10am-4pm. £3, seniors and children £2, families £8. Tours May-Aug. 4 per day; 50p, children free.)

Pembroke swells with churches, the only havens surviving the village desertions during the Black Plague. Have a look at the 12th-century **St. Daniel's Church,** St. Daniel Hill by the train station; the 13th-century windows of **St. Mary's Church,** Main St.; or **Monkton Priory Church,** Church Terr., which has a hagioscope—a wall-slit that enabled leprous monks to watch the service at the altar.

ST. DAVID'S (TYDDEWI)　　　　　　　　　　☎ 01437

St. David's (pop. 1700) was once the largest and richest diocese in medieval Wales; it now stands proudly as Britain's smallest city, nearly out of reach on the western extremity of the Pembrokeshire coast. While you may have to plan ahead with bus schedules in hand to avoid being stranded, it's well worth the time and effort. There is an almost magical serenity about St. David's; the hill sweeps down from the tiny village through quiet fields to a quiet shore. In the Middle Ages, St. David's was considered so holy that two pilgrimages here equaled one to Rome, and three equaled one to Jerusalem. Today's pilgrims, while also drawn to the cathedral, come for peace amidst coves and fiery sunsets far out over the deep Atlantic.

🕿🔢 GETTING THERE AND PRACTICAL INFORMATION. The **Richards Bros.** (☎ (01239) 613756) **Haverfordwest-Fishguard bus** hugs the coast, stopping at St. David's from both towns (#411, 50min., M-Sa 5 per day with many other buses going only to St. David's). A day-long **Explorer Pass** may be the cheapest return fare at £3.40. **Tony's Taxis** (☎ (0860) 967058) come when you call. The **National Park Information Centre**, The Grove, will book you a bed. (☎ 720392; fax 720099; www.stdavids.co.uk. Open Easter-Oct. daily 9:30am-5:30pm; Nov.-Easter M-Sa 10am-4pm.) Services include: **Barclays**, corner of High St. and New St. (open M-F 9:30am-4pm); the **police** (☎ 764545), High St., or the **Haverfordwest police** (☎ 763355); and the **post office**, 13 New St. (☎ 720283; open M-F 9am-5:30pm, Sa 9am-1pm). **Postal code:** SA62 6SW.

🔢🔢 ACCOMMODATIONS AND FOOD. The **YHA Youth Hostel** in St. David's lies two miles northwest of town at the foot of a rocky outcrop near the ancient St. David's Head (see p. 450). **B&Bs** in the city charge £14-20. **Pen Albro Bed and Breakfast,** 18 Goat St., has TVs and stereos in every room; the doubles have art deco fireplaces and wedding-cake canopies on the beds. (☎ 721865. £14.50 per person.) **Norma's,** 45 Nun St., is a cheerful family-run B&B, warmly accommodating to groups or singles. The proprietress also opens for home-cooked Welsh dinners, and is happy to share her expertise in holistic and aroma therapy. (☎/fax 721781; mel.davies@virgin.net. £16.50 per person, group and student rates lower.)

For excellent Welsh food, head for the elegant interiors of **Cartref,** in Cross Sq. Their imaginative menu features both traditional and vegetarian items; the terrific Celtic Pie (wholemeal and oat flan, laverbread, veggies and cheese, £8.50) combines the two. Starters and sandwiches are available for £2-3, with a children's menu at £2.85. (☎ 720422. Open June-Aug. 11am-3pm, 6-9pm; closed Sept.-May.) Join the crowd at **Prices,** Nun St., for delicious takeaway sandwiches, breads, and pasties. Doubling as a food store, it serves up a double burger at an unbeatable £2.40. (☎ 720219. Cooked food from 5pm. Open 7am-11pm in the summer, until 10pm the rest of the year.)

🔢 SIGHTS. ▨ **St. David's Cathedral,** perhaps the finest in Wales, stands majestically in a hollow by a sloping, grassy graveyard below the village. A great diversity of styles and periods are represented in its ancient crumbling arches, massive stone buttresses, and slanting floors; a few remnants of the 6th-century church linger on in the 12th-century structure. Like lakes on a lucid day, the tiled floors at times seem to mirror the painted ceiling, whose wooden timbers exude a live smell into the airy chambers. The contents of the reliquary betray the cathedral's importance as a religious site: a chest holds the bones of St. David, the patron saint of Wales, and his comrade St. Justinian, who was killed on nearby Ramsey Island but managed to carry his own head back to the mainland for burial. In the St. Thomas à Becket chapel, the stained-glass window portrays three rather surly knights jabbing with their swords at poor old prostrate Becket. (Open 6am to around 9pm, after evening services. Suggested donation £2, children £1.)

The **Bishop's Palace,** a few yards away across a bridged brook, eschewed frugality and proclaimed the wealth of the medieval bishops when it was Wales's largest palace. (☎ 720517. Open Oct. and Apr.-May 9:30am-5pm; June-Sept. 9:30am-6pm; Nov.-Mar. M-Sa 9:30am-4pm, Su noon-2pm. £2, concessions £1.50, families £5.50.) A half a mile south of town, the ruined seaside walls of **St. Non's Chapel** mark the site of St. David's birth around AD 500. According to *Historia o Uuched Dewi (The Life of St. David)*, at the moment of his birth, the saint split a rock poised to fall on his mother, saving them both. Water from the nearby well supposedly cures all ills; take Goat St. downhill from the town and follow signs to health and happiness. Tours run to **Ramsey Island,** off the coast (see p. 451).

FISHGUARD ☎ 01348

The victim of pirate attacks and privateers, star of the film *Moby Dick*, and harbor of the late *Lusitania*, modest Fishguard hasn't let its several moments of celebrity go to its head. A town in three parts, its roots lie in Lower Town's herring trade, where merchants and smugglers made the money that moved the town up the cliff to Upper Fishguard, and later down to the region of Goodwick around an international harbor. At its height, the wealth and limelight of Fishguard attracted smugglers, pirates, and travelers; when they departed they left the town to recede backstage, where it took on its current role as ferry port. Still, rumors of passageways from Upper Town basements to smugglers' caves, cannon balls wedged in hotel walls, and local pride in its history keep Fishguard quietly vital and solidly grounded on its perch and ports looking out to the teal blue Cardigan Bay.

🖸 GETTING THERE AND GETTING AROUND. Although history saw a time when Fishguard was *the* connection point to distant lands, public transport to Fishguard now takes some maneuvering. **Trains** (☎ (08457) 484950) pull into **Fishguard Harbor,** Goodwick, from **London** via **Bristol, Cardiff, Newport,** and **Whitland** (4½hr., 1 per day). **Buses** stop at **Fishguard Square,** off Vergam Terrace. From the north, take **Richards Bros.** (☎ (01239) 613756) buses from **Aberystwyth** to **Cardigan** (#550/551, 2hr., 11 per day) and then from **Cardigan** to **Fishguard** (#412, 1½hr., 1 per hour, £3-4). Take **First Cymru** (☎ (08706) 082608) buses from **Tenby** or **Pembroke** to **Haverfordwest** (#349; 1hr.; M-Sa 1 per hour, Su 6 per day; £2-4) and from **Haverfordwest** to **Fishguard** (#412, 45min., 1 per hr., £1.98). Two **ferries** (☎ (08475) 707070) run daily from **Rossiare, Ireland: Stena Lynx** (£20-29, children £10-14) and **Superferry** (£16-20, children £8-10). Call for reservations (see **By Ferry,** p. 35). **Town bus** #410 shuttles the mile between the Fishguard Harbor and Fishguard Square, and **Merv's Taxis** (☎ 875129) are on call 24 hours a day.

🖸 PRACTICAL INFORMATION. The **tourist information centre** (TIC), Town Hall, Main St., sells National Express tickets and books rooms for 10% of the first night's stay. (☎ 873484; fax 875246. Open daily Easter-Oct. 10am-4:30pm., M-Sa Nov.-Easter 10am-4pm.) Across the square from the TIC, **Barclays** has a 24hr. cash machine. (☎ 822400; fax 402999. Open M-T and Th-F 9am-4:30pm, W 10am-4:30pm.) Services include: **Dyfed Cleaning,** Brodog Terr. (☎ 872140; wash £1.75, dry 75p per 15min., soap 45p per cup; open M-Sa 8:30am-4:30pm); **Internet access** at **Cyber Café,** The Parrog (£2 per 30min.); the **police** (☎ 872835), Brodog Terr.; the **hospital** (☎ 873041), The Ropewalk; and the **post office,** 57 West St. (☎ 873863; open M-F 9am-5:30pm, Sa 9am-12:30pm). **Postal Code:** SA65 9NG.

🖸🖸 ACCOMMODATIONS AND FOOD. Pricey B&Bs (£16-20) run up **High St.** in Upper Fishguard. Weary travelers and wayward backpackers run home to the 🖸 **Harlton Guest House & Backpackers Lodge,** 21-23 Hamilton St. The beds and atmosphere are hugely comfortable, and the couches in the book-lined TV lounge aren't bad either. Enjoy toast and tea breakfasts, or the occasional backyard barbecue while swinging in the garden hammocks. Laundry, cooking, and Internet facilities. No lockout or curfew. (☎ 874797; stephenism@ukgateway.net. Dorms £10; singles £12; doubles £24; group discounts.) Peaceful **Avon House,** 76 High St., has inviting interiors and proprietors. The rooms are large and fresh, as are the breakfasts. (☎ 874476. £16 per person, £8 under 12 with family, £4 supplement for singles.)

If you come to Fishguard with dreams of fish and chips, rest easy: **Bursco's** (☎ 872008), Market Square, fries up good spuds and fins. **Y Pantri,** 31 West St., rolls chicken and cheese sandwiches, corned beef pasties, and crusty pizza boats for under £3. (☎ 872637. Open M-Sa 9am-5:30pm.) **Taj Mahal,** 22 High St., has a full menu of Indian and Tandoori, with especially celebrated cardamom-rich curry. Main dishes range from £3.50 to £7.50. (☎ 874593. Open M-Su 6-11:30pm, takeaway until midnight.) Not just your average pub and converted barn, **The Old Coach House,** High St., serves a mammoth menu of traditional or Italian creations in its spacious, solid-beamed restaurant. (☎ 875429. Open M-Sa 11am-11pm, Su noon-10:30pm; food served noon-2pm and 6-9pm.)

FRENCH MISS In 1797, the last-ever invasion of Britain took place, when three frigates landed on the shores just outside Fishguard. Led by the Irish-American General Tate, this band of 1500 Frenchmen (all convicts) gallantly aimed to recapture the glory days of 1066. But when the warriors landed, they set up headquarters in a farmhouse that was stocked for a wedding—and the party favors more than quenched the soldiers' thirst. Tate's force, now a drunken mob, couldn't hold out long enough to recover from the hangover. When the gallant heroes emerged from the farmhouse onto the fields of battle, they were met by hundreds of red-cloaked women in the surrounding hills who had assembled to witness the spectacle. Thinking himself vastly outnumbered by British soldiers, a disillusioned Tate surrendered. Jemima Nicholas, a 47-year-old cobbler, captured 14 Frenchmen single-handedly. *La gloire*, indeed.

◙ ♫ SIGHTS AND ENTERTAINMENT. The **Marine Walk,** an undulating paved path running along the ocean cliffs of the three regions of Fishguard, has exquisite overlooks on town and sea, as well as interesting plaques reporting the town's rich history. Peer down, as Richard Burton and Gregory Peck did, on **Lower Town,** where both *Under Milk Wood* and *Moby Dick* were filmed. One can see **Goodwick Harbor,** where the flagship *Lusitania* began its monthly sails to America, and where the first flight from Britain to Ireland took off. Near the shores that saw the last invasion of Britain, the Bayeux style **Last Invasion Tapestry,** in St. Mary's Church Hall, Market Sq., recounts the story. Stitched by local women, the 100 ft. long canvas depicts the unsuccessful French invasion of 1797, colored by local legends that have evolved since. (☎ 873484. Open Apr.-Oct. M-Sa 10am-5pm, Su 2-5pm; Nov.-Mar. M-Sa 11am-4pm, Su 2-4pm. £1.50, children 50p, under 8 free.)

In a glassy building overlooking the beach, **Ocean Lab,** The Parrog, features a 15-minute show by the Henson Creature Shop, famous for their muppeteering. The simulation of a submarine time trip to view prehistoric sea creatures is particularly suited to young children. The lab also has a few hands-on exhibits of show-relevant phenomena. (☎ 874737. Open daily Easter-Oct. 10am-6pm. Call for winter times.) During the day, picnickers and sun gluttons pebble the protected **Goodwick Beach.** If you have a whole day, enquire at the TIC about walks and tours into the **Preseli Hills**, ancient sacred grounds that still support stone circles and a mysterious **standing stone.**

Fishguard nightlife can be a bit dodgy early in the week, but weekends erupt into a pub scene of festival proportions. **The Old Coach House** (above) is the place to be, but all pubs along **High St.** see some action.

NORTH WALES

Since the 14th century, when Welsh rebel leaders plotted their campaigns against the English from headquarters deep in Snowdonia, the mountains, valleys, and towns of North Wales have rung with cries of a nationalism historically more fierce than in the south. Although the English King Edward I designed a ring of spectacular fortresses to keep the rebels in the mountains, Welsh pride never wavered and remains strong despite (or perhaps due to) centuries of union with England. With the guttural sounds of the Welsh language ringing in their ears, monolinguists will struggle to get their tongues around the markedly un-Anglicized town names, and to make sense of streets whose names appear in Welsh on maps but in English on signs, or vice versa. Even the topography of the region seems to pronounce its distinctiveness: tall, jagged Welsh hills and cliffs contrast sharply with the placid English flatlands to the east.

   If you want to escape the crowds that invariably flock to Edward I's castles on the north coast, head to the mountain footpaths, lakes, and hamlets of Snowdonia National Park, which covers the larger part of northwest Wales. Mount Snowdon itself, at 3560 ft., is the highest and most precipitous peak in England and Wales. Other ranges, such as the Glyders or the mountains around Cader Idris, challenge blissfully smaller numbers of serious hikers. To the west, the largely unspoiled Llŷn Peninsula invites visitors to its sandy beaches; to the northwest, the Isle of Anglesey beckons with prehistoric remains; to the east languishes the peaceful Vale of Conwy. Near the English border, Llangollen hosts the annual International Musical Eisteddfod, attended by performers from around the world (see p. 422).

NORTH WALES

HIGHLIGHTS OF NORTH WALES

SNOWDONIA Dash (okay, hike) up **Mount Snowdon,** the highest peak in England and Wales and the center of **Snowdonia National Park** (p. 467), land of craggy peaks, high moors, dark pine forests, and deep glacial lakes.

LLYN PENINSULA Go Mediterranean at the Italianate village of **Portmeirion** (p. 464) before heading for the quiet beaches of this unhurried peninsula (p. 463).

CASTLES Lord it over townsfolk and peasants, as well as tourists storming the city walls, from the towers of the majestic castles at **Beaumaris** (p. 479), **Caernarfon** (p. 473), **Conwy** (p. 480), and **Harlech** (p. 461).

ANGLESEY Wave your flashlight about in the eerie Celtic burial mounds and other prehistoric ruins on the ancient **Isle of Anglesey** (p. 477).

ABERYSTWYTH
☎ **01970**

Ever since a bevy of academics moved in—the University College of Wales was established here in 1874, and the National Library of Wales in 1909—the crowded streets of Aberystwyth (Abber-RIST-with) have been packed with students. Though salt-stained buildings, a hotel-lined quay, and the inevitable camera-toting tourists betray Aberystwyth's hybrid role as a resort town, it's the would-be scholars who fill seaside flats, raucous pubs, and innumerable veggie cafes. Firmly situated in the sweeping curve of the Cardigan Bay coastline, halfway between St. David's and the Llŷn Peninsula, Aberystwyth is a pleasant stop for travelers heading north towards mountain valleys and craggy peaks.

◨ GETTING THERE AND GETTING AROUND

A transport hub for all of Wales, Aberystwyth sits at the end of a rail line running from Shrewsbury, England.

456

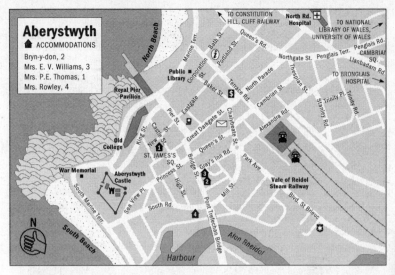

Aberystwyth

🏠 ACCOMMODATIONS

Bryn-y-don, 2
Mrs. E. V. Williams, 3
Mrs. P.E. Thomas, 1
Mrs. Rowley, 4

NORTH WALES

Trains: Alexandra Rd. Office open M-F 6:20am-5:25pm, Sa 6:20am-3:20pm. Trains from **Machynlleth** (30min.; M-Sa 10 per day, Su 6 per day; £4.60) and **Shrewsbury** (2hr.; M-Sa 7 per day, Su 5 per day; £8.40). Machynlleth is the southern terminus of the **Cambrian Coaster** line running up the northern coast to **Pwllheli**. The **Cambrian Coaster Day Ranger** (☎ (01766) 512340) covers travel the length of the line (£6.40; after 4:30pm, £3.60). The **Vale of Rheidol Railway** (☎ 625819) runs to sites in the mountains (see p. 459).

Buses: Alexandra Rd., in front of the train station. **National Express** (☎ (08705) 808080) from **London** via **Birmingham** (#420, 7hr., 1 per day, £19.25). **TrawsCambria** bus #701 from **Cardiff** (4hr., 1 per day, £10.90) and **Holyhead** (4hr., 1 per day, £14.50). **Arriva Cymru** (☎ (08706) 082608) operates jointly with **Richards Bros.** from **Machynlleth** (#2; 1hr.; M-Sa 5 per day, Su 2 per day; £3.80) and **Cardigan** via **Synod Inn** (#550; 1½hr.; M-Sa 7 per day, Su 2 per day; £4). **Day Rover** tickets (£5), valid on all Arriva buses, are available from the driver. The **North and Mid-Wales Rover,** available for 1 day, 3 days, or a week, is valid on all buses and trains north of the imaginary Aberystwyth-Shrewsbury line as well as Arriva Cymru buses south of Aberystwyth.

Taxis: Express (☎ 612319). Open 24hr.

ℹ PRACTICAL INFORMATION

Tourist Information Centre: Lisburne House (☎ 612125; fax 626566), Terrace Rd., on the corner of Bath St. Chipper, helpful staff doles out dossiers of B&B photos and rates. Room bookings £1. Open daily July-Aug. 9am-6pm; Sept.-June M-Sa 10am-5pm.

Financial Services: Barclays, North Parade. Open M and W-F 9am-5pm, Tu 10am-5pm, Sa 10am-12:30pm. **Lloyds TSB,** Terrace Rd. Open M-T and Th-F 9am-5pm, W 9:30am-5pm.

Launderette: Wash 'n' Spin 'n' Dry, 16 Bridge St. Bring change. Wash £2, dry 20p per cycle, soap 10p. Open daily 7am-9pm, last wash 8:30pm.

Market: Market Hall, St. James Sq. Open M-Sa 8am-5pm.

Police: (☎ 612791), Blvd. St. Brieuc, at the end of Park Ave.

Hospital: Bronglais General Hospital (☎ 623131), Caradog Rd., 5min. walk up Penglais Rd. 24hr. switchboard.

Internet access: Biognosis, 21 Pier St. (☎ 636953). £2.50 per hr., £1 min. charge. Open M-Th 9am-9pm, F 9am-5pm, Sa 10am-6pm, Su noon-6pm.

Post Office: 8 Great Darkgate St. (☎ 632630). **Bureau de change.** Open M-F 9am-5:30pm, Sa 9am-12:30pm. **Postal Code:** SY23 1DE.

ACCOMMODATIONS

Expensive B&Bs (£16-30) snuggle up with student housing on the waterfront. **Bridge St.** has a small B&B community, and a few cheap establishments are scattered on **South Rd.** and **Rheidol Terr.**

Mrs. E. V. Williams, 28 Bridge St. (☎ 612550). Large rooms with staggeringly comfortable beds. Kind proprietress bakes heavenly Welsh cakes and gladly shares the secrets of the mysterious *bara brith.* £15 per person.

YHA Borth (☎ 871498), 9 mi. north of Aberystwyth in Borth. Beautifully set among beaches, the hostel is often full. Take the train to Borth (10min.; M-Sa 12 per day, Su 8 per day; £1.50) or Crosville bus #511 or 512 (30min., 1 per hr.). From the train station, turn right onto the main road and walk 5min. Kitchen available. Open Apr.-Aug. daily; Sept. M-Sa; Oct. and Mar. Tu-Sa. Dorms £9.80, under 18 £6.75.

Mrs. P. E. Thomas, 8 New St. (☎ 617329), off Pier St. Digest the mammoth breakfast amid Chinese paintings and a giant harp. All rooms have TVs. £15 per person.

Mrs. Rowley, 28 South Rd. (☎ 612115), off Bridge St. TVs and washbasins share space with ten thousand stuffed animals. £15 per person.

Bryn-y-don, 36 Bridge St. (☎ 612011; fax 636678). Large rooms with TV. £16 per person.

Camping: Midfield Caravan Park (☎ 612542), 1½ mi. from town center on the A4120, 200 yd. uphill from the junction with the A487. From Alexandra Rd. take any bus going to Southgate. One of the most pleasant campsites in the area, with a view of town and the hills. £4.50 per person; £9.40 for two.

FOOD

On **Pier St.**, takeaway spots are cheap and open on Sunday. **Spar,** 32 Terrace Rd. (open daily 24hr.) sells sundries. **The Academy** and **Lord Beechings** serve pub grub to hungry travelers; see **Pubs, Nightlife, and Entertainment,** p. 459.

Gannets Bistro, St. James Sq. (☎ 617164). The former head of British Airways' catering department runs the place; if only airline food was half this good. Main courses may stretch the budget (£6.50-10), but a few starters can make a satisfying meal (£1.50-3); the ravioli au gratin (£1.25) is first class, and the hot smoked mackerel (£1.25) makes economy dining delicious. Vegetarian items abound. Open M and W-Sa noon-2pm and 6-9:30pm, last orders 1:30pm and 8:30pm.

The Treehouse Cafe, 14 Baker St. (☎ 615791). Summery tablecloths and wood floors atop the Treehouse Organic Shop. Cool your carnivorous cravings with beef burgers (£3.10), or terrorize chick-peas the world over by ordering hummus with pita (£1.30). The ginger beer (£1.10) and guava juice are both divine. Open M-W 9:30am-5:30pm, Th-Sa 9:30am-5:30pm and 6:30-9:30pm.

Sunclouds, 25 North Parade (☎ 617750). Sit at the wooden counters of this cafe and watch the world go by as you bite into a tasty baguette (£2-2.50) or sip a flavored coffee (£1.25). Takeaway available. Open M-Sa 10am-4:30pm.

The Ancient Rain Vegetarian Eatery, 13 Cambrian Pl. (☎ 612363), on the corner of Union St. Arrayed in bright blue and yellow, they serve pancakes (£2.75) and vegan and vegetarian meals from £4.50. Takeaway available. Open M-Sa 10am-4:30pm.

SIGHTS

PIER. Aberystwyth's charming *fin-de-siècle* pier has been battered by the tourist trade. The beachfront and promenade remain much as they were in Victorian times, and pastel townhouses still lend the town a tamed, aristocratic air. At the south end of the promenade stands the university's **Old College,** a neo-Gothic structure opened in 1877 as a hotel and restored in 1885 as Wales's first university. Prince Charles was drilled in Welsh here before being crowned Prince of Wales in 1969. For fishing trips, check at the pier or call **Sunshine Boat Trips** (☎ 828844).

ABERYSTWYTH CASTLE. Just south of the Old College on a hilly peninsula, the castle has witnessed centuries of Welsh rebellion and English repression. Before Edward I built the present castle in 1277, previous forts had burned down nearly half a dozen times, the fifth at the hands of the last Welsh Prince of Gwynedd, Llewelyn ap Gruffydd. Oliver Cromwell made quick work of the diamond-shaped fortress in 1649. When night falls, the crumbling walls are often silhouetted against fiery sunsets over the shimmering Atlantic. *(Partial wheelchair access. Free.)*

ELECTRIC CLIFF RAILWAY. At the northern end of the promenade, the railway creaks up an angle normally associated with roller coasters to the top of **Constitution Hill.** At the top lies the wide lens of the camera obscura, a popular Victorian amusement which acts as a giant pinhole camera onto the whole city. You can also walk across the small series of wooden bridges to the camera. *(☎ 617642. Open daily July-Aug. 10am-6pm; mid-Mar. to June and Sept.-Oct. 10am-5pm. Trains 6 per hr., return £2, students and seniors £1.75, children £1, under 5 free, families £5.80. Camera obscura free.)*

NATIONAL LIBRARY OF WALES. An imposing classical structure sitting on a bluff overlooking the bay, the National Library of Wales, off Penglais Rd. past the hospital, houses almost every book or manuscript written in, or pertaining to, Wales. The well-designed **Gregynog Gallery** displays the first Welsh written text (c. 800), the first Welsh printed book (1546), the first Welsh dictionary (1547), the first Welsh map (1573), the first Welsh "Beibl" (1588), and the first Welsh magazine (1735), which managed one issue before it folded. In another corner, scalded toutes and lusty bachelors rise from the pages of the earliest surviving manuscript of the *Canterbury Tales*, dating to the early 15th century. *(☎ 632800. Open M-F 9:30am-6pm, Sa 9:30am-5pm. Free.)*

🎵🎶 PUBS, NIGHTLIFE, AND ENTERTAINMENT

There are over 50 pubs in Aberystwyth, and the owners all tell tales of the student swarms that keep them buzzing. **The Academy,** St. James Sq., takes the pub scene to school. It's a converted chapel where sports are cast over a 16-ft. screen and breakfast is served all day. *(☎ 636852. Open M-Sa noon-11pm, Su noon-10:30pm. Food served noon-3pm and 6-8:30pm).* **Lord Beechings,** Alexandra Rd., is fit for a king and priced for a poor man, serving huge, cheap meals. *(☎ 625069. Open M-Sa 11am-11pm, Su 11am-10:30pm. Food served noon-2pm and 6-8:45pm).* A vine-covered beer garden and reveling students make **Rummer's,** Pont Trefechan Bridge, at the end of Bridge St., a choice stop for a round. *(Open M-W and Sa 7pm-midnight, Th-F 7pm-1am, Su 7-10:30pm.)* Smashed mirrors quake and smashed clubbers shake n' bake at **Pier Pressure,** The Royal Pier, Marine Terr. Thursdays rocks to 60's, 70's and 80's, while the weekend's "Cheese Factory" pulls in younger tastes. *(☎ 136100. Cover £1-4. Open M-W 10:30pm-1am, Th-F 10pm-1am, Sa 9pm-1am.)*

Up Penglais Rd., in the University of Wales at Aberystwyth campus, stands the **Aberystwyth Arts Centre,** which sponsors Welsh drama and film in Welsh and English. *(☎ 623232. Box office open daily 10am-5pm.)*

📸 DAYTRIPS FROM ABERYSTWYTH

🏰 DEVIL'S BRIDGE

Trains from Aberystwyth run mid-July to Aug. 4 per day some weekdays, 2 per day weekends and some weekdays, M-Th 10am-4pm, F-Su 10am-2:30pm; Apr. to mid-Jul. and Sept.-Oct. 2 per day, 10am-2:30pm. Rides £10.50, accompanied child £1, 2 accompanied children £1.50, dogs £1.

Originally built to serve the lead mines, the **Vale of Rheidol Railway** *(☎ (01970) 625819)* chugs and twists its way on tracks less than 2 ft. apart from Aberystwyth station to the waterfalls and gorges of Devil's Bridge. The **three bridges** *(☎ (01970) 890233)* were inexplicably built on top of one another; the lower bridge, attributed to the Architect of Evil, was probably built by Cistercian monks from the nearby **Strata Florida Abbey** in the 12th century. (Abbey open daily 10am-5pm. Admission charged May-Sept., Oct.-Apr. free.) The paths are turnstile-operated, so take some change. The rungs of **Jacob's Ladder** (£1.20) descend into the depth of the **Devil's Punchbowl** gorge, cross the torrent on an arched footbridge, and climb back beside the waterfall to the road.

MACHYNLLETH   ☎ 01654

And so 'twas to Machynlleth (mach-HUN-hleth) that Owain Glyndŵr, that great 15th-century Welsh rebel and the hero of our story, summoned four men from every commote in the territory to a vast open-air parliament. There it was explained that a commote corresponds roughly to 50 hamlets, each typically containing 9 houses, 1 plow, 1 oven, 1 churn, 1 cat, 1 cock, and 1 herdsman. When the delegates departed, the rebellion quickly unraveled, and the town collapsed into a slumber from which it has yet to fully awaken (even though the number of cocks in some hamlets has grown to at least two). However, modernity has begun to rouse the tiny mountain town, combining displays of cutting-edge technology with traditional Welsh character and ancient Celtic history.

▛ GETTING THERE AND GETTING AROUND. The **train station** (☎ 702311), on Doll St., receives **trains** (☎ (08457) 484950) from: **Aberystwyth** (30min.; M-Sa 12 per day, Su 6 per day; £3.90); **Shrewsbury** (1½hr.; M-Sa 8 per day, Su 5 per day; £10.50); and **Birmingham** (2½hr.; M-Sa 8 per day, Su 5 per day; £11.70). The **Cambrian Coaster Day Ranger** covers routes from **Aberystwyth** (£6.40; £3.50 after 4:30pm). **Buses** (☎ 702239) stop by the clock tower. **Arriva Cymru** (☎ (08706) 082608) bus #701 travels along the scenic A487 from **Aberystwyth** and **Dolgellau** (1hr.; M-Sa 5 per day, Su 2 per day; £5.10); bus #32 swerves inland from **Dolgellau** on an even lovelier route (7 per day, Su 1 per day in summer only, £4.80). **TrawsCambria** rolls in from: **Aberystwyth** and **Dolgellau** (#701, 1hr., £5.10); **Holyhead** (3½hr., £11.70); and **Cardiff** (5½hr., £14.50). Mountain **bikes**—perfect for exploring the nearby hills—can be rented at **Greenstiles,** 7 Penrallt St., next to the clock tower. (☎ 703543. £8 per half-day, £12 per day, £60 per week. 50% discount for Centre for Alternative Technology visitors. Open M-Sa 9:30am-5:30pm; Apr.-Sept. also Su 10am-4pm.)

▞▟ ORIENTATION AND PRACTICAL INFORMATION. The unmistakable heart of town is the **clock tower,** standing Eiffel-like where **Pentrerhedryn St., Penrallt St.,** and **Maengwyn St.** form a T. From the train station, turn left onto Doll St., veer right at the church onto Penrallt St., and continue until you see the clock tower; Maengwyn St. is on the left. The **tourist information centre** is in the Owain Glyndŵr Centre, Maengwyn St. (☎ 702401; fax 703675. Open M-Sa 9:30am-5:30pm, Su 10am-5pm.) A **Barclays bank** lies under the shadow of the tall timepiece. (Open M-W and F 9am-4:30pm, Th 10am-4:30pm.) Around the corner, find **Nigel's Launderette** on New St. (Wash £2, dry cycle 20p, no soap. Open M-Sa 8:30am-8pm, Su 9am-4:30pm.) Other services include: the **police** (☎ 702215), Doll St.; **Chest Hospital** (☎ 702341), Newton Rd.; and the **post office,** 51-53 Maengwyn St., inside the **Spar** store (☎ 702323; open M-F 8:30am-6pm, Sa 8:30am-3pm). **Postal code:** SY20 8AE.

▛▛ ACCOMMODATIONS AND FOOD. Machynlleth lacks a hostel, but **YHA Corris,** in the old school on Corris Rd. in Corris, is 15 minutes away on buses #30 or 32. Reminders of nature abound, from the hostel's position on the southern side of the Cader Idris mountain to its conservation motif. (☎/fax 761686. Laundry facilities. Lockout 10am-5pm. Open Jan.-Feb. and Nov. Th-Sa, mid-Feb. to Oct. daily. Dorms £9, under 18 £6.20.) Machynlleth has a fair number of **B&Bs,** but you'd be hard pressed to find a budget-friendly location. **Melin-y-Wig,** Aberystwyth Rd., near Celtica, has TVs in each room and an ark of a bathtub. (☎ 703933. Doubles £32.) **Haulfryn,** next door to Melin-y-Wig on Aberystwyth Rd., blooms with large, flowery bedrooms and a breakfast room packed with plates from around the world. (☎ 702206. £15 per person.) **Campers** can seek out the riverside **Llwyngwern Farm,** off the A487 next to the Centre for Alternative Technology. (☎ 702492. Open Apr.-Sept. £4 per person, £6.50 per 2 people.)

Machynlleth pubs offer nothing spectacular in the way of affordable gluttony, although tasty dishes are served alongside the massive stone hearth at the **Skinners Arms,** 10 Penrallt St., near the clock tower. Come nightfall, it's the liveliest pub in town. (☎ 702354. Open M-Sa 11am-11pm, Su noon-10:30pm; food served M-Sa noon-2pm and 6-9pm.) Cheap, healthy feasts can be had at the pine tables of the **Quarry Shop Café and Wholefoods,** 13 Maengwyn St. (☎ 702624. Open M-W and F-Sa 9am-5pm, Th 9am-2pm.) Craft your own menu from the groceries at **Spar,** 51-53 Maengwyn St. (open M-Sa 7am-11pm, Su 7am-10:30pm), or at the weekly **market** on the town's two main streets (open W 9am-4pm).

🗑 **SIGHTS.** From the gargoyled clock tower, a two-minute downhill walk along Aberystwyth Rd. (the A487) will bring you to **Celtica,** in Y Plas. The exhibit uses advanced high-tech wizardry to trace the millennia-old story of the Celtic peoples. Darkened chambers shrouded in mist feature rising cauldrons, rotating stone masks, and startling flashes of light, all to the thundering echo of a narrator's voice. In a bizarre but entertaining denouement, a druid atop a gnarled tree whisks you on a whirlwind video tour of Celtic history, bringing you back to the present. (☎ 702702; www.celtica.wales.com. Open daily 10am-6pm, last entrance 4:40pm. Wheelchair access. £4.95, concessions £3.80, families £13.75. YHA members 30% off. Half price with joint train/admission ticket.)

High on a hill three miles north of town along the A487, the **Centre for Alternative Technology** is like a giant summer camp whose counselors never leave. A funicular railway, powered by nifty water counterbalancing, draws visitors up a 200 ft. cliff into a green village of lily ponds, wind turbines, and energy-efficient houses, including the best-insulated house and the largest solar panel roof in Britain. Glimpse into the lifestyles of those living here communally, or climb into the Mole Hole with giant insect replicas. Crosville buses #30 and 34 (10min., M-Sa 8 per day) run to the entrance, or ride bus #32 (10min., M-Sa 5 per day) to Pantperthog and walk 200 yd. north and across a bridge. (☎ 702400. Open daily Easter-Oct. 10am-5:30pm; Nov.-Easter 10am-4pm. Water-powered railway open Easter-Oct. Wheelchair access. £6.90, students and seniors £4.90, children £3.50, families £19.50, under 5 free. YHA members and bus riders get a 10% discount; cyclists and pedestrians get a 50% discount. Joint admission and train ticket with a 50% discount can be purchased in staffed railway stations.)

Bringing the present into focus, or sometimes strikingly out of focus, the **Welsh Museum of Modern Art** in Y Tabernacl on Penrallt St., houses continuously rotating exhibits such as Peter Blake's *Prints* and John Meirion Morris's *Presence* sculptures. Summer evenings often hear music floating from the performance hall. (☎ 703355. Open M-Sa 10am-4pm. Free.) For a robustly informative walk through history, visit the **Owain Glyndŵr Interpretive Centre,** Maengwyn St., which occupies a primitive stone building on the site of Glyndŵr's parliament house; placards place the rebel's career in the context of Welsh mythology. (☎ 702827. Open Easter-Sept. M-Sa 10am-5pm; Su and winter by appointment. Free.)

HARLECH ☎ 01766

On the Cambrian coast just south of the Llŷn Peninsula and the foothills of Snowdonia, the tiny town of Harlech clings to a steep, rocky hillside that commands panoramic views of sea, sand, and summits. Harlech's castle, its chief attraction, ranks among the most spectacular in Wales, perched 200 ft. above the sea on an utterly impenetrable cliff outcropping. The grassy dunes far below its parapets attract those seeking solitude and cool sea breezes. While fair weather reveals craggy Snowdonia peaks by day and Llŷn town lights sparkling like diamonds along the bay by night, mist and rolling dark clouds (often the norm) lend an even more haunting texture to the scene.

🗐🗗 **GETTING THERE.** Harlech lies midway on the Cambrian Coaster line. The uphill walk to town from the unstaffed **train station** is quite a calf-burner; the stairs up the castle hill may look easier but are equally demoralizing. **Trains** arrive from **Machynlleth** (1½hr.; M-Sa 12 per day, Su 3 per day; £8.20) and connect to **Pwllheli** and other spots on the **Llŷn Peninsula** (M-F 5 per day, Sa 6 per day, Su 3 per day). The **Cambrian Coaster Day Ranger** (£6.40, evening version £3.50) is cheaper than the single fare from Machynlleth. **Arriva Cymru** (☎ (08706) 082608) **bus** #38 links Harlech to the southern beach town of **Barmouth** (M-Sa 10 per day, £1.80) and northern **Blaenau Ffestiniog** (M-Sa 4 per day, £1.80), stopping at the station and the car park, just past the tourist information centre on Stryd Fawr.

◼◪ ORIENTATION AND PRACTICAL INFORMATION. The castle opens out onto **Twtil;** slightly uphill is the town's major street, **Stryd Fawr** (High St.). The **tourist information centre** (TIC), Gwyddfor House, Stryd Fawr, doubles as a **Snowdonia National Park Information Centre.** The staff will help you stock up on Ordnance Survey maps and pamphlets detailing mountain walks. (☎/fax 780658. Open daily Easter-Oct. 10am-1pm and 2-6pm.) Services include an **HSBC bank** on Stryd Fawr (open M, W, and F 9:30-11:30am, Tu and Th 12:45-3pm) and the **post office** on Stryd Fawr (☎ 780231; open M-T and Th-F 9am-12:30pm and 1:30-5:30pm, W and Sa 9am-12:30pm). **Postal code:** LL46 2YA.

▐◌ ACCOMMODATIONS AND FOOD. The closest hostel is **YHA Llanbedr,** four miles south of town; take the train to the Llanbedr stop (10min.) or ride bus #38 and ask to be let off at the hostel. (☎ (01341) 241287; fax 241389. Open May-Aug. daily; mid-Feb. to Apr. and Sept.-Oct. Th-M; Jan. to mid-Feb. F-Su. Dorms £8, under 18 £5.35.) Revel in spacious rooms and what may be the best view in Harlech (spanning the castle, Snowdonia, and the Llŷn Peninsula) at ◪ **Arundel,** Stryd Fawr. From Barclays head north along High St. and take a right before the Yr Ogof Bistro. Sunny Mrs. Stein (pronounced Steen) will come pick you up if the climb from the train station does not appeal. (☎ 780637. £14 per person.) The **Byrdir Hotel,** on Stryd Fawr near the TIC, has comfortable rooms with TVs and washbasins, and a nearby water trough for your thirsty horse. (☎/fax 780316. £16.50 per person, with bath £21; single with bath £28.) **Camp** at **Min-y-Don Park,** Beach Rd., with showers and laundry. (☎ 780286. Open Mar.-Oct. £3 per person, children £1.)

Spar supermarket greets travelers next to the Plâs Café. (Open M-Sa 8am-8pm, summer until 10pm, Su 9am-8pm.) **Yr Ogof Bistro,** left from the castle on Stryd Fawr, offers some of the best cuisine for miles around, with a wide range of vegetarian dishes (£6.95), an interesting salad bar, and an extremely satisfying three-course Welsh menu for £10.95. (☎ 780888. Open daily 10am-10:30pm.) The sweeping ocean view from the grassy patio of the **Plâs Café,** Stryd Fawr, demands a long afternoon tea with gorgeous desserts (85p-£3.50) or a £7 sunset dinner. (☎ 780204. Open daily Mar.-Oct. 9:30am-8pm, Nov.-Dec. 9:30am-5:30pm.) The **Lion Hotel's** bar offers cheap, simple food (£4-6) and reigns as the top place for an evening pint in this virtually publess town. (Open M-Su noon-11pm, food served until 9pm.)

◼◪ SIGHTS AND ENTERTAINMENT. ◪ **Harlech Castle,** a World Heritage Site and arguably the most spectacularly located of Edward I's many fortresses, crowns a 200 ft. rock with sweeping views of Snowdonia, brown-sugar sand dunes, and the bay. From the outer bailey, 151 steps descend the cliff to the train station, where the sea once lapped at the boat gate. Built on legéndary King Bendigeidfran's favorite resting spot, the castle also served as the insurrection headquarters of Welsh rebel Owain Glyndŵr after he captured the castle from Edward I in 1404. (☎ 780552. Open Apr.-May and Oct. daily 9:30am-5pm; June-Sept. daily 9:30am-6pm; Nov.-Mar. M-Sa 9:30am-4pm, Su 11am-4pm. Last admission 30min. before closing. £3, concessions £2, families £8.) Public **footpaths** snake in and around Harlech, running from the grassy dunes to the forested hilltops above the town; pick up brochures at the TIC. **Theatr Ardudwy,** Coleg Harlech, is the town's cultural axis, hosting films, plays, and exhibitions. (☎ 780667. Wheelchair access. Some concerts are free; other performances £2.50-6; concessions £1-2 discount.)

LOVE YOUR CUTLERY Some suitors bring flowers, others serenade with a guitar and a ballad, but in old time Wales, wooing often involved a large wooden spoon. Making and giving a lovespoon to one's beloved is a centuries-old Welsh custom. The oldest known lovespoon dates from the 17th century, but lovespoons have been around much longer. The romantic eating utensils, extremely popular during the 18th and 19th centuries, were often carved as a pastime on long winter evenings. Gentlemen wooers tried to convey the extent of their love through fancy designs, which made for some ridiculously enlarged, elaborate spoons. Acceptance of the spoon meant courting could begin, and the term "spooning" has found its way into the English language, implying what might follow. Although the custom has languished, lovespoons can still be found in homes and tourist traps across Wales.

LLŶN PENINSULA (PENRHYN LLŶN)

The Llŷn has been a tourist hot spot since the Middle Ages, when religious pilgrims tramped through on their way to Bardsey Island. Now 25 miles of sandy beaches lining the southern coast draw pilgrims of a different faith—sun worshippers coddled by the uncharacteristically good weather of the towns between Pwllheli and Abersoch. A hilly region of simple beauty, the Llŷn holds green fields spreading down to the coast, bounded by hedges filled with bright *blodau wylltion* (wildflowers). The farther west you venture, the more unsullied the Llŷn becomes and the more scarce certain conveniences grow—stock up at the cash machines in Porthmadog, Pwllheli, and Criccieth.

▐ GETTING THERE AND GETTING AROUND

The northern end of the Cambrian Coaster rail line reaches through **Porthmadog** and **Criccieth** (KRIK-key-ith) to **Pwllheli** (poohl-HEL-ly), stopping at smaller towns in between. **Trains** begins in mid-Wales at **Aberystwyth** and change at **Machynlleth** or **Dyfi Junction** for northern destinations **Porthmadog** (M-F 5 per day, Sa 6 per day, Su 3 per day; £11.80, return £12.30) and **Pwllheli** (same freq., £13.70, return £15.10). The **Cambrian Coaster Day Ranger** (☎ (01766) 512340) offers unlimited travel all along the line (£6.40 per day, evening version £3.50). The Conwy Valley line's western end is at **Blaenau Ffestiniog**, inland east of the peninsula, and continues via **Betws-y-Coed** to **Llandudno** on the northern coast; this line in turn connects to **Chester** and **Bangor** (M-Sa 6 per day, Su 3 per day).

National Express (☎ (08705) 808080) bus #545 arrives in **Pwllheli** from **London** via Birmingham, Bangor, Caernarfon, and Porthmadog (1 per day leaving 10:30am, 9hr., £21). **TrawsCambria** bus #701 connects **Porthmadog** once a day with **Aberystwyth**, **Swansea, Holyhead** (2hr.), and **Cardiff** (7hr.). **Express Motors** (☎ (01286) 881108) bus #1 stops in **Porthmadog** on its winding route between **Blaenau Ffestiniog** (30min.; M-Sa 1 per hr. until 9:40pm, in summer also Su 5 per day as bus #2; £1.60-£2.20) and **Caernarfon** (1hr.; same freq., £1.60-2.20). **Berwyn** (☎ (01286) 660315) and **Clynnog & Trefor** (☎ (01286) 660208) run bus #12 between **Pwllheli** and **Caernarfon** (1hr.; M-Sa 1 per hr., Su 3 per day; £2).

A smattering of bus companies, most prominently **Arriva Cymru** (☎ (01248) 750444), serves most spots on the peninsula with reassuring haste for £1-2. Check bus schedules in *Gwynedd Public Transport Maps and Timetables*, available from tourist information centres. Arriva and **Caelloi** (☎ (01758) 612719) share the running of bus #3, which is often open-top in the summer, from **Porthmadog** to **Pwllheli** via **Criccieth** (30min.; M-Sa 2 per hr. until 6pm, 1 per hr. until 10:20pm, Su 6 per day). Arriva buses #17, the circular 17B, and 18 all leave Pwllheli to weave around the western tip of the peninsula. A **Gwynedd Red Rover,** bought from the driver, is good for a day of travel throughout the peninsula and the rest of Gwynedd and Anglesey counties (£4.60, children £2.30).

NORTH WALES

PORTHMADOG
☎ 01766

Don't get bogged down by Porthmadog's banal town center; this travel hub is ideally situated for touring the Llŷn Peninsula and hiking into Snowdonia, and is just minutes away from mountain walks and world-class climbing rocks. Its principal attraction is the ▓ **Ffestiniog Railway,** which departs from Harbour Station on High St. This justly famous but expensive narrow-gauge railway rumbles and shakes along the slate-lined hillsides of the Ffestiniog Valley into the hills of Snowdonia, terminating in Blaenau Ffestiniog, where it connects to the Conwy Valley Line and the Slate Caverns of Llechwedd. (☎ 512340. 1hr., 2-10 per day mid-Feb. to Nov., sporadic departures in Dec. £13.80, seniors £10.35, one child with adult free, additional children half price, families £27.60, bikes £3.) At the other end of town, the more modest **Welsh Highland Railway** and Russell, their dogged 1906 locomotive, are trying to recapture a little of the glory days of train travel. Once the longest narrow-gauge railway in Wales, the track now runs ¾mi. to Pen-y-mount, with every effort made to reconstruct the atmosphere of a Victorian steam line. (☎ 513402. Mid-Apr. to Sept. 6 per day. also runs some days in Oct. £2, children £1.50, seniors £1.75, families £6.) You can also torture clay behind the largest mural in Wales at **Porthmadog Pottery,** five minutes down Snowdon St., which crosses High St. near the bus stop. (☎ 510910. Open July-Aug. M-F 9am-5pm, Sa-Su 10am-4pm; Sept.-June M-F 9am-5pm. £3 to throw a pot or paint a plate.)

From Porthmadog's unstaffed **train station,** a right turn onto High St. will bring you into town; further up the street are Bank Pl. and Snowdon St. **Buses** stop at various points along High St., most commonly outside the Australia Inn (see below) or across the street in front of the park. Holler for **Port Taxis** (☎ 514244) if you need a lift. The well-stocked **tourist information centre** is at the end of High St., opposite the community center by the harbor. (☎ 512981. Open daily Easter-Oct. 10am-6pm; Nov.-Easter 9:30am-5pm.) **Barclays,** 79 High St., has a **cash machine.** (Bank open M and W-F 9am-4:30pm, Tu 10am-4:30pm.) Services include: the **launderette,** 34 Snowdon St. (open M-Sa 7:30am-5pm, Su 9am-5pm; sells soap, bleach, and softener); the **police** (☎ 512226), Avenue Rd. opposite the Sportsman Hotel; **Bron y Garth Hospital** (☎ 770310), in Minffordd; and the **post office,** at the corner of High St. and Bank Pl., which has a **bureau de change** (☎ 512010; open M-F 9am-5:30pm, Sa 9am-12:30pm). **Postal code:** LL49 9AD.

Ten minutes down Church St. in neighboring Tremadog, the hugely comfortable, **Snowdon Backpackers hostel** has a TV and fireplace lounge, large dining room, and kitchen. The fun owners impress with lots of local insight. (☎ 515354; fax 515364; snowdon@backpackers.fsnet.co.uk. Continental breakfast included. Internet access. Open year-round. £12.50 per person.) Small signs in windows along **Madoc St.** and **Snowdon St.** mark **B&Bs,** although you may not always be allowed to look before you commit. **Llys Caradog,** 12 Snowdon St., has well-kept rooms, TVs, dressing gowns, and much-celebrated breakfasts, but may not book single nights in the summer. (☎ 512635. July-Aug. £17 per person, Sept.-June £16.) **Mrs. Skellern,** 35 Madoc St., has rooms with TVs. (☎ 512843. £15 per person.)

Not a haven for gourmets, Porthmadog does have a great **Castle Bakery,** 105 High St., where *bara brith,* sandwiches, and salads are made fresh every morning. (☎ 514932. Open from 9am.) Scatter sandwich crumbs along the stool-lined counter at **Jessie's,** 75 High St. (☎ 512814. Open M-Sa 9am-5pm.) The **Australia Inn,** 31-33 High St., features good grub (£2-6) and a wide-screen TV. (Open M-Sa 11am-11pm, Su noon-10:30pm; food served M-F noon-2:30pm and 6-8:30pm, Sa-Su noon-2:30pm.)

NEAR PORTHMADOG

PORTMEIRION

Bus #98 leaves Porthmadog for Minffordd, an easy and scenic 30min. walk from Portmeirion (M-Sa 3 per day); some also go directly to Portmeirion (10min.; M-Sa 3 per day, Su 2 per day; return £2). Minffordd is also a stop on the Cambrian Coaster train line. ☎ (01766) 770000. Open daily 9:30am-5:30pm. £4.50, students and seniors £3.60, children £2.25; reduced admission Nov.-Mar. Admission tickets list the times for incoming tides so you can know when it is safe to wade in the estuary.

An eccentric landmark of Italy-fixation, the private village of **Portmeirion** rises from the woods by a quiet estuary two miles east of Porthmadog. Mediterranean court-yards, whorls of pastel buildings, and the occasional palm tree provide an other-worldly diversion from the standard castles and cottages. The village was built between 1925 and 1972 by Sir Clough Williams-Ellis, whose sole concern was beauty, "that strange necessity," and who wanted to show "how a naturally beauti-ful place could be developed without defiling it." The very real threat of Disneyfi-cation has been narrowly averted, but it would still not seem out of character if a Munchkin or Oompa-loompa tottered out of a sun-baked building into one of the pooled gardens. Dogs can't enter the village, but they go the way of all flesh at the **dog cemetery** in the nearby woods, where Dearest Darling Woofy (1977-94, "a very exceptional dog and mother of Softy") slumbers peacefully. In the Ghost Garden nearby, the wind whispers through eucalyptus leaves.

CRICCIETH ☎ 01766

Above the coastal town of Criccieth (KRIK-key-ith), five miles west of Porthma-dog, stand the remains of **Criccieth Castle,** built by Llewelyn the Great in 1230, taken by the Normans in 1283, destroyed by Owain Glyndŵr in 1404 (check out some scorch marks still on the walls), and now a World Heritage Site. The castle still puzzles architectural historians, who debate which portion was English and which was Welsh. Its gatehouse, silhouetted against the skyline, glowers over Tremadog Bay, with views of Snowdonia to the northeast and Harlech across the water. (☎ 522227. Castle open Apr.-Sept. daily 10am-6pm; grounds also open Oct.-Mar. 9:30am-4pm. Castle £2.20, concessions £1.70, families £6.10; grounds free.)

Trains (☎ (08457) 484950) stop in town from **Pwllheli** on the Cambrian Coaster line. From the station, turn right onto High St. to reach the town center. **Arriva** bus #3 arrives from **Porthmadog** and **Pwllheli** (M-Sa every half-hour, Su 6 per day). The **tourist information centre,** High St., across from Spar, books beds for £1 and a 10% deposit. (☎ 523457. Open Apr.-Sept. M-F 10:30am-1pm and 1:30-6:30pm, Sa-Su 2-6pm.) **HSBC** and its **cash machine** sit on 51 High St. (Open M-F 10:30am-1pm.) Near the bus stop on High St. lies the **post office.** (Open M-Tu and Th-F 9am-5:30pm, W and Sa 9am-12:30pm.) **Postal code:** LL52 0BV.

B&Bs (£15-25) are scattered on **Tan-y-Grisiau Terr.,** just across the rail track from the bus stop, and on **Marine Terr.** and **Marine Crescent,** by the beach near the castle. From **Dan-Y-Castell,** 4 Marine Crescent, you can watch the surf batter the castle's hill. (☎ 522375. £14 per person.) Dinner-seekers head to **Poachers Restaurant,** 66 High St., downhill from the bus stop; classy main courses go for £6.75-12. (☎ 522512. Open daily 6-9pm; Su book ahead.) Two doors down, **Spar** stocks shelves of groceries in a closet-sized store. (Open M-Sa 8am-10pm, Su 9am-10pm.) The beer garden of **The Bryn Hir Arms,** along High St. in the opposite direction, provides the ideal setting for a quiet pint. (☎ 522493. Open M-F 3-11pm, Sa noon-11pm, Su noon-10:30pm.) Branches of **Cadwalader's** ice cream store dot the Llŷn, but the original lies on Castle St. Grab a tasty cone (75p-£2) to complement a beach walk. (Open M 11am-9pm, T-F 10:30am-9pm, Sa 10am-9:30pm, Su 10am-9:30pm.)

LLANYSTUMDWY ☎ 01766

Arriva bus #3 also stops at **Llanystumdwy,** a tiny town a walkable 1½ mi. north of Criccieth. Llanystumdwy was the boyhood home of **David Lloyd George,** British Prime Minister between 1916 and 1922. The town preserves Highgate (his boyhood home), the school where he first made mischief, and his simple grave along the banks of the Dwyfor. In the cottage, his long-winded tape-recorded uncle takes a break from cobbling to give you some historical background and family anecdotes in either English or Welsh. The **Lloyd George Museum** displays relics from his career, including his working copy of the Treaty of Versailles and the pen he used to sign it. (☎ 522071. Open July-Sept. daily 10:30am-5pm; June M-Sa 10:30am-5pm; Apr.-May M-F 10:30am-5pm; Oct. M-F 11am-4pm. £3, concessions £2, families £7.)

466 ■ NORTH WALES

OH FATHER It may surprise some to know that as recently as 1922, Britain
had a Prime Minister whose mother tongue wasn't English. Called by Winston Churchill
"the greatest Welshman which that unconquerable race has produced since the age of
the Tudors," David Lloyd George, the lad who rose from humble origins on the Llŷn Peninsula to the position of Prime Minister (1916-22), enjoyed a distinguished tenure in
office, introducing pensions and universal suffrage, granting (partial) independence to
Ireland, and leading Britain to victory in the First World War. So well-connected had he
become during his years in politics that he inspired the never-ending song with one
line, "Lloyd George knew my father, father knew Lloyd George." But Lloyd George was
not known as the "Welsh mountain goat" for his gruff manner and rousing oratory
alone. So legendary was his philandering that the song rang with new lyrics through the
valleys of Wales, "Lloyd George was my father, father was Lloyd George, Lloyd George
was my father, father was Lloyd George," and so on forever.

PWLLHELI ☎01758

The last stop on the Cambrian Coaster rail line, Pwllheli (poohl-HEL-ly), eight
miles west of Criccieth, has little to attract the traveler besides the station that
spews buses to every corner of the peninsula and beyond. Its two **beaches**—sandy
Abererch Beach to the east, and pebbly South Beach—are hardly spectacular, and
both are farther away than the tourist information centre's brochures imply.

The **train station** hugs the corner of Y Maes and Ffordd-y-Cob at Station Sq., with
the **bus station** at the first right a little further down Ffordd-y-Cob. For **taxis** call
☎ 740999. The **tourist information centre** (TIC), Station Sq., books B&Bs. (☎ 613000.
Open Apr.-Oct. daily 10am-6pm; Nov.-Mar. Tu-Sa 10:30am-4:30pm.) **HSBC** and its
cash machine take the corner of High St. and Penlan St. (Open M-F 9am-5pm.)
There are Welsh cakes and a wealth of fruit and vegetables at the sprawling open-
air **market** in front of the bus station. (W 9am-5pm.) The **Spar** and **Iceland** supermarkets nearby pick up the slack the rest of the week. Services include the **police** (☎
701177) and the **post office**, opposite the station at the back of a general store
(open M-F 9am-5:30pm, Sa 9am-1:30pm). **Postal code:** LL53 5HL.

Mrs. Jones, 26 High St., lets out comfortable rooms. From the TIC, cross the
street and follow Penlan St. until it meets High St., where a right will take you to
her door. (☎ 613172. £12 per person.) Across the street, **Bank Place Guest House**,
29 High St., safeguards spacious rooms and huge breakfasts. (☎ 612103. £13 per
person.) **Camping** is good in the area. **Hendre**, 1½ mi. down the road to Nefyn at
Efailnewidd, offers camping near Pwllheli. (☎ 613416. Laundry facilities and
showers. Open Mar.-Oct. £8 per tent.) The **Bodawen Cafe**, on Y Maes near the bus
station, serves tasty sandwiches for £1.50-2 and sells local maps. (Open M-Su
8:30am-late.)

ABERDARON AND TRE'R CEIRI ☎01758

Tucked in a sandy cove close to the peninsula's western tip, the peaceful village
of **Aberdaron** blends subtly into the misty mystical blue of sea and sky, where
winds brush hillside houses and skittish white sheep. Down by the beach, the
plain stone **Church of Saint Hywyn** surrounds the oldest doorway in northern
Wales and two 5th-century gravestones carved in Latin. Water in the **wishing well**,
1½ mi. west of town, stays fresh even when the tide crashes over it. Follow road
signs from Aberdaron two miles to what may be the finest sands in the Llŷn,
Porthor. If conditions are right, the sands live up to their nickname, the
"Whistling Sands." (Admission £1.50.) Off the southwest corner of the peninsula,
20,000 saints somehow find the space to sleep beneath **Bardsey Island,** one of the
last Welsh Druid strongholds and a seaswept haven for migratory birds. A
National Trust information point lodges in an old Coast Guard hut overlooking
Bardsey at the Uwchmynydd headland, also known as the Welsh Land's End.
(Open Eater-Sept. most weekends.)

Bus #17 runs from **Pwllheli** (40min., M-Sa 7 per day, return £2.40); #17B follows a more scenic, circular coastal route (2 per day). Bus #10 from **Pwllheli** to Aberdaron also stops at **Porthor** (M-Sa 1 per day). Rest in elegant rooms with sea views (and TV) at **Bryn Mor,** which crowns a hill above Aberdaron. (☎ 760344. £17 per person). Since 1300, pilgrims to Bardsey have fended off hunger at **Y Gegin Fawr** cafe. Tear into the large salads for £4-5 or the tasty Welsh rarebit for £3. (☎ 760359. Open daily July-Aug. 10am-6pm; Easter-June and Sept.-Oct. 10am-5:30pm.)

Tre'r Ceiri (trair-KAY-ree: "town of the giants"), on the peninsula's north shore, is Britain's oldest fortress, dating back some 4000 years. Take the Pwllheli-Caernarfon bus #12 to **Llanaelhaearn,** seven miles from Pwllheli (15min.; M-Sa 1 per hr., Su 4 per day), then look for the public footpath signpost one mile southwest of town on the B4417. At its upper reaches, keep to the stony track, which is more or less a direct uphill route (elevation 1600 ft.). The remains of 150 circular stone huts are clustered within a double defensive wall. The wall isn't good protection against the windy weather, though, so wear warm clothing.

SNOWDONIA NATIONAL PARK

Rough and handsome, misty purple and mossy green, the highest mountains in Wales dominate horizons across the 840 square miles of Snowdonia National Park (Parc Cenedlaethol Eryri), stretching from forested Machynlleth in the south to sand-strewn Conwy in the north. Known in Welsh as Eryri, Place of Eagles, Snowdonia's upper reaches, barren and lonesome at their craggy peaks, are as dramatic and powerfully graceful as their name suggests. Where sheep don't carpet the landscape, dark pine forests run into precipitous gorges, and sun-pierced coves open to shimmering estuaries. Welsh is still the dominant tongue here, from valley hamlets to farmhouses scattered between Celtic hillforts and Roman camps. Though these lands, as in most British National Parks, lie largely in private hands, endless public footpaths accommodate the droves of visitors who come to scale the heights or descend into dormant slate mines. Even in peak season, the park's broad expanses provide untrammeled corners for those in search of a quiet hike.

NORTH WALES

GETTING THERE AND GETTING AROUND

Trains (☎ (08457) 484950) stop at several large towns on the park's outskirts, including **Bangor** and **Conwy.** The **Conwy Valley Line** runs through the park from **Llandudno** through **Betws-y-Coed** to **Blaenau Ffestiniog** (2-10 per day, return £14.20). **Buses** run to the interior from those towns, and from other towns near the edge of the park such as **Caernarfon.** Consult the indispensable *Gwynedd Public Transport Maps and Timetables,* free in tourist information centres throughout the region. Blue **Snowdon Sherpa** buses maneuver between the park's towns and trailheads with somewhat irregular service, but will stop at any safe point in the park on request. A Gwynedd **Red Rover ticket** (£4.60, children £2.30) buys unlimited travel for a day on the Sherpa buses and any other bus in Gwynedd and Anglesey counties: individual trips cost about £2. Most routes are serviced every two hours, and Sunday service can often be sporadic at best. Tell the driver if you plan to switch buses, since connections sometimes fail due to impatient buses.

Narrow-gauge railway lines running through Snowdonia let you enjoy the countryside in a few select locations without enduring a hike. The **Ffestiniog Railway** (☎ (01766) 512340) romps through the mountains from Porthmadog (see p. 464) to Blaenau Ffestiniog, where the mountains of discarded slate rival those of Snowdonia. You can travel part of its route to Minffordd, Penrhyndeudraeth, or Tan-y-bwlch. At Porthmadog, the narrow-gauge rail meets the Cambrian Coaster service from Pwllheli to Aberystwyth; at Blaenau Ffestiniog, it connects with the Conwy Valley Line. The **Snowdon Mountain Railway** and the **Llanberis Lake Railway** both make short trips from Llanberis (see p. 470).

> **MINE EYES HAVE SEEN THE GLORY** Those purple mountains' majesty painting the horizons across Northern Wales aren't just a tint of light and atmosphere; the closer you get to their faces, the clearer it becomes that the rocks are in fact plum purple in places, and bared bonnie blue in others. These are the slate mountains that fueled the industrial revolution in Northern Wales and, according to some proud Welsh miners, roofed the world. The slate also fueled a few local egos, as miners regularly held slate-splitting competitions with highly publicized results. The London Exhibition of 1862 featured a 10 ft. by 1 ft. slate sheet 1/16 in. thick; in 1872 a 2½ in. block was split into 45 layers; today, less fanfare is made about the 35 sheets per inch regularly split for decorations like fans and wall ornaments.

◪ PRACTICAL INFORMATION

Tourist information centres (TICs) and National Park Information Centres stock leaflets on walks, drives, and accommodations, as well as Ordnance Survey maps. For details, contact the **Snowdonia National Park Information Headquarters,** Penrhyndeudraeth (pen-rin-DAY-dryth), Gwynedd, Wales LL48 6LF (☎ (01766) 770274). The annual glossy *Snowdonia—Mountains and Coast*, stacked to the roof at TICs across North Wales, contains fistfuls of information on the park and accommodations, as well as overly enthusiastic write-ups of selected attractions. If you're cyber-savvy, sneak a peak at www.gwynedd.gov.uk for bus schedules and tourist info. The following are Snowdonia's **National Park Information Centres:**

Aberdyfi: Wharf Gdns. (☎/fax (01654) 767321). Open Easter-Oct. daily 10am-1pm and 2-6pm.

Betws-y-Coed: The busiest and best stocked. See p. 484.

Blaenau Ffestiniog: Isallt Church St. (☎ (01776) 830360). In the shadow of the Ffestiniog Railway's steam clouds. Open Easter-Sept. daily 10am-6pm.

Dolgellau: See p. 472.

Harlech: See p. 461.

◤ ACCOMMODATIONS

This section lists only **YHA Youth Hostels** in Snowdonia; B&Bs are listed under individual towns. The eight hostels in the mountain area are some of the best in Wales. They are marked clearly on Gwynedd bus schedules and on the general Wales transport map. School excursions can make getting a space in the hostels a challenge. All have kitchens, and meals are available except where noted.

Bryn Gwynant: (☎ (01766) 890251; fax 890479), ¾ mi. from the Watkin path, above Llyn Gwynant and along the Penygwryd-Beddgelert road (4 mi. from Beddgelert). Take Sherpa bus #95 from Caernarfon (40min., M-Sa 5 per day) or Llanberis (20min.; M-Sa 5 per day, Su 3 per day). Sherpa summer express #97A comes from Porthmadog or Betws-y-Coed (30min. each way, June-Sept. 3 per day). Lockout 10am-1pm. Curfew 11pm. Open Mar.-Oct. daily; Jan.-Feb. F-Sa. Dorms £9.80, under 18 £6.75.

Capel Curig: (☎ (01690) 720225; fax 720270), 5 mi. from Betws-y-Coed on the A5. Sherpa buses #19, 65, 96, and 97A from Betws and Llanberis stop nearby. At the crossroads of many mountain paths; a favorite with climbers and school kids. Spectacular view of Mt. Snowdon across a lake. Lockout 10am-5pm. Curfew 11pm. Open mid-Feb. to Aug. daily; Sept.-Dec. F-Sa. Dorms £9.80, under 18 £6.75; doubles £22.50.

Idwal Cottage: (☎ (01248) 600225; fax 602952), just off the A5 at the foot of Llyn Ogwen in northern Snowdonia. Within hiking distance of Pen-y-Pass, Llanberis, and Capel Curig. Bus routes here are less plentiful—take Sherpa bus #66 from Bangor, changing to #65 at Bethesda (M-Sa 6 per day, Su 5 per day), or #7 directly from Bangor on Su (3 per day). Self-catering only. Lockout 10am-5pm. Curfew 11pm. Open mid-Feb. to Aug. daily; Jan. and Sept. to mid-Dec. F-Sa. Dorms £8.10, under 18 £5.65.

Kings (Dolgellau): (☎ (01341) 422392; fax 422477), Penmaenpool, 4 mi. from Dolgellau. Take Arriva bus #28 from Dolgellau (5min.; M-F 7 per day, Sa 5 per day, Su 3 per day). Endure the walk uphill to this large house in the Vale of Ffestiniog. Lockout 10am-5pm. Curfew 11pm. Open mid-Apr. to Aug. daily; mid-Feb. to mid-Apr. F-Sa. Dorms £8.10, under 18 £5.65.

Llanberis: (☎ (01286) 870280); fax 870936), ½ mi. up Capel Goch Rd., with views of Llyn Peris and Llyn Padarn below and Mt. Snowdon above. Curfew 11:30pm. Open Apr.-Aug. daily; Sept.-Oct. and Jan.-Mar. Tu-Sa. Dorms £9.80, under 18 £6.75.

Lledr Valley: (☎ (01690) 750202; fax 750410), on a bluff 5 mi. west of Betws-y-Coed, ¾ mi. past Pont-y-Pant train station, 2 mi. from the majestic tower of Dolwyddelan Castle. No laundry facilities. Lockout 10am-5pm. Curfew 11pm. Open Easter-May, Jul.-Aug., and Oct. daily; Feb.-Easter, June, and Sept. F-Sa. Dorms £9, under 18 £6.20.

Pen-y-Pass: (☎ (01286) 870428; fax 872434), in Nant Gwynant, 6 mi. from Llanberis and 4 mi. from Nant Peris. Take Sherpa bus #19 from Llanberis or Llandudno (3 per day); #95 from Caernarfon (1hr.; M-Sa 5 per day, Su 3 per day); or #96 from Betws-y-Coed (25min.; M-Sa 6 per day, Su 9 per day). Commands an unusual and splendid position: 1170 ft. above sea level at the head of Llanberis Pass between the Snowdon and Glyders peaks. The doors opens onto the Pyg track, or the Llyn Llydaw miner's track to the Snowdon summit. Rents hiking boots, waterproofs, and ice axes. Lockout 10am-1pm. Open Feb.-Oct. daily; Nov.-Jan. F-Sa. Dorms £9.80, under 18 £6.75.

Snowdon Ranger: Llyn Cwellyn (☎ (01286) 650391; fax 650093). The base for the Ranger Path, the grandest Snowdon ascent. Take Sherpa bus #95 from Caernarfon (20min.; M-Sa 7 per day, Su 4 per day). No washers. Lockout 10am-5pm. Curfew 11pm. Open Easter-Aug. daily; Sept.-Oct. W-Su; mid-Feb. to Easter and Nov.-Dec. F-Su. Dorms £9.80, under 18 £6.75.

In the high mountains, **camping** is permitted as long as you leave no mess, but the Park Service discourages it because of recent and disastrous erosion. In the valleys, owner's consent is required to camp. Public campsites dot the roads in peak seasons; check listings below for sites in specific towns.

▮ HIKING AND OTHER OUTDOOR PURSUITS

Weather on Snowdonia's exposed mountains shifts quickly, unpredictably, and wrathfully. No matter how beautiful the weather is below, *it will be cold and wet* in the high mountains. Dress as if preparing for an armed confrontation with the Abominable Snowman: bring a waterproof jacket and pants, gloves, a hat, and wool sweater. You can peel off the layers as you descend. (See **Wilderness Safety,** p. 53.) Pick up the Ordnance Survey Landranger Map #115: *Snowdon and Surrounding Area* (scale 1:50,000; £5.25) and Outdoor Leisure Map #17: *Snowdonia, Snowdon, and Conwy Valley Areas* (scale 1:25,000; £6.50), as well as individual path guides (40p each). Maps are available at Park Centres and most bookstores. Call **Mountaincall Snowdonia** (☎ (0891) 500449; 36-48p per min.) for a local 3-to-5-day forecast and ground conditions. Weather forecasts are also tacked outside park information centers. Park rangers lead day-walks; ask at the centers. The land in Snowdonia is privately owned—stick to public pathways, or ask the owner's consent to hike through.

Snowdonia National Park Study Centre (☎ (01766) 590324), Plas Tan-y-Bwlch, Maentwrog, Blaenau Ffestiniog, Gwynedd LL41 3YU, conducts courses on naturalist favorites such as wildlife painting. **YHA Pen-y-Pass**, Nant Gwynant (☎ (01286) 870428; see above, p. 469) can put groups in touch with guides for mountaineering, climbing, canoeing, and sailing.

Guided cycle tours leave from Caernarfon for multi-night forays in the park, thanks to **Beics Eryri Cycle Tours,** 44 Tyddyn Llwydyn. (☎ (01286) 676637. From approximately £42 per night including bike and accommodations; call ahead.) Guided horse and pony rides canter from the **Snowdonia Riding Stables,** three miles from Caernarfon, just off the A4085 near Waunfawr. Take Sherpa bus #95

(10min.; M-Sa 7 per day, Su 3 per day) and ask to be let off at the turn-off road. (☎ (01286) 650342. Rides £12 per hr., £26 per half-day; £45 per day.) The brave can paraglide off the peaks of Snowdonia with the help of Llanberis-based **Enigma: The Snowdonia School of Paragliding** (☎ (01248) 602103). Myriad aquatic, equestrian, and artistic adventures are detailed in the *The Snowdon Peninsula: North Wales Activities* brochure, available in TICs and National Park Information Centres.

LLANBERIS   ☎01286

One of the few small Welsh villages lively even on Sundays, Llanberis owes its outdoorsy bustle to the popularity of Mt. Snowdon, whose ridges and peaks unfold before you as you ascend the arduous path that starts just south of town.

🔃 GETTING THERE AND PRACTICAL INFORMATION. Situated on the western edge of the park, Llanberis is a short ride from Caernarfon on the A4086. Catch **KMP** (☎ 870880) **bus #88** from **Caernarfon** (25min.; M-Sa 2 per hr., Su 1 per hr.; £1.60); or **Arriva** bus #77 from **Bangor** (40min.; M-Sa 1 per hr., Su 5 per day; £1.55). **Sherpa** bus #96, operated by Arriva, winds past Capel Curig and Pen-y-Pass on its way from **Betws-y-Coed** (1½hr.; M-Sa 6 per day, Su 9 per day), while Sherpa bus #95, operated by KMP, stops at the Bryn Gwynant and Pen-y-Pas **YHAs** on its way from **Beddgelert** (45min., M-Sa 5 per day, £2).

The **tourist information centre** (TIC), 41a High St., doles out hiking tips and books accommodations. (☎ 870765; fax 871951. Open Easter-Oct. daily 10am-6pm; Nov.-Easter W and F-Su 10:30am-4:30pm.) You can't have it all—either you get the **HSBC bank** without a cash machine, 29 High St. (open M-F 10am-2pm), or the bank-less cash machine of **Barclays,** at the entrance to the Electric Mountain Railway on the A4086, near its fork with High St. Pick up hiking gear at **Joe Brown's Store,** Menai Hall, High St., owned by one of the world's greatest pioneer climbers. (☎ 870327. Open M-F 9am-1pm and 2-5:30pm; Sa 9am-1pm and 2-6pm; Su 9am-1pm and 2-5pm.) The **post office** is at 36 High St. (Open M-T and Th-F 9am-1pm and 2-5:30pm, W and Sa 9am-5:30pm.) **Postal code:** LL55 4EU.

🏠🍴 ACCOMMODATIONS AND FOOD. Those looking for a group experience have two choices in Llanberis. Plenty of sheep and cows keep hostelers company at the **YHA Llanberis** (see p. 469). The **Heights Hotel,** 74 High St., has 24 bunk beds packed into big rooms. Half the town crowds into the bar on weekends. (☎ 871179; fax 872507. June-Aug. dorms £9, with breakfast £12.50; Sept.-May dorms £7, with breakfast £10.50.)

The town also has flocks of **B&Bs** starting at around £15 a little way out of town, although more expensive ones can be found on **High St.** A cozy 19th-century temperance house, **Snowdon Cottage,** Pentre Castell, sits between a mossy rock-filled hillside and the shadow of Dolbadarn Castle. Follow High St. and its extension, the A4086, toward the park and past the Victoria Hotel for five minutes. Tired climbers can ask the proprietors for relief: one is a sports therapist, the other an aromatherapist. (☎ 872015. £14-18 per person.) Head two miles north to find camping at the **Snowdon View Caravan Park,** which has excellent facilities, including a heated swimming pool. (☎ 870349. £5-6 per tent.)

Llanberis's restaurants have adapted their fare to the healthy demands (and appetites) of hikers. Though cooked breakfasts are in high demand at **Pete's Eats,** 40 High St., opposite the TIC, you can also get a vegetarian mixed grill for £4.80 or hot, hot chili for £5. (☎ 870358. Open Easter-Oct. M-F 9am-8pm, Sa-Su 8am-8pm; Nov.-Easter M-F 9am-6:30pm, Sa-Su 8am-8pm.) **The Pannier,** 50 High St., will pack a roll full of anything from peanut butter and banana (£1.20) to egg mayo and bacon (£1.15), and top it off with a selection of drinks, nuts, and fruits. (☎ 870301. Open Easter-Oct. M-Sa 10:30am-4pm.) The **Spar** store is on the corner of High St. and Capel Goch Rd. (Open M-Sa 7am-11pm, Su 7am-10:30pm.)

SIGHTS. Most local attractions lie near the fork where the A4086 meets High St. The immensely popular but immensely expensive **Snowdon Mountain Railway** is an easy way to lose yourself in the clouds on the summit of Snowdon. The locomotives, some still steam-operated, whisk you up Mt. Snowdon from the terminus on the A4086. The 2hr. round-trip stops at the peak for 30 short minutes, so snap those panoramic summit shots in a hurry. If you miss your return train you aren't guaranteed a seat on another, and the path down feeds on tender human knees. Weather conditions and passenger demand dictate the schedule from July to early September; on a clear day the first train leaves Llanberis at 9am (if there are at least 25 passengers), with subsequent trains about every half-hour until 5pm (Sa 3:30pm). Line up early to get a ticket. (☎ 870223. Runs mid-Mar. to Oct. Return £15.80, children £11.30; one-way £11.30, children £8.10; standby for return £11.20.)

Most other attractions lie near **Parc Padarn.** The **Llanberis Lake Railway,** near the entrance, takes a short, scenic route from Gilfach Ddu station at Llanberis through the woods along the lake. (☎ 870549. 40min., Apr.-Sept. 4-11 per day, Oct.-Mar. 4 per day. Wheelchair access. £4.20, children £2.50.) Nearby, the **Welsh Slate Museum** houses live demonstrations and exhibits on the importance of slate to Welsh history. (☎ 870630. Open Easter-Oct. daily 10am-5pm, Nov.-Easter Su-F 10am-4pm. £3.50, students £2, seniors and children free.) Within the park lies **Llŷn Padarn,** a needle-shaped. Follow the road into the park until a footbridge off the right brings you to the ruins of **Dolbadarn Castle,** where Prince Llewelyn of North Wales imprisoned his brother for 23 years. Only a single tower of the castle remains. (Free.) For an eye-level view of **Ceunant Mawr,** a plummeting, angled waterfall, follow the well-marked footpath on Victoria Terr. by the Victoria Hotel; (¾ mi.).

MOUNT SNOWDON AND VICINITY

By far the most popular destination in the park, Mount Snowdon (*Yr Wyddfa*, "the burial place") is the highest peak in Wales (and higher than any in England, too, mind you), measuring in at 3560 ft. Over half a million hikers ramble around the mountain each year. Future hikes were almost scuttled when a plot of land including the summit of Mt. Snowdon was put up for sale a few years ago, but fortunately celebrated Welsh actor Sir Anthony Hopkins sprang to the rescue and contributed a vast sum to the National Trust to help save the pristine wildness of the mountain. Much travel by enthusiasts of all abilities has in past years disrupted Snowdon's ecosystem and eroded some of its face; park officers request that all hikers stick to the well-marked trails to avoid further damage. Six principal paths of varying degrees of difficulty wend their way up Snowdon; TICs and National Park Information Centres stock guides on these ascents (50p each).

Though Mt. Snowdon is the main attraction in the northern part of the park, experienced climbers cart pick-axes and ropes to the **Ogwen Valley.** There, climbs to **Devil's Kitchen** (*Twll Du*), the **Glyders** (*Glyder Fawr* and *Glyder Fach*), and **Tryfan** all begin from **Llyn Ogwen.** Those attempting the climbs should pick up both the appropriate Ordnance Survey maps and the card-sized *Walk About Guides* (50p), which give directions, map references, and severity ratings for the climbs.

NEVER CRY DOG Not only did Llewelyn the Great imprison his brother (see Dolbadarn Castle, p. 471), but he also did his dog a great wrong. According to legend, Llewelyn left his infant son in the custody of his trusty dog, Gelert, while he went out hunting. A hungry wolf, sensing tasty baby nearby, entered Llewelyn's tent, only to be slaughtered by the canine babysitter. On returning home, however, Llewelyn saw the blood, and immediately speared Gelert, only to hear his baby's healthy cry. He saw the mangled wolf and the untouched child and immediately realized his mistake; Gelert—faithful to the end—licked his master's hand as he died. It is said that the prince never smiled again, and he erected a memorial to his pooch in the mountain village of Beddgelert, which in Welsh means "tomb of Gelert."

DOLGELLAU   ☎ 01341

Deep in the conifers of the Idris mountain range, the dark stone buildings of Dolgellau (dol-GECTH-lee) are grim and roughly cut, glaring with callous severity at the wildness around them. Dolgellau has been populated since Roman times, when three roads met here and legionnaires scoured the surrounding hills for gold. Huddled in the shadow of Cader Idris, the town's main function for travelers is the easy access it offers to the mountain and to local walks.

🖪🗈 GETTING THERE AND PRACTICAL INFORMATION. Buses stop in Eldon Sq. near the tourist information centre. **Arriva** (☎ (08706) 082608) bus #94 stops in Dolgellau (M-Sa 9 per day, Su 4 per day) from: **Barmouth** (20min., £1.75); **Llangollen** (1½hr., £3.30); and **Wrexham** (2hr., £4.05). Arriva bus #2 follows a winding, scenic route through the mountains from **Caernarfon** via **Porthmadog** (2hr.; M-Sa 6 per day, in summer also Su 4 per day). A lone **TrawsCambria** bus stops daily from **Holyhead** (3hr., £11.70) and **Cardiff** (6hr., £16.20).

The **tourist information centre** (TIC), Eldon Sq., in Tŷ Meirion by the bus stop, doubles as a **Snowdonia National Park Information Centre.** (☎ 422888; fax 422576. Open Apr.-Sept. 10am-1pm and 2-6pm; Oct.-Mar. Th-M 10am-1pm and 1:30-5pm.) **HSBC,** Eldon Sq., caters to money mavens. (Open M-F 9am-5pm.) Equip yourself with warm and waterproof clothing or grab Ordnance Survey maps (£5.25-£6.50) from **Cader Idris Outdoor Gear,** at Eldon Sq. (☎ 422195. Open M-Sa 9am-5:30pm; May-Sept. also Su 1-4pm.) Other services include **Dolgellau Launderette,** Smithfield St. (no soap; open daily 9am-7pm, last wash 6:30pm) and the **post office,** inside **Spar** at Plas yn Dre St. (open M-F 9am-5:30pm, Sa 9am-12:30pm). **Postal code:** LL40 1AD.

🏠🗈 ACCOMMODATIONS AND FOOD. Four miles away at **Kings** is a **YHA Youth Hostel** (☎ 422392; see p. 468). Lodging is scarce and expensive in Dolgellau; expect to pay at least £18. Two **B&Bs** with spectacular views of the Idris range cling to the hills just north of town. **Arosfyr,** Pen-y-Cefn St., an old farmhouse in a blooming dimple of the mountains, has plush furniture and lush views. From the bus stop, walk with the HSBC on your right, down over the bridge, turn left, then right at the school, and follow the steep road until a sign directs you past some tractors. (☎ 422355. Singles £18; doubles £30-32.) **Dwy Olwyn,** Coed-y-Fronallt, will provide a big breakfast following a comfortable night's sleep. Cross the Bont Fawr bridge, turn right, then left after you pass the Kwik Save; it's five minutes uphill. (☎ 422822. Singles £21; doubles £32-34.) Camping is available at the hostel and at the deluxe **Tanyfron Caravan and Camping Park,** a 10-minute walk south on Arron Rd. onto the A470. (☎/fax 422638. Open year-round. £10 for small tent, 2 people, and 1 car; £1 per additional person. £2 electricity.)

Spar, Plas yn Dre St., stocks groceries. (Open daily 8am-10pm.) Duck under the low portal at **Y Sospan,** Queen's Sq., behind the TIC, for sandwiches (£2-6) or savory quiche with a salad. A sign on a side wall proclaims the escape of Rowland Lloyd, a "stoutly made" forger of bank notes, from the local jail in 1808—catch him and you'll cash in on the £100 reward. (☎ 423174. Cafe open daily from 9am; restaurant upstairs open F-Sa 7-9pm.) A heavenly aroma greets those who descend into the **Popty'r Dref** bakery and delicatessen, Smithfield St., just off Eldon Sq., where homemade jams, large filled rolls (85p-£2), and delectable spongy pastries (£1-2) crowd the shelves. (☎ 422507. Open M-Sa 8am-5pm.)

🕓 SIGHTS. The famous three-mile **Precipice Walk** rewards with views of the Mawddach Estuary and **Cader Idris** (see below), while the 2½ mi. **Torrent Walk** circles through mossy woodlands past waterfalls. Pamphlets for treks are available at the TIC (40p). In town, the free **Quaker Interpretive Centre,** above the TIC and open the same times, details the history of this hotbed of nonconformity and the circumstances that fueled Quaker emigration to the United States.

CADER IDRIS

The origin of the mountain name Cader Idris ("Chair of Idris") remains a mystery. One story has it that in AD 630, a national hero named Idris was killed in battle here by a host of marauding Saxons, while another maintains that Idris was a giant who kept house here. Mystic legends abound in this region: the Cwn Annwn, "Hounds of the Underworld," are said to fly around the peaks of the Idris range. This portion of Snowdonia National Park offers scenic walks less crowded than those of Mt. Snowdon to the north. A number of paths catering to all levels of experience cover Cader Idris (all cross privately owned farm and grazing land). The five-mile pony track from **Llanfihangel y Pennant** is the easiest but also the longest way to the summit. A rather complicated route, the path climbs steadily after a relatively level initial one-third. The pony track from **Tŷ Nant** begins at Tŷ Nant farm, three miles from Dolgellau. While the trail is eroded in spots, it is also not particularly strenuous, and offers the most striking views of the surrounding countryside. The **Minffordd Path** (about 3 mi.) is the shortest but steepest ascent, not to be taken lightly. On its way to the summit, the path traverses an 8000-year-old oak wood and rises above the lake of **Llyn Cau**, the "Bearded Lake." An 18th-century story holds that a young man swimming in the lake was ingested by a grotesque monster and was never seen again. Another legend claims that anyone who sleeps by the lake for one night will awaken either a poet or a madman. (*Let's Go* does not recommend sleeping by haunted lakes.) Allow five hours for any of these three walks. Individual booklets charting each are available at the National Park Information Centre in Dolgellau (40p). For longer treks, the Ordinance Survey Outdoor Leisure #23 (£5.25) or Landranger #124 maps (£6.50) are essential.

If you need a base to climb Cader Idris, stay either in **Dolgellau** or at the **Corris YHA** (see p. 460). The 6000 hectares of the **Coed-Y-Brenin Forest Park** crawl with fine biking trails, in addition to miles of trails reserved exclusively for hikers. Covering the peaks and valleys around the Mawddach and Eden Rivers, the forest is best entered seven miles north of Dolgellau off the A470, near the **visitor center**. (☎ (01341) 440666. Open Apr.-Oct. daily 10am-5pm; Nov.-Mar. Sa-Su 10am-4pm.)

CAERNARFON ☎ 01286

Strikingly well preserved and festively majestic, the walled city of Caernarfon (car-NAR-von) sails on the shifting tides of the Menai Strait that separate it from the Isle of Anglesey, with its world-famous castle at the helm and mountains in its wake. Occupied since pre-Roman times and once the center of English government in northern Wales, Caernarfon has been a hotspot of struggle for regional political control. During a tax revolt in 1294 the Welsh managed to break in, sack the town, and massacre the English settlers. Vestiges of English domination remain (a young Prince Charles, looking like a scared rabbit caught in bright headlights, was invested as Prince of Wales at the castle in 1969), but Caernarfon is thoroughly Welsh in character—visitors can hear the town's own dialect of Welsh in the flower-bedecked streets and inviting pubs of this friendly walled city.

⌐ GETTING THERE. The nearest **train station** is in **Bangor** (see p. 475). The city is, however, the well-greased pivot for **buses** from mid-Wales and the Llŷn Peninsula swinging north to Bangor and thence to Anglesey. Buses arrive on **Penllyn** in the city center. **Arriva Cymru** (☎ (08706) 082608) buses #5, 5A, 5B, and 5X roll into Caernarfon from **Bangor** (25min., every 10 min., £1.55, return £2.65) and **Conwy** (1hr.; M-Sa 2 per hr., Su 1 per hr.; £2.85, return £3.50). **Express Motors** (☎ 881108) bus #1 drifts in from **Porthmadog** (1hr., M-Sa 1 per hr., £1.80, return £2.40). On Sundays, Arriva's #2 runs the same route (5 per day). **Clynnog & Trefor** (☎ 660208) and **Berwyn** (☎ 660315) run bus #12 from **Pwllheli** (1hr.; M-Sa 1 per hr., Su 3 per day; £2.60). **KMP** (☎ 870880) bus #88 zooms from **Llanberis** (25min.; M-Sa 2 per hr., Su 1 per hr.; return £1.60), while its Sherpa bus #95 passes through **Beddgelert** (£2) and by many YHA hostels on its way to **Llanberis** (1½hr.; M-Sa 5 per day, Su 3 per day). **TrawsCambria**

bus #701 arrives daily from **Cardiff** (7½hr.) and **Holyhead** (1½hr). **National Express** (☎ (08705) 808080) bus #545 arrives daily from **London** via **Chester** (8hr., 1 per day, £21). A Gwynedd **Red Rover ticket** earns unlimited bus travel for a day in the county (£4.60, children £2.30); the handy *Gwynedd Public Transport Maps and Timetables* offers info on the routes between major towns in Gwynedd.

⊿🗏 ORIENTATION AND PRACTICAL INFORMATION. The heart of Caernarfon is the area within and just outside the town walls. Buses arrive on **Penllyn,** which runs perpendicular to **Bridge St.** To the right, Bridge St. becomes **Bangor St.,** while a left onto Bridge St. opens into the wide expanse of **Castle Sq.** Turning right from the square's entrance leads to **Castle Ditch,** which holds the tourist information centre (TIC). **Eastgate St.** is perpendicular to the point where Bridge St. meets Bangor St. and continues through a gate onto **High St.** inside the city walls.

The **tourist information centre** (TIC) is on Castle St., in Oriel Pendeitsh opposite the castle gate. Pick up the helpfully illustrated street map within the free *Visitor's Guide to Caernarfon,* or browse their huge lists of accommodations. (☎ 672232. Open Apr.-Oct. daily 10am-6pm; Nov.-Mar. Th-Tu 9:30am-4:30pm.) **Barclays bank,** 5-7 Bangor St., dispenses filthy lucre. (☎ 672386. Open M-Tu and Th-F 9am-4:30pm, W 10am-4:30pm). **Camping supplies** can be found at **14th Peak,** 9 Palace St., with excellent student discounts. (☎ 675124. Open M-W and F-Sa 9am-5:30pm, Th 9am-5pm, Su 1-4pm.) Services include: **Pete's Laundrette,** Skinner St., off Bridge St., (☎ 678395; full- and self-service; open daily 9am-6pm; last wash 5:30pm); the **police** (☎ 673333 ext. 5242), Maes Incla Ln.; **Vale Cabs** (☎ 676161 or 881345), Palace St.; **Internet access** at **Dimensiwn 4,** 4 Bangor St. (☎ 678777; open M-F 10am-6pm, Sa 10am-5:30pm); and the **post office,** Castle Sq. (☎ 672116; open M-F 9am-5:30pm, Sa 9am-12:30pm). **Postal code:** LL55 2ND.

⌐ ACCOMMODATIONS. Budget travelers, do not pass up the chance to stay at ▨ **Totter's Hostel,** 2 High St. Sunlight off the strait ignites the town wall where this Plas-Porth-Yr-Aur (Grand House of the Golden Gate) reigns king of hostels, thanks to fun owners Bob and Henryette and their lively pup Lucia. The rooms are huge, the wooden bunks are comfortable, and the living room is bright and well-equipped with sofas, books, and videos. The medieval stone arch in the cellar stands nonchalantly amidst a full kitchen, breakfast toasts and cereals, and a banquet table perfect for post-pub gatherings. (☎ 672963, mobile ☎ (07979) 830470; www.applemaps.co.uk/totters. Free lockers and bikes to borrow. No curfew or lockout. Dorms £10.) Budget-busting **B&Bs** (£20 and up) line **Church St.** inside the old town wall; for cheaper options, walk 10min. from the castle to **St. David's Rd.,** off the Bangor St. roundabout. The welcoming proprietress of **Bryn Hyfryd,** St. David's Rd., cares for guests in style with well-furnished rooms with bath, TVs, and a boundless breakfast. Dote on the friendly pair of tiny dogs and a duo of Persian cats. (☎ 673840. July to mid-Sept. £17-20 per person; mid-Sept. to June £15-16.) Or try **Marianfa,** St. David's Rd., which has a collection of statues, spacious rooms all with TVs and bathrooms, and great lounge chairs. (☎ 675589; fax 673689. Singles £18; doubles £34, with bath £40.) **Camp** half a mile from town at **Cadnant Valley,** Llanberis Rd.; expect caravans in the summer. (☎ 673196. £4-8 per person.)

SOMEDAY MY PRINCE WILL COME
While there is today a Prince of Wales, not since the slaying of Llewellyn ap Gruffydd has there been a Welsh prince. Fully aware that, no matter how many intimidating castles he constructed along the northern coast, the Welsh would not be settled until they once again had a Welsh prince and English dominion withdrawn, Edward I made them a promise: their very own Prince of Wales, born in Wales, and speaking not a word of English. When his son, later Edward II, was born, Edward I carried the baby to the window of Caernarfon Castle on the Welsh shield, and presented him as the next Prince of Wales: son of an English king, true, but born in Wales, and speaking not a word of English.

◻◻ FOOD AND PUBS. Cafes and pubs crowd the area within the town walls. Groceries abound at **Safeway,** the Promenade (open M-F 8am-10pm, Sa 8am-8pm, Su 8am-4pm), and at the **market,** Castle Sq., on Saturdays. Cast off at the **Floating Restaurant,** Slate Quay, where you're sure to get a bite. With windows to port, starboard, and aft, views of strait, castle, and mountains complement swordfish steaks (£5.95) and burgers and chipped potatoes (£4.10), or any number of fish dishes. (☎ 672896. Open Easter to mid-Sept. 10:30am-7:30pm.) **Crempogau,** at the corner of Palace St. and High St., cooks up sweet and savory dinner pancakes: try the chicken supreme (£2.20), Bavarian apple (£1.70), or a dessert pancake, only £1. (☎ 672552. Open daily Apr.-Oct. 10:30am-5pm.) **Stones Bistro,** 4 Hole-in-the-Wall St., near Eastgate, is candlelit and crowded. The £10 Welsh lamb is worth it—you get a vast limb, sweet and tender. Vegetarian main courses go for £8. (☎ 671152. Open Tu-Sa 6-11pm.) **Bechdan Bach,** Castle Sq., serves up tasty toasties for £1.50-2.50. (☎ 677222. Open M-Sa 9am-5pm.) The stout wooden doors of the ◪ **Anglesey Arms** open onto the Promenade just below the castle; pretty much the whole town gathers here every summer evening, pint in hand and spirits high, to watch the sunset over the shimmering Menai Strait. (Open M-Sa 11am-11pm, Su noon-10:30pm.)

◻ SIGHTS. In a nod to Caernarfon's Roman past (and, no doubt, to his own ego), Edward I built ◪ **Caernarfon Castle,** featuring eagle-crowned turrets and polygonal towers in imitation of Byzantine Constantinople. Starting in 1283, Edward spent a fortune constructing this grandest in his ring of North Welsh fortresses; a resentful Welshman called it "this magnificent badge of our subjection." Despite its swagger, the fortress was left unfinished (note the masonry jutting out at points in the castle) thanks to an empty royal pocket and distractions from unruly Scots. Summer sees performances of scenes from the great Welsh epic *The Mabinogi*. The "tradition" of holding the investiture of the Prince of Wales here is a 20th-century creation, which has led to the castle's restoration and growing international prominence. Entertaining and cynical tours run about once an hour for £1.50, and a 20-minute video recounts the castle's history twice an hour for free. The castle also houses the **regimental museum** of the Royal Welsh Fusiliers. (☎ 677617. Open June-Sept. daily 9:30am-6pm; Apr.-May and Oct. daily 9:30am-5pm; Nov.-Mar. M-Sa 9:30am-4pm, Su 11am-4pm. £4.20, concessions £3.20, families £11.60.)

Most of Caernarfon's 13th-century **town wall** survives, and a short stretch between Church St. and Northgate St. is open for climbing during the same hours as the castle. To see what today's youth hostels will look like in 2000 years, inspect the ruined barracks at **Segontium Roman Fort.** Plundered down to its foundations by zealous builders stealing stones for Caernarfon Castle, the fort impresses with thorough displays of archaeological excavations. Ignore the misleading road signs and cross under the A487 at the end of Pool St., then follow Ffordd Cwstenin until the fort appears on the left. (☎ 675625. Open Apr.-Oct. M-Sa 10am-5pm, Su 2-5pm; Nov.-Mar. M-Sa 10am-4pm, Su 2-4pm. £1.25, concessions 75p.)

Atop **Twt Hill,** alongside the Bangor St. roundabout, lie the scattered remains of a Celtic settlement; the jutting peak also offers sweeping vistas of the town and castle. Check at Slate Quay opposite the Castle Gift Shop for 40-minute **cruises** to the southwest entrance of the Menai Strait and back. (☎ 672902, evening ☎ 672772. £3.50, seniors £3, under 16 £2.) Across the Aber bridge near the castle, **Parc Coed Helen** is a peaceful, green spot to picnic.

BANGOR ☎ 01248

After spending time in Snowdonia or on the Llŷn, travelers may find Bangor's relative urbanity both reviving and disappointing. Crowded into a valley by the Menai Strait, Bangor (pop. 12,000) draws travelers by virtue of its status as a rail and bus hub. The city also forms a convenient (and cheap) base for exploring the nearby Isle of Anglesey. Perched gracefully over the city, the stately buildings of the University of Wales remind visitors of Bangor's role as a city of learning, a point also brought home by the masses of students who fill the pubs on High St.

NORTH WALES

F GETTING THERE. Bangor is the transport depot for the Isle of Anglesey to the west, the Llŷn Peninsula to the southwest, and Snowdonia to the southeast. The **train station** is on Holyhead Rd., up a hill at the end of Deiniol Rd. (☎ (01492) 585151. Ticket office open daily in high season 5:30am-6:30pm; in low season 11:30am-6:30pm.) Trains (☎ (08457) 484950) run into town on the north Wales train line from: **Llandudno Junction** (20min., £3.50); **Holyhead** (30min., £5.05); and **Chester** (1¼hr., £11.90). The **bus station** is on Garth Rd., down the hill from the town clock. **Arriva Cymru** (☎ (08706) 082608) **bus** #4 travels from **Holyhead** via **Llangefni** and **Llanfair P.G.** (1¼hr.; M-Sa 2 per hr., Su 6 per day; £2.75); buses #53 and 57 head from **Beaumaris** (30min.; M-Sa 2 per hr., Su 6 per day; £1.65). Arriva bus #5 and its cousins 5A, 5B, and 5X come from **Caernarfon** (25min.; M-Sa every 10min., Su 1 per hr.; £2.35); #5 and 5X continue east to **Conwy** (40min.; M-Sa 2 per hr., Su 1 per hr.; £2.35). Transfer at **Caernarfon** for the **Llŷn Peninsula,** including **Pwllheli** and **Porthmadog.** A solitary **TrawsCambria** bus #701 follows the coast all the way from **Cardiff** (7¾hr., £19.80); and the other way to **Holyhead** (1hr., £7.50). **National Express** (☎ (08705) 808080) buses arrive from **London** (7½hr., 2 per day, £21).

◼▮ ORIENTATION AND PRACTICAL INFORMATION. An age-old street plan and roads that don't advertise their names might leave you scratching your head. Bangor sprawls over hills, but its two main streets—**Deiniol Rd.** and the extraordinarily long **High St.**—run parallel to each other and sandwich the city on a relatively flat expanse. **Garth Rd.** starts from the town clock on High St., and, perpendicular to Deiniol Rd., winds past the bus station; when it finally meets Deiniol Rd., it makes a right angle turn to the east and takes over the main thoroughfare that had been Deiniol Rd. **Holyhead Rd.** begins its ascent at the rail station, also the starting point for Deiniol Rd. The **University of Wales at Bangor** sits on both sides of **College Rd.,** a right off Holyhead Rd. as it reaches the summit.

The **tourist information centre** (TIC) is in the Town Hall on Deiniol Rd., opposite Theatr Gwynedd, and provides a free booklet with an essential town map. They also keep an index of local bus fares. (☎ 352786. Open Easter-Sept. daily 10am-1pm and 2-6pm; Oct.-Easter F-Sa 10am-1pm and 2-6pm.) **HSBC,** 274 High St., proffers banking services. (Open M-F 9am-5pm, Sa 9:30am-12:30pm.) Find camping equipment at **The Great Arete,** 307 High St. (☎ 352710. Open M-Sa 9am-5:30pm.) The **Internet** is accessible both at the YHA (see below) and at the local library across from the TIC. Be forewarned that the computers are very busy during the school year. (Open M and Th-F 10am-7pm, T 10am-5pm, W 10am-1pm, Su 9:30am-1pm.) Bangor's **post office,** 60 Deiniol Rd., has a **bureau de change.** (☎ 373329. Open M-F 9am-5:30pm, Sa 9am-12:30pm.) **Postal code:** LL57 1AA.

▮◪ ACCOMMODATIONS AND FOOD. Finding a room in Bangor during the University of Wales's graduation (the second week of July) is a nightmarish prospect unless you book many months ahead. The **YHA Youth Hostel,** Tan-y-Bryn, lies half a mile from the town center. Follow High St. to the water and turn right at the end onto the A5122 (which masquerades as Beach Rd.), turning right again at the hard-to-spot Youth Hostel sign. The rich wood paneling of the entrance hall and vaulted wide-beam ceilings betray its former role as country estate, though the packed bunks are probably not original furnishings. Vivien Leigh and Sir Laurence Olivier always chose Room 6. (☎ 353516; fax 371176. Meals, Internet access, and laundry facilities available. Reception open 7am-11pm. Open Jan.-Nov. Dorms £9.80, under 18 £6.75.) The most agreeable **B&Bs** occupy the Victorian townhouses on **Garth Rd.** and its extensions. TVs are among the creature comforts provided by **Mrs. Jones,** who resides in Bro Dawel near the end of Garth Rd. (☎ 355242. £15 per person.) **Mrs. S. Roberts,** 32 Glynne Rd., between Garth Rd. and High St., has TVs and 13 choices for breakfast, including omelettes. (☎ 352113. £14 per person.) **Dinas Farm,** on the banks of the River Ogwan, offers camping and showers. Follow the A5 past Penrhyn Castle and then turn left off the A5122.

High St. holds a wide array of fruit shops and cafes, as well as a **Kwik Save** supermarket. (Open M-W and Sa 8:30am-6pm, Th-F 8:30am-7pm, Su 10am-4pm.) The friendly **Royal Tandoori,** 111 High St., dishes up standard tandoori fare. If your stomach is growling like a tiger, try the Bengal-style curry (£8.95); for smaller appetites, biriani (£5.45) comes in vegetable and meat varieties, with a 10% takeaway discount. (☎ 364664. Open daily noon-2pm and 5:30-11:30pm.) Munch sandwiches (£2.25-3.25) at the **Penguin Café,** 260 High St., as you people-watch from the sidewalk tables. (☎ 362036. Open M-Sa 7am-5:30pm.)

🔲 **SIGHTS AND ENTERTAINMENT.** The gray bleakness of 🔳 **Penrhyn Castle,** George Hay Dawkins-Pennant's 19th-century neo-Norman grotesquerie, squats over two acres just outside of Bangor. Its chiseled square towers glare across a 40-acre estate, testament to the staggering wealth accumulated by the owners of Gwynedd's slate mines. Picnickers will find the grounds a brilliant location. Inside, Penrhyn's opulence makes Versailles seem tastefully understated; the intricately carved stone staircase took 10 years to complete, and even the servants' version manages to seem pretentious. A fine collection of Old Masters and some historical artifacts are also housed inside. The luxury contrasts starkly with the poverty and toil known to the residents of nearby mining towns, a point stressed on the audio tour. To get to Penrhyn, walk up High St. toward the pier, then turn right onto the A5122 and go north for 1 mi., or catch bus #5 or one of its #5A/B//X spawn from the town center; the castle is an additional mile from the gate. (☎ 353084. Open July-Aug. W-M 11am-5pm; late Mar. to June and Sept.-Oct. W-M noon-5pm. Castle and grounds £5, children £2.50, families £12.50; grounds only £3, children £1.50.)

The venerable **St. Deiniol's Cathedral,** on Gwynedd Rd. just off High St., with its humble, steepleless stature, has been the ecclesiastical center of this corner of Wales for 1400 years; its Bible Garden, with plants mentioned in the Good Book, provides a haven for weary shoppers. (☎ 353983. Open daily 8am-6pm.) The **Museum of Welsh Antiquities and Art Gallery,** also on Gwynedd Rd., houses an authentic man-trap, used as an anti-poaching device. (☎ 353368. Open Tu-F 12:30-4:30pm, Sa 10:30am-4:30pm. Free.) Watch tides ebb and flow at the long, onion-domed Victorian **pier** at the end of Garth Rd. (Open daily until sunset. 20p.)

The modern **Theatr Gwynedd,** on Deiniol Rd. at the base of the hill, houses a thriving troupe that performs in both Welsh and English. (☎ 351708. Box office open M-Sa 9:30am-5pm; on performance days M-Sa 9:30am-8:30pm, Su 6-8:30pm. Films £4.20, students and seniors £3.20, children £2.10; plays £6-18.) Incredibly for at student town, Bangor doesn't offer much by way of a nightlife scene, but there are rumors of a club opening sometime in 2001.

ISLE OF ANGLESEY (YNYS MÔN)

The Isle of Anglesey, connected to mainland Wales by the massive Menai and Britannia Bridges, feels more like a parallel landscape than an island. Once a center of Celtic druidic culture, the flat, arable land has provided both spiritual and physical sustenance for the entire region. The isle's old name is *Mona mam Cymru* (Mona the mother of Wales), and, appropriately, Anglesey hosted the last Royal National Eisteddfod of the millennium in August 1999 (see Ffestivals, p. 422). While Beaumaris Castle is what attracts most visitors, the well-preserved prehistoric sites and gentle coastline should not be neglected.

🔲 **GETTING THERE AND GETTING AROUND**

Bangor, on the mainland, is the best hub for the island. **Trains** (☎ (08457) 484950) run along the north Wales train line to **Holyhead** from **Bangor** (30min., 1-3 per hr., £5.05); some of these trains stop at **Llanfair P.G.** The main bus company is **Arriva Cymru** (☎ (08706) 082608), which spins a web of buses around most of the island; a handful of smaller bus companies fill in the gaps. Arriva bus #4 travels north from **Bangor** to **Holyhead** via **Llanfair P.G.** and **Llangefni** (1¼hr.; M-Sa 2 per hr., Su 6 per day; £2.75); buses #53 and 57 hug the southeast coast in a scenic run from **Bangor** to **Beaumaris** (30min.; M-Sa 2 per hr., Su 6 per day; £1.65). Bus #62 sputters to **Amlwch,** on the northern coast, from **Bangor** (50min.; M-Sa 1 per hr., Su 3 per day; £1.75); bus #42 curves along the southwest coast up to **Aberffraw** before cutting north to **Llangefni** (1hr.; M-Sa 8 per day, Su 2 per day; £1.75). From **Amlwch, Lewis y Llan** (☎ (01407) 832181) bus #61 cruises into **Holyhead** (50min., M-Sa 8 per day, £1.80). **Gwynfors** (☎ (01248) 722694) #32 shuttles north from **Llangefni** to **Amlwch** (40min.; M-Sa 2 per hr., Su 5 per day; £1.50). Pick up the *Isle of Anglesey Public Transport Guide* in tourist information centres; the Gwynedd **Red Rover ticket** (£4.60, children £2.30) covers a day's bus travel in all of Anglesey, as well as Gwynedd, including Bangor.

◼ ISLAND SIGHTS

From prehistory, people fancied living on Anglesey. Burial chambers, cairns, settlement remains, and more recent constructions are scattered on Holyhead and both the eastern and western coasts. Explore with Ordnance Survey Landranger Map #114, available at most TICs (scale 1:50,000; £5.25). Most ancient monuments sit quietly in farmers' fields; a map detailing exactly how to reach them (without walking through a herd of cows) is your best bet. *Anglesey: A Guide to Ancient and Historic Sites on the Isle of Anglesey* (£2.25), produced by CADW, gives good directions to 22 sites.

■**BRYN CELLI DDU.** Bryn Celli Ddu (bryn kay-HLEE thee), "The Mound in the Dark Grove," is a burial chamber dating from the late Neolithic period and the most famous of Anglesey's remains. The nonchalance of it all is amazing—this 4000-year-old construction looks just like any old mound of earth from out the outside, and sits quietly in the middle of a sheep pasture. A flashlight helps illuminate the etchings on the walls inside. *(Take Bangor-Holyhead bus #4, which sometimes stops at Llandaniel (M-Sa 9 per day), and walk about a mile from there. You can also walk there from Llanfair P.G. past Plas Newydd; ask at the TIC.)*

PLAS NEWYDD. The 19th-century country home of the Marquess of Anglesey, two miles south of Llanfair P.G., is now run by the National Trust. The 58 ft. Rex Whistler painting that covers an inside room is certainly impressive, but admission is expensive. *(Take bus #42 from Bangor. ☎ 714795. House open Apr.-Oct. Sa-W noon-5pm, garden 11am-5:30pm. £4.50, children £2.25, families £11; garden only £2.50, children £1.25.)*

PENMON PRIORY. The late medieval priory of Penmon is perhaps the most readily accessible of Anglesey's sights. St. Seiriol's Well, found here, is reputed to have healing qualities, certainly has at least £4.20 in coins in the water, and may have magnetic powers on clumsy clamberers. After curing yourself of that pesky rheumatism, scamper like a sprite into the church itself, where an elaborately carved cross stands. *(Take Arriva Cymru bus #57 from Beaumaris to Penmon (20min.; M-Sa 1 per hr., Su 3 per day; 90p); from there it's a short walk to Penmon Point, where the priory lies.)*

LLANALLGO. Three sets of remains cluster near the town of Llanallgo, but getting to them requires a bit of effort. Follow the minor road (to the left of the Moelfre road) to the ancient **Ligwy Burial Chamber.** Between 15 and 30 people are entombed in this squat enclosure, covered with a 25-ton capstone. Farther on stand the 12th-century chapel **Hen Capel Ligwy** and the remains of the Roman **Din Ligwy Hut Group.** *(Arriva bus #62 hits Llanallgo on its Benllech-Moelfre route, M-Sa 1 per hr., Su 3 per day. Ask the driver to stop at the roundabout heading to Moelfre.)*

LLANFAIRPWLL...

Llanfairpwllgwyngyllgogerychwyrndrobwllllantysiliogogogoch (HLAN-vire-poohl-gwin-gihl—ah, screw it), the longest-named village in the world, is linked to Bangor by the Britannia Bridge. Devised by a 19th-century humorist to attract attention, the name translates roughly as "Saint Mary's Church in the hollow of white hazel near the rapid whirlpool and the Church of Saint Tysillio near the red cave" (or, alternatively, "we-couldn't-find-a-compelling-reason-to-get-you-to-come-here-so-we-just-created-a-ridiculous-name"). Sensibly, the town's war memorial reads "Llanfair P.G." so as not to overwhelm the roll call of the dead. The town is also known locally as "Llanfairpwll." Llanfair P.G. holds Anglesey's sole **tourist information centre.** (☎ (01248) 713177; fax 715711. Open Apr.-Oct. M-Sa 9:30am-5:30pm, Su 10am-5pm; Nov.-Mar. M-F 9:30am-1pm and 1:30-5pm, Su 10am-5pm.) The James Pringle **woollens factory** in town is mobbed by tourists taking photos under the sign with the name. Puts antiecclesiodisestablishmentarianism in the lexicographical dustbin, doesn't it?

BEAUMARIS ☎01248

Four miles northeast of the Menai Bridge on the A545, the main street of Beaumaris (bew-MAR-is; don't you dare say it the French way) runs quietly along the coastline. Yachts dot the harbor, surveying the mountains of Snowdonia. In town, savor the magnificent (albeit unfinished) symmetry of 🏰 **Beaumaris Castle,** the last of Edward I's Welsh fortresses and now a World Heritage site. Begun in 1295 and built on a marsh, the moat-ringed castle couldn't depend on rugged geography to discourage would-be invaders. Edward's architect relied instead on a concentric design, with an inner gate off-center from the outer one to force would-be attackers to turn and expose their left flanks. (☎ 810361. Open June-Sept. daily 9:30am-6pm; Apr.-May and Oct. daily 9:30am-5pm; Nov.-Mar. M-Sa 9:30am-4pm, Su 11am-4pm. £2.20, concessions £1.70, families £6.10.)

On Bunkers Hill, off Steeple Ln., the cells of the former **Beaumaris Gaol** show what it meant to be a prisoner in Victorian times. Reform meant hard time on the treadwheel, supplying running water; for the rest, a chilling walk down Death Row ended at the courtyard gallows. (☎ 810921. Open Apr.-Sept. daily 10:30am-5pm. £2.75, concessions £1.75.) The lighter side of the Victorian experience is captured in the **Museum of Childhood Memories,** 1 Castle St., where legions of tin wind-ups, round-eyed dolls, and pea-shooting piggy banks sing the sweet and silly song of nostalgia. (☎ 712498. Open Easter-Oct. M-Sa 10:30am-5:30pm, Su noon-5pm. £3, students and seniors £2.50, children £1.75, families £8.50.) A catamaran cruise down the Menai Strait to **Puffin Island** leaves from the Starida booth on the pier, as do longer trips. (☎ 810379; before 10:30am or after 5pm ☎ 810251. Cruises 1hr.; £4.50, seniors £4, children £3.50.) The week-long **Gŵyl Beaumaris Music Festival** at the end of May features concerts, opera, theater, and street performances.

Buses stop on Castle St. An independently run **tourist information centre,** Town Hall, on Castle St., provides brochures and accommodation info. (☎ 810040. Open Easter-Oct. daily 10am-5:30pm.) The **HSBC bank** is on Castle St. (Open M-F 11am-2pm.) The **post office** is at 10 Church St. (Open M-Tu and Th-F 9am-12:30pm and 1:30-5:30pm, W and Sa 9am-12:30pm.) **Postal code:** LL58 8AB.

The closest **YHA Youth Hostel** to Beaumaris is in Bangor (☎ 353516; see p. 476). Only three **B&Bs** reside in Beaumaris; accommodations are mostly provided by pubs, and beds come at high prices. Budget travelers should sleep across the strait in Bangor or nearby Caernarfon. Institutionalized camping is best at **Kingsbridge Caravan Park,** two miles out of town toward Llangoed. At the end of Beaumaris's main street, follow the coastal road two miles past the castle until you come to the crossroads. Turn left for Llanfaes; Kingsbridge is 400 yd. down on the right. (☎ 490636; kingsbridge@hotmail.com. Showers available. £4 per adult, £1 per child, £1.50 per car.) Gratify gluttony at the stocked shelves of **Spar,** 11 Castle St. (Open M-Sa 8am-11pm, Su 8am-10pm.)

HOLYHEAD (CAERGYBI) ☎01407

A narrow strip of land attached to Anglesey by a causeway and a bridge, Holyhead (pop. 12,000) has only one real lure for the traveler: ferries to Ireland. **Irish Ferries** and **Stena Sealink** operate ferries and catamarans to **Dublin** and its suburb, **Dún Laoghaire.** Only car-ferry parties leave from the docks; foot passengers embark at the train station. Arrive 30 minutes early and remember your passport. (See **By Ferry,** p. 35, for more details.) There are a few sights on Holyhead, but it takes some effort to reach most them. **Caer Gybi,** the Roman walls that surround St. Gybi's church, are in the middle of the city, between Stanley St. and Victoria Rd. If you have time, explore the many paths of **Holyhead Mountain** near town. Its North and South Stacks are good for birdwatching, and the lighthouse looks longingly to sea. **Caer y Tŵr** and **Holyhead Mountain Hut Group** sit at the mountain's base. The former is an Iron Age hillfort, the latter a settlement inhabited from 500 BC until Roman times.

Holyhead can be reached from land by hourly **trains** from: **Bangor** (30min., £5.05); **Chester** (1½hr., £16.15); and **London** (6hr., £57.30). **Arriva Cymru** (☎ (08706) 082608) **bus #4** comes from **Bangor** via **Llanfair P.G.** and **Llangefni** (1¼hr.; M-Sa 2 per hr., Su 6 per day; £2.75). **National Express** (☎ (08705) 808080) hits Holyhead from most major cities. **TrawsCambria bus** #701 arrives from and departs for **Cardiff** once a day (9hr.). For a **taxi**, call ☎ 765000. An **HSBC bank** sits on the corner of William St. and Market St. (Open M-F 9am-5pm.) The **post office**, 13a Stryd Boston, off Market St., has a **bureau de change.** (Open M-F 9am-5:30pm, Sa 9am-12:30pm.) **Postal code:** LL65 1BP.

Holyhead **B&Bs** are accommodating to passengers arriving and departing at the beck and call of boat schedules. Holyhead has no tourist information centre to help you find a bed, but the ferry staff at the car dock and train station have a B&B list. If you call ahead, B&B owners can usually arrange to greet you in the middle of the night, but don't go ringing doorbells unannounced in the wee hours. Some will provide B&PL (beds and packed lunches) for ferry riders. **Roselea,** 26 Holborn Rd., the closest B&B to the station and the ferries, will pack you a lunch for the day after you sleep in their orthopedic beds and watch their TVs. (☎/fax 764391. Singles £20; twins £32.) To get to **Orotovia**, 66 Walthew Ave., go up Thomas St., which becomes Porth-y-Felin Rd. as it passes the school, and turn right onto Walthew Ave., not to be confused with Walthew St. All the rooms have TVs, and the dining room offers woodcrafts for sale. The kind proprietress serves scrumptious breakfasts, with every possible cereal on offer. (☎ 760259. £16 per person with *Let's Go*.) A little way down the road, the proprietress of **Witchingham,** 20 Walthew Ave., totes a Toto named Jody but is hardly the broom-riding-pointy-hat-wearing type. Comfortable beds and TVs in rooms, not poppies, lull you to sleep here. Just think before you book for St. David's Day, when a ghost has been known to drop by. (☎ 762426. £17 per person; £19.50 with bath.)

CONWY ☎ 01492

With a 13th-century castle towering over narrow lanes and a pleasant quayside, Conwy bears its tiring role as modern tourist mecca well. Edward I, who seemed never to tire of constructing the damn things, had the town's solemn castle built as another link in his ring of North Wales fortresses. It now stands guard over a fine city wall, elegant houses, and a gaggle of eclectic attractions.

▣ GETTING THERE

Trains (☎ (08457) 484950) only stop at Conwy station, off Rosehill St., by request, even though Conwy lies on the north Wales train line linking Holyhead to Chester. Trains stop instead at the nearby, fully staffed **Llandudno Junction** station, one of the busiest in Wales, which connects to the scenic Conwy Valley line. (Llandudno Junction booking office open M-Sa 5:30am-6:30pm, Su 11:30am-6:30pm.) Not to be confused with Llandudno proper (a resort town about a mile north; see p. 483), Llandudno Junction is a 20-minute walk from Conwy. Turn left onto a little side road after exiting the station, walk past a supermarket on your left, pass under a bridge, and then climb the stairs to another bridge that will lead you past pretty gardens and across the estuary to Conwy castle and town. If you haven't the energy for such a hike, hop on Arriva bus #22 from the stop down the ramp from the station (M-Sa 1 per hr., Su 4 per day as #22A; 60p).

Buses are the best way of getting directly to Conwy, and they stop at various points, with the two main stops at Lancaster Sq. and Castle St. just before the corner of Rosehill St.; check posted schedules. **National Express** (☎ (08705) 808080) comes from: **Chester** (2hr., 1 per day, £15); **Manchester** (3½hr., 1 per day, £10.75); and **London** (7hr., 1 per day, £19). **Arriva Cymru** (☎ (08706) 082608) buses #5, 5A, and 5X stop in Conwy as they climb the northern coast from **Caernarfon** via **Bangor** (1hr.; M-Sa 3 per hr., Su 1 per hr.; £2.85). Bus #19 takes in Conwy on its **Llandudno-Llanrwst** journey down the Vale of Conwy (40min.; M-Sa 2 per hr., Su 7 per day; £1.10). The comprehensive *Conwy Public Transport Information* booklet has schedules and maps and is available at the tourist information centre.

✴️🛈 ORIENTATION AND PRACTICAL INFORMATION

The town wall squeezes old Conwy into a roughly triangular shape. The castle lies in one corner, by the Conwy and Gyffin Rivers; **Castle St.**, which becomes **Berry St.**, runs from the foot of the fortress parallel to the Quay on the other side of the wall. **High St.** stretches from the Quay's edge to **Lancaster Sq.**, crossing Castle St. en route. From Lancaster Sq., **Rosehill St.** circles back to the castle, while in the opposite direction **Bangor Rd.** scrunches northward through a small arch in the wall.

The **tourist information centre** (TIC), at Castle Entrance, hands out clear street maps and books beds for £1 plus a 10% deposit. (☎ 592248. Open daily Mar.-Oct. noon-6pm; Nov.-Mar. 10am-4pm.) **Conwy Outdoor Shop,** 9 Castle St., has an extensive, if slightly overpriced, selection of camping supplies. (☎ 593390. Open daily 9am-6pm.) The weekly **market** takes place in the train station parking lot. (Open Sa 8:30am-5pm; Apr.-Aug. also Tu.) Services include: **Barclays bank,** 23 High St. (☎ 616616; open M-F 10am-4pm); the **police** (☎ 511000), Lancaster Sq.; **Llandudno Hospital,** Maesdu Rd. (☎ 860066; take Arriva bus #19); **Internet access** at the **library** (£2.50 per 30min.; open M and Th-F 10am-5:30pm, Tu 10am-7pm, W and Sa 10am-1pm); and the **post office,** Lancaster Sq. at High St., in The Wine Shop (☎ 573990; open M-F 8:30am-6pm, Sa 9am-5:30pm). **Postal code:** LL32 8DA.

🛏 ACCOMMODATIONS

B&Bs crowd the **Cadnant Park** area, a 10-minute walk from the castle. Head from the castle down Rosehill St., past Lancaster Sq., through the arch down Bangor Rd., then turn left into a sea of well-tended gardens.

YHA Conwy, Larkhill, Sychnant Pass Rd. (☎ 593571; fax 593580; conwy@yha.org.uk). From Lancaster Sq., head down Bangor Rd., turn left up Mt. Pleasant, and right at the top of the hill. The hostel is on the left after 150 yd. This sprawling YHA is well-equipped with a huge self-catering kitchen, laundry facilities, TV room, and luggage lockers (£1). Showers in all rooms. Wheelchair access. Internet access £2.50 per 30min. Reception and facilities open from 1pm. Open mid-Feb. to Dec. Dorms £11.90, under 18 £8.20.

Llwyn Guest House, 15 Cadnant Park (☎ 592319). Lose yourself in the downy duvets while vegging in front of your personal TV, or doze in the carefully cultivated garden in a quiet neighborhood. £16 per person.

Glan Heulog, Llanrwst Rd., Woodlands (☎ 593845). Go under the arch before the Visitor Centre on Rosehill St., down the steps, and across the carpark. Turn right and walk 5min. down Llanrwst Rd. Huge house on a hill with TVs and a "healthy option" breakfast of fresh fruit and yoghurt available. Singles £22; doubles and twins £34-40.

Swan Cottage, 18 Berry St. (☎ 596840). One of the few B&Bs within the city walls. Cozy rooms with timber ceilings and TVs. Loft room with view of the estuary. £15 per person.

Camping: Conwy Touring Park, Llanrwst Rd. (☎ 592856). A steep mile or so out of town. Follow Llanrwst Rd. and posted signs. Launderette and showers. Families and couples only; no large groups. Open Easter-Oct. 2-person tent £5-7.

🍴 FOOD

Most Conwy restaurants serve ordinary grub, but the name of High St., along which many are found, might well be a reference to the inflated prices. Fear not, thrifty gourmands, for the ever-reliable **Spar** grocery also defends its territory here next to Barclays. (Open daily 8am-10pm.) Fine vegetarian and vegan fare (£2-7) awaits at **The Wall Place,** on Chapel St. off Berry St. On some evenings, traditional Welsh music wafts across the light grain wood floor; on winter afternoons, the cafe hosts creative workshops. (☎ 596326. Open Easter-June F-Sa noon-3pm and 7-10pm, Su noon-3pm, some weekdays noon-3pm; July to mid-Sept. daily noon-3pm and 7-10pm; mid-Sept. to Easter F-Sa noon-3pm and 7-10pm.) For light meals (£2.80-4.30) and sandwich snacks (£1.70), open the doors of the **Pantri Conwy,** Lancaster Sq. (☎ 592436. Open M-Su 9am-5pm.) Above-average pub grub (£2.25-4.50) in a bright, homey atmosphere awaits at **Ye Olde Mail Coach** on High St. (Open M-Sa 11am-11pm, Su noon-10:30pm.)

■ SIGHTS

CONWY CASTLE. More compact than Edward I's colossal fortresses at Caernarfon and Beaumaris, Conwy Castle's menacing stone stance was still challenge enough for would-be attackers. Invaders would need to scale the slippery rock promontory, shielded by water on three sides, before somehow breaching one of two massive barbicans amid a shower of crossbow bolts. And that's just to get to the grim walls and turreted towers of the inner curtain. The prison tower saw many prominent Normans rot beneath its false bottom, and the castle chapel witnessed Henry "Hotspur" Percy's betrayal of Richard II in 1399; two years later Welsh rebel Owain Glyndŵr and his band of armed nationalists seized the ramparts. The turrets and nooks occasionally house seagulls' nests. *(☎ 592358. Open June-Sept. daily 9:30am-6pm; Apr.-May and Oct. daily 9:30am-5pm; Nov.-Mar. M-Sa 9:30am-4pm, Su 11am-4pm. Tours £1. £3.50, concessions £2.50, families £9.50.)*

TOWN WALL. Almost a mile long, the wall was built at the same time as the castle and shielded burghers with its 22 towers and 480 arrow slits—the twelve latrine shoots may have been useful, too. Many sections are open for climbing; the steep section bordering Mt. Pleasant rewards the fit traveler with a magnificent view.

TELFORD SUSPENSION BRIDGE. Next to a rather unsightly rail bridge, Telford's elegant 1826 suspension bridge stretches across the Conwy River from the foot of the castle's grassy east barbican; at the end stands the tollmaster's house, carefully recreated. Both bridge and castle can be seen by boat; vigorous bellowing heralds the departure of the **Queen Victoria** from the quay at the end of High St. *(☎ 573282. Bridge and house open July-Aug. daily 10am-5pm; Apr.-June and Sept.-Oct. W-M 10am-5pm. Last admission 4:30pm. £1, children 50p. Cruises 30min.; £3, children £2.)*

THE SMALLEST HOUSE. Bang your head into what's billed as Britain's smallest house, another one of Conwy's oddities. With a frontage of 6 ft., the 380-year-old two-floor edifice housed an elderly couple and then one 6-foot 3-inch fisherman before it was condemned in 1900. *(Head down High St. and onto the quay. ☎ 593484. Open July-Aug. 10am-9pm; Easter-June and Sept.-Oct. 10am-6pm. 50p, concessions 30p.)*

CONWY BUTTERFLY JUNGLE. Some 400 butterflies flutter by in the Conwy Butterfly Jungle, a swarming greenhouse in Bodlondeb Park outside the town wall. Some frightening specimens, including a "giant armored jungle nymph" measuring a spiky 8 in., mean-looking tarantulas, and scorpions, are locked in cages for safety. Your safety. *(☎ 593149. Open Apr.-Sept. 10am-5:30pm; Oct. 10am-4pm. £3.50, students £2, seniors £3. YHA members 20% off.)*

ABERCONWY HOUSE. Walk along tilted floors past displays of armor and period furnishings in the 14th-century Aberconwy House, the oldest house in Conwy, which has survived numerous wars and Welsh uprisings in such guises as a sea captain's house and a temperance center. *(Castle St. ☎ 592246. Open Apr.-Oct. W-M 10am-5pm. Last admission 4:30pm. £2, children £1, families £5.)*

TEAPOT MUSEUM. Two grand British traditions—tea and eccentricity—meet at the Teapot Museum, which displays 300 years of teapots—some short, some stout, and some shaped like a craggy Lloyd George, a dour Thatcher, and a roomy Pavarotti. Don't knock over the Humpty Dumpty pot; the nearest savior is not a King's horse or a King's man, but the King of Rock and Roll himself, who warns that only fools rush in this packed little room. Glimpses of *risqué* teapots reward the diligent museum-goer. *(Castle St. ☎ 593429. Open Easter-Oct. M-Sa 10am-5:30pm, Su 11am-5:30pm. £1.50, concessions £1. YHA members 10% off.)*

OTHER SIGHTS AND ENTERTAINMENT. Plas Mawr, on High St., is the best-preserved Elizabethan house in Britain. Lovingly restored, it sports exquisite plasterwork and a pantry with (faux) rabbit and deer hanging from the walls. *(☎ 580167. Open Tu-Su Apr.-May and Sept. 9:30am-5pm; June-Aug. 9:30am-6pm; Oct. 9:30am-4pm. £4, concessions £3, families £11.)* Most of the tranquility in Conwy has migrated to **St. Mary's Church.** Just outside the South Porch rests the grave that inspired Wordsworth's poem "We are Seven." In September, the **Conwy Festival** draws local musicians and dancers into the streets and castle courtyard.

LLANDUDNO   ☎01492

Until 1849, the flatlands between the Great Orme and the Little Orme bore only indigenous wildflowers and whatever crops farmers could grow in the shadow of the two rock heads. The Mostyn family, however, had grander schemes in mind for the sheltered strip flanked by two beaches, and planted the seeds of a resort town that now blooms with colorful rows of Victorian and Edwardian buildings. The streets just outside the city center are crammed with tourist housing, but the sidewalks and promenades are wide, the wrought iron awnings decorative and tasteful, and the atmosphere cheerful and perpetually on holiday. Llandudno offers a happy mix of elegant charm and good old-fashioned relaxation, with escape to nature as easy as a trip to the theater.

GETTING THERE AND GETTING AROUND. In the very north of Wales, Llandudno is the terminus of several lines of transport. Llandudno's **train station** is at the end of Augusta Rd. (Ticket office open M-Sa 8:40am-3:30pm, July-Aug. also Su 10:15am-5:45pm.) **Trains** (☎ (08457) 484950) arrive on the single-track Conwy Valley train line from **Blaenau Ffestiniog** via **Betws-y-Coed** (1hr.; M-Sa 6 per day, Su 3 per day); and into **Llandudno Junction,** a mile south of town on the Conwy Valley line, eastward from **Holyhead** (50min.) and **Bangor** (20min.), and westward from **Chester** (40min.), all on the north Wales train line. **National Express** (☎ (08750) 808080) **buses** arrive at Mostyn Broadway from: **London** (7½hr., 1 per day, £19); **Chester** (1¾hr., 1 per day, £5.50); and **Manchester** (3¼hr., 1 per day, £8.75). **Arriva Cymru** (☎ (08706) 082608) buses #5, 5A, and 5X power in from **Conwy** (15min.; M-Sa 3 per hr., Su 1 per hr.; £1.10), **Bangor** (40min., £2.70); and **Caernarfon** (1¼hr., £3.25). Bus #19 arrives from **Llanrwst** in the Vale of Conwy (1hr.; M-Sa 2 per hr., Su 7 per day; £1.20). Bus #96 travels from **Betws-y-Coed** (M-Sa 4 per day, £3). Bus #70 runs the same trip Su (3 per day). Bikes rented from **West End Cycles,** 22 Augusta St., make the promenades and the trip down the Orme a breeze. (☎ 876891. £10 per day; £25 deposit. Open M-Sa 9am-5:30pm.)

ORIENTATION AND PRACTICAL INFORMATION. Llandudno is flanked by two pleasant beaches; the West Shore is less built up than the North, which is decorated with Victorian promenades and tipped by a long pier. On the left as you come out of the train station is the **tourist information centre** (TIC), Chapel St., which houses a library of free pamphlets and books rooms for a 10% deposit. (☎ 876413. Open daily Easter-Oct. 9:30am-5:30pm, Nov.-Easter 10am-4pm.) Services include: Kings Cabs **taxis** (☎ 878156); **Barclays bank,** on the corner of Mostyn St. and Market St. (open M-T and Th-F 9:30am-4:30pm, W 10am-4:30pm, Sa 10am-12:30pm); **Internet access** at **CyberSkills,** 50 Madoc St. (☎ 874627; £2.50 per 30min.; open M-Th 9am-5pm, F 9am-4:30pm, Sa 10am-3pm); and the **post office,** 14 Vaughn St., with a **bureau de change** (☎ (0345) 223344; open M-F 9am-5:30pm, Sa 9am-12:30pm). **Postal code:** LL30 1AA.

ACCOMMODATIONS AND FOOD. Designed for visitors, Llandudno has no shortage of places to eat and sleep. Budget travelers should seek out B&Bs (£12-14) on **Chapel St., Deganwy Ave.,** and **St. David's Rd**. Try **Walsall House,** 4 Chapel St. (☎ 875279. £14 per person, £11 without breakfast.) The popular **YHA Conwy** (see p. 481) is only 15min. away by bus. Eateries accommodate all appetites. Busy **Ham Bone,** Clonmel St. off Mostyn St., fixes sandwiches with loads of fixings (£1.55), baps with hot pork stuffing and apple sauce (£2), and meat or cheese pies (75p-£1) for takeaway. (Open M-Sa 8:30am-5pm.) **The Fat Cat Cafe-Bar,** 149 Mostyn St., offers a varied menu in an academic atmosphere, including Mexican nachos (£3.55), vegetarian Thai rice (£4.95), and Scottish pancakes for £2.45. (☎ 871844. Open M-Sa 10am-11pm, Su 10am-10:30pm.) The good **Habit,** 12 Mostyn St., won't break your budget. Main courses run around £5, with hot sandwiches from £1.95-3.50 and a table full of baked and sweet things to top it all off. (☎ 875043. Open daily 9:30am-5:30pm.) **The Cottage Loaf,** Market St. off Mostyn St., next to Barclays, exudes a village pub atmosphere in its blooming beer garden, and serves up really good grub, too. (☎ 876121. Open M-Sa until 11pm, Su until 10:30pm.)

NORTH WALES

◉ SIGHTS. Llandudno's two pleasant beaches, Victorian North Shore and quieter West Shore, are both outdone by the looming **Great Orme**. At the 679 ft. summit, wildflowers run amok amid prehistoric remains and a modern visitor center, accessible by foot or by the **Great Orme Tramway,** starting at Church Walks. (☎ 574237. Runs Apr.-Oct. 10am-6pm. Return £3.80, children £2.60; single £2.60, children £1.80.) The two counter-balanced cable cars also stop halfway up at the **Bronze Age Copper Mines,** where audio-visual exhibits and tunnels lead to a 3,500-year-old cavern. (☎ 870447. Open Feb.-Oct. 10am-5pm. Joint tram tickets available.) Llandudno pays tribute to one of its famous summer visitors with **The Rabbit Hole** at the Alice in Wonderland Centre, 3-4 Trinity Sq. Alice Liddell, the inspiration for Lewis Carroll's fantastical story, spent her childhood summers here, but this audio and walk-through trip down the rabbit hole sticks to Cheshire Cats and Mad Hatters. (☎/fax 860062. Open Easter-Oct. M-Sa 10am-5pm, Su 10am-4pm. Audio tour available in multiple languages. £2.95, seniors £2.75, children £2.50.)

📺🎵 NIGHTLIFE AND ENTERTAINMENT. It all depends what you're looking for, kids. **Annabelle's,** St. George's Pl. off Mostyn St., is all about the beer and fun times, and you can go in a t-shirt. Drinks flow freely for £1.49-1.89 a pint. (☎ 877630. Open M-Su from 7pm.) If you want to disco, you'll have to dress. **Broadway Boulevard,** Mostyn Broadway, pumps and grinds the night away. (☎ 879614. Smart casual; no trainers. W and Sa 21+, Th 18+, F 19+. Open 9pm-2am, last admission midnight; bar closes 1:30am.) For a bit of culture, spend an evening at the **North Wales Theatre,** sandwiched between Mostyn Boulevard and the Promenade. (Box office ☎ 872000. Tickets £7-15; call box office for shows and prices.)

VALE OF CONWY

Well-watered by river and rain, the lush Vale of Conwy hosts walkers, cyclists, and innumerable waterfowl. The undulating hills that peter out of the lofty Snowdonia mountains slope down to the tidal Conwy River. In the thick woods around Betws-y-Coed, tripping tributaries converge excitedly, then relax and meander lazily north to Llandudno. Cyclists take advantage of the scenic terrain here: views are glorious and gear-changes infrequent. Pick up the excellent brochure *Walks from the Conwy Valley Line* at local tourist information centres and train stations for information on the area's splendid hiking opportunities.

▐ GETTING THERE AND GETTING AROUND

The single-track, 27-mile **Conwy Valley** line (☎ (08457) 484950) offers unparalleled views as its **trains** hug the river banks between the seaside resort of **Llandudno** and the mountain town of **Blaenau Ffestiniog,** stopping at **Llandudno Junction** (near Conwy) and **Betws-y-Coed** on the way (1hr.; M-Sa 6 per day, Su 3 per day). The **North & Mid Wales Rover ticket** gives virtually unlimited bus and train travel as far south as **Aberystwyth** (day £17.30, 3-day £26.30, week £40.90). Most **buses** stop at Betws-y-Coed and Llanrwst; the rest of the valley is relatively untouched. The main bus along the Conwy River is **Arriva Cymru** (☎ (08706) 082608) #19, which winds from **Llandudno** and **Conwy** down to **Llanrwst** (M-Sa 2 per hr., Su 7 per day). Some of those services continue as **Sherpa** bus #96 to Llanberis via Betws-y-Coed (8 per day). Arriva sells a one-day **Explorer** pass good for unlimited travel on any of its buses (£5, children £3.50; longer options available).

BETWS-Y-COED   ☎01690

At the southern tip of the Vale of Conwy and the eastern edge of the Snowdonia mountains, the crowded but picturesque village of Betws-y-Coed (BET-iss uh COYD), often called just Betws, exudes adventurism; *everyone* seems to be communing with the great outdoors, even the solid rock houses lining the town's one road, which were quarried from the cliffs directly behind them. Coursing through town, the Conwy and Llugwy rivers crash over rocks and foamy rapids, while brooding conifers darken the hills and lend to the scene a distinctly Alpine air.

GETTING THERE. Trains (☎ (08457) 484950) stop in Betws-y-Coed on the Conwy Valley line (see above). **Sherpa** bus #96, operated by Arriva Cymru, connects Betws-y-Coed with **Llanrwst** and **Llanberis**, stopping at most area hostels (8 per day). Connect for buses to Conwy in Llanrwst. Arriva bus #70 runs west twice a day from **Llangollen** (£3.80) via **Corwen** (£2); sometimes you have to change buses in Corwen. Rent **bikes** from the laid-back cyclists at **Beics Betws** (☎ 710766), beside the tourist information centre. (£4 per hr., £12 per half-day, £16 per day; reduced group rates. Helmet included. Open M-F 9am-5:30pm, Su 10am-5:30pm.)

◪ PRACTICAL INFORMATION. The main (and only real) street is Holyhead Rd., which is also the A5. The self-proclaimed busiest **tourist information centre** (TIC) in north Wales, also a **National Park Information Centre,** is at the Old Stables, next to a park between the station and Holyhead Rd. The spirited and tireless staff provides information on sights and bus and train timetables, and there's also a well-stocked bookshop. (☎ 710426; fax 710665; www.betws-y-coed.co.uk. Open daily Easter-Oct. 10am-6pm; Nov.-Easter 9:30am-12:30pm and 1:30-4:30pm.) Between April and September, **guided walks** around Betws leave from the TIC. (All walks 6-8 mi., 5-6hr. Walks leave Th-Su 9:55am. £3.50, children 50p.) An **HSBC bank** hides at the southern edge of Holyhead Rd. (Open M and F 9:15am-2:30pm, Tu-Th 9:15am-1pm.) Three emporia on Holyhead Rd. sell mountaineering supplies and canoe equipment: **Ultimate Outdoors** (☎ 710555; open M-Th 9am-5:30pm, F-Su 9am-6pm) and two **Cotswold** outlets, one next to the Royal Oak Hotel (☎ 710710), the other just south of town (☎ 710234; both open M-Th 9am-5:30pm, F-Su 9am-6:30pm). The friendly staff at the **post office,** at the T-junction of Holyhead Rd. and Station Rd. near St. Mary's Church, can simultaneously **exchange currencies** and pleasantries. (Open M-F 9am-1pm and 2-5:30pm, Sa 9am-7:30pm.) **Postal code:** LL24 0AA.

⌨ ACCOMMODATIONS AND FOOD. Two hostels rest conveniently near town: **YHA Lledr Valley** and **YHA Capel Curig** (see p. 468). Most B&Bs in town charge £16 and up, and cluster along Holyhead Rd. **Riverside,** just past the Ultimate Outdoors store, offers comfortable beds and TVs and an old-fashioned flavor above the family restaurant downstairs. (☎/fax 710650; riverside4u@talk21.com. Singles £16-20; doubles £32, with bath £40.) For a comfy lounge and large, TV-endowed rooms with fine views of lambs by a river, head for **Glan Llugwy,** on the western edge of town. If it's raining, the friendly owners, Jean and Graham Brayne, will come and pick you up at the station (☎ 710592. £15-18 per person.) **Riverside Caravan Park** suns itself beside a cemetery behind the train station. (☎ 710310. Open Mar.-Oct. Electricity £2. Showers and hot water included. Tents or caravans £5 per adult, £2.50 per child. Families and couples only; no large groups.)

For a supermarket experience, head for **Spar** at the northern bend of Holyhead Rd. (Open daily 8am-9:30pm.) Most of the restaurants in Betws-y-Coed cater to tourists, and are priced accordingly. The staff at **Dil's Diner,** Station Rd., in front of the train station, cheerfully dishes out greasy platters of eggs and sausages (£3-6) and giant burgers. (☎ 710346. Open 8am-9pm.) Golden oldies quietly accompany your meal at **Three Gables,** Holyhead Rd. Top off a meal of homemade pizza, vegetarian dishes, or seafood (£4-6) with a wide hunk of hot apple pie for £2.50. (☎ 710328. Open Easter-Oct. M-Su 11:30am-9:30pm, Nov.-Easter F-Su.)

◩ SIGHTS. Betws is known for its eight **bridges,** especially Telford's 1815 cast-iron **Waterloo Bridge** at the village's southern end, built the year the famous battle ensured Napoleon's political demise. Near St. Michael's Church, the miniature **suspension footbridge,** which sways when trod upon, crosses the Conwy. **Pont-y-Pair Bridge,** "the bridge of the cauldron" and the most serene in Betws, crosses the Llugwy to the north. The first bridge was built in 1475; Inigo Jones may have contributed to building the second, which consists of eleven stone arches hopping from rock to rock. Behind the train station, weathered gravestones surround the humble, ivy-covered 14th-century **St. Michael's Church,** whose sobriety is tempered by the fragments of stained glass that remain in the east and west windows.

Two miles west of town, signposted off the A5, the swift waters of the Llugwy crash furiously over descending plateaus of rocks at **Swallow Falls,** whose original

Welsh name, Rhaeadr Ewyrnol, means "foaming falls". (Open daily Easter-June and Sept. 9am-6pm; July-Aug. 9am-8pm; Oct.-Easter 24hr. turnstile-operated. £1.) Sherpa bus #96 between Betws and Llanberis stops at the falls. Further along the A5 lies "the Ugly House," **Tŷ Hyll,** whose uncarved stone facade is due to its hasty construction. At the time, a house constructed in a day and a night (with smoke wafting out of the chimney in the morning) earned the builder the right to live there. (☎ 720287. Open Apr.-Sept. daily 9:30am-5:30pm; call for winter hours.)

VALLEY VILLAGES ☎01492

The Vale of Conwy is still largely untouched by coach-bound tourists, leaving walkers, cyclists, and *Let's Go* loyalists to explore its gorgeous scenery.

BODNANT GARDENS. At the 80-acre Bodnant Gardens, eight miles south of Llandudno off the A470, Chilean Fire Bush flirts shamelessly with eucrypheas and hydrangea. The gardens often host summer evening events, including plays. The entrance is by Eglwysbach Rd. To get there, take Arriva bus #25 from Llandudno (30min.; M-Sa 10 per day, Su 4 per day); or the Conwy Valley train to the Tal-y-Cafn stop 2 mi. away (M-Sa 6 per day, Su 3 per day). (☎ 650460. Open mid-Mar. to Oct. daily 10am-5pm. £5, children £3.60.)

TREFRIW. To the south, the town of Trefriw sleeps along the River Crafnant. **Lake Crafnant,** three miles uphill from town (along the road opposite the Fairy Hotel), is surrounded by some of the highest peaks in Snowdonia. A 1½ mi. walk from town north along the main road, a rust grotto offers up the world's only fully licensed spa water medicine at the **Trefriw Wells Spa.** Originally used to treat rheumatism and skin diseases, today the spa water eases iron deficiency as well. A month's supply goes for £6.49. (☎ 640057. Open 9:30am-5:30pm. £2.65, seniors £2.50, children £1.50, under 10 free.)

To reach Trefriw and Rowen, take **Arriva bus** #19 from Conwy, Llandudno, or Llandudno Junction (M-Sa 2 per hr., Su 7 per day).B&Bs (£15-18) line Trefriw's long main street. The rustic **YHA Rowen,** halfway between Trefriw and Conwy, is a superb place to rest your weary bones after the mile uphill hike from the bus stop. (☎ 650089. Lockout 10am-5pm. Open May-Aug. Dorms £8.10, under 18 £5.65.)

LLANRWST. A useful transit town, Llanrwst has banks, and a **market** on Tuesdays. Cramped beside the Conwy River, just across the 1636 Old Bridge built by Inigo Jones, the 15th-century stone **Tu-Hwnt-i'r-Bont** hides a tea room beneath a roof that is level to the road. Before banging your head, check the timbers for multilingual graffiti. (Open Easter-Oct. Tu-Su 10am-5:30pm.) A 10-min. walk past the tea house deposits you at **Gwydir Castle,** the 16th-century manor house of Sir John Wynne. The grounds shelter peacocks and a selflessly-named yew tree. (☎ 641687. Open daily 10am-4:30pm. £3, children £1.50.)

LLANGOLLEN ☎01978

Set in a hollow in the hills near the English border, Llangollen (hlan-GO-hlen) hosts the annual International Musical Eisteddfod, which draws thousands from all over the world every summer. Apart from the cultural extravaganza, all of the town's attractions spawn from nature. Walkers gently tread the surrounding hills on their way to Horseshoe Pass, and weekends bring whitewater canoeists slashing through neighboring streams and into the River Dee, which tumbles through town under a 14th-century bridge.

🖥🚻 GETTING THERE AND PRACTICAL INFORMATION. For a booming tourist town, Llangollen can be difficult to reach for the carless. Most public transport from outside Wales only gets as far as **Wrexham,** 30 minutes away; **Bryn Melyn** (☎ 860701) bus #5 connects Wrexham and Llangollen (M-Sa 2 per hr., £2.20). On Sundays, **Arriva Midland** (☎ (01691) 652402) runs a winding version of bus #5 (50min., 6 per day). From Wrexham, **trains** (☎ (08457) 484950) connect with **Chester, Shrewsbury,** and **London.** A closer train station to Llangollen, though less well-served, is **Ruabon,** from which B&B owners may transport weary backpackers. **National Express** (☎ (08705) 808080) **bus** #420 comes from **London** (5½hr., 1 per day, £19.75). **Arriva Cymru** (☎ (08706) 082608) bus #94 connects Llangollen to **Dolgellau** (£3.30) and the west coast of Wales at **Barmouth** (2½hr.; M-Sa 7 per day, Su 4 per day; £4.90). Arriva Cymru's bus #70 runs twice a day from **Llanrwst** and **Betws-y-Coed** via **Corwen;** sometimes you have to change in Corwen, where various buses such as the #94 connect to Llangollen (1hr., £2.20).

Both the **tourist information centre** (TIC), Town Hall, Castle St., and the Eisteddfod office (see below) keep an emergency list of accommodations, although some are as far as 15 mi. away. (☎ 860828; fax 861563; www.llangollen.org.uk. Open daily Easter-Oct. 10am-6pm; Nov.-Easter 9:30am-5pm.) Services include: **Barclays bank,** Castle St., opposite the TIC (open M-F 10am-4pm); **Blue Bay Launderette,** Regent St. (wash £2, soap 30p; open M-W and F-Sa 9am-7pm, Th 9am-6pm); **Internet access** at **The Gallery Computer World,** 22 Chapel St., in an old garage opposite the restaurant of the same name (☎ 869384; £3 per 30min; open M-F 9am-5pm, Sa-Su 9am-noon; ask at the restaurant if no one's around); and the **post office,** 41 Castle St., with a **bureau de change** and the only post office museum in Wales (open M-F 9am-5:30pm, Sa 9am-1pm). **Postal code:** LL20 8RW.

⌂ ACCOMMODATIONS AND FOOD. The Victorian manse that is the **YHA Llangollen,** Tyndwr Hall, Tyndwr Rd., lies 1½ mi. out of town. Expect to share this 124-bed activity center with a group of some sort. From town, follow the A5 towards Shrewsbury, bear right up Birch Hill, and after ½ mi. take a right at the Y-junction. (☎ 860330; fax 861709. No lockout or curfew. Internet access. Open mid-Feb. to Oct. Dorms £9.80, under 18 £6.75.) **B&Bs** (£15-20) are numerous in Llangollen, especially along Regent St. Expect a warm greeting from the proprietress of **Bryant Rose,** 31 Regent St., where TVs glow in comfortable, large rooms. (☎ 860389. Singles £20; twins £35; doubles £36; student discounts available). **Campsites** abound; investigate **Tower Farm,** Tower Rd., at the far end of the Eisteddfod campgrounds. (☎ 860798. £2.50 per person, £10 per caravan.)

The most exciting of Llangollen's many restaurants is **Robbin's Nest,** Market St., which serves healthy portions for £5.25 or less. (☎ 861425. Open M-Sa 10am-2pm and 6:30pm-late, Su noon-8pm.) At **Café and Books,** 17 Castle St., you can thumb hundreds of used volumes upstairs while they boil your peas and fry your fish and chips downstairs. (☎ 861963. Open daily Apr.-Sept. 9am-7pm; Oct.-May 9am-5pm.) Nearby **Spar** sells fruits, vegetables, and refreshments. (Open daily 8am-11pm.)

SIGHTS. Up Hill St. from the town center stands **Plas Newydd,** former home of two noblewomen who fled Ireland in 1778. Charmed by Llangollen, they settled into village life, dividing their time between charitable works and the elaborate decoration of this house, including the carved oaken walls. Wellington and Sir Walter Scott visited, as did Wordsworth, who was moved to pen a poem in their honor. (☎ 861314. Open Easter.-Oct. daily 10am-5pm. £2.50, children £1.25, families £6.) Perched on a steep mount high above town are the lyrical ruins of **Dinas Brân** (Crow's Castle). The panoramic drop-away view spans from the peaks of Snowdonia to the flat English midlands. Two main paths access the castle; a 40min. gravel path zig-zags directly up the side, while an hour-long walk runs along a pastoral road and up the grassy hillside. Both are steep, scoff at weak shoes, and begin behind the canal museum on Dinbryn Rd. A 30-minute walk from Llangollen along Abbey Rd., the ruins of 13th-century **Valle Crucis Abbey** grace a leafy valley. Its empty arches serenely frame trees and sky, along with an unfortunate cluster of caravans in the park next door. (☎ 860326. Open daily Apr.-Sept. 10am-5pm; Oct.-Mar. 9:30am-dusk. £2, concessions £1.50, families £5.50. Free in winter.)

THE EISTEDDFOD. Every summer, the town's population of 3,000 swells to 80,000 during the **International Musical Eisteddfod** (ice-TETH-vod), not to be confused with the roaming Royal National Eisteddfod (see **Ffestivals,** p. 422). From July 2-7 in 2001, the hills will be alive with the singing and dancing of competitors from 50 countries—much to the chagrin of groggy livestock. Book tickets and rooms *far in advance* through the **Eisteddfod Box Office,** Llangollen International Musical Eisteddfod Office, 1st floor, Royal International Pavilion, Abbey Road, Llangollen, LL20 8SW. (☎ 862000; fax 862002; www.internationaleisteddfod.co.uk. Phone bookings M-F 9am-5pm. Box office open from Feb. 2001 M-Th 9am-4pm, F 9am-3pm. Unreserved seat and admission to grounds on day of show £5, seniors £4, children £3, families £12; concert tickets £7-13.)

SCOTLAND

A distinct nation within the United Kingdom, Scotland at its best is a world apart. Its cities revel in a culture and world view all their own, from the rampant nightlife of Glasgow to the festival activities of Edinburgh. A little over half the size of England but with a tenth of its population, Scotland possesses open spaces and natural splendor its southern neighbor cannot rival—the Scottish highlands contain some of the last great wilderness in Europe. The craggy, heather-sloped mountains and silver beaches of the west coast and the luminescent mists of the Hebrides demand any traveler's awe, while the farmlands to the south and the peaceful fishing villages of the east coast display a gentler beauty.

A native of Scotland is a Scot; a Scot may be British, but *never* English. Most Scots will welcome you with geniality and pride; as in the other few unharried corners of the world, hospitality and conversation are valued highly. Before reluctantly joining with England in 1707, the Scots defended their independence for hundreds of years. Since the union, they have nurtured a separate identity, retaining control over schools, churches, and the judicial system. In 1999, Scots finally regained a separate parliament, which gave them more control over domestic tax laws and strengthened the independent Scottish identity. While the kilts, bagpipes, and find-your-own-clan kits of Glasgow, Edinburgh, and Aberdeen may quickly grow annoying, a visit to the less touristed regions of Scotland will allow you to encounter inheritors of ancient traditions: a B&B proprietor talking to her grandchildren in soft Gaelic cadences, a crofter cutting peat, or a fisherman setting out in his skiff at dawn.

GETTING THERE

The easiest and cheapest way to Scotland from outside Britain is usually through London. Before you leave London, visit the **Scottish Tourist Board** office, 19 Cockspur St., SW1 Y5BL. They stock gads of books and brochures and can book train, bus, and plane tickets. (☎ (020) 7930 8661. Tube: Charing Cross or Piccadilly Circus. Open M-F 9am-6pm, Sa 10am-5pm.)

BY PLANE. Flights are predictably expensive. **British Airways** (☎ (08457) 773 3377) sells a limited number of APEX return tickets starting at £70. **British Midland** (☎ (08706) 070555) offers a Saver fare from **London** to **Glasgow** (from £70 return). Book as far in advance as you can (2 weeks if possible) for the cheapest fare. Scotland is also linked by **ferry** (see **p. 35**) to **Northern Ireland** and to the **Isle of Man.**

BY TRAIN. From London, trains (☎ (08547) 484950) to **Edinburgh** and **Glasgow** take only six hours, but fares are steep—trains can cost up to £90. Overnight trains offer sleeper berths for an extra £30. Book cheaper APEX fares early if you can.

BY BUS. Although the bus trip from **London** takes more than seven hours, it is significantly cheaper than train travel. **National Express** (☎ (08705) 808080) services connect England and Scotland via **Glasgow** and **Edinburgh;** see those cities' **Getting There** listings for journey times, frequencies, and prices.

GETTING AROUND

The *Touring Map of Scotland* (£3.50) and the *Touring Guide of Scotland* (£5), available at tourist information centres, provide fodder for planning any sojourn.

BY BUS AND TRAIN

In the Lowlands (south of Stirling and north of the Borders), train and bus connections are frequent. In the Highlands, **trains** snake slowly on a few restricted routes, bypassing the northwest almost entirely. Many stations are unstaffed or nonexistent—purchase tickets on board. In general, **buses** are the best way to travel.

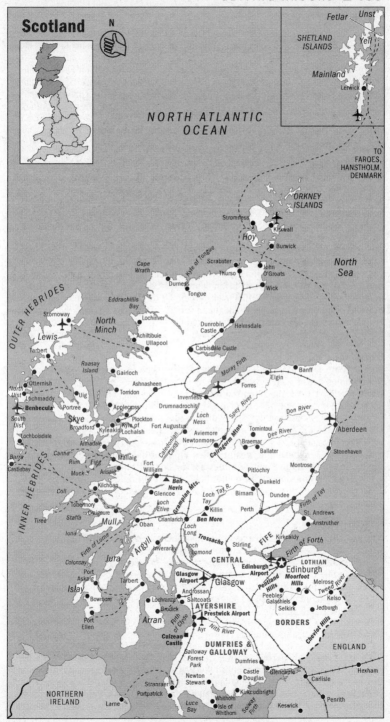

Scotland

N

NORTH ATLANTIC OCEAN

SHETLAND ISLANDS

Fetlar *Unst*

Yell

Mainland

Lerwick

TO FAROES, HANSTHOLM, DENMARK

ORKNEY ISLANDS

Stromness

Kirkwall

Hoy

Burwick

North Sea

Cape Wrath

Kyle of Tongue

Scrabster

Thurso

John O'Groats

Durness

Tongue

Wick

Eddrachillis Bay

Lochinver

Dunrobin Castle

Helmsdale

OUTER HEBRIDES

Stornoway

Lewis

North Minch

Achiltibuie

Ullapool

Carbisdale Castle

Moray Firth

Banff

Raasay Island

Gairloch

Ashnasheen

Forres

Elgin

Tarbert

Otternish

North Uist

Lochmaddy

Uig

Torridon

Inverness

Spey River

Don River

Benbecula

Portree

Applecross

Drumnadrochit

South Uist

Skye

Broadford

Plockton

Fort Augustus

Loch Ness

Tomintoul

Dee River

Aberdeen

Lochboisdale

Kyleakin

Kyle of Lochalsh

Aviemore

Newtonmore

Braemar

Barra

Canna

Armadale

Cairngorm Mtns.

Ballater

Stonehaven

Castlebay

Rum

Eigg

Mallaig

Caledonian Canal

Muck

Arisaig

Fort William

▲ *Ben Nevis*

Pitlochry

Montrose

Coll

Kilchoan

Glencoe

Grampian Mtns.

Dunkeld

Loch Etive

Birnam

Dundee

Tobermory

Craignure

Loch Tay R.

Loch Tay

Perth

Firth of Tay

Tiree

Staffa

Mull

Killin

▲ *Ben More*

St. Andrews

Iona

Oban

Loch Long

Crianlarich

Trossachs

Anstruther

Firth of Lorne

Loch Lomond

Stirling

FIFE

Kirkcaldy

Jura

Argyll

Inveraray

CENTRAL

Firth of Forth

Colonsay

Edinburgh Airport

Edinburgh

LOTHIAN

Port Askaig

Glasgow Airport

Glasgow

Pentland Hills

Moorfoot Hills

Melrose

Islay

Bowmore

Lochranza

Androssan

Saltcoats

Peebles

Galashiels

Tweed River

Kelso

Brodick

Firth of Clyde

Selkirk

Jedburgh

Port Ellen

Arran

Prestwick Airport

AYRSHIRE

BORDERS

Cheviot Hills

Ayr

Nith River

▲ *Culzean Castle*

DUMFRIES & GALLOWAY

ENGLAND

Galloway Forest Park

Dumfries

Castle Douglas

Glencaple

Carlisle

Hexham

NORTHERN IRELAND

Stranraer

Portpatrick

Newton Stewart

Kirkcudbright

Solway Firth

Keswick

Penrith

Larne

Luce Bay

Whithorn

Isle of Whithorn

SCOTLAND

They're usually more frequent and far-reaching than trains and always cheaper, although non-smokers may find smoggy buses less hospitable than non-smoking train cars. **Scottish Citylink** (☎ (08705) 505050) provides most inter-city service. Bus service declines in the northwest Highlands and grinds to a halt on Sundays.

A great money-saver is the **Freedom of Scotland Travelpass,** which allows unlimited train travel and transportation on all Caledonian Macbrayne ferries. The pass also allows travel on some Scottish Citylink buses and on the Glasgow Underground, and provides discounts on some P&O ferries. Purchase the pass at almost any train station or order through Rail Europe (see **By Train,** p. 37; June-Sept. £79 for 4 within 8 days, £109 for any 8 within 15 days, £119 for any 12 within 20 days; Oct.-May £69, £89, £99).

BUS TOURS

If you have limited time in Scotland, or if you want to be thrown together with a group of backpackers, there is a thriving industry of backpacker tour companies eager to whisk you away into the Highlands. The two main companies are **Mac-Backpackers** (☎ (0131) 558 9900; www.macbackpackers.com) and **HAGGiS** (☎ (0131) 557 9393; www.radicaltravel.com), whose offices literally stare each other in the face across Edinburgh's High Street. Both cater to the young and adventurous with a number of 1-7 day tours of the Highlands departing from Edinburgh. Especially cool are their hop-on, hop-off tours, which let you travel Scotland at your own pace, but with the convenience of transportation and good company. See **Bus Tours,** p. 41, for prices. **Celtic Connection** (☎ 225 3330; www.thecelticconnection.co.uk) covers Scotland in a variety of 3-7 day tours, with one-way, return, or jump on-jump off options. Book ahead for all companies. Other, less youth-oriented companies also provide day and half-day bus tours. **Scotline Tours,** 87 High St. in Edinburgh (☎ 557 0162), charges £10-20, with student and child concessions.

BIKING

Scotland offers scenic, challenging biking terrain. You can usually rent bikes even in very small towns and transport them by ferry for little or no charge. In the Highlands, however, even major roads often have only one lane, and locals drive at high speeds—keep your eye out for the passing zones. Bringing a bike to the Highlands by public transportation can be as difficult as pedaling there. Many trains can carry only four or fewer bikes; reservations (£3) are essential.

Fife and regions south of Edinburgh and Glasgow offer gentle country pedaling, and both the northern and western isles are negotiable by bicycle. Touring or mountain biking in the Highlands allows a freedom of access to the area's remote beauty, which compensates for the demanding cycling. Harry Henniker's *101 Bike Routes in Scotland* (£10) and *101 Mountain-Bike Routes* (£15) are worth a look before you set out.

HITCHHIKING

Many hitchhike in Scotland, except in areas such as the northwest and Inverness, where cars packed with families of tourists make up a large percentage of the traffic. Hitchhikers report that drivers tend to be most receptive in the least-traveled areas. Far to the northwest and in the Western Isles, the sabbath is strictly observed, making it difficult or impossible to get a ride on Sundays. Hitchhiking in Scotland, as in many places, is accompanied by many risks, and *Let's Go* does not recommend it as a safe mode of transport.

HIKING

Two long-distance footpaths were planned and marked by the Countryside Commission under the Countryside Act of 1967. The **West Highland Way** begins just north of Glasgow in Milngavie and snakes 95 mi. north along Loch Lomond, through Glen Coe to Fort William and Ben Nevis ("from Scotland's largest city to its highest mountain"). The **Southern Upland Way** runs 212 mi. from Portpatrick on the southwest coast to Cockburnspath on the east coast, passing through

> **MUNRO BAGGING** Scottish mountaineering is dominated by the fre-
> quently obsessive practice of Munro Bagging. Hugh T. Munro compiled the original list
> of Scottish peaks over 3000 ft. in 1891; today about 280 are recorded. Any addition
> sends thousands of hikers scrambling up previously unnoticed peaks to maintain their
> distinction of having "bagged every Munro." Some people accomplish this feat over a
> lifetime of hiking; others do it in a frenetic six months. Thankfully, only one Munro, the
> Inaccessible Pinnacle on Skye, requires technical rock-climbing skills. *The Munros*
> (£17), produced by the Scottish Mountaineering Club, presents a list of the peaks
> along with climbing information. In *The First Fifty: Munro Bagging Without a Beard*
> (£9), the irreverent Muriel Gray presents a humorous account of this compulsive sport.

Galloway Forest Park and the Borders. Most tourist information centres distribute
simple maps of the Ways as well as a list of accommodations along the routes. For
information on these paths, write or call the **Scottish Tourist Board,** 23 Ravelston
Terr., Edinburgh EH4 3EU (☎ (0131) 332 2433). Detailed guidebooks for both are
available at most bookstores.

Mountain areas like the Cuillins, the Torridons, Glen Nevis, and Glen Coe all
have hostels situated in the midst of the ranges, providing bases for spectacular
round-trip hikes or bike rides. You can also walk along mainland Britain's highest
cliffs at Cape Wrath or ramble across the eerie moors of the Outer Hebrides.

One of the most attractive aspects of hiking in Scotland is that you can often
pick your own route across the heather (you should check first with the local
ranger or landowner). The wilds do pose certain dangers. Stone markers can be
unreliable, and expanses of open heather will often disorient. Heavy mists are
always a possibility, and blizzards can surprise you even in July. Never go up into
the mountains without proper equipment (see **Wilderness Safety,** p. 53, for details).
Leave a copy of your planned route and timetable at the hostel or nearest mountain rescue station, and, from mid-August to mid-October, always ask the hostel
warden about areas in which deer hunters might be at work. For information on
walking and mountaineering in Scotland, consult Poucher's *The Scottish Peaks*
(£13) or the introductory Tourist Board booklet, *Walk Scotland*.

LIFE AND TIMES

HISTORY

The beginnings of Scottish history are shrouded in mist. Little is known of the
early people who inhabited Scotland, save that their strength allowed them to
repel Roman incursions in their land. **Emperor Hadrian** built a wall across the north
of England to protect against attacks from the north (see **Early Invaders,** p. 66).
Other invading tribes were more successful, and by AD 600 the Scottish mainland
was inhabited by four groups. The **Picts,** originally the most powerful of the bunch,
are also the most mysterious—nothing remains of their language, and only a
collection of carved stones and references to them in Latin histories provide information. The Celtic **Scots** arrived from Ireland in the 4th century, bringing their
Gaelic language and Christian religion. The Germanic **Angles** invaded Scotland
from northern England in the 6th century. In AD 843, the Scots, under **King Kenneth
MacAlpin** (Kenneth I), decisively defeated the Picts and formed a joint kingdom.
United by the threat of encroaching **Vikings,** various groups were led by the first
king of all Scotland, **Duncan,** who was killed by a certain Macbeth in 1040.

The House of Canmore (literally "big-headed" after Duncan's son Malcolm, who
was cranially well-endowed) reigned over Scotland until the close of the 13th
century. Allied through marriages with the Norman lords who had come to dominate England, the Scottish monarchs found their independence considerably

threatened by the increasingly powerful nation to the south. The 13th-century reigns of **Alexander II** and **Alexander III** were characterized by an uneasy peace punctuated with periodic skirmishes, while the Scottish kings successfully contained both civil revolts and Scandinavian attacks.

SQUABBLES WITH ENGLAND

Alexander III died without an heir, and the ensuing contest over the Scottish crown fueled the territorial ambitions of **Edward I** of England. **John Balliol** took the kingship, only to be subjugated by Edward and lose control over most of Scotland to the English monarch. The **Wars of Independence** bred heroic figures like William Wallace (yes, the *Braveheart* guy), who bravely, and for a time successfully, led a company of Scots against the English. But it was the patient and cunning **Robert the Bruce** who emerged as Scotland's leader; against all odds, he led the Scots to victory over Edward II's forces at the **Battle of Bannockburn** in 1314, which won Scotland her independence from the English crown.

In the next centuries the monarchy set rebellious nobles against each other in an attempt to preserve its own waning position. The Scottish kings frequently capitalized on the "Auld Alliance" with France and prevented the English crown from exploiting the monarchy's difficulties with dissatisfied barons. The reigns of **James IV** (1488-1513) and **James V** (1513-42) witnessed the Renaissance's arrival in Scotland just as the effects of the **Reformation** began to appear throughout the country.

The death of James V left the infant **Mary, Queen of Scots** (1542-67), on the throne. The Queen was promptly sent to France, where she later married the future François II. Scottish nobles and commoners were drawn to the appeal of Protestantism, embodied in the form of iconoclastic preacher **John Knox.** Lacking a strong ruler during Mary's absence, Scotland was vulnerable to passionate Protestant revolts, as much political as they were religious. In 1560, the monarchy capitulated. The Protestant **Scottish Parliament** denied the Pope's authority in Scotland and established the Presbyterian Church as Scotland's new official church.

In 1561, after the death of her husband, staunchly Catholic Mary returned to Scotland. Never accepted by Scottish nobles or Protestants, Mary's rule fanned the flames of discontent, and civil war resulted in her forced abdication and imprisonment in 1567. She escaped her Scottish captors only to find another set of shackles across the border; as the Queen languished in an English prison, her son **James VI** was made King. Nine years later, with Catholic Spain a rising threat, Queen Elizabeth of England made a tentative alliance with the nominally Protestant James while executing his mother Mary in 1587.

UNION WITH ENGLAND

Elizabeth's death without an heir in 1603 left James VI to be crowned **James I** of England, uniting both countries under a single crown. James ruled from London, while his half-hearted attempts to reconcile the Scots to British rule were tartly resisted. Scottish Presbyterians supported Cromwellian forces against James's successor **Charles I** during the **English Civil War.** Nonetheless, when the English Parliament executed Charles in 1649, the Scots again switched allegiance and declared the headless king's heir to be King Charles II. **Oliver Cromwell** handily defeated him as well, but in a conciliatory gesture gave Scotland representation in the English Parliament. Though Cromwell's governing body eventually dissolved, the political precedent of Scottish representation in Parliament endured.

Two more Stuart monarchs, Charles II and James II, reigned in London after the Civil War. Wide discontent with James's rule led to the Glorious Revolution of 1688, which put the Dutchman **William of Orange** on the English throne. The **War of the Spanish Succession** (1701-1714) convinced Scotland's leaders that its Presbyterian interests were safer with the Anglicans than with long-standing ally Catholic France, and in 1707 the Scottish and English Parliaments were officially united, formally joining the two countries politically, while allowing Scotland to retain significant control over its own ecclesiastical, legal, and judicial affairs.

THE JACOBITE REBELLION
The Scottish supporters of **James II** never accepted the 1707 Union, and after a series of unsuccessful uprisings, they launched the "Forty-Five," the events of 1745 that have captured the imagination of Scots and romantics alike ever since. James's grandson **Bonnie Prince Charlie** landed in Scotland, where he succeeded in mustering unseasoned troops from various Scottish clans. From Glenfinnan, Bonnie Prince Charlie rallied his troops, marching to Edinburgh, where he kept court and prepared for full rebellion. On the march to London, however, the venture was hampered by desertions and the uncertainty of French support, prompting a return to Scotland. Modest French support did materialize, and with new troops under the Scottish standard, Charles led his troops to victory at Stirling and Falkirk in 1746. After that, the rebellion once again collapsed; although Charles eventually escaped to France, his Highland army fell on the battlefield of Culloden.

ENLIGHTENMENT AND THE CLEARANCES
Aside from Jacobite political turmoil, the 18th century proved to be the most economically and culturally prosperous in Scotland's history. As agriculture, industry, and trading all boomed, a vibrant intellectual environment produced such luminaries as **Adam Smith** and **David Hume.** In the 19th century, although political reforms did much to improve social conditions, economic problems proved disastrous. The Highlands were particularly affected by a rapidly growing population combined with lack of available land and food, archaic farming methods, and the demands of rapacious landlords. The resulting poverty resulted in mass emigration, mostly to North America, and the infamous **Clearances.** Between 1811 and 1820, the Sutherland Clearances, undertaken by the Marquis of Stafford, forcibly relocated poor farmers from their lands to the coasts, where farming could be supplemented by fishing. Resistance to the relocations was met with violence—homes were burned and countless people killed. Other Clearances occurred throughout the Highlands; in 1853, the Clearances at Glengarry evicted entire families from their homes and land, whereupon they were not just relocated to another area in Scotland, but forcibly packed on boats and shipped overseas. Meanwhile, the **Industrial Revolution** led to urban growth in southern Scotland and increasingly poor working and living conditions for new industrial laborers.

THE 20TH CENTURY
Scotland, like the rest of Britain, lost a generation of young men in **World War I**, after which the economic depression of the 1930s only exacerbated economic difficulties. Organized labor gained clout in factories and in politics, leading to strong Scottish support for the Labour Party and, later, the **Scottish National Party (SNP),** founded in 1934. Surprisingly, a 1979 referendum on devolution from England was unsuccessful due to an insufficient number of favorable Scottish votes.

Today, Scotland has 72 seats in the United Kingdom's **House of Commons** and is largely integrated into the British economy. The May 1997 elections swept the Conservatives in Scotland out of power, and accrued support for the SNP, which bases its platform on devolution for the Scottish nation. September of 1997 brought a victory for the proponents of home rule; Scottish voters supported devolution by an overwhelming 3:1 margin, and the first elections for the new Assembly occurred in 1999. Though the Assembly is able to levy taxes and legislate in other areas, Westminster still controls foreign affairs and fiscal policy. With many Scottish politicians more closely tied to London than to their own constituents, only time will tell whether Scotland is truly on the road to greater independence.

LANGUAGE
Although the early Picts left no record of their language (aside from some influence in place names), settlers in southern Scotland well into the 7th century heard a **Celtic** language related to Welsh. These settlers also brought their native tongues—Celtic Gaelic from Ireland, Norse from Scandinavia, and an early form of

English (Inglis) brought by the Angles from northern England. By the 11th century, **Scottish Gaelic** (pronounced GAL-ick), subsuming Norse and the earlier Celtic and Pictic languages, had become the official language of Scottish law. As the political power of southern Scotland began to rise in the late 11th and early 12th centuries, Gaelic speakers migrated primarily to the Highlands and Islands in northwest Scotland, and Inglis became the language of the Lowlands, and, eventually, of the Scottish monarchy. Beginning as a dialectical variation of the English developing in England, Inglis, or **Scots** as it is known, was influenced by Flemish, French, and Latin, and developed into a distinctive linguistic unit.

While a number of post-1700 Scottish literati, most notably Robert Burns and the contemporary Hugh MacDiarmid, have composed in Scots, union with Britain and the political and cultural power of England in the 18th and 19th centuries led to the rise of England's language in Scotland. Today, though **standard English** is spoken throughout Scotland, Scots influences the English of many Scottish men and women. You may not understand a word or two in a sentence. In the Highlands, for example, the "ch" becomes a soft "h," as in the German "ch" sound. Modern Scottish Gaelic, a linguistic cousin of Modern Irish, is spoken by at least 65,000 people in Scotland today, particularly in the western islands. Recent attempts to revive Gaelic have led to its introduction in the classroom, ensuring that some form of the language will continue to exist in Scotland for years to come. For a glossary of Scottish Gaelic and Scots words and phrases, see p. 748.

LITERATURE

Spanning the centuries and including composition in three languages—Scottish Gaelic, Scots, and English—Scottish literature embodies a complexity of experience. In a nation where stories and myths have long been recounted by the fireside, **oral literature** is as much a part of Scotland's literary tradition as novels. Most traces of medieval Scottish manuscripts have unfortunately been lost—not surprising, since raids on monastic centers of learning during this period were fierce and frequent, effectively erasing pre-14th-century literary records. **John Barbour** is the best-known writer in Early Scots—his *The Bruce* (c. 1375) preceded Chaucer, and favorably chronicled the life of King Robert I in an attempt to strengthen national unity. **William Dunbar** (1460-1521) composed Middle Scots verse under James IV, and is today considered the representative of Scots poetry.

In 1760, **James Macpherson** published versions of **"Ossian,"** supposedly an ancient Scottish bard to rival Homer; Macpherson was widely discredited when he refused to produce the manuscripts that he claimed to be translating. **James Boswell** (1740-95), the biographer of Samuel Johnson, composed Scots verse as well as voluminous journals detailing his travels through Great Britain and the Continent. "Scotland's National Bard," **Robert Burns** (1759-96), was acutely aware of his heritage as he bucked pressure from the south that urged him to write in English, instead composing in his native Scots. **Sir Walter Scott** (1771-1832) was among the first Scottish authors to achieve international accolades for his work. *Ivanhoe*, a chivalrous tale of knights and damsels, is one of the best-known, if sappy, novels of all time. **Robert Louis Stevenson** (1850-94) is most famous for his tales of high adventure, including *Treasure Island* and *Kidnapped*, which still fuel children's imaginations. His *Strange Case of Dr. Jekyll and Mr. Hyde* is nominally set in London, but any Scot would recognize the familiar setting as Edinburgh.

Scotland's literary present is as vibrant as its past. In the twentieth century, poets **Hugh MacDiarmid** and **Edwin Morgan** have attracted the most attention, while novelists **Lewis Grassic Gibbon** and **Nell Gunn** used their pens to develop the nation's prose tradition. More recent novelists include **Alasdair Gray, Tom Leonard, Janice Galloway,** and **James Kelman,** who won 1995's Booker Prize for his controversial, sharp-edged novel *How Late It Was, How Late. Trainspotting*, the 1993 novel about Edinburgh drug-addicts by **Irvine Welsh,** and its 1996 film adaptation have been both condemned as amoral and hailed as chronicles of a new generation.

MUSIC

The Gaelic music of the West has its roots in the traditional music of Scotland's Irish settlers; as in Ireland, **ceilidhs,** spirited gatherings of music and dance, bring jigs, reels, and Gaelic songs to halls and pubs. Although there are no extant scores of Gaelic music prior to the 17th century, evidence suggests the *clarsach,* a Celtic harp, was the primary medium for musical expression until the 16th century, when the Highlander's **bagpipes** and the violin introduced new creative possibilities. Scots musical heritage centers around **ballads,** dramatic narrative songs. Scotland today possesses a quality national symphony orchestra and opera company.

In the 1970s and 80s, Scotland has played a significant role in the development of popular music, launching **The Rezillos, The Skids, Average White Band,** Glasgow's **Orange Juice,** Edinburgh's **Josef K,** and the record label Postcard, which favored Byrdsy guitar chimes and winsome, coy-boy singers. Although mainstream rock was popular during the early 1990s, with groups such as **The Wake, The Proclaimers,** and Aberdeen's **Kitchen Cynics,** Scottish punk rages once again. Slampt and Vesuvius record labels promote Scottish punk bands, including the suggestively named **Yummy Fur** and **Lung Leg.** The quiet folk-rock of **Belle and Sebastian** wails throughout Edinburgh and Glasgow, and Scotland has also mastered the ubiquitous Britpop genre with **Texas** and **Travis,** bands popular on both sides of the border and abroad.

YOU OUGHTA BE IN THE MOVIES: A GUIDE TO RE-ENACTING YOUR FAVORITE SCOTTISH FILMS

If Scotland looks familiar, it's probably because you've seen parts of it in a slew of movies. Go figure: grand, sweeping landscapes like the Highlands make for a nice cinematic backdrop. But some people are obsessive and want to know the exact places where Mel Gibson, Ewan McGregor, and that dude from Highlander slew Englishmen, shot heroine, and in general screamed until they were blue in the face. For those of you who insist on viewing life through a movie screen, *Let's Go* here provides a handy how-to and where-to on re-enacting your favorite big-screen versions of Scotland:

Highlander: So there can be only one castle, and it's **Eilean Donan Castle** (see p. 612) at the heads of Loch Long, Loch Alsh, and Loch Duich, near Dornie. (Where's that? It's near Kyle of Lochalsh.) If you haven't seen the movie, you've seen the castle on just about every calendar, tourist brochure, and shortbread tin related to Scotland. Prance around on the photogenic stone bridge and try not to behead any tourists.

Trainspotting: Grab three buddies and a bottle of vodka and head out to **Rannoch Moor,** east of Glen Coe (see p. 588). After stepping off the train, walk about 100 ft. toward Buchuaille Etive Mor, and then come to the realization that Scotland has been "colonized by wankers." Or run frantically down Princes St. in **Edinburgh** (see p. 498) after breaking into cars and stealing car radios. *Let's Go* does not recommend shooting heroine after selling stolen goods, and wouldn't know where to get some anyway.

Braveheart: Hike out to **Glen Nevis,** east of **Fort William** (see p. 590), and run up to the summit of one of the mountains while a rotating helicopter films a 360-degree panorama of your striking image against the horizon. Pretend that the English have killed your father and brother and recently slit your wife's throat, but comfort yourself with the knowledge that you'll get to sleep with the really hot French princess.

Monty Python and the Holy Grail: Rent a boat and row out to the Castle of the Holy Grail, which is actually **Castle Stalker** (see p. 564), on Loch Linnhe, by Appin. You might need to ask the family that owns the castle for permission; otherwise, like King Arthur, you could end up getting arrested by the police.

Hamlet: To follow in Mel Gibson's footsteps as the famous Dane, climb the dramatic cliffs by **Dunnottar Castle** (see p. 576), in Stonehaven south of Aberdeen, and recite the "to be or not to be" soliloquy. Bring a human skull for dramatic effect.

HAGGIS: WHAT'S IN THERE? Although restaurants throughout Scotland produce steamin' plates o' haggis for eager tourists, we at *Let's Go* believe all should know what's inside that strange-looking bundle before taking the plunge. An age-old recipe calls for the following ingredients: the large stomach bag of a sheep, the small (knight's hood) bag, the pluck (including lights (lungs), liver, and heart), beef, suet, oatmeal, onions, pepper, and salt. Today's haggis is available conveniently canned and includes: lamb, lamb offal, oatmeal, wheat flour (healthy, no?), beef, suet, onions, salt, spices, stock, and liquor (1%).

FOOD AND DRINK

The frequenter of B&Bs will encounter a glorious **Scottish breakfast,** including oat cakes, porridge, and marmalade. In general, however, Scottish cuisine greatly resembles English food. Aside from delicious, buttery **shortbread,** visitors are unlikely to take a shine to most traditional Scottish dishes, most notably the infamous **haggis,** made from a sheep's stomach. Though the food might be a let-down, Scotland's **whisky** (spelled without the "e") certainly is not. Scotch whisky is either "single malt" (from a single distillery), or "blended" (a mixture of several different brands). The malts are excellent and distinctive, the blends the same as those available abroad. Due to heavy taxes on alcohol sold in Britain, Scotch may be cheaper at home or from duty-free stores than it is in Scotland. The Scots know how to party: more generous licensing laws than those in England and Wales keep drinks served later and pubs open longer.

FESTIVALS

Weekend clan gatherings, bagpipe competitions, and Highland games occur frequently in Scotland, especially in summer. Check for events at tourist information centres and in the local newspapers for the area in which you end up. In addition, the Scottish Tourist Board publishes the annual *Scotland Events*, which details happenings across Scotland. Traditional **Scottish games** originated from competitions in which participants could use only common objects, such as hammers, rounded stones, and tree trunks. Although "tossing the caber" (a pine trunk) may look simple, it actually requires a good deal of talent and practice. *Let's Go* does not recommend participating in caber-tossing for the uninitiated tourist.

Each year a slew of events and festivals celebrates Scotland's distinctive history and culture. June and July's **Common Ridings** in the Borders (see p. 516) and the raucous **Up-Helly-A'** in Shetland on the last Tuesday in January (see p. 624) are among the best known. Above all events towers the **Edinburgh International Festival** (Aug. 12-Sept. 1 in 2001; ☎ (0131) 473 2001), the largest international festival in the world. The concentration of musical and theatrical events in the space of three weeks is dizzying; Edinburgh's cafes and shops open to all hours and pipers roam the streets. Be sure to catch the **Fringe Festival** (Aug. 5-27 in 2001; ☎ (0131) 226 5257), the much less costly sibling of the International Festival. There are literally hundreds of performances every day, including drama, comedy acts, jazz, and a bit of the bizarre. For more information, see p. 514.

SOUTHERN
SCOTLAND

Stark contrasts distinguish southern Scotland: just to the west of major cities lies the beautiful, desolate Isle of Arran, an island with more deer than people. Until the 17th century, southern Scotland was characterized by skirmishes with its southern neighbors, from the Romans who battled the Picts to the interminable wars with England. The Borders region to the southeast contains monuments and ruins marking these struggles, and Dumfries and Galloway in the southwest is rich in tales of local-born Robert the Bruce, who led Scotland to independence at Bannockburn in 1314. Both areas have long since calmed down: walkers and cyclists arrive to admire their serenity, while literary buffs visit the various sites dedicated to national literary icon Robert Burns. Southern Scotland's true draws, though, are the great cities of Edinburgh and Glasgow; nearly 80% of Scotland's population lives in the cities' greater metropolitan areas by the rivers Forth and Clyde. A fountainhead of the Enlightenment, Edinburgh—Scotland's capital—preserves its classical beauty and old buildings, and draws in the crowds each summer during its famous festival. Not to be outdone, Glasgow showcases formidable art collections and spectacular architecture by day and a kinetic club and pub scene by night.

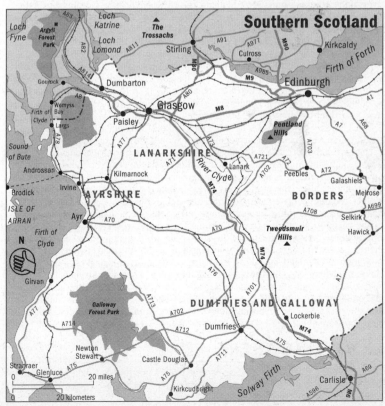

HIGHLIGHTS OF SOUTHERN SCOTLAND

EDINBURGH AND THE FESTIVAL Don't miss out on the military fireworks, theater, opera, jazz and blues, and literary readings which enchant audiences throughout the month of August. The festival season draws artists from all over the world to noble **Edinburgh,** Scotland's invigorating capital (p. 498).

THE BORDERS Visit Sir Walter Scott's grave at majestic Dryburgh Abbey, one of many, not to mention castles and homes, that pepper the Borders (p. 518).

GLASGOW Survey the magnificent architecture of Glasgow, with free museums, hundreds of pubs—and Britain's highest concentration of Indian restaurants (p. 529).

ISLE OF ARRAN Delight in Brodick Castle on the Isle of Arran, "Scotland in miniature," or take on the challenge of climbing up Goatfell (p. 540).

EDINBURGH ☎0131

This profusion of eccentricities, this dream in masonry and living rock is not a drop-scene in a theatre, but a city in the world of reality.
—Robert Louis Stevenson

A city of impressive stone elegance amidst rolling hills and ancient volcanoes, Edinburgh (ED-din-bur-ra; pop. 500,000) is truly the jewel of Scotland. It's next to impossible to have a bad time here, where friendliness thrives, festivals bubble over, and rollicking pubs buzz beneath the regal shadow of Edinburgh Castle. Since David I granted it burgh (town) status in 1130, Edinburgh has been the site of literary and cultural milestones. In the reign of the medieval Stuarts, it was the poetic and musical center of the royal court, and later, the seeds of the Scottish Reformation were sown here when John Knox became minister of St. Giles Cathedral. In the 18th century, the dark, twisting alleys of this Calvinist Kingdom of God gave way first, briefly, to Bonnie Prince Charlie's premature victory celebration, then more permanently to the brilliance of the Scottish Enlightenment. Towering intellectuals such as David Hume and Adam Smith mingled with writers and artists in a heady literary atmosphere, transforming Edinburgh into a hotbed of genius.

The modern city continues to shine as a cultural beacon, and today its crusty medieval spires soar above streets infused with a glowing cosmopolitan verve. August is Edinburgh's unparalleled festival season, when the city becomes a cultural magnet, drawing in international talent and enthusiastic crowds. These days, new youth hostels, museums, dance clubs, and government buildings are springing up all over Edinburgh, and this productivity owes itself largely to the tourists who flood its streets, looking, oddly enough, for an Edinburgh of the past. But the city is not all bagpipe music and tartan heritage shops; indeed, the city's millennial banners proclaim: "Edinburgh on-line to the Future." Thus, a controversial new Parliament Building slowly rises at the foot of the Royal Mile, while the reinstated Scottish Parliament, operating since July 1999, reclaims a bit of the sovereignty which had been missing from Scotland since 1707. But paradox has always been an essential part of Edinburgh. Here, the Old Town's twisting tenements, closes and wynds, immortalized in Robert Louis Stevenson's *Dr. Jekyll and Mr. Hyde*, contrast starkly with the graceful symmetry and orderly gridwork of the Georgian New Town. Visitors, locals, and students alike explore the city's storied history, beautiful walks, and vibrant culture; these are exciting times for Edinburgh. You, too, won't want to miss it.

✈ GETTING THERE

Edinburgh lies 45 mi. east of Glasgow and 405 mi. northwest of London on Scotland's east coast, on the southern bank of the Firth of Forth. It's easy enough to reach—after all, it is the Scottish capital.

Airport: Edinburgh International Airport (☎ 333 1000), 7 mi. west of the city center. Bus rides to the airport run by LRT's **Airlink 100** (☎ 555 6363; 25min.; every 10min. until 11:35pm; £3.30, children £2) and the **Edinburgh Airbus Express** (☎ 556 2244; £3.60). Both depart from Waverley Station.

Trains: Waverley Station, in the center of town, straddles Princes St., Market St., and Waverley Bridge. Free **bike storage** at the back of the main travel center. Office open M-Sa 8am-8pm, Su 9am-8pm; Su-F until 11pm only for same-night travel reservations. Trains (☎ (08457) 484950) from: **Stirling** (45min., 2 per hr., £5); **Glasgow** (1hr., 2 per hr., £7.30); **Aberdeen** (2½hr., 1 per hr., £28.90); **Inverness** (4hr., every 2hr., £29.90-42.60); **Oban** via Glasgow (4½hr., 3 per day, £24.40); **London King's Cross** (5hr., every 30min. 9am-3pm, £76-86); and **Thurso** (7½hr., 2 per day, £37.30-50.80).

Buses: While the St. Andrew Bus Station (☎ 663 9233) gets a face-lift, the south side of **St. Andrew Square** is being used by **Scottish Citylink, National Express,** and all buses from **Fife,** while buses from **West Lothian, the Borders,** and **Dumfries and Galloway** leave from **Waterloo Pl.,** at the east end of **Princes St.** Call the **Traveline** (☎ 0800) 232323) for information. Edinburgh is a major hub of Scotland's bus network. **National Express** (☎ (08705) 808080) from **London** (2 per day, £22). **Scottish Citylink** (☎ (08705) 505050) from: **Glasgow** (1hr.; M-Sa 4 per hr., Su 2 per hr.; £3); **Aberdeen** (4hr., at least 1 per hr., £14.50); **Inverness** (4½hr., 8-10 per day, £13.40); **Thurso** via Inverness (8hr., 4-6 per day, £18); **Belfast** (by bus/ferry, 2 per day, £28); and **Dublin** (by bus/ferry, 1 per day, single £36).

▐ GETTING AROUND

Public Transportation: Although your feet will suffice, and are often faster, Edinburgh does have an efficient, comprehensive bus system. **Lothian Regional Transport** or **LRT** (☎ 555 6363), with a fleet of maroon double-deckers, provides the best service. Be sure to carry coins; drivers do not carry much change for the 80p-£1 fares. You can buy a one-day **Day-Saver Ticket** (£2.40, children £1.50; off-season as low as £1.50 for adults; includes discounts at a number of tourist attractions) and longer-term passes from any driver or from the **main office,** 1-4 Shrub Pl., on the Old Town side of Waverley Bridge. LRT also sells the **Family Saver Ticket** (£6 for 2 adults and up to 4 children) and the **AirSaver Ticket** (£4.20, children £2.65, unlimited travel in the city and 1 trip to or from the airport). After midnight, hop on a **Night Bus** for £1.50.

Taxis: Taxi stands are at both stations and on almost every corner on Princes St. Call **City Cabs** (☎ 228 1211) or **Central Radio Taxis** (☎ 229 2468).

Car Rental: The tourist information centre (TIC) has a list of rental agencies. Most have a minimum age of 21 or 23. Rates from £19 per day. Try **Carnie's Car Hire** (☎ 346 4155) which rents for min. 3 days (£64) to customers 21 and over. The **Radical Travel Centre,** 60 High St. (☎ 557 9393), will help you get the best rates around.

Bike Rental: Edinburgh Rent-a-Bike, 29 Blackfriars St. (☎ 556 5560; cycle.safaris@virgin.net; www.cyclescotland.co.uk;), off High St. One of the grooviest bike rental shops on the planet, owned by a funky former music promoter. 10-speed city bikes £5-10 per day, and 21-speed mountain bikes from £10-15 per day. Cheaper rates after 3 days. Also arranges city tours (£15) and "Scottish Cycle Safaris" in the Highlands from £40 per day. Open daily July-Sept. 9am-9pm; Oct.-June 10am-6pm.

Hitching: Hitchers often take public transit to the outskirts of Edinburgh, though there are many risks involved; *Let's Go* does not recommend hitchhiking. For points south (except Newcastle and northeast England), most hitchers ride bus #4 or 15 to Fairmilehead and then catch a ride on the A702 to Biggar. For Newcastle, York, and Durham, many take bus #15, 26, or 43 to Musselburgh and then the A1. Hitchers seeking to go north catch bus #18 or 40 to Barnton for the Forth Rd. Bridge and beyond.

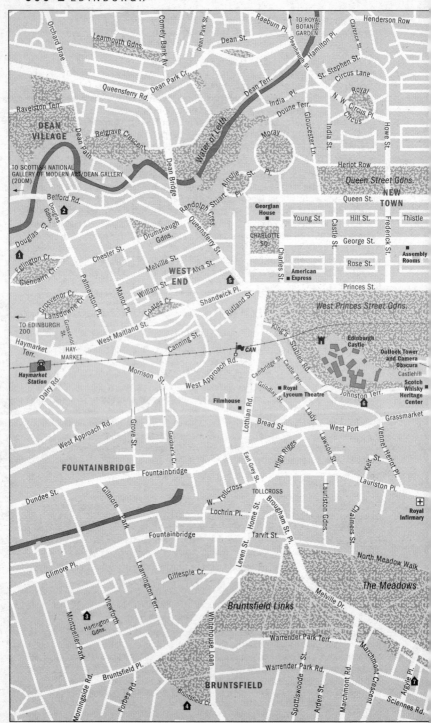

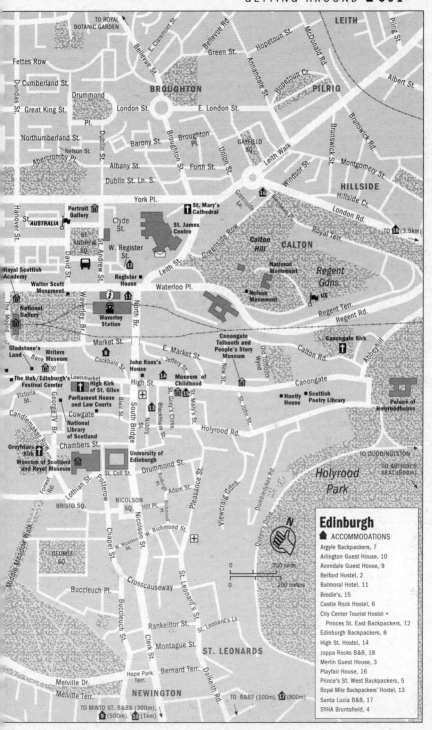

TO ROYAL
BOTANIC GARDEN

Fettes Row

Cumberland St.

Dundas St.

Great King St.

Drummond Pl.

London St.

E. London St.

BROUGHTON

Bellevue St.

E. Claremont St.

Bellevue Rd.

Green St.

Hopetoun St.

McDonald Rd.

LEITH

Pilrig St.

Albert St.

Northumberland St.

Abercromby Pl.

Nelson St.

Dublin St.

Barony St.

Broughton Pl.

Albany St.

Forth St.

Dublin St. Ln. S.

GAYFIELD SQ.

Leith Walk

Windsor St.

Brunswick Rd.

Montgomery St.

HILLSIDE

PILRIG

Hopetoun Cr.

Amandale St.

Annandale St.

Brunswick St.

Hanover St.

York Pl.

Portrait Gallery

AUSTRALIA

Clyde St.

St. ANDREW SQ.

David St.

St. Andrew St.

W. Register St.

St. James Centre

St. Mary's Cathedral

Greenside Ln.

16

Blenheim Pl.

Calton Hill

CALTON

Hillside Cr.

London Rd.

Royal Terr.

TO 18 (3.5km)

Royal Scottish Academy

Walter Scott Monument

National Gallery

The Mound

Register House

Waterloo Pl.

National Monument

Nelson Monument

Regent Gdns.

US

Regent Terr.

Regent Rd.

Gladstone's Land

Writers Museum

Bank St.

i

North Br.

Waverley Station

Waverley Br.

Market St.

E. Market St.

Cockburn St.

Jeffery St.

New St.

Canongate Tolbooth and People's Story Museum

Old Tolbooth Wynd

Calton Rd.

Canongate Kirk

Abbeyhill

The Hub/Edinburgh's Festival Center

Lawnmarket

High Kirk of St. Giles

John Knox's House

Museum of Childhood

High St.

Canongate

Huntly House

Scottish Poetry Library

Palace of Holyroodhouse

Victoria St.

George IV Br.

Candlemaker Row

Parliament House and Law Courts

Cowgate

National Library of Scotland

Chambers St.

Blair St.

South Bridge

Niddry St.

Blackfriars St.

St. Mary's St.

St. John St.

Holyrood Rd.

Greyfriars Kirk

Museum of Scotland and Royal Museum

University of Edinburgh

St. Coll St.

Drummond St.

Forrest Rd.

Lothian St.

Potterow

St. Coll St.

Adam St.

Pleasance

Roxburgh Pl.

Richmond Pl.

Viewcraig Gdns.

Dumbiedykes Rd.

Queen's Drive

Holyrood Park

TO DUDDINGSTON

TO ARTHUR'S SEAT (500m)

BRISTO SQ.

NICOLSON SQ.

Hill Pl.

Nicolson St.

W. Richmond St.

Chapel St.

GEORGE SQ.

Buccleuch Pl.

Crosscauseway

Middle Meadow Walk

Rankeillor St.

St. Leonard's St.

St. Leonard's Ln.

Montague St.

Clerk St.

Buccleuch St.

Bernard Terr.

Dalkeith Rd.

ST. LEONARDS

Melville Dr.

Melville Terr.

Hope Park Terr.

NEWINGTON

TO MINTO ST. B&BS (300m),
9 (500m), 10 (1km)

TO B&BS (100m), 17 (800m)

N

0   200 yards
0   200 meters

Edinburgh

▲ ACCOMMODATIONS

Argyle Backpackers, 7
Arlington Guest House, 10
Avondale Guest House, 9
Belford Hostel, 2
Balmoral Hotel, 11
Brodie's, 15
Castle Rock Hostel, 6
City Center Tourist Hostel +
  Princes St. East Backpackers, 12
Edinburgh Backpackers, 8
High St. Hostel, 14
Joppa Rocks B&B, 18
Merlin Guest House, 3
Playfair House, 16
Prince's St. West Backpackers, 5
Royal Mile Backpackers' Hostel, 13
Santa Lucia B&B, 17
SYHA Bruntsfield, 4

✦ ORIENTATION

A glorious city for walking, Edinburgh is quite a feat of engineering. Its short distances, quiet streets, and many shops disguise the steep hills and massive bridges that span its urban valleys. **Princes St.** is the main thoroughfare in **New Town,** the northern section of Edinburgh. From here you can view the impressive stone facade of the towering Old Town, the southern half of the city across the valley. **The Royal Mile** (Castlehill, Lawnmarket, High St., and Canongate) is the major road in the Old Town and connects **Edinburgh Castle** and the **Palace of Holyroodhouse. North Bridge, Waverley Bridge,** and **The Mound** connect the Old and New Towns.

🛈 PRACTICAL INFORMATION

TOURIST AND FINANCIAL SERVICES

Tourist Information Centre: Edinburgh and Scotland Information Centre, Waverley Market, 3 Princes St. (☎ 473 3800), on the north side of the Waverley Station complex (look for the blue triangular sign). Slickly helpful, but mobbed. Expect to wait in amusement park-like lines. Books rooms for a £3 fee and 10% refundable deposit. Sells bus, museum, tour, and theater tickets, and hands out excellent free maps and pamphlets. **Bureau de change.** Glitzy souvenir shop. In summer, look out for the **City Centre Representatives** around the city—yellow-slicker-wearing folk who can answer questions (about Edinburgh only) in several languages.

Tours: Edinburgh offers a vast number of tours, both by foot and by vehicle; see **Tours** in the **Entertainment** section (p. 506).

Budget Travel: Edinburgh Travel Centre, Potterow Union, Bristo Sq. (☎ 668 2221). For flight information call the **branch** at 92 South Clerk St. (☎ 667 9488). Both open M-W and F 9am-5:30pm, Th 10am-5:30pm, Sa 10am-1pm. **usit Campus Travel,** 53 Forrest Rd. (☎ 225 6111), issues ISIC cards as well. Open M-Tu and Th-F 9am-5:30pm, W 10am-5:30pm, Sa 10am-5pm. The **Radical Travel Centre,** 60 High St. (☎ 557 9393), is affiliated with Haggis Tours; it books hostels for free, arranges tours and car hire, and offers advice for young independent travelers. Open daily 8am-7pm, later in summer.

Financial Services: Banks are everywhere; try **Barclays,** 18 South St. Andrews St. Open M-Tu and Th-F 9:30am-4:30pm, W 10am-4:30pm.

American Express: 139 Princes St. (☎ 718 2503 or ☎ (08706) 001600), at the west end of Princes St. Open M-F 9am-5:30pm, Sa 9am-4pm.

LOCAL SERVICES

Camping Supplies: Camping and Outdoor Centre, 77 South Bridge (☎ 225 3339). All the essentials, but no rentals. Open M-Sa 9am-5:30pm.

Bisexual, Gay, and Lesbian Services: Edinburgh holds a multitude of gay-oriented establishments and events—pick up the *Gay Information* pamphlet at the TIC. At bookstores, pick up a copy of *Gay Scotland,* or better yet, drop by the **Nexus Café-Bar,** 60 Broughton St. (☎ 478 7069), which is also the site of the **Centre for Lesbians, Gays and Bisexuals** and the new **Atomix** gay and lesbian shop. Open daily 11am-11pm. The nearby **Blue Moon Café** (☎ 557 0911), on the corner of Broughton St. and Barony St., dispenses pastries, coffee, and friendly, up-to-date advice. Open M-F 11am-11pm, Sa-Su 9am-11pm. Just next door is the women-only cafe **Dolls.** For more information, see **Gay and Lesbian Nightlife,** p. 514.

Disabled Services: The tourist information centre has info on disabled access to restaurants and sights, as well as *The Access Guide* and *Transport in Edinburgh.* **Shopmobility** (☎ 225 9559), at The Mound by the National Gallery, lends motored wheelchairs for free. Open M-Sa from 10am.

Public Showers: In the "Superloo" at the train station. Super clean, for a train station. Shower £2, toilet 20p, free towel with £1 deposit. Open daily 4:15am-1am.

EMERGENCY AND COMMUNICATIONS

Emergency: Dial ☎ 999 or ☎ 112; no coins required.

Police: 5 Fettes Ave. (☎ 311 3131).

Hospital: Royal Infirmary of Edinburgh, 1 Lauriston Pl. (emergencies ☎ 536 4000, otherwise call ☎ 536 1000). From The Mound take bus #23 or 27, or from Hanover St. take bus #23, 27, 28, or 45.

Internet Access: No one is cheaper than the ultra-convenient, corporate **easyEverything**, 58 Rose St. (☎ 220 3577). Prices fluctuate; £1 can give you 200min.-6hr. of access. You can come and go as you please and use your £1's worth over the course of 28 days. Open 24hr. For *much* less value, but much more panache, try **Café Cyberia,** 88 Hanover St. (☎ 220 4403). Open M-Sa 10am-10pm, Su noon-7pm. £2.50 per 30min., students and seniors £2. Or try **Web 13 Internet Café,** 13 Broad St. (☎ 229 4403). The no-frills **International Telecom Centre,** 52 High St. (☎ 558 7114), has some 20 coin-operated computers, £1 per 15-20min. It also offers cheap **international phone calls,** prepaid international phone cards, fax services, and free coffee. Open daily 9am-10pm. **connect@edinburgh**, at the tourist information centre. Open July-Aug. M-Sa 9am-8pm, Su 10am-8pm, May-June and Sept. closes at 7pm, Oct.-Apr. closes at 6pm. Most hostels also offer Internet access.

Post Office: Edinburgh's main post office is at 8-10 St. James Centre (☎ 556 9546). Open M 9am-5:30pm, Tu-Fr 8:30am-5:30pm, Sa 8:30am-6pm. **Postal Code:** EH1.

▟ ACCOMMODATIONS

HOSTELS AND CAMPING

Edinburgh is a backpacker's paradise, offering a bevy of cheap and convenient youth hostels, many of them smack-dab in the middle of town, and ranging from the small and cozy to the huge and party-oriented. In some of the larger, more central hostels, security can be an issue, so watch your stuff. Also expect cliques of long-term residents who may swallow you into their midst. The tourist information centre (TIC) can book you into a hostel for a nominal fee; the more backpacker-oriented **Radical Travel Centre** (see **Tourist and Financial Services,** above) will do it for less. Still, you should call early in summer if you're coming during the Festival (late July to early Sept.).

🛏 **Brodies Backpackers,** 12 High St. (☎/fax 556 6770; www.brodieshostels.co.uk), right next to The World's End pub on the corner of High St. and St. Mark's St. A relaxing good-times environment, with guests congregating in the small, rustic interior. Friendly, helpful management. Only 56 beds, so book ahead in summer and on weekends. Laundry service. Internet access. Reception open 7am-midnight. Dorms £11.90 M-Th, £13.50 F-Su. Prices higher in August, lower for long-termers.

🛏 **Argyle Backpackers,** 14 Argyle Pl. (☎ 667 9991; fax 662 0002; argylr@aol.co.uk), south of the Meadows and the Royal Mile. Take bus #40 or 41 from The Mound to Melville Dr. Two cozy, renovated townhouses with a relaxing back patio. Some rooms with TV. Check-out 10:30am. Dorms £10; doubles and twins £15 per person. £5 more August.

Edinburgh Backpackers, 65 Cockburn St. (☎ 220 1717, reservations ☎ 221 0022; www.hoppo.com). From North Bridge, turn right onto High St. and right again onto Cockburn St. (uh, that's pronounced "Coburn"). Good location, just off the Royal Mile. Great showers. 110 comfy beds in 6-person, co-ed rooms. Guests get a 10% discount at the trendy Southern Cross Café downstairs. "Legendary" guided pub crawls Tu in the summer. Pool table, ping-pong, TV, and Internet access (£1.50 per 15min.). Reception 24hr. Check-out 10am. Dorms £12, £14 during the festival. Doubles and twins with kitchen access at 34a Cockburn St., £38.50.

City Centre Tourist Hostel, 5 West Register St. (☎/fax 556 8070); ccth@hostel1.fsnet.co.uk; www.touristhostel.freeserve.co.uk). Close to Waverley Station, in the same building as the Princes Street East Hostel. Small, new, and super-clean. Towel and linens provided. Full kitchen. Reception 24hr. Free luggage storage. 4 rooms with showers. Dorms Oct.-Feb. £10, 7th night free; Mar.-Sept. at least £12.

Scotland's Top Hostels (hostels@scotlands-top-hostels.com; www.scotlands-top-hostels.com). This chain has a triple presence in Edinburgh with the following three well located hostels. Great sense of community, with communal events such as movie screenings, city walking tours, and even techno-ceilidhs. The hostels also form the base for the MacBackpackers Tours which snake into the Highlands (see **Tours,** p. 506). For all, dorms are single-sex, £10.50 (£11 in July, £12 in August). 30p credit card surcharge. 7th night free in the off-season. Reception open 24hr.

Castle Rock Hostel, 15 Johnston Terr. (☎ 225 9666). Walking toward the castle on the Royal Mile, turn left onto Johnston Terr. A gigantic hostel with regal views of the castle. All the pros and cons of serving as home to hundreds of travelers. 250 beds in spacious single-sex rooms of 8-12. Laundry service. Ping pong, jukebox, fireplace, and Internet access (£1.80 per 30min.). Breakfast £1.60. Book ahead (*months* ahead for Aug.).

Royal Mile Backpackers, 105 High St. (☎ 557 6120). Walk down High St. from Cockburn St.; the hostel is directly opposite the red Telecom Centre. Head up the stairs and veer left. This spiffy 38-bed facility is smaller and calmer, although there are still unofficial pub crawls. Laundry £2.50.

High St. Hostel, 8 Blackfriars St. (☎ 557 3984). Edinburgh's original hostel lacks a bit of the polish sported by its sister hostels. Still, the 140 beds are spread out spaciously. Pool table, TV, movies, continental breakfast £1.60.

SYHA Youth Hostels (www.syha.org.uk). They may not have the party atmosphere of some other hostels, but they're certainly clean.

SYHA Eglinton, 18 Eglinton Crescent (☎ 337 1120). A mile west of the town center, near Haymarket train station. Walk on Princes St. away from Calton Hill as it becomes Shandwick Pl. Turn right onto Palmerston Pl. and take the second left onto Eglinton Crescent, and buzz in at the front gate. Or take bus #3, 4, 28, 33 or 44 from Princes St. to Palmerston Pl. (look for the Scottish flag). This one has 160 beds in 3- to 14-bed dorms and an elegant, dark-wood first floor. Continental breakfast included, dinner £4.20. Reception 7am-midnight. Check-out 9:30am. Curfew 2am. Pre-aid reservations urged Easter-Sept. Open Jan.-Nov. Dorms July-Aug. £13.75, under 18 £12.25; Sept.-June £12.75, under 18 £11.25.

SYHA Bruntsfield, 7 Bruntsfield Crescent (☎ 447 2994). The tidy hostel offers dorms, quads and cubicle-like spaces within larger rooms. Dorms July-Aug. £12.75, under 18 11.50; Sept.-June £11.75, under 18 £10.50. Sony PlayStation access £1!

SYHA Central 4 Robertson Close, Cowgate (beds £14), and **SYHA Pleasance,** on New Arthur Pl. near the university (beds £16.50). Reservations ☎ 337 1120 for both. Open July-Aug.

Belford Hostel, 6-8 Douglas Gdns. (☎ 225 6209, reservations ☎ 221 0022; fax 476 7139). Take bus #2, 26, 31, 36, 85, or 86 from Princes St. Get off at Haymarket Station, cross the road and head back towards Princes St. Take the second left onto Palmerston Pl., and go to the end. Belford is the church on the corner, converted into a bizarre clash of the sacred and the profane. Gothic stone ceilings soar over pastel bunk-beds. A bit far from most things, but it's got a great bar area and a TV room. Dorms £11-13.50; doubles and twins £37.50-42.50.

Princes St. East Backpackers, 5 West Register St. (☎ 556 6894). Only one floor above the City Centre Tourist Hostel, but it's an entirely different world. Up lots of steps, with lots of long-term, party-prone guests. Rooms with 4-6 beds, and a couple of doubles. Private showers. Laundry service and a well-stocked movie room. Internet access £3 per ½hr. Breakfast £2. Dorms £9-10. £7.50 for long-termers; £13 in August. Doubles £26.

Camping: Edinburgh Caravans, Marine Dr. (☎ 312 6874), by the Forth. Take bus #28A from Frederick St. off Princes St. (90p). Recently revamped. Toilets, showers, and shop. Arrive before 8pm. Open Apr.-Oct. Tents £3, £4 per person, £1.50 per car.

BED AND BREAKFASTS

During festival season (late July to early Sept.), there are few free rooms anywhere in the city; singles are especially rare. Try to book a few months in advance. B&Bs ($20-30 per person) cluster in three well-stocked colonies. Try Gilmore Pl., Viewforth Terr., or Huntington Gdns., in the **Bruntsfield** district south of the west end of Princes St.; Dalkeith Rd. and Minto St. in **Newington,** south of the east end of Princes St.; or Pilrig St. in **Leith,** northeast of the east end of Princes St. All three areas are fairly easy to walk to, and numerous buses run from Princes St. Some B&Bs open only between May and September. The TIC has a $3 booking service.

■**Joppa Rocks Guest House,** 99 Joppa Rd. (☎/fax 669 8695; www.freepages.co.uk/
joppa_rocks). About 3 mi. from the city center on the coast, 50 yd. from the beach;
take the frequent buses #26 or 26A from the Marks and Spencer on Princes St.
(20min., 85p). The sounds of gentle rolling waves replace the noise of the city in this
fully stocked B&B. An amazing bargain. All rooms with bath, bathrobes, TV, and slip-
pers! Single £20; twins £37; doubles £46.

■**Merlin Guest House,** 14 Hartington Pl. (☎ 229 3864). Just under a mile southwest of
the Royal Mile, directly off Viewforth which intersects with Bruntsfield Pl.; take Morning-
side-bound buses #11, 15, 16, or 17 from Princes St. Comfortable rooms in an elegant
Victorian house in a leafy-green neighborhood close to the city center. TVs and French
wallpaper. £16-22.50 per person. Student discounts in winter.

Avondale Guest House, 10 South Gray St. (☎ 667 6779; isabel.fraser@breathemail.net).
From Waverley Station, turn right onto Princes St. and again onto North Bridge St., or
catch bus #69 or any Newington-bound bus to the corner of Minto St. and West Mayfield.
Turn right onto West Mayfield and again onto South Gray St. Friendly proprietors welcome
you to their small, comfortable, smartly decorated house. Free **Internet access;** all rooms
with TV. Singles £20-23; doubles £40-46; £5 extra with bath.

Arlington Guest House, 23a Minto St. (☎ 667 3967; fax 662 9605; www.the-arling-
ton.co.uk). Straight down North Bridge a little over a mile south of the city center; take
buses #8, 8A, 9, 9A, 80, 80A, or 80B. A stately but warm house on a major thoroughfare. Singles £17-23, doubles £30-40.

Santa Lucia Guest House, 14 Kilmaurs Terr. (☎ 667 8694). Off Dalkeith Rd., 1½mi.
south of the city center; take buses #14, 21, 33 or 82. A relaxed atmosphere in a quiet
neighborhood. Backpackers can feel right at home in surprisingly spacious rooms, all
with TV. £18 per person; £2 cheaper without breakfast. Prices vary by season, and are
negotiable for *Let's Go* readers.

◘ FOOD

As the capital of Scottish tourism, Edinburgh serves traditional fare with much
ceremony and expense. You can get cheap haggis in a number of pubs; many
places offer student and hosteler discounts in the early evening. Sandwich shops
abound near the Royal Mile. Takeaway shops on South Clerk St., Leith St., and
Lothian Rd. offer reasonably priced Chinese or Indian fare. For groceries, try
Sainsbury's Central on South St. David St., just north of the Scott monument. (Open
M-Sa 7am-9pm, Su 9am-8pm.)

■**The Basement,** 10a-12a Broughton St. (☎ 557 0097). The menu of this cheap, high
quality restaurant changes daily, with plenty of vegetarian courses. Well-known for Mexican fare on weekends, but Thai cuisine every W is equally potent. Oh, and the sticky
toffee pudding (£2.25) is a gift from the gods. Draws a lively mix of students, musicians, and members of the gay and lesbian community in its candlelit, cavernous environment. It gets crowded on weekends; try to make reservations. Food served daily
noon-10pm; drinks served until 1am.

■**The City Café,** 19 Blair St. (☎ 220 0125). Right off the Royal Mile behind the Tron Kirk,
this Edinburgh institution is popular with the young and tightly-clad. Pool tables in the
back and a blinking Smirnoff bottle display behind the bar accompany venison burgers
(£4-6) and nachos. Incredible shakes, immortalized in the movie *Trainspotting*. Dance
club downstairs (see p. 514). Food served until 10pm. Open daily 11am-1am.

The Black Medicine Coffee Co., 2 Nicolson St. (☎ 622 7209). Proximity to the university and cool Native American interior design pack this place with sophisticated students most afternoons. Lots of sandwiches (£1-3) and smoothies. Live music (mainly
acoustic guitar) Th and Su afternoons. Open daily 8am-8pm.

The Last Drop, 72-74 Grassmarket (☎ 225 4851). Just outside the old gallows (hence
the name), this tourist-friendly pub serves very good "haggis, tatties, and neeps" (haggis, potatoes, and turnips) in carnivorous and vegetarian versions. Nearly everything on
the menu is £2.95 for students and hostelers before 7:30pm. Packed and comfortable;
order a Guinness with a gallows carved into the head. Open daily 10am-2am.

Lost Sock Diner, 11 East London St. (☎ 557 6097). *My Beautiful Launderette* goes a step further here, where you can order a delicious meal for £3.50 while your clothes finish drying. Open M 9am-4pm, Tu-F 9am-10pm, Sa 10am-10:30pm, Su 11am-5pm.

Ndebele, 57 Home St. (☎ 221 1141). Named for a tribe from Swaziland in southern Africa, this atmospheric restaurant serves copious amounts of grub for under £5. Try an avocado, mushroom, and cucumber sandwich (£2.60), or sample the daily African specialty. Mind-numbing array of African and South American coffees and fresh juices. African art gallery downstairs; try to find the secret drawer. Open daily 10am-10pm.

Kebab Mahal, 7 Nicolson Sq. (☎ 667 5214). This unglamorous, student-filled hole-in-the-wall will stuff you with huge portions of great Indian food such as tandoori, curries, chicken tikka, and biryani, all for under £5. Worth the wait. Open Su-Th noon-midnight, F-Sa until 2am.

Blue Moon Café (☎ 557 0911), on the corner of Broughton St. and Barony St. This gay-friendly place is also extremely friendly to everyone. Cushy booths, tasteful decor, and charming staff make this coffee shop hard to leave. Breakfast served until 5pm for hungover late risers. Open M-F 11am-11pm, Sa-Su 9am-11:30pm.

The Elephant House, 21 George IV Br. (☎ 220 5355). The perfect place to chill, chat, smoke, or pore over the stack of available newspapers. Slowly take in their exotic teas and coffees, munch on a pastry or two, or turn to more filling fare (quiche, nachos, or baked potatoes for under £5) while 600 elephants on the wall look on. The sunny back room has great views of the Castle and Old Town. Happy hour drink specials M-Sa 9-10pm. Live music Th 7pm. Open M-F 8am-11pm, Sa-Su 10am-11pm.

◧ SIGHTS

TOURS. A mind-boggling plethora of Edinburgh tour companies tout themselves as "the original" or "the scariest," but the most worthwhile is ▨ **McEwan's 80/- Edinburgh Literary Pub Tour** (that's "McEwan's eighty shilling" in case you were wondering). Led by professional actors, this 2hr. alcohol-friendly crash course in Scottish literature meets outside the Beehive Inn in the Grassmarket. (☎ 226 6665;www.scot-lit-tour.co.uk. June-Sept. daily 7:30pm; April-May and Oct.-Nov. Th-Su 7:30pm; Dec.-March F only. £7, children and students £5.) Then there are the myriad "scary" tours (with the emphasis on the quotation marks). The newish **City of the Dead Tour** has been getting lots of press for poltergeist encounters during its sojourns into Greyfriars graveyard. (☎ 447 2230. 10pm daily. £5, children £4.) The older **Mercat Tours,** leaving from Mercat Cross in front of St. Giles Cathedral, can take you into Edinburgh's spooky underground vaults. (☎ 557 6464. £4-6.)

Edinburgh is really best explored by foot, but if you get lazy, **Guide Friday** has an open-top bus tour that lets you jump on and off as you please. Tours leave Waverley Bridge every 10-15min.; tickets get you discounts at many sights and may be used all day. (☎ 556 2244. £7.50, concessions £7.) Similar bus tours with similar prices include the **Edinburgh Classic Tour,** which offers multilingual narration. (☎ 555 6363. £7.50, students and seniors £6, children £2.50, after 5pm £4.)

THE OLD TOWN AND THE ROYAL MILE

The Royal Mile (Castlehill, Lawnmarket, High St., and Canongate) defines the length of the Old Town—the medieval center of Edinburgh—and passes many of Edinburgh's classic old houses and attractions. Defended by Edinburgh Castle at the top of the hill and by Holyrood Palace at the bottom, the Old Town once packed thousands of inhabitants into a scant few square miles. This limited space resulted in narrow shopfronts and slum buildings towering as high as thirteen stories (Europe's first skyscrapers, some might argue). That dodgy history isn't apparent in the now-fashionable Royal Mile—today, the walk from the castle to the palace is more tourist trap than tenement.

CASTLEHILL AND LAWNMARKET

EDINBURGH CASTLE. Overlooking the city from the peak of an extinct volcano, the castle holds the 15th-century Scottish Crown Jewels and has a view north all the way to Fife, but you have to pay royally at the gate. Still, there is only one Edinburgh Castle. The intricate structures of the castle are mostly the result of recent centuries of rebuilding. Tour guides revel in recounting how many Englishmen fell in various attempts to take the stronghold. A comprehensive audio guide of the castle's history is also provided. Inside the castle, St. Margaret's Chapel, a Norman church that dates back to the 12th century, is believed to be the oldest structure in Edinburgh. Also on display are the royal scepter, sword and crown, as well as the storied but unimpressive Stone of Scone (see **Near Perth,** p. 557). The state apartments include Queen Mary's bedroom. One massive cannon (called Mons Meg) and the Scottish National War Memorial await further contemplation, while working cannons continue to boom at 1pm everday. If you're low on funds, the view is also available at other spots, such as the Nelson Monument (see p. 510), without the high admission fee and the hour-long wait common on summer afternoons. The view from the embankment below the castle isn't bad either. *(At the top of the Royal Mile.* ☎ *225 9846. Castle open daily Apr.-Oct. 9:30am-6pm; Nov.-Mar. 9:30am-5pm; last admission 45min. before closing. Tours every 15min. £7, seniors £5, children £2, under 5 free.)*

THE SCOTTISH PARLIAMENT. While controversy rages over the incomplete new building for the Scottish Parliament *(Pàrlamaid na h-Alba)*, the Members themselves have been raging over various domestic issues in a temporary **Debating Chamber,** located right near the Castle. For a glimpse of the new Scottish Parliament in action, go to the former **Church of Scotland Assembly Hall,** accessible through Milne's Close, off the Royal Mile and across from Johnson's Terrace. Security to enter is not as strict as for the British Parliament at Westminster in London. The fiery Thursday afternoon questioning session is always the most popular; for busy times, you'll want to reserve tickets ahead of time, which can be picked up at the Information Desk in the nearby **Visitor Centre** *(Ionad Tadhail)*, at the corner of the Royal Mile and the George IV Bridge. The Parliament's **Committee Rooms** *(Seomraichean Comataidh)* are in the same building; to observe the committees, consult the Information Desk. Stroll through a high-tech exhibit, then buy your very own Scottish Parliament chocolate bars, whisky, and mousepads. *(Parliament meets in Debating Chamber Sept.-June W 2:30-5:30pm, Th 9:30am-12:30pm and 2:30-5:30pm. Free.* ☎ *348 5000; sp.info@scottish. parliament.uk; www.scottish.parliament.uk. Bookings* ☎ *348 5411. Visitor Centre open Sept.-June M and F 10am-5pm, Tu-Th 9am-5pm; July-Aug. M-F 10am-5pm, Sa same hours for August and early September. Free.)*

THE WRITER'S MUSEUM. This excellent tribute to literary personae, established in Lady Stair's House, contains a reliquary of memorabilia and manuscripts belonging to three of Scotland's greatest literary figures—Robert Burns, Sir Walter Scott, and Robert Louis Stevenson, as well as a plaster cast of Burns's skull. Nearby is the Makar's Court, where stone tables carved with quotations from Scottish writers lead down to Market St. *(Through the passage at 477 Lawnmarket.* ☎ *529 4901. Open M-Sa 10am-5pm; during Festival also Su 2-5pm. Free.)*

OTHER SIGHTS IN THE AREA. The magnetic power of the Castle is undeniable, and tourist attractions cluster around it the way midges do a sweaty backpacker. Their target: the eager tourist. Most of these attractions are quite expensive, although they do offer concessions: the **Scotch Whisky Experience** at the Scotch Whisky Heritage Centre *(£5.50)*, **Outlook Tower and Camera Obscura** *(£4.25)*, and the **Tartan Weaving Mill and Experience** *(exhibition £4, access to massive tartan store free)*. Less glitzy is **Gladstone's Land,** the oldest surviving house (c. 1617) on the Royal Mile, which has been carefully preserved and staffed with knowledgeable guides. *(483 Lawnmarket.* ☎ *226 5856. Open Apr.-Oct. M-Sa 10am-5pm, Su 2-5pm. £3.50, students £2.50.)*

508 ■ EDINBURGH

THE HIGH STREET

HIGH KIRK OF ST. GILES. The kirk is Scotland's principal church, sometimes known as **St. Giles Cathedral.** From its pulpit, John Knox delivered the fiery Presbyterian sermons that drove the Catholic Mary, Queen of Scots into exile. Spectacular stained-glass windows illuminate the structure; its crown spire is one of Edinburgh's hallmarks. St. Giles hosts a number of free organ and choral concerts throughout the year; pick up a schedule. The cathedral is flanked on the east side by the stone **Mercat Cross**, marking the site of the medieval market (hence, "mercat"), and on the other by the **Heart of Midlothian** inlaid in the pavement. Spit on the latter. It'll bring you good luck. *(Where Lawnmarket becomes High St., directly across from Parliament.* ☎ *225 4363. Open Easter to mid-Sept. M-F 9am-7pm, Sa 9am-5pm, Su 1-5pm; mid-Sept. to Easter M-Sa 9am-5pm, Su 1-5pm. Requested donation in the Thistle Chapel £1.)*

TRON KIRK. Just a block downhill from St. Giles, another church pops up on the south side of the High St.: the high-steepled Tron Kirk, built to deal with the overflow of 16th-century religious zealots from St. Giles. Today, it functions as a valuable **information centre** for tourists who are baffled by the myriad sights and tourist traps of the Royal Mile. There's also an interesting archaeology exhibit on the Old Town, including the excavated **Marlin's Wynd,** the buried close which runs underneath the church. *(Open daily July-Aug. 10am-7pm, June and Sept.-Oct. 10am-5pm. Free.)*

MUSEUMS ON THE HIGH STREET. The **Museum of Childhood,** offers a bizarre display of old-school games, toys, and dolls, like the "creeping baby automata." *(42 High St.* ☎ *529 4142. Open M-Sa 10am-5pm; during Festival also Su 2-5pm. Free.)* Across the street and down Chalmer's Close is the **Brass Rubbing Centre.** Artsy folks might appreciate the chance to replicate some fascinating medieval, Celtic, and Gothic designs. Entrance is free, but if you've got the urge to rub the brass, it'll cost you anywhere from £1.20-16 depending on the design. You'll end up with a very nice souvenir, though. *(*☎ *556 4364. Open M-Sa 10am-4:45pm. Last rubbing 3:45.)* Nearby is the picturesque **John Knox House,** 43 High St., which offers a small but engaging look at its former inhabitants, John Knox and James Mossman, and the heated Protestant-Catholic conflicts which engulfed them. *(*☎ *556 9579. Open M-Sa 10am-4:30pm. £1.95, students and seniors £1.50, children even less.)*

CANONGATE

Canongate, the steep hill that constitutes the last segment of the Royal Mile, was once a separate burgh and part of the Augustinian abbey that gave the royal palace its ecclesiastical name. These days, this last downhill stretch shows a welcome dwindling of the Royal Mile's furious tourism.

■ **SCOTTISH POETRY LIBRARY.** Located to your right as you proceed down the hill, this fantastic new building houses an equally fantastic collection of Scotland's poetry in Scots, Gaelic, and English, and also has international poetry, a children's section, and audio and video recordings. It's a relaxing refuge from the main tourist drag in an award-winning piece of expansive modern architecture. The library loans materials out to anyone for a month, free of charge. *(5 Crichton's Close.* ☎ *557 2876; www.spl.org.uk. Open M-F noon-6pm, Sa noon-4pm. Longer Festival hours. Free.)*

CANONGATE KIRK. Yet another church on the Royal Mile, this 17th-century chapel provides the royals with a place to worship when in residence. Its sloping graveyard deserves a contemplative stroll; here lies Adam Smith, founder of modern economics. Here, too, is the famous joint effort of three literary Roberts: Robert Louis Stevenson commemorated the monument erected by Robert Burns in memory of Robert Fergusson.

MUSEUMS ON THE CANONGATE. **Canongate Tolbooth** (c. 1591), with its beautiful clock face and hangman's hook projecting over the Royal Mile, once served as a prison and gallows for "elite" criminals. Now, it houses **The People's Story Museum,** an eye-opening, vaguely Marxist look at "the ordinary people of Edinburgh" across the centuries. *(163 Canongate.* ☎ *529 4057. Open M-Sa 10am-5pm; during Festival also Su*

2-5pm. Free.) Across the street, 16th-century **Huntly House,** a nobleman's mansion, contains a hodgepodge of Edinburgh artifacts, including the key to the Canongate Tolbooth. *(142 Canongate. ☎ 529 4143. Hours as for The People's Story Museum. Free.)*

FUTURE SITE OF THE NEW SCOTTISH PARLIAMENT. There's not much to see right now, and it's all behind the walls at the bottom of the Canongate. But at least the walls are significant: they are covered with the drawings of schoolchildren from around Scotland, a poignant and symbolic reminder of the progress and plurality of 21st-century Scotland. It's a striking juxtaposition to the ancient, monarchial Palace of Holyroodhouse across the street.

THE PALACE OF HOLYROODHOUSE. This Stewart palace abuts Holyrood Park and the peak of Arthur's Seat (see **Gardens and Parks,** p. 510), and dates from the 16th century. It was home to Mary, Queen of Scots, whose antechamber bears the "bloodstain" of her murdered secretary. Behind the palace lies the 12th-century abbey ransacked during the Reformation. The palace remains Queen Elizabeth II's official Scotland residence. *(At the east end of the Royal Mile. ☎ 556 7371. Open Apr.-Oct. daily 9:30am-5:15pm; Nov.-Mar. M-Sa 9:30am-3:45pm; closed during official residences in late May and late June to early July. £6, seniors £4.50, under 17 £3, families £13.50.)*

ELSEWHERE IN THE OLD TOWN

GREYFRIARS KIRK. Off George IV Bridge, the kirk, built in 1620, rests in a beautiful, quiet churchyard that, while lovely, is estimated to contain 250,000 bodies and has long been considered haunted. A few centuries ago, body-snatchers like the infamous Burke and Hare dug up their precious corpses here. Linguistics mavens can listen to Gaelic services inside. Look for the grave of loyal pooch Greyfriars Bobby in front of the Church, as well as the famous statue at the corner. *(Beyond the gates atop Candlemakers Row. ☎ 225 1900. Gaelic services Su 12:30pm, English services 11am. Open Easter-Oct. M-F 10:30am-4:30pm, Sa until 2:30pm. Wheelchair access. Free.)*

NATIONAL LIBRARY OF SCOTLAND. The library has excellent rotating exhibitions of its vast store of material, which includes a Gutenberg Bible, the last letter of Mary, Queen of Scots, and the only surviving copy of "The Wallace," a wildly popular epic poem which then inspired a certain wildly popular Hollywood movie. Alas, these items are not always on display, but the exhibits are generally quite interesting for literary folk. *(George IV Bridge. ☎ 226 4531; www.nls.uk. Exhibition open M-Sa 10am-5pm, Su 2-5pm; during Festival M-F until 8pm. Free.)*

THE NEW TOWN

Edinburgh's New Town is a masterpiece of Georgian planning. James Craig, a 23-year-old architect, won the city-planning contest in 1767, and his rectangular, symmetrical gridiron of three main parallel streets (Queen, George, and Princes) linking two large squares (Charlotte and St. Andrew) reflects the Scottish Enlightenment's belief in order. Queen St. and Princes St., the outer streets, were built up on only one side to allow views of the Firth of Forth and the Old Town, respectively. On your way in or out, wander through **Charlotte Square,** Edinburgh's most elegant 18th-century square.

THE WALTER SCOTT MONUMENT. Statues of Scott and his dog preside inside the spire of this Gothic "steeple without a church." Climb the winding 287 steps for an eagle's-eye view of the Princes St. Gardens, the castle, and Old Town's Market St. *(On Princes St. between The Mound and Waverley Bridge. Open March-May and Sept. daily 9am-6pm; June-Aug. M-Sa 9am-8pm and Su 10am-6pm; Nov.-Feb. daily 9am-4pm. £2.50.)*

CALTON HILL. The other hill at the eastern end of New Town provides as fine a view of the city and the Firth of Forth as Edinburgh Castle. It's also free! Get 143 steps higher inside the castellated **Nelson Monument.** *(☎ 556 2716. Open Apr.-Sept. M 1-6pm, Tu-Sa 10am-6pm; Oct.-Mar. M-Sa 10am-3pm. £2.)* Calton Hill also supports an ersatz Parthenon, built to commemorate those killed in the Napoleonic Wars. If it looks incomplete, that's because they ran out of funding before finishing it.

SOUTHERN SCOTLAND

OTHER SIGHTS. The **Georgian House** makes an interesting stop in a stroll through New Town. A guide staffs each room in this elegantly restored townhouse—ask one of them about the speaking tubes that connect the upstairs hall to the kitchen. *(7 Charlotte Sq. From Princes St., take a right onto Charlotte St. and then your second left; the discreetly labeled house is in the middle of the block.* ☎ *226 3318. Open Apr.-Oct. M-Sa 10am-5pm, Su 2-5pm; last admission 4:30pm. £5, students and seniors £3.50, children free.)* For more posh architecture, try the **Assembly Rooms,** which embody Classical-era Edinburgh complete with lavishly chandeliered theaters. They are generally busy hosting all kinds of performances in the Festival and during the summer, but ask the Duty Manager if you can take a peek at the architecture. *(Near the corner of Frederick St. and George St. Box office* ☎ *220 4349. Box office open M-Sa 10am-5pm.)*

GARDENS AND PARKS

Just off the eastern end of the Royal Mile, you can wink at the Highlands with a stroll through **Holyrood Park,** or by a manageable 45 min. climb up **Arthur's Seat** (823 ft.)—the exposed summit offers a stunning view. The hill was considered to be a holy place by the Picts because it appeared and disappeared in the frequent fogs. **Radical Rd.,** named for the politically extreme, unemployed weavers who built it, allows a shorter walk up to the steep Salisbury Crags on the city-facing side of Arthur's Seat. The best access to the park is from Holyrood Rd., by the Palace, where a small TIC displays information on the history, geology, and wildlife of the park. The **Scottish Wildlife Trust** (☎ 312 7765) has info on guided tours of the park.

Hidden away from the city, the sleepy village of **Duddingston,** at the foot of Arthur's Seat, makes a great grazing stop. You can also take bus #42 there from The Mound, and visit the nearby **Craigmillar Castle.** *(Craigmillar Castle Rd.* ☎ *661 4445. Open Apr.-Sept. M-Su 9:30am-6:30pm, Oct.-March M-Su 9:30am-4:30pm. £2, seniors £1.50, children 75p.)* A smaller refuge, located directly in the city center, is the **Princes St. Gardens,** a lush green park where Edinburghers used to drown their accused witches and fetch their drinking water from the now-drained Nor' Loch. Now, visitors soak in the view of the Old Town and listen to the bands that perform on summer afternoons. Public football fields and tennis courts can be found at the tranquil **Meadows,** an enormous grassy park south of the Old Town. The **Water of Leith** winds its way through the northern part of town; you can follow its lush path all the way to the historic **Port of Leith.** Try starting in the picturesque **Dean Village,** accessible by Queensferry St. from the west end of Princes St.

Edinburgh's requisite romantic oasis is the **Royal Botanic Gardens,** on Inverleith Row. Take bus #23 or 27 from Hanover St. and stroll around the splendid rock garden and plant houses, including a new Scottish Heath Garden. (☎ 552 7171. *Open daily Apr.-Aug. 9:30am-7pm; Mar. and Sept. 9:30am-6pm; Feb. and Oct. 9:30am-5pm; Nov.-Jan. 9:30am-4pm.)* The **Edinburgh Zoo,** 134 Corstorphine Rd., lies just outside the city to the west. Penguins parade every day in the summer at 2pm (when they feel like it), and three new tiger cubs have recently been getting lots of attention. Take red bus #12, 26, or 31 from Princes St. *(☎ 334 9171; www.edinburghzoo.org.uk. Open Apr.-Sept. M-Sa 9am-6pm, Su 9am-6pm; Mar. and Oct. M-Sa 9am-5pm, Su 9am-5pm; Nov.-Feb. daily 9am-4:30pm. £7, students and seniors £5, children £4.)*

🏛 GALLERIES AND MAJOR MUSEUMS

The *Edinburgh Gallery Guide* at the TIC will lead you through the marble halls of Edinburgh's vast and varied collections, most of which are free.

NATIONAL GALLERIES OF SCOTLAND

www.natgalscot.uk. Free shuttle bus on the hour between the galleries. All open M-Sa 10am-5pm and Su noon-5pm. Some may have longer hours during the Festival. Wheelchair accessible. And they're all free.

There are four such galleries in Edinburgh, and they form an elite group, all excellent collections housed in stately buildings. There may be fees for special exhibits.

NATIONAL GALLERY OF SCOTLAND. The prize gallery stashes a superb collection of works by Renaissance, Romantic, and Impressionist masters including Raphael, Titian, Gauguin, Degas, and Monet, as well as a remarkable collection of Italian and French icons. The basement houses a fine spread of Scottish art. *(On The Mound between the two halves of the Princes St. Gardens. ☎ 624 6516.)*

SCOTTISH NATIONAL PORTRAIT GALLERY. Past the lavishly gilt entrance hall, the gallery mounts the mugs of famous Scots, including the definitive portraits of Robert Burns, Bonnie Prince Charlie, and Mary, Queen of Scots. *(1 Queen St., north of St. Andrew Sq. ☎ 624 6200.)*

SCOTTISH NATIONAL GALLERY OF MODERN ART. In the west end of town, the gallery has an excellent rotating collection that includes works by Braque, Matisse, Kokoschka, and Picasso. If you won't wait for the free Galleries shuttle, take bus #13 from George St., or walk—several picturesque paths take you along the Water of Leith to Belford Rd. *(75 Belford Rd. ☎ 556 8921.)*

DEAN GALLERY. Dedicated to Surrealist and Dadaist art, the newest addition to the National Galleries also has a massive collection of work by landmark sculptor Eduardo Paolozzi, best known for his machine-like human figures. A towering, three-story Paolozzi statue dominates the museum. Recent exhibitions featured Dali and Klee. *(Across the road from the National Gallery of Modern Art at 73 Belford Rd. ☎ 624 6200.)*

OTHER MUSEUMS

▩ MUSEUM OF SCOTLAND AND ROYAL MUSEUM. These two connected museums and their stunning architecture are not to be missed. The spanking new **Museum of Scotland** houses a large collection of decorative art and exhibits devoted to Scottish history, from the first Scots through today. The building's architecture is impressive, though the collection is somewhat of a hodgepodge. Objects include the Monymusk Reliquary (said to have once contained St. Columba's bone and been present at the Battle of Bannockburn) and the Maiden (Edinburgh's pre-French Revolution guillotine, used on the High St. around 1565). Gallery tours and audio guides in various languages (even Gaelic) are free. Less modern and more hodgepodge is the **Royal Museum,** with exhibits on natural history and international art. Watch the **Millennium Clock** chime every hour—it's a towering nightmarish display of mechanized Gothic figures. *(Chambers St. ☎ 225 7534. Open M and W-Sa 10am-5pm, Tu 10am-8pm, Su noon-5pm. Admission for both museums £3, seniors and students £1.50, children free. Year-long pass £5.50. Free Tu 4:30-8pm.)*

OUR DYNAMIC EARTH. Edinburgh is proud of its newest museum, which is generally billed as an "experience." It's a glitzy, high-tech, high-priced educational lesson in geology, natural history, and ecology, part amusement park, part science experiment. Computerized time machines take you back to various simulated environments, including a prehistoric volcano and an elaborate rainforest. Kids and science buffs should have a blast. Look for the huge white tent-like structure next to the Palace of Holyroodhouse. *(Holyrood Rd. ☎ 550 7800; www.dynamicearth.co.uk. Open Easter-Oct. daily 10am-6am, Nov.-Easter W-Su 10am-5pm. £6.95, students and disabled £4.95, seniors and under 15 £3.95, families £8.50.)*

MODERN ART GALLERIES. Beneath The Mound down Market St. are galleries of a newish bent. The **Fruitmarket Gallery** flaunts cheeky modern artwork. *(☎ 225 2383. Open M-Sa 11am-6pm, Su noon-5pm. Free.)* Explore material and space at **The City Art Centre,** where exhibits of Scottish modern artwork slip away faster than Dalí's clocks. *(2 Market St. ☎ 529 3993. Open M-Sa 10am-5pm. Admission from free to £5, depending on exhibit.)* Don't miss **i2 art and design,** a New Town venue whose shows have included works by Picasso, Miró, and David Hockney. *(66 Cumberland St. ☎ 557 1020. Open M-F 10am-6pm, Sa 10am-4pm. Free.)* Meanwhile, the wonderful **Royal Scottish Academy** is undergoing long-term reconstruction at its permanent location on The Mound. At time of publishing, it was still looking for a place to house its annual exhibits of modern Scottish art in 2001. *(Call ☎ 556 8921 to find out.)*

🎵 ENTERTAINMENT

The summer season sees an especially joyful round of events—music in the gardens, plays and films, and *ceilidhs*—and that's all *before* the festival comes to town. In winter, shorter days and the crush of students promote a flourishing nightlife. For details, no one does it better than *The List* ($1.95), a bi-weekly comprehensive guide to events in Edinburgh and Glasgow, available at any local newsstand. Numerous tours can also introduce you to some of Edinburgh's lesser-known or scarier nooks and crannies.

THEATER AND FILM

Festival Theatre, 13-29 Nicholson St. (tickets ☎ 529 6000). Offers ballet and opera. Open daily 11am-6pm. Box office open daily 10am-6pm. The Festival sometimes offers drastically reduced day seat tickets (£5.50), which go on sale at 10am for the show that night. The affiliated **King's Theatre,** 2 Leven St., promotes serious and comedic fare, musicals, opera, and pantomime. Box office open daily 1-6pm.

Royal Lyceum Theatre, 30 Grindlay St. (☎ 248 4848). Scottish, other British, and international theater. Box office open M-Sa 10am-6pm. £7-16; students half-price.

Bedlam Theatre, 11b Bristo Pl. (☎ 225 9893). The Edinburgh University theater presents excellent student productions of both traditional and experimental drama in a converted church with a bedlam-red door.

Traverse Theatre, 10 Cambridge St. (☎ 228 1404). Performs innovative, sometimes controversial drama. £1-2.

Stand Comedy Club, 5 York Pl. (☎ 558 7272). Presents laugh-inducing acts every night and a special, 15-shows-a-day program for the Fringe Festival. £1-7.

The Filmhouse, 88 Lothian Rd. (☎ 228 2688). European and art house films, though quality Hollywood fare appears as well. £3.20-5.20; F bargain matinee £1.20-2.20.

LIVE MUSIC

Thanks to an abundance of university students who never let books get in the way of a good night out, Edinburgh's live music scene is alive and well. Excellent impromptu and professional folk sessions abound at pubs (see p. 513), and many of the university houses also sponsor live shows; look for flyers near Bristol Sq. Free live jazz can be found W-Sa 9:30pm-1am at the **Jazz Joint,** 8 Morrison St. (☎ 538 7385), and daily except Mondays 10am-1am at the **Cellar Bar,** 1a Chambers St. (☎ 220 4298). For a complete run-down of Edinburgh's jazz scene, pick up the *Jazz News* at the International Jazz Festival Office, 116 Canongate.

For rock and progressive shows, try **The Venue** (☎ 557 3073). **Ripping Records,** 91 South Bridge (☎ 226 7010), lists and sells tickets to rock, reggae, and pop performances. **Negociant's,** 45-47 Lothian St. (not Lothian Rd.), is a pub with frequent live shows downstairs. (☎ 225 6313. Open daily 9am-3am.) Quality Scottish music hasto be weeded out from the bad: "Scottish Evenings" sponsored by many of the larger hotels are about as authentic as vegan haggis. You can find Scottish bands at most local pubs, and country dancing at the **Ross Open-Air Theatre.** Edinburgh occasionally has a **Folk Festival** in the spring; for more information, contact the TIC.

🛍 SHOPPING

One step out of Waverley Station and you'll realize that Edinburgh is also a thriving mecca of consumer culture. If you're out to get souvenirs, the shops along the **Royal Mile** and **Princes St.** will provide a lifetime's worth of tartans, shortbread, and plush sheep. If you're a mainstream culture maven, the stores along Princes St., in **Princes Street Mall** (underground, connected to Waverley Station), and in the massive **St. James Shopping Centre** (on the east end of Princes St.) will sound pleasingly familiar. (Gap? Virgin Megastore, anyone?) And if you delight in the funky, vintage,

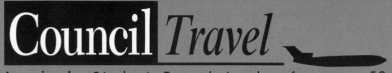

Call the USA

"feel free to call"

1-800-COLLECT

When in Ireland
Dial: 1-800-COLLECT (265 5328)

When in N. Ireland, UK & Europe
Dial: 00-800-COLLECT USA (265 5328 872)

Member of
Dublin Tourism

Australia	0011	800 265 5328 872
Finland	990	800 265 5328 872
Hong Kong	001	800 265 5328 872
Israel	014	800 265 5328 872
Japan	0061	800 265 5328 872
New Zealand	0011	800 265 5328 872

and secondhand, Edinburgh's got that, too. The shops along **Victoria St.,** the **Grassmarket,** and **Cockburn St.** are eccentric enough. Bookstores also abound, selling everything from first edition literary classics to sex guides to glossy postcards (of Edinburgh). And the venerable **Jenner's,** the dignified-looking department store on Princes St., is the Harrod's of Scotland.

◪ NIGHTLIFE

PUBS

If you can't find a pub in Edinburgh, well, then, we won't say what you are. Edinburgh claims to have the highest density of pubs anywhere in Europe, and we at *Let's Go* don't doubt it. *The List* (£1.95), available from any news agent, directs you to the most authentic pubs, the best live bands, the hippest clubs, and the centers of student nightlife. Scottish licensing laws are more liberal than in England, so you can sample a pint of McEwan's any time of day; most pubs open at 11am and close some point between 11pm and 4am.

Pubs directly on the **Royal Mile** usually attract an older crowd, while students tend to loiter in the **Old Town** pubs just south. Casual pub-goers gallivant to live music on the **Grassmarket, Candlemaker Row,** and **Victoria St.** The New Town also has its worthy share of pubs, some historical, and most strung along **Rose St.,** parallel to Princes St. Gay-friendly **Broughton St.** is becoming increasingly popular for nightlife, though its pubs are more trendy and less traditional.

▨ **The Tron,** 9 Hunter Sq. (☎ 226 0931), behind the Tron Kirk. A convenient location and incredible student deals make this place wildly popular. Students and hostelers get £1 drinks on W nights in term (£1 cover), and burgers with a pint for £3.95 year-round 3-7pm. 3 floors of carousing. Frequent live music. Open daily 11:30am until at least 1am.

The Three Sisters, 139 Cowgate. This popular pub offers copious space for dancing, drinking, and socializing—a bit of a meat-market, so the young crowd tends to be slickly dressed. The beer garden provides a delightful outdoor setting. Open daily 9am-1am.

Whistle Binkie's, 4 Niddry St. (☎ 557 5114), off High St. A windowless, vaulted interior packs 'em in for live music. Open daily until 3am.

The World's End, 4 High St. (☎ 556 3628), on the corner of St. Mary's St. A typical pub that has open-mike Sundays (10pm-midnight) with free pints for extroverts willing to show off their prowess. Great pub food. Open M-F 11am-1am, Sa-Su 10am-1am.

The Last Drop, 72-74 Grassmarket (☎ 225 4851). Great pub with great grub (see **Food,** p. 505). Open daily 10am-2am.

Bannermans Bar, 59 Niddry St., near the Royal Mile. Often has live music on weekends. Try the excellent fruit-flavored beer. Open daily noon-1am.

Peartree House, 38 West Nicolson St. (☎ 667 7796). With a large outdoor courtyard and great lunch buffet, Peartree House is a great option for a daytime meal or a quick drink outdoors. Open daily noon-midnight.

Finnegan's Wake, 9b Victoria St., and its similarly popular neighbor **Biddy Mulligan's** both promote the Irish way of life with several stouts on tap and live Irish music every weekend. Finnegan's is open M-Sa noon-1am, Su 1pm-1am.

Sheep's Heid Inn, in the sleepy village of Duddingston, at the foot of Arthur's Seat, bus #42 from The Mound. Scotland's oldest licensed drinking establishment, with an ancient outdoor garden. Open M-Sa 11am-11pm, Su 12:30-11pm.

Pop Rokit, corner of Broughton St. and Picardy Pl. (☎ 556 4272). More London chic than Edinburgh cozy, this new Euro-trendy bar is a favorite pre-club hangout before a night of dancing. The black-clad clientele dine on Mediterranean food amidst the smoked glass and concrete interior. DJs spin House and soft funk, Th-Su starting at 9pm. Open 11am-1am daily. Food served until 9:30pm.

CLUBS

Edinburgh may be best known for her pubs, but her club scene ain't so shabby, either. It is, however, constantly in flux, with clubs constantly closing down and reopening under new management. You're best off consulting the weekly magazine *The List* (£1.95), available at any newsstand. Beyond that, clubs tend to cluster around Edinburgh's historically sleazy and disreputable Cowgate, just downhill from and parallel to the Royal Mile.

Espionage Bar and Club Complex, Victoria St. (☎ 477 7007). A new, throbbing mecca for the young and fashionable. Its 5 floors attempt to recreate different brands of the exotic: the Lizard Lounge goes for Native American chic, the Casbah for Moroccan, and Pravda for Eastern European (over 100 vodkas available), while Club Matahari is a modern dance club with Indian flourishes. No cover, but arrive before 10:30pm weekends, or you might wait in line for an hour. Open daily 5pm-3am, until 4am weekends.

Bertie's, end of Merchant St. off Candlemaker Row, under the bridge. Music tends toward the cheesy, but its "Sabotage" nights (M, Th, and Su) feature all drinks under £1.20 with a £2.50 cover. 50p drinks Tu nights, with £5.50 cover. Open 7pm-3am.

An as-yet-unnamed superclub, 36 Blair St. (☎ 220 6176). Scheduled to open in late 2000 with a whopping capacity of 1,500. Even if you don't know the name, you should be able to hear it.

The City Café, 19 Blair St. (☎ 220 0125). Combines a mellow pool room-restaurant top floor (see p. 505) with a hip dance floor downstairs. Open daily 11am-1am.

The Attic, Dyer's Close (☎ 225 8382), off Cowgate. Provides a dance floor with basic pop tunes, and has a £4 cover on Sunday nights with shots for just 20p.

GAY AND LESBIAN NIGHTLIFE

In 1995, Edinburgh hosted Scotland's first Gay Pride March, a testament to its growing role as a center of lesbian, gay, and bisexual life. The Broughton St. area of the New Town (better known as the **Broughton Triangle**) is the center of the lesbian, gay, and bisexual community of Edinburgh. **Planet Out,** 6 Baxter's Pl., is a frequent stopover on the way to **C.C. Bloom's,** 23-24 Greenside Pl. on Leith St., a super-friendly, super-fun gay club, with no cover. (☎ 556 9331. Open daily 6pm-3am; until 5am during the Festival.) The **Nexus Bar and Café,** also in the Broughton Triangle, is another local favorite. (Open daily 10am-11pm.)

FESTIVALS

EDINBURGH INTERNATIONAL FESTIVAL

For a few weeks in August, Edinburgh is *the* place to be in Europe. Prices go up, pubs and restaurants stay open late, and viewing stands overrun the streets. No, it's not a royal visit (though you just might see that as well), it's the Edinburgh International Festival (Aug. 12-Sept. 1 in 2001), with a kaleidoscopic program of music, drama, dance, and art. A flurry of other cultural events and festivals (see below) take place at the same time during "Festival season," but the International Festival proper encompasses higher-brow events such as classical music, ballet, opera, and drama. Nevertheless, it acts as an umbrella structure for the other festivals. Tickets for the International Festival (£4-44) are sold by phone and at The HUB (see below) starting the third week of April, and by post or fax beginning in the second week of April. You can purchase tickets at the door for most events. Ask about half-price tickets after 1pm on the performance day. For International Festival tickets and a full schedule of events for all festivals, head for the Gothic church just below the Castle on the Royal Mile, now dubbed **The HUB, Edinburgh's Festival Centre,** Castlehill, Edinburgh EH1 2NE. (Inquiries ☎ 473 2001, bookings ☎ 473 2000; fax 473 2003; www.eif.co.uk; www.edinburghfestivals.co.uk.)

▓FRINGE FESTIVAL

Around the established festival has grown a less formal **Fringe Festival** (Aug. 5-27 in 2001), which now includes over 500 amateur and professional companies presenting theater, comedy, children's shows, folk and classical music, poetry, dance, mime, opera, revue, and various exhibits. Budget travelers may find the Fringe better suited to their wallets than official offerings; most tickets hover in the £5 area or are free. Get the scoop on the best shows at some main haunts, including the Fringe Club at the Teviot Row Union, the Pleasance Theatre on Pleasance St., the Gilded Balloon on Cowgate, the Assembly Rooms, the Theatre Workshop, and the Traverse Theatre. The *Fringe Programme* (available from mid-June) and the *Daily Diary* list performances; get brochures and tickets by mail from the **Fringe Festival Office,** 180 High St., Edinburgh EH1 1QS (☎ 226 5257; bookings 226 5138; www.edfringe.com). For programs, go online or call ☎ (0906) 557 5577 (£1 per min.). Bookings can be made online, by post starting in mid-June, by phone (with a credit card) from late June, and in person from July 28. (Box office open 10am-6pm Aug. daily; July M-Sa; Sept.-May M-F.)

MORE FESTIVITIES

Other festivals that take place during the five-week period surrounding the Edinburgh International Festival include the **Military Tattoo,** the **Film Festival,** the **Jazz and Blues Festival,** and the **Book Festival.**

Military Tattoo: Tattoo Ticket Sale Office, 32 Market St. (☎ 225 1188; fax 225 8627). A spectacle of military bands, bagpipes, and drums performed M-Sa nights in the Esplanade. Sa performances followed by fireworks. £8.50-20. Phone and mail bookings from early Jan. Open M-F 10am-4:30pm; on performance days, open until the show.

Edinburgh International Film Festival: Film Festival, The Filmhouse, 88 Lothian Rd., Edinburgh EH3 9BZ (☎ 228 4051, bookings 623 8030). Box office sells tickets starting at the end of July. Runs Aug. 12-26 in 2001.

Edinburgh International Jazz and Blues Festival: (☎ 467 5200; www.jazzmusic.co.uk). Opens with a day of free jazz at the Princes St. Gardens. Tickets (£3-9) go on sale in May, and can be purchased over the phone (☎ 668 2019) or from the HUB. Runs July 27-Aug. 5 in 2001.

Edinburgh Book Festival: Scottish Book Centre, 137 Dundee St., Edinburgh, EH11 1BG (☎ 228 5444; www.edbookfest.co.uk). The largest book celebration in Europe. In Charlotte Square Gardens. Tickets £3-9; some free events. Runs Aug. 11-27 in 2001.

Months before the August madness of full-on festival fever hits, May Day sparks the **Beltane Fires.** This pagan event begins with coal jumping around Calton Hill and then moves to Arthur's Seat at sunrise where, legend has it, those who wash their face with the morning dew will receive eternal youth.

HOGWILD ON HOGMANAY

There's always the insanity of **Hogmanay,** Edinburgh's traditional New Year's Eve festival (☎ 473 3800; www.edinburghshogmanay.org), a hefty annual street party which depends heavily on booze. The millennial Hogmanay consisted of a week-long festival, with street performers, torch-lit processions, and bagpipers, as well as the traditional street party. This year, tickets will be available to 180,000 lucky revellers; to reserve, call the Hogmanay Information Hotline. (☎ (09069) 150150; 2 ticket limit per person.) Or you could join the **First Foot Club** (☎ 473 2056), which will guarantee you a pass (£15) to the street party section of the festival.

▌ DAYTRIPS FROM EDINBURGH

The hills just outside Edinburgh's moderate urban sprawl provide myriad opportunities for rural excursions. Here are just a few.

SOUTHERN SCOTLAND

BRAID HERMITAGE NATURE TRAIL. South of the city, enjoy the Lowland countryside at **The Braids,** where a trail cuts through the woods around Braid Burn. Go through the red archway and up **Blackford Hill** for a piquant view of the city (15min.). Here you'll find telescope viewing Oct.-Mar. on Friday nights at 7:30pm (£1), and various summer exhibitions on astronomy and ecology. *(Bus #40 or 41 from The Mound. Alight at Blackford Ave. and walk away from the city. ☎ 668 8405. Open M-Sa 10am-5pm, Su noon-5pm £3.50, children £2.50, families £8.)*

LAURISTON CASTLE. The placid fishing village of **Cramond** holds Lauriston Castle, a mansion whose 16th-century tower house and 19th-century additions exude privilege. Its gardens look over the Firth of Forth. *(Bus #41 from Frederick St. to 2a Cramond Rd. South. ☎ 336 2060. Guided tours only. 5 tours per day, 11:20am-4:20pm. Open Apr.-Oct. Sa-Th 11am-5pm; Nov.-Mar. Sa-Su 2-4pm. £4.50, concessions £3.)*

HOPETOUN HOUSE. In **South Queensferry,** about 10 mi. west of the city center, stand two grandiose homes. Hopetoun House is the more spectacular, considered by most to be Scotland's stateliest "Adam" mansion, designed by 18th-century Scottish architect William Adam and his sons Robert and John. The house has a rooftop viewing platform which provides a panoramic vista of the Firth of Forth and its bridges. *(Bus #43 from town to South Queensferry or the train to Dalmeny Station; take a taxi (☎ 331 5050) the remaining distance. ☎ 331 2451; www.hopetounhouse.com. Open Apr.-Sept. daily 10am-5pm, last admission 4:30pm. £5.30, students and seniors £4.70, children and disabled £2.70, families £15; grounds only £2.90, children £1.70.)*

DALMENY HOUSE. The first Tudor Gothic building in Scotland, Dalmeny includes the **Napoleon Room,** which holds furniture that propped up the emperor both at the height of his glory and in the despair of his exile. The **Rothschild Collection** includes remarkable 18th-century French furniture, tapestries, and porcelain. *(Take a bus from St. Andrew Sq. to Chapel Gate in Dalmeny, then walk a mile up the drive. ☎ 331 1888. Open July-Aug. Su-Tu 2-5:30pm. £4, students £3, seniors £3.50, under 16 £2, under 10 free.)*

ROSSLYN CHAPEL. The exotic stone carvings of Rosslyn Chapel, in the village of Roslin, raised eyebrows in late medieval Scotland. Filled with occult symbols, the chapel became important to the Knights Templar, and there are even rumors that the Holy Grail lies beneath it. The most famous visible part of the church is the pier known as the Apprentice Pillar, supposedly the work of an apprentice who was later killed by the jealous master mason. Just outside the chapel are footpaths leading to the ruined Roslin Castle in the midst of the peaceful Roslin Glen. Roslin lies by the **Pentland Hills,** a superb hiking area and haunt of Robert Louis Stevenson. *(Take a Penicuik-bound bus (#64 and 87, among others) from Waverley Bridge. Alight at Bilston and head left, following road signs to Roslin. ☎ 440 2159. Chapel open M-Sa 10am-5pm, Su noon-4:45pm. £4, students and seniors £3.50, children £1.)*

THE BORDERS

From the time that Hadrian and his legions repelled in the 2nd century until just 200 years ago, this 1800 sq. mi. region was continually caught in a tug-of-war between Scotland and England. Relics of this past strife remain: fortified houses and castles dot the area, and spectacular abbeys at Dryburgh, Jedburgh, Kelso, and Melrose lie in ruins. These grim reminders of war stand in contrast to a landscape where winding roads and spectacular hill paths reward walkers and cyclists, and where gentle rivers such as the Tweed, which runs eastward through the center of the Borders, provided the setting for Sir Walter Scott's works. Nevertheless, the tradition of conflict remains strong, if only in the rugby matches for which the Borders are famous, and to which the locals are fanatically devoted.

SOUTHERN SCOTLAND

GETTING THERE AND GETTING AROUND

Ask the local tourist information centre (TIC) for the essential *Scottish Borders Travel Guide* (free), which summarizes all bus information. There are seven "areas" in the Borders, and each has a more detailed *Travel Guide* of its own. There are no **trains** in the Borders, but **buses** are frequent. From **Edinburgh**, take an hourly **Lowland** bus #62 to **Peebles** (1hr.), **Galashiels** (1¾hr.), or **Melrose** (2¼hr.); #95 to **Galashiels** or **Hawick** (2hr., 1 per hr.); or #29 and 30 to **Jedburgh** and **Kelso** (2hr., 8 per day). **National Express** (☎ (08705) 808080) #383 travels once a day between **Newcastle** and **Edinburgh** via **Jedburgh** and **Melrose;** #394 also hits **Galashiels** and **Glasgow.** **McEwan's** bus #195 runs from the train station in **Carlisle** to **Galashiels** (2hr.; M-Th 8 per day, F-Sa 9 per day, Su 4 per day). No routes lead directly from **Dumfries and Galloway** in the west; either come through Carlisle or change at **Biggar** or **Lanark.**

Within the Borders, buses run frequently, if not always promptly. Several **taxi services** operate in the Borders. Three or four people can share a cab for the same price as bus fare; ask at TICs for more information.

Hitchhikers report that the lethargy of Border hitching is least painful along the main roads; the A699 runs east-west between Selkirk and Kelso, the A68 connects Edinburgh to Newcastle via Jedburgh, and the A7 runs south through Galashiels and Hawick. The labyrinth of B roads—smaller highways—is less traveled. As always, *Let's Go* does not recommend hitchhiking as a safe mode of travel.

HIKING AND BIKING

The Borders welcome hikers of all levels; take a late afternoon stroll in the hills or wander the wilds for days at a time. Be sure to pick up the superb *Walking in the Scottish Borders*, free at TICs, which details many scenic half-day walks based around towns. The same series includes booklets on cycling, golf, and fishing. Trails weave through the **Tweedsmuirs** (all over 2500 ft. high) to the west along the A708 towards Moffat, as well as the **Cheviot Hills** to the southeast. Closer to Edinburgh, the **Moorfoots** and **Lammermuirs** offer gentler day walks. Eighty-two of the 212 mi. **Southern Upland Way,** Scotland's longest footpath, wind through the Borders. The Way is clearly marked (with a thistle in a hexagon), and the Countryside Commission for Scotland publishes a free annual pamphlet with route and accommodations info. **St. Cuthbert's Way** rambles for 62 mi. from Melrose to Lindisfarne on the English coast. Retrace ancient footsteps along **Dere St.** (an old Roman road), **Girthgate** (a pilgrimage from Edinburgh to Melrose Abbey), or **Minchmoore;** for info trails, pick up the helpful *Scottish Hill Tracks—Southern Scotland.*

The annual regional **Walking Festival** is held in early September; for more information, contact Roger Smith, Walking Development Officer (☎ (01896) 758991). Local TICs provide plenty of trail guides, leaflets on walks (45p), and Ordnance Survey 1:50,000 Map Sheets (£5). Consult the **Scottish Borders Tourist Board** office in Jedburgh at Murrays Green (see **Jedburgh,** p. 521).

Both on- and off-trail **bikers** can enjoy the Borders. The essential *Cycling in the Scottish Borders* includes routes, accomodations, cycle shops, and contact numbers. The *Tweed Cycleway* pamphlet, free from any TIC, describes an 89 mi. route that hugs the Tweed River from Biggar to Berwick and lists bike shops in the Borders. The new **Four Abbeys Cycle Route** connects the abbeys at Melrose, Dryburgh, Jedburgh, and Kelso. See the free pamphlet from TICs. *Let's Go* lists bike rental shops in Galashiels and Peebles. **Hawick Cycle Centre,** 45 North Bridge St., Hawick, also rents bikes. (☎ (01450) 373352. £5 per 8hr., £10 per day, £50 per week. £20 deposit. ID required. Open M-Sa 9am-5pm.)

ACCOMMODATIONS

The *Scottish Borders Holiday Guide*, free at TICs, lists a wide range of Borders accommodations, including campsites. All TICs can help you find a bed, usually for a 10% deposit on the first night's stay. To book rooms in advance, call the Jedburgh

TIC with a credit card (☎ (01835) 863435). The following **SYHA Youth Hostels** in the Borders are strategically dispersed—a fourth is in **Melrose** (see below).

SYHA Broadmeadows (☎/fax (01750) 76262), 5 mi. west of Selkirk off the A708, and 1¼ mi. south of the Southern Upland Way. Opened in 1931 as the first SYHA hostel and provides footholds for an ascent into the Tweedsmuir Hills. Reception closed 10:30am-5pm. Curfew 10:45pm. Open late Mar. to Sept. Dorms £6.75, under 18 £6.

SYHA Coldingham (☎/fax (01890) 771298), just outside Coldingham at St. Abbs Head near the ocean. Surveys the entire east coast and the eastern end of the Southern Upland Way. Reception closed 10:30am-5pm. Curfew 11:30pm. Open late Mar. to Oct. Dorms £8.25, under 18 £7.25.

SYHA Kirk Yetholm (☎ (01573) 420631), at the junction of the B6352 and B6401. Watch hikers collapse at the northern terminus of the Pennine Way. Buses run from Kelso (1hr.; M-Sa 5-7 per day, Su 3 per day; £2.65). Reception closed 10:30am-5pm. Curfew 11:30pm; open late Mar. to Oct. Dorms £8.25, under 18 £7.25.

MELROSE ☎01896

Among the loveliest of the region's towns, Melrose (pop. 2400) draws many visitors to its abbey, and is also within convenient reach of Dryburgh Abbey and Sir Walter Scott's country home of Abbotsford.

🛈 PRACTICAL INFORMATION. Buses stop at Market Sq. The **tourist information centre** (TIC), next to a small park and across from the abbey on Abbey St., gives quirky insights on the area's colorful history. (☎ 822555. Open July-Aug. M-Sa 9am-6pm, Su 10am-5pm; June and Sept. M-Sa 10am-5:30pm, Su 10am-2pm; Apr.-May M-Sa 10am-5pm, Su 10am-1pm; Oct. M-Sa 10am-4pm, Su 10am-1pm.) A **Bank of Scotland** is at Market Sq. (Open M-Tu and Th-F 9am-12:30pm and 1:30-5pm, W 10:30am-12:30pm and 1:30-5pm.) The **post office** is on Buccleuch St. (☎ 822040. Open M-F 9am-1pm and 2-5:30pm, Sa 9am-12:30pm.) **Postal code:** TD6 9LE.

📷🍴 ACCOMMODATIONS AND FOOD. The comfortable **SYHA Melrose,** off High Rd., is a superb base for exploring the Borders. One minute from the town center, the hostel resembles a stately manor more than a backpackers' abode, with 86 beds, an excellent kitchen, laundry facilities, and a relaxing yard. Grab a trashy romance novel from the shelves and gaze at the abbey's Gothic ruins out the window. (☎ 822521; fax 823505; melrose@syha.org.uk. Continental breakfast included. 9 showers. Reception 7am-11pm. Curfew 11:45pm. Open year-round. Dorms £11.25, under 18 £10.) Or try **Birch House,** down High St., which offers homey, pine-furnished rooms. (☎ 822391. Singles £25; doubles £36-44.) Camp at the deluxe **Gibson Park Caravan Club Park,** St. Dunstan's Park, off High St., featuring the cleanest bathrooms you'll ever see at a campsite, and excellent facilities for the disabled. (☎ 822969. Tent and car £3.50, plus £4 per adult, under 17 £1.20.)

Though not known for its budget fare, Melrose does offer farm-fresh food, including gourmet cheeses and wholefoods, at **The Country Kitchen,** Market Sq., at Palma Pl. (☎ 822586. Open M-F 9am-5pm, Sa 9am-1pm and 2-5pm.) The award-winning **Melrose Station Restaurant,** Palma Pl., in a renovated railway station, serves wholemeal sandwiches (£2.35-3.25) and exquisite main courses for excruciating prices. (☎ 822546. Lunch around £6, 2-course dinner £15.50. Lunch served W-Su noon-2pm; dinner served Th-Sa from 6:45pm.)

📷🥾 SIGHTS AND HIKING. The centerpiece of the town, Cistercian 🏰 **Melrose Abbey** was begun in 1136, destroyed by the English, rebuilt in an ornate and Gothic style, then destroyed again by the English in 1549. Some walls remain remarkably intact, while others provide good ventilation. Search the extensive grounds for the tombstone of Robert the Bruce's embalmed heart (see p. 492). On the lighter side, the monastery is also home to some amusing gargoyles. Search the south wall for a pig playing bagpipes and a cow with wings. (☎ 822562. Open Apr.-Sept. daily

9:30am-6:30pm; Oct.-Mar. M-Sa 9:30am-4:30pm, Su 2-4:30pm. Audio tour included. £3, seniors £2.30, under 16 £1.) Admission to the Abbey includes the **Abbey Museum,** displaying objects unearthed from the abbey and regional Roman forts. The museum also details Sir Walter Scott's life, death, and poetic dishonesty. Come, see, and briskly conquer the **Trimontium Exhibition,** in Market Sq., which jams information about the large ancient Roman fort upon the three Eildon Hills into one small room. Don't be shy; sit in the replica Roman saddle—you know you want to. (☎ 822651. Open Apr.-Oct. daily 10:30am-4:30pm, Sa-Su closed for lunch. Audio tour included. Museum £1.50, concessions £1, families £4.)

Bike routes fan out from town, and the **Eildon Hills,** an easy five-mile hike, supply sweeping views from three volcanic summits. Legend has it that King Arthur and his knights lie in an enchanted sleep (fully armed, of course) within a cavern deep beneath the Hills, and will someday awake when the country needs to be saved. To reach the Hills, walk 200 yd. south of Market Sq. on the Dingleton Rd.; after passing Newlyn Rd. on the right, look for the footpath on the left.

NEAR MELROSE

DRYBURGH ABBEY. For those with time and the willingness to walk, the real treasure of the area is Dryburgh Abbey, which has extensive ruins, the graves of Sir Walter Scott and World War II commander Earl Haig, and serene grounds (visitors rave about the trees). A 22 ft. statue of William Wallace and the spectacular **Scott's View** are nearby. *(5 mi. southeast of Melrose; take a bus that goes through St. Boswell's and ask the driver to drop you off. Follow the marked road, cross the footbridge, then turn right (about a 20min. walk).* ☎ *(01835) 822381. Open Apr.-Sept. 9:30am-6:30pm; Oct.-Mar. 9:30am-4:30pm. £2.50, seniors £1.90, children £1.)*

ABBOTSFORD. Sir Walter Scott settled into this mock-Gothic estate, three miles west of Melrose, to write most of his Waverley novels, and died here in 1832. The house is stuffed with Scott's collections of books, armor, and knick-knacks, including a lock of Bonnie Prince Charlie's hair and a piece of the gown worn by Mary, Queen of Scots at her execution. *(Buses between Galashiels and Melrose via Tweedbank stop nearby. Ask the driver to drop you at the stop on the east side of the River Tweed bridge; from the Galashiels side of the road, a dirt path dips down, then climbs uphill to the entrance.* ☎ *(01896) 752043. Open June-Sept. daily 10am-5pm; mid-Mar. to May and Oct. M-Sa 10am-5pm, Su 2-5pm. £3.80, children £1.90.)*

THIRLESTANE CASTLE. Ten miles north of Melrose on the A68 near Lauder stands Thirlestane Castle, the ancient seat of the Earls and Duke of Lauderdale. Its beautiful restoration hides its bloody history—jealous nobles hanged a host of King James III's low-born supporters here in 1482. There are also historic toys on display for the delight of your inner child. *(☎ (01578) 722430. Open Apr.-Oct. M-F and Su 10:30am-5pm. £5.20, children £3, families £13.)*

GALASHIELS ☎ 01896

Birthplace of tartan and tweed and center of the wool-weaving industry since the 13th century, welcoming "Gala" is to be thanked for the garb of tweed-bound professors around the world. Start (and end) your exploration of the town with a visit to **Lochcarron's Scottish Cashmere and Wool Centre,** Huddersfield St. The museum informs, but the tour of the 19th-century water-powered loom and modern working wool factory enthralls. (☎ 752091. Open June-Sept. M-Sa 9am-5pm, Su noon-5pm; Oct.-May M-Sa 9am-5pm. Free 40min. tours M-Th every hr. 10:30am-2:30pm, F 10:30am and 11:30am; £2.50, under 15 free.)

At the **bus station,** across Gala Water, the helpful staff sells National Express and Citylink tickets, and **stores luggage** during office hours for 50p. (☎ 752237. Open M-F 9am-12:30pm and 1:30-5pm, Sa 9am-noon.) **Gala Cycles,** 38 Island St., **rents bikes** for £5 per half-day and £10 per day. (☎ 757587. Open M-Tu and Th-F 10am-5pm, W 10am-noon, Sa 10am-5pm.) The **tourist information centre,** 3 St. John's St., off Bank

SOUTHERN SCOTLAND

St., assists with beds and buses. (☎ 755551. Open July-Aug. M-Sa 10am-6pm, Su 11am-1pm; Apr.-June and Sept.-Oct. M-Sa 10am-5pm.) **Banks** abound on Bank St. The **post office** is at 1 Channel St. (☎ 754731. Open M-F 9am-5:30pm, Sa 9am-12:30pm.) **Postal code:** TD1 1AA.

Morven Guest House, 12 Sine Pl., around the corner from Poundstretcher on High St., has spacious rooms with bath at a bargain. (☎ 756255. £17 per adult, £8.50 per child.) Tasty sandwiches (brie-and-apple £1.30) await at the **Supa-Fresh** grocery-deli, 7 Overhaugh St. (☎ 757307. Open M-Sa 9am-4:30pm.) Groceries can be found at **Tesco,** Paton St. (☎ 610400. Open M-F 8am-9pm, Sa 8am-8pm, Su 9am-7pm.)

12th-century **Traquair House,** the oldest inhabited house in Scotland, stands 12 mi. west of Galashiels off the A72 and 1½ mi. from Innerleithen on the B709. The treasures of the Stewarts of Traquair are displayed upstairs. The main gates are permanently closed; legend has it that the Earl of Stair swore after Prince Charlie's defeat in 1745 that they would not be reopened until another Stewart took the throne. Catherine Stewart, the present resident, brews ale in the 200-year-old brewery below the chapel and has tastings on summer Fridays. (☎ (01896) 830323. Open June-Aug. daily 10:30am-5:30pm, Apr.-May and Sept. daily 12:30-5:30pm, Oct. F-Su 12:30-5pm. £4.50, seniors £4, children £2.25, families £11.)

PEEBLES   ☎01721

Eighteen miles west of Galashiels, Peebles nurtures the River Tweed with gentle grass and restful benches along its banks. A 20min. sally upstream yields **Neidpath Castle,** a small but sturdy fortress with something for everyone—crumbling rooms, river views (one of the best from the bathroom), batik art depicting the life of Mary, Queen of Scots, and a tartan display. The castle inspired many a 19th-century bard, including Sir Walter Scott. (☎ 720333. Open Easter-Sept. M-Sa 11am-5pm, Su 1-5pm. £3, students and seniors £2.50, children £1, families £7.50.) The **Tweeddale Museum and Gallery,** in the Chambers Institute on High St., houses constantly changing exhibitions and the well-marked Chamber's Room, containing Greek friezes placed here in 1859 to "ennoble and enlighten" the viewer. (☎ 724820. Open M-F 10am-noon and 2-5pm, Easter-Oct. also Sa 10am-1pm and 2-4pm.) On Cross Rd. in a small wooded park, the ruins of **Cross Kirk**—supposedly founded in 1262 when Alexander III and his pals discovered a 4th-century cross here—represent one of the two remaining Trinitarian monasteries in Scotland. The **Beltane Festival** takes place on the third Saturday in June. Formerly a pagan holiday of random sexual encounters, the ceremonies now celebrate not fertility, but the work of elementary school children. Near Peebles, the forests of the Tweed Valley, such as **Glentross** and **Cardrona,** have hiking and cycling paths. *Forests of the River Tweed,* free from the tourist information centre, has the details.

Said **tourist information centre,** 23 High St., sells a slew of local maps; their town walk (25p) is a great way to make the most of your visit. (☎ 720138; fax 724401. Open July-Aug. M-F 9am-8pm, Sa 9am-7pm, Su 10am-6pm; off-season hours vary slightly, but often closed Su.) **Banks** along High St. dispense cash. **Crossburn Caravan Park,** Edinburgh Rd., rents bikes. (☎ 720501. £7 per half-day, £14 per day. Helmets £1. Deposit £60. Open M-Sa 8:30am-6pm.) Get **Internet access** from the library, in the Chambers Institute on High St. (☎ 720123. £2.50 per 30min.; concessions £1.25. Open M, W, and F 9:30am-5pm, Tu and Th 9:30am-7pm, Sa 9am-12:30pm.) The **post office** is at 14 Eastgate. (☎ 720119. Open M-F 9am-5:30pm, Sa 9am-12:30pm.) **Postal code:** EH45 8AA.

Stay with **Mrs. Mitchell,** Viewfield, 1 Rosetta Rd., for fresh, spacious, clean rooms above a wonderful front garden. (☎ 721232. Singles £18.50; twins £35.) Campers find comfort at the **Rosetta Camping and Caravan Park,** Rosetta Rd., 15min. from the town center on the wooded grounds of Rosetta House, with laundry facilities, showers, and an amenity complex with a bar. (☎ 720770; fax 720623. Open Apr.-Oct. £4.50 per person, under 17 50p; per week £27 and £3.) At **Big Eg's,** just outside the center at 14-16 Northgate, the proprietor ladles out a healthy dollop of travel experience with his tasty fish and chips, which go for £2.95 takeaway or £4.10 sit-down, tea and bread included. (☎ 721497. Open M-Sa 11:45am-11pm, Su 1-8pm.)

JEDBURGH   ☎ 01835

Thirteen miles south of Melrose bustles the town of Jedburgh (JED-burra), known to locals as "Jethart." Founded in 1138 by King David I and located smack in the middle of town, **Jedburgh Abbey** was a statement to both the Scots and English that the monarch was not afraid to place magnificent monuments on the fringes of his realm. Nearly a century later the abbey was derisively dismantled in the 1540s by the English Earl of Hertford—take that, King David. One of the remarkable surviving relics is a small yet intricately decorated ivory comb which lies at the heart of a 12th-century murder mystery. An advantage of demolition is that you can see almost everything from the outside for free—the best view is from Abbey Close St. off Castlegate. (☎ 863925. Open Apr.-Sept. daily 9:30am-6:30pm; Oct.-Mar. M-Sa 9:30am-4:30pm, Su 2-4:30pm. £3, seniors and students £2.30, under 16 £1.)

Now a fascinating museum chronicling the monarch, the **Home of Mary, Queen of Scots,** down Smiths Wynd on Queen St., is one of the few remaining examples of a 16th-century fortified house. While in Jedburgh she became so gravely ill due to childbirth, tough marriages, and riding accidents that her doctor thought she had died. Long after, facing death after years of imprisonment, she is said to have wished aloud, "Would that I had died at Jedburgh." On her gruesome death mask, look for signs of the bandaging used to hold her head together after it was messily hacked off. Surrounding the house are the most beautiful gardens in Jedburgh, and the area's best picnic spot. (☎ 863331. Open June-Aug. M-Sa 10am-4:30pm, Su 10am-4:30pm; Apr.-May and Oct. M-Sa 10am-4:45pm, Su noon-4:30pm; Mar. and Nov. M-Sa 10:30am-3:30pm, Su 1-4pm. £2, concessions £1, disabled free but access limited.) The 18th-century **Jedburgh Castle Gaol** stands atop a hill on Castlegate over the original Jethart Castle, which was destroyed in 1409 to prevent the English from taking it. Enter between two cannons to learn about prison history. (☎ 863254. Open Apr.-Oct. M-Sa 10am-4:45pm, Su 1-4pm. £1.25, concessions 75p.)

The **bus stand** on Canongate does not have an office, but is located behind that shrine to Borders info, the Jedburgh **tourist information centre** (TIC), Murrays Green, opposite the abbey. The TIC dispenses information, books National Express tickets, reserves rooms for a deposit, and exchanges currency for free. Pick up the free publications *Jedburgh Town Trail*, *Jedburgh Mini-guide*, or *What's On: Scottish Borders*, or your favorite Scottish romance novel. (☎ 863435; fax 864099; info@scot-borders.co.uk. Open July-Aug. M-F 9am-8pm, Sa 9am-7pm, Su 10am-7pm; June-Sept. M-Sa 9:30am-6pm, Su 10am-6pm; off-season hours reduced.) The **Royal Bank of Scotland** stands on the corner of Jeweller's Wynd and High St. (☎ 862563. Open M-Tu and Th-F 9:15am-4:45pm, W 10am-4:45pm; closed 12:30-1:30pm for lunch.) The **post office** rests at 37 High St. (☎ 862268. Open M-F 9am-5:30pm, Sa 9am-12:30pm.) **Postal code:** TD8 6DG.

B&Bs pepper the town. At 7 Queen St., near the house of Mary, Queen of Scots, **Mrs. Elliott** serves fresh fruit salad for those weary of bacon and eggs. Rumor has it that Mrs. Elliott makes a majestic plum jam. The rooms are small and cozy. (☎ 862482. Singles £15; twins £27.) Stargazers can camp at the **Jedwater Caravan Park,** four miles south of the town center off the A68; watch for the signs and a side road. (☎/fax 840219. Open Easter-Oct. Showers available. Tent and two people £8, extra adult £1, children 50p.) For groceries, visit the **Co-op Superstore,** on the corner of Jeweller's Wynd and High St. (☎ 862944. Open M-Sa 8am-8pm, Su 9am-6pm.) For quick snacks, try the sweet **Brown Sugar Coffee Shop and Bakery,** 12 Canongate, including burgers (£1.50-3), teacakes (95p), and toasted sandwiches for £1.25-2. (☎ 863399. Open M-Sa 8am-5pm.)

KELSO   ☎ 01573

In the busy transport hub of Kelso, one of the larger towns in the Borders, palatial **Floors Castle** endures tourist masses. This home is still used as a residence, as the Duke of Roxburgh will attest, and Prince Andrew is known to drop by for the annual charity golf tournament. The castle has nearly 400 windows, allowing spectacular views of the Tweed. A holly in the gardens marks the site where James II

> **MARY, MARY, QUITE CONTRARY** Mary, Queen of
> Scots (1542-87) endured a flurry of spicy rumors during her lifetime. Her first husband,
> King François II of France, reportedly had a shriveled male organ. Wits at the French
> court speculated on the King's ability to have intercourse, and remarked that if the
> Queen were to become pregnant, the child could not be the King's. In any case, Mary
> experienced a "hysterical" (false) pregnancy during her year as Queen of France before
> François died. Mary's later marriage to the wicked Lord Darnley did bear fruit. During
> the long and agonizing birth, Mary's companion Lady Reres moaned and thrashed in
> empathy beside Mary, as a lady-in-waiting supposedly drew Mary's pains into the Lady
> Reres through witchcraft. Rumor has it that Mary's son was stillborn, and that the future
> King James VI of Scotland (also James I of England) was actually another infant smug-
> gled in to replace the dead child—a story made more tantalizing by the discovery years
> later of an infant's skeleton hidden between the walls of Mary's apartments.

was killed while inspecting a cannon. Try not to make the same mistake. Scores of
turrets and vast grounds make this the most impressive sight in the area. (☎
223333. Open Easter-Oct. daily 10am-4:30pm. House and gardens £5, seniors and
students £4.50, under 16 £3, families £14; grounds only £3, students and seniors
£1.50, children free.) Like Jedburgh's abbey, Kelso's **abbey,** near the Market Sq., is
King David-raised, Earl of Hertford-razed. (Open Apr.-Sept. M-Sa 9:30am-6pm, Su
2-6pm; Oct.-Mar. M-Sa 9:30am-4pm, Su 2-4pm. Free.)

The **bus station** is off Roxburgh St., near Market Sq., and **stores luggage** for 50p
per bag. (☎ 224141. Open M-F 8:45am-5pm, Sa 8:45-11am.) Kelso's **tourist information centre** is in the old town hall in Market Sq., and books rooms for a 10% deposit
on the first night's stay. (☎ 223464. Open July-Aug. M-Sa 9am-6pm, Su 10am-5pm;
June and Sept. M-Sa 9:30am-5pm, Su 10am-5pm; Apr.-May M-Sa 10am-5pm, Su
10am-1pm; Oct. M-Sa 10am-4:30pm, Su 10am-1pm.) The **post office** is at 13 Wood-
market. (Open M-F 9am-5:30pm, Sa 9am-12:30pm.) **Postal code:** TD5 7AT.

Stay with **Mr. Watson,** Clashdale, 26 Inchmead Dr., for simple, spacious rooms.
(☎ 223405. £15 per person.) **The Home Bakery,** 50 The Square, near Hosemarket,
sells pies and sandwiches for around £1.50. (☎ 226782. Open daily 7:30am-5pm.)
Restock your supplies at **Safeway,** Roxburgh St. (☎ 225641. Open M-W and F 8am-
8pm, Th 8am-9pm, Sa 8am-6pm, Su 9am-6pm.)

Near Kelso on the A6089 sits **Mellerstain House,** one of the finest Georgian
houses in Scotland, begun in 1725 by William Adam and completed by his son Robert. More impressive than the house itself is the perfectly symmetrical garden with
a picturesque view of the distant Cheviot Hills. (☎ (01573) 410225. Open Easter-
Sept. M-F and Su 12:30-5pm. House and gardens £4.50, seniors and students £3.50,
children £2; gardens only £2.)

DUMFRIES AND GALLOWAY

Galloway, the southernmost region of Scotland, derives its name from medieval
Welsh neighbors who dubbed the area *Galwyddel* ("Land of the stranger Gaels").
Today, there are few strangers here, since Galloway receives few tourists compared to the well-trodden paths to the north and south. Over the centuries, Dumfries, name to both the neighboring county and the largest town in the area, has
passed through the hands of Romans, Vikings, and English feudal lords; each of
these owners has left behind at least a few sights to visit. Castles, gardens, and
local heroes (among them Robert the Bruce, Robert Burns, and Mary, Queen of
Scots) are plentiful; good public transportation is not. Although the region is
known as Scotland's "quiet country," locals know how to celebrate as well as any

bunch of Scots. On the 25th of January of every year, folks get together to eat, drink, and celebrate the anniversary of the birth of their favorite son, Robert Burns—a little bit of poetry is even thrown around in drunken splendor.

⌐ GETTING AROUND

Buses run with relative frequency, but it's difficult to know when and where they leave. The Dumfries and Galloway Council publishes six free essential regional Public Transport Guides; the free *Dumfries and Galloway Visitor Guide* also provides useful info on transport services; all are available from tourist information centres (TICs). Several bus companies criss-cross the area; call **Western Buses** (☎ (01387) 253496), **MacEwan's Service** (☎ (01387) 710357), **McCulloch's Coaches** (☎ (01776) 830236), or the **Travel Information Line** (☎ (0345) 090510; open M-F 9am-5pm) for schedule information. A **Day Discoverer Ticket,** available on buses, allows unlimited travel in Dumfries and Galloway, and on Stagecoach buses in Cumbria (see **Lake District: Getting Around,** p. 358; £5, children £2).

▚ HIKING AND BIKING

Dumfries and Galloway stock a magnificent stretch of coastline, with a reserve supply of fields, forests, and hills. Two peninsulas—the **Machars** and the **Rhins of Galloway**—jut southward; hikers can follow the 30 mi. **Pilgrim's Way** down the Machars from Glenluce Abbey in the north to the Isle of Whithorn at the southern tip, where St. Ninian founded a chapel in the 4th century. For those with leisure and ambition, the **South Upland Way** begins at Portpatrick, then snakes its way in a northeasterly direction, passing SYHA hostels in **Kendoon, Wanlockhead, Broadmeadows,** and **Melrose.** For shorter walks, ask a TIC for the free guide *Walking in Dumfries and Galloway,* which describes over 30 possible walks. Also pick up the free *Ranger Led Walks and Events.* If you're planning a strenuous hike, check the weather (☎ (0891) 500420; premium rate call) and bring the necessary survival supplies, maps, and compass (see **Wilderness Safety,** p. 53).

Cyclists will find *Cycling in Dumfries and Galloway* (free at TICs) equally useful. The Forest Enterprise also puts out smaller leaflets describing on- and off-trail routes in some of the area's forests—ask at the TIC. For bike rental, try **Ace Cycles,** Church St., Castle Douglas. (☎ (01556) 504542. £8 per 8hr., overnight hire £10. Open M-W and F-Sa 9am-5pm, Th 9am-4pm.) You can also rent from **Deprato's Bike Hire,** Zebra Crossing, Victoria St., Newton Stewart, but call ahead and reserve a rental in the summer months. (☎ (01671) 402656. £6 per half day, £10 per day. Open Th-Tu 9:30am-6:30pm, W 9:30am-2:30pm.)

DUMFRIES ☎ 01387

Dumfries (pop. 30,000) hangs its tam upon tales of two famous Roberts. Robert the Bruce proclaimed himself King of Scotland in Dumfries after stabbing throne-contender Red Comyn at Greyfriars. Robert Burns lived and wrote in Dumfries from 1791 until his death in 1796. Lest its auld acquaintance be forgot, the town has devoted many a site to Burns. Along with its historical claims, the town's central location and transportation connections make it the unofficial capital of southwest Scotland. Even so, Dumfries fails to catch—let alone hold—one's interest; hurry through to reach the charm of the countryside.

⌐▟ GETTING THERE AND PRACTICAL INFORMATION

Trains (☎ (08457) 484950) come in from: **Carlisle** (35min.; M-Sa every 2 hr., Su 4 per day; £6.20); **Glasgow Central** (1¾hr.; M-Sa 8 per day, Su 2 per day; £9.20); and **London Euston** (change in Carlisle, 5hr., 9 per day, £66.20). **Stagecoach Western Scottish** (☎ 253496) **buses** run from **Glasgow Buchanan St.** (#X74; 2hr.; M-Sa 5 per day, Su 2 per day; £6.30, return £8.50) and **Edinburgh St. Andrew Sq.** (#100 or X73; 2hr.; M-Sa 5 per day, Su 1 in the evening; £6.30, return £8.50).

The Dumfries **tourist information centre,** 64 Whitesands Rd., books accommodations for £1 plus a 10% deposit and sells National Express bus tickets. Pick up the free *Dumfries and Galloway Visitors Guide.* (☎ 253862; fax 245555. Open June-Sept. M-Sa 10am-5:30pm, Su noon-5pm; Oct.-May M-Sa 10am-5pm, Su 10am-4pm.) The **Royal Bank of Scotland** resides in Queensberry Sq. off High St. (Open M-Tu and Th-F 9:15am-4:45pm, W 10am-4:45pm.) **Dumfries IT Centre,** 26-28 Brewery St., provides **Internet access** and drinks. (☎ 259400. £4 per hr. Open M-F 9am-6pm, Sa 10am-5pm.) The **post office** is at 7 Great King St. (☎ 256690. Open M-F 9am-5:30pm, Sa 9am-12:30pm.) **Postal code:** DG1 1AA.

ACCOMMODATIONS AND FOOD

The closest **hostels** are miles away in Newton Stewart (Minigaaff) and Castle Douglas (Kendoon; p. 525). **B&Bs** are easy to find with the help of the TIC's *Accommodations Guide;* a number of reasonably priced abodes lie along **Lockerbie Rd.,** to the north of the city across the tracks. The friendly proprietors and unique decor of **Knock Guest House,** 1 Lockerbie Rd., more than make up for the noisy street. (☎ 253487. £15 per person). Try **Selmar House,** 41 Cardoness St., off Lockerbie Rd., for simple, refreshing rooms in a family environment. (☎ 250126. £16 per person.)

Cafes, bakeries, and fish and chip shops line **High St.,** and **Whitesands Rd.** also has some options for cheap grub. Fresh fruits and veggies are sold at **Loreborn Fruit and Vegetables,** Loreborn Rd. (Open M-Sa 9am-5pm.) At night, choices are scarce; however, a hot evening meal can be found at **The Queensberry Hotel,** 16 English St. Listen to the local football team extol their exploits as you gulp down a bowl of their excellent soup for £2. (☎ 253526. Open M-Sa 9am-9pm, Su noon-8pm; food served noon-3pm and 5-9pm.) If you're out for the night, grab a pint at the **Flesher's Arms,** Newell Terr. off Loreborn Rd. (Open M-W 10am-midnight, Th-Sa 10pm-1am.) You can dance off the calories across the street at **Chancers Night Club,** Munches St. (☎ 263170. Cover F-Sa £1-2. Open Th-Su 10pm-3am.)

SIGHTS AND FESTIVALS

It's all Robbie Burns. Pick up a free copy of *Dumfries: A Burns Trail* in the TIC; this helpful map has an easy-to-follow walking tour that covers all the major sights. Across the river, the **Robert Burns Centre,** Mill Rd., contains an uninspiring scale model of 18th-century Dumfries Town, and, of course, Robert Burns memorabilia, including a cast of his skull. A twenty-minute film runs through a sentimental version of Burns's life; the 10 million Burns songs make it worth the small fee. (☎ 264808. Open May.-Sept. M-Sa 10am-8pm, Su 2-5pm; Oct.-Mar. Tu-Sa 10am-1pm and 2-5pm. Free; film £1.50, concessions 75p.) In an ornate **mausoleum** in St. Michael's Kirkyard, St. Michael St., the poet rests in peace; an immaculate white marble Burns leans on a plow and seems surprised to see an attractive muse inspiring him overhead. The mausoleum was built in 1815 after admirers decided Burns's former grave was too ordinary. (☎ 255297. Free.) The wee **Burns House** on Burns St. contains many of the poet's original manuscripts and editions. Burns died here after aggravating an illness by bathing—on a doctor's advice—in a nearby well. (☎ 255297. Open Apr.-Sept. M-Sa 10am-5pm, Su 2-5pm; Oct.-Mar. Tu-Sa 10am-1pm and 2-5pm. Free.)

The **Dumfries Museum,** Church St., is yet another local museum with old tools, stuffed birds, and images of Dumfries through the ages. The top floor of the museum offers panoramic views from Britain's oldest camera obscura. (☎ 253374. Open Apr.-Sept. M-Sa 10am-5pm, Su 2-5pm; Oct.-Mar. Tu-Sa 10am-1pm and 2-5pm. Free. Camera obscura £1.50, concessions 75p, weather permitting.) The **Old Bridge House Museum,** Mill Rd., at the end of the bridge, packs eclectic period paraphernalia into four tiny rooms. Attractions include a chair once sat upon by Grierson of Lag, who had women tied to stakes on the beach while the tide came in because they wouldn't become Episcopalians. The fake teeth in the dentistry collection, juxtaposed with nightmarishly primitive equipment, conjure up scenes of gore. (☎ 256904. Open Apr.-Sept. M-Sa 10am-5pm, Su 2-5pm. Free.)

Dumfries's **Guid Nychburris Festival** (pronounced "good neighbors"), starting on the third Saturday in June, is a week-long celebration with performances and riding reenactments.

⚡ DAYTRIPS FROM DUMFRIES

CAERLAVEROCK CASTLE. Eight miles south of Dumfries on the B725 just beyond Glencaple is the moated, triangular Caerlaverock Castle (car-LAV-rick), one of Scotland's finest medieval ruins. No one is sure whether this strategic marvel was built for Scottish defense or English offense; it was seized by England's Edward I in 1300 and passed around like a hot kipper thereafter. *(Western Bus #371 runs to the castle from the Loreburn Shopping Centre, off Irish St. (not Loreburn Rd.), in Dumfries (M-Sa 12 per day, Su 2 per day; £1, return £1.80). ☎ (01387) 770244. Open Apr.-Sept. daily 9:30am-6:30pm; Oct.-Mar. M-Sa 9:30am-4:30pm, Su 2-4:30pm. £2.50, seniors £1.90, children £1.)*

SWEETHEART ABBEY. Also within easy reach is **Sweetheart Abbey,** seven miles southwest along the A710. The abbey was founded by Lady Devorguilla Balliol in memory of her husband John. She was later buried in the abbey with her husband's embalmed heart clutched to her breast—how romantic. *(Take MacEwan's bus #372 (M-Sa 15 per day, Su 5 per day; £1.30, return £2.35) to New Abbey from Dumfries's White-sands depot stand 5. ☎ (0131) 668 8800. Open Apr.-Sept. daily 9:30am-6:30pm; Oct.-Mar. M-W and Sa 9:30am-4:30pm, Th 9:30am-1pm, Su 2-4:30pm. £1.20, seniors 90p, children 50p.)*

RUTHWELL CHURCH. Nine miles southeast of Dumfries, the **Ruthwell Church** contains the magnificent 7th-century **Ruthwell Cross,** which bears dense carvings of vine scrolls and beasts of Celtic art, plus everyone's favorite Anglo-Saxon poem, *The Dream of the Rood*, in the margins—it's the oldest surviving fragment of written English in Scotland. Call Mrs. Coulthard (☎ (01387) 870249) to get the key to the church. *(Take a Western Buses bus to Annan via Clarencefield and get off at Ruthwell (30min.; M-Sa 1 per hr., Su every 2hr.; £1.40, return £2.55). Church free.)*

DRUMLANRIG CASTLE. Eighteen miles north of Dumfries off the A76 is the home of the Duke of Buccleuch. After perusing the art collection, enjoy the castle's marvelous grounds and country park. *(☎ (01848) 330248. Castle open by guided tour daily Apr.-Sept. 11am-5pm. Grounds open Apr.-Sept. daily 11am-5pm. Castle and grounds £6, students and seniors £4, children £2, families £14; grounds only £3, students and seniors, £2.)*

WANLOCKHEAD. One of Scotland's highest villages comes complete with nose-bleeds and a 28-bed **SYHA Youth Hostel.** (☎/fax (01659) 74252. Reception closed 10:30am-5pm. Open Apr.-Sept. daily, Mar. and Oct. F-Sa. Dorms £8.25, under 18 £7.25.) You can reach Wanlockhead by walking along the Southern Upland Way; there is an **Information Shelter** here. Some opt to hitch the B797, which branches off the A76 two miles south of Sanquhar, miles downhill from Wanlockhead.

CASTLE DOUGLAS ☎01556

Halfway between Dumfries and Kirkcudbright, Castle Douglas resembles every town in Scotland's southwest in that it has marvelous gardens and a castle within its reach; however, there's nothing in the town itself. One mile west, the 60-acre **Threave Garden** bursts with blooms gingerly pruned by students of the School of Gardening. (☎ 502575. Garden open daily 9:30am-sunset, walled garden and glasshouses open daily 9:30am-5pm. £4.50, children £3.) Buses #500 and 501 between Kirkcudbright and Castle Douglas pass the Garden turnoff; ask the driver to stop, and walk for 10 minutes. A mile or two farther west, the ruins of ▓ **Threave Castle** command an island on the River Dee. Threave was the last stronghold of the Earls of Douglas to surrender to James II in 1453; it was taken again and ravaged in 1640 by Covenanters. The Kirkcudbright-Castle Douglas bus can drop you off at the roundabout on the A75; follow signs for Threave Castle on the road that ends at

Kelton Mains Farm. Follow the path until you see the roofless keep; when you ring the ship's bell nearby, a boatman should arrive to ferry you across the river. (Open Apr.-Sept. daily 9:30am-6:30pm; last boat 6pm. £2, seniors £1.50, children 75p; ferry included.) Southeast from Castle Douglas, through the town of Dalbeattie, lie the **beaches** at **Sandyhill** and **Rockcliffe**.

MacEwan's buses #500 and 501 zip to Castle Douglas from Kirkcudbright (12 per day, £1.40); check the return schedule before heading to the castle. For beds nearby, ask the staff at the **tourist information centre**, Market Hill, to help you find a room. (☎ 502611. Open June-Aug. M-Sa 10am-5:30pm, Su 11am-5pm; Apr.-May and Sept.-Oct. M-Sa 10am-5pm.) A **Royal Bank of Scotland** rules on King St. To reach the simple but charming **SYHA Kendoon Hostel**, take the A713 north to Dalry, turn off and follow the A702 towards Moniaive for less than a quarter mile, then make a left onto the B700 north towards Carsphairn; the hostel is three miles ahead on your left. (☎ (01644) 460680. Self-catering only. Open mid-Mar. to Sept. Dorms £6.75, under 18 £6.) **Mrs. Laidlaw**, 33 Abercromby Rd., a five-minute walk from town, runs a B&B close to bird watching, fishing and walking trails. (TV lounge. Doubles £36.)

KIRKCUDBRIGHT ☎01557

Attractive and dignified, Kirkcudbright (car-COO-bree) gracefully occupies its coastal spot in the center of Dumfries and Galloway. Old Scottish buildings and Georgian homes line the angular High Street of this small town. Artists and dreamers have fled here for centuries, and if you are in the region, you should too.

GETTING THERE AND PRACTICAL INFORMATION. Buses #500, 501, and 505 travel from **Dumfries** (1 per hr.) and bus #431 comes from **Newton Stewart** (1hr.; M-Sa 7-8 per day, Su 2 per day; £2.65), sometimes beginning in **Stranraer**. The **tourist information centre**, Harbour Sq., books rooms for £1. (☎ 330494; fax 332416. Open daily mid-June to mid-Sept. 9:30am-5:30pm; mid-Sept. to Oct. 10am-4:30pm; Apr.-June 10am-5pm.) The **Royal Bank of Scotland**, 37 St. Mary St., lies at the corner of St. Cuthbert St. (☎ 330492. Open M-Tu and Th-F 9:15am-4:45pm; W 10am-4:45pm.) Services include: **Shirley's Laundrette**, 20 St. Cuthbert St. (☎ 332047; wash £2, dry £2); **Internet access** at the library, Sheriff Court House, High St. (☎ 31240; £3 per 30min., £5 per hr.; open M and W 2:30-7:30pm, Tu and F 10am-12:30pm and 2:30-7:30pm, Th 10am-12:30pm and 2:30-5:30pm, Sa 10am-12:30pm and 2-5pm); and the **post office**, 5 St. Cuthbert's Pl. (☎ 330578; open M-F 9am-12:30pm and 1:30-5:30pm, Sa 9am-12:30pm). **Postal code:** DG6 4DH.

ACCOMMODATIONS AND FOOD. Fabulous **Mrs. McIlwraith**, 22 Millburn St., runs a bright blue house with a fountained garden, oh-so-comfortable beds, and oh-so-hearty breakfasts. From the bus stop, turn left onto St. Cuthbert St., walk past the Safeway, and make a left onto Millburn St. at the school sign. (☎ 330056. Singles £16; twins £32.) **Mrs. McGeough**, 109 St. Mary St., offers beds in a house surrounded by roses, and a common room with a TV. If travelling by bus, ask the driver to stop at the garage on St. Mary St. and walk four houses to the left. (☎/fax 331885. Singles £18; doubles £32.) Pick up groceries at the **Safeway supermarket**, 52 St. Cuthbert St., at Millburn St. (☎ 330516. Open M-W and Sa 8:30am-6pm, Th-F 8:30am-8pm, Su 10am-4pm.) **The Royal Hotel**, St. Cuthbert St., offers an all-you-can-eat lunch buffet for £5, and a multi-course dinner for £6.50. A live band entertains on Sunday nights. (Lunch buffet M-Sa noon-2:30pm. Dinner F-Sa 6:30-9pm, Su noon-3pm. Open M-Sa 11am-11pm, Su noon-10:30pm.)

SIGHTS. The town's colorful harbor and idyllic surrounding countryside attracted a circle of prominent Scottish painters and designers who took residence in Kirkcudbright in the 1890s, transforming it into a hotbed of artistic creativity. Aspiring and established artists still frequent the town. An excellent gallery show details the town's history at the ▧ **Tolbooth Art Centre**, High St. An audio-visual show on the life of Jessie King, a preeminent Scottish artist, lasts about 15 minutes. The exhibit is housed in the oldest surviving tollbooth in Scotland (c. 1629-1762), which once imprisoned mariner John Paul Jones. (☎ 331556. Open July-Aug. M-Sa 10am-6pm, Su 2-5pm; Mar.-Apr. and Sept.-Oct. M-Sa 11am-4pm; May-June M-Sa 11am-5pm; Nov.-Feb. Sa 11am-4pm. £1.50, students and children 75p.)

Broughton House, 12 High St., displays the artwork (mostly carefree girls cavorting amidst wildflowers) of E.A. Hornel. The backyard is everything a British garden could hope to be, with bright green lawns, lily ponds, sundials, and greenhouses. Peek through the bushes over the wall for a splendid view of the harbor. (☎ 330437. Open daily Apr.-Oct. 1-5:30pm; July-Aug. from 11am. £2.50, concessions £1.70, families £6.70.) **MacLellan's Castle,** a 16th-century tower house, dominates the town from Castle St. near Harbour Sq. Sneak into the "Laird's Lug," a secret chamber behind a fireplace from which the Laird could eavesdrop on conversations in the Great Hall. It's not a bad ruin, but you'll spend 20 minutes here at most. (☎ 331856. Open Apr.-Sept. daily 9:30am-12:30pm and 1:30-6:30pm; Oct.-Nov. M-Sa 9:30am-4:30pm, Su 2-4:30pm. £1.80, seniors and children £1.30.)

About a mile west of town on the A75 is **Cardoness Castle,** a rocky stronghold of the McCullochs for five centuries. This is the only castle in Scotland with a two-seat toilet; if you ask nicely, the castle curator may let you try it out with a close friend. (☎ (0131) 668 8800. Castle open Apr.-Sept. daily 9:30am-6:30pm; Oct.-Mar. Sa 9:30am-4:30pm and Su 2-4:30pm. £2, seniors £1.50, children 75p. Toilet free.)

STRANRAER ☎01776

On the westernmost peninsula of Dumfries and Galloway, Stranraer (stran-RAHR) provides ferry access to Northern Ireland. Locals have a unique accent; most of the early inhabitants came from Ireland, and they are still often referred to as the Galloway Irish.

GETTING THERE AND SAILING AWAY. Trains (☎ (08457) 484950) come from **Glasgow** (2½hr.; M-Sa 4-7 per day, Su 2 per day; £15.30) and **Ayr** (M-Sa 7per day, Su 2 per day; £10.20). **Citylink** (☎ (08705) 505050) **buses** run from: **Ayr** (1½hr., 2 per day, £4.30); **Glasgow** (#923, 2½hr., 2 per day, £8.50); and **Dumfries** (#500; 3hr.; M-Sa 4-5 per day, Su 3 per day; £4.50). **National Express** (☎ (08705) 808080) lumbers from: **Carlisle** (2½hr., £14, students £10); **Manchester** (5½hr., 1 per day, £26, students £18); and **London** (9hr., 2 per day, £32, students £22). **Ferries** travel to Northern Ireland across the North Channel. **Stena Line** (☎ (0990) 707070; www.stenaline.co.uk) sails to **Belfast** (1¾hr., 5 per day, £25, students and seniors £20, children £13). Five miles up the coast at **Cairnyan, P&O Ferries** (☎ (0870) 242 4777) depart for **Larne** (1-2¼hr., 8 per day, £25, concessions £18). Sea passage is sometimes discounted with a rail ticket. See **By Ferry**, p. 35, for more information.

PRACTICAL INFORMATION. The tourist information centre, Harbour St., posts a list of B&Bs and books rooms for a deposit. Pick up the handy *What's On* guide as well. (☎ 702595; fax 889156. Open June-Sept. M-Sa 9:30am-5:30pm, Su 10am-4:30pm; Apr.-May and Oct. M-Sa 10am-5pm; Nov.-Mar. M-Sa 11am-4pm.) **Internet access** is available at the **Stranraer Public Library,** North Strand St., for £3 per 25min. or £5 per 55min. (☎ 707400. Open M-W and F 9:30am-7:30pm, Th 9:30am-5pm, Sa 9:30am-1pm and 2-4:30pm.) **Banks** are everywhere. The Tesco on Charlotte St. houses Stranraer's **post office.** (☎ 702587. Open M-W 8:30am-6pm, Th-F 8:30am-8pm, Sa 8am-6pm, Su 11am-2pm.) **Postal code:** DG9 74F.

ACCOMMODATIONS AND FOOD. If you're marooned, check B&Bs on the A75 (London Rd.) towards the castles, or try the ▨ **Jan Da Mar Guest House,** 1 Ivy Pl., on London Rd, whose owners supply nice rooms with fabulous new furniture and even better stories. (☎/fax 706194. Singles £18; twins £32.) If they're full, call **The Old Manse,** Lewis St., also near the ferries and town center. (☎ 702135. Singles £14; doubles £28.) The **Tesco** supermarket, on Charlotte St. at Port Rodie near the ferry terminal, burgeons with goods. (Open M-F 8:30am-8pm, Sa 8am-6pm, Su

10am-5pm.) When the sun starts to fade, the hip head to the creatively-named **The Pub,** 3 Hanover St. (☎ 705518. Open M-W 4pm-midnight, Th 4-10pm, Sa noon-1am, Su 12:30pm-midnight.)

🆑 **SIGHTS.** In town, the only sight is the **Castle of St. John,** George St., a 1510 edifice which looks more like an ill-designed building than a castle. (☎ 705544. Open Apr.-Sept. M-Sa 10am-1pm and 2-5pm. £1.20, children 60p.) Four miles east of Stranraer on the A75 lie the ivy-clad ruins of **Castle Kennedy,** which burned down in 1726. Bring a picnic and walk through the splendid gardens to the **Lochinich Castle,** present day home of the Earl of Stair. You can't enter his mansion of a home, but you can trample around his flower beds. Frequent buses run from Stranraer past the castle; it's about a mile off the main road. (☎ 702024. Open Apr.-Oct. daily 10am-5pm. Wheelchair access. £3, students and seniors £2, children £1.) Six miles out of Stranraer on the A75 you'll find the **Glenwahn Gardens,** replete with foreign and domestic plants and flowers, a man-made pond, and a pagoda with a view of the peninsula. (Open daily 10am-5pm. £2.50, students and seniors £2, children £1.)

WESTERN GALLOWAY

The two peninsulas of Western Galloway provide extensive coastlines with cliffs, beaches, and great views. The western peninsula, a north-south hammerhead, lies just 25 miles from Ireland across the North Channel.

PORTPATRICK. Eight miles southwest of Stranraer on the A77 is the quiet family vacation village of Portpatrick, one end of the **South Upland Way** (see p. 517). On weekends, wealthy yacht owners sail here from Northern Ireland for Sunday lunch—stroll by the harbor with your crusty bread and yearn for the good life. Sixteenth-century **Dunskey Castle** lies secluded on a spectacular cliff overlooking the ocean, a 20min. walk from Portpatrick harbor. On the left side of the harbor as you face the water, a long flight of steps leads up to the path to the castle. Dunskey might be the most secluded, romantic castle you'll visit; beautiful wildflowers and stunning sea views await. Unfortunately, the castle was recently purchased by a German entrepreneur and access to the ruins themselves has been restricted.

   Bus #367 makes it to Portpatrick from **Stranraer** (Tu and Th also #411; 20min.; M-F 5-8 per day, Sa 7 per day; return £2.10). Several **caravan parks** back onto the castle and cliffs; to reach them, turn left after the war memorial on the A77 from Stranraer. The **Castle Bay Caravan Park,** the farthest down the road, has a breathtaking stretch of lawn and excellent facilities, including showers, bathrooms, and a giant amusement room. (☎ (01776) 810462. £5 per tent.)

SANDHEAD, PORT LOGAN, AND DRUMMORE. At **Sandhead,** south of Stranraer on the eastern shore of the peninsula, the eerie **Kirkmadrine Stones,** three of the earliest Christian monuments in Britain, stand on a windswept hill. The *chi-rho* symbol (the first two Greek letters of Christ's name) and other inscriptions date from the 5th or 6th century. Bus #407 on the Stranraer-Stoneykirk-Drummore line stops at Sandhead (4 per day, return £2.20); from Sandhead follow the signposts for about 2 mi. off the A716. In **Port Logan,** between Sandhead and Drummore, you'll find the **Logan Botanic Garden.** Audio tours guide you through their famous Walled Garden and tranquil Woodland Garden. (Open daily Mar-Oct. 9:30am-6pm. £3, students and seniors £2.50, children £1, families £7.) Four miles south of **Drummore** you'll reach Scotland's southernmost point. Follow the footpath beyond the lighthouse to a grassy cliff.

GLENLUCE AND GALLOWAY FOREST PARK. The **Pilgrim's Way** (see p. 523) begins at **Glenluce Abbey,** just northwest of the peninsula. The abbey has deteriorated since its founding in 1192 by Roland, Earl of Galloway; only the chapterhouse retains a roof (and some killer acoustics). Legend has it that a wizard lured the Black Plague into the abbey's cellar and starved it to death. Take bus #500 from Stranraer to Glenluce and walk 1½ mi. north along the road to New Luce. (☎ (0131) 668 8800. Open Apr.-Sept. daily 9:30am-6:30pm; Oct.-Mar. Sa 9:30am-4:30pm, Su 2-4:30pm. £1.80, seniors £1.30, children 75p.) Northeast of Stranraer is **Galloway Forest Park,** which surrounds **Glen Trool.** A 240-square-mile inland reserve with peaks over 2000 ft., the park offers superb day-hikes and camping. Call the Newton Stewart Forest District (☎ (01671) 402420).

GLASGOW ☎0141

Competing with Edinburgh for the title of cultural heart of Scotland, Glasgow, Scotland's largest city (pop. 675,000), teems with free museums, extensive galleries, and first-rate theaters. Though previously thought of as less-than-attractive, Glasgow was named UK City of Architecture and Design in 1999, and rightfully so: the professional city center is a grid of structural wonders, while the West End, a mile northwest, overflows with artistic energy. A small town until the union of the Scottish and English crowns in 1603, Glasgow grew through exploiting new markets—first tobacco, then heavy industry. It became the greatest center of shipbuilding and steel production in the world, and eventually, a Victorian city second in importance only to London. Modern Glasgow remains self-assured and urbane—less touristy than its rival to the east, its energy comes from spirited locals. With millions of pounds poured into the arts, a flourishing economy, and a passion for football (Glasgow's two clubs, Celtic and Rangers, have long dominated the Scottish league), the city remains unforgettable.

✈ GETTING THERE

Glasgow lies on the Firth of Clyde, 45 minutes west of Edinburgh. The M8 motorway links east and west coasts and Scotland's two largest cities.

Flights: Glasgow Airport (☎ 887 1111), 10 mi. west in Abbotsinch. Scotland's major airport, served by **Aer Lingus, British Airways,** and others. Scottish Citylink buses run to Buchanan Station (20min., 2 per hr., £3) and to Edinburgh (1¾hr., 2 per hr., £8).

Trains: Bus #398 runs between Glasgow's two main stations (4 per hr., 50p, children 30p), but it's only a 10min. walk.

Central Station, Gordon St. U: St. Enoch. Serves trains from southern Scotland, England, and Wales. Open daily 5:30am-midnight. Travel center open M-Sa 5:30am-10pm, Su 8am-10pm. Bathrooms 20p; shower with soap and towel £2; open M-Sa 5am-midnight, Su 6am-midnight. Lockers £2-4, for up to a day; all luggage is searched; open daily 6am-midnight. Trains (☎ (08457) 484950) from: **Ardrossan,** connecting to ferries to Brodick on the Isle of Arran (1hr., 10-12 per day, £4.40); **Dumfries** (1¾hr.; M-Sa 7 per day, Su 2 per day; £9.20); **Stranraer** (2½hr.; M-Sa 8 per day, Su 3 per day; £15.30); **Liverpool** (4hr., 1 per hr., £51, return £39.90); **Manchester** (4hr., 1 per hr., £51, return £39.90); and **London King's Cross** (5-6hr.; M-F 16 per day, Sa 20 per day, Su 5 per day; £50).

Queen St. Station, beside Copthorne Hotel, George Sq. U: Buchanan St. Serves trains from the north and east. Open M-Sa 5am-12:30am, Su 7am-12:30am. Travel center open M-Sa 5:15am-11:15pm, Su 7am-11pm. Bathrooms 20p. Lockers £2-4; all luggage is scanned; open M-Sa 7:30am-9:15pm, Su 11:15am-7pm. Trains (☎ (08457) 484950) from: **Edinburgh** (50min., 2 per hr., £7.30); **Aberdeen** (2½hr.; M-Sa 1 per hr., Su 11 per day; £36); **Inverness** (3¼hr., 5 per day, £30); and **Fort William** (3¾hr.; M-Sa 3 per day, Su 2 per day; £20).

Buses: Buchanan Station (☎ 332 7133), 2 blocks north of Queen St. Station on North Hanover St. The station houses National Express and Scottish Citylink buses. Bathrooms 20p. **Luggage storage** £2-4 per item. Lockers open daily 6:30am-10:30pm. Ticket office open M-Sa 6:30am-10:30pm, Su 7am-10:30pm. **Scottish Citylink** (☎ (08705) 505050) from: **Edinburgh** (1hr.; M-Sa 4 per hr., Su 2 per hr.; £3); **Perth** (1½hr., 1 per hr., £7.50); **Oban** (3hr.; M-Sa 3 per day, Su 2 per day; £10.70); **Inverness** (3½-4½hr., 1 per hr., £12.80); and **Aberdeen** (4hr., 1 per hr., £14.50). **National Express** (☎ (08705) 808080) arrives daily from **London** (8-18hr., 1 per hr., £22, return £31).

⊟ GETTING AROUND

Travel Center: Strathclyde Transport Authority runs an immensely useful travel center, St. Enoch's Sq., two blocks from Central Station, dishing out transport advice, passes, and Underground maps. (☎ 332 7133. U: St. Enoch. Open M-Sa 8:30am-5:30pm.)

Public Transportation: Glasgow's transportation system includes suburban rail, a variety of private local bus services, and the circular **Underground (U)** subway line, a.k.a. the "Clockwork Orange." U trains run M-Sa 6:30am-midnight, Su 11am-6pm; 80p, children 40p. **Underground Season Tickets** are a good deal at £6 for 7 days (children £3), or £20 for 28 days (children £10); bring a photo and ID to the Underground office at St. Enoch station. The **Day Discovery Pass** can be used on the Underground after 9:30am (£2.50). For a whirlwind tour, see if you can travel fast and far enough to get your money's worth from a **Roundabout Glasgow ticket,** which covers one day of unlimited Underground and train travel (£3.50, children £1.75). The **Daytripper Ticket** gives families unlimited travel throughout the Strathclyde region (which includes Glasgow) by rail, Underground, most buses, and some ferries (1 adult and 2 children £7.50, 2 adults and 4 children £13). Wave your hand to ensure that **buses** stop for you, and carry exact change (fares usually 45-95p, depending on destination).

Taxis: Wide TOA Taxis (☎ 429 7070). **Albany Cars** (☎ 556 3111 or 554 4469).

❄ ORIENTATION

George Sq. is the center of town; the stations, tourist information centre (TIC), and cathedral are within a few blocks. Sections of **Sauchiehall St.** (SAW-kee-hall), **Argyle St.,** and **Buchanan St.** are pedestrianized, forming busy shopping districts in the city center. As an old Glasgow saying has it, "if you go up Sauchie and down Bucky, you will have shopped your heart out." **Charing Cross,** in the northwest where Bath St. crosses the M8 Motorway, is used as a locator. The vibrant **West End** revolves around **Byres Rd.** and **Glasgow University,** a mile northwest of George Sq.

⁊ PRACTICAL INFORMATION

TOURIST, FINANCIAL, AND LOCAL SERVICES

Tourist Information Centre: 11 George Sq. (☎ 204 4400; fax 221 3524), off George Sq. south of Buchanan and Queen St. Stations, northeast of Central Station. U: Buchanan St. Travel bookshop, accommodations bookings £2 (local) or £3 (national) plus 10% deposit, theater tickets, car rental, Cal-Mac ferry tickets, Western Union money transfers, and a **bureau de change.** Pick up the free *Essential Guide to Glasgow, City Live!* (entertainment), and *Where to Stay.* Open July-Aug. M-Sa 9am-8pm, Su 10am-6pm; June and Sept. M-Sa 9am-7pm, Su 10am-6pm; Oct.-May M-Sa 9am-6pm.

Tours: Glasgow City Walk (☎ 579 7976) sets off from the TIC M-Sa 6pm, Su 10:30am. Historic 1½hr. tours leave at 2pm and ghost tours at 7pm and 9pm. £5, concessions £4. **Discovering Glasgow** (☎ 204 0444) buses leave from George Sq., 2 per hr. 9:30am-4pm. £7, students and seniors £5.50, under 14 £2, families £15. The green-and-cream **Guide Friday** buses also run from George Sq., 2 per hr. 9:30am-5pm. £7, students and seniors £5.50, under 12 £2, families £15.

Financial Services: Banks are easily found. **Thomas Cook,** 15-17 Gordon St. (☎ 204 4484), rests inside Central Station. Open M-W and F-Sa 8:30am-6:30pm, Th 8:30am-7:30pm, Su 10am-4pm.

American Express: 115 Hope St. (☎ (08706) 001060). Open Jul.-Aug. M-F 8:30am-5:30pm, Sa 9am-5pm; Sept.-June M-F 8:30am-5:30pm, Sa 9am-noon.

Launderette: Coin-Op Laundromat, 39-41 Bank St. (☎ 339 8953). U: Kelvin Bridge. Soap and change available. Open M-F 9am-7:30pm, Sa-Su 9am-5pm.

Glasgow

▲ ACCOMMODATIONS
Alamo Guest House, 2
Backpackers Hostel, 4
Baird Hall, 9
Berkeley Globetrotters
& Blue Sky, 8
Bunkum Backpackers, 7
Cairncross House, 1
Campus Village, 12
Glasgow Euro Hostel, 11
Hillview Guest House, 6
Kelvin Lodge, 5
McLay's Guest House, 10
Seton Guest House, 14
SYHA Youth Hostel, 3
YMCA Aparthotel, 13

EMERGENCY AND COMMUNICATIONS

Emergency: ☎ 999 or ☎ 112; no coins required.

Police: (☎ 532 3000), Stewart St.

Hospital: Glasgow Royal Infirmary, 84-106 Castle St. (☎ 211 4000).

Internet Access: Internet Exchange Internet Cafe, 136 Sauchiehall St. (☎ 353 0535). Non-members £5.50 per hr. Members £1.80-4.20 per hr., depending on time of day. Free membership—join! **The Internet Cafe,** 569 Sauchiehall St. (☎ 564 1052). £3 per 30min., £5 per hr. (plus an extra 30min. free if you pay for an hour in advance). Concessions £2.50 for 30min. Open M-Th 9am-11pm, F 9am-7pm, Sa-Su noon-7pm.

Post Office: Post offices are sprinkled about the city center on Bothwell St., Sauchiehall St., Hope St., and Renfrew St. near George Sq. The main one is at 47 St. Vincent St. (☎ 204 3688). Open M-F 8:30am-5:45pm, Sa 9am-5:30pm. **Postal Code:** G2 5QX.

⌐ ACCOMMODATIONS

Glasgow undergoes a bed shortage in the warmer months. Book guesthouses, B&Bs, and hostels at least a month in advance, especially in August. Last-minute planners will probably have to stay on the outskirts, particularly at the accessible and elegant **SYHA Loch Lomond** (see p. 548) or the **SYHA New Lanark** (see p. 538). If you enjoy paying £16-20 for mediocre urban B&Bs, the TIC can often find you a room. If you'd rather wander, come early; most of Glasgow's B&Bs scatter to either side of the **Great Western Rd.** in the university area or east of the Necropolis near **Westercraigs Rd.** The universities have a lot of summer housing, but the available dorms often change from year to year; check at the offices listed below.

HOSTELS

▧ **Bunkum Backpackers,** 26 Hillhead St. (☎/fax 581 4481). Friendly proprietors Jim and Jean provide a fun hostel and excellent advice about the city. Though located away from the city center, Bunkum is minutes away from the West End and its infamous pubs and museums. Dorm rooms have more space than you can imagine as well as comfy beds, and many have wall-length windows. Common room with TV, a large selection of movies, and a pianola. Free lockers (deposit required), laundry facilities (£1.50 wash), kitchen and Internet access. Some parking available. Dorms £9, weekly £45.

Glasgow Backpackers Hostel, 17 Park Terr. (☎ 332 9099). U: St. George's Cross or Charing Cross. Good location in the West End, just minutes away from the lively party scene. Clean, friendly, and extremely social hostel. Laundry service (£2.50 for wash, dry and fold), Internet access, self-catering kitchen, and you get your own bed—no bunks! Open July-Sept. Dorms £10.50; twins £24.

SYHA Glasgow, 7-8 Park Terr. (☎ 332 3004; fax 331 5007), in a lovely residential area overlooking Kelvingrove Park. U: St. George's Cross. From Central Station, take bus #44 from Hope St. and ask for the first stop on Woodlands Rd. (at Lynedoch St.), then follow the sign. From Queen St. Station or Buchanan Station, catch bus #11 on Bath St. Once the residence of an English nobleman and later an upscale hotel, this hostel maintains an air of luxury. All rooms with shower. TV and game rooms, bike shed, laundry facilities, kitchen. Breakfast included. Dorms July-Aug. £13.75, under 18 £12.25; Sept.-June £12.25, under 18 £11.25.

Kelvin Lodge Backpackers Hostel/B&B, 8 Park Circus, (☎ 331 2000; contact@backpackersglasgow.co.uk). The hostel has large rooms, comfy beds, a kitchen, a common room with TV, laundry, and parking. Occupied by students during term, many of the B&B rooms are quite large, with plenty of shelf and desk space, and some incredible views over the city. All come with TV and telephone. Hostel open year-round: dorms £11, twins £15 per person. B&B available July-Sept.: doubles £40, with bath £46.

Glasgow Euro Hostel (☎ 446 0066; info@euro-hostels.com), corner of Clyde St. and Jamaica St. opposite Central Station. In an excellent location in the city center, this hostel used to be University of Strathclyde housing. 378 beds, 4-14 people per room; **Internet access,** laundry, kitchen, breakfast included. Dorms £13.75.

UNIVERSITY DORMS

University of Strathclyde, Office of Sales and Marketing, 50 Richmond St. (☎ 553 4148). B&B in summer at a number of campus dorms. **Baird Hall,** 460 Sauchiehall St. (☎ 332 6415). Small kitchen on each floor, nicely furnished rooms in a grand location, laundry facilities, and towels. No lockout or curfew. Available mid-June to Sept. Singles £19; twins £33. Also 11 **guest rooms** usually filled by visiting professors. Available year-round. Wheelchair access. Singles £20.50; twins £34.

University of Glasgow, 52 Hillhead St. (☎ 330 5385; fax 334 5465). Summer housing at several dorms. Office open M-F 9am-5pm. **Cairncross House,** 20 Kelvinhuagh Pl. (☎ 221 9334), offers housing off Argyle St., near Kelvingrove Park. Tea and coffee, soap, towels, and linen provided. Self-catering. Student dorms £13.50.

B&BS

Seton Guest House, 6 Seton Terr. (☎ 556 7654; fax 402 3655; passway@seton.prestelco.uk). A 20min. walk east of George Sq., or hop on bus #6, 6A, or 41A. Kindly hosts keep immaculate large rooms with ornate chandeliers. Out of the way, but all the quieter for it. Singles £17; twins £32.

Alamo Guest House, 46 Gray St. (☎ 339 2395), across from the Kelvingrove Museum. Gracious proprietors and spacious, quiet rooms. Singles £20-22; doubles from £34.

Hillview Hotel, 18 Hillhead St. (☎ 334 5585), near Glasgow University, on a street lined with B&Bs. U: Hillhead. Convenient for reaching Byres Rd. Comfortable rooms, each with TV and telephone. Light wood breakfast room, red carpets and walls everywhere else. Parking available. Singles £23; doubles £38.

McLay's Guest House, 268 Renfrew St. (☎ 332 4796; fax 353 0422), near the Glasgow School of Art and Sauchiehall St. With satellite TV and phones in each of the 62 rooms and 3 dining rooms, it looks and feels more like a hotel than a B&B. Singles £22, with bath £27; doubles £38, with bath £46; family room (sleeps 4) £51, with bath £60.

YMCA ApartHotel, David Naismith Court, 33 Petershill Rd. (☎ 558 6166; fax 558 2036). Take bus #12A or 16 from Queen St. Station, or #12 from Central Station. Comfortable rooms in a 30-floor monstrosity. TV lounge, game room. Restaurant and bar. Reception open 24hr. Kitchen flats available. B&B singles £20; doubles £30.

ⓘ FOOD

If you're in town for a while you might want to invest in the *Eating & Drinking Guide* ($3.50 from news agents or the TIC). Glasgow is often called "the curry capital of Britain," and for good reason. The area bordered by **Otago St.** in the west, **St. George's Rd.** in the east, and along **Great Western Rd., Woodlands Rd.,** and **Eldon St.** brims with cheap kebab 'n' curry joints. The presence of university students has bred a number of cheap hole-in-the-wall restaurants with excellent food. **Byres Rd.** and **Ashton Ln.,** a tiny hard-to-find cobblestone alley parallel to Byres Rd., thrive with cheap, trendy cafes and bistros. Bakeries along **High St.** below the cathedral serve scones for as little as 20p. For self-caterers, **Woodlands Grocers,** 110 Woodlands Rd. (☎ 353 3820), is open 24hr.

Insomnia Cafe, 38-40 Woodlands Rd. (☎ 564 1530), in the West End. The place to gorge, day or night, with eclectic dishes and a hip atmosphere. Dine on pasta with Italian sausage (£4.95) or satisfy a 4:30am craving for stuffed red peppers and leek risotto (£4.75)—all amidst energetic students and a bathtub/fishtank. The adjoining deli, **Crispins,** serves fresh sandwich platters for £2.95. Both open 24hr.

The Bay Tree Vegetarian Café, 403 Great Western Rd. (☎ 334 5898), at Park Rd. in the West End (cut through Kelvingrove Park). This popular, cramped cafe serves delicious vegan dishes in mid-sized portions. Pita bread with excellent hummus and salad £3.50-4.50. Wide variety of cakes 50p per piece. 10% student discount, 15% senior discount. Open M-Sa 9am-9pm, Su 9am-8pm.

Cafe Antipasti, 337 Byres Rd. (☎ 337 2737) and 305 Sauchiehall St. (☎ 332 9002). Excellent Italian food in a bustling but intimate atmosphere. Try the spinach and ricotta cannelloni. Pizzas, pastas, and fancy caesar salads with swordfish are all £5.45-7.45. Open daily 8am-11pm.

La Focaccia, 291 Byres Rd. (☎ 337 1642). Excellent pizzas and sandwiches on fresh focaccia for £3.95, takeaway £2.90. Not much room—grab your grub and hit the park.

The Willow Tea Rooms, 217 Sauchiehall St. (☎ 332 0521), upstairs from Henderson the Jewellers. A Glasgow landmark, designed by famed local architect Charles Rennie Mackintosh; everything in the building matches, down to the antiquated bathroom. Admire the silver and purple elegance of the well-preserved Mackintosh room while you sip one of 28 kinds of tea (£1.20-1.45 per pot), or snack on meringues with strawberries and cream for £2.10. 3-course afternoon tea £7.75. Open M-Sa 9:30am-4:30pm, Su noon-4:15pm.

Grosvenor Café, 31-35 Ashton Ln. (☎ 339 1848). Stuff yourself silly from the endless menu, but beware of the long lines. Desserts and stuffed rolls 95p-£1.20, bigger dishes £3-4. A more elaborate dinner menu (main courses £5.25-8.45) is available Tu-Sa 7-11pm. Open M 9am-7pm, Tu-Sa 9am-11pm, Su 10:30am-5:30pm.

🔆 SIGHTS

Glasgow is a budget sightseer's paradise, with grand museums, chic modern-art galleries, and splendid Georgian and Victorian constructions. Observe the ornate architectural detail of the buildings and sculptures from the view of a double-decker bus, or strain your neck as you walk by. Many of the best sights are part of the **Glasgow Museums** group, whose museums are scattered across the city and are all free. Pick up a free guide at the TIC. *The List* reviews current exhibitions and lists galleries (£1.95 from newsagents).

THE CITY CENTER

GEORGE SQUARE. This red-paved respite, with small patches of grass, lies in the busiest part of the city. Named for George III, the square's 80 ft. column was originally designed to support a statue of His Royal Highness. But, in the ultimate snub, Glaswegians replaced George with a statue of Sir Walter Scott. The author wears his plaid, as he always did, over the wrong shoulder (the right). The square is guarded on every side by several statues (12 in total, one of which usually has an orange traffic cone placed on its head by a student from Glasgow's School of Art). The **City Chambers,** on the east side of George Sq., conceal an ornate marble interior in Italian Renaissance style. Pop into the lobby for 30 seconds, or take a free tour starting at the main entrance. *(☎ 287 4017. Tours M-F 10:30am and 2:30pm.)* **The Gallery of Modern Art,** south of George Sq. on Queens St., is housed in a beautiful classical building, once the Royal Exchange, and displays not-so-classical art. *(☎ 229 1996. Open M-Th and Sa 10am-5pm, F and Su 11am-5pm. Wheelchair access. Free.)*

THE ST. MUNGO MUSEUM OF RELIGIOUS LIFE AND ART. The museum surveys every religion you can think of, from Hindu to Native American faiths to Yoruba. It features a fascinating exhibit on the intersection of sex, marriage, gender roles, and religion. Its prized possession is the spectacular *Christ of St. John's Cross* painting by Dalí. *(2 Castle St. ☎ 553 2557. Open M-Sa 10am-5pm, Su 11am-5pm. Free.)*

GLASGOW CATHEDRAL. This Gothic cathedral was the only full-scale cathedral spared the fury of the mid-16th-century Scottish Reformation. The cathedral's lime-green slanted roof and blackened exterior, reminding everyone of Glasgow's industrial past, contrast sharply with the ornate carvings and marvelous stained glass of the interior. Its stained glass is mostly post-war: look for the purple Adam and Eve in the western window, rendered in graphic detail. The Victorians would not have been amused. *(Castle St.; walk to the eastern end of Cathedral St. behind Queen St. Station. ☎ 552 6891. Open Apr.-Sept. M-Sa 9:30am-6pm, Su 2-5pm; Oct.-Mar. M-Sa 9:30am-4pm, Su 2-4pm. Organ recitals held some Tu in July and Aug. 7:30pm. Free.)*

NECROPOLIS. In this spectacular and terrifying hilltop cemetery, inspired by Paris's Père Lachaise, tombstones, statues, and obelisks lie aslant, broken and flat on the ground. A 50 ft. high statue of John Knox, leader of the Scottish Reformation, tops the hill where amazing views of the city await, interlaced through silhouettes of crosses and markers. Wander amid the 20 ft. tall tombs of most of the city's 19th-century industrialists and remember where all paths of glory lead. At night, visit at your own risk, and watch out for wandering spirits. *(Behind the cathedral. Free. And very cool.)*

OTHER CENTRAL SIGHTS. Built in 1471 and the oldest house in Glasgow, **Provand's Lordship,** near the St. Mungo Museum, now preserves a collection of heavy old furniture in musky air. The garden features some of Glasgow's finest healing herbs. *(3-7 Castle St. ☎ 553 2557. Open M-Th and Sa 10am-5pm, F and Su 11am-5pm. Free.)* In their eagerness to join the Industrial Revolution, Glaswegians destroyed most remnants of their medieval past, only to recreate it later on the ground floor of the **People's Palace** museum, which now recounts the city's history. *(On Glasgow Green by the river. ☎ 554 0223. Open M-Th and Sa 10am-5pm, F and Su 11am-5pm. Free.)*

THE WEST END

▧ KELVINGROVE PARK AND ART GALLERY. Starting one block west of Park Circus is Kelvingrove Park, a large wooded expanse on the banks of the River Kelvin, where locals tan on the grassy slopes, students read books, and senior citizens rest beneath the trees. In the southwest corner of the park sits the magnificent, spired **Kelvingrove Art Gallery and Museum.** The excellent art collection includes works by Rembrandt, Monet, van Gogh, Renoir, and Cezanne. The museum includes a display on arms and armor (from medieval knights to imperial stormtroopers), as well as silver, clothing, and natural history exhibits. The building, which is rumored to have been built back to front (the true entrance faces the park, not the street), often houses marvelous temporary exhibits. *(On the corner of Argyle St. and Sauchiehall St. U: Kelvin Hall. ☎ 287 2699. Tours of art collection at regular intervals. Open M-Th and Sa 10am-5pm, F and Su 11am-5pm. Free.)*

MUSEUM OF TRANSPORT. Housing old cars, trains, horse-drawn carriages, fire engines, ambulances, and bicycles, the Museum of Transport is a must for everyone who has been caught saying "Do we really have to walk all the way there?" *(On Argyle St., near the Kelvingrove Museum. Wheelchair access off Old Dunbarton Rd. ☎ 221 9600. Open M-Th and Sa 10am-5pm, F and Su 11am-5pm. Free.)*

UNIVERSITY OF GLASGOW. The central spire of the university, a Gothic revival building devised by Gilbert Scott, is visible from afar. The main building is on University Ave., which runs into Byres Rd., a busy thoroughfare in the West End. The best overall view of the university buildings is from Sauchiehall St. by the Kelvingrove Park, but the structures are worth a zoomed-in look as well. *(U: Hillhead.)* While you're walking the campus that has churned out 57 Nobel laureates, stop by the **Hunterian Museum.** The oldest museum in Scotland includes a death mask of Bonnie Prince Charlie. There is a huge coin collection upstairs, which was second only to the King of France's when it was established. *(☎ 330 4221. Open M-Sa 9:30am-5pm. Free.)* The **Hunterian Art Gallery,** across the street, displays 19th-century Scottish art, a sizeable Whistler collection, and reconstructed rooms from the house of Charles Rennie Mackintosh. *(☎ 330 5431. Open M-Sa 9:30am-5pm. Free.)*

BOTANIC GARDENS. At the end of Byres Rd. lie the beautiful, serene Botanic Gardens. The drab, glorified greenhouse **Kibble Palace** houses a fish pond and some exotic but unimpressive plants, though the Neoclassical statues lend the palace an air of elegance. **Main Range,** another greenhouse, contains hot and humid rooms with gorgeous, impressive orchids, ferns, palms, and cacti. *(Great Western Rd. ☎ 334 2422. Gardens open daily 7am-10pm. Kibble Palace and Main Range open daily Apr. to late Oct. 10am-4:45pm; late Oct. to Mar. 10am-4:15pm; Main Range opens Sa 1pm, Su noon. All free.)*

SOUTHERN SCOTLAND

THE GALLERY FOR CONTEMPORARY ART. The gallery is temporarily housed in the **McLellan Galleries,** 270 Sauchiehall St., until its building is finished being renovated in late 2001. It holds temporary visual art displays, as well as numerous musical and theater performances. *(☎ 332 7521, box office ☎ 332 0522. Open M-F 10am-6pm, Su 11am-6pm. Gallery free. Performances £4-10, some student discounts.)*

CHARLES RENNIE MACKINTOSH BUILDINGS. Several buildings designed by Charles Rennie Mackintosh, Scotland's most famous architect, are open to the public. Pick up the free leaflet *Charles Rennie Mackintosh: Buildings & Tours Guide* at the TIC or any Mackintosh sight and plan your route. The best place to start is probably the **Glasgow School of Art,** 167 Renfrew St., completed in 1898. Here, Mackintosh fused wrought iron, sweeping bay windows, Scottish Baronial styles, and Art Nouveau influences to create a uniquely Glaswegian Modernist style. *(☎ 353 4526. Interior tours M-F 11am and 2pm, Sa 10:30am; July-Aug. also Sa-Su 10:30am, 11:30am, and 1pm. £5, students £3.)* The Charles Rennie Mackintosh Society is based at the stark **Willow Tea Rooms;** stop by to imbibe in Mackintosh surroundings (see **Food,** p. 534).

POLLOK COUNTRY PARK. In the large Pollok Country Park, 3½ mi. south of town but worth the trek, **Pollok House,** a lovely 18th-century mansion, has a fine array of Spanish paintings. Take bus #45, 48, or 57 (£1.20) from Jamaica St. *(☎ 616 6410. Open M-Th and Sa 10am-5pm, F and Su 11am-5pm. Free.)* Also in the park, the **Burrell Collection,** Sir William Burrell's personal collection of 19th-century French paintings, Chinese ceramics, and Persian tapestries, is housed in an award-winning patchwork building. *(☎ 287 2550. Open M-Th and Sa 10am-5pm, F and Su 11am-5pm. Free.)*

SHOPPING. Princes Square is a gorgeous high-end shopping mall—the classiest place to shop outside London. *(48 Buchanan St. ☎ 221 0324.)* A new shopping center, the **Buchanan Galleries,** is at the end of Buchanan St. If your wallet has any life left, hit **Sauchiehall Street,** which has shops and art galleries as well.

◪ NIGHTLIFE

Glaswegians have a reputation for partying hard. Three universities and the highest student-to-resident ratio in Britain guarantee a kinetic nightlife scene.

PUBS

There are hundreds of pubs in the city, and you'll never find yourself much more than half a block from a frothy pint. The infamous **Byres Rd.** pub crawl slithers past the Glasgow University area, beginning at Tennant's Bar and proceeding toward the River Clyde. Drinks are cheap to start with, but watch for happy hours, when many pubs reduce prices to a joyous £1.

▨ **Uisge Beatha,** 232 Woodlands Rd. (☎ 564 1596). A Scottish bar with blackened wood furnishings, old paintings, and red velvet seats one step away from kilt-clad bartenders. "Uisge Beatha" (oos-ga BAY-uh) is Gaelic for "water of life" (read: whisky). Over 100 malt whiskys, costing between £1.85 and £35; make sure you order the right one. Sip the national drink as you listen to Gaelic tunes. Open M-Th 11am-11pm, F-Sa 11am-midnight, Su 12:30-11pm.

Cul de Sac Bar, 46 Ashton Ln. (☎ 334 4749). Various floors suit all sorts of styles. Ground floor sells expensive but tasty crepes (£7.95, half-price daily 5-7pm). First floor has an artsy, fun crowd of pre-clubbers. Top floor "attic" is where the pretentious escape the students. Happy hour 5-7pm. Open M-Sa 9am-midnight, Su noon-midnight.

Russell Bar-Cafe, 77 Byres Rd. (☎ 334 4973). The wood paneling outside makes this place seem like a log cabin in the middle of a blond sandstone building, but the Scottish pies (including haggis), live DJs, and meal deals make everything fine. All pasta dishes £1 after 8pm Su. Open Su-Th 11am-11pm, F-Sa 11am-midnight.

The Ark, 42-46 North Frederick St. (☎ 559 4331), near George Sq. File in two by two, and then drink plenty of beer amidst the bright colors, funky signs, and other animals. 4-pint pitcher £6. Cover some weekend nights. Open daily noon-midnight.

Nice 'n' Sleazy, 421 Sauchiehall St. (☎ 333 9637). Eclectic live music downstairs Sa-W, £2.50-3. Upstairs, it almost gets too loud for a bar, believe it or not. Happy hour Sa-Th 5-10pm, F 5-8pm; £6 gets you a 4-pint pitcher. Occasional cover Th-Sa. Open daily 11:30am-midnight.

Horseshoe Bar, 17-21 Drury St. (☎ 204 4056), one block north of Gordon St., off Reinfield St. This Victorian, horseshoe-shaped pub, with etched mirrors and carved wooden walls, is a Glasgow institution. The place boasts the longest continuous bar in the UK; up to 15 bartenders staff it when the mostly older male crowd begins to swell by mid-afternoon. Head upstairs for a hearty and popular 3-course lunch (£2.80; served M-Sa noon-2:30pm). Open M-Sa 8am-midnight, Su 12:30pm-midnight.

Variety Bar, 401 Sauchiehall St. (☎ 332 4449). Older men's pub by day, art student hangout by night. Cheap drinks make it a popular destination for backpackers. No frills, just a quality pub. Tu reggae, Th techno, F guest DJs, Sa Mystic Beats. Happy hour M-Sa 11am-8pm, Su 12:30-8pm: pints of lager £1.50; Guinness £1.60; vodka, rum, whisky dashes £1.35. Open M-Sa 11am-11:45pm, Su 12:30-11:45pm.

CLUBS

Most clubs are open 11pm-3am, but the bacchanalia reaches a fevered pitch after the pubs close. *The List* (£1.95 from newsagents) lets you know which club is best each night, but there is always a wild, wild party Thursday through Saturday.

Archaos, 25 Queen St. (☎ 204 3189). Look for two skeletons just outside the second floor windows. Frequent student discounts and musical variety pack in the punters. Thursday is the busiest student night in Glasgow; on Saturday put on your best, blackest, tightest duds to dance on the domed floor. Cover £3-9. Open W-Su until 3am.

Sub Club, 22 Jamaica St. (☎ 248 4600). All types grind to house and techno in the purple basement. Their "sub-culture Saturdays" have been running strong for over a decade. Cover £3-6, Sa £8. Open Th-F and Su 11pm-3am, Sa 11pm-3:30am.

Velvet Rooms, 520 Sauchiehall St. (☎ 332 0755). Where young 'uns get down. When you get tired of the funky hip-hop in one room, go enjoy the grunge in the other. Smart casual is usually OK, but most people dress up a bit. Cover £6, students £5. Open F-Sa 10pm-3am; W-Th, Su 11pm-3am.

The Garage, 490 Sauchiehall St. (☎ 332 1120). Beckons with Mad Hatter decor; look for the yellow truck hanging over the door. Dance club classics blast from downstairs; The Attic, upstairs, is indie. Cover £4-6; student discounts usually available. Open Sa 10:30pm-3am, Su-F 11pm-3am.

Cathouse, 15 Union St. (☎ 248 6606) Grunge and indie please mostly student crowds in the three floors. Cover £3-5; student £1-2 less. Open W-Su 10:30pm-3am.

♫ ❊ ENTERTAINMENT AND FESTIVALS

The dynamic student population of Glasgow ensures constant film, theater, and music offerings. *The List*, an excellent resource for the entertainment seeker, details the scenes in both Glasgow and Edinburgh (£1.95 from newsagents and the TIC). The **Ticket Centre,** City Hall, Candleriggs, will tell you what's playing at the city's dozen-odd theaters. Get the free *City Live* guide, which has great advice. (☎ 287 5511. Phones answered M-Sa 9am-9pm, Su noon-5pm; office open M-Sa 9:30am-6:30pm, Su 10am-5pm.) Theaters include the **Theatre Royal,** Hope St. (☎ 332 9000) and the **Tron Theatre,** 63 Trongate (☎ 552 4267). The **Cottier Theatre,** 935 Hyndland St. (☎ 357 3868) hosts a wide variety of musical and theatrical events, from avant-garde plays to opera (£4-25). The **Royal Concert Hall,** Sauchiehall St., is frequently the venue for concerts by the Royal Scottish National Orchestra. (☎ 353 8000. Box office open M-Sa 10am-6pm.) The **Glasgow Film Theatre,** 12 Rose St., screens sleeper hits and cult classics and also features a bar with food and art exhibitions. (☎ 332 8128. Call for wheelchair access. Box office open M-Sa noon-9pm, Su 30min. before first film. £4.75, matinees £3.75; concessions £3.25, £2.25.)

Among Glasgow's constant flow of musical shows, temporary art exhibitions, and festivals is the annual **Glasgow International Jazz Festival** (☎ 552 3552), in the first week in July, which draws jazz greats from all over the world. During mid-August, over 100 of the top kilt-clad bagpipe bands compete for glory and honor on the Glasgow Green at the **World Pipe Championships** (☎ 221 5414).

NEAR GLASGOW: LANARK   ☎01555

Thirty miles southwest of Glasgow, in the peaceful Clyde valley, the recreated village of **New Lanark** allows tourists to experience 19th-century utopian dreams of the Industrial Revolution. Founded in 1785, it was the most productive manufacturing site in Scotland for much of the 19th century. This was partly due to the somewhat socialist tendencies of the cotton-mill owner. Instead of sending 8-year-olds to work 12-hour days, Robert Owen sent them to school. He also paid workers decent wages, founded an Institute for the Formulation of Character, and started the first semi-cooperative village store and infant school. Visitors can walk through the restored store, a millworker's house, and Owen's own abode, which, despite his beliefs, was somewhat posh. The visitor center also lets you try out cloth production yourself. Admission to New Lanark includes the *New Millennium Experience*, a ride through scenes in New Lanark's colorful history. (☎ 661345. Open daily 11am-5pm. £3.95, concessions £2.95, families £10.95-12.95.) The river valley has lovely, free hikes. Walk a mile upstream past the hydro-power plant to the **Falls of Clyde**, where the waters turn white with foamy fury as they rocket down vertical drops.

To reach New Lanark, you'll need to go through **Lanark. Trains** (☎ (08457) 484950) from **Glasgow Central** (45min., 1 per hr., return £5) run to Lanark's **station.** (Ticket office open M-Sa 6:10am-10:10pm.) **Irvine's Coaches** (☎ (01698) 372452) shuttle from **Glasgow Buchanan St.** to **Lanark Interchange** (1hr., 5 per day). From Lanark, **Stuart's Coaches** (☎ 773533) run to New Lanark from the tourist information centre (1 per hr., 55p); otherwise, it's a 20min. walk. The **tourist information centre** is next to the train station. (☎ 661661; fax 666143. Open Apr.-Sept. M-Sa 10am-6pm, Su noon-5pm; Oct.-Mar. M-Sa 10am-5pm.) Pick up the free *Lanark Heritage Trail* guide, which details **Old St. Kentigern's Church,** where William Wallace supposedly married Marion Braidfute. The **post office** is at 28 St. Leonard St. (☎ 662230. Open M-F 9am-5:30pm, Sa 9am-12:30pm.) **Postal code: ML11 9AB.**

Stay at the **New Lanark Youth Hostel,** Wee Row, Rosedale St., a restored mill workers' dwelling with river views and modern luxuries only dreamed of by earlier occupants: laundry facilities, and attached baths in all rooms. Socialize with Paddy the dog—hey, traveling can be lonely. (☎ 666710; fax 666719. Continental breakfast included. Reception closed 10:30am-5pm. Curfew 11:45pm. Dorms £11.25, under 18 £10.) **Bankhead Farm,** near the corner of Braxfield Rd. and Lanark Rd., tenders spacious rooms with thick carpets, TVs, desks, and comfortable beds in a converted farmhouse. Take Braxfield Rd. out of the town center. (☎/fax 666560. £16-18 per person.)

THE PLAID FAD The tourist's desperate quest for his or her ancestral tartan has brought lots of business—and lots of amusement—to modern Scots. Tartans originally had no clan affiliation, but indicated only the geographic base of the weaver. It wasn't until the 19th century's mounting romanticization of the Scottish medieval past that the kilt craze really began. King George IV, who was fat, kicked it all off by buying £1354 worth of the Regal Stuart tartan and wearing most of it during his 1822 visit to Edinburgh. Very few clans actually had any defining plaid, but the shortage was solved by the happy 1842 publication of *Vestiarium Scotium* (a fraudulent "discovery" of an ancient manuscript revealing all). Today, tartans are mostly used for ceremonial occasions—and for milking tourists.

AYRSHIRE

AYR
☎01292

The city of Ayr (as in fresh AIR; pop. 49,500) makes a good base from which to explore the rolling hills and seaside cliffs of Ayrshire. The Scottish weather usually prevents you from getting a sunburn on the marvelous sandy beaches that line the coast; you will, however, be scorched with Robert Burns, the city's local hero. Home to his birthplace, the lovely—but unexciting—countryside of Ayrshire is full of first- to third-degree Burns sights.

GETTING THERE AND PRACTICAL INFORMATION. The **train station** is at the crossroads of Station Rd., Holmston Rd., and Castle Hill Rd. **Trains** (☎ (08457) 484950) travel from **Glasgow** (1hr., about 2 per hr., £5) and **Stranraer** (M-Sa 7 per day, Su 3 per day; £10.20). **Stagecoach** (☎ 613500) **buses** arrive from **Stranraer** (£5.85) and **Glasgow** (£3.30). For local transport info, call the **bus station,** 73 Sandgate, near Wellington Sq. (☎ 613500. Open M-Sa 8am-5pm.) The **tourist information centre** (TIC), 22 Sandgate, near the bus station, **changes currency** and provides free guides to history, cycling, and water sports. Pick up their version of *Let's Go*, a guide to events in Ayrshire and Arran. (☎ 288688. Open July-Aug. M-Sa 9am-6pm, Su 10am-5pm; Sept.-June M-Sa 9am-5pm.) **Banks** reside across from the Robert Burns statue on High St. Get **Internet access** at Carnegie Library, 12 Main St. (☎ 618492. £3 per hr. Open M-Tu and Th-F 10am-7:30pm, W and Sa 10am-5pm.) A **post office,** 65 Sandgate, stands near the TIC. (☎ 287264. Open M-Sa 9am-5:30pm.) **Postal code:** KA7 1AB.

ACCOMMODATIONS AND FOOD. The ▧ **SYHA Ayr,** Cragweil House, in a prime location at the corner of the Esplanade, offers breathtaking second-story views. The hostel is 15 minutes by foot from the town center; take a right off Racecourse Rd. onto Blackburn Rd. and then a right onto Cragweil Rd. (☎ 262322; fax 289061. Self-catering only. Laundry facilities; £1 wash, £1 dry, soap 20p. Curfew 11:45pm. Open Feb.-Dec. Dorms £9.25, under 18 £8.) If the hostel is full, try the **Tramore Guesthouse,** 17 Eglinton Terr. A few hundred meters from the town beach, this guesthouse has high ceilings and Moroccan decorations. (☎/fax 266019. £17 per person.) A gargantuan **Safeway** rests on Castlehill Rd. across the street from the train station. (☎ 283906. Open M-Th 8am-8pm, F 8am-9pm, Sa 8am-6pm, Su 9am-5pm.) For cheap sandwiches (£2.70-3.30) and other baked delights, head for **Café Ginger,** 57 Fort St., near the bus station. (☎ 264108. Open M-Sa 7:30am-5:30pm.) Drink at the most popular pub in town, the tartan-filled, proud-to-be-Scottish ▧ **Chapman Billie's,** near the town center on Dallair Rd. at Barnes St. (☎ 618161. Open M-Sa 1pm-12:30am, Su 1pm-12:30am.)

FESTIVALS. For horseracing fans, the **Ayr Racecourse,** host of the **Scottish Grand National** in April and the **Ayr Gold Cup** in September, promises untold equine thrills. (☎ 264179. Tickets £10-25; call for race dates.)

NEAR AYR

ALLOWAY

From Ayr's bus station, take Western bus #57 to Alloway (10min., 1 per hr., £1.60). The hop-on hop-off Burns Country Open Top Bus Tour takes you on an extended ride before reaching Alloway 30min. later (1 per hr. 10am-5pm from bus station; £3, children £1.50).

Two miles south of Ayr, the village of Alloway blazes with Burns sites. Visit the **Burns Cottage and Museum,** built by you-know-who's dad, where guess-who was born. The museum's excellent collection of Burns memorabilia redeems the too-touching tableaux of family life and realistic barnyard smells. (☎ (01292) 441215. Open Apr.-Oct. daily 9am-6pm; Nov.-Mar. M-Sa 10am-5pm, Su noon-4pm. £1.70, seniors and children 80p, families £4.) The **Tam o' Shanter Experience** supplies a presentation on the life of the poet as well as a multimedia enactment full of the lyricism of its namesake poem. (☎ (01292) 443700. Open daily Apr.-Oct. 9am-6pm, Nov.-Mar. 9am-5pm. £2.80, seniors and children £1.40, families £8; joint ticket with the Cottage and Museum £4.50, seniors and children £2.20, families £12.) The nearby **Burns Monument and Gardens** are free, and superb on a sunny summer day. Climb up for a view of the **Brig o' Doon,** a bridge featured in the "Tam o' Shanter" poem. Stop by the ruined **Alloway Kirk,** where, according to Burns, the devil played the bagpipes.

CULZEAN CASTLE

From Ayr take bus #60 to Culzean (30min., M-Sa 6 per day, day return £3.40); tell the driver where you're going, and follow the signs from the main road for about a mile. ☎ (01655) 760274. Castle open Apr.-Oct. daily 10:30am-5:30pm; park open year-round. Free tours daily July-Aug. 11am and 3:30pm. £7, seniors and children £5, families £18; park only £3.50, seniors and children £2.50, families £9.

Twelve miles south of Ayr, Culzean Castle (cul-LANE) perches on a coastal cliff. According to legend, one of the cliff's caves shelters the Phantom Piper who plays to his lost flock when the moon is full. The castle's famed oval staircase, designed by Robert Adam, looks more impressive in brochures than in real life, but there is a stunning armory. The top floor was given to Dwight Eisenhower for use during his lifetime, and lesser persons are not allowed up. The park can be accessed for free by walking north along the beach from the nearby town of Maidens and climbing an unguarded stairway.

ISLE OF ARRAN ☎ 01770

The glorious Isle of Arran (AH-ren; pop. 4750) justifiably bills itself as "Scotland in Miniature." Gentle lowland hills and majestic Highland peaks coexist on an island less than 20 mi. long. In the north, the gray, craggy peaks of Goatfell and the Caisteal range surge above the pine-filled foothills. Amid the bog-grass near the western coast, prehistoric stone circles and lone standing stones rise suddenly out of the mist. The eastern coastline winds south from Brodick Castle past the conical hump of Holy Island into meadows and white beaches. On sunny days, the waters turn crystalline, providing an enchanting view of the marine life below.

▐ GETTING THERE AND GETTING AROUND

To reach Arran, take a **train** (☎ (08457) 484950) to **Ardrossan** from **Glasgow Central** (45min.; M-Sa 5 per day, Su 4 per day; £4.40). From Ardrossan the **Caledonian-MacIntyre ferry** (☎ 302166) makes the crossing to **Brodick** on Arran in sync with the train schedule (1hr.; M-Sa 5 per day, Su 4 per day; £4.25). There's also ferry service to **Lochranza** on Arran from **Claonaig** on the Kintyre Peninsula (30min., usually mid-Apr. to mid-Oct. 8 per day, £3.90, bikes £1). When returning to Claonaig, be sure of your connection. Pick up a timetable at the tourist information centre (TIC).

Buses on the island run frequently, and for every ferry there is a connection to and from every part of the island. There are bus stops, but drivers will pick you up anywhere if you flag them down. The **Rural Day Card** grants a full day of travel on Arran's buses (available on the bus; £3, children £1.50). Pick up bus timetables at a TIC or on a bus. The **Stagecoach Western** office is at Brodick pier. (☎ 302000. Open daily 8am-5pm.) Stagecoach's **full-day tour** from Brodick Pier travels the perimeter of the island, stopping in Lochranza, Blackwaterfoot, and Whiting Bay. (Departs daily June-Sept. 11am, returns 4:20pm; £6, children £4.) The 45min. **open-top tour,** with taped commentary, passes some beautiful scenery from Brodick to Whiting Bay. (June-Sept. 6 per day, £3, children £2.)

⚠ HIKING AND BIKING

Despite Arran's proximity and excellent connections to Glasgow, large swaths of wilderness in the northwest and southeast remain untouched, and some of the villages in these areas are quiet and untouristed. The best walks on the island are well marked, but more demanding hikes are detailed in *Seventy Walks in Arran* (£2.50) and *My Walks of Arran* (£2.25), both available at the TIC. The Forestry Commission arranges various **guided walks** on the island (2-5hr.; £2-4, children free) as does the National Trust for Scotland (☎ 302462); schedules are at the Brodick TIC. The well-marked path up popular **Goatfell** (2866 ft.), Arran's highest peak, begins on the road between the Arran Heritage Museum and Brodick Castle. The hike averages 4-5 hours, but the view from the cold and windy peak is worth it; on a clear day, it includes the jagged Caisteal range to the north and Holy Island to the southeast. If you don't want to go back down the same way you came up, try descending through the village of **Corrie**. As always when mountain-climbing, be sure to wear warm, waterproof gear.

Biking on the hilly island is a rewarding challenge; the full circuit takes about 9 hours. Pick up a free copy of the SYHA's *Cycling on Arran. Let's Go* lists bike rental stores in Brodick and Blackwaterfoot. Rent cycles from **Whiting Bay Hires**, which deposits a rental van on the shore on nice days. (☎ 700382. £8 per day.) **Hitchhikers** report that getting rides out of Brodick isn't hard, though *Let's Go* never recommends hitching; elsewhere, locals are friendly, but pass infrequently.

BRODICK

Be sure to stay in Brodick for longer than the walk from the ferry pier to the bus stop. In addition to its major transportation connections, Arran's main town (pop. 2000) holds a glorious castle and some tasty restaurants—all against a backdrop of rugged mountains and a peaceful bay.

⎕ GETTING AROUND. Mini-Golf Cycles, behind the miniature golf course on Shore Rd., rents mountain and touring bikes. (☎ 302272. 21-speed bikes £8.50 per day, 10-speeds £7.50 per day, children's bikes £3.50 per day; helmets included. Deposit £10 plus ID. Open daily 9am-7pm.) **Brodick Cycles,** farther down Shore Rd., opposite the village hall and just past the post office, rents all kinds of bikes. (☎ 302460. £3-5.50 per 2hr., £5-9.50 per day, £17-36 per week; deposit £5-50. Open Easter-Sept. M-Sa 9am-1pm and 2-6pm, Su 10am-1pm and 2-6pm.)

⚠ PRACTICAL INFORMATION. The center of Brodick is along Shore Rd., to the right as you disembark from the ferry. A **Cal-Mac** office is at Brodick Pier. (☎ 302166. Open M-Sa 7:40am-5pm and 6:30-7:20pm, Su 10am-5pm and 6:30-7:20pm.) Arran's only **tourist information centre** answers questions at the base of the pier. The staff distributes free maps, updates a handy "What's On" bulletin board, and books local B&Bs for £1.50 plus a 10% deposit. (☎ 302140; fax 302395. Open June-Sept. M-Sa 9am-7:30pm, Su 10am-5pm; Oct.-May roughly M-F 9am-5pm, Sa 10am-5pm.) The **Royal Bank of Scotland** is on Shore Rd. (☎ 302222. Open M-Tu and Th-F 9am-5pm, W 10am-5pm.) The **launderette** is at the western end of Shore Rd., next door to Collins' Good Food Shop. (☎ 302427. Soap 45p, wash £2.40, dry 90p-£2. Open Th-Tu 9am-5pm, last wash 4:15pm; W 9am-4pm, last wash 3:15pm.) The **post office** is set back from Shore Rd. on Mayish Rd. (☎ 302245. Open M-F 9am-5:30pm, Sa 9am-12:45pm.) **Postal code:** KA27 8AA.

▟▙ ACCOMMODATIONS AND FOOD. Brodick B&Bs fill quickly, so call ahead. To reach the TV-equipped rooms of **Mrs. Macmillan,** Glenard House, Manse Rd., head away from the pier on Shore Rd. and turn left just after the Heathfield Hotel; it's the fourth house on the left. (☎ 302318. Open Apr.-Oct. Singles £18; doubles £36.) The ideally located seafront **Glenfloral B&B,** Shore Rd., has spacious rooms with TVs and a great vegetarian breakfast. (☎ 302707. £17 per person.) Mrs. Rayburn's **Crovie** promises a great view if you take a pleasant (if challenging) hike.

Take a left from the pier, and walk away from town on the main road; turn onto Crovie Rd. after a mile, and follow it for half a mile; Crovie is on your right. (☎ 302193. £17 per person.) The **Glen Rosa Farm,** two miles north of Brodick on the coastal road to Corrie (the B880), lets campers pitch tents. (☎ 302380. £2.50 per person; toilets and cold water available.) You can also look for grassy spots by the beach, but the golf course is off-limits.

At the **Co-op,** across from the ferry terminal, you can stock up on groceries. (☎ 302515. Open M-Sa 8am-10pm, Su 9am-7pm.) **Collins' Good Food Shop,** at the western end of Shore Rd. just past the bridge on your left, has outdoor seating next to a stream. Try the mouthwatering quiche (£1.05) and vegetarian haggis-filled rolls (£1.50); the shop also vends fruits and veggies. (☎ 302427. Open Th-Tu 9am-5pm, W 9am-4pm.) Cheap traditional fare (most main dishes £4-8) will find you at the **Stalkers Restaurant,** on Shore Rd. (☎ 302579. Open daily Apr.-Oct. 9am-9pm; Nov.-Mar. 9am-5pm.)

■ ▓ **SIGHTS AND FESTIVALS.** Shore Rd. becomes Low Glencloy Rd., which reaches the splendid ▓ **Brodick Castle** that surveys the harbor above fantastic wild and walled gardens. Built on the site of an old Viking fort and the ancient seat of the Dukes of Hamilton, the castle contains a fine porcelain collection, paintings, and scores of dead beasties. The Dukes supposedly shot everything that ran or flew, including 89 stags' heads that all ended up in the entrance hall. That's 178 baleful eyes waiting to greet you. Friendly guides wait in every room to share history lessons. If you can't visit the castle, look on the back of a Royal Bank of Scotland £20 note. Stagecoach runs a Vintage Coach service (June-Sept. 9 per day, return £2, children £1) to the castle from Brodick Pier. (☎ 302202. Castle open Apr.-June and Oct. daily 11am-4:30pm; July-Aug. daily 11am-5pm; gardens open daily 9:30am-dusk. Castle and gardens £6, concessions £4; gardens only £2.50, concessions £1.70.) The wooded **country park** around the castle has marked trails for walks. The rangers run **guided walks** 3 times per week from April to September. (☎ 302462. 1½-7hr.; £2.50-10, children £1.25-5. Call to book ahead.)

Also on Low Glencloy Rd., closer to town, the **Arran Heritage Museum** features a working forge (the beloved "Smiddy"), and a cottage stuffed with 19th-century household and farming implements (if you can get up the wee stairs). On some summer Sundays, the museum explodes into a flurry of activity; blacksmiths fire up the forge for a demonstration of horseshoeing while woolly sheep are shorn. (☎ 302636. Open Apr.-Oct. daily 10:30am-4:30pm. £2.25, seniors £1.50, children £1, families £6.) The **Arran Highland Games,** replete with unusual sports and bagpipe parades, arrive in Brodick in early August. The **Isle of Arran Folk Festival** spreads merriment in early June.

NEAR BRODICK: WHITING BAY. Eight miles south of Brodick, the shores of Whiting Bay harbor a stone **SYHA Youth Hostel** amid rolling hills. (☎/fax 700339. Lockout 10:30am-5pm. Curfew 11:45pm. Dorms £8, under 18 £7.) Take the easy one mile path to **Glenashdale Falls.** Afterwards, sit outside at **The Coffee Pot,** Golf Course Rd., and enjoy a bowl of scrumptious home-made soup (£1.50) and the spectacular view of Holy Island. (☎ 700382. Open daily 10am-5pm, July-Aug. 10am-6pm.) Between Brodick and Whiting Bay lies **Lamlash,** Arran's most populated town and one of the best natural harbors in Europe. The bay is protected by the steep form of Holy Island, to which ferries run frequently.

LOCHRANZA

Idyllic Lochranza, 14 mi. from Brodick at the island's northern tip, shelters a serene harbor ringed by high hills and guarded by the ruins of a 13th-century **castle.** Pick up the key to the castle from the post office, unlock the iron gate, explore the ancient ruins, and let your imagination fly in solitary splendor. (Open Apr.-Sept. Free.) Lochranza is also a popular base for avid walkers and exlorers. An excellent half-day walk is the seven-mile **Cock of Arran** route, which circles the northern tip of the island. The beach section takes you past **Fairy Dell,** a small, lushly ferned sandstone ravine, the bard **Ossian's Cave,** a hole-in-the-cliff with no historical importance, and the now-headless **Cock of Arran,** whose features are hard to spot unless you bring along a magic spyglass, a local, or your own stone rooster. Alternatively, you can head south up **Glen Catacol** to **Loch Tanna,** passing several waterfalls and several muddy, rather dreary segments on your way (4 mi. each way). Before setting out, buy the waterproof *Walker's Map: Arran North* (£6.95) or the Ordnance Survey *Isle of Arran* (£5.25), both available at the Brodick TIC. The third weekend in July brings the **Lochranza Gala Weekend,** when boats with silly themes compete in a down-and-dirty race.

Lochranza Golf Caravan Camping Site (see below) provides **bike rentals** for £4.50 per day. (☎ 830273; fax 830600. £2 min. Open daily 8am-8pm.) The **post office** is located in Primrose's, the town's grocery store, overlooking the castle ruins. (☎ 830641. Open M-Tu and Th-Sa 8:30am-1:30pm and 2:30-5:30pm, W 8:30am-1:30pm and 5-6pm; supermarket only Su 10am-2pm and 5-6pm.) **Postal code:** KA27 8EU.

In the former town church across from the castle, the ▨ **Castlekirk B&B** has high, arched ceilings, a lounge with stained-glass windows, and enchanting quietude. The talented proprietress fills the ground floor with her own artwork and that of other local artists, forming a splendid gallery that's open W-Su noon-6:30pm. (☎ 830202. £18-20 per person.) Minutes inland of the castle, the **SYHA Lochranza** graces the town on the main road. This peaceful white mansion has 68 beds, 5 showers, and 2 friendly and helpful wardens. (☎/fax 830631. Laundry facilities; wash £1, dry £1. Kitchen lockout 10:30am-5pm. Curfew 11:30pm. Open Mar.-Oct. Dorms £9.25, under 18 £8.) Campers can pitch at the **Lochranza Golf Caravan Camping Site,** half a mile inland of town on the main road, with laundry, hot water, and disabled facilities. (☎ 830273; fax 830600. Open Apr.-Oct. £3 per person, £2-4 per tent.) The waterfront **Lochranza Hotel** has a varied menu; the veggie pasta (£5.60) or the lunch baguettes (£3) will surely hit the spot. (☎ 830223. Open daily 11am-9:45pm.)

CATACOL BAY. One mile down the coast from Lochranza, the village of Catacol Bay harbors the **Twelve Apostles,** 12 connected white houses that differ only in the shapes of their windows. The fisherfolk residents would turn on a light at night so that their returning comrades could tell who was still out at sea. The **Machrie Stones,** various Bronze-Age arrangements of upright stones and boulders, are 10 mi. down the road. Ask the bus driver on the Lochranza-Blackwaterfoot bus to drop you off. A mile down the main road brings you to a footpath signposted to **King's Cave,** where Robert the Bruce allegedly passed time watching the spiders while still in hiding. Now fenced off, the cave holds ancient carvings and modern graffiti. It's open for tours on some summer days; ask at the Lochranza TIC.

CENTRAL
SCOTLAND

Though less dramatic than the lofty Highlands to the north and more subdued than Glasgow and Edinburgh to the south, central Scotland has its charms. The eastern shoulder extends northwards from Tayside and Fife to the Highland Boundary Fault and chilly curve of the North Sea. Descending from snow-covered mountains, the countryside flattens into the coastal plains of the Central Lowlands, giving the A82 road from Loch Lomond to Glen Coe some of the best views in Scotland. Castles of all vintages and sizes are testament to the region's past strategic importance, as is proud, ancient Stirling. To the west, separated by mountains and a thin strip of sea, lies the remote, natural splendor of the Inner Hebrides.

HIGHLIGHTS OF CENTRAL SCOTLAND

STIRRING STIRLING Admire the 5½ ft. sword of William Wallace and one of Britain's grandest castles in the historic royal capital of Scotland (p. 546).

THE BONNY BONNY BANKS Hike along the shores of beautiful **Loch Lomond,** the inspiration for the haunting ballad of the same name (p. 548).

FIRE BURN AND CAULDRON BUBBLE Walk along gloriously isolated **Loch Tay** in Dunkeld and Birnam, home to sites immortalized in Shakespeare's *Macbeth* (p. 557).

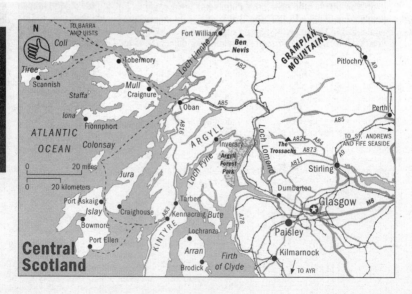

STIRLING
☎01786

Sitting atop a triangle completed by Glasgow and Edinburgh, Stirling has historically presided over north-south movement in the region; it's been said that he who controlled Stirling controlled Scotland. At the 1297 Battle of Stirling Bridge, William Wallace outwitted and overpowered the English army, enabling Robert the Bruce to lead Scotland to independence 17 years later. When James VI took the English throne, he declared a new in capital Edinburgh, leaving Stirling to languish. Despite its development into a bustling settlement, Scotland's former capital has not forgotten its heroes. The city's rich history and stirring architecture have been rediscovered, and it now swarms with tourists and *Braveheart* fans set on capturing the glorious Scotland of old.

⌐ GETTING THERE

The **train station** is on Goosecroft Rd. (Travel center open M-F 6am-9pm, Sa 6am-8pm, Su 8:30am-10pm. Luggage storage ₤2-4; open M-Sa 10am-6pm.) **Trains** (☎ (08457) 484950) arrive from: **Glasgow** (30min.; M-Sa 2-3 per hr., Su 1 per hr.; ₤4.20); **Edinburgh** (50min., 2 per hr., ₤5); **Aberdeen** (2hr.; M-Sa 1 per hr., Su 6 per day; ₤30); **Inverness** (3hr., 4 per day, ₤28.90); and **London King's Cross** (5½hr., 1 per hr., ₤81.50). The **bus station** is also on Goosecroft Rd. (☎ 446474. Ticket office open M-F 8:30am-6pm, Sa 8:30am-5pm. Luggage storage ₤1; open M-Sa 7am-9pm, Su 12:30-7:30pm.) **National Express** (☎ (08705) 808080) buses run from **Glasgow** (2-3 per hr., ₤3.40) and **Inverness** (1 per hr., ₤11.20).

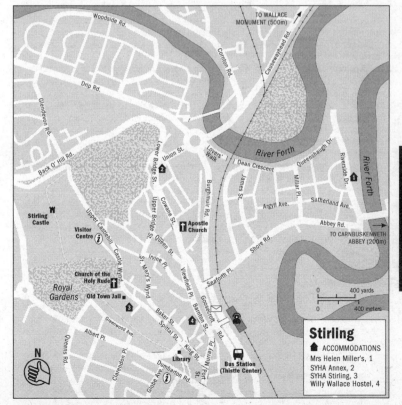

Stirling

▲ ACCOMMODATIONS
Mrs Helen Miller's, 1
SYHA Annex, 2
SYHA Stirling, 3
Willy Wallace Hostel, 4

ℹ PRACTICAL INFORMATION

Tourist Information Centre: 41 Dumbarton Rd. (☎ 475019). Open July-Aug. M-Sa 9am-7:30pm, Su 9:30am-6:30pm; June and Sept. M-Sa 9am-6pm, Su 10am-4pm; off-season open roughly M-Sa 10am-5pm. More helpful is the **Stirling Visitor Centre** (☎ 462517), next to the castle. High-altitude, high-tech with exhibits and a 12min. movie. The staff exchanges currency (£3 commission), and books accommodations for £1. Open daily July-Aug. 9am-6:30pm; Apr.-June and Sept.-Oct. 9:30am-6pm; Nov.-Mar. 9:30am-5pm. Both offices provide the free *What's On* and *Royal Stirling Events* calendars, as well as bus timetables.

Tours: If you balk at walking up Stirling's hills, **Guide Friday** (☎ (0131) 556 2244) operates 70min. open-top bus tours that begin at the castle esplanade, and offer hop-on/hop-off service throughout the town and to the Wallace Monument. Tours 10am-5pm. £6.50, students and seniors £5, children £2, families £15.

Internet Access: Network Cafe, 68 Barnton St. (☎ 471122). £2.50 per 30min. **Library** (☎ 432107), Corn Exchange Rd. £2.50 per 30min., concessions £1.25.

Post Office: 84-86 Murray Pl. (☎ 465392). **Bureau de change.** Open M-F 9am-5:30pm, Sa 9am-12:30pm. **Postal Code:** FK8 2BP.

🏠 ACCOMMODATIONS AND FOOD

B&Bs abound near the train station and the university. **SYHA Stirling,** on St. John St., halfway up the hill to the castle, occupies the shell of the first Separatist Church in Stirling. Each of the 2- to 5-bed rooms has its own shower and toilet. In July and August, overflow singles are used in the **Union St. Annexe,** known in cooler months as University of Stirling housing, with the same prices as the hostel. (☎ 473442; fax 445715. Reception open 7am-11:30pm, bedroom lockout 10am-2pm, curfew 2am. Dorms July-Aug. £13.75, under 18 £12.25; Sept.-June £12.75, under 18 £11.25.) The **Willy Wallace Hostel,** 77 Murray Pl., is a mere two-minute walk from the bus or train stations, and has a kitchen and a full laundry services for only £3.50. (☎ 446773; willywallacehostel@scottishhostels.co.uk. Dorms £10; twins £24; doubles £26.) **Mrs. Helen Miller's,** 16 Riverside Dr., offers two spotless singles—one with a view of the Wallace Monument—and a breakfast that will hold you until dinner. Turn right from the train station, cross the bridge, go down Seaforth Pl. and Abbey Rd. until the road ends, and turn left onto Riverside Dr. (☎ 461105. £11 per person.)

Tucked in an alley, **The Greengrocer,** 81 Port St., offers some of the freshest fruits and veggies in town (☎ 479159. Open M-F 9am-5:30pm, Sa 8:30am-3:30pm.) Head to **Iceland,** 5 Pitt Terr., for the rest of your grocery needs. (☎ 464300. Open M-F 8:30am-8pm, Sa 8:30am-6pm, Su 10am-5pm.) **Paco's Restaurant,** 21 Dumbarton Rd., has a dish for every taste bud and a price for every budget, with main courses ranging £4.45-11.45. (☎ 446414. Open M-Sa noon-late and Su 5pm-late.) For burgers under £2.50, or for a pleasant tea, try **Sarah Jane's,** 2 Pitt Terr. (☎ 470139).

👁 SIGHTS

STIRLING CASTLE. Planted atop a defunct volcano, and embraced on all sides by the scenic Ochil Hills, the castle possesses prim gardens and superb views of the Forth Valley that belie its militant and occasionally murderous past. Robert the Bruce determined the castle was the cause of too much bloodshed and had it destroyed. It was rebuilt nonetheless in the 1380s, and Robert's statue ironically stands guard in front of the present structure. The castle's hideous gargoyles glowered over the 14th-century Wars of Independence, a 15th-century royal murder, and the 16th-century coronation of the infant Mary, Queen of Scots; its final military engagement came in 1746, when Bonnie Prince Charlie besieged it while retreating from England (then gave up and kept retreating). After years of use as an army barracks (a practice begun when King James I housed his new "British Army" in the Great Hall), the castle is currently undergoing renovation. Beneath the cannons pointed at Stirling Bridge lie the 16th-century **great kitchens;** visitors can walk among the recreated chaos of cooks, dogs, bakers, and large slabs of meat. Free 30min. **guided tours,** leaving every 30min., give a background for further exploration. (☎ 450000. Open Apr.-Oct. 9:30am-6pm; Nov.-Mar. 9:30am-5pm; last admission 45min. before closing. £6, seniors £4.50, under 16 £1.50.)

The castle also contains the **Regimental Museum of the Argyll and Sutherland Highlanders,** a fascinating military museum including men in kilts, of course. (Open Easter-Sept. M-Sa 10am-5:45pm, Su 11am-4:45pm; Oct.-Easter daily 10am-4:15pm. Free.) The highlight of **Argyll's Lodging,** a 17th-century townhouse on the castle esplanade, is the purple and gold toilet box in the main bedroom. (Open Apr.-Sept. 9:30am-6pm; Nov.-Mar. 9:30am-5pm. £2.80, seniors £2, children £1.20; free with castle admission.)

WALLACE MONUMENT. This 19th-century tower offers incredible views to those bravehearted enough to climb the 246-step, wind-whipped spiral staircase to the top. It houses the 5½ ft. sword William Wallace wielded against King Edward I of England, and provides exhibits on Wallace's capture: Wallace was hanged until semi-conscious, then disemboweled, castrated, beheaded, and quartered, his entrails burnt, and parts of his body dispersed to the corners of Scotland. (Hillfouts Rd., 1½ mi. from town center; buses run from train and bus stations to the base. ☎ 472140. Open daily July-Aug. 9:30am-6:30pm; June and Sept. 10am-6pm; Mar.-May and Oct. 10am-5pm; Nov.-Feb. 10am-4pm. £3.30, students £3.05, seniors and children £2.30, families £9.70.)

OTHER SIGHTS. On the east side of town, cross the Abbey Rd. footbridge over the River Forth to find the ruins of the 12th-century **Cambuskenneth Abbey,** where an occasional black-faced sheep may eyeball you across the graves of James III and his wife Margaret. (Open Apr.-Sept. M-Sa 9:30am-6pm, Su 2-6pm; grounds open all year. Free.) Down Castle Hill Wynd, the high walls and timbered roof of the **Church of the Holy Rude** witnessed the coronation of James VI, and shook under the fire and brimstone of John Knox; bullet holes can still be seen in the church walls. It's the only church in Scotland still being used for regular worship in which a coronation once took place. (Open May-Sept. daily 10am-5pm; Su service July-Dec. 10am, Jan.-June 11:30am. Frequent organ recitals. Donations requested.) **Ladies Rock,** a lookout point where ladies could find out local happenings while keeping a healthy distance, is located in **Valley Cemetery** behind the church. Next to the church lies the 17th-century **Cowane's Hospital,** built as an almshouse for poor members of the merchant guild. Legend has it that at the stroke of midnight each New Year, the statue of founder John Cowane descends from its niche over the front door and dances a jig in the courtyard. (Open M-Sa 9am-5pm, Su 1-5pm. Free.)

Two miles south of Stirling at **Bannockburn,** a statue of a battle-ready Robert the Bruce overlooks the field where his men decisively defeated the English in 1314, after which Scotland was independent for 393 years. (☎ 812664. Heritage Centre open daily Apr.-Oct. 10am-5:30pm; Mar. and Nov.-Dec. 11am-4:30pm; grounds open year-round.)

CROMWELL'S STOLEN LAUNDRY
Much like the Scottish sun, the Scottish Crown Jewels have been hidden for extended periods of time. The regalia owe their continuing existence to two brave Scotswomen who lived in the 17th century. As Oliver Cromwell stormed his way to Stirling, Catherine, the wife of the minister of Moneydie, covertly transported the items to Dunnator Castle. Dressed as a peasant woman, she crossed through Cromwell's lines with the jewels in sacks of wool. Later, when Dunnotar Castle itself was under siege, a second woman, Christian Fletcher, smuggled them out again, trotting them through the castle on horseback. If only Cromwell had decided to rummage through bags of dirty pillows, the crown, scepter, sword, and scabbard would have been his.

INVERARAY   ☎01499

The most obvious reason for visiting comely and unpretentious Inveraray is its splendid lochside setting; none of its tourist attractions is particularly captivating. The **Inveraray Jail** is possibly the town's most interesting sight. Visitors are greeted by the "Torture, Death and Damnation" exhibit, while the Old Prison (1820) and New Prison (1849) are stuffed with interactive displays such as the "Crank Machine," on which prisoners carved out 14,400 revolutions a day as a form of useless labor. Guests are invited to "please try" the Whipping Table. (☎ 302381. Open daily Apr.-Oct. 9:30am-6pm; Nov.-Mar. 10am-5pm. £4.75, students and seniors £3, children £2.30, families £12.95.)

Home to the Duke and Duchess of Argyll, cultivated **Inveraray Castle** contrasts strikingly with the rugged mountains that surround it. The castle seems to hold enough weapons to defend all Scotland. (☎ 302203. Open July-Aug. M-Sa 10am-5:45pm, Su 1-5:45pm, Apr.-June and Sept.-Oct. M-Sa 10am-1 and 2-5:45pm, Su 1-5:45pm. £4.50, students and seniors £3.50, under 16 £2.50, families £12; grounds free.) The 126 ft. **Bell Tower** has the second-heaviest bells in the world, weighing nearly 8 tons. The free bell-ringing exhibit does not include the rooftop view. (Open daily May-Sept. 10am-1pm and 2-5pm. Tower £2, concessions 75p.) The fun-packed **Fortnight Festival** parties between July and August.

Buses #926 and 976 run to Inveraray from **Glasgow** (1¾hr.; M-Sa 9 per day, Su 4 per day; £6). The town has a small **tourist information centre** on Front St. that books accommodations for a £1 fee. (☎ 302063. Open July to mid-Sept. daily 9am-6pm; May-June M-Sa 9am-5pm, Su 11am-5pm; Apr. and mid-Sept. to late Oct. M-Sa 9am-5pm, Su noon-5pm; Nov.-Mar. M-F 10am-4pm, Sa-Su noon-4pm.) The **Bank of Scotland** is at Church Sq. (☎ 302068. Open M-Tu and Th-F 9:15am-12:30pm and 1:30-4:45pm, W 10:30am-12:30pm and 1:30-4:45pm.) The **post office** is on Black's Land. (☎ 302062. Open M-Tu and Th-F 9am-1pm and 2-5:30pm, W 9am-1pm, Sa 9am-12:30pm.) **Postal code:** PA32 8UD.

The small **SYHA Inveraray** is just north of town on Dalmally Rd.; take a left through the arch next to the Inveraray Woollen Mill onto Oban Rd. and walk past the gas station. The super-clean hostel is small, so don't expect frills, but know that the silverware is sparkling. (☎/fax 302454. Self-catering. 38 beds, 2 showers. Lockout 10:30am-5pm. Curfew 11pm. Open mid-Mar. to Sept. Dorms £8.25, under 18 £7.25.) Inveraray hides a stash of **B&Bs** up the road past the post office. The **Old Rectory,** Main St. South, is home to nine large rooms with fluffy beds and a beautiful glass-ceilinged breakfast room. (☎ 302280. £17.50 per person.) **Lorona Guest House,** on the same street by the gas station, has six soothing rooms and a lounge with a great loch view. (☎ 302258. Open Easter-Oct. £17 per person.)

LOCH LOMOND AND BALLOCH   ☎01389

With Scotland's largest lake as its base, the landscape of Loch Lomond is filled with lush bays, thickly wooded islands, and bare hills immortalized by the famous ballad. Even the lochside towns that shamelessly commercialize "The Bonnie Bonnie Banks" (we'll take the high road and not make jokes about the ballad) are mostly unpolluted by tourists. Visitors who undertake challenging hikes in such roadless areas as the northeastern edge of Loch Lomond or most of Loch Katrine are rewarded with stunning views and the quiet splendor of untrammeled swaths of space. A number of small, rough beaches dot the shores. Hikers adore the West Highland Way, which snakes along the entire eastern side of the Loch, and in full measure stretches 95 mi. from Milngavie north to Fort William.

At the southern tip of Loch Lomond, Balloch is the area's major town, the word "major" being used loosely: with the exception of the youth hostel, everything you need is within a casual three-minute walk of the tourist information centre.

⚆⁊ GETTING THERE AND PRACTICAL INFORMATION. The **train station** is on Balloch Rd., across the street from the tourist information centre (TIC). **Trains** (☎ (08457) 484950) arrive from **Glasgow Queen St.** (45min., at least 2 per hr., £3.10). The **bus stop** is a few minutes down Balloch Rd., across the bridge to the left of the TIC, but buses bypassing the town center pick up passengers on the A82 near the roundabout. **Scottish Citylink** (☎ (08705) 505050) buses #926, 975, and 976 arrive from **Glasgow** (M-Sa 5 per day, Su 3 per day). **First Midland** (☎ (01324) 613777) travels from **Stirling** (1½hr.; M-F 3 per day, Sa 3 per day, Su 1 per day; £4.60). To reach the eastern side of the loch, take bus #309 or 9 from Balloch to **Balmaha** (40min., 6 per day). Buses #305 and 307 head for the village of **Luss** (15min., 7 per day).

The **tourist information centre,** Old Station Building, Balloch Rd., books rooms for a £1 fee, stocks bus schedules, hands out the useful *In and Around Loch Lomond,* and shows a short film on the loch. (☎ 753533. Open daily July-Aug. 9:30am-7pm; June 9:30am-6pm; Sept. 9:30am-7pm; Apr.-May and Oct. 10am-5pm.)

⚐ ACCOMMODATIONS. B&Bs congregate on Balloch Rd., conveniently close to the TIC. The ⚄ **SYHA Loch Lomond** is one of Scotland's largest hostels, with 9 entrances, 53 chimneys, and 180 beds in a stunning 19th-century castle-like building 2 mi. north of Balloch. The hostel retains its original splendor—the high-ceilinged common room is astounding. Other amenities include the ghost of Veronica, who, pregnant with the child of a stable boy, took a steep dive from the window of the tower in which her family had locked her. Book ahead in summer. (☎ 850226. Dorms July-Aug. £13.25, under 18 £11.75; Sept.-Oct. and early Mar. to June £12.25, under 18 £10.75.) The **SYHA Rowardennan** is the first hostel along the West Highland Way. Huge windows put the loch in your lap. (☎ (01360) 870259. Curfew 11:30pm. Open Mar.-Oct. Dorms £9.25, under 18 £8.) To reach it, take the Inverberg ferry to Rowardennan. (☎ (01301) 702356. May-Sept. daily; leaves Rowardennan at 10am, 2, and 6pm, Inverberg 30min. later. £4, children £1.50.)

The **Tullichewan Caravan and Camping Site** is on Old Luss Rd., up Balloch Rd. from the TIC. At this Club Med of campsites, you can luxuriate in a sauna or spa bath, or rent **mountain bikes.** (☎ (01389) 759475; fax 755563. Reception open 8:30am-10pm, but may be open later for *quiet* campers. Open year-round. Bikes £7.50 per 4hr., £10 per 8hr.; deposit of £100. Tent and 2 people £6.50-9, with car £8.50-12.50; additional guests free in winter, otherwise £2; children £1.)

⚆ SIGHTS. Across the River Leven, **Balloch Castle Country Park** provides 200 acres of gorgeous beach lawn, woods, and gardens, as well as a 19th-century castle that houses a **Visitor's Centre.** If the weather is good, don't miss the opportunity to walk around and look for the pixies in **Fairy Glen.** (Park open daily dawn-dusk. Visitor's Centre, doubling as a Loch Lomond Park Ranger Station, open Easter-Oct. daily 10am-6pm. Free.) One of the best introductions to the area is **Sweeney's Cruises** boat tours, from the TIC's side of the River Leven. (☎ 752376. Cruises 1hr., 1 per hr. 10am-4pm, £4.80, children £2.50.) Cruises also sail to Luss, with half an hour ashore (2½hr., departs 2:30pm; £7.50, children £3.50), and there's even an evening cruise with onboard bar (1½hr., departs 7:30pm; £6.50, children £3). Avert your eyes (or don't) from the nudist colony on one of the islands in the lake's center (brrr!). Ruins of the **Lomond Castle Hotel** are also visible; the owner burnt it down in an insurance scam. The **Glasgow-Loch Lomond Cycleway** covers 21 mi. between the two areas; get info at the TIC.

LOCH LONG

Loch Long stretches like a salty finger northeast toward Loch Lomond. The **Ardgartan Forest Park,** on the northern side of Loch Long, has excellent cycling potential. The park lies beneath the "Arrochar Alps," a series of rugged mountains including five Munro peaks and the 289 ft. **Cuckolded Cobbler.** Also known as Ben Arthur, The Cobbler is unmistakable for its unusual, jagged rock formations—the peak appears to have sprouted horns befitting a cuckold. A leisurely trail with some rocky parts near the tip begins in the town of Arrochar, halfway between Tarbet and Ardgartan (inquire in town or at the hostel about the exact location of the trailhead). Once at the top, enjoy the view from the Eye of the Needle, an opening in one of the horny rock-stacks. To tackle the hike knowledgably, pick up the Ordnance Survey Pathfinder Map 368 (£4.50) or Landranger Map 56 (£5) from a TIC.

The easiest way to enter the area is via the **Arrochar-Tarbet** train station. **Trains** (☎ (08457) 484950) run from **Glasgow** (1¼hr.; M-Sa 5 per day, Su 3 per day; £7.30) and **Fort William** (2½hr.; M-Sa 4 per day, Su 3 per day; £12.50). Pick up the *Cycling In The Forest* pamphlet (30p) in the Ardgartan **tourist information centre,** off the A83 at the north end of the loch. (☎ (01301) 702432. Open daily July-Aug. 10am-6pm; Apr.-June and Sept.-Oct. 10am-5pm.) Half a mile away, the **SYHA Ardgartan** has glorious views. Citylink bus #976 passes the hostel. (☎/fax (01301) 702362. Lockout 11am-5pm. Curfew 11:45pm. Open Apr.-Dec. £11.25, under 18 £10.)

THE TROSSACHS

The gentle mountains and lochs of the Trossachs (which means "bristly country") form the northern boundary of central Scotland. Sir Walter Scott and Queen Victoria lavished praise on the region, the only easily accessible Scottish wilderness before the 20th century. The Trossachs today are less accessible; only a few buses each day link Glasgow and Stirling to **Aberfoyle** and **Callander,** the two main towns. The A821 winds through the heart of the Trossachs between Aberfoyle and Callander, passing near majestic **Loch Katrine,** the Trossachs' original lure and the setting of Scott's "The Lady of the Lake." A road for walkers and cyclists traces the Loch's shoreline; unfit tourists drop like flies after a half mile, leaving the Loch's joys to more hardy travelers. The **Steamship Sir Walter Scott** steams between Loch Katrine's Trossachs Pier and Stronachlachar. The scenery is arresting, but in July and August, the crush of passengers may make the trip a hassle. (☎ (01877) 376316. Cruises Apr.-Oct. Su-F 11am, 1:45pm, and 3:15pm, Sa 1:45pm and 3:15pm. £4.60-6, seniors and children £3.20-4.20.) Nearby, **Ben A'an'** (1207 ft.) hulks over the Trossachs; the rocky one-hour hike up begins a mile from the pier, along the A821.

Getting to this area is tough: **Scottish Citylink** bus #974, running from **Edinburgh** and **Stirling** to **Fort William,** stops in **Callander** (2 per day in each direction). Or try **The Trossachs Trundler,** a 1950s-style bus that creaks to **Callander, Aberfoyle,** and **Trossachs Pier** in time for the sailing of the *Sir Walter Scott* (July-Sept. Su-F 4 per day, Day Rover £5.50, seniors and children £3.50). Bus #59 from Stirling connects with the Trundler in **Callander** (Stirling-Trossachs Rover £8, seniors and children £5.50). Or try **postbuses,** which wind their way through selected towns. Grab timetables at TICs, or call the **Stirling Council Public Transport Helpline** (☎ (01786) 442707). **Trossachs Cycle Hire,** on the pier in Callander, rents quality bikes. (☎ (01877) 382614. £3 per hr., £7.50 per half-day, £12 per day. Open Apr.-Oct. daily 8:30am-5:30pm.)

ST. ANDREWS   ☎ 01334

Would you like to see a city given over,
Soul and body to a tyrannising game?
If you would, there's little need to be a rover,
For St. Andrews is the abject city's name.
   —Robert F. Murray

The "tyrannising game" of golf overruns the small city of St. Andrews. It was here, at the Royal and Ancient Golf Club (the R&A), that the rules of the game were formally established. The windows of the club look out over the Old Course, the sport's world headquarters. But beyond the tradition that attracts millions of pompom clad putt-putt enthusiasts, there is also the beauty of St. Andrews' other glories: the gray stone buildings of Scotland's oldest university, the cathedral remnants of the seat of pre-Reformation Christianity, and the restored medieval streets that lead to castle ruins overlooking the North Sea. Sadly, golf tourism and the influx of students from England and America have driven the prices in St. Andrews sky-high, turning it into a gentrified town with few bargains for the budget traveler (though providing many opportunities for guidebook golf puns).

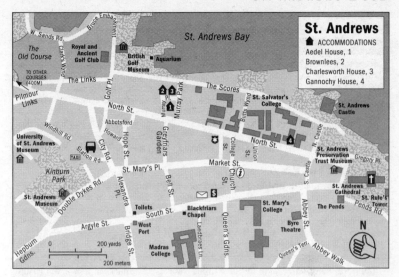

St. Andrews
🏠 ACCOMMODATIONS
Aedel House, 1
Brownlees, 2
Charlesworth House, 3
Gannochy House, 4

GETTING THERE AND GETTING AROUND

Trains: Trains (☎ (08457) 484590) stop 5 mi. away at **Leuchars** (LU-cars) on the London-Edinburgh-Aberdeen line. From **Edinburgh** (1hr., 1 per hr., £8.10). From Leuchars, buses #93-96 go to St. Andrews (5 per hr. 7am-8pm, £1.45).

Buses: St. Andrews Bus Station (☎ 474238), City Rd. **Stagecoach Express Fife Buses** (☎ (01383) 621249, ☎ 474238) from **Edinburgh** (#X59 or X60; 2hr.; M-Sa 2 per hr. until 6:45pm, fewer on Su; £5.70, students £3.60) and **Glasgow** (#X24, change at Glenrothes to #X59; 2½hr.; M-Sa 1 per hr., fewer on Su; £5.50). From **Aberdeen, Perth,** and **Inverness,** first take **Scottish Citylink** to Dundee (2 per hr.) and then **Stagecoach Fife** #95, 96, or 96A to St. Andrews (£2.40, students £1.60 on #95 only).

Hitchhiking: Hitchers often approach from Leuchars in the north on the A919 to the A91. Hitchers report the route from Edinburgh or Glasgow is tricky because of the manic crisscrossing of roads outside these cities; once reaching the A91 or the A915, they usually hitch straight to town. *Let's Go* does not recommend hitchhiking.

ORIENTATION AND PRACTICAL INFORMATION

The three main streets in St. Andrews—**North St., Market St.,** and **South St.**—run nearly parallel east to west, culminating near the cathedral at the town's east end. Manicured golf greens and shops rule the northwest part of town.

Tourist Information Centre: 70 Market St. (☎ 472021; fax 478422; www.standrews.co.uk). Provides the free *Kingdom of Fife* guide, which includes an extensive list of local B&Bs, and books accommodations within Fife for a 10% deposit (plus a £3 fee for listings outside Fife). Open July-Aug. M-Sa 9:30am-7pm, Su 11am-6pm; May-June and Sept. M-Sa 9:30am-6pm, Su 11am-5pm; Oct.-Apr. M-Sa 9:30am-5pm.

Financial Services: Royal Bank of Scotland, 119 South St. (☎ 472181). Changes currency. Open M-Tu and Th-F 9:15am-4:45 pm, W 10am-4:45 pm.

Launderette: 14b Woodburn Terr. (☎ 475150). Open M-Sa 9am-7pm, Su 9am-5pm; last wash 1½hr. before closing.

Internet Access: Costa Coffee, 83 Market St., across from the TIC. £1.50 per 15min., 75p for students. Open M-Sa 8am-8pm, Su 10am-8pm.

Hospital: St. Andrew's Memorial (☎ 472327), Abbey Walk, southeast of town.

Post Office: 127 South St. (☎ 472321). Open M-Sa 10am-5:30pm. **Postal code:** KY16 9UL.

ACCOMMODATIONS

Golfers with chubby wallets have made prices in St. Andrews above par. Near the golf links, **Murray Park** and **Murray Place** greet the backpacker with expensive B&Bs (£17-24 per person). Summer housing at the university provides cheap lodging, but is not always offered; inquire at the tourist information centre (TIC). Otherwise, you can make St. Andrews a daytrip from Glasgow, Edinburgh, or the nearby Anstruther Bunkhouse (see p. 554).

Aedel House, 12 Murray Pl. (☎ 472315). Attractive doubles and one single with bath. Book ahead. Open Feb.-Nov. Singles £18; doubles £26.

Brownlees, 7 Murray Pl. (☎ 473868). Elegant housing only a few blocks from the Old Course. TV. £18-25 per person.

Charlesworth House, 9 Murray Pl. (☎/fax 476528; charlesworth@talk21.com). New, near the Old Course, but pricey. All non-smoking, with bath and TV. £22-27 per person.

FOOD

Housing may be pricey, but at least the university has caused many cheap, greasy takeaways to spring up. The **Tesco** supermarket sits at 130 Market St. (☎ 472448. Open M-W 8:30am-7pm, Th-F 8:30am-8pm, Sa 8am-7pm, Su 10am-6pm.)

The North Point Cafe, North St. (☎ 473997). Makes light snacks in view of the castle ruins. Tea steeped in bone china (£1 per pot) and gingerbread (£1.20). Open daily Easter-Oct. 10am-5pm, Nov.-Easter 10am-4:30pm.

Brambles, 5 College St. (☎ 475380). Anything but prickly. Vegetarian-friendly menus await, as do long lines of locals. Try the home-baked scones for a warm treat (£1.65 with coffee) if you don't want their full dinners. Open M-Sa 9am-10pm, Su 11am-10pm.

The Eating Place, 177-9 South St. Serves tasty breakfasts all day (under £5), including Scottish drop pancakes. Open M-Sa 9:30am-5pm, Su 11:30am-5pm.

B. Jannetta, 31 South St. (☎ 473285). Their business card says "Ice Cream Specialist," and 52 flavors of award-winning ice cream, including Nutella, show they're not kidding. Overrun by sticky-chinned children when school gets out. 60p per scoop. Open daily in spring 9am-6pm; in summer 7:30am-6:30pm; in winter 9am-5:30pm.

PUBS

St. Andrews's pubs are worth a 19th-hole stop, although they close quite early. **The Central,** stereotyped as a Yah hangout ("yes" to the commoner; "yah" mocks the English and Scottish public school accent), attracts a student clientele to its digs on Market St. and College St. Pub meals go for £2 to £4. (☎ 478296. Open M-Sa 11am-11:45pm, Su 12:30-11:45pm.) **The Victoria,** 1 St. Mary's Pl., looks like the love-child of a Scottish pub and a Western saloon. Sip whisky at the two adjoining bars. (☎ 476964. Happy hour 8-10pm. Open Sa-W 11am-midnight, Th-F 11am-1am.) For great pub grub (burgers £5) as well as the usual pints, drop by **Drouthy Neebors**, 209 South St. (Open Su-Th until 11pm, F-Sa until midnight.) The **Lizard Lounge,** 127 North St., in the basement of the Argyle House Hotel, has great atmosphere and drink specials (£1 shots, £1.30 lager pints) from 8:30-9:30pm. (☎ 473378. Open M-W and Sa 11am-midnight, Th-F 11am-1am, Su noon-midnight.)

SIGHTS AND ACTIVITIES

GOLF, OF COURSE. If you love golf, play golf, have played golf, or even think that you might want to golf at some point, this is your town. The game was so avidly practiced here that Scotland's rulers outlawed the sport three times, fearing for the national defense ("the men neglected their archery for golf!"). The TIC has a free *Golfer's Information* brochure. At the northwest edge of town, the **Old Course,** the golf pilgrim's Canterbury, stretches regally to a gorgeous beach as manicured as the greens. According to the 1568 *Book of Articles*, Mary, Queen of

Scots, played here just days after her husband was murdered. Nonmembers must present a handicap certificate or a letter of introduction from a golf club. Make Old Course reservations a year in advance (yeah, no kidding), or enter your name into a near-impossible lottery by 2pm the day before you hope to play. (☎ 466666; fax 477036. Apr.-Oct. £80 per round; Nov.-Mar. £56.) Call the same line to reserve a time at the **New, Jubilee, Eden,** or **Strathtyrum** courses. Try to book at least a day in advance, although walk-ins are possible. The budget option is **Balgove Course,** nine holes of fun for £7. (Info line ☎ 466666; fax 477036. Courses Apr.-Oct. £17-40; Nov.-Mar. £15-28.) July 2000 also saw the opening of the newest R&A-associated course, the **Kingsbarns Golf Links,** further east along the coast. (☎ 880222; www.kingsbarns.com.)

BRITISH GOLF MUSEUM. Even if you left your clubs at home, you can still learn about the origins of the sport. Papier-maché mannequins whittle putters and stitch balls into eternity. Golf enthusiasts will find the exhibits fascinating; others, less so. (Bruce Embankment. ☎ 478880. Wheelchair access. Open Easter-Oct. daily 9:30am-5:30pm; Nov.-Easter Th-M 11am-3pm. £3.75, students and seniors £2.75, under 15 £1.50.)

ST. ANDREWS CATHEDRAL. In the Middle Ages, thousands of pilgrims journeyed here to pray at the Saint's Shrine. During the Reformation, iconoclast Protestants defaced the interior of the church, which was later pillaged by locals. Only the shell of the once-huge structure remains, while a plush carpet of grass has replaced the original stone. According to legend, the cathedral's stones make up the foundations of many of St. Andrews's houses. Nearby, **St. Rule's Tower,** 157 steps up a square building that was part of the original 12th-century church, provides stunning views. (☎ 472563. Open daily Apr.-Sept. 9:30am-6:30pm; Oct.-Mar. 9:30am-4:30pm. Cathedral free; tower £1.80, seniors £1.30, children 75p.)

ST. ANDREWS CASTLE. The high stone walls of the castle now tumble down to the North Sea. Once the local bishop's residence, it maintains explorable secret tunnels, bottle-shaped dungeons, and high stone walls to keep out (or in) rebellious heretics. (At the end of North Castle St. ☎ 477196. Open daily Apr.-Sept. 9:30am-6:30pm; Oct.-Mar. 9:30am-4:30pm. £2.50, seniors £1.90, children £1; joint ticket with cathedral £3.75, seniors £2.80, children £1.25.)

UNIVERSITY OF ST. ANDREWS. Scotland's oldest university was founded in the 15th century. Following in the royal footsteps of many Scottish kings who studied here, Prince William will begin his undergraduate course in art history in the fall of 2001. The university's well-heeled student population participates in a strong performing arts program. While it is possible to meander into placid quads through the parking entrances on North St., the one-hour **official tour** is your key to the interiors of most university buildings. Buy a ticket from the Admissions Reception, Butts Wynd, beside St. Salvator's Chapel Tower on North St. (Between North St. and The Scores. ☎ 462245. Tours mid-June to Aug. M-F 11am and 2:30pm. £4.50, concessions £3.50, under 6 free.) Newly opened last summer in conjunction with the 2000 Open Championship, the glassy, round **University of St. Andrews Museum & Information Centre** details the five-century history of the University in a modern, high-tech building. (The Gateway, on your way into town. ☎ 470070. Open June-Sept. daily 10am-6pm, Oct.-May daily 10am-5pm. £4, concessions £2.)

OTHER SIGHTS AND ACTIVITIES. The baronial **St. Andrews Museum,** in Kinburn Park, down Doubledykes Rd., travels back in time to the arrival of St. Regulus and points out that golf is but "a small dot" (a tee, perhaps?) in the town's history. (☎ 412690. Open Apr.-Sept. daily 10am-5pm; Oct.-Mar. M-F 10:30am-4pm, Sa-Su 12:30-5pm. Free.) A wax chemist distills elixirs among the reproductions of early 20th-century shops at the tiny **St. Andrews Preservation Trust Museum,** North St. (☎ 412690. Open early June to Sept. daily 2-5pm. Donations welcome.) A break from local history, the **St. Andrews Aquarium,** The Scores, displays massive eels and orphaned seals, a putt away from the golf museum. (☎ 474786. Open daily 10am-5pm. £4.50, students £3.35, seniors £3.85, children £3.50. Seal feeding daily 11am and 3pm.) The **Byre Theatre,** Abbey St., recently reopened. (☎ 474 6101. Student tickets £3-7.50.)

FIFE SEASIDE
☎ 01333

The fiefdom of Fife fills the fields fanning from the Firth of Forth and the Firth of…Tay. South of St. Andrews, a series of sun-warmed fishing villages cling along the coast of Fife like barnacles to the hull of a weathered fishing boat, making up The East Neuk. The scenic Fife Coastal Walk strings these villages together, while those with a car can cruise down the A917, which stretches from St. Andrews to Elie. Bus service #95 (St. Andrews-Leven) goes every hour along the A917 with frequent stops, including Crail, Anstruther, Elie, and Pittenween. For the most up-to-date info, call the Fife Council's Public Transport Information Line. (☎ (01592) 416060. Open M-F 9am-4pm.) Alas, Fife suffers from minimal train service and a lack of budget accommodations. Budget-paranoid backpackers might be best off making the Bunkhouse in Anstruther (see below) their base, or making Fife a day trip from Edinburgh.

CRAIL. Considered by many the bonniest of Fife's villages, Crail and its harbor offer the snap-happy tourist the perfect Kodak moment. It's a fitting place to relax and gnaw on freshly caught crab claws sold at stalls by the harbor. In the last week of July, things get more interesting with the **Crail Festival,** featuring various concerts, parades, and craft shows. Crail's **tourist information centre,** 62-64 Marketgate, also houses a small local history museum. (☎ 450869. Open Apr.-May Sa-Su 2-5pm; June-Sept. M-Sa 10am-1pm and 2-5pm, Su noon-5pm. Free.) **Guided walks** of town leave every Sunday at 2:30pm in July and August from the museum (1½-2hr., £3).

ANSTRUTHER. About 5 mi. west of Crail along the A917 (or 9 mi. southeast of St. Andrews along the B9131) lies Anstruther. The busiest of the seaside's towns is home to 12 pubs, a great fish and chip shop, and the **Scottish Fisheries Museum.** (☎ 310628. Open Apr.-Oct. M-Sa 10am-5:30pm, Su 11am-5pm; Nov.-Mar. M-Sa 10am-4:30pm, Su noon-4:30pm. Last entry 45min. before closing. £3.20, students and seniors £2.20.) Off the coast, the **Isle of May,** home to Scotland's first lighthouse (built in 1636), rises from the Firth of Forth. A nature reserve, the Isle is home to puffins, gray seals, and the 2000-year-old remains of human inhabitants. In summer, **The May Princess** sails from Anstruther to the Isle. (☎ 310103. July-Aug. 1 per day; May-June and Sept. W-M 1 per day. £12.50, children £5.50.) Times depend on weather and tides; call ahead or check with Anstruther's **tourist information centre,** located right next to the museum. (☎ 311073. Open Easter-Oct. M and F-Sa 10am-5pm, Tu-Th 10am-1pm and 2-5pm, Su noon-5pm.) Landlubbers can rent bikes at **East Neuk Cycles,** 63 James St., for £4 per day. (☎ 312179. Open M-Sa 9:30am-5pm.)

Anstruther has the only budget hostel in the area, the comfortable **Bunkhouse,** 1 mi. outside town; call a taxi (☎ 310085; about £2) or take bus #61 to West Pitkirie. This 700-year-old fortified farmhouse, run by the Pennington family, is home to a few Vietnamese pigs and a squawking parrot. (☎ 310768. Sheets 50p. Dorms and twins £7.50 per person.) Join the queue at the **Anstruther Fishbar and Restaurant,** 42-44 Shore St., for a pile of greasy goodness. (Open daily 11:30am-10pm.)

SECRET BUNKER. Halfway between Anstruther and St. Andrews, the (not so) Secret Bunker crouches hidden below a farmhouse. This subterranean shelter was prepared as a home for British leaders during a nuclear war. Locals claim they knew what it was all along. Take bus #61 (Anstruther-St. Andrews) and ask to get off near the bunker, then walk a mile. (☎ 310301; www.secretbunker.co.uk. Open Apr.-Oct. 10am-5pm. £6, students and seniors £5, children £3.25.)

ELIE. The village of **Elie** (EEL-y), five miles west of Anstruther, has become a somewhat posh resort and retirement community, perhaps because of beautiful **Ruby Bay,** named for the garnets occasionally (if rarely) found on its sands. While Elie boasts excellent bathing waters, among the purest in Britain, you can command a better, quieter view of sporting seals, tidal-pool marine life, and slippery yellow rocks from the headland by the lighthouse. Down the coast lies the **Lady's Tower,** built in the 18th century as a bathing box for Lady Jane Anstruther, who reportedly sent a bell-ringing servant through the streets to warn the village of her presence to prevent (or promote?) anyone seeing her scantily clad.

SO YOU WANT TO BE A LADY On the road from St. Monans, look to the shore to see the very brief remnants of Newark Castle. It may not look like much, but it is the seat of a barony and it is for sale. Therefore, anyone (including YOU) could purchase this pile of rocks and become a bona fide member of the ruling class. Years ago, a local madam put in for the property thinking she could turn the former castle into a brothel. She was turned down. Clearly, the British nobility is unwilling to tarnish its impeccable reputation.

TENTSMUIR POINT NATURE RESERVE. In Fife's northeastern nook lies the Nature Reserve, a young forest park hemmed in from the sea by a 10-mile beach. Reach the park from **Leuchars,** on the St. Andrews-Dundee road and on the Edinburgh-Dundee train line (see **Getting There,** p. 551).

FALKLAND. Further inland in the Kingdom of Fife, **Falkland Palace and Gardens,** once the hunting lodge of the Stewarts, epitomizes outstanding early Renaissance architecture. It features a tennis court built in 1539 and still in use. (☎ (01337) 857397. Open Easter-July and Sept.-Oct. M-Sa 11am-4:30pm, Su 1:30-4:30pm; July-Aug. M-Sa 10am-4:30pm, Su 1:30-4:30pm, grounds daily until 5:30pm. £5, concessions £3.50; grounds only £2.50, concessions £1.70.) The surrounding town shows off some well-preserved 17th-century architecture. Getting to Falkland is tricky: you'll need to get to **Glenrothes** by a **Stagecoach Fife bus** (from St. Andrews £3.55, from Edinburgh slightly more), and then transfer to a Falkland-bound bus.

PERTH   ☎01738

Frequently referred to as "The Fair City," Perth is exactly that: fair. Pretty, yes. Peaceful, too. But this placid city of 43,000 is not particularly extraordinary either, catering primarily to residents and mild-mannered guests. Perth served as Scotland's capital until 1452, and there are a few decent reasons to visit—beautiful walks, the Black Watch Museum, and the historical significance of nearby Scone Palace—but travelers pressed for time could easily move on.

▐ GETTING THERE

The **train station** is on Leonard St. (Ticket office open M-Sa 6:45am-8:45pm, Su 8:15am-8:25pm.) **Trains** (☎ (08457) 484950) arrive from: **Glasgow** (1hr., 1 per hr., £9.30); **Aberdeen** (1½hr., 2 per hr., £20.20); **Edinburgh** (1½hr., 2 per hr., £9.30); and **Inverness** (2½hr., 8-9 per day, £15.40). Just a block away on Leonard St. sits the **bus station.** (Ticket office open M-F 7:45am-5pm, Sa 8am-4:30pm). **Scottish Citylink** (☎ (08705) 505050) buses run from most major towns in Scotland, including: **Dundee** (45min., 16 per day, £3.40); **Pitlochry** (45min., 1 per hr., £4.80); **Edinburgh** (1½hr., 16 per day, £5); **Glasgow** (1½hr., 1 per hr., £7.50); **Aberdeen** (2½hr., 1 per hr., £10.20); and **Inverness** (2½hr., 1 per hr., £9.80).

▐ PRACTICAL INFORMATION

The **tourist information centre** (TIC), Lower City Mills, offers an unparalleled selection of maps, and books rooms for £1 plus a 10% deposit. From the bus station, turn right on Leonard St., continue along South Methven St., then take a left onto Old High St., following signposts all the way. (☎ 450600; fax 444863; www.perthshire.co.uk. Open Apr.-Aug. M-Sa 9am-7pm, Su 11am-5pm; Sept.-Nov. M-Sa 9am-6pm, Su 11am-4pm; Nov.-Mar. M-Sa 10am-4pm.) **Guide Friday** runs **open-top bus tours** in summer, making transport easy to far-away places like Scone Palace and Kinnoull Hill. Buy tickets at the TIC or on the bus at the Mill St. stop. (☎ (0131) 556 2244. Daily June-Aug. 1 per hr. 10am-4pm. £5.50, seniors and students £4, under 12 £2.) The **Royal Bank of Scotland,** South St., is next to the post office. (Open M-Tu and Th-F 9:15am-4:45pm, W 10am-4:45pm, Sa 10am-2pm.) **Internet access** is available at the **A.K. Bell Library,** Glasgow Rd. Either call ahead to book a terminal in the upstairs reference section, or use the computer in the **A.K. Bell Incredible Cafe,** at the front entrance. (☎ 477061. Library £2.50 per 30min.; open M, W, and F 9:30am-5pm, Tu and Th 9:30am-8pm, Sa 9:30am-4pm. Cafe £1 per 15min.; open M-F 9:30am-4:30pm, Sa 9:30am-3:30pm.) The **post office** is at 109 South St. (☎ 624413. Open M-Sa 9am-5:30pm.) **Postal code:** PH2 8AF.

◢◖◗ ACCOMMODATIONS AND FOOD

There used to be fun and music, but all's quiet now at **SYHA Perth,** off Glasgow Rd. Take Hillend bus #7 from the post office, or walk 15 minutes up South St. as it becomes County Pl., York Pl., and Glasgow Rd. Near the crest of the hill, turn right on Rosebank. This 64-bed hostel also has one five-bed cottage for families. (☎ 623658. Lockers available. Laundry. Reception open 7-11am and 5-11:30pm. Check-out 9:30am. Lockout 9:30am-1:30pm. Curfew 11:30pm. Open Mar.-Oct. Dorms £9.25, under 18 £8.) Affordable **B&Bs** line Glasgow Rd. below the hostel (around £14-20 per person), including **Mrs. Glennie,** 54 Glasgow Rd. (☎ 626723; £16 per person); and **Almond Villa,** 81 Glasgow Rd. (☎ 620334; TV; £17.50 per person).

There's an enormous **Safeway** supermarket on Caledonian Rd. (Open M-Tu and Sa 8am-8pm, W-Th 8am-9pm, F 8am-10pm, Su 9am-6pm.) **The Lemon Tree,** 29-41 Skinner Gate, serves up aubergine bake (£4.75), as well as other savory wholefoods. (☎ 442689. Open M-Sa 9:30am-5pm.) A spicy three-course Indian lunch costs £4 (M-Sa) at **Shezan Restaurant,** 21 Princes St. (☎ 620415. Open M-Th noon-2pm and 5pm-midnight, F-Sa noon-2pm and 5pm-1am, Su 4pm-midnight.)

◉ SIGHTS

Balhousie Castle, off Hay St., was once the 16th-century home of the Earls of Kinnoull and now accommodates the **Black Watch Regimental Museum.** It includes weapons, medals from the 18th century, the key to the back door of Spandau prison in Berlin, and the occasional real-life member of the Watch. (☎ 621281. Open May-Sept. M-Sa 10am-4:30pm; Oct.-Apr. M-F 10am-3:30pm. Free.) In 1559, John Knox delivered an incendiary sermon from the pulpit of **St. John's Kirk,** on St. John's Pl., resulting in the destruction of churches and monasteries during the Reformation. Unfortunately, nothing interesting happened here in the next 441 years. (Open M-F 10am-noon and 2-4pm. Tours and laminated leaflet available.)

The **Perth Museum and Art Gallery,** at the intersection of Tay St. and Perth Bridge, houses a random but extensive collection of local history objects, ranging from Pictish stones to antique clocks to the biggest fish which didn't get away in the River Tay. (Tours M-F in the summer. Open M-Sa 10am-5pm. Free.) The **Fergusson Gallery,** in the Old Perth Water Works on Marshall Pl., houses an excellent collection of watercolors by artist J.D. Fergusson, a local lad heavily influenced by his companion, dancer Margaret Morris. (☎ 441944. Open M-Sa 10am-5pm. Free.)

Strolling along the swiftly flowing River Tay lets you peek under the arches of the **Perth Bridge.** Across the bridge, a nature trail in ▨ **Kinnoull Hill Woodland Park** leads to a panoramic view near a ruined tower. A walk across the Queen's Bridge, near the Fergusson Gallery, will take you right to the Rodney Gardens on the opposite bank, where you can start the mile-long **Perth Sculpture Trail.** Survey 24 pieces of modern art while wandering through Perth's riverside greenery. The new **Bell's Cherrybank Centre** is best known for the 900-plus types of heather that bloom in its gardens, but it also provides a glossy look at Perth and a certain native, Arthur Bell, who went into the whisky business. Visitors receive a free dram of whisky, plus free admission into Pitlochry's Blair Athol Distillery (see p. 561) To reach Bell's, catch the #7 bus from South St. (every 20min.) or walk 20 minutes uphill from the youth hostel along Glasgow Rd. (☎ 627330. Open Easter-Oct. M-Sa 9am-5pm, Su noon-4pm; Oct.-Easter M-F 10am-4pm. £3, children free.)

🖤🎵 NIGHTLIFE AND ENTERTAINMENT

Talk Turkey till the wee hours at **Istanbul Kebab,** 1 County Pl., on South St. (☎ 449911. Open daily 5pm-1am.) For a bit of Irish fun, **Mucky Mulligans,** 97 Canal Crescent, hosts live music on Wednesdays and Saturdays. (☎ 636705. Open W-Th noon-12:30am, F noon-1:30am, Sa noon-1am, Su-Tu 12:30-11pm. Cover £1-2 W-Sa after 10:30pm.) **Scaramouche,** 103 South St., is the other classic nightlife spot. Next door to the post office, it has a live DJ Thursday through Sunday nights. (☎ 637479. Open M-Th 11am-11pm, F-Sa 11am-11:45pm, Su 12:30-11pm.) After Scaramouche closes, a free shuttle (Th-Su) will whisk you to **The Ice Factory,** a dance club located outside of town. The **Dewar's Rink** (☎ 624188), Glasgow Rd., stays open all summer and on alternate weekends in winter. Skate or watch a game of curling.

🏛 DAYTRIPS FROM PERTH

SCONE PALACE. Less than three miles northeast of Perth on the A93, sumptuous Scone (SKOON) Palace witnessed the coronation of many a Scottish monarch on the famous Stone of Scone. The English stole the stone in the 13th century (perhaps they mistook it for an English pastry), but returned it some 700 years later on St. Andrew's Day in 1996. Many Scots believe this stone is a fake (see **Stoned,** p. 118). Surrounded by peacock-strewn gardens, the present palace is the lavish Georgian/Neo-Gothic home of the Earl of Mansfield. *(Take bus #3 from South St. (1 per hr., tell the driver where you're going) or a Guide Friday bus tour (see Practical Information, above). ☎ (01738) 552300. Open Apr.-Oct. daily 9:30am-4:45pm. £5.60, seniors and students £4.80, under 16 £3.30; grounds only £2.80, seniors and students £2.40, under 16 £1.70.)*

GLAMIS CASTLE. Macbeth's purported home (pronounced GLOMZ) and childhood playground of the Queen Mum pokes its dozen storybook turrets into the sky 35 mi. northeast of Perth on the A94. It houses collections of armor, paintings, and furniture. *(Take Scottish Citylink from Perth to Dundee, then catch Strathtay bus #22 or 22A to Glamis (30min.; 5 per day). Call the Perth & Kinross Public Transport Traveline (☎ (0845) 301 1130) for updated info. Castle ☎ (01307) 840393. Open Apr.-Oct. daily 10am-4:45pm. £6, students and seniors £4.50, children £3.)*

DUNKELD AND BIRNAM   ☎01350

Huddled amid the forested hills of Perthshire on either side of the River Tay, the wee medieval twin towns of Dunkeld and Birnam (15min. walk apart) provide easy access to one of Scotland's most blessedly isolated regions. The region has long welcomed walkers and hikers to its snow-capped mountains, while artists now find a burgeoning cultural community here as well. The scintillating waters of Loch Tay reflect hilltop forts, 16th-century castles, and the occasional osprey.

🔄 GETTING THERE AND PRACTICAL INFORMATION

The unstaffed **train station** in Birnam is on the main Edinburgh-Inverness line. **Trains** run from: **Perth** (15min., £4.40); **Inverness** (1½hr., £15.40); **Edinburgh** (2hr., £9.30); and **Glasgow** (2hr., £19.30). **Scottish Citylink** (☎ (08705) 505050) **buses** stop by the car park of the Birnam train station, and run fairly frequently from: **Perth** (25min., 6 per day, £4.10); **Pitlochry** (20min., 6 per day); **Edinburgh** (£7); **Glasgow** (£7.50); and **Inverness** (£8.80). If you're coming from Perth or Pitlochry, **local buses** are cheaper and may get you closer to your destination. Grab an essential and free *Public Transport Guide (Highland Perthshire and Stanley Area)* from your nearest tourist information centre or transport centre, or call the Public Transport Traveline (☎ (0845) 301 1130). Local buses stop at the Birnam House Hotel. Find **bike rentals** at **Dunkeld Cycles,** below the Tay Bridge. In summer, you should be able to rent canoes, rowboats, and kayaks here as well. (☎ 728744. Mountain bikes £13 per day. Open daily 9am-5:30pm.)

Nearly all public transport arrives in Birnam (once a popular vacation spot for Victorians), but most amenities are in the quainter Dunkeld. The **Dunkeld tourist information centre** (TIC), in the center of town by the fountain, about a mile from the train station, books accommodations for £1 plus a 10% deposit. There's also a small exhibition upstairs on local history. (☎ 727688. Open July-Aug. M-Sa 9am-7pm, Su 11am-5pm; Apr.-June and Sept.-Oct. M-Sa 9:30am-5:30pm, Su 11am-4pm; Nov.-Dec. Tu-Sa 10am-4pm). Services include Dunkeld's **Bank of Scotland,** High St. (open M-Tu and Th-F 9am-12:30pm and 1:30-5pm, W 10am-12:30pm and 1:30-5pm) and the Dunkeld **post office,** Bridge St. (open M-W and F 9am-1pm and 2-5:30pm, Th 9am-1pm, Sa 9am-12:30pm). **Postal code:** PH8 0AH.

▐▝ ACCOMMODATIONS AND FOOD

The ▓ **Wester Caputh Independent Hostel,** the dreamy masterpiece of three musically-inclined former hostelers, splits into cozy B&B-type rooms or rustic hostel dorms (with incredible showers) and sometimes witnesses impromptu jam sessions. It's out of town on the A984, and then right on the road to Caputh, but if you give them notice they'll pick you up from the train or bus station. (☎/fax (01738) 710617. Breakfast £1.50. Laundry £2-4 per load. Internet access £1 per 15min. Bike rental £6 half day, £10 full day. Dorms £8; B&B £10.) Birnam and Dunkeld have dozens of **B&Bs;** the TIC has a complete listing on its door. The happening **Taybank Hotel** (owned by the legendary folk musician Dougie Maclean of "Caledonia" fame), is right by the Dunkeld Bridge and offers simple, comfy rooms themed around Scottish musicians. (☎ 727340; fax 728606; www.taybank.com. Breakfast included. £17.50 per person; single £5 extra.) Two people looking for unusual luxury can try the twin annexes at the posh **Royal Dunkeld Hotel,** Atholl St. (☎ 727322; fax 728989. Breakfast and luxury included. Twins £35.) **Campers** should head for **Inver Mill Caravan Park,** across the river from Dunkeld and north, with toilets and showers. (☎ 727477. Open Apr.-Oct. Electricity not included. £8-10 for 2 people, tent, and car; £1 each additional person.)

The **Co-op** supermarket, Bridge St., is in Dunkeld. (Open M-Sa 8am-8pm, Su 9am-6pm.) ▓ **Maclean's Real Music Bar,** in the Taybank Hotel, Dunkeld (see above), serves amazing chocolate pudding (£2) and hosts casual gatherings of local and visiting musicians—sometimes even Dougie himself. Spare instruments on the walls let you join in. Thursday's the best night for music, but it gets crowded in the summer. Friday also features live folk music upstairs, often with surprise guests or open mike sessions. (☎ 727340. Open M-W 6-11pm, Th-Su noon-11pm. Cover F £4, open mike £2.) For great date and walnut bread (80p), head down to the **Tappit Hen,** 7 Atholl St., in Dunkeld. (☎ 727472. Open summer M-Sa 10:30am-5pm; July-Aug. also Su. 11:30am-4:30pm; winter M-Sa 10:30am-4:30pm.)

◉▐ SIGHTS AND ACTIVITIES

Painstakingly restored 18th-century houses line the way to the partially charred 13th-century **Dunkeld Cathedral,** High St., whose choir is now a restored parish church. Alexander Stewart, the "Wolf of Badenoch" and illegitimate son of English king Robert II, sought revenge for his excommunication by razing several Tayside villages and pilfering the gold chalices from the cathedral. (Open Apr.-Sept. M-Sa 9:30am-6:30pm, Su 2-6:30pm; Oct.-Mar. M-Sa 9:30am-4pm, Su 2-4pm. Free.) In the summer, a perennial **Amateur Art Exhibition** in nearby Duchess Anne Hall is certainly worth a look (open mid-June to Aug. daily until 9pm); also be sure to stroll through the tranquil meadows of **Stanley Hill** just behind it.

Over the arched Telford Bridge in Birnam, catch a flimsy claim to literary fame: Beatrix Potter spent most of her childhood holidays in the area, drawing on her experiences in *The Tale of Peter Rabbit.* The **Beatrix Potter Garden,** across from the Birnam Hotel, recreates the setting of the bunny's escapades, including Mrs. Tiggywinkle's house and Peter's burrow. Next door, the **Birnam Institute** also celebrates the author. (Open M-Sa 10am-4pm, Su 2-4pm. Garden Free.)

The TIC's *Dunkeld & Birnam Walks* (50p) provides maps of lovely walks around the area. Paths lead north from Birnam to the great **Birnam Oak,** the remnant of Shakespeare's fabled Birnam Wood, while the brisk and savage waterfalls of the **Hermitage** tumble 1½ mi. away, with a well-marked ¾ mi. path that takes you to all the designated photo ops. (Free walking tours July to mid-Sept. Contact the Dunkeld TIC.) Birdwatchers will enjoy the **Loch of the Lowes,** a wildlife reserve 2 mi. east of Dunkeld just off the A923. For the past eight years, this has served as the summer retreat for some travel-happy ospreys, who fly all the way from Gambia, and boy, are their wings tired. (☎ 727337. Visitor center open daily mid-July to mid-Aug. 10am-6pm; Apr. to mid-July and mid-Aug. to Sept. 10am-5pm.) It's also possible to **fish** in the River Tay. A trout-fishing license costs only £3-4 per day and can be bought from **Kettles,** 15 Atholl St. (☎ 727556). They or the TIC can also point you toward tackle hire. Trout season last from mid-March to mid-October.

NEAR DUNKELD AND BIRNAM: THE CATERAN TRAIL

Highland Perthshire, in the area northeast of Dunkeld and Birnam, is also home to the newly-established Cateran Trail, a user-friendly 60 mi. hike "in the heart of Scotland." Cairns and ruins line the loop between the Bridge of Cally, Alyth, Blairgowrie, and the Spittal of Glenshee. The theme is romanticized cattle-rustling of yore (caterans were cattle-rustlers, as the map, available in most local TICs, will tell you). The trail splits into five easy sections, each a day's hike with comfy B&Bs at the end. Call the **Cateran Trail Company** (☎ (08000) 277200) to book accommodations; if you're really a wimp, they'll even cart your pack around for you.

LOCH TAY

As one might expect, the most beautiful part of Perthshire is also the most remote. **Aberfeldy** is accessible by various Perthshire local buses from Pitlochry, Perth, and Dunkeld and Birnam. The **Perthshire Public Transport Traveline** (☎ (0845) 3011130) has the most updated information. From Aberfeldy you can travel to other towns around Loch Tay by post bus. The folks at the **Postbus Helpline** (☎ (01246) 546329) can help you sort out the confusion.

The remarkable village of **Fortingall,** about 4 mi. northwest of Kenmore (beyond Aberfeldy on the A827), has two claims to fame: it's home to a 3000-year-old yew tree, the oldest living organism in Europe, and it's the supposed birthplace of Pontius Pilate, whose father was purportedly a Roman soldier stationed here. **Post buses** arrive from **Aberfeldy** (#211, 50min., M-Sa 9am). At the opposite end of Loch Tay, the village of **Killin** is a good base for hiking, with many reasonably priced B&Bs and a green-gabled **SHYA Youth Hostel.** (☎ (01567) 820546. Open Mar.-Oct. F-Sa. Dorms £8.50, under 18 £7.50.) Killin is also home to the **Breadalbane Folklore Centre,** located in the same building as the **tourist information centre,** by the Falls of Douchart on Main St. Learn about Gaelic mythical characters while you soak up information on countless hill walks and water-sports on the surrounding lochs. (☎ (01567) 820254. Open July-Aug. daily 9:30am-6:30pm; Mar.-June and Sept. daily 10am-6pm; Mar-Apr. and Oct. daily 10am-5pm; Feb. Sa-Su 10am-4pm. £1.55, concessions £1.05.) One of the best short hikes starts from behind the schoolyard on Main St. and leads to a marvelous sheep's eye view of the loch. **Post buses** arrive from: **Aberfeldy** (#212, 3hr., M-Sa 9am); **Crianlarich** (#025, M-Sa 10:32am); and **Tyndrum** (#025, M-Sa 10:22am). Midway between Kenmore and Killin on the west shore of Loch Tay, 7 mi. northeast of town, is the **Ben Lawers Visitors Centre.** (☎ (01567) 820397. Open Easter-Sept. daily 10am-1pm and 2-5pm.) The center marks the trailhead of a 5-6hr. hike up Britain's tenth-highest peak. Postbus #212 swings near Ben Lawers on its way from **Aberfeldy** to **Killin.**

CENTRAL SCOTLAND

PITLOCHRY   ☎01796

Snuggled in the "Heart of Scotland," amid the foliage and mist of the Grampian Mountains, Pitlochry and its environs have attracted travelers since the mid-19th century. Summer theater, a dam and salmon ladder, two distilleries, and a web of hill walks continue to make visits worthwhile, although you might be better off staying in the nearby town of Moulin and making quick incursions into Pitlochry to avoid the tour buses. A bulging trade in whisky, shortbread, and knitwear has turned this picturesque town into just a place to shop.

▐ GETTING THERE AND GETTING AROUND

Trains (☎ (08457) 484950) stop alongside the town center from: **Perth** (35min., 9 per day, £8); **Glasgow** (1¾hr., 7 per day, £18.70); **Inverness** (1¾hr., 9 per day, £13.10); and **Edinburgh** (2hr., 7 per day, £18.70). The yellow phone on the platform connects to the information office at Inverness Station. **Scottish Citylink** (☎ (08705) 505050) **buses** stop outside the Fishers Hotel on Atholl Rd. from: **Perth** (40min., 1 per hr., £4.80); **Inverness** (2hr., 1 per hr., £7.70); **Edinburgh** (2hr., 10 per day, £7); and **Glasgow** (2½hr., 8 per day, £7.50). In the summer, **Stagecoach Bluebird** (☎ (01224) 212266) "Heather-hopper" #201 flies from **Aberdeen** via **Braemar** (1 per hr., £14). From Perth you can also take various local bus services; call the **Public Transportation Traveline** (☎ (0845) 301 1130) for the most up-to-date info. Rent **bikes** at **Escape Route,** 8 West Moulin Rd., for £14 per day (☎ 473859; open Su-F 10am-5pm, Sa 9:30am-5pm) or **The Well House,** 11 Toberargan Rd., for £5 per day (☎ 472239; opens 7am).

▐ PRACTICAL INFORMATION

A mammoth selection of postcards awaits at the **tourist information centre** (TIC), 22 Atholl Rd., as does the £1 *Perthshire: The Essential Guide.* (☎ 472215; fax 474046. Open June to mid-Sept. daily 9am-8pm; Apr.-May and mid-Sept. to Oct. M-Sa 9am-6pm, Su 11am-5pm; Nov.-Mar. M-F 9am-5pm, Sa 11am-3pm.) The **Royal Bank of Scotland** is at 76 Atholl St. (Open M-Tu and Th-F 9am-5pm, W 10am-5pm.) Services include: **Internet access** at the **Computer Services Centre,** 67 Atholl Rd., next to the Gem Box jewelry store (☎ 473711; 10p per min.; open M-F 9am-5:30pm, Sa 9am-noon) or at **Perth College Pitlochry Learning Centre,** 123 Atholl Rd. (☎ 473828; £5 per hr.; open M-F 9am-5pm, Tu also 6-9pm); **Pitlochry Laundrette,** 3 West Moulin Rd. (☎ 474044; wash £2.60 per load, £1.50 to dry, soap 20p; open M-W and F 7:30am-5pm, Th and Sa 9am-5pm; June-Sept. also Tu until 8pm), and the **post office,** 92 Atholl Rd. (open M-F 9am-5:30pm, Sa 9am-12:30pm). **Postal code:** PH16 5AH.

▐ ACCOMMODATIONS AND FOOD

The inviting **SYHA Pitlochry,** Knockard Rd. and Well Brae Rd., provides mountain views and a shower in each room. From the train and bus stations, it's a 10-minute walk for the spry, or a 20-minute trek for the rest of us. Turn right on Atholl Rd., and then left uphill onto Bonnethill Rd., where the hostel is signposted. (☎ 472308; fax 473729. Breakfast included. Reception open 7am-11pm. Laundry £2 per load. Internet access £5 per hr. Checkout 9:30am. Curfew 11:45pm. Dorms £11.25, under 18 £10.) The brand-new **Pitlochry Backpackers,** 134 Atholl St., converted from a former hotel, has all twin rooms with bath. (☎ 470044. £11 per person.) On the west end of town, **Bowmore Cottage,** 145 Atholl Rd., is a cheery B&B with a sunny backyard patio less than five minutes from the city center. Turn left from the train and bus stations onto Atholl Rd. (☎ 473314; dougie@bowmore.oik.co.uk. £15 per person.) One mile up West Moulin Rd., the wee village of **Moulin** provides the perfect base for an escape into the hills. There, **Mrs. Currie's B&B,** Baringa, Craiglunie Gdns., offers a spectacular view. (☎ 472868. Open June-Sept. £16 per person; discount if you flash your *Let's Go.*) Two miles past town on Atholl Rd., you can **camp** at **Faskally Home Farm** at one of their 255 sites. (☎ 472007; fax 473896. Electricity, sauna, pool, and jacuzzi cost extra. Open mid-Mar. to Oct. £6 per person and tent.)

It's only a 5min. walk from Mrs. Currie's to the 300-year-old **Moulin Inn,** Moulin Sq., which brews its own "Braveheart ale" and serves affordable grub until 9:30pm. (☎ 472196. Open Su-Th noon-11pm, F-Sa noon-11:45pm.) On West Moulin Rd., back in Pitlochry, the **Pitlochry Co-op** provides groceries. (Open daily 8am-10pm.) At **Bamboo House,** 48 Atholl Rd., sweet-and-sour chicken with chips costs £4.50. (☎ 472036. Open Su-Th 3:30pm-midnight, F noon-12:30am, Sa noon-midnight.)

🏛 🎭 SIGHTS AND FESTIVALS

Since the word "whisky" comes from an old Gaelic term meaning "the water of life," Pitlochry may live forever. Down the main road, a half mile from the TIC, is **Blair Athol Distillery,** where enough alcohol evaporates daily to intoxicate the entire town. Tours leave from the gift shop; kilted guides take you from flowing water to mashing malt to a free dram. (☎ 472234. Open Easter-Sept. M-Sa 9am-5pm, Su noon-5pm; Oct.-Easter M-F 9am-4pm. Last full tour 1 hr. before closing. £3.) ◾ **The Edradour** is Scotland's tiniest distillery, and still employs old-fashioned techniques to turn out 15 casks a week. The 2½ mi. walk from Pitlochry (past Moulin along the A924) is rewarded with a free tour and gulp of a single malt upon arrival. Get there before 3pm, when distilling finishes. (☎ 472095. Open Mar.-Oct. M-Sa 9:30am-5pm, Su noon-5pm; Nov. to mid-Dec. M-Sa 10am-4pm.)

Those walking should arm themselves with a copy of *Pitlochry Walks,* available at the TIC for 50p. Footpaths connect the Edradour Distillery with the 15th-century **Black Castle ruins,** burned way back for fear of the plague. Beyond that lies the charming village of Moulin, which has a reputed **Crusader's grave** in its ancient churchyard. For a quick jaunt, take the path over the suspension footbridge to the **Pitlochry Dam** and **salmon ladder.** From the dam's observation chamber, voyeurs watch spawning future fillets struggle ceaselessly against the current. The unromantic may get a fishing permit and head 100 yd. upstream. An electronic fish counter keeps tally. (☎ 473152. Open Apr.-Oct. daily 10am-5:30pm. Observation chamber and dam free; visitor center £2, students £1.20, under 16 £1.) Observe more weird processes at the **HeatherGems Factory and Visitor Centre,** right behind the TIC. Craftsmen cut and polish vacuum-packed heather stems into tourist-pleasing jewelry. Eh? (☎ 474391. Open June-Sept. M-F 9am-5:30pm, Sa 9am-5pm, Su 9:30am-5pm; Oct.-May M-F 9am-5pm, Sa 9:30am-5pm.)

The glitzy **Pitlochry Festival Theatre,** just over the Aldour Bridge, boasts a cinema as well as international performers. The 2001 season opens in May. (Tickets £13.50-17.50, students and hostelers half price.) Last year saw the first-ever **Pitlochry Fringe,** a program of rotating small theater and other cultural events. For information and tickets for both the Fringe and the Festival Theatre, visit the box office on Bonnethill Rd. or call ☎ 484626. In the field down Tummel Crescent, **Highland Nights** feature excellent local pipe bands and traditional dancing. (May-Sept. M nights. Tickets available at the gate; £3, students and seniors £2.50, children 50p.) Pick up the free *What's On in Perthshire* at the TIC for entertainment ideas.

🏞 DAYTRIPS FROM PITLOCHRY

HIKING. If you're feeling fit, a 4hr. hike will allow you to charge up the 2757 ft. **Ben-y-Vrackie,** which gives views of Edinburgh on a clear day. From Moulin, turn left onto the road directly behind the Moulin Inn and follow the curve until you reach a fork (note the standing stones in the field nearby). Taking the right-hand road brings you to Ben-y-Vrackie; continue along the left-hand road about two hours to explore **Craigower Hill.** A 2½ mi. walk from the Pitlochry dam leads to the Pass of Killiecrankie (see below).

PASS OF KILLIECRANKIE. A few miles north of Pitlochry, the valley of the River Garry narrows into a stunning pass, laced with historical significance. In 1689, a

Jacobite army slaughtered William III's troops here in an attempt to reinstall James VII of Scotland on the English throne. One stranded government soldier by the name of Donald MacBean vaulted 18 ft. across **Soldier's Leap,** preferring to risk the steep fall rather than surrender. For information or a guided walk, stop in at the **National Trust Visitors Centre.** (☎ 473233. Open Apr.-Oct. daily 10am-5:30pm.) The area affords spectacular views, especially over the River Garry at sunset. *(Elizabeth Yule bus #87 runs from the West End Car Park to the pass in summer (4 per day; £1).*

◼ **BLAIR CASTLE.** Seven miles north of Pitlochry on the A9, the well-groomed lawns of Blair Castle are used as training grounds for the Duke of Atholl's army, the only private army in Western Europe. Prepared to fight in both the American Revolution and World War I, the farthest the troops have ever gone is Ireland. Today the army is about 80 men strong and limited mostly to ceremonial duties. *(Take the train to Blair Athol (about £3) and walk 10min., or hop on bus #26 or 87 from the West End Car Park.* ☎ 481207. Open Apr.-Oct. daily 10am-6pm, last admission 5pm. £6, seniors and students £5, children £4, families £18.)

OBAN   ☎ 01631

Oban (OH-ben; pop. 8500), the busiest ferry port on Scotland's west coast, has managed an unabashed embrace of tourism without a Faustian sale of its soul. Lacking notable attractions, Oban endears itself with sporadic outbursts of small-town warmth; it is also an excellent base from which to explore the nearby islands and the Argyll countryside. As the sun sets over the blue hills of Mull and the port workers turn in for the day, the streets of Oban fill with people strolling along the scenic harbor, chatting with neighbors, or heading to the pub for a dram.

▐ **GETTING THERE AND GETTING TO THE HEBRIDES.** The **train station** is on Railway Pier. (☎ 563083. Ticket office open M-Sa 7am-6:10pm, Su 11am-6:10pm.) **Trains** (☎ (08457) 484950) run from **Glasgow Queen St.** (3hr., 3 per day, £17) and from **Fort William** via **Crianlarich** (4hr., 3 per day, £18.50). The **bus stop** is near the train station. The **Oban District Bus Office,** 1 Queens Park Pl., provides timetables, sells tickets, and stores luggage for £1.50. (☎ 562856. Open June-Aug. M-Sa 8:30am-5pm; Sept.-May daily 8:30am-1pm and 2-5pm.) **Scottish Citylink** (☎ (08705) 505050) arrives from: **Fort William** (1¾hr., 5 per day, £6.60); **Glasgow** (3hr.; M-Sa 3 per day, Su 2 per day; £10); and **Inverness** via Fort William (4hr., 4 per day, £10.90).

Caledonian MacBrayne Ferries (☎ 566688, reservations ☎ (0990) 650000) sail from Railway Pier to the southern Hebrides. Pick up a copy of the *Cal-Mac 2001 Timetable* at the ferry station or tourist information centre. Ferries head to **Craignure,** Mull (45min.; M-Sa 6 per day, Su 5 per day; £3.45); **Lismore** (50min., M-Sa 3-5 per day, £2.35); **Colonsay** (2½hr.; M, W, and F 1 per day; £9.85); **Coll** and **Tiree** (2¾hr. to Coll, 3¾hr. to Tiree; 5 per week; £11.10); and **Barra** and **South Uist** (5hr. to Barra, 7hr. to South Uist; M and W-Sa 1 per day; £18.25). If you have a car, book ahead and be prepared to pay exorbitant sums. Foot passengers rarely need to book, but you should call to confirm times. In winter, ferry travel is very limited.

◼▐ **ORIENTATION AND PRACTICAL INFORMATION.** Fronting the harbor, **George St.** is the heart (and much of the torso) of Oban. **Argyll Sq.,** actually a roundabout, is a block inland, northeast of the pier. **Corran Esplanade** runs along the coast north of town, **Gallanach Rd.** along the coast to the south. A vaulted **tourist information centre** (TIC) inhabits an old church on Argyle Sq. Browse books or the extensive display board, reserve a bed for £1 and a 10% deposit, and pick up travel timetables in the bright, cheery interior. (☎ 563122. Open May-June M-Sa 9am-6:30pm, Su 10am-5pm; July-Aug. M-Sa 9am-9pm, Su 9am-7pm; Sept. M-Sa 9am-6:30pm, Su 10am-5pm; Oct. M-Sa 9am-5:30pm, Su 10am-4pm; Nov.-Mar. M-F 9:30am-5pm, Sa-Su noon-4pm; Apr. M-F 9am-5pm, Sa-Su noon-5pm.) **Internet access** is available at the Oban Backpacker's Lodge (see below). The **post office** is in the **Tesco** supermarket, Lochside St. off Argyll Sq. (☎ 565676. Store open M-Th and Sa 8am-8pm, F 8am-9pm, Su 9am-6pm.) **Postal code:** PA34 4AA.

▌ ACCOMMODATIONS. The spacious **Oban Waterfront Lodge**, Corran Esplanade, about ½ mi. from the train station on the waterfront, holds the biggest beds around. The friendly staff and ideal location next to Markie Dan's Pub make for a very social atmosphere. (☎ 566040. No curfew. Breakfast £1.85, 10% discount vouchers for all-you-can-eat dinner at Markie Dan's. Dorms £10.) To reach the glorious peach bunks and super-pressure showers of **Oban Backpacker's Lodge**, 21 Breadalbane St., take George St. from Railway Pier until it forks; it's on the right prong. Shoot pool, browse through *Cosmo*, and surf the web in the all-purpose lounge. (☎ 562107. Internet access £5 per hr. Checkout 10:30am. Curfew 2:30am. Continental breakfast £1.60. Dorms £11.) The **SYHA Oban**, Rassay Lodge, Corran Esplanade, hugs the waterfront ¾ mi. north of the train station, just past St. Columba's Cathedral. Rooms in the new annex all come with bath, but a bit more expensive. (☎ 562025. Lockout 10:30am-1pm. Reception until 11:30pm. Checkout 10:30am. Curfew 2am. Open Mar.-Dec. Dorms £12.25-13.25, under 18 £10.75-11.75.)

B&Bs (£15-17) line **Ardonnel Rd.** and **Dunollie Rd.** Eight rooms, all with bath and TV, welcome you to bright blue **Maridon House**, Dunuaran Rd. Guests have full use of the kitchen. From Argyle Sq., walk to the end of Albany St. and look up. (☎ 562670; maridonhse@aol.com. July-Aug. £19 per person; Sept.-June £16). **St. Anne's B&B**, Dunollie Rd., provides 6 clean rooms. (☎ 562743. July-Aug. £15 per person; Sept.-June £13.50). Ask at the TIC about **campsites** around town.

▐▐ FOOD AND PUBS. Harborside **George St.,** beginning near the train station, is Oban's food center and nightlife strip. Seafood shops cluster around the ferry terminal. **Mussels** are atypically cheap in Oban; grab some delicious steamed ones. **Cafe Forty-One,** 41 Combie St., provides inexpensive meals with nary a tourist in sight. (All-day breakfast £3.95, sandwiches 80p-£1.30. Open daily 10am-2:30pm and 6:30-9:30pm.) For fresh fish and chips pulled straight out of Oban waters, stop by **Hungry Macs,** 116 George St. (☎ 562426). Or try **McTavish's Kitchens,** 34 George St. (☎ 563064), with shows of traditional Scottish singing and dancing; of course, the tourist-packed room makes the whole thing rather *un*traditional. The downstairs cafeteria serves good, cheap food. (Shows May-Sept. 8:30pm and 10:30pm. £3.50, children £1.75. Open daily in summer 9am-10pm; in winter 9am-6pm.)

Pints go for about £2 in Oban. **O'Donnell's Irish Pub,** Breadalbane St., draws in the young, with live music Thursday through Monday nights. (☎ 566159. Open daily noon-1am.) Also competing for local drinkers and cheery hostelers is **Markie Dan's,** next door to the Oban Waterfront Lodge on the Esplanade. Frequent live music, drink specials, and a friendly bar staff make for a great atmosphere. Step outside for a marvelous view of the water. (Open daily 11am-1am.)

▐▐ SIGHTS AND ENTERTAINMENT. The structure that awkwardly dominates the Oban skyline is **McCaig's Tower.** A free climb leads to a great view overlooking the harbor. To get to the tower, take the steep Jacob's Ladder stairway at the end of Argyll St., then walk to your left along Ardconnel Rd. and right up Laurel St. to the tower's grassy entrance. Past the north end of town, the ivy-eaten remains of 7th-century **Dunollie Castle**—Oban's oldest building—loom atop a cliff. Dunollie is the seat of the MacDougall family, who once owned a third of Scotland. From town, walk 20min. north along the water until you've curved around the castle; then take the path to the right. Look out or the stinging nettles that line the path. (Always open. Free.) Just 2½ mi. outside town on Glencruitten Rd., **Achnilarig Farms** offers guided horse rides to people of all levels of experience. (☎ 562745. Open all year, usually Su-F; hours vary. £12 per hr., children £10.)

NEAR OBAN

LOCH ETIVE AND TAYNUILT. To the north gapes the mouth of Loch Etive, where the unduly famed **Falls of Lora** change direction with the shifting of the tides. From **Taynuilt,** off the A85, seven miles east of the loch mouth, the family-run **Loch Etive Cruises** runs 3hr. tours up the loch into beautiful and otherwise inaccessible countryside. Call the night before you arrive to arrange a free shuttle from your bus to the pier. (☎ (01866) 822430. May-Sept. M-F 10:30am and 2pm, Sa-Su 2pm; Apr. and early to mid-Oct. daily 2pm only. £8, children £4, families £20.) **Scottish Citylink** buses stop at Taynuilt on their **Oban-Glasgow** and **Oban-Edinburgh** routes; **Strathclyde Transport** bus #976 also stops at Taynuilt from Oban (£2.50).

LOCH AWE AND KILCHURN CASTLE. Fourteen miles beyond Taynuilt on the A85 is **Loch Awe,** renowned for its salmon and trout fishing and for the ruins of massive 15th-century **Kilchurn Castle.** At the loch's north end, the castle is one of Scotland's most photographed. Its broad, gray stone towers sit right on the water, with majestic hills looming behind. (Always open. Free.)

CASTLE STALKER. To reach **Appin,** cross Connel Bridge over the mouth of Loch Etive. The hauntingly beautiful **Castle Stalker** is 10 mi. down the A828 in Portnacroish. This 16th-century Stewart stronghold sits on an islet in Loch Linnhe. Perhaps best known as "Castle Aaaaaaaaa" in *Monty Python and the Holy Grail,* it can only be visited by arrangement during the last three weeks of August. (☎ (01631) 730234. £6, children £3. 1½hr. tours Tu and W 9:30am.) Take bus #918 to Appin from **Oban** (M-Sa 4 per day, Su 2 per day; £3.50).

SEIL, EASDALE AND LUING. South of Oban, four miles off the A816 (take the B844 Kilninver turn-off for eight miles), are the islands of **Seil, Easdale,** and **Luing.** Until the opening of the Skye Bridge, Seil was the only Hebridean island connected to the mainland; crossing **The Bridge Across the Atlantic** allows tourists to cross the Atlantic without leaving Scotland. Just across the bridge is the **Tigh an Truish Hotel** (☎ (01852) 300242), with good pub lunches and Guinness (£2.80). The name means "House of Trousers"; after kilt-wearing was forbidden on the mainland, Highlanders would change at the inn before and after crossing. Bus #418 scampers to Seil from Oban (M-Sa 1-4 per day, £2). **Hitchhikers** report success in the area, although *Let's Go* does not recommend hitchhiking. **Easdale,** less than one mile across, offers spectacular views of the sea.

KERRERA. Five minutes across the bay from Oban is the beautiful, nearly-deserted island of **Kerrera** (CARE-er-uh). A ferry comes to Kerrera from **Ganlochhead,** two miles south of Oban. Turn the board to the black side to signal the ferryman; call for winter sailings. (☎ (01631) 563665. Daily 2 per hr. 10:30am-noon and 2-6pm, also M-Sa 8:45am. Return £3, children £1.50, bike 50p.) Wander over for the day, or stay the night at the **Gylen Bothy** on the island's south tip, two miles from the pier. (☎ (01631) 570223. Kitchen. Bedding provided. Bunkhouse space £7.50.)

ISLE OF ISLAY

West of the Kintyre Peninsula, the Isle of Islay (EYE-luh) receives relatively few visitors, for good reason. Islay's two ports are hardly enticing: Port Askaig, on the northeast coast, offers little but a hotel, a shop, and a ferry terminal; similarly, Port Ellen, in the south, has one cafe, a few B&Bs, and two shut-down, boarded-up hotels. Those who do make it here are usually living *la vida agua,* drowned in the whisky of Islay's scattered distilleries. Near Islay, the tiny **Isle of Jura** ("Deer Island") is one of the most isolated Scottish islands and a walker's heaven, possessing rugged hills and just one wee road.

THE WHISKY TRAIL Islay is famed for its fine malt whiskys and possesses seven distilleries; Jura has another for good measure. The malts are known for their peaty flavor—not surprising, considering half of Islay is peat bog. Islay's sparse population, clean and fertile environment (very little farming results in very little pollution), and fresh water supply (numerous lochs and rivers), are all ideal for a flourishing whisky trail. So what gives each malt a distinctive flavor? A plethora of determinants: the water supply, the type and quality of the barley, the temperature, the air quality, the type of wood in which the whisky is stored—even the shape of the pot-still (the large kettle-like structure in which whisky is distilled) matters. Pick up *The Islay and Jura Whisky Trail* leaflet, free from tourist information centres, to aid you in your quest for that perfect dram. Better yet, use our condensed guide:

Ardbeg: (☎ (01496) 302244). On the southeast coast, 4 mi. from Port Ellen. Tours by appointment. £2.

Bowmore: (☎ (01496) 810441), right in town. The oldest distillery on Islay, brewing since 1779. Tours year-round M-F 10:30am and 2pm; in summer also 11:30am and 3pm and Sa 10:30am. £2.

Bunnahabhainn (Bunna-HAV-en): (☎ (01496) 840646). The northernmost distillery. Tours year-round M-Th 10:30am, 1:30pm, and 2:45am; F 10:30am. Free.

Caol Ila (Cool-EE-la): (☎ (01496) 840207), 1 mi. from Port Askaig. Tours year-round M-Tu and Th-F 10am, 11:15am, 1:30pm, and 2:45pm; W 10am and 11:15am. £3.

Jura: (☎ (01496) 820240), near Craighouse village. Tours by appointment only.

Lagavulin: (☎ (01496) 302400), 3 mi. from Port Ellen. Tours in summer M-F by appointment only. £3.

Laphroaig (La-FROYG): (☎ (01496) 302418), beside Port Ellen, the peatiest of peaty malts. Tours M-F 10:15am and 2:15pm. Free.

F GETTING THERE AND GETTING AROUND. Ferries leave from **Kennacraig Ferry Terminal,** seven miles south of **Tarbert** on the Kintyre Peninsula, running either to Port Askaig or to Port Ellen (M-Tu and Th-Sa 7:15am, 12:50pm, and 6pm, W 8:15am, Su 12:50pm; either route £6.65). Travelers from **Arran** can catch bus #448 at the **Claonaig** ferry landing to Kennacraig (M-Sa 3 per day). A combination bus-ferry ticket for travel between **Glasgow** and **Islay** is £20 from **Scottish Citylink** or **Cal-Mac** offices. Every Wednesday in summer, a boat leaves **Oban,** stops on **Colonsay,** and continues to Port Askaig (4 hr., £9.60). Check times in the Strathclyde Transport *Area Transport Guide* (to Arran or the Kintyre Peninsula), available at any TIC or from bus drivers. Most bus schedules follow ferry times quite closely, but call to verify your connection or risk being stranded. **Western Ferries** (☎ 840681) runs a little blue car ferry to **Jura** from Port Askaig across the Sound of Islay (5min.; in summer M-Sa 14 per day, Su 6 per day; in winter M-Sa 12 per day, Su 2 per day; 90p)

Islay Coaches (☎ (01496) 840273) bounce frequently around the island. Bus #451 connects **Port Ellen** and **Port Askaig** via **Bowmore** (M-Sa about 4 per day, Su 1 per day); #450 runs from **Bowmore** to **Port Charlotte** (M-Sa 3 per day). **Postbuses** also travel between the towns a few times per day. It is easiest to get to and around the island on a Wednesday, and many of the bus times apply to one day only, so read bus schedules carefully. Purchase single tickets because returns aren't cheaper, and tickets on different buses are not interchangeable.

PORT ELLEN   ☎01496

The beauty of Port Ellen is not in the solitude of the pub-less streets, but in the solitude of the nearby coastline. To the west, the windswept **Mull of Oa** drops dramatically to the sea. For a taste of its beauty, walk along the Mull of Oa Rd. toward the solar-powered Carraig Fhada lighthouse 1½ mi. away. To the east, a more substantial journey passes the distilleries, standing stones, the ruins of the 16th-century **Dunyveg (Dun-Naomhaig) Castle,** and **Loch an t-Sailein,** otherwise known as "Seal Bay." Seven miles east is the **Kildalton Chapel;** its holds the miraculously preserved **Kildalton High Cross,** a piece of blue stone thought to date from the 9th century.

CENTRAL SCOTLAND

Port Ellen's tiny **Kildalton and Oa Information Centre,** next to the post office, is not an official tourist information centre, but stocks bus schedules and leaflets on the area's attractions. (Open Mar.-Dec. M-Sa 9am-noon.) The **post office** is at 54 Frederick Crescent near the ferry terminal, on the corner of Charlotte St. (☎ 302382. Open M-F 9am-1pm and 2-5:30pm, Sa 9am-12:30pm.) **Postal code:** PA42 7BD.

In town, Mrs. Hedley's **Trout Fly Guest House,** 8 Charlotte St., has decent rooms. If you're hungry, you may have to pay for their £12.50 three-course meal, since there are no restaurants in town. (☎ 302204; fax 300076. Singles £18.50; doubles £41.) Three miles away in Kintra, the **Kintra Independent Hostel** stands in solitary coastal splendor on a full-fledged working farm. (☎ 302051. Self-catering only. No curfew. Open Apr.-Sept. Dorms £6.50.) Kintra welcomes **campers** as well, who perch at the southern end of a seven-mile white-sand beach. From Port Ellen, take the Mull of Oa Road 1 mi., then follow the right fork marked "To Kintra." (Showers and toilets. £2 per person; £2.50 per tent.) In Port Ellen, Frederick Crescent rings the harbor and holds a **Co-op Foodstore.** (☎ 302446; open M-Sa 8am-8pm, Su 12:30-6pm.)

NEAR PORT ELLEN: PORT CHARLOTTE. In West Islay, the town of Port Charlotte holds the **Port Charlotte Field Centre,** in a former distillery warehouse on the beach. The center tells all about the island's famed wildlife, which includes several rare bird species. (☎ 850288. Open Apr.-Oct. M-Tu and Th-Sa 10am-3pm, Su 2-5pm. £2, students and seniors £1.20, children £1.) Across the road, the **Museum of Islay Life** reveals Islay's history of Viking raids, clans, and—of course—whisky. (☎ 850358. Open June-Sept. M-Sa 10am-5pm, Su 2-5pm. £2, students and seniors £1.20, children £1, families £5.) The **SYHA Islay** youth hostel stands above the Field Centre. (☎/fax 850385. Curfew 11:45pm. Open Mar.-Oct. Dorms £8.75, under 18 £7.75.)

BOWMORE ☎01496

Bowmore, Islay's largest town, is 10 mi. from both Port Ellen and Port Askaig. Arranged in a grid-like, practical design, Bowmore is not exactly laden with architectural splendors. The 18th-century **Bowmore Round Church** on Main St. (also called Kilarrow Parish Church) was built perfectly round to keep Satan from hiding in the corners. (Open daily 10am-5pm. Free.) Sprawling behind the town square, **Morrison's Bowmore Distillery,** School St., is the oldest distillery in full-time operation. Drain your complimentary dram after the £2 tour. The coast between Bowmore and Port Ellen is graced by the **Big Strand,** 7 mi. of sandy beach.

Islay's only **tourist information centre** (TIC) calls Bowmore home, and books accommodations for £1. If you plan to explore, pick up *Walks in Islay, Jura, and Colonsay* for £2. (☎ 810254. Open July to mid-Sept. M-Sa 9:30am-5:30pm, Su 2-5pm; June M-Sa 9:30am-5pm, Su 2-5pm; Apr. M-Sa 10am-5pm; mid-Sept. to Oct. M-Sa 10am-4:30pm; Nov.-Mar. M-F noon-4pm.) Services include: a **cash machine** at the **Royal Bank of Scotland,** next to the TIC (☎ 810555; open M-Tu and Th-F 9:15am-4:45pm, W 10am-4:45pm); the only **launderette** on the island, in the **Mactaggart Leisure Centre,** School St., where you can go for a swim (£2.10) while your clothes take a spin (☎ 810767; wash £2.80, dry £2.80; open Tu-F 12:30-9pm, Sa 10:30am-4pm, Su 10:30am-5:30pm); and the **post office,** just up the hill on Main St., next to the Round Church. (☎ 810366; open M-W and F 9am-1pm and 2-5:30pm, Th 9am-1pm, Sa 9am-12:30pm). The post office also **rents bicycles** for £10 per day; discounts for longer rentals. **Postal code:** PA43 7JH.

Mrs. Omand's B&B, Tiree House, offers accommodations on Jamieson St. (☎ 810633; £16 per person), or try **Lambeth Guest House,** on the other side of the gas pump on Jamieson St. (☎ 810597; £17 per person). You can **camp** on the grounds of **Craigens Farm,** a few miles outside town at Gruinart by Bridgend. (☎ 850256. No facilities. £2 per tent.) A **Co-op Foodstore** is on Main St. (☎ 810201. Open M-Sa 8am-8pm, Su 12:30-7pm.) The **Lochside Hotel,** Shore St., serves varied, large main courses (£6-10). Try the famous smoked Islay cheese, renowned for its aphrodisiacal qualities. (☎ 810244. Food served daily noon-2:30pm and 5:30-8:45pm.) Schmooze with the locals at the only pub in town, the **Bowmore Hotel Pub,** Jamieson St., a.k.a. "Lucci's"—ask for an explanation. (☎ 810416. Open daily 11am-1am.)

ISLE OF MULL

Even on the brightest days, mist lingers in the cracks of Mull's blue hills. Perhaps that's why the island's population clings to the shoreline. Tiny isles fortify Mull to the west and south, including the captivating Erraid, the focus of Robert Louis Stevenson's *Kidnapped*. Scenic in its own right, Mull is also a stepping-stone to the isles of Iona and Staffa. Mull's Gaelic heritage has largely given way to the pressure of English settlers, who now comprise over two-thirds of the population, but local craftsmen and itinerant fishermen keep tradition and culture alive.

■ GETTING THERE AND GETTING AROUND

Ferries: Caledonian MacBrayne ("Cal-Mac"; ☎ (01631) 566688) runs a ferry from **Oban,** east of Mull, to **Craignure** (45min.; M-Sa 6 per day, Su 5 per day; foot passengers £3.45). A smaller car and passenger ferry runs from **Lochaline** on the Morvern Peninsula, just north of Mull, to **Fishnish** (15min.; M-Sa 14-15 per day, Su 9 per day; £2). Note that these ferry times are for summer; winter sailings are few and far between.

Buses: R.N. Carmichael (☎ (01688) 302220), **Bowman Coaches** (☎ (01680) 812313), and **Highland and Islands Coaches** (☎ (01680) 812510) share tour duties and regular routes. Bus #496 meets the Oban ferry at **Craignure** and carries passengers to **Fionnphort** (1¼hr.; M-F 6 per day, Sa 3 per day, Su 1 per day). #495 runs between **Craignure** and **Tobermory** (1hr.; M-F 7 per day, Sa 4 per day, Su 1 per day; £3.80). Ask at a tourist information centre (TIC) for a timetable. R.N. Carmichael #494 connects **Tobermory** and the western village of **Calgary** (45min.; M-F 4 per day, Sa 2 per day). Of course, you can also jump on the friendly **postbus** (schedules at the TIC).

Tours: Daytrip tickets can be purchased at the Cal-Mac office (☎ (0990) 650000) in Oban for the **Mull Experience.** The price includes return ferry, coach transport, Mull Railway, and entry to Duart and Torosay Castles. Tour leaves May-Sept Su-F 10am and noon, also M-Th 2pm. £17, children £8.50.

Bike Rental: A good way to see the island is by bike; wheels can be rented from **Mull Travel and Crafts** ☎ (01680) 812487) in Craignure, two doors from the TIC. £7 per half-day, £12 per day. They also **rent cars,** 23+. £26.50-29.50 per day; £100 deposit.

Hitchhiking: Many travelers hitchhike on Mull, despite sparse traffic; *Let's Go* does not recommend hitchhiking as a safe mode of transport.

✳ ORIENTATION

Mull's three main hubs, **Tobermory** (northwest tip), **Craignure** (east tip), and **Fionnphort** (southwest tip), form a triangle bounded on two sides by the A849 and the A848. A left turn off the **Craignure Pier** takes you 35 mi. down Mull's main road along the southern arm of the island to **Fionnphort** (FINN-a-furt), where the ferry leaves for **Iona,** a tiny island off the southwest corner of Mull. A right turn leads 21 mi. along Mull's northwestern arm to **Tobermory,** Mull's pocket metropolis.

CRAIGNURE   ☎01680

Craignure, Mull's main ferry port, is a wee town with one nameless street. Make like its 10¼ in. gauge miniature **steam train** and toot out of town. (☎ 812494. Leaves near the campsite. Late Apr. to early Oct. 5-12 per day 11am-5pm. Limited wheelchair access. Return £3.30, children £2.20, families £8.75.) The little trooper rolls one mile south through woodlands to the inhabited ▓ **Torosay Castle,** a Victorian mansion filled with Edwardian artifacts, which has stunning views of the ocean and 12 splendid acres of gardens. It's one of the few castles around where you can actually sit on the furniture. (☎ 812421. Open Apr. to mid-Oct. daily 10:30am-5:30pm; gardens open year-round 9am-dusk. £4.50, students and seniors £3.50, children £1.50, families £10; gardens only £3.50, students and seniors £2.75, children £1.) Lacking a tiny train but otherwise worth your money is the spectacular 700-year-old stronghold of the clan Maclean,

THE TOBERMORY GALLEON It was originally called the "Santa Maria della Grazia e San Giovanni Battista," but by the time it exploded and sunk to the bottom of Tobermory Bay, this member of the not-so-invincible Spanish Armada had shed several syllables, dying as "San Juan de Sicilia". Soon after the sinking, a legend emerged: the daughter of the Spanish king Philip II came to Tobermory in search of the perfect man; when she found him on board the San Juan de Sicilia, his jealous wife blew the ship sky-high (and then sea-deep). Divers expert and crackpot have long been captivated with the wreck and continually explore it for treasure—perplexing, since there's no reason to expect treasure on a warship. Still, they beat on against the current: in the 1910s and 20s, explorers found some guns, and in 1950 the Royal Navy made a valiant effort, bringing up a cannonball, oak timber, and some coins from the reign of Philip II. The latest search, in 1982, unearthed lead.

Duart Castle, 3 mi. west of Torosay. Guide yourself through the state bedroom, the dungeon, and the cell where Spanish sailors were kept for ransom after the Armada's destruction. Take the bus to the end of Duart Rd. and walk the remaining 1½mi. (☎ 812309. Open May to mid-Oct. daily 10:30am-6pm. £3.50, students and seniors £3, children £1.75, families £8.75.) **Boat tours** from Oban to the castles leave in summer twice daily. (☎ (01866) 822280. £6, students and seniors £5, children £3, families £11.)

The **tourist information centre,** by the ferry terminal, books accommodations for £1 and exchanges money for a £3 commission. (☎ 812377. Open May-Sept. M-Th and Sa 9am-7pm, F 9am-5pm, Su 10:30am-7pm; Oct.-Apr. M-Sa 9am-5pm, Su 10:30am-5pm.) The **post office** is in the **Spar** store. (Open M-W and F 9am-1pm and 2-5pm, Th and Sa 9am-1pm.) **Postal code:** PA65 6AY.

You can camp at **The Shielings Holidays Campsite.** From the ferry terminal, turn left, then left again at the sign opposite the church. It's past the dilapidated town hall. Enjoy showers, laundry, and a mattress in a carpeted, well-lit PVC tent. (☎/fax 812496. Open Apr.-Oct. 2 people and tent £10, with car £11.50.) Laden with groceries, a **Spar** waits across from the ferry terminal. (☎ 812301. Open M 7:30am-7pm, Tu-F 8:15am-7pm, Sa 8:30am-7pm, Su 10:30am-1pm and 2:30-5:30pm.)

TOBERMORY ☎01688

Colorful cafes and bars line an attractive harbor in Tobermory (pop. 1000), Mull's main town. The tiny **Mull Museum** chronicles the island's history with local artifacts and folklore. (Open Easter-Oct. M-F 10:30am-4pm, Sa 10:30am-1:30pm. £1, children 10p.) Local artists display creative pieces at the **An Tobar Arts Centre,** Argyll Terr., which also hosts musical performances. (☎ 302211. Open Mar.-Dec. M-Sa 10am-6pm; also Su 1pm in summer; pick up a schedule at the Centre or the tourist information centre.) The **Tobermory Distillery,** on the opposite side of the harbor from the tourist information centre, conducts 30min. tours, with a generous swig of the final product. Watch for the kitty who greets you at the window. (☎ 302645. Tours Easter-Sept. M-F 10:30am-4pm, every 30min. Visitor center open Easter-Oct. M-F 10am-4pm. £2.50, seniors £1, children free.) For the very freshest in Scottish seafood, rent your own fly rod (£3) from **Tackle and Books,** 10 Main St., a combination angling center and bookstore. They also arrange three-hour **fishing trips** in season. (☎ 302336. 2-3 trips per week; £15, children £12. Store open July-Aug. M-Sa 9am-5:30pm, Su 11am-4pm; Sept. to June M-Sa 9am-5:30pm.) In the third weekend of April, Tobermory hosts the **Mull Music Festival,** with lively Scottish music. Early July brings the **Mendelssohn Festival.** The **Mull Highland Games** offer caber-tossing and *ceilidhs* on the third Thursday of July.

The **tourist information centre** (TIC), on a pier across the harbor from the bus stop, books rooms for £1 (£3 off-island), and sells boat-tour tickets. (☎ 302182. Open July to mid-Sept. M-Sa 9am-6pm, Su 10am-5pm; Apr. M-Sa 9am-5pm, Su 10am-5pm; May-June daily 9am-5pm; mid-Sept. to Oct. M-Sa 9am-5pm, Su 10am-5pm.) Services include: a **Cal-Mac** ferry office next to the TIC (☎ 302017; open M-F 9am-6pm; Mar.-Oct. also Sa 9am-4pm); **bike rental** at **Archibald Brown & Son,** 21 Main St. (☎ 302020, ask for Bryan; £13 per day, £8 per half-day); **Clydesdale Bank,** Main

St., the only bank and **cash machine** on the island (bank open M-W and F 9:15am-4pm, Th 9:15am-5:30pm); a full-service **launderette,** by the youth hostel (☎ 302669; £5.95 for up to 9 lb; open daily 9am-1pm and 2-5pm, closed some winter Su); **Internet access** at the An Tobar Arts Centre (£1.50 per 15min.; see above); and the **post office,** 36 Main St., on the harbor strip next to the supermarket (open M-Tu and Th-F 9am-5:30pm, W and Sa 9am-1pm). **Postal code:** PA75 6NT.

The small **SYHA Tobermory** youth hostel, on the far end of Main St. from the bus stop, has a homey kitchen/dining room and a lounge. (☎/fax 302481. Lockout 10:30am-5pm. Curfew 11:45pm. Open Mar.-Oct. Dorms £8.75, under 18 £7.75.) The **Harbor Guest House,** 59 Main St., conveniently opposite the bus stop, offers green-tartaned B&B in bright rooms with great harbor views. (☎ 302209. £19.50 per person, with bath £22.) **Ach-na-Craoibh,** on Erray Rd., has a wide range of accommodations, both B&B and self-catering. Walk up the footpath by the post office, then follow the road as it curves around to the right. (☎ 302301. B&B from £20-25 per night. Self-catering rooms from £90 per week.)

The **Co-op Supermarket,** by the harbor between the hostel and the post office, cures Hobnob cravings. (☎ 302004. Open M-W and Sa 8:30am-6pm, Th-F 8:30am-8pm, Su 12:30-6pm.) Most local restaurants cater to wealthy yacht owners; one exception is the **Tobermory Fish Company,** Main St., which serves up delicious smoked trout sandwiches for £1.45 and has attention-grabbing seashells in every shape and size—buy one for your mom and tell her you found it on the beach. (☎ 302120. Open M-F 9am-5pm, Sa 9am-1pm and 2-5pm.) Fishermen, tourists, and locals crowd the spacious pub at the **Mishnish Hotel,** near the TIC. (☎ 302009. Lunch £2-4, dinner £4-10. Live folk music from 9:30pm most summer nights. Open daily 11am-1am. Lunch served noon-2pm, dinner 6-8:30pm.)

IONA AND STAFFA

These tiny islands off Mull's west coast offer religious contemplation, geological marvels, and splendid isolation.

E GETTING THERE. Cal-Mac Ferries (☎ (01631) 566688) run to Iona from **Fionnphort,** (2 per hr., return £3.20, children £1.60). The friendly captain at **Turus Mara** (☎ (01688) 400242; mobile ☎ (0831) 638179) leaves from **Ulva Ferry,** Mull, and floats over to Iona, Staffa, and the Treshnish Isles. (Full- and half-day tours £11-32.50, children £6-16.25; £35 including transport from Oban.) Other tour companies offer similar services from different ports. **Gordon Grant Marine** (☎ (01681) 700338; reservations ☎ (0800) 783 8470) chugs to Mull, Staffa, and the Treshnish Isles from **Oban.** (Tours mid-Apr. to July; £19-35, seniors £17-35, children £10-17.50.) **The Kirkpatricks** (☎ (01681) 700358), on Iona, run Staffa tours from Iona and Fionnphort. Book tours directly, or at the Oban TIC. (£12.50, children under 14 £5.)

IONA   ☎01861

The sacred isle of Iona (pop. 150) is awash in an otherworldly purity of color—rocks the hue of Mars, waters the color of the Carribean, all draped with a very Scottish mist. Iona's crooked coastline shelters sandy beaches, and rocky knolls rise out of fertile grasslands in the island's center. All of Iona's manmade attractions cluster within a few hundred yards of the ferry terminal. More than 140,000 pilgrims visit Iona each year to pay homage to the tiny outcropping of land, a center of Christianity since Irish-bred St. Columba landed his coracle in AD 563.

⑦ PRACTICAL INFORMATION. To the left of the pier, **Ross Finlay** rents all kinds of **bicycles.** (☎ 700357. £4.50 per half-day, £8 per day; £10 deposit. Open M-Sa 9:15am-6pm, Su 10:15am-6pm; in winter daily 11am-1pm and 2-4pm.) In summer, Iona fills with daytrippers from Mull and Oban, so the best way to savor the island's beauty is to spend a night. The small village of **Baile Mor** holds a few shops and B&Bs, and a score of well-manicured gardens. To the right of the ferry landing, the **post office** offers **Internet access** for £2 per 30min. (☎ 700515. Open M-Tu and Th-F 9am-1pm and 2-5pm, W 9am-1pm, Sa 9am-12:30pm.) **Postal code:** PA76 6SJ.

ACCOMMODATIONS AND FOOD. Pick up a list of **B&Bs** from the post office (10p). The **Iona Community** has unique accommodations, allowing visitors to experience Iona more as St. Columba did, without worldy vanities such as televisions and electricity. Regular six-day retreats in the Abbey or the more modern, wheelchair-accessible MacLeod Centre on themes of religion and community take place from late June to mid-September, combining work and activities. Outside of summer, the retreats are often replaced with open weeks, when guests can stay with no theological requirements. (☎ (01681) 700404. Vegetarian cuisine. Abbey £185 per week, students £108, youths £98, children £87, under 5 £24; MacLeod Centre £175 per week, students £98, youths £88, children £78, under 5 £21.50. 3 days minimum stay for both.) If the Scottish Episcopal Church is more your style, stay in their **Bishop's House,** a shoreside building with a chapel and decorative windows at the end of the village street. (☎ 700800. B&B £18; 10% student discount, 15% for religious affiliates.) Through some miracle, groceries bless the island at **Spar,** uphill from the ferry landing. (☎ 700321. Open Easter-Oct. M-Sa 9am-6pm, Su 10:30am-6pm; Nov.-Easter M-Sa 11am-1pm and 2-4pm.)

SIGHTS. The ecumenical **Iona Community** lies outside the village, where it cleaves to the massive **Benedictine Abbey,** built on the site of St. Columba's original monastery. Walk up through the village and bear right to reach the abbey, which lies at the center of your view as you arrive on the ferry. As you enter, be prepared to forfeit £2 at the behest of threatening signs. Visitors are welcome to attend one of the 10min. services. (Open Apr.-Sept. daily 9:30am-6:30pm, Oct.-Mar. daily 9:30am-4:30pm. Services M-Th and Sa 9am and 9pm, F 8:15am and 9pm, Su 10:30am and 9pm, and daily 2pm in summer.) On your way, you'll pass through the ruins of a 13th-century **nunnery,** one of the better-preserved medieval convents in Britain. Derelict for over 300 years, its walls now sprout flowers. Signs will get thee from the nunnery to the **Iona Heritage Centre,** located in the "old manse." Here you can learn intriguing snippets about Iona's history, such as what happened "the year the potato went away." (☎ 700576. Open Easter-Oct. M-Sa 10:30am-4:30pm. £1.50, concessions £1, under 12 free.) To visit the tiny 12th-century **St. Oran's Chapel,** turn right just before the abbey. The surrounding burial ground contains the remnants of more than 60 kings of Scotland, Ireland, and Norway, including the pious Macbeth. Of course, given that the gravestones are over a millennium old, they're a trifle hard to read. On Wednesdays, guides lead an open **pilgrimage** around the island, leaving at 10:15am from St. Martin's Cross. Tuesday nights bring rousing *ceilidhs* to the Village Hall at 10:15pm. On the far side of the island (a 10min. walk), the **Spouting Cave** spews salt water when the waves are high enough.

If you're coming through Fionnphort, visit the **Columba Centre,** which charts St. Columba's story, and the spread of Christianity and monastic life. The sleek exhibition is uphill from the ferry port. (☎ (01681) 700660. Open Easter-Oct. M-Sa 10am-6pm, Su 11am-6pm. £2, students and seniors £1.50, under 16 £1, families £5.)

STAFFA

The incredible island of Staffa, composed of hexagonal basalt columns and rimmed with tidal caves, lies eight miles north of Iona. At a weak point in the earth's crust, liquid rock spewed upward and was cooled by ocean water to form columns. Surrounded by treacherous cliffs (particularly slippery in the rain; use of the guardrails is essential along the base), Staffa is ruled by an imperial council of six sheep and four cows. Puffins nest on the cliff edge and allow the curious to examine their personal space. When the tide is low, you can walk far inside the infamous ■ **Fingal's Cave** to be surrounded by water and basalt. Wait for the rest of your tour group to go through the cave first so that you can take your time alone, wondering at its formation. When rough seas roar into the cave, the sound reverberates around the island; the pounding of wave against rock inspired the surging strings in Mendelssohn's *Hebrides Overture.*

The nearby **Treshnish Isles** offer sanctuary to seals, seabirds, and ferrets. Wander along the cliffs as guillemots, razorbills, shags, and other ornithologist favorites land on **Lunga's** only remnant of human inhabitance—a 13th-century chapel. Legend holds that monks from the Iona Abbey buried their library on one of the isles to save it from the pillages of the Reformation. Many have tried digging under the third ferret from the left, as yet without luck.

HIGHLANDS AND ISLANDS

Long live the weeds and the wilderness yet.
—Gerard Manley Hopkins, S.J.

Misty, sublime, and remote, the Scottish Highlands have long been the stuff of fantasy. If we see them as wild outposts of untouched nature and nobility—the real, heather-clad heart of the Scottish spirit—it is only because countless movies, postcards, and stereotypes have told us so. And yet, somehow, the Highlands and Islands do not fail us. A ride on the West Highland Railway reveals these long-romanticized landscapes as one of the last stretches of genuine wilderness in Europe. Sheep-dotted emerald moors and towering granite mountains are sliced by the narrow lochs of the Great Glen (most famously Loch Ness) and girded by innumerable islands. Off the coast, the pristine Hebrides arch to the west, a thriving outpost of Gaelic culture, while the Norse-influenced Orkney and Shetland Islands stretch northeasterly off Scotland's horn at John O'Groats. The mainland towns of Inverness, Fort William, and Ullapool are access points for further exploration: from here, trains, buses, and ultimately ferries stretch outward to the islands and imposing mountain ranges such as the Cairngorms and the Cuillins.

The Highlands have not always been so vacant. Three centuries ago, almost one in three Scots lived north of the Great Glen in fiercely Gaelic, clan-based societies. The defeat of the 1745 Jacobite rising, which had been largely supported by the clans in opposition to the English king, dealt a heavy blow to Highland society. Following this, profit-seeking landlords turned from tenant farming to sheep farming and evicted entire communities in the infamous Highland Clearances of the 18th and 19th centuries. Many Scots, forcibly turned out of their homes, emigrated to Canada, Australia, New Zealand, and the United States. Today, the events of the past continue to haunt the nostalgia-steeped Highlands, and the once-universal Gaelic language (rhymes with "Alec," unlike the Irish "GALE-ick") is spoken only in the Hebrides. Nevertheless, a recent move to teach Gaelic in schools has begun to reinvigorate the language.

The region's economic fuel now comes mainly from tourism, the industry which transformed the Highlands into a playground for the rich and pleasure-seeking after the population was cleared. The Highlanders themselves make ends meet through self-employment, typically by crofting (small, independent farming; a croft is a tenant farmer's plot of land), fishing, or running B&Bs. Ever a cultural paradox, the stunning Highland wilderness continues to inspire imaginations, postcard photographers, and wistful wandering.

HIGHLIGHTS OF THE HIGHLANDS AND ISLANDS

BEN NEVIS Dash up the highest peak in the British Isles, which at 4406 ft. hides its height in a layer of clouds. On a clear day, you can see all the way to Ireland (p. 592).

ORKNEY ISLANDS Seek an unparalleled wealth of ancient ruins with the company of sheep, sky, and ocean (p. 618).

SKYE Explore the mighty Cuillin Hills and sparkling waters of the most accessible of the Hebrides (p. 596).

NORTHWEST HIGHLANDS Trek far from the reaches of the rails to find impossibly remote fingers of sea-lochs reaching deep into the rugged mountains.

☞ GETTING AROUND THE HIGHLANDS AND ISLANDS

Traveling in the Highlands requires a great deal of planning. You can't count on making more than one or two journeys a day on any form of transportation, even in high season. Transport services are, as a rule, drastically reduced on Sundays and during the winter. If you're spending serious time here, get the *Public Transport Travel Guide* (£1) from tourist information centres for your region of travel—it's absolutely essential. The **train** (☎ (08457) 484950), while offering the best views, will only get you so far in the Highlands, and **Scottish Citylink** (☎ (08705) 505050) **buses** do not travel much beyond the main rail routes. Scottish Citylink's unlimited **"Explorer Pass"** (from £30) is somewhat pricey and not too helpful, though it provides a 50% discount on Cal-Mac ferry fares. To reach some of the more remote and rewarding places, you will have to depend on small, local bus companies, which are listed in the *Public Transport Travel Guide.*

Most **ferries** are run by **Caledonian MacBrayne** (☎ (01475) 650100; www.calmac.co.uk), known as "Cal-Mac," which publishes a free, widely available timetable. Special 8- to 15-day **"Island Rover"** tickets provide discounts on ferry trips, but require substantial travel on consecutive days and are not valid on some sailings during peak times. **"Island Hopscotch"** tickets can provide modest savings for certain well-planned routes. Bikes can cross without reservations (for a fee of up to £2), but advance booking for cars is strongly recommended.

NORTHEASTERN SCOTLAND

ABERDEEN ☎01224

Whoever dubbed Aberdeen (pop. 210,000) "The Granite City" wasn't far off the mark: on a standard cloudy Scottish day, the gray hues of the city's buildings flow seamlessly into the grayness of the skies. Perpetually haunted by seagulls, this melancholy mecca of the North Sea oil industry nevertheless shelters the unmistakeable din of students partying, the hum of a vibrant arts community, and a dazzling array of pubs and museums. Many visitors use Aberdeen solely as a base for exploring the castles nearby; those who stay longer will realize that Aberdeen itself—cosmopolitan, gritty, and melodramatic—should not be ignored.

☞ GETTING THERE AND GETTING AROUND

Flights: Aberdeen Airport (☎ 722331). Stagecoach Bluebird #10/Scottish Citylink #996 runs to the airport from the bus station (1 per hr., last bus 11:55pm; £1.20) and First Aberdeen (☎ 650065) #27 runs from the Guild St. stop (13 per day, last bus 5:20pm; £1.35). **British Airways** (☎ (08457) 733377) flies from **Heathrow** and **Gatwick** (2 per hr., standard return £112 plus tax, advance purchase return from £47).

Trains: Guild St. Ticket office open M-Sa 6:15am-8pm, Su 8:45am-7:15pm. **Luggage storage,** 24hr., £2-4. Trains (☎ (08457) 484950) from: **Glasgow** (1½hr., 16 per day, £36.40); **Inverness** (2¼hr., 10 per day, £17.80); **Edinburgh** (2½hr., 17 per day, £28.90); and **London King's Cross** (7½hr.; 12 per day, 1 overnight sleeper; £90).

Buses: Guild St. (☎ 212266), next to the train station. Ticket office open M-F 7am-5:45pm, Sa 7am-4:30pm, Su 9:30am-3:30pm. **National Express** (☎ (08705) 808080) from **London** (2 per day, £28). **Scottish Citylink** (☎ (08705) 505050) from **Edinburgh** (4hr., at least 1 per hr., £14.50) and **Glasgow** (3½hr., at least 1 per hr., £14.50). **Stagecoach Bluebird** (☎ 212266) #10 and **Scottish Citylink** #996 from **Inverness** (3½hr. 1 per hr., £9).

Highlands and Islands

Ferries: The Aberdeen Ferry Terminal (☎ 572615), Jamieson's Quay. Turn left at the traffic light off Market St., past the P&O Scottish Ferries building. Office open M-F 9am-6pm, Sa 9am-noon. **P&O Scottish Ferries** run to **Stromness, Orkney** (see p. 618), and head from Stromness straight to **Lerwick, Shetlands** (in summer Tu and Su noon, in winter Sa only). Fares are cheap, but bring motion-sickness pills.

Taxis: Mairs City Taxis (☎ 724040). Open 24hr.

Car Rental: Nearly all major car rental companies have offices at the airport and in town. **Budget** is one of the cheapest at £40 per day, £160 per week.

🔢 PRACTICAL INFORMATION

Tourist Information Centre: St. Nicholas House (☎ 632727; fax 620415; www.agtb.org), Broad St. From the bus and train stations, turn right on Guild St., left on Market St., right on Union St., and left again at Broad St. Books rooms for £1.50 plus a 10% deposit. **Bureau de change.** Open July-Aug. M-F 9am-7pm, Sa 9am-5pm, Su 10am-4pm; Sept.-June M-Sa 9am-5pm, Su 10am-2pm.

Tours: Grampian Coaches (☎ 650024) runs various day tours to nearby castles, Royal Deeside, the Whisky Trail, and beyond. Jul.-Sept., £8-12, seniors and children £6-10.

Financial Services: Banks line Union St., including **The Royal Bank of Scotland,** 201 Union St. (☎ 804100). Open M-Tu and Th-F 9am-5pm, W 9:30am-5:30pm, Su 9am-noon. **ChequeCenter** (☎ (0800) 243028) has a **bureau de change** at the train station. Open M-F 9am-5:30pm. **Thomas Cook,** Bon Accord Shopping Centre. Open M, W, and F-Sa 9am-5:30pm, Tu 10am-5:30pm, Th 9am-8pm, Su noon-5pm.

American Express: 3-5 St. Nicholas St., 2nd fl. (☎ 633119). Housed in Lunn Poly Holiday and Flight Shop. Open M-F 9am-5:30pm, Sa 9am-5pm.

Launderette: A1, 555 George St. (☎ 621211). Open daily 10am-5pm.

Wheelchair Loan Service: Contact Peter or Irene (☎ 663180). Open M-F 11am-2pm.

Police: (☎ 386000), Queen St.

Hospital: Aberdeen Royal Infirmary (☎ 681818), Foresterhill Rd.

Internet Access: Costa Coffee, 31-33 Loch St. (☎ 626468), opposite the Bon Accord Shopping Centre's George St. entrance. 5p per min. Open M-W and F-Sa 8am-6pm, Th 8am-7:30pm, Su 10am-5pm.

Post Office: St. Nicholas Centre, Upperkirkgate (☎ 633065). Open M-Sa 9am-5:30pm. **Postal Code:** AB10 1HW.

▚ ACCOMMODATIONS

Rich and oily businessmen have slicked up Aberdeen's accommodation prices. An area with reasonable **B&Bs** is conveniently near the train station, between **Crown St., Springbank Terr.,** and **Bon Accord St.** From the bus and train stations, head left up Guild St., turn right on Bridge St., left on Union St., and look for Crown St. on your left. To get to Springbank Terr. more directly, turn left from Guild St. onto College St., then right onto Wellington Pl. which melds into Springbank Terr.

SYHA King George VI Memorial Hostel, 8 Queen's Rd. (☎ 646988). Reachable by a long walk on Union St. and Albyn Pl., or a short ride on bus #14, 15, or 27 from Union St. to Queen's Rd. Tidy, with spacious dorms and a large backyard. Continental breakfast included. Kitchen and laundry facilities. Reception open 7am-11pm. Check-out 9:30am. Lockout 9:30am-1pm. Lights out 11:30pm. Curfew 2am. Dorms June-Sept. £13.25, under 18 £11.75; Oct.-May £11.75, under 18 £10.25.

Roselodge Guest House, 3 Springbank Terr. (☎/fax 586794). All rooms have TV. Singles £18-22; doubles £30-34.

Greyholme, 35 Springbank Terr. (☎ 587081; fax 212287). TV in each room. Singles £19-22; doubles £32-34.

Stewart Lodge Guest House, 89 Bon Accord St. (☎ 573823; fax 592624). Singles £19-22; doubles £30-36.

FOOD AND PUBS

Tins and boxes lure the thrifty to **Tesco,** in the court in front of the St. Nicholas Centre on Union St. (Open M-W and Sa 7:30am-7pm, Th 7:30am-8:30pm, F 7:30am-7:30pm, Su 10am-5pm.)

The Ashvale, 42-48 Great Western Rd. (☎ 596981). Hailed by many as the best fish and chips in the UK, this restaurant now has a takeaway around the back. A delicious haddock supper costs only £3.50. Open daily 11:45am-1am.

Lucky Boat, 12-16 Guild St. (☎ 213392), across from the bus station. Chinese dishes served until 3pm (£3.60-4.20); eat in or takeaway. Other evening specialities run £4 to £5.60. Open M-Sa 11:45am-10:30pm, Su 4-10:30pm.

Shezan Tandoori, 53 Holburn St. (☎ 590810). An late-night stop where friendly staff whip up a mean korma. Chips, dinner and salad £3.70. Open daily 5pm-3am.

⊠ The Wild Boar, 19 Belmont St. (☎ 625 5357), off Union St. A one-stop center for food, drink, and fun. All the desserts are homemade (try the 95p chocolate chip cookie), the specials change daily, and if you hang around into the night, the DJs show up and drink specials start. Th nights Latin, F-Sa more up-tempo. Open M-Sa 10am-midnight, Su noon-11pm; food served until 8:45pm, F-Sa until 7:45pm.

The Malt Mill, 82 Holburn St. (☎ 573830). Live music downstairs Tu-Su night. Younger local groups perform during the week, while bigger names play on the weekend. An older, more sedate crowd drinks upstairs. Student drink specials 7-9pm daily. No food served. No admission after 11:45pm. No cover. Open M-Th 11am-midnight, F-Sa 11am-1am, Su 12:30pm-11pm.

SIGHTS

Aberdeen's stony architecture is not to be missed, especially when viewed against a melodramatic gray sky. For the best in gloomy turrets, **Old Aberdeen** and **Aberdeen University** are a short bus ride (#1, 2, 3, 4, or 15) from the city center, or a long walk through commercial and residential districts along King St. Once there, the **King's College Visitor Centre,** just off High St., greets you with an interesting exhibit on how students used to live. It hasn't always been pints and discos, you know. (☎ 273702. Open M-Sa 10am-5pm, Su noon-5pm. Free.) Peaceful **King's College Chapel** dates from the 16th century and features intricately carved "misery seats," so called because students had to sit in these extremely un-comfy chairs for hours before going to class. (☎ 272137. Open daily 9am-4:30pm. Guided tours July-Aug. Su 2-5pm. Free.) The twin-spired **St. Machar's Cathedral,** with a heraldic ceiling and stained glass, was built in the 14th century. (Services Su 11am and 6pm. Open daily 9am-5pm.) After your visit, take a walk through **Seaton Park** to the Brig O' Balgownie—a gift from Robert the Bruce.

The **Aberdeen Art Gallery,** on Schoolhill, houses a wide range of English, French, and Scottish paintings; its 20th-century British collection is particularly worthwhile. (☎ 523700. Open M-Sa 10am-5pm, Su 2-5pm. Free.) Close to the pier, the **Aberdeen Maritime Museum,** Shiprow, offers a fascinating look at the city's relationship with the sea. (☎ 337700. Open M-Sa 10am-5pm, Su noon-3pm. Free.) Just up Broad St., next to the tourist information centre (TIC), the historic **Provost Skene's House** recreates its 16th-century past. (☎ 641086. Open M-Sa 10am-5pm, Su 1-4pm. Free.) Across the street the imposing Gothic hulk of **Marischal College** houses the anthropology-heavy **Marischal Musuem.** (☎ 274301. Open M-F 10am-5pm, Su 2-5pm. Free.) The **Gordon Highlanders Museum,** St. Lukes, Viewfield Road has a comprehensive display on the pomp, circumstance, and bloody heroism of the kilted fighting regiment. To get there, walk farther down Queens Rd. from the hostel, or take bus #14 or 15 from Union St. (☎ 311200. Open Apr.-Oct. Tu-Sa 10:30am-4:30pm, Su 1:30-4:30pm. £2.50, students and seniors £1.50, children £1.)

Believe it or not, quite a bit of greenery thrives in the midst of Aberdeen's grayness. **Duthie Park** (DA-thee), by the River Dee at Polmuir Rd. and Riverside Dr., has a huge rose garden, birds and reptiles, and the **Winter Gardens Hothouse.** (Hothouse open daily 9:30am-dusk. Free.) A ride on the ever-handy bus #14 or 15 will take you to sprawling **Hazlehead Park,** off Queen's Rd. on the western edge of the city, with an aviary and extensive woodlands. A garden for the visually impaired with strong-scented flowers and Braille plaques blooms in the more centrally located **Victoria Park,** west of the city center on Westburn Rd. The city also sports a fine sandy **beach,** stretching north for about two miles from the old fishing community of Footdee (fi-TEE, foot of the River Dee) to the Don estuary. Two **amusement parks** rear over the southern end, while the northern sands are cleaner and often quieter. Take bus #14 from the bus station.

🎵 ENTERTAINMENT

Seagulls aren't the only things to listen to in Aberdeen—five main entertainment venues and assorted other hangouts ensure a steady stream of live music and the-ater. **The Lemon Tree Café Theatre,** 5 West North St., near Queen St., presents folk, jazz, rock, and drama in its two theaters. (☎ 642230. Tickets £5-9, students and seniors £2-3.) The **Music Hall** (☎ 641122), on Union St., is your best bet for finding out about current performances. The hall itself hosts pop bands and orchestra recitals. **His Majesty's Theatre,** Rosemount Viaduct, hosts opera, ballet, and theater; book tickets through the Music Hall box office. The **Aberdeen Arts Centre,** 33 King St., offers fine avant-garde and traditional theater. (Book through Music Hall. Tick-ets £3-6, students and seniors £1-2.) Pubs like **The Wild Boar** and **The Malt Mill** fre-quently host hip live bands in an alcohol-friendly atmosphere (see p. 575). For info on all venues, snag *What's On in Aberdeen* from the TIC or the art gallery.

Aberdeen also has pumping nightlife, courtesy of student throngs forced indoors by the cold weather. **Langstane Pl.,** south of Union St., is the place to prowl for **dance clubs** weekend nights. **The Triple Kirks,** 12 Schoolhill, just below the Aber-deen Art Gallery, is a ruined church where you can groove to everything from jazz to disco to techno in its **Exodus Nightclub,** or listen to stand-up at its monthly **Com-edy Cafe.** £1 drink promotions are frequent at the bar. (☎ 619921. Cover £2-4. Club open Th-Su 10:30pm-2am, bar open M-Sa 11am-midnight, Su noon-11pm.)

NEAR ABERDEEN: THE EAST GRAMPIAN COAST

The Grampian coast is dotted with some of the most dramatic castles in Scotland, from well-preserved residences to crumbling ruins.

DUNNOTTAR CASTLE. The splendidly decrepit Dunnottar Castle stands a romantic half-hour walk from seaside **Stonehaven,** 15 mi. south of Aberdeen. Built in the 12th century by Earl Marischal's family, the castle was the backdrop of Franco Zeffirelli's *Hamlet* (starring Mel Gibson), and has been the locus of many impressive historical events, such as the burning of a poor Englishman at the hands of William Wallace in 1297. The castle commands a gut-wrenching view of the crashing sea, and if you crawl through the tunnel at the base of the castle's cliff, you'll find a pebbly beach that rattles with the receding waves. (☎ (01569) 762173. Open Easter-Oct. M-Sa 9am-6pm, Su 2-5pm; Nov.-Mar. M-F 9am-dusk. £3.50, children £1.) **Trains** (20min., 17-25 per day, £2.90), and **Bluebird Northern** bus #101 (30min., 2 per hr., return £3.65) connect Aberdeen to Stonehaven.

FYVIE CASTLE. Northwest on the inland A947, 25 mi. from Aberdeen, the amaz-ingly intact 13th-century Fyvie Castle endures a brace of curses: a disgruntled medieval seer by the name of Thomas the Rhymer declared that the castle would never pass to the first son of the family until three stones were retrieved from its structure and returned to the stream from which they were taken. There is also a sealed chamber in one of the towers that, if opened, causes the laird to die and his wife to go blind—it's happened…twice! (☎ (01651) 891266. Open June-Aug. daily 11am-5:30pm; May and Sept. daily 1:30-5:30pm; Oct. Sa-Su 1:30-5:30pm; last admis-sion 4:45pm. Grounds open daily 9:30am-dusk. £6, seniors and children £4.) **Stage-coach Bluebird** (☎ (01224) 212266) runs from Aberdeen (#305, 1hr., 1 per hr.).

WORLDWIDE CALLING MADE EASY

The MCI WorldCom Card, designed specifically to keep you in touch with the people that matter the most to you.

MCI WORLDCOM — WORLDPHONE.

1·800·888·8000

J. L. SMITH

www.wcom.com/worldphone

Please tear off this card and keep it in your wallet as a reference guide for convenient U.S. and worldwide calling with the MCI WorldCom Card.

HOW TO MAKE CALLS USING YOUR MCI WORLDCOM CARD

> When calling from the U.S., Puerto Rico, the U.S. Virgin Islands or Canada to virtually anywhere in the world:

1. Dial 1-800-888-8000
2. Enter your card number + PIN, listen for the dial tone
3. Dial the number you are calling :
   Domestic Calls: Area Code + Phone number
   International Calls:
   011+ Country Code + City Code + Phone Number

> When calling from outside the U.S., use WorldPhone from over 125 countries and places worldwide:

1. Dial the WorldPhone toll-free access number of the country you are calling from.
2. Follow the voice instructions or hold for a WorldPhone operator to complete the call.

> For calls from your hotel:

1. Obtain an outside line.
2. Follow the instructions above on how to place a call.
   Note: If your hotel blocks the use of your MCI WorldCom Card, you may have to use an alternative location to place your call.

RECEIVING INTERNATIONAL COLLECT CALLS*

Have family and friends call you collect at home using WorldPhone Service and pay the same low rate as if you called them.

1. Provide them with the WorldPhone access number for the country they are calling from (In the U.S., 1-800-888-8000; for international access numbers see reverse side).
2. Have them dial that access number, wait for an operator, and ask to call you collect at your home number.

For U.S. based customers only.

START USING YOUR MCI WORLDCOM CARD TODAY. MCI WORLDCOM STEPSAVERS℠

Get the same low rate per country as on calls from home, when you:

1. **Receive international collect calls to your home** using WorldPhone access numbers

2. **Make international calls with your MCI WorldCom Card** from the U.S.*

3. **Call back to anywhere in the U.S. from Abroad** using your MCI WorldCom Card and WorldPhone access numbers.

An additional charge applies to calls from U.S. pay phones.

WorldPhone Overseas Laptop Connection Tips —
Visit our website, www.wcom.com/worldphone, to learn how to access the Internet and email via your laptop when traveling abroad using the MCI WorldCom Card and WorldPhone access numbers.

Travelers Assist® — When you are overseas, get emergency interpretation assistance and local medical, legal, and entertainment referrals. Simply dial the country's toll-free access number.

Planning a Trip?—Call the WorldPhone customer service hotline at 1-800-736-1828 for new and updated country access availability or visit our website:

www.wcom.com/worldphone

MCI WorldCom Worldphone Access Numbers

Easy Worldwide Calling

MCI WORLDCOM.

The MCI WorldCom Card.

The easy way to call when traveling worldwide.

MCI WORLDCOM   WORLDPHONE

1·800·888·8000

J. L. SMITH

The MCI WorldCom Card gives you...

• Access to the US and other countries worldwide.

• Customer Service 24 hours a day

• Operators who speak your language

• Great MCI WorldCom rates and no sign-up fees

For more information or
to apply for a Card call:

1-800-955-0925

Outside the U.S., call
MCI WorldCom collect
(reverse charge) at:

1-712-943-6839

COUNTRY	WORLDPHONE TOLL-FREE ACCESS #
Argentina (CC)	
Using Telefonica	0800-222-6249
Using Telecom	0800-555-1002
Australia (CC) ♦	
Using OPTUS	1-800-551-111
Using TELSTRA	1-800-881-100
Austria (CC) ♦	0800-200-235
Bahamas (CC) +	1-800-888-8000
Belgium (CC) ♦	0800-10012
Bermuda (CC) +	1-800-888-8000
Bolivia (CC) ♦	0-800-2222
Brazil (CC)	000-8012
British Virgin Islands +	1-800-888-8000
Canada (CC)	1-800-888-8000
Cayman Islands +	1-800-888-8000
Chile (CC)	
Using CTC	800-207-300
Using ENTEL	800-360-180
China ♦	108-12
Mandarin Speaking Operator	108-17
Colombia (CC) ♦	980-9-16-0001
Collect Access in Spanish	980-9-16-1111
Costa Rica ♦	0800-012-2222
Czech Republic (CC) ♦	00-42-000112
Denmark (CC) ♦	8001-0022
Dominica+	1-800-888-8000
Dominican Republic (CC) +	
Collect Access	1-800-888-8000
Collect Access in Spanish	1121

COUNTRY	ACCESS #
Ecuador (CC) +	999-170
El Salvador (CC)	800-1767
Finland (CC) ♦	08001-102-80
France (CC) ♦	0-800-99-0019
French Guiana (CC)	0-800-99-0019
Germany (CC)	0800-888-8000
Greece (CC) ♦	00-800-1211
Guam (CC)	1-800-888-8000
Guatemala (CC) ♦	99-99-189
Haiti +	
Collect Access	193
Collect access in Creole	190
Honduras +	8000-122
Hong Kong (CC)	800-96-1121
Hungary (CC) ♦	06*-800-01411
India (CC)	000-127
Collect access	000-126
Ireland (CC)	1-800-55-1001
Israel (CC)	1-800-920-2727
Italy (CC) ♦	172-1022
Jamaica +	
Collect Access	1-800-888-8000
From pay phones	#2
Japan (CC) ♦	
Using KDD	00539-121 ▶
Using IDC	0066-55-121
Using JT	0044-11-121

COUNTRY	ACCESS #
Korea (CC)	
To call using KT	00729-14
Using DACOM	00309-12
Phone Booths +	
Press red button ,03,then*	
Military Bases	550-2255
Luxembourg (CC)	8002-0112
Malaysia (CC) ♦	1-800-80-0012
Mexico (CC)	01-800-021-8000
Monaco (CC) ♦	800-90-019
Netherlands (CC) ♦	0800-022-91-22
New Zealand (CC)	000-912
Nicaragua (CC)	166
Norway (CC) ♦	800-19912
Panama	00800-001-0108
Philippines (CC) ♦	
Using PLDT	105-14
Filipino speaking operator	105-15
Using Bayantel	1237-14
Using Bayantel (Filipino)	1237-77
Using ETPI (English)	1066-14
Poland (CC) +	800-111-21-22
Portugal (CC) +	800-800-123
Romania (CC) +	01-800-1800
Russia (CC) + ♦	
Russian speaking operator	
	747-3320
Using Rostelcom	747-3322
Using Sovintel	960-2222
Saudi Arabia (CC)	1-800-11

COUNTRY	WORLDPHONE TOLL-FREE ACCESS #
Singapore (CC)	8000-112-112
Slovak Republic (CC)	08000-00112
South Africa (CC)	0800-99-0011
Spain (CC)	900-99-0014
St. Lucia +	1-800-888-8000
Sweden (CC) ♦	020-795-922
Switzerland (CC) ♦	0800-89-0222
Taiwan (CC) ♦	0080-13-4567
Thailand (CC)	001-999-1-2001
Turkey (CC) ♦	00-8001-1177
United Kingdom (CC)	
Using BT	0800-89-0222
Using C & W	0500-89-0222
Venezuela (CC) + ♦	800-1114-0
Vietnam + ●	1201-1022

KEY
Note: Automation available from most locations. Countries where automation is not yet available are shown in *Italic*.
(CC) Country-to-country calling available.
+ Limited availability.
★ Not available from public pay phones.
● Public phones may require deposit of coin or phone card for dial tone.
● Local service fee in U.S. currency required to complete call.
▶ Regulation does not permit Intra-Japan Calls.
* Wait for second dial tone.
■ Local surcharge may apply.
Hint: For Puerto Rico and Caribbean Islands not listed above, you can use 1-800-888-8000 as the WorldPhone access number.

ROYAL DEESIDE

Tourist industry wizards have dubbed the area between Aberdeen and Braemar "Royal Deeside." It's royal since this is where Queen Victoria decided to build her Highland retreat at Balmoral Castle, and it's Deeside because it runs along the River Dee. The same folks behind the curtain have also churned up a ridiculous number of tourist trails through the area, including the Castle Trail and the Victorian Heritage Trail, which are nice activities for mindless motorists. If you don't have a car, use the efficient **Bluebird "Heather-hopper" bus** #201 that runs hourly between Aberdeen and Braemar (day-long rover pass £6, children £3). The route hits a number of great castles as it moves from Aberdeenshire, traditionally a stronghold of "Lowland" Scots culture, to the edge of the Highlands, where Gaelic may no longer thrive, but hill-walking, fishing, and skiing opportunities do.

The first castle along the Bluebird bus route (30min. from Aberdeen) is modest **Drum Castle,** which may not be the most stunning of the lot but is nicely undertouristed. The Scots ballad "The Laird of Drum" immortalizes the long-gone master of this house who, at over 70 years of age, wooed and married a 16-year-old milkmaid on his estate. Hmm.... Hop off the #201 bus at Drumoak, then walk a mile to the castle and its fragrant Garden of Historic Roses. (☎ (01330) 811204. Open late Apr.-May and Sept. daily 1:30-5:30pm; June-Aug. daily 11am-5:30pm; Oct. Sa-Su 1:30-5:30pm. Grounds open daily 9:30am-dusk. £5, students and seniors £3.50, children free. Joint ticket with Crathes Castle available; see below.)

Considerably more crowded is the impressive 16th-century **Crathes Castle,** just a few miles down the #201 route. The castle houses the ancient ivory Horn to Leys, which was given as a "horn of tenure" to the family patriarch, Alexander Burnett, by Robert the Bruce in 1323. It's a good thing the castle was never attacked—the fierce cannons projecting from the towers shoot only water. A "Green Lady" allegedly haunts the castle, perhaps contributing her thumb to the spectacular gardens. (☎ (01330) 844525. Castle open Apr.-Sept. daily 11am-5:30pm; Oct. daily 10:30am-4:30pm; last admission 45min. before close; gardens open year-round daily 9:30am-sunset. £6, concessions £4. Garden or castle only £4, concessions £2.50. Joint ticket with Drum Castle can be bought only at Crathes; £8.50, concessions £5.80.)

Just over an hour farther along, the town of **Crathie** contains **Balmoral Castle,** the Queen's holiday palace. The castle was a gift to Queen Victoria from Prince Albert in 1852, who helped redesign it as it stands today. (☎ (013397) 42334. Open mid-Apr. to July M-Sa 10am-5pm. £4, seniors £3, under 16 £1.) **Horseback riding** (pony trekking) is also available on the Balmoral Estates. Call ahead for the two hour treks. (At 9:30am and 1:30pm; £20 per person.) If you continue up the hill from Balmoral, you'll eventually reach the **Royal Lochnagar Distillery Visitor Centre,** with the inevitable tour, free dram, and gift shop, as well as a £4 voucher off any bottle of the golden stuff. (☎ (013397) 42273. Open Easter-Oct. M-Sa 10am-4pm, Su noon-3pm; Nov.-Easter M-F 10am-4pm. £4.)

BRAEMAR   ☎013397

Situated along the glorious River Dee, Braemar is the southern gateway to the Cairngorm Mountains and a hiker's paradise. The fully furnished 17th-century **Braemar Castle** was once a stronghold of the Farquharson clan. (☎ 41219. Open Apr.-Oct. Sa-Th 10am-6pm. Last entry 5:30pm. £3, students and seniors £2.50, children £1.) Behind the butcher shop in town lie the ruins of **Kindrochit Castle,** now but a pile of rocks with an interesting historical placard. Braemar is renowned for the annual highland games of the **Braemar Gathering,** held on the first Saturday in September. Braemar's population swells from 410 to 20,000 during the festivities, including the Queen, who almost always attends. Advance bookings are essential for a seat; otherwise, uncovered stand tickets will cost you about £12, and you'll just have to plant your bum on the damp grass. (Information ☎ 55377, bookings ☎ (01330) 825917.) The second week of July is **Braemar's Gala Week,** featuring such random events and activities as battle reenactments, a mountain rescue display, and "children's activities with bouncy castle."

Reach Braemar by the **Bluebird "Heather-hopper" bus** #201 (from Crathie and Balmoral 15min., from Aberdeen 2¼hr.; 1 per hr.; £6 day-long rover pass, children £3). For **bike rental,** head to the **Mountain Sports Shop,** just around the bend on Invercauld Rd. (☎ 41242. £15 per day.) The **tourist information centre** (TIC), Mar Rd., at the Mews, can give you a comprehensive list of places to stay in and around the town. (☎ 41600. Open daily mid-May to Sept. 10am-6pm; Nov.-May M-Sa 10am-1pm and 2-5pm, Su noon-5pm.) Stock up on hiking grub at the **Alldays food store** across the street (open M-Sa 7:30am-9pm, Su 9am-9pm), which is also home to the **post office** (open M-F 9am-noon and 1-5:30pm, Sa 9am-1pm). **Postal code:** AB35 5YL.

The 64-bed **SYHA Braemar** lies just south of town in an old stone house on Glenshee Rd., near the Glenshee ski area and surrounded by a thicket of Scotland's oldest pine trees. (☎ 41659. Dorms £9.25, under 18 £8.) The **Rucksacks Bunkhouse,** 15 Mar Rd., behind the TIC and across the road from Alldays, has room for 26 (although 10 of those spaces require sleeping bags), with showers, kitchen facilities, and central heating. (☎ 41517. Dorms £8.50, bunkhouse £7.) The **Invercauld Caravan Club Site,** just a five-minute walk past the hostel on Glenshee Rd., also welcomes tent campers. (☎ 41373. Open Dec.-Sept. £5 per person.)

HIKING NEAR BRAEMAR

Just outside Braemar, the mountains teem with fantastic **hiking trails.** Victorians once swarmed to the hypnotic **Linn of Dee,** a curious waterfall which has managed to carve out its own mini-Grand Canyon. It's five miles west of town along a gorgeous road, so you'll need to either walk, cycle, or hop on the **postbus** that leaves the Braemar post office around 1pm (M-Sa route 072, 15min.). From the Linn, the thrilling **Lairig Ghru trail** stretches 20 mi. north to Aviemore. The name means "gloomy pass" in Gaelic, and that's exactly what this path is: heartbreakingly desolate as it winds between steep mountainsides and past Ben Macdui. It's also quite challenging, so don't overestimate your own ability or underestimate your need for an Ordnance Survey map (Outdoor Leisure #3).

Hikers will want to start early in the day to finish the whole Lairig Ghru; consider spending the previous night at the nearby **SYHA Inverey,** where there are usually more deer than guests. The daily postbus stops at the hostel right before swinging by the Linn of Dee. (☎ (013397) 41969. No showers. Open mid.-May to Sept. Dorms £6.75, under 18 £6.) The **SYHA Glendoll** is a difficult 13 mi. hike from Braemar. Follow the A93 two miles south to the Glen Callater turn-off, then take the Jock's Rd. footpath. Be sure to take an Ordnance Survey map and compass and notify the Braemar police of your plans. (☎ (01575) 550236. Open Apr.-Sept. Dorms £8.25, under 18 £7.25.)

ELGIN ☎ 01343

Elgin (pronounced with a hard "g"—like Guinness, not gin; pop. 20,000) is a relatively urban town halfway between Aberdeen and Inverness, famed for the spectacular **Elgin Cathedral,** which was regarded in the 14th century as the most beautiful of Scottish cathedrals. Sadly, it was looted and burned by the Wolf of Badenoch just as that century ended. The cathedral was further tormented by fire, Edward III, the Reformation, and Cromwell's bullets. Thanks to careful restoration and repair, however, the grand church remains a breathtaking sight. (☎ 547171. Open Apr.-Sept. daily 9:30am-6pm; Oct.-Mar. M-Sa 9:30am-4pm, Su 2-4pm. £2.50, seniors £1.90, children £1.) Just next door, the **Biblical Garden** merits a pious stroll: all 110 plants mentioned in the Bible thrive here, amidst Bibilical statues and proverbs. (Open May-Sept. daily 10am-7:30pm. Free.) The **Elgin Museum** displays spoils collected by local notables in the Age of Empire, including a shrunken head from Ecuador and a mummy from Peru. (☎ 543675. Open Easter-Oct. M-F 10am-5pm, Sa 11am-4pm, Su 2-5pm; in winter for groups only. £2, students and seniors £1, children 50p.) A working mill creates tourist-pleasing sweaters at the **Johnstons of Elgin Cashmere Visitor Centre,** east of the Elgin Cathedral on Newmill Rd. (☎ 554099. Open M-Sa 9am-5:30pm, June-Oct. also Su 11am-5pm. Tours M-Th 10am-4pm and F 10am-noon. Free.)

The **train station,** five minutes from town along South Guildry St., greets **trains** (☎ (08457) 484950) from **Inverness** (45min., 11 per day, £7) and **Aberdeen** (1½hr., 10 per day, £11.30). **Buses** stop behind High St. and the St. Giles Centre. **Stagecoach Bluebird** (☎ (01343) 554222) #10 and **Citylink** #996 arrive from **Inverness** (1¼hr., 27 per day, £6.20) and **Aberdeen** (2¼hr., 20 per day, £7.20). The **tourist information centre,** 17 High St., provides accommodations listings and bookings. (☎ 542666; fax 552982. Open Apr.-Oct. M-Sa 10am-5:30pm, June-Sept. also Su 10am-2pm; Nov-Mar. M-F 10am-4pm, Sa 10am-2pm.) Services include: **Internet access** at **Elgin Library,** north of town (☎ 562600; £2 per 30min., £3.50 per hr.; open M-F 10am-8pm, Sa 10am-noon); and the **post office,** in the **Tesco** supermarket on Batchen Ln. (open M-F 8:30am-8pm, Sa 8am-6pm, Su 10am-5pm). **Postal code:** IV30 1LY.

Elgin's only hostel, the small **Saltire Bunkhouse,** Pluscarden Rd., is a 30-minute walk west of town. Check out the World War II bunker and surrounding livestock. (☎ 550624. Laundry facilities and kitchen. Open Easter to mid-Sept. Dorms £8.50.) Elgin is full of B&Bs; the friendly Rosses will set you up in a room with TV at **The Bungalow,** 7 New Elgin Rd., a five-minute walk from the train station, or 15 minutes along New Elgin Rd. from the town center. (☎ 542035. £15 per person.) Eat a two-course lunch for only £3 (noon-2:30pm) at the **Thunderton House** pub, Thunderton Pl. off the High St. (☎ 554921. Karaoke Th and Su nights. Open Su-W until 11pm, Th until 11:45pm, F-Sa until 12:30am.) For more bump and grind action, there's **Joanna's Nightclub** across the High St. in City Arms Close, next to the cinema. (No entry to club after 12:30am.)

NEAR ELGIN

FORRES. The rival village of Forres, quieter than Elgin and a perennial winner in the cutthroat Britain in Bloom competition, boasts the magnificent **Sueno's Stone,** a richly-carved Pictish cross-slab (Scotland's tallest) viewable for free day and night in a locked glass house. On a nearby heath, Shakespeare's sisters three revealed Macbeth's destiny; these days tea rooms flower along High St. Elgin blossoms 20 minutes from Elgin by **bus** (Stagecoach Bluebird #10 or Citylink #996, 2 per hr., £2.30) or 15 minutes by **train** (10 per day, £3). The **tourist information centre,** 17 High St., lists area **B&Bs.** (☎ (01309) 672938. Open July-Aug. daily 10am-6pm; Apr.-June and Sept.-Oct. M-Sa 10am-1pm and 2-5pm.)

LOSSIEMOUTH. The secluded seaside village of Lossiemouth, six miles north of Elgin on the A941, is linked by frequent bus service on the #329 (20min., 3 per hr.). Two sandy, windswept beaches are nearby: **East Beach** is connected to the mainland by a narrow footbridge and has grassy dunes; **West Beach** is cleaner, less crowded, and leads to a lighthouse. The weary find a haven at **Mrs. Stephen's,** 54 Queen St. (☎ (01343) 813482. £16 per person.) Campers pitch their tents at **Silver Sands Leisure Park.** (☎ (01343) 813262. Open Apr.-Oct. £7.50-12 per tent.) Between Elgin and Lossiemouth, on the same #329 bus route, sits **Spynie Palace,** once the digs of the Bishops of Moray. (☎ (01343) 546358. Open Apr.-Sept. daily 9:30am-6pm; Oct.-Mar. Sa 9:30am-4pm and Su 2-4pm. £1.80, seniors £1.30, children 75p. Joint ticket with Elgin Cathedral £3, seniors £2.25, children £1.20.)

THE MALT WHISKY TRAIL. The world-famous Speyside area has 57 working distilleries, making it prime territory for dram-drinking. The 62 mi. **Malt Whisky Trail** staggers past seven famous distilleries, all of which offer free booze. Stagecoach Bluebird #10/Scottish Citylink #996 covers Keith, Elgin, and Forres (all key Speyside stopovers) twice per hour on its way from Aberdeen to Inverness and back. Always tell the driver where you want to go. The **Stagecoach** (☎ (01343) 544222) **Bluebird Day Rover** ticket gives unlimited one-day travel on Stagecoach (£9, children £4.50), and the **Off Peak Day Rover** includes unlimited travel M-F after 9am or all day on the weekends (£6, children £3).

The best (and only free) tour is at the **Glenfiddich Distillery** in Dufftown, 17 mi. south of Elgin. It's also the only distillery in the highlands where you can see whisky bottled on the premises. Note the black fungus on the trees—when brewing was illegal, it was a dead giveaway to police. Take Bluebird bus #336 from Elgin (40min., 6 per day) right to the distillery. (☎ (01340) 820373. Open Jan. to mid-Dec. M-F 9:30am-4:30pm; Easter to mid-Oct. also Sa 9:30am-4:30pm and Su noon-4:30pm.) If you ask the driver, the #336 bus to Glenfiddich will stop at **The Speyside Cooperage,** where casks are still handmade. The Cooperage is ¼ mi. south of Craigellachie on the A941. (☎ (01340) 871108. Open Jan. to mid-Dec. M-F 9:30am-4:30pm; June-Sept. also Sa 9:30am-4pm. Tours £2.95, seniors £2.45, children £1.75.) A self-guided tour takes you to **Strathisla Distillery,** the "home and heart" of Chivas Regal, and the oldest working distillery in the Highlands (est. 1786). It's a 10 minute crawl from the Keith bus or train station. (☎ (01542) 783044. £4. Open Feb. to mid-March M-F 9:30am-4pm; mid-March to Nov. M-Sa 9:30am-4pm, Su 12:30-4pm.)

TOMINTOUL AND THE SPEYSIDE WAY. If your view of Scotland is broader than single malts, the area around Elgin affords more interactive activities. Walkers enjoy the **Speyside Way,** a 84 mi. trail along the river from Buckie at Spey Bay to Aviemore in the Cairngorms. Grab a trail map at the Elgin tourist information centre. The trail takes you through the small but charming village of **Tomintoul,** set amidst the Highland hills of the **Glenlivet Estate.** Here you can hike the seven miles to the famed **Glenlivet Distillery,** Ballindalloch. (☎ (0154) 278322. Open July-Aug. M-Sa 10am-6pm, Su 12:30-6pm; mid-March to June and Sept.-Oct. M-Sa 10am-4pm, Su 12:30-4pm. £2.50, under 18 free.)

If you're not driving, biking, or long-distance hiking, Tomintoul is difficult to get to. **Roberts Buses** (☎ (01343) 544222) runs from Keith and Dufftown (#362, Tu and Sa 1 per day), and Elgin (#363, Th 1 per day, about £3.75). The **tourist information centre,** The Square, can give hikers information on various trails around town. (☎ (01807) 580285. Open July-Aug. M-Sa 9:30am-6:30pm; Apr.-June and Sept.-Oct. 9:30am-1pm and 2-5pm.) Cheap accommodations abound in Tomintoul, starting with the basic **Gordon Hotel Bunkhouse,** The Square. See the hotel reception to check in, and bring your own sleeping bag. (☎ (01807) 580206. Overnight stay £7.) The equally basic **SYHA Tomintoul** will be moving at some undetermined point from its old haunts down the Main St., so call the SYHA Central Reservations Service to find out. (☎ (08701) 553255. Open mid-May to Sept. £6.75, under 18 £6.)

CAIRNGORM MOUNTAINS ☎ 01479

The towering Cairngorms, 120 mi. north of Edinburgh, are real Scottish wilderness: misty, mighty, and arctic even in the summer. Unfortunately, these mountains have also witnessed the gradual deforestation that nearly stripped Scotland of its native pine and birch forests. While the peaks are bare, covered only with heather, reindeer, and, for much of the year, the snow that attracts skiers and dogsledders to the region, the area does contain Britain's largest expanse of nature preserves. Careful reforestation is not only blanketing the slopes of the Cairngorms with pine and juniper, but is also increasing the pine marten, capercaillie (a rooster-like bird), and red squirrel populations. For humans, this means wildlife-viewing may one day be just as much an attraction as the superb hiking, mountain biking, and skiing.

⌨ GETTING THERE AND GETTING AROUND

The largest town in the Cairngorms, **Aviemore** is conveniently located on the main Inverness-Edinburgh rail and bus lines. **Trains** (☎ (08457) 484950) arrive at the station on Grampian Rd., just north of the tourist information centre, from **Inverness** (45min., 7 per day, £9.10) and **Edinburgh** and **Glasgow** (2¾hr., 7 per day, £28). Southbound **buses** stop at the shopping center just north of the train station; northbound buses brake before the Cairngorm Hotel. **Scottish Citylink** (☎ (08705) 505050) runs nearly every hour from: **Inverness** (40min., £4.50); **Glasgow** (3½hr., £10.90); and **Edinburgh** (3½hr., £12.50). **Kincraig,** six miles south of Aviemore on the A9, is accessible by **Scottish Citylink** #957 from **Perth.**

The area's prettiest road trip is a 10 mi. jaunt through the heather moors of the **Ski Rd.** into the interior. The principal path into the **Glen More Forest Park,** the Ski Rd. begins just south of Aviemore (on the B970) and jogs eastward, merging into the A951. The road passes the sandy beaches of **Loch Morlich** before carrying on to **Glenmore** and ending at the Cairngorm chairlift. From Aviemore's train station, **Highland Country** "Munro Bagger" **bus** #37 and 337 travel this route, running past **Kincraig, Loch Morlich,** and **Glenmore** to **Cairngorm** (summer, 10 per day). A similar winter service whisks away all-too-eager skiers wanting to hit the slopes.

The **Cairngorm Service Station,** on Aviemore's Main St., offers **car rentals.** (☎ 810596. £34-42 per day; £185-235 per week.) **Bike rental** (½ day £8, full day £14) is available from **Bothy Bikes** (☎ 810111) and **Inverdruie Bikes** (☎ 810787) in Aviemore. **The Glenmore Shop and Café,** near the Loch Morlich Youth Hostel, rents bikes, skis, and mountain boards. (☎ 861253. Bikes £13 per day, £8 per half day, £3 per hr. Open daily 8:30am-5:30pm.)

⚡❓ ORIENTATION AND PRACTICAL INFORMATION

While the Cairngorms themselves are refreshingly quiet, their largest town, **Aviemore,** is unfortunately not. This concrete roadside strip entertains tourists with its clutter of pricey resort hotels; once you've used its urban amenities, escape into the mountains. **Glenmore** offers the most intimate access, and **Kincraig,** though farther away, sustains visitors with a welcome breath of non-touristed air on the tranquil shores of Loch Insh.

The **Aviemore and Spey Valley tourist information centre** (TIC), on Grampian Rd., Aviemore's main artery, books local B&Bs, sells bus tickets, and exchanges currency (£2.50 commission) during peak season. (☎ 810363. Open July to mid-Sept. M-Sa 9am-7pm, Su 10am-6pm; mid-Sept. to June daily 9am-5pm.) The **Rothiemurchus Estate Visitors Centre** lies nearly a mile down the Ski Rd. from Aviemore toward the Cairngorms. (☎ 812345. Open daily 9am-5:30pm.) **Kincraig Stores** serves as the Kincraig **post office** and unofficial tourist information centre. (☎ (01540) 651331. Post office open M-Tu and Th-F 9am-1pm. Store open M-Sa 8am-6pm, Su 8:30am-1pm.) Services include: **Bank of Scotland,** Grampian Rd., across from the Tesco (open M-Tu and Th-F 8am-5pm, W 10am-5pm); **Internet access** at SYHA Aviemore (see below) or **The Illicit Still,** a bar in the Highlands Hotel, off Grampian Rd. (☎ 810771; access until 10:30pm; £4 per 30min., £7 per hr.); and the **post office,** Grampian Rd. (open M-F 9am-5:30pm, Sa 9am-12:30pm). **Postal code:** PH22 1RH.

▌ ACCOMMODATIONS

Check the tourist board's *Aviemore and Spey Valley* publication for a complete listing of seasonal hostels and year-round B&Bs (£15-25).

SYHA Loch Morlich (☎ 861238), Glenmore. Superb accommodations on Loch Morlich, with sublime views of the mountains. The Highland Country Bus departs from Aviemore train station and stops in front of the hostel, both summer and winter. Curfew 11:30pm. Dorms £9.25, under 18 £8.

SYHA Aviemore (☎ 810345). This hostel 100 yd. south of the TIC has scorching showers and sinks in every suite. 115 beds with 4-8 beds to a room. No lockout. Curfew 2am. Internet access. Breakfast included. Dorms £12, under 18 £10.75; July-Aug. £1 extra.

Glen Feshie Hostel (☎ (01540) 651323), 11 mi. south of Aviemore, 5 mi. from Kincraig. Call ahead and they might get you from the station. Close to numerous walks and hikes. Showers, kitchen. No curfew. Linen, and porridge breakfast included. Dorms £8.

Insh Hall Lodge (☎ (01540) 651272), 1 mi. downhill from Kincraig on Loch Insh; Scottish Citylink #957 runs to the hostel from Kincraig. Year-round accommodations with bath for skiers and hikers. Sauna and gym. Stay at least 2 nights to get free use of watersports equipment. Rooms from £17.50; full board £35.50.

Lazy Duck Hostel (☎ 821642; lazy.duck@virgin.net), Badanfhuarain, in nearby Nethy Bridge. Catch Highland Country bus #334 from Aviemore (20min.; 8 per day). Dorms £8.50 per person.

Camping: Glenmore Forest Camping and Caravan Park (☎ 861271), across from the SYHA Loch Morlich. Ample space and good facilities, though crowded in summer. Open

Dec.-Oct. £3.70-5 per person with tent. **Rothiemurchus Camp and Caravan Park** (☎ 812800), 1½ mi. south of Aviemore on the Ski Rd. £3.50 per person with tent.

◗ FOOD

The local **Tesco** supermarket lies just north of the Aviemore train station. (Open M-W and Sa 8:30am-8pm, Th-F 8:30am-9pm, Su 9am-6pm.) At the Aviemore station, the modestly-titled **Number One Restaurant** lets you watch the trains rattle by while you have High Tea (£5.85 for 3 courses, late afternoon). For chic, upmarket (read: expensive) eats, enter the world of **Café Mambo**, 12-13 Grampian Rd., which serves burgers (£5-7), "fetish" cocktail pitchers (£10), and less sinful but still outstanding hot chocolate (£1.50). Stick around to groove in their dance club if you've had too many fetish cocktails. (☎ 811670. Restaurant and bar open Su-W 11am-11pm, Th-Sa 11am-1am; food served until 9pm. Club open F-Sa 10pm-1am.)

◤ HIKING, SKIING, AND OTHER REINDEER GAMES

The Cairngorm region has Scotland's highest concentration of ski resorts. In winter, alpine skiers from throughout Britain converge at the **Cairngorm Ski Place**, currently undergoing a monstrous overhaul while a nifty **funicular railway** is constructed to replace the old double-legged chairlift. The forthcoming eco-friendly railway will *not* allow hikers to depart on walks from its stations, so enjoy that privilege this summer with the doomed chairlift, scheduled to run until late 2001. (Bottom to top and return £6, seniors and children £3.60; middle to top and return £4.20, seniors and children £2.50.) The first ride ascends a quite walkable 368 ft.; the second lift covers the remaining 1056 ft. to a summit near the peak of Cairngorm Mt. (4084 ft.). Arrive early (the first chairlift runs at 9am in summer, the last at 3:55pm) or your view of the surrounding snow-capped peaks and silver lochs may be obstructed by hordes of Teutonic prepubescents. Call ahead; winds and the ongoing construction shut down the lift with some regularity.

To enjoy the mountains in peace, descend The Saddle into **Glen Avon** or traverse the southern ridge of Cairngorm to **Ben Macdui**, the second-highest peak in Britain (4296 ft.). On a clear day, you can see the first 100 mi. of infinity; if you're lucky, you may even run into the reindeer (see below). The Ben Macdui hike will take at least six hours; for something less challenging, you can take the **Northern Corries Path:** depart from the chairlift car park and follow any of the left-branching paths to explore quiet mountain sanctuaries and clear-running streams. Closer to Aviemore, the daunting but renowned **Lairig Ghru** path heads south through 20 mi. of gloomy valleys to Braemar. This one's only for the bravest of souls, so make sure you have your Ordnance Survey Outdoor Leisure map (#3) and your stamina.

Once at the base of the mountains, the **Cairngorm Rangers** offer guided walks for both experienced and novice hikers; walks vary in length. For skiers, a day ticket at Cairngorm including lift passes costs £20 (students £16, children £10). Several local companies run ski schools and rent equipment; pick up a copy of *Skiing Information* at the Aviemore TIC for details. Down the hill three miles from the chairlift, the **Cairngorm Reindeer Centre** is home to 150 velvet-horned creatures. For a fee, visitors are entitled to a 1½hr. frolic amid the herd. Smaller paddock visits are possible from Easter to December. (☎ 861228. Open daily 10am-5pm. Visits daily at 11am; May-Oct. also at 2:30pm. Call ahead to confirm availability of afternoon visit. £5, seniors and children £3; paddock £1.50.) Next door, the **Glenmore Forest Park Visitors Centre** disburses information on walks and conditions. (☎ 861220. Open daily 9am-5pm.) In the summer, the **Highland Country** bus service runs from Aviemore to the chairlift and the Reindeer Centre (see **Getting There and Around**, p. 580). Otherwise, if you have the energy, you can bike the 10 mi. back and forth. The **Highland Wildlife Park** in Kincraig is dedicated to preserving local beasties. Scottish Citylink #957 stops there from Aviemore en route to Edinburgh, Perth, and Pitlochry (☎ (01540) 651270. Open daily June-Aug. 10am-7pm, last admission 5pm; Apr.-May and Sept.-Oct. 10am-6pm, last admission 4pm; Nov.-Mar. 10am-4pm, last admission 2pm.)

SAFETY PRECAUTIONS. Although the Cairngorms rise only 4000 ft., the weather patterns of the **Arctic tundra** characterize the region. Explorers may be at the mercy of bitter winds and unpredictable mists *any day of the year*. Furthermore, many trails are not posted and trekkers must be able to rely on their own proficiency with a map and compass. Make sure to use an Ordnance Survey map (Landranger #35 and 36), or preferably, yellow Outdoor Leisure map #3. Both are available at the tourist information centre. Be prepared to spend a night in **sub-freezing temperatures** no matter what the temperature is when you set out. Leave a description of your intended route with the police or at the mountain station, and learn the locations of the shelters (known as bothies) along your trail. See **Wilderness Safety**, p. 53.

THE GREAT GLEN

INVERNESS   ☎01463

To reach just about anything in the Highlands, you'll have to pass through the transport hub of Inverness (pop. 40,000), a city of somewhat superficial charms. Inverness is comfortably cosmopolitan, with shops, pubs, and amenities—plus Gaelic street signs, to remind you that you're in the Highlands. No trip to Inverness would be complete without taking in nearby Loch Ness. You don't need to be a Nessie nut to appreciate Britain's largest inland body of water, and even if you don't see the real monster, vendors are all too happy to sell you a cute stuffed one.

⌐ GETTING THERE AND GETTING AROUND

Trains: Academy St., in Station Sq. Travel center open M-Sa 6:25am-8:30pm, Su 9:15am-8:30pm. **Luggage storage,** 24hr., £2-4. Trains (☎ (08457) 484950) from: **Aberdeen** (2¼hr., 7-10 per day, £17.80); **Kyle of Lochalsh** (2½hr., 2-4 per day, £15); **Thurso** (3½hr., 2-3 per day, £13); **Edinburgh** (3½-4hr., 5-7 per day, £29.90-42.60); **Glasgow** (3½hr., 5-7 per day, £29.90-42.60); and **London** (8hr., 1 per day, £81).

Buses: Farraline Park (☎ 233371), just off Academy St. **Highland Bus and Coach** sells tickets for almost all companies and stores luggage (£1). Office open M-Sa 8:30am-6pm, Su 10am-6pm. **Scottish Citylink** (☎ (08705) 505050) from: **Kyle of Lochalsh** (2½hr., 2 per day, £9); **Aberdeen** (3½hr., 1-2 per hr., £9); **Thurso** (3½hr., 4-5 per day, £9); **Edinburgh** (4½hr., 8-10 per day, £13.40); **Glasgow** (4½hr., 10-12 per day, £12.80); and **London** (10hr., 1 per day, £42). Both Citylink and **Rapsons Coaches** (☎ (01463) 222244) from **Ullapool** (1½hr., M-Sa 2-6 per day, £5).

Taxis: Rank Radio Taxis (☎ 220222).

Car Rental: Ken's Garage, 15b Harbour Rd. (☎ 717606). Also **Arnold Clark Car Hire** (☎ 713322), Harbour Rd. From £16-18 daily, £80-90 per week. Minimum age 23.

Bike Rental: Barney's convenience store, 35 Castle St. (☎ 232249). £12 per day. Open daily 7:30am-10:30pm.

✦ ❷ ORIENTATION AND PRACTICAL INFORMATION

The River Ness divides Inverness; most of what you need is on the east bank. A huge suspension bridge bounces travelers between the two banks.

Tourist Information Centre: (☎ 234353; fax 710609), Castle Wynd. The staff can tell you how to track the monster by bus, boat, or brochure; books non-hostel beds (£1.50); and exchanges currency. Open roughly mid-June to Aug. M-Sa 9am-7pm, Su 10am-6pm; Sept. to mid-June M-Sa 9am-5pm, Su 10am-4pm.

Tours: Guide Friday (☎ 224000) hop-on/hop-off open-top bus tours leave every 45min. daily May-Sept. from the tourist information centre (TIC). Inverness and Culloden tour,

£7, seniors and students £5.50, children £2.50; Inverness city tour £5, £4, £2.50. Numerous tours depart for **Loch Ness;** see p. 587. **Puffin Express** (☎ 717181) runs daily summer minibus tours to John O'Groats and the North (£20; students, hostelers, and seniors £18; children £12) and Cawdor Castle, Clava Cairns, and Culloden battle-field (£7.50, concessions £6.50). Pick up *Day Trips from Inverness* from the TIC to find out how to get virtually anywhere in the Highlands.

Financial Services: Royal Bank of Scotland, 38 Academy St. Open M-Tu and Th-F 9:15am-4:45pm, W 10am-4:45pm. **Branch,** 60 Union St., also open Sa 10am-2pm. **Thomas Cook,** across the street from the train station, exchanges money. Open M and W-Sa 9am-5:30pm, Tu 10am-5:30pm.

American Express: 43 Church St. (☎ 718008). Open M-F 9am-5:30pm, Sa 9am-1pm.

Launderette: 17 Young St. (☎ 242507). Open M-F 8am-8pm, Sa 8am-6pm, Su 10am-4pm. Last wash 1hr. before close. £3 per wash, £1.40 per dry.

Police: (☎ 715555), Burnett Rd.

Hospital: Raigmore Hospital (☎ 704000), Old Perth Rd.

Internet Access: MTC, 2 Grant St. (☎ 715450), on the west side of Waterloo Bridge. £5 per hr. Open M-Th 9am-5pm, F 9am-4:30pm. Also **The Gate** cafe (see below).

Post Office: 14-16 Queensgate. Open M-F 9am-5:30pm, Sa 9am-6pm. Send Post Restante to **Royal Mail Enquiry Office,** Inverness, 7 Strothers Ln., IV1 1AA. ☎ 256240. Open M-F 7am-5:30pm, Sa 7am-12:30pm. **Postal Code:** IV1 1AA.

▌ ACCOMMODATIONS

▨ **Wits End,** 32 Ardconnell St. (☎ 239909). Bright, airy rooms, all with TVs, in a restored Victorian house. The owners love backpackers. Soak your cares away in the skylit bath-room, complete with a tub. No smoking. No breakfast. Dorms £10; twin rooms £24.

Inverness Student Hotel, 8 Culduthel Rd. (☎ 236556). The capable and friendly staff might even take you out to the local pubs. 57 beds in rooms of 6-10, free coffee and tea all day, small kitchen. Great views. Breakfast £1.60. Laundry £2.50. Bike hire £6 per half day. Internet access £5 per hr. Reception open 6:30am-2:30am. Check-out 10:30am. Credit card reservations accepted. Dorms July-Sept. £11, Oct.-June £10. Credit card surcharge 30p.

Bazpackers Backpackers Hotel, 4 Culduthel Rd. (☎ 717663). A down-home smoke-free atmosphere next to the Student Hotel. 36 beds in rooms of 4-8; 2 doubles also avail-able. Kitchen, cozy fireplace, co-ed rooms and bathrooms. Reception 7:30am-midnight. Check-out 10:30am. No curfew. Credit card reservations accepted, 50p surcharge. Mid-June to Sept. dorms £10, doubles £14; Oct. to mid-June £8.50, £12.

SYHA Inverness Millburn, Victoria Dr. (☎ 231771). State-of-the-art hostel, but a bit of a trek, especially if you're pub-crawling. From the train station walk 10-15min. up Millburn Rd.; Victoria Dr. is on your right. 166 beds in rooms of 2-6. Lockers, laundry (£1), kitchen, TV room, and hairdryers in the women's bathroom. Internet access £5 per hr. Continental breakfast included. Check-out 10:30am. Curfew 2am. Wheelchair access. Dorms July-Aug. £13.75, under 18 £12; Sept.-June £12.75, £11.75.

Ho-Ho Hostel, 23a High St. (☎ 221225). 76 beds in rooms of 8-10, some with bath. Large Victorian lounge often crawls with rowdy long-termers. Frequent pub crawls and monthly live music. Internet access £4 per hr. Laundry. Check-out 10am. No curfew. Dorms £8.90; doubles and twins £20. An **annex** at 28 Ardconnell St. has larger rooms (as many people as you can cram in) for £24 a night

Eastgate Backpackers Hostel, 38 Eastgate (☎ 718756), above a Chinese restaurant. 38 beds in rooms of 6-8. Bike hire, free tea and coffee. Dorms £8.90; twins £11; less in winter. The **Church Hall annex** across the river has very basic dorm beds for £7.

Mr. and Mrs. Lyall, 20 Argyll St. (☎ 710267). Handsome rooms with TVs, tea, and cof-fee. Don't miss the antics of the Lyalls' latest parrot. Continental breakfast included. Bed and shower deluxe, an amazing value at £10 per person.

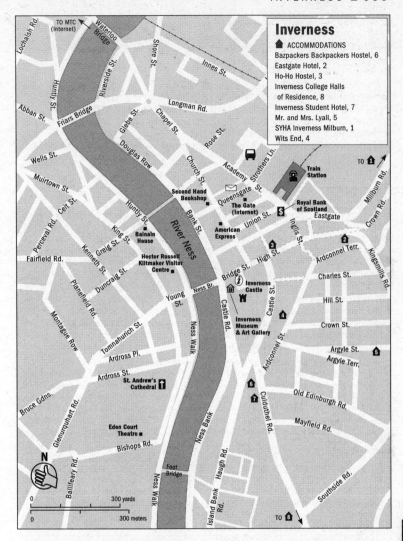

Inverness

🏠 ACCOMMODATIONS

Bazpackers Backpackers Hostel, 6
Eastgate Hotel, 2
Ho-Ho Hostel, 3
Inverness College Halls
    of Residence, 8
Inverness Student Hotel, 7
Mr. and Mrs. Lyall, 5
SYHA Inverness Milburn, 1
Wits End, 4

Inverness College Halls of Residence, 23 Culduthel Rd. (☎ 713430). Walk 10min. past the Castle and Student Hotel; it's on your left; Or take bus #5 or 7 from the city center. These quiet singles and doubles each have their own desk, sink, and wardrobe. Breakfast £1.50. No curfew. Open July–Aug. £11 per person; singles sometimes £16.

Camping: Most grounds fill with caravans in summer. The closest one to town is the **Bught Caravan and Camping Park** (☎ 236920), in the southern part of town near the Ness Islands. About 90 pitches. £4.10 per tent, cars £5.90.

🍴🍺 FOOD AND PUBS

Across from the bus station, buy groceries at **Safeway.** (Open M-F 8am-10pm, Sa 8am-8pm, Su 9am-6pm.) Inverness holds a range of fairly unexceptional restaurants, though there are some diamonds in the rough. One of these is **Shapla Tandoori Restaurant,** 2 Castle Rd., perhaps pricier than usual for the budget traveler,

HIGHLANDS/ISLANDS

but the sizzling curry dishes (£5-9) and great views of the River Ness make it worthwhile. (☎ 241919. Open daily noon-11:30pm.) For home-baked goods and fabulous soups (£1.75), try the **Lemon Tree,** on Inglis St., just off High St. (☎ 241114. Open M-Sa 8:30am-5:45pm.) **The Gate,** 21 Queensgate, is a hip haunt with frothy mochas and Internet access for £3 per 30min. (☎ 711700. Open M-F 10am-12:45am, Sa 10am-11:45pm, Su noon-11:30pm.)

A wide array of pubs invigorates Inverness with live music. The place to be seen is the big and crowded **Johnny Foxes,** 26 Bank St., near the main bridge. (☎ 236577. Open M-Sa 11am-1am, Su 12:30pm-midnight.) **Lafferty's,** 96 Academy St., has loud and lively Irish music. (☎ 712270. Open M-W noon-11pm, Th-F noon-1am, Sa noon-midnight, Su 2-11pm.) Across the River Ness on Young St., play pool or darts at **Glenalbyn,** which sometimes features R&B bands on Friday nights and Sunday afternoons. (☎ 231637. Open Tu-W and F 11am-1am, M and Th 11am-11pm, Sa 11am-11:45pm, Su 12:30-11pm.)

▣ SIGHTS

Disillusion awaits those who remember Inverness as the home of Shakespeare's *Macbeth.* Nothing of the "Auld Castlehill" remains; the present reconstructed **Inverness Castle,** home to the sheriff's courts, looks like it was made out of pink Legos this very morning. That doesn't deter the tourism machine from luring gullible travelers into "joining the government army": the 40-minute castle tour is highlighted by verbal abuse from your commanding officer. (Tours Easter-Nov. M-Sa 10:30am-5:30pm. £3, students and seniors £2.70, children £2.) Down the hill lurks the **Inverness Museum and Art Gallery,** in Castle Wynd, which focuses on things local, from wildcats to Pictish lifestyles. (☎ 237114. Open M-Sa 9am-5pm. Free.) If you have an ear for Highland music, visit the fascinating ▧ **Balnain House,** 40 Huntley St., and try your hand at the bagpipe, fiddle, or *clarsach.* A museum, music store, cafe, and bar all rolled into one, it has frequent live music, *ceilidhs* on summer Wednesdays, and jam sessions Monday through Thursday nights. (☎ 715757. Open July-Aug. M-F 10am-10pm, Sa-Su 10am-6pm; Sept.-June daily 10am-5pm. Cellar Bar open M-Th until 1am, F-Sa until 1:30am. Exhibit £2.50, students and seniors £2, children £1.) Just up the road, the **Hector Russell Kiltmaker Visitor Centre,** 4-9 Huntly St., offers a glance at live plaid production. (☎ 222781. Open mid-May to Sept. M-Sa 9am-9pm, Su 10am-5pm; Oct. to mid-May M-Sa 9am-5pm. £2, concessions £1.) **Leakey's Secondhand Bookshop** deals with more cerebral matters. Located at the end of Church St. in atmospheric Greyfriar's Hall, it claims to be Scotland's largest secondhand bookshop. (☎ 239947. Open M-Sa 10am-5:30pm.)

Upstream from the city center, the Highlands' greenery is only a ten minute stroll away, over the Ness Bridge and along **Ness Walk.** There, the shallow, swiftly flowing River Ness forks and forks again, forming the **Ness Islands**—narrow islets connected to both banks by small footbridges and blanketed with virgin forest.

♫ ❧ ENTERTAINMENT AND FESTIVALS

The **Eden Court Theatre,** Bishop's Rd., puts on surprisingly urbane productions throughout the year; in the summer, casts are often dotted with British soap stars. Beyond theater, the venue also hosts dance and music performances, and screens films. (☎ 234234. Tickets £5-9.) If Inverness's intellectual stimulants tire you out, you can search idly for dolphins on the **Moray Firth Cruises.** Boats leave from the quay on Shore St., downstream from the city center. (☎ 717900. 90min., 5-6 cruises per day, Mar.-Oct. £10, students and seniors £8, children £5.)

Inverness has its share of summertime fêtes. In late July, strongmen hurl cabers during the **Inverness Highland Games.** (☎ 724262. Tickets £2-3.50.) Pipe-and-drum bands and daredevil display teams dominate the **Inverness Tattoo Festival** at the end of July. (☎ 235571. Tickets £3-5.) In mid-August, the **Marymas Fair** recreates 19th-century street life with craft stalls, concerts, and proletarian strife. (☎ 715760.) The **Northern Meeting,** the world's premier piping competition, comes to the Eden Court Theatre in early September. (☎ 234234. Tickets £8-15.)

▐ DAYTRIPS FROM INVERNESS

Those planning to visit numerous spots in a day should invest in either Stagecoach Inverness **Off Peak Rover** or Highland Country **Tourist Trail Day Rover** tickets. These allow unlimited bus travel to and from Inverness and sights like Culloden Battlefield, Cawdor Castle, Nairn, Fort George, and Castle Stuart. Buses leave from the Inverness bus station or Queensgate. (Both summer only. £6, concessions £4.)

CULLODEN BATTLEFIELD. In 1746 the Jacobite cause died on Culloden, east of Inverness, as Bonnie Prince Charlie, charismatic but no genius in battle, lost 1200 men to the King's army in a 40-minute bloodbath. A pretty 1½ mi. south of Culloden, the stone circles and chambered cairns (mounds of rough stones) of the **Cairns of Clava** recall the Bronze Age. *(Highland Country bus #12 (return £2) leaves from the post office at Queensgate. Visitor center ☎ (01463) 790607. Open daily Apr.-Oct. 9am-6pm; Feb.-Mar. and Nov.-Dec. 10am-4pm. Battlefield free; center £3.50, concessions £2.50.)*

MONIACK CASTLE. Built in 1580 as the home of the Frasers, Moniack Castle, seven miles west of Inverness, still houses the family and their wine-making business. The castle offers guided tours of the winery every 20 minutes. *(☎ (01463) 831283. Open Mar.-Oct. M-Sa 10am-5pm; Nov.-Feb. M-Sa 11am-4pm. £2.50, children free.)*

CAWDOR CASTLE. The castle has been the residence of the Thane of Cawdor's descendants since the 15th century and is still inhabited for much of the year. The late Lord Cawdor IV detailed its priceless items in a series of humorous and witty signs. Don't miss the garden maze and nature walks. *(Highland Country bus #12 (return £4.50) leaves from the post office at Queensgate. ☎ (01667) 404615. Open May-Sept. daily 10am-5:30pm. £5.50, students and seniors £4.50, children £2.80.)*

LOCH NESS   ☎01456

Unfathomably deep and mysterious, Loch Ness guards its secrets five miles south of Inverness. In AD 565, St. Columba repelled a savage sea beast as it attacked a monk; whether a prehistoric leftover, giant seasnake, or cosmic wanderer, the Loch Ness monster has captivated the imagination of the world ever since. The loch is shaped like a wedge, 700 ft. deep just 70 ft. from its edge. The caverns at its floor extend down so far that no one has definitively determined how vast it really is, or what life exists at its bottom.

One of the easiest ways to see the loch is with tour groups, which are a dime a dozen. The popular **Jacobite Cruises,** Tomnahurich Bridge, Glenurquhart Rd., Inverness, can whisk you around any number of ways, to Urquhart Castle or on coach and boat trips. (☎ (01463) 233999. £9.50-13.50, students £7.50-10. Prices include castle admission.) **Ken White's Tours** take you around the entire loch and back to Inverness on a minibus from 10:30am-5pm. (☎ (01463) 223168. £12, students and hostelers £10.) Not to be outdone, **Guide Friday** offers a three-hour bus and boat tour departing from the Inverness TIC. (☎ (01463) 224000. May-Sept. daily 10:30am and 2:30pm. £10.50, students and seniors £8.50, children £4.) A slew of boat trips leave from touristy Drumnadrochit, on the northwest shore of the loch; most last one hour and cost £8-10 per adult, with concessions available.

Sixteen miles down the western shore road (the A82), a lone bagpiper drones from the ruined ramparts of lovely **Urquhart Castle** (URK-hart), one of the largest in Scotland before it was blown up in 1692 to prevent Jacobite occupation. Most tours from Inverness stop at these ruins, and a number of photos of Nessie have been fabricated at this spot. (☎ 450551. Open Apr.-May and Sept. daily 9:30am-5:45pm; June-Aug. M-Sa 9:30am-7:45pm, Su 9:30am-5:45pm; Oct.-Mar. M-Sa 9:30am-3:45pm. £3.80, seniors £2.80, children £1.20.) In nearby **Drumnadrochit,** not one but two visitor centers expound on the legend that is Nessie. The better of the two, the **Official Loch Ness Exhibition Centre,** features a 40-minute audio-visual display. (☎ 450573. Open daily July-Aug. 9am-8pm; June and Sept. 9am-6pm; Easter-May 9:30am-5pm; Oct. 9:30am-5:30pm; Nov.-Easter 10am-5:30pm. £5.95, students and seniors £4.50, children £3.50.) The **Great Glen Cycle Route** careens past the loch on its way to Fort William. You can also **bike** down the eastern side of the loch, where the narrow B582 runs close to the water. Eighteen miles down the road, the River Foyers empties into the loch in a series of idyllic waterfalls.

Near Drumnadrochit, the hip **Loch Ness Backpackers Lodge,** Coiltie Farm House, East Lewiston, is served by several buses from Inverness (ask for Lewiston) and within walking distance of Loch Ness. It has cozy cabin-like rooms and runs boat trips for £4.50. The rooms in the annex are larger, but you have to step outside for all facilities. (☎ 450807; hostel@lochness-backpackers.com. Continental breakfast £1.50. Dorms £9-9.50; doubles £24.) The **SYHA Loch Ness** stands on the western shore of the loch, 7½ mi. south of the castle. (☎ (01320) 351274. Open mid-Mar. to Oct. Reserve in advance July-Aug. Dorms £8.25, under 18 £7.25.) Both hostels lie on the Scottish Citylink bus routes between Inverness and Fort William (#917-919; roughly £4.50 from Inverness).

GLEN AFFRIC AND GLEN CANNICH ☎ 01456

West of Loch Ness, amidst stands of evergreens and gleaming waterfalls, Glen Affric and Glen Cannich stretch away into the mountainous distance. This is prime hiking country, and a welcome respite from the throngs of tourists in Inverness and Drumnadrochit. The gorgeous **Plodda Falls** and **Dog Falls** attract oglers, and with a 400-year-old Caledonian-pine forest, Glen Affric is often considered one of Scotland's most beautiful glens. The main access points for the glens are the villages of **Cannich**, at a turn in the A831, and **Tomich**, farther on. For recommended hikes, pick up *Fifty Walks Near Tomich and Cannich* (£2), which actually lists 60 walks. In Cannich, paths into Glen Cannich depart behind the Glen Affric Hotel; walks into the more popular Glen Affric depart a few miles down the road at the Fasnakyle power station or the Dog Falls car park. Be sure to pick up the Ordnance Survey map Landranger 25, especially for the walks that extend westward.

In the summer, **Highland Country** (☎ (01463) 233371) **buses** run from **Inverness** to **Cannich** (1hr.; M-F 4 per day, Sa 1 per day); some extending to **Tomich** (M-F 2 per day). **Ross Minibuses** (☎ (01463) 761250) also run to Cannich and Tomich from **Inverness** and **Beauly** a few times a week. Cannich's two **hostels** are located next to each other in nearly identical low brown buildings. From the Glen Affric Hotel, head directly down the road lined with pine trees, away from the Spar. **Glen Affric Backpackers** sleeps 70, all in twin rooms. (☎ (01456) 415263. £6 per person.) The **SYHA Cannich** is a bit cozier. (☎ 415244. Open Apr.-Oct. Dorms £8.25, under 18 £7.25.) Next door, at the **Cannich Caravan & Camping Park,** you can also **rent bikes.** (☎ 415364. Open Apr.-Oct. Bikes £7.50 per day. Tent pitch £3.50-6.50.) **Slater's Arms,** down the road toward Glen Affric, serves standard meals with chips for £2-7. (☎ 415215. Open daily 9am-11pm.) The **Spar** right next door is the only shop for miles, and contains the Cannich **post office.** (Open M-Sa 9am-8pm, Su 10am-6pm.)

Tomich, 5 miles further into Glen Affric, has closer access to the trails, but less amenities and no budget accommodations. The basic **Cougie Lodge** is a six-mile hike away. (☎ 415459. Open Apr.-Sept. Dorms £8.) Even farther and quite basic is the **SYHA Glen Affric,** Allt Beithe, buried amidst mountains and located at a crossroad of trails to Tomich, Ratagan, and Clunie. (No phone. Open Apr.-Oct. Dorms £7.75, under 18 £7.) Bring a sleeping bag when staying at either of these hostels.

GLEN COE ☎ 01855

Stunning in any weather, Glen Coe is best seen in the rain, when a slowly drifting web of mist over the valley laces the innumerable rifts and crags of the steep slopes, and silvery waterfalls cascade into the River Coe. Only on rare days is the view marred by shining sun; the glen records over 100 inches of rain a year. Glen Coe is infamous as the site of the 1692 massacre, when the Clan MacDonald welcomed a company of Campbell soldiers, henchmen of William III, into their chieftain's home. After enjoying the MacDonalds' hospitality for over a week, the soldiers proceeded to slaughter their hosts. Neither the rain nor the dramatic history, however, deter hikers and skiers from passing time in this beautiful valley.

E7 GETTING THERE AND PRACTICAL INFORMATION. Scottish Citylink (☎ (08705) 505050) **buses** arrive in Glencoe village from **Glasgow** (4 per day, £9.80) and **Edinburgh** (2 per day, £13.40.) The **Oban-Fort William** bus #918 stops at nearby **Ballachulish** (M-Sa 4 per day, Su 1 per day; £6.40.) **Postbuses** putter daily in the area but at irregular times; get a schedule from the tourist information centre (TIC) or hostel. For bike rental, try **Mountain Bike Hire,** at the Clachaig Inn, across the river from the Visitors Centre (☎ 811252; £8.50 per half-day, £12 per day), or the **Strathassynt Guest House,** next to the TIC (☎ 811261; £8 per half-day, £12 per day).

Glencoe village, essentially one street, rests at the edge of Loch Leven, at the mouth of the River Coe and the western end of the Glen Coe valley. The A82 runs the length of the valley. **Glencoe Visitors Centre,** three miles southeast of Glencoe village on the A82, gives hiking advice, sells maps, and shows a film on the Massacre of Glencoe. (☎ 811307. Open daily mid-May to Aug. 9:30am-5:30pm; Apr. to mid-May and Sept.-Oct. 10am-5pm. Film 50p, concessions 30p). The **tourist information centre** in Ballachulish, one mile west of the village, books accommodations for a £1.50 fee. (☎ 811296. Open July-Aug. M-Sa 9am-6:30pm, Su 10am-5pm; Apr.-June M-Sa 10am-5pm, Su 10am-5pm; Sept.-Oct. M-Sa 9am-5pm.) There are no **cash machines** in Glencoe village or Ballachulish, and the **Royal Bank of Scotland** is only open Tu and F 9:30am-4:30pm. The **Spar** supermarket (see below) offers a cashback service with a minimum £5 purchase. On the A82, **Glencoe Guides and Gear** rents rock- and ice-climbing gear. (☎ 811402. Open daily 9am-5:30pm.) The **post office** in Glencoe village is in the Spar. (☎ 811367. Open M-F 9am-12:30pm and 1:30-5:30pm, W 9am-12:30pm, Sa 9am-12:30pm.)

F.G ACCOMMODATIONS AND FOOD. The agreeable, brown-clapboard **SYHA Glencoe** rests two miles southeast of Glencoe village on the east side of the river. Book ahead—the 62 beds fill up fast. (☎ 811219; fax 811284. Laundry facilities. Reception 7am-midnight. Curfew midnight. Internet access. Dorms £9.25, under 18 £8.) If you hike to the hostel and find it full, you can backtrack 500 yd. to the white-walled **Leacantium Farm Bunkhouse.** The farm includes three bunkhouses, ranging from the basic Alpine barn to the super-cozy Ben End suite. (☎ 811256. £6.50-7.50; per week £45.) Follow the painted white rocks to the farm's riverside **Red Squirrel Camp Site** next door, where you can pitch your tent. (£4.50 per person, under 12 50p; hot showers 50p.)

Small but sufficient supermarkets in the area include **Spar,** in Glencoe village (☎ 811367; open M-Sa 8am-9pm, Su 9am-5pm), and **The Co-op,** in Ballachulish (☎ 811253; open M-W and Sa 8:30am-6pm, Th-F 8:30am-7pm). The **Clachaig Inn,** one mile southeast of the hostel and a five-minute walk across a footbridge from the Visitors Centre, serves the area's best food for £6-10, including some vegetarian dishes. The public bar is a lively gathering point, especially for nearby campers and hostelers. A sign outside the inn proclaims that no Campbells are allowed inside. (☎ 811252. Open F 11am-midnight, Sa 11am-11:30pm, Su-Th 11am-11pm; food served noon-9pm.)

⬛Ⱥ SIGHTS AND HIKING. Glen Coe provides a range of challenges. Walkers stroll the floor of the magnificent cup-shaped valley, climbers head for the cliffs, and winter ice-climbers hack their way up frozen waterfalls. Well-equipped and sure-footed hikers prepared to use hands, knees, and hindquarters can scramble up the 3766 ft. **Bidean nam Bian** or try the four-mile traverse of the **Aonach Eagach** ridge on the north side of the glen. Saner walkers can find the **Lost Valley,** once called the Coire Gubhail—Corrie of Plunder—because the MacDonalds hid pilfered stuff there. The trail follows the stream on the south side of the glen, just west of the Coe Gorge (3hr. round-trip). You can avoid the 1000 ft. climb by hopping on the **Glen Coe Ski Centre Chairlift,** off the A82 in the middle of Glen Coe. (☎ 851226. Open June-Aug. daily 9:30am-4:30pm, depending on weather. £4, seniors £3, children £2.50, families £11.) For a cruise around the loch, perhaps to see some seals, **Boat Trips and Fishing Trips** leave from Ballachulish West Pier (☎ 811658). Call for details; sailing times are subject to demand and weather.

HIGHLANDS/ISLANDS

FORT WILLIAM AND BEN NEVIS ☎01397

In 1654, General Monck built the town of Fort William among Britain's highest peaks to keep out "savage clans and roving barbarians." These days, the largest town in the Highlands has let down its guard, and the surrounding mountains induce seasonal tidal waves of skiers and hikers. Packed with outdoor-equipment outfitters, Fort William makes an excellent base camp for mountain excursions or other outdoor activities. Thousands each year pass through Fort William on their way to Ben Nevis, the highest peak in Britain at 4406 ft. After a hard day of canyoning, hiking, or anything else, tired tourists can massage their sorry feet in the green grass of the town park before heading to the local pubs at night.

▐ GETTING THERE AND GETTING AROUND

The **train station** is just beyond the north end of High St. **Trains** (☎ (08457) 484950) arrive from **Glasgow Queen St.** (3¾hr.; M-Sa 3 per day, Su 2 per day; £20) and **London Euston** (12hr., 1 per day, £89) on the magnificent ▨ **West Highland Railway.** Built at the turn of the old century, the Railway is a triumph of Victorian engineering, crossing glens, moors, and rivers while skirting mountain ranges and presenting some of the best scenery in Scotland. **Buses** arrive at High St. or at the stand opposite the Safeway by the train station. **Skye-Ways** (☎ (01599) 534328) runs from **Glasgow** (3hr., 4 per day, £11.20). **Scottish Citylink** (☎ (08705) 505050) arrives from: **Mallaig** (1½hr., M-Sa 2 per day, £4.80); **Oban** (1½hr., 2-4 per day, £6.20); **Kyle of Lochalsh** (1¾hr., 1 per day, £9.50); **Inverness** (2hr., 5-6 per day, £6.50); and **Edinburgh** (6hr., 2 per day). Pick up schedules at the tourist information centre. **Alba Taxi** (☎ 701112) is open 24hr. **Offbeat Bikes,** 117 High St., rents bikes. (☎ 704008. £8.50 per half-day, £12.50 per day, including helmet, map, and tool kit; child seat £6.)

▐ PRACTICAL INFORMATION

Through the underpass at the train station lies the north end of **High St.**, Fort William's main street. The friendly **tourist information centre** (TIC) dispenses info on the West Highlands and **exchanges money.** (☎ 703781; fortwilliam@host.co.uk. Open mid-June to mid-July M-Sa 9am-7pm, Su 10am-6pm; mid-July to Aug. M-Sa 9am-8:30pm, Su 9am-6pm; Sept.-Oct. M-Sa 9am-6pm, Su 10am-5:30pm; Nov.-Mar. M-Sa 9am-5pm, Su 10am-4pm; Mar.-June M-Sa 9am-6pm, Su 10am-4pm.) **Lloyds TSB** is on North High St. (☎ 702029. Open M-Tu 9:30am-4pm, W 10am-4pm, Th 9:30am-5:30pm, F 9:30am-5pm.) For equipment, maps, and weather reports from the summits, head to **Nevisport,** a cathedral of the outdoors at the north end of High St. (☎ 704921. Hiking boots for £3.50 per day; winter climbing boots £5 per day; deposit required. Open June-Sept. daily 9am-7pm; Oct.-May M-Sa 9am-5:30pm, Su 9:30am-5pm.) **West Coast Outdoor Leisure Centre,** 102 High St., rents boots for £5. (☎ 705777. Open M-Sa 9am-5:30pm, Su 10am-5pm.) The **mountain rescue post** (☎ 702361), in the **police station** at the south end of High St., has forms that need to be filled out before you climb Ben Nevis. **Internet access** can be had at the **Fort William library;** you usually need to book ahead a day or two. (Open M and Th 10am-8pm; Tu and F 10am-6pm; W and Sa 10am-1pm. Free.) The **post office** is at 5 High St. (☎ 702827. Open M-F 9am-5:30pm, Sa 9am-12:30pm.) **Postal code:** PH33 6AR.

▐ ACCOMMODATIONS

Fort William abounds with budget-friendly bunkhouses and hostels. A morning walk down Fassifern Rd., behind the Alexandra Hotel, will overpower you with the smell of breakfasts drifting from B&Bs. Other B&Bs roost farther up the hill on **Alma Rd.** and **Argyll Rd.**

▨ **Farr Cottage Accommodation and Activity Center** (☎ 772315; fax 772247), in Corpach. By far the best place to stay within reach of Ben Nevis. Corpach is two train stops north of Fort William or a 10min. bus ride from High St. (M-Sa 3 per hr., Su 1 per hr.;

80p). Comfortable rooms with 4-10 beds and TVs in each. Stuart Nicol and his hilarious staff (mostly travelers who have refused to move on and are now employees), will keep you entertained at the in-house bar. Stuart puts on his kilt almost every night and gives Scottish history lessons and whisky talks (and samples). If you're lucky, some of the locals will drop by to really add to the Scottish flavor. Staff will also drive guests to outdoor activities in the region (small charges for rides), including canyoning, whitewater rafting, and horse trekking. Continental breakfast £2. Internet access. Laundry and kitchen facilities. Mountain bikes £10 per day. Dorms £11; less for longer stays.

Fort William Backpackers Guesthouse (☎ 700711), Alma Rd., just a 5min. walk from the Fort William train station. The snug and fun-loving 30-bed guesthouse welcomes you with a hot cup of tea and a cozy bed. The big windows fill the rooms with light and offer excellent views of the mountains. Continental breakfast £1.60. Curfew 2am. Dorms £11, in winter £10.

SYHA Glen Nevis (☎ 702336), 3 mi. east of town on the Glen Nevis Rd., across from the trail up Ben Nevis. Highland Bus and Coach and West Highland Motor Service bus #42 run from Fort William to the hostel and back in summer (M-Sa 14 per day, Su 7 per day, £1.05). Book well in advance in July and August. Continental breakfast included. Reception 24hr. Bedroom lockout 9:30am-12:30pm. Open Dec.-Oct. Dorms July-Aug. £13.25, under 18 £11.75; Sept.-Oct. and Dec.-June £12.25, under 18 £10.75.

Ben Nevis Bunkhouse (☎ 702240), at Achintee Farm, a 2 mi. walk along the Achintee Rd. Sleeps 24 in a 200-year-old barn with full kitchen and bathing facilities. Book ahead in July and August. Lockout 10:30am-4pm. No curfew. Dorms £9; twins £22.

Smiddy Bunkhouse (☎ 772467), across the street from the Farr Cottage. Quiet, clean and comfortable, and immaculately clad in Swedish wood paneling. Dorms £8.50.

Glen Nevis Caravan & Camping Park (☎ 702191), on the Glen Nevis Rd., ½ mi. before the SYHA hostel. Free showers. Open mid-Mar. to Oct. 2-person tent £8.70, with car £11.20; less in the off-season.

FOOD AND PUBS

Stock up at the **Tesco** supermarket at the north end of High St. (Open M-W 8:30am-6:30pm, Th-F 8:30am-7pm, Sa 8:30am-6pm, Su 10am-5pm.) Those eschewing the wilderness can make for the **Garrison,** also at the north end of High St., which offers sandwiches from £2.30, cooked dishes for £3-4, and daily specials. (Open daily 9am-8pm.) Before striking out for the hills, grab a packed lunch of juice, 2 filled rolls, cake, fruit, and a candy bar (£2.90) at the **Nevis Bakery,** 49 High St. (☎ 704101). As you wander the quiet streets of Fort William, follow the crowd to one of the few hot nightspots—the justifiably popular **Ben Nevis Bar,** 103-109 High St. You'll find beer drinkers every night and live music at least once a week. The pub serves food from its fairly extensive menu (from salmon to haggis) between noon and 10pm. (☎ 702295. Open M-Sa 11am-12:15am, Su 12:30pm-12:15am.)

SIGHTS AND ENTERTAINMENT

The best sights around Fort William are all natural, so don't expect too much frilly indoor excitement during the day. Rock jocks should visit **Treasures of the Earth,** in Corpach, where a fine collection of minerals, gemstones, exotic crystals, and fossils awaits. (☎ 772283. Open daily July-Sept. 9:30am-7pm; Feb.-June and Oct.-Dec. 10am-5pm. £3, seniors £2.75, children £1.50.) Slickly tourist-oriented as Fort William is, its **West Highland Museum,** next to the TIC, is a rustic treasure, with a room full of taxidermy, displays on mountaineering of yore, and a stirring Bonnie Prince Charlie exhibit. (☎ 702169. Open M-Sa 10am-5pm; July-Aug. also Su 2-5pm; shorter off-season hours. £2, students and seniors £1.50, children 50p.)

For the rock-weary, **Marco's An Aird,** behind Safeway, holds a 10-pin bowling alley, pool tables, and a bar. (☎ 700707. Open M-Sa 11am-10pm, Su 11am-8pm. Bowling £7 for lane rental. Pool tables £4.60 per hr.) Past Smiddy Alpine Lodge in Corpach sits **Kilmallie Hall,** host of dancing, folk-singing, and other traditional entertainment several times a week. (Open June-Sept. From 8pm.)

HIGHLANDS/ISLANDS

⚠ OUTDOOR ACTIVITIES

BEN NEVIS. Of course, most tourists will first want to hike the highest peak in the British Isles before they do anything else—and justifiably so. On the 65 days a year when **Ben Nevis** deigns to lift the veil of cloud from its peak, the unobstructed view spans from Scotland's western coast all the way to Ireland. The interminable switchbacks of the tourist trail ascend from the Fort William town park to Ben Nevis's summit; go north ½ mi. along the A82 and follow signs. The hike up takes about 3hr. and the descent 2-3hr. You will be cold, so dress accordingly. A much more arduous **ridge walk** deviates from the tourist trail. When the tourist trail makes a sharp turn to the right near Lochan Meall an t-Suidhe, the experienced can walk parallel to the loch instead, following a small path by the stream. Leave the path where it descends to Coire Leis and clamber up the steep grass slopes to Carn Dearg Meadhonach; continue to the summit of Carn Mór Dearg. Along the ridge, a trail veers right towards the southeastern slopes of Ben Nevis by a lovely mountain lake; scramble the final 1000 ft. up steep terrain and claim the top of the world. Leave a full 8½ hours of daylight for the 9½ mi. round trip, and don't set foot on the trail without weather information, an Ordnance Survey map, a hat, gloves, and warm clothes, a windbreaker, proper footwear, a tank, and plenty of food and drink. Okay, maybe not the tank. Remember to register with the **mountain rescue post** (☎ 702361), in the **police station** at the south end of High St. in Fort William, before you head out. See **Wilderness Safety**, p. 53, for more info.

INCHREE FALLS. For more than just great views, try canyoning down the 500 ft. **Inchree Falls** with the guides at **Vertical Descents.** The adrenaline buzz is worth the expense. Say goodbye to stories about Scottish museums and castles—instead, tell your friends tales about the flumes, rocks, and 20 ft. jumps you braved with a wetsuit, helmet, and some other protective gear (well, leave out the part about the protective gear when you retell the story). The trip down the falls takes two hours. (☎ (01855) 821593. Canyoning May 15-Sept., bookings flexible. £30, including all necessary equipment.) For another wet and thrilling experience, call **Free Spirits,** which takes groups down whitewater trails (grades II-V) whose difficulty depends on the season and the experience of the rafters. Expect to be curled over laughing from the jokes he tells in between shouts of "paddle left." (☎ (01887) 830633. Flexible scheduling. Most trips £25.) Don't let the temperature or crying skies keep you away—in both canyoning and rafting you are lent wetsuits that keep you surprisingly warm.

SKIING. Speaking of warmth (or lack thereof), Fort William offers some of the best skiing and snowboarding in Scotland. Four miles north of Fort William along the A82, the slopes of **Aonach Mor** (4006 ft.) cushion the **Nevis Range** ski area. Though smaller than the Cairngorm facility, the range features Scotland's longest ski runs and a state-of-the-art cable car, which lifts you 2150 ft. to a restaurant at the base of the trails. (☎ 705825. Ski range open May-June daily 10am-5pm; July-Aug. Th-F 9:30am-9pm, Sa-W 9:30am-6pm. Cable car and marked hiking trails open all year. Return £6.75, children £4.15.) **Buses** run from Fort William to the slopes (5 per day, return £3.25). Aonach Mor (a 10min. drive from Fort William) is also open for skiing and snowboarding Dec.-Apr. (Day tickets £19.75, children £11, families £17.75.)

GAMES AND RACES. A few miles up the road past the SYHA hostel splash the falls where, on the first Saturday in August, hundreds of businessmen who base their virility on being daredevils rocket down the rapids on homemade rafts during the **Glen Nevis River Race.** On the first Saturday in September, the area hosts the **Ben Nevis Race,** a punishing event in which runners sprint up and down the mountain (you, too, can pick up an entry form at the TIC). The record time for the grueling 5 miles up, 5 miles down is an incredible 82 minutes. Fort William dons kilts and tosses cabers at the **Lochaber Highland Games** on the last Saturday in July.

ROAD TO THE ISLES

The scenic Road to the Isles (*"Rathad Iarainn nan Eilean,"* now the A830) traverses lochside and mountain valleys on its breathtaking westward journey from Fort William to Mallaig, on the Sound of Sleat. Beyond having a catchy name to attract eager tourists, the Road to the Isles was the route crofters traveled to sell their wares in the larger towns. Today, the road is more important for bringing visitors up close and personal with sundry attractions.

The train ride on the ◪ **West Highland Railway** offers sublime panoramas at a fast clip (June-Sept. M-Sa 4 per day, Su 3-4 per day; Oct.-May M-Sa 2 per day, Su 1 per day; £11.80). In the summer, "The Jacobite" steam train chugs from **Fort William** in the morning to **Mallaig** (stopping at Glenfinnan) and back in the afternoon, in an attempt to restore the romance of the grand old days; however, on a rainy day you might do as well to take the cheaper modern version. (☎ (01524) 732100. June-Sept. daily 1 per day in either direction. £16, day return £21. BritRail passes not valid.) **Buses** make the same trip, but only once a day (90min.; M-F, July-Sept. also Sa; £5.50). To get to the Road to the Isles, **hitchhikers** usually walk north and try the intersection of the Fort William road (A82) and the Mallaig road (A830); most report nothing but sore thumbs. *Let's Go* doesn't recommend hitchhiking.

GLENFINNAN. The road sets off westward from Fort William along Loch Eil, arriving after 12 mi. at spectacular Glenfinnan, on the head of Loch Shiel. A **monument** recalls August 19, 1745, the day Bonnie Prince Charlie rowed up Loch Shiel and rallied the clans around the Stewart standard to signal the rebellion of '45 (see **Jacobite Revolution,** p. 493). Trains often stop atop the famously photogenic **Glenfinnan Viaduct** to give passengers a sentimental gaze. After you climb the narrow spiral staircase and squeeze through the hatch at the top, a knee-high railing is all that lies between you and the end of your trip—be careful! A worthy ◪ **visitor centre** provides the accompanying history lesson and postcards. (☎ 722250. Centre and monument open daily mid-May to Aug. 9:30am-6pm, Sept.-Oct. and Apr. to mid-May 10am-5pm. £1.50, concessions £1.) The cramped but interesting **Glenfinnan Station Museum** stands at the train station. (Open June-Sept. daily 9:30am-4:30pm. 50p; free for Sleeping Car guests.) If you're feeling lazy, drift on **Loch Shiel Cruises** as far as Acharacle, at the far end of the loch. Trips depart from the Glenfinnan House Hotel, up the road from the visitor centre. (☎ 722235. Various 1-3½hr. cruises June-Sept. Su-F; Apr.-May and Oct. Su-M, W, and F. £5-12.)

Glenfinnan is 30 minutes from Fort William by train (£3.70) and 50 minutes from Mallaig (£4.90); by bus it's roughly the same (£2.50 and £4 respectively). The **phone code** is 01397. You can rest in cramped but authentic quarters at the **Glenfinnan Sleeping Car,** a vintage railway-car-turned-hostel at the train station. (☎ 722295. Claustrophobic bunk £8, with bedding £10.) For a pint, a meal, and a twilight view of the loch, stop at the **Glenfinnan House Hotel pub.** (Open M-W 11am-midnight, Th-Su 11am-1am.)

SOUTH OF THE ROAD. Ten miles west of Glenfinnan, the village of **Lochailort** sits near the **Loch Nan Uamh** (Loch of the Caves), where a shattered Prince Charlie fled in September 1746 after his brave bid for the crown ended in a whimper. From here, **Shiel buses** (☎ (01967) 431272) from Fort William (M-F morning and afternoon, Sa afternoon only) head southward into the desolate districts of **Moidart, Ardnamurchan** (see below), and **Morvern,** all virtually emptied by the Highland Clearances. Those who venture south to brave ridiculous roads and nonexistent budget accommodations will be duly rewarded with stunning coastal views and a genuinely peaceful solitude. The village of **Acharacle,** 19 mi. south of Lochailort, is Moidart's main settlement, with a handful of eateries, B&Bs, a hotel, and a shop by the shores of Loch Shiel. **Loch Moidart,** 2½ mi. from Acharacle and a mile from the nearest bus stop in Dorlinn, opens onto one of western Scotland's most beautiful bays, studded with islets and graced with beaches. The abandoned 13th-century **Castle Tioram,** on an island in the middle of the loch, was destroyed in 1715 by its owner in an ill-conceived plan to keep anti-Jacobites from moving in while he was off at war. The castle is connected to the shore by a strip of land.

ARDNAMURCHAN PENINSULA. Even more remote, the Ardnamurchan Peninsula stretches to the west, anchored by the village of **Kilchoan.** The daily Fort William-Acharacle Shiel bus extends to Kilchoan on request. Along the harrowing single-track way, the **Ardnamurchan Natural History Centre** near Glenborrodale is a great animal- and kid-friendly attraction, owned by famous photographer Michael MacGregor—you might see some of his postcards on sale at the gift shop. (☎ (01972) 500209. Open Apr.-Oct. M-Sa 10:30am-5pm, Su noon-5pm.) In Kilchoan, beneath the shadow of crumbling Mingarry Castle, a **Cal-Mac ferry** runs to Tobermory on the Isle of Mull (May-Oct. M-Sa 7 per day; July-Aug. also Su 5 per day; £3.30). A **tourist information centre** just up the road can help you find B&Bs and sell you maps. (☎ (01972) 510222. Open Apr.-Oct. M-Sa 9am-5pm.) Ten miles farther at lonely Ardnamurchan Point, the **Ardnamurchan Lighthouse** marks the westernmost spot on the British mainland. (Visitor centre open Apr.-Oct. daily 9am-5pm.)

ARISAIG AND LOCH MORAR. The road finally meets the west coast at the sandy beaches of Arisaig. **Murdo Grant** (☎ (01687) 450224) operates ferries and day cruises from Arisaig to Rum, Eigg, and Muck and can go to Skye, Mull, and Canna by charter (May-Sept. daily 11am, return £13-17). The trips allow for a few hours on the island of your choice. Arisaig is 30 minutes from Mallaig by rail (£2). A three mile walk along the A830 from Arisaig or Morar Station will bring you to the placid **Camusdarach campsite** near the beach. (☎ (01687) 450221. £5 per tent, £1 per person.) **Dr. Ian Pragnell** (☎ (01687) 450272) rents **bikes** (£10 per day) and willingly shares his knowledge of local cycling routes. Across the road and down a short footpath from the campsite, brilliantly white beaches afford views of the Inner Hebrides. Rocky outcrops cut across the sand, creating secluded beach coves accessible only by foot. Don't let nasty stinging jellyfish catch you skinny-dipping. Another fine walk follows the banks of **Loch Morar,** Britain's deepest freshwater loch (1017 ft.), complete with its own monster, Morag, cousin to Nessie.

MALLAIG ☎01687

Past Morar looms the relative megalopolis of Mallaig (MAL-ig), the small fishing village where cruises and ferries leave for the Inner Hebrides. Tourists, not fishermen, visit the nifty **Mallaig Marine World,** where you can pet the rays and wee sharks. A tankful of ballan wrasse fish change sex and color every now and then. Kinky. (☎ 462292. Open July-Aug. M-Sa 9am-9pm, Su 10am-6pm; Apr.-June and Sept.-Oct. M-Sa 9am-7pm, Su noon-5:30pm. Nov.-Mar. and mid-Jan. to mid-Feb. M-Sa 9am-5:30pm. £2.75, students and seniors £2, children £1.50, families £7.50.) The **Mallaig Heritage Centre** is right at the train station. (☎ 462085. Open M-F 11am-4pm. £1.80, students and seniors £1.20, under 17 90p.)

Bruce Watt (☎ 462320) runs ferries and day cruises from Mallaig along lovely Loch Nevis to **Tarbert** and **Inverie** (M, W, and F; June to mid-Sept. also Tu and Th; £7-12). The one village in Great Britain which is reachable by water only, Inverie (pop. 60) sits on the wild and roadless **Knoydart peninsula,** emptied by the Highland Clearances. **Cal-Mac** (☎ 462403) skips along from Mallaig to Armadale on **Skye** (M-Sa 6-7 per day, June-Aug. also Su; £2.70, 5-day return £4.60) and to the **Small Isles. Morar Motors** rents cars for explorations into the surrounding area. (☎ 462118. Min. age 21. £32-38 per day.) The **tourist information centre** angles around the block from the train station. (☎ 462170. Open Apr.-June and Sept.-Oct. daily 10am-6:30pm; July-Aug. M-Sa 9am-8pm, Su 10am-5pm; Nov.-Mar. M, W, and F 9am-2pm.) Services include: **Bank of Scotland,** near the station (open M-Tu and Th-F 9:15am-1pm and 2-4:45pm; W 10am-1pm and 2-4:45pm); **Internet access** across the street in the Lochaber College Library; and the **post office,** in the **Spar** shop up the road from Sheena's (☎ 462419; open M-F 9am-5:30pm, Sa 9am-1pm). **Postal code:** PH41 4PU.

Sheena's Backpackers Lodge, with beds roomy enough to sleep two, fills fast after early train and ferry arrivals in the summer, so book ahead. To reach Sheena's, turn right from the train station—the lodge is past the bank, above the restaurant. (☎ 462764. Dorms £9.50.) For more privacy in a tastefully decorated B&B, continue down the street to the **Half Moon Bay B&B,** Main St. (☎ 462988. £15 per person.) The **Spar** and **Nevis Stores,** Station Rd. across from the hostel, sell groceries.

(Nevis ☎ 462240. Open M-F 9am-9pm, Sa 9am-5:30pm.) The **Fisherman's Mission Café,** across from the train station, serves filling grub, including a £3 burger and chips and a £4 lasagna with chips and peas. (☎ 462086. Open M-F 8:30am-10pm, Sa 8:30am-noon; hot meals served M-F 8:30am-1:45pm and 5:30-10pm.) Just up Davie's Brae, the **Central Bar** is the hang-out for locals, with live music on summer weekends. (Open M-Th 11am-11pm, F-Su 11am-midnight.)

THE INNER HEBRIDES

THE SMALL ISLES ☎01687

From the water, they form silent gray-green silhouettes—remote, rugged, and seemingly uninhabited. Lacking vehicle-landing facilities and almost untouched by tourism, **Canna, Muck, Rum,** and **Eigg** often require visitors to jump from their ferry to a small dinghy before setting foot on solid land. Those who make the trip are rewarded with a true taste of island life—jalopies cruise the roads instead of tourist caravans, electricity is provided by generators, seabirds jostle the cattle, and coastline stretches everywhere the eye can see.

Caledonian MacBrayne (☎ 462403) ferries sail from **Mallaig** to Rum, Eigg, Canna, and back. There are both non-landing cruises (M 10:30am and Sa 12:30pm, £12.30), and cruises that allow time on the isles (Eigg Tu and Th 10:30am, £7.80; Rum W 10:30am, £12; Canna W 10:30am, £13.45). For daytrips, you're better off with **Murdo Grant** (☎ 450224), which usually allows at least two hours ashore. Boats sail from **Arisaig** (2 train stops from Mallaig) May-Sept. at 11am to: **Rum** (Tu and Th, June-Aug. also Sa-Su; return £17); **Eigg** (F-W, return £13); and **Muck** (M, W, and F, return £13). Murdo Grant also runs summer cruises from Arisaig to **Canna** by request.

RUM. Rum (also spelled Rhum), the largest island, is owned by the National Trust of Scotland and is carefully managed by Scottish Natural Heritage. Deer, highland cattle, golden eagles, and rarer creatures are the main residents; the entire human population emigrated in 1826 during the Highland Clearances. Today, the grand total of full-time residents has risen to about 25. With clearly marked trails, Rum is an excellent place to spend an afternoon (or a week) hiking. A wealthy Lancashire mill owner built the lavish **Kinloch Castle** in 1901. (☎ 462037. Excellent tours usually daily in summer, £4.) Behind the castle is **Kinloch Castle Hostel,** where advance booking is essential. (☎ 462037. Dorms £13 per person; singles and doubles also available.) To **camp** on Rum (tent pitch £5), obtain prior permission from the Chief Warden, Scottish Natural Heritage, Isle of Rum, Scotland PH43 4RR (☎ 462026).

EIGG. The isle of Eigg (pop. 78) shelters the largest community of the Small Isles, amidst vertical cliffs, sandy beaches, and lush green hills. In **Massacre Cave,** the island's entire population (all 395 MacDonalds) were slaughtered by rival MacLeods in the 16th century, all after St. Donnan and 52 companions were martyred by the warrior women of the pagan Queen of Moidart at **Kildonnan** in 617. In the summer, ranger John Chester offers weekly **guided walks** that reveal the island's bloody history. (☎ 482477. £2.) For **bike hire** inquire at the craft shop by the pier. (☎ 482417. £7 per day.) If you call ahead, you can stay at the **Glebe Barn** (☎ 482417; £9.50, twins £22), or the **Lageorna Guesthouse** (☎ 482405; B&B £15, with dinner £34). **Kildonan Guesthouse** (☎ 482446; B&B with dinner £34) and **Laig Farm Guest House** (☎ 482412; full board with packed lunch £30) are all two miles away along the main road; call ahead for a taxi (☎ 482494; return £3.50). There's a **shop** (open Apr.-Sept. daily), a **tearoom** (open Apr.-Sept. daily roughly 11am-4pm) and Saturday night *ceilidhs,* where everybody knows your name.

MUCK AND CANNA. Muck, the tiny (1½ mi. by 5 mi.) southernmost isle, is an experiment in communal living. The entire island is a single farm owned by the MacEwens, who handle farming, transport along the Muck 1 road, and shopping on the mainland. Stay with **Mrs. Harper,** who may pick you up from the pier (☎ 462371; B&B £15, with dinner £25), or at **Port Mor Guesthouse** (☎ 462365; dinner and B&B £30).

If you intend to muck about outside, bring food, as places to eat or shop are open very sporadically. The miniature isle of Canna ("porpoise" in Gaelic) offers a few miles of trails for hikers and seabird enthusiasts, but no shops or budget accommodations.

ISLE OF SKYE

Skye is often raining, but also fine: hardly embodied; semi-transparent; like living in a jellyfish lit up with green light. Remote as Samoa; deserted, prehistoric. No room for more.
—postcard from Virginia Woolf

Often described as the shining jewel in the Hebridean crown, Skye radiates unparalleled splendor from the serrated peaks of the Cuillin Hills to the rugged northern tip of the Trotternish Peninsula. As elsewhere in the Highlands, the 19th-century Clearances saw entire glens emptied of their ancient settlements. Today, as northern migration pushes the English population of the island towards 40%, Skye's traditional Gaelic culture survives mostly in museums and local music events. The island's natural beauty is by no means a secret; an endless cortege of family-filled Ford Fiestas lines Skye's bridge. But most visitors keep to the main roads, and vast swaths of terrain remain unscarred—there are no fast food chains on Skye, and there are only three cash machines (in Portree and Broadford). Skye's large landmass and spotty transportation will probably force you to concentrate your travels in certain areas of the island, so use the extra time to listen to the sheep talking amongst themselves on the verdant hills of this famously beautiful isle.

✈ GETTING THERE

With the **Skye Bridge** firmly in place between Skye and **Kyle of Lochalsh** on the mainland, the tradition of ferries carrying passengers "over the sea to Skye" has come to an end. **Trains** (☎ (08457) 484950) arrive at the Kyle of Lochalsh terminus from **Inverness** (2½hr.; M-Sa 4 per day, Su 2 per day; £15). **Skye-Ways** (☎ (01599) 534328), in conjunction with **Scottish Citylink**, runs **buses** every day from: **Fort William** (2hr., 3 per day, £10.70); **Inverness** (2½hr., 2 per day, £9.80); and **Glasgow** (5½hr., 3 per day, £17.50). **Pedestrians** may now traverse the 1½ mi. footpath on the Skye Bridge, or take the **shuttle bus** (2 per hr., 65p). **Cars** no longer need wait in ferry lines, but the one-way bridge toll is a weighty £5.70.

From the Outer Hebrides, **Cal-Mac** ferries sail to **Uig** from **Tarbert** on Harris or **Lochmaddy** on North Uist (1¾hr., M-Sa 1-2 per day, £8.30, 5-day return £14.20). Ferries also run to **Armadale** in southwestern Skye from **Mallaig** on the mainland (30min.; M-Sa 6-7 per day, June-Aug. also Su 6 per day; £2.70, 5-day return £4.60). For reservations and schedules, call the offices in Tarbert (☎ (01859) 502444) or Mallaig (☎ (01687) 462403).

⬛ GETTING AROUND

Touring Skye without a car takes either effort or cash. To avoid headaches and long unplanned hikes along the highway, pick up the handy *Public Transport Guide to Skye and the Western Isles* (£1) at any tourist information centre (TIC).

Buses: Buses on Skye are run by different operators; get that golden transport guide, and be careful not to pay twice when making connections, which are infrequent and somewhat pricey (Kyleakin-Uig £7.50; Kyleakin-Armadale £4). The only decent service hugs the coast from Kyleakin to Broadford to Portree on the A87. On **Sundays**, nothing runs except **Skye Ways/Scottish Citylink** and the buses that meet the Armadale ferry.

Biking: Always an option, provided you have plenty of raingear and enjoy miles of steep hills and roads with nearly nonexistent shoulders. Note that buses will not carry bikes. To **rent** bikes in Kyleakin, try the **Dun Caan Hostel** (☎ (01599) 534087; £7.50 per day); in Broadford, **Fairwinds Cycle Hire** (☎ (01471) 822270; £6 per day, £5 deposit); in Portree, **Island Cycles** (☎ (01478) 613121; £10-12 per day); and in Uig, **Uig Cycle Hire** (☎ (01470) 542311; £8-10 per day).

Car Rental: Sutherland's Garage (☎ (01471) 822225), Broadford, rents cars to those over 21. Free collection at Kyleakin. From £35 per day; £250 deposit. **MacRaes Car Hire** (☎ (01478) 612554), Portree, rents cars to those over 21 with an international driver's license from £30 per day. In Kyleakin, you can rent the one car at the Dun Caan Hostel (☎ (01599) 534087) for £35 per day; £150 deposit.

Tours: To see Skye's highlights, take a minibus tour from Kyleakin, such as **Nick's Tour** out of the Dun Caan Hostel (☎ (01599) 534087; 8hr., daily, £15) or **MacBackpackers** tours (☎ (01599) 534510; 9hr., daily, £15). **Walking tours** are offered free by Scottish National Heritage and the Highland Council Ranger Service (☎ (01599) 524270). Better yet, for those who really want a piece of the action but left their proper hiking boots at home, join the fantastic ■ **MacBackpackers Skye Trekker Tour,** departing from Kyleakin. It's a two-day, eco-conscious hike into the magnificent Cuillin Hills, and the MacBackpackers folks provide you with all the necessary camping gear (including midge nets), plus a free dinner and £5 toward camping grub. Boot hire is an extra £15. For the eager and adventurous, it's perhaps the best way to spend £30 on Skye. (☎ (01599) 534510. Weekly departing on Tuesdays. Call ahead.)

Hitchhiking: Fairly easy, and many report that it is the most efficient way to see Skye, although *Let's Go* does not recommend hitchhiking.

🎵 🎿 ENTERTAINMENT AND FESTIVALS

In an effort to evade the midges, Skye has developed a vigorous indoor nightlife. Lively traditional music in English and Gaelic is abundant if you know where to look. Snag a copy of the weekly *What, Where and When* leaflet or *The Visitor* newspaper for a list of special events, and look for signs posted in TICs. There are frequent local dances—half folk, half rock—in the village halls, usually starting after 11pm. The **Highland Games,** a mirthful day of bagpipes, foot races, and boozing in Portree on the first Wednesday of August, and the **Skye Folk Festival,** featuring *ceilidhs* in Portree, Broadford, and Dunvegan during the second week of August, liven up an already lively crowd. Contact the TICs in Kyle of Lochalsh, Portree, Broadford, or Dunvegan for information.

KYLE OF LOCHALSH AND KYLEAKIN　　　　☎01599

Though you can almost reach out and touch Kyle of Lochalsh (the nickname is Kyle) on the mainland from Kyleakin (Kyle-ACK-in) on Skye's southeastern tail fin, there are some real differences between the two hamlets. Coming across the bridge from Kyle, you might feel a weight come off your chest—the feeling of leaving the hustle (and the convenience) of mainland Scotland behind.

🛈 PRACTICAL INFORMATION. The Kyle **train station** (☎ 534205) stands near the pier. Turn left out of the train station, and the **bus station** is on your left, after a minute's walk. Highland Country **buses** meet incoming trains to head for Kyleakin across the bridge. The Kyle **tourist information centre** (TIC) is on the hill right above, overlooking the pier. The staff books beds on either side of the channel for £1.50. (☎ 534276. Open Apr.-Oct. M-Sa 9am-5:30pm, July-Sept. also Su 10am-4pm.) Get **Internet access** at the chip shop in Kyleakin. (£1.49 per 20min. Open Tu-Sa 5-9:30pm, Su 5-8pm.) The last **cash machine** for miles stands at the **Bank of Scotland,** Main St., in Kyle. (Open M-Tu and Th-F 9am-12:30pm and 1:30-5pm, W 10am-12:30pm and 1:30-5pm.) You can buy Citylink bus tickets at the **post office** next door. (Open M-F 9am-5:30pm, Sa 9am-12:30pm.) **Postal code:** IV40 8AA.

⌂ ACCOMMODATIONS. In Kyle of Lochalsh, **Cu'chulainnsis Backpackers Hostel,** over one of the town's more popular pubs, has all the typical amenities, only newer and with especially cozy beds. (☎ 534492. Sheets 50p. Dorms £9.) Over the bridge in Kyleakin, there are a slew of hostels a few hundred yards from the pier. On the pier itself, the **Dun Caan Hostel** is a hub of backpacker activity. The small lounge is replete with a TV and VCR; the wood-paneled bathrooms invite you to relax in the oversized bathtubs. (☎ 534087; fax 534795. Book ahead. Dorms £10.)

On the village green where buses stop, the comfy and relaxed ■ **Skye Backpackers** has expanded to two buildings. Both have stone fireplaces, kitchen facilities, free tea and coffee, and all the friendly amenities of the Scotland's Top Hostels chain. (☎ 534510. Laundry £2.50. Breakfast £1.60. Curfew 2am. Dorms July-Aug. £11, Sept.-June £10; doubles and twins £25.) A Scrabble-whiz warden presides over the large, modern **SYHA Kyleakin.** The hostel fills *extremely* quickly in the summer, so book weeks ahead. Ask to rent the hostel's canoe (£5)—a half-hour paddle across the bay and under the bridge takes you to seal territory. The merry mammals may even approach you. (☎ 534585. Laundry facilities. Continental breakfast included. Dorms July-Aug. £13.25, under 18 £11.75; Sept.-June £12.25, £10.75.)

📷📧 **FOOD AND PUBS.** Grab groceries at the **Co-op,** beside the Kyle bus station. (Open M-Sa 8am-10pm.) Cooked food is available at the **Pier Coffee Shop** in Kyleakin, which serves toasties for £2, haggis in batter for £3, and chocolate cake for £1.25. (☎ 534641. Open daily 9am-8pm.) Kyleakin boasts great nightlife, thanks to a steady stream of backpackers and tourists. The **King Haakon Bar,** at the end of the village green, has a free juke box and frequent live music on weekend nights. (☎ 534164. Open M-Th noon-midnight, F noon-1am, Sa noon-11:30pm, Su 12:30-11pm.) Live music is also common at **Saucy Mary's.** (Open M-Th 5pm-12am, F 5pm-1am, Sa 5-11:30pm, Su 5-11pm.)

📷 **SIGHTS.** The **Bright Water Visitor Centre** on the pier offers a kid-oriented look at local natural history and folklore. (☎ 530040. Open Apr.-Oct. M-Sa 9am-6pm. Free.) The center also runs boat trips to **Eilean Ban,** the island under the Skye Bridge, which has an old lighthouse and frequent seal, otter, and bird sightings. Sailing times depend on tides, so call ahead. (M-Sa 2-3 trips per day; £10, under 16 £5.) Quiet **Kyleakin** harbor is resplendent in beautiful hues of orange, pink, and purple every day at sunset—grab a drink and sit on the grass by the water, or climb to the memorial on the hill behind Castle Moil Restaurant for the best views. A more slippery scramble takes you to the small ruins of **Castle Moil** itself. Cross the little bridge behind the SYHA hostel, turn left, follow the road to the pier, and take the gravel path. Legend relates that the original castle on this site was built by "Saucy Mary," a Norwegian princess who stretched a stout chain across the Kyle and charged ships a fee to come through the narrows. She also used to flash ships who paid the toll—hence the name Saucy Mary and not Entrepreneurial Mary. (Castle Moil open all the time. Free. Hey, it's a ruin.)

SOUTHERN SKYE   ☎01471

BROADFORD. Located on a silent rocky bay eight miles west of Kyleakin, Broadford is remarkable only for its 24hr. convenience store and for being the bus transport hub for the southern half of Skye. The **tourist information centre** (TIC) sits in a parking lot along the bay south of the bus stop. (☎ 822361; fax 822141. Open M-Sa 9am-5:30pm, Apr.-Aug. also Su 10am-4pm.) Five minutes up the road is a blessed **cash machine** at the **Bank of Scotland.** (Open M-Tu and Th-F 9:30am-12:30pm and 1:30-5pm, W 10am-12:30pm and 1:30-5pm.) A second cash machine is by **Skye Surprises,** the massive 24hr. convenience store/petrol station/car rental/launderette by the TIC. It's open seven days a week; look for the hairy Highland coo model out front. (Laundry £3 per load.) The **post office** is open M-Tu and Th-F 9am-1pm and 2-5:30pm, W and Sa 9am-1pm. **Postal code:** IV49 9AB.

Two hostels grace the Broadford area. The **SYHA Broadford** has soothing harbor views half a mile from Broadford's main bus stop, along a signposted side road. (☎ 822442. Reception after 5pm. Check-out 9:30am. Curfew midnight. Open Feb.-Oct. Dorms £9.25, under 18 £8.) Three miles east of Broadford, the funky **Fossil Bothy Hostel,** 13 Lower Breakish, is a renovated stone bunkhouse with room for 8 on a tranquil coast. It's very badly signposted, but any Broadford-Kyleakin bus can drop you off at the Lower Breakish turnoff on the A87; it's a 15min. walk from there. A taxi from Broadford costs about £3. Book ahead. (☎ 822644. Dorms £8.) For food in Broadford, stock up at the **Co-op.** (Open M-Sa 8am-10pm.) **The Fig Tree,** near the post office, has a selection of filled baguettes (£2), fish and chips (£3.50), and chicken curries (£5.50). Their takeaway at the back has the same grub, only cheaper. (☎ 822616. Open M-Sa 10:15am-8pm.)

SLEAT PENINSULA AND ARMADALE. Two miles south of Broadford, the single-lane A851 veers southwest through the thick foliage of the Sleat Peninsula (SLATE), also fondly dubbed "The Garden of Skye." Both **Skye-Ways** and **Highland Country** buses run along this route between Armadale and Broadford (4-6 per day, about £3). To the south, past 17 mi. of hills, is the town of **Armadale,** from which the Mallaig ferries depart. The **Armadale Castle Gardens** and **Museum of the Isles** is the site of a disintegrating MacDonald castle, expansive gardens, and an excellent if somewhat pro-MacDonald exhibit on the Hebrides. Formerly the Clan Donald Centre, its Study Centre is still one of the best places around for genealogical research. They even give free consultations. (☎ 844305. Open Apr.-Oct. daily 9:30am-5pm. Research from £5 per half day. Gardens and museum £4, concessions £2.60.) One such MacDonald, Peter, runs the **Sleat Independent Hostel,** which has incredible views of the Sound of Sleat. He'll pick you up from the Armadale ferry and eagerly tell you about his ancestor, the famous Flora MacDonald. (☎ 844272. Kitchen and TV. No curfew. Dorms £8.) The **SYHA Armadale,** 10min. around the bay from the pier, overlooks the water. (☎ 844260. Lockout 10:30am-5pm. Curfew 11:30pm. Open Apr.-Sept. Dorms £8.25, under 18 £7.25.) Farther inland along the A851, **Hairy Coo Backpackers,** Knock Bay, has a bar, restaurant, and all rooms with bath. Watch for Colonel Campbell's ghost. Buses on the Armadale-Broadford route can drop you off. (☎ 833231. Dorms £9; twins and doubles £25; tent pitch £1.50 per person.) North of Armadale at Ostaig, the famous Gaelic college, **Sabhal Mor Ostaig,** offers one-week summer courses in piping, Gaelic, and fiddling. They can provide B&B lodging while you pretend to be Scottish for a week. (☎ 844373. Courses £110-125. Singles £20 per night; twins £16.)

THE CUILLINS AND CENTRAL SKYE ☎01478

The Cuillin Hills, the highest peaks in the Hebrides, dominate central Skye from Broadford to Portree. They are renowned for hiking paths and fantastic formations of cloud and mist. Legend says the warrior CuChulainn was the lover of the Amazon ruler of Skye, who named the hills for him when the ill-fated hero returned to Ireland to die. The smooth, conical Red Cuillins and the rough, craggy Black Cuillins meet in **Sligachan** (SLIG-a-han). The Kyleakin-Portree road wends its way through the Red Cuillins, which rise at dramatic angles from the road and present a bleak and foreboding face to the aspiring hill walker.

■ **ACCOMMODATIONS AND FOOD.** If you plan to scale some peaks, stay at the **SYHA Glenbrittle** near the southwest coast, where expert mountaineers can give you advice on exploring the area. (☎ 640278. Open Apr.-Sept. Dorms £8.25, under 18 £7.25.) Campers should head to one of the 200 sites at **Glenbrittle Campsite,** which has a small shop. (☎ 640404. Open Mar.-Oct. Shop open 8:30am-8:30pm. £3.50 per person). Glenbrittle can be reached by Highland Country bus #360 from Portree and Sligachan (M-Sa 2 per day, last bus from Portree at noon). Below the mountains at the junction of the A863 to Portree and the A850 to Dunvegan, the village of Sligachan is little more than a hotel, a pub, and a campsite in a jaw-dropping setting. The trail through Glen Sligachan departs south from here (see below), and hikers often stay at the **Sligachan Campsite,** with 80 pitches and showers in an open field by the sea. (☎ 650333. Open Easter-Oct. £4 per person.) Across the street in the hotel, **Seumas' Bar** brews its own "Slig 80/-" beer (pints £2) and serves lovely meals from £3-5 to exhausted hill walkers. (Open daily 10:30am-11:30pm, food served noon-9pm.)

■ **HIKING AND CLIMBING.** The Cuillin Hills are good for both rock climbing and hiking. The booklet *Walks from Sligachan and Glen Brittle* (£2), by the Skye Mountain Rescue Team and available at tourist information centres, suggests hiking routes. Don't even try hiking without warm, waterproof clothing and the Ordnance Survey Outdoor Leisure map 8 (1:25,000; £6.50); consult **Wilderness Safety,** p. 53, for advice on safety precautions to take in the outdoors. Expect sopping wet feet; the treacherously pitted peat is always drenched. If you don't want to go it alone, **MacBackpackers Skye Trekker Tour** hikes the gorgeous coastal path from Elgol, camping overnight at Camasunary, and moving north through Glen Sligachan the next day. A guide, fellow backpackers, and transport to and from trailheads are all part of the deal. (☎ (01599) 534510. £30. See **Getting Around,** p. 596.)

A short but scenic path follows the stream from Sligachan near the campsite to the head of **Loch Sligachan.** After crossing the old bridge, fork right off the main path through the gate and walk upstream along the right-hand bank. The narrow and often boggy path leads past pools and miniature waterfalls (3 mi. round-trip). In 1899, a fit (and barefoot!) Gurkha soldier ascended and descended **Glamaig,** the 775 yd. oversized anthill to the left, in just 55 minutes. Give yourself 3½ hours, and even then do so only if you feel at ease on steep slopes with unsure footing. The smaller trail, which branches off the main trail after about 15min., leads up the ridge between the higher peaks, granting views of the ocean and offshore isles.

Experienced climbers might try the ascent into the **Sgurr nan Gillean Corrie,** to the southwest of Glamaig, which rises 3167 ft. above a tiny mountain lake. For more level terrain, take the eight-mile walk down **Glen Sligachan** through the heart of the Cuillins to the beach of **Camasunary,** with views of the isles of Rum and Muck. From Camasunary, you can hike five miles along the coast to Elgol.

A less intimate view of the Cuillins unfolds at **Elgol,** 14 mi. southwest on the A881 from Broadford. From Elgol, a sailing trip to **Loch Coriusk** with **Bella Jane Boat Trips** reveals an extraordinary panorama of mountains and water. (☎ (01471) 866244. Runs Apr.-Oct. M-Sa; call in off-season. Reservations recommended. Return £12.50; Maxi Day Return allowing you to go onshore for 4½hr. £19.) From Camasunary beach, you can also hike to Loch Coriusk (1½hr.) along a coastal trail which traverses steep rocks at the intimidating "Bad Step." **Postbuses** (service 106) rumble into Elgol from Broadford (M-F 2 per day, Sa 1 per day).

THE MINGINISH PENINSULA   ☎01478

Ten miles west of the Cuillins, arresting but less rugged views continue to surround the B8009. This is the Minginish Peninsula, a peaceful, secluded place, where you can escape most tourists, though not the midges. **Nicolson buses** run here from Portree and Sligachan (M-F 3 per day, Sa 1 per day), stopping at **Carbost,** where most tourists will get off to see the **Talisker Distillery** alongside serene Loch Harport. (Open Apr.-Oct. M-F 9:30am-4:30pm, July-Aug. also Sa; Nov.-Mar. 2-4:30pm. £3.) Buses continue to **Portnalong,** where two hostels bless the area. The **Skyewalker Independent Hostel,** on Fiskavaig Rd., is a recently renovated old schoolhouse with 34 beds, a cafe, campsites, a post office, free pick-up from Sligachan, and occasional Jedi Knight training. Bet you didn't see that one coming. (☎ 640250. Dorms £7, tent pitch £2.50.) The **Croft Bunkhouse,** in a converted cowshed, sleeps 14 in a gigantic two-tiered platform-style bed—bring a sleeping bag—and sports a ping-pong table and a dart board. (☎ 640254. Dorms £6.50.) A footpath from Sligachan over the pass to the hostel skirts the seven-mile walk on the main road.

PORTREE   ☎01478

Skye's capital Portree (pop. 2500), with its busy shops and attractive harbor, is a welcome cosmopolitan respite (relatively speaking) from the surrounding rugged wilderness. Bonnie Prince Charlie took shelter with Flora MacDonald here in 1746, Samuel Johnson and James Boswell paid a visit to the divine Miss M. several years later, and tourists have put Portree in motion ever since, hoping for similar hospitality. Indeed, Portree brims with accommodations, food, and services.

🛈 **PRACTICAL INFORMATION. Buses** stop at Somerled Sq. From the Square, face the Portree Hotel, then turn right down the narrow lane, and left onto Bridge Rd. to reach the busy **tourist information centre,** Bayfield Rd. The staff directs tourists to the right buses and books accommodations for £1.50 on Skye (£3 elsewhere) and a 10% deposit. (☎ 612137. Open July-Aug. M-Sa 9am-8pm, Su 10am-6pm; Sept.-Oct. and Apr.-June M-F 9am-5:30pm, Su 10am-5pm; Nov.-Apr. M-F 9am-5pm, Sa 10am-4pm.) Services include: the **Bank of Scotland,** Somerled Sq. (open M-

Tu and Th-F 9am-12:30pm and 1:30-5pm, W 10am-12:30pm and 1:30-5pm); a **laun-derette,** next to the hostel (open M-Sa 9am-9pm; £3 per load); and the **post office,** Gladstone Buildings, on Quay Brae by the harbor (☎ 612533; open M-Sa 9am-5:30pm). **Postal code:** IV51 9DB.

▐ ACCOMMODATIONS. An enthusiastic staff, comfy beds, and a massive common area await at **Portree Backpackers Hostel,** 6 Woodpark, Dunvegan Rd., across from the Co-op. It's a 10min. walk from the center of town along Bridge Rd. and then Dunvegan Rd. (☎ 613641. Laundry facilities. Dorms July-Aug. £9, Sept.-June £8.50; doubles and twins £18.) The **Portree Independent Hostel,** The Green, has a prime location and a spacious kitchen. (☎ 613737. Dorms May-Sept. £9.50, Oct.-Apr. £8.50; twins £21.) One mile north of town along the A855 to Staffin, you can pitch your tent at the **Torvaig campsite.** (☎ 691 1209. Open Apr. to mid-Oct. £3.)

☐⊠ FOOD AND PUBS. The **Safeway** supermarket on Bank St. (open M-Sa 8:30am-8pm) and super-cheap ⊠ **The Bakery** on Somerled Sq. (open M-F 9am-5pm, Sa 9am-4:45pm) should satisfy your budget culinary needs. Near the Portree Backpackers Hostel, the cafe at the **An Tuireann Arts Centre** offers scrumptious culinary concoctions made with organic local produce. Walk up Bridge Rd., then Dunvegan Rd., and turn left past the Co-op (about 15min.). There's also a free contemporary art gallery. (☎ 613306. Open M-Sa 10am-5pm. 10% student discount.) Seafood restaurants line the **harbor.** For a pint and good fun, head to the **Royal Hotel Lounge Bar,** on Bank St. near the harbor (☎ 612525; open M-Sa 11am-midnight, Su 12:30-11pm; live music W-Sa in summer), or the *upstairs* pub at the **Caledonian Hotel** (☎ 612641; open Su-F 11am-1am, Sa 11am-12:30pm; live music F-Sa).

NORTHERN SKYE   ☎01470

Thanks to two scenic circular roads and miles of quiet shoreline, the northern part of Skye allows you to travel in blissful ignorance of the thousands of other tourists running amuck on the island. The northwestern circuit follows the A850 from Portree to Dunvegan Castle, then down the A863 along the gorgeous west coast; the northeastern circuit hugs the A855 and A856 around the Trotternish Peninsula through Uig and Staffin and back to Portree. From Portree, **Nicolson buses** (M-Sa 4 per day) and **postbuses** (M-Sa 9:45am) leave for the northwest route; the northeast is covered by **Scottish Citylink** and **Highland Country** buses on the Portree-Flodigarry Circular route (M-Sa 4-8 per day, June-Sept. also Su 3 per day).

DUNVEGAN CASTLE. Buses run from Portree to Dunvegan Castle, the seat of the clan MacLeod (whose chief is featured in a movie in the basement). The castle holds the **Fairy Flag,** more than 1300 years old and swathed in clan legend, although looking rather tattered of late. Samuel Johnson paid a visit here in 1773 and sent a nice thank you note: "The kind treatment which I have found wherever I go makes me leave with some heaviness of heart an island which I am not likely to see again." Present-day travelers leave with only a lightness of wallet. (☎ 521206. Open daily late Mar. to Oct. 10am-5:30pm; Nov.-Mar. 11am-4pm. £5.20, students and seniors £4.60, children £2.60. Gardens only £3.70, children £1.80.)

TROTTERNISH PENINSULA. Northeast of Portree, the A855 snakes along the east coast of the Trotternish Peninsula, past the **Old Man of Storr,** a finger of black rock visible for miles around, and the **Quirang,** a group of spectacular rock pinnacles readily accessible by foot. Nearby **Staffin Bay** offers remarkable views of Skye and the mainland, while **Kilt Rock** bears lava columns similar to those on the Isle of Staffa. Strong, well-shod walkers can try the challenging and rewarding 12 mi. hike along the **Trotternish Ridge,** which runs the length of the peninsula from the Old Man of Storr to Staffin. The less mighty can take the buses from Portree to Staffin.

DUNTULM CASTLE. The ruins of Duntulm Castle guard the tip of the peninsula. The castle was the MacDonalds' formidable stronghold until a nurse dropped the chief's baby boy from the window to the rocks below, thereby drawing a curse onto the house. The one remaining room is now sealed off, perhaps to deflect bad karma. (Always open. Free, but watch your step.)

Near Duntulm at Kilmuir, the **Skye Museum of Island Life** recreates old crofter life in a village of tiny, 200-year-old black houses. (☎ 552206. Open Easter-Oct. M-Sa 9:30am-5:30pm. £1.75, students £1.50, seniors £1.25, children 75p.) Nearby along the same turn-off from the highway lies **Flora MacDonald's Monument,** which pays tribute to the Scottish folk hero who sheltered Bonnie Prince Charlie. Get some R&R at the **Dun Flodigarry Backpackers Hostel,** five miles north of Staffin. The hostel is situated on a bluff overlooking the water, and has a large kitchen, a small shop, and a common area. Take the bus bound for Staffin from Portree and ask to be let off at the hostel. (☎/fax 552212. Dorms £8-9.)

UIG ☎ 01470

The town of Uig (OO-ig) flanks a windswept bay on the peninsula's west coast, the terminus for ferries to the Outer Hebrides and the final resting place for most long-distance buses from Glasgow and Inverness. The **SYHA Uig** is a tough 45min. walk along the A586 from the ferry—you can just see it across the bay from the ferry office. If you ask politely, the bus driver might cut down the walking time for you. Once there, gaze at the stunning views of the bay from the kitchen as a dozen fellow hostelers crash into you, trying to use the sink. (☎ 542211. Lockout 9:30am-5pm. Open mid-Mar. to Oct. Dorms £8.25, under 18 £7.25.) **The Pub at The Pier** gives discounts to hostelers on standard pub grub, supplemented by a selection of rather nice puddings. (☎ 542212. Open M-Sa 11am-11pm.)

THE OUTER HEBRIDES

The landscape of the magical Outer Hebridean archipelago is not just extraordinarily beautiful, but astoundingly ancient. Much of its exposed rock has been around for more than half as long as the planet itself, and inhabitants of the island in the distant past have left behind a rich sediment of tombs, standing stones, and Neolithic antiquities. The culture and customs of the Hebridean people are rooted in religion and a love of tradition, and scattered family crofts remain the norm on many islands. While television and tourism have inevitably diluted traditional ways of life, it is still here, in the Western Isles, where you are most likely to hear Gaelic spoken on the streets, and the isles boast an active arts community. The sabbath retains its powerful hold on the strongly Calvinist islands of Lewis, Harris, and North Uist, where most establishments and even public transportation grind to a halt on Sundays. Still, there are one or two places that may quietly serve lunch or an afternoon pint to some poor lost souls. On the islands of Benbecula, South Uist, and Barra to the south, tight-shuttered Protestant sabbatarianism gives way to Catholic chapels and commemorative plates of the Pope on living room walls. While many young Hebrideans leave to escape what they see as the rural isolation of these islands, just as many city-sick "Inlanders" are beginning to migrate westward to seek the seclusion and quiet of the Western Isles.

▐ GETTING THERE AND GETTING AROUND

Four major **Caledonian MacBrayne** (☎ (01475) 650100) **ferries** serve the Western Isles—from Oban to Barra and South Uist, from Mallaig to South Uist, from Skye to Harris, and from Ullapool to Lewis. Once in the archipelago, ferries and infrequent buses connect the islands. If you know ahead of time which islands you will visit, consider buying an **Island Hopscotch ticket** from Cal-Mac; it will save you money on ferry rides over a month, plus you can bring along your bike for free. **Cycling** is excellent provided you like the challenge of the hills in the wind and don't melt in the rain. Though traffic is light, **hitchhikers** report frequent rides.

(*Let's Go* does not recommend hitchhiking.) If you have the money, you can rent a car inexpensively (from £20 per day) at several places throughout the isles, but they'll probably prohibit you from taking it on ferries. Except in bilingual Stornoway and Benbecula, all road signs are now in Gaelic only. Tourist information centres (TICs) often carry translation keys, and *Let's Go* lists Gaelic equivalents after English place names where necessary. For up-to-date transport information, consult the *Skye and Western Isles Public Transport Travel Guide* (£1 at TICs).

ACCOMMODATIONS

Since ferries arrive at odd hours, try to book a bed ahead. An area TIC will book you **B&Bs** for £1. **Camping** is allowed on public land in the Hebrides, but freezing winds and sodden ground often make it miserable. Lewis has one SYHA Youth Hostel, in the remote South Lochs area: the **SYHA Kershader,** Ravenspoint, Kershader, South Lochs. It's your standard SYHA, with laundry and even a shop next door. (☎ (01851) 880236. Dorms £8.25, under 18 £7.25.) A. Macdonald (☎ (01851) 830224) runs the W9 **bus** service to here from Stornoway, but you must call ahead.

The Outer Hebrides are home to the unique **Gatliff Hebridean Trust Hostels,** four 19th-century thatched croft houses turned into simple year-round hostels. Authenticity and atmosphere compensate for the basic facilities—bring a sleeping bag, knife, fork, and the ability to shower *fast* before the hot water runs out (if the shower is working). Affiliated with the SYHA, the hostels accept no advance bookings, but they never turn travelers away. Refer to the SYHA handbook for more details. All £6 per person, under 18 £5, camping with use of facilities £3.

> **Berneray** (Bhearnaraigh), off North Uist. A beautifully thatched and whitewashed affair set on the windswept eastern tip of the island. Frequent buses on the W19 route shuttle between the hostel, the Otternish pier (where ferries from Harris arrive), the Lochmaddy pier on North Uist, and the Sollas Co-op food store (30 min., M-Sa 6-9 per day, £1).

> **Garenin** (Na Gearranan), Lewis, 1½ mi. from Carloway. A converted black croft house, this 14-bed hostel has a kitchen and hot shower. Buses on the W2 "West Side Circular" route from Stornoway (M-Sa 10-11 per day) will take you to Carloway, if not Garenin village itself. A free taxi service meets some buses at Carloway.

> **Howmore** (Tobha Mòr), South Uist, about 1hr. from Lochboisdale. 8 beds. Coin-operated electricity! W17 buses from Lochboisdale to Lochmaddy will stop at the Howmore Garage (M-Sa 5-8 per day, £1); from there, follow the sign 1 mi. west from the A865.

> **Rhenigidale** (Reinigeadal), a substantial hike from Tarbert in North Harris. A taxibus service (☎ (01859) 502221) is available from Tarbert *only if you call ahead* (2 per day, last bus at 4:40pm); they will also take just your pack if you want to venture the tough 6 mi. hike. From Tarbert, take the road towards Kyles Scalpay for 2 mi., then follow the signposted path left to Rhenigidale. The path takes you up 850 ft. for stunning views and a sore back before zig-zagging down very steeply (3hr. total). To get to the hostel by road, follow the turn-off to Maaruig (Maraig) from the A859 (13 mi. from Tarbert).

LEWIS (LEODHAS)   ☎ 01851

Traveling through Lewis can be frustrating, because you may never be able to put your finger on exactly why you love it. Photographs fail to convey its strange aura. Relentlessly remote and desolate, the landscape is flat, treeless, and speckled with quiet lochs. Drifting mists shroud untouched miles of moorland and half-cut fields of peat. The unearthly setting is fitting for exploring Lewis's many archaeological sites, most notably the Callanish Stones. Somewhat incongruously, the island is also home to "the most consistent surf in Europe," and hosted an international surfing competition in 1999. The island's relatively flat roads are good for biking— Pentland Rd., starting in the main town of Stornoway, earns raves. Check the weather forecasts; on a gusty day you may have to pedal hard even downhill. Make sure you rent your bike on a Saturday—otherwise, you'll have nothing to do on Sunday, when virtually everything in Lewis grinds to a halt. See **The Outer Hebrides: Getting There and Getting Around,** p. 602, for information on how to reach Lewis.

HIGHLANDS/ISLANDS

STORNOWAY ☎ 01851

Stornoway (Steornobhaigh), Lewis's main town, is unlike anything else in the Outer Hebrides. Its artificially forested bay, well-kept castle, and small industrial and fishing centers contrast vividly with the rolling countryside around it. With a population of 8000, it's the largest town in northwestern Scotland, and hosts the Hebridean festival in mid-July.

🖃🖩 GETTING THERE AND PRACTICAL INFORMATION. Cal-Mac ferries sail in from **Ullapool** (M-Sa 2-3 per day, £12.70, 5-day return £21.75). **Buses** from Stornoway run frequently around Lewis; the bus station has schedules. Destinations include **Tarbert** (An Tairbeart) on Harris (M-Sa 3-4 per day, £2.65); and **Ness** (Nis), **Callanish** (Calanais), and **Carloway** (Carlabhaigh) on Lewis. Car hire companies abound and are cheaper than on the mainland; try **Lochs Motors,** across from the bus station (☎ 705857; 21+; from £18 per day), or **Mackinnon Self Drive,** 18 Inaclete Rd. (☎ 702984; 21+; from £24 per day). Most places offer a special weekend rate of Sa 5pm to M 9am for the cost of a single day. Rent bikes at **Alex Dan's Cycle Centre,** 67 Kenneth St. (☎ 704025. £2 per hr., £6 per day, £29 per week. Open M-Sa 9am-6pm.) To get to the Stornoway **tourist information centre** (TIC), 26 Cromwell St., turn left from the ferry terminal, then right onto Cromwell St. The TIC books **coach tours** of Lewis. (☎ 703088. Open Mar.-Sept. M-Sa 9am-6pm and to meet late ferries; Oct.-Feb. M-Sa 9am-5pm.) **Stornoway Trust** organizes free **walks** of Stornoway and the countryside, as well as private vehicle tours. (☎ 704733. Apr.-Oct.) Services include: the **Bank of Scotland,** across from the TIC (open M-Tu and Th-F 9am-5pm, W 10am-5pm); **Erica's Laundrette,** 46 Macaulay Rd., the only one in Harris and Lewis, and a bit of a walk (☎ 704508; open M-Tu and Th-Sa 9am-3pm); and **Internet access** at the Stornoway Library (☎ 703064; £2 per 30min., £3.50 per hr.; open M-Th and Sa 10am-5pm, F 10am-7pm). The **post office** is at 16 Francis St. (open M-F 9am-5:30pm, Sa 9am-12:30pm), but send **poste restante** to the Royal Mail Delivery Office, Sandwick Rd. **Postal code:** HS1 2AA.

🖪 ACCOMMODATIONS. The best place to lay your head and wax your board is the new ▨ **Fair Haven Hostel,** a comfortable mecca for wayward surfers, over the surf shop at the intersection of Francis St. and Keith St. From the pier, turn left onto Shell St., which becomes South Beach, then turn right on Kenneth St. and right again onto Francis St. They cook up fresh seafood dinners and offer surfing discounts to hostel guests. (☎ 705862. Dinners £4.50. Dorms £10, with cooked breakfast £12.50, with full board £20.) The **Stornoway Backpackers Hostel,** 47 Keith St., welcomes travelers just two minutes farther up Keith St. This relaxed 18-bed hostel has free tea, coffee, and cereal, and is always open. (☎ 703628. Dorms £9.) The **Laxdale Bunkhouse,** Laxdale Holiday Park, 6 Laxdale Ln., is 1½ mi. north of town on the A857; to get there, hop on any of the Stornoway town service buses (M-Sa 2 per hr.) to New Valley. (☎ 706966. Dorms May-Sept. £8.50, Oct.-Apr. £7.50.) For those departing on early ferries, many **B&Bs** oblige with a crack-of-dawn breakfast. **Mr. and Mrs. Hill** run a comfortable B&B at "Kerry Croy" on Robertson Rd. From the TIC, head up Church St. and turn left onto Matheson Rd.; Robertson Rd. is on the right. (☎ 706553. £17-19 per person.)

🖺🖬 FOOD AND NIGHTLIFE. Cheap food is easy to come by in Stornoway, inclduing groceries at the **Co-op,** on Cromwell St. (Open M-Sa 8am-7pm.) For an unexpectedly good taste of Asia, try the excellent ▨ **Thai Café,** 27 Church St. They do a cheap takeaway as well, but the restaurant (mouth-watering main dishes £4-6) is a lovely candlelit affair. (☎ 701811. Open M-Sa noon-2:30pm and 5-11pm.) The **Bank Street Deli** has everything from curries (£4) to pizza (£3.40) for takeaway. (☎ 706419. Open M-W 9am-6pm, Th-F 9am-2pm, Sa 9am-11:30pm.) The **An Lanntair Gallery** (below) also houses the town's best cafe (smoked salmon roll £2, jacket potatoes from £2; closes 30min. before gallery). Don't miss out on Stornoway's vibrant **nightlife** when you're in town. Pubs and nightclubs crowd the area between Point

> **CHECK, MATE** In 1831, a man was walking along the dunes of West Lewis, bracing himself against a heavy wind. Suddenly a hard gale tripped him up and, as he regained balance, he witnessed a tribe of small, grim figures rising menacingly from the sand at his feet. Dashing off in fright, he returned to tell his family and friends about his perilous encounter in the Kingdom of Fairies. The "tribe" was actually a set of 78 walrus-tooth gamepieces left behind by ancient Vikings, who apparently were avid chess players when not sacking the country. Today the **"Lewis Chessmen"** can be seen at the British Museum (see p. 128). A native exhibit on the subject is found in Stornoway, on Francis St. at the Museum nan Eilean. (☎ 703773. Open Apr.-Sept. M-Sa 10am-5:30pm; Oct.-Mar. Tu-F 10am-5pm, Sa 10am-1pm.)

St., Castle St. and the two waterfronts. Check out the **Crown Inn** on North Beach St. (open M-W until 11pm, Th-F until midnight, Sa until 11:30pm); the **Caley Bar** on South Beach St. (Th and Sa "Karaoke-Disco" nights); or **The Heb,** a hip club/bar/cafe (Th-Sa disco starting at 10pm, 18+, cover £2; open M-W 11am-8pm, Th 11am-1am, F 11am-2am, Sa 11am-11:30pm).

🔲 **SIGHTS.** The **An Lanntair Gallery,** in the Town Hall on South Beach St., hosts art exhibits and events including musical and historical evenings. (☎ 703307. Open M-Sa 10am-5:30pm. Free.) The free **Museum nan Eilean** on Francis St. (see below) has fascinating Hebridean exhibitions. If the volume of human companionship is too much, meander through the shell of **Lewis Castle,** northwest of town. Built in the 19th century by a merchant and opium smuggler, the castle now sequesters a college. The castle entrance is on Cromwell St., but you can admire it from across the water at the end of North Beach St., or from a clearing reached by turning left after the footbridge from New St.

LEWIS SIGHTS AND SURF

Most of Lewis's big tourist sights, including the Callanish Stones, Dùn Carloway Broch, and the Arnol Black House, are ranged along the west coast and can be reached with the **W2 bus service,** which operates on a circuit beginning at the Stornoway bus station (M-Sa 5 per day in either direction). Maclennan Coaches offer a £5 day-rover pass for this route, or a return ticket to see one, two, or three of the sights May-Oct. (£3.50, £4, and £4.50 respectively). Alternatively, travel with a minibus tour company, such as **Out & About Tours** (☎ 612288; half-day tour from £7) or **Albannach Guided Tours** (☎ 830433; from £8).

🔲 **CALLANISH STONES (CALANAIS).** The impressive Callanish Stones, 14 mi. west of Stornoway on the A858, are second only to Stonehenge in grandeur and a thousand times less overrun. The speckled greenish-white stones were hewn from Lewisian gneiss, the three-billion-year-old rock hidden beneath the island's peat bogs. Local archaeologists believe that prehistoric peoples used the stones to track the movements of the moon, employing complex trigonometry and displaying a level of technical knowledge unavailable to the Greeks 2000 years later. Others are skeptical, but admit that the circle may have been designed by primitive astronomers. The Visitor Centre has a comprehensive exhibit. (☎ 621422. Visitor Centre open M-Sa Apr.-Sept. 10am-6pm; Oct.-Mar. 10am-4pm. Exhibit £1, students and seniors 75p, children 40p. Stones themselves always open and free.)

Local writer Gerald Ponting has published guides to Callanish and 20 neighboring sites with explicit directions (40p-£4); get them from the Stornoway tourist information centre. A mile before Callanish, postbuses snake off along the B8011 across the bridge to **Great Bernera** (Bearnaraigh). Now joined to Lewis by a causeway, this former island has the **Bostadh Iron Age House** on the site of an Iron Age village. *(Open Tu-Sa noon-4pm. £1-2.)* Perhaps more spectacular are the idyllic **white beaches** nearby. Twenty miles farther west stand the surprisingly lush **Glen Valtos** and the expansive sands at **Timsgarry,** flanked by dozens of deserted islets.

CARLOWAY BROCH (DÙN CHARLABHAIGH). On the A858 five miles north of Callanish is **Carloway** (Carlabhaigh), a crofting town dominated by the imposing Carloway Broch, an Iron Age tower with a partially intact staircase and a breath-taking view of the surrounding hills and lochs. Once it would have protected farmers and their cattle from Viking raiders—now it shelters tourists from high winds. Watch your footing on the broch; a sudden gust of wind may bring you closer to the surrounding landscape than you'd like. (Visitor Centre open Apr.-Oct. M-Sa 10am-6pm. Broch always open and free.) The **Garenin Hebridean Trust Hostel,** 1½ mi. from Carloway (see p. 603), stands within the restored **Gearrannan Blackhouse Village.** (☎ 643416. Open M-Sa 10am-4pm. Guided tours £1.50. £1, concessions 50p.)

ARNOL BLACK HOUSE. On the A858, beyond Shawbost, a small town north of Carloway, stands this restored thatched-roof crofter's cottage. A chimney was intentionally left out, as smoke from the peat fire was supposed to conserve heat and improve the thatch by seeping through the roof—hence the name. Inhale a hearty lungful of peat smoke and get a watery-eyed glimpse of the dim interior. (☎ 710395. Open Apr.-Sept. M-Sa 9:30am-1pm and 2-6:30pm; Oct.-Mar. M-Th and Sa 9:30am-1pm and 2-4:30pm. £2.50, seniors £1.90, children 75p.)

SURF'S UP. Farther north, across splashes of grassy moors and scattered villages, lies the **Butt of Lewis** (Rubha Robhanais), the island's northernmost point. A lighthouse on the disintegrating cliffs overlooks beaches below. It is a bleak but beautiful Butt, and at night you can hear the growl of the corncrake, a rare and elusive bird. Just around the corner from the Butt is the **Port of Ness,** home to a popular surf beach. Another occasional option for the wave-seekers is **Uig,** the central western area of Lewis. **Kneep Reef** sometimes gets good swells, and if the surf's not up, the endless deserted beach will cheer even the most eager sports enthusiast. Search the sands for Neolithic artifacts, or the little pink shells that are fabled to be mermaid fingernails. The most frequented surf on the island is at **Dalmor beach,** near the town of Dalbeg, site of an international surf competition in 1999. Head to **Hebridean Surf Holidays** (☎ 705862), on the corner of Keith St. and Francis St. in Stornoway by the hostel, and ask for Derek—he'll tell you where the swells are. His all-inclusive **surfing lessons** are £35 per day, or he can just rent you the equipment and will usually transport you out to the beach (from £3).

If you don't ride with Derek, the ever-handy **W2 bus route** runs past Dalbeg and Dalmor beach, while buses operating the **W4 route** (2-4 per day) from Stornoway and Garynahine pass Kneep Reef and other spectacular surf spots in the Uig district. The Galson Motors bus on the **W1 route** can whisk you from Stornoway along the northwest coast to the Butt and the Port of Ness (M-F 9-10 per day, Sa 6 per day). En route, it'll also stop by the village of Galson, where budget travelers can rest up at the **Galson Farm Hostel,** a quarter-mile from the A857 with 8 beds and great ocean views. (☎ (01851) 850492. Dorms £9.)

HARRIS (NA HEARADH)

Harris is technically part of the same island as Lewis, but in all other respects, it's an entirely different world. Here, the flat, desolate landscape of Lewis gives way to another kind of desolation, more rugged and spectacular, with steely-gray mountains ranged one against the other. Towards the west coast, the barricade of the Forest of Harris (ironically enough, a treeless mountain range splotched with heather) descends to brilliant crescents of yellow beaches bordered by indigo waters and *machair*—sea meadows of soft green grass and summertime flowers. In the 19th century, these idyllic shores were cleared for sheep grazing and the islanders moved to the boulder-strewn waste of the east coast. They responded to the east's complete lack of arable land by developing still-visible "lazybeds," furrowed masses of seaweed and peat compost laid on bare rock. The island's main road, the A859, bumps through the mountains from

Tarbert to Stornoway. The Golden Road (so named because of the king's ransom spent in blasting it from the rock) twists from Tarbert to Harris's southern tip via the desolate east coast, making a harrowing bus trip or grueling bike ride. Small roads branch from Tarbert west to the small fishing community on the island of Scalpay (Scalpaigh), now connected to Harris by a new causeway. See **The Outer Hebrides: Getting There and Getting Around,** p. 602, for information on how to reach Harris.

HIKING. With its astounding boulder-strewn stretches and heathery slopes, Harris makes for a near-orgasmic hiking experience. The largest peaks on Harris lie within the Forest of Harris, whose main entrances are off the B887 to Huisinish Point, at **Glen Meavaig,** and farther west at **Amhuinnsuidhe Castle,** a Victorian building erected in 1863 (about 15 mi. from Tarbert). All of these points can be reached by the **W12 bus** service from Tarbert, which is infrequent in summer (Tu and F only, 3 per day). An excellent 4hr. hike runs down through to Glen Meavaig from Ardvourlie in the north and past Loch Bhoisimid. Ardvourlie lies on the **W10 bus** route from Tarbert to Stornoway (Harris Coaches, M-Sa 3-4 per day). If you don't have time for exhaustive exploration, hop any fence just outside Tarbert and hike up **Gillaval** (1554 ft.), which overlooks the town and harbor islands. The view from the top is stupendous; allow yourself at least an hour for the trip up. The hills of South Harris are smaller, but just as rugged. In any case, always be sure to have the proper Ordnance Survey map with you in these remote parts.

TARBERT   ☎01859

Tarbert (An Tairbeart) straddles a narrow isthmus that divides the island into North Harris and South Harris. As the population center (roughly 500) of Harris, the town offers the greatest concentration of amenities, including B&Bs. **Ferries** serve Tarbert from **Uig, Skye** (M-Sa 1-2 per day, £8.30, 5-day return £14.20). Check with **Caledonian MacBrayne** (☎ 502444), in Tarbert at the pier, for ferry schedule information. **Buses** (☎ 502441) run from both **Stornoway** and **Leverburgh** (45min. in either direction, M-Sa 3-5 per day, £2.65) and stop in the car park behind the tourist information centre (TIC). Prices at **Gaeltech Car Hire** (☎ 520460) average £20 a day. The beguiling nothingness of the Harris landscape is best seen by foot or **bike;** rent from **D.M. Mackenzie** in the hairdresser's behind the TIC. (☎ 502271. Mountain bike £7 per day, £25 per week; touring bike £6 per day, £20 per week.) **Hiking** is agreeable; there's little risk of getting lost in the treeless landscape. Still, marked trails are scarce, so bring a compass, sturdy boots, and a map.

A **tourist information centre** sits on Pier Rd. (☎ 502011. Open early Apr. to mid-Oct. M-Sa 9am-5pm and for late ferry arrivals). Ask them for the hours for **Internet access** at the Sir E. Scott School library, a 10min. walk from town along the A859 to Stornoway. The **Bank of Scotland** sits uphill from the pier, sadly without a cash machine. (Open M-Tu and Th-F 9am-12:30pm and 1:30-5pm, W 10am-12:30pm and 1:30-5pm.) The **post office,** Main St., is up the hill and to the right. (Open M-Tu and Th-F 9am-1pm and 2-5:30pm, W 9am-1pm, Sa 9am-12:30pm.) **Postal code:** HS3 3BL.

The bright and comfy **Rockview Bunkhouse,** Main St., is less than five minutes from the pier. Walk uphill past the TIC and hang a left at the grocer's. It'll be on your right. It's run by two postal clerks, so you can also check in at the post office. (☎ 502211. Dorms £9.) Effie MacKinnon's huge rooms rest in **Waterstein House,** across from the TIC. (☎ 502358. £14 per person.) **A.D. Munro,** Main St., just up from the TIC, serves Tarbert as grocer, butcher, and baker. (☎ 502016. Open M-Sa 7:30am-6pm.) The **Firstfruits Tearoom,** next door to the TIC, ladles out tasty soups of the day. (☎ 502439. Open Apr.-Sept. 10:30am-4:30pm.) The **Harris Hotel** serves lunches (£5) and pints (£1.80) in its bar across the road from the main hotel building. It has average food and service, but come Sunday, it's all you've got. (☎ 502154. Meals served daily noon-2:15pm and 7-8:45pm.) Bill Lawson presents **Evenings of Song, Story, and Slides** at the hotel, for those interested in local history and culture. (☎ 520258. May-Sept. W at 8:30pm. £3.)

RODEL AND LEVERBURGH. After exploring Tarbert and the mountains, head down to Rodel (Roghadal), at Harris's southern tip, site of **St. Clement's Church.** Peek at the three MacLeod tombs; the principal one, built in 1528, is hewn from local black gneiss (volcanic rock). Up the road is Leverburgh, where a **Cal-Mac** (☎ (01876) 500337) **ferry** sails to Otternish on North Uist (M-Sa 3-4 per day, £4.60, 5-day return £7.30). **Buses** (☎ 502441) run from **Tarbert** (45min., M-Sa 3-5 per day, £2.65). The upscale, funky **Am Bothan Bunkhouse** is conveniently located near the ferry—the bus passes it about ¼ mi. up the road. (☎ (01859) 520251. Wheelchair access. Dorms £12.)

THE UISTS (UIBHIST)

Coming from anywhere in the peak-strewn Highlands, the extreme flatness of the Uists (YOO-ists) will be a shock. Save for a thin strip of land along the east coast, these islands are almost completely level, packed with so many lochs that it's difficult to distinguish where the islands end and the water begins. A rare shard of sunlight reveals a world of thin-lipped beaches, crumbling black houses, wild jonquils, and quiet streams hiding some of Europe's best salmon-fishing spots.

The population is tiny and decentralized, scattered across small crofts. The main villages of **Lochmaddy** (Loch nam Madadh) on North Uist (Uibhist a Tuath) and **Lochboisdale** (Loch Baghasdail) on South Uist (Uibhist a Deas) are but glorified ferry hubs. Small **Benbecula** (Beinn na Faoghla) lies between its two larger neighbors, and possesses the Uists' sole airport. If you think that this spread-out arrangement will make backpacking difficult, you're absolutely right. There are only five hostels in the Uists, and transportation to them is tricky; prepare to walk or hitch. Crossing from North Uist to South Uist, Calvinism gives way to Roman Catholicism. Although Sunday remains a day of church-going, secular public activity is much more acceptable here than in the north.

▐ GETTING THERE AND GETTING AROUND

Cal-Mac ferries float to **Lochmaddy** from **Uig, Skye** (1¾hr., 1-2 per day, £8.30, 5-day return £14.20); the ferry also connects with **Tarbert, Harris** (see p. 607). Ferries also drift to **Otternish** from **Leverburgh, Harris** (M-Sa 3-4 per day, £4.60, 5-day return £7.80); and to **Lochboisdale** from **Oban** (7hr., M and W-Sa 1 per day, £18.25) and **Mallaig** (3½hr., 1 on Tu, £13.50), sometimes via **Castlebay, Barra.**

All modes of transportation are scarce. **Bus** #W17 runs along the main road from Lochmaddy to the airport in **Balinavich** and **Lochboisdale** (2hr., M-Sa 4-6 per day, £3.10). Buses also connect to meet at least one ferry per day in **Otternish** for departures to Harris, and **Ludag** in the South for connections to Barra (5-9 per day, £1). If you are arriving on a late ferry, there may not be a bus until the next day. Call ahead to book with a B&B that will pick you up, or prepare to camp. Pick up a schedule in the Lochmaddy or Lochboisdale tourist information centre. For **car rental,** call **Maclennan's Self Drive Hire,** Balivanich, Benbecula. (☎ (01870) 602191. From £22.50 plus tax and gas.) The Uists' few drivers are often friendly to **hitchhikers,** but it's rude to ask on Sundays; *Let's Go* never recommends hitchhiking.

▐ PRACTICAL INFORMATION

Tourist information centres (TICs) on the piers at **Lochmaddy** (☎ (01876) 500321) and **Lochboisdale** (☎ (01878) 700286) book accommodations for £1 within the Western Isles, £3 elsewhere. (Both open Apr. to mid-Oct. M-Sa about 9am-5pm and to meet late ferries.) Lochboisdale has a **Royal Bank of Scotland** (open M and Th-F 9:15am-4:45pm, W 10:00am-4:45pm) and Lochmaddy a **Bank of Scotland** (open M and Th-F 9:30am-12:30pm and 1:30-4:30pm, W 10:30am-12:30pm and 1:30-4:30pm); both have **cash machines.** Benbecula also boasts a cash machine-blessed bank (☎ (01870) 602044), along with the Uists' sole launderette, **Uist Laundry,** by Balivanich Airport (☎ (01870) 602876; open M-F 8:30am-5pm, Sa 9am-1pm). **Internet access** is near impossible to find, though North Uist has the **Claddach Kirkibost Centre,** 20 minutes by bus from Lochmaddy. (☎ (01876) 580390. Open M-Sa 10am-5pm.)

ACCOMMODATIONS

The only **hostel** on North Uist near Lochmaddy is the **Uist Outdoor Centre,** which also offers courses in **rock climbing, canoeing,** and **water sports** during the day. Bring a sleeping bag, and book ahead. It's a mile walk up the road from the pier, following signposts and turning right. (☎ (01876) 500480. Linen £2. Dorms £7.) The other hostels are far from town and reachable only by clever navigation. For **Taigh Mo Sheanair** (☎ (01876) 580246), near Clachan, ride any of the buses that travel the main stretch from Lochmaddy to Lochboisdale. The bus driver can let you off at the Clachan shop on Balishare Rd., from where it's about a mile signposted walk. Easier to reach but more primitive is the **Gatliff Hebridean Trust-SYHA croft house** on **Berneray** (see p. 610), serviced directly by bus from Lochmaddy (30min., M-Sa 6-9 per day, £1). Another very basic **Gatliff Hebridean Trust-SYHA croft house** on South Uist at **Howmore** (Tobha Mòr), a mile from the Lochmaddy-Lochboisdale bus route (see p. 603). The bus also passes through **Balinavanich,** Benbecula, where the **Taigh-na-Cille Bunkhouse,** 22 Balinavanich, sleeps 10. (☎ (01870) 602522. Dorms £10-11.)

B&Bs are scarce and difficult to reach. In Lochmaddy, **Mrs. Morrison** greets guests at the Old Bank House. (☎ (01876) 500275. £18-20 per person.) In Lochboisdale, **Mrs. MacLellan's,** Bay View, is right above the ferry terminal (☎ (01878) 700329; £16-18 per person), and **Mrs. MacDonald's,** Kilchoan Bay, is just a mile along the main bus route (☎ (01878) 700517; pick-up from pier possible; £15 per person). You can **camp** almost anywhere, but, as always, ask the crofters.

FOOD

The cheapest **food stores** on the islands are the **Co-ops** in Sollas (Solas) on North Uist, Creagorry (Creag Ghoraidh) on Benbecula, and Daliburgh (Dalabrog) on South Uist. For supper in either ferry hub, your only option is somewhat pricey, but tasty pub grub ($4-10) at the **Lochmaddy Hotel (**☎ (01876) 500331) or the **Lochboisdale Hotel.** Food served in both noon-2pm and 6-9pm.) Across the street from the Lochmaddy Hotel, the small **Café Taigh Chearsabhagh** sells baked goods and sandwiches for £2-3. (☎ (01876) 500293. Open M-Sa 10am-5pm.) In Lochboisdale, the **All Seasons Coffee Shop & Store** offers cattle feed (£6) along with cappuccinos. (Open M-F 9am-6pm, Sa 9:30am-5:30pm, Su 12:30-5pm.) If you're going out to Bharpa Langass, follow the signs to **Langass Lodge** (☎ (01876) 580282) for a post Cairn pint. Halfway between Lochmaddy and Clachan, this classy hunting lodge holds some down and dirty drinking sessions. Mention *Let's Go* and get Niall to make you his special Pimms.

SIGHTS

The vibrant ◪ **Taigh Chearsabhagh Museum & Arts Centre** in Lochmaddy has an ever-rotating gallery of contemporary Scottish artists and an extensive photo exhibit in its museum on North Uist life. They also offer 2-3 day art courses from £10 per day. (☎ (01876) 500293. Open mid-Feb. to Nov. 10am-5pm. Gallery free. Museum £1, students and seniors 50p.) Elsewhere on North Uist, the A865 runs past wide beaches at **Sollas,** sea-carved arches and a Victorian folly at **Scolpaig,** and the site of Sloc a'Choire, a spouting cave and hollow arch, at **Tigharry.** It is said that a young lass once hid in the arch rather than marry the man to whom her parents had betrothed her; listen carefully and you might still hear her echoing cries. Two miles past Locheport Rd. on the A867 is the chambered cairn **Barpa Langass,** which dates back 3000 years, and the nearby standing stone circle **Pobull Fhinn.** On North Uist's southern tip at **Carinish** lie the ruins of 13th-century **Trinity Temple,** probably the islands' most noteworthy building. Bus #W17 from Lochmaddy swings near Langass and Carinish. Birdwatchers enjoy the **Balranald Reserve** on western North Uist, north of Bayhead (signposted "RSPB"). May and June are the best months for observation, but you'll almost always see lapwings, oyster-catchers, and rare red-necked phalaropes. Bus #W18 passes by from Lochmaddy (M-Sa 3-4 per day).

HIGHLANDS/ISLANDS

The A865 (and W17 bus) continues its run southward into Benbecula, past historical sites visually indistinguishable from the surrounding landscape. In north Benbecula, the B892 forks off, passing splendid beaches to the west, and arriving at **Nunton,** former spiritual home to nuns massacred during the Reformation. In Culla Bay, where the nuns were tied and left to drown, the seaweed seems to grow on the rocks in the shape of hands. The newly-restored **Nunton Steadings** (☎ (01870) 602039) provides information on crofting and natural and local history. Further south crumble the scanty remains of the 14th-century **Borve Castle.**

South Uist has paltry attractions, centered around the birthplace of Flora Mac-Donald in Milton, where a commemorative cairn stands by the A865. The nearby **Kildonan Museum** houses some local artifacts and a showcase for Uist Craft Producers. (☎ (01878) 710343. Open M-Sa 10am-5pm, Su 2-5pm.) Access to the **moorland** in the Uists is free, but there are few well-marked footpaths. For vistas of loch and moor, hop over the roadside fence and climb **Blashaval Hill,** a short walk west of Lochmaddy on the A865. TICs offer handy *Western Isles Walks* leaflets (50p), as well as a summertime *Out & About* schedule of **guided walks** offered by the Southern Isles Amenity Trust. (☎ (01870) 602039. Free-£2.)

NEAR THE UISTS

BERNERAY. The tiny island of Berneray (Beàrnaraigh), connected to North Uist's north coast by a brand-new causeway, is a rare gem. A favorite rustic retreat of Prince Charles and home to the best-equipped **Gatliff Hebridean Trust SYHA croft house** (see p. 603), it offers a gorgeous west coast of white beach and *machair* (sea meadow), a thriving seal population, and a friendly, slightly larger human population of 140 that first saw electricity in 1969. You can easily walk the eight mile circumference of the island, maybe passing a standing stone or two along the way. Berneray is a five-minute walk from the Otternish pier (where Harris ferries arrive), and frequent **buses** run from Lochmaddy (M-Sa, 30 min., 6-9 per day, £1).

ERISKAY. On February 4, 1941, with strict wartime alcohol rationing in effect all over Scotland, the *S.S. Politician* foundered on a reef off the isle of Eriskay (Eiriosgaigh), between South Uist and Barra, while carrying 207,000 cases of whisky to America. The concerned islanders mounted a prompt salvage operation, and Eriskay hasn't been the same since. The local pub, named after the ship, displays some of the original bottles. By 2001, a causeway linking Eriskay to South Uist should be completed. Once ready, the frequent **ferries** from Ludag (20min., £1) will be replaced with a bus service; call the Lochboisdale TIC for updated information.

BARRA (BARRAIGH)   ☎ 01871

Little Barra, the southern outpost of the Outer Isles, is unspeakably beautiful, a composite of moor, *machair*, and beach. On sunny days, the island's colors are unforgettable; sand dunes crown waters flecked with shades of light-dazzled blue, wreathed below by dimly visible red, brown, and green kelp. The best times to visit are May and early June, when the primroses bloom. Believed to be named after St. Findbar, the island is also the ancient stronghold of descendants of the Irish O'Neils. As late as the 16th century, islanders returned to Ireland for religious festivals. Though the primroses and beaches beckon, be warned that Barra is not the most easily accessible, or budget-friendly, of the Outer Hebrides.

◪ GETTING THERE AND GETTING AROUND. Cal-Mac (☎ (01878) 700288) **ferries** stop at **Castlebay** (Bagh A Chaisteil), Barra's main town, from **Oban** (5hr., M, W-Th, and Sa 1 per day, £18.25) and **Lochboisdale, South Uist** (1¾hr., Tu, Th-F, and Su 1 per day, £5.15). A small 60-passenger ferry (☎ (01878) 720265) runs to **Eoligarry** (Eolaigearraidh) on Barra from **Ludag, South Uist** (M-Sa 2 per day, £5, children and bicycles £2.50). Times change daily, and the monthly schedule is difficult to read, so phone the tourist information centre for additional help (☎ (01878) 720233). **Hebridean Coaches** (☎ (01870) 620345) runs to **Ludag** from the **airport** on Benbecula and Lochboisdale (M-Sa 4-9 per day).

You can see almost all of Barra in a day. Those without cars can take the **postbus** around the island (☎ 810312; departs Castlebay for Eoligarry M-Sa, £2) or **H. Mac-Neil's minibus** (☎ 810262; 4 per day, £2.75). **Barra Car Hire** (☎ 810243) rents from £20 per day. By far the best way to see Barra is on a **bike**. To rent from **Castlebay Cycle Hire,** drop by the long wooden shed on the main road. (☎ 810284. From £11 per day, less for 2 or more days. Open daily 10am-1pm.)

🛈 PRACTICAL INFORMATION. **Castlebay** is Barra's primary town, and holds a helpful **tourist information centre** (TIC), around the bend and to the right from the pier. They'll find you a B&B for a £1 fee, but book ahead—a wedding, a festival, or even a positive weather forecast can fill every bed for miles. (☎ 810336. Open mid-Mar. to mid-Oct. M-Sa 9am-5pm, Su 10-11am; also 1hr. before and after late ferry arrivals.) Be forewarned: there is **no cash machine** on the island, and the only **bank** is across from the TIC. (Open M-F 9:15am-12:30pm and 1:30-4:45pm, W opens at 10am.) **Internet access** is available at the **Castlebay School library,** 10 minutes past the Castlebay Hotel. Book ahead, as there's only one terminal. (☎ 810471. £3 per hr. Open M-F 9am-1pm and 2-4:30pm, Tu and Th also 6-8 pm, Sa 10am-12:30pm.)

To use your money wisely, stay at **Mrs. Clellan's,** 47 Glen—she runs the cheapest B&B around Castlebay. (☎ 810438. £17 per person.) Next is Mrs. MacKechnie's **Ravenscroft,** in Nask. (☎ 810574. Open May-Sept. £20 per person.) For a drink and solid cheap eats, hit the **Castlebay Bar** up the hill from the harbor. (☎ 810223. Live music Sa-Su. Open M-Sa 11:30am-11:30pm, Su 12:30pm-midnight.) Just below is the **Co-op food store.** (Open M-Sa 8:30am-6pm.)

🔟 SIGHTS. **Kisimul Castle,** bastion of the old Clan MacNeil, inhabits the island in Castlebay Harbor. It lay in ruins for two centuries, and last year was given to Historic Scotland for reconstruction. At some undetermined point in the future, the castle will be open to the public (via a boat trip); inquire at the TIC for an update. Less grand but still quite interesting are the rotating local exhibitions at the **"Dualchas" Barra Heritage & Cultural Centre,** near the school. (☎ 810413. Open Apr.-Sept. M-F 11am-4pm. £1, children 50p.) The road west from Castlebay passes the brooding, cloud-topped mass of **Ben Tangasdale** before reaching an amazing white beach at **Halaman Bay.** From there the road extends northward past turquoise waters and more white sand. Near the village of **Borve** (Borgh), one squat standing stone remains visible on the left. While an excavation near here did reveal a skeleton and Nordic armor, the stone itself has become a favorite spot for cattle defecation. Opposite Allasdale, **Seal Bay** makes an excellent picnic spot, so bring some herring and make a friend. A detailed map of Barra can reveal numerous standing stones and cairns dotting the hills east of the road.

On the north coast, the huge beach of **Traigh Mhor** provides a spectacular landing spot for daily Loganair flights to Glasgow; planes land only at low tide. Farther north in **Eoligarry** is **Cille Bharra Cemetery.** Still in use, it contains "crusader" headstones thought to have served as ballast in the warship of a clan chief. Inside the neighboring **St. Barr's Church,** step through shrines, Celtic crosses, and Norman stones, as pilgrim candles flicker through the dust. To see the whole island, follow the single-lane **A888,** which makes a 14 mi. circle around the rather steep slopes of Ben Heavel. An excellent road for biking, it follows the coast past stunning beaches and mountains; a detour north to **Eoligarry** winds by ponds and dunes.

NEAR BARRA: VATERSAY AND MINGULAY

A causeway connects Barra to **Vatersay** (Bhatarsaigh), the small, southernmost inhabited island in the Outer Hebrides. Check out its scenic beaches and the monument to the *Annie Jane,* a ship that sunk off Vatersay in 1853 while carrying 400 would-be emigrants to Canada. Buses run to Vatersay from the Castlebay post office, by the pier (M-Sa 3-4 per day). Bird watchers should visit the deserted island of **Mingulay,** still farther south. Call Mr. Campbell to inquire about boat trips from Castlebay in the summer (☎ 810223; 2 per week in good weather, £20).

HIGHLANDS/ISLANDS

THE NORTHWEST HIGHLANDS

If you don't mind comically limited public transport options, a trip to Scotland's northwest will reward you with a place of priceless, pristine beauty. The region's spectacular isolation is occasionally punctuated by small hamlets, dominated by black, jagged mountains and heather-covered hills, threaded with lochs and water-falls, and lapped by ocean waves. Grand expanses of mountain and moor stretch along the coast, from the imposing Torridon Hills to the eerie volcanic rock forma-tions of Inverpolly near Ullapool and finally to Cape Wrath, where waves crash against the highest cliffs in mainland Britain.

▐ GETTING AROUND

Without a car, traipsing around the northwestern coast is tricky in summer and nearly impossible the rest of the year. Inverness is the area's main transport hub, with Ullapool a distant second. **Trains** (☎ (08457) 484950) run to **Kyle of Lochalsh** and **Thurso. Scottish Citylink** (☎ (08705) 505050) and **Rapson Buses** serve the same routes, and also go to **Ullapool** on the northwest coast (1½hr.; in sum-mer M-Sa 4-6 per day, Apr.-May and Sept. to mid-Oct. 4 per day; £5), from where ferries leave for the Outer Hebrides. From April to October, the **Northern Explorer Ticket** provides decent bus transportation, looping from Inverness to Ullapool, Durness, Tongue, and Thurso—if you're lucky, you'll even get a bit of a tour guide. The ticket covers a week of unlimited travel (£25), but you can also ride and pay somewhat pricey single fares. (1 bus per day. Ullapool-Durness £10; Durness-Thurso £7; 10% SYHA discount). **Postbuses** are another convenient option—as always, consult the public transport guide, or call a local hostel war-den for specific routes in outlying regions. Those who **hitchhike** dance with fate. The few locals drive like devils on the area's narrow, winding roads, but pick up hikers if they don't run them over first. *Let's Go* never recommends hitchhiking in the first place.

NEAR KYLE OF LOCHALSH   ☎01599

Despite the masses of tourists rushing onwards to Skye, the region just east of Kyle of Lochalsh is quite spectacular in its own right. Best-known is the made-for-postcard **Eilean Donan Castle** (EL-len DOE-nin or "that KA-sil in HI-lan-der"), the restored 13th-century seat of the MacKenzies that perches on an islet in Loch Duich. Photographs of this castle adorn more shortbread boxes and souvenir ash-trays than any other Scottish monument, though the view from the parking lot is more memorable than its restored interior. The castle stands beside the main A87 between Inverness and Kyle; take a Scottish Citylink bus and get off at Dornie. (☎ 555202. Open daily Apr.-Oct. 10am-5:30pm, Mar. and Nov. 10am-3pm. £3.75, con-cessions £3, families £9.)

If you miss the bus back, you can stay in the nearby village of **Dornie,** which stretches peacefully along the reflective waters of Loch Long. The small **Silver Fir Dornie Bunkhouse,** Carndubh, only sleeps 4 and is a five-minute walk along the loch. (☎ 555264. Breakfast included. £8.50.) If you call ahead, the owner of the **Tigh Iseabail Bunkhouse,** Camushunie, Killilan, might pick you up from Dornie or Kyle; otherwise, it's impossible to get there without a car. (☎ 588205. Free-range eggs included. Dorms £7.50.) The bunkhouse is located near the 370 ft. **Falls of Glomach,** an amazing but otherwise tough 1½ hour hike from up Glen Elchig. Farther east, the 3505 ft. **Five Sisters of Kintail** tower above the A87, and on the other side of the highway, the spectacular **Mam Ratagan pass** leads to secluded Glenelg.

Immediately south of Kyle, the **Lochalsh Woodland Gardens** offer a peaceful place to stroll and from which to view the Isle of Skye across the water. (☎ 56632. Open daily 9am-sunset. £2, concessions £1.) The lovely **SYHA Ratagan** is 1½ mi. west of Shiel Bridge and the A87, on Loch Duich in the treeless, Munro-laden Glenshiel. Get off at Shiel Bridge, on the Glasgow-Kyle bus route. Postbuses (☎ (01463) 256228) and Diana Norris buses (☎ 522233; M-Sa 2-3 per day) also run to the hostel from Kyle and Dornie. (☎ 511243. Open Feb.-Oct. Dorms £9.25, under 18 £8.)

PLOCKTON ☎ 01599

Six miles north of Kyle of Lochalsh, the village of Plockton has been drawing a lot of tourists lately, thanks to its prominent role in a recent British TV show. With palm trees, a rocky beach, and green mountains surrounding a tranquil harbor, Plockton certainly deserves the starry-eyed tourists who gape at its picturesque perfection. A bit like an unspoilt Ullapool, it still has a few years before it acquires the souvenir shops and rowdy school groups of its larger neighbor to the north; for now, the trip is definitely worth it. Float on the clear waters in a **boat** (canoe, rowboat, motorboat) from the Leisure Marine Office on the waterfront (£5-12 per hr.). Hop on **Callum's Seal Trips** which are free if no seals show up. (☎ 544306. 1hr.; Apr.-Oct. daily at 10am, noon, 2pm, 4pm and sometimes evenings. £5, children £3.)

The comfy **Station Bunkhouse** is located right across from the train station, and a five-minute walk from the famous waterfront. (☎ 544235. Dorms Apr.-Oct. £10, Nov.-Mar. £8.50.) The owners also run a small B&B, **Nessun Dorma,** next door. (£15 per person.) Watch trains roll in at **Off the Rails Restaurant** (☎ 544423; open daily 10:30am-9:30pm) or party by the harbor at the **Plockton Hotel's pub** (open M-F until midnight, Sa-Su closes earlier). **Duncraig Castle,** across the water, is being developed into the newest of the Scotland's TopHostels chain. The future hostel should be ready by Easter 2001, and will be serviced by its own rail station; call to find out details. (☎ 544444; Edinburgh headquarters ☎ (0131) 5576120. Dorms £10.)

BETWEEN INVERNESS AND KYLE OF LOCHALSH

Moving northeast from Lochalsh, the land loses the spectacular coastal setting of Torridon and Applecross, but it's still great hill-walking country. Three weekly **Westerbuses** (☎ (01445) 712255) travel from Inverness to **Achnasheen,** the region's main town, which also lies on the Inverness-Kyle rail line. From Achnasheen, a train makes a request stop at **Achnashellach** (1¼hr.; M-Sa 4 per day, May-Sept. also Su 2 per day; £8.90). The **Achnashellach Independent Hostel,** two miles from the rail stop, is in good hill-walking territory. (☎ (01520) 766232. Linen £1. Dorms £9.)

APPLECROSS ☎ 01520

The adventurous can try the trip from Kishorn up **Bealach-na-Ba Pass,** leading 13 mi. west to the remote coastal village of Applecross. The highest road in Britain, this single lane winds steeply to an altitude of 2054 ft. On a clear day, one point near the peak allows views of Skye and the Small Isles. Shortly after this, the welcome sight of a double-track road causes more accidents among pedal-happy motorists than the harrowing ascent. Once safely in Applecross, picnic on the small, sheltered beach, or go for the ultimate in outdoors action with **Mountain & Sea Guides.** They offer beginner full- and half-day kayaking and trekking trips (£22-35), in addition to longer sea kayaking and mountaineering courses. (☎ 744393. 3 days to 1 week; from £145.) At the head of Applecross Bay, a signposted **hiking trail** departs for Inverbain and Kenmore, eight miles away. Applecross is serviced by **postbus** #92 (M-Sa) from Torridon (10:30am) and Shieldaig (11:30am).

Directly above town lies the placid **Applecross Campsite.** (☎ (01520) 744268. £9 for a tent and 2 people; third night free.) The campsite boasts a fragrant tearoom in the **Flower Tunnel.** (Open Apr.-Oct.) At the excellent ▓ **Applecross Inn** on the waterfront (☎ 744262), you can feast on anything from lobster curry to venison burgers (£2-7), and listen to live music Mondays and Fridays.

TORRIDON
☎ 01445

Just north of Applecross Peninsula (entire pop. 230), the tiny village of Torridon crouches between Loch Torridon and the Torridon Hills, which are second in cragginess only to the Cuillins of Skye. This small, beautiful place has a beach full of perfect skipping stones. There's also a range of hiking in the immediate area, and off-trail nordic skiing in the winter. The highest and closest peak is **Liathach** (3456 ft.), considered by some the most bullying mountain in Britain.

From Inverness, **trains** (☎ (08457) 484950) run to **Achnasheen** (1¼hr.; M-Sa 4 per day, Su 2 per day); there, **postbus** #91 (12:10pm) connects to Torridon. Buses do not meet every train; call ahead (☎ (01463) 234111) to confirm times. **Duncan Maclennan** (☎ (01520) 755239) shuttle buses connect with the Inverness train at **Strathcarron** station (1hr.; June-Sept. M-Sa 12:30pm, Oct.-May M, W, and F only). The **Ranger Station and Countryside Centre,** at the crossroads into Torridon, 200 yd. from the Torridon hostel, stocks maps and books that detail area walks. There's also a **Deer Museum** and **Deer Park;** July-Aug., the Torridon Ranger Service conducts walks. (☎ 791221. Open May-Sept. M-Sa 10am-5pm, Su 2-5pm. Suggested donation £1-2.50.) The large **SYHA Torridon** crouches at the base of the daunting Liathach. (☎ 791284. Open Mar.-Oct. Dorms £9.25, under 18 £8.) If you're really game for some exploring, venture 13 mi. west of Torridon along the B8021 to the remote, coastal **SYHA Craig** with no phone or bedding—bring a sleeping bag. It's a 1hr. hike from the end of the road at **Diabaig,** which **postbus** #91 reaches after Torridon. (Open mid-May to Sept. Dorms £6.50, under 18 £5.75.) Between the Torridon hostel and the ranger office is the **Torridon Campsite.** (☎ 791313. Showers £1 per 30min. £3 per tent.) The small **general store** 15min. down the road is your only bet for supplies, and also sports a notice board outside with pertinent local information. (Open M-Sa 9:30am-6pm, Su 10am-noon and 4-6pm.)

GAIRLOCH AND BADACHRO
☎ 01445

Flanked by magnificent coastal scenery and inland mountains, the peaceful village of **Gairloch** is 20 winding miles north of Torridon. Gairloch holds little for visitors, save the impressive but cluttered **Gairloch Heritage Museum,** and a gorgeous sandy **beach** out toward the pier, where the occasional seal appears. (Museum ☎ 712287. Open M-Sa 10am-5pm. £2.50, seniors £2, children 50p.) You can ride your rump sore at the **Gairloch Trekking Centre** (☎ 712652), where horseback rides start at £5 per 30min. Six miles north along the coast road from Gairloch grow the **Inverewe Gardens,** a glorious profusion of flowers and shrubs from all over the world. **Westerbus** (☎ 712255) runs from Gairloch to the gardens twice on Saturdays and less frequently during the week. (☎ 781229. Open daily mid-Mar. to Oct. 9:30am-9pm; Nov. to mid-Mar. 9:30am-5pm; visitor center open Apr.-Oct. daily 9:30am-5:30pm. £5, concessions and SYHA hostelers £3.40.)

Gairloch is served by direct **Westerbuses** from **Inverness** (2¾hr., M-Sa 5:05pm, £7). The accommodating **tourist information centre** will help you find **B&Bs** in Gairloch and Dundonnell, just east of the Ardessie Gorge. (☎ 712130. Open mid-July to Aug. daily 9am-6pm; mid-Apr. to mid-July daily 9am-5:30pm; Sept.-Oct. daily 9am-5:30pm; Nov. to mid-Apr. M-Sa 9am-5:30pm.) For a quiet, lochside bed, the **SYHA Carn Dearg** welcomes visitors two miles northwest of town. Get off the Gairloch bus at the village of **Strath** and walk towards the sea from there. (☎ 712219. Open mid-May to Oct. Dorms £8.25, under 18 £7.25.) Just beyond the hostel, campers can pitch at the beachside **Sands Holiday Centre** (☎ 712152; £8-9 per tent); right in Strath at the **Gairloch Caravan & Camping Holiday Park** (☎ 712373; £8 per tent); or even near the gardens at the **Inverewe Campsite** (☎ 781249; £9 per tent, National Trust members £4).

ULLAPOOL
☎ 01854

The mountain-ringed fishing port of Ullapool has recently been invaded by hordes of European tourists and souvenir shops, drawing visitors for its breathtaking views, for its position in some of Scotland's most arresting countryside, and for its transport links to the Outer Hebrides. At the **Ullapool Museum,** housed in an old church on West Argyle St., visitors can sit in the pews and watch a display on the history of Ullapool and the surrounding region. (☎ 612987. Open M-Sa 9:30am-5:30pm. £2, students and seniors £1.50, children free.)

Except for 1am arrivals, **ferries** from **Stornoway, Lewis** (M-Sa 2-3 per day, £12.70, 5-day return £21.75) are met by **Scottish Citylink** and **Rapsons buses** to and from **Inverness** (1½hr., £5). Ullapool's **tourist information centre,** Argyle St., books rooms for a £1 fee. (☎ 612135; fax 613031. Open Apr.-Oct. M-Sa 9am-5:30pm, Su noon-4:30pm; Nov.-Mar. M-Sa 2-5:30pm.) **Caledonian MacBrayne** (☎ 612358) runs a variety of day-long summer **cruise tours** to Lewis (from £15). Smaller boats run daily wildlife-watching **tours** (☎ 613126) to the nearby **Summer Isles** (£8-15); inquire at the booths by the pier. **Scotpackers West House** (see below) runs half- and full-day minibus **tours** of the area (£10-15, for guests £9-13.50). The **post office** sits at West Argyle St. (☎ 612228. Open M-Tu and Th-F 9am-1pm and 2-5:30pm, W and Sa 9am-1pm.) **Postal code:** IV26 2TY.

Scotpackers West House, West Argyle St., has comfy bunks and a sunny kitchen. (☎ 613126. Internet access £1 per 10min. Bike rental £10 per day. Dorms £10.) The affiliated **Crofton House** has double rooms. (☎ 613216. £25 per room.) The well-situated **SYHA Youth Hostel,** Shore St., lies 100 yd. right of the pier, with splendid views of mist rolling in over the harbor. Book ahead. (☎ 612254. Laundry facilities. Dorms £9.25, under 18 £8.) Pitch your tent for only £5 at the **Broomfield Holiday Park** (☎ 612026), right at the west end of town. Grab groceries galore at **All-Days,** West Argyle St. (open M-Sa 7am-10pm, Su 8am-10pm), or at the **Safeway** farther up the hill. **The Seaforth** by the pier fries up super-fresh fish (£6); it's also the most happening pub in town, with frequent live music. (Open daily 10am-midnight.) For a cheaper option, head to the **takeaway shop** around the corner. **The Ceilidh Place,** 14 West Argyle St. (☎ 612103), is a hotel, cafe, bar, bookstore, and gallery; it serves coffee until 9pm, and stomps to Celtic music several nights a week in summer.

ACHILTIBUIE AND CORRIESHALLOCH GORGE ☎01854

Northwest of Ullapool washes the secluded beauty of **Achiltibuie,** a small village flanked by two alluring nature reserves and a trio of sandy beaches. **Spa Coaches** leave from Ullapool (M-F 2 per day, Sa 1 per day, £2.50). If driving, take the A835 north 10 mi., then turn left at the well-marked one-lane road and follow it west 15 mi. The idyllic ▓ **SYHA Achininver** occupies an old cottage ¼ mi. from a sandy beach and three miles from Achiltibuie. If you ask the bus driver politely, he'll take you to the end of the road; it's half a mile from there. (☎ 622254. Open mid-May to Sept. Dorms £6.75, under 18 £6.) It's worth walking into Achiltibuie proper for the ▓ **Lily Pond Cafe,** which serves a 3-course Sunday roast dinner for £6 (12:30-5pm) in a tranquil greenhouse. (Open mid-Apr. to Sept. daily 10am-6pm, June-Aug. also Th-Su 7-9pm.) The Cafe is part of the odd **Hydroponicum,** the self-proclaimed "garden of the future," where plants are grown without soil. (☎ 622202. Tours Easter-Sept. 10am-5pm. £4, students and seniors £3.25, children £2.50.)

Twelve miles south of Ullapool on the A835, the **Falls of Measach** cascade down 150 ft. through the lush, mossy forest of **Corrieshalloch Gorge.** The gorgeous gorge is conveniently on the bus route from Inverness—just make sure that there's another bus coming to pick you up on your return journey.

LOCHINVER ☎01571

Thirty miles up the rugged northwest coast, the otherwise unexciting town of Lochinver is a necessary outpost in the wild region of **Assynt.** North of here, the mountains and lochs form an ever more daunting landscape, breathtaking but also empty and desolate. The only public transport to enter this forbidding country are the daily **Northern Explorer buses, Rapsons Coaches,** and **Spa Coaches** from Ullapool (1 hr., 2-3 per day, £3-4), as well as **postbus** #123 from the Lairg train station (M-Sa 1pm). The excellent **Assynt Visitor Centre** on the waterfront in Lochinver provides an informative exhibit on the local area, and also serves as a **tourist information**

centre, with a £1.50 local booking service. (☎ 844330. Open Easter-Oct. daily 10am-5pm.) The **Ranger Service** based here (☎ 844654) offers **free guided walks** during the summer. To do some walking of your own, turn left from the Visitor Centre. The signposted second left leads to Glencanisp Rd. and up the River Inver; if you turn left after reaching the Glencanisp Lodge, it'll make for a nice 3hr. **hike.** Shorter is the **Culaig Wood Walk,** departing just beyond the green field near the pier.

Assynt is best known for its longer-distance treks up the imposing mountains of **Suilven** and **Canisp** (8-10 hours); get advice from the Visitor Centre and supplies from **Assynt Adventures,** just up the road in Lochinver. The **Spar** supermarket at the entrance to town (open M-Sa 8am-6:30pm, Su 9am-5:30pm) is just across from the Esso **petrol station.** At the other end of town, just before the pier and behind the stone wall, the **Royal Bank of Scotland** even boasts a **cash machine.** (Bank open M-Tu and Th-F 9:15am-12:30pm and 1:30-4:45pm, W open at 10am.) The cheapest **B&Bs** in town are **Tigh-Lios** (☎ 844316; £15-17), next to the police station, and **Ardglas Guesthouse** (☎ 844257; £16), across the stone bridge.

Hostels are far away, but located in dramatic places with great access to hiking and cycling trails. The **SYHA Achmelvich,** Recharn, is three miles away along a stunning footpath, or 20min. by the 11:15am postbus. (☎ 844480. Open Apr.-Oct. Dorms £6.75, under 18 £6.) Mr. Macleod runs the **Achmelvich campsite** nearby. (☎ 844393. Tent pitch £4.) Farther inland, the heart-rending ruins of **Ardvreck Castle** on Loch Assynt sit opposite the hiking-friendly **Inchnadamph Lodge,** Assynt Field Centre. (☎ 822218. Breakfast included. Dorms from £9, doubles and twins from £14.) Ullapool-Lochinver buses, including the Northern Explorer, will stop here on request. The Northern Explorer **bus,** along with **postbus** #129 from Lochinver (M-Sa 12:50pm), will also take you past **Kylesku Backpackers** farther north. (☎ (01971) 502003. Open Mar.-Oct. £10.) Nearby is the award-winning (and awe-inspiring) **Kylesku Bridge.** This is great hiking country, but be sure to bring food.

DURNESS   ☎01971

A quiet village on Scotland's north coast, Durness holds a beautiful beach that travelers can usually enjoy all by themselves. A 10-minute walk west of town takes you to the secluded **Balnakeil Beach** with a puffin colony farther out on **Faraid Head.** Once you're tired of writing your name in the sand, head a mile up the road from the town center to the ▧ **Smoo Caves.** These eerie caverns take their name from *smuga,* the Viking word for hiding place—legend has it that centuries ago the bastard son of a McKay chieftain hid the bodies of 18 men here. When the cave isn't flooded, you can float via rubber dinghy past the interior waterfall. (☎ 511704; ask for Colin. 15min. tours depart from cave entrance Apr.-Sept. daily 10am-5pm. £2.50, children £1.) Britain's highest cliffs tower at **Cape Wrath,** 12 mi. west of Durness. **Iris MacKay** runs a ferry and minibus service from the Cape Wrath Hotel, two miles from Durness. It's the only way to Cape Wrath, unless you're up for a thrilling, but boggy, hike. (☎ 511343. May-Sept. daily from 9:30am, on demand. Ferry return £3.65; minibus return £6.50.) Incidentally, the Cape closes every now and then so that the Royal Air Force can practice blowing stuff up.

To reach Durness, hop on **postbus** #44, 105, or 134 from the **Lairg** train station. **Highland Country** bus #387 arrives from **Thurso** (2½hr., June to mid-Sept. M-Sa 1 per day, £7) and **Tim Dearman** coaches in from **Inverness** and **Ullapool** (same freq., at least £10). The **tourist information centre** books local B&Bs for £1.50. (☎ 511259. Open mid-July to mid-Aug. M-Sa 9am-6pm, Su 10am-6pm; Mar. to mid-July and mid-Aug. to Oct. daily 10am-5pm.) The **post office** is down the road. (Open M-Tu and Th-F 9am-5:30pm, W and Sa 9am-12:30pm.) The brand-new **Lazycrofter Bunkhouse** has cheery bunks. (☎ 511366. £8.50-9.) Alternatively, visit the simple **SYHA Durness,** a mile from town along the A838. (☎ 511244. Open Apr.-Sept. Dorms £6.75, under 18 £6.) **Sango Sands Camping Site** is right next to the visitor centre, overlooking the sea. (Showers 50p. Tent pitch £4.) **Mace supermarket** stocks essentials in town. (☎ 511209. Open M-F 8am-5:30pm, Sa 9am-12:30pm, 1:30-5:30pm.)

TONGUE
☎ 01847

The town of Tongue twists east of Durness on the kyle (strait) bearing the same name. **SYHA Tongue** perches at Tongue's tip, ¾ mi. toward the causeway of Loch Eriboll. (☎ 611301. Open Apr.-Sept. Dorms £8.25, under 18 £7.25.) To the north, empty beaches ring the turquoise waters. Gorgeous ridges and mountains rise from the loch's south end, where the 14th-century ruins of **Castle Varrish** stand precariously above the water. The **Northern Explorer** presses into Tongue (June-Sept., M-Sa) on its way between Thurso and Durness; a **postbus** reaches town from the Lairg train station (M-Sa); and **school buses** lap from Thurso (M-F).

THURSO AND SCRABSTER
☎ 01847

Surrounded by oil refineries, Scrabster is nothing more than a ferry port to the Orkney Islands, while Thurso is the nearest town, just 2½ mi. away. Unfortunately, there are no museums to alleviate the tedium of waiting for a ferry in Thurso. Head to the waterfront and gaze across at the misty blue Orkneys or work off aggression at the riverbank obstacle course. **ScotRail** strikes Thurso from **Inverness** (3¼hr.; M-Sa 3 per day, Su 2 per day; £13), as do **Scottish Citylink buses** (3½hr., 4-6 per day, £9.50). Buses to **Scrabster** (£2.10) usually meet the trains. Services include: the **tourist information centre,** Riverside Rd. (☎ 892371; open June-Sept. daily 10am-6pm; May and Oct. M-Sa 9am-5pm, Su 11am-5pm; Apr. M-Sa 10am-5pm); and free **Internet access** at the **Thurso Library,** Davidsons Ln., at one end of the city centre (☎ 893237; open M and W 10am-6pm, Tu and F 10am-8pm, Th and Sa 10am-1pm).

The friendly **Sandra's Backpackers,** 24 Princes St., has the best budget beds in town, with bathrooms and TVs in each room. Chill out in the snack bar downstairs. They'll even take you to Scrabster Pier for the midday ferry. (☎ 894575. Breakfast pack included. Internet access 75p per 15min. Dorms £8.50.) The independent **Thurso Youth Club Hostel,** stashed in a converted mill, is open only in July and August. From the train station, walk down Lover's Ln., turn left on Janet St., cross the footbridge over the river, and follow the footpath to the right. (☎ 892964. Breakfast and linen included. Dorms £8.) **Borlum,** 26 Sinclair St., provides soft beds and hearty breakfasts. (☎ 895830. £15-17 per person.)

JOHN O'GROATS
☎ 01955

While you may have heard of the town—it's traditionally considered the northern tip of Great Britain—John O'Groats is hardly pretty, having been systematically robbed of all vestiges of Scottish culture and re-inhabited with large, touristy shops. While John O'Groats allows shorter **ferry** rides to the Orkneys, Thurso is the lesser of two evils if you get stuck for a night on the mainland. Fortunately, the surrounding areas are breathtaking. **Dunnet Head,** about halfway between Thurso and John O'Groats, is the true northernmost point of mainland Britain, but **Duncansby Head,** about two miles outside John O'Groats, has a more impressive view overlooking the Pentland Firth. The **tourist information centre** (TIC), by the pier, can plan escapes to the prettier surrounding area. (☎ 611373. Open June-Sept. daily 10am-6pm; Apr.-May and Oct. daily 10am-5pm.) From May to August, **Orkney Bus** (run by John O'Groats Ferries) rides from **Inverness** (daily at 2:20pm, June-Aug. also 7:30am; £12). **Highland Country buses** run from the **Wick** train station (#77 and 960; 50min.; M-Sa 6-7 per day, Su 2 per day). **Harrold Coaches** run from **Thurso** (1hr., M-Sa 2-4 per day). Both routes ignore the train schedules, but they do swing by the **SYHA John O'Groats,** three miles out of town at Canisbay. (☎ 611424. Open Apr.-Sept. Dorms £8.25, under 18 £7.25.)

BETWEEN INVERNESS AND THE FERRY PORTS

Across the districts of Caithness and Sutherland, the moors and mountains mellow to rolling farmlands before the lonely Pentland Firth to the north. The most popular stop between Inverness and Caithness is the legendary **SYHA Carbisdale Castle,** in a 20th-century castle not far from the A836. Walk a ¼ mi. uphill from the Culrain train stop to stay in the building's fading grandeur. In 1945, Captain

Salvesen donated this castle—great hall, marble statuary, and oil paintings included—to the SYHA. Book ahead. (☎ (01549) 421232. Continental breakfast included. Dinner £4.95. Open Mar.-Oct. Dorms July-Aug. £13.75, under 18 £12.25; Sept.-Oct. and Mar.-June £12.75, £11.25.) The Culrain **train** request stop connects from Inverness (1¼hr., 2-3 trains per day, £10.40).

Located five miles south of the **Ord of Caithness,** a hilly area that jumps sharply from the ocean and supports a sizable herd of red deer, the **SYHA Helmsdale** makes a good base for fossil-hunting and gold-panning. (☎ (01431) 821577. Open May-Sept. Dorms £6.50, under 18 £5.75.) Trains drop passengers at the gates of **Dunrobin Castle,** the spectacular seat of the Dukes of Sutherland. Though sections of the house date back to the 1300s, most of the architecture is ecstatically Victorian: ambitious, gaudy, and lavish. Birds of prey fly to gloved hands at the **Falconry Display** on the magnificent castle grounds. (☎ (01408) 633177. Open Apr. to mid-Oct. daily 10:30am-5pm. £5.50, students £4.50, seniors and children £4, families £16.) Getting to Helmsdale or Dunrobin Castle by **train** from **Inverness** costs £11.40.

ORKNEY ISLANDS ☎01856

Björn was here.
  —ancient rune carved into Orcadian standing stone

Across the broad and occasionally rough Pentland Firth, the emerald villages, red sandstone cliffs, and iris-studded farmlands of the Orkneys (pop. 19,500) are treasures. The landscape between villages is a timeless assemblage of paddocks, beaches, and gardens trod by Orcadians for millennia. Traces of the ancients are everywhere; the 70-island archipelago has some of the best-preserved Stone Age, Pictish, and Viking villages, monuments, and burial chambers in Europe.

Mainland (sometimes called Pomona) is Orkney's main island, with its two largest towns. The small capital city of Kirkwall encases a dramatic 12th-century cathedral, still in use, and a fine medieval and Renaissance palace. Quieter still, Stromness whispers its invitation to wander down small wynds to the waterside. That seaside holds secrets as well—at low tide, broken prows and sterns of sunken blockships rear up from the sea foam along the World War II Churchill Barriers. A careful walk along the cliffs of the West Mainland displays elderducks, fulmar petrels, and even the occasional puffin in summer. The islands of Westray, Papa Westray, Copinsay (all pronounced to rhyme with "see"), and the Pentland Skerries are sacred to ornithology pilgrims—337 species of birds alight on or inhabit Orkney, and birds outnumber people 100 to 1.

⚔ GETTING THERE

Ferries connect Orkney to mainland Scotland. **John O'Groats Ferries** (☎ (01955) 611353) travels from **John O'Groats** to **Burwick, Orkney** (45min.; June-Aug. 9am, 10:30am, 4pm, and 6pm; May 9am and 6pm; Sept. 9am and 4:30pm; return £27, off peak afternoon departure and morning return £24). A free bus runs from **Thurso** train station to John O'Groats. The multi-faceted **Orkney Bus,** which departs daily from **Inverness** bus station's Platform 1 (May to mid-Sept. 2:20pm, June-Aug. also 7:30am), connects to the John O'Groats Ferry, then continues by bus from Burwick past the Churchill Barriers to **Kirkwall.** A £39 return or £27 single fare (buy onboard) includes all connections between Inverness and Kirkwall.

P&O Scottish Ferries (☎/fax (01224) 572615) depart from **Scrabster** (near Thurso) for **Stromness, Orkney.** The longer ride takes you past the famous Old Man of Hoy (see p. 622); these ferries are a bit cozier than their John O'Groats counterparts (2hr.; Apr.-Oct. daily at noon, M-F also 6am, M and F-Sa also 5:45pm; Nov.-Mar. M-Sa at noon, M and F also 6am; return £32, low season £30, 5-day return £22, 10% student and senior discount). A bus departs from **Thurso** train station for Scrabster before each crossing (85p). P&O also sails from **Aberdeen** to **Stromness** every Saturday (8hr., June-Aug. also Tu at noon, single from £42, return from £84).

☐ GETTING AROUND

Orkney Coaches (☎ 870555) run between **Kirkwall** bus station and **Stromness Pier Head** (30min., M-Sa 8 per day, £2.20). **Orkney Ferries** (☎ 872044) take you to the outer islands. Ferries leave from **Kirkwall** to: **Shapinsay** (45min., 5-6 per day, £2.50); **Sanday** (1½hr., 2 per day, £5); **Westray/Papa Westray** (1½hr., 2-3 per day, £5); **Eday** (2hr., 2 per day, £5); **Stronsay** (2hr., 1-2 per day, £5); and **North Ronaldsay** (2¾hr., occasional F service in summer only, £5). Ferries leave from **Houton Pier,** accessible from Kirkwall by bus (30min., 5 per day, £1.40) to **Hoy** (Tu-Th 3 per day, M and F 5 per day, Sa-Su 2 per day; £2.50) and **Flotta** (M-Sa 3 per day, occasional Su service in summer; £2.50). Ferries leave from **Tingwall** (catch a bus from Kirkwall bus station, 35min., 5 per day) to **Rousay/Egilsay/Wyre** (30min., M-Sa 6 per day, £2.50). For exact times, get the *Islands of Orkney* from the Stromness or Kirkwall tourist information centres. Winter ferries are far less frequent. It's also possible to fly to many of the islands from Kirkwall Airport; call **British Airways** (☎ 872494).

Car rental, if you can afford it, is by far the most convenient way of getting around Orkney; for rental agencies, see **W.R. Tullock** and **Peace's Car Hire** in Kirkwall (below), and **Stromness Car Hire** (p. 620). The less profligate should consider **biking,** though the rain and wind can be a problem. Bikes can be rented in Stromness at **Orkney Cycle Hire** (p. 620) and in Kirkwall from **Bobby Cycle Centre** (below).

KIRKWALL   ☎01856

Established in the 11th century, the city of Kirkwall (pop. 7000) is the administrative and social center of the Orkney Islands. A few ancient structures at the town center testify to its age.

☑ PRACTICAL INFORMATION. For **car rental, W.R. Tullock** (☎ 876262) and **Peace's Car Hire** (☎ 872866) will meet you at the airport or ferry port. **Bobby Cycle Centre,** Tankerness Ln., off Broad St., rents **bikes.** (☎ 873777; £8-10 per day; open M-Sa 9am-5:30pm). The **tourist information centre,** 6 Broad St., gives out the free *Heritage Guide to Kirkwall* and books B&Bs for £1.50. Ask about details on **Internet access** at Orkney College, East Rd. (☎ 872856. TIC open Apr.-Sept. daily 8:30am-8pm; Oct.-Apr. M-Sa 9:30am-5pm.) Services include: **Bank of Scotland,** 56 Albert St. (open M-Tu and Th-F 9am-5pm, W 10am-5pm); **Kelvinator Launderama,** Albert St. (open M-F 8:30am-5:30pm, Sa 9am-5pm); and the **post office,** 15 Junction Rd. (☎ 874249; open M-Tu and Th-F 9am-5pm, W 9am-4pm, Sa 9:30am-12:30pm). **Postal code:** KW15 1AA.

☑☐ ACCOMMODATIONS AND FOOD. Kirkwall holds a **SYHA Youth Hostel** on Old Skapa Rd. To reach it, turn left and follow the main road from the TIC for ½ mi. as it evolves from Broad St. into Victoria St. Cross over Union St., Main St., and then High St., where SYHA signs will carry you home. Located behind blackened old buildings and machinery, the hostel has all the standard facilities, including a laundry and a drying room. (☎ 872243. Open Apr.-Oct. Dorms £8.75, under 18 £7.75.) Sleep on the tidy bunkbeds of **Peedie Hostel,** 1 Ayre Rd., near the pier, if you're catching an early ferry out of Kirkwall. (☎ 875477. Dorms £9.50.) For quiet rooms and an occasional harbor view, try the B&B provided by Mrs. Hume at **Vanglee,** Weyland Park off Cromwell Rd. (☎ 873013. £14-15 per person.) **Camping** is available on Pickaquoy Rd. off the A965 at the **Pickaquoy Centre Caravan & Camping Site.** (☎ 879900. £3.50-4.65 per person.) You can pitch a tent almost anywhere on the islands, but ask the landowner first.

Safeway stands on the corner of Broad St. and Great Western Rd. (☎ 228876. Open M-F 8am-9pm, Sa 8am-8pm, Su 9am-6pm.) **Buster's Diner,** 1 Mounthoolie Ln., is draped in Americana and cooks up amazing pizza for under £5. (☎ 876717. Open M-F noon-2pm and 5-10pm, Sa noon-2am, Su noon-10pm.) At **Trenabies Cafe,** 16 Albert St., coffee lovers can get a cappucino fix. (☎ 874336. Open M-F 8am-6pm, Sa 9:30am-6pm.) **The Bothy Bar,** across from Buster's, offers pints in a windowless interior with a coal fire and plenty of locals. (☎ 876000. Open M-W 11am-midnight, Th-Sa 11am-1am, Su noon-midnight; food until 9:30pm.)

HIGHLANDS/ISLANDS

SIGHTS. South of the TIC on Broad St., the impressive **St. Magnus Cathedral,** begun in 1137, houses the bones of its founder's uncle, St. Magnus himself. Grave markers dating from the 16th and 17th centuries line the aisles; their grim *memento mori* ("Remember Death") and halting poetry are poignant reminders of the past. (Open Apr.-Sept. M-Sa 9am-6pm, Su 2-6pm; Oct.-Mar. M-Sa 9am-1pm and 2-5pm. Free.) Across Palace Rd. from the cathedral, the **Bishop's and Earl's Palaces** once housed the Bishop of Orkney and his enemy, the wicked Earl Patrick Stewart, who was later executed for treason. Now roofless, the Earl's Palace has brightly illustrated plaques that convey an accurate impression of a 17th-century earl and his domestic affairs. (Both buildings open Apr.-Sept. daily 9:30am-6pm, Oct.-Nov. M-Sa 9:30am-4pm, Su 2-4pm. £2, seniors £1.50, children 75p. £7.50 combination ticket allows entry into both palaces as well as Skara Brae, Maes Howe, and the Broch of Gurness.)

Opposite St. Magnus Cathedral, the **Orkney Museum,** Tankerness House, introduces visitors to the island's remote and recent past, displaying finds from the chief archaeological sites in Orkney and paintings by native son Stanley Cursiter. The skulls from the Tomb of the Eagles are intriguingly ghastly—check out those still-gleaming teeth! (☎ 873191. Open May-Sept. M-Sa 10:30am-5pm, Su 2-5pm; Oct.-Apr. M-Sa 10:30am-5pm. Free.) Twenty minutes south of town lies the **Highland Park Distillery Visitor Centre,** Holm Rd., the world's northernmost whisky distillery and purveyors of damn good single malts. Walk to the end of Broad St./Victoria St., turn left on Clay Loan, right on Bignold Park Rd., and take the right fork onto Holm Rd. (☎ 874619. Open Apr.-Oct. M-F 10am-4pm, July-Sept. also Sa-Su noon-4pm; Nov.-Mar. M-F tours at 2pm. £3, students and seniors £2, children £1.50.)

STROMNESS   ☎01856

Founded in the 16th century as a fishing and whaling port, Stromness (pop. 2000) is a town of narrow cobblestone streets and beautiful open vistas. The **P&O Ferry** floats here from Scrabster (see p. 618); almost everything is along the harbor on Victoria St. The **Pier Arts Centre** is right at the start of Victoria St., and worth a walk-through to view the work of contemporary Scottish artists. (☎ 850209. Open Tu-Sa 10:30am-12:30pm and 1:30-5pm; July-Aug. also Su 2-5pm. Free.) The **Stromness Museum,** 52 Alfred St., tackles the history of the sea with artifacts from the whaling and fishing industries and a photo exhibit on the German High Seas Fleet in Scapa Flow during World War II. (☎ 850025. Open May-Sept. daily 10am-5pm; Oct.-Apr. M-Sa 10:30am-12:30pm and 1:30-5pm. £2.50, students and seniors £2, children 50p.)

Stromness Car Hire, 75 Johns St., **rents cars** from £25 a day, less after 2 days. (☎ 850973. £12.50 deposit. Min. age 21.) Rent **bikes** at **Orkney Cycle Hire,** 54 Dundas St. (☎ 850255; £5.50-6.50 per day; open daily 8:30am-9pm). The **tourist information centre** (TIC), in an 18th-century warehouse on the pier, provides the free *Stromness Heritage Guide.* (☎ 850716. Open Apr.-Oct. M-W and F-Sa 8am-8pm, Th 8am-6pm, Su 9am-4pm; Nov.-Mar. M-F 9am-5pm; also open to meet most late ferry arrivals.) Services include: **Bank of Scotland,** Victoria St. (open M-F 9:45am-12:30pm and 1:30-4:45pm, W opens at 10:45am); and the **post office,** 37 Victoria St. (☎ 850225; open M-F 9am-1pm and 2-5:15pm, Sa 9am-12:30pm). **Postal code:** KY16 3BS.

BA'… NOT JUST FOR SHEEP
Amid all the puffin sightings and archeological digs is a more lively Orkney tradition—the Ba'. Best described as a large rugby game with no rules and no limit on time or team size, the Ba' takes place on New Year's Day. Two teams take to the streets of Kirkwall, the Uppies (from the upper part of town) and the Doonies (you figure it out). The ranks of the competitors have been known to swell to 400. The action begins in front of St. Magnus Cathedral, in Kirkwall, when a specially crafted Ba' ball is thrown to the waiting throngs. The massive scrum can continue for hours, ending at nightfall. There are no time-outs or penalties, although the once-tried practice of smuggling the Ba' in a car is frowned upon. The Uppies quest to chuck the ball into the harbor, while the Doonies labor to hit the side of the town hall: the hardy soul deemed most valuable player gets to keep it.

A half-mile from the TIC (make a left onto Victoria St., then a right onto Helli-hole Rd.) rests the well-kept **SYHA Stromness,** which is hospitable and not nearly as infernal as the address suggests. (☎ 850589. Lockout 10:30am-5pm. Open mid-Mar. to Oct. Dorms £8.25, under 18 £7.25.) The small rooms at the 14-bed **Brown's Hostel,** 45-47 Victoria St., are just a five-minute walk down the same route. (☎ 850661. Dorms £8.) The **Point of Ness Caravan and Camping Site** is a mile from the pierhead. (☎ 875353, ext. 2404 851235. Open May to mid-Sept. £3-5.25.) On the pier, ▨ **Julia's Coffee Shop,** 20 Ferry Rd., has delicious home baking and sandwiches for £2-5. (☎ 850904. Open M-Sa 9am-5pm, Easter-Sept. also Su 10am-4pm.) Next to it, the tour-isty **Ferry Inn Bar** dishes up main courses (including vegetarian items) for £5-6. (☎ 850280. Open daily noon-2pm and 5:30-10pm.) The **Stromness Hotel** bar on Victoria St. is a popular nightspot with frequent live music.

OTHER MAINLAND SIGHTS

Mainland is endowed with an astonishing wealth of Stone Age and Viking remains, particularly around Stromness and Kirkwall—not to mention the billowing mist, rocky promontories, and expanses of primroses that cover the islands. Excellent walks abound, but getting to many sights without a car or superhuman stamina can be tricky, since public transport is scant or absent. In the summer, **bus** #8A runs twice a day in either direction from Kirkwall to Stromness, hitting three main archaeological sites: the Standing Stones of Stenness, the Ring of Brodgar, and Skara Brae. Despite endless uphills and winds that make downhills take forever, however, **cycling** may be the best and cheapest way to do Orkney justice.

If you want guidance, ranger-naturalist Michael Hartley of **Wildabout Tours** squires visitors around Mainland and Hoy in his minibus on half- and full-day tours. With a vigorous imagination and encyclopedic knowledge of Orkney, Michael helps visitors to envision the Orkney of over 5000 years ago. (☎ 851011. Tours March-Oct. daily. From £10; student and hosteler discounts.) Orkney native John Grieve leads **Discover Orkney Tours** (☎ 872865), which crafts trips to meet your interests (from £10). John will also take you to the other islands—a great way to see some smaller islands if you lack time or transport (from £29). Both guides leave from the TICs in Kirkwall and Stromness.

▨ **SKARA BRAE.** Dating back 4000 years, Skara Brae was once a bustling Stone Age village. As the ocean crept farther in, waves gradually consumed the village houses; after approximately 600 years of continuous habitation, the villagers aban-doned the settlement. Preserved in sand, the village slept quietly until 1850, when a violent storm ripped out the side of the cliff and revealed nine houses, a work-shop, and covered town roads, all perfectly preserved. While the visitor center is open only during the day, the site remains accessible until nightfall—a trip at dusk evades the tourists and the admission fee. The **Skaill House** is the 17th-century home of the lairds of Breckness, the family who rediscovered the island. *(By the Bay of Skaill.* ☎ *841501. Open Apr.-Sept. daily 9:30am-6:30pm; Oct.-Mar. M-Sa 9:30am-4:30pm, Su 2-4:30pm. Skara Brae and Skaill House £4.50, seniors £3.30, children £1.30.)*

RING OF BRODGAR. Nearby on the A965, the sedimentary sandstones of the Ring of Brodgar once witnessed gatherings about which no two archaeologists can agree. Some believe the upright ring marked a meeting place for local chieftains; others propose that dead bodies were left here to the elements and the birds. Now filled in for the safety of visitors, a deep ditch around the circle would have warded off dogs and wild predators. Of the original 60 stones, only 36 remain.

STANDING STONES OF STENNESS. Close to the Ring, on the A965, the Standing Stones of Stenness once numbered twelve, but by 1760 only four remained—no one knows what became of the other eight, but some suggest that they were knocked down by locals angered at the monument's pagan origins. Recently, pos-sible evidence of a priests' settlement has been found near the site.

MAES HOWE TOMB. Accessible from the A965, the tomb may have held the bones of the earliest settlers in the area from approximately 2700 BC. According to runic graffiti, Viking raiders broke through the roof and spent three glorious days hauling treasure out of the chamber. The runes are almost more of an attraction than the tomb itself—the largest collection of runic inscriptions in the world, they enabled linguists to crack the runic alphabet and read profound statements such as "This was carved by the greatest rune carver" and "Ingigerth is the most exquisite of women." *(☎ 761606. Open Apr.-Sept. daily 9:30am-6:30pm; Oct.-Mar. M-Sa 9:30am-4:30pm, Su 2-4:30pm. £2.50, seniors £1.90, children £1.)*

THE BROUGH OF BIRSAY. An island showing evidence of early Christian and Viking habitation, the Brough is just off the northwest of Mainland. Once the administrative and religious center of Orkney, the island's kirkyard holds a Pictish stone engraving of a royal figure with a crown, suggesting that Orcadian kings once ruled from Birsay. The Brough is accessible by foot only in the hour before and the hour after low tide. Bird-watching from the cliffs may be absorbing, but linger too long and the puffins may become your bedfellows. *(Open mid-June to Sept. £1.50, seniors £1.10, children 50p.)*

CHURCHILL BARRIERS. After the sinking of the *HMS Royal Oak* in October 1939 by a German submarine, Churchill erected the famous barriers of **Scapa Flow.** Today, the Churchill Barriers allow motorists access to the smaller southeast islands of **Lamb Holm, Glimps Holm, Burray,** and **South Ronaldsay.** In these same waters, plucky Rear Admiral Ludwig von Reuter ordered his 74-ship German fleet to be scuttled during World War II, earning him a *Guinness Book of World Records* mention for most ships sunk at one time. Much to the delight of scuba divers, seven German vessels remain. You don't need to be a certified diver to go into the deep—give it a go with **Scapa Scuba.** *(☎ 851218. £55.)* If you don't want to get wet, **Roving Eye Enterprises** does the dirty work for you, with the benefit of a roaming underwater camera. *(☎ 811360. Tours leave Houton Pier daily 1:20pm.)*

SMALLER ISLANDS

BEYOND THE BARRIERS. On tiny **Lamb Holm** rests the **Italian Chapel,** one of the few buildings remaining from the World War II prison camps on Orkney. The Italian prisoners of war who designed and decorated it made do with such materials as bathroom tiles, stair rails, and wood from a wrecked ship. (Open daily Apr.-Sept. 9am-10pm; Oct.-Mar. 9am-4:30pm. Free.) During the summer, **Orkney Coaches** chug daily over the Churchill Barriers from Kirkwall to the Burwick Ferry (#10, 2-4 per day); **Rosie Coaches** go nearly as far, to St. Margaret's Hope on the north coast of South Ronaldsay (year-round M-Sa 3-5 per day). A tiny 8-bed hostel, **Wheems,** stands on South Ronaldsay. It's an organic farm; call ahead and they might pick you up. *(☎ 831537. Open Apr.-Oct. Dorms £6.50.)*

HOY. The landscape of Hoy ("High Island"), the second largest island in Orkney, is surprisingly rocky and mountainous. All visitors to Orkney should glimpse the **Old Man of Hoy,** a famous 450 ft. sea stack off the West Coast of the island. On a clear day, the P&O ferry from Scrabster to Stromness gives an excellent view of the landmark; a careful walk along the coast affords the hiker a look down on the Old Man himself. A steep marked footpath leads from Rackwick two miles away (3hr. round-trip). The hefty **North Hoy Bird Reserve** offers respite for guillemots and a host of other species. Dedicated puffin-scouts should see several here during breeding season, from late June to early July—the rest of the year the pudgy birds rough it on the seas. The **SYHA Hoy** near the pier and the eight-bed **SYHA Rackwick** farther south, two miles from the Old Man of Hoy, offer accommodations and share a telephone number. These hostels do not provide linen, and there are no sleeping bags available on the island. *(☎ 873535. Hoy open May to mid-Sept.; Rackwick open mid-Mar. to mid-Sept. Dorms £6.75, under 18 £6.)* Food and supplies are also difficult to procure, especially on Sundays.

SHAPINSAY. A mere 45 minutes from Kirkwall, with frequent ferry service, Shapinsay is the most accessible of the outer isles. Mostly a big, wide-open space, Shapinsay's landscape is defined by **Ward Hill,** the island's highest point at 210 ft., from where you can see almost all the Orkney Isles on a clear day, as well as the **Storm beaches.** Formerly home to the lairds of Balfour, **Balfour Castle** was completed in 1848 and is now a posh B&B. The big house opens its doors to the public weekly from May to September. Romantics can rent the castle and its chapel for weddings. For those who don't want to see inside, the castle is perfectly visible from the ferry. (☎ 711282, tours ☎ 872856. Tours leave Kirkwall pier W 2:15pm, £15.) **Burroughston Broch,** an Iron Age fortified shelter, lies five miles from the ferry pier. Archeology buffs will be thrilled by the ancient round home, which was excavated in the 1860s. For bird fans, the **Bird Hide,** about one mile from the ferry, looks out over Royal Society for the Protection of Birds wetland reserve, home to various breeds of birds. (Open daily dawn-dusk. Free.) There are no youth hostels on Shapinsay, but the Kirkwall TIC (☎ 872856) can provide information on B&Bs.

PAPA WESTRAY. The "isle of the priests" once supported an early Christian Pictish settlement. Most pilgrims to the island now content themselves with bird-watching or archaeology. The rare Scottish primrose, thought to grow only in Orkney and isolated spots in the Highlands, can be found in fields. On the south coast, the **Knap of Howar** is the location of the earliest standing houses in northern Europe (c. 3500 BC). The **Bird Sanctuary** at North Hill sports the largest colony of Arctic terns in Europe. Two miles from the pier, **SYHA Papa Westray,** Beltane House, is open year-round. (☎ (01857) 644267. Dorms £8, under 18 £7.)

WESTRAY. The largest of Orkney's northern isles sits just next to Papa Westray, and boasts ruined **Noltland Castle** and the **Knowe O'Burristae Broch,** along with other ancient ruins and magnificent cliffs. Legend holds that the Castle is linked underground to the Gentlemens' Cave, where Jacobite supporters of Bonnie Prince Charlie once hid. Bird-watchers rejoice on **Noup Head Reserve,** and budget travelers can rejoice over the island's two hostels. **The Barn,** Chalmersquoy, is practically a B&B, minus one B. (☎ (01857) 677214. £11.75, children £8.80.) 2001 should see the opening of the **Bis Geos Hostel** near Pierowall. (☎ (01857) 677786. Dorms £10.)

EDAY. The peat-covered hills of Eday hide Stone Age field walls, chambered tombs like **Vinquoy and Huntersquoy Cairns,** the towering **Stone of Setter,** and on the Calf of Eday, the remnants of an Iron-Age roundhouse. **SYHA Eday Hostel,** London Bay, on the main north-south road four miles from the pier, also welcomes campers. (☎ (01857) 622206. Open Apr.-Sept. Dorms £6.75, under 18 £6; camping £2.)

ROUSAY. Some will argue that Orkney's finest archaeological sights lie not on the Mainland, but on the isle of Rousay. Here the **Midhowe Broch and Cairn** features not only a Bronze and Iron age dwelling, but also the largest Stone Age cairn known of its kind. The **Knowe of Yarso Cairn** stands on a high cliff overlooking Eynhallow Sound, and the **Westness Walk** winds past archaeological sights from the Neolithic, Pictish, Viking, medieval, and crofting eras. Stay at the **Rousay Hostel** on Trumland Farm near the pier. (☎ 821252. Dorms £6.)

NORTH RONALDSAY. The most remote of Orkney's islands is not lacking in archaeological sights, with the **Broch of Burrian,** the **Brae of Stennabreck,** and an unusual standing stone with a hole through it. Better yet, the island's famous seaweed-eating sheep graze on the beaches. Nesting birds are all over the place—you can even stay at the **North Ronaldsay Bird Observatory Hostel.** An unreal £10 return flight to and from the island is available if you spend the night here. (☎ (01857) 633200. No kitchen. Dorms £8; full board and lodging £17.)

HIGHLANDS/ISLANDS

SHETLAND ISLANDS ☎01595

The Shetlands and Orkneys only became part of Scotland in the 15th century when King Christian I of Denmark and Norway mortgaged them in order to pay for his daughter's dowry, and in many ways Shetland, closer to Norway than to Great Britain, is still a country unto itself. Shetlanders still look proudly to their Viking heritage, rather than to Scotland or Britain, an influence that lingers in their Nordic craftsmanship, in their Scandinavian architecture, and in festivals such as the longship-burning Up-Helly-A'. Most Shetlanders will look askance at you if you imply that their homeland is part of the UK—"Scotland," they will tell you, "is down there." Local poet Hugh MacDiarmid aptly describes the difference between Orkney and Shetland: "The Orcadian is a farmer with a boat, the Shetlander is a fisherman with a croft." Besides fish, the hardy crops and animals that can survive here—peat, ponies, and sheep, sheep, sheep—support agriculture, while North Sea oil drilling has brought new prosperity. The Shetlands are an alluring destination, but unless you're an oil tycoon, watch your cash—after London, Shetland is the priciest place in Britain.

✈ GETTING THERE AND CROSSING THE NORTH SEA

The fastest way to Shetland, if the weather cooperates, is **flying. Sumburgh Airport** lies on the southern tip of the mainland right near the town of Sumburgh. Leasks buses run from the airport to **Lerwick** (1hr.; M-F 6 per day, Sa 4 per day, Su 2 per day; £1.90), arriving at the **Viking Bus Station** (☎ 694100), in the city center on Commercial Rd. Flights arrive from **Orkney** (35min.; 1 per day; £83, £65 if booked one 1 week ahead; must stay over Sa night, otherwise prices are in the hundreds). **Ridgeway Travel** (☎ (01856) 873359), by the Kirkwall tourist information centre (TIC) in Orkney, can get you tickets in a jiffy. **British Airways** (☎ (08457) 773 3377) also flies from: **Aberdeen** (£99); **Edinburgh** (£168); and **Glasgow** (£168).

Ferries arrive at **Holmsgarth Terminal,** a 20min. walk northwest of Lerwick town center, and the smaller **Victoria Pier,** across from the TIC downtown. **P&O Scottish Ferries** (☎ (01224) 572615) arrive from **Aberdeen** (14hr.; M-F 6pm; June-Aug. also Tu noon, 20hr.; £58, berth from £85, return from £104) and **Stromness, Orkney** (8hr.; Apr.-Dec. Su noon, June-Aug. also Tu 10pm, Jan.-Mar. variable; £39, return £78). **P&O Smyril Line** runs mid-May to mid-Sept. from Lerwick to **Bergen, Norway** (13½hr.; M 11:30pm; £68, berth from £77), and to **Iceland** (W 2am, 31hr., £150) via the **Faroe Islands** (13hr., £68). 10% student discount, lower in early June and late August.

⌂ GETTING AROUND

Infrequent public transport makes getting around the Shetlands difficult. **Ferries** within the archipelago are heavily subsidized; the longest trips cost about £2. All except those to Fair Isle transport bikes for free. Shetland's main **bus** lines are **John Leask & Son** (☎ 693162) and **Shalder Coaches** (☎ 880217). The TIC stocks the vital *Shetland Transport Timetable* (80p) with bus, ferry, and plane schedules. To reach remote areas on the decent road system, try **Bolts Car Hire** (☎ 693636; 21+) or **Grantfield Garage** (☎ 692709; 23+), both on North Rd. (Both from £23.95 per day.) Bolts also has a branch at Sumburgh Airport (☎ (01950) 460777). **Eric Brown's Cycle Hire,** at Lerwick's Grantfield Garage, North Rd., 500 yd. past the ferry terminal, rents fully equipped touring bikes. (☎ 692709. £7.50 per day, £45 per week. Open daily 8am-9pm.) Remember that the strong winds can make biking difficult.

Various **tour** companies offer painfully pricey ways of seeing more of the Shetlands. The most affordable are the **Leasks Coach Tours,** on the Esplanade in Lerwick, which run £8.50-12 for Mainland tours and £20 for tours to Yell and Unst. (☎ 693162. Open M-Sa 7:30am-5pm, Su 9:30am-2pm.) Other pricier options are the folklore-oriented **Island Trails** (☎ (01950) 422408), the **Shetland Wildlife Tours** (☎ (01950) 422483), and the artsy **See Shetland** (☎ 693434; £30 for a day tour).

★ 7 ORIENTATION AND PRACTICAL INFORMATION

Lerwick is on the eastern coast of the main island (called Mainland) and is served by the A970, which runs the length of the island. The **Shetland Islands Tourism** information centre, Market Cross, will book you a bed anywhere in the islands for £3. (☎ 693434; fax 695807. Open Apr.-Sept. M-F 8am-6pm, Sa 8am-4pm, Su 10am-1pm; Oct.-Apr. M-F 9am-5pm.) For a hot shower (80p), quick swim (£2.25), or sauna (£4), try one of the **Shetland's Leisure Centres;** the one in Lerwick is the **Clickimin Leisure Complex** (☎ 741000), Lochside, on the south side of town. Services include: the **Royal Bank of Scotland,** 81 Commercial St. (☎ 694520; open M-F 9:15am-4:45pm, W 10am-4:45pm); **Lerwick Laundry and Dry Cleaners,** 36 Market St. (☎ 693043; £4.11 per load; open M-F 8:30am-1pm and 2-5:30pm, Sa 9am-1pm); free **Internet access** at the **Shetland Library,** in the church on Lower Hillhead (☎ 694430; open M, W, and F 10am-7pm, Tu, Th, and Sa 10am-5pm), at **The Computer Shop** (☎ 694744), Commercial St., and at **Zet-Tech,** 22 Commercial Rd. (☎ 694643), near the bus station; and the **post office,** 46-50 Commercial St. (☎ 693372; open M-F 6:30-8am and 8:45am-5:30pm, Sa 6:30-8am, 8:45-11am, and 1-3pm). **Postal code:** ZE1 0AA.

▌ ACCOMMODATIONS

The ■ **SYHA Youth Hostel,** Islesburgh House at King Harald St. and Union St., has fabulous facilities such as elegant curtains, strong showers, and a cafe. (☎ 692114. Reception open 9-9:30am, 4-4:30pm, and 9:45-10:15pm; at other times try the neighborly Community Centre. Curfew 11:30pm. Open Apr.-Sept. Dorms £9.25, under 18 £8.) Harbor views are yours at **Mrs. Nicholson's** B&B, 133 North Rd. (☎ 693362. £16-20 per person.) There are three **campgrounds** on Mainland, but you can camp almost anywhere with the landowner's permission. **Clickimin Caravan and Camp Site** is closest to the Lerwick ferry terminal; turn left on Holmsgarth Rd. (the A970), then through the roundabout and right on North Lochside. If you're arriving by bus, just ask the driver to drop you off. (☎ 741000. Open May-Sept. Pitches £6-7.)

Camping **böds** (Old Norse for barns) are another Shetland accommodations alternative. They are, to put it bluntly, very, very basic. There are four böds on Mainland (available Apr.-Sept.): **Betty Mouat's** near the airport, **The Sail Loft** next to the pier in Voe, the **Voe House** in Walls, and **Johnnie Notions** (no electricity) at Hamnavoe, Eshaness in the far northeast. The **Windhouse Lodge,** on Yell, is the best equipped. All böds cost £5 per night and must be booked in advance through the Lerwick TIC. Bring sleeping bags, a camping stove, and 50p coins for electricity (when available); the roof, grass, and sky are already there.

◐ ▦ FOOD AND PUBS

Inexpensive eats cluster in the center of **Lerwick.** Head to **D.G. Leslie's,** on the Esplanade, for groceries. (☎ 693073. Open M-Th 8am-8pm, F-Sa 8am-7pm, Su 10am-7pm.) **Osla's Cafe,** up Mounthooly St., has pancakes and a beer garden for those rare times when the weather is calm, warm, and dry. (☎ 696005. Open May-Aug. M-Sa 9am-7pm; Sept.-Apr. M-Sa 10am-5pm.) Lerwick's cheapest food (everything under £2!) awaits at the **Islesburgh Community Centre Café,** King Harald St., next to the hostel. (☎ 692114. Open M-Sa 10am-5pm.) On the Esplanade, the **Peerie Shop Cafe** serves massive sandwiches, baked goods, and organic cider in a bright, lively setting. (☎ 692817. Open July-Aug. M-Sa 9am-9pm; Sept.-June M-Sa 10am-6pm.) **The Lounge,** 4 Mounthooly St., is the town's busiest pub. (☎ 692231. Open M-Sa 11am-1am.) Musicians congregate upstairs Saturday afternoons and some Wednesday nights. For a friendly crowd, try the **Thule Bar** on the Esplanade. (☎ 692508. Open M-Sa 8am-1am, Su 12:30pm-1am.)

WOOL

Shetland is one of the best places in the world to buy woollens (you may have noticed a few sheep here and there). To avoid paying relatively high prices in Lerwick's tourist shops, get bargains upstairs at the **Shetland Woollen Company,** 68 Commercial St., where leftover sweaters can be found for as low as £5. (☎ 693610. Open May-Sept. M-Sa 9am-5pm; Oct.-Apr. M-F 9am-5pm.) There are also branches in Sandwick, Yell, and Scalloway, on Castle Rd. (☎ 880243). Huge piles of cheap sweaters (£11-22) sit at the **Judane Shetland Limited Knitwear Factory,** Blackhill Mills, Gremista Industrial Estate (☎ 693724), 1½ mi. north of Lerwick town center on the A970, opposite the huge factory stack. **The Spider's Web,** 41 Commercial St., showcases high-quality knitwork done by individuals from their homes. (☎ 693299. Open M-Sa 9am-5pm, and Su if there is a cruise ship in port.) On northerly **Unst,** you can simultaneously shop for knitwear and enjoy apple pie at **NorNova Knitwear** in Muness. (☎ (01957) 755373. Open daily 10am-4pm.)

MAINLAND SIGHTS

LERWICK SIGHTS. Not much of a sight in itself, the giant, pentagonal **Fort Charlotte,** a relic of the Cromwellian era just off Commercial Rd. at the north end of town, supplies the best views of Lerwick and its harbor. *(Open daily 9am-10pm. Free.)* Only one mile west of the city center on Clickimin Rd., the ruins of **Clickimin Broch,** a stronghold from the 4th century BC, still look tough enough to repel invaders. *(Always open. Free.)* More modern (by Shetland standards) is the **Town Hall** on Hillhead, built in 1882. The clock tower is closed, but the main hall contains a lovely series of stained-glass windows depicting scenes from Shetland's Viking past. *(☎ 693535. Open M-Th 9am-5pm, F 9am-4pm. Free.)* **The Shetland Museum,** in the library building on Lower Hillhead, focuses on local archaeology and marine history. *(☎ 695057. Open M, W, and F 10am-7pm, Tu, Th, and Sa 10am-5pm. Free.)*

SCALLOWAY. There's not much to see in Shetland's ancient capital, seven miles west of Lerwick, except 17th-century **Scalloway Castle.** Once home to the villainous Earl Patrick Stewart, the crumbling edifice can now be yours. Get the key from the Shetland Woolen Company (next door) or the Scalloway Hotel. *(Open M-Sa 9:30am-5pm, Su by appointment only. Free.)* **Shalder Coaches** leave from the Viking Bus Station in Lerwick. *(M-Sa 5-6 per day, £2 return.)*

JARLSHOF AND SOUTH MAINLAND. At the southern tip of Mainland, next to Sumburgh Airport, lies Jarlshof, one of the most remarkable archaeological sites in Europe. Stacked here are the remains of layers of human settlement from Neolithic times to the Renaissance, discovered in 1896 when a storm uncovered the site. *(☎ 460112. Open Apr.-Sept. daily 9:30am-6:30pm. £2.50, seniors £1.90, children £1.20.)* Just a mile up the road, the **Old Scatness Broch** is the fascinating scene of an ongoing excavation. Archaeological remains were discovered here in 1975 during airport construction; since then an entire Iron Age village and over 20,000 artifacts have been found. It should still be open to the public in the summer of 2001. *(☎ (01595) 694688. Open M-Th 10:30am-5pm, Sa-Su 10:30am-5:30pm. Free.)* On nearby **Sumburgh Head,** thousands of gulls, guillemots, and puffins rear their young each year. All South Mainland sights can be reached by the **Leasks bus** that runs to Sumburgh Airport from Lerwick. *(1 hr., 2-6 per day, £3.50 return.)*

NORTH MAINLAND. The northern part of the Mainland has the wildest and most deserted coastal scenery, much of which is accessible only by car. At **Mavis Grind,** northwest of Brae, Mainland is almost bisected; this 100-yard-wide isthmus is flanked by the Atlantic Ocean and the North Sea. Farther northwest stand the jagged volcanic sea-cliffs on **Eshaness,** where you can view nesting birds, oceansprayed stacks, and the standing arch of **Dore Holm.** On Sundays, when buses and ferries are rare, **Leask Coach Tours** runs three different tours of the mainland. *(☎ 693162. Tours leave at 2:15pm. £8.)*

🌁 SMALLER ISLANDS

BRESSAY AND NOSS. Hourly ferries (5min., £1.25) sail from Lerwick to the west coast of the island of Bressay. Hike to the summit of conical **Ward of Bressay** (743 ft.) for a sweeping view of the sea. From Bressay's east coast, three miles from the Lerwick ferry port (follow the "To Noss" signs), dinghies go to the tiny isle of Noss; just stand at the "Wait Here" sign and wave. (Mid-May to Aug. Tu-W and F-Su 10am-4pm. £2.50 return, seniors and children £1.) Great skuas (a.k.a. bonxies), large primeval birds, will dive-bomb you at this spectacular bird sanctuary; wave a hat over your head to ward them off. (Noss is open to visitors Tu-W and F-Su 10am-5pm; overnight stays are forbidden.)

MOUSA. The tiny, uninhabited island of Mousa, just off the east coast of the Mainland, holds the world's best preserved Iron-Age broch, a 50 ft. drystone fortress that has endured 1000 years of Arctic storms. Available flashlights help you climb the still-intact staircase onto the broch's roof. Catch a Sumburgh-bound Leask bus at the Viking Bus Station in Lerwick and ask the driver to let you off at the Setter Junction for Sandsayre (£2.60 return); it's a 15-min. walk from there to the ferry. (☎ (01950) 431367. Ferry departs mid-Apr. to mid-Sept. M-Th and Sa noon, F and Su 12:30pm and 2pm. £7, children £3.50.) During the week in the summer, **Leask Coach Tours** leads tours of Mousa, leaving from the Esplanade in Lerwick. (☎ 693162. £10, including ferry).

ST. NINIAN'S ISLE. Only six miles away on the west side of the Mainland, an unusual tombolo—a sandbar washed by waves on both sides—links St. Ninian's Isle, site of an early monastery, to the west coast of the Mainland. Inhabited from the Iron Age to the late 18th century, the isle is now home to a ruined church, and tons of rabbits and sheep. The ever-helpful Sumburgh-bound bus takes you from Lerwick to Bigton, from where you can walk.

YELL. If you tire of bird- and seal-watching on starkly remote Yell, head for the north end of the main road at Gloup; a three-mile hike from here takes you to the desolate eastern coast. The remains of an Iron Age fort on the Burgi Geos promontory have held tenaciously to a perfect defensive position—jagged outcroppings face the sea and a 3 ft. ridge leads between cliffs to the mainland. Killer whales are occasionally spotted in Bluemull Sound between Yell and Unst. **Ferries** run from Toft on the Mainland to Ulsta on Yell (20 min., 2 per hr., £1.25).

UNST. Unst is home to the northernmost everything in Britain. The **Muness Castle** (Britain's northernmost) was built in the late 16th century; the key-keeper at the white cottage will give you a flashlight to illuminate its spooky darkness. At **Haroldswick Beach,** gannets crash the ocean near crumbling, abandoned air-raid shelters. The celebrated northernmost bird reserve at **Hermaness** is graced by a pair of black-browed albatross and countless puffins. Ferries from Belmont on Unst and Gutcher on Yell divert routinely to Oddsta on the island of **Fetlar,** where birdwatchers view the crimson-tailed finch. **Ferries** run from **Gutcher** on northern Yell to **Belmont** on Unst (10 min., 1-2 per hr., £1.25). A daily **Leask bus** leaves Lerwick at 8am and connects with ferries to Haroldswick on Unst, stopping by Unst's Gardiesfauld Hostel along the way. (Bus and ferry £10.)

Find a gorgeous coastal view and a sunny indoor patio at the **Gardiesfauld Hostel,** in Uyeasound in the south of Unst—the northernmost hostel in Britain. (☎ (01957) 755259. Dorms £8, under 18 £6.50. Tent pitch for 2 people £6.) The **Baltasound post office** (open M-Tu and F 9am-1pm and 2-5:30pm, W 9am-1pm and 2-4:30pm, Th and Sa 9am-1pm) lets you experience Britain's northernmost **postal code:** ZE2 9DP.

OTHER ISLANDS. Shetland's outermost islands are the most remote in Britain. **Planes** depart for the outer islands from **Tingwall** on the Mainland, but ferries, at an unbelievable £2.15 per single journey (except for Whalsay, which is only £1.25),

HIGHLANDS/ISLANDS

are a cheaper choice. Rooms and transport are hard to come by, and booking several weeks in advance is a must. Bring supplies to last at least a week, as the ferries often do not operate in inclement weather. Many ferries operate from **Walls, Vidlin,** or **Laxo** on the Mainland, all of which can be reached by bus from Lerwick (bus generally under 1hr. and £2; consult the *Shetland Transport Timetable*).

Whalsay, a relatively huge fishing community (pop. 1000), is accessible by bus and ferry from Lerwick. Talk to the Lerwick TIC for bookings of the primitive **Grieve House** böd (roof under which to sleep £5). The **Out Skerries** support 85 hardy fishermen. Planes (5 per week, £18) swoop down from Tingwall, while ferries converge from Lerwick (2½hr., 2 per week) and Vidlin (1½hr., 10 per week). **Papa Stour** (pop. 35) has a frothy coastline with abundant bird life and sea-flooded cliff arches. The only place to stay is **Mrs. Holt-Brook's.** (☎ 873238. £18 per person.) To get to Papa Stour, take a plane (Tu only, £16) from Tingwall, or a boat (call ☎ 810460 to book in advance; 7 per week, £2.15).

Far to the west, rugged **Foula** is home to 40 humans, 2000 sheep, and the highest sheer cliff in Britain at 1220 ft. Barely Scottish, the inhabitants of Foula had their own monarch until the late 17th century, and spoke the now-extinct Nordic language of Norn until 1926. From April to October, ferries (☎ 753226) drift from Walls (Tu, Sa and every other Th) and Scalloway (every other Th), while planes fly from Tingwall (15 min., 7 per week, £21.30).

Fair Isle, midway between Shetland and Orkney and home of the famous Fair Isle knit patterns, is billed as the most remote island in Britain. In summer, a **ferry** (☎ 760222) runs every other Thursday from Lerwick and two to three times a week from Sumburgh (Apr.-Sept., £2.15). Planes (☎ 840246) depart from Tingwall (25min.; Apr.-Oct. M, W, and F 2 per day, May to mid-Oct. also Sa 1 per day; £37.20) and Sumburgh (May-Oct. Sa, £37.20). Lodging is available at the **Fair Isle Bird Observatory Lodge.** (☎ 760258. Open Apr.-Oct. Room and full board £25-40.)

❄ FESTIVALS AND VIKING LONGSHIPS

The **Shetland Folk Festival** in early May lures fiddlers from around the world, while the **Shetland Fiddle and Accordion Festival** takes place in Lerwick in mid-October; call the TIC for details. The famous **Up-Helly-A' Festival,** on the last Tuesday in January, is a Viking extravaganza with outlandish costumes, a torchlit procession through the streets, and a ship-burning in the town park. Shetlanders plan months in advance for this impressive light-bearing event—after the bonfire dies out blackness settles in again (with only short reprieves of daylight) until late spring. If you miss the real thing, the permanent **Up-Helly-A' Exhibition** is in the Galley Shed, Saint Sunniva St., Lerwick. (Open mid-May to Sept. Tu 2-4pm and 7-9pm, F 7-9pm, Sa 2-4pm. £2.50, concessions £1.) Weather permitting, cruise around the bay on the **Dim Riv,** a full-scale replica of a Viking longship which launches every summer Monday at 7pm. Riders may be asked to row. (☎ 693471. Advance booking at the TIC is a must. Cruises £5, children £2.)

NORTHERN IRELAND

The predominantly calm tenor of life in Northern Ireland has been overshadowed overseas by media headlines concerning politics and bombs that, while disturbing and accurate, fail to reflect that the North is a society of mostly peaceful citizens, however divided they might be. There is much to savor: Northern Ireland's natural beauty includes the green Glens of Antrim and Giant's Causeway, one of the world's strangest geological sights, while the ceasefires of recent years have allowed Belfast and Derry to develop into hip, pub-loving cities. The deeper problem than the violent fringe groups on both sides is the huge division in civil society that sends Protestants and Catholics to separate neighborhoods, separate pubs, and separate schools, with separate, though similar, traditional songs and slang. The widespread support of the 1998 Peace Agreement raised hopes for a resolution to the struggles that have divided the North for centuries, but the agreement's success continues to hang in the balance.

HIGHLIGHTS OF NORTHERN IRELAND

BELFAST Take in the compelling political murals on a black cab tour (p. 636).

GLENS OF ANTRIM Stroll through tiny villages harbored between mountains, forests, and lush valleys, then go for a hike along the nearby coast (p. 649).

GIANT'S CAUSEWAY Marvel at the 60-million-year-old volcanic rock formations, the stuff of Irish myth and legend (p. 651).

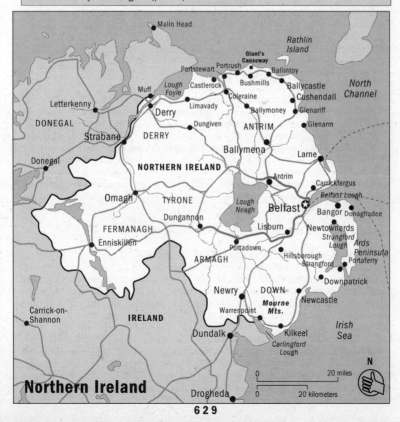

Northern Ireland

The phone code for all of Northern Ireland is 028.

MONEY. Legal tender in Northern Ireland is the British pound. Northern Ireland has its own bank notes, which are identical in value to English and Scottish notes of the same denominations, but are not accepted outside Northern Ireland. All British notes are accepted in the North. The Republic of Ireland's pounds are generally not accepted in the North, with the exception of some border towns which will calculate the exchange rate and add an additional surcharge.

SAFETY AND SECURITY. Overall, Northern Ireland has one of the lowest tourist-related crime rates in the world. Although sectarian violence is dramatically less common than in the height of the Troubles (see p. 631), some neighborhoods and towns still experience turmoil during sensitive political times. It's best to remain alert and cautious while traveling during **Marching Season,** July 4-12 (see **Orange Day,** p. 630). August 12, when the **Apprentice Boys** march in Derry, is also a testy period during which urban areas should be avoided or treated with circumspection. The most common form of violence is property damage, and tourists are unlikely targets. In general, when traveling during Marching Season, be prepared for possible transport delays, and for some shops and services to be closed. Vacation areas such as the Glens and the Causeway Coast are less affected. Use common sense in conversation, and, as in dealing with any issues of a culture not your own, be respectful of locals' religious and political perspectives.

   Border checkpoints have been removed, and armed soldiers and vehicles are less visible in Belfast and Derry. Do not take **photographs** of soldiers, military installations, or vehicles; your film will be confiscated and you may be detained for questioning. Taking pictures of political murals is not a crime, although many people feel uncomfortable doing so in residential neighborhoods. Unattended luggage is always considered suspicious and worthy of confiscation. It is generally unsafe to hitch in Northern Ireland. *Let's Go* never recommends hitchhiking.

HISTORY AND POLITICS

Northern Ireland is a region that lacks a collective cultural identity. Its citizens still recognize themselves by their political allegiances as Unionists and Nationalists. The 950,000 Protestants are generally Unionists, who want the six counties of Northern Ireland to remain part of the UK; the 650,000 Catholics tend to identify with the Republic of Ireland, not Britain, and many are Nationalists, who want the six counties to be part of the Republic. Extremists bring violence into the argument; they are referred to as Loyalists and Republicans, respectively. The conflict between them has seemed intractable. In 1998, the world felt a tentative optimism descend upon the North when its two communities collectively voted into being the monumental Peace Agreement, but the passage of 1999 and 2000 has proven that internal challenges are far from over. For more information on the geographic region of Northern Ireland before the formation of the Republic, see p. 656.

BRITISH RULE AND THE DIVISION OF IRELAND

The 17th-century **Ulster Plantation** systematically set up English and Scottish settlers on what had been Gaelic-Irish land. Over the following two centuries, merchants and working-class immigrants from nearby Scotland settled in northeast Ulster. Institutionalized religious discrimination limited Catholic access to land ownership, making it profitable for Scottish Protestants to settle here. The British developed an industrial economy in Cos. Antrim and Down while the rest of the island remained agricultural. By the end of the 19th century, Belfast had thriving textile and ship-building industries, but most refused to hire Catholic workers.

   As the Republican movement gained fervor in the South in the late 19th century, the picture looked very different in the Northeast. The Ulster Plantation and Scottish settlement, over the course of 300 years, had created a working- and middle-class population in Ulster who identified with the British Empire and did not support Irish Home Rule. The **Orange Order,** named after King William of Orange who had won victories over Catholic James II in the 1690s (see p. 660), organized the Ulster Protestants in local lodges. They ordained **July 12th** as an annual holiday to celebrate William's defeat of James at the Battle of the Boyne.

Lawyer and politician **Edward Carson** and his ally **James Craig** translated Ulster Unionism into terms the British elite understood. When Home Rule looked likely in 1911, Carson held a mass meeting, and Unionists signed the **Ulster Covenant of Resistance to Home Rule** (1912). In 1914, when Home Rule appeared imminent, the Unionist **Ulster Volunteer Force (UVF)** (see p. 661) armed itself by smuggling guns in through Larne—an act that prompted fearful Nationalists to smuggle their own guns in through Howth. World War I gave Unionists more time to organize and gave British leaders time to see that the imposition of Home Rule on all of Ulster would mean havoc: the UVF intended to fight the **Irish Republican Army** (IRA; see p. 661), who in turn would fight the police. The **1920 Government of Ireland Act** created two parliaments for North and South. The Act of Union went nowhere in the south and was quickly superseded by the **Anglo-Irish Treaty** and Civil War (see p. 661), but the measure—intended as a temporary one—became the basis of Northern Ireland's government until 1973. The new Parliament met at **Stormont,** near Belfast.

The new statelet included only six of the nine counties in the province of Ulster. This arrangement suited the one million Protestants in the six counties. Discrimination against the half-million Catholics was widespread. The **Royal Ulster Constabulary** (RUC), the mostly Protestant police force, filled its ranks with part-time policemen called Bs and **B-Specials,** a major source of Catholic casualties.

The 1930s sent the Northern economy into the dumps, requiring more and more British subsidies, while the Stormont Cabinet aged and withered. **World War II** gave Unionists a chance to show their loyalty. The Republic of Ireland stayed neutral and stayed out, but the North welcomed Allied troops, ships, and air force bases. Building and repairing warships raised employment in Belfast and allowed Catholics to enter the industrial workforce for the first time.

The North's standard of living stayed higher than the Republic's, but discrimination and joblessness persisted. The government at Stormont neglected to institute social reform, and parliamentary districts were drawn to favor Protestants. Large towns were segregated by religion, perpetuating the cultural separation. After a brief, unsuccessful try at school desegregation, Stormont ended up granting subsidies to Catholic schools. As the Republic gained a sure footing, violence receded on the island, and, barring the occasional border skirmish, the IRA was seen as finished by 1962. **Capt. Terence O'Neill,** who became the third Stormont Prime Minister in 1963, tried to enlarge the economy and soften discrimination, meeting in 1965 with the Republic's Prime Minister (Taoiseach), Sean Lemass. O'Neill epitomized the liberal Unionist attitude when he said, "If you treat Roman Catholics with due kindness and consideration, they will live like Protestants."

THE TROUBLES

The economy grew, but the bigotry festered, as did the Nationalist community's resentment at being left unemployed and unrepresented. The American civil rights movement inspired the 1967 founding of the **Northern Ireland Civil Rights Association** (NICRA), which worked to end anti-Catholic discrimination in public housing. NICRA leaders tried to distance the movement from constitutional concerns. Protestant extremists included the acerbic **Dr. Ian Paisley,** whose **Ulster Protestant Volunteers (UPV)** overlapped in membership with the illegal, paramilitary UVF. The first NICRA march was raucous but nonviolent. The second, in Derry in 1968, was a bloody mess disrupted by Unionists and then by the RUC's water cannons.

Catholic **John Hume** and Protestant **Ivan Cooper** formed a new civil rights committee in Derry but were overshadowed by Bernadette Devlin's student-led, radical **People's Democracy** (PD), which encouraged a four-day peaceful march from Belfast to Derry starting on New Year's Day, 1969. Paisleyite harassment along the way was nothing compared to the RUC's physical assault on Derry's Catholic

Bogside once the marchers arrived. After that, Derry authorities agreed to keep the RUC out of the Bogside, and this area became **Free Derry.** O'Neill, granting more civil rights concessions in hopes of calming everyone down, was deserted by more of his hardline Unionist allies. On August 12, 1969, Catholics based in Free Derry threw rocks at the annual Apprentice Boys parade along the city walls. The RUC attacked the Bogside residents, and a two-day siege ensued. Free Derry retained its independence, but the violence showed that the RUC could not maintain order alone. At the invitation of Catholics, who sought protection from Unionists, the British Army arrived—and hasn't left yet.

O'Neill resigned in 1969. Between 1970 and 1972, Stormont leaders alternated concessions and crackdowns to little effect. The rejuvenated IRA split in two, with the Socialist "Official" faction practically fading into insignificance as the new **Provisional IRA,** or **Provos** (the IRA we primarily hear about today), took over with less ideology and more arms. In 1970, John Hume founded the **Social Democratic and Labour Party** (SDLP), with the intension of bringing about social change through the support of both Catholics and Protestants; by 1973, it had become the moderate political voice of Northern Catholics. British policies of **internment without trial** outraged Catholics and led the SDLP to withdraw from government.

On January 30, 1972, British troops fired into a crowd of non-violent protesters in Derry, killing 14 Catholics; the famous event, called **Bloody Sunday,** and the ensuing reluctance of the British government to investigate, increased Catholic outrage. Catholics said the soldiers shot at the backs of unarmed, fleeing marchers. Only in 1999 did official re-examination of the event begin. On February 2, 1972, the British embassy in Dublin was burned down. Soon thereafter, the IRA bombed a British army barracks. After further bombings, Stormont was dissolved and replaced by the **Sunningdale executive,** which split power between Catholics and Protestants. This policy was immediately crippled by a massive Unionist work stoppage, and a policy of **direct British rule** from Westminster began. A referendum that year, asking if voters wanted Northern Ireland to remain part of the United Kingdom, showed that voters supported the Union at a rate of ninety to one—Catholics had boycotted the polls. The violence continued with an average of 275 deaths per year between 1970 and 1976.

In 1978, 300 Nationalist prisoners in the Maze Prison in Northern Ireland began a campaign to have their special category as political prisoners restored. The campaign's climax was the 10-man **hunger strike** of 1981, led by **Bobby Sands.** He was elected to Parliament from a Catholic district in Tyrone and Fermanagh even as he starved to death. Sands died after 66 days, becoming a martyr; his face is still seen on murals in the Falls section of Belfast (see p. 642). The hunger strikes galvanized Nationalists, and support for **Sinn Féin,** the political arm of the IRA, surged in the early 80s. British Prime Minister Margaret Thatcher and Taoiseach Garret FitzGerald signed the **Anglo-Irish Agreement** at Hillsborough Castle in November 1985, granting the Republic of Ireland a "consultative role" but no legal authority in the governance of Northern Ireland. It improved relations between London and Dublin but infuriated extremists on both sides. In 1991 and 1992, the Brooke Initiative led to the first multi-party talks in the North in over a decade, but they did not include Sinn Féin. In December 1993, the **Downing Street Declaration,** issued by Prime Minister John Major and Taoiseach Albert Reynolds, invited the IRA to participate in talks if they refrained from violence for three months.

THE 1994 CEASEFIRE

On August 31, 1994, the IRA announced a complete cessation of violence. While Loyalist guerillas cooperated by announcing their own ceasefire, Unionist leaders bickered over the meaning of the IRA's statement; in their opinion, it did not go far enough—only the IRA's disarmament could signify a commitment to peace. Nonetheless, **Gerry Adams,** Sinn Féin's leader, defended the statement and called for direct talks with the British government. The peace held for over a year. In February 1995, John Major and Taoiseach John Bruton issued the **joint framework** proposal. The document suggested the possibility of a new Northern Ireland

Assembly that would include the "harmonizing powers" of the Irish and British governments and the right of the people of Northern Ireland to choose their own destiny. Subsequently, the British government began talks with both Loyalists and, for the first time, Sinn Féin.

In 1996, a flurry of tragic events left the future of Northern Ireland as tenuous as ever. The IRA ended their ceasefire on February 9, with the bombing of an office building in London's Docklands. The stalled peace talks, to be chaired by US diplomat **George Mitchell,** were slated for June 10, 1996. Ian Paisley, now leader of the extreme **Democratic Unionist Party (DUP),** objected to Mitchell's appointment, calling it a "dastardly deed," but did not boycott the talks. The talks proceeded sluggishly and precariously. Sinn Féin did not participate in these talks because it did not agree to the **Mitchell Principles,** which included the total disarmament of all paramilitary organizations. The credibility of Sinn Féin was jeopardized on June 15, 1996, when a blast in a Manchester shopping district injured over 200 people.

As the peace process continued, the Orangemen's July and August marches grew increasingly contentious. The government created a **Parades Commission** to oversee the rerouting of parades and encourage the participation of both sides in negotiations. Protestants see the Commission's decisions as infringing on their rights to practice their culture. Catholics argue that the marches are a form of harassment and intimidation from which they deserve protection. Violence flared around **Orange Day, 1996,** when the Parades Commission banned an Orange Order march through the Catholic Garvaghy Rd. in Portadown, a staunchly Protestant town. Nightly rioting by both sides also took place in Belfast, where RUC policemen were wounded, and in Derry, where Catholic Dermot McShane died after being run over by a jeep. On Oct. 7, the IRA bombed British army headquarters in Belfast, killing one soldier and injuring thirty in the first bombing in Northern Ireland in two years. In early 1997, the IRA tried to make Northern Ireland an issue in the upcoming elections in Great Britain by making several bomb threats, including one that postponed the Grand National horse race. No one was injured, but public ire was aroused and John Major condemned Sinn Féin.

In May of 1997, the Labour party swept the British elections and **Tony Blair** became Prime Minister, bringing hope for peaceful change. Sinn Féin made its most impressive showing yet: Gerry Adams and member Martin McGuinness won seats in Parliament but were barred from taking their seats by their refusal to swear allegiance to the Queen. Despite this act, the government ended its ban on talks with Sinn Féin. Sinn Féin, however, still refused to join the talks.

THE GOOD FRIDAY AGREEMENT

The British government's Northern Ireland Secretary **Mo Mowlam** had a rough introduction to her new job: **marching season** in 1997 was the most violent in recent years. The Orange Order held a large march through Portadown a week before Orange Day. More than 80 people were hurt in the ensuing rioting and looting. On July 10, the Orange Order called off and re-routed a number of contentious parades. On July 19, the IRA announced an "unequivocal" **ceasefire** to start the following day. In September 1997, Sinn Féin joined the peace talks. Members of the **Ulster Unionist Party (UUP),** the voice of moderate Protestants, joined shortly thereafter and were attacked by Ian Paisley and the DUP for sitting with terrorists. **David Trimble,** leader of the UUP, assured Protestants that he wouldn't negotiate directly with Sinn Féin. Other groups still opposed the peace process. In January 1998, 12 people were killed by sectarian violence, mostly committed by extremist Loyalists against Catholic civilians. After two Protestants were killed by Catholic extremists in early February, Unionist leaders charged Sinn Féin with breaking its pledge to support only peaceful actions toward political change and tried to oust party leaders from the talks. Mitchell, Mowlam, Blair, and Taoiseach Bertie Ahern continued to push for progress, holding the group to a strict deadline in April. Mowlam made the unprecedented move of visiting Republican and Loyalist prisoners in the maximum-security Maze prison to encourage their participation in the peace process.

After an interminable week of late-night negotiations, the delegates approved a draft of the **1998 Northern Ireland Peace Agreement** in the early morning after April 10, Good Friday. The agreement emphasized above all that change in Northern Ireland could come only with the consent of the majority of its people. It declared that the "birthright" of the people is the right to choose whether to personally identify as Irish, British, or both; even as the status of Northern Ireland changes, the agreement lets residents retain the right to hold Irish or British citizenship. On Friday, May 22, in the first island-wide vote since 1918, a resounding 71% of the North and 94% of the Republic voted yes to the agreement, including a majority of Protestants. Under the agreement, governing responsibilities of Northern Ireland are divided into three strands. The main body, a new 108-member **Northern Ireland Assembly,** assigns committee posts and chairs proportionately to the parties' representation. Catholics see this body as an opportunity for reclaiming the political power they were long denied. On June 25, the UUP and the SDLP won the most seats, and Sinn Féin garnered more support than ever before, winning 18 assembly seats. David Trimble of the UUP and Seamus Mallon of the SDLP were elected First Minister and Deputy First Minister, respectively, by the new assembly. The second strand, a **North-South Ministerial Council,** serves as the cross-border authority. At least 12 possible areas of focus were under consideration by them in 1998, including social welfare issues such as education, transportation, urban planning, tourism, and EU programs. The final strand, the **British-Irish Council,** approaches issues similar to those considered by the North-South Council, but operates on a broader scale, concerning itself with the entire British Isles.

While most felt that Northern Ireland was finally on the verge of lasting peace, a few controversial issues remain unresolved. Sinn Féin called for disbanding the still largely Protestant RUC, which was cited in an April 1998 United Nations report for its systematic intimidation and harassment of lawyers representing those accused of paramilitary crimes. Blair declared that the RUC would continue to exist, but in June appointed Chris Patten, the former governor of Hong Kong, to head a small one-year commission to review the RUC's recruiting, hiring, and training practices, as well as its culture and symbols.

The 1998 marching season brought challenges and tragedy to the newly arrived peace. The beginning of July saw a wave of violence that included hundreds of bombings and attacks on security forces as well as a slew of arson attacks on Catholic churches. A stand-off began over the fate of the **Drumcree** parade. The parade was not given permission to march in the Catholic section in Portadown. Angered by the decision but encouraged by a history of indecision by the government, thousands of people participated in a week-long standoff with the RUC that affected the whole country. Neither the Orangemen nor the Parade Commission would budge, and the country looked with anxiety toward Orange Day, July 12, the expected climax of the tense situation. On July 11, however, a Catholic home in almost entirely Protestant Ballymoney was firebombed in the middle of the night by local hooligans, and three young boys were killed. Marches still took place the following day; but instead of rioting against the Orangemen who passed though their neighborhoods, Catholics looked on at the marches in silence, holding black balloons and carrying signs that read "for shame." The seemingly intractable Drumcree stand-off gradually subsided.

On August 15, 1998, a bombing in the religiously mixed town of **Omagh,** County Tyrone, left 29 dead and 382 injured. A tiny splinter group calling itself the "Real IRA" claimed responsibility for the attack. The terrorists' obvious motive for the worst atrocity of the Troubles was to undermine the Good Friday Agreement. Sinn Féin's Gerry Adams unreservedly condemned the attack. In October of 1998, Catholic John Hume and Protestant David Trimble received the **Nobel Peace Prize** for their participation in the peace process. The coming year, however, saw the failure to form the Northern Ireland Assembly, the fundamental premise of the agreement. Two major provisions of the pact became the source of irreconcilable differences between Catholic and Protestant politicians: the gradual decommissioning of all paramilitary groups' arms, and the early release of political prisoners. Tensions rose out of the **Northern Ireland (Sentences) Bill,** voted against by members of the UUP, the DUP, and the British Conservative Party, splitting the UK Parliament for the first time during the talks. The bill was to have released all political prisoners, including those convicted of murder, by May 2000; dissenters feared that the bill did not sufficiently link the releases of prisoners to their organizations' full disarmament. Of greatest concern for most Unionists was the issue of decommissioning: the military wings of political parties, most notably Sinn Féin, were expected to disarm themselves in time for the June elections, but the agreement lacked a time frame for decommissioning.

The 1999 marching season started well, with little trouble in July. Violence began in August as the Apprentice Boys marched through Derry and Belfast. Catholics in Belfast staged a sit-down protest in the marchers' path, only to be removed by the RUC. In Derry, the streets fell prey to petrol bombs and riot gear.

CURRENT EVENTS

In December 1999, London signed the devolution bill and returned home rule to Northern Ireland after 27 years of direct rule. A power-sharing 12-member cabinet and government was formed under the leadership of Trimble and Mallon, but the IRA's hidden weapon caches remained a central conflict and threatened the collapse of the new assembly, made up of four parties: the Democratic Unionist Party, the UUP, the Labour Party, and the controversial inclusion of Sinn Féin.

In late January 2000, Trimble gave the IRA an ultimatum to put its weapons "beyond use," and predicted a return to British rule if his demands were not met. The February peace talks were hamstrung by the IRA's unwillingness to comply, and further complications arose when the dissident IRA Continuity group bombed a rural hotel in Irvinestown on February 6 in protest of the IRA's 1997 truce. Every Irish political group, including Sinn Féin, condemned the attack. Though the blast injured no one, it was an unwelcome reminder of the past during the stalled peace talks. Soon after, Britain suspended the power-sharing experiment just 11 weeks after its implementation and reintroduced direct British rule.

On midnight of May 29, 2000, Britain restored the power-sharing scheme after the IRA promised to begin disarmament. In June, two ambassadors inspected the secret weapon caches. The monumental advances did little to dispel conflict throughout the rest of the summer. "Teflon" Taoiseach Bertie Ahern scraped out an 84-80 victory against a vote of no confidence put by the opposition Labour Party on June 30, defending his Fianna Fail-led government's role in the peace process, as well as the dubious appointment of a disgraced former judge to a high-ranking European Union job. Marching season was, again, a violent, widespread affair, although Tony Blair and Ahern expressed satisfaction over its containment by security. Reacting against the prevention of a march by the Parades Commission through a Catholic section of Portadown, the Orange Order shut down both Belfast and Portadown, barricading streets and rioting with police. The marching season concluded after 10 successive days of violence and at least one casualty. Soon after, on July 28, the last prisoners in Maze Prison, near Belfast, walked free under the highly criticized provisions of the 1998 accord. The jail, an intimidating symbol of conflict, is to be closed and possibly used as a museum or monument. While supporters gave the prisoners heroes' welcomes, other civilians and relatives of the deceased found the early release of convicted murderers, often given life sentences, appalling. Many men expressed remorse for the past and stated that their war was over, but others refused to apologize. Though this provides the North with new hope, party disputes are inevitable. More debates remain unresolved, such as the overhaul of the RUC, urged on by Catholics and opposed by Protestants. This promises to be one of many political jousts—Protestant hard-liners have vowed to remove Sinn Féin from the government, while the DUP plans to lock horns with the UUP. The UUP, the Labour Party, and Sinn Féin appear enthusiastic about the peace process in the face of these problems. Northern Ireland is still trying to awake from its nightmarish history.

NORTHERN IRELAND

RECENT LITERATURE

Many recent Northern writers have attempted to create works of relevance to members of both the Catholic and Protestant communities. Protestant poet **Louis MacNeice** (1907-63) infused his lyric poems with a modernist concern for struggle and social upheaval, but he took no part in the sectarian politics. His *Valediction* masterfully attacks an idealized Ireland. Novelist **Brian Moore's** *The Emperor of Ice Cream* (1965) is a coming-of-age story set in wartime Belfast. Born in rural Co. Derry, **Seamus Heaney,** a Nobel laureate in 1995, is the most prominent living Irish poet. While his tone is often lyrical, Heaney writes in an anti-pastoral mode, and his fourth book, *North* (1975), tackles the Troubles head-on.

BELFAST

Despite Belfast's reputation as a terrorist-riddled metropolis, the city feels more neighborly than most international and even Irish visitors expect. The second-largest city on the island, Belfast (pop. 330,000) is the center of the North's cultural, commercial, and political activity; for several hundred years it has been a cosmopolitan and booming center of mercantile activity, in brazen contrast to the rest of the island (until the "Celtic Tiger" began its own boom over the last decade). Renowned writers and the annual arts festival maintain Belfast's reputation as a thriving artistic center. Such luminaries as poet and Nobel laureate Seamus Heaney and poet Paul Muldoon have haunted the halls of Belfast's esteemed Queen's University, giving birth to a modern, distinctive Northern Irish literary *esprit* that grapples with—and transcends—the difficult politics of the area. The Belfast bar scene, a mix of Irish-British pub culture and international trends, entertains locals, foreigners, and a student population as lively as any in the world.

■ GETTING THERE

Flights: Belfast International Airport (☎ 9442 2888) in Aldergrove. **Aer Lingus** (☎ (0845) 973 7747), **British Airways** (☎ (0845) 722 2111), **Jersey European** (☎ 9045 7200), **British Midland** (☎ 9024 1188), and **Sabena** (☎ 9448 4823) land here. **Airbus** (☎ 9033 3000) runs to Belfast's Europa and Laganside bus stations in the city center (M-Sa every 30min. 5:45am-10:30pm, Su about every hr. 7:10am-8:45pm; £5, £8 return). **Belfast City Airport** (☎ 9045 7745), at the harbor, is the destination of **Manx Airlines** (☎ (0845) 7256 256) and **Jersey European. Trains** run from the City Airport **(Sydenham Halt)** to Central Station (M-Sa 25-33 per day, Su 12 per day; £1).

Trains: Central Station, East Bridge St. (☎ 9089 9400; inquiries M-Sa 7:30am-6pm, Su 9:30am-6:30pm). Some trains also stop at **Botanic Station** (☎ 9089 9400) on Botanic Ave. in the center of the University area, or the **Great Victoria Station** (☎ 9043 4424; open M-Sa 7:30am-6:30pm), next to the Europa Hotel. Trains from: **Bangor** (33min.; M-F 39 per day, Sa 25 per day, Su 9 per day; £3); **Larne** (50min.; M-F 20 per day, Sa 16 per day, Su 6 per day; £3.20) **Derry** (2½hr.; M-F 7 per day, Sa 6 per day, Su 3 per day; £6.70); and **Dublin, Republic of Ireland** (2hr.; M-F 8 per day, Sa 8 per day, Su 5 per day; £17). To get to Donegall Sq. from Central Station, turn left and walk down East Bridge St. Turn right on Victoria St. then left after 2 blocks onto May St., which runs into Donegall Sq. South. A better option for those encumbered with luggage is the **Centrelink** bus service, free with train tickets (see **Local Transportation,** below).

Buses: There are 2 main stations in Belfast. Buses traveling to and from the west, the north coast, and the Republic operate out of the **Europa Station** off Great Victoria St. behind the Europa Hotel (☎ 9032 0011; inquiries M-Sa 7:30am-6:30pm, Su 12:30-5:30pm). From **Derry** (1hr.40min.; M-Sa 19 per day, Su 6 per day; £6.50) and **Dublin, Republic of Ireland** (3hr.; M-Sa 7 per day, Su 4 per day; £10.50). Buses to and from Northern Ireland's east coast operate out of **Laganside Station** off Donegall Quay (☎ 9033 3000; inquiries M-Sa 8:30am-5:45pm). Take a left when you exit the terminal onto Queen's Sq. and walk past the clock tower. Queen's Sq. becomes High St. and runs into Donegall Pl.; a left here will get you to City Hall and Donegall Sq. (at the end of the street). The **Centrelink** bus connects both stations with the city center and the hostels and B&Bs near Queen's University (see **Local Transportation,** below).

Ferries: For information on ferries and hovercraft to Belfast from **England** and **Scotland,** see **By Ferry,** p. 44. To reach the city center from the **Belfast SeaCat terminal** (☎ (08705) 523523; www.seacat.co.uk), off Donegall Quay, you have 2 options. Late at night or early in the morning, a **taxi** is your best bet; the docks can be somewhat unsafe at these times. Take a left when you exit the terminal onto Donegall Quay. Turn right onto Albert Sq. about 2 blocks down at the Customs House (a large Victorian stone building). After 2 more short blocks, turn left on Victoria St. (not Great Victoria St.). Turn right again at the clock tower onto High St., which runs into Donegall Pl. Here, a left will lead you to the City Hall and Donegall Sq. (at the end of the street), where you can catch a **Centrelink** bus (see **Local Transportation,** below). SeaCat arrives more or less daily from **Troon** in Scotland (2½hr.); **Heysham** in England (3¾hr.); and the **Isle of Man.** Fares £10-30 without car, cheapest if booked 4 weeks in advance. **Norse Irish Ferries** (☎ 9077 9090) run from **Liverpool** in England. **P&O Ferries** in **Larne** (☎ 0870 2424 777) run from **Cairnryan** in Scotland, and from **Fleetwood**.

Hitchhiking: Notoriously hard in and out of Belfast—most people take the bus out as far as Bangor or Larne before they stick out a thumb. *Let's Go* does not recommend using your thumb or any other part of your body for this activity, as it is not safe.

⊟ GETTING AROUND

Local Transportation: The red **Citybus Network** (24hr. recorded info ☎ 9024 6485), is supplemented by **Ulsterbus's** "blue buses" to the suburbs. Travel within the city center 50p, seniors and children under 16 free. Citybuses going south and west leave from Donegall Sq. East; those going north and east leave from Donegall Sq. West (80p). **4-journey tickets** £2.70, seniors and children £1.35. 7-day **"gold cards"** allow unlimited travel in the city (£11.50). 7-day **"silver cards"** permit unlimited travel in either North Belfast, West/South Belfast, or East Belfast (£7.50). All transport cards and tickets can be bought from the kiosks in Donegall Sq. West (open M-Sa 8am-6pm) and around the city. The **Centrelink** bus connects all the major areas of Belfast in the course of its shamrock-shaped route: Donegall Sq., Castlecourt Shopping Centre, Europa and Lagan-side Bus Stations, Central Station, and Shaftesbury Sq. The buses can be caught at any of 24 designated stops (every 12min.; M-F 7:25am-9:15pm, Sa 8:36am-9:15pm; 50p, free with bus or rail ticket). Late **Nightlink** buses shuttle the tipsy from Donegall Sq. West to various small towns outside of Belfast F-Sa 1am and 2:30am (£3, payable on board or at the Donegall Sq. W. kiosk).

Taxis: 24hr. metered cabs abound: **Value Cabs** (☎ 9023 0000), **City Cab** (☎ 9024 2000; wheelchair accessible), **Fon a Cab** (☎ 9023 3333), and **Abjet Cabs** (☎ 9032 0000). Residents of West and North Belfast utilize the huge **black cabs** you'll see in the city center; some are metered, but some follow set routes, collecting and discharging passengers along the way (under £1).

Car Rental: McCausland's, 21-31 Grosvenor Rd. (☎ 9033 3777; fax 9024 1255), is Northern Ireland's largest car rental company. From £20 per day, £95 per week, less for longer rentals. Ages 21-70. Open M-Th 8:30am-6:30pm, F 8:30am-7:30pm, Sa 8:30am-5pm, Su 8:30am-1pm. 24hr. car return at all offices. **Branches** at Belfast International Airport (☎ 9442 2022) and Belfast City Airport (☎ 9045 4141). **Budget,** 96-102 Great Victoria St. (☎ 9023 0700). Ages 23-70. Open M-F 9am-5pm, Sa 9am-noon. Belfast International Airport Office (☎ 9442 3332). Open daily 7:30am-11:30pm; Belfast City Airport Office (☎ 9045 1111). Open M-Sa 8am-9:30pm, Su 10am-9:30pm.

Bike Rental: McConvey Cycles, 10 Pottingers Entry (☎ 9033 0322) and 467 Ormeau Rd. (☎ 9049 1163). Locks supplied. Open M-Sa 9am-5:30pm. £7 per day, £40 per week; deposit £30. Panniers £5 per week.

⊕ ORIENTATION

To the northeast is the City Hall in **Donegall Sq.** A busy pedestrian shopping district extends north for four blocks between City Hall and the enormous Castlecourt Shopping Centre. **Donegall Pl.** becomes **Royal Ave.**, and runs from Donegall Sq. through the shopping area. In the eastern part of the shopping district is the **Cornmarket** area. South of the bus station, Great Victoria St. meets **Dublin Rd.** at **Shaftesbury Sq.** The stretch of Great Victoria St. between the bus station and Shaftesbury Sq. is known as the **Golden Mile. Botanic Ave.** and **Bradbury Pl.** (which becomes **University Rd.**) extend south from Shaftesbury Sq. into the **Queen's University area.** In this southern area of the city, the busiest neighborhoods center around **Stranmillis, Malone,** and **Lisburn Rd.**

Divided from the rest of Belfast by the Westlink Motorway, working-class **West Belfast** retains a sharp division between sectarian neighborhoods. The Protestant neighborhood stretches along **Shankill Rd.**, just north of the Catholic neighborhood, centered around **Falls Rd.** The two are separated by the **peace line.** The **River Lagan** divides industrial **East Belfast** from the rest of the city. The shipyards and docks that brought Belfast fame and fortune extend north on both sides of the river as it grows into **Belfast Lough.**

The **M1** and **M2** motorways join to form a backwards "C" through Belfast. The **A1** branches off from the M1 around Lisburn and heads south, changing into the N1 before continuing on to **Dublin.** The M2 merges into the A6 then heads northwest to **Derry. Larne** is connected to Belfast by the **A8.**

⊠ PRACTICAL INFORMATION

TOURIST AND FINANCIAL SERVICES

Tourist Information Centre: 59 North St., St. Anne's Court (☎ 9024 6609). Supplies a great booklet on Belfast and an excellent map of the city with bus schedules (free). 24hr. computerized info kiosk outside. Open July-Aug. M-F 9am-7pm, Sa 9am-5:15pm, Su noon-4pm; Sept.-June M 9:30am-5:15pm, Tu-Sa 9am-5:15pm.

Irish Tourist Board (Bord Fáilte), 53 Castle St. (☎ 9032 7888). Provides info on the Republic and makes reservations for accommodations in the south. Open June-Aug. M-F 9am-5pm, Sa 9am-12:30pm; Sept.-May M-F 9am-5pm.

Financial Services: Most banks, the HINI on Donegall Rd., and post offices provide bureaux de change and travelers check cashing services for a small fee. **Northern Bank,** 14 Donegall Sq. West (☎ 9024 5277). Open M-F 9am-4:30pm. **Thomas Cook,** 22-24 Lombard St. (☎ 9088 3800). Cashes Thomas Cook traveler's checks with no commission, others 2% commission. Open May-Oct. M-Tu and Th 5:30am-10pm, W 5:30am-11pm, F-Su 5:30am-midnight; Nov.-Apr. daily 5:45am-8pm. **Bureau de change** at Belfast International Airport office (☎ 9444 7500). Open May-Oct. daily M 5:30am-midnight; Nov.-Apr. Sa-Th 5:30am-9pm.

LOCAL SERVICES

Counseling and Support: Samaritans (☎ 9066 4422). 24hr. line for depression.

Women's Resources: Ardoyne Women's Group, Butler St. (☎ 9074 3536).

Bisexual, Gay, and Lesbian Information: Rainbow Project N.I., 33 Church Ln. (☎ 9031 9030). Open M-F 10am-4pm. **Lesbian Line** (☎ 9023 8668). Open Th 7:30-10pm.

Disability Resources: Disability Action (☎ 9049 1011). Open M-F 9am-5pm.

Launderette: The Laundry Room (Duds 'n' Suds), Botanic Ave. (☎ 9024 3956). Open M-F 8am-9pm, Sa 8am-6pm, Su noon-6pm. Last load 1½hr. before closing.

EMERGENCY AND COMMUNICATIONS

Emergency: ☎ 999 or ☎ 112; no coins required.

Police: 65 Knock Rd. (☎ 9065 0222).

Hospitals: Belfast City Hospital, 9 Lisburn Rd. (☎ 9032 9241). From Shaftesbury Sq. follow Bradbury Pl. and take a right at the fork.

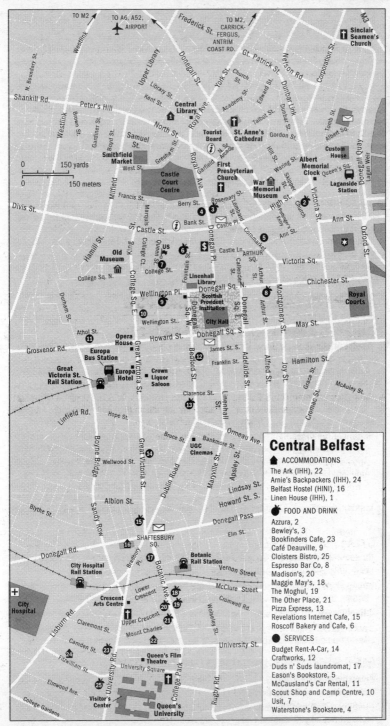

Central Belfast

♠ ACCOMMODATIONS
The Ark (IHH), 22
Arnie's Backpackers (IHH), 24
Belfast Hostel (HINI), 16
Linen House (IHH), 1

🍓 FOOD AND DRINK
Azzura, 2
Bewley's, 3
Bookfinders Cafe, 23
Café Deauville, 9
Cloisters Bistro, 25
Espresso Bar Co, 8
Madison's, 20
Maggie May's, 18
The Moghul, 19
The Other Place, 21
Pizza Express, 13
Revelations Internet Cafe, 15
Roscoff Bakery and Cafe, 6

● SERVICES
Budget Rent-A-Car, 14
Craftworks, 12
Duds n' Suds laundromat, 17
Eason's Bookstore, 5
McCausland's Car Rental, 11
Scout Shop and Camp Centre, 10
Usit, 7
Waterstone's Bookstore, 4

NORTHERN IRELAND

Internet Access: Revelations Internet Cafe, 27 Shaftesbury Sq. £4 per hr., students and hostelers £3 per hr. Open M-F 10am-10pm, Sa 10am-6pm, Su 11am-7pm.

Post Office: Central Post Office, 25 Castle Pl. (☎ 9032 3740). Open M-Sa 9am-5:30pm. Poste Restante comes here. **Postal code:** BT1 1NB.

ACCOMMODATIONS

Nearly all Belfast's budget accommodations are near Queen's University, south of the city center. If you have a lot of baggage you may want to catch a **Centrelink** bus to Shaftesbury Sq., or **Citybus** #59, 69, 70, 71, 84, or 85 from Donegall Sq. East. A walk to these accommodations takes 10-20min. from the bus or train station. Reservations are recommended in the summer.

HOSTELS AND DORMS

The Ark (IHH), 18 University St. (☎ 9032 9626). 10min. from the Europa bus station. Great sense of community. Owner John leads informative, if somewhat talky, tours of Belfast (£8) and Giant's Causeway excursions (£15). Weekend luggage storage. Internet access £2 per 30min. Laundry. Curfew 2am. Dorms £6.50-£7.50; doubles £28.

Arnie's Backpackers (IHH), 63 Fitzwilliam St. (☎ 9024 2867). Friendly atmosphere. Key deposit £2. Luggage storage during the day. Dorms £7.50.

Belfast Hostel (HINI), 22 Donegall Rd. (☎ 9031 5435; www.hini.org.uk), off Shaftesbury Sq. Clean, modern rooms with 2 to 6 beds, some with bath. Located near Sandy Row, a Loyalist area that has seen violence during the July marching season. Books city and Causeway tours. Breakfast £2. Laundry £3. No kitchen. 24hr. reception. Book ahead for weekends. Wheelchair accessible. Dorms £8-10.

The Linen House Youth Hostel (IHH), 18-20 Kent St. (☎ 9058 6400; info@belfasthostel.com; www.belfasthostel.com) in West Belfast. This converted 19th-century linen factory now houses scores of weary travelers (about 160 beds total). Downtown location is a good or bad thing, depending on the time of night and year. Books black cab (£8) and Causeway tours (£15). 24hr. secure parking. **Internet access** £3 per hr. Laundry £3. No curfew. Dorms £6.50-8.50; singles £12; doubles £28.

Queen's University Accommodations, 78 Malone Rd. (☎ 9038 1608). Bus #71 from Donegall Sq. East or a 25min. walk from Europa. University Rd. runs into Malone Rd.; the residence halls are on your left. An undecorated, institutional dorm providing spacious singles or twin rooms with sinks and desks. Strong, reliable showers. Open mid-June to mid-Sept. and Christmas and Easter vacations. Singles and doubles £8 per person for UK students, £9.40 for international students, £11.75 for non-students.

B&BS

Marine House, 30 Eglantine Ave. (☎ 9066 2828). This mansion defies the stereotypes of B&B architecture, overcomeing the alienating implications of its size. Hospitality and housekeeping standards as high as the ceilings. Singles £22; doubles £40, with bath £45; triples £57.

The George, 9 Eglantine Ave. (☎ 9068 3212). Immaculately clean rooms, all with shower and TV. Bring cash; no credit cards accepted. Singles £22; doubles £44.

Botanic Lodge, 87 Botanic Ave. (☎ 9032 7682), on the corner of Mt. Charles Ave. B&B comfort with as short a walk to the city center as possible. Singles £22; doubles £40.

Liserin Guest House, 17 Eglantine Ave. (☎ 9066 0769). Comfy beds and a huge velvet-covered lounge make the Liserin an inviting abode. Watch TV while taking a shower; they're both in the room. Singles £22; doubles £40; triples £60.

Eglantine Guest House, 21 Eglantine Ave. (☎ 9066 7585). The owner is the sister of the Liserin's proprietor, and treats her guests with equal hospitality. Small but comfortable rooms. Singles £22; doubles £38; triples £57.

⚪ FOOD

Dublin Rd., Botanic Rd., and the **Golden Mile** have the highest concentration of restaurants. Bakeries and cafes dot the shopping areas; nearly all close by 5:30pm with later hours on Thursday. **Tesco Supermarket** is at 2 Royal Ave. (☎ 9032 3270. Open M-W and Sa 8am-7pm, Th 8am-9pm, F 8am-8pm, Su 1-5pm.)

☒ **The Other Place,** 79 Botanic Ave. (☎ 9020 7200), 133 Stranmillis Rd. (☎ 9020 7100), and 537 Lisburn Rd. (☎ 9029 7300). Stomping grounds for the backpacker's unicorn, the mythic 99p breakfast, served 8-10am. Features an array of ethnic foods, from Thai to Cajun, accompanied by an eclectic soundtrack. Open daily 8am-11pm.

☒ **Azzura,** 8 Church Ln. (☎ 9024 3503). This tiny cafe dishes out pizzas and gourmet sandwiches for £2-3, and mountains of pasta for about £4. Open M-Sa 9am-5pm.

Bookfinders, 47 University Rd. (☎ 9032 8269). Smoky bookstore/cafe with mismatched dishes and retro counter-culture paraphernalia. Open M-Sa 10am-5:30pm.

Maggie May's Belfast Cafe, 50 Botanic Ave. (☎ 9032 2622). Walls covered with brown newsprint depicting the Belfast of yesteryear. Relax with a cup of tea and a free newspaper; order food when you feel like it. Sandwiches £2-3. 3-course meals £4-6. Open M-Sa 8am-10:30pm, Su 10am-10:30pm.

Pizza Express, 25-27 Bedford St. (☎ 9032 9050). It sounds like your typical franchise, but the grandeur of its spiral staircase and Tuscan decor belie its mundane name. Plus, it's one of the few places in town that actually serves real pizza. 1- to 2-person pizzas £4-6. Open M-Sa noon-11:30pm.

🔲 SIGHTS

Black Cab Tours are led by residents of West Belfast and provide the best introduction to the city's sectarian neighborhoods. Cab tours provide a fascinating, if biased commentary that highlights the murals, paraphernalia, and sights on both sides of the peace wall. Backpackers and locals alike arrange tours through the hostels; these are your best bet for a good tour at a fair price. (£6-7per person.)

DONEGALL SQUARE AND CORNMARKET

BELFAST CITY HALL. The administrative and geographic center of Belfast is distanced from the downtown streets by a grassy square. Its green copper dome (173 ft.) is visible from any point in the city. Inside A. Brunwell Thomas's Neoclassical 1906 design, portraits of the city's Lord Mayors somberly line the halls. The **City Council's** oak-paneled chambers are deceptively austere, considering the council's reputation for rowdy meetings that sometimes devolve into fist fights. In front of the main entrance, an enormous marble **Queen Victoria statue** stares down at visitors with a formidable grimace. The interior of City Hall is accessible only by tour. (☎ 9032 0202, ext. 2346. 1hr. tours June-Sept. M-F 10:30am, 11:30am, and 2:30pm; Sa 2:30pm. Oct.-May M-Sa 2:30pm. Free.)

LINEN HALL LIBRARY. The library was originally located across the street in the linen hall that became present-day City Hall; it was moved to its present location in 1894. It contains a famous collection of political documents relating to Northern Ireland. (17 Donegall Sq. North. ☎ 9032 1707. Open M-F 9:30am-5:30pm, Sa 9:30am-4pm.)

CORNMARKET ENTRIES. Cornmarket has been a marketplace since Belfast's early days and is named after one of its original commodities. Although the Cornmarket area is dominated by modern buildings, relics of old Belfast remain in the tiny alleys, or **entries,** that connect some of the major streets. Between Ann and High St. runs **Pottinger's Entry.** Off Lombard and Bridge St., **Winecellar Entry** is the site of Belfast's oldest pub, **White's Tavern** (see **Pubs and Clubs,** p. 644).

THE GOLDEN MILE

"The Golden Mile" refers to a strip along Great Victoria St. containing many of the jewels in the crown of Belfast's establishments.

GRAND OPERA HOUSE. Belfast's pride and joy, the opera house was cyclically bombed by the IRA, restored to its original splendor at enormous cost, and then bombed again. Ask at the stage door on Glengall St. if a rehearsal is on; if not, they'll give you a tour. (☎ 9024 0411. *Booking office open M-Sa 9:45am-5:30pm.*)

THE CROWN LIQUOR SALOON. The National Trust has restored this highly frequented pub to make it a showcase of carved wood, gilded ceilings, and stained glass. Box-like snugs fit groups of 2-10 comfortably (see **Pubs**, p. 644).

QUEEN'S UNIVERSITY AREA

BOTANIC GARDENS. Behind the university, meticulously groomed gardens offer a welcome green respite from traffic-laden city streets. Inside the gardens lie two 19th-century greenhouses, the toasty **Tropical Ravine House,** and the more temperate Lanyon-designed **Palm House.** Don't forget to stop and smell the rose gardens. (☎ 9032 4902. *Open daily 8am-dusk. Tropical House and Palm House open Apr.-Sept. M-F 10am-noon and 1-5pm, Sa-Su 2-5pm; Oct.-Mar. M-F 10am-noon and 1-4pm, Sa-Su 2-4pm. Free.*)

ULSTER MUSEUM. This national-caliber museum has developed a variety of exhibits to fill its huge display halls. Irish and modern art, local history, antiquities, and the Mummy of Takabuti are all subjects for investigation. The treasure salvaged from the *Girone*, a Spanish Armada ship that sank off the Causeway Coast in 1588, is also on display. (*In the Botanic Gardens, off Stranmillis Rd.* ☎ 9038 3000. *Open M-F 10am-5pm, Sa 1-5pm, Su 2-5pm. Free, except for some traveling exhibitions.*)

WEST BELFAST AND THE MURALS

Separated from the rest of the city by the Westlink motorway, the neighborhoods of West Belfast have historically been at the heart of the political tensions in the North. The Catholic area (centered on **Falls Rd.**) and the Protestant neighborhood (centered on the **Shankill**) are grimly separated by the **peace line,** a gray and seemingly impenetrable wall. The most dominant feature of the neighborhoods is their family community. West Belfast is not a center of consumer tourism or a "sight" in the traditional sense. The streets display political murals, which you will soon come across as you wander among the houses. It is best to visit the Falls and Shankill during the day, when the murals can be seen. To see both the Falls and Shankill, the best plan is to visit one then return to the city center before heading to the other, as the area around the peace line is still desolate.

THE FALLS. This Catholic neighborhood is much larger than Shankill and houses a younger, rapidly multiplying population. On Divis St., the **Divis Tower,** a high-rise apartment building, is an ill-fated housing development built by optimistic social planners in the 1960s that soon became an IRA stronghold. The British army still occupies the top three floors, and Shankill residents refer to it as "Little Beirut." Continuing west, Divis St. turns into the **Falls Rd.** The **Sinn Féin** office is easily spotted: one side of it is covered with an enormous portrait of Bobby Sands (see **The Troubles,** p. 631) and an advertisement for the Sinn Féin newspaper, *An Phoblacht*. Continuing down the Falls you will see a number of murals with Celtic art and the Irish language. They display scenes of traditional music and dance, or grimmer portraits of Famine victims. Murals in the Falls, unlike those of the Shankill, are becoming less militant in nature, though there are a few left in the Lower Falls that refer to specific acts of violence.

SHANKILL. North St., to the left of the tourist information centre, turns into Shankill Rd. as it crosses the **Westlink** and then arrives in Protestant **Shankill,** once a thriving shopping district. Turning left (coming from the direction of North St.) onto most side roads leads to the peace line. Some murals in Shankill seem to glorify the UVF and UFF rather than celebrate any aspect of Orange culture. The densely decorated **Orange Hall** sits on the left at Brookmount St. The side streets on the right guide you to the **Shankill Estate** and more murals. Through the estate, Crumlin Road heads back to the city center past an army base, the courthouse, and the jail, which are linked by a tunnel. The oldest Loyalist murals are found here. The Shankill area is shrinking as middle-class Protestants leave, but a growing Protestant population lives on Sandy Row. This stretch is a turn off of Donegall Rd. at Shaftesbury Sq. An orange arch topped with King William marks its start.

SYMBOLS IN THE MURALS OF WEST BELFAST: A PRIMER

PROTESTANT MURALS

Red, White, and Blue: The colors of the British flag; often painted on curbs, signposts, etc., to demarcate Unionist murals and neighborhoods.

The Red Hand: The symbol of Ulster (found on Ulster's crest), usually used by Unionists to emphasize the separation of Ulster from the rest of Ireland. Symbolizes the hand of the first Viking King, which he supposedly cut off and threw on a Northern beach to establish his primacy.

King Billy/William of Orange: Sometimes depicted on a white horse, crossing the Boyne to defeat the Catholic King James II at the 1690 Battle of the Boyne. The Orange Order was later founded in his honor.

The Apprentice Boys: A group of young men who shut the gates of Derry to keep out the troops of James II, beginning the great siege of 1689. They have become Protestant folk heroes, inspiring a sect of the Orange order in their name. The slogan **"No Surrender,"** also from the siege, has been appropriated by radical Unionists, most notably Rev. Ian Paisley.

Lundy: The Derry leader who advocated surrender during the siege; now a term for anyone who wants to give in to Catholic demands.

Taig: Phonetic spelling of the Irish given name Teague; Protestant slang for a Catholic.

Scottish Flag: Blue with a white cross; recalls the Scottish-Presbyterian roots of many Protestants whose ancestors were part of the Ulster Plantation.

CATHOLIC MURALS

Orange and Green: Colors of the Irish Republic's flag; often painted on curbs and signposts in Republican neighborhoods.

Landscapes: Usually imply Republican territorial claims to the North.

The Irish Volunteers: Republican tie to the earlier (nonsectarian) Nationalists.

Saiorsche: "Freedom"; the most common Irish term found on murals.

Éireann go bráth: "Ireland forever"; a popular IRA slogan.

Tiocfaidh ár lá: (CHOCK-ee-ar-LA) "Our day will come."

Slan Abnaile: (slang NA-fail) "Leave our streets"; directed at the primarily Protestant RUC police force.

Phoenix: Symbolizes united Ireland rising from the ashes of British persecution.

Lug: Celtic god, seen as the protector of the "native Irish" (Catholics).

Green ribbon: IRA symbol for "free POWs."

Bulldog: Britain.

Bowler Hats: A symbol for Orangemen.

♫ ENTERTAINMENT

Belfast's many cultural events are covered in the monthly *Arts Council Artslink*, free at the tourist information centre. The **Crescent Arts Centre**, 2 University Rd., supplies general arts info. (☎ 9024 2338. Open M-Sa 9:30am-5pm.) Belfast's theater season runs from September to June. July and August are slow months for Belfast arts; around July 12 the whole city shuts down. The **Grand Opera House** is on Great Victoria St. (☎ 9024 0411; ☎ 9024 1919 for reservations; 24hr. info line ☎ 9024 9129. Open M-W 8:30am-8pm, Th 8:30am-9pm, F 8:30am-6:30pm, Sa 8:30am-5:30pm. Wheelchair accessible. Tickets ₤8 and up. 50% off student standby tickets available after noon for M-Th performances.) **Ulster Hall,** Bedford St. (☎ 9032 3900), brings Belfast everything from classical to pop. Try the independent box offices **Our Price** (☎ 9031 3131) or the **Ticket Shop** at Virgin (☎ 9032 3744) for tickets. **Waterfront Hall,** 2 Lanyon Pl., is Belfast's newest concert center, hosting a series of performances. (☎ 9033 4400. Tickets ₤10-35, average ₤12; student discounts available.)

■ PUBS AND CLUBS

Lavery's, 12 Bradbury Pl. (☎ 9087 1106). 3 floors of unpretentious socializing: unlike nightclubs, you don't have to dress up to get noticed (some do anyway). Live music W nights in the back bar, DJs on weekends (no cover); disco in the upstairs Gin Palace (£1 cover); 3rd floor "Heaven" club (£5 cover). Open until 1am.

The John Hewitt, 51 Lower Donegall St. (☎ 9023 3768). A new pub suited for business lunches and named after the late Ulster poet. It's run by the Unemployment Youth Resource Centre, to which half the profits go, so drink up. Really great food, too. Take a cab after dark. Live music W and Su nights (open until 2am) and Sa afternoons.

The Botanic Inn (the "Bot"), 23 Malone Rd. (☎ 9066 0460). Huge and hugely popular student bar. Pub grub daily £4-5, Su carvery meal £4.50, students £3.50. Trad on Tu, no cover. Th-Sa 60s-80s music. Cover £2. 21+. Open until 1am.

Robinson's, 38-40 Great Victoria St. (☎ 9024 7447), has 4 floors of theme bars, but is most renowned for **Fibber McGees** in the back, which hosts incredible trad sessions Tu-Sa twice daily (no cover). Non-trad F evening and Sa afternoons. Decent nightclub on top 2 floors Th-Sa (cover £5-7).

White's Tavern, 2-4 Winecellar Entry (☎ 9024 3080), off Lombard and Bridge St. Belfast's oldest tavern, serving drinks since 1630. An excellent stop for an afternoon pint. W is gay night. Open daily noon-1am, W until 2:30am.

Crown Liquor Saloon, 46 Great Victoria St. (☎ 9024 9476). This National Trust-owned pub has been bombed 32 times, but you'd never know it; the stained glass and gas lamps seem original. It's more to impress tourists—the locals go elsewhere.

The Fly, 5-6 Lower Crescent (☎ 9023 5666). Look for the big torches. Extremely popular, with an entomological decor geared towards its namesake. Downsairs bar for the pints, upstairs bar for mingling, and an Absolut lounge. No cover.

The Manhattan, 23-31 Bradbury Pl. (☎ 9023 3131). Huge 3-story dance club that's packed with a younger crowd clad in Brit-pop fashions. Dress to impress. Events are sporadic, but F is often 70s night. No cover for downstairs bar; nightclub cover £4-6.

Katy Daly's and **The Limelight,** 17 Ormeau Ave. (☎ 9032 5942). High-ceilinged, wood-paneled, antique pub, with strobe-filled nightclub next door. Tu disco, F funk, Sa "helter skelter." Cover £3. Has a knack for hiring bands before their time, but don't come with a sore throat—it's LOUD.

The Kremlin, 96 Donegall St. (☎ 9080 9700). Look for the imposing statue of Stalin above the entrance. Belfast's newest and hottest gay nightspot with too many different events to list, from foam parties to internationally renowned drag queens. Mixed crowd, but mostly men. Theme night F; "Kink" night once a month. Tight security. Open M-Sa 7:30pm-late, Su 5pm-late. Cover varies, but free Su, M, W, and before 9pm.

🎌 DAYTRIP FROM BELFAST

ULSTER FOLK AND TRANSPORT MUSEUMS. In Holywood, the Ulster Folk Museum and Transport Museum stretches over 176 acres. Established by an Act of Parliament in the 1950s, the 🎌 **Folk Museum** contains over 30 buildings from the past three centuries and all nine Ulster counties. Most of the buildings are transplanted originals, reconstructed stone by stone in the museum's landscape. The Transport Museum and the Railway Museum are across the road from the Folk Museum. Inside the **Transport Museum,** horse-drawn coaches, cars, bicycles, and trains display the history of moving vehicles. The hangar-shaped **Railway Museum** stuffs in 25 old railway engines. *(Take the Bangor Rd. 7 mi. east of Belfast on the A2. Buses and trains stop on their way to Bangor. ☎ 9042 8428. Open July-Aug. M-Sa 10:30am-6pm, Su noon-6pm; Apr.-June and Sept. M-F 9:30am-5pm, Sa 10:30am-6pm, Su noon-6pm; Oct.-Mar. M-F 9:30am-4pm, Sa-Su 12:30-4:30pm. Some wheelchair access. £4, students and seniors £2.50.)*

DOWN AND ARMAGH

NEWCASTLE AND THE MOURNES

The 15 rounded peaks of the Mourne Mountains sprawl across the southeastern corner of Northern Ireland. Volcanic activity pushed up five different kinds of granite beneath a shale crust 50 million years ago. No road penetrates the center of the mountains, leaving hikers in welcome solitude. Outdoorsy types often spend the night in Newcastle, where arcades and waterslide parks line the waterfront.

📠 **GETTING THERE AND GETTING AROUND.** Newcastle's **bus station** is at 5-7 Railway St. (☎ 4372 2296), at the end of Main St., away from the mountains. Buses run from: **Downpatrick** (40min.; M-F 12 per day, Sa 11 per day, Su 6 per day; £2.30); **Newry** (1hr.; M-F 12 per day, Sa 10 per day, Su 3 per day; £3.60); **Belfast** (80min.; M-F 24 per day, Sa 18 per day, Su 10 per day; £4.60); and **Dublin, Republic of Ireland** (3hr.; M-Sa 4 per day, Su 2 per day; £9.90). **Rent bikes** at **Wiki Wiki Wheels,** 10B Donard St., beside the Xtra-Vision building to the left of the bus station. (☎ 4372 3973. £6.50 per day, £30 per week; children £5 per day; ID deposit. Open M-Sa 9am-6pm, Su 2-6pm). For **taxis,** call **Donard Cabs** (☎ 4372 4100 or 4372 2823). **Hitchhikers** stand at either end of the main road. *Let's Go* does not recommend hitchhiking.

🔧🎌 **ORIENTATION AND PRACTICAL INFORMATION.** Newcastle's main road stretches along the waterfront, changing from **Main St.** (where it intersects with Railway St., where Ulsterbuses stop) to **Central Promenade** to **South Promenade.**

The **tourist information centre** is on 10-14 Central Promenade, in a blue-and-white building 10min. down the main street from the bus station. Free map and visitor's guides are available. (☎ 4372 2222. Open July-Aug. M-Sa 9:30am-7pm, Su 1-7pm; Sept.-June M-Sa 10am-5pm, Su 2-6pm.) **Rent camping equipment** at **Hill Trekker,** 115 Central Promenade. (☎ 4372 3842. Hiking boots £1.50 per day, £10 per week, deposit £10. Open Tu-W and Sa-Su 10am-5:30pm, Th 10am-4:45pm, F 10am-6:15pm.) Services include: **First Trust Bank,** 28-32 Main St. (☎ 4372 3476; open M-Tu and Th-F 9:30am-4:30pm, W 10am-4:30pm); the **police,** on South Promenade (☎ 4372 3583); **Internet access** at the **Anchord Bar** (see below), free if you buy a pint; and the **post office,** 33-35 Central Promenade (☎ 4372 2418; open M-W and F 9am-5:30pm, Th and Sa 9am-12:30pm). **Postal code:** BT33 OAA.

🏠🍴🍺 **ACCOMMODATIONS, FOOD, AND PUBS.** B&Bs in this summer resort town range in price from affordable to sky high; fortunately, there is a hostel. The Mournes are a free and legal camping alternative. Follow Railway St. toward the water and take a right onto Downs Rd. at the Percival Arms to reach **Newcastle Youth Hostel (HINI),** 30 Downs Rd. Quarters are tight, but such discomforts are appeased by the prime location. (☎ 4372 2133. Dorms £8.50, under 18 £7.50.) **Castlebridge House,** 2 Central Promenade, is understandably popular, with cozy rooms and an ideal location over the bay. (☎ 4372 3209. £15 per person.) **Drumrawn House,** 139 Central Promenade, is about a 15min. walk from the bus station. This Georgian townhouse has a marvelous sea view. (☎ 4372 6847. £21.50 per person with breakfast.) There are excellent **camping** facilities at **Tollymore Forest Park,** 176 Tullybrannigan Rd. (☎ 4372 2428), a two-mile walk along the A2, or take the "Busybus" (10min., 75p) from the Newcastle Ulsterbus station at 10am and noon, more often during the high season. (Easter-Sept. £10 per tent or caravan; Oct.-Easter £6.50.)

The nougat-like density of takeaways, sweet shops, and ice cream shops on the waterfront could keep you on a permanent grease and sugar high. **Seasalt,** 51 Central Promenade, is a stylish deli and cafe with a Mediterranean edge. F-Sa nights, it transforms into an expensive, reservations-only 3-course bistro (£15 per person) that has to be experienced to be believed. (☎ 4372 5027. Open M-Tu 9am-6pm, W-Su 9am-9pm.) **The Cookie Jar,** in the Newcastle Shopping Centre on Main St., has sandwiches made to order (under £2) and a wide selection of baked goods. (Open M-Sa 9am-5:30pm.) **Sea Palace,** 136 Main St., serves memorable Chinese fare in a forgettable dining room. (☎ 4372 3626. Most dishes around £7, £5-6 takeaway. Open M-Th 5pm-midnight, F-Sa 4pm-1am, Su 4pm-midnight.) **Anchor Bar,** 9 Bryansford Rd., is a century-old pub, with stained-glass windows depicting the ferocious Irish sea. (☎ 4372 3344. Lunch £2-4, served noon-7pm.)

◪ THE MOURNE MOUNTAINS. Before heading for the hills, stop at the **Mourne Countryside Centre,** 91 Central Promenade. A friendly and knowledgeable staff leads hikes and offers a broad selection of guides and maps of the mountains. Those planning short excursions can purchase *Mourne Mountain Walks* (£6), which describes 10 one-day hikes. Those planning to stay in the Mournes overnight should buy the topographical *Mourne Country Outdoor Pursuits Map* for £4.55. (☎ 4372 4059. Centre open July-Aug. M-F 9am-5pm; winter hours vary.) The **Mourne Heritage Trust** just two doors down is also worth a stop.

The **Mourne Wall,** built between 1904 and 1923, encircles 12 of the mountains just below their peaks. Following the length of the 22 mi. wall takes a strenuous eight hours. The Mourne's highest peak, **Slieve Donard** (850m.), towers above Newcastle. The trail to it is wide and well maintained, and paved in many places with flag and cobblestones (5hr. return). **Donard Park** provides the most direct access to the Mournes from Newcastle; it's convenient to both Slieve Donard and nearby **Slieve Commedagh.** The park lies on the corner of Central Promenade and Bryansford Rd. Follow the dirt path at the back of the car park carefully (it crosses 2 bridges). It eventually joins the Glen River Path for about 1½ mi. to reach the Mourne Wall. At the wall, turn left for Slieve Donard, right for Slieve Commedagh. Most of the land in and around the Mournes is privately owned. Visitors should bear this in mind and treat the environs with respect (close those sheep gates!).

Wilderness **camping** is legal and popular. Common spots include the **Annalong Valley,** the shores of **Lough Shannagh,** and near the **Trassey River.** While camping around the Mourne Wall is allowed, camping in the forest itself is strictly prohibited because of the risk of forest fires. Remember to bring warm clothing since the mountains get cold and windy at night. Weather conditions can change suddenly.

ARMAGH

The pagan worshippers who built huge ceremonial mounds at Navan Fort named their city Ard Macha (Macha's Height) after the legendary Queen Macha. Since then, Armagh has become Ireland's ecclesiastical capital, with cathedrals for both the Catholic Church and the Church of Ireland.

■? GETTING THERE AND PRACTICAL INFORMATION. Buses (☎ 3752 2266) stop at Lonsdale Rd. from: **Belfast** (1hr.; M-F 20 per day, Sa 15 per day, Su 8 per day; £5) and **Enniskillen** (2hr., M-Sa 3 per day, £5.50). **Brown's Bikes,** 21A Scotch St., **rents bikes** for £7 per day, £30 per week. (☎ 3752 2782. Open M-Sa 9am-5:30pm.)

English St., Thomas St., and **Scotch St.** comprise Armagh's city center. Just to the east lies the **Mall.** West of the city center, two cathedrals sit on neighboring hills. To reach the **tourist information centre** (TIC), Old Bank Building, 40 English St., from the bus stop, face the Mall, turn left, walk past the Mall, and turn left up the hill onto College St. The office is a short way down the first street. (☎ 3752 1800. Open M-Sa 9am-5pm, Su 1-5pm.) Two refurbished 1940s-style **coaches** cart tourists around in summer; schedules are available at the TIC. Services include: **Northern Bank,** 78 Scotch St. (☎ 3752 2004; open M 9:30am-5pm, Tu-F 10am-3:30pm); the **police** on Newry Rd. (☎ 3752 3311); the **hospital** at Tower Hill (☎ 3752 2341), off College Hill; **Internet access** at **Armagh Computer World,** 43 Scotch Street (☎ 3751 0002; £3 per 30min.; open M-Sa 9am-6pm); and the **post office,** 31 Upper English St. (☎ 3751 0313; open M-F 9am-5:30pm, Sa 9am-12:30pm). Poste Restante is across the street at 46 Upper English St. (☎ 3752 2856). **Postal code:** BT61 7AA.

▼ ACCOMMODATIONS. Armagh's huge **hostel (HINI),** behind the old health clinic, is sparklingly clean. From the TIC, turn left twice and follow Abbey St. for two blocks until the hostel appears on your right. (☎ 3751 1800. Dorms £9.75-10.75; doubles £11.50.) The **Padua Guest House,** 63 Cathedral Rd., is just past the Catholic Cathedral. Mrs. O'Hagen greets guests with a cup of tea. (☎ 3752 2039. Doubles £32.) Make a right on Desart Rd., then turn left to reach **Desart Guest House,** 99 Cathedral Rd. It's a formidable mansion, and the rooms are sunny, clean, and plush. (☎ 3752 2387. Singles £20; doubles £30.) **Gosfard Forest Park,** off the A28, offers **camping** seven miles southeast of town. Take bus #40 to Market Hill. (☎ 3755 1277; ranger ☎ 3755 2169. Easter-Sept. £8.50 per 2-person tent, Oct.-Easter £5.50.)

◖▣ FOOD AND PUBS. On weekdays, it's hard to find a restaurant in Armagh that stays open after 6pm. Armagh's few eateries are scattered across English and Scotch St. Your best bet may be to pick up groceries at **Emerson's** on Scotch St. (☎ 3752 2846. Open M-W 8:45am-5:30pm, Th-F 9am-9pm, Sa 8:45am-6pm.) The **Basement Cafe** (☎ 3752 4311) sits under the Armagh Film House on English St. next to the library and serves cheap sandwiches for £1.85. (☎ 3752 4311. Open M-Sa 9am-5:30pm.) **Hong Kong Chef,** English St., serves up tasty Chinese takeaway and is open later than most places. (mobile ☎ (01861) 511047. Open until midnight on weekdays, 1am on weekends.) **The Station Bar,** 3 Lower English St. (☎ 3752 3731) is one of Armagh's most popular pubs, with trad twice a week in winter and good conversation year-round. **Harry Hoots,** Railway St. (☎ 522103), sounds and is fun.

◙▓ SIGHTS AND FESTIVALS. Armagh's twin cathedrals preside grandly over the city. The Protestant Church of Ireland **Cathedral of St. Patrick** is a 19th-century restoration of a 13th-century structure that enlarged upon the 5th-century original attributed to Patrick himself. It's also the final resting place of the great Irish King Brian Ború. (☎ 3752 3142. Open daily Apr.-Sept. 10:30am-5pm; Oct.-Mar. 10:30am-4pm. Tours June-Aug. M-Sa 11:30am and 2:30pm. Free.) The Catholic **Church of St. Patrick** raises its spires from Cathedral Rd. Opened in 1873, the cathedral's imposing exterior and exquisite mosaic interior are marred only by the ultra-modern granite sanctuary. (Open daily 9am-6pm. Free.)

Up College Hill north of The Mall is the **Armagh Observatory,** where you can observe the modern weather station and an 1885 refractory telescope. (☎ 3752 2928. Free.) Celestial wonders await in the **Planetarium,** College Hill, where a 3cm chunk of Mars is on display. Book ahead because seating is limited. (☎ 523 689. £3.50, students £2.50.) On Friary Rd., south of the town center, the ruins of the 13th-century **Franciscan Friary** occupy a peaceful green corner of the **Palace Demesne.** Although the palace itself is closed to the public, the **Palace Stables**

Heritage Centre puts on a slick multimedia show about "A Day in the Life" of the closed palace. (☎ 3752 9629. Open Apr.-Sept. M-Sa 10am-7pm, Su 1-7pm; Oct.-Mar. M-Sa 10am-5pm, Su 2-5pm. £2.80, students £2.20.) Peek at a first edition of *Gulliver's Travels*, covered with Swift's scrawls, at the **Armagh Public Library,** built on Abbey St. in 1771. (☎ 3752 3142. Open M-F 10am-12:30pm and 2-4pm.)

On the outskirts of Armagh, the mysterious **Navan Fort,** also called Emain Macha (AHM-win maka), was the capital of the Kings of Ulster for 800 years. It may look like a grassy mound but with a little imagination, you might see extensive defensive fortifications. ■ **Navan Centre** presents a fascinating 1hr. program of interactive exhibits on the archaeological evidence and legends associated with the site. The Centre is on Killylea Rd. (the A28), two miles west of Armagh, and a 10min. walk from the fort. (☎ (01861) 525 550. Open M-Sa 10am-6pm. £3.95, students £3.)

In mid-August, the Ulster **Road Bowls Finals** are held throughout Armagh. In this popular local game, contestants compete to see who can throw an 8 oz. solid ball 4km in the fewest throws. **The Apple Blossom Festival** (☎ 3752 9600), in the second week of May, culminates in a lavish May Ball. On March 17, people come from far and near for the feast of the city's patron on **St. Patrick's Day.**

ANTRIM AND DERRY

A coastal road skirts the northern edge of Co. Antrim and Derry, traveling across a long distance of rapidly changing geological, commercial, and cultural phenomena. As the road meanders west from Belfast, stodgy and industrial Larne gives way to lovely little seaside towns. Near the midpoint of the island's northern coast, the fantastic Giant's Causeway spills out into the ocean. The road finally arrives at Derry, the North's second-largest city, where a turbulent history and recent redevelopment projects contribute to a fascinating cityscape.

LARNE

The **ferries** that depart for Scotland from the harbor are the only worthwhile reason to pass through industrial Larne. This route is less frequented since the institution of the more convenient SeaCat service to Belfast (see **By Ferry,** p. 33). **P&O Ferries** (☎ (0990) 980777) operates passages from Larne to Cairnryan, Scotland. Travelers should book ahead and arrive 45min. early, as there are always standby passengers waiting for your seat.

Trains (Belfast office ☎ 9089 9411 or 9023 0671, Larne office ☎ 2826 0604) chug from Central Station in **Belfast** to **Larne Harbour** (50min.; M-F 20 per day, Sa 16 per day, Su 6 per day; £3.20). Frequent **buses** (☎ 2827 2345) pull into Station Rd. from Laganside Station in **Belfast** (1½hr., express 50min.; M-F 14 per day, Sa 15 per day, Su 2 per day). Those departing on a ferry from Larne should ensure that their train or bus terminates in Larne Harbour rather than in Larne Town, a 15min. walk away. The **bus and train stations** lie adjacent to a roundabout two minutes from the town center; the tourist information centre and town center are well signposted from the roundabout. To reach town, take the first right outside of the ferry port. As the road curves left, it becomes Curran Rd. and then Main St. The **tourist information centre** (TIC), Narrow Gauge Rd., has a free town map and **Internet access.** (☎/fax 2826 0088. Open July-Aug. M-F 9am-6pm, Sa 9am-5pm; Sept.-Easter M-F 9am-5pm; Easter-June M-Sa 9am-5pm. 24hr. computerized info kiosk outside.) **Northern Bank** is at 19 Main St. (☎ 2827 6311. Open M 9:30am-5pm, Tu-F 10am-3:30pm, Sa 9:30am-12:30pm.) Larne's **post office** is at 98 Main St. (☎ 2826 0489. Open M-F 9am-5:30pm, Sa 9am-12:30pm.) **Postal code:** BT40 1RE.

While you're lingering for your ferry, there are a few food options. **Caffe Spice,** 7 Dunluce St., is especially popular with the younger crowd. (☎ 2826 9633. Open M-W 10am-10pm, Th-Sa 10am-10pm.) **Chekker's Wine Bar,** 33 Lower Cross St., serves a broad selection of bistro food in a take-your-time atmosphere. (☎ 2827 5305. Most meals £5; food served daily noon-9pm.)

GLENS OF ANTRIM

North of Larne, nine lush green valleys, or "glens," slither from the hills and high moors of Co. Antrim down to the seashore. The villages along the coast provide beds and basic sustenance for glen-wanderers. The A2 connects the small towns at the foot of each glen. The area's only hostel is in Cushendall.

GETTING AROUND. Bus service in the Glens is limited. Two **Ulsterbus** (Belfast ☎ 9032 0011, Larne ☎ 2827 2345) routes serve the area year-round. Bus #162 from **Belfast** stops in **Larne, Ballygally, Glenarm,** and **Carnlough** (M-F 7 per day, Sa 6 per day, Su 3 per day) and sometimes continues to **Waterfoot, Cushendall,** and **Cushendun** (M-F 5 per day, Sa 3 per day). Bus #150 connects to **Belfast** via **Waterfoot** and **Glenariff** (M-Sa 3 per day). The **Antrim Coaster** (#252) runs year-round, following the coast road from **Belfast** to **Coleraine,** stopping at every town along the way (daily 2 per day). **Cycling** in the Glens is fabulous. The coast road from Ballygally to Cushendun is scenic and flat; once the road leaves Cushendun, however, it becomes hilly enough to make even motorists groan. **Hitchhiking** is difficult, and the winding, narrow road between the cliffs and the sea wall make drivers feel less guilty about not stopping. *Let's Go* doesn't feel guilty for not approving of hitchhiking.

GLENARIFF

The village of Waterfoot guards Antrim's broadest glen, Glenariff, often deemed the most beautiful of the nine. Thackeray dubbed Glenariff "Switzerland in miniature." The glen is within the very large **Glenariff Forest Park,** four miles south of the village along Glenariff Rd. (the A43 toward Ballymena). The **bus** between **Cushendun** and **Ballymena** stops at the official park entrance (#150; M-F 5 per day, Sa 3 per day), where cars can park. (☎ 2175 8769. Open daily 10am-8pm. £3 per car or £1.50 per adult pedestrian, 50p child.) Once inside the park, you are confronted with a wealth of trails ranging from a ½ mi. to five-mile round-trip. The most stunning walk is the **Waterfall Trail,** marked by blue triangles: it follows the cascading, fern-lined Glenariff River from the park entrance to the Manor Lodge (1 mi. from entrance to lodge, 3 mi. round-trip). All of the walks officially begin and end at the car park, where you will also find the **Glenariff Tea House.** This bay-windowed restaurant offers fresh snacks (sandwiches £1.75), exotically seasoned meals (£5-6), and free **maps** of the park's trails. (☎ 2565 8769. Open daily Easter-Sept. 11am-6pm.) **Glenariff Forest Park Camping,** 98 Glenariff Rd., encourages travelers to pitch a tent. (☎ 2175 8232. Tents £10, off-season £7.)

CUSHENDALL

Cushendall is nicknamed the capital of the Glens, most probably because its village center consists of *four* streets instead of just one. The additional storefronts house a surplus of goods, services, and pubs. Moors and hills border the town.

GETTING THERE AND PRACTICAL INFORMATION. Ulsterbus comes in from **Larne,** bus #162 (M-F 5 per day, Sa-Su 1 per day). From July to August, the **Antrim Coaster** bus #252 runs through Cushendall toward **Portrush, Larne,** and Belfast (2 per day). **Ardclinis Activity Centre,** 11 High St. (☎ 2177 1340), **rents bikes** (£10 per day; deposit £50) and wetsuits for £5 per day. They also provide advice on hillwalking, canoeing, and gorge-walking.

The **tourist information centre,** 25 Mill St., sits near the bus stop at the Cushendun end of town. (☎ 2177 1180. Open July-Sept. M-F 10am-1pm and 2:30-5pm, Sa 10am-1pm; Oct. to mid.-Dec. and Feb.-June Tu-Sa 10am-1pm.) **Northern Bank** is at 5 Shore St. (☎ 2177 1243. Open M 9:30am-12:30pm and 1:30-5pm, Tu-F 10am-12:30pm and 1:30-3:30pm.) The **post office** is on Mill St. (☎ 2177 1201. Open M and W-F 9am-1pm and 2-5:30pm, Tu and Sa 9am-12:30pm.) **Postal code:** BT44.

ACCOMMODATIONS, FOOD, AND PUBS. Cushendall Youth Hostel (HINI), 42 Layde Rd., occupies a lovely spot just half a mile from town. Layde Rd. is the left-hand (uphill) fork from Shore Rd. (☎ 2177 1344. Continental breakfast £2.

Laundry £2. Bike rental £6 per day, £4 per half-day. Reception 7:30-10:30am and 5-11pm. 11:30pm curfew. Dorms £8.50-9.50, under 18 £7.50-8.50.) It's hard to imagine a warmer welcome than that of Mrs. O'Neill at ■ **Glendale,** 46 Coast Rd. (☎ 2177 1495. £16 per person. All rooms with bath.)

Spar Market, 2 Coast Rd., just past Bridge Rd., has a plentiful fruit and veggie selection. (☎ 2177 1763. Open daily 7:30am-10pm.) **Harry's,** 10-12 Mill St., serves bar snacks (around £5) and vegetarian main courses on request. (☎ 2177 2022. Food served daily noon-9:30pm.) ■ **Joe McCollam's,** 23 Mill St., a.k.a. "Johnny Joe's," features impromptu ballads: musicians usually gather Friday through Sunday nights.

🔘 **SIGHTS.** The sights are really in the miniscule, picturesque seaside village of **Cushendun,** five miles north of Cushendall on the A2. Buses head to Cushendun from Cushendall. In 1954, the National Trust bought the entire village, a white-washed and black-shuttered set of buildings lying by a vast beach and perforated by wonderful, murky **caves** carved within red sea cliffs. The largest cave, just past the Bay Hotel, serves as the only entrance to **Cave House,** which was built in 1820 and is currently closed to the public. **Mary McBride's,** 2 Main St. (☎ 2176 1511), used to be the *Guinness Book of World Records*'s "smallest bar in Europe." Today the original bar is still there, but it has been vigorously expanded to create a lounge.

CAUSEWAY COAST

Past Cushendun, 600 ft. sea-battered cliffs tower over white wave-lapped beaches and then give way to the spectacular Giant's Causeway. The A2, suitable for cycling, is the major thoroughfare between the main towns along the Causeway.

📧 **GETTING AROUND. Ulsterbus** #172 runs along the coast to **Ballycastle** (1hr., 7 per day). In good summer weather, the open-topped orange **Bushmills Bus** outlines the coast between **Coleraine,** 5 mi. south of Portrush, and **Giant's Causeway.** (Coleraine bus station, ☎ (01265) 7043 3334. July-Aug. 5 per day.) The summertime **Antrim Coaster** bus (Belfast Bus Station, ☎ 9033 3000) runs up the coast from **Belfast** to **Portstewart** via just about every town in *Let's Go* (late June to early July M-Sa 2 per day; early July to late Sept. daily 2 per day). Those **hitchhiking** along the A2 or the marginally quicker inland roads find that the lack of cars and high ratio of tourists slows them down. *Let's Go* is not slow to discourage hitchhiking.

BALLYCASTLE

The Causeway Coast leaves the sleepy Glens behind when it hits Ballycastle, a bubbly seaside town that shelters Giant's Causeway-bound tourists. Warm summer weekends bring carloads of locals to its beaches; music-lovers flock to its pubs every summer weekend.

📧 **GETTING THERE. Ulsterbus** stops at the Marine Hotel on the waterfront, coming from: **Cushendall** (50min., M-F 1 per day) and **Belfast** (3hr., 6 per day). In summer, Ulsterbus's **Antrim Coaster** runs through the **Glens of Antrim** from **Belfast** (full trip 3½-4hr.; 2 per day). **Argyll and Antrim Steam Packet Co.** (☎ (08705) 523523) runs **ferries** between Ballycastle and **Campbeltown, Scotland** (3hr.; July-Oct. 19 2 per day in each direction; £20-25, vehicles and driver £80-105). **Northern Auto Factors,** 41 Castle St., **rents bikes.** (☎ 2076 3748. £6 per day.) For a **taxi,** call ☎ 2076 2822.

📧 **ORIENTATION AND PRACTICAL INFORMATION.** Ballycastle's main street runs perpendicular to the waterfront. It starts at the ocean as **Quay Rd.,** becomes **Ann St.,** and then turns into **Castle St.** as its passes **The Diamond.** As Quay Rd. meets the water, the road takes a sharp left onto **North St.,** where more stores and food await; a right from Quay puts you on **Mary Rd.,** site of the tourist information centre. A park sits on the harbor; to its west is the ferry service.

The **tourist information centre** is in Sheskburn House, 7 Mary St., with 24hr. computerized information outside. (☎ 2076 2024. Open July-Aug. M-F 9:30am-7pm, Sa 10am-6pm, Su 2-6pm; Sept.-June M-F 9:30am-5pm.) Services include: **First Trust**

Bank, Ann St. (☎ 2076 3326; open M-Tu and Th-F 9:30am-4:30pm, W 10am-4:30pm); the **Dalriada Hospital,** Coleraine Rd. (☎ 2076 2666); and the **post office,** 3 Ann St. (☎ 2076 2519; open M-Tu and Th-F 9am-1pm and 2-5:30pm, W 9am-1pm, Sa 9am-12:30pm). **Postal Code:** BT54 6AA.

▓▓▓ ACCOMMODATIONS, FOOD, AND PUBS. Watch out for the Ould Lammas Fair on the last Monday and Tuesday in August. **B&Bs** fill almost a year in advance, and hostel beds fill weeks before the big event. The 40-bed **Castle Hostel (IHH),** 62 Quay Rd., slightly out of town, next to the Marine Hotel, has a relaxed atmosphere. (☎ 2076 2337. Laundry £1. Dorms £7; private rooms £8.50 per person.) **Cúchulainn House,** 56 Quay Rd., provides fresh fruit and local baked goods for breakfast. (☎ 2076 2252. Singles £16.50, doubles with bath £39.) At **Fragrens,** 34 Quay Rd., Mrs. Greene offers a fruit bowl at breakfast in her 17th-century home, one of Ballycastle's oldest. (☎ 2076 2168. £15 per person, with bath £17.)

Brady's Supermarket, 54 Castle St., is a 10min. walk from the hostels. (☎ 2076 2268. Open daily 8am-10pm.) **Herald's,** 22 Ann St., kindly doles out huge portions at cheap prices. (☎ 2076 9064. Main courses £2-3. Open daily 8am-9pm.) **Wysner's,** 16 Ann St., sets its sights on healthy meals. (☎ 2076 2372. Lunch around £5, dinner special £8-9. Open M-Tu and Th-F 9am-5pm, plus 7-9pm F-Sa.)

Trad is in vogue year-round in Ballycastle, but summer nights promise several venues nightly. Tourists head for tiny, fire-warmed **House of McDonnell,** 71 Castle St. (☎ 2076 2975), for trad on Fridays; it also features folk on Saturday and spontaneous trad other days of the week. Guinness guzzlers fill the **Boyd Arms,** 4 The Diamond (☎ 2076 2364), to enjoy trad on Friday nights.

NEAR BALLYCASTLE: RATHLIN ISLAND. Just off the coast at Ballycastle, bumpy, boomerang-shaped **Rathlin Island** ("Fort of the Sea") is the ultimate in escapism for 20,000 puffins, the odd golden eagle, 100 human inhabitants, and four daily ferryloads of tourists. Its windy surface supports few trees, but it's a paradise of orchids and purple heather. For a more complete presentation of the island's intricately intertwined history and myths, visit the island's own **Boat House Heritage Centre** at the opposite end of the harbor from the ferry. (☎ 2076 3951. Open May-Aug. daily 11:30am-4:30pm, other months by arrangement. 50p, children free.) The **lighthouse** is the best place from which to view birds, but it's accessible only with the warden's supervision; call Liam McFaul (☎ 2076 3948) in advance. **Caledonian MacBrayne** ("Cal-Mac") runs a ferry service from Ballycastle to the island. The small office at the Ballycastle pier, open before each departure, sells tickets. (☎ 2076 2024.) **McCuaig's Bar** (☎ 2076 3974) sometimes allows free **camping** on its grounds. The bar is the single entertainment center and food source for the entire island. (Sandwiches and toasties £1.60-2, burgers £1.90, a limited selection of main courses around £5. Served 9am-9pm.) The head of Duncan, a bull who went crazy and was shot in 1880, is the showpiece of the pub's interior.

▓ GIANT'S CAUSEWAY

Advertised as the eighth natural wonder of the world, the Giant's Causeway is Northern Ireland's most famous sight. Be warned that 2000 visitors arrive each day in July and August. A spillage of 40,000 hexagonal columns of basalt form a 60-million-year-old honeycomb path from the foot of the cliffs far into the sea. Geologists have decided that the Causeway resulted from an unusually steady cooling of lava that stimulated crystallization. **Giant's Causeway Visitors Centre** sits at the pedestrian entranceway to the Causeway from the carpark. Besides offering the usual tourist information, a bureau de change, and a post office, it sells an excellent leaflet of walks (75p) that will guide you the eight miles back to Whitepark Bay or along several shorter circular walks. (☎ 2073 1855. Center open daily June 10am-6pm; July-Aug. 10am-7pm; Mar.-May and Sept. 10am-5pm; Nov.-Feb. 10am-4:30pm. Parking £3 per car.) Every 15min., it runs Causeway Coaster minibuses the half-mile to the columns (60p, £1 return). Many paths loop to and from the Causeway. Two begin at the Visitors Centre, one passing along the high cliffs and another along the low coast close to the Causeway. The paths meet after one mile.

652 ■ ANTRIM AND DERRY

DERRY (LONDONDERRY)

Derry competes with Dublin for the most long-lasting contribution to Irish political history. The city itself was built at the beginning of the 17th century, when the English seized land from native Catholic residents for Protestant settlers from England and Scotland. Derry itself was renamed on the maps as "Londonderry" to assert its new Anglo-Irish identity. When King James II approached the city in 1689, the Protestant inhabitants of the city rallied around the cause of his opponent, King William of Orange; the ensuing Siege of Derry lasted 105 days. The creation of the Republic made Derry a border city, and a Catholic majority made it a headache for Unionist leaders; it became the locus of some of the most blatant civil-rights violations and religious discrimination. The civil rights marches that sparked the Troubles originated here in 1968 (see p. 631).

Modern Derry is in the middle of a largely successful effort to cast off the legacy of the Troubles. Violence still erupts occasionally during the marching season and other contentious sectarian events, but recent years have seen more peaceful coexistence among its residents. The depiction of Derry's history in murals makes for fascinating sights, as do less contentious aspects of the city, including its brilliant music scene, thriving artistic community, and irrepressible pub life.

▐ GETTING THERE AND GETTING AROUND

Trains: Duke St., Waterside (☎ 7134 2228), on the east bank. From **Belfast** (3hr., M-Sa 6-7, Su 3 per day, £6.40). A free **Rail-Link bus** connects the bus and train stations.

Buses: Most buses stop on Foyle St. between the walled city and the river. **Ulsterbus** (☎ 7126 2261) comes from all destinations in the North and some in the Republic, including **Belfast** (1½-3hr.; M-Sa 15 per day, Su 8 per day; £7.50) and **Dublin, Republic of Ireland** (M-Sa 5 per day, Su 3 per day; £11). **Lough Swilly** (☎ 7126 2017) heads from Co. Donegal, including **Malin Head** (1½hr.; M-F 2 per day, Sa 3 per day; £6); and **Letterkenny** (1hr., M-Sa 11 per day, £4.20). **Northwest Busways** (☎ (077) 82619) comes into Patrick St. from **Inishowen** and **Malin Head** (2 per day, £4.20).

Taxis: City Cabs, William St. (☎ 7126 4466).

Car Rental: Ford Rent-a-Car, 173 Strand Rd. (☎ 7136 0420). 25+. Open July-Aug. M-F 9am-5:30pm, Sa 9am-4pm; Sept.-June M-F 9am-5:30pm, Sa 9am-1pm.

Bike Rental: Rent-a-Bike, 245 Lone Moor Rd. (☎ 7128 7128). Sells a range of accessories and offers a pick-up service. £9 per day, £35 per week; passport or £50 deposit.

✦ ❼ ORIENTATION AND PRACTICAL INFORMATION

Derry straddles the **River Foyle**. The **city center** lies on the Foyle's western banks. The old city within the medieval walls is now Derry's center, with a pedestrian shopping district around **Waterloo St.** In the center of the old city lies **The Diamond,** from which radiate four main streets: **Shipquay St.** to the northeast, **Butcher St.** to the northwest, **Bishop St.** to the southwest, and **Ferryquay** to the southeast. The famous Catholic **Bogside** neighborhood is west of the city walls. The residential areas of the Foyle's western bank are primarily Catholic, while most Protestants live on the housing estates known as the **Waterside,** on the eastern bank.

Tourist Information Centre: 44 Foyle St. (☎ 7126 7284), inside the Derry Visitor and Convention Bureau. Books accommodations throughout the island. **Bord Fáilte** (☎ 7136 9501) keeps a desk here, too. Open July-Sept. M-F 9am-7pm, Sa 10am-6pm, Su 10am-5pm; Oct.-Easter M-F 9am-5pm; Easter-June M-F 9am-5pm, Sa 10am-5pm.

Tours: Walking tours provide an introduction to the city's history-laden geography. **Derry Visitor and Convention Bureau Guided Walking Tours** (☎ 7126 7284), **Northern Ireland Tours and Guides Limited** (☎ 7128 9051), and **Foyle Civic Bus Tours** (☎ 7126 7284) all run good tours.

Budget Travel: usit, Ferryquay St. (☎ 7137 1888). ISICs, TravelSave stamps, and other discount cards and tickets. Open M-F 9:30am-5:30pm, Sa 10am-1pm.

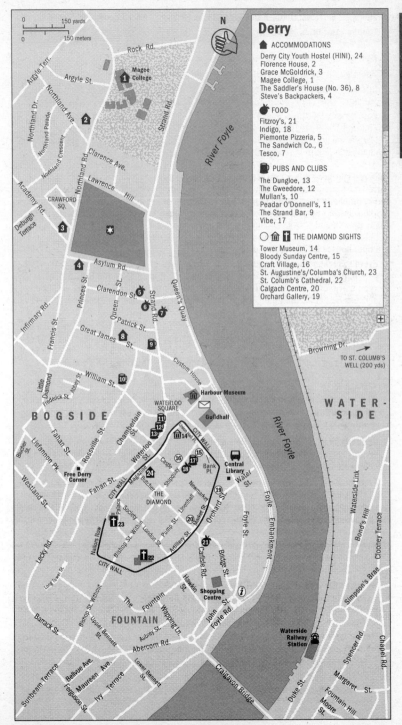

Derry

ACCOMMODATIONS

Derry City Youth Hostel (HINI), 24
Florence House, 2
Grace McGoldrick, 3
Magee College, 1
The Saddler's House (No. 36), 8
Steve's Backpackers, 4

FOOD

Fitzroy's, 21
Indigo, 18
Piemonte Pizzeria, 5
The Sandwich Co., 6
Tesco, 7

PUBS AND CLUBS

The Dungloe, 13
The Gweedore, 12
Mullan's, 10
Peadar O'Donnell's, 11
The Strand Bar, 9
Vibe, 17

THE DIAMOND SIGHTS

Tower Museum, 14
Bloody Sunday Centre, 15
Craft Village, 16
St. Augustine's/Columba's Church, 23
St. Columb's Cathedral, 22
Calgach Centre, 20
Orchard Gallery, 19

Financial Services: Ulster Bank, Guildhall Sq. (☎ 7126 1882). Open M-F 9:30am-4:30pm.

Launderette: Duds 'n' Suds, 141 Strand Rd. (☎ 7126 6006). Pool table and TV. Wash and dry £3.60. Open M-F 8am-9pm, Sa 8am-6pm. Last wash 1½hr. before closing.

Police: Strand Rd. (☎ 7136 7337).

Hospital: Altnagelvin Hospital, Glenshane Rd. (☎ 7134 5171).

Internet Access: Central Library, Foyle St. (☎ 7127 2300). Free until 1pm, £2.50 per hr. after. Open Tu-W and F 9:15am-5:30pm, M and Th 9:15am-8pm, Sa 9:15am-5pm.

Post Office: 3 Custom House St. (☎ 7136 2563). Open M 8:30am-5:30pm, Tu-F 9am-5:30pm, Sa 9am-12:30pm. Unless addressed to 3 Custom House St., Poste Restante letters will go to the Postal Sorting Office (☎ 7136 2577) on the corner of Great James and Little James St. **Postal Code:** BT48 6AA.

ACCOMMODATIONS

▨ **The Saddler's House (No. 36),** 36 Great James St. (☎ 7126 9691). Friendly, historically knowledgeable owners make their Victorian house into your ultimate comfort zone. Fresh fruit and cheese and homemade jam at breakfast. The same couple also runs **The Merchant's House,** an award-winning, restored Georgian townhouse at 16 Queen St. Both houses £20, with bath £25.

Steve's Backpackers, 4 Asylum Rd. (☎ 7137 7989 or 7137 0011). Down Strand Rd. 7min. from the city center; Asylum Rd. is on the left just before the RUC station. Once you stay, you'll have a hard time leaving—the 5th night is free. Laundry £3. Internet access £3 per hr. 6pm-8am, £4 per hr. 8am-6pm. £2 key deposit. Dorms £7.50.

Derry City Youth Hostel (HINI), Magazine St. (☎ 7128 4100). A sky-high mural on the side of the building identifies this large and institutional hostel located within the city walls. 24hr. access with night watchman. Lockers available; bring your own lock. Wheelchair accessible. Breakfast £1.50-2.50. Towels 50p. Laundry £3.50. Check-out 10am. 8- to 10-bed dorms £7.50; 3- to 10-bed dorms with bath £8.50; B&B with bath £15.

FOOD

Tesco supermarket, in the Quayside Shopping Center, is a few minutes walk from the walled city along Strand Rd. (Open M-Sa 8:30am-9pm, Su 1-6pm.)

▨ **Rhubarb and Custard,** Custom House St. (☎ 7137 7977), near the Guildhall. This colorfully rustic cafe sells sandwiches (£2) and a filling 2-course lunch special (£3). Lots of vegetarian dishes. Open M-Sa 9am-5pm.

Cappuccinos, 31 Foyle St. (☎ 7137 0059). Green paisley wallpaper makes you wax nostalgic for Grandma's. £2.95 breakfast special (8am-noon). Open M-Sa 8am-6pm.

Indigo, 27 Shipquay St. (☎ 7127 1011), serves tasty international foods in a stylish interior. Main courses £7-9, Su-W 2-course for 2 £15. Open daily 11am-11pm.

SIGHTS

THE WALLS. Derry's city walls, 18 ft. high and 20 ft. thick, were erected between 1614 and 1619. They have never been breached, hence Derry's nickname "the Maiden City." A walk along the top of this mile-long perimeter takes about 20 minutes. The stone tower along the southeast wall past New Gate was built to protect **St. Columb's Cathedral,** the symbolic focus of the city's Protestant defenders. Stuck in the center of the southwest wall, **Bishop's Gate** was remodeled in 1789 into an ornate triumphal gate in honor of William of Orange.

ST. COLUMB'S CATHEDRAL. Built between 1628 and 1633, this was the first purpose-built Protestant cathedral in Britain or Ireland (all the older ones were confiscated Catholic cathedrals). The original lead-coated wood spire was in disrepair at the time of the Great Siege, so the city's defenders removed its lead and smelted it into bullets and cannonballs. Like many Protestant churches in the North, St. Columb's is bedecked with war banners, including flags from the Crimean War, the World Wars, and the two yellow flags captured from the French at the Great Siege. A tiny, museum-like **chapterhouse** at the back of the church displays the original locks and keys of the four main city gates, and relics from the 1689 siege. *(Off Bishop St. in the southwest corner of the city. ☎ 7126 7313. Open Apr.-Oct. M-Sa 9am-5pm, Nov.-Mar. M-Sa 9am-4pm. £1 suggested donation for cathedral; chapterhouse 50p.)*

TOWER MUSEUM. Engaging walk-through dioramas and audiovisual displays relay Derry's long history. A series of short videos illustrate Derry's economic, political, and cultural past. The whole museum deserves at least two hours. *(Union Hall Place, just inside Magazine Gate. ☎ 7137 2411. Open July-Aug. M-Sa 10am-5pm, Su 2-5pm; Sept.-June Tu-Sa 10am-5pm. Last entrance 4:30pm. £3.75, students and seniors £1.25.)*

THE FOUNTAIN ESTATE. The Protestant Fountain estate is reached from the walled city by exiting through the left side of Bishop's Gate; it is contained by Bishop St., Upper Bennett St., Abercorn St., and Hawkin St. This small area of only 600 residents holds the more interesting Protestant murals.

THE BOGSIDE. This famous Catholic neighborhood is easily recognizable. A huge sign just west of the city walls at the junction of Fahan St. and Rossville Sq. declares "You Are Now Entering Free Derry." It was originally painted in 1969 on the end of a row-house; the houses of the block have since been knocked down, but this endwall remains with a frequently repainted but never reworded message. This powerful mural is surrounded by other striking nationalist artistic creations, and the spot is referred to as **Free Derry Corner.** Nearby, a stone monument commemorates the 14 protesters shot dead on Bloody Sunday.

PUBS AND ENTERTAINMENT

▓ **Peadar O'Donnell's,** 53 Waterloo St. (☎ 7137 2318). Named for the famous Donegal Socialist who organized the Irish Transport and General Workers Union and took an active role in the 1921 Irish Civil War. Banners and sashes of all nationalities and orders cover the ceiling, while *craic* covers the ground level. Live trad nightly. The back door has connected to **The Gweedore,** 59-61 Waterloo St. (☎ 7126 3513), since Famine times. Hosts rock, bluegrass, and funk venues nightly.

▓ **Mullan's,** corner of William and Rossville St. An incredible pub with idiosyncratically lavish decor, from stained-glass ceilings and bronzed lion statues to plasma flat-screen TVs. Hosts excellent jazz many nights of the week.

  The Townsman, 33 Shipquay St. (☎ 7126 0820). Attracts a young and colorful crowd to its surreal decorative scheme. 20 purple pool tables and an open ceiling (in nice weather) over the bar. DJs nightly. Weekend cover £5-6.

The Playhouse, 5-7 Artillery St., specializes in the work of young playwrights. (☎ 7126 8027. £3-7.) St. Columb's Hall, Orchard St., houses the **Orchard Cinema,** which screens cult and classic films. (☎ 7126 7789. £3.50, students £2.50.)

REPUBLIC OF IRELAND (ÉIRE)

Literary imaginations have immortalized Ireland's natural scenery from the ancient times of Celtic bards to Yeats and Joyce. The largely agricultural and sparsely populated island has experienced little physical change over thousands of centuries, yet amid stunning seascapes and misty mountains lie pockets of civilization, ranging in size from one-street villages to small market towns to Dublin and a handful of cities, all inspiration for some of the finest writing ever to grace the English language. For international visitors, today's Ireland promises an old-world welcome alongside the edge of urban countercultures.

It's useful to know that the island is traditionally divided into four provinces: Leinster, the east and southeast; Munster, the southwest; Connacht, the province west of the river Shannon; and Ulster, the north. Six of Ulster's nine counties make up Northern Ireland, part of the United Kingdom. "Ireland" can mean the whole island or the Republic, depending on who's listening. It's best to refer to "Northern Ireland" or "the North" and "the Republic." "Southern Ireland" is not a viable term.

For even more detailed coverage of the Emerald Isle, run—don't walk—to your nearest book emporium for a copy of the lovely *Let's Go: Ireland 2001*.

HIGHLIGHTS OF THE REPUBLIC OF IRELAND

DUBLIN Admire the **Book of Kells** at **Trinity College** (p. 677), windowshop on **Grafton Street** (p. 684), then head around the corner to **Temple Bar** for a night of tomfoolery in its pubs and clubs (p. 678).

WICKLOW MOUNTAINS Hike through the splendid vistas of the Wicklow Way (p. 691).

RING OF KERRY Run the peninsula's circuit (p. 711), taking in exquisite mountains, lakes, and forests in **Killarney National Park** (p. 711).

DINGLE PENINSULA Explore the stunning coastline by bike (p. 714).

ARAN ISLANDS Glimpse an older way of life, from the ringforts of pre-Christian settlers to the *curraghs* of today's fishermen (p. 722).

CO. CLARE Shudder at the sheer drop from the spectacular **Cliffs of Moher** (p. 721), then head for the otherworldly landscape of the **Burren** (p. 722).

GALWAY Down pints of Guinness while you enjoy the musical vigor and copious *craic* of the city's myriad pubs (p. 725).

CO. DONEGAL Brush up on your Gaelic in **Gweedore**, Ireland's largest *gaeltacht* (p. 741), and hike past Europe's highest sea cliffs at **Slieve League** (p. 739).

LIFE AND TIMES

HISTORY

> Books about Ireland that begin with its history have a tendency to remain unread.
> The misunderstandings are so many.
> —attributed to Frank O'Connor (1903-1966)

ANCIENT HISTORY

What little knowledge historians have of ancient Irish culture they have gleaned from the fragile remains of its stone structures, landscaping, and metalware.

Ireland's first settlers came from Britain in about 7000 BC. These Neolithic mound-builders founded an agrarian civilization, and left behind various structures still visible on the Irish landscape. **Dolmens,** arrangements of enormous stones to create table-like forms, were probably created as shrines. **Passage graves** are orna-mented underground stone hallways and chambers containing corpses and ciner-ary urns (see **Newgrange,** p. 694). **Stone circles** are rings of pint-sized gravestones probably marking spots of religious importance, including passage graves. Bronze blazed into Ireland around 2000 BC, and with it the rise of a warrior aristocracy. In the first two centuries of the **Bronze Age** (900-700 BC), known as the Irish Golden Age, Irish culture flowered, and the old stone structures evolved into new types, including **ringforts** (see **Dún Aengus,** p. 723), protective walls that circled encamp-ments and are still scattered across Ireland and many of its islands. The **Celts** began their main migration to Ireland from central Europe around 600 BC, and kept coming for the next 600 years. Probably initially named by the Greeks as *Keltoi* or "hidden people" (because of their reluctance to write down their great stores of scholarship and knowledge), the Celts settled Ireland as the remotest extremity of a pan-European migration that stretched east to Asia Minor. They prospered on the peaceful isle, speaking Old Irish and living in small farming communities organized under regional chieftains.

THE MIDDLE AGES

Ireland was Christianized in piecemeal fashion by a series of hopeful missionaries, starting most famously with **St. Patrick** in the 5th century. Missionaries and monks entering Ireland after the 5th century introduced a new architectural style that included the Viking-inspired **round tower.** Built as fortifications against invaders, the sturdy towers survive in the dozens. **High crosses,** or Celtic crosses, are a hybridization of Christian and Celtic esthetics: their form combined the cross with a circle to win the devotion of the native sun-worshipping pagans. The enormous **monastic cities** of the 6th to 8th centuries earned Ireland its reputation as the "land of saints and scholars." The monks wrote illuminated gospels, including the early 9th-century **Book of Kells.** Irish missionaries converted (and reconverted) much of Europe to Christianity, although the Early Irish Church remained decidedly inde-pendent of Rome. The golden age of Irish scholasticism was interrupted by **Viking invasions** in the 9th and 10th centuries. The Vikings founded Dublin, and many eventually settled in Ireland after long periods of raiding.

In the following years, the clans of Ireland fought ferociously amongst them-selves. **Dermot MacMurrough** fought for the crown of High King and made the mis-take of seeking the assistance of Norman nobles from England in reconquering Leinster. Richard de Clare, known popularly as **Strongbow,** was all too willing to help. Strongbow and his Anglo-Normans arrived in 1169 and cut a bloody swath through south Leinster. Strongbow married Dermot's daughter **Aoife** after Der-mot's death in 1171, and he seemed ready to proclaim an independent Norman kingdom in Ireland. Instead, he affirmed his loyalty to King Henry II and gener-ously offered to govern Leinster on England's behalf, beginning English control of Irish land. The feudal period that followed saw constant power struggles between Gaelic and Norman-descended English lords. The fiefdoms were hardly divided culturally: they built similar castles, ate similar foods, appreciated the same poets, and hired the same mercenaries. Overseas, the English crown fretted over this cul-tural cross-pollination, and in 1366 it sponsored the notorious **Statutes of Kilkenny** that banned English colonists from speaking Irish, wearing Irish styles of dress, or marrying natives, and forbade the Irish from entering walled cities.

When Henry VIII broke with the Catholic Church to create the Church of England, a newly convened Dublin Parliament passed the 1537 **Irish Supremacy Act,** which declared Henry head of the Protestant **Church of Ireland,** and effectively made the island property of the Crown. The lords of Ireland, however, both Old English and Gaelic, wished to remain loyal both to Catholicism and to the Crown—a near-impossible order to fill. A reactionary uprising in Munster in 1579 planted in English heads the idea that Irish land had to be directly controlled by

REPUBLIC OF IRELAND

The Counties of the Republic and Northern Ireland

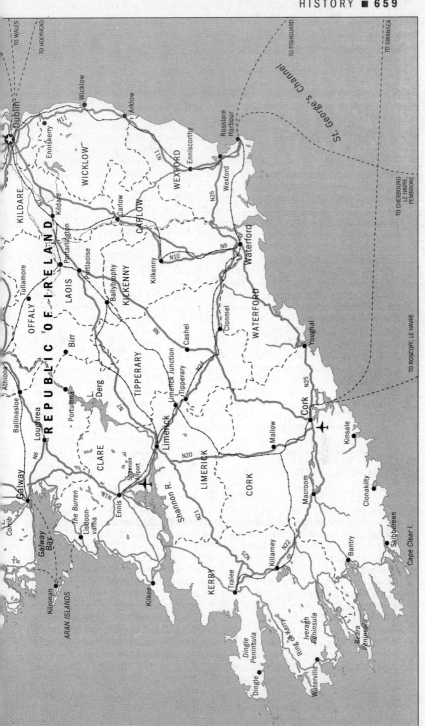

Protestants if it were to be considered safe and loyal. In defiance of the crown, **Hugh O'Neill,** an Ulster earl, raised an army of thousands in open rebellion in the late 1590s. Gaelic lords supported him, but the Old English lords were divided. Their power ultimately broken, O'Neill and the rest of the major Gaelic lords soared out of Ireland in 1607 in what came to be known as the **Flight of the Earls.** The English took control of the land and parceled it out to Protestants.

PLANTATION

The English project of dispossessing Catholics of their land and "planting" Ireland with Protestants was most successful in Ulster. Scottish Presbyterian tenants and laborers joined the expected mix of adventurers, ne'er-do-wells, and ex-soldiers. The project in the North became known as the **Ulster Plantation.** The now landless Irish revolted in Ulster in 1641 under a loose group of Gaelic-Irish leaders. The rebels advanced south, and in 1642 formed the **Confederation of Kilkenny,** an uneasy alliance of Irish and Old English lords. Negotiations between the Confederation and King Charles ended with **Oliver Cromwell's** victory in England and his arrival in Ireland at the head of a Puritan army. Catholics were massacred and whole towns razed as the Confederation dwindled away. Entire tracts of land were confiscated and handed out to soldiers and Protestant adventurers. The native Irish landowners had the options of going "to hell or to Connacht," the desolate and infertile region in Ireland's west. By 1660, the vast majority of Irish land was owned, maintained, and policed by Protestant immigrants.

Thirty years after the English Civil War, English political disruption again resulted in Irish bloodshed. Catholic **James II,** driven from England by the Protestant **William of Orange** in the Glorious Revolution of 1688, came to Ireland with his army, intending to gather military support to reclaim his throne. James's actions spurred vicious battles between Jacobites (James's supporters) and Williamites. In 1689, James attempted to take the northern city of Derry, where a young band of **Apprentice Boys** (now Loyalist icons) closed the gates at his approach. The ensuing **Siege of Derry** lasted 105 days. The war between William and James ended on July 12, 1690 at the **Battle of the Boyne,** with James's defeat and exile. The battle is still celebrated by many Northern Protestants in marches that take place on July 12, Orange Day. The war's end delivered the **Treaty of Limerick,** which ambiguously promised Catholics undelivered civil rights. Instead, the **Penal Laws,** enacted in the 18th century, further limited Catholics economically and banned the public practice of their religion, even though they comprised 90% of the island's population.

THE ASCENDANCY

The newly secure Anglo-Irish elite built their own culture in Dublin and the surrounding Pale. The term **"Ascendancy"** was coined to describe a social elite whose distinction depended upon Anglicanism. Within this exclusive social structure, such thinkers as **Bishop George Berkeley** and **Edmund Burke** rose to prominence, and **Trinity College, Dublin** flourished as the quintessential institution of the Ascendancy. Despite their cultural ties, many aristocrats felt little political allegiance to England. **Jonathan Swift** campaigned for Irish rights and against dependency upon England, and the American and French Revolutions inspired notions of independence in small political organizations such as the **United Irishmen.** Their Protestant leader, **Theobald Wolfe Tone,** hoped that a general uprising would create an independent, non-sectarian Ireland. In May 1798, the rebels made their last stand at **Vinegar Hill,** near Enniscorthy in Co. Wexford (see p. 699); they fell by the thousands. The rebels' actions ended any hopes England had held of making Irish society less volatile by relaxing anti-Catholic laws. The 1801 **Act of Union** dissolved the Dublin Parliament and created "The United Kingdom of Great Britain and Ireland."

Union meant Irish representatives now held seats in the British parliament. The Irish elected Catholic **Daniel O'Connell** to Parliament in 1829, essentially forcing Westminster to repeal the remaining anti-Catholic laws that would have barred him from taking his seat. O'Connell acquired the nickname "The Liberator," and his efforts within Parliament allotted money to improve Irish living conditions, health care, and trade. The 1830s brought the passage of the **Irish Poor Law Act,** which established workhouses to provide services for impoverished citizens. In 1836, the police force was centralized under the title **Royal Irish Constabulary,** which later became the model for the British Empire's colonial police forces.

THE FAMINE AND INDEPENDENCE MOVEMENTS

In the first half of the 19th century, the potato was the only crop capable of supporting the Irish population. This reliance had devastating effects when the potato fell prey to fungal disease. The **Great Famine,** which was far harsher than any blight or crop failure earlier that century, lasted roughly from 1847 to 1851. In that short time, an estimated two to three million people died, and another million emigrated. While the Irish were eating grass, the British shipped thousands of pounds of grain from the island. The depopulation of the island continued after the 1840s as **emigration** became an Irish way of life. The **Encumbered Estates Act** began the 50-year process of removing the landlord class—a process which was continued by a series of Land Acts and the Congested Districts Board, which converted Ireland, with the exception of Dublin and northeast Ulster, into a nation of conservative, culturally uniform, Catholic smallholders.

British injustice fueled the formation of angry nationalist groups. 1858 saw the founding of the **Fenians,** a secret society aimed at the violent removal of the British. In 1870, Isaac Butt founded the **Irish Home Rule Party.** Its members adopted obstructionist tactics. Home Ruler **Charles Stewart Parnell** was a charismatic Protestant aristocrat, and backed by Parnell's invigorated Irish party, British Prime Minister Gladstone introduced a **Home Rule Bill,** which was defeated. Meanwhile, various groups tried to revive what they took to be essential "Gaelic" culture, unpolluted by foreign influence. Arthur Griffith, who advocated Irish abstention from British politics, began a tiny movement and little-read newspaper, which went by the name **Sinn Féin** (SHIN FAYN), meaning "Ourselves Alone." As the Home Rule movement grew, so did resistance to it. Between 1910 and 1913, thousands of Northern Protestants opposing Home Rule joined mass rallies and organized into a quasi-militia named the **Ulster Volunteer Force (UVF).** Nationalists led by **Eoin MacNeill** in Dublin responded in 1913 by creating the **Irish Volunteers.**

THE EASTER RISING AND INDEPENDENCE

In the summer of 1914, Irish Home Rule seemed imminent and Ulster ready to go up in flames. However, domestic concerns were subsumed by World War I, at least until the arrival on the political scene of poet and schoolteacher **Padraig Pearse.** Pearse believed that if a small cache of committed men died publicly and violently as martyrs for Ireland, then the entire population of the island would join in the struggle for independence. Fenian leaders planned to receive a shipment of German arms for use in a nationwide revolt on **Easter Sunday, 1916**. MacNeill and most Fenian leaders had been thinking in terms of military success, which at that point was clearly impossible, but Pearse's followers wanted martyrdom. On Sunday the Pearse group met and decided to stage the uprising on the following Monday, April 24, in Dublin. Pearse, James Connolly, and about one thousand others seized the **General Post Office** on O'Connell St., read aloud a "Proclamation of the Republic of Ireland," and held out through five days of fighting in downtown Dublin. Dubliners initially saw the Easter rebels as criminals, since their only tangible accomplishment was massive property damage.

The harsh reaction of the British martial-law administration to Easter Sunday turned popular opinion on its head. Over ten days in May, fifteen "ringleaders" received the death sentence, among them Pearse and Connolly. **Éamon de Valera** was spared because the British wrongly thought him an American citizen. By June Pearse's prophecy proved true: the public had grown sympathetic to the martyrs and increasingly anti-British. In 1917, the Volunteers reorganized under master spy and Fenian bigwig **Michael Collins.** The Sinn Féin party, falsely associated with the Rising, became the political voice of military Nationalism. Collins brought the Volunteers to Sinn Féin, and de Valera became the party president. Extremist Irish

Volunteers became known as the **Irish Republican Army (IRA),** which functioned as the military arm of the Sinn Féin government. The new government fought the **War of Independence** against the British, who reinforced their police with the notoriously brutal **Black and Tans**—demobilized soldiers whose nickname referred to their patched-together uniforms.

In 1920 British Prime Minister Lloyd George, supported by US President Wilson, passed the **Government of Ireland Act,** which divided the island into Northern Ireland and Southern Ireland, two partially self-governing areas within the UK. Hurried negotiations produced the **Anglo-Irish Treaty,** which created a 26-county Irish Free State while recognizing British rule over the northern counties. The population split on whether to accept the treaty. Collins said yes; de Valera said no. When the representative parliament voted yes, de Valera resigned and Arthur Griffith assumed the presidency. A portion of the IRA, led by **General Rory O'Connor,** opposed the treaty. Two years of **civil war** followed, tearing up the countryside and dividing the population. The pro-treaty government won, but Griffith died suddenly and Collins was assassinated before the end of 1922. The dwindling minority of anti-treaty IRA officers went into hiding.

THE DE VALERA ERA

Under the guidance of Éamon de Valera, the government ended armed resistance by May 1923, imprisoned Republican insurgents, and executed 77 of them. In 1927 de Valera founded his own political party, **Fianna Fáil,** in order to participate in government and oppose the treaty nonviolently. Fianna Fáil won the 1932 election, and de Valera held power for much of the next 20 years. De Valera and the voters approved the permanent Irish Constitution in 1937. It declared the state's name to be Éire and established the country's legislative structure, which consists of two chambers, both with five year terms. The **Taoiseach** (TEE-shuch; Prime Minister) and **Tánaiste** (tah-NESH-tuh; Deputy Prime Minister) lead a Cabinet, while the **President** is the ceremonial head of state, elected to a seven-year term.

Ireland maintained neutrality during World War II, despite German air raids on Dublin and pressure from US President Roosevelt. While the young government lacked the monetary and military strength to have a large effect on the war, Éire's expression of neutrality effectively assisted the Allies. When the Germans fire bombed Belfast in 1941, Dublin's fire brigade came to the rescue. A government under **John Costello**'s Fine Gael party in 1948 officially proclaimed "the Republic of Ireland," ending British Commonwealth membership. Britain recognized the Republic in 1949 but declared that the UK would maintain control over Ulster.

RECENT HISTORY (1960-1998)

By reaching out Ireland has kept its young people in. In the 1960s, increased contact with the rest of the world meant slowed emigration and accelerated economic growth, resulting in increased national confidence. In 1967, the government introduced free secondary education, including state grants for privately owned schools; in 1968, it introduced free university education for those below a certain income level. Tourism became a major source of employment. Ireland entered the European Economic Community, now the **European Union** (EU), in 1973. In 1985, the **Anglo-Irish agreement** granted the Republic an official role in Northern negotiations. In 1990 the Republic broke progressive social and political ground when it elected its first female president, **Mary Robinson.** The new Taoiseach, **Albert Reynolds** of the small, leftist Labour Party, declared that his top priority was to stop violence in Northern Ireland. In August 1994, he announced the nearly miraculous cease-fire agreement with Sinn Féin and the IRA. In June 1997, Fianna Fáil won the general election, making **Bertie Ahern,** the 45-year-old party leader, the youngest Taoiseach in the history of the state. Ahern joined the peace talks that produced the **Northern Ireland Peace Agreement** in April of 1998 (see p. 633). On May 22, 1998, in the first island-wide election since 1918, an overwhelming 94% of voters in the Republic voted for the enactment of the Agreement. (For the recent status of the Peace Agreement and Northern Ireland peace negotiations, see p. 633.)

CURRENT ISSUES

In November 1995, the closest vote in Irish history—50.3% to 49.7%—passed the **Divorce Bill,** allowing divorce if spouses have lived apart for four years with "no reasonable prospect of a reconciliation." Equally encouraging to progressives and disturbing to the Catholic Church is the **gay and lesbian rights** movement, which is slowly gaining legal ground. In 1980, the first legal challenge to laws against homosexuality was brought before the High Court. In June 1993, the age of consent between gay men was set at age 17. A large and relatively open gay scene has developed in Dublin. Another controversial issue is **abortion:** policies have changed little over the decades. In 1983, voters approved a constitutional amendment securing "the right to life of the unborn." A High Court decision in 1995 made it legal for centers to give advice on where to go abroad.

Ireland's **economy** is booming, in large part due to increased foreign investment over the past decade. Huge incentives have drawn foreign investors, boosting Ireland's economy at one of Europe's fastest rates. According to a report completed in 1999, unemployment should fall to 3% by the year 2005. This is indicative of a drastic change in Ireland's pattern of emigration. 1999 was the first year in recent history in which the rate of immigration to Ireland surpassed the rate of emigration away from it. For current events in Northern Ireland, see p. 630.

LITERATURE AND LANGUAGE

HISTORY OF THE IRISH LANGUAGE

The constitution declares Irish the national language of the Republic, yet there are only 60,000 individuals in the exclusively Irish-speaking communities, or **gaeltacht** (GAYL-tacht). The most prominent *gaeltacht* are in Connemara, Co. Donegal, the Dingle Peninsula, and the Aran Islands, and these geographically disparate communities are further divided by three almost mutually incomprehensible dialects: **Donegal** Irish, **Connemara** Irish, and the southern **Munster** Irish. Donegal Irish, like its traditional music, retains traces of past contact with Scottish Gaelic. The oldest vernacular literature and the largest collection of folklore in Europe are both Irish.

The language reentered the lives of the privileged classes with the advent of the Gaelic Revival. In 1893, **Douglas Hyde** (who later became the first president of Éire) founded the **Gaelic League** in order to inspire enthusiasm for Irish among people who didn't grow up speaking it. The revolutionaries of 1916 and the political leaders of the 20s were almost without exception excited about reinvigorating the Irish language, and they tried to use the government to strengthen it: the civil service exam included an Irish test, and Irish became a compulsory school subject. Preoccupied with economic development, the people of the postwar Republic resented these policies. Today, Irish has lost its stigma, and has grown in popularity among native English speakers. The modern Irish-literature community produces dozens of novels, poetry collections, and critical essays every year. At the same time, the area of the *gaeltacht* continues to shrink. Long-term trends in most *gaeltacht* still point to depopulation and dispersal, as Ireland's strengthening economy brings improvements in roads and communications to the previously isolated regions.

LEGENDS AND FOLKTALES

In early Irish society, language equaled action. What the bard sang about battles, valor, and lineage was the only record a chieftain had by which to make decisions. Poetry and politics of the Druidic tradition were so intertwined that the *fili* (trained poets) and *breitheamh* (BREH-huv; judges of the Brehon Laws) were often the same people. Poets living in the chieftains' households invented the art of verse satire. These poets had the power to curse and lay a *geis*, a magic compulsion or prohibition. Several "cycles," or collections, of tales narrate the life stories of a set of heroes and villains. The most extensive is the **Ulster Cycle,** which includes the adventures of King Conchobar, or Conor, of Ulster and his clan, the **Ulaid,** and his archenemy, his ex-wife Queen Medbh of Connacht. Ulster's champion is **Cúchulainn** (KOO-hu-lin), the king's nephew, an athlete extraordinare known as the Hound of Ulster whose adventures begin at the age of five. Literati have periodically compiled Ireland's **folktales.** These tales include other-worldly creatures such as **banshees,** still believed to forecast an imminent death when they are heard wailing outside the house of an ailing individual, and the **faeries,** descendants of the Túatha de Danann. **Leprechauns,** a degenerate conflagration of Ireland's mythic creatures, are embraced mainly by foreign cultures.

SWIFT, WILDE, AND SHAW

In long-colonized Dublin, **Jonathan Swift** (1667-1745), Dean of St. Patrick's Cathedral, wrote some of the most sophisticated, misanthropic, and marvelous satire in the English language, towering above his Anglo-Irish contemporaries with his mix of moral indignation, bitterness, and wit. Swift felt compelled to write about the sad condition of starving Irish peasants, while defending the Protestant Church of Ireland. "A Modest Proposal" (1729) satirically suggests that the overpopulated and hungry native Irish sell their children as food.

In the mid-19th century, cosmopolitan Dublin managed to breed talent, but young writers moved on from Trinity to London to make their names. **Oscar Wilde** (1856-1900) produced one novel and many sparklingly witty plays, including *The Importance of Being Earnest* (1895). Prolific playwright **George Bernard Shaw** (1856-1950) was also born in Dublin but moved to London in 1876, where he became an active socialist. Shaw won the Nobel Prize for Literature in 1925 for a body of work that includes *Candida* (1905) and *Pygmalion* (1938).

YEATS AND THE REVIVAL

Towards the end of the nineteenth century, a portion of Ireland's crop of young writers no longer turned to London to cultivate their talent. Rather, a vigorous and enduring effort known today as the **Irish Literary Revival** took over. Members of this movement turned to Irish culture, from its ancient mythology to contemporary folktales, for inspiration, overturning the assumption that the indigenous culture was less sophisticated than that of England. The early poems of **William Butler Yeats** (1865-1939) create a dreamily rural Ireland of loss and legend. Yeats's vision changed remarkably after he realized the role of the Gaelic Revival in promoting the nationalism that led to the violence of the Irish Civil War. In 1923, he became the first Irishman to win the Nobel Prize for Literature. In 1904, Yeats and Lady Gregory founded the **Abbey Theatre** in Dublin (see p. 683), in order to "build up a Celtic and Irish school of dramatic literature." But conflict arose almost immediately: was this new body of drama to be written in verse or prose, in the realistic or the fantastic mode? A sort of compromise was found in the work of **John Millington Synge.** Yeats advised Synge to look for inspiration on the Aran Islands. His experiences led him to write *The Playboy of the Western World* (1907), which destroys the pastoral myth about Irish peasantry and portrays a class-ridden rural society. **Sean O'Casey's** plays were well received by Dublin's middle class, as they were the first portrayals of gritty urban life in their fair city; examples of his work include *Juno and the Paycock* (1924) and *The Shadow of a Gunman* (1923).

JOYCE, BECKETT AND RECENT AUTHORS

The most famous of Ireland's expatriates is **James Joyce** (1882-1941); his novels are recognized as some of the seminal works of modernism. Joyce's writing never did leave Ireland, as his novels and stories exclusively describe the lives of Dubliners, and obsessively detail the city's geography and establishments. Joyce's most accessible writing is the collection of short stories titled *Dubliners* (1914). In *Ulysses* (1922) and *Finnegan's Wake* (1939), Joyce falls into a reverie of allusion, puns, and onomatopoeia that defy all attempts at light reading, but sound fantastic. Like Joyce, **Samuel Beckett** (1906-89) fled to Paris to pursue his writing career; unlike Joyce, he left most of vernacular Ireland behind. His three novels (*Molloy, Malone Dies,* and *The Unnameable*), world-famous plays (*Waiting for Godot, Endgame*), and bleak prose poems convey a deathly pessimism about language, society, and life. Beckett won the Nobel Prize in 1969, but did not accept it on the grounds that Joyce had never received it. Other authors felt the influence of modernism without needing to turn their back on Ireland. **Flann O'Brien** (1912-66) let loose an unrestricted literary inventiveness in celebrated novels such as *At Swim Two Birds* (1939), a comedy combing ancient Irish mythology with the fantasies of a foppish university student in early 20th-century Dublin.

After the 1940s, Irish poetry once again commanded widespread appreciation. **Patrick Kavanaugh** (1906-67) debunked a mythical Ireland in such poems as "The Great Hunger" (1945). The works of both **Thomas Kinsella** and **John Montague** display a keen awareness of the history of Irish poetry with a sensitivity to mid-19th century civil strife, while being intensely introspective. **Paul Muldoon** adds quirk and confusion to the hum-drum existence of today's Ireland. The dirt of Dublin continues to provide fodder for generations of writers beyond O'Casey and Joyce. Notorious wit, playwright, poet, and terrorist **Brendan Behan** created semi-autobiographical works about delinquent life such as his play *The Quare Fellow* (1954). Mild-mannered schoolteacher **Roddy Doyle** wrote the well-known *Barrytown Trilogy* about good times in down-and-out Dublin and won the Booker Prize in 1994 for *Paddy Clarke Ha Ha Ha*.

MUSIC

Irish traditional music is alive and kicking. Commonly called **"trad,"** it is the centuries-old array of dance rhythms, cyclic melodies, and embellishments that has been passed down through generations of musicians. These tunes can be written down, yet a traditional musician's training consists largely of listening to and innovating from the work of others. The same tune will produce a different result every session. Irish traditional music may be heard in two ways: recordings and impromptu pub sessions. Best-selling recording artists include **Altan, De Danann,** and the **Chieftains.** Other excellent groups that are available on CD are the **Bothy Band** and **Planxty** of the 1970s, and, more recently, **Nomos, Solas, Dervish,** and **Deanta.** Most traditional musicians are accustomed to playing before smaller, more intimate audiences of locals at a pub. *Let's Go* lists many pubs with regular trad sessions, but you'll find the best music by asking local trad enthusiasts.

The instruments with which Irish trad music is most frequently played are the fiddle, the wooden flute, the button accordion or smaller concertina, the tin whistle, and the *uilleann* pipes (elbow pipes). These pipes appear similar to the Scottish bagpipes, but are played differently: the bellows are held under the arm. The resulting sound is far more melodic and resembles a sweet fiddle. The *bodhrán* (BAU-ron) is a hand-held drum played with either with both ends of a stick or the bare hand. Sessions in pubs typically alternate between fast-paced traditional instrumental music and folk songs. Ireland's favorite traditional songsters include **Dominick Behan, The Dubliners, Christy Moore,** and **Sean Tyrell.**

In Ireland there is surprisingly little distinction between music types—a fine musician is one who uses materials from a wide variety of resources. Like The Dubliners, the London-based **Pogues** also fused rock and trad, to far different effect. In albums such as *Rum, Sodomy, and the Lash*, they whipped out reel and jigs of drunken, punk-damaged revelry, accompanied by MacGowan's poetic descriptions of Irish emigrant sorrows, and the horrors of sectarian violence. **My Bloody Valentine** weaved shimmering distortions to land them in the outskirts of grunge. Ireland's rock musicians have also set their sights on mainstream super-stardom, and achieved that goal often enough. **U2** is Ireland's biggest rock export. **Sinéad O'Connor** stood her own as an independent female rock star with attitude long before the lauded American phenomenon of the late 1990s. In recent years, **The Cranberries** and **The Corrs** have achieved great success abroad.

SPORTS

The Irish take enormous pride in their two native sports: hurling and Gaelic football. Attending a pub the day of that county's game will leave you happy, deaf, drunk, and counting down the days to the next round. In 1884, the **Gaelic Athletic Association (GAA)** was founded to establish official rules and regulations for hurling, Gaelic football, and other ancient Irish recreations. **Gaelic football** seems like a cross between football and rugby, although it pre-dates both of them. According to the GAA, "played well, Gaelic football is a fast, skillful game striking to the eye. Played badly, it is an unimpressive spectacle of dragging and pulling!" The ball is shorter and fatter than a rugby ball, and players may run holding the ball for no more than four paces, after which they must bounce, kick, or punch it in any direction. At each end of the field is a set of rugby-like goalposts, and below the crossbar there is a net resembling a football net. One point is scored for putting the goal over the crossbar between the posts, three for netting it. The game is played in teams of 15, for two 30-minute periods. Charging is within the rules.

As fans like to say, if football is a game, then **hurling** is an art. This fast and dangerous-looking game was first played in the 13th century. Perhaps best imagined as a blend of lacrosse and field hockey, the game is named after the stick with which it is played, the *caman* or "hurley." The hurley—like a hockey stick with a shorter and wider blade—is used to hit the ball along the ground or overhead. Players may also kick the ball or hit it with the their hands. The ball, or *sliothar*, is leather-covered and can be caught for hitting, or carried along on the stick. A goal is worth three points and is scored by hitting the ball under the crossbar. **Football** enjoys an equally fanatical following as hurling and gaelic football. The Irish are also fiercely devoted to the football clubs of England. **Horse racing** maintains a devoted following in the Republic, thanks to Co. Kildare's well-appreciated place as a breeding ground for champion racehorses.

FOOD AND DRINK

Food in Ireland can be fairly expensive. The basics are simple: the specialties are *Colcannon* (a potato, onion, and cabbage dish), Guinness stew, and Irish stew. Loud and long will the Irish bards sing the praises of the Clonakilty man who first concocted **black pudding.** This delicacy was invented during a food shortage and makes the most of the pig. As one local butcher put it, it's "some pork, a good deal of blood, and grains and things—all wrapped up in a tube." **White pudding** uses milk instead of blood. Regional specialties include **crubeen** (tasty pigs' feet) in Cork, **coddle** (boiled sausages and bacon with potatoes) in Dublin, and **blaa** (sausage rolls) in Waterford. The main culinary merit of the Irish resides in their bread. Most famous is **soda bread,** a heavy white bread especially tasty when fried. Another indigenous bread is **barm brack**; perfect for picnics, it is a spicy mixture of dried fruits and molasses mixed to a lead-like density. **Seafood** can be a real bargain in smaller towns; Guinness-marinated mussels and oysters are splendid.

A 1998 study found that Irish students spend roughly £80 a month on **drinks,** which is no wonder considering the centrality of pubs in Irish culture. Locals of all ages from every social milieu head to pubs for conversation, food, singing and dancing, and **craic** (crack), an Irish word meaning "a good time." In the evening, most pubs host traditional music. In rural pubs, there's also the chance that a *seanachaí* (SHAN-ukh-ee), or travelling storyteller, might demand an audience. Pubs are generally open Monday through Saturday from 10:30am to 11:30pm (11pm in winter) and Sunday from 12:30 to 2pm and 4 to 11pm (closed 2-4pm). Many pubs lock the doors at closing time and let you stay inside, but many pubs (especially in Dublin) are now able to obtain licenses that allow them to stay open officially until midnight-2am. Some pubs, especially ones catering to a clientele of fishermen, have been granted special "early" licenses allowing them to open at 7:30am.

Beer wins a landslide victory as the drink of choice in Irish pubs. **Guinness** inspires a reverence otherwise reserved for the Holy Trinity. Known variously as "the dark stuff," "the blonde in the black skirt," or simply "I'll have a pint, please," it's a rich, dark brew with a head thick enough to stand a match in. **Murphy's** is a similar, slightly creamier Cork-brewed stout. Cork also produces **Beamish,** a tasty "economy" stout. **Smithwicks** is a hoppy, English-style bitter commonly perceived of as an old man's drink. Two more popular domestic lagers are **Kilkenny** and **Harp. Irish whiskey,** which Elizabeth I once claimed was her only true Irish friend, is sweeter than its Scotch counterpart (spelled "whisky"). Irish monks invented whiskey, calling it *uisce beatha,* meaning "water of life." **Jameson** is popular everywhere. **Irish coffee** is sweetened with brown sugar and whipped cream and laced with whiskey, though it's more popular with the tourists than the natives. In the west, you may hear locals praise "mountain dew," a euphemism for **poitín** (put-CHEEN), an illegal distillation sometimes given to cows in labor that ranges in strength from 115 to 140 proof.

MEDIA

The largest **newspapers** in the Republic are the *Irish Times* (www.ireland.com) and the *Irish Independent* (www.independent.ie). The *Times* takes a liberal voice and is renowned for its excellent coverage of international affairs. The *Independent* is more internally focused, and often maintains a chatty writing style. Neither the *Times* nor the *Independent* comes out with a Sunday paper, but their readership is generally satisfied with an Irish edition of the British newspaper *The Times*. A large number of regional papers offer in-depth local news; the largest is *The Cork Examiner*. **British papers** are sold throughout Ireland. In 1961, the Republic's national radio service made its first television broadcast, naming itself **Radio Telefís Éireann (RTE).** The Irish government's most recent developments include the start of Irish-language radio and TV stations, called Telifis na Gaelige, aimed at promoting the use of Irish in modern media forms.

DUBLIN ☎01

In a country known for its relaxed pace of life and rural sanctity, Dublin stands out for its international style and boundless energy. The Irish who live outside of Dublin worry that it has taken on the characteristics of big cities everywhere: crime, rapid social change, and a weakness for short-lived trends. Yet, while Dublin may seem harsh by Irish standards, it's still as friendly a major city as you'll find. Zooming cultural and economic growth has led to the rocket ship success of Temple Bar as the new nightlife hub. Still, the image of old Ireland persists in the castles and cathedrals that saturate the city, as well as in the pubs that continue to shelter much of Dublin's public life and world-renowned music scene. The capital of Ireland since the late 17th century, Dublin has occasioned extraordinary intellectual and literary communities. From Swift and Burke to Joyce and Beckett, Dublin has produced so many great writers that nearly every street has a literary landmark.

◧ GETTING THERE

Rail lines, bus lines (both state-run and private), and the national highway system radiate from Dublin. Major highways **N5** and **N6** lead to **N4**, while **N8, N9,** and **N10** all feed into **N7,** dumping buses and cars into Dublin's vehicular sphere. Because intercity transport is so Dublin-centric, you may find it more convenient to arrange your travel in other parts of the Republic while you're in the capital.

Flights: Dublin Airport (☎ 844 4900). **Dublin Bus** #41, 41B, and 41C run from Eden Quay in the city center with stops along the way (3 per hr., £1.20). The **Airlink** shuttle begins at Heuston Station (50min., £3.50) and stops at Busáras Central Bus Station and O'Connell St. (30-40min., 4-5 per hr., £3). **Airport Express** buses (☎ 844 4265) go to Busáras and O'Connell St. (30min.; 2-4 per hr. M-Sa 6:30am-10:50pm, Su 7:10am-11pm; £2.50). **Taxis** from the city center cost £12-15. Wheelchair-accessible cabs may be available; call ahead (see **Taxis**, p. 669).

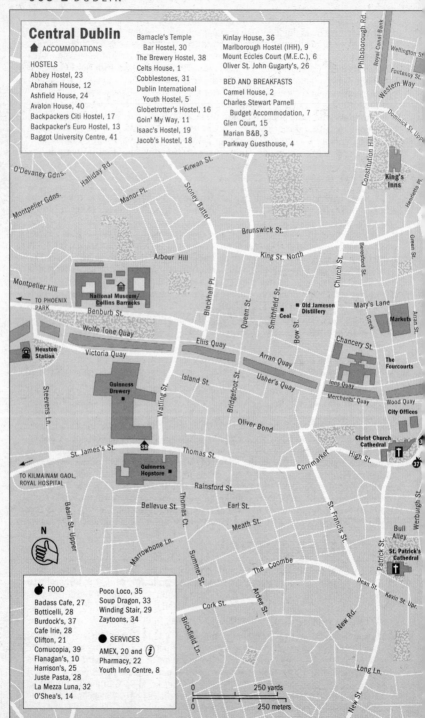

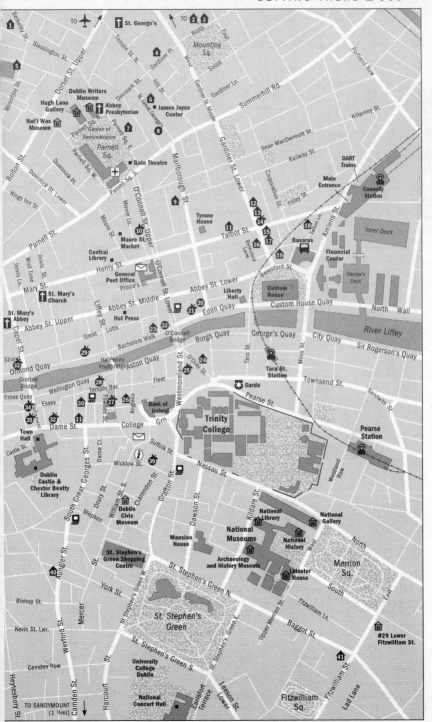

Trains: Irish Rail/Iarnród Éireann Travel Center (EER-ann-road AIR-ann), 35 Lower Abbey St. (☎ 836 6222). Sells advance rail tickets. Spews data on DART, suburban trains, and cross-channel ferries. Open M-F 9am-5pm, Sa 9am-1pm. 24hr. "talking timetables" recite schedules of trains from Belfast (☎ 855 4477), Cork (☎ 855 4400), Galway/Westport (☎ 855 4422), Killarney/Tralee (☎ 855 4466), Limerick (☎ 855 4411), Sligo (☎ 855 4455), Waterford (☎ 855 4433), and Wexford/Rosslare (☎ 855 4488). Bus #90 (every 10min., 60p) makes the circuit of Connolly, Heuston, and Pearse Stations, as well as Busáras Central Bus Station. Connolly and Pearse are also DART stations serving the north and south coasts.

Connolly Station, Amiens St. (☎ 836 3333; night ☎ 703 2358), north of the Liffey and close to Busáras Bus Station. Buses #20, 20A, and 90 at the station head south of the river, and the DART runs to Tara on the south quay. Open M-Sa 5:30-9pm and Su 4:30-8:30pm. **Luggage storage** £2 per item; open M-Sa 7:40am-9:15pm, Su 9:10am-9:45pm. Trains from **Belfast** (2¼hr.; 8 per day, Su 5 per day; £18) and **Wexford** via **Rosslare** (3hr.; 3 per day, Su 2 per day; £11).

Heuston Station (☎ 703 2132; night ☎ 703 2131), south of Victoria Quay, well west of the city center, a 25min. walk from Trinity College. Buses #26, 51, and 79 go from Heuston to the city center. Open M-Sa 5:30-8pm and 9-10pm, Sa 7:30am-8pm and 9-10pm, Su 8am-10pm. **Luggage storage** £1.50-3.50 per item; open daily 6:30am-10:30pm. Trains from **Cork** (3½hr.; M-Th and Sa 8 per day, F 11 per day, Su 6 per day; £ 33.50).

Pearse Station, just east of Trinity College on Pearse St. and Westland Row. Receives southbound trains from Connolly Station.

Buses: Busáras Central Bus Station, Store St. (☎ 836 6111; lost property ☎ 703 2489). Open M-Sa 8am-7:45pm, Su 10am-5:45pm. **Luggage Storage** £2 per item, backpacks £3. **Bus Éireann** (☎ 62121) ticket window at Dublin Bus Office (see **Local Buses,** below). Open M-F 9am-5pm, Sa 9am-1pm. From: **Belfast** (3hr.; 7 per day, Su 4 per day; £10.50); **Rosslare Harbour** (3hr.; 10 per day, Su 7 per day; £10); and **Shannon Airport** via a shuttle connection every 30min. from **Limerick** (4½hr., 13 per day, £14). Bus Éireann window open M-F 9am-5pm, Sa 9am-1pm.

Ferries: Book at **Irish Rail office** (see below). Dun Laoghaire is Dublin's major port. See **By Ferry,** p. 35, for more information.

Dún Laoghaire terminal (☎ 204 7777), in the suburbs (see p. 688). DART connects it to Connolly Station, Pearse Station, or Tara St. Station in the city center (£1.30). Buses #7, 7A, and 8 go to Eden Quay from Georges St. in Dún Laoghaire (£1.30). **Stena Line** from **Holyhead, Wales.**

Dublin Port (☎ 607 5665). Buses #53 and 53A run from Busáras (1 per hr., 80p); Dublin Bus also runs timed to fit the ferry schedule (£2-2.50). **Irish Ferries** (☎ (1890) 313 131, 24hr.) from **Holyhead, Wales. Merchant Ferries** from **Liverpool** (8hr., 2 per day, £40, car £150-170); book from **Gerry Feeney,** 19 Eden Quay (☎ 819 2999).

▐ GETTING AROUND

Travel passes were not designed for the casual traveler; each pass requires several trips a day to save money. **Travel Wide** passes offer unlimited bus rides (day £3.50; week £13, students with TravelSave stamp £10). However, a Dublin Bus week runs from Sunday to Saturday inclusive, no matter when you purchase the pass. Dublin Bus months, similarly, are calendar months. Other tickets allow for both bus and suburban rail/DART travel (adult one-day short hop £5.20, weekly £17, monthly £63). All special tickets are available at the bus office and at newsagents around the city; an ISIC card is required for student rates. Students may wish to get a **TravelSave** stamp for bus and rail discounts (see **Budget Travel,** below).

DART: Electric DART trains run frequently up and down the coast to the suburbs. The trains put buses to shame in terms of cost and speed, but only reach a limited number of destinations. From **Connolly, Pearse,** and **Tara St.** stations in the city center, the DART shoots south past **Dún Laoghaire** and north to **Howth.** The DART runs every 10-15min. roughly 6:30am-11:30pm; a ride costs £0.55-1.10. Tickets are sold in stations and usually must be presented at the end of the trip.

Suburban Rail: The orange suburban rail trains all leave from Connolly Station and continue north to **Drogheda,** south to **Wicklow,** and west to **Mullingar.** The north and south lines also stop at Tara St. and Pearse Stations. Trains are frequent M-Sa (roughly 30 per day). Complete DART/suburban rail timetables available at many stations (50p).

Local Buses: Dublin Bus Office, 59 O'Connell St. (☎ 873 4222 or ☎ 872 0000, lost property ☎ 703 3055). Lime-green **Dublin Buses** run 5am-11:30pm and comprehensively cover the city and suburbs north to **Howth** and **Dún Laoghaire** (buses every 8-20min. 8am-6pm, off-hours every 30-45min.; 55p-£1.10). Most routes begin or end at city center stops located near Christ Church, the Trinity College facade, St. Stephen's Green, O'Connell St., or Parnell St. Bus stands along the quays post timetables; the *Map of Greater Dublin* (£4.10) and the *Dublin Bus Timetable* (£1.50) are sold by newsagents and the Dublin Bus Office; and the important pamphlet, *Which Ticket Type Are You?*, is free at the office. Dublin Bus runs the **NiteLink** service to the suburbs (Th-Sa 1 per hr. 12:30-3:30am; £3, no passes valid). **Wheelchair-accessible buses** are limited: the only options are the OmniLink service (#300), which cruises around Clontarf (60p), and the #3 bus from Whitehall to Sandymount via O'Connell St.

Taxis: National Radio Cabs, 40 James St. (☎ 677 2222). **Blue Cabs** (☎ 676 1111), **ABC** (☎ 285 5444), and **City Group Taxi** (☎ 872 7272). Call for wheelchair-accessible taxis. All 24hr. £2.20 plus 90p per mi.; 80p call-in charge. It's easiest to pick up cabs at taxi stands, such as spots in front of Trinity, on Lower Abbey St., and on Parnell St.

Car Rental: Budget, 151 Lower Drumcondra Rd. (☎ 837 9611), and at the airport. Summer from £35 per day, £165 per week; winter £30, £140. Ages 23-75. **Alamo,** Dublin Airport (☎ 844 4086). Summer from £35 per day, £195 per week; winter £30, £175. Ages 21-75; additional insurance cost for ages 21-24. Many rental agencies offer free pickup or delivery for cars booked early.

Bike Rental: Dealers close to city center are **MacDonald Cycles,** 38 Wexford St. (☎ 475 2586), and **Cycle Ways,** 185-186 Parnell St. (☎ 873 4748; limited one-way rental system, £10 surcharge; £10 per day, £40 per week; deposit £50). **Dublin Bike Tours** (☎ 679 0889), behind the Kinlay House hostel on Lord Edward St., rents and provides advice on route planning. £10 per day, £40 per week; students £8, £35; ID deposit. Bicycles are not allowed on DART trains, sometimes on suburban rail lines (ask first), and usually on main-line trains for a small fee (£6 single, £12 return).

Hitchhiking: Since Dublin is well served by bus and rail, there is no good reason to hitch, nor does *Let's Go* recommend it. Hitchers coming to Dublin generally ask drivers to drop them off at one of the bus and DART stops outside the city. Those leaving Dublin ride a bus to the city outskirts where the motorways begin.

◆ ORIENTATION

The **River Liffey** is the natural divide between Dublin's North and South Sides. The more famous sights and posh businesses are on the **South Side.** The majority of hostels, the bus station, and Connolly Station sprout up on the **North Side.** The streets running alongside the Liffey are called **quays** ("keys"); their names change every block. Streets change names as they cross the river; if a street is split into "Upper" and "Lower," then the "Lower" is always the part of the street closer to the mouth of the Liffey. The core of Dublin is circumscribed by **North Circular Rd.** and **South Circular Rd.,** which have their own assortment of name changes. Almost all sights are located within this area, and you can walk from one end to the other in about 40 minutes. **O'Connell St.,** three blocks west of Busáras Central Bus Station, is the primary link between north and south Dublin. South of the Liffey, O'Connell St. becomes **Westmoreland St.,** passes **Fleet St.** on the right, curves around Trinity College Dublin on the left, and then becomes **Grafton St.** One block south of the Liffey, **Fleet St.** becomes **Temple Bar.** While Temple Bar is the name of a street, it usually applies to the surrounding neighborhood of pubs and trendy shops. **Trinity College** functions as the nerve center of Dublin's cultural activity, drawing legions of bookshops and student-oriented pubs into its orbit. The college touches **Grafton St.,** a pedestrian shopping district. Grafton's southern end opens onto the public park **St. Stephen's Green.** On the North Side, **Henry St.** and **Mary St.** comprise a shopping zone that intersects with O'Connell just after the **General Post Office (GPO)**. The North Side has the reputation of being a rougher area after sunset. Avoid walking in unfamiliar areas on either side of the Liffey at night, and it's wise to steer clear of Phoenix Park at night.

⁊ PRACTICAL INFORMATION

TOURIST, FINANCIAL, AND LOCAL SERVICES
Tourist Information:

Dublin Tourist Centre, Suffolk St. (Ireland ☎ (1850) 230 330, UK ☎ (0171) 493 3201, elsewhere ☎ (066) 979 2083; www.visitdublin.com). Books Dublin accommodations for £1 and a 10% non-refundable deposit; outside Dublin £2 and deposit. Credit card bookings by phone (☎ (0800) 6686 6866; reservations@dublintourism.ie). **Bus Éireann** and **Irish Ferries** have representatives to provide info and tickets. Open July-Aug. M-Sa 9am-7pm, Su 10:30am-2:30pm; Sept.-June M-Sa 9am-6pm; reservation desk closes 1 hr. earlier.

Northern Ireland Tourist Board: 16 Nassau St. (☎ 679 1977). Books accommodations in the North. Open M-F 9am-5:30pm, Sa 10am-5pm.

Temple Bar Information Centre: 18 Eustace St. (☎ (1850) 260 027). Heading away from Trinity College, turn right off Dame St. where it intersects both Eustace St. and Great Georges St. Open June-Sept. M-F 9am-6pm, Sa 11am-4pm, Su noon-4pm; Oct.-May M-F 9am-6pm, Sa noon-6pm.

Budget Travel: usit NOW, 19-21 Aston Quay (☎ 679 8833), near O'Connell Bridge. Ireland's main usit branch. **TravelSave** stamps £7. Open M-W and F 9am-6pm, Th 9am-8pm, Sa 10am-5:30pm.

An Óige Head Office (Irish Youth Hostel Association/HI), 61 Mountjoy St. (☎ 830 4555), Wellington St. Follow O'Connell St. north, continuing through its name changes. Mountjoy St. is on the left, about 20min. from O'Connell Bridge. Book and pay for hostels. Sells package bike and rail tours. Open M-F 9:30am-5:30pm, Sa 10am-12:30pm.

Financial Services: Bank of Ireland, AIB, and **TSB** banks with **bureaux de change** cluster on Lower O'Connell St., Grafton St., and in the Suffolk St. and Dame St. areas. Most banks open M-F 10am-4pm.

American Express: 41 Nassau St. (☎ 679 9000). Traveler's check refunds (☎ 618 5588). Open M-F 9am-5:30pm. **Branch** in the Dublin Tourist Centre.

Camping Store: The Great Outdoors, Chatham St. (☎ 679 4293), off Grafton St. An Óige/HI 10% discount. Open M-W and F-Sa 9:30am-5:30pm, Th 9:30am-8pm.

Launderette: The Laundry Shop, 191 Parnell St. (☎ 872 3541). Closest to Busáras and the North Side hostels. Wash and dry £4.20-5. Open M-F 8am-7pm, Sa 9am-6pm.

EMERGENCY AND COMMUNICATIONS

Police (*Garda*): Dublin Metro Headquarters, Harcourt Sq. (☎ 478 5295); Store St. Station (☎ 855 7761); Fitzgibbon St. Station (☎ 836 3113). *Garda* **Confidential Report Line** (☎ (1800) 666 111).

Helplines: Tourist Victim Support, Parliament St. (☎ 478 5295, 24hr. helpline ☎ (1800) 661771). If you are robbed, this organization helps you find accommodations and puts you in contact with your embassy or family; a loss or crime report must first be filed with a Garda station. **Samaritans,** 112 Marlborough St. (☎ (1850) 609 090 or 872 7700).

Gay, Lesbian, and Bisexual Information: Gay Switchboard Dublin (☎ 872 1055, Su-F 8-10pm). A good resource for events and updates. **Lesbians Organizing Together (LOT),** 5 Capel St. (☎ 872 7770). Resource center and library open Tu-Th 10am-5pm. **Outhouse,** 65 William St. (☎ 670 6377). Gay and lesbian community resource center, with library, cafe, and info. Organizes support groups, seminars, and info sessions.

Hospital: St. James's Hospital, James St. (☎ 453 7941). Served by bus #123. **Mater Misericordiae Hospital,** Eccles St. (☎ 830 1122), off Lower Dorset St. Served by buses #10, 11, 13, 16, 121, and 122.

REPUBLIC OF IRELAND

Internet Access: Free Internet research (not email) available at the **central library,** Henry and Moore St. (☎ 873 4333), in the ILAC Centre. **The Internet Exchange** has branches at 146 Parnell St., the Dublin Tourist Centre, and in the Granary at Temple Bar South, in addition to two others in Temple Bar. Membership entitles users to low rates. Open daily 9am-11pm. **Global Internet Cafe,** 8 Lower O'Connell St. (☎ 878 0295), a block north of the Liffey and on the right. £1.25 per 15min., students £1. **usit NOW** (see **Budget Travel,** opposite). With ISIC card £1 per 15min., £2.50 per 45min.

Post Office: General Post Office (GPO), O'Connell St. (☎ 705 7000). Dublin is the only city in Ireland with postal codes. Poste Restante pickup at the **bureau de change.** Open M-Sa 8am-8pm, Su 10am-6:30pm. **Postal code:** Dublin 1.

▟ ACCOMMODATIONS

Dublin has a handful of marvelous accommodations, but the high demand for lodging keeps lesser places open, too. Reserve as early as possible, particularly around holiday weekends, sporting weekends, St. Patrick's Day, around the New Year, and from July through August. The Dublin Tourist Office books local accommodations for £1, but they only deal in Bord Fáilte-approved B&Bs and hostels; they aren't necessarily better than unapproved ones but, in the case of hostels, are usually cleaner. Camping in Phoenix Park is a terrible idea: if the Garda and park rangers don't get you to leave, the threat of thieves and drug dealers should. If the accommodations listed below are full, consult Dublin Tourism's annually updated *Dublin Accommodation Guide* (£3), or ask hostel and B&B staff for referrals.

HOSTELS

To deal with the crowds, Dublin's hostels lean toward the institutional, especially in comparison to their country cousins. Dorms range from £9 to £17 per night. The beds south of the river, closest to the city's sights and nightlife, are most expensive and fill up fastest. The hostels in **Dún Laoghaire** (see p. 688), a DART ride away, are an alternative to the city. All listed hostels have 24hr. reception unless noted.

▓**Barnacle's Temple Bar House,** 19 Temple Ln. (☎ 671 6277; templebar@barna-cles.iol.ie). The burning hot center of everything. A new, well-kept hostel right in Temple Bar. All rooms with bath. Excellent security. Small continental breakfast included. June-Sept. 10-bed dorms £11; 6-bed dorms £13; 4-bed dorms £15; doubles and twins £40; Mar.-May and Oct. about £1 cheaper; Nov.-Feb. £2-3 cheaper.

▓**The Brewery Hostel,** 22-23 Thomas St. (☎ 453 8600). Follow Dame St. past Christ Church through its name changes, or take bus #123. Next to Guinness and a 20min. walk to Temple Bar. Excellent facilities with a personable feel. The distinct Guinness odors waft through the whole neighborhood, which, unfortunately, isn't the safest. All rooms with bath. Continental breakfast included. Free luggage storage. Laundry £3.50. 8- to 10-bed dorms £10-12; 4-bed dorms £15 per person; singles £28; doubles £44.

Avalon House (IHH), 55 Aungier St. (☎ 475 0001). Temple Bar is within stumbling distance. Co-ed showers, toilets, and dorms. Small continental breakfast included. Free luggage storage opened every 2hr., or get a personal luggage cage (£1). Towels £1 with £5 deposit. Non-smoking. Wheelchair accessible. Large dorms June-Sept. £12.50, Mar.-May and Oct. £9.50, Nov.-Feb. £8; 4-bed dorms with bath £16.50, £14, £11.50; doubles Mar.-Oct. £36, Nov.-Feb. £28; doubles with bath £40. Singles also available.

Abbey Hostel, 29 Bachelor's Walk, O'Connell Bridge (☎ 878 0700; www.indigo.ie/~abbeyhos). An emphatic yellow addition to Dublin's hostel scene. A little pricey, but clean, comfy, and well-kept. Great location. Internet access £1 per 7min. Continental breakfast included. Luggage storage free; "super-security" (for guests and non-guests) £2.50. Big dorms June-Sept. £15, Oct. and Mar.-May £11; 6-bed dorms £16, £14, with bath £17; 4-bed dorms £18, £15; doubles £40-60. Some prices higher on weekends.

Abraham House, 82-3 Lower Gardiner St. (☎ 855 0600; ☎/fax 855 0598; stay@abra-ham-house.ie). Respectable, tidy rooms. Bureau de change. Internet access. Kitchen open until 10pm. Light breakfast and towels included. Laundry £4. June-Sept. 12-bed dorms £9; 4-bed £15; doubles £40; more for rooms with bath.

Globetrotter's Tourist Hostel (IHH), 46-7 Lower Gardiner St. (☎ 873 5893; www.iol.ie/globetrotters). Beds are snug, but there's plenty of room to stow your travel debris. Excellent bathrooms and superb showers—just too few of them. Internet access. Hearty, healthy breakfast included. Free luggage storage. Safety deposit boxes £1.50. Towels 50p. Dorms July to mid-Sept. £15, mid-Sept. to June £12.

Jacobs Inn, 21-28 Talbot Pl. (☎ 855 5660; jacobs@isaacs.ie). Spacious rooms, all with bath, are clean. Luggage storage accessible every 30min. Towels £1. Laundry £5. Bed lockout 11am-3pm. Bureau de change. Bike storage at Isaacs (see p. 674). Breakfast £2.50. Wheelchair accessible facilities. Dorms Apr.-Oct. £11.25; 3-bed dorms £17.50; doubles £43; Nov.-Mar. £2 less per person.

Ashfield House, 19-20 D'Olier St. (☎ 679 7734; ashfield@indigo.ie). In the center of Dublin, this "guest accommodation" has a variety of bedrooms. Good security. Luggage storage. Bureau de change. Kitchen open until 10pm. Internet access. Laundry £4. Light breakfast included. 6-bed dorms £14; 4-bed £16; triples £18; doubles £28; singles £40. Weekend prices £1-2 higher, Nov.-Apr. £1-2 lower.

An Óige Dublin International Youth Hostel, 61 Mountjoy St. (☎ 830 4555; www.irelandyha.org). Welcome to the mothership. Beds are decent, and rooms and bathrooms are clean. Cafe has cheap meals (£3.50) and packed lunches (£2). Shuttles to Temple Bar. Breakfast included. Luggage storage £1. Towels £1. Self-service laundry £4. Carpark. Wheelchair accessible. Big dorms June £11, July-Aug. £13; 6- to 8-bed £12, £13.50; 4-bed £13.50, £14; doubles £29, £30. Oct.-May £1-2 cheaper.

Celts House, 32 Blessington St. (☎ 830 0657; res@celtshouse.iol.ie). 38 comfy, solid, wooden bunk beds in a brightly-painted atmosphere. 15min. walk from the city center. Key deposit £5. Internet access. 8-bed dorms May-Sept. £10.50, Sept.-May £9; 6-bed £12; 4-bed £12.50; doubles £36.

Mount Eccles Court (M.E.C.), 42 North Great Georges St. (☎ 878 0071; fax 874 6472; meccles@iol.ie). A former convent with large dorms. Small continental breakfast included. Free luggage storage and car park available. Towels £1. With bath add 50p-£1. 16-bed dorms Apr.-Sept. £8.50, Oct.-Mar. £8; 12-bed £10.15, £9; 10-bed £11, £9; 6-bed £11.50, £10; 4-bed £13.50, £12.50; doubles £36, £28.

Marlborough Hostel (IHH), 81-82 Marlborough St. (☎ 874 7629; fax 874 5172; marlboro@internet-ireland.ie), between O'Connell and Gardiner St. Mega-renovations will be complete by 2001. Large rooms and a nice barbecue patio in back. Bike shed. Internet access. Continental breakfast included. Sheets 50p. Check-out 10:30am. 4- to 10-bed dorms July-Sept. £8.50-10, Oct.-June £7.50-8.50; doubles £30, £26.

Isaacs Hostel, 2-5 Frenchman's Ln. (☎ 855 6215; fax 855 6574; hostel@issacs.ie). Rooms are comfortable enough, but save the begatting for the singles. Heavy timber ceilings and a split log-furnished common area give a rough-hewn feel. Cafe. Internet access. Towels £1. Laundry £5. Bedroom lockout 11am-2:30pm. Large dorms £8-9.25; 4-bed dorms £14; singles £20; doubles £34; Nov.-Mar. £1 cheaper per person.

Cobblestones, 29 Eustace St. (☎/fax 677 5614). In the middle of Temple Bar action, this smaller hostel has a friendly staff and bright rooms, but uncomfortable beds and no kitchen. Free towels and small breakfast. Dorms £14-16; doubles £37.

Other Dublin Hostels: In our opinion, these aren't as good as the hostels above, but they're still decent places to stay.

Kinlay House (IHH), 2-12 Lord Edward St. (☎ 679 6644), the continuation of Dame St. 15- to 24-bed dorms £10.50; 20-bed dorms partitioned into 4-bed nooks £11.50, 4- to 6-bed dorms £14.50, with bath £16; singles £22; doubles £34, with bath £36. Oct.-June prices £1-2.50 less.

Oliver St. John Gogarty's Temple Bar Hostel, 18-21 Anglesea St. (☎ 671 1822). Dorms June-Sept. £16, Mar.-May and Oct. £14, Nov.-Feb. £12-13; twins £42, £36, £32; triples £51, £48, £42. Weekends always £1 more.

Baggot University Centre, 114 Baggot St. (☎ 661 8860), by the intersection with Fitzwilliam St. 5- to 8-bed dorms £12-13; doubles £30.

BED AND BREAKFASTS

A blanket of quality B&Bs covers Dublin and the surrounding suburbs. On the north side, B&Bs cluster along **Upper** and **Lower Gardiner St.** and near **Parnell Sq.** Be warned: these can be a budget traveler's hell. Many travelers arrive late at night by bus or train and, knowing no better, are charged exorbitant fees. Both Lower and Upper Gardiner St. are within walking distance of Busáras and Connolly; buses #41, 41A, 41B, and 41C from Eden Quay will take you to the farthest reaches of the road. **Clonliffe Rd.** has a few friendly empty-nests-turned-B&Bs. Take bus #51A from Lower Abbey St., or make the 20-minute walk from the city center up O'Connell St., right on Dorset St., across the Royal Canal, and right onto Clonliffe Rd. Buses #41A, 41B, and 41C all serve the area from the airport.

Suburban B&Bs are more likely to be decent and available. **Sandymount** is a peaceful neighborhood near Dublin Port, 1¾ mi. south of the city center, and famous for its Joycean associations. Take bus #3 from Clery's on O'Connell St. or the 10-minute DART ride to Landsdowne Rd. or Sandymount. The view along the **Clontarf Rd.** includes coastal grass, the harbor, some industrial smokestacks of the Dublin Port facility, and the impressive Dublin Mountains in the backdrop. Bus #130 runs from Lower Abbey St. to Clontarf Rd. (15min.). B&Bs in **Howth** (see p. 690) and **Dún Laoghaire** (see p. 688) are just as accessible by DART from Dublin.

Rita and Jim Casey, Villa Jude, 2 Church Ave. (☎ 668 4982), off Beach Rd. Bus #3 to the first stop on Tritonville Rd.; Church Ave. is back a few yards. Call for directions from the Lansdowne Rd. DART stop. Clean rooms and big breakfasts for the best B&B price in Dublin. Not a very quiet street by day. Singles £16; doubles £32.

Parkway Guest House, 5 Gardiner Pl. (☎ 874 0469). Rooms are plain but high-ceilinged and immaculate, and the location just off Gardiner St. is excellent. Singles £23; doubles £36-40, with shower £44-48.

Mona B&B, 148 Clonliffe Rd. (☎ 837 6723). Firm beds in rooms kept tidy by a proprietress who offers tea and cakes upon arrival. Open May-Oct. Singles £17; doubles £36.

The White House, 125 Clontarf Rd. (☎ 833 3196). Sink into your bed and look out at pristine rose gardens. Singles £25, off-season £24; doubles £44, with bath £48.

Charles Stewart Budget Accommodation, 5-6 Parnell Sq. (☎ 878 0350). Continue up O'Connell St. past Parnell St. and look on your right. Technically a hostel but much more like a guesthouse. Laundry £3. Singles £20; twins £40, with bath £45; doubles £50, with bath £60; triples with bath £84. Rates 10% lower in winter.

St. Aidan's B&B, 150 Clonliffe Rd. (☎ 837 6750). Good beds, non-smoking rooms, and a friendly proprietor. Open Apr.-Sept. Singles £17; doubles £34, with bath £40.

Mrs. Dolores Abbot-Murphy, 14 Castle Park (☎ 269 8413). Ask the #3 bus driver to drop you off at Sandymount Green; continue past Browne's Deli and take the 1st left. At the end of the road, look right. 5min. walk from Sandymount DART stop. Cheerful rooms look onto a peaceful cul-de-sac with flowers blooming everywhere. The dining room adds elegance to every meal. Singles £23; doubles £38, with bath £44.

Bayview, 98 Clontarf Rd. (☎ 833 3950). The Barry family provides fresh, airy rooms, with every sort of wallpaper imaginable. Singles £25; doubles £45, with bath £50.

Mrs. Molly Ryan, 10 Distillery Rd. (☎ 837 4147), off Clonliffe Rd., on the left if you're coming from the city center. A yellow house attached to #11. The unsinkable Molly Ryan, in her countless years, has never marked the B&B with a sign. Small rooms, small prices. Singles £17, £11 without breakfast; doubles £30, less without breakfast.

Carmel House, 16 Upper Gardiner St. (☎ 874 1639; fax 878 6903). An elegant breakfast room and a generally high comfort factor. Rooms £27.50-30 per person.

CAMPING

Most campsites are far from the city center. **Phoenix Park** is **not safe** for camping.

Camac Valley Tourist Caravan & Camping Park, Naas Rd., Clondalkin (☎ 464 0644), near Corkagh Park. Accessible by bus #69 (35min. from city center, £1.10). Food shop and kitchen. Laundry £3.50. Showers 50p. Wheelchair accessible. No dogs. 2 people with tent and car June-Aug. £10, Sept.-May £9; pedestrians £5, cyclists £4.

Shankill Caravan and Camping Park (☎ 282 0011; fax 282 0108). The DART and buses #45 and 84 from Eden Quay run to Shankill, as does bus #45A from the Dún Laoghaire ferryport. Middle-aged tourists in caravans alternate with shrubs and tents. Showers 50p. £4.50-5 per tent plus £1 per adult, 50p per child.

⬛ FOOD

Dublin's many **open-air markets** sell fresh and cheap fixings. Actors head to **Moore St. Market** to try to perfect a Dublin guttural accent, and get fresh veggies to boot. (Open M-Sa 7am-5pm.) The cheapest **supermarkets** around Dublin are **Dunnes Stores,** with branches at St. Stephen's Green Shopping Centre, the ILAC Centre off Henry St., and on North Earl St. off O'Connell St. (Open M-W and F-Sa 8:30am-7pm; Th 8:30am-9pm; Su noon-6pm.) **Temple Bar** and **Grafton St.** have more ethnic diversity in their selection of restaurants than the neighboring counties combined. **O'Connell St.** sports blocks of neon fast-food chains, and side streets overflow with fish-and-chip shops. Of course, pub grub is always an option (see **Publin,** p. 684).

⬛ Cafe Irie, 11 Fownes St. (☎ 672 5090), above the colorful Sé Sí Progressive. Probably the best value in Temple Bar. Lip-smackingly good sandwich concoctions under £3. Vegan-friendly. Great coffee. Open M-Sa 9am-8pm, Su noon-5:30pm.

⬛ Cornucopia, 19 Wicklow St. (☎ 677 7583). This vegetarian horn of plenty spills huge portions onto your plate. If you can find a table, sit down for a rich meal (about £5) or just a snack (about £1.50). Takeaway. Open M-W and F-Sa 9am-8pm, Th 9am-9pm.

La Mezza Luna, 1 Temple Ln. (☎ 671 2840), corner of Dame St. Celestial food; roast pepper and chicken crepe £8.50. Daily lunch specials £5 (served noon-5pm). Delicious desserts £3.50. Open M-Th noon-11pm, F-Sa noon-11:30pm, Su noon-10:30pm.

Poco Loco, 32 Parliament St. (☎ 679 1950), between Grattan Bridge and City Hall. Good Mexican food with a wide variety of choices. Even the appetizers are filling.

Juste Pasta, 12 Fownes St. (☎ 670 3110), next to Cafe Irie. A mighty selection of hearty pasta dishes for less than £7. Vegetarians will have more than juste a good time. Open daily noon-midnight. In winter 5pm-midnight.

Wed Wose Cafe, 18 Exchequer St. (☎ 672 7323), off South Great Georges St., near the red-brick market. My wove is wike the filling all-day breakfasts in Dubwin's swickest gweasy spoon. Iwish breakfast £3. Open M-Sa 8am-5pm, Su 10am-4pm.

Leo Burdock's, 2 Werburgh St. (☎ 454 0306), uphill from Christ Church Cathedral. Takeaway only. Burdock's fish and chips is a religious experience that's a holy ritual for many Dubliners. Fish £3; chips £1.20. Open M-Sa noon-midnight, Su 4pm-midnight.

Bewley's Cafes. A Dublin institution. Dark wood paneling, marble table tops, and mirrored walls. Decadent pastries (£1), variable coffee. Meals are plain but inexpensive. 78 Grafton St. (☎ 635 5470), was recently renovated for the worse, but the room for its most famous patron, James Joyce, still charms. Open daily 7:30am-11pm, later weekends. **Branches:** 12 Westmoreland St. (☎ 677 6761; open M-Sa 7:30am-7:30pm, Su 9:30am-8pm); 13 South Great Georges St. (open M-Sa 7:45am-6pm); and on Mary St., past Henry St. (open M-W 7am-9pm, Th-Sa 7am-2am, Su 10am-10pm).

⬛ SIGHTS

TOURS. Guided tours generally last about two hours, but entertaining anecdotes and continuous movement preclude boredom. **Dublin Bus** (see p. 670) also runs a number of tours through and around the city, departing from the main office.

The Historical Walking Tour (☎ 878 0227). A 2hr. crash course in Dublin's history from the Celts to the present, stopping at 9 points of historical interest and laying emphasis on the "gritty" lives of ordinary Dubliners. Meet at Trinity front gate May-Sept. M-F 11am and 3pm, Sa-Su 11am, noon, and 3pm; Oct.-Apr. F-Su noon. £6, students £5.

Trinity College Walking Tour (☎ 608 1000). Moderately irreverent and hugely pretentious, this tour concentrates on University lore and glances slightly at Dublin's history. Leaves roughly every 45min. from the info booth inside the front gate. 30min. tours £6; includes admission to the Old Library and the Book of Kells.

1916 Rebellion Walking Tour (☎ 676 2493). Shows you the scars the rebellion left and the state it created. 2hr. Meet at the International Bar, 23 Wicklow St. mid-May to Aug. Tu-Sa 11:30am. £6, students and seniors £5.

The Literary Pub Crawl (☎ 670 5602). References Dublin's literary history to its liquid history. Meet at The Duke, 2 Duke St. Easter-Oct. M-Sa 7:30pm, Su noon and 7:30pm; Nov.-Easter Th-Sa 7:30pm, Su noon and 7:30pm. £6.50, students £5.50. Book at the door or at the Dublin Tourist Centre for 15p extra.

The Musical Pub Crawl (☎ 478 0193). An enjoyable jaunt led by two musicians, who'll teach you how to differentiate between trad sessions by the end. Show up early upstairs at Oliver St. John Gogarty's, on the corner of Fleet St. and Anglesea St. May-Oct. daily 7:30pm, Nov. and Feb.-Apr. F-Sa 7:30pm. £6, students and seniors £5.

TRINITY COLLEGE AND ENVIRONS

TRINITY COLLEGE

The main entrance fronts College Green. ☎ *608 1000. Grounds always open. Free.*

Ancient walls contain Trinity's sprawling expanse of stone buildings, cobblestone walks, and green grounds. The British built Trinity in 1592 as a Protestant religious seminary that would "civilize the Irish and cure them of Popery." The college became part of the accepted path that members of the Anglo-Irish elite tread on their way to high government and social positions. Jonathan Swift, Oscar Wilde, and Samuel Beckett are just a few of the famous Irishmen who studied here. Until the 1960s, the Catholic church deemed it a cardinal sin to attend Trinity; once the church lifted the ban, the size of the student body more than tripled.

THE OLD LIBRARY. The star exhibit in this 1712 chamber's collection of ancient manuscripts is the magnificent **Book of Kells.** Around AD 800, four Irish monks squeezed multicolored ink from bugs and plants to illuminate this four-volume edition of the Gospels. Each page holds a dizzyingly intricate latticework of Celtic designs, into which images of animals and Latin text are interwoven. For preservation purposes, the display is limited to two volumes, of which one page is turned each month. The **Book of Durrow,** Ireland's oldest manuscript, is also on display here periodically. Upstairs, the **Long Room** contains "Ireland's oldest harp," the so-called **BrianBorú Harp** (the model for Irish coins), and one of the few remaining 1916 proclamations of the Republic of Ireland. *(From the main gate, go straight; it's on the southern side of Library Sq. Open June-Sept. M-Sa 9:30am-5pm, Su noon-4:30pm; Oct.-May M-Sa 9:30am-5pm, Su noon-4:30pm. £4.50, students and seniors £4.)*

OTHER SIGHTS

BANK OF IRELAND. Built in 1729, the building originally housed the 18th-century **Irish parliament,** a body that represented the Anglo-Irish landowning class. After the Act of Union, the British sold the building to the bank on the condition that the bank blot out any material evidence of the parliament. Enormous curved walls and pillars were erected around the original structure to make the whole thing look more impressive; the bank inside is much smaller. *(☎ 677 6801. Open M-W and F 10am-4pm, Th 10am-5pm. 45min. guided talks Tu 10:30am, 11:30am, and 1:45pm. Free.)*

AROUND KILDARE STREET

LEINSTER HOUSE. The Duke of Leinster built his home on Kildare Street back in 1745, when most of the urban upper-crust lived north of the Liffey. By erecting his house so far south, where land was cheaper, he was able to front it with an enormous lawn. Now Leinster House provides chambers for the **Irish parliament,** or **An tOireachtas** (on tir-OCH-tas). The Dáil meets, very roughly, from October to Easter (with lots of breaks), Tuesdays and Wednesdays 3-9pm, and Thursdays 10am-3pm. When the Dáil is in session, visitors can view the proceedings by contacting the Captain of the Guard, who conducts **tours** of the Dáil's galleries. *(☎ 678 9911. Passport necessary for identification. Tours meet Sa 1 per hr. in the adjacent National Gallery.)*

ST. STEPHEN'S GREEN AND MERRION SQUARE

ST. STEPHEN'S GREEN. The 22-acre park was a private estate until the Guinness clan bequeathed it to the city. Today it's a hotbed of activity, crowded with an artificial lake, punks, swans, a waterfall, and statues. During the summer, all enjoy the outdoor musical and theatrical productions near the old bandstand. *(Kildare, Dawson, and Grafton St. all lead to it. Open M-Sa 8am-dusk, Su 10am-dusk.)*

MERRION SQUARE. The square and adjacent **Fitzwilliam Street** visually stimulate with Georgian buildings fronted by elaborate doorways. W.B. Yeats moved from 18 Fitzwilliam St. to 82 Merrion Sq. Farther south on **Harcourt Street,** playwright George Bernard Shaw and Dracula's creator, Bram Stoker, once lived at #61 and #16, respectively. **#29 Lower Fitzwilliam Street** demonstrates the lifestyle of the 18th-century Anglo-Irish elite. A short audio-visual show leads to a 25-minute tour of the house. *(☎ 702 6165. Open Tu-Sa 10am-5pm, Su 2-5pm. £2.50, students and seniors £1.)* The prim Georgian townhouses continue up **Dawson Street,** which connects St. Stephen's Green to Trinity College one block west of Leinster House. Dawson St. has the honor of providing an address to the **Mansion House,** home of the Lord Mayors of Dublin since 1715. The Irish state declared its independence here in 1919; the Anglo-Irish truce was signed here in 1921.

NEWMAN HOUSE. A fully restored building that was once the seat of **University College Dublin,** the Catholic answer to Trinity (see p. 677). Joyce's years here are chronicled in the latter part of *Portrait of the Artist as a Young Man.* The poet Gerard Manley Hopkins spent the last years of his life teaching classics at the college. *(85-86 St. Stephen's Green South. ☎ 706 7422. Tours on the hour. Open June-Sept. Tu-F noon-5pm, Sa 2-5pm, Su 11am-2pm. £3, students and seniors £2.)*

THE SHAW BIRTHPLACE. Suitable for viewing as either a period piece or a glimpse into the childhood of George Bernard Shaw. Mrs. Shaw held recitals here, sparking little George's interest in music, and kept a lovely Victorian garden, sparking George's interest in landscape painting—until socialism, that is. *(33 Synge St. ☎ 475 0854. Stroll down Camden, turn right on Harrington, and then left onto Synge. Or take buses #16, 19, or 122 from O'Connell St. Open May-Oct. M-Sa 10am-5pm, Su 11am-5pm. £2.60, students and seniors £2.10; joint ticket with Dublin Writers Museum £4.60, or with the Writers Museum and the James Joyce Museum £6.50.)*

THE IRISH JEWISH MUSEUM. A restored former synagogue chronicles the history of the small Jewish community in Ireland from 1079 (five arrived and were sent away) through later waves of European migration. The most famous Dublin Jew covered is Leopold Bloom, hero of *Ulysses. (3-4 Walworth Rd., off Victoria St. South Circular Rd. runs to Victoria St.; from there follow signs. Take buses #16, 20, or any others to South Circular Rd. ☎ 490 1857. Open May-Sept. Tu, Th, and Su 11am-3:30pm, Oct.-Apr. Su 10:30am-2:30pm. Access at other times fairly easily arranged.)*

TEMPLE BAR, DAME ST., AND THE CATHEDRALS

DUBLIN CASTLE. King John of England built the castle in 1204 on top of the first Viking settlement of *Dubh Linn;* more recently, a series of structures from various eras have covered the site, dating mostly from the 18th and 19th centuries and culminating in a rather uninspired 20th-century office complex. For 700 years after its construction, Dublin Castle was the seat of British rule in Ireland. The **State Apartments,** once home to English viceroys, now entertain EU representatives and foreign heads of state. Next door, the **Dublin City Hall,** designed as the Royal Exchange in 1779, boasts an intricate inner dome and statues of national heroes. *(Dame St. ☎ 677 7129. State Apartments open M-F 10am-5pm, Sa–Su and holidays 2-5pm, except during official functions. £3, students and seniors £2; grounds free.)*

CHRIST CHURCH CATHEDRAL. Dublin's cathedrals are considered works of art more than centers of worship in the 20th century. Built centuries ago for Catholic worship, they were forced to convert to the Anglican Church of Ireland in the 16th century. Stained glass sparkles above the raised crypts, one of which supposedly belongs to Strongbow. The cavernous crypt once held shops and drinking houses, but now cobwebs hang down from the ceiling, fragments of ancient pillars lie about like bleached bones, and a mummified cat is caught in the act of chasing a mummified mouse. *(At the end of Dame St. ☎ 677 8099. Take buses #50 from Eden Quay or 78A from Aston Quay. Open daily 10am-5:30pm except during services. £2 donation strongly encouraged, concessions £1.)* **Dublinia,** a recent appendage to Christ Church Cathedral, recreates medieval Dublin, with life-sized reconstructions. It's informative, if a little underwhelming. *(☎ 679 4611. Open Apr.-Oct. daily 10am-5pm; Sept.-Mar. 11am-4pm. £4, students and children £3, with cathedral £4.95, students and children £3.50.)*

ST. PATRICK'S CATHEDRAL. This 12th-century cathedral measures 300 ft. from stem to stern, making it Ireland's largest. St. Patrick allegedly baptized converts in the park next door. Jonathan Swift spent his last years as Dean of St. Patrick's; his crypt rises above the south nave. *(Patrick St. Take bus #49, 49A, 50, 54A, 56A, 65, 65B, 77, or 77A from Eden Quay. ☎ 475 4817. Open Apr.-Sept. M-F 9am-6pm, Oct.-Mar. Sa 9-5. Su closed 11am-12:45pm and 3-4pm. £2, concessions £1.)*

GUINNESS BREWERY AND KILMAINHAM

GUINNESS HOPSTORE. Guiness perpetuates the legend of the world's best stout at its Hopstore, which has displays on the historical and modern processes of brewing and a short promotional film. Best of all is the bar, where visitors get a complimentary pint of dark and creamy goodness. Don't even ask if it's "good for you." *(St. James's Gate. Take bus #51B or 78A from Aston Quay or bus #123 from O'Connell St. ☎ 408 4800; www.guinness.ie. Open Apr.-Sept. M-Sa 9:30am-5pm, Su 10:30am-4:30pm; Oct.-Mar. M-Sa 9:30am-4pm, Su noon-4pm. £5, students and seniors £4, under 12 £1.)*

KILMAINHAM GAOL. Almost all the rebels who fought in Ireland's struggle for independence from 1792 to 1921 spent time here. Today the former prison is a museum that traces the history of penal practices since the 19th century. *(Inchicore Rd. Take bus #51 from Aston Quay, #51A from Lower Abbey St., or #79 from Aston Quay. ☎ 453 5984. Open Apr.-Sept. daily 9:30am-5pm; Oct.-Mar. M-F 9:30am-4pm, Su 10am-5pm. Tours every 35min. £3.50, seniors £2.50, students and children £1.50.)*

DUBLINESE Mastering the Dublin dialect has been a persistent challenge to writers and thespians of the 20th century. James Joyce, Brendan Behan, and Roddy Doyle are just a few ambitious scribes who have tried to capture the nuances of this gritty, witty city. The following is a short introduction to Dubliners' favorite phrases.

Names for Outsiders: The rivalry between Dubliners and their country cousins is fierce. For Dubliners, all counties outside their own blur into one indiscriminate wasteland populated with "culchies," "plonkers," "turf-gobblers," and "muck-savages."

In Times of Difficulty: Dublinese is expeditious in keeping others in line. Idiots are rebuked as "eejits"; in dire situations, they are called "head-the-ball." Total exasperation calls for "shite and onions." When all is restored to order, it's said that "the job's oxo and the ship's name is murphy."

Affectionate Nicknames for Civic Landmarks: Over the past couple decades, the government has graced the city with several public artworks that personify the Irish spirit in the female form. Dubliners have responded with poetic rhetoric. Off Grafton St., the statue of the fetching fishmongress Molly Malone is commonly referred to as "the dish with the fish" and "the tart with the cart." The goddess of the River Liffy sits in a fountain on O'Connell St. and is popularly heralded as the "floozy in the jacuzzi," "Anna Rexia," and even "the whore in the sewer" (pronounced HEW-er).

O'CONNELL ST. AND PARNELL SQUARE

Dublin's biggest shopping thoroughfare starts at the Liffey and leads to Parnell Square. At 150 ft., it was once the widest street in Europe. The center traffic islands contain monuments to the Irish leaders who organized the heroic Dublin general strike of 1913 (see p. 661). **O'Connell's statue** faces the Liffey and the O'Connell Bridge; the winged women aren't angels but Winged Victories, although one has a bullet hole in a rather inglorious place. At the other end of the street, **Parnell's statue** points towards nearby Mooney's pub while Parnell's famous words "Thus far and no further" are engraved below his feet. A block up O'Connell St., where Cathedral St. intersects, the 1988 statue of a woman lounging in water is officially named the Spirit of the Liffey or **Anna Livia**. Not just a place to send a letter, the **General Post Office** on O'Connell St. was the nerve center of the 1916 Easter Rising (see p. 661). When British troops closed in, mailbags became barricades.

ALONG THE QUAYS

THE CUSTOM HOUSE. Dublin's greatest architectural triumph was designed and built in the 1780s by James Gandon, who gave up the chance to be St. Petersburg's state architect to settle in Dublin. Carved heads along the frieze represent the rivers of Ireland; the Liffey is the only girl in the bunch. *(Custom House Quay. ☎ 878 7660. Visitor Center open mid-Mar. to Nov. M-F 10am-12:30pm, Sa-Su 2-5pm; Nov. to mid-Mar. W-F 10am-12:30pm, Su 2-5pm.)*

FOUR COURTS. This Gandon work appears monumentally impressive from the front, but the back and sides reveal 20th-century ballast. On April 14, 1922, General Rory O'Connor seized the Four Courts on behalf of the anti-Treaty IRA; two months later, the Free State government of Griffith and Collins attacked the Four Courts garrison, starting the Irish Civil War (see p. 661). The building now houses the highest court in Ireland. *(Inn's Quay, several quays to the west of the Custom House.)*

ST. MICHAN'S CHURCH. The dry atmosphere in the church has preserved the corpses in the vaults, which inspired Bram Stoker's *Dracula*. Of particular interest is a 6½ ft. tall crusader (dead) and the hanged, drawn, and quartered bodies (very dead) of two of the 1798 rebels. *(Church St. Open Mar.-Oct. M-F 10am-12:45pm and 2-4:45pm, Sa 10am-12:45pm; Nov.-Feb. M-F 12:30-3:30pm, Sa 10am-12:45pm. Church of Ireland services Su 10am. £2, students and seniors £1.50, under 16 50p.)*

SMITHFIELD

OLD JAMESON DISTILLERY. Learn how science, grain, and tradition come together to create the golden fluid called whiskey. The tour ends with a glass of the Irish whiskey of your choice; be quick to volunteer in the beginning and you'll get to sample a whole tray of different kinds. Feel the burn. *(Bow St. ☎ 807 2355. Tours daily 9:30am-5:30pm. £3.95, students and seniors £3.)*

CEOL IRISH TRADITIONAL MUSIC CENTRE. Computers and interactive media provide extensive demonstrations of the various instruments, songs, and dances that make up trad as we now know it. *(Next to Jameson, at the base of the large chimney between North King St. and Arran Quay. ☎ 817 3820. Open M-Sa 10am-6pm, Su 11am-6pm. £5, students and seniors £4, children £3. Chimney open M-Sa 10am-6pm, Su 11am-6pm; £5, £4 student. Combined music and chimney £10, £8.)*

DISTANT SIGHTS

PHOENIX PARK. Europe's largest enclosed public park (1760 acres) is home to the residences of the President *(Áras an Uachtaraín)* and the US Ambassador, as well as cricket pitches, cattle, and red deer. The **Phoenix Column**, a Corinthian column capped with a phoenix rising from flames, is something of a pun—the park's name actually comes from the Irish *Fionn Uísce*, "clean water." *(Take bus #10 from O'Connell St. or #25 or 26 from Middle Abbey St. west along the river. Free.)*

Dublin Zoo, one of the world's oldest zoos and Europe's largest, is in the park along with 700 non-indigenous animals. *(Bus #10 from O'Connell St. ☎ 677 1425. Open M-Sa 9:30am-6pm, Su 10:30am-6pm. £6.30, students £4.80, families £18.50-22.)*

CASINO MARINO. It's an architectural gem and house of tricks. You can gambol here, but you can't gamble; it's a casino only in the sense of "small house," built for the Earl of Charlemont in 1758 as a seaside villa. Roof-top funeral urns are chimneys, the columns are hollow and serve as drains, the casino has secret tunnels and trick doors, and the lions standing guard are made of stone. *(Off Malahide Rd. Take bus #123 from O'Connell St. or #27 or 42 from the quays by Busáras. ☎ 833 1618. Open daily June-Sept. 9:30am-6:30pm, May and Oct. 10am-5pm, Nov. W and Su noon-4pm, Feb.-Apr. Th and Su noon-4pm. Admission by guided tour. £2, seniors £1.50, students and children £1.)*

🏛 MUSEUMS AND GALLERIES

THE NATIONAL MUSEUMS

General Information Line for all three museums (☎ 677 7444). All open Tu-Sa 10am-5pm, Su 2-5pm. All free. Museum Link bus runs hourly from the Natural History and Archaeology museums to Collins Barracks. Single trip 85p, all-day pass £2.

Dublin's three national museums cover a broad slice of Irish life, history, and scholarship. The new National Museum at Collins Barracks is the farthest out geographically, while the Museum of Natural History is the farthest out conceptually.

▮THE NATURAL HISTORY MUSEUM. A museum within a museum, this creepily fascinating collection of world wildlife displays not so much the natural world as how museums used to interpret their role in it. A skeleton of the ancient Irish Elk, glass cases of stuffed animals, amoebae replicas, and jars of Irish tapeworms are mysteriously compelling. *(Merrion Square West. Free.)*

THE NATIONAL MUSEUM OF ARCHAEOLOGY AND HISTORY. The largest of Dublin's museums contains a number of beautiful artifacts spanning the last two millennia. The museum contains extraordinary reminders of ancient Ireland. One room gleams with the **Tara Brooch,** the **Ardagh Hoard** (including the great chalice), and other Celtic goldwork. Another section is devoted to the Republic's founding years, and shows off the bloody vest of nationalist hero **James Connolly.** *(Kildare St., adjacent to Natural History Museum. ☎ 677 7444. Guided tours £1. Call for times.)*

THE NATIONAL MUSEUM OF DECORATIVE ARTS AND HISTORY, COLLINS BARRACKS. The most sophisticated of the three, the baby of the National Museum family gleams with exhibits that range from the traditional to the multidisciplinary. The Curator's Choice room displays a range of objects in light of their artistic importance, cultural context, and historical significance. *(Benburb St., off Wolfe Tone Quay. Take the Museum Link, or bus #10 from O'Connell. #90 to Heuston Station stops across the street. 1-2 guided tours daily. £1.)*

OTHER MUSEUMS AND GALLERIES

THE NATIONAL GALLERY. A collection of over 2400 canvases includes paintings by Brueghel, Carravaggio, El Greco, Goya, Rembrandt, and Vermeer. Works by 19th-century Irish artists comprise a major part of the collection; of special interest are the works of **Jack Yeats,** the brother of William. A new Millennium wing housing a Centre for the Study of Irish Art and new gallery space will be completed in 2001. *(Merrion Square West. ☎ 661 5133; www.nationalgallery.ie. Free guided tours Sa 3pm, Su 2:15pm, 3pm, and 4pm. Open M-Sa 10am-5:30pm, Th 10am-8:30pm, Su 2-5pm. Free.)*

THE DUBLIN CIVIC MUSEUM. This pint-sized, two-story townhouse holds photos, antiquities, and knick-knacks relating to the whole range of Dublin life, from the accessories of the Vikings to the shoes of Patrick Cotter, the 8½ ft. "giant of Ireland." *(58 South William St. ☎ 679 4260. Open Tu-Sa 10am-6pm, Su 11am-2pm. Free.)*

THE ROYAL HOSPITAL KILMAINHAM. Built in 1679 as a hospice for retired or disabled soldiers, the compound now houses the **Irish Museum of Modern Art.** Modern Irish artists are intermixed with others as the gallery builds up a permanent collection. *(Military Road. ☎ 612 9900. Bus #90 and 91 from Heuston Station, #78A and 79 from the City Center. Guided tours W and F 2:30pm, Su 12:15pm. Call for events. Museum and building open Tu-Sa 10am-5:30pm, Su noon-5:30pm. Free.)*

BEST OF THE REST. The **Dublin Writers' Museum** has rare editions, manuscripts, and memorabilia of Swift, Shaw, Wilde, Yeats, Beckett, Brendan Behan, Patrick Kavanagh, and Sean O'Casey. *(18 Parnell Sq. North. ☎ 872 2077. Open June-Aug. M-F 10am-6pm, Sa 10am-5pm, Su 11am-5pm; Sept.-May M-Sa 10am-5pm. £3.10, students and seniors £2.89; combined ticket with Shaw birthplace or James Joyce Centre £4.60.)* The new **James Joyce Centre** offers Joyceana ranging from portraits of individuals who inspired his characters to more arcane delights. Feel free to mull over Joyce's works in the library or the tearoom. *(35 North Great Georges St. ☎ 873 1984. Open Sept.-June M-Sa 9:30am-5pm, Su 12:30-5pm; July-Aug. M-Sa 9:30am-5pm, Su 11am-5pm. £3, students and seniors £2.)* Dublin's sparkling new anthem to its musical wonders, the **Hot Press Irish Music Hall of Fame,** offers aheadset tour takes you through memorabilia-laden displays on the history of Irish music, from bards to the modern studio. *(57 Middle Abbey St. ☎ 878 3345. Open daily 10am-6pm last entry. £6; concessions £4.)*

SHOPPING

LITERARY SHOPPING

Eason, 80 Middle Abbey St. (☎ 873 3811), off O'Connell St. A floorspace behemoth. Lots of serious tomes and an extensive "Irish interest" section. Their bargain shelves are in the cleverly named **Bargain Books,** and reside diagonally across Abbey St. Open M-W and Sa 8:30am-6:45pm, Th 8:30am-8:45pm, F 8:30am-7:45pm, Su 1:45-5:45pm.

Winding Stair Bookstore, 40 Ormond Quay (☎ 873 3292), on the North Side. 3 atmospheric floors of good tunes, great views, and cheap food. New and used books, contemporary Irish literature, and literary periodicals. Open M-Sa 10am-6pm, Su 1-6pm.

Fred Hanna's, 27-29 Nassau St. (☎ 677 1255), across from Trinity College at Dawson St. Intelligent staff answers all questions about contemporary Irish writing. Open M-W and Sa 8:30am-6:45pm, Th 8:30am-8:45pm, F 8:30am-7:45pm, Su 1:45-5:45pm.

Books Upstairs, 36 College Green (☎ 679 6687), across from Trinity Gate. Extensive sections on gay literature and women's studies. The principal distributor for *Gay Community News.* Open M-F 10am-7pm, Sa 10am-6pm, Su 1-6pm.

An Siopa Leabhar, 6 Harcourt St. (an SHUP-a LAU-er; ☎ 478 3814). Irish historical and political books, as well as tapes and books on traditional music. Specializes in literature and resources in Irish. Open M-F 9:30am-5:30pm, Sa 10am-1:30pm and 2-4pm.

RECORDS, TAPES, AND CDS

Claddagh Records, 2 Cecilia St. (☎ 677 0262), Temple Bar, between Temple Ln. and Crow St. Best selection of trad and a variety of music from other countries. Open M-F 10:30am-5:30pm, Sa noon-5:30pm.

Freebird Records, 1 Eden Quay (☎ 873 1250), on the North Side facing the river. Crowded basement has perhaps Dublin's best selection of indie rock. Proprietors can recommend local bands. Open M-W and Sa 10:30am-6pm, Th-F 10:30am-7:30pm.

🎵 ENTERTAINMENT

Be it poetry or punk you fancy, Dublin is equipped to entertain you. The *Event Guide* (free) is available at the Dublin Visitor Centre, Temple Bar restaurants, and the Temple Bar info center. It comes out every other Friday with ads in the back, fawning reviews in the front, and reasonably complete listings of museums and literary, musical, and theatrical events in between. The glossier *In Dublin* (£1.95) comes out every two weeks with feature articles and listings for music, theater, art exhibitions, clubs, and gay venues. *Events of the Week* is a much smaller, free booklet, also jammed with ads, but there's good info buried in it.

MUSIC

Pubs are the scene of much of the musical action. There is often a cover charge of £3-4 on better-known acts. *Hot Press* (£1.50) has the most up-to-date music listings, particularly for rock. Scheduled concerts tend to start at 9pm, impromptu ones later. Traditional music (trad) is not a tourist gimmick but a vibrant and important element of the Dublin music scene. Some pubs in the city center have trad sessions nightly, others nearly so: **Hughes', Oliver St. John Gogarty,** and **McDaid's** are all good choices (see **Publin,** p. 684). The best pub for trad in the entire city is ▨ **Cobblestones** (☎ 872 1799), King St. North, in Smithfield. Another great small venue for live music, from rock to folk, is **Whelan's,** 25 Wexford St. (☎ 478 0766), the continuation of South Great Georges St., with music nightly. Next door, **The Mean Fiddler,** Wexford St., has rollicking shows. Big-deal bands frequent the **Baggot Inn,** 143 Baggot St. (☎ 676 1430). **The Temple Bar Music Centre,** Curved St. (☎ 670 9202), has events and concerts virtually every night. The **National Concert Hall,** Earlsfort Terr. (☎ 671 1533), provides a venue for classical concerts and performances. July and August bring nightly shows (tickets £6-12, students half-price). Programs for the **National Symphony** are available at the Dublin Tourist Centre.

THEATER

Off Dame St. and Temple Bar, smaller theater companies thrive, presenting new plays and innovative interpretations of the classics. The ▨ **Abbey Theatre,** 26 Lower Abbey St., was founded by Yeats and Lady Gregory in 1904 to promote Irish cultural revival and modernist theater. Today it is the National Theatre. (☎ 878 7222. Box office open M-Sa 10:30am-7pm. Tickets £10-17.50, matinees Sa 2:30pm £8; students M-Th £8.) More experimental productions are put up downstairs at the **Peacock Theatre,** 26 Lower Abbey St. (☎ 878 7222. Lunch events £8, students £5; theater tickets £8-10, matinee £6.) The **Gate Theatre,** 1 Cavendish Row, specializes in international period drama. (☎ 874 4045. Box office open M-Sa 10am-7pm. Tickets £13-15; M-Th student discount with ID at curtain £6, subject to availability.)

FILM

Ireland's well-supported film industry reeled with the arrival of the **Irish Film Centre,** 6 Eustace St., Temple Bar. You must be a "member" to buy tickets. (☎ 679 3477; www.fii.ie. Weekly membership £1; yearly membership £10, students £7.50. Membership must be purchased at least 15min. before start of show; each member can buy only 4 tickets per screening. Matinees £2; 5pm showing £2.50; after 7pm £4, students £3. 18 and older.) **The Screen,** D'Olier St. (☎ 672 5500), also runs artsy reels. First-run cinemas cluster on O'Connell St., the quays, and Middle Abbey St.

SPORTS AND RECREATION

Dubliners aren't as sports-crazy as their country cousins tend to be, but that's not saying much. The season for **Gaelic football** and **hurling** (see **Sports,** p. 666) runs from mid-February to November. Provincial finals take place in July, national semifinals on Sundays in August (hurling the 1st week, football the 2nd and 3rd weeks), and All-Ireland Finals in either late August or early September. Games are played in **Croke Park** and on **Phibsborough Rd.** Tickets are theoretically available at the turnstiles, but they tend to sell out quickly; your best bet is to hit the Dublin pubs on game day and see who's selling. Home games of the Irish **rugby** team are played in **Lansdowne Road Stadium,** with the peak of the season spanning from February to early April. **Camogie** (women's hurling) finals occur in September. For sports information, check the Friday papers or contact the GAA (☎ 836 3232).

⊠ PUBLIN

James Joyce once proposed that a "good puzzle would be to cross Dublin without passing a pub." As in the rest of Ireland, most pubs close at 11:30pm, but the laws that dictate these hours are changing. An increasing number of Dublin pubs have permits for late hours, at least on some nights; drink prices at these watering holes tend to rise around 11pm. Bars will post their closing time as "late," meaning after midnight. The *Let's Go* **Dublin Pub Crawl** aids in discovering the best pint of Guinness. We recommend that you begin your crawl at the gates of Trinity College, then stroll up Grafton St., teeter to Camden St., stumble to South Great Georges St., and triumphantly drag your soused self to Temple Bar. Start early (say, noon).

GRAFTON STREET AND VICINITY

Sinnott's, South King St. (☎ 478 4698). Classy twentysomethings gather in this basement with wooden rafters. Portrays itself as a pub for readers and writers, but let's be honest, it's for drinkers. Chart music packs the dance floor until 2am.

McDaid's, 3 Harry St. (☎ 679 4395), off Grafton St. across from Anne St. The center of Ireland's literary scene in the 50s. Book-adorned walls pack in a yuppie crowd downstairs and a more sedate set above. W blues; Su blues and jazzier tunes.

Café en Seine, 40 Dawson St. (☎ 677 4369). Built to impress. A chic cafe with dainty pastries in front. A very long bar undulates through the hall's super-nouveau decor. A large crowd of mixed ages. Late bar W-Sa until 2am; Su jazz 1-3:30pm.

M. J. O'Neills (☎ 679 3614), Suffolk St., across from the Dublin Tourist Centre. The maze of staircases is quiet by day, but a fun young crowd meets here at night. Sports screen. Late closing Th-F 12:30am, Sa midnight.

Davy Byrne's, 21 Duke St. (☎ 677 5217), off Grafton St. A lively, middle-aged crowd throngs at the pub that Joyce chose as the setting for the Cyclops chapter in Ulysses. The images of Joyce himself on the walls hint at some redecorating since then.

The Pavilion, Trinity College (☎ 608 1000), head to the far right corner of the campus from the main gate. Watch a summer cricket match over Guinness at the Pav. Open all year, daily noon-11pm. You can also join the Trinity students Oct.-May under the vaults of **The Buttery**, in a basement to the left as you enter the campus. Open M-F 2-11pm.

HARCOURT AND CAMDEN ST.

The Bleeding Horse, 24 Upper Camden St. (☎ 475 2705). You can't beat it, 'cause it ain't dead yet. All sorts of little nooks for private affairs. Late bar with DJ Th-Sa.

The Odeon, the Old Harcourt Train Station (☎ 478 2088). The Odeon has the second longest bar in Ireland. The upstairs is cozier (but still huge). DJ on Sa. Late bar Th-Sa.

WEXFORD ST. AND SOUTH GREAT GEORGES

⊠ **The Stag's Head**, 1 Dame Ct. (☎ 679 3701). The subtle and ancient entrance has a mosaic of a stag's head on the sidewalk. Beautiful Victorian pub with stained glass, mirrors, and yes, a stag's head. The crowd dons everything from t-shirts to tuxes and spills out into the alleys. Excellent grub. Main courses around £5-7; served M-F 12:30-3:30pm and 5:30-7:30pm, Sa 12:30-2:30pm. Late bar Th-F till 12:30am. Closed Su.

⊠ **Whelan's**, 25 Wexford St. (☎ 478 0766). Continue down South Great Georges St. The stage venue in back hosts big-name trad and rock groups. Cover £5-8. Gigs followed Th-Su by pop and dance music. Open Th-Su until 1:30am.

Mono, 26 Wexford St. (☎ 475 8555), next door to Whelan's. A neon club scene. Late bar every night. Occasional theme nights. Cover £5-7.

The Globe, 11 South Great Georges St. (☎ 671 1220). Pretentious clientele? "Wankers," the barman corrects, "not pretentious. Arty-farty wannabe artists." Maybe so, but it's a fine spot for a Guinness or cappuccinos. **Rí Rá** nightclub attached (see p. 687).

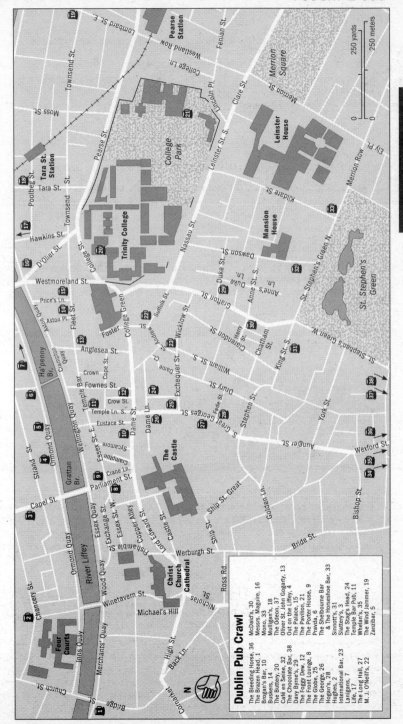

Dublin Pub Crawl

The Bleeding Horse, 36
The Brazen Head, 1
Brogan's Bar, 10
Buskers, 14
The Buttery, 20
Café en Seine, 32
The Chocolate Bar, 38
Davy Byrne's, 29
The Foggy Dew, 12
The Front Lounge, 8
The Globe, 25
The George, 26
Hogan's, 28
Hughes, 2
International Bar, 23
Lanigans, 7
Life, 17
The Long Hall, 27
M. J. O'Neill's, 22
McDaid's, 30
Messrs. Maguire, 16
Mono, 33
Mulligan's, 18
The Odeon, 37
Oliver St. John Gogarty, 13
Out on the Liffey, 4
The Palace, 15
The Pavilion, 21
The Porter House, 9
Pravda, 6
The Shelbourne Bar
    & The Horseshoe Bar, 33
Sinnott's, 31
Slattery's, 3
The Stag's Head, 24
Temple Bar Pub, 11
Whelan's, 35
The Wind Jammer, 19
Zanzibar, 5

TEMPLE BAR

■ **The Palace,** 21 Fleet St. (☎ 677 9290), behind Aston Quay. This classic, neighborly Dublin pub has old-fashioned wood paneling and close quarters; head for the comfy seats in the skylit back room. The favorite of many a Dubliner.

The Porter House, 16-18 Parliament St. (☎ 679 8847). The largest selection of world beers in the country, and 8 self-brewed kinds of porter, stout, and ale. Their excellent sampler tray includes a sip of ale brewed with oysters and other oddities (£6). Late bar Th-F to 1:30am, Sa to midnight. Occasional trad, blues, and rock gigs.

The Foggy Dew, Fownes St. (☎ 677 9328). A big, mellow neighborhood pub. A great spot for a pint or two without the flash of other Temple Bar pubs. Live rock Su nights.

Oliver St. John Gogarty (☎ 671 1822), at Fleet and Anglesea St. Also see the hostel (**Other Dublin Hostels,** p. 674). Lively and convivial atmosphere in a traditional, but touristed, pub. Named for Joyce's nemesis and onetime roommate, who appears in *Ulysses* as Buck Mulligan (see p. 689). Stately, plump trad sessions daily from 2:30pm. Open M-F until 1:30am, Sa until midnight, Su until 1am.

Messrs. Maguire, Burgh Quay (☎ 670 5777). You'll still find new rooms here after hours inside, especially if you've been quaffing the microbrews. Late bar W-Sa. Trad Su-Tu.

BEST OF THE REST

Mulligan's, 8 Poolbeg St. (☎ 677 5582), behind Burgh Quay off Tara St. Upholds its reputation as one of the best pint pourers in Dublin. The crowd consists mainly of middle-aged men. A taste of the typical Irish pub: low-key and nothing fancy. Really.

The Brazen Head, 20 North Bridge St. (☎ 679 5186), off Merchant's Quay. Dublin's oldest pub, established in 1198 as the first stop after the bridge on the way into the city. The courtyard is a pickup scene. Nightly Irish music, F-Sa late bar until 12:30am.

The Shelbourne Bar, the Shelbourne Hotel (☎ 676 6471), at the corner of Kildare St. and St. Stephen's Green North. The best place for cocktails in Dublin; their Bloody Mary is a divine hangover remedy. Also the center of Ireland's media culture—political cartoons decorate the walls, and journalists chat it up. The hotel's other bar, the **Horseshoe Bar,** attracts the bigwig politicians, who gripe about the journalists. Open M-Sa.

Lanigans, Clifton Court Hotel, Eden Quay (☎ 874 3535). Imagine a pub with Irish singers that actually attracts more Dubliners than tourists: this happy pub is it. Live music nightly at 9pm breaks down generational barriers and breaks into Irish dancing M-Th.

Slattery's, 129-31 Capel St. (☎ 872 7971). Trad and pop nightly downstairs. Upstairs rock and blues Th-Su (£3-4 cover).

The Wind Jammer, Townsend St. (☎ 677 2576), at East Lombard St. For mornings when you need a pint with your porridge, this "early house" opens at 7:30am every day.

Pravda, (☎ 874 0090), at the north side of the Ha'penny Bridge. The Russian late bar and Russian DJ action lasts until a Russian 1:30am. Actually there's nothing Russian about the place other than the Cyrilic on the wall murals. This theme bar is trendy, popular, and gay-friendly. Probably Russian-friendly, too.

Life, Lower Abbey St. (☎ 878 1032), next to the Irish Life Mall. The young and the beautiful head here after work to talk about important things, like image. Decently priced menu for lunch. Late bar Th-F until 1:30am, Sa until midnight.

GAY, LESBIAN, AND BISEXUAL PUBS

The George, 89 South Great Georges St. (☎ 478 2983). This throbbing, purple man o' war is Dublin's first and most prominent gay bar. A mixed-age crowd gathers throughout the day to chat and sip. The attached nightclub opens W-Su. Cover £5-7 after 10pm. Look spiffy—no effort, no entry. Frequent theme nights.

Out on the Liffey, 27 Upper Ormond Quay (☎ 872 2480). Ireland's second gay bar; its name plays on the more traditional Inn on the Liffey a few doors down. Comfortably small. The short hike from the city center ensures a more local crowd on most nights. Late bar W until 12:30am, F until 1:30am, and Sa until midnight. F-Su nights filled with music and a variety of live acts and dancing. Cover £2-3.

🎵 CLUBLIN

As a rule, clubs open at 10:30pm or 11pm, but the action starts up after 11:30pm when the pubs start to close. Clubbing is an expensive way to end the night, since covers run £5-12 and pints are £3. **Concessions,** available at many pubs, provide discounts with varying restrictions. Most clubs close between 1:30am and 3am.

Gay Community News (GCN), 6 South William St. (☎ 671 0939), is a free monthly that offers the most comprehensive and up-to-date information on gay life and nightlife in Dublin. It's available at Books Upstairs (p. 682), the George, and venues around Temple Bar. The "queer" pages of *In Dublin* list pubs, dance clubs, saunas, gay-friendly restaurants, bookshops, hotlines, and organizations.

🎵**The Kitchen,** The Clarence Hotel (☎ 677 6635), Wellington Quay, Temple Bar. Entrance is behind hotel on Essex St. With 2 bars and a dance floor, this U2-owned club is the coolest spot in town. Half of it is impossible to get into on most nights because it's filled with "VIPs." Dress as a model. Cover £8-10, students £3-4 on Tu.

Rí-Rá, 1 Exchequer St. (☎ 677 4835), in the back of the Globe Pub (see p. 684). Generally good music that steers clear of pop and house extremes. 2 floors, several bars, and more nooks and crannies than a crumpet. Open daily 11pm-2:30am. Cover £6-7.

PoD, 35 Harcourt St. (☎ 478 0225). Spanish-style decor meets hard-core dance music. As trendy as The Kitchen. The truly brave venture upstairs to **The Red Box** (☎ 478 0225), a separate, more intense club with a warehouse atmosphere, brain-crushing music, and an 8-person-deep crowd at the bar to winnow out the weak. Often hosts the big name DJs—cover charges skyrocket. Cover £8-10; Th ladies free before midnight; Th and Sa £5 with ISIC card. Start the evening at the Chocolate Bar or the Odeon, which also share the building (see **Pubs,** p. 684).

Velur, at the Vicar St. theater, (☎ 454 6656). Funk, soul, and a little bit of Austin Powers sound mixed with people who wear multiple shades of gray, black, and brown. Live bands and DJs. Cover Th-Sa £6.

Club M, Blooms Hotel, Anglesea St. (☎ 671 5622), Temple Bar. One of Dublin's largest clubs, attracting a crowd of diverse ages and styles, with multiple stairways and a few bars in the back. Pseudo-dance cages by the DJ occasionally host "exotic dancers" who try mightily to inject an aura of debauched celebration. Cover around £6.

Velvet, 60 Harcourt St. (☎ 478 3677). A smaller venue, usually blasting house and glam-girly sounds; looks up to the PoD and Kitchen crowd. Open nightly. Cover Th £6, F-Sa £8, W student night £3 or free.

🎊 FESTIVALS AND EVENTS

Dublin returns to 1904 each year on June 16, **Bloomsday,** the day on which the 18-hour journey of Joyce's *Ulysses* takes place. Festivities are held all week long, starting before the big day and continuing after it. The James Joyce Cultural Centre (☎ 873 1984; see p. 682) sponsors a reenactment of the funeral and wake, a lunch at Davy Byrne's, and a breakfast with Guinness. The **Feis Ceoil** music festival (☎ 676 7365) goes trad in mid-March. The **Guinness Blues Festival** (☎ 497 0381; www.guinnessbluesfest.com.) is a three-day extravaganza in mid-July, getting bigger and broader each year. The half-week leading up to **St. Patrick's Day** (☎ 676 3205; www.paddyfest.ie.), Mar. 17, occasions a city-wide carnival of concerts, fireworks, street theater, and intoxicated madness.

The **Dublin Theatre Festival,** held the first two weeks of October, is a spree of about 20 works of theater from Ireland and around the world. Tickets may be purchased all year at participating theaters, and, as the festival draws near, at the Festival Booking Office. (47 Nassau St. ☎ 677 8439. Tickets £10-16; student discounts vary by venue). The **Dublin Film Festival** (☎ 679 2937; www.iol.ie/dff) screens two weeks of Irish and international movies in March.

DUBLIN SUBURBS   ☎01

Strung along the Irish Sea, Dublin's suburbs (reachable by DART, suburban rail, or
Dublin buses) offer a calm alternative to the voracious human tide on Grafton
Street; at the same time, they host far too many crowds to fit the bill of Ireland's
romanticized rural villages. Two regions that stand out from the uniform suburban
sprawl are the tranquil Howth Peninsula to the north and the area around Dún
Laoghaire, south of Dublin Bay. Both can be seen in an afternoon.

DÚN LAOGHAIRE

As Dublin's major out-of-city ferry port, Dún Laoghaire (dun-LEER-ee) is the first
peek at Ireland for many tourists. Fortunately, it makes a good spot to begin a ramble along the coast south of Dublin. Literary buffs may want to investigate the
James Joyce Tower, where the artist once stayed as a young man. Summer evenings are the best time to visit, when couples stroll down the waterfront and the
whole town turns out for weekly sailboat races.

GETTING THERE AND PRACTICAL INFORMATION. Reach Dún Laog-
haire by **DART** from Dublin (£1.10), or southbound **buses** #7, 7A, 8 or (on a longer,
inland route) 46A from Eden Quay. From the ferry port, **Marine Rd.** climbs up to
the center of town. **George's St.**, at the top of Marine Rd., holds most of Dún
Laoghaire's shops, many right at the intersection in the **Dún Laoghaire Shopping Centre.** The **tourist information centre** (TIC), is in the ferry terminal. (Open M-Sa 10am-
5:30pm.) Ferry travelers can change money at the terminal's **bureau de change.** (☎
280 4783. Open M-Sa 9am-5pm, Su 10am-5pm.) Services include: the **Bank of Ireland,** 101 Upper George's St. (☎ 280 0273; open M-W and F 10am-4pm, Th 10am-
5pm); and **Internet access** at the **Dun Laoghaire Youth Info Centre,** in the church on
Marina St. (☎ 280 9363; free by appointment; M-F 9:30am-5pm, Sa 10am-4pm), and
at **Net House,** 28 Upper George's (☎ 230 3085; open M-F 8am-midnight, Su 10am-
midnight; £6 per hr., students £5).

ACCOMMODATIONS. As the port for the Stena ferries and a convenient
DART stop on the way to Dublin, Dún Laoghaire is prime breeding ground for
B&Bs, only a portion of which are modestly priced. Three hostels are also within
walking distance. To reach **Belgrave Hall,** 34 Belgrave Sq., from the Seapoint
DART station, head left down the coast, then zigzag right, left, right, left at each
intersection to Belgrave Sq. It's a top-tier hostel with ornamented ceilings, wood
and marble floors, and old furniture. (☎ 284 2106; info@dublinhostel.com. Continental breakfast included. Internet access. Laundry £3-6. Bike rental £10 per day.
Free parking. Summer F-Sa 10-bed dorm £15, Su-Th £13.) **Marina House,** 7 Old
Dunleary Rd., has the most solid, comfy beds you'll find. Owners Donagh and Mike
will join you for drinks out back at night and then get up early to bake *pain au
chocolat* for your breakfast. Head left out of Salthill and Monkstown DART station; it's next to the Purty Kitchen. (☎ 284 1524. Internet access. Large dorms £12
in summer, £10 in winter; 4-bed dorms £14; doubles £35.) Next to the DART station and ferry terminal stands **Marleen,** 9 Marine Rd., a 200-year-old stint with
friendly owners. (☎ 280 2456. Singles £20; doubles £36.)

FOOD AND PUBS. Tesco Supermarket vends downstairs in the Dún
Laoghaire shopping center. (☎ 280 8441. Open M-W and Sa 8:30am-7pm, Th-F
8:30am-9pm, Su 11am-6pm.) **Patrick St.,** which continues Marine Rd.'s path uphill
on the other side of George's St., offers cheap eateries. **Bits and Pizzas,** 15 Patrick
St., wins local approval for good value. (☎ 284 2411. Lunch special of pizza, coleslaw, and tea £4.35. Open M-Sa noon-midnight.) Next door to the Marina Hostel,
the **Purty Kitchen** pub opens its loft for a purty little nightclub with poppy music
and jazz on Wednesdays. (☎ 280 1257. No cover Th and Su; W and F-Sa £5.) The

ULYSSES PRIMER So, you've meant to read *Ulysses* but were intimidated by its 700 pages, thousands of allusions, and dense verbal puzzles. Despite is status in several polls as greatest book of the 20th century, very few people have read it in its entirety. *Let's Go*, a far more accessible book, is here with some trivia to help you bluff your way through a literary pub crawl:

The first and last letters of the book are both "s"; other than symmetrizing the novel, the "s" stands for "Stephen" (Daedalus, one of the three main characters), while "P" stands for "Poldy" (nickname of Leopold Bloom, the central figure), and "M" for "Molly" (Poldy's wife). The first words of the novel—"Stately, plump Buck Mulligan"—also incorporate these letters. Taken together, S-M-P stands for subject-middle-predicate, or logical sentence structure. The form (a syllogism) suggests a logical and narrative structure which readers can grasp, but which eludes the central characters.

Ulysses uses 33,000 different words, and 16,000 are used only once. Shakespeare was known to have used 25,000 different words throughout all his plays.

Since Molly calls Leopold "Poldy," she takes the "Leo" out of him—de-lionizing him. Her first sounds in the novel are "Mn." The word "melon" echoes in Leopold's mind throughout the day. Why? The word recalls Molly's voluptuous figure while reconfiguring "Leo" and "Mn" in a palatable way through anagram. (He also carries around a bar of lemon soap.)

Joyce once said he expected readers to devote nothing less than their entire lives to figuring out his epic. For the less ambitious and less masochistic, this primer Suffices.

best *craic* is at the **Cultúrlann na hÉireann,** next door to the Belgrave Hall hostel. The headquarters of Comhaltas Ceoltóirí Eireann, a huge international organization for Irish traditional music, the Cultúrlann houses bona fide, non-tourist oriented trad sessions, as well as *céilí* dancing. (☎ 280 0295. Mid-June to Sept. M-Th sit-down performances 9pm. Tickets £6; F *céilí* £4.50, Sa sessions £2.)

🔯 SIGHTS. 🔳 James Joyce Tower. is a fascinating retreat, especially for tourists with a specific interest. Joyce stayed in the tower for a tense six days in August 1904 as a guest of Oliver St. John Gogarty, a Dublin surgeon, poetic wit, man-about-town, and the first civilian tenant of the tower. Unfortunately, Gogarty's other guest was an excitable Englishman with a severe sleepwalking problem. The Englishman, Samuel Trench, dreamt there was a panther in the tower and fired his pistol into the fireplace. Gogarty mockingly seized the pistol, shouted "Leave him to me!" and fired his own shotgun overhead into a row of saucepans that fell onto Joyce. Not as amused, Joyce left that morning, and later infamously immortalized Gogarty in the first chapter of *Ulysses*. The novel is partially set in and around the tower, with Gogarty transformed into Buck Mulligan, Trench into Haines, and Joyce into Stephen Daedalus, who meditates on the "snotgreen" sea from the gun platform at the top of the tower. The two-room museum contains Joyce's death mask and personal effects, including his guitar, bookshelves, some of his correspondence, a page of the original manuscript of Finnegan's Wake, and lots of editions of *Ulysses*, including one illustrated by Henri Matisse. (From Sandycove DART station, go left at either the green house or Eagle House down to the coast, turn right and continue to the Martello tower; or take bus #8 from Burgh Quay in Dublin to Sandycove Ave. ☎ 872 2077. Open Apr.-Oct. M-Sa 10am-1pm and 2-5pm, Su 2-6pm; Nov.-Mar. by appointment. £2.70, seniors and students £2.20.)

At the foot of the tower lies the **Forty Foot Men's Bathing Place** the infamous aquatic spot of Joycean fame. A wholesome crowd with plenty of toddlers splashes in the shallow pool facing the road. But behind a wall, on the rocks below the battery and adjacent to the Martello Tower, men traditionally skinny-dip year-round; apparently, they don't mind that they're a tourist attraction. Joyce's host, Oliver St. John Gogarty, once took the plunge here with a reluctant W.B. Yeats in tow. Yeats failed to apply to his epic poems the principles of shrinkage he learned in the cold waters. The **harbor** itself is a sight, filled with yachts, boat tours, car ferries, and fishermen. Frequent summer evening boat races draw much of the town. For more organized sightseeing, try the **National Maritime Museum.** The massive lens from the Bailey Lighthouse in Howth rotates majestically in front of a large stained-glass window. (In Mariners' Church. From the ferry port, turn left on Queen's Rd. to the stone steps that lead up to Haigh Terr. ☎ 280 0969. Open May-Sept. Tu-Su 1-5pm; Apr. and Oct. Sa-Su 1-5pm. £1.50, children 80p.)

HOWTH
The affluent peninsula of Howth (rhymes with "both") dangles from the mainland in Edenic isolation, less than 10 mi. from the center of Dublin. Howth offers a brief look-in at many of Ireland's highlights: rolling hills, pubs, a literary landscape, and a castle. Man-made structures from various millennia pepper the rest of the island, connected by quiet paths around hills of heather and stunning cliffs.

GETTING THERE AND PRACTICAL INFORMATION. The easiest way to reach Howth is by **DART,** on a northbound train (30min., 6 per hr., £1.15). **Buses** arrive from Dublin's Lower Abbey St.: #31 runs every hour to the center of Howth, near the DART station, and #31B adds a loop that climbs Howth Summit. Turn left out of the station to get to the harbor and the **tourist information centre,** in the Old Courthouse on Harbour Rd. (☎ 832 0405 Open May-Aug. M-F 11am-1pm, 1:30-5pm.) When the tourist office is closed, head for the hand-drawn map of the peninsula posted at the harbor entrance across from the St. Lawrence hotel. There is an **cash machine** at the **Bank of Ireland** (☎ 839 0271), on Main St. (Open M-F 10am-4pm, Th 10am-5pm.) The **post office** is at 27 Abbey St. (☎ 831 8210).

ACCOMMODATIONS AND FOOD. Howth's pricey B&Bs concentrate around **Thormanby Rd.,** which forks off upper Main St. and heads for the summit; bus #31B goes up the hill every hour. **Gleann na Smól,** on the left at the end of Nashville Rd. off Thormanby Rd., is the closest affordable option to the harbor, and has firm beds for the weary, cable TV for the post-literate, and a supply of books to suit wormier guests. (☎ 832 2936. Singles £25; doubles £38-42; ask about student discounts). At **Hazelwood,** at the end of the cul-de-sac in the Thormanby Woods estate, a mile up Thormanby Rd., Mrs. Rosaleen Hobbs serves breakfast around a large table. Bus #31B runs up Thormanby Rd., or call from the DART station for a lift. (☎ 839 1391. Singles £30; doubles £42; all rooms with bath.)

The hungry head to **Spar supermarket,** St. Laurence Rd. (☎ 832 6496), off Abbey St. (Open M-Sa 8am-10pm, Su 8am-9pm.) Quash your monstrous traveler's appetite with fabulous pizza and sundaes at **Porto Fino's,** on Harbour Rd. (☎ 839 3054. Open M-F 5pm-midnight, Sa-Su noon-midnight.) The **St. Lawrence Hotel** drops trad in the Anchor Bar in summer. (☎ 832 2643. Music M-F from 9pm.) For more local flavor, join the fishermen at the **Lighthouse,** Church St., and relax with a pint and frequent trad. (☎ 832 2827. Sessions Su, M, W, and F from about 9pm.)

SIGHTS. A three-hour **cliff walk** rings the peninsula and passes heather and thousands of seabird nests. The trail is well-trodden, but narrow; its best section is a one-hour hike that runs between the harbor and the lighthouse at the southeast tip of the peninsula. At the harbor end, **Puck's Rock** marks the spot where the devil fell when St. Nessan shook a Bible at him. The nearby **lighthouse,** surrounded by cliffs, housed Salman Rushdie for a night during the height of the *fatwa* against him. To get to the trailhead from town, turn left at the DART and bus station and follow Harbour Rd. around the coast 20 minutes. From the lighthouse, hike downhill. Bus #31B from Lower Abbey St. in Dublin makes it to the cliffs; from the bus stop, make your way to the lower path, or stay and admire the magnificent view.

In town, the ruins of 14th-century **St. Mary's Abbey** stand peacefully surrounded by a cemetery at the bend in Church St. Get the key to the courtyard from the caretaker, Mrs. O'Rourke, at 13 Church St. For more sights, turn right as you exit the DART station and then left after ¼ mi. at the entrance to the Deer Park hotel. Up this road lies the private **Howth Castle,** an awkwardly charming patchwork of different styles and degrees of upkeep. At the end of the driveway to the side of the castle and up the hill, an uncertain path leads around the right side of the Deer Park Hotel to the **Rhododendron Gardens,** in which Molly remembers romance and such at the end of Joyce's *Ulysses.* Yes. At the top of the path, you emerge into an astounding floral panorama overlooking Howth and Dublin to the south. Turn right as soon as you enter the gardens (or cut beforehand through the golf course to tee 4) to see a collapsed **portal dolmen** with a 90-ton capstone that marks the grave of someone much more important in 2500 BC than now. (Always open. Free.)

Just offshore, **Ireland's Eye** once provided both religious sanctuary for monks, as seen in the ruins of **St. Nessan's Church,** and one of the coast's many **Martello towers.** The island's long beach is now primarily a bird haven. **Ireland's Eye Boat Trips** jets passengers across the water. Their office is on the East Pier, toward the lighthouse. (☎ 831 4200; mobile ☎ (087) 267 8211. Trips 15min., 2 per hr. weather permitting. £5 return, students £3, children £2.50.)

EASTERN IRELAND

WICKLOW MOUNTAINS

Over 2000 ft. high, covered by heather, and pleated by rivers, the Wicklow summits are home to grazing sheep and few villagers. Public transportation is severely limited, so driving is the easiest way to connect the scattered sights and towns. The climbs can be rough for hikers, but their efforts are rewarded by the best-kept trail in Ireland, the Wicklow Way. Stop by the tourist information centres at Bray, Wicklow Town, Arklow, and Rathdrum for advice and free, colorful maps.

⬛ GETTING THERE AND GETTING AROUND

Several **bus** companies can drop you off at various spots in the mountains. **Dublin Bus** (☎ (01) 873 4222) runs frequently from Marlay Park in **Rathfarnham** (#47B and 48A) and **Enniskerry** (#44, or 85 from **Bray**), and less frequently from **Glencullen** (#44B). **Bus Éireann** (☎ (01) 836 6111) comes somewhat near the Wickloy Way farther south, with infrequent service from **Dublin** to **Aughrim, Tinahely, Shillelagh,** and **Hackettstown. St. Kevin's** (☎ (01) 281 8119) runs two shuttles daily from St. Stephen's Green West, **Dublin,** to **Roundwood** and **Glendalough** (£6, return £10).

Bus Éireann runs **tours** to Glendalough and through the mountains (depart Dublin Apr.-Oct. daily 10:30am, return by 5:45pm; £17, children £9). **Wicklow Tours** (☎ 67671) runs a fairly reliable van between **Glendalough** (departs from Glendalough Hotel), **Rathdrum** (Avondale), and **Wicklow** (June-Aug. 1 per day, return £4).

🧗 HIKING THE WICKLOW WAY

Founded in 1981, Ireland's oldest marked hiking trail is also its most spectacular. Stretching from Marlay Park at the border of Dublin to Clonegal, Co. Carlow, the 76 mi. **Wicklow Way** meanders south through Ireland's largest highland expanse. Yellow arrows and signs keep the trail well-marked along various footpaths, dirt roads, and even paved roads that weave over heathered summits and through steep glacial valleys. Civilization is rarely more than 3km away, but appropriate wilderness precautions should still be taken. Bring warm, windproof layers and raingear for the exposed summits, and while the terrain never gets frighteningly rugged, sturdy footwear is still a must (see **Wilderness Safety,** p. 53). Water is best taken from farmhouses (with permission), not streams. Open fires are illegal within a mile of the forest. Most of the county's tourist information centres sell the invaluable *Wicklow Way Map Guide* (£4.50), which is the best source for information about the trail and sights along the way.

692 ■ EASTERN IRELAND

Six days of hiking for seven to eight hours will carry you from one end to the other, though many side trails around the Way make excellent day hikes; *Wicklow Way Walks* (£4.50) outlines a number of these loops. The northern 44 mi. of the Way, from Dublin to Aghavannagh, attract the most people with the best scenery and all of the hostels; An Óige publishes a pamphlet detailing four- to five-hour hostel-to-hostel walks. (Available at An Óige hostels in Co. Wicklow and Dublin.)

In order to avoid trail erosion, bikes are only allowed on forest tracks and paved sections of the Way, but plenty of off-Way roads provide for equal beauty. For a particularly scenic route, take R759 to **Sally Gap,** west of the Way near Lough Tay, and then head south on R115 past **Glenmacnass Waterfall** to Glendalough (roughly 15 mi.). For further information about the Way, contact the **National Park Information Office** (☎ (01) 45425) between Glendalough's lakes (see Glendalough, p. 692); if they're closed try the **ranger station** nearby (☎ 45338 or 45561). Forestry lands are governed by **Coillte** (KWEEL-chuh, ☎ (01) 286 7751), though much of the Way is simply on a right-of-way through private lands.

ACCOMMODATIONS

Camping is feasible along the Way but requires planning ahead. Many local farmhouses will let you pitch a tent on their land if you ask. National Park lands are fine for short-term camping; pitching a tent in state forest plantations is prohibited. All bookings are handled through the An Óige head office in Dublin (see p. 672). Hostels line the Wicklow Way from north to south in the following order:

An Óige Glencree, Stone House, Enniskerry (☎ (01) 286 4037). From Enniskerry, 12km out on the Glencree Rd. 3½km off the Way and a bit too remote. Dorms June-Sept. £7, Oct.-May £6.50.

An Óige Knockree, Lacken House, Enniskerry (☎ (01) 286 4036), on the Way. 4 mi. from the village and 2 mi. from Powerscourt Waterfall. From Enniskerry, take the right fork road leading uphill from the village green, take a left at Buttercups Newsagent, and begin a steep walk, following signs for Glencree Dr. Fireplace in the dining area. Lockout 10am-5pm (unless it's raining). Dorms June-Sept. £7, Oct.-May £6.50.

An Óige Tiglin, a.k.a. **Devil's Glen,** Ashford (☎ 0404 40259), 5 mi. from the Way by the Tiglin Adventure Centre. From Ashford, follow Roundwood Rd. for 3 mi., then follow the signs for the Tiglin turnoff and R763 on the right; a hilly 8 mi. from Powerscourt. 50 beds in basic, single-sex dorms; mattresses are droopy, but sleepable. Towels 50p. 11pm curfew. June-Sept. £7, Oct.-May £6.

Wicklow Way Hostel (☎ (0404) 45398). See **Glendalough,** p. 692.

An Óige Glendaloch, (☎ (0404) 45342). See **Glendalough,** p. 692.

An Óige Glenmalure, Glenmalure. At the end of a dead-end road, 12km south from Glendalough. Head from Glendalough to Laragh and take every major right turn. Back-to-nature lodging; not even connected by telephone. June-Sept. £6.50, Oct.-May £5.50.

The following few **B&Bs** will both allow camping and pick-up hikers if necessary. **Coolakay House** is 2½ mi. outside Enniskerry, neighbors the Powerscourt Waterfall, and even has a small cafe. (☎ (01) 286 2423. £23 per person.) In Knockananna, **Hillview B&B,** Tinahely, sits a mile from the Way. (☎ (0508) 71195. Singles £16; doubles £30. Camping £3-5 per person.) **Rosbane Farmhouse,** Rosbane, is a seven-minute walk from the Way, near the summit of Garryhoe. (☎ (0402) 38100. £19 per person. Camping £4 per tent.) **Orchard House,** Tinahely, is within earshot of the trail. (☎ (0402) 38264. Singles £22-24; doubles £36-40. Camping £10 per tent.)

GLENDALOUGH   ☎0404

In the 6th century, a vision told St. Kevin to give up his life of ascetic isolation and found a monastery. He offset the austerity of monastic life by choosing one of the most spectacular valleys in Ireland and founded Glendalough (GLEN-da-lock, "glen of two lakes"). Today the valley is known for its monastic ruins, excellent hikes, and swarms of tourists. Glendalough consists of just St. Kevin's habitat, a hostel, and an overpriced hotel and restaurant; for more affordable food, B&Bs, and groceries, travelers should head to Laragh (LAR-a), a mile up the road (10min. walk from the Wicklow Way; 15 mi. from Powerscourt, 7 mi. from Roundwood).

GETTING THERE AND PRACTICAL INFORMATION. Most pilgrims to Glendalough come by car; a few hike into town; and the rest take buses run by the private **St. Kevin's Bus Service** (☎ (01) 281 8119). Buses run from St. Stephen's Green West, **Dublin** (M-Sa at 11:30am and 6pm, Su 11:30am and 7pm; £6, return £10) via **Bray** (M-Sa 12:10pm and 6:30pm, Su 12:10pm and 7:30pm; return £6). Buses return from the glen in the evening (M-F 7:15am and 4:15pm, Sa 9:45am and 4:15pm, Su 9:45am and 5:30pm; 9:45am departure F year-round and daily July-Aug.). **Hitchhiking** to Glendalough is reported to be fairly easy from Co. Wicklow towns, though from Dublin much of the Glendalough-bound traffic is bus tours. Hitchers starting at the beginning of N11 in southwest Dublin hop to the juncture of N11 with Glendalough's R755. *Let's Go* does not recommend hitchhiking.

Various vendors offer tourist information. The Board Failté **tourist information centre** (TIC), across from the Glendalough Hotel, provides info about the area and Dublin, and can book accommodations. (☎ 45688. Open mid-June to Sept. Tu 11am-1pm and 2-6pm, W-Su 10am-1pm and 2-6pm.) The **Glendalough Visitor Centre** (see **Sights**) picks up the slack when the TIC is closed. The **National Park Information Office,** between the two lakes, is the best source for hiking information in the region. (☎ 45425. Open May-Aug. daily 10am-6pm, Apr. and Sept. Sa-Su 10am-6pm.) When closed, call the **ranger office.** (☎ 45338 or ☎ 45561.) **Laragh IT,** in the parking lot next to Lynham's pub, has **Internet access.** (☎ 45600. £5 per hr.)

ACCOMMODATIONS AND FOOD. An **Óige Glendaloch** is a five-minute walk past the Glendalough visitor center. Prices are high, but with good beds, excellent security, and an in-house cafe, it's the best choice in the area. (☎ 45342. Breakfast £2.25, £4.50 full Irish; dinners £6.50; always a vegetarian dish. Towels 50p. Laundry £4. Internet access. Bike rental. Wheelchair accessible. Dorms £11; doubles £30; £1-2 less per person in off-season.) In nearby Laragh, the **Wicklow Way Hostel** offers a less comfortable and less expensive stay. The showers are exposed, but the private rooms are cleaner and more agreeable. The cafe serves inexpensive breakfasts. (☎ 45398. Dorms £7.) **B&Bs** abound in Laragh. One of the most welcoming is **Gleann Albhe,** next to the post office. Bathrooms, TVs, and tea facilities are found in every room, and you can look out a spectacular bay window while you choose your breakfast. (☎ 45236. Singles £25; doubles £36-40.) Part of the view is **Oakview B&B,** down the driveway by the Wicklow Heather, where excellent flowered rooms await. (☎ 45453. Open Mar.-Oct. Singles £24; doubles £32, with bath £38.)

The **Wicklow Heather,** 75m up the road toward Glendalough, serves marvelous concoctions, especially for well-behaved vegetarians. (☎ 45157. Open daily 8:30am-10pm. Breakfast £4.25. Most main courses under £8. Baguette sandwiches £4.95.) **Lynham's** also piles plates high with hot edibles. (☎ 45345. Entrees £7-10. Open daily 12:30-3:30pm and 5:30-9pm.) The attached **Lynham's Pub** attracts travelers with cover bands and rock sessions most weekend nights.

SIGHTS. Glendalough is a single, multifold sight. Smooth glacial valleys embrace the two lakes and the monastic ruins. The **Visitor Centre** presents everything that's known about them, an exhibition, a 17-minute audiovisual show on the history of Irish monasteries in general, and a tour of the ruins. (☎ 45324. Wheelchair accessible. Tours every 30min. on peak days. £2, students and children £1. Open daily June-Aug. 9am-6:30pm, Sept. to mid-Oct. 9:30am-6pm, mid-Oct. to mid-Mar. 9:30am-5pm, mid-Mar. to May 9:30am-6:30pm.)

The centerpiece is **St. Kevin's Tower,** a 100 ft. round tower with a mere 3 ft. foundation, built in the 10th century as a watchtower, belltower, and retreat. The entrance is 12 ft. from the ground: when Vikings approached, the monks would climb the inside of the tower floor by floor, drawing up the ladders behind them. The **Cathedral,** constructed in a combination of Greek and Roman architectural styles, was once the largest in the country. In its shadow is **St. Kevin's Cross,** an early high cross. It was carved before the monks had tools to cut holes clean through the stone. The 11th-century **St. Kevin's Church,** with an intact stone roof, acquired the misnomer "St. Kevin's Kitchen" because of its chimney-like tower.

The **Upper and Lower Lakes,** across the bridge and to the right, are a rewarding sidetrip from the monastic site. Hikers and bikers can cross the bridge at the far side of the monastery and head right on the paved path for five minutes to reach the serene **Lower Lake.** Twenty-five minutes farther, the path hits the National Park Information Office (see **Practical Information**) and the magnificent **Upper Lake.** Drivers should continue past the hotel and park in the lot by the Upper Lake.

BOYNE VALLEY

The thinly-populated Boyne Valley safeguards Ireland's greatest archaeological treasures, and is about a one-hour bus ride from Dublin. Massive passage tombs like Newgrange create subtle bumps in the landscape that belie the cavernous underground chambers they cover. They are older than the Pyramids and at least as puzzling: virtually nothing is known about the rituals and design on which they are based. The Celtic High Kings once ruled from atop the Hill of Tara, leaving a wake of mysterious folklore.

BRÚ NA BÓINNE: NEWGRANGE, KNOWTH, AND DOWTH

Along the curves of the river between Slane and Drogheda sprawls Brú na Bóinne (broo na BO-in-yeh, "homestead of the Boyne"). The 10 sq. km landscape swells with no fewer than 40 passage tombs dating from the 4th millennium BC. The Neolithic architects' mind-boggling engineering constructed Newgrange, Dowth, and Knowth within walking distance of one another. One explanation for their existence suggests that farming improvements gave people extra time to build structures that would remain intact, even waterproof, 5000 years later. The larger mounds took a good half-century to build, by men with only 30-year lifespans. Hundreds of enormous kerbstones were moved by raw manpower from 10km away, and countless smaller rocks were boated in from Wicklow, 80km away.

The most impressive of the three, for archaeologists if not for visitors, is **Knowth** (rhymes with "mouth"). Long-term excavations and the demands of preservation prevent visitors from actually entering the tomb, but the visitor center's tour offers a peek. In the 1960s, a roof box was discovered over the **Newgrange** passage entrance. At dawn on the shortest day of the year (Dec. 21), and for two days to either side, 17 minutes of golden sunlight reach straight to the back of the 19m passageway and illuminate the burial chamber. The calendar alignment, while impressive, is quite common in passage tombs; Newgrange is unique in having a separate entrance exclusively for the worshipped golden orb. Because the passage is shorter and a little wider than Knowth, you can actually enter into the cool bowels of the one-acre mound and see two-thirds of all the Neolithic art in Western Europe. Amidst the intricately carved patterns, diamonds, and spirals, you can read graffiti from 18th-century visitors who clearly didn't have the brains of their distant ancestors. The tour's highlight is a simulation of the golden winter solstice. **Dowth** (rhymes with "Knowth") has been closed to the public for several years, because of ongoing excavations. To gain admission, get a PhD in archaeology.

To access Knowth and Newgrange, it's necessary to pay admission into the ▨ **Brú na Bóinne Visitors Centre,** located near Donore on the south side of the River Boyne, across from the tombs. Do not try to go directly to the sites—a guard minds the gate. Instead, head to the Centre and immediately book a tour. The place is mobbed in the summer, and Sundays are manic; from June through August, you'll most likely be turned away if you get there after 2:30pm. The center has an excellent exhibit on how gifted and talented Stone Agers lived. A nifty film on the winter solstice runs every 15 minutes. (☎ (041) 988 0300. 1hr. tours 2 per hr. until 1½hr. before closing. Open Mar.-Apr. 9:30am-5:30pm, May 9am-6:30pm, June to mid-Sept. 9am-7pm, rest of Sept. 9am-6:30pm, Oct. 9:30am-5:30pm, Nov.-Feb. 9:30am-5pm. Center only £2, seniors £1.50, students and children £1; center and Newgrange £4, £3, £2; center and Knowth £3, £2, £1.25; center, Newgrange, and Knowth £7, £5, £3.25. Last admission to center 45min. before closing.)

To reach the center from Drogheda, turn left by the bus station and head straight on the uphill road. It's a pleasant five-mile bike ride, and hitchers report successful journeys, despite *Let's Go*'s non-recommendation. **Bus Éireann** (☎ (01) 836 6111) shuttles to the Visitors Centre from **Dublin** (1½hr.; M-F 5 per day, Sa-Su 4 per day; £10 return), stopping at **Drogheda** (10min., £3 return). Several guided bus tours from Dublin include admission to the sights. Bus Éireann covers Newgrange and either Tara/Trim or Mellifont/Monasterboice (Sa-Th, £19). A **tourist information centre,** on the ground floor of the Visitors Centre, can give you a free area map. (☎ (041) 980305. Open daily 9am-7pm.)

HILL OF TARA

From prehistoric times until at least the 10th century, Tara was the political and often religious center of Ireland. Three of the 70 sites strewn around the hill have been excavated, revealing that ancient peoples built a Stone Age tomb and an Iron-Age fort here. Ownership of the hill was disputed until the 10th century, but the arrival of St. Patrick around 400 deposed Tara from its position as the Jerusalem of Ireland. In modern times, the hill's aura persists: Daniel O'Connor gathered "a million" people here for a Home Rule rally in 1843. A cult destroyed one site a century ago in its fervent search for the Arc of the Covenant. History has left a strong legacy of myth and legend, much of which is refuted by archaeological findings.

The enormous site is about five miles east of Navan on the N3. The actual buildings—largely wattle, wood, and earthwork—have long been buried or destroyed; what you'll see are grassy, windswept dunes forming concentric rings. They are always open for exploration, but to make any sense of them you have to hit the **visitor center,** in the old church at the site. The center displays aerial photos of Tara, and shows a good 20-minute slideshow about Tara's history. After the film, your ticket entitles you to an excellent guided tour (35min.) that circles the site. The full site encompasses 100 acres of many smaller mounds and ringforts. (☎ (046) 25903. Center open daily early-May to mid-June and mid-Sept. to Oct. 10am-5pm, mid-June to mid-Sept. 9:30am-6:30pm. £1.50, seniors £1, students and children 60p.) Take any local (not express) **bus** from Dublin to **Navan** (1hr.; M-Sa 37 per day, Su 15 per day; £5.50) and ask the driver to let you off at the turnoff, to the left and marked by a small brown sign. The site is about a mile straight uphill.

SOUTHEAST IRELAND

Historically the power base of the Vikings and then the Normans, the influence of the Celts is faintest in southeast Ireland. Town and street names in this region are likely derived from Viking, Norman, and Anglo-Saxon origins. Wexford is a charismatic town, packed with historic sites and convenient to many of the Southeast's finest attractions, while Waterford has the resources, nightlife, and grit of a real city. Cashel boasts a superbly preserved cathedral complex. Continue your hunt for raging nightlife south from Dublin through Kilkenny; alternatively, the daylight hours are most enjoyably spent exploring the pretty paths through Wexford and its surrounding area. Travelers stuff themselves into cars speeding to and from Europe via Rosslare Harbour on the southeastern tip of the island.

KILKENNY   ☎056

As the economy of the Celtic Tiger roars, the best-preserved medieval town in Ireland has launched a historical preservation campaign to draw more visitors; the town's population of 25,000 doubles during the high season. Kilkenny's streets, nine churches, and 80 pubs are all cloaked in the architecture of past eras.

☞ GETTING THERE AND GETTING AROUND

Trains: Kilkenny Station (☎ 22024), Dublin Rd. Open M-Sa 8am-9:30pm, Su 9am-9pm. Always staffed, but ticket window open only around departures. From **Dublin** (2hr., £11) and **Waterford** (45min., £5). Connections to western Ireland can be made at **Kildare Station,** 1hr. north on the Dublin-Waterford line.

Buses: Kilkenny Station (☎ 64933), Dublin Rd. and Patrick St. in the city center. **Bus Éireann** (☎ 62121) from: **Dublin** (2hr.; M-Sa 6 per day, Su 5 per day; £7); **Waterford** (1½hr.; M-Sa 2 per day, Su 1 per day; £5); and **Rosslare Harbour** via Waterford (2hr.; M-Sa 5-6 per day, Su 3 per day; £10.50); and **Galway** (5hr.; M-Sa 5 per day, Su 3 per day; £17). **J.J. Kavanagh's Rapid Express** (☎ 31106) has routes in the area with prices that routinely beat Bus Éireann's; from **Dublin** (M-Sa 5 per day, Su 1 per day).

Car Rental: Barry Pender, Dublin Rd. (☎ 65777). Ages 23+. From £50 per day, £250 per week. Open M-F 9am-5:30pm, Sa 9am-1pm.

Bike Rental: The thriftiest place is **Kilkenny Cycles** (☎ 64374), Michael St. £7 per day, £35 per week; £50 or passport deposit. Open M-Sa 9am-6pm.

Hitchhiking: They take N10 south to Waterford, and N10 past the train station toward Dublin. *Let's Go* does not recommend hitchhiking as a safe mode of travel, although hitchers report that patience is required.

✴☞ ORIENTATION AND PRACTICAL INFORMATION

From Kilkenny Station, turn left on John St. to reach a large intersection with **High St.** and **The Parade.** A busy triangle is formed by **Rose Inn St., High St.,** and **Kieran St.**

Tourist Information Centre: (☎ 51500), Rose Inn St. Open July-Aug. M-Sa 9am-8pm; Apr.-Sept. M-Sa 9am-6pm, May-Sept. also Su 11am-1pm and 2-5pm; Oct.-Mar. M-Sa 9am-5pm.

Financial Services: Bank of Ireland (☎ 21155), Parliament St. The High St.-Parade intersection has 4 other banks. All open M 10am-5pm, Tu-F 10am-4pm.

Launderette: Brett's Launderette, Michael St. (☎ 63200). Soap 70p. Wash and dry £5.70. Open M-Sa 8:30am-8pm; last wash 6:30pm. No self-service drying.

Police (*Garda*): (☎ 22222), Dominic St.

Hospital: St. Luke's, Freshford Rd. (☎ 51133). Continue down Parliament St. to St. Canice's Cathedral, then turn right and veer left onto Vicars St., then left again onto Freshford Rd. The hospital is down on the right.

Post Office: (☎ 21891), High St. Open M-Tu, Th-Sa 9am-5:30pm, W 9:30am-5:30pm.

Internet Access: Web Talk, Rose Inn St. 2 shops closer to The Parade than the tourist information centre. £1 per 10min, £5 per hr. Open M-Sa 10am-9pm, Su 2-8pm.

☞ ACCOMMODATIONS

Housed in a 15th-century castle, ▨ **An Óige Foulksrath Castle,** Jenkinstown, is one of Ireland's nicest hostels. It's eight miles north of town on N77 (Durrow Rd.). Turn right off N77 at signs for Connahy; it's ¼ mi. down on the left. **Buggy's Buses** (☎ 41264) run from The Parade to the hostel M-Sa at midday and 5:30pm and leave the hostel for Kilkenny shortly after 8:25am and around 3pm The 20 minute trip costs £1; call the hostel for exact times. (☎ 67674. Continental breakfast £2.50. Sheets £1. Laundry £4. Kitchen open 8am-10pm. Dorms £5.50-7.50.) In town, **Kilkenny Tourist Hostel (IHH),** 35 Parliament St., isn't luxurious, but at least it's close to the pubs. (☎ 63541; kilkennyhostel@tiniet.ie. Kitchen with microwave open 7am-11pm. Check-out 10:30am. 6- to 8-bed dorms £7; doubles £20; add £1 May-Sept.; Sept.-June 50p discount for *Let's Go* readers.) Spacious rooms and friendly proprietors characterize **Demsey's B&B,** 26 James's St., in a little old house by the Superquinn, off High St. (☎ 21954. Singles £20; doubles £36-40.)

◯ FOOD

Dunnes Supermarket sells housewares and food on Kieran St. (☎ 61655. Open M-Tu and Sa 8:30am-7pm, W-F 8:30am-10pm, Su and bank holidays 10am-6pm.) At **Langton's**, 69 John St., an eccentric owner cooks fantastic pub grub. (☎ 65123. Lunch ₤5, served daily noon-6pm. Dinner in the double digits, served daily 6-10:30pm.) **Pordylo's**, Butterslip Ln., between Kieran St. and High St., has zesty, vegetarian-friendly dinners from across the globe. (Some meals under ₤8. Open daily 6-11pm.) Couples enjoy mood lighting and romantic music at **Ristorante Rinuccini**, 1 The Parade, opposite the castle. (☎ 61575. Lunch ₤5-6; dinner ₤7-9; early evening specials ₤6-7, 6-7:30pm. Food served noon-3pm and 6-10:30pm.)

◉ SIGHTS

Kilkenny itself is a sight, since the government preserved (or recreated) most of the buildings' medieval good looks. The belle of the ball is 13th-century **Kilkenny Castle**, The Parade. Ogle the Long Room, reminiscent of a Viking ship, which displays portraits of English bigwigs. (☎ 21450. Castle and gallery open June-Sept. daily 10am-7pm; Oct.-Mar. Tu-Sa 10:30am-12:45pm and 2-5pm, Su 11am-12:45pm and 2-5pm; Apr.-May daily 10:30am-5:30pm. Castle access by guided tour only. ₤3.50, students ₤1.50.) Across the street, the internationally known **Kilkenny Design Centre** fills the castle's old stables with expensive Irish crafts. (☎ 22118. Open Apr.-Dec. M-Sa 9am-6pm, Su 10am-6pm; Jan.-Mar. M-Sa 9am-6pm.) For the down-and-dirty on Kilkenny's folkloric tradition, take the **Tynan Walking Tours.** Besides conjuring some animated lore, the tour is the only way to see the old city jail. Tours depart from the tourist information centre (TIC). (☎ 65929, mobile ☎ (087) 2651745; tynantours@eircom.net. 1hr.; Mar.-Oct. M-Sa 6 per day, Su 4 per day; Nov.-Feb. Tu-Sa 3 per day. ₤3, students and seniors ₤2.50.)

13th-century **St. Canice's Cathedral** sits up the hill off Dean St. The name "Kilkenny" itself is derived from the Irish Cill Chainnigh, "Church of St. Canice." The thin, 100 ft. tower next to the cathedral was somehow built without scaffolding, in pre-Norman times, and still stands on its 3 ft. foundations. ₤1 and a bit of faith let you climb the series of six steep ladders inside to behold a panoramic view of the town and its surroundings. (☎ 64971. Open Easter-Sept. M-Sa 9am-1pm and 2-6pm, Su 2-6pm; Oct.-Easter M-Sa 10am-1pm and 2-6pm; Su 2-6pm. Donation requested.) It is rumored that crafty 14th-century monks brewed a light ale in the **St. Francis Abbey** on Parliament St.; the abbey is in ruins but its industry survives in the abbey's yard at the **Smithwicks Brewery.** Commercial use started in 1710, making it the oldest brewery in Ireland. Unfortunately, the company profanes the abbey by brewing Budweiser as well. Show up at 3pm outside the green doors on Parliament St. for a free audio-visual tour and ale tasting. (Tours July-Aug. M-F.)

♪ ❀ ENTERTAINMENT AND FESTIVALS

The TIC can provide a bimonthly guide to the town's happenings, and *The Kilkenny People* (₤1) is a good newsstand source for arts and music listings. **The Watergate Theatre,** Parliament St., stages shows year-round. (☎ 61674. Tickets usually ₤7, student discounts available. Booking office open M-F 11am-7pm, Sa 2-6pm, Su 1hr. before curtain.) **The Pump House,** 26 Parliament St., is loud, conveniently located, and generally packed. (☎ 63924. Trad M-Th in summer, rock and blues Su.) Thespians from the theater across the street converge during intermission at **Cleere's**, 28 Parliament St. (☎ 62573), for a pint. A black box theater at the back hosts vivacious musical and theatrical acts. Be as cool as a Parisian and as crowded as cattle in **Paris, Texas** (☎ 61822), High St., an extremely popular bar where over-23s shake, shimmy, smoke, and lasso themselves some good times with vim and vigor. Crowds bury themselves in **Maggie's,** Kieran St., a superb wine cellar. (☎ 62273. Trad most nights of the week, rock on summer weekends.) Not a Canterbury Tale, **Matt the Miller's,** 1 John St., at the bridge, will suck you in and force you to dance to silly Euro pop. (☎ 61696. Cover M ₤2 for rock music and late bar hours.)

During the second or third week of August, Kilkenny holds its annual **Arts Festival**, which has a daily program of theater, concerts, and readings by famous European and Irish artists. (☎ 63663. Tickets sold at 92 High St., or by phone; free-£12, student and senior discounts vary.) Kilkenny's population increases by over 10,000 for the **Cat Laughs** (☎ 51254), a festival held on the first weekend of June, featuring international comedy acts.

CASHEL   ☎062

Tucked between a series of mountain ranges, the town of Cashel lies halfway between Limerick and Waterford. Legend has it that the devil furiously hurled a rock from above the Tipperary plains when he discovered a church being built, thus explaining the commanding 300 ft. Rock of Cashel.

█🛈 GETTING THERE AND PRACTICAL INFORMATION. Bus Éireann (☎ 62121) arrives at Bianconi's Bistro on Main St., from: **Dublin** (3hr., 3 per day, £9); **Cahir** (15min., 4 per day, £2.40); **Cork** (1½hr., 3 per day, £8); **Limerick** (1hr., 4 per day, £8.80); and **Waterford** via Cahir. Cashel's efficient **tourist information centre** (TIC), shares space with the Heritage Centre in the recently renovated Cashel City Hall on Main St. (☎ 61333. Open July-Aug. M-Sa 9:15am-6pm, Su 11am-5pm, Apr.-June and Sept. M-Sa 9:15am-6pm.) **AIB,** Main St., has a **bureau de change.** (Open M-W and F 10am-12:30pm and 1:30-4pm, Th 10am-12:30pm and 1:30-5pm.) The **post office** rocks the Cashel on Main St. (☎ 61418. Open M and W-F 9am-1pm and 2-5:30pm, Tu 9:30am-1pm and 2-5:30pm, Sa 9am-1pm.)

█🛈 ACCOMMODATIONS AND FOOD. A few hundred yards from the ruins of Hore Abbey lies the stunning █ **O'Brien's Farm House hostel.** A five-minute walk from Cashel on Dundrum Rd., the hostel has an incredible view of the Rock and cheerful rooms. (☎ 61003. Serviced laundry £6. 6-bed dorms £9-10; doubles/twins £30. **Camping** £4.50-5.) Back in town, the plush **Cashel Holiday Hostel (IHH),** 6 John St., just off Main St., has a gorgeous kitchen crowned with a glass pyramid skylight. Spacious bedrooms are named after Irish heroes. (☎ 62330; cashel@iol.ie. Laundry £3.50. Key deposit £3. Internet access. 4- to 8-bed dorms £8.50; 4-bed dorms with bath £10; singles £14; doubles £24.) Just steps from the Rock on Dominic St. is **Rockville House,** a fantastic bargain with elegant and fully equipped bedrooms; turn past the TIC and pass the model village museum. (☎ 61760. Singles £24.50; doubles £34; triples £51.)

SuperValu Supermarket, Main St., offers a selection of groceries. (Open M-Sa 8am-9pm, Su 8am-6pm.) **The Bake House,** across from the Heritage Centre on Main St., is the town's best spot for coffee and light meals with pseudo-elegant upstairs seating. (Open M-Sa 8am-7pm, Su 9am-6pm.) Superior pub grub is served up at **O'Sullivan's** on Main St. (£4.50-5.50; food served M-Sa noon-3pm.) The *craic* is nightly and the atmosphere timeless at **Feehan's,** Main St. The bartenders at the well-appointed **Dowling's,** 46 Main St., make it their business to pour the best pint in town. Innocuous-looking **Mikey Ryan's,** Main St. (☎ 61431), hides a multilevel beer garden.

🛈 SIGHTS. The **Rock of Cashel** (also called **St. Patrick's Rock**) is a huge limestone outcropping topped by medieval buildings. Periodic guided tours are informative if a bit dry; a less erudite but equally awe-inspiring option is to explore the rock's buildings yourself. (Open daily mid-June to mid-Sept. 9am-7:30pm, mid-Sept. to mid-Mar. 9:30am-4:30pm, mid-Mar. to mid-June 9:30am-5:30pm. Last admission 45min. before closing. £3.50, students £1.50.) Two-towered **Cormac's Chapel,** consecrated in 1134, holds semi-restored Romanesque paintings, disintegrating stone-carved arches, and a barely visible, ornate sarcophagus once thought to be in the tomb of King Cormac. A highlight of Cashel's illustrious history was the reported burning of the 13th-century **cathedral** by the Earl of Kildare in 1495; when Henry VII demanded an explanation, the Earl replied, "I thought the Archbishop was in it." Henry made him Lord Deputy. The cathedral survived the Earl and today's visitors can inspect its vaulted Gothic arches.

The small **Heritage Centre,** in the same building as the TIC on Main St., features permanent exhibitions, including "The Rock: From 4th to 11th Century" and its sequel, "The Rock: 12th-18th Century," as well as temporary exhibitions on such themes as Hore Abbey, Cashel Palace, life in Cashel, and "The Rock: 21st-Century Wrestler Extraordinare." (☎ 32511. Open May-Sept. daily 9:30am-5:30pm, Oct.-Apr. M-F 9:30am-5:30pm. Free.) The **GPA-Bolton Library,** John St., past the hostel, has a musty collection of books and silver that once belonged to an Anglican archbishop of Cashel, Theophilus Bolton. The collection harbors ecclesiastical texts and rare manuscripts, including a 1550 edition of Machiavelli's *The Prince*, the first English translation of *Don Quixote*, and what is locally reputed to be the smallest book in the world. (☎ 61944. Open July-Aug. Tu-Su 9:30am-6pm, Sept.-Dec. and Mar.-June M-F 9:30am-5:30pm. £1.50, students and seniors £1.)

THE EAST MUNSTER WAY

The East Munster Way footpath starts in Carrick-on-Suir, hits Clonmel, skirts the Comeragh Mountains, and runs full-force into the Knockmealdowns, ending 43 mi. later in Clogheen. The best maps to use are Ordnance Survey 74 and 75 (1:50,000). The *East Munster Way Map Guide* (£4) provides a written guide and an accurate but less detailed map, and is available at the **tourist information centre** (TIC) in Clogheen across from the Vee Rd. turnoff (☎ (052) 65258; open M-Sa 9am-5pm), and at the **Powers-the-Pot Hostel** (☎ (052) 23085). The route contact is the Tipperary Co. Council (☎ (052) 25399). **Parsons Green,** part garden and part **campsite,** offers river walks, boat rides, and pony rides. (☎ (052) 65290. Kitchen. Laundry £4. £3 per small tent. £2 per person.) The **Kilmorna Farm Hostel** (☎ (058) 54315) in Lismore is a more luxurious, less convenient base for hiking in the range.

The **Comeragh Mountains** are more like large hills; not even the highest peaks are very steep. The ground is usually soft and wet; most of the terrain is manageable in sneakers. With map in hand, head east and follow the ridges south. Guided walking is also available; inquire with Niall at Powers-the-Pot. The technical term for the mountain hollows common in the Comeraghs is "cwms" (KOOMS).

Straddling the Tipperary-Waterford border 12 mi. south of Cahir, the **Knockmealdown Mountains** are roughly contoured, like the inside of an Aero bar. *Knockmealdown Walks 1* to *4* (50p each) are available at local TICs. All four walks start in the town of Clogheen; walks 2 and 4 assume transportation to nearby car parks. Sights to head for include the spectacular **Vee Road** south from Clogheen, which erupts with purple rhododendrons on its way to the **Knockmealdown Gap. Knockmealdown Peak** (2609 ft.), is the highest in the range. Beautiful (and supposedly bottomless) **Bay Loch,** on the way to Lismore, is the stuff of legend.

WEXFORD ☎053

Gaels, Vikings, and Normans all worked together—well, against each other—to create the winding, narrow streets of modern Wexford. The town's main attraction for visitors is undoubtedly its abundance of quality pubs and restaurants. The prominent Bull Ring and surrounding Norman ruins remain visual reminders of a history that featured the likes of Henry II and Oliver Cromwell.

▐ GETTING THERE AND GETTING AROUND

Trains: O'Hanranhan (North) Station (☎ 22522), Redmond Sq., a 5min. walk along the quays from Crescent Quay. From **Dublin Connolly** (2¾hr., 3 per day, £11, Friday £14.50) and **Rosslare Harbour** (30min., 3 per day, £2).

Buses: Buses stop at the train station. If the station office is closed, get info at the Station Cafe (☎ 24056) across the street. **Bus Éireann** (☎ 62121) from **Dublin** (2½hr.; M 8 per day, Tu-Sa 7 per day, Su 4 per day; £10) and **Rosslare Harbour** (20min.; M-Sa 10 per day, Su 9 per day; £2.65).

Taxis: Walsh Cabs (☎ 41449; mobile ☎ (088) 567 489). **Noel Ryan** (☎ 24056). A list of taxi companies is posted in the train station.

Bike Rental: Bike Shop, 9 Selskar St. (☎ 22514; gordon@iol.ie). £8 per day, £30 per week; £50 cash or credit card deposit. £12 extra to drop off elsewhere in the country. Open M-Sa 9am-6pm.

Hitchhiking: Hitchers report that the odds of getting a ride are highest from 5-7pm. Hitchhikers to **Dublin** (via N11) stand by the Wexford Bridge off the quays; those bound for **Rosslare** head south along the quays to Trinity St. Hitchers heading to **Cork, New Ross,** or **Waterford** go to Upper John St. (N25). *Let's Go* does not recommend hitching.

✳🛈 ORIENTATION AND PRACTICAL INFORMATION

The town's new marina is located by the **Crescent Quay** in the center of the waterfront. Most of the town's action takes place one block inland and uphill, on **Main St.** A plaza called the **Bullring** is near the center of town.

Tourist Information Centre: (☎ 23111), Crescent Quay. Open Apr.-Oct. M-Sa 9am-6pm; July-Aug. M-Sa 9am-6pm, Su 11am-5pm; Nov.-Mar. M-F 9:30am-5:30pm.

Financial Services: Bank of Ireland (☎ 23022), the Bullring. Open M 10am-5pm, Tu-F 10am-4pm.

Launderette: My Beautiful Launderette, St. Peter's Sq. (☎ 24317), up Peters St. from South Main St. Full- or self-service; pickup and delivery available. Wash up to 10 lbs. £6.50, self-service £5; dry £6. Open M-Sa 9:30am-6pm.

Police *(Garda):* (☎ 22333), Roches Rd.

Hospital: Wexford General Hospital (☎ 42233), New Town Rd., on N25/N11.

Internet Access: Wexford Library (☎ 053 2163) offers free access. Call ahead to reserve a 1hr. slot.

Post Office: Anne St. (☎ 22123). Open M and W-Sa 9am-5:30pm, Tu 9:30am-5:30pm. Smaller offices on South Main St. (☎ 45177) and at Main St. and Monck St.

▌ ACCOMMODATIONS

If you're planning to be in town during the opera festival, book as far in advance as possible; some rooms are reserved a year ahead of time. ▨ **Kirwan House Hostel (IHH),** 3 Mary St., is short of space, but not good feelings. (☎ 21208; kirwanhostel@tinet.ie. Internet access £1.50 per 20min. Bike rental £6 per day. Dorms £7.50-8.50; doubles £38-44.) **Abbey House,** 34 Abbey St., flaunts a fantastic location and comfy quarters. Call ahead, as the owner is often out. (☎ 24408. Singles £20; doubles with bath and TV £32.) On the east edge of town, on Dublin Rd., is **Ferrybank Caravan and Camping Park.** Take the bridge and continue straight to the camping site. (☎ 44378. Open Easter-Oct. £5 per 1-person tent; £7 per 2-person tent.)

◖ FOOD

The **Dunnes Store,** Redmond Sq., has everything from food to clothes to lampshades. (☎ 45688. Open M-Tu and Sa 9am-7pm, W-F 9am-9pm, Su 9am-6pm.) Head to the **The Sky and the Ground,** 112 South Main St., before 6pm for scaled-down versions of the pricier upstairs restaurant. (☎ 21273. Pub grub £5-7. Music Su-Th, usually trad.) **Greenacres,** 56 N. Main St., is Wexford's gourmet grocery, with a gem of a cafe in back, a special find for vegetarians. (☎ 21788. Cafe open M-Sa 9am-5:30pm.) There's nothing too fancy at the **Tack Room,** 38 N. Main St., right by the Bullring, but the food will stick to your ribs. Prices swell after 6pm. (☎ 21669. Main courses around £5. Food served until 8:30pm.)

SIGHTS

The remains of the Norman **city wall** run the length of High St. **Westgate Tower,** near the intersection of Abbey and Slaney St., is the only one of the wall's six original gates that still stands. The tower gate now holds the **Westgate Heritage Centre,** where an excellent 27-minute audio-visual show recounts the history of Wexford. (☎ 46506. Open M-F 10am-4pm. £1.50, children 50p.)

Three miles outside of Wexfod on the N11, the **Irish National Heritage Park,** lets you stroll through 9000 years of Irish history in just a few hours. From a Stone Age campsite to an early Norman tower, check out replicas of houses, tombs, and fortifications that archaeologists have discovered across Ireland. There's a restaurant with main courses for around £6. (☎ (053) 20733. Main trail wheelchair accessible. Open daily 9:30am-6:30pm. £5, students £4. Restaurant open 12:30-5:30pm.)

ENTERTAINMENT AND FESTIVALS

The two halves of **Mooney's Lounge,** Commercial Quay (☎ 24483), by the bridge, comprise *the* late-night hot spot in Wexford. All sorts of live music Th-Su, in one half or the other. The crowd looks young for 21+, but the bouncers are not decorations. (☎ 21128. Occasional cover.) A classy crowd of twentysomethings flocks to **The Centenary Stores,** Charlotte St., a pub and dance club housed within a former warehouse. (☎ 24424. Blues and folk Tu nights. DJ spins Th-Su 11pm-2am. Club cover £5.) **O'Faolain's** (oh FWAY lans), 11 Monck St., is a bar for all generations, with live music almost every night. A nightclub spins F-Su nights, with DJ, dance floor, and 60s-80s music. (☎ 23877. Club cover £5; £3 if in the pub before 11pm.)

The **Theatre Royal,** High St., produces performances throughout the year, culminating in the internationally acclaimed **Wexford Festival Opera** (www.wexfordopera.com), held annually in late October and early November. (☎ 22400; box office ☎ 22144. Box office open May-Sept. M-F 9:30am-5:30pm and during performances; Oct. daily 9:30am-11pm. Opera tickets £42-52, available from early June.)

ROSSLARE HARBOUR ☎053

Rosslare Harbour is an over-equipped seaside village providing ferry service to France and Wales.

GETTING THERE AND GETTING AROUND. Trains (office ☎ 33114; open daily 6am-10pm) arrive in the ferry port from: **Dublin** (3hr., 3 per day, £11); **Wexford** (20min., 3 per day, £2); **Waterford** (1¼hr.; M-F 2 per day, Sa-Su 1 per day; £6); and **Limerick** (2½hr.; M-F 2 per day, Sa-Su 1 per day; £12.50). **Buses** (call train office for info) stop in front of the Catholic church. **Bus Éireann** (☎ 62121) from: **Dublin** (3hr., 7-10 per day, £9); **Wexford** (20min., 10-14 per day, £2.65); **Waterford** (M-Sa 4 per day, Su 3 per day; £9.20); **Cork** (M-Sa 4 per day, Su 3 per day; £13); and **Limerick** (M-Sa 3 per day, Su 2 per day; £13.50).

The **ferry terminal** has a port authority desk (☎ 33114; open daily 6:30am-9:30pm), as well as a **bureau de change,** and Bus Éireann and Irish Rail desks (☎ 33592). **Stena Line** (☎ 33115) and **Irish Ferries** (☎ 33158; www.irishferries.com) serve the ferry port. For info on ferries from **England, Wales,** and **France,** see **By Ferry,** p. 35. Trains and buses often connect with the ferries. **Car rental** is offered by Europcar (☎ 33634) and **Hertz** (☎ 33238); prices hover around £40 per day (includes insurance), £154-175 for a week. **Taxis** can be hailed from **Dermot O'Hagan** (☎ 33777). **Hitchhikers** report that rides are hard to come by. *Let's Go* does not recommend hitchhiking.

PRACTICAL INFORMATION AND ACCOMMODATIONS. The mediocre Rosslare-Kilrane **tourist information centre** is a mile from the harbor on Wexford Rd. in Kilrane. (☎ 33622. Open daily 10:30am-8pm.) Services include the **Bank of Ireland** (☎ 33304; open M-F 10am-1:30pm and 2:30-4pm), and the **post office** (☎ 33201; open M-F 9am-1pm and 2-5:30pm, Sa 9am-1pm), in the **SuperValu supermarket** (open M-F 8am-7pm, Sa 8am-6pm, Su 9am-1pm).

REPUBLIC OF IRELAND

Those wanting a hostel should try **An Óige Rosslare Harbour,** Goulding St. Take a right at the top of the cliff, then go left around the Hotel Rosslare; the hostel is to the left, with decent showers and cinderblock walls. (☎ 33399; fax 33626. Dorms £8; June-Aug. quads £40, Sept.-Apr. £36.) For an overnight stay, ⊠ **Mrs. O'Leary's Farmhouse,** Killilane, off N25 in Kilrane, is a 15-minute drive from town, set beside a secluded beach. Call for pickup. (☎ 33134. £16.50 per person, with bath £18.50.)

WATERFORD   ☎051

Huge metal silos and harbor cranes greet the visitor to Waterford. Fortunately, behind this industrial facade lies a city with 10 centuries of history. The grandson of the Viking Ivor the Boneless founded Vadrafjord around AD 914 to harbor his longships, making it the oldest city in Ireland. Traces of the Viking settlement persist in Waterford's streets, despite the massive freighters that have since replaced the longships. Scores of pubs and shops make Waterford an indulgent break from touring the small towns that sleep over the rest of the county.

🄴 **GETTING THERE AND GETTING AROUND.** JFK's ancestors grew up in Waterford, and the city is still well connected. **Planes** fly into **Waterford Airport** (☎ 875589). Follow The Quay, turn right at Reginald's Tower, then left at the sign (20min. from town). No city buses head that way, so take a taxi if you aren't driving. **British Airways** fly from locations in England and Europe. **Trains** arrive at **Plunkett Station,** across the bridge from The Quay (☎ 317889, 24hr. recorded timetable ☎ 876243; staffed M-Sa 9am-6pm, Su at departure times) from: **Dublin** (2¾hr.; M-Sa 7 per day, Su 4 per day; £7); **Kilkenny** (40min.; M 5 per day, T-Sa 4 per day, Su 3 per day; £5); **Rosslare Harbour** (1¼hr.; 4 per day, Su 3 per day; £9.20); and **Limerick** (2½hr.; 5 per day, F 7 per day, Su 6 per day; £10.50). **Buses** stop on the Quay, near the bridge. (☎ 879000. Office open M-Sa 8:15am-6pm.) **Bus Éireann** (☎ 62121) runs from: **Dublin** (2¾hr.; M-Sa 7 per day, Su 4 per day; £7); **Kilkenny** (1hr.; M-Sa 2 per day, Su 1 per day; £5); and **Rosslare Harbour** (1¼hr.; 4 per day, Su 3 per day; £9.20).

For **taxis** call **7 Cabs** (☎ 877777), or **Five-O Cabs** (☎ 850000). **Car rental** is available at **Enterprise** (☎ 304804. Ages 25+. £35 per day.) For **bike rental,** check **Wright's Cycles,** 19-20 Henrietta St. (☎ 874411). £12 first day, £10 per day after; £52 per week; £50 deposit. Open Tu-F 9:30am-1pm and 2-6pm, Sa 9:30am-1pm and 2-5:30pm. **Hitchhikers** place themselves on the main routes, away from the city center. To reach N24 (Limerick), N10 (Kilkenny, Dublin), or N25 (Wexford, Rosslare), they head over the bridge toward the train station. Those heading to **Cork** take a bus out to the Crystal Factory. *Let's Go* does not recommend hitchhiking as a method of travel.

🄴🄽 **ORIENTATION AND PRACTICAL INFORMATION.** The quays on the River Suir and Barranstrand St. (through its many name changes) form a crooked triangular city center. Services include: the **Bank of Ireland** (☎ 872074; open M 10am-5pm, Tu-F 10am-4pm); the **police** (*Garda*; ☎ 874888), Patrick St.; **Waterford Regional Hospital** (☎ 873321), follow The Quay east to the Tower Hotel, turn left, then follow signs straight ahead to the hospital; **Internet Access** at **Voyager Internet Cafe,** Parnell St., in Parnell Court shopping center (☎ 843843; £1.50 per 15min, 10p per add. min.; open M-Sa 11am-9pm, Su 3-9pm); and the **post office,** The Quay (☎ 874321; open M and W-F 9am-5:30pm, Tu 9:30am-5:30pm, Sa 9am-1pm).

🄲🄲 **ACCOMMODATIONS AND FOOD.** Most B&Bs in the city are nothing special; those outside town on the Cork Rd. are better; the hostels are best of all. **Barnacle's Viking House (IHH),** Coffee House Ln., Greyfriars, The Quay, has spacious quarters and top-notch security. Follow The Quay east past the Clock Tower and post office; the hostel is on the right. (☎ 853827; viking@barnacles.iol.ie. Laundry £4 per load. Luggage storage 50p per day. Kitchen open 6am-midnight. Wheelchair accessible. Dorms £7.50-9; doubles with bath £29-31.) **Mayor's Walk House,** 12 Mayor's Walk, is a 15-minute walk from the train station with quiet rooms and a bottomless pot of tea. (☎ 855427. Open Feb.-Nov. Singles £16; doubles £30.) From the Quay, go up Henrietta St. to reach **Beechwood,** 7 Cathedral Sq. Mrs. Ryan invites you into her charming home on a silent street. (☎ 876677. Doubles £32.)

You might want to try Waterford's contribution to Irish cuisine, the *blaa* ("blah"), a floury white sausage roll of Huguenot origins. Pick up groceries at **Dunnes Stores,** in the City Square Mall. (☎ 853100. Open M-W 9am-7pm, Th-F 9am-9pm, Sa 9am-6pm, and Su noon-6pm.) The late-night **Cafe Luna,** 53 John St., serves creative pastas, salads, and sandwiches. (☎ 834539. Most dishes £3-5. Open M-W until 12:15am, Th-Su until 3:30am.) Vegetarians, carnivores, and newspaper-readers live in harmony at **Haricot's Wholefood Restaurant,** 11 O'Connell St. (☎ 841299. Most main courses £5-7. Open M-F 9:30am-8pm, Sa 9:30am-6pm.) **Gino's,** John St., at the Apple Market, is a busy family restaurant that serves pizza made right before your eyes. (☎ 879513. Reservations recommended on F-Sa nights, or get takeaway. Individual pizza £2.70. Open daily until 10:45pm for seating or 11pm for takeaway.)

🔲 **SIGHTS.** The **Waterford Crystal Factory** is two miles from the city center out on N25 (Cork Rd.). Witness master craftsmen transform molten goo into sparkling crystal. Catch the City Imp bus (10-15min., every 15-20min., 70p) along Parnell St. and request the factory stop. (☎ 373311. 1hr. tours every 15min., audio-visual shows on demand. Wheelchair accessible. Apr.-Oct. showroom open 8:30am-6pm, tours daily; Nov.-Mar. showroom open 9am-5pm, call ahead to check tour times; Jan.-Feb. showroom only 9am-5pm. Tours £3.50, students £2.) The remnants of the old **city walls,** both Viking and medieval, surround the city center. One excellent way to sort out Waterford's many architectural eras is the **Walking Tour of Historic Waterford** (☎ 873711). These one-hour tours depart from the Granville Hotel on the Quay and the Granary museum at a quarter to the hour, providing a thorough introduction to Waterford's mongrel history. (Mar.-Oct. daily at noon and 2pm. £3.)

🔲 **ENTERTAINMENT.** The Quays are loaded with pubs; even more reside on John St. A number run discos on weekend nights, so there's always somewhere open late. **T&H Doolan's,** George's St., has been serving crowds for 300 years in a fantastic building. (☎ 841504. Trad nightly. Open M-Sa until 11:30pm, Su until 11pm.) At **The Gingerbread Man,** Arundel Lane, authentic trad sessions jam at the front tables as the good time spills over to the back of this small bar. (☎ 875041. Food served noon-6pm.) The **Waterford Show** (☎ 358397, mobile ☎ (087) 681 7191) at City Hall is an entertaining performance of Irish music, stories, and dance. Tickets cost £7, but also get you a glass of Baileys or wine. (May-Sept. Tu, Th, and Sa at 9pm. July-Aug. also W at 9pm. Call for reservations or make them at the TIC.)

SOUTHWEST IRELAND

CORK   ☎021

As Ireland's second-largest city, Cork (pop. 150,000) is the center of the southwest's sports, music, and arts. Wise travelers will exploit the city's sources of food and shelter while exploring the exquisite scenery outside the city.

🔲 **GETTING THERE AND GETTING AROUND**

Flights: Cork Airport (☎ 431 3131), 5 mi. south of Cork on Kinsale Rd. **Aer Lingus** (☎ 432 7155) and **British Airways** (☎ 1 (800) 626 747) fly from various points in Britain.

Trains: Kent Station (☎ 450 6766), Lower Glanmire Rd., across the river from the city center. **Luggage storage** £1. Open M-Sa 7am-8:30pm, Su 7am-8pm. From: **Dublin** (3hr.; M-Sa 7 per day, Su 5 per day; £33.50); **Limerick** (1½hr.; M-Sa 7 per day, Su 4 per day; £14); **Killarney** (2hr.; M-Sa 7 per day, Su 4 per day; £14); and **Tralee** (2½hr.; M-Sa 3 per day, Su 3 per day; £18).

Buses: (☎ 450 8188), Parnell Pl., east of Patrick's Bridge on Merchants' Quay. Enquiries open daily 9am-5pm. **Bus Éireann** (☎ 62121) from: **Dublin** (4½hr., 4 per day, £13); **Killarney** (2hr.; M-Sa 8 per day, Su 6 per day; £9.40); **Limerick** (2hr.; M-Sa 6 per day, Su 5 per day; £9.60); and **Belfast** (7½hr.; M-Sa 4 per day, Su 2 per day; £20).

Ferries: Ringaskiddy Terminal (☎ 427 5061), 8 mi. south of the city. A 30min. bus ride from the Parnell Pl. station (£3). **24hr. ferry information** (☎ (01) 661 0715). Tickets can be bought on Bridge St. at the **Irish Ferries** office (☎ 455 1995). Open M-F 9am-5pm, Sa 9:15am-12:45pm.

Local Transportation: Downtown **buses** run every 10-30min. M-Sa 7:30am-11:15pm, reduced service Su 10am-11:15pm. Fares from 70p. The main bus station at Parnell Pl. offers free timetables (☎ 450 8188).

Car Rental: Budget Rent-a-Car, Tourist House, Grand Parade (☎ 427 4755). Ages 23+. £33 per day, £90 for 3 days, £195 per week.

Bike Rental: The Bike Shop, 68 Shandon St. (☎ 430 4144). £7 per day, £30 per week.

Hitchhiking: Hitchers headed for West Cork and County Kerry walk down Western Rd. past both the An Óige hostel and the dog track to the Crow's Nest Pub. Those hoping to hitch a ride to Dublin or Waterford should stand on the hill next to the train station on the Lower Glanmire Rd. *Let's Go* doesn't recommend hitchhiking as a method of travel.

✴🛈 ORIENTATION AND PRACTICAL INFORMATION

The **River Lee** runs through the city with downtown Cork lying on the island, the southern side filled with quiet avenues, and the north side dominated by the sight-filled **Shandon** district. Downtown action concentrates on **Oliver Plunkett St., Saint Patrick St.,** and **Paul St.** Heading west from the Grand Parade, **Washington St.** becomes **Western Rd.** and then the N22 to Killarney; to the north, **MacCurtain St.** flows east into **Lower Glanmire Rd.,** which becomes N8 and N25.

Tourist Information Centre: Tourist House (☎ 427 3251), Grand Parade, across from National Monument. Open M-Sa 9:15am-5:30pm.

Financial Services: TSB, 4-5 Princes St. (☎ 427 5221). Open M-W and F 9:30am-5pm, Th 9:30am-7pm.

Launderette: Duds 'n' Suds (☎ 431 4799), Douglas St., around the corner from Kelly's Hostel. TV and snack bar. Wash £1.50, dry £1.80. Open M-F 8am-9pm, Sa 8am-8pm.

Police *(Garda):* (☎ 452 2000) Anglesea St.

Hospital: Mercy Hospital (☎ 427 1971), Grenville Pl. £20 fee for access to emergency room. **Cork Regional Hospital** (☎ 454 6400), Wilton St., on bus #8.

Internet Access: Favourite, 122 Patrick St. (☎ 427 2646), near Merchant Quay. Bring coins. £1 per 10min. Open daily 10am-midnight.

Post Office: (☎ 427 2000), Oliver Plunkett St. Open M-Sa 9am-5:30pm.

▌ ACCOMMODATIONS

B&Bs are clustered along Western Rd. near University College. The other concentration of accommodations is in the slightly more central area along MacCurtain St. and Lower Glanmire Rd., near the bus and train stations.

▨ **Sheila's Budget Accommodation Centre (IHH),** 3 Belgrave Pl. (☎ 450 5562). Centrally located, Sheila's offers a kitchen and summer barbecues. Internet access £1 per 10 min., video rental £1, sauna £1.50 for 40 min. All rooms non-smoking. Rooms available with bath. Free luggage storage. Sheets 50p. Key deposit £5. Check-out 10:30am. Bike rental £6. 6-bed dorms £7; 4-bed dorms £8.50; doubles £21.

An Óige Cork, 1-2 Redclyffe, Western Rd. (☎ 454 3289), a 15min. walk from the Grand Parade. Bus #8 stops (requested) across the street. Spacious rooms in a brick Victorian townhouse. All rooms with bath. Continental breakfast £2. Check-in 8am-midnight. Bike rental £5 per day, £30 per week. 10-bed dorms £8-9.50; 6-bed dorms £12.50-14.50; 4-bed dorms £10.50-12; doubles £25. Rates seasonal, less for under 18.

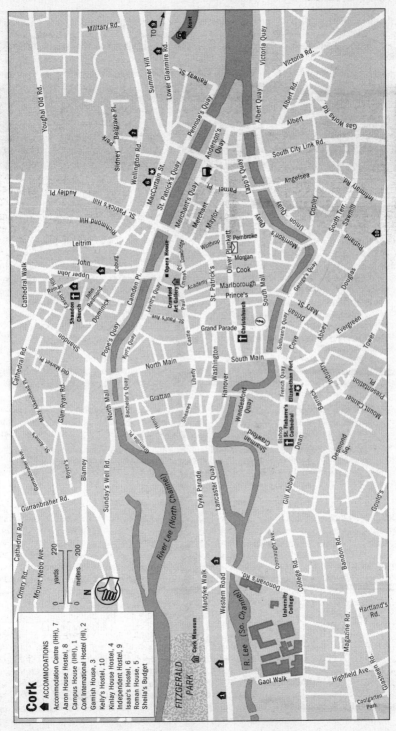

REPUBLIC OF IRELAND

Cork

♦ ACCOMMODATIONS
Accommodation Centre (IHH), 7
Aaron House Hostel, 8
Campus House (IHH), 1
Cork International Hostel (HI), 2
Gamish House, 3
Kelly's Hostel, 10
Kinlay House Hostel, 4
Independent Hostel, 9
Isaac's Hostel, 6
Roman House, 5
Sheila's Budget

REPUBLIC OF IRELAND

Kinlay House (IHH), Bob and Joan Walk (☎ 450 6927; kincork@usit.ie), down the alley to the right of Shandon Church. Located in less-than-posh but convenient Shandon, Kinlay House is large and clean, if motel-like. Each of the modern rooms has a locker and wash basin. Video library and game room. 10% ISIC discount. Continental breakfast included. Laundry £3.60. Internet access £1.50 per 15min. 50p key deposit. Free parking. 10- to 14-bed dorms £8; singles £15; doubles £25.

Isaac's (IHH), 48 McCurtain St. (☎ 450 8388). Located near the bus and train stations. Cafe open for breakfast and lunch. 24hr. reception. Dorm lockout 11am-3pm. 14- to 16-bed dorms £7.95; 6- to 10-bed dorms £8.95, 4-bed dorms £9.25.

Aaran House Tourist Hostel, Lower Glanmire Rd. (☎ 455 1566). A casual atmosphere and convenient location, near the train station. Continental breakfast included. 8-bed dorms £7.50. 4-bed dorms £8, with bath £8.50; 2-bed dorms £9.50.

Garnish House, Western Rd. (☎ 427 5111). Gorgeous rooms, fluffy duvets, fruit, and flowers. Free laundry. Singles from £25; doubles from £40, with jacuzzi from £50.

Roman House, St. John's Terrace, Upper John St. (☎ 450 3606, rhbb@ircom.net). Cork's only B&B catering specifically to gay and lesbian travelers, Roman House is decorated decadently. Singles from £20; doubles £36.

◖ FOOD

The **English Market,** accessible from Grand Parade, displays a wide variety of meats, cheeses, and fruits. Cork's historic role as a meat-shipping center meant that residents got stuck eating leftovers: feet, snouts, and other delectable goodies. Cork's local specialties include crubeen (pig's feet), drisheen (blood sausage, a hybrid of liver and gelatin), and Clonakilty black pudding. **Tesco,** Paul St., deals in groceries. (☎ 427 0791. Open M-W and Sa 8:30am-8pm, Th-F 8:30am-10pm.)

Scoozi, in the alley just off Winthrop Ave. (☎ 427 5077). Follow the tomato signs to this expansive, brick-and-wood-lined establishment. It's the perfect spot for enjoying burgers, pizza, grilled chicken, and pasta with wild abandon amongst crowds. Pesto chicken breast on a bun with fries and coleslaw £6.85. Open M-Sa 9am-11pm, Su noon-10pm.

The Gingerbread House, Paul St. (☎ 429 6411). Huge windows, cool jazz, and heavenly breads, pastries, and quiche all made fresh on the premises. Eat in or take out. Open M-W, Sa 8:15am-7pm, Th-F 8:15am-9pm, Su 8:15am-6pm.

Quay Co-op, 24 Sullivan's Quay (☎ 431 7660). Nary a creature was sacrificed for the scrumptious vegetarian dishes in this classy establishment. Open M-Sa 9am-9pm. The store downstairs caters to all organic and vegan needs. Store open M-Sa 9am-6:15pm.

Gino's, 7 Winthrop St. (☎ 427 4485), between Patrick St. and Oliver Plunkett St. Primo pizza draws crowds. Lunch special includes pizza and Cork's best ice cream for £4.50. Open M-Sa noon-11pm, Su 1-11pm.

◣ SIGHTS

CORK CITY GAOL. The museum is a reconstruction of the gaol as it appeared in the 1800s. Visitors are treated to displays of Cork's social history and miserable punishments, like the "human treadmill" used to grind grain. *(Sunday's Well Rd. From Fitzgerald Park, cross the white footbridge at the western end of the park, turn right onto Sunday's Well Rd., and follow signs. ☎ 430 5022. Open daily Mar.-Oct. 9:30am-6pm, Nov.-Feb. 10am-5pm. Last admission 1hr. before closing. £4.50, students and seniors £3.)*

ST. ANN'S CHURCH. Commonly called **Shandon Church,** after its steeple, Shandon Tower. The now barely visible red-and-white strips on the steeple inspired the "Rebel" flag, still ubiquitous throughout Cork. Construction of the current church began in 1722. Admission to the tower promises a spectacular view. *(Walk up Shandon St., take a right down unmarked Church St., and go straight. ☎ 450 5906. Open in summer M-Sa 9:30am-5:30pm. £5 adults, students and seniors £4, group rates available.)*

CRAWFORD MUNICIPAL ART GALLERY. The gallery specializes in the paintings of Irish masters like James Barry and Jack Yeats, along with contemporary work by aspiring artists of all nationalities. Adjacent is the monstrous cement Opera House, erected 20 years ago after the older, more elegant opera house went down in flames. (*Emmet Place. Over the hill from Shandon Church and across the north fork of the Lee. ☎ 427 3377. Gallery open M-Sa 10am-5pm. Free.*)

🍺 🎵 PUBS AND CLUBS

Along Oliver Plunkett St., Union Quay, and South Main St., there are more pubs than you can shake a stick at. Nearly all stop serving at 11:30pm.

The Lobby, 1 Union Quay (☎ 431 9307). Arguably the most famous venue in Cork, the Lobby has given some of Ireland's biggest folk acts their start. Live music nightly at 9:30pm, from trad to acid jazz. Two floors overlook the river. Occasional cover £4.

An Spailpín Fanac (uhn spal-PEEN FAW-nuhk), 28 South Main St. (☎ 427 7949). One of Cork's more popular pubs, with live trad complementing the decor and tourists most nights. Pub grub (Irish stew £3.75) served M-F noon-3pm.

Gallaghers, McCurtain St. A traditional pub conveniently located to welcome tourists, especially on "Backpacker Nights" (M-Tu), when a three-pint pitcher sells for £6. Also features an array of filling pub grub, with most meals costing around £4.50.

The Western Star (☎ 454 3047), Western Rd. A 25min. walk from the town center, this largely student bar rocks with the chart toppers nightly. If you're staying nearby in summer, enjoy the outdoors bar on the patio by the River Lee. Free barbecue F-Sa.

Rosie O'Grady's (☎ 427 8253), N. Main St. Brace yourself. A wild, swelling crowd and pulsing trad render the Rosie's experience one of Cork's liveliest. Largely student crowd in the winter. Live trad Su, M, W. Lunch served M-F noon-3pm.

Gorbys (☎ 427 0074), Oliver Plunkett St. Track lighting illuminates young groovers. The £2-5 cover allows access to the lower dance floor and the retro-flavored upstairs.

🎭 ENTERTAINMENT

Everyman's Theatre (a.k.a. "the Palace"), MacCurtain St., stages big-name musicals, plays, operas, and concerts. (☎ 450 1673. Box office open M-F 9am-5:30pm, Sa 10am-5:30pm, until 7pm on show dates. Tickets £8-18.) **Hurling** and **Gaelic football** take place every Sunday afternoon at 3pm from June to September; for additional details, call the GAA (☎ 439 5368) or consult *The Cork Examiner*. Tickets to big games are £13-15 and scarce, but Saturday, Sunday, and Wednesday evening matches are cheap (£1-4) or free. You can buy tickets to these local games at the **Pairc Uí Chaoimh** (park EE KWEEV) stadium; take bus #2 to Blackrock.

🌄 DAYTRIPS FROM CORK

THE BLARNEY STONE. Blarney Castle, with its Blarney Stone, is the quintessential tourist spot. You might just find yourself bending over backwards to kiss the stone in hopes of acquiring the legendary eloquence bestowed on those who smooch it. The term "blarney" refers to the supposedly Irish talent of stretching, or even obstructing, the truth. More impressive than the stone is the castle itself, built in 1446. Bus Éireann runs buses from Cork to Blarney (return £2.50). To avoid the crowds, go early in the morning. (*☎ 385 252. Open June-Aug. 9am-7pm, Su 9:30am-5:30pm; Sept. M-Sa 9am-6:30pm, Su 9:30am-sundown; Oct.-Apr. M-Sa 9am-6pm, Su 9:30am-sundown; May M-Sa 9am-6:30pm, Su 9:30am-5:30pm. Last admission 30min. before closing. £3.50, seniors and students £2.50, children £1.*)

NEAR CORK: CAPE CLEAR ISLAND (OILEÁN CHLÉIRE)

The rugged landscape seen from the bumpy ferry docking at Cape Clear Island seems incapable of providing for its sparse population of 150 individuals. The main industry of this wild and beautiful island, however, is still farming. A 25-minute walk up a steep hill from the pier is the island's **Heritage Centre**. Since over half of the exhibits are in Irish, it's a quick trip for the Gaelically-challenged. (Open daily June-Aug. 2-5:30pm. £1.80, students £1, under 18 50p.) The **bird observatory**, the white house on North Harbour, is one of the most important in Europe.

Ferries run to and from **Baltimore** (£9 return). Call Capt. Conchúr (Conner) O'Driscoll (☎ 39135) for more information. The **Co-op office** (☎ 39119) hands out free maps. **An Óige Cléire Lasmuigh,** the Cape Clear Island Adventure Centre and Hostel, is a 10-minute walk from the pier (keep to the left on the main road). The hostel often fills up in the summer, so call ahead. (☎ 39144. Dorms June-Sept. £8, Oct.-May £7.) **Cuas an Uisce campsite,** on the south harbor, is a five-minute walk from the harbor: go up the main road, turn right, then bear left. (☎ 39136. Open June-Sept. Showers 50p. Tent rental £10. £2.70 per person.)

The one grocery store, **An Siopa Beag,** stocks the essentials in a white building a few hundred yards down the pier to the right. (☎ 39099. Open Jun.-Aug. M-Sa 9:30am-1:30pm and 2:30-6pm; Sept.-May 9:30am-4pm.) The island has no resident authorities to regulate after-hours drinking, and 150 people support two pubs: **The Night Jar's** (☎ 39012) and **Ciarán Danny Mike's** (☎ 39172).

BEARA PENINSULA

For unspoiled scenery and solitude, the Beara is superb; if you're looking for pubs, people, and other signs of civilization, you might be happier on the Iveragh or Dingle Peninsulas. The spectacular Caha and Slieve Miskish Mountains march down the center of the peninsula, while West Beara is even more remote.

BANTRY   ☎027

According to the *Book of Invasions,* Ireland's first human inhabitants landed just a mile from Bantry. Today's invaders come in the form of tourists eager to sample Bantry's elegance and relive its history or to start off on a trek to the more remote areas westward. Bantry's biggest tourist attraction is **Bantry House,** a Georgian manor with an imposing garden overlooking Bantry Bay. The long and shaded driveway to the house is a 10-minute walk from town on Cork Rd. (☎ 50047. Open mid-Mar. to Oct. daily 9am-6pm. House and garden £6, students £4. Garden £2.)

Buses stop in Wolfe Tone Sq. **Bus Éireann** (☎ 62121) comes from: **Glengarriff** (M-Sa 3 per day, Su 2 per day; £2.25); **Cork** (M-Sa 3 per day, Su 2 per day; £8.80); and **Killarney** via **Kenmare** (June-Sept. only, 2 per day). **Rent bikes** from **Kramer's** on Glengarriff Rd., Newtown. (☎ 50278. £8 per day, £40 per week; ID deposit. Open M-Sa 9am-6pm.) Cars and cyclists stay on N71 to get in or out of town. The **tourist information centre** (TIC) in Wolfe Tone Sq. has a **bureau de change.** (☎ 50229. Open July-Aug. M-Sa 9:30am-7pm, Su 10am-6pm.) Services include: **AIB**, Wolfe Tone Sq. (☎ 50008; open M-W and F 10am-4pm, Th 10am-5pm); the **police** (*garda;* ☎ 50045), Wolfe Tone Sq.; **St. Joseph's Bantry Hospital** (☎ 50133), Dromleigh; and the **post office,** 2 William St. (☎ 50050; Open M and W-Sa 9am-5:30pm, Tu 9:30am-5:30pm).

To find the **Bantry Independent Hostel (IHH),** Bishop Lucey Pl., head away from town on Glengarriff Rd. (Marino St.), take the left fork, and walk ¼ mi. (☎ 51050. Laundry £4. Open mid-Mar.-Oct. 6-bed dorms £8; private rooms £10 per person.) Four miles from town in Ballylickey, the **Eagle Point Camping and Caravan Park,** Glengarriff Rd., has private beach and tennis courts, a TV room, and free showers. (☎ 50630. Laundry £3. Open May-Sept. £4 per person.) **O'Siochain,** Bridge St., serves well-prepared food in a comfy, kitschy coffeehouse. (☎ 51339. Open daily 9am-10pm.) Aside from being exceedingly popular, **The Snug,** Wolf Tone Sq. (☎ 50057), serves up grub at great prices (burgers £4-6) and occasional bursts of trad.

CASTLETOWNBERE   ☎027

Castletownbere is a reluctant hub with energetic downtown pubs and restaurants to revitalize weary trekkers on their way to and from the Beara. Castletownbere's seat at the foot of hefty **Hungry Hill** (2245 ft.) makes it a fine launch pad for daytrips up the mountain. The best scenery on the Beara is on **Dursey Island,** reached by Ireland's only cable car. Walks around the island expose you to a stark combination of sea, sky, land, and sheep. The cables begin five miles out from Allihies, off the Casteltownbere Rd., and stretch across the water. (☎ (027) 73017. Cable car runs M-Sa 9-10:30am, 2:30-4:30pm, and 7-7:30pm, depending on demand; Su hours vary depending on which church has mass that morning; £2.50 return.)

Bus Éireann (☎ 62121) offers service to **Cork** (3hr., 9-11 per day, £14), and summer service between Castletownbere and **Killarney** via **Kenmare** (M-Sa 1 per day, £8.80). The closet-sized **tourist information centre** is behind O'Donoghue's by the harbor. (☎ 70054. Open June-Sept. M-F 10:30am-5pm.) **Bank** at **AIB,** Main St. (☎ 70015. Open M 10am-12:30pm and 1:30-5pm, Tu-F 10am-12:30pm and 1:30-4pm.)

Two miles west of town on Allihies Rd., just past the fork to Dunboy Castle, the **Beara Hostel** hands out "welcome cakes" upon arrival, but be warned that the rural location may involve more of an outdoorsy experience than you bargained for. (☎ 70184. Bike rental £7 per day, £35 per week; passport deposit. Dorms £7; private rooms £8.50 per person, with bath £9.50. Camping £4 per person.) **Castletown House,** Main St., above the Old Bank Seafood Restaurant, offers lovely rooms and lots of advice. Be sure to show the friendly owner your *Let's Go* guide. (☎ 70252. £15, with bath £17.) **SuperValu,** Main St., sells the largest selection of groceries. (☎ 70020. Open M-Sa 8am-9pm, Su 9am-9pm.) **The Old Bakery,** Main St., serves piping-hot pizzas and an extensive menu of top-quality curries, sandwiches, and pasta (£4-6). (☎ 70901. Open daily 9am-9pm.) **MacCarthy's,** Main St. (☎ 70014), the most popular pub in town and a well-stocked grocery, serves food all day. Sandwiches are under £2 and there's trad and ballads on the weekends.

KILLARNEY   ☎064

Just a short walk away from some of Ireland's most extraordinary scenery, Killarney celebrates tourism. You'll find all you need in town, plus lots of trinkets to weigh down your pack as you hike nearby.

▐ GETTING THERE AND GETTING AROUND

Trains: Killarney Station (☎ 31067, recorded info ☎ (066) 26555), off East Avenue Rd. Open M-Sa 7:30am-10pm, Su 30min. before train departures. From: **Dublin** (3½hr., 4 per day, £33.50); **Cork** (2hr., 5 per day, £9.50); and **Limerick** (3hr.; M-Sa 4 per day, Su 3 per day; £15).

Buses: (☎ 30011), Park Rd., in a trailer next to the mall. Open M-Sa 8:30am-5pm. **Bus Éireann** (☎ 62121) from: **Dublin** (6hr., 4-5 per day, £15); **Cork** (2hr., 3-7 per day, £9.40); **Dingle** (2hr., 4-6 per day, £9.20); and **Galway** (7hr., 2-3 per day, £13.50).

Bike Rental: O'Sullivans (☎ 31282), Bishop's Ln., next to Neptune's hostel. £7 per day, £35 per week. Free panniers, locks, and park maps. Open daily 8:30am-6:30pm.

▐▐ ORIENTATION AND PRACTICAL INFORMATION

Killarney packs into three crowded major streets. **Main St.,** in the center of town, begins at the town hall, and becomes **High St. New St.** and **Plunkett St.** both intersect Main St. New St. heads west toward Killorglin. Plunkett St. becomes **College St.** and then **Park Rd.** on its way east to the bus and train stations.

Tourist Information Centre: (☎ 31633), Beech St., off New St. Open July-Aug. M-Sa 9am-8pm, Su 10am-1pm and 2:15-6pm; June and Sept. M-Sa 9am-6pm, Su 10am-1pm, 2:15-6pm; Oct.-May M-Sa 9:15am-5:30pm.

Financial Services: Allied Ireland Bank (☎ 31047), Main St. Open M-Tu and Th-F 10am-4pm, W 10am-5pm.

American Express: East Avenue Rd. (☎ 35722). Open May-Sept. M-F 8am-7:30pm, Sa 9am-6pm; Jul.-Aug. also Su 9am-7pm; Feb.-Apr. M-F 9am-5pm.

Launderette: J. Gleeson's Launderette (☎ 33877), next to Spar Market on Brewery Lane off College St. £5 per load. Open M-W and Sa 9am-6pm, Th-F 9am-8pm.

Police (*Garda*): (☎ 31222), New Rd.

Hospital: District Hospital (☎ 31076), St. Margaret's Rd. Follow High St. 1 mi. from the town center. Nearest **emergency facilities** are in **Tralee.**

Internet Access: PC Assist (☎ 37288), at the corner of High St. and New Rd. (not New St.). £1.50 per 15min., £5 per hr. Open M-Sa 9am-6pm.

Post Office: (☎ 31288), New St. Open M-F 9am-5:30pm, Sa 9am-1pm.

▮ ACCOMMODATIONS

Call ahead to the three hostels in town during the summer months. Camping is not allowed in the National Park, but there are excellent campgrounds nearby.

IN TOWN

The Súgán (IHH), Lewis Rd. (☎ 33104), 2min. from the bus or train station. Make a left onto College St.; Lewis Rd. is the 1st right. Somewhat cramped quarters are compensated for by exuberant management and impromptu storytelling and music. Dorms £9.

Neptune's (IHH), Bishop's Ln. (☎ 35255), the first walkway off New St. on the right. Immense and clean with good showers, smaller rooms, but numerous amenities. Breakfast £1.50-3.50. Free luggage storage; £5 locker deposit. Laundry £5. Internet access £2 per 15min. Tour booking: Dingle £12, Ring of Kerry £8. 8-bed dorms £7.50-8; 6-bed dorms £8-8.50; 3- to 4-bed dorms £9-9.50; doubles £20; 10% ISIC discount.

The Railway Hostel (IHH), Park Rd. (☎ 35299), the first lane on your right as you head towards town from the bus station. Skylights, modern kitchen, and pool table. Internet access £1 per 8 min. 3am curfew. 4- to 8-bed dorms £8.50-9; doubles £25.

Orchard House B&B (☎ 31879), Fleming's Ln., off High St. Make yourself at home in the center of town. This friendly and immaculate place is hard to beat. All rooms come with TV, tea, coffee, and hair dryer. Singles £18; doubles £34-36.

OUTSIDE TOWN

▨ **Peacock Farms Hostel (IHH;** ☎ 33557). Take Muckross Rd. out of town and turn left just before the Muckross post office. After 2 mi., follow the signposts. A less taxing alternative is to call for a ride from the bus station. Surrounded by Killarney's slopes, this hostel is home to a collection of homing pigeons. Skylights, hand-painted showers, and comfy rooms. 2 free buses to town daily at 9:30am and 6:30pm. Open Apr.-Oct. Wheelchair accessible. 8-bed dorms £7; twins £18.

An Óige Aghadoe (☎ 31240). In Aghadoe, 3 mi. west of town on the Killorglin Rd. Call for free van ride to and from bus and train stations. Well-equipped hostel in a stone mansion surrounded by forests and a mountain view. Laundry £4. Internet access £1 per 10min. Reception 7:30am-midnight. Bike rental £6 per day. Dorms July-Aug. £9.50; Sept.-June £8.50. Singles July-Aug. £12, Sept.-June £10.

Fossa Caravan and Camping Park (☎ 31497), 3½ mi. west of town on the Killorglin Rd. Kitchen, tennis, and restaurant. Bike rental £7. Showers 50p. Laundry. Open mid-Apr. to Oct. July-Aug. £4 per person, mid-Apr. to June and Sept. £3.50.

◖▨ FOOD AND PUBS

Tesco, in an arcade off New St., is the town's largest supermarket. (Open M-W and Sa 8am-8pm, Th-F 8am-10pm, Su 10am-6pm.)

▨ **O'Connor's Traditional Pub,** 7 High St. (☎ 31115). Tourists and locals mingle in this upbeat, comfortable pub. Trad M and Th.

The Stonechat (☎ 34295), Fleming Ln. A stone cottage just far enough from High St. for a quiet meal. Specializes in vegetarian food. Open 11:30am-3pm and 5:30-10pm.

Celtic Cauldron, 27 Plunkett St. (☎ 36821). Feast on the foods of the ancient Celts, then wash it all down with a tall glass of mead. Open daily mid-Mar. to Nov. 6-10pm.

Cyrano's, Innisfallen Center (☎ 35853). Lower level of the plaza between Main St. and Car Park. Cyrano's knows variety, including tasty vegetarian meals. Sate that silver tongue with a dangerous dessert and a cappuccino. Open M-Sa 9:30am-6pm.

Courtney's Bar (☎ 32688), Plunkett St. Locals and a few well-informed tourists (pat yourself on the back) come here for occasional unplanned trad sessions but mainly for the good company and good beer.

FESTIVALS

In mid-March, Killarney hosts the **Guinness Roaring 1920s Festival,** for which pubs, restaurants, and hostels bust out in jazz, barbershop singing, and flapper regalia. In mid-May and mid-July, horses gallop in the **Killarney Races** at the racecourse on Ross Rd. (tickets available at gate, £3-5). The **Killarney Regatta,** the oldest regatta in Ireland, draws spectators to Lough Leane in early to mid-July (tickets £5).

NEAR KILLARNEY: KILLARNEY NATIONAL PARK

Ice Age glaciers sliced up the Killarney region, scooping out a series of lakes and glens and scattering silk-smooth rocks and precarious boulders. The 37 sq. mi. park, stretching west and south of Killarney toward Kenmare, incorporates a string of forested mountains and the famous **Lakes of Killarney.** Biking is a great way to explore, and **bike rentals** are readily available in town (see **Practical Information,** p. 709). The park's size demands a map, available at the **Information Centre** behind Muckross House. (☎ 31440. Open daily June-Sept. 9am-7pm.)

The most frequented destinations are the **Ross Castle** area, **Muckross House** on Middle Lake, and the **Gap of Dunloe** just west of the park area, bordered on the southwest by **Macgillycuddy's Reeks,** Ireland's highest mountain range (most peaks are under 3000ft.). The Gap of Dunloe is a full-day excursion. The others can be managed in several hours or stretched out over a full day, depending on transport.

RING OF KERRY

The Southwest's most celebrated peninsula holds majestic views of the Iveragh Peninsula, rarely disappointing the droves of tourists who cruise through the region in private buses with tour guides. A set of roads circumnavigates the peninsula: N71 from Kenmare to Killarney, R562 from Killarney to Killorglin, and the long loop of N70 west and back to Kenmare. **Bus Éireann** runs a regular summer circuit through all the major towns on the Ring (2 per day).

KENMARE ☎064

A bridge between the Ring of Kerry and Beara, Kenmare has adapted to a continuous stream of visitors. Busloads of tourists can dilute Kenmare's appeal, but services and pleasant surroundings overshadow the postcard stands.

🖃🖬 GETTING THERE AND PRACTICAL INFORMATION. Bus Éireann (☎ 62121) arrive at Brennan's Pub on Main St. from **Sneem** (35min., June-Sept. M-Sa 2 per day) and **Killarney** (1hr., M-Sa 3 per day, Su 2 per day), for connections to **Cork** and **Tralee.** Kenmare's streets form a triangle: **Henry St.** is the lively base, while **Main** and **Shelbourne St.** connect on either side. The intersection of Henry and Main St. forms **The Square,** which contains a small park and the **tourist information centre.** (☎ 41233. Open daily July-Oct. 9am-6pm.) Services include: **Allied Ireland Bank,** 9 Main St. (☎ 41010; open M-Tu and Th-F 10am-4pm and W 10am-5pm); the **hospital** (☎ 41088), Old Killarney Rd., down Henry St. past The Square; **Internet access** at **Bean and Leaf,** Rock St., off Main St. (☎ 40026; £1.50 per 15min; open Mar.-Nov. Tu-Sa 10am-6pm); and the **post office,** Henry St., at the corner of Shelbourne St. (☎ 41490; open M-F 9am-1pm and 2-5:30pm, Sa 9am-1pm).

712 ■ SOUTHWEST IRELAND

ACCOMMODATIONS AND FOOD. Fáilte Hostel (IHH), on the corner of Henry St. and Shelbourne St., is not the white building that says "private hostel," but the one across the street. (☎ 42333. Curfew 1am. Dorms £8.) **Keal Na Gower House B&B,** The Square, is near a babbling brook. One room has a bathtub; the other two have brook views. (☎ 41202. Doubles £36.) **Ring of Kerry Caravan and Camping Park,** Sneem Rd., 3 mi. west of Kenmare, overlooks mountains and a bay. (☎ 41648. Kitchen, TV room, and small shop. Open May-Sept. £4 per person.)

The Pantry, Henry St., sells wholefoods and organic produce. (☎ 42233. Open M-Sa 9:30am-6pm.) **An Leath Phingin,** 35 Main St., makes its pasta and smokes its salmon on-site. (☎ 41559. Most pizzas £7. Open Th-Tu 6-10pm.) **The New Delight,** 18 Main St., has veggies at unbeatable prices. (☎ 42350. Open June-Nov. High season M-Sa 10am-8pm, low season M-Sa 10am-5pm.) Kenmare's pubs attract a hefty contingent of tourists. Still, native Guinness guzzlers hear too much good music to quibble over "Kiss me, I'm a leprechaun" hats. **Ó Donnabháin's,** Henry St. (☎ 42106), is a favorite among natives, with a beer garden out back. **Murty's,** New Rd. (☎ 41453), just off Henry St., features live bands (W, F-Sa) and disco (Th, Su).

CAHERSIVEEN   ☎066

Even those immune to history lessons will enjoy the coastal location of Cahersiveen (CARS-veen), best known as the birthplace of patriot Daniel O'Connell (see p. 660). Its two hostels are excellent bases for exploring the nearby beach and historical sites. There's no shortage of nightlife—Cahersiveen has 30 pubs, and once had 52 to its name.

GETTING THERE AND PRACTICAL INFORMATION. The Ring of Kerry **bus** stops in front of Banks Store on Main St. (June-Sept. 2 per day) and continues to **Caherdaniel** (1½hr., £3.10) and **Killarney** (2½hr., £9); one route heads directly east to **Killarney** (M-Sa 1-2 per day). **Casey's,** Main St., **rents bikes.** (☎ 947 2474. £7 per day, £35 per week; helmet and lock included. Open daily 9am-6pm.) The **tourist information centre** (TIC) is in former barracks on the road to Ballycarbery Castle. (☎ 947 2589. Open May to mid-Sept. M-F 10am-1pm, 2:15-6pm.) Main St. has an **AIB** bank (☎ 947 2022; open M 10am-5pm, Tu-F 10am-3pm). The **post office** is at the end of Main St. (☎ 947 2010. Open M-F 9:30am-1pm and 2-5:30pm, Sa 9:30am-1pm.)

ACCOMMODATIONS AND FOOD. The **Sive Hostel (IHH),** 15 East End, Main St., has a welcoming and well-informed staff, comfortable beds, and a third-floor balcony that overlooks the castle across the river. (☎ 947 2717. Sheets 50p. Wash and dry £4. 4- to 8-bed dorms £8; doubles £20-25. Camping £5 per person.) **Mortimer's Hostel,** Main St., competes with the Sive in friendliness. (☎ 947 2338. Dorms £7.) Mortimer himself is unsurpassed in local knowledge. He also runs the **Mannix Point Caravan and Camping Park** (☎ 947 2806), located at the west end of town. One of the best campsites in the country, the site adjoins a waterfront nature reserve and faces the romantic ruins of Ballycarbery Castle. (☎ 947 2806. Open mid-Mar. to mid-Oct. Kitchen. Free showers. £4 per person.)

You'll find the juiciest steaks at **QC's Chargrill Bar & Restaurant,** Main St. The colorful, modern restaurant also specializes in seafood and is home to Ireland's first indoor barbecue, imported from Spain. Lunch costs £5-9, dinner £12-16. (☎ 947 2244. Open daily 11:45am-midnight.) The casual **Cupan Éile** (☎ 947 3200), Main St., meets all sandwich needs (£1.60-3.50) and cooks a filling breakfast with vegetarian choices for £3.75 to £4. Cahersiveen's long Main St. still has several **pubs** of the early 20th-century variety: these establishments are both watering holes and the proprietor's "main" business, whether it be general store, blacksmith, leather shop, or farm goods retail. The **Anchor Bar** (☎ 947 2049), toward the west end of Main St., sells Guinness alongside fishing tackle. Don't come before 10pm, and when you do, take your drink into the kitchen for friendly conversation.

SIGHTS. O'Connell's Church in town is the only one in Ireland named for a layperson. "The Liberator" and other aspects of Irish history are celebrated at the **Old Barracks Heritage Centre,** in the TIC. (☎ 947 2589. Open M-Sa 10am-6pm, Su 1-6pm. £3, £2.50.) Turn left past the bridge, then left off the Main Rd. to reach the ruins of 15th-century **Ballycarbery Castle,** once held by O'Connell's ancestors. Two hundred yards past the castle turnoff, two of Ireland's best-preserved stone forts spread over a small stretch of land. You can walk atop the 10 ft. thick walls of **Cahergall Fort,** or visit the small stone dwellings of **Leacanabuaile Fort.** A few minutes beyond the second fort is **Cuas Crom** beach, known as the best swimming spot in the area.

CAHERDANIEL   ☎066

There's delightfully little in the village of Caherdaniel to attract the Ring's drove of travel coaches, but this hamlet (two pubs, a grocer, a restaurant, and a takeaway) has the advantage of proximity to one of Ireland's best beaches and one of the region's finest hostels. **Derrynane House,** signposted just up from the beach, was the residence of Daniel "The Liberator" O'Connell, who won Catholic representation in Parliament in 1829. (☎ 947 5113. Open May-Sept. M-Sa 9am-6pm, Su 11am-7pm; Apr. and Oct. Tu-Su 1-5pm; Nov.-Mar. Sa-Su 1-5pm. Last admission 45min. before closing. £2, students and children £1.) The largest stone fort in Ireland, **Staigue Fort** stands high on a hill overlooking the sea 6 mi. west of town and protects you from Pictish invaders. Skip the **heritage center** devoted to the fort, which runs the danger of being an over-hyped tourist attraction. (☎ 947 5288. Heritage center open Easter-Oct. daily 10am-10pm. £2, students £1.50.)

The **bus** stops in Caherdaniel twice a day at the junction of the Ring of Kerry Rd. and Main St., picking up passengers for **Killarney** (1½hr., June-Sept. 2 per day, £7.30). The new **tourist information centre** is a mile east of town at the Wave Crest Camping Park. (Open May-Sept. daily 8am-10pm.)

Guests have the run of the house at ▓ **The Travellers' Rest Hostel,** with a relaxed sitting room, fireplace, and small B&B-like dorms. (☎ 947 5175. Continental breakfast £3. 4- to 6-bed dorms £8.50; doubles £20.) The **Caherdaniel Village Hostel,** across the street from Skellig Aquatics, resides in the first British police building to be deserted in the Civil War. (☎ 947 5277. Open Mar.-Nov. 8-bed dorms £8.) Campers lodge a mile east of town on the Ring of Kerry road at **Wave Crest Camping Park,** overlooking the beach. (☎ 947 5188. Showers 50p. Open mid-Mar. to Oct. and off-season by arrangement. £3.25 per person.) The **Courthouse Cafe,** which serves the most affordable food in town, has both sit-down and takeaway menus. (☎ 947 5005. Sandwiches under £2. Open daily 5-11:30pm.) **Freddy's Bar** (☎ 947 5400) sells groceries and serves pints to locals. The **Blind Piper** (☎ 947 5126) is a popular local meeting place and occasional folk and trad spot with outdoor tables by a stream.

THE DINGLE PENINSULA   ☎066

On the Dingle Peninsula, green hills interrupted by rough stone walls and occasional sheep suddenly break off into the foam-flecked sea, and glorious **Slea Head** impresses with jagged cliffs and plunging waves. The best way to see Slea Head and the scattered stone settlements of Dunquin (Dún Chaoin) in a day or less is to bike along the predominantly flat **Slea Head Drive.**

Past Dingle Town (see below) towards Slea Head, the village of **Ventry** (Ceann Trá) is home to the **Ballybeag Hostel,** on an inland turn just past the sandy beach. Huge beds, soothing sitting rooms, and regular shuttle buses into downtown Dingle make it an ideal shelter for explorers. (☎ 915 9876; balybeag@iol.ie. **Bike rental** £2.50-5 per day. Laundry £4. Dorms £9 May-Oct., off-season £7.50.) Farther down the road, the laid-back proprietor of the ▓ **Celtic and Prehistoric Museum** will take you on a tour of his astounding collection, ranging from 300-million-year-old seaworm fossils to Iron Age tools and jewelry to an electric sheep. (☎ 915 9941; Open daily Apr.-Oct. 10am-5pm, for other months call ahead. £3, children £2.)

REPUBLIC OF IRELAND

Evacuated in 1953, the six **Blasket Islands** off the peninsula's coast were once inhabited by proud but impoverished villagers, poet-fishermen, and memoirists. Early 20th-century islanders' memoirs bemoan the decline of the *gaeltacht* culture; among them are Maurice O'Sullivan's *Twenty Years A-Growing*, Thomas O'Crohan's *The Islander*, and Peig Sayers's *Peig*. One author reluctantly warned that "after us, there will be no more." Mists, seals, and occasional fishing boats may continue to pass the Blaskets, but the islands' unique way of life is extinct. **Boats** for the Blaskets depart from Dunquin. (☎ (066) 915 6422. Daily Apr.-Oct. every 30min. 10am-3pm, weather permitting. £12 return.) A shuttle runs from Dingle to the Blasket ferry and back (2 per day, £6; ask at the Mountain Man for details). **Blasket Island Ferries** runs 2-3hr. **cruises** that circle the islands without landing (2 per day, £20). Outstanding writings and photographs of the Great Blasket authors can be found at the **Blasket Centre,** just outside Dunquin on the road to Ballyferriter. (☎ 915 6444. Open daily July-Aug. 10am-7pm; Easter-June and Sept.-Nov. 10am-6pm. Last admission 45min. before closing. £2.50, students £1.) Also along the Ballyferriter road, **An Óige Hostel** provides bunk rooms and a dining room overlooking the sea. (☎ 915 6121. Midnight curfew. Breakfast £2. Sheets £1. June-Sept. dorms £7-8; twins £19; Oct.-May £6-7 and £17.)

DINGLE ☎ 066

Though the *craic* in bayside Dingle is still homegrown, increasing armadas of tourists crowd the docks, pubs, and smart pubs. Visitors are indulged with music sessions, fantastic hostels, and the gregarious dolphin Fungi, who charms the whole town from his permanent residence in Dingle Bay.

▐ GETTING THERE

Bus Éireann stops on Ring Rd. by the harbor, behind Garvey's SuperValu, from **Tralee** (1¼hr.; June-Sept. 6 per day, Su 3 per day; Oct.-May 6 per day, Su 4 per day; £5.90) and **Dunquin** and **Ballyferriter** (summer M and Th 4 per day, Tu-W and F-Sa 2 per day; £2.30). From June to September additional buses tour the south of the peninsula (M-Sa 2 per day). **Rent bikes** from Paddy's Bike Shop, Dykegate St. (☎ 915 2311. £6 per day, £30 per week. Open daily 9am-7pm.) **Hitchhikers** report that rides are scarce. *Let's Go*'s approval of hitchhiking is even more scarce.

◀▶ ▐ ORIENTATION AND PRACTICAL INFORMATION

Dingle dangles in the middle of the of the Dingle Peninsula's southern coast. The **R559** heads east to Killarney and Tralee, and west to Ventry, Dunquin, and Slea Head. **Strand St.** runs next to the harbor along the marina; **Main St.** is its parallel counterpart farther uphill. **The Mall, Dykegate St.,** and **Green St.** connect the two, running perpendicular to the water. On the eastern edge of town, Strand St., the Mall, and **Tralee Rd.** converge in a roundabout.

The crowded **tourist information centre** is on Strand St. (☎ 915 1188. Open June-Aug. M-Sa 9am-6pm, Su 10am-6pm; Sept.-Oct. and mid-Mar. to May M-Sa 9am-5pm.) Services include: **Allied Ireland Bank,** Main St. (☎ 915 1400; open Tu-F 10am-12:30pm and 1:30-5pm, M closes 4pm), and **Bank of Ireland,** Main St. (☎ 915 1100; same hours); the **police** (*Garda*), The Holy Ground (☎ 915 1522); **Internet access** at **Dingleweb,** Main St. (☎ 915 2477; £1.50 per min., £5 per hr.); and the **post office,** Upper Main St. (☎ 915 1661; open M-F 9am-1pm and 2-5:30pm, Sa 9am-1pm).

▐ ACCOMMODATIONS

▨ **Ballintaggart Hostel (IHH;** ☎ 915 1454), a 25min. walk east of town on Tralee Rd. Set in the grand stone mansion where the Earl of Cork strangled his wife after a poisoning attempt went awry. Her ghost supposedly haunts the enormous bunk rooms, enclosed cobbled courtyard, and elegant, fire-heated common rooms. Free shuttle to town. Laundry service £4.50. Bike rental £7 per day. Dorms £8-10; doubles £30; off-season £1-2 less. Camping £4 per person.

Rainbow Hostel (☎ 915 1044; info@net-rainbow.com). Walk 15min. west out of town on Strand St.; bear right and inland at the corner of Dunquin Rd. One of Ireland's best-decorated hostels. Free lifts to and from town in the rainbow-mobile. Laundry £4. Internet access £5 per hr. Bike rental £6 per day. Dorms £8; doubles £20. Camping £4.

Grapevine Hostel, Dykegate St. (☎ 915 1434), off Main St. Smack in the middle of town, just a short stagger from Dingle's finest pubs. Laundry £4. Dorms £8.50-10.50.

Old Mill House, Avondale Rd. (☎ 915 1120; verhoul@iol.ie), off Dykegate St. Comfortable pine beds in this bright house outdone only by the vivacious owner. All rooms with bathroom, TV, and hair dryer. Singles £15-22; doubles and triples from £16 per person.

Kirrary House, Avondale Rd. (☎ 915 1606), across from Old Mill House. Mrs. Collins puts guests up in her delightful rooms. Book archaeological tours here with Mr. Collins's *Sciuird* Tours (see **Sights**). Bike rental £6 per day. Doubles £40; all rooms with bath.

🁢🁢 FOOD AND PUBS

SuperValu supermarket, The Holy Ground, stocks a SuperSelection of groceries and juicy tabloids. (☎ 915 1397. Open M-Sa 8am-9pm, Su 9am-6pm.)

The Oven Door, The Holy Ground (☎ 915 1056), across from SuperValu. Crispy pizzas (£4-7) and incredible cakes draw droves. Open Mar.-Christmas daily 9am-10:30pm.

The Forge, The Holy Ground (☎ 915 2590). This large green-and-red family restaurant serves lunches from £5, and pricier but delightful dinners. Open Mar.-Oct. M, W-Su noon-2:30pm and 6-9:30pm.

An Droichead Beag (The Small Bridge), Lower Main St. (☎ 915 1723). The most popular, crowded pub in town unleashes the best trad around—401 sessions a year.

Danno's, Strand St. (☎ 915 1855). Popular pub can't be beat for hearty burgers and cold pints. Main courses £5-9. Food served M-Sa noon-2:30pm and 6-9pm.

O'Flaherty's Pub, The Holy Ground (☎ 915 1913), a few doors up from the traffic circle. Trad masters have the pub filled by 9pm.

🁢🁢 SIGHTS AND ENTERTAINMENT

Fungi the Dolphin swam into Dingle Bay one day in 1983 with his mother, and the pair immediately became local celebrities. Mom has gone on to the great tuna can in the sky, but egomaniacal Fungi remains fond of humans. **Boat trips** to see the dolphin leave from the pier in summer. (Most around £7, free if Fungi is a no-show.) You can rent a **wetsuit** from **Flannery's,** just east of town off Tralee Rd. (☎ 915 1967. £14 per 2hr., £22 overnight.) The closest look at sea creatures is available at **Dingle Ocean World,** Strand St., where you can observe fish in an underwater tunnel and pet and prod skates and rays in the touch tank. (☎ 915 2111. Open daily July-Aug. 9am-9:30pm; Apr.-July and Aug.-Sept. 10am-6pm; Oct.-Mar. 10am-5pm. £5, students £4.) **Sciúird Archaeology tours** take you from the pier on a 3hr. whirlwind bus tour of the area's ancient spots. (☎ 915 1606. 2 per day. £8. Book ahead.) The **Dingle Regatta** hauls in the salty mariners on the third Sunday in August. In early September, the **Dingle Music Festival** (☎ 915 2477; www.iol.ie/~dingmus) lures big-name trad groups and others from across the musical spectrum.

TRALEE ☎066

While tourists tend to identify Killarney as the core of Kerry, Tralee (pop. 20,000) is the county's economic capital. Though industrial development renders some neighborhoods a bit dreary, multimillion-pound projects have added splashy tourist attractions to the cosmopolitan city center. The annual Rose of Tralee festival is a centuries-old pageant that has Irish eyes glued to their TV sets every August.

✕ ⏏ GETTING THERE AND GETTING AROUND

Flights: Kerry Airport (☎ 64644), off the N22 halfway between Tralee and Killarney. **Ryanair** (☎ (01) 609 7999) flies in daily from **London.**

Trains: Edward St. and John Joe Sheehy Rd. (☎ 712 3522). Ticket office open daily with sporadic hours. From: **Dublin** (4hr.; M-Sa 4 per day, Su 3 per day; £33.50); **Killarney** (40min.; M-Sa 5 per day, Su 4 per day; £5.50); **Cork** (2½hr.; M-Sa 5 per day, Su 3 per day; £17); **Galway** (3 per day, £33.50); **Waterford** (4hr., M-Sa 1 per day, £33.50); and **Rosslare Harbour** (5½hr., M-Sa 2 per day, £33.50).

Buses: Edward St. and John Joe Sheehy Rd. (☎ 712 3566). Station open in summer M-Sa 8:30am-6pm, Su 9am-3:30pm; in winter M-Sa 9am-5:15pm. Buses from: **Killarney** (40min., £4.40); **Dingle** (1¼hr., £5.90); **Limerick** (2¼hr., £9); **Cork** (2½hr., £9.70), and **Galway** (£13).

Taxi: Call-A-Cab (☎ 712 0333). **EuroCabs** (☎ 712 7111). Cabs park at the intersection of Denny St. and The Mall. £1 per mi., less for longer distances.

Bike Rental: O'Halloran, 83 Boherboy (☎ 712 2820). £6 per day, £30 per week; helmet £1 per day. Open M-Sa 9:30am-6pm.

✲✱ ⏏ ORIENTATION AND PRACTICAL INFORMATION

Tralee's streets are hopelessly knotted; it's wise to arm yourself with a free map from the tourist information centre. The main street—variously called **The Mall, Castle St.,** and **Boherboy**—holds many stores and restaurants along its roughly east-west path; **Edward St.** connects it to the train and bus stations.

Tourist Information Centre: Ashe Memorial Hall (☎ 712 1288), at the end of Denny St. From the station, head into town on Edward St., turn right on Castle St., and then left onto Denny St. Open July-Aug. M-Sa 9am-7pm, Su 9am-6pm; May-June and Oct. M-Sa 9am-6pm; Nov.-Apr. M-F 9am-5pm.

Financial Services: Bank of Ireland, Castle St. Open M 10am-5pm, Tu-F 10am-4pm.

Launderette: Kate's Launderette, Boherboy (☎ 712 7173). Open M-Sa 8:45am-6pm.

Police (*Garda*): High St. (☎ 712 2022).

Hospital: Tralee County General Hospital, off Killarney Rd. (☎ 712 6222).

Internet Access: Cyberpost, 26 Upper Castle St. (☎ 718 1284). £2 first 10min., £1 per each additional 20min. Open July-Sept. M-Sa 10am-9pm, Oct.-June 10am-6pm.

Post Office: Edward St. (☎ 712 1013), off Castle St. Open M and W-Sa 9am-5:30pm, Tu 9:30am-5:30pm.

▮ ACCOMMODATIONS

Tralee's several hostels can barely contain festival-goers in late August. The new **Courthouse Lodge (IHH),** 5 Church St., off Ashe St., is centrally located but hidden on a quiet street. You'll find a clean bed, shower, kitchen, and TV room with VCR; and all rooms come with full bath. (☎ 712 7199. Laundry £4. Internet access £1 per 10min. Dorms £9; singles £17; doubles £24.) Near-perfect **Collis-Sandes House (IHH)** is far from town. Call for pick-up, or follow Oakpark Rd. (the N69) one mile, take the first left after Spar Market, and follow signs another ½ mi. to the right. Free lifts to and from town and pub runs. (☎ 712 8658. Continental breakfast £1. Laundry £3. Wheelchair accessible. Dorms £7.50-9.50; singles £15; doubles £23-25; triples £30-33. Camping £4 per person.) **Finnegan's Hostel (IHH),** 17 Denny St., a majestic 19th-century townhouse, contains part of the old town castle and has a great common room. (☎ 712 7610. Laundry £3. Dorms £10; doubles £25.)

◉🍴 FOOD AND PUBS

There's a **Tesco** in the Square. (☎ 712 2788. Open M-W and Sa 8:30am-8pm, Th-F 8:30am-10pm, Su 10am-6pm.) 🍴 **Pocott's,** 3 Ashe St., has quality Irish food, fast and cheap. (☎ 712 9500. Open July-Sept. 9am-9:30pm, Oct.-June 9am-7pm.) **Mozart's,** 4 Ashe St., has a range of well-prepared delights, from stuffed baguettes (£3-4) in the afternoon to stir-frys and steaks in the evening for under £12. (☎ 712 7977. Open mid-May to Sept. M-Sa 9am-9:30pm; Oct. to mid-May 9am-7pm.) **The Skillet,** Barrack Ln., off the Mall, serves stew and other Irish specialties. Lunch is £4-7, but dinner is pricier. (☎ 712 4561. Open M-Sa 9am-10pm, Su noon-10pm.) Tasty, well-prepared vegetarian food with mostly organic ingredients fills plates at **Brat's Place,** 18 Milk Market Ln., a pedestrian walkway off The Mall. (Open M-Sa 12:30-2:30pm, later if food lasts.)

With its impressive fireplace and lots of trad, **Seán Óg's,** the Square (☎ 712 8822), generates a lively following. A tough crowd comes to hear live rock most weekends at the **Abbey Inn,** the Square. When U2 played here in the 70s, the manager thought they were so bad that he made them clean the floors to pay for their drinks. Meatloaf, however, drank for free. (☎ 712 3390. Open Su-F until 1am.) Kerry's Gaelic-football legacy hangs on the walls while real-life players join an older crowd for trad at **Baily's Corner Pub** (☎ 712 3230), at Ashe and Castle St.

◉🎵 SIGHTS AND ENTERTAINMENT

Tralee is home to Ireland's second-largest museum, 🏛 **Kerry the Kingdom,** Ashe Memorial Hall, Denny St. The Kingdom marshals all the resources of display technology to tell the story of Co. Kerry from 8000 BC to the present. You can even sample the old city's stench. (☎ 712 7777. Open Mar.-Oct. daily 10am-6pm; Nov.-Dec. noon-4:30pm. £5.50, students £4.75.) The building on the Prince's Quay traffic circle looks like a cross between a Gothic castle and a space-age solarium, but it's actually Tralee's £4.5-million **Aquadome,** complete with whirlpools, steam room, sauna, and gym. (☎ 712 8899. Open daily 10am-10pm. £6, students £4.) Recalling Blenneville's status as Kerry's main port of emigration during the Famine, a small **museum** focuses on the "coffin ships" that sailed from Ireland at the time. (☎ 712 1064. Open Apr.-Oct. daily 10am-6pm. £2.75, students £2.25.)

The **Siamsa Tíre Theatre,** next to the museum at the end of Denny St., is Ireland's national folk theater. (☎ 712 3055. Productions July-Aug. M-Sa; May-June and Sept. M-Th and Sa. Shows start at 8:30pm. Box office open M-Sa 9am-8:30pm. Tickets £8-12.) Lovely, marriageable Irish lasses from around the world come to town during the last week of August for the nationally beloved **Rose of Tralee Festival** (☎ 712 1322). A maelstrom of entertainment surrounds the event, a personality competition to earn the title "Rose of Tralee."

WESTERN IRELAND

Even Dubliners will tell you that the west is the "most Irish" part of Ireland. In recent centuries, Connacht mostly meant poor soil and frequent emigration. When Cromwell uprooted the native Irish landowners in Leinster and Munster and resettled them west of the Shannon, the popular phraseology for their plight became "To hell or Connacht." The potato famine was devastating here: today, every western county has less than half of its 1841 population. Western Ireland's gorgeous desolation and traditional culture are now its best features.

LIMERICK CITY   ☎ 061

Despite a thriving trade in off-color poems, Limerick City (pop. 60,000) has never had much status as a tourist town. During much of the 20th century, hard economic times spawned poverty and crime, and what little attention was paid to Limerick seemed to celebrate squalor. Today the republic's third-largest city sports a top-notch museum and a prospering student arts scene, adding to a wealth of cultural treasures that have long gone unnoticed.

▐ GETTING THERE AND GETTING AROUND

Trains: Colbert Station (☎ 315555), off Parnell St. Inquiries desk open M-F 9am-6pm, Sa 9am-5:30pm. Luggage storage. Trains from: **Dublin** (2hr.; M-Sa 10 per day, Su 9 per day; £27); **Ennis** (M-Sa 2 per day, £5.70); **Cork** (2½hr.; M-Sa 6 per day, Su 5 per day; £14); **Killarney** (2½hr.; M-Sa 4 per day, Su 3 per day; £15); **Tralee** (3hr.; M-Sa 6 per day, Su 3 per day; £16) and **Rosslare** (3½hr., M-Sa 1 per day, £21).

Buses: Colbert Station, off Parnell St. (☎ 313333; 24hr. timetable ☎ 319911). Open June-Sept. M-F 8:10am-6pm, Su 9am-6pm; Oct.-May M-Sa 8:10am-6pm, Su 3-7pm. The city is easily navigable by foot; to reach the suburbs, catch a city bus from Boyd's or Penney's on O'Connell St. (M-Sa 7:30am-11pm, 2 per hr.; Su 10:30am-11pm, 1 per hr.; 75p) Buses #2 and 8 access the university, while bus #6 follows Ennis Rd.

Taxi: Top Cabs, Wickham St. (☎ 417417). Takes you most places in the city for under £3 and to the airport for about £15.

Bike Rental: Emerald Alpine, 1 Patrick St. (☎ 416983). £12 per day, £50 per week; deposit £40. £14 for return at other locations. Open M-Sa 9:15am-5:30pm.

◼▐ ORIENTATION AND PRACTICAL INFORMATION

The city's streets form a grid bounded by the **River Shannon** to the west and the **River Abbey** to the north. Most activity takes place on blocks around **O'Connell St.**

Tourist Information Centre: Arthurs Quay (☎ 317522). **Bureau de change.** Open July-Aug. M-F 9am-7pm, Sa-Su 9am-6pm; May-June and Sept.-Oct. M-Sa 9:30am-5:30pm; Nov.-Apr. M-F 9:30am-5:30pm, Sa 9:30am-1pm.

Tours: Walking tours (☎ 318106) cover the King's Island neighborhood (daily 11am and 2:30pm) and the more decrepit locations described in Frank McCourt's *Angela's Ashes* (daily 2:30pm). Both depart from St. Mary's Action Centre, 44 Nicholas St. £4.

Budget Travel: usit, O'Connell St. (☎ 415064), near Ulster Bank. Open M-F 9:30am-5:30pm, Sa 10am-1pm. Also at University of Limerick (☎ 332 079).

Financial Services: Bank of Ireland (☎ 415055), O'Connell St. **Allied Ireland Bank** (☎ 414388), O'Connell St.

Police (*Garda*): Henry St. (☎ 414222).

Hospital: Regional (☎ 301111), follow O'Connell Rd. past the Crescent southward.

Internet Access: Webster's, Thomas St. (☎ 312066). £1 per 10min. Fruit drinks and coffee available. Open M-Sa 9am-9pm, Su 1-9pm.

Post Office: Main office on Lower Cecil St. (☎ 315777), just off O'Connell St. Open M and W-Sa 9am-5:30pm, Tu 9:30am-5:30pm.

▐ ACCOMMODATIONS

Limerick has two hostels and several budget accommodation centers geared toward term-time university students. For those seeking refuge from the bustle of the city, **Ennis St.** is a B&B bonanza in the £19-22 price range.

An Óige Hostel, 1 Pery Sq. (☎ 314672). A pleasant Georgian house, a cheerful staff, and park views. Sheets £1. Continental breakfast £2. Lockout 10am-2pm. Midnight curfew. June-Sept. Dorms £6.50-8.50.

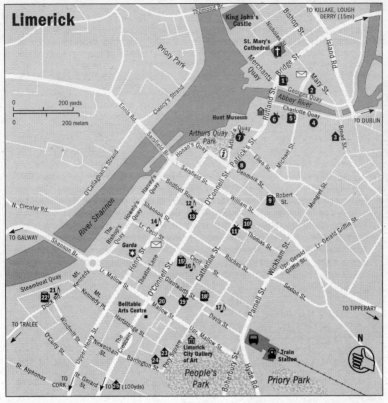

Limerick

ACCOMMODATIONS	FOOD AND DRINKS	PUBS	MUSIC AND CLUBS	SERVICES
Alexandra House, 25	Cafe Furze Bush, 19	Doc's, 5	BPs, 17	Charlotte Quay Pharmacy, 4
An Óige Hostel (HI), 24	The Green Onion Cafe, 6	The Doghouse, 10	The George Hotel, 14	Emerald Alpine Bike Rental, 8
Barrington Hostel (IHH), 2	Java's Beat Café, 11	Dolan's, 22	The Globe, 16	Laundrette, 20
Broad St. Hostel, 3	Nature's Way and Tesco	The Glen Tavern, 18	The Warehouse, 21	
Finnegan's (IHH), 23	O'Grady's Cellar Restaurant, 13	Locke Bar 1	The Works, 12	
		Nancy Blake's, 9		
		Tom Collins, 15		

Barrington Hostel (IHH), George's Quay (☎ 415222). Far from the train and bus station, but very close to city action. Large, but relatively private dorms. Laundry £3-4. Dorms £7.50; singles £11; doubles with bath £25.

Finnegan's (IHH), 6 Pery Sq. (☎ 310308). High-ceilinged common rooms and a convenient location, but somewhat crowded. Dorms £8-12; private rooms £12 per person.

Broad St. Hostel, Broad St. (☎ 317222; broadstreethostel@tinet.ie). Vigilant security and remarkable cleanliness. Continental breakfast included. Laundry £4. Wheelchair accessible. Dorms £10.50; singles £15; doubles and twins £34.

FOOD

Gather groceries at **Tesco** in Arthurs Quay Mall. (☎ 412399. Open M-W 8:30am-8pm, Th-F 8:30am-10pm, Sa 8:30am-8pm, Su noon-6pm.) **The Glen Tavern,** Lower Glentworth St., prides itself on Irish specialties for great value. (☎ 411380. Most meals £3-5. Open M-F 8am-9pm.) In the faux thatch of the subterranean **O'Grady's Cellar**

Restaurant, O'Connell St., Irish meals are the substance of the menu. (☎ 418286. Most meals £5-7. Open daily 9:15am-10:30pm.) **The Green Onion Cafe,** 3 Ellen St., just off Patrick's St., serves elite bistro fare at egalitarian prices during lunch (£5-7). Meal prices rise to £10-12 after 6pm. (☎ 400710. Open M-Sa noon-10pm.)

◉ SIGHTS

King John's Castle is on Nicholas St.; walk across the Abbey River and take the first left after St. Mary's Cathedral. The castle's history as a military fortification remains evident outside, where the **mangonel** is on display. Easily recognizable from its use in *Monty Python's Quest for the Holy Grail*, the mangonel was used to catapult pestilent animal corpses into enemy cities and castles. (☎ 411201. Open Mar.-Dec. daily 9:30am-6pm. Last admission 5pm. £4.20, students £3.20.) The rough exterior of nearby **St. Mary's Cathedral** was built in 1172 on the site of a Viking meeting place. Fold-down seats, built into the wall on the side of the altar, display elaborate carvings that depict the struggle between good and evil. They are called *misericordia*, Latin for "acts of mercy," and are used in long services during which sitting was prohibited. (☎ 416238. Open daily 9:15am-5pm.)

The fascinating **Hunt Museum,** Custom House, Rutland St., houses the largest collection of medieval, Stone Age, and Iron Age artifacts outside the National Museum in Dublin. It also contains what may be one of Leonardo da Vinci's four "Rearing Horses" sculptures, and a coin reputed to be one of the infamous 30 pieces of silver paid to Judas by the Romans. (☎ 312833. Open M-Sa 10am-5pm, Su 2-5pm. £4.20, seniors and students £3.20.)

◪ PUBS AND NIGHTLIFE

For pubs, ▨ **Dolan's,** Dock Rd. (☎ 314483), is worth a Shannon-side walk from the city center to hear nightly trad played for rambunctious local patrons. **Nancy Blake's,** Denmark St. (☎ 416443), has the best of both worlds—an older crowd huddles in the sawdust-floored interior for periodic trad, while boisterous students take in nightly rock in the open-air "outback." Heal your ale-ing body at **Doc's,** Michael St. (☎ 417266), at the corner of Charlotte's Quay in the Granary. The outdoor beer garden lures festive young folks. College bands often play in the school year, and DJs bust out chart-toppers most weekend nights.

Nightclubs thump from 11:30pm until 2am nightly. Cover charges can be steep (£5-8), but clubs spread fliers good for £2-3 discounts throughout the city's pubs. **The Globe,** Cecil St., has three floors of manic clubbery, with suggestive artwork and flashing video screens. Only members are allowed on the top floor, where the Cranberries and U2 periodically stop by to sip £135 champagne. (☎ 313533. Cover £5.) The snazzy **Warehouse,** behind Dolan's on Dock Rd., draws big-name bands and rising stars. (☎ 314483. Music Th-Sa. Cover £5-9, higher for well-known acts.) The circular dance floor and balcony of **The George Hotel,** O'Connell St., are always packed, with nightly musical-decade themes. (☎ 414566. Open Th-Sa; cover £6-7.)

SHANNON AIRPORT ☎061

Fifteen miles west of Limerick off Ennis Rd. (the N18), Shannon Airport (☎ 471444; Aer Lingus info ☎ 471666) sends jets to North America and Europe. Arriving travelers descend into a blend of cottages, industrial office complexes, and housing developments. **Bus Éireann** picks up passengers here on its way to **Dublin** (4½hr., 5 per day, £10); **Limerick** (40min.; M-Sa 9 per day, Su 7 per day); **Ennis** (45min.; M-Sa 22 per day, Su 13 per day; £3.50); **Waterford,** and **Tralee.** Inexpensive **Alamo** (☎ 75061) **rents cars** for £22 per day. **Dan Dooley Rent-A-Car** is the only 21+ rental agency. (☎ (062) 53103. From £32 per 2-5 days.)

If you need a place to stay, nearby **Sixmilebridge** is a gem. **Bus Éireann** runs from **Shannon Airport** (M-Sa 2 per day, £2.50) and **Limerick** (M-Sa 2 per day, £2.50). A taxi to the airport is around £10. The best reason for coming is the ▨ **Jamaica Inn** hostel, with amenities and multi-talented proprietors. (☎ 369220. Internet access £1 per 8min. Laundry £4. Luggage and bike storage. Open Feb.-Oct. Dorms £9-12; singles £15-17; doubles with bath £26-30.) The hostel also houses the only restaurant in town. (Open M-Sa 8:30am-6pm, Su 8:30am-3:30pm.)

DOOLIN   ☎065

Something of a national shrine to Irish traditional music, the little village of Doolin (pop. 200) draws thousands of visitors every year to its pubs, and several of Doolin's restaurants have won coveted national culinary awards. The eight-mile paved and bicycle-friendly segment of the Burren Way links Doolin to the Cliffs of Moher, and boats leave the pier on the other end of town for the Aran Islands, though boats from Galway (p. 725) and Rossaveal are almost always cheaper.

⬛ GETTING THERE AND GETTING AROUND. Buses stop at the Doolin Hostel and the campsite (see **Accommodations,** below), and advance tickets can be purchased at the hostel. Route #15 runs from **Kilkee** and from **Dublin** via **Ennis** and **Limerick** (M-Sa 1 per day in off-season, summer 2 per day; Su 1 per day). Bus #50 runs from **Galway** (1½hr.) via multiple other **Burren** destinations on its way to the **Cliffs of Moher** 15min. away, (in summer M-Sa 5 per day, Su 2 per day; off-season M-Sa 1 per day). The **Doolin Bike Store,** outside Aille River Hostel, **rents bikes.** (☎ 707 4282. £7 per day. Open M-Su 9am-8pm.)

⬛⬛ ORIENTATION AND PRACTICAL INFORMATION. Doolin is shaped like a barbell, made up of two villages about a mile apart. Close to the shore is the **Lower Village,** connected to the **Upper Village** by **Fisher St.,** where it turns into **Roadford.** The nearest **cash machine** is in Ennistymon, five miles southeast. There's a **bureau de change** at the **post office,** in the Upper Village. (☎ 74209. Open M-F 9am-1pm and 2-5:30pm, Sa 9am-1pm.)

⬛ ACCOMMODATIONS. Tourists pack Doolin in the summer, so book ahead. In a cottage by the river, ⬛ **Aille River Hostel (IHH)** has clean, well-maintained rooms, and local musicians often stop by to warm up before pub gigs. (☎ 707 4260. Free laundry. Open mid-Mar. to mid-Nov. Dorms July-Aug. £7.50, Sept.-May £7; doubles £16; triples £24. Camping £4.) The new and expanded **Flanaghan's Village Hostel,** a half mile up the road from the Upper Village, has spacious rooms and a back garden with farm animals. (☎ 707 4564. Dorms £7.50; doubles £17-20.) The small **Rainbow Hostel (IHH),** Upper Village, has pastel rooms and a casual atmosphere. The owners give free 1½hr. walking tours of the Burren for hostelers. (☎ 707 4415. Dorms July-Aug. £7.50; doubles £17.) Geared toward large groups, the **Doolin Hostel (IHH),** Lower Village, has clean, comfortable rooms. (☎707 4006. Reception 7:30am-9pm. Dorms £7.50-8, doubles £20-21). The spotless ⬛ **Doolin Cottage B&B** is one door down from the Aille. (☎ 707 4762. Open Mar.-Nov. Doubles £26, with bath £30.) Doolin has a **campsite,** near the harbor, with kitchen, laundry facilities, and a view of the Cliffs of Moher. (☎ 707 4458. £4 per tent plus £1.50 per person.)

⬛⬛ FOOD AND PUBS. The **Doolin Deli,** near O'Connor's in the Lower Village, packs overstuffed sandwiches (£1.30) and stocks groceries. (☎ 707 4633. Open June-Sept. M-Sa 8:30am-9pm, Su 9:30am-9pm.) Doolin's few restaurants are a bit pricey, but **Bruach na hAille** has delicious, creative home-grown dishes in addition to a working antique phonograph player. (☎ 707 4120. £10 early-bird special until 7:30pm. Open daily St. Patrick's Day to Oct. 6-9:30pm.) If Doolin looks like a ghost-town at first glance, have no fear: the people are all in the pubs, which serve good, cheap food. **McGann's** (☎ 707 4133), Upper Village, has music nightly in summer, and weekends in winter, at 9pm. Muscle your way in for a plate of fresh wild mussels (£5.50). **O'Connor's** (☎ 707 4168), Lower Village, is the busiest and most-touristed pub, with drink and song nightly and Sunday afternoons all year.

NEAR DOOLIN: CLIFFS OF MOHER AND THE BURREN

■**CLIFFS OF MOHER.** The Cliffs of Moher are justifiably one of Ireland's most famous sights, dropping 700 ft. straight down into the open sea. American poet Wallace Stevens based his poem "The Irish Cliffs of Moher" on photographs, as he'd never been. Don't make his mistake. On a clear day, the views from the majestic cliffs include Loop Head, the Kerry Mountains, the Twelve Pins of Connemara, and the Aran Islands. Three miles south of Doolin, the R478 skirts the Cliffs; cars pay £1 for parking. **Bus Éireann** clangs by on the summer-only **Galway-Cork** route (M-Sa 3 per day). The **tourist information centre,** by the parking lot, houses a **bureau de change** and a tea shop. (☎ (065) 81171. Open daily Apr.-Oct. 9:30am-5:30pm.) **Aran Ferries** operates a fantastic cruise that leaves from the pier in nearby Liscannor and sails along directly under the cliffs. (☎ 81368. 55min., 1 per day. £10.)

THE BURREN. If there were wild orchids, cantankerous cows, and B&Bs on the moon, it would probably look a lot like the Burren. Comprising nearly 100 sq. mi. and almost one third of Co. Clare's coastline, the Burren's lunar beauty includes jagged gray hills resembling skyscrapers turned to rubble, hidden depressions opening into labyrinths of caves, and wildflowers found nowhere else. The best way to see the Burren is by **foot** or **bicycle;** be forewarned that the dramatic landscape makes for exhausting climbs. George Cunningham's *Burren Journey* series is worth a look ($4.50), as are Tim Robinson's meticulous maps ($5) and the detailed *Burren Rambler* maps ($2), all available at the tourist information centres at the Cliffs of Moher and in Galway. **Bus** service in the Burren is as confused as the geography. **Bus Éireann** (☎ (065) 682 4177) connects Galway to towns in and near the Burren a few times a day in the summer, but infrequently in the colder months. Full-day bus tours from **Galway** are another popular way to see the Burren (see p. 722). The region is a strenuous but hugely rewarding **bike** ride from Doolin. **Hitchhiking** involves patience, but *Let's Go* has no patience for it as a safe mode of transport, and does not recommend it.

ARAN ISLANDS (OILEÁIN ÁRANN)   ☎099

The three Irish-speaking Aran Islands—Inishmore, Inishmaan, and Inisheer—rest in Galway Bay 15 mi. southwest of Galway City. Sections of the islands are covered with slabs of limestone that resemble the stark landscape of the Burren in Co. Clare, and the green fields that compose the rest of the islands' surface are the result of centuries worth of farmers' piling acres of stones into the maze-like walls. Iron Age peoples appreciated the Arans' isolation and built awe-inspiring ringforts on the edges of precipices to preserve it. Early Christians flocked to the Arans in search of spiritual seclusion; the ruins of their ancient churches and monasteries now litter the islands. The islands' cultural isolation has also drawn artistic attention in the 20th century: both writer John Millington Synge (see p. 664) and filmmaker Robert Flaherty memorialized the islands' folk culture. During July and August, crowds of curious visitors surround every monument and fill every pub on Inishmore. Visitors are fewer on Inishmaan and Inisheer, the two smaller islands, but their numbers are rising as inter-island ferries become more frequent.

◧ GETTING THERE AND GETTING AROUND

Three ferry companies—**Island Ferries, O'Brien Shipping/Doolin Ferries,** and **Liscannor Ferries**—operate boats to the Aran Islands (30min.-1½hr.). Ferries serving Inishmore are reliable and leave daily. Even in the summer, ferries to the smaller islands are less certain. There is no charge to bring bicycles on board. If the ferry leaves from Rossaveal, the company making the trip will provide a shuttle bus from Galway City to Rossaveal, usually for £3.

Island Ferries (☎ (091) 561767, after hours ☎ 72273). Based in the **Galway** tourist information centre. The **Aran Sea Bird** serves all 3 islands year-round from **Rossaveal,** west of Galway (35min., £15 return). A bus connects the tourist information centre with the ferry port (departs 1½hr. before sailing time, £4 return). The **Sea Sprinter** connects Inishmore with Inisheer via Inishmaan (£10 return per island). They also offer a package deal: the bus from Galway, return ferry to Inishmore, and one night's B&B at the Mainistir House Hostel (see below) for £24.

O'Brien Shipping/Doolin Ferries (☎ (065) 74455 in Doolin, ☎ (091) 567283 in Galway, after hours ☎ (065) 71710). Year-round service connects **Doolin** and **Galway** to the Aran Islands. Galway to any island £12 return. Cars always £100.

Liscannor Aran Ferries (☎ (065) 81368). Ferries depart twice a day from **Liscannor** and stop at Inishmaan and Inisheer. £17 return.

INISHMORE (INIS MÓR)

The archaeological sites of Inishmore (pop. 900), the largest and most touristed of the Aran Islands, include the Dún Aengus ringfort, where a semicircular wall surrounds a sheer 300 ft. drop off the sea cliffs of the island's southern edge. The village of Kilronan (Cill Rónáin), above the pier where the ferry lands on the north shore, is the only place to buy supplies.

⌨ ☎ GETTING AROUND AND PRACTICAL INFORMATION. Minibuses roaming the island can be flagged down (return £5 to Dún Aengus), and the drivers can organize 2hr. tours (about £5). **Aran Bicycle Hire** rents bikes. (☎ 61132. £5 per day, £21 per week; deposit £9. Open Mar.-Nov. daily 9am-5pm.) Bike theft is a problem—lock it up, or don't leave it. The Kilronan **tourist information centre** (TIC) stores luggage (75p), **exchanges currency,** and sells the *Inis Món Way* (£1.50) and other maps. (☎ 61263. Open Feb.-Nov. daily 10am-6:15pm.) Get **Internet access** at the Heritage Centre (see **Sights,** below). The **post office,** uphill from the pier, has a **bureau de change.** (☎ 61101. Open M-F 9am-5pm, Sa 9am-1pm.)

⌂ ACCOMMODATIONS. A free bus to the hostels meets all ferries. The huge, sunny, and spotless ◪ **Kilronan Hostel** is just seconds from the pier and directly upstairs from the *craic* at Joe Mac's pub. (☎ 61255. Dorms July-Aug. £9, Sept.-June £8.) **Mainistir House (IHH)** has earned a reputation as a haven for writers, musicians, and yuppies. Esthete Joël dishes up creative, organic, all-you-can-eat buffet dinners (£8), and morning porridge and fresh scones for all. Book ahead. (☎ 61169. Laundry £5. Bike rental £5 per day. Dorms £8.50; singles £15; doubles £22.) **St. Brendan's House** is an ivy-covered house across the street from the ocean. (☎ 61149. Apr.-Oct. £13 per person, with continental breakfast £11; Nov.-Mar. £8, £10.) **Beach View House,** three miles west of Kilronan, is a great outpost for hiking. Some rooms have views of Dún Aengus. (☎ 61141. Open May-Sept. Singles £23; doubles £34.)

⌂ ☒ FOOD AND PUBS. Spar Market, past the hostel in Kilronan, often seems to be the island's social center. (☎ 61203. Open M-Sa 9am-8pm, Su 10am-6pm.) The **Ould Pier,** up the hill from the town center, serves up great, cheap grub. (☎ 61228. Fish and chips £4.95). ◪ **Tigh Nan Phaidt,** in a thatched building at the turn-off to Dún Aengus, specializes in home-baked bread with home-smoked fish. (☎ 61330. Smoked salmon sandwich £4.50. Open daily July-Aug. 10am-9pm; Mar.-June and Sept.-Dec. 10am-5pm.) For organic lunches, try **The Man of Aran Restaurant,** just past Kilmurvey Beach to the right. (☎ 61301. Toasties £2; lunch daily 12:30-3:30pm.) Trad musicians occasionally strum on the terrace at **Tí Joe Mac** (☎ 61248), a pub overlooking the pier. West of the harbor on the main road, **Joe Watty's** offers food, music to accompany thick pints. **The American Bar** (☎ 61303) attracts younger islanders and droves of tourists with music most summer nights.

▨ SIGHTS. The sights themselves are crowded, but since so many tourists hop on the minibus tour, the paths between them are usually pleasantly desolate. Cycling or walking makes for a hugely rewarding day-long excursion. The TIC sells £1.50 maps of the **Inis Mór Ways** that outline the yellow trail arrows system; the arrows sometimes vanish in the fog, so invest in a good map. The island's most famous monument is magnificent 1st-century-BC **Dún Aengus,** four miles west of the pier at Kilronan. The fort's walls are 18 ft. thick and form a semicircle around the sheer drop of Inishmore's northwest corner. **Be very careful:** strong winds have blown tourists off the edge and to their deaths. Left off the main road a half-mile past Kilmurvey is **Dún Eoghanachta,** a huge circular fort with 16 ft. walls; to the right past Eoghanachta are the **Seven Churches.** Both sites are evidence of the island's earliest inhabitants. The island's best beach is at **Kilmurvey.** The **Black Fort** (Dún Dúchathair), a mile south of Kilronan over eerie terrain, is larger than Dún Aengus, a millennium older, and an unappreciated beauty. Uphill from the pier in Kilronan, the new, expertly designed **Aran Islands Heritage Centre** (Ionad Árann) beckons to the inquisitive. Soil and wildlife exhibits, old Aran clothes, a cliff rescue cart, and *curraghs* combine for a fascinating introduction to the island's natural and human life. (☎ 61355. Open Apr.-Oct. daily 10am-7pm. £2, students £1.50.)

INISHEER (INIS OÍRR)

The Arans have been described as "quietness without loneliness," but Inishmaan can get damn lonely, and Inishmore isn't always quiet. Inisheer (pop. 300), the smallest Aran, is a compromise that lives up to the famous phrase. The **Inis Oírr Way** covers the island's major attractions on a four-mile path. The first stop is in town at **Cnoc Raithní,** a Bronze Age tumulus (stone burial mound), from 4000 BC. Walking along the **An Trá** shore leads to the romantic, overgrown graveyard of **St. Kevin's Church** (Teampall Chaomhain). Below the church, a pristine, sandy beach stretches back to the edge of town. Farther east along the beach, a grassy track leads to **An Loch Mór,** a 16-acre inland lake where wildfowl prevail. The stone ringfort **Dún Formna** is above the lake. The walk back to the island's center leads through **Formna Village** and on out to **Cill na Seacht nInníon,** a small monastery with a stone fort. The remains of the 14th-century **O'Brien Castle,** razed by Cromwell in 1652, sit atop a nearby knoll. On the west side of the island, **Tobar Einne,** St. Enda's Holy Well, is believed to have curative powers.

Inisheer's town **tourist information** is cheerfully given in English or Irish from the small wooden hut on the beach near the main pier. (☎ 75008. Open July-Aug. daily 10am-6pm.) **Rothair Inis Oírr** rents **bikes.** (☎ 75033. £5 per day, £25 per week.) The **post office** is farther up the island to the left of the pier in the cream house with turquoise trim. (☎ 75001. Open M-F 9am-1pm and 2-5:30pm, Sa 9am-1pm.) **Tigh Ruairí,** an unmarked pub and shop in a white building just up the road, sells groceries. (☎ 75002. Shop open July-Aug. daily 9am-8:30pm; Sept.-June M-Sa 9am-7:30pm, Su 10:45am-12:30pm.) Monkfish leap from the sea into the kitchen of ▨ **Fisherman's Cottage,** 350 yd. to the right of the pier, whereupon they are expertly cooked and served. They also rent **kayaks** and have **Internet access.** (☎ 75703. Catch of the day £7. Open daily 11am-4pm and 7-9:30pm.) **Tigh Ned's** pub lies next to the hostel and caters to a younger crowd, while the pub at the **Ostan Hotel,** just up from the pier, is exceptionally crowded and dark. (☎ 75020. Food served daily 11am-9:30pm.)

INISHMAAN (INIS MEÁIN)

Seagulls circle the cliffs while goats chew their cud, but there's little human activity in the limestone fields of scenic Inishmaan (pop. 300). The *Inishmaan Way* brochure (£1.50) describes a five-mile walking route to all of the island's sights. The thatched cottage where John Millington Synge wrote much of his Aran-inspired work from 1898 to 1902 is a mile into the island on the main road. Across the road and a bit farther down is **Dún Chonchúir** (Connor Fort), an impressive 7th-century ringfort. At the western end of the road is **Synge's Chair,** where the writer came to think and compose. To the left of the pier are the shore remains of the 8th-century **Cill Cheannannach** church. A mile north of the pier is Inishmaan's safest beach, **Trá Leitreach.** For **tourist info** and a chance to buy a variety of local crafts, try the **Inishmaan Co-op** (☎ 73010). Take the turn-off for the knitwear factory, continue straight, and then turn right after the factory. The **post office** (☎ 73001) is in Inishmaan's tiny village, which spreads out along the road west of the pier and divides the island in half. The **An Dún Shop** (☎ 73067) sells some food at the entrance to Dún Chonchúir. **Padraic Faherty's** thatched pub is the island's center of life, and serves a small selection of grub until 6:30pm.

GALWAY

☎091

In the past few years, the city's reputation as Ireland's cultural capital has brought young Celtophiles flocking to Galway (pop. 60,000). Mix over 13,000 students at Galway's two major universities and a large population of international backpackers, and you have a small college town on *craic*.

✗ ▐ GETTING THERE AND GETTING AROUND

Flights: Three small **Aer Lingus** planes fly from **Dublin** daily.

Trains: Eyre Sq. (☎ 561444). Open M-Sa 7:40am-6pm. Trains from **Dublin** (3hr.; M-F 5 per day, Sa-Su 3-4 per day; £15-21) with a stop in **Athlone** (£7.50-13.50); transfer at Athlone from all other lines.

Buses: Eyre Sq. Open July-Aug. M-Sa 8:30am-7pm, Su 8:30am-6pm; Sept.-June M-Sa 8:30am-6pm, Su 8:30am-noon and 1:40-6pm. From **Dublin, P. Nestor Coaches** (☎ 797144) arrives at the Imperial Hotel (£5-£8), and **Citylink** (☎ 564163) at Supermac's (5 per day, £5-£8). A **shuttle** to **Doolin** and other Burren destinations leaves various Galway hostels on request (£5). **Michael Nee Coaches** (☎ 51082) arrive at Forester St. from **Cleggan** via **Clifden,** meeting the **Inishbofin** ferry (£5, return £7).

Local Transportation: City buses (☎ 562000) leave Eyre Sq. for all parts (every 20min., 70p). Buses go to each area of the city: #1 to **Salthill,** #2 to **Knocknacarra** (west) or **Renmare** (east), #3 to **Castlepark,** and #4 to **Newcastle** and **Rahoon.** Service M-Sa 8am-9pm, Su 11am-9pm. Commuter tickets £8 per week, £29 per month.

Taxis: Big O Taxis, 21 Upper Dominick St. (☎ 585858).

Car Rental: Budget Rent-a-Car, Eyre Sq. (☎ 566376).

Bike Rental: Europa Cycles, Hunter Buildings, Earls Island (☎ 563355), opposite the cathedral. £5 per day, £6 per 24hr., £25 per week; deposit £30. Open M-F 9am-6pm.

Hitchhiking: Dozens of hitchhikers wait on Dublin Rd. (the N6) scouting rides to **Dublin** and **Limerick.** Most catch bus #2, 5, or 6 from Eyre Sq. to this main thumb-stop. University Rd. leads drivers to **Connemara** via the N59. *Let's Go* does not recommend hitchhiking as a safe mode of transport.

✦ ▐ ORIENTATION AND PRACTICAL INFORMATION

Eyre Square is a central block of lawn and monuments with the train and bus station on its east side. Many B&Bs are to the square's northeast along **Prospect Hill.** The town's commercial zone spreads out to the south and west in the flashy and recently pedestrianized medieval area around **High St., Shop St., Cross St.,** and **Quay St.** Fewer tourists venture over the bridges into the more bohemian **left bank** of the Corrib, the site of Galway's best pubs. Just south of the left bank is the **Claddagh,** Galway's original fishing village. A road stretches west past the quays to **Salthill,** a tacky beachfront resort with row houses and skyrocketing property values.

Tourist Information Centre: Victoria Pl. (☎ 563081). A block southeast of Eyre Sq. Open July-Aug. daily 8:30am-7:45pm; May-June and Sept. daily 8:30am-5:45pm; Oct.-Apr. M-F and Su 9am-5:45pm, Sa 9am-12:45pm.

Travel Agency: usit, Mary St. (☎ 565177). Open May-Sept. M-F 9:30am-5:30pm, Sa 10am-3pm; Oct.-Apr. M-F 9:30am-5:30pm, Sa 10am-1pm.

Financial Services: Bank of Ireland, 19 Eyre Sq. (☎ 563181). Open M-W and F 10am-4pm, Th 10am-5pm.

Bookstore: Kenny's (☎ 562739), between High and Middle St., has an enormous collection of Irish interest books, an art gallery, and artsy postcards. Open M-Sa 9am-6pm.

Police (*Garda*): Mill St. (☎ 563161).

Hospital: University College Hospital (☎ 524222), on Newcastle Rd.

Internet Access: Cyberzone, the Old Malte Arcade, High St., (☎ 569772). £5 per hr., £4 with student ID. Spacey murals to get you in the mood, free coffee when you log in.

Post Office: Eglinton St. (☎ 562051). Open M, W-Sa 9am-5:30pm, Tu 9:30am-5:30pm.

ACCOMMODATIONS

Reservations are near necessary in July and August, when rates rise 10-20%. Large, custom-built hostels gather around Eyre Square. Smaller, friendlier ones clump westwards at Woodquay, or across the river around Dominick Street.

HOSTELS

Barnacle's Quay Street Hostel (IHH), Quay St. (☎ 568644). Shop St. becomes Quay St. Bright, spacious rooms and a peerless location in the city center make this hostel the place to be, especially for pub-crawlers. Excellent security. Laundry £5. Dorms £8-13.50; doubles with bath £35; less in the off-season.

Woodquay Hostel, 23-24 Woodquay (☎ 562618). Huge living room with potted plants and comfy couches. Marie's paintings of butterflies and flowers adorn the walls and bathrooms. The roomy candlelit dining area makes even the skimpiest of budget-conscious meals romantic. Clean and close to the pubs. Dorms £10; twins £12.50.

Great Western House (IHH), Eyre Sq. (☎ 561150 or ☎ (800) 425929), in a mammoth building across from the station. Somewhat impersonal, even with the pool room and sauna. Bureau de change. Small breakfast included, full breakfast £2.50. Laundry £5. Internet access £2 per 20min. 24hr. reception. Wheelchair accessible. July-Aug. dorms £10-12.50; singles £18; doubles with bath £32. Off-season £1.50-3 cheaper.

Archview Hostel, Dominick St. (☎ 586661). The cheapest, most laid-back accommodations in town, in the heart of Galway's bohemian district. This place has seen some wear and tear over the years, but it's comfortable, and a short stumble home from your big night on Dominick St. Dorms £7, off-season £6; £30 per week for long-term stays.

Kinlay House (IHH), Merchants Rd. (☎ 565244), across from the tourist information centre. Megalithic, and a bit sedate. Security monitors at reception remind you they're watching. Small breakfast included. Laundry £3.50. Internet access £5 per hr. Bureau de change. Co-ed dorms. Wheelchair accessible. July-Sept. dorms £10-12.50; singles £20; doubles £29, with bath £33; Oct.-June dorms 50p-£1 less, private rooms £2 less.

The Galway Hostel, Eyre Sq. (☎ 566959), across from the station. Burren Shale tiles lead up past the soft-yellow walls to dorms with super-clean bathrooms. The kitchen fills fast in this 80-bed hostel. June-Sept. 14-bed dorms £8; 8-bed dorms £8.50; 4-bed £15; doubles £32; Sept.-May dorms £1 cheaper, doubles £2 less.

An Óige Galway Hostel (☎ 527411). Follow Dominick St. to the west and turn left onto St. Mary's Rd. When school lets out for the summer, St. Mary's school for boys, an imposing building surrounded by playing fields, puts bunks in its classrooms and gyms to form a 180-bed hostel. Close to Galway's best bars, but far from the station. Open late June to Aug. Breakfast included. Dorms £9-10; twins £11.

B&BS AND CAMPING

St. Martin's, 2 Nuns' Island (☎ 568286), on the west bank of the river at the end of Dominick St. (visible from the Bridge St. bridge). Gorgeous riverside location with a grassy lawn. Singles £20; doubles £36.

Mrs. E. O'Connolly, 24 Glenard Ave. (☎ 522147), Salthill, off Dr. Mannix Rd. Bus #1 from Eyre Sq. Excellent B&B for super-cheap prices. £10 with continental breakfast, £12 with full Irish breakfast.

Mrs. Ruth Armstrong, 14 Glenard Ave. (☎ 522069), close to Salthill. Full Irish breakfast and friendly chatter. £17 per person.

Camping: Salthill Caravan and Camping Park (☎ 523972). Beautiful location on the bay, ½ mi. west of Salthill. A good hour's walk from Galway along the shore. Open May-Oct. Crowded in summer. £3 per hiker or cyclist.

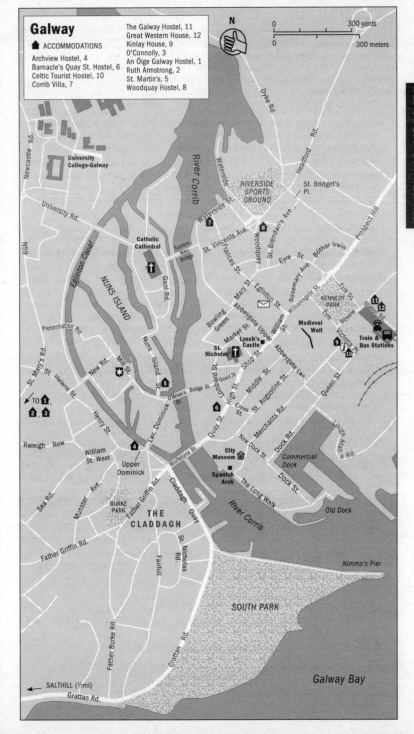

Galway

▲ ACCOMMODATIONS

Archview Hostel, 4
Barnacle's Quay St. Hostel, 6
Celtic Tourist Hostel, 10
Corrib Villa, 7

The Galway Hostel, 11
Great Western House, 12
Kinlay House, 9
O'Connolly, 3
An Óige Galway Hostel, 1
Ruth Armstrong, 2
St. Martin's, 5
Woodquay Hostel, 8

N

0   300 yards
0   300 meters

FOOD

The east bank has the greatest concentration of restaurants. The **Supervalu,** in the Eyre Square mall, is a chef's playground. (☎ 567833. Open M-W and Sa 9am-6:30pm, Th-F 9am-9pm.) **Evergreen Health Food,** 1 Mainguard St., has just the healthy stuff. (☎ 564215. Open M-Sa 8:45am-6:30pm.) On Saturday mornings, an **open market** sets up in front of St. Nicholas Church on Market St. with seafood, pastries, and fresh fruit. The crepes are a steal at £3. (Open 8am-1pm.)

🖾 **Anton's** (☎ 582067). A bit off the beaten path: a 3min. walk up Father Griffin Rd. over the bridge near the Spanish Arch. Amazing, cheap sandwiches make it worth the walk. Ham, tomato, and onion marmalade on foccacia £2.50; salad and bread £3; creative sandwiches £2-2.50. Open Tu-Sa 11am-6pm.

🖾 **Apostasy,** Dominick St. (☎ 561478). A hip coffee shop with an unbelievable after-hours scene. New-age regulars fill the place pretending to talk art until 4am each morning. Pub crawlers half-heartedly try to sober up with cups of strong coffee. Garlic bread with olives and mozzarella £2.20. Cappuccino £1.20.

Da Tang, Middle St. (☎ 561 43). Businessmen and hipsters alike crowd together in this busy Chinese noodle house. Pickled mustard with shredded pork in a lovely broth £6, tofu and veggies in a yellow sauce £5.50. Some of the best food in town. Takeaway available. Open Su-Th noon-10pm, F-Sa noon-11pm.

The River God Cafe, Quay St. (☎ 565811). French and Asian flavors combine in subtle seafood curries and salmon steaks with seaweed pasta. The champagne sorbet makes bubbly heavenly. Lunch special £5, dinners at least £10. Open noon-10pm.

Mocha Mania, High St. (☎ 566146). A bright, friendly, smoke-free coffee shop with good coffee. Lovely Normandy apple tarts £2.50, tasty toasted panini £2.50-3. Espresso £1. Open M-Sa 9:30am-6pm, Su noon-6pm.

McDonagh's, 22 Quay St. (☎ 565809). Locals and tourists flock here for world-class fish and chips. Certificates, newspaper clippings, and magazine articles line the wall to prove its popularity. Takeaway cod and chips £4.10. Restaurant open daily noon-11pm; takeaway M-Sa noon-midnight, Su 5-11pm.

SIGHTS

Rededicated as John F. Kennedy Park, **Eyre Square** has a small collection of monuments around its grassy common stand. Across the river to the south of Dominick St., **Claddagh** was an Irish-speaking, thatched-cottage fishing village until the 1950s. Stone bungalows replaced the cottages, but a bit of the small-town appeal and atmosphere still persists. The famous Claddagh rings, traditionally used as wedding bands, are mass-produced today. The **Nora Barnacle House** is the home of James Joyce's life-long companion. The table where he composed a few lines to Nora draws the admiration of Joyce addicts. (8 Bowling Green. ☎ 564743. Open mid-May to mid-Sept. M-Sa 10am-1pm and 2-5pm. £1.) By the river, the **Long Walk** makes a pleasant stroll, bringing you to the **Spanish Arch.** Built in 1584 as a defensive bastion for the port, this worn, one-story stone curve is revered by townspeople despite its unimpressive stature.

PUBS AND CLUBS

Galway's pubs come in all flavors. Trad blazes across town nightly, but Dominick St. is the best place to hear it. Only big gigs have cover charges. For schedules check *The List,* free and available at most pubs and newsstands.

🖾 **Roisín Dubh** ("The Black Rose"), Dominick St. (☎ 586540). Big-name Irish and international musicians light up the stage in this large, dark pub—mostly rock, but also folk, blues, and trad. Irish record labels, including the pub's own, promote new artists, and music enthusiasts of all ages turn out in numbers. Occasional M and Tu cover £5-10.

▨ **The Crane,** 2 Sea Rd. (☎ 587419). Well known as the best place to hear trad in Galway. Enter through the side door and hop up to the 2nd-floor loft. Two musicians quickly become 6, 6 become 10, 10 become 20. Trad "whenever."

▨ **The King's Head,** High St. (☎ 566630). A locus for many pub-goers and a crawl in itself. Check out the modern club room on the 3rd floor. Huge stage area with funky lighting hosts live bands nightly. Several bars make the wait for a pint no wait at all. Occasional trad. Lunchtime theater M-Sa 1-2pm, £2. Popular jazz brunch Su noon-1:45pm.

▨ **The Hole in the Wall,** Eyre Sq. A large pub (not at all befitting its name) that fills up fast with lots of singles and the occasional high-profile celebrity. Ideal meat-market conditions with huge booths, 3 bars for mingling, and tables to dance on.

La Graal, 38 Lower Dominick St. (☎ 567614). A candlelit wine (only) bar and restaurant, La Graal is the center for Galway's Latin community. A diverse crowd; gay-friendly. Exquisite staff. Salsa dancing Th. Open until 1:15am.

The Quays, Quay St. (☎ 568347). Popular with the younger crowd and scamming yuppies. The massive, multi-floored interior was built with carved wood and stained glass from an old church. Worth a visit for the interior alone. Cover bands electrify the equally impressive upstairs extension nightly 10pm-1:30am. Cover £5.

Seaghan Ua Neachtain (called **Knockton's**), Quay St. (☎ 568 820). One of the oldest and most genuine pubs in the county. An older crowd trades personal space for warmth and energy. Trad nightly. 21+.

Padraig's, (☎ 563 696), at the docks. Opens daily at 7:30am for fishermen, and plain ol' die-hards. You know who you are.

McSwiggin's, Eyre St. (☎ 568 917), near Eglinton St. A sprawling mess of small rooms and stairwells spanning 3 stories, McSwiggin's holds hundreds of tourists at a time. The *craic* is good, though, and so is the food.

Between 11pm and midnight, the pubs empty out, and the tireless go dancing. Unfortunately, Galway's clubs lag far behind the pubs. **GPO,** Eglinton St., doesn't look good, but it draws a high-energy crowd nonetheless. (☎ 563073. 21+. Cover £5.) With its finger firmly on the pulse of the European dance scene, **The Blue Note,** William St. West (☎ 589116), throbs with the spins of guest DJs every night of the week. The more adventurous and mobile head out to the **Liquid Club,** King's Hill, in Salthill. Expect a provocative dance mix that will fuel your engine well into morning. A taxi is the best way to get there and back. (☎ 522715. Open Th-Su. Cover £6.)

🎵 ▨ ENTERTAINMENT AND FESTIVALS

Dancers, singers, musicians, and actors routinely stun audiences with their showcase of traditional Irish art at **Siamsa na Gaillimhe,** at the Galway Folk Theatre, University College. (☎ 755479. Performances June 22-Aug. 28 M-F 8:45 pm. Tickets from £7.) The **Galway Arts Centre,** 47 Dominick St., hosts rotating art and photography exhibits and frequent workshops on dance, writing, and painting. (☎ 565886. Open M-Sa 10am-5:30pm.) The **Town Hall Theatre,** Courthouse Sq., hosts everything from the Druid Theatre Company's Irish-themed plays and original Irish films to international hit musicals. (☎ 569777. Shows daily in summer; most performances 8pm. Tickets £5-15, student discounts most shows.) In 1928, a group of academics from Galway University founded **An Taibhdhearc** (An TIVE-yark), Middle St., as a mostly Irish-language theater. Poetry readings, musicals, and other events alternate with full-blown plays. (☎ 562024. 7 performances per year. Box office open M-F 10am-6pm, Sa 1-6pm. Tickets £6-9.)

Festivals rotate through Galway all year long, with the greatest concentration in the summer. For two crazed weeks in mid-July, the **Galway Arts Festival** (☎ 583800) reels in famous trad musicians, rock groups, theater troupes, and filmmakers. The gates go up for the **Galway Races** at the end of July. Those attending the races celebrate horses, money, and stout, not necessarily in that order. The grandstand bar at the 23,000 capacity Ballybrit track holds the record for the longest bar in

Europe, measuring over 70 yd. from end to end. (☎ 753870. Tickets £8-10 at the gate.) The 45-year-old **Galway International Oyster Festival** (☎ 566490) takes place in late September, with street theater, parades, and free concerts. Also known as the Cúirt, the **Galway Poetry and Literature Festival** (☎ 565886) gathers the highest of the nation's brows at the end of April. The **Galway Film Fleadh** is Ireland's biggest film festival; it screens its stuff in early July.

CONNEMARA

With Ireland's largest *gaeltacht* stretching along it, Connemara's jagged southern coastline teems with beaches, sinuous estuaries, and tidal causeways connecting to rocky offshore islands. English-speaking Clifden, the largest town, hosts the largest crowds. Squishy bogs spread between the coast and two major mountain ranges, the Twelve Bens and the Maamturks, which rise up like little green hills that just forgot to stop growing. Cycling is a particularly rewarding way to absorb Connemara; the 60 mi. rides from Galway to Clifden via Cong or to Letterfrack are the most popular, although the roads become a bit difficult near the end. Along the seaside route through Inverin and Roundstone to Galway and in north Connemara, each of the dozens of loops and backroads is as spectacular as the next. Hiking through the boglands and along the coastal routes is also popular; the Western Way footpath offers dazzling views as it winds 31 mi. from Oughterard to Leenane through the Maamturks. Buses regularly service the main road from Galway to Westport, with stops in Clifden, Oughterard, Cong, and Leenane. The N59 from Galway to Clifden is the main thoroughfare; the R336, R340, and R341 make more elaborate coastal loops. Hitchhikers report that locals are likely to stop; nonetheless, *Let's Go* does not recommend hitchhiking as a safe mode of transport.

CLIFDEN (AN CLOCHÁN)   ☎091

Clifden is called the capital of Connemara because of its size, not because of any cultural membership in the *gaeltacht*; this busy English-speaking town has more amenities and modernities than its Irish-speaking neighbors. Clifden's proximity to the region's scenic bogs and mountains attracts crowds of tourists, who enjoy the frenzied pub scene that starts up at nightfall.

█ GETTING THERE AND GETTING AROUND. The N59 makes a U-turn at Clifden; most traffic is from Galway, 1½hr. southeast, but the road continues northeast to Letterfrack and Connemara National Park. **Bus Éireann** pulls into the library on Market St. from **Westport** via **Leenane** (1½hr., late June to Aug. 1-2 per day) and **Galway** via **Oughterard** (2hr.; June-Aug. M-Sa 5 per day, Su 2 per day; Sept.-May 1 per day; £6.50). **Michael Nee** (☎ 51082) runs a private bus to the courthouse from **Galway** (June-Sept. 3 per day, £5) and **Cleggan** (June-Sept. 1-2 per day; Oct.-May 2 per week; £3). **Rent bikes** from **Mannion's,** Bridge St. (☎ 21160, after hours ☎ 21155. £7 per day, £40 per week; deposit £10. Open M-Sa 9:30am-6:30pm, Su 10am-1pm and 5-7pm.) **John Ryan,** Sky Rd., **rents boats.** (☎ 21069. Prices negotiable.) For a **taxi,** call **Joyce's** (☎ 21076). **Hitchhikers** reportedly wait at the Esso station on N59; *Let's Go* reports with certainty that hitchhiking is not a safe mode of transport.

█▊ ORIENTATION AND PRACTICAL INFORMATION. Market St. meets **Main St.** and **Church Hill** at **The Square.** The **tourist information centre,** Galway Rd., has info on all of Connemara. (☎ 21163. Open July-Aug. M-Sa 9:45am-5:45pm and Su noon-4pm; May-June and Sept. M-Sa 9:30am-5:30am.) An **AIB bank** is in The Square. (☎ 21129. Open M-Tu and Th-F 10am-12:30pm and 1:30-4pm, W 10am-12:30pm and 1:30-5pm.) Call the **police** (*Garda*) at ☎ 21021, or the **hospital** at ☎ 21301. The **post office** is on Main St. (☎ 21156. Open M-F 9:30am-5:30pm, Sa 9:30am-1:30pm.)

▌ ACCOMMODATIONS. B&Bs litter Clifden's streets, and charge around £18-20 per person. Reservations are necessary in July and August. **The Clifden Town Hostel (IHH),** Market St., has great facilities, spotless rooms, and a quiet atmosphere close to the pubs. Despite the modern decor, stone walls remind you that the house is

180 years old. (☎ 21076. Dorms £8; doubles £24; triples £30-33; quads £36; off-season private rooms £1-2 less.) The roomy dorms of **Brookside Hostel,** Hulk St., overlook fat sheep in the backyard. Head straight at the bottom of Market St. (☎ 21812. Dorms £7-8; doubles £18.) Centrally located **Ard Rí Bay View,** Market St., behind King's Garage, is a small, comfortable hostel. (☎ 21866. July-Aug. dorms £5-6; private rooms £8 per person.) **Kingston House,** Mrs. King, Bridge St., has friendly staff, huge breakfasts, and spiffy rooms with a partial view of the church. (☎ 21470. Singles £20; doubles £34-40.) The tranquility of **Shanaheever Campsite,** a little over a mile outside Clifden on Westport Rd., compensates for its distance from the pubs. (☎ 21018. Showers and kitchen. £8 per 2-person tent, £3 per additional person.)

FOOD AND PUBS. O'Connor's SuperValu, Market St., has groceries. (Open M-F 9am-7pm, Su 10am-6pm.) Get homecooked meals at compassionate prices at **An Tulan,** Westport Rd. (☎ 21942. Sandwiches from £1.20, main coursers around £4. Open daily 10am-10:30pm.) Cozy, candlelit **Mitchell's Restaurant,** the Square, serves hearty plates for all palates. (☎ 21867. Burgers £5.95. Open daily noon-10:30pm.) The lunch specials of **Derryclare Restaurant,** the Square, quell pangs of shopper's guilt. (☎ 21440. Six oysters £4.50; pasta around £7. Open daily 8am-10:30pm.) To join in the music at **Mannion's,** Market St., bring your own instrument, or just pick up some spoons when you get there. (☎ 21780. Music nightly in summer, F-Sa in winter.) The town's best pint by consensus is at **King's,** the Square (☎ 21800), while **Malarkey's,** on Church Hill, is perpetually packed and jiggity jammin' most nights.

SIGHTS. There are no cliffs in Clifden itself, but 10 mi. long **Sky Rd.** leads the way to some dizzying ones. It's best covered by bicycle, but involves several strenuous climbs. A mile down Sky Rd. stand the ruins of **Clifden Castle,** once home to Clifden's founder, John D'Arcy. The **Connemara Walking Center,** Market St., offers tours that explore the history, folklore, geology, archaeology, and, most importantly, bogs of the region. (☎ 21379. Open Mar.-Oct. M-Sa 10am-6pm. One full-day or two half-day tours daily Easter-Oct.; call for a schedule. £15-25.)

CONNEMARA NATIONAL PARK

Outside Letterfrack and composed of bogs thinly covered by a screen of grass and flowers, Connemara National Park occupies 7¾ sq. mi. of mountainous countryside that is home to thousands of birds. Guides lead free 2hr. walks over the hills and through the bogs (July-Aug. M, W, and F 10:30am) and tell about the history, breeding, and feeding of the Connemara ponies (July-Aug. M, W, and F 2pm; free). The Visitors Centre excels at explaining blanket bogs, raised bogs, turf, and heathland. (☎ (095) 41054. Open daily June 10am-6:30pm; July-Aug. 9:30am-6:30pm; May and Sept. 10am-5:30pm. £2, students £1.) The **Snuffaunboy Nature Trail** features alpine views, while the **Ellis Wood Trail** submerges walkers in an ancient forest; both teem with wildflowers. A guidebook mapping out 30min. walks (50p) is available at the Visitors Centre, where the staff helps plan longer hikes. More experienced hikers often head for the **Twelve Bens** (*Na Benna Beola,* a.k.a. the Twelve Pins), a rugged range that reaches 2400 ft. heights and is not recommended for solo or beginning hikers. Hikers often base themselves at the **An Óige Ben Lettery Hostel,** which overlooks sheep and postcard-quality stretches of scenery in Ballinafad. The turn-off from the N59 is eight miles east of Clifden. (☎ (095) 51136. Dorms June-Aug. £7.50; Easter-May and Sept. £6.50.)

WESTPORT ☎098

One of the few planned towns in Ireland, Westport (pop. 4300) still looks marvelous in her Georgian-period costume. In summer, droves of visitors traipse through the town's tree-lined mall, central Octagon, and shop-encrusted Bridge Street.

GETTING THERE AND GETTING AROUND. Trains puff into **Altamont St. Station** (☎ 25253) from **Dublin** via **Athlone** (M-Th and Sa 3 per day; F and Su 2 per day; £15). **Rent bikes** from **Breheny & Sons,** Castlebar St. (☎ 25020. £5 per day, £7 per

24hr., £35 per week. £30 deposit. Bikes can be dropped off in Galway.) The N60 passes through **Clifden, Galway,** and **Sligo** on its way to Westport, and **hitchhikers** report it to be an easy route; *Let's Go* as easily states that hitchhiking is not safe.

⚠️🔧 ORIENTATION AND PRACTICAL INFORMATION. The tiny **Carrowbeg River** runs through **Westport's Mall** with **Bridge St.** and **James St.** extending south. **Shop St.** connects Bridge St. to James St. on the other end. The **tourist information centre** (TIC) is on James St. (☎ 25711. Open Apr.-Oct. M-Sa 9am-12:45pm and 2-5:45pm, July-Aug. also Su 10am-6pm.) The **Bank of Ireland** is at North Mall. (☎ 25522. Open M-W and F 10am-4pm, Th 10am-5pm.) For **Internet access,** try **Dunning's Cyberpub,** The Octagon. (☎ 25161. £5 per 30min. Open daily 9am-11:30pm.) The **police** (*Garda*) are at Fair Green (☎ 25555), while the **post office** is at North Mall (☎ 25475; open M-Sa 9am-noon and 2-5:30pm).

🏠🍴🍺 ACCOMMODATIONS, FOOD, AND PUBS. The ◾ **Granary Hostel,** a mile from town on Louisburgh Rd., near the main entrance to Westport House, is flanked by a peaceful garden and conservatory. (☎ 25903. Closed Dec. Dorms £6.) The **Old Mill Holiday Hostel (IHH),** James St., between The Octagon and the TIC, has character and comfort in a renovated mill and brewery. (☎ 27045. Kitchen and common-room lockout 11pm-8am. Dorms £8.) The small, family-run **Slí na h-Óige,** North Mall, has comfortable beds and frequent trad. (☎ 28751. Open June-Sept. Internet access £1 per hr. Dorms £7.) For quiet, private rooms above a bustling pub, try the central **Dunning's Pub,** The Octagon. (☎ 25161. £17 per person.)

Peruse local art while waiting for a table at ◾ **McCormack's,** Bridge St. Locals praise the exemplary teas and pastries. (☎ 25619. Hot bacon bap £2.80, pasta salad £3.75. Open M-Tu and Th-Sa 10am-6pm.) Owned by the flautist of the Chieftains, ◾ **Matt Molloy's,** Bridge St. (☎ 26655), officially runs trad sessions nightly at 9:30pm, but really anytime of the day is deemed appropriate. A run-down exterior hides **Henehan's Bar,** Bridge St. (☎ 25561), and its beer garden, ripe for people-watching. It has music nightly in summer, on weekends in winter.

📷🥾 SIGHTS AND HIKING. While the museum at **Westport House** is hardly worth the entrance fee, the grounds are beautiful and free. To get to them, take James St. above The Octagon, bear right, and follow the signs to the Quay (45min.). The narrow interior of the **Clew Bay Heritage Centre,** at the end of the Quay, crams together a pair of James Connolly's gloves and a stunning original photograph of Maud Gonne. (☎ 26852. Open July-Sept. M-F 10am-5pm, Su 2-5pm; Oct.-June M-F noon-3pm. £1.)

The summit of conical **Croagh Patrick,** rising 2510 ft. over Clew Bay, has been revered as a holy site for thousands of years. St. Patrick worked it here in AD 441, praying and fasting for 40 days and nights, arguing with angels, and then banishing snakes from Ireland. Climbing the mountain takes four hours round-trip; be forewarned that the ascent can be quite steep and the footing unsure. Well-shod climbers start their excursion from the 15th-century **Murrisk Abbey,** several miles west of Westport on the R395 toward Louisburgh. **Buses** go to Murrisk (July-Aug. M-F 3 per day, Sept.-June M-Sa 2 per day), but a **taxi** (☎ 27171) is cheaper for three people and more convenient. Pilgrims and hikers also set out for Croagh Patrick along the Tóchar Phádraiga path from **Ballintubber Abbey** (☎ (094) 30709), several miles south of Castlebar and 22 mi. from Croagh Patrick. Founded in 1216 by King of Connacht Cathal O'Connor, the abbey still functions as a religious center.

ACHILL ISLAND   ☎ 098

Two decades ago, Achill (AK-ill) Island was Co. Mayo's most popular holiday refuge. Its popularity has inexplicably dwindled, but Ireland's biggest little island is still one of its most beautiful and personable. Ringed by glorious beaches and cliffs, Achill's interior consists of acres of bog and a few mountains. The town of Achill Sound, the gateway to the island, has the best hostel and the most amenities, while Keel has more promising nightlife. Achill's most potent vistas are farther west in Keem Bay and at Croaghaun Mountain.

Buses run infrequently over the bridge to **Achill Sound, Dugort, Keel,** and **Dooagh** from **Westport, Galway,** and **Cork** (summer M-Sa 5 per day, off-season M-Sa 2 per day), and from **Enniskillen** and **Belfast** in **Northern Ireland** (summer M-Sa 3 per day, off-season 2 per day). **Hitchhikers** report relative success in July and August, but **cycling** is more reliable, and *Let's Go* does not recommend hitchhiking. The **tourist information centre** is next to the Esso station in Cashel, on the main road from Achill Sound to Keel. (☎ 47353. Open daily 10am-5pm.) There's **no bank** on the island, so change money on the mainland or suffer rates worthy of Grace O'Malley.

Achill Sound's convenient location at the island's entrance warrants the high concentration of shops and services in its center. Practicality isn't the only reason to stop in Achill Sound: an internationally famous stigmatic and faith healer sets up her House of Prayer here, drawing thousands to the attention-starved town each year. About six miles south of Achill Sound and left at the first crossroads stand two sets of ruins. The ancient **Church of Kildavnet** was founded by St. Dympna when she fled to Achill Island to escape her father's incestuous desires. The remains of **Kildavnet Castle,** really a fortified tower house dating from the 1500s, proudly crumble nearby. Grace O'Malley, the swaggering, seafaring pirate of medieval fame, once owned the castle. The spectacular Atlantic Drive, which roams along the craggy south coast past beautiful beaches to **Dooagh,** makes a fantastic bike ride.

The town has a **post office** with a **bureau de change** (☎ 45141; open M-F 9am-12:30pm and 1:30-5:30pm, Sa 9am-1pm), a **SuperValu supermarket** (open daily 9am-7pm), and a **pharmacy** (☎ 45248; open July-Aug. M-Sa 9:30am-6pm, Sept.-June Tu-Sa 9:30am-6pm). **Achill Sound Hotel** rents **bikes.** (☎ 45245. £6 per day, £30 per week; deposit £40. Open daily 9am-9pm.) **The Wild Haven Hostel,** a block left past the church, glows with polished floors and antique furniture. (☎ 45392. Breakfast £3.50; candlelit dinner £12.50. Sheets £1. Laundry £5. Lockout 11am-3:30pm, except on rainy days. Dorms £7.50, private rooms £10 per person. Camping £4.) The **Railway Hostel,** just before the bridge to town, is a simple affair in the old station (the last train arrived in the 1930s). The proprietors with the keys can be found at Mace Supermarket in town. (☎ 45187. Sheets £1. Laundry £1.50. Dorms £7.50; doubles £18.) Opposite the Railway Hostel, **Alice's Harbour Bar** flaunts gorgeous views, a stonework homage to the deserted village, and a boat-shaped bar. (☎ 45138. Bar food £4-6; served noon-6pm. Music on weekends.)

BALLINA   ☎096

Hordes in olive-green waders invade Ballina (bah-lin-AH) each year during the February-September salmon season. Ballina has non-ichthyological attractions as well, though, including lovely vistas, river walks, and a raging weekend pub scene.

🖥🛈 GETTING THERE AND PRACTICAL INFORMATION. The **train station** is on Station Rd. (☎ 71818. Open M-F 7:30am-6pm, Sa 9am-1pm and 3:15-6pm.) **Trains** arrive from **Dublin** (M-Sa 3 per day, £15). The **bus station** is nearby. (☎ 71800. Open M-Sa 9:30am-6pm.) **Buses** arrive from: **Dublin** (4hr., 3 per day, £8); **Westport** (1½hr.; M-Sa 3 per day, Su 1 per day; £6.30); **Donegal** (M-Sa 3 per day, Su 1 per day; £10); and **Sligo** (2hr., M-Sa 3-4 per day, £7.30). **Gerry's Cycle Centre,** 6 Lord Edward St., **rents bikes.** (☎ 70455. £7 per day, £30 per week. Collection service available. Open M-Sa 9am-7pm.) **Mulherin Taxi Service** is on the Brook (☎ 22583).

Ballina's commercial center is on the west bank of the **River Moy.** A bridge crosses to the cathedral and tourist information centre (TIC). The bridge connects to **Tone St.,** which turns into **Tolan St.** This strip intersects **Pearse St.** and **O'Rahilly St.,** which run parallel to the river, to form Ballina's center. The **tourist information centre** (TIC) is on Cathedral Rd., on the river by St. Muredach's Cathedral. (☎ 70848. Open Mar.-May and Sept. M-Sa 10am-1pm and 2-5:30pm; June-Aug. 10am-5:30pm.) Services include: a **Bank of Ireland,** Pearse St. (☎ 21144; open M-W and F 10am-4pm, Th 10am-5pm); **Internet access** at **Moy Valley Resources,** in the same building as the TIC (☎ 70905; £6 per hr.; open M-Th 9am-1pm and 2-5:30pm, F 9am-

1pm and 2-5pm); the **police** (*Garda*) at Walsh St. (☎ 21422); and the **post office**, Casement St. (☎ 21498; open M-Sa 9am-5:30pm).

▊▊ ACCOMMODATIONS AND FOOD. Much to the budget traveler's chagrin, there are no hostels in Ballina. but dozens of **B&Bs** line the main approach roads into town. The river, the lake, and sea fishing are just a cast away from Ms. Corrigan's **Greenhill**, on Cathedral Close behind the TIC. Spacious, bright rooms look out onto rose gardens. (☎ 22767. Singles £23-25; doubles £38-34.) Or try Breda Walsh's **Suncraft** two doors down. (☎ 21573. Doubles with bath £34.) **Hogan's American House,** a restful, family-run place with a dated but dignified interior, is conveniently located just up from the bus station. (☎ 70582. Breakfast £5. Singles £20; doubles £35.) **Belleek Camping and Caravan Park** is two miles from Ballina toward Killala on the R314, behind the Belleek Woods. (☎ 71533. Laundry and kitchen. Open Mar.-Oct. £4 per person with tent.)

Aspiring gourmets can prepare for a feast at the **Quinnsworth** supermarket on Market Rd. (☎ 21056. Open M-W 9am-7pm, Th-F 9am-9pm, Sa 9am-6pm.) Pubs and restaurants tend to go hand in hand in Ballina; get the same food for half the price by sitting in the pub. **Cafolla's,** just up from the bridge, is fast, cheap, and almost Italian. The milkshakes tingle tongues. (☎ 21029. Open M-Sa 10am-12:30pm.) **Tullio's,** Pearse St., exudes elegance and has pleasantly surprising prices; pizzas, burgers, and pasta dishes go for around £5-7. (☎ 70815. Restaurant open daily noon-3pm and 6-10pm; bar food served noon-10pm.) **Duffy's,** Pearse St. (☎ 22576), is a local coffee and tea shop that provides cheap eats for £2-5.

▊▊ OUTDOOR ACTIVITIES AND FESTIVALS. The bird-rich **Belleek Woods** (bah-LEEK) around Belleek Castle are a fairy-tale forest with an astonishing bird-to-tree ratio. To reach the entrance, cross the lower bridge near the cathedral on Pearse St. and keep Ballina House on your right. Behind the train station is the **Dolmen of the Four Maols,** locally called "Table of the Giants." The lonely **Ox Mountains** east of Ballina are cyclable; dirt and asphalt trails crisscross up the slopes. The 44 mi. **Ox Mountain Drive** traces the scenic perimeter of the mountains and is well signposted from Tobercurry, 21 mi. south of Sligo on the N17. The **Western Way** footpath begins in the Ox Mountains and winds its way past Ballina through Newport and Westport, ending up in Connemara. TICs sell complete guides. Equestrian enthusiasts can ride at the **Ardchuan Lodge,** five miles north of Ballina on the road to Sligo. (☎ 45084. Pony trekking £15 per hr.)

The annual, week-long **Ballina Street Festival** (☎ 70905) has been swinging mid-July since 1964. All of Co. Mayo turns up for the festival's **Heritage Day,** when the streets are closed off and life reverts to the year 1910. All the flashier aspects of traditional Irish life are staged, including greasy-pig contests.

▊ PUBS AND CLUBS. Gaughan's has been pulling the best pint in town since 1936. No music or TV—just conversation, great food, and homemade snuff. Jolly musical drinkers are fixtures of **The Parting Glass** on Tolan St. (☎ 72714. Weekly trad sessions.) Down by the river on Clare St., **Murphy Bros.** (☎ 22702) serves pints to twentysomethings amongst dark wood furnishings. They also dish out superb pub grub. **Doherty's,** by the bridge, revels in the angling lifestyle. (☎ 21150. Trad Th and Sa.) **An Bolg Bui** (☎ 22561) next door is Irish for "the yellow belly." The pub calls itself a "young fisherperson's pub" and sells tackle and licenses along with pints. Belleek Castle is an expensive hotel, but its **Armada Bar,** supposedly built from an actual 500-year-old Spanish wreck, is accessible and affordable. Downstairs, another bar occupies a medieval banquet hall. Of Ballina's four clubs, **Longneck's,** behind Murphy's, is the most popular. (☎ 22702. Open July-Aug. Tu-Su. 21+. Cover £3-5.) **The Pulse,** behind the Broken Jug, is a close and throbbing second. (Cover £3-5. Open W and F-Su.)

NORTHWEST IRELAND

SLIGO   ☎071

Gray and relentless, the Garavogue River gurgles through the industrial and market center of Sligo Town (pop. 18,000), but the town brightens up at night with one of Ireland's most colorful pub scenes. Urban Sligo is surrounded by an impressive natural pageant, memorialized in the poetry of William Butler Yeats.

⬅ GETTING THERE AND GETTING AROUND

Trains: McDiarmada Station (☎ 69888), Lord Edward St. Open M-Sa 7am-6:30pm, Su 20min. before departures. From **Dublin** via **Carrick-on-Shannon** and **Mullingar** (3 per day, £13.50).

Buses: Also at **McDiarmada Station** (☎ 60066). Open M-F 9:15am-6pm, Sa 9:30am-5pm. **Luggage storage** £1.50 per bag; open M-F 9:30am-1:30pm and 2:30-6pm. From: **Dublin** (4hr., 4 per day, £9); **Galway** (2½hr., 3-4 per day, £11); **Westport** (2½hr., 1-3 per day, £9.70); **Derry, Northern Ireland** (3hr., 3-6 per day, £10); and **Belfast, Northern Ireland** (4hr., 1-3 per day, £12.40).

Taxis: Cab 55 (☎ 42333) or **Finnegan's** (☎ 77777). At least £3 in town, 50p per mile.

Bike Rental: Flanagan's Cycles, Market Sq. (☎ 44477, after hours ☎ 62633). £7 per day, £30 per week; deposit £35.

✳🔋 ORIENTATION AND PRACTICAL INFORMATION

To reach the main drag from the bus/train station, take a left and follow Lord Edward St. straight onto **Wine St.**, then turn right at the post office onto **O'Connell St.** To reach the tourist information centre (TIC), head to Lord Edward St., then follow the signs right onto Adelaid St. and around the corner to Temple St. More shops, pubs, and eateries beckon from **Grattan St.**, left off O'Connell St.

Tourist Information Centre: Temple St. (☎ 61201), at Charles St. Open M-Sa 9am-8pm, Su 10am-6pm. Less crowded **info booth** on O'Connell St. Open M-Tu 10am-7pm, W-F 10am-9pm, Sa 10am-6pm.

Financial Services: Allied Ireland Bank, 49 O'Connell St. (☎ 41085). Open M-W and F 10am-4pm, Th 10am-5pm.

Bookstore: The Winding Stair, Hyde Bridge (☎ 41244). Fiction, Irish interest, used books, and *Exploring Sligo and North Leitrim* (£7). Open daily 10am-6pm.

Launderette: Pam's Laundrette, 9 Johnston Ct. (☎ 44861), off O'Connell St. Wash and dry from £6. Open M-Sa 9am-7pm.

Police (*Garda*): Pearse Rd. (☎ 42031).

Hotlines: Samaritans crisis line (24hr. ☎ 42011).

Hospital: On The Mall (☎ 42161).

Internet Access: Cygo Internet Cafe, 19 O'Connell Street (☎ 40082). £5 per hour; students £4. Open M-Sa 10am-7pm.

Post Office: Wine St. (☎ 42646). Open M and W-Sa 9am-5:30pm, Tu 9:30am-5:30pm.

🏠 ACCOMMODATIONS

There are plenty of hostels in Sligo, but they fill up quickly, especially while the Yeats International Summer School is in session in mid-August. Over a dozen B&Bs cluster along **Pearse Rd.** on the south side of town; less refined ones are near the station.

Harbour House, Finisklin Rd. (☎ 71547). A 10min. walk from the bus station. The plain stone front hides a luxurious hostel. Big pine bunks have individual reading lights. Irish breakfast £3, continental £1.50. Bike rental £7. Dorms £10; private rooms £10.50 per person; singles £17.

Railway Hostel, 1 Union Place (☎ 44530). Signposted from the train station. From the main station entrance take three lefts, *et voilà*, you're there! An old train station gracefully converted into nice digs. Plus, there's Socks the Friendly Hostel Dog. Limited kitchen utensils. Dorms £6.50; private rooms £8 per person.

The White House Hostel (IHH), Markievicz Rd. (☎ 45160). Take the first left off Wine St. after the bridge. The reception is in the brown house. A little run-down, but spacious dorms, some with river views. Sheets 50p. Key deposit £2. Dorms £7.

Yeats County Hostel, 12 Lord Edward St. (☎ 46876), across from the bus station. Its location can make it crowded. Liam, the man in charge, was once butler to the Kennedy family. Spacious rooms and private backyard. Key deposit £5. Dorms and triples £7 per person; doubles £21.

Eden Hill Holiday Hostel (IHH), Pearse Rd. (☎ 43204). Entrance via Marymount or Ashbrook St., 10min. from town, at the opposite end from the train station. Cozy rooms and a Victorian parlor in a grand but aging house. Huge backyard, and a common room with VCR. Laundry facilities. Dorms £7; private rooms £8.50 per person. Camping £4.

Renaté House, Upper Johns St. (☎ 62014). From the station, go straight 1 block and left half a block. Businesslike and spotless, with elegant burgundy leather furnishings. Singles £23.50, with bath £25.50; doubles £34, with bath £38.

◨▨ FOOD AND PUBS

Yeats's "faery vats / Full of berries / And of reddest stolen cherries" are not to be found in Sligo today, but **Quinnsworth Supermarket,** O'Connell St., sells neatly packaged berries as well as other assorted items. (☎ 62788. Open M-Tu 8:30am-7pm, W-F 8:30am-9pm, Sa 8:30am-7pm, Su 10am-6pm.) ▨ **Kate's Kitchen,** Market St. (☎ 43022), offers sophisticated pates and other deli delicacies. Frozen homemade soups are a steal at £1.20. **Hy-Breasil,** Bridge St. is a utopia of coffee and fresh-squeezed juice, just over the river, with local art on the walls. (☎ 61180. Juice £1.50. Open M-F 8:30am-6pm, Sa 10am-6pm.) **Ho Wong,** Market St., offers Cantonese and Szechuan takeaway with an Irish-Asian flair. (☎ 45718. Dishes £4-7. Open daily 4-11pm.)

Over 70 pubs crowd Sligo's main streets, filling the town with live music during the summer. ▨ **Shoot the Crows,** Castle St., is a small, murky joint where millennial hipsters and white-haired characters compete for bar stools. Dark fairy-folk dangle from the ceiling. Weird skulls and crazy murals look on in amusement. (Music Tu and Th 9:30pm.) Across the river from the footbridge, modern **Garavogue** (☎ 40100) has a spacious, wooden interior, twentysomething crowd, and palm trees. **Hargadon Bros.,** O'Connell St., is a pub worth spending your day in, with open fires, old Guinness bottles, and *poitín* jugs in a maze of dark and intimate nooks, not to mention perfect pints unfettered by the modern audio-visual distractions found elsewhere. (☎ 70933. Occasional blues nights.) At **McGarrigle's,** O'Connell St., 18th-century lanterns light the cave-dark interior. Upstairs is just as dark, with new-age murals, blaring techno, and young faces. (☎ 71193. Live trad Th and Su.)

◨ SIGHTS

In town, at the well-preserved 13th-century **Sligo Abbey,** Abbey St., the **Dominican friary** boasts cloisters and ornate coupled pillars that, though old, can hardly be called ruins. A defaced monument stone, which bore the names of a mother and her child, graces the sacristy. Tradition claims that the mother's descendants, not wanting a public reminder of their forbearers' illegitimacy, hired a stonemason to chisel away the names in secret. (☎ 46406. Open daily in summer 9:30am-6:30pm; last admission 45min. before closing. If it's closed, ask for the key from Tommy

McLaughlin, 6 Charlotte St. £1.50, students 60p.) Next door, the 1874 **Cathedral of the Immaculate Conception,** on John St., is best visited at dawn or dusk, when the sun streams through 69 magnificent stained-glass windows.

The **Niland Gallery,** Stephen St., houses one of the finest collections of modern Irish art, including a number of works by Yeats's brother Jack, and contemporaries Nora McGinness and Michael Healy. Other treasures include some Yeats first editions and Countess Markievicz's prison apron. (Rotating exhibits. Open Tu-Sa 10am-noon and 2-5pm. Free.) The **Sligo County Museum** preserves small reminders of Yeats, including his funeral pictures. (Open Tu-Sa June-Sept. 10:30am-12:30pm and 2:30-4:50pm; Oct.-May 10:30am-12:30pm. Free.) The **Sligo Art Gallery,** Yeats Memorial Building, Hyde Bridge, rotates exhibitions of Irish art with an annual northwest Ireland exhibit in November. (☎ 45847. Open daily 10am-5pm.)

🎵 ENTERTAINMENT

Hawk's Well Theatre, Temple St., beneath the TIC, presents modern and traditional dramas, ballets, and musicals. (☎ 61526. Box office open M-Sa 9am-6pm. £7-10, students £4.) The **Blue Raincoat Theatre Company,** Lower Quay St., is a traveling troupe covering a wide range of material in their Quay St. "factory space" 16 weeks a year. Look for flyers or call for show dates. (☎ 70431. £5-7.) The final weekend of the June **Sligo Arts Festival** (☎ 69802) focuses on world music. In the first two weeks of August, the internationally renowned **Yeats International Summer School** (☎ 42693) opens some of its poetry readings, lectures, and concerts to the public.

🎭 NEAR SLIGO: YEATS, YEATS, YEATS

DRUMCLIFF. Yeats composed his own epitaph a year before his death in France in 1939. The churchyard bearing his grave is in Drumcliff, four miles northwest of Sligo. His grave is to the left of the church door. On Sunday evenings in the summer, the church sponsors concerts (☎ 56629). **Buses** from Sligo toward Derry stop at Drumcliff (10min.; in summer M-Sa 4 per day, Su 3 per day, in winter M-Sa 3 per day; return £2.60). A few miles northeast of Drumcliff, **Glencar Lake,** mentioned in Yeats's "The Stolen Child," is the subject of more literary excursions. The lake is marked by a sign about one mile north of Drumcliff on the N15.

BENBULBEN. Farther north of Drumcliff, eerie Benbulben, rich in mythical associations, protrudes from the landscape like the keel of a foundered boat. In AD 574, St. Columcille founded a monastery on top, and it continued to be a major religious center until the 16th century. The climb up the 1729 ft. peak is inevitably windy, and the summit can be downright gusty. Standing at the very point of Benbulben, where the land inexplicably drops 5000 ft., can be a watershed experience for even the most weathered hiker. Signs guide travelers to Benbulben from Drumcliff Rd. Ask at the Drumcliff petrol station for directions to the trailheads.

LISSADELL HOUSE. Four miles west of Drumcliff is Lissadell House, where poet Eva Gore-Booth and her sister Constance Markievicz, second in command in the Easter Rising and later the first woman elected to the Dáil, entertained Yeats and his circle. The gaunt house has lost some of its lustre, but Constance's great-nephew still lives here and allows tours. Take the first left after Yeats Tavern Hostel on Drumcliff Rd. and follow the signs. (☎ 63150. House open M-Sa June to mid-Sept. 10:30am-12:15pm and 2-4:15pm. £2.50. Grounds open year-round. Free.)

DONEGAL TOWN ☎ 073

Donegal takes its name from the Irish *Dun na nGall,* meaning "fortress of the foreigners." Many travelers use Donegal Town as the entrance to the county, taking advantage of the helpful tourist information centre, wealth of accommodations, many bus routes that stop in the town, and marvelous trad sessions.

▐ GETTING THERE AND GETTING AROUND

Buses stop outside the Abbey Hotel on the Diamond, where timetables are posted. **Bus Éireann** (☎ 21101) arrives from: **Dublin** (4hr., 5 per day, £12); **Sligo**, (1hr.; M-Sa 7 per day, Su 3 per day); and **Galway** (4hr.; M-Sa 5 per day, Su 3 per day; £10). **McGeehan Coaches** (☎ (075) 46150) arrive from **Dublin** via **Enniskillen** and **Cavan** (2 per day). **Feda O'Donnell** (☎ (075) 48114) arrives at the tourist information centre from **Galway** (M-Sa 9:45am and 5:15pm). **Rent bikes** at **The Bike Shop**, Waterloo Pl., the first left off Killybegs Rd. from the Diamond. (☎ 22515. £7 per day, £45 per week; deposit £30. Panniers £1 per day, £5 per week. Locks and repair equipment included. Open M-Sa 10am-6pm.)

▐✹ ORIENTATION AND PRACTICAL INFORMATION

The center of town is **The Diamond,** a triangular area bordered by Donegal's main shopping streets. At the top of the hill lies **Main Street,** which leads to **Killybegs Rd.** The **tourist information centre** (TIC) is on Quay St. With your back facing the Abbey Hotel, turn right; it's just outside The Diamond on Sligo Rd. It's one of only a few TICs in the county, and thus a wise stop. (☎ 21148; www.donegaltown.ie. Open July-Aug. M-Sa 9am-8pm, Su 10am-4pm; Sept.-Oct. and Easter-June M-F 9am-5pm, Sa 10am-2pm.) Services include: a **Bank of Ireland,** on the Diamond (☎ 21079; open M-W and F 10am-4pm, Th 10am-5pm); the **police** (*Garda*; ☎ 21021); the **hospital** (☎ 21074); **Internet Access** on the second floor of **The Blueberry Tea Room** (see below; £5 per hr., £3 for 15-30min; open daily 11am-11pm); and the **post office,** Tirconaill St., past Donegal Castle and over the bridge (☎ 21007; open M-F 9am-1pm and 2-5:30pm, Sa 9am-1pm).

▐ ACCOMMODATIONS

The family-run ▧ **Donegal Town Hostel (IHH),** half a mile out on Killybegs Rd., is popular, so call ahead. (☎ 22805. Laundry £4. Dorms June-Aug. £7.50, Oct.-May £7; doubles £18. Camping £4 per person. Separate showers for campers.) **Ball Hill Youth Hostel (An Óige),** three miles from town, has a plethora of activities, including horse riding, swimming, and day hikes. Go 1½ mi. out of Donegal on the Killybegs Rd., turn left at the sign, and continue 1½ mi. towards the sea. Buses leaving from the Abbey Hotel (£1) often go as far as Killybegs Rd. (☎ 21174. June-Aug. £7.50, Sept.-May £5; youth discounts.) **Atlantic Guest House,** Main St., has an unbeatable location. Despite being on a busy street, this 16-room guest house offers the undisturbed privacy of a fancy hotel. Each room has TV, telephone, and sink. (☎ 21187. Singles £15, with bath £20.)

▐ FOOD

A good selection of £4-5 cafes and takeaways occupy the Diamond and nearby streets. For groceries, head to the **SuperValu,** minutes from the Diamond down Sligo Rd. (☎ 22977. Open M-W and Sa 9am-7pm, Th-F 9am-9pm.) **Simple Simon's,** the Diamond, sells fresh baked goods, local cheeses, and homeopathic remedies for the organic farmer in you. (☎ 22687. Open M-Sa 9am-6pm.) **Sam's Deli,** Main St., is that rare spot where you can relax with a cup of tea and read the paper for hours. Delicious sandwiches cost around £2, main courses £4. (☎ 23174. Open July-Aug. M-Sa 9am-6pm, Sept.-June 9am-5:30pm.) **The Blueberry Tea Room,** Castle St., on the Killybegs Rd. corner of the Diamond, sells popular sandwiches and an all-day breakfast, and has a cybercafe upstairs. (☎ 22933. Main courses around £5. Open M-Sa 9am-7pm.) The family-run **Harbour Restaurant,** Quay St., across from the TIC, has a menu ranging from £4-8 pizza to £10 steaks. (☎ 21702. Open M-Th 4-10:30pm, F-Su 11am-10:30pm.)

PUBS AND CLUBS

Almost every bar has nightly live music, and many pubs host national acts during the Donegal Summer Festival in early July (see below). **The Schooner Bar and B&B,** Upper Main St. (☎ 21671), has the best trad and contemporary sessions in town on weekends. **McGroarty's,** the Diamond, packs in the young and the young at heart for live bands on weekends. (☎ 21049. No cover.) In **The Coach House,** Upper Main St. (☎ 22855), spontaneous sing-alongs are known to break out at any point in this wooden-beamed locals' hangout. At **Baby Joe's,** Main St., you'll find lots of wrought iron and electric blue, and an equally funky crowd. (☎ 22322. Live bands often on weekends.) **Charlie's Star Bar,** Main St., sparkles for young crowds, with live rock, country, and blues. (☎ 21158. Music Th-Su in summer, F-Su in winter.)

SIGHTS AND FESTIVALS

Originally the seat of several chieftains, Donegal was torn apart by Irish-English conflicts in the 17th century. Evidence of this turmoil remains at **Donegal Castle,** Castle St., the former residence of the O'Donnell clan, and, later, various English nobles. The recently refurbished ruins of the clan's 1474 castle stand adjacent to the manor built by English rulers in 1623. Some rooms include displays detailing the history of the castle and the genealogy of the O'Donnells. (☎ 22405. Open Apr.-Sept. daily 9:30am-5:45pm. Guided tours on the hour. £3, seniors £2, students and children £1.25.) The stones and doorways of the grand manor were taken from the ruins of the 15th-century Franciscan Friary, known as the **Old Abbey,** just a short walk from the TIC along the south of town. Four of its monks went on to write the *Annals of the Four Masters,* the first narrative history of Ireland and the source of many extant myths.

Just a mile south of Donegal Town on Sligo Rd., eight craftspeople open their workshops to the public at the **Donegal Craft Village.** The work of an Invereske potter, a batik artist, an *uileann* pipe maker, and a porcelain crafter make great gift alternatives to the mass-produced leprechauns sold in stores. (☎ 22015. Open July-Aug. M-Sa 10am-6pm, Su noon-6pm; Sept.-June M-Sa 10am-6pm.) The **Donegal Summer Festival,** held on the first weekend of July, brings such diverse activities as craft fairs, the Bonny Baby show, and trad sessions to town.

SLIEVE LEAGUE PENINSULA ☎073

To the west of Donegal Town lies the Slieve League Peninsula, where every bend in the road brings more dramatic views of windswept heather fields, lonely thatched cottages, and dramatic coastline. The few villages on the peninsula all lie along the busy N56, which turns into the R63 as it approaches the peninsula's western tip. Though most easily covered by car, the peninsula is a spectacular opportunity for cycling (expect to walk your bike on frequent serious hills). Only a few buses go by the hostels on the N56.

KILCAR AND SLIEVE LEAGUE

A breathtaking eight miles past Killybegs along the N56 is tiny **Kilcar,** the gateway to Donegal's *gaeltacht* and a commercial base for many Donegal tweed weavers. **Spar Market** on Main St. sells groceries and fishing tackle. (Open M-Sa 9am-10pm, Su 9:30am-1pm and 7-10pm.) The new owners of **Piper's Rest Pub & Restaurant,** Main St., have stripped the stone walls of their musical instruments, so the *craic* has yet to be established. Expect a mixture of young and old folk inside. (☎ 38205. Soup and sandwich £3.80. Food served daily 11:30am-6pm.)

One-and-a-half miles out on the coast road from Kilcar to Carrick and five minutes from the beach, Shaun at the ■ **Derrylahan Hostel (IHH)** welcomes guests like long-lost cousins. Call for pickup from Kilcar or Carrick. Buses pass daily on the way to Killybegs and Glencolmcille. Call ahead to book a bed in July and August. (☎ 38079; derrylahan@eircom.ie. Laundry £5. Dorms £7; private rooms £10. Camping £4, with separate showers and kitchen.) On the way to Derrylahan, just under one mile from Killybegs, ■ **Dun Ulun House** is a luxurious alternative to hostel life at virtually the same price. The flowery beds, hardwood floors, and gorgeous views in the two- to four-bed rooms are turned into small dorms, if you're willing to share. (☎ 38137. Laundry £5. Triples and quads £9.50 per person; doubles £25; B&B £16-20 per person. All with bath. Rooms in cottage across road £5 per person, with linens £6.50. Camping £3, with separate facilities.)

Slieve League claims the hotly contested (in Ireland) title of having the highest sea cliffs in Europe. Undoubtedly, the sheer face of the cliffs' drop into the Atlantic is spectacular. Most Slieve League hikers stay in Kilcar, from which they can comfortably drive, bike, or walk (about 6hr. return) to the mountain. In clear weather it'd be unconscionable *not* to visit Slieve League, a mountain set along a precipitous, beautiful coastline rimmed with 1000 ft. cliffs. To reach the mountain, turn left halfway down Carrick's main street and follow signs for Teelin. At the **Rusty Mackerel Pub** (☎ 39101), you can turn left for the inland route to Slieve League. Alternatively, a turn to the right (the most popular decision) leads along the sea cliffs on the way up to Bunglass. From the car park at the end of the road at Bunglass, a cliff path heads west along the coast. It should take 1½hr. to walk from Carrick to the car park. About half an hour along the path continuing from the car park, the mountain top narrows to 2 ft. On one side of this pass—called **One Man's Pass**—the cliffs drop 1800 ft. to the sea. On the other side, the cliffs drop a measly 1000 ft. to a rocky floor. There are no railings, and the acrophobic sometimes slide across the 30m pass on their behinds or hands and knees. The path then continues all the way along the cliffs to **Rossarrel Point,** near Glencolmcille. **Never go to Slieve League in poor weather.** Use extreme caution if you plan to cross the pass; it is not a necessary part of the hike across Slieve League. (You can still enjoy a steep climb by walking along the inland face of the mountain.) People have died here under poor conditions; several hikers have been blown off the pass by the strong winds. It's always a good idea to ask a local expert for advice.

GLENCOLMCILLE (GLEANN CHOLM CILLE)

The parish on the western top of the Slieve League peninsula, Glencolmcille (glen-kaul-um-KEEL) is the base of several tiny towns and huge natural wonders; its land consists of rolling hills and sandy coves that lie between two huge sea cliffs. This Irish-speaking area and pilgrimage site centers around the street-long village of Cashel, which lies just off the N56 on, Cashel St. The road leads past the village's several storefronts and down to the coast, where most of the area's accommodations and attractions are located. Though less dramatic than the mountain paths, the N56 is the convenient route to most of Glencolmcille.

■ **GETTING THERE AND PRACTICAL INFORMATION. Bus** Éireann (☎ 21101) arrives at the village corner from **Donegal Town** via **Killybegs** and **Kilcar** (3 per day). Glencolmcille's tiny **tourist information centre** (TIC) is on Cashel St. (☎ 30116. Open July-Aug. M-Sa 9:30am-9pm, Su noon-6pm; Apr.-June and Sept. to mid-Nov. M-Sa 10am-6pm, Su 1-5pm.) The nearest **banks** and **cash machines** are in Killybegs and Ardara. A **bureau de change** can be found at the **post office,** east of the village center. (Open M-F 7:30am-1pm and 2-5:30pm, Sa 9am-1pm.)

■ **ACCOMMODATIONS, FOOD, AND PUBS.** To get to the ■ **Dooey Hostel (IHO),** turn left at the end of the village and follow the signs ¾ mi. uphill. The hostel is built into the hillside overlooking the sea, and a wide spectrum of flowers grows into the rocky face that is the hostel's corridor. (☎ 30130; fax 30339. Wheelchair accessible. Dorms £7; doubles £14. Camping £4 with use of hostel facilities.) Mrs. Ann Ward's **Atlantic Scene,** the next house after the hostel, lives up to its name. (☎ 30186. Open May-Sept. £15 per person.)

The **Lace House Restaurant,** above the TIC on Cashel St., has a large menu of fried foods and small windows to admire the cliffs. (☎ 30444. Main courses £4-9. Open daily 9:30am-10pm.) **Byrne and Sons Food Store,** Cashel St., supplies the basics in solids, liquids, and printed matter. (Open M-Sa 9:30am-10pm, Su 9:30am-1pm and 7-9pm.) Cashel's pubs have a dark, dusty 1950s Ireland feel and are primarily a haven for locals. Irish speakers congregate at **Biddy's,** at the mouth of Carrick Rd. (☎ 30016. Trad at least 3 times a week during the summer.) **Roarty's** (☎ 30273), the next pub down Cashel St., welcomes guests with trad several times a week.

■■ **SIGHTS AND FESTIVALS.** Glencolmcille's craft movement began in the 1950s under the direction of the omnipresent Father James McDyer, who was also responsible for getting electricity in Glencolmcille, founding the Folk Village, and building the local football field. Close to town is the **Foras Cultúir Uladh** (FOHR-us KULT-er UH-lah; "The Ulster Cultural Institute"), which runs the Oideas Gael institute for the preservation of the Irish language and culture. (☎ 30248. Open daily 9am-6pm.) A bit past the village center is Father McDyer's **Folk Village Museum and Heritage Centre,** the town's attraction for non-hiking, non-Irish speaking tourists. The museum is housed in stone cottages with immaculately thatched roofs, which date from 1700, 1850, and 1900. (☎ 30017. Open Easter-Sept. M-Sa 10am-6pm, Su noon-6pm. Tours July-Aug. every 30min., Apr.-June and Sept. every hr. £2; concessions £1.25.) A great walk from town begins at the Protestant church and climbs over a hill to the ruins of the ghostly "famine village" of **Port** in the valley on the other side (3hr. walk). The gargantuan phallic rock rising from the sea is just what it appears to be: the only part of the Devil still visible after St. Colmcille banished him to the ocean. The beginning of July brings the two-day **Glencolmcille Folk Festival,** a lively and occasionally raucous celebration.

GWEEDORE (GAOTH DOBHAIR) ☎075

Quilted with sheep and stone fences, the ragged, grassy mountains of Irish-speaking Gweedore welcome walking enthusiasts. Cyclists are enthralled by the challenging but quiet roads.

ERRIGAL MOUNTAIN AND GLENVEAGH NATIONAL PARK

The N56 intersects with the coastal road at a small bridge; the coastal road twists and bends along the jagged edges where Donegal meets the sea, leading you through spectacular scenery dotted with small Irish-speaking villages. Smart travelers stop at **Crolly,** just past the N56 bridge, for a pint and groceries. Several buses stop in front of Paddy Oig's pub. **Feda O'Donnell** (☎ 48114) provides a daily coach service to and from **Galway** and **Donegal Town** via **Letterkenny; Swilly** (☎ 21380) passes on its route from **Dungloe** to **Derry, Northern Ireland. John McGinley Coaches** (☎ (074) 35201) makes Crolly its starting point for a **Dublin** journey; and **O'Donnell Trans-Ulster Express** (☎ 48356) goes by on its way to **Belfast, Northern Ireland.** The **Crolly Filling Station,** next to the post office, provides everything from groceries and petrol to bike repairs and car rental. (Open M-Sa 9am-11pm, Su 9am-10pm.) The postmistress at the Crolly **post office** is a good source of area information. (☎ 48120. Open M-F 9am-5:30pm, Sa 9am-1pm.)

Just past Paddy Oig's pub, a weather-beaten sign will point you toward ■ **Screagan an Iolair Hill Hostel** (SCRAG an UH-ler), which lies four miles up a mountain road at **Tor** in Glenveagh National Park. Turn left off the coastal road at the sign and follow Tor Road past breathtaking scenery and climbs; when you pass Lough Keel, the road divides. Continue straight ahead to reach one of the best hostels in Ireland, which makes a good base for exploring the pristine heath lands of the Derryveagh Mountains. (☎ 48593. Open all year, but call ahead Nov.-Feb. Laundry £3. Dorms £7.50; private rooms £9.) **Coillín Darach Caravan & Camping Park,** just behind the pub, has modern facilities, a convenience store with the basic commodities, and the odd tennis court. (☎ 32000. Store open daily 9am-10pm. Electricity £1. Laundry £2. July-Aug. £7 tent, Sept.-June £5.) **Paddy Oig's** pub (☎ 31306) has everything a body could need: camping, pub grub (sandwiches £1.40), and Tuesday and Thursday night trad sessions in the summer.

One mile north of Crolly, the N56 and the coastal road diverge, the N56 turning inland and reaching the R251 after about five miles. This road leads east through **Dunlewey** past the foot of conical **Errigal Mountain** (2466 ft.), Ireland's second-highest mountain, and eventually to Glenveagh National Park. A few minutes up the road is a turn-off to **Dunlewey Lake** and the **Poison Glen.** Within the wooded area of the glen is a former manor of the English aristocracy. Continue along the paved road around a few curves; you will reach an unmarked car park that signals the beginning of the trail up Errigal Mountain. You must follow this trail in order to scramble through the loose scree to the summit. Expect the climb to take 2-3hr. total. A dangerous, narrow ridge must be traversed to reach the summit. Be sure to keep an eye on the clouds—they've been known to congregate suddenly.

On the eastern side of the Derryveagh Mountains, **Glenveagh National Park** is 37 sq. mi. of forest glens, bogs, and mountains. One of the largest herds of red deer in Europe roams the park; deer-watching is best done at dusk and in the winter months after October, when the deer come down to the valley to forage. Make sure to hold on to the free map handed out at the Visitor Centre. Park rangers lead guided walks. The **Visitor Centre** has more information about these or self-guided hikes. (☎ (074) 37090 or 37262. Open Mar.-Nov. daily 10am-6:30pm. £2, students £1, seniors £1.50.)

BUNBEG AND BLOODY FORELAND

Where the N56 moves inland, the R257 continues along the coast to **Bunbeg.** The coastal road traverses a strip of continuously stunning scenery, perfect for cyclists, since there's little traffic. Bunbeg's harbor is one of two docking places for **Donegal Coastal Cruises'** (a.k.a. **Turasmara**) ferry service for Tory Island; in the summer, it makes a morning and an afternoon trip once a day, weather permitting. (☎ 31991. £15 return, students £13.) The **Bunbeg House** (☎ 31305), on the waterfront, serves sandwiches and seafood.

If you continue past the Bunbeg turn-off, you will immediately see the irresistible 🖾 **Hudi Beag's** pub (☎ 31016). On Monday nights, only the completely tone-deaf could walk past the intense session taking place within. A stone's throw away is **An Chisteanach** (an KEESH-nach), a cozy sit-down deli with stomach-stretching portions for about £5. (Open M-Sa 8:30am-7pm.) On the streets of nearby **Derrybeg** are several banks, but only the **Allied Ireland Bank** has both a **bureau de change** and a **cash machine.** (Open M-W and F 10am-12:30pm and 1:30-4pm, Th until 5pm.) The **post office** is also on the main street. (Open M-F 9am-1pm and 2-5:30pm.) About seven miles north of Bunbeg, **Bloody Foreland,** a short length of rough scarlet rock, juts into the sea. At sunset, the sea reflects the deep red hue of the sky and rocks.

LETTERKENNY (LEITIR CEANNAN) ☎074

Letterkenny is the center of action in Donegal, but that's not saying much. Most tourists arrive in Letterkenny to make bus connections, but Letterkenny's relative urbanity does also bring in pub-goers for weekend revelry.

📳 **GETTING THERE AND GETTING AROUND. Buses** stop at the junction of Port Rd. and Derry Rd. in front of the Quinnsworth Supermarket. **Bus Éireann** (☎ 21309) runs from: **Dublin** (5hr., 4 per day, £11); **Derry, Northern Ireland** (40min.; M-Sa 12 per day, Su 3 per day; £5), **Sligo** (2hr., 3 per day, £9.50), and **Donegal Town** (50min., £5.50) on the way to **Galway** (5hr., 3 per day, £12.50). **Feda O'Donnell Coaches** (☎ (075) 48114) arrive from **Galway** (M-Th and Sa 2 per day, F and Su 3 per day; £10) via **Donegal Town** (£5) and from **Crolly** via **Dunfanaghy** (2 per day, more F and Su; £5). A Bus Éireann "Hills of Donegal" **tour,** including Dungloe, Glenveigh National Park, and Gweedore, departs from town M-Sa at 11am (£10). **Rent bikes** at **Starlight Garage.** (☎ 22248. £7 per day, £35 per week, deposit £10. Open M-Sa 9am-6pm.)

☑ PRACTICAL INFORMATION. Bord Fáilte, ¾ mi. past the bus station and out of town on Derry Rd., has info on Co. Donegal and accommodations bookings. (☎ 21160. Open July-Aug. M-Sa 9am-7pm, Su 10am-2pm; Sept.-June M-F 9am-5pm.) The closer **Chamber of Commerce Visitors Information Centre,** 40 Port Rd., has a slightly smaller selection of info. (☎ 24866. Open M-F 9am-5pm.) Services include: **banks** clustering on Main St., including **AIB,** 61 Upper Main St. (☎ 22877; open M-W and F 10am-4pm, Th 10am-5pm); **Letterkenny General Hospital** (☎ 25888); **Internet access** at **Cyberworld,** Main St., in the Courtyard Shopping Centre (☎ 20440; £5 per hr., students £3.50 per hr.); and the **post office,** halfway down Main St. (☎ 22287; open M, W, and F 9am-5:30pm, Tu and Th 9:30am-5pm, Sa 9am-5:30pm).

☐☐☐ ACCOMMODATIONS, FOOD, AND PUBS. The ▨ **Arch Hostel,** Upper Corkey, is six miles out of town in Pluck. Take the Derry (Port) Rd. from the roundabout near the bus station. Continue straight at the next roundabout onto the dual carriageway. At the first break, turn right across the way and then head left, following signs for Pluck. Stay on the same road until it passes under an archway, then fork right. The hostel is on the right. Better yet, call for pickup. The Gallagher family welcomes hostelers to the six beds in a refinished loft above their stable. (☎ 57255. Open May-Oct. £7.50 per person.) Mrs. McConnellogue's **White Gables,** Lower Dromore, is the third exit from the roundabout three miles out on Derry Rd.; the house is half a mile along Lower Dromore, around a bend, with cheery rooms. Call for pick-up. (☎ 22583. £16, with bath £17.)

Tesco, in the Letterkenny Shopping Centre behind the bus station, sells groceries. (Open M-W 9am-7pm, Th-F 9am-9pm, Sa 9am-6pm, Su noon-6pm.) **Galfees** has two locations: the nicer one is at 63 Main St. (☎ 28535), near the High Rd. fork, but the one in the basement of the Courtyard Shopping Centre (☎ 27173) transcends its location with Irish illustrations and wooden walls. Both will serve an evening main course for £4-5. (Main St.: open M-Sa 9am-10pm, Su noon-7pm. Courtyard: open 8:30am-7:30pm, cheaper evening menu served from 5pm.) **Cafe Rico,** 3-4 Oliver-Plunkett Rd., at the end of Main St., serves full breakfasts and sandwiches for £2 to £4. (☎ 29808. Open M-F 8:30am-5:30pm, Sa until 6pm, Su 11am-4pm.)

INISHOWEN PENINSULA ☎077

An untouristed mosaic of pristine mountains, forests, meadows, and white-sand beaches, the Inishowen Peninsula is dotted with villages and plotted by a winding road. The clearly posted **Inish Eoghin 100** road takes exactly 100 mi. to navigate the peninsula's perimeter.

☐ GETTING THERE AND GETTING AROUND. Lough Swilly (Derry head office ☎ (028) 7126 2017; Buncrana depot ☎ (077) 61340) **buses** head from **Derry, Northern Ireland** to the following points on the Inishowen: **Buncrana** (35min.; M-F 10 per day, Sa 12 per day, Su 3 per day); **Moville** and **Greencastle** (50min.; M-F 5 per day, Sa 6 per day); **Carndonagh** (55min.; M-F 6 per day, Sa 4 per day); **Malin** (1hr.; M, W, and F 2 per day, Sa 3 per day); and **Malin Head** (1½hr.; M, W, and F 2 per day, Sa 3 per day). Swilly also connects **Buncrana** directly with **Carndonagh** (50min., M-Sa 3 per day). **Northwest Buses** (Moville office ☎ 82619) runs from **Moville** through **Culdaff, Carndonagh, Ballyliffin, Clonmany, Buncrana, Fahan,** and on to **Letterkenny** (M-Sa 2 per day); from **Shrove** to **Derry** via **Moville** (1hr., M-Sa 2 per day); from **Buncrana** to **Derry** (M-Sa 5 per day); and from **Malin Head** to **Derry** via **Culdaff** and **Muff** (M-Sa 1 per day). The last bus of the day also stops in Malin Head if you request so in Derry.

MALIN HEAD

Inishowen's most popular attraction is Malin Head, Ireland's northernmost tip. Aside from its latitude, the stretch is remarkable for its rocky, wave-tattered coast and sky-high sand dunes. Inish Eoghin 100 runs east from Cardonagh to Malin Head, passing through the tiny town of Malin on its way. High above the beach,

Knockamany Bens provide fantastic views of the whole peninsula. The scattered town of **Malin Head** includes **Bamba's Crown,** the exact northernmost tip of Ireland, a tooth of dark rock rising up from the ocean spray. Written in whitewashed stones on a nearby lower cliff and readable from thousands of feet above, "S. S. EIRE" (*Saor Stát Éire;* "Irish Free State") identified Ireland as neutral territory to Nazi would-be bombers. The raised beaches around Malin Head (the result of glaciers' passage millions of years ago) are covered with semi-precious stones.

To reach the ■**Sandrock Holiday Hostel (IHO/IHH),** Port Ronan Pier, take the left fork off the Inish Eoghain 100, just before the Crossroads Inn (also a bus stop). This hostel is right on the water with huge views and potential glimpses of seals, dolphins, and puffins. (☎ 70289. Sheets £1. Wash £3, dry £1.50. Dorms £7.) On the Inish Eoghain 100, after the phone booth and across from the post office, the **Malin Head Hostel (IHO/IHH)** welcomes guests with an open fire, reflexology, aromatherapy, homemade elderflower cordial, and carraigan moss jam (made from a local seaweed). The rooms are impeccably clean, and Mary's garden yields fresh, cheap veggies for hostelers' consumption. (☎ 70309. Wash £2, dry £1.50. Bike rental £6 per day. Dorms £7; twins and doubles £20.) All of Malin Head's pubs have late hours and sell groceries. Trad sessions, fishing tackle, and revitalizing brew are all sold at **Farren's,** Ireland's northernmost pub. (Music nightly July-Aug.) **Seaview Tavern and Restaurant** (☎ 70117), commonly referred to as "Vera Dock's," pours your pint in its 12 ft. by 12 ft. space beneath shelves full of corn flakes and motor oil. It opens at 8am and closes (supposedly) at 1am. The **restaurant** next door serves tasty local seafood for £5-9. (Open daily 9am-10pm.)

CULDAFF. In Culdaff, the ■ **Pines Hostel,** Bunagee Rd., houses guests in a spiffy owner-built house with a hearth-warmed common room. (☎ 79060. Sheets £1. Dorms £7.50; doubles £20.) Anyone on a trad pilgrimage should stop in at ■ **McGrory's,** where sessions sometimes last until dawn and the fresh food attracts half the town at dinner time. (☎ 79104. Meat and vegetarian dishes £5-8.) Attached to McGrory's is possibly the best live music venue in the northwest, **Mac's Backroom Bar.** Chummy owners Neil and John McGrory play regularly in sessions. Wednesday nights are the wildly popular "country jam" (£4), where you're likely to hear tongue-in-cheek covers of anything from Al Green to Prince. (Trad Tu and Sa, in summer Th as well. Cover £5 on Sa.)

MOVILLE. Heading back from the tip of the peninsula, small Moville is located at the intersection of the R239 (from Derry) and the R238 (from Culdaff). An **Allied Ireland Bank** with a **cash machine** is on Main St. (☎ 82050. Open M-W, and F 10am-12:30pm and 1:30-4pm, Th 10am-12:30pm and 1:30-5pm.) Mrs. McGuinness's **Dunroman B&B,** off Derry Rd. across from the football field, serves breakfast in a sunny conservatory overlooking the River Foyle. Green plants and murals painted by the eldest daughter complete the splendid setting. (☎ 82234. £17.50, with bath £18.50.)

APPENDIX

CLIMATE

SEASONAL	JANUARY			APRIL			JULY			OCTOBER		
TEMP. (HI-LO), **precipitation**	°C	°F	**mm**	°C	°F	**mm**	°C	°F	**mm**	°C	°F	**mm**
London	2/6	36/43	**77**	6/13	43/55	**56**	14/22	57/72	**59**	8/14	46/57	**70**
Cardiff	2/7	36/45	**108**	5/13	41/55	**65**	12/20	54/68	**89**	8/14	46/57	**109**
Edinburgh	1/6	34/43	**57**	4/11	39/52	**39**	11/18	52/64	**83**	7/12	45/54	**65**
Dublin	1/8	34/46	**67**	4/13	39/55	**45**	11/20	52/68	**70**	6/14	43/57	**70**

BANK HOLIDAYS IN 2001

Government agencies, post offices, and banks are closed on the following days (hence the term "Bank Holiday"), and businesses—if not closed—may have shorter hours. Transportation in rural areas grinds to a halt, while traffic congestion can reach ridiculous levels. Sights, on the other hand, are more likely to be open, but can get crowded with tons of holidaymakers.

DATE	HOLIDAY	AREAS
January 1	New Year's Day	UK and Republic of Ireland
January 2	New Year's Holiday	Scotland
March 17	St. Patrick's Day	Republic of Ireland and Northern Ireland
April 13	Good Friday	UK and Republic of Ireland
April 16	Easter Monday	UK and Republic of Ireland
May 7	May Day Bank Holiday (first Monday in May)	UK and Republic of Ireland
May 28	Spring Bank Holiday (last Monday in May)	UK
June 4	First Monday in June	Republic of Ireland
July 5	Tynwald Fair Day	Isle of Man
July 12	Orange Day	Northern Ireland
August 6	Summer Bank Holiday (first Monday in August)	Republic of Ireland and Scotland
August 27	Summer Bank Holiday (last Monday in August)	UK except Scotland
October 29	Halloween Weekend	Republic of Ireland
December 25	Christmas Day	UK and Republic of Ireland
December 26	Boxing Day/St. Stephen's Day	UK and Republic of Ireland

TELEPHONE CODES

CITY CODES		COUNTRY CODES	
London	020	**United Kingdom**	44
Manchester	0161	**Ireland**	353
Cardiff	029	**Australia**	61
Edinburgh	0131	**Canada**	1
Glasgow	0141	**New Zealand**	64
Belfast	028	**South Africa**	27
Dublin	01	**United States**	1

Northern Ireland can also be reached from the Republic of Ireland by dialing 048.

TIME ZONES

From late Mar. to late Oct., Britain and Ireland use British Summer Time, one hour ahead of **Greenwich Mean Time (GMT);** in winter, both countries revert to GMT. This means that, most of the time, Britain and Ireland are one hour earlier than (most of) continental Europe; five hours later than New York City (EST); six hours later than Chicago (CST); eight hours later than Seattle (PST); ten hours later than Nanakuli, Hawaii; eight hours earlier than Perth, Australia; ten hours earlier than Sydney; and twelve hours earlier than Auckland, New Zealand.

MEASUREMENTS

Britain and Ireland operate on the metric system, though Britain's conversion is as yet incomplete: while the weather report will give the temperature in Celsius, road signs still indicate distances in miles. It should be noted that gallons in the US are not identical to those across the Atlantic; one US gallon equals 0.83 Imperial gallons. Pub aficionados will want to note that a US pint (16 ounces) likewise equals 0.83 Imperial pints (which are 20 ounces each). The following is a list of Imperial units and their metric equivalents.

MEASUREMENT CONVERSIONS

1 inch (in.) = 25.4 millimetres (mm)	1 millimetre (mm) = 0.039 in.
1 foot (ft.) = 0.30m	1 metre (m) = 3.28 ft. = 1.09 yd.
1 yard (yd.) = 0.914m	1 kilometre (km) = 0.62 mi.
1 mile = 1.61km	1 gram (g) = 0.035 oz.
1 ounce (oz.) = 28.35g	1 kilogram (kg) = 2.202 lb.
1 pound (lb.) = 0.454kg	1 millilitre (ml) = 0.034 fl. oz.
1 fluid ounce (fl. oz.) = 29.57ml	1 litre (L) = 0.264 gal.
1 UK gallon (gal.) = 4.546L	1 square mile (sq. mi.) = 2.59km²
1 acre (ac.) = 0.405ha	1 square kilometre (km²) = 0.386 sq. mi.

In Britain and Ireland, **electricity** is 240 volts AC, enough to melt your favorite 110V American curling iron, although probably compatible with your 220V European toaster. 240V appliances won't function on 120V, either. See **Packing,** p. 26, for specific information.

LANGUAGE

The varieties of world English can sometimes lead to bewilderment. The vocabulary of American English, in particular, diverges from British English to a considerable extent. Here's a list of British words travelers are most likely to encounter.

BRITISH ENGLISH	AMERICAN ENGLISH	BRITISH ENGLISH	AMERICAN ENGLISH
all over the shop	in disarray	boot	car trunk
aubergine	eggplant	boozer	pub
bap	a soft bun	braces	suspenders
barmy	insane, erratic	brilliant	awesome, cool
bathroom	room with a bathtub	busker	street musician
bed-sit, or bed sitter	studio apartment	cashpoint	ATM or cash machine
biro	ballpoint pen	caravan	trailer, mobile home
biscuit	a cookie or cracker	car park	parking lot
bobby	police officer	cheeky	mischievous
give a bollocking to	shout at	cheers, cheerio	thank you, goodbye

BRITISH ENGLISH	AMERICAN ENGLISH	BRITISH ENGLISH	AMERICAN ENGLISH
bonnet	car hood	chemist, chemist's	pharmacist, pharmacy
chips	french fries	mate	pal
chuffed	happy	motorway	highway
circle	theater balcony	mobile phone	cellphone
coach	inter-city bus	naff	cheap, in poor taste
concession	discount on admission	petrol	gasoline
courgette	zucchini	phone box, call box	telephone booth
crisps	potato chips	take the piss	make fun
dear	expensive	pissed	drunk
dicey, dodgy	problematic, sketchy	plaster	Band-Aid
the dog's bollocks	the best	prat	stupid person
dosh	money	prawn	large shrimp
dual carriageway	divided highway	props	pub regulars
dustbin	trash can	pudding	dessert
ensuite	with attached bathroom	pull	to "score"
fag	cigarette	public school	private school
fanny	vagina	punter	average person
first floor	second floor	quid	pound (in money)
geezer	man	queue up, queue	line up
fortnight	two weeks	quay	river bank
full stop	period (punctuation)	return ticket	round-trip ticket
gob	mouth	ring up	to phone
grotty	grungy	roundabout	rotary road interchange
half-six in the morning	6:30am	rubber	eraser
high street	main street	sack	to fire someone
hire	rental, to rent	self-catering	with kitchen facilities
hoover	vacuum cleaner	self-drive	car rental
holiday	vacation	serviette	napkin
ice-lolly	popsicle	a shag, to shag	sex, to have sex
interval	intermission	single carriageway	non-divided highway
"in" a street	"on" a street	single ticket	one-way ticket
jam	jelly	snogging	making out
jelly	Jell-O	sod it	forget it
jumble sale	yard sale	stalls	orchestra seats
jumper	sweater	sultana	a type of raisin
kip	sleep	sweet(s)	candy
kit	sports team uniform	swish	swanky
knackered	tired, worn out	ta-ta	goodbye
lavatory, "lav"	restroom	tariff	cost
lay-by	roadside turnout	toilet	restroom
leader (in newspaper)	editorial	torch	flashlight
wanker	masturbator; see prat	tosser	term of abuse; see prat
way out	exit	trainers	sneakers
W.C. (water closet)	toilet, restroom	trunk call	long-distance phone call
legless	intoxicated	vest	undershirt
to let	to rent	waistcoat (weskit)	men's vest
lift	elevator	wellies	waterproof rubber boots
loo	restroom	yob	prole
lorry	truck	"zed"	the letter Z

BRITISH PRONUNCIATION

Berkeley	BARK-lee	Maryleborn	MAR-lee-bun
Berkshire	BARK-sher	Magdalen	MAUD-lin
Birmingham	BIRM-ing-um, not "ham"	Norwich	NOR-ich
Derby	DAR-bee	Salisbury	SAULS-bree
Dulwich	DULL-idge	Shrewsbury	SHROWS-bree
Edinburgh	ED-in-bur-ra	Southwark	SUTH-uk
Ely	EEL-ee	Thames	TEMS
Gloucester	GLOS-ter	Warwick	WAR-rick
Greenwich	GREN-ich	Woolwich	WOOL-ich
Hertfordshire	HART-ford-sher	Worcester	WOO-ster
Grosvernor	grovnor	gaol	JAIL
Holborn	HO-bun	quay	KEY
Leicester	LES-ter	scones	SKONS

WELSH WORDS AND PHRASES

Consult **Llanguage,** p. 421, for the basic rules of Welsh pronunciation. Listed below are a number of words and phrases you may encounter on the road.

WORD/PHRASE	PRONUNCIATION	MEANING
allan	ahl-LAN	exit
ar agor	ahr AG-or	open
ar gau	ahr GUY	closed
bore da	boh-RA DAH	good morning, hello
cyhoeddus	cuh-HOY-this	public
diolch yn fawr	dee-OLCH uhn VOWR	thank you
dydd da	DEETH dah	good day
dynion	dihnion	men
Ga i peint o cwrw?	gah-EE pint oh coo-roo?	Can I have a pint of beer?
hwyl	huh-will	cheers
ia	eeah	yes (sort of—it's tricky)
iawn	eeown	well, fine
llwybr cyhoeddus	hlooee-BIR cuh-HOY-this	public footpath
merched	mehrch-ED	women
nage	nahgah	no (sort of—it's tricky)
nos da	nos dah	good night
noswaith dda	nos-WAYTHE tha	good evening
os gwelwch yn dda	ohs gwell–OOCH uhn tha	please
perygl	pehr-UHGL	danger
preifat	"private"	private
safle'r Bus	savlehr boos	bus stop
stryd Fawr	strihd vahor	High Street
Sut mae?	sit my? or shoo my?	How are you?

SCOTTISH GAELIC WORDS AND PHRASES

Consult **Language,** p. 493, for information on Scottish Gaelic. Listed below are a number of words and phrases you may encounter on the road.

WORD/PHRASE	PRONUNCIATION	MEANING
Ciamar a tha sibh?	KI-mer a HA shiv?	How are you?
Tha gu math	HA gu MA	I'm fine
Gle mhath	GLAY va.	very well

WORD/PHRASE	PRONUNCIATION	MEANING
Gabh mo leisgeul	GAV mo LESH-kul	excuse me
Tapadh leibh	TA-pa LEEV	thank you
De an t-ainm a th'oirbh?	JAY an TEN-im a HO-riv?	what's your name?
Tha mi ag iarraidh uisge-beatha.	HA mee ag EAR-ee OOSH-ka BAY-ha.	give me whisky
Slainte mhath	SLAN-che VA	cheers, good health
Is mise...	ISH MISH-uh	My name is...
Seo	SHAW	this is... (to introduce someone)
Madainn mhath	MA-ting VA	good morning
Latha ma	LA-huh MA	good day
Oidhche mhath	a-HOY-chuh VA	good night
Failte gu...	FAL-chuh goo	welcome to...
taigh	TAI	house
ionad	EE-nud	place, visitor centre
sraid	SRAHJ	street
rathad	RAH-hud	road
beinn	BEN	mountain
gleann	GLAY-ahn (smooshed together)	valley
coire	COH-ruh	corry
baile	BAL-eh	town
dubh	DOOV	black
ruadh	ROO-ah	red
buidhe	BOO-ye	yellow
allt	ALT	stream

SCOTS WORDS AND PHRASES

Consult **Language**, p. 493, for more info on Scots, a distinct dialect of English. Listed below are some of the many Scots words and phrases used in standard Scottish English:

WORD/PHRASE	PRONUNCIATION	MEANING
ben		mountain
brane	BRAY	slope, hill
the bonny		awesome, cool (Glasgow only)
braw		bright, strong, great
burn		stream
craic	CRACK	great fun, "it's a craic"
glen		valley
Haud yer weesht		shut up, be quiet
ken		to know
kirk		church
lad		boy
lass		girl
Sassenach	SAS-uh-nach	Lowlander
strath		broad valley
Teuchter	TYOOCH-ter	someone from north Scotland
tipple		a drink
wee		little
Weegie	WEE-gee	Glaswegian
Yer gleachit!	YER GLEEch-it	You're falling apart!

IRISH WORDS AND PHRASES

The following bits of the Irish language are either used often in Irish English or are common in Irish place names. Spelling conventions almost never match English pronunciations: for example, "mh" sounds like "v," and "dh" sounds like "g."

WORD/PHRASE	PRONUNCIATION	MEANING
aisling	ASH-ling	vision or dream, or a poem or story thereof
An Lár	on lahr	city center
Baile Átha Cliath	BAL-yah AW-hah CLE-ah	Dublin
bodhrán	BOUR-ohn	traditional drum
Bord Fáilte	bored FAHL-tshuh	Irish Tourist Board
Conas tá tú?	CUNN-us thaw too?	How are you?
céilí	KAY-lee	Irish dance
craic	krak	good cheer, good pub conversation
Dáil	DOY-il	House of Representatives
Dia dhuit	JEE-a dich	goodday, hello
Dia's Muire dhuit	JEE-as MWUR-a dich	reply to "goodday"
dún	doon	fort
Éire	AIR-uh	Ireland; official name of the Republic of Ireland
fáilte	FAWLT-cha	welcome
feis	fesh	an assembly, Irish festival
fir	fear	men
fleadh	flah	a musical festival
gaeltacht	GAYL-tokt	a district where Irish is the everyday language
garda, Garda Síochána	GAR-da SHE-och-ANA	police
go raibh maith agat	guh roh moh UG-ut	thank you
inch, innis, ennis	inch, innis, ennis	island; river meadow
kil	kill	church; cell
knock	nok	hill
lei thras	LEH-hrass	toilets
lough	lohk	lake
mná	min-AW	women
mór	more	big, great
ní hea	nee hah	no (sort of—it's tricky)
oíche mhaith dhuit	EE-ha woh ditch	good night
Oifig an Phoist	UFF-ig un fwisht	Post Office
poitín	po-CHEEN	moonshine; sometimes-toxic homemade liquor
rath	rath *or* rah	earthen fort
sea	shah	yes (sort of—it's tricky)
seanachaí	SHAN-ukh-ee	storyteller
Seanad	SHAN-ud	Senate
Sinn Féin	shin fayn	"Ourselves Alone"; the political wing of the IRA
sláinte	SLAWN-che	cheers, to your health
slán agat	slawn UG-ut	goodbye
sraid	shrawd	street
Tá mé i mo idirgalacht-ach bhithiúnach.	ta-MAY imah va-HOO-nock idder gah-lachtach	I am an inter-galactic space criminal.
Taoiseach	TEE-shukh	Prime Minister
teachta dála (TD)	TAKH-ta DAH-lah	member of Irish parliament
trá	thraw	beach
uilleann	ILL-in	"elbow"; bagpipes played with the elbow

INDEX

INDEX

If I had my life to live over again,

I would relax. I would limber up. I would take more chances.

I would take more trips.

I would climb more mountains, swim more rivers, and watch more sunsets.

I would go places and do things and travel lighter than I have.

I would ride more merry-go-rounds.

Excerpt from Nadine Stair, 85 years old / photo> John Norris

technical packs & apparel

Find Yourself. Somewhere Else.

Don't just land there, do something. Away.com
is the Internet's preferred address for those
who like their travel with a little something
extra. Our team of travel enthusiasts and
experts can help you design your ultimate
adventure, nature or cultural escape. Make
Away.com your destination for extraordinary
travel. Then find yourself. Somewhere else.

away.com
1.877.769.2929

Will you have enough stories to tell your grandchildren?

Yahoo! Travel

Do You
Yahoo!
?